NEW ERA OF MANAGEMENT

RICHARD L. DAFT

Vanderbilt University

NEW ERA OF MANAGEMENT

RICHARD L. DAFT

Vanderbilt University

Second Edition

THOMSON

SOUTH-WESTERN

AUSTRALIA ▪ BRAZIL ▪ CANADA ▪ MEXICO ▪ SINGAPORE ▪ SPAIN ▪ UNITED KINGDOM ▪ UNITED STATES

New Era of Management, Second Edition

Richard L. Daft

With the assistance of Patricia G. Lane

VP/Editorial Director:
Jack W. Calhoun

Editor-in-Chief:
Melissa Acuña

Sr. Acquisitions Editor:
Joe Sabatino

Sr. Developmental Editor:
Emma Guttler Newsom

Editorial Assistant:
Ruth Belanger

Sr. Content Project Manager:
Cliff Kallemeyn

Marketing Manager:
Kimberly Kanakes

Marketing Coordinator:
Sarah Rose

Sr. Marketing Communications Manager:
Jim Overly

Technology Project Manager:
Kristen Meere

Art Director:
Tippy McIntosh

Sr. First Print Buyer:
Doug Wilke

Photo Manager:
John Hill

Photo Researcher:
Rose Alcorn

Internal Design:
John Walker Design

Printer:
China Translation and Printing Services

Library of Congress Control Number: 2007920212

For more information about our products, contact us at:

Thomson Learning Academic Resource Center

1-800-423-0563

Thomson Higher Education
5191 Natorp Boulevard
Mason, OH 45040
USA

With deep appreciation to Dorothy,
the playwright and partner in my life,
and to my parents, who started my life
toward outcomes that I could not understand at the time.

ABOUT THE AUTHOR

Richard L. Daft, Ph.D., is the Brownlee O. Currey, Jr., Professor of Management in the Owen Graduate School of Management at Vanderbilt University. Professor Daft specializes in the study of organization theory and leadership. Dr. Daft is a Fellow of the Academy of Management and has served on the editorial boards of *Academy of Management Journal, Administrative Science Quarterly,* and *Journal of Management Education.* He was the Associate Editor-in-Chief of *Organization Science* and served for three years as associate editor of *Administrative Science Quarterly.*

Professor Daft has authored or co-authored 12 books, including *Organization Theory and Design* (South-Western, 2007), *The Leadership Experience* (South-Western, 2005), and *What to Study: Generating and Developing Research Questions* (Sage, 1982). He recently published *Fusion Leadership: Unlocking the Subtle Forces That Change People and Organizations* (Berrett-Koehler, 2000, with Robert Lengel). He has also authored dozens of scholarly articles, papers, and chapters. His work has been published in *Administrative Science Quarterly, Academy of Management Journal, Academy of Management Review, Strategic Management Journal, Journal of Management, Accounting Organizations and Society, Management Science, MIS Quarterly, California Management Review,* and *Organizational Behavior Teaching Review.* Professor Daft has been awarded several government research grants to pursue studies of organization design, organizational innovation and change, strategy implementation, and organizational information processing.

Dr. Daft also is an active teacher and consultant. He has taught management, leadership, organizational change, organizational theory, and organizational behavior. He served as associate dean, produced for-profit theatrical productions, and helped manage a start-up enterprise. He has been involved in management development and consulting for many companies and government organizations, including the American Banking Association, Bell Canada, the National Transportation Research Board, NL Baroid, Nortel, TVA, Pratt & Whitney, State Farm Insurance, Tenneco, the United States Air Force, the U.S. Army, J. C. Bradford & Co., Central Parking System, Entergy Sales and Service, Bristol-Myers Squibb, First American National Bank, and the Vanderbilt University Medical Center.

PREFACE

Managing in Turbulent Times: Unlocking Innovative Solutions

In light of the dramatic and far-reaching events of the early twenty-first century, the central theme being discussed in the field of management is the pervasiveness of turbulent change and its impact on organizations. This edition of *New Era of Management* was revised to help current and future managers find innovative solutions to the problems that plague today's organizations—whether they are everyday challenges or once-in-a-lifetime crises. The world in which most students will work as managers is undergoing a tremendous upheaval. The emergence of crisis management, ethical turmoil, e-business, rapidly changing technologies, globalization, outsourcing, global virtual teams, knowledge management, global supply chains, and other changes place demands on managers that go beyond the techniques and ideas traditionally taught in management courses. Managing in today's turbulent times requires the full breadth of management skills and capabilities. This text provides comprehensive coverage of both traditional management skills and the new competencies needed in a turbulent environment characterized by economic turmoil, political confusion, and general uncertainty.

The traditional world of work assumed the purpose of management was to control and limit people, enforce rules and regulations, seek stability and efficiency, design a top-down hierarchy to direct people, and achieve bottom-line results. To unlock innovative solutions and achieve high performance, however, managers need different skills to engage workers' hearts and minds as well as take advantage of their physical labor. The new workplace asks that managers focus on leading change, harnessing people's creativity and enthusiasm, finding shared visions and values, and sharing information and power. Teamwork, collaboration, participation, and learning are guiding principles that help managers and employees maneuver the difficult terrain of today's turbulent business environment. Managers focus on developing, not controlling, people to adapt to new technologies and extraordinary environmental shifts, and thus achieve high performance and total corporate effectiveness.

My vision for the second edition of *New Era of Management* is to explore the newest management ideas for turbulent times in a way that is interesting and valuable to students while retaining the best of traditional management thinking. To achieve this vision, I have included the most recent management concepts and research and have showed the contemporary application of management ideas in organizations. I have also added a feature for "new managers" to give students a sense of what will be expected when they become managers. The combination of established scholarship, new ideas, and real-life applications gives students a taste of the energy, challenge, and adventure inherent in the dynamic field of management. The Thomson South-Western staff and I have worked together to provide a textbook better than any other at capturing the excitement of organizational management.

I revised *New Era of Management* to provide a book of utmost quality that will create in students both respect for the changing field of management and confidence that they can understand and master it. The textual portion of this book has been enhanced through the engaging, easy-to-understand writing style and the many in-text examples, boxed items, and short exercises that make the concepts come alive for students. The graphic component has been enhanced with several new exhibits and a new set of photo essays that illustrate specific management concepts. The well-chosen photographs provide vivid illustrations and intimate glimpses of management scenes, events, and people. The photos are combined with brief essays that explain how a specific management concept looks and feels. Both the textual and graphic portions of the textbook help students grasp the often abstract and distant world of management.

Focus on Innovation: New to the Second Edition

The second edition of *New Era of Management* is especially focused on the future of management education by identifying and describing emerging ideas and examples of innovative organizations and by providing enhanced learning opportunities for students.

Learning Opportunities

The second edition has taken a leap forward in pedagogical features to help students learn what it is like to manage in an organization today. New to this edition is a New Manager Self-Test in each chapter. These short feedback questionnaires give students insight into how they respond to situations and challenges typically faced by real-life managers. End-of-chapter questions have been thoroughly and carefully revised to encourage critical thinking and application of chapter concepts. The end-of-chapter cases and ethical dilemmas that help students sharpen their diagnostic skills for management problem solving have also been updated. This edition contains 11 new cases and 9 new ethical dilemmas. Seven additional cases and dilemmas have been substantially revised.

Chapter Content

Within each chapter, many topics have been added or expanded to address the current issues managers face. Text content has been sharpened to provide greater focus on the key topics that count for management today.

Chapter 1 includes a new section on making the leap from being an individual contributor in the organization to becoming a new manager and getting work done primarily through others. The chapter introduces the skills and competencies needed to effectively manage organizations, including issues such as managing diversity, coping with globalization, and managing crises. In addition, a new section discusses the emphasis within organizations on innovation as a response to today's turbulent environment.

Chapter 2 continues its solid coverage of the historical development of management and organizations and examines new management thinking for turbulent times. The chapter also looks at the shifting world of e-business and effective management of the technology-driven workplace, including trends such as supply chain management, outsourcing, and customer relationship management.

Chapter 3 contains an updated look at current issues related to the environment and corporate culture, including a section illustrating how managers shape a high-performance culture as an innovative response to a shifting environment.

Chapter 4 includes a new discussion of the growing power of China and India in today's global business environment and what this means for managers around the world. In addition, the complex issues surrounding globalization are discussed, including a consideration of the current globalization backlash. A new section in Chapter 4 looks at the importance of *cultural intelligence* for managers working in foreign countries or interacting with people from different cultures.

Chapter 5 has an expanded discussion of ethical challenges managers face today and the business case for incorporating ethical values in the organization. The chapter also considers global ethical issues, including a discussion of corruption rankings of various countries and a consideration of the growing sustainability movement.

Chapter 6 takes a look at entrepreneurial activity on a global basis and examines the reasons entrepreneurship and small business are booming. The chapter continues its focus on practical information regarding small business formation, including a look at the challenges of entrepreneurial startups. In addition, a new section discusses the growing interest in *social entrepreneurship*, sometimes called *social capitalism.*

Chapter 7 provides an overview of planning and goal setting, including a close look at crisis planning and how to use scenarios. The chapter's final section on planning for high performance has been enhanced by a discussion of the use of executive dashboards to help managers plan in a fast-changing environment.

Chapter 8 continues its focus on the basics of formulating and implementing strategy and includes a consideration of the challenges of implementing strategy during turbulent times.

Chapter 9's overview of managerial decision making has an expanded discussion of intuition in decision making and the refined use of brainstorming for group decision making.

Chapter 10 discusses basic principles of organizing and describes both traditional and contemporary organization structures in detail. The chapter includes a discussion of organic versus mechanistic structures and when each is more effective and also contains a description of the virtual network organization form.

Chapter 11 has been thoroughly updated and reorganized to reflect the critical role of managing change and innovation today. The chapter includes new or expanded material on exploration and creativity, the importance of internal and external cooperation, and the growing trend toward open innovation.

Chapter 12 includes a discussion of changes in the social contract between employers and employees. A new section looks at how organizations apply strategic human resource management to help the organization become an employer of choice to attract and retain the best human capital.

Chapter 13 has been revised and updated to reflect the most recent thinking on organizational diversity issues. The chapter looks at the challenges women and minorities face in organizations, including the current debate about women opting to leave the corporate workforce (the opt-out trend). The chapter also has an expanded discussion of using diversity training to give people the interpersonal and communication skills they need to reap the benefits of diversity.

Chapter 14 provides an overview of financial and quality control, including Six Sigma, ISO certification, and a new application of the balanced scorecard, which views employee learning and growth as the foundation of high performance. The chapter also addresses current concerns about corporate governance and finding a proper balance of control and autonomy for employees.

Chapter 15 has been thoroughly updated to incorporate recent trends in information technology, including user-generated content through wikis, blogs, and social networking sites. The chapter explores how these new technologies are being applied within organizations along with traditional information systems. The chapter also discusses e-commerce strategies, the growing use of business intelligence software, and how new IT affects the manager's job.

Chapter 16 has been enhanced by a discussion of the organization as a value chain and a consideration of the four major outcomes managers focus on for building an effective operations system. The chapter also talks about new technology used for operations and service management, such as product life-cycle management software, radio frequency identification (RFID) for logistics and supply chain management, and location scouting software for facilities location planning.

Chapter 17 contains updated coverage related to personality traits and the use of personality and other assessment tests in organizations. Exercises throughout the chapter enhance students' understanding of organizational behavior topics and their own personalities and attitudes.

Chapter 18 has been reorganized to focus on the styles of leadership that are highly effective today. The chapter emphasizes that leadership can make a difference, often through subtle everyday actions. The discussion of power has been expanded to discuss how leaders exercise power through various interpersonal influence tactics.

Chapter 19 covers the foundations of motivation and also incorporates recent thinking about motivational tools for today, such as the importance of helping employees achieve work-life balance, incorporating fun and learning into the workplace, giving people a chance to fully participate, and helping people find meaning in their work.

Chapter 20 begins with a discussion of how managers facilitate strategic conversations by using communication to direct everyone's attention to the vision, values, and goals of the organization. The chapter explores the foundations of good communication and includes a new section on effective written communication in recognition of the growing use of e-mail and the need for managers to write clearly and concisely.

Chapter 21 discusses how to lead work teams to effectiveness and includes a new section on using negotiation to manage conflict, including how to reach a win-win solution. The final section of the chapter takes a new look at the positive outcomes of effective teams.

In addition to the topics listed above, this text integrates coverage of the Internet and new technology into the various topics covered in each chapter. Each chapter also contains a valuable application in an *Unlocking Innovative Solutions* box. Approximately half of these boxes feature a technologically savvy company or highlight a manager who is using technology to meet the challenges of today's environment. The other half of the *Unlocking Innovative Solutions* boxes describe various unique, innovative, or interesting approaches to managing people for high performance and innovative response, in recognition that human capital is essential for solving today's complex organizational problems.

Organization

The chapter sequence in *New Era of Management* is organized around the management functions of planning, organizing, controlling, and leading. These four functions effectively encompass both management research and characteristics of the manager's job.

Part One introduces the world of management, including the nature of management, issues related to today's turbulent environment, the learning organization, historical perspectives on management, and the technology-driven workplace.

Part Two examines the environments of management and organizations. This section includes material on the business environment and corporate culture, the global environment, ethics and social responsibility, the natural environment, and the environment of entrepreneurship and small business management.

Part Three presents three chapters on planning, including organizational goal setting and planning, strategy formulation and implementation, and the decision-making process.

Part Four focuses on organizing processes. These chapters describe dimensions of structural design, the design alternatives managers can use to achieve strategic objectives, structural designs for promoting innovation and change, the design and use of the human resource function, and the ways managing diverse employees are significant to the organizing function.

Part Five describes the controlling function of management, including basic principles of total quality management, the design of control systems, information technology, and techniques for control of operations management.

Part Six is devoted to leadership. The section begins with a chapter on organizational behavior, providing grounding in understanding people in organizations. This foundation paves the way for subsequent discussion of leadership, motivation of employees, communication, and team management.

Innovative Features

A major goal of this book is to offer better ways of using the textbook medium to convey management knowledge to the reader. To this end, the book includes several innovative features that draw students in and help them contemplate, absorb, and comprehend management concepts. South-Western has brought together a team of experts to create and coordinate color photographs, video cases, beautiful artwork, and supplemental materials for the best management textbook and package on the market.

Chapter Outline and Objectives. Each chapter begins with a clear statement of its learning objectives and an outline of its contents. These devices provide an overview of what is to come and can also be used by students to guide their study and test their understanding and retention of important points.

Manager's Challenge. The text portion of each chapter begins with a real-life problem faced by organization managers. The problem pertains to the topic of the chapter and will heighten students' interest in chapter concepts. At the end of each challenge, students are asked to "**Take a Moment**" to ponder the situation and think about how they would handle it. The Take a Moment questions posed in the Manager's Challenge are resolved in the **Manager's Solution** at the end of the chapter, where chapter concepts guiding the management's actions are highlighted.

Take a Moment. The Take a Moment feature has been expanded throughout the chapter. This new feature for the second edition provides a call to action that helps students apply the concepts discussed in the text and see how they would use the idea as a practicing manager. Some of the Take a Moment features also refer students to the associated New Manager Self-Test, or direct students from the chapter content to relevant end of chapter materials, such as an experiential exercise or an ethical dilemma.

New Manager Self-Test. A New Manager Self-Test in each chapter of the text provides opportunities for self-assessment as a way for students to experience management issues in a personal way. The change from individual performer to new manager is dramatic, and these self-tests provide insight into what to expect and how students might perform in the world of the new manager.

Concept Connection Photo Essays. A key feature of the book is the use of photographs accompanied by detailed photo essay captions that enhance learning. Each caption highlights and illustrates one or more specific concepts from the text to reinforce student understanding of the concepts. Although the photos are beautiful to look at, they also convey the vividness, immediacy, and concreteness of management events in today's business world.

Contemporary Examples. Every chapter of the text contains a large number of written examples of management incidents. They are placed at strategic points in the chapter and are designed to illustrate the application of concepts to specific companies. These in-text examples—indicated by an icon in the margin—include well-known U.S. and international companies such as Sony, UPS, Kraft Foods, Lenova, Wal-Mart, BMW, eBay, and LG Electronics, as well as less-well-known companies and not-for-profit organizations such as Remploy Ltd. and Strida (United Kingdom), Barbara K! Enterprises and Manchester Bidwell (U.S.), Esquel Group (Hong Kong), Unión Fenosa (Spain), Mississippi Power Company, the *Los Angeles Times*, and the U.S. Federal Bureau of Investigation (FBI). These examples put students in touch with the real world of organizations so that they can appreciate the value of management concepts.

Unlocking Innovative Solutions Boxes. Each chapter contains an Unlocking Innovation Solutions box. Some of the boxes focus on using technology to unlock innovative solutions, whereas a comparable number look at the importance of people in innovation. Describing real managers and companies, these boxes reflect the dual emphasis that today's most successful managers use to unlock innovative solutions and increase organizational performance: the technology side and the human capital side. These boxes provide students with an in-depth analysis of the various issues facing today's organizations and managers.

Manager's Shoptalk Boxes. A Manager's Shoptalk box in each chapter addresses a specific topic straight from the field of management that is of special interest to students. These boxes may describe a contemporary topic or problem that is relevant to chapter content, or they may contain a diagnostic questionnaire or a special example of how managers handle a problem. The boxes heighten student interest in the subject matter and provide an auxiliary view of management issues not typically available in textbooks.

Video Cases. The six parts of the text conclude with video cases, one per chapter, that illustrate the concepts presented in that part. The 21 videos enhance class discussion, because students can see the direct application of the management theories they have learned. Companies discussed in the video package include Yahoo!, Caterpillar, Cold Stone Creamery, Ford, McDonald's, and Allstate. Each video case explores the issues covered in the video, allowing students to synthesize the material they've just viewed. The video cases culminate with several questions that can be used to launch classroom discussion or as homework.

Exhibits. Many aspects of management are research based, and some concepts tend to be abstract and theoretical. To enhance students' awareness and understanding of these concepts, many exhibits have been included throughout the book. These exhibits consolidate key points, indicate relationships among concepts, and visually illustrate concepts. They also make effective use of color to enhance their imagery and appeal.

Glossaries. Learning the management vocabulary is essential to understanding contemporary management. This process is facilitated in three ways. First, key concepts are boldfaced and completely defined where they first appear in the text. Second, brief definitions are set out in the margin for easy review and follow-up. Third, a glossary summarizing all key terms and definitions appears at the end of the book for handy reference.

Chapter Summary and Discussion Questions. Each chapter closes with a summary of key points that students should retain. The discussion questions are a complementary learning tool that will enable students to check their understanding of key issues, to think beyond basic concepts, and to determine areas that require further study. The summary and discussion questions help students discriminate between main and supporting points and provide mechanisms for self-teaching.

Management in Practice Exercises. End-of-chapter exercises called "Management in Practice: Experiential Exercise" and "Management in Practice: Ethical Dilemma" provide a self-test for students and an opportunity to experience management issues in a personal way. These exercises take the form of questionnaires, scenarios, and activities, and many also provide an opportunity for students to work in teams. There are seven new ethical dilemmas in this edition. The exercises are tied into the chapter through the Take a Moment feature that refers students to the end-of-chapter exercises at the appropriate point in the chapter content.

Case for Critical Analysis. Also appearing at the end of each chapter is a brief but substantive case that provides an opportunity for student analysis and class discussion. Some of these cases are about companies whose names students will recognize; others are based on real management events but the identities of companies and managers have been disguised. These cases allow students to sharpen their diagnostic skills for management problem solving. There are 11 new cases in this edition.

Continuing Case. Located at the end of each part, the Continuing Case is a running discussion of management topics as experienced by one company as it is relevant to the material discussed in that part. Focusing on one company, Costco, allows students to follow the managers' and the organizations' problems and solutions in a long-term way.

Supplementary Materials

Instructor's Manual. Designed to provide support for instructors new to the course, as well as innovative materials for experienced professors, the Instructor's Manual includes Chapter Outlines, annotated learning objectives, Lecture Notes, and sample Lecture Outlines. Additionally, the Instructor's Manual includes answers and teaching notes to end-of-chapter materials, including the video cases and the continuing case.

Test Bank. Scrutinized for accuracy, the Test Bank includes more than 2,000 true/false, multiple-choice, short-answer, and essay questions. Page references are indicated for every question, as are designations of either factual or application so that instructors can provide a balanced set of questions for student exams. Each question is also tagged based on AACSB guidelines.

ExamView. Available on the web site www.thomsonedu.com/aise. ExamView contains all of the questions in the printed Test Bank. This program is an easy-to-use test creation software compatible with Microsoft Windows. Instructors can add or edit questions, instructions, and answers, and select questions (randomly or numerically) by previewing them on the screen. Instructors can also create and administer quizzes online, whether over the Internet, a local area network (LAN), or a wide area network (WAN).

PowerPoint Lecture Presentation. Available on the Web site, the PowerPoint Lecture Presentation enables instructors to customize their own multimedia classroom presentation. Containing approximately 350 slides, the package includes figures and tables from the text, as well as outside materials to supplement chapter concepts. Material is organized by chapter and can be modified or expanded for individual classroom use. PowerPoint slides are also easily printed to create customized Transparency Masters.

Video Package. The video package for *New Era of Management*, Second Edition, contains three options: On the Job videos from the first edition of Daft's *New Era of Management*, Biz Flix videos, and On the Job videos created specifically for the second edition of Daft's *New Era of Management*. Biz Flix are film clips taken from popular Hollywood movies and integrated into the second edition of Daft. Clips are supported by short cases and discussion questions at the end of each chapter. On the Job videos within the text were created to accompany *New Era of Management*, First Edition, or *New Era of Management*, Second Edition, and utilize real-world companies to illustrate management concepts as outlined in the text. Focusing on both small and large business, the videos give students an inside perspective on the situations and issues that corporations face. Video cases in an appendix, two per chapter, reinforce what the student has just seen, and provide an opportunity for critical analysis and discussion.

Acknowledgments

A gratifying experience for me was working with the team of dedicated professionals at South-Western who were committed to the vision of producing the best management text ever. I am grateful to Joe Sabatino, Sr. Acquisitions Editor, whose enthusiasm, creative ideas, assistance, and vision kept this book's spirit alive. Emma Guttler Newsom, Sr. Developmental Editor, provided superb project coordination and offered excellent ideas and suggestions to help the team meet a demanding and sometimes arduous schedule. Kimberly Kanakes, Marketing Manager, provided keen market knowledge and innovative ideas for instructional support. Cliff Kallemeyn, Sr. Content Project Manager, cheerfully and expertly guided me through the production process. Tippy McIntosh contributed her graphic arts skills to create a visually dynamic design. Ruth Belanger, Editorial Assistant, and Sarah Rose, Marketing Coordinator, skillfully pitched in to help keep the project on track. Anne Williams and the team at Graphic World deserve a special thank you for their layout expertise and commitment to producing an attractive, high-quality textbook.

Here at Vanderbilt I want to extend special appreciation to my assistant, Barbara Haselton. Barbara provided excellent support and assistance on a variety of projects that gave me time to write. I also want to acknowledge an intellectual debt to my colleagues, Bruce Barry, Ray Friedman, Neta Moye, Rich Oliver, David Owens, Bart Victor, and Tim Vogus. Thanks also to Deans Jim Bradford and Joe Blackburn who have supported my writing projects and maintained a positive scholarly atmosphere in the school.

Another group of people who made a major contribution to this textbook are the management experts who provided advice, reviews, answers to questions, and suggestions for changes, insertions, and clarifications. I want to thank each of these colleagues for their valuable feedback and suggestions:

David C. Adams
Manhattanville College

Erin M. Alexander
University of Houston–Clear Lake

Hal Babson
Columbus State Community College

Reuel Barksdale
Columbus State Community College

Gloria Bemben
Finger Lakes Community College

Pat Bernson
County College of Morris

Art Bethke
Northeast Louisiana University

Thomas Butte
Humboldt State University

Peter Bycio
Xavier University, Ohio

Diane Caggiano
Fitchburg State College

Douglas E. Cathon
St. Augustine's College

Jim Ciminskie
Bay de Noc Community College

Dan Connaughton
University of Florida

Bruce Conwers
Kaskaskia College

Byron L. David
The City College of New York

Richard De Luca
William Paterson University

Robert DeDominic
Montana Tech

Linn Van Dyne
Michigan State University

John C. Edwards
East Carolina University

Mary Ann Edwards
College of Mount St. Joseph

Janice M. Feldbauer
Austin Community College

Daryl Fortin
Upper Iowa University

Michael P. Gagnon
New Hampshire Community Technical College

Richard H. Gayor
Antelope Valley College

Dan Geeding
Xavier University, Ohio

James Genseal
Joliet Junior College

Peter Gibson
Becker College

Carol R. Graham
Western Kentucky University

Gary Greene
Manatee Community College

Ken Harris
Indiana University Southeast

Paul Hayes
Coastal Carolina Community College

Dennis Heaton
Maharishi University of Management, Iowa

Jeffrey D. Hines
Davenport College

Bob Hoerber
Westminster College

James N. Holly
University of Wisconsin–Green Bay

Genelle Jacobson
Ridgewater College

C. Joy Jones
Ohio Valley College

Kathleen Jones
University of North Dakota

Sheryl Kae
Lynchburg College

Jordan J. Kaplan
Long Island University

J. Michael Keenan
Western Michigan University

Gloria Komer
Stark State College

Paula C. Kougl
Western Oregon University

Cynthia Krom
Mount St. Mary College

Mukta Kulkarni
University of Texas–San Antonio

William B. Lamb
Millsaps College

Robert E. Ledman
Morehouse College

George Lehma
Bluffton College

Cynthia Lengnick-Hall
University of Texas–San Antonio

Janet C. Luke
Georgia Baptist College of Nursing

Jenna Lundburg
Ithaca College

Walter J. MacMillan
Oral Roberts University

Myrna P. Mandell
California State University, Northridge

Daniel B. Marin
Louisiana State University

Michael Market
Jacksonville State University

James C. McElroy
Iowa State University

Dennis W. Meyers
Texas State Technical College

Alan N. Miller
University of Nevada–Las Vegas

Irene A. Miller
Southern Illinois University

James L. Moseley
Wayne State University

Micah Mukabi
Essex County College

David W. Murphy
Madisonville Community College

Nora Nurre
Upper Iowa University

Nelson Ocf
Pacific University

Tomas J. Ogazon
St. Thomas University

Allen Oghenejbo
Mills College

Linda Overstreet
Hillsborough Community College

Ken Peterson
Metropolitan State University

Clifton D. Petty
Drury College

James I. Phillips
Northeastern State University

Linda Putchinski
University of Central Florida

Kenneth Radig
Medaille College

Gerald D. Ramsey
Indiana University Southeast

Barbara Redmond
Briar Cliff College

William Reisel
St. John's University–New York

Terry Riddle
Central Virginia Community College

Walter F. Rohrs
Wagner College

Meir Russ
*University of Wisconsin–
Green Bay*

Marcy Satterwhite
Lake Land College

Don Schreiber
Baylor University

Kilmon Shin
Ferris State University

Daniel G. Spencer
University of Kansas

Gary Spokes
Pace University

M. Sprencz
David N. Meyers College

Shanths Srinivas
*California State Polytechnic
University, Pomona*

Jeffrey Stauffer
Ventura College

William A. Stower
Seton Hall University

Mary Studer
Southwestern Michigan College

James Swenson
Moorhead State University, Minnesota

Irwin Talbot
St. Peter's College

Andrew Timothy
Lourdes College

Frank G. Titlow
St. Petersburg Junior College

John Todd
University of Arkansas

Philip Varca
University of Wyoming

Dennis L. Varin
Southern Oregon University

Gina Vega
Merrimack College

George S. Vozikis
University of Tulsa

Bruce C. Walker
Northeast Louisiana University

Mark Weber
University of Minnesota

Emilia S. Westney
Texas Tech University

Stan Williamson
Northeast Louisiana University

Alla L. Wilson
*University of Wisconsin–
Green Bay*

Ignatius Yacomb
Loma Linda University

Imad Jim Zbib
Ramapo College of New Jersey

Vic Zimmerman
Pima Community College

I'd like to pay special tribute to my long-time editorial associate, Pat Lane. I can't imagine how I would ever complete such a comprehensive revision on my own. Pat provided truly outstanding help throughout every step of writing the second edition of *New Era of Management*. She skillfully drafted materials for a wide range of chapter topics, boxes, and cases; researched topics when new sources were lacking; and did an absolutely superb job with the copyedited manuscript and page proofs. Her commitment to this text enabled us to achieve our dream for its excellence.

I also feel a special debt to Jane Woodside, who came on board for this edition to renew and revise the end-of-chapter materials and Concept Connections. She worked creatively and diligently to find just the right idea to make the new cases and ethical dilemmas fit the content for each chapter. She also developed new, more applied discussion questions, and drafted new Concept Connections. Jane's contributions have improved the pedagogy in every chapter.

Finally, I want to acknowledge the love and contributions of my wife, Dorothy Marcic. Dorothy has been very supportive during this revision as we share our lives together. I also want to acknowledge my love and support from my five daughters, Danielle, Amy, Roxanne, Solange, and Elizabeth, who make my life special during our precious time together. Thanks also to B. J. and Kaitlyn, and Kaci and Matthew for their warmth and smiles that brighten my life, especially during our days together skiing and on the beach.

Richard L. Daft
Nashville, Tennessee
December 2006

BRIEF CONTENTS

PART 1 INTRODUCTION TO MANAGEMENT 2

  1 Innovative Management for Turbulent Times 4
  2 The Evolution of Management Thinking 36

PART 2 THE ENVIRONMENT OF MANAGEMENT 68

  3 The Environment and Corporate Culture 70
  4 Managing in a Global Environment 104
  5 Ethics and Social Responsibility 138
  6 Managing Small Business Start-Ups 172

PART 3 PLANNING 206

  7 Managerial Planning and Goal Setting 208
  8 Strategy Formulation and Implementation 236
  9 Managerial Decision Making 270

PART 4 ORGANIZING 304

  10 Designing Adaptive Organizations 306
  11 Managing Change and Innovation 346
  12 Human Resource Management 378
  13 Meeting the Challenge of Diversity 414

PART 5 CONTROLLING 450

  14 Managerial and Quality Control 452
  15 Information Technology and E-Business 486
  16 Operations and Value Chain Management 516

PART 6 LEADING 550

  17 Dynamics of Behavior in Organizations 552
  18 Leadership 588
  19 Motivation 620
  20 Communication 656
  21 Teamwork 692

Appendix: Video Case Library 728
Glossary 778
Indexes 791

CONTENTS

PART 1 INTRODUCTION TO MANAGEMENT 2

1 Innovative Management for Turbulent Times 4

Manager's Challenge 5

The Definition of Management 7

The Four Management Functions 8

Planning 8 ▪ Organizing 8 ▪ Leading 9 ▪ Controlling 9

Organizational Performance 10

Management Skills 11

Conceptual Skills 11 ▪ Human Skills 11 ▪ Technical Skills 12
▪ When Skills Fail 12

Management Types 13

Vertical Differences 14 ▪ Horizontal Differences 15

What Is It Like to Be a Manager? 16

Making the Leap: Becoming a New Manager 16 ▪ Manager Activities 17
▪ Manager Roles 20

Managing in Small Businesses and Nonprofit Organizations 23

Management and the New Workplace 25

Forces on Organizations 26 ▪ The Innovative Response 26
▪ New Management Competencies 27 ▪ Turbulent Times: Managing Crises
and Unexpected Events 28

Manager's Solution 29

Discussion Questions 30

Management in Practice: Experiential Exercise 31

Management in Practice: Ethical Dilemma 32

Case for Critical Analysis 32

Endnotes 33

Manager's Shoptalk
Do You Really Want to Be a
Manager? 18

New Manager Self-Test
Manager Role and
Reality 20

**Unlocking Innovative
Solutions Through
Technology** Click Here for
Lower Taxes 24

2 The Evolution of Management Thinking 36

Manager's Challenge 37

Management and Organization 38

Classical Perspective 40

Scientific Management 41 ▪ Bureaucratic Organizations 42
▪ Administrative Principles 44

Humanistic Perspective 46

Human Relations Movement 46 ▪ Human Resources Perspective 47
▪ Behavioral Sciences Approach 50

Management Science Perspective 50

Recent Historical Trends 52

Systems Theory 52 ▪ Contingency View 53 ▪ Total Quality Management 54

Innovative Management Thinking for Turbulent Times 54

The Learning Organization 55 ▪ Managing the Technology-Driven Workplace 56

**Unlocking Innovative
Solutions Through
Technology** Of Railroads
and Web Sites 40

New Manager Self-Test
Evolution of Style 48

Manager's Shoptalk
Ebbs and Flows of
Management Innovations,
1950–2000 51

Manager's Solution   59

Discussion Questions   60

Management in Practice: Experiential Exercise   61

Management in Practice: Ethical Dilemma   61

Case for Critical Analysis   62

Endnotes   62

CONTINUING CASE   66

PART 2   THE ENVIRONMENT OF MANAGEMENT   68

3   The Environment and Corporate Culture   70

Manager's Challenge   71

The External Environment   72

General Environment   73   ■   Task Environment   78

The Organization–Environment Relationship   81

Environmental Uncertainty   81   ■   Adapting to the Environment   82

The Internal Environment: Corporate Culture   85

Symbols   87   ■   Stories   87   ■   Heroes   87   ■   Slogans   88   ■   Ceremonies   88

Environment and Culture   89

Adaptive Cultures   89   ■   Types of Cultures   90

Shaping Corporate Culture for Innovative Response   92

Managing the High-Performance Culture   93   ■   Cultural Leadership   94

Manager's Solution   96

Discussion Questions   97

Management in Practice: Experiential Exercise   98

Management in Practice: Ethical Dilemma   99

Case for Critical Analysis   99

Endnotes   100

4   Managing in a Global Environment   104

Manager's Challenge   105

A Borderless World   106

Getting Started Internationally   108

Outsourcing   109   ■   Exporting   109   ■   Licensing   110   ■   Direct Investing   111
■   China Inc.   112

The International Business Environment   113

The Economic Environment   114

Economic Development   115   ■   Infrastructure   115   ■   Resource and Product
Markets   115   ■   Exchange Rates   116

The Legal-Political Environment   116

Political Risk and Instability   116   ■   Laws and Regulations   117

The Sociocultural Environment   117

Social Values   117   ■   Other Cultural Characteristics   121

International Trade Alliances   122

GATT and the World Trade Organization   122   ■   European Union   123
■   North American Free Trade Agreement (NAFTA)   124
■   Other Trade Alliances   125   ■   The Globalization Backlash   126

Multinational Corporations   126

Managing in a Global Environment   127

Developing Cultural Intelligence   127   ■   Managing Cross-Culturally   129

Manager's Shoptalk
The Ties That Bind   75

New Manager Self-Test
Manager Mind and the
Environment   83

**Unlocking Innovative
Solutions Through People**
It's Power (and Respon-
sibility) to the People   95

**Unlocking Innovative
Solutions Through
Technology** Nighthawks
to the Rescue   110

Manager's Shoptalk How
Well Do You Play the
Culture Game?   120

New Manager Self-Test
Cultural Intelligence   128

Contents

Manager's Solution   130

Discussion Questions   131

Management in Practice: Experiential Exercise   132

Management in Practice: Ethical Dilemma   133

Case for Critical Analysis   133

Endnotes   134

5   Ethics and Social Responsibility   138

Manager's Challenge   139

What Is Managerial Ethics?   140

Criteria for Ethical Decision Making   142

　　Utilitarian Approach   142 ▪ Individualism Approach   143

　　▪ Moral-Rights Approach   143 ▪ Justice Approach   144

Factors Affecting Ethical Choices   144

　　The Manager   145 ▪ The Organization   149

What Is Social Responsibility?   150

Organizational Stakeholders   151

The Ethic of Sustainability and the Natural Environment   153

Evaluating Corporate Social Responsibility   155

　　Economic Responsibilities   155 ▪ Legal Responsibilities   156

　　▪ Ethical Responsibilities   156 ▪ Discretionary Responsibilities   157

Managing Company Ethics and Social Responsibility   157

　　Ethical Individuals   157 ▪ Ethical Leadership   158

　　▪ Organizational Structures and Systems   159

Ethical Challenges in Turbulent Times   162

　　The Business Case for Ethics and Social Responsibility   162

　　▪ Economic Performance   164

Manager's Solution   165

Discussion Questions   166

Management in Practice: Experiential Exercise Ethical Work Climates   166

Management in Practice: Ethical Dilemma   167

Case for Critical Analysis   167

Endnotes   168

Manager's Shoptalk
Challenging the Boss on
Ethical Issues   145

New Manager Self-Test
Manager Courage   148

**Unlocking Innovative
Solutions Through People**
South Mountain Prac-
tices Community
Entrepreneurism   163

6   Managing Small Business Start-Ups   172

Manager's Challenge   173

What Is Entrepreneurship?   174

Entrepreneurship and the Environment   175

　　Entrepreneurship Today   176 ▪ Definition of Small Business   179

　　▪ Impact of Entrepreneurial Companies   179

Who Are Entrepreneurs?   181

　　Diversity of Entrepreneurs   182 ▪ Personality Traits   183

Social Entrepreneurship: An Innovative Approach to Small Business   185

Launching an Entrepreneurial Start-Up   186

　　Starting with the Idea   187 ▪ Writing the Business Plan   187

　　▪ Choosing a Legal Structure   189 ▪ Getting Financing   190

　　▪ Tactics for Becoming a Business Owner   191

Managing a Growing Business   194

　　Stages of Growth   194 ▪ Planning   195 ▪ Organizing   196 ▪ Leading   196

　　▪ Controlling   197

New Manager Self-Test
Improvisation   176

**Unlocking Innovative
Solutions Through People**
White Dog Enterprises:
Doing Well by Doing
Good   186

Manager's Shoptalk
Helpful Hints for Writing
the Business Plan   188

Manager's Solution   197
Discussion Questions   198
Management in Practice: Experiential Exercise   199
Management in Practice: Ethical Dilemma   199
Case for Critical Analysis   200
Endnotes   201
CONTINUING CASE   204

PART 3   PLANNING   206

New Manager Self-Test
Does Goal-Setting Fit Your
Management Style?   211

Manager's Shoptalk
Regulating E-mail in the
Workplace   223

**Unlocking Innovative
Solutions Through
Technology** Fighting Fires
at Symantec   229

7   **Managerial Planning and Goal Setting   208**
Manager's Challenge   209
Overview of Goals and Plans   210
Purposes of Goals and Plans   211
Goals in Organizations   213
   Organizational Mission   213   ▪   Goals and Plans   214   ▪   Alignment of Goals   216
Criteria for Effective Goals   217
Planning Types   219
   Management by Objectives   219   ▪   Single-Use and Standing Plans   221
   ▪   Contingency Plans   222
Planning in a Turbulent Environment   223
   Building Scenarios   224   ▪   Crisis Planning   224
Planning for High Performance   226
   Traditional Approaches to Planning   227   ▪   High-Performance Approaches
   to Planning   227
Manager's Solution   230
Discussion Questions   231
Management in Practice: Experiential Exercise   232
Management in Practice: Ethical Dilemma   232
Case for Critical Analysis   233
Endnotes   234

**Unlocking Innovative
Solutions Through People**
Four Seasons Hotels:
Managing by the Golden
Rule   254

New Manager Self-Test
What Is Your Strategy
Strength?   259

Manager's Shoptalk Tips
for Effective Strategy
Implementation   260

8   **Strategy Formulation and Implementation   236**
Manager's Challenge   237
Thinking Strategically   238
   What Is Strategic Management?   239   ▪   Grand Strategy   239
   ▪   Global Strategy   240   ▪   Purpose of Strategy   242   ▪   Levels of Strategy   244
The Strategic Management Process   246
   Strategy Formulation Versus Implementation   247   ▪   Situation Analysis   247
Formulating Corporate-Level Strategy   249
   Portfolio Strategy   249   ▪   The BCG Matrix   249
Formulating Business-Level Strategy   251
   Porter's Competitive Forces and Strategies   251   ▪   Partnership Strategies   255
Formulating Functional-Level Strategy   257
Strategy Implementation and Control   258
   Leadership   259   ▪   Structural Design   261   ▪   Information and Control
   Systems   261   ▪   Human Resources   262
Implementation During Turbulent Times   262
   Global Mind-Set   262   ▪   Corporate Culture   262   ▪   Information Technology   263
Manager's Solution   263
Discussion Questions   264

Management in Practice: Experiential Exercise   265
Management in Practice: Ethical Dilemma   265
Case for Critical Analysis   266
Endnotes   267

9   **Managerial Decision Making   270**

Manager's Challenge   271
Types of Decisions and Problems   272
   Programmed and Nonprogrammed Decisions   272   ▪   Certainty, Risk, Uncertainty,
   and Ambiguity   273
Decision-Making Models   275
   Classical Model   275   ▪   Administrative Model   277   ▪   Political Model   279
Decision-Making Steps   281
   Recognition of Decision Requirement   282   ▪   Diagnosis and Analysis of Causes   282
   ▪   Development of Alternatives   283   ▪   Selection of Desired Alternative   283
   Implementation of Chosen Alternative   285   ▪   Evaluation and Feedback   285
Personal Decision Framework   286
Increasing Participation in Decision Making   288
   The Vroom-Jago Model   288   ▪   New Decision Approaches for Turbulent
   Times   292
Manager's Solution   295
Discussion Questions   295
Management in Practice: Experiential Exercise   296
Management in Practice: Ethical Dilemma   297
Case for Critical Analysis   298
Endnotes   299
CONTINUING CASE   302

**Unlocking Innovative
Solutions Through
Technology** Southwest
Uses Technology to Keep a
Hawk's Eye on Costs   277

Manager's Shoptalk
Decision Biases to
Avoid   284

New Manager Self-Test
Your Decision-Making
Behavior   287

PART 4   ORGANIZING   304

10   **Designing Adaptive Organizations   306**

Manager's Challenge   307
Organizing the Vertical Structure   308
   Work Specialization   309   ▪   Chain of Command   309   ▪   Span of Management   311
   ▪   Centralization and Decentralization   313
Departmentalization   314
   Vertical Functional Approach   316   ▪   Divisional Approach   316   ▪   Matrix
   Approach   318   ▪   Team Approach   320   ▪   The Virtual Network Approach   321
   ▪   Advantages and Disadvantages of Each Structure   323
Organizing for Horizontal Coordination   326
   The Need for Coordination   326   ▪   Task Forces, Teams, and Project Management   327
   ▪   Reengineering   329
Factors Shaping Structure   331
   Structure Follows Strategy   332   ▪   Structure Reflects the Environment   333
   ▪   Structure Fits the Technology   335
Manager's Solution   338
Discussion Questions   339
Management in Practice: Experiential Exercise   340
Management in Practice: Ethical Dilemma   341
Cases for Critical Analysis   341
Endnotes   342

Manager's Shoptalk How
to Delegate   312

**Unlocking Innovative
Solutions Through People**
Teams Work at Imagination
Ltd.   321

New Manager Self-Test
Authority Role Models   331

New Manager Self-Test
Taking Charge of
Change 356

**Unlocking Innovative
Solutions Through People**
The Spies Who Came in
from the Cold 360

Manager's Shoptalk
Making Change Stick 366

Contents

xxvi

**Unlocking Innovative
Solutions Through
Technology** TopCoder to
the Rescue 394

New Manager Self-Test
People on the Bus 396

Manager's Shoptalk The
Right Way to Interview a Job
Applicant 398

Manager's Shoptalk
A Guide for Expatriate
Managers in America 421

New Manager Self-Test
Subtle Biases 429

**Unlocking Innovative
Solutions Through People**
Google Chow 436

11 **Managing Change and Innovation 346**

Manager's Challenge 347
Turbulent Times and the Changing Workplace 348
Changing Things: New Products and Technologies 348
  Exploration 349 ▪ Cooperation 351 ▪ Entrepreneurship 354
Changing People and Culture 357
  Training and Development 357 ▪ Organization Development 358
Model of Planned Organizational Change 362
  Forces for Change 363 ▪ Need for Change 364
Implementing Change 365
  Resistance to Change 365 ▪ Force-Field Analysis 367
  ▪ Implementation Tactics 368
Manager's Solution 371
Discussion Questions 372
Management in Practice: Experiential Exercise 372
Management in Practice: Ethical Dilemma 373
Case for Critical Analysis 374
Endnotes 374

12 **Human Resource Management 378**

Manager's Challenge 379
The Strategic Role of Human Resource Management 380
Environmental Influences on HRM 381
  Competitive Strategy 381 ▪ Federal Legislation 384
The Changing Nature of Careers 385
  The Changing Social Contract 385 ▪ HR Issues in the New Workplace 386
Attracting an Effective Workforce 389
  Human Resource Planning 390 ▪ Recruiting 391 ▪ Selecting 395
Developing an Effective Workforce 399
  Training and Development 399 ▪ Performance Appraisal 401
Maintaining an Effective Workforce 404
  Compensation 404 ▪ Benefits 406 ▪ Termination 406
Manager's Solution 407
Discussion Questions 408
Management in Practice: Experiential Exercise 409
Management in Practice: Ethical Dilemma 409
Case for Critical Analysis 410
Endnotes 411

13 **Meeting the Challenge of Diversity 414**

Manager's Challenge 415
Valuing Diversity 417
  Dimensions of Diversity 418 ▪ Attitudes Toward Diversity 419
The Changing Workplace 420
  Challenges Minorities Face 422 ▪ Management Challenges 422
Current Debates About Affirmative Action 424
The Glass Ceiling 425
  The Opt-Out Trend 426 ▪ The Female Advantage 427
Current Responses to Diversity 428
  Changing the Corporate Culture 428 ▪ Changing Structures and Policies 430
  ▪ Diversity Training 432

Defining New Relationships in Organizations   434
    Emotional Intimacy   434   ■   Sexual Harassment   434
Global Diversity   435
    Selection and Training   436   ■   Communication Differences   437
Diversity in a Turbulent World   438
    Multicultural Teams   438   ■   Employee Network Groups   439
Manager's Solution   440
Discussion Questions   441
Management in Practice: Experiential Exercise   441
Management in Practice: Ethical Dilemma   442
Case for Critical Analysis   443
Endnotes   444
CONTINUING CASE   448

PART 5   CONTROLLING   450

14   Managerial and Quality Control   452
Manager's Challenge   453
The Meaning of Control   454
Organizational Control Focus   455
    Feedforward Control   455   ■   Concurrent Control   456   ■   Feedback Control   456
Feedback Control Model   458
    Steps of Feedback Control   458   ■   Application to Budgeting   460
Financial Control   462
    Financial Statements   462   ■   Financial Analysis: Interpreting the Numbers   463
The Changing Philosophy of Control   465
Total Quality Management   468
    TQM Techniques   468   ■   TQM Success Factors   472
Trends in Quality and Financial Control   472
    International Quality Standards   473   ■   New Financial Control Systems   473
Innovative Control Systems for Turbulent Times   474
    Open-Book Management   474   ■   The Balanced Scorecard   476
    ■   New Workplace Concerns   478
Manager's Solution   479
Discussion Questions   480
Management in Practice: Experiential Exercise   481
Management in Practice: Ethical Dilemma   481
Case for Critical Analysis   482
Endnotes   483

15   Information Technology and E-Business   486
Manager's Challenge   487
Information Technology Has Changed Everything   488
    Boundaries Dissolve; Collaboration Reigns   488
    ■   People Do Better Work   489   ■   Things Are More Efficient   489
    ■   Employees Are Engaged   490   ■   People Can Suffer from Information
    Overload   491
The Evolving World of Information Technology   492
    A New Generation of IT   492   ■   Applying New IT Within Organizations   493

Manager's Shoptalk
Cyberslackers Beware: The
Boss Is Watching   457

Unlocking Innovative
Solutions Through People
Controlling With Love, Not
Fear   467

New Manager Self-Test
Freedom Versus
Regulation   469

New Manager Self-Test
Brain Hemispheric Domi-
nance   491

Manager's Shoptalk
Putting Performance
Dashboards to Work   497

Unlocking Innovative
Solutions Through People
Grant J. Hunt Co. Likes the
Personal Touch   506

Types of Information Systems   493
   Data Versus Information   494   ▪   Operations Information Systems   494
   ▪   Management Information Systems   494
The Internet and E-business   497
   E-Business Strategies   500   ▪   E-Marketplaces   503   ▪   Enterprise Resource
   Planning Systems   504   ▪   Customer Relationship Management   507   ▪   Turning
   Data and Information into Knowledge   508
Manager's Solution   510
Discussion Questions   511
Management in Practice: Experiential Exercise   511
Management in Practice: Ethical Dilemma   512
Case for Critical Analysis   513
Endnotes   514

New Manager Self-Test
Political Skills   524

Manager's Shoptalk A
German Factory Shows How
to Be Fast and Flexible   528

**Unlocking Innovative
Solutions Through
Technology** At PrairieStone
Pharmacy, Smaller Is
Better   530

16   **Operations and Value Chain Management**   516
Manager's Challenge   517
The Organization as a Value Chain   518
   Manufacturing and Service Operations   519   ▪   Operations Management and
   Competitive Strategy   520   ▪   The Integrated Enterprise   521
Designing Operations Management Systems   523
   Product and Service Design   523   ▪   Procurement   525   ▪   Facilities Layout   526
   ▪   Technology Automation   529   ▪   Facility Location   532   ▪   Capacity
   Planning   533
Inventory Management   533
   The Importance of Inventory   534   ▪   Economic Order Quantity   535
   ▪   Material Requirements Planning   536   ▪   Just-in-Time Inventory   536
   ▪   Logistics and Distribution Management   538
Lean Manufacturing and Productivity   538
   Lean Manufacturing   538   ▪   Measuring Productivity   539
   ▪   Improving Productivity   540
Manager's Solution   542
Discussion Questions   542
Management in Practice: Experiential Exercise   543
Management in Practice: Ethical Dilemma   543
Case for Critical Analysis   544
Endnotes   545
CONTINUING CASE   548

PART **6**   LEADING   550

**Unlocking Innovative
Solutions Through
Technology** Can Success
Be Guaranteed in Affairs of
the Heart?   566

New Manager Self-Test
Self-Confidence   568

Manager's Shoptalk
What's Your Crisis
EQ?   569

17   **Dynamics of Behavior in Organizations**   552
Manager's Challenge   553
Organizational Behavior   554
Attitudes   554
   Components of Attitudes   555   ▪   High-Performance Work Attitudes   557
   ▪   Conflicts Among Attitudes   559
Perception   560
   Perceptual Selectivity   560   ▪   Perceptual Distortions   561   ▪   Attributions   562
Personality and Behavior   563
   Personality Traits   564   ▪   Emotional Intelligence   565   ▪   Attitudes and Behaviors
   Influenced by Personality   567   ▪   Person–Job Fit   572

Learning 573
  The Learning Process 573 ▪ Learning Styles 574 ▪ Continuous Learning 575
Stress and Stress Management 576
  Type A and Type B Behavior 576 ▪ Causes of Work Stress 577 ▪ Innovative
  Responses to Stress Management 578
Manager's Solution 579
Discussion Questions 580
Management in Practice: Experiential Exercise 581
Management in Practice: Ethical Dilemma 584
Case for Critical Analysis 584
Endnotes 585

18 Leadership 588
Manager's Challenge 589
The Nature of Leadership 590
Leadership for Contemporary Times 590
  Level 5 Leadership 591 ▪ Women's Ways of Leading 592
Leadership Versus Management 593
Leadership Traits 594
Behavioral Approaches 595
  Ohio State Studies 595 ▪ Michigan Studies 596 ▪ The Leadership Grid 596
Contingency Approaches 598
  Hersey and Blanchard's Situational Theory 598 ▪ Fiedler's Contingency Theory 600
  ▪ Matching Leader Style to the Situation 601 ▪ Path–Goal Theory 602
  ▪ Substitutes for Leadership 604
Leading Change 605
  Charismatic and Visionary Leadership 605 ▪ Transformational Leaders 607
Power and Influence 608
  Position Power 609 ▪ Personal Power 609 ▪ Interpersonal Influence
  Tactics 610
Enduring Leadership Approaches 611
  Servant Leadership 612 ▪ Moral Leadership 612
Manager's Solution 613
Discussion Questions 614
Management in Practice: Experiential Exercise 614
Management in Practice: Ethical Dilemma 615
Case for Critical Analysis 616
Endnotes 617

19 Motivation 620
Manager's Challenge 621
The Concept of Motivation 622
Foundations of Motivation 624
  Traditional Approach 624 ▪ Human Relations Approach 624 ▪ Human
  Resource Approach 624 ▪ Contemporary Approach 624
Content Perspectives on Motivation 625
  Hierarchy of Needs Theory 625 ▪ ERG Theory 626 ▪ Two-Factor Theory 628
  ▪ Acquired Needs Theory 629
Process Perspectives on Motivation 630
  Equity Theory 630 ▪ Expectancy Theory 632 ▪ Goal-Setting Theory 633
Reinforcement Perspective on Motivation 635
  Reinforcement Tools 635 ▪ Schedules of Reinforcement 636

New Manager Self-Test
Interpersonal Patterns 593

Unlocking Innovative
Solutions Through People
The De La Salle Spartans
Win with Soul 597

Manager's Shoptalk Are
You a Charismatic
Leader? 607

New Manager Self-Test
Employee Engagement
623

Manager's Shoptalk The
Carrot-and-Stick Contro-
versy 639

Unlocking Innovative
Solutions Through People
Nucor: Giving People a
Stake in the Business 644

Job Design for Motivation 639
    Job Simplification 640 ▪ Job Rotation 640 ▪ Job Enlargement 641
    ▪ Job Enrichment 641 ▪ Job Characteristics Model 641
Innovative Ideas for Motivating 643
    Empowering People to Meet Higher Needs 645 ▪ Giving Meaning to Work 646
Manager's Solution 648
Discussion Questions 649
Management in Practice: Experiential Exercise 650
Management in Practice: Ethical Dilemma 651
Case for Critical Analysis 651
Endnotes 652

**Unlocking Innovative
Solutions Through People**
Managers at Kwik-Fit Learn
That It Pays to Listen 666

New Manager Self-Test
Personal Networking 674

Manager's Shoptalk
Leaping over Language
Barriers 682

Contents

xxx

20 **Communication 656**
Manager's Challenge 657
Communication and the Manager's Job 658
    What Is Communication? 659 ▪ The Communication Process 659
Communicating Among People 661
    Communication Channels 661 ▪ Communicating to Persuade and Influence
    Others 663 ▪ Nonverbal Communication 664 ▪ Listening 665
Organizational Communication 668
    Formal Communication Channels 668 ▪ Team Communication Channels 672
    ▪ Personal Communication Channels 673
Communicating During Turbulent Times 677
    Open Communication 677 ▪ Dialogue 678 ▪ Crisis Communication 679
    ▪ Feedback and Learning 679
Managing Organizational Communication 680
    Barriers to Communication 681 ▪ Overcoming Communication Barriers 682
Manager's Solution 684
Discussion Questions 685
Management in Practice: Experiential Exercise 685
Management in Practice: Ethical Dilemma 686
Case for Critical Analysis 687
Endnotes 688

**Unlocking Innovative
Solutions Through
Technology** MySQL:
Creating a Twenty-
First–Century Global
Team 701

New Manager Self-Test
Managing Conflict 713

Manager's Shoptalk
How to Run a Great
Meeting 718

21 **Teamwork 692**
Manager's Challenge 693
Teams at Work 694
    What Is a Team? 694 ▪ Model of Work Team Effectiveness 695
Types of Teams 696
    Formal Teams 696 ▪ Self-Directed Teams 698
    ▪ Teams in the New Workplace 699
Team Characteristics 702
    Size 702 ▪ Diversity 703 ▪ Member Roles 703
Team Processes 705
    Stages of Team Development 705 ▪ Team Cohesiveness 707
    ▪ Team Norms 709
Managing Team Conflict 711
    Balancing Conflict and Cooperation 711 ▪ Causes of Conflict 712 ▪ Styles to
    Handle Conflict 713 ▪ Negotiation 715
Work Team Effectiveness 717
    Productive Output 717 ▪ Satisfaction of Members 717 ▪ Capacity to Adapt
    and Learn 719

Manager's Solution   719
Discussion Questions   720
Management in Practice: Experiential Exercise   720
Management in Practice: Ethical Dilemma   721
Case for Critical Analysis   722
Endnotes   723
CONTINUING CASE   726

Appendix: Video Case Library   728
Glossary   778
Indexes   791

NEW ERA OF MANAGEMENT

RICHARD L. DAFT

Vanderbilt University

PART 1

INTRODUCTION TO MANAGEMENT

Innovation can be used to adapt changes, such as new materials, ideas, or fashions, to shifting needs and to bring those components into harmony. Of the countless changes that came from the Industrial Revolution, cast iron emerged as a new alternative to wood or stone, which made it possible to build tall structures with thin walls. This, in turn, led Sir Joseph Paxton to design the Crystal Palace, a building with a frame of cast iron and walls of glass to house the Great Exhibition of 1851. The first of its kind, the Crystal Palace was considered by many to be a symbol of modernity and civilization.

Architecture is a blend of art and science, and since the time of Caesar Augustus it has been held that a structure must have "firmness, commodity, and delight," also commonly known as fit, function, and form. Firmness is typically understood to mean a structure's stability; commodity or value pertains to how well a structure performs its function. Delight is commonly understood as the structure's aesthetics: It must be pleasing to the eye, as well as the other senses, in the context of its use.

Management can be judged by much the same standards. Whether small or large, a whole company or simply one department, proper management will result in a business that is structurally fit, functions as intended, and is a desirable place to work or conduct business.

There is not one particular step where the architect or the manager concentrates on firmness, another for commodity, and another for delight. All stages and aspects must be considered because they are mutually intertwined, not mutually exclusive. A structure without firmness will by nature lack commodity and, lacking both, not long hold delight. A business that does not produce will not be stable, and the uncertainty and stress will not create a desirable place to work or do business. Bringing these three qualities into balance requires imagination, innovation, and adaptation.

CHAPTER 1

CHAPTER OUTLINE

Manager's Challenge

The Definition of Management

The Four Management Functions

Planning

Organizing

Leading

Controlling

Organizational Performance

Management Skills

Conceptual Skills

Human Skills

Technical Skills

When Skills Fail

Management Types

Vertical Differences

Horizontal Differences

What Is It Like to Be a Manager?

Making the Leap: Becoming
  a New Manager

Manager Activities

Manager Roles

**Managing in Small Businesses and
Nonprofit Organizations**

Management and the New Workplace

Forces on Organizations

The Innovative Response

New Management Competencies

Turbulent Times: Managing Crises
  and Unexpected Events

LEARNING OBJECTIVES

After studying this chapter, you should be able to:

1. Describe the four management functions and the type of management activity associated with each.

2. Explain the difference between efficiency and effectiveness and their importance for organizational performance.

3. Describe management types and the horizontal and vertical differences between them.

4. Describe conceptual, human, and technical skills and their relevance for managers and employees.

5. Define 10 roles that managers perform in organizations.

6. Understand the personal challenges involved in becoming a new manager in an organization in today's world.

7. Discuss the management competencies needed to deal with today's turbulent environment, including issues such as diversity, globalization, and rapid change.

8. Explain the leadership skills needed for effective crisis management.

INNOVATIVE MANAGEMENT FOR TURBULENT TIMES

MANAGER'S CHALLENGE

Imagine that you are a mid-level marketing manager at a public utilities company. One day you're reviewing next year's advertising campaign. A day later, you're responsible for coordinating the feeding, housing, and health care of 11,000 repair workers from around the country. That's the situation Melvin Wilson, a marketing manager for Mississippi Power, found himself in when Hurricane Katrina hit the state in August 2005, wiping out 1,000 miles of power lines, destroying 65 percent of the company's transmission and distribution facilities, damaging 300 transmission towers, and knocking out power for all 195,000 customers. The company had a disaster recovery plan in place, but managers were suddenly thrust into a situation that was twice as bad as the worst case scenario. Mississippi Power's corporate headquarters was totally destroyed, its disaster response center flooded and useless. Early recovery work had to be done without access to computers, phones, or basic sanitary facilities. Confusion and chaos reigned. "My day job did not prepare me for this," Wilson told a reporter in a choked voice as he struggled to find nurses, beds, tetanus shots, laundry service, showers, security services, and food for repair workers. Other managers, from all levels and divisions, were dealing with similar predicaments. One compared the process to managing an Army division at war. Amazingly, Mississippi Power employees got the job done smoothly and efficiently, restoring power in just 12 days, thus meeting the bold target of getting power back on by the symbolic date of September 11. The tale of how they did it is one of the great crisis management stories of modern times, and a lesson for managers in how much can be accomplished quickly when it's managed right.[1]

■ TAKE A MOMENT

Think about the situation Melvin Wilson and other managers at Mississippi Power were in and try to imagine what you would do. What management style and systems do you think would enable the kind of rapid, flexible response needed to accomplish seemingly impossible goals amid chaos and confusion? Jot down two or three elements that you think might play a role in this success story.

In today's turbulent world, managing in times of crisis and confusion is becoming a critical skill for managers in all kinds of organizations, not just companies that have to get the power back on after a hurricane. Certainly, the example of Mississippi Power is exceptional, but many managers deal with uncertainty and crisis to a lesser extent on an almost daily basis. Consider the strife and confusion in the music industry, where traditional recording labels and music stores are battling with the iPod and with online file sharing services that let people download music for free. The once-hot Tower Records declared bankruptcy due to the steep decline in music sales through traditional stores.[2] Managers in all organizations deal with uncertainty and unexpected events, whether it is something as small as the loss of a key employee or something as large and dramatic as a plant explosion. Moreover, the frequency and intensity of crises have increased over the past couple of decades, with a sharp increase in the rate of intentional acts such as product tampering, workplace violence, or terrorism.[3] Solid management skills and actions are the key to helping any organization weather a crisis and remain healthy, inspired, and productive.

The nature of management is to cope with diverse and far-reaching challenges. Managers have to keep pace with ever-advancing technology, find ways to incorporate the Internet and e-business into their strategies and business models, and strive to remain competitive in the face of increasingly tough global competition, uncertain environments, cutbacks in personnel and resources, and massive worldwide economic, political, and social shifts. The growing clout, expertise, and efficiency of China and India, in particular, have many U.S. companies worried. To gain or keep a competitive edge, companies have renewed their emphasis on innovation, shifting away from a relentless focus on controlling costs toward investing in the future. In a recent survey of nearly 1,000 executives in North America, Europe, South America, and Asia, 86 percent agreed that "innovation is more important than cost reduction for long-term success."[4]

The shift toward new ways of working, enabled by technology, puts additional demands on today's managers. Many employees are always on the move, juggling laptops, mobile phones, and Blackberrys to keep in electronic touch with customers, teammates, and managers who may have limited face-to-face contact. In the new world of work, managers need a new approach that relies less on command and control and more on coordination and communication. The field of management is undergoing a revolution that asks managers to do more with less, to engage whole employees, to see change rather than stability as the nature of things, and to inspire vision and cultural values that allow people to create a truly collaborative and productive workplace. This approach differs significantly from a traditional mind-set that emphasizes tight top-down control, employee separation and specialization, and management by impersonal measurement and analysis.

Making a difference as a manager today and tomorrow requires integrating solid, tried-and-true management skills with innovative approaches that emphasize the human touch, enhance flexibility, and engage employees' hearts and minds as well as their bodies. Successful departments and organizations don't just happen—they are managed to be that way. For example, the success of rock groups from the Rolling Stones to U2 to Green Day relies not just on good songs, musical talent, and performance skills but also on solid business management. "We always said it would be pathetic to be good at the music and bad at the business," said Paul McGuinness, U2's band manager. The Irish rock band is still selling out concerts and moving millions of albums a year after nearly three decades by paying attention to some business basics, such as forming a partnership with Apple for a special edition iPod and collaborating with iTunes to produce the industry's first downloadable version of a box set.[5] Managers in every organization have the opportunity to make a difference. Heather Coin made a difference at the Sherman Oaks, California, branch of The Cheesecake Factory when she implemented management changes that reduced turnover from 25 percent to below 10 percent and dramatically increased customer traffic to serve as many as 16,000 customers a week.[6]

Managers like Heather Coin and Paul McGuinness are not unusual. Every day, managers solve difficult problems, turn organizations around, and achieve astonishing performances. To be successful, every organization needs skilled managers.

This textbook introduces and explains the process of management and the changing ways of thinking

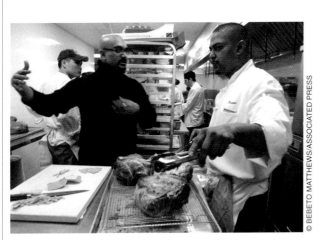

© BEBETO MATTHEWS/ASSOCIATED PRESS

CONCEPT
CONNECTION If there was ever a business that emerged out of crisis, it is New York City's Colors, a project of the Restaurant Opportunities Center. Many of the restaurant's employee-owners, immigrants hailing from about 25 different nations, worked in the World Trade Center's North Tower Windows on the World restaurant before its destruction on September 11, 2001. They share a strong commitment to a mission of honoring the 73 Windows employees who died, and improving the restaurant industry's working conditions. Yet, it still takes **good management** to keep people motivated, focused, and productive. General manager Stefan Mailvaganam, shown here with head chef Raymond Mohan, says the goal of Colors is to be "a restaurant with a conscience."

about the world that are becoming critical for managers of today and tomorrow. By reviewing the actions of some successful and not-so-successful managers, you will learn the fundamentals of management. By the end of this chapter, you will already recognize some of the skills managers use to keep organizations on track, and you will begin to understand how managers such as those at Mississippi Power can achieve astonishing results through people. By the end of this book, you will understand fundamental management skills for planning, organizing, leading, and controlling a department or an entire organization. In the remainder of this chapter, we will define management and look at the ways in which roles and activities are changing for today's managers. The final section of the chapter talks about a new kind of workplace that has evolved as a result of changes in technology, globalization, and other forces, and examines how managers can meet the challenges of this new environment.

THE DEFINITION OF MANAGEMENT

What do managers such as Melvin Wilson, Heather Coin, and Paul McGuinness have in common? They get things done through their organizations. Managers create the systems, conditions, and environment that enable organizations to survive and thrive beyond the tenure of any specific supervisor or manager. Jack Welch was CEO of General Electric through 20 amazingly successful years, and some observers worried that GE would falter without him. Yet the leadership transition to Jeff Immelt in 2001 was as smooth as silk, and in 2005–2006 GE once again topped *Fortune* magazine's list of "Most Admired Companies," as well as ranking number one on the *Financial Times* "most respected" survey, and *Barron's* ranking of most admired companies. People who have studied GE aren't surprised. The company has thrived for more than a century because managers throughout the years created the right environment and conditions: a shared sense of purpose and pride, a passion for change and willingness to take risks, and most importantly an obsession with people and making them the best they can be. The obsession with developing leaders at all levels began in the late 1800s with CEO Charles Coffin, who emphasized that GE's most important product was not lightbulbs or transformers, but managerial talent. Every manager at GE is required to spend a huge amount of time on human resources issues—recruiting, training, appraising, mentoring, and developing leadership talent for the future.[7]

A key aspect of managing is recognizing the role and importance of other people. Early twentieth-century management scholar Mary Parker Follett defined management as "the art of getting things done through people."[8] More recently, noted management theorist Peter Drucker stated that the job of managers is to give direction to their organizations, provide leadership, and decide how to use organizational resources to accomplish goals.[9] Getting things done through people and other resources and providing leadership and direction are what managers do. These activities apply not only to top executives such as Bill Gates of Microsoft or Steve Jobs of Apple, but also to the leader of an airport security team, a supervisor of an accounting department, or a director of sales and marketing. Moreover, management often is considered universal because it uses organizational resources to accomplish goals and attain high performance in all types of profit and nonprofit organizations. Thus, our definition of management is as follows:

> **Management** is the attainment of organizational goals in an effective and efficient manner through planning, organizing, leading, and controlling organizational resources.

This definition holds two important ideas: (1) the four functions of planning, organizing, leading, and controlling, and (2) the attainment of organizational goals in an effective and efficient manner. Managers use a multitude of skills to perform these functions. Management's conceptual, human, and technical skills are discussed later in the chapter. Exhibit 1.1 illustrates the process of how managers use resources to attain organizational goals. Although some management theorists identify additional

management The attainment of organizational goals in an effective and efficient manner through planning, organizing, leading, and controlling organizational resources.

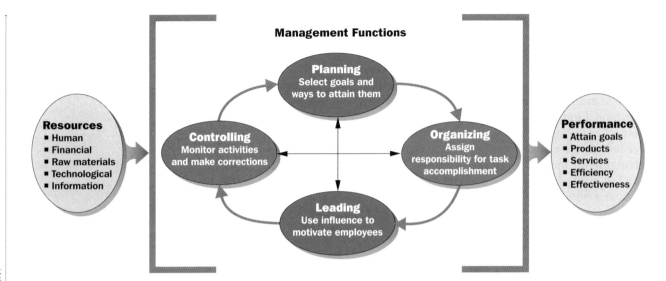

Management Functions

Planning
Select goals and
ways to attain them

Resources
- Human
- Financial
- Raw materials
- Technological
- Information

Controlling
Monitor activities
and make corrections

Organizing
Assign
responsibility for task
accomplishment

Leading
Use influence to
motivate employees

Performance
- Attain goals
- Products
- Services
- Efficiency
- Effectiveness

E X H I B I T   1.1

The Process of
Management

management functions, such as staffing, communicating, or decision making, those additional functions will be discussed as subsets of the four primary functions in Exhibit 1.1. Chapters of this book are devoted to the multiple activities and skills associated with each function, as well as to the environment, global competitiveness, and ethics, which influence how managers perform these functions. The next section begins with a brief overview of the four functions.

■ TAKE A MOMENT

As a new manager, remember that management means getting things done through other people. You can't do it all yourself. As a manager, your job is to create the environment and conditions that engage other people in goal accomplishment.

THE FOUR MANAGEMENT FUNCTIONS

Planning

Planning defines where the organization wants to be in the future and how to get there. **Planning** means defining goals for future organizational performance and deciding on the tasks and use of resources needed to attain them. At Time Warner, Inc., the marketing chiefs of the various divisions—HBO, Time Inc., Turner Broadcasting, Warner Bros., AOL, New Line Cinema, and Time Warner Cable—get together every three weeks to talk about future projects and how the divisions can work together to make them more successful. Thanks to careful planning, for example, almost every division was involved in promoting the final film in *The Lord of the Rings* trilogy.[10]

A lack of planning—or poor planning—can hurt an organization's performance. For example, despite a cult-like following, Krispy Kreme Doughnuts is struggling to survive as a result of poor planning. Top managers' lack of vision in perceiving market direction and weak planning efforts regarding rapid expansion and franchisee relationships has seriously damaged the once successful firm.[11]

Organizing

Organizing typically follows planning and reflects how the organization tries to accomplish the plan. **Organizing** involves assigning tasks, grouping tasks into departments, delegating authority, and allocating resources across the organization. Organizations as diverse as IBM, the Catholic Church, Microsoft, Motorola, and the Federal Bureau of Investigation have all undergone structural reorganizations to

planning The management function concerned with defining goals for future organizational performance and deciding on the tasks and resources needed to attain them.

organizing The management function concerned with assigning tasks, grouping tasks into departments, and allocating resources to departments.

accommodate their changing plans. Voyant Technologies, a maker of teleconferencing equipment, revised its structure to meet goals of increased sales and faster product development. By creating a new position specifically to bridge the gap between product managers and engineers, Voyant realized a 25 percent increase in sales, a 20 percent reduction in development costs, and a 40 percent improvement in time to market.[12]

Leading

Leading is the use of influence to motivate employees to achieve organizational goals. Leading means creating a shared culture and values, communicating goals to employees throughout the organization, and infusing employees with the desire to perform at a high level. Leading involves motivating entire departments and divisions as well as those individuals working immediately with the manager. In an era of uncertainty, global competition, and a growing diversity of the workforce, the ability to shape culture, communicate goals, and motivate employees is critical to business success.

One doesn't have to be a well-known top manager such as Michael Dell of Dell Inc. or Meg Whitman of eBay to be an exceptional leader. Many managers working quietly in both large and small organizations around the world also provide strong leadership within departments, teams, nonprofit organizations, and small businesses. Cara Kakuda is an area general manager in Hawaii for Nextel Partners, the rural-market division of Nextel Communications. Only eight other people nationwide hold that title, which Kakuda was awarded because of her ability to motivate people. "Cara's people give her 150 percent," said a Nextel executive. "When someone believes in you, it makes you want to work harder, and Cara does that for her people."[13] Greg Mortenson runs the Central Asia Institute, a nonprofit organization he founded to promote secular education for girls in northern Pakistan and neighboring Afghanistan. Mortensen's vision, determination, courage, and enthusiasm encouraged others to join him in this innovative long-term approach to fighting terrorism.[14]

CONCEPT CONNECTION PaeTec Communications provides voice and data services for mid-sized businesses. The company has increased to more than 1,000 employees while most telecommunications businesses have struggled. This dramatic growth is the result, in part, of a corporate culture that revolves around respect for employees. CEO Arunas Chesonis believes in **leading** PaeTec by putting employees first and then watching those employees voluntarily put customers before themselves. Placing high value on employees is successful for the company: although dealing with 4,000 problem calls a month, the company always answers the phone by the second ring, and the monthly customer retention rate is 99.5% or better since the company was founded in 1998. Every Friday morning, Chesonis demonstrates employee value by communicating with half of his employees.

Controlling

Controlling is the fourth function in the management process. **Controlling** means monitoring employees' activities, determining whether the organization is on target toward its goals, and making corrections as necessary. Managers must ensure that the organization is moving toward its goals. Trends toward empowerment and trust of employees have led many companies to place less emphasis on top-down control and more emphasis on training employees to monitor and correct themselves.

Information technology is also helping managers provide needed organizational control without strict top-down constraints. Companies such as Cisco Systems and Oracle use the Internet and other information technology to coordinate and monitor virtually every aspect of operations, which enables managers to keep tabs on performance without maintaining daily authoritarian control over employees. Cisco employees have amazing freedom to make decisions and take action, but they also know that top managers keep a close eye on what's going on throughout the company with just a few mouse clicks.[15]

leading The management function that involves the use of influence to motivate employees to achieve the organization's goals.

controlling The management function concerned with monitoring employees' activities, keeping the organization on track toward its goals, and making corrections as needed.

Organization failure can result when managers are not serious about control or lack control information. Particularly in turbulent times, managers need effective control systems to help them make fast, difficult decisions.

ORGANIZATIONAL PERFORMANCE

The other part of our definition of management is the attainment of organizational goals in an efficient and effective manner. Management is so important because organizations are so important. In an industrialized society where complex technologies dominate, organizations bring together knowledge, people, and raw materials to perform tasks no individual could do alone. Without organizations, how could technology be provided that enables us to share information around the world in an instant; electricity be produced from huge dams and nuclear power plants; and thousands of videogames, compact discs, and DVDs be made available for our entertainment? Organizations pervade our society. Most college students will work in an organization—perhaps Cingular Wireless, Toronto General Hospital, Office Depot, or Hollywood Video. College students already are members of several organizations, such as a university, junior college, YMCA, church, fraternity, or sorority. College students also deal with organizations every day: to renew a driver's license, be treated in a hospital emergency room, buy food from a supermarket, eat in a restaurant, or buy new clothes. Managers are responsible for these organizations and for seeing that resources are used wisely to attain organizational goals.

Our formal definition of an **organization** is a social entity that is goal directed and deliberately structured. *Social entity* means being made up of two or more people. *Goal directed* means designed to achieve some outcome, such as make a profit (Old Navy, Starbucks), win pay increases for members (AFL-CIO), meet spiritual needs (United Methodist Church), or provide social satisfaction (college sorority). *Deliberately structured* means that tasks are divided and responsibility for their performance is assigned to organization members. This definition applies to all organizations, including both profit and nonprofit. Small, offbeat, and nonprofit organizations are more numerous than large, visible corporations—and just as important to society.

Based on our definition of management, the manager's responsibility is to coordinate resources in an effective and efficient manner to accomplish the organization's goals. Organizational **effectiveness** is the degree to which the organization achieves a *stated goal*, or succeeds in accomplishing what it tries to do. Organizational effectiveness means providing a product or service that customers value. Organizational **efficiency** refers to the amount of resources used to achieve an organizational goal. It is based on how much raw materials, money, and people are necessary for producing a given volume of output. Efficiency can be calculated as the amount of resources used to produce a product or service.

Efficiency and effectiveness can both be high in the same organization. During the tough economy of the early 2000s, companies such as Eaton Corporation, which makes hydraulic and electrical devices, struggled to wring as much production as they could from scaled-back factories and a reduced workforce. Managers initiated process improvements, outsourced some work to companies that could do it cheaper, streamlined ordering and shipping procedures, and shifted work to the most efficient assembly lines. At Eaton, these adjustments enabled the company to cut costs and hold the line on prices as well as meet its quality and output goals.[16]

Sometimes, however, managers' efforts to improve efficiency can hurt organizational effectiveness, especially in relation to severe cost cutting. Some years ago, a former CEO at Delta Airlines dramatically increased cost efficiency by cutting spending on personnel, food, cleaning, and maintenance. The moves temporarily rescued the company from a financial tailspin, but they also precluded Delta from meeting its effectiveness goals. The airline fell to last place among major carriers in on-time performance, the morale of employees sank, and customer complaints about dirty planes and long lines at ticket counters increased by more than 75 percent.[17]

organization A social entity that is goal directed and deliberately structured.

effectiveness The degree to which the organization achieves a stated goal.

efficiency The use of minimal resources—raw materials, money, and people—to produce a desired volume of output.

The ultimate responsibility of managers is to achieve high **performance**, which is the attainment of organizational goals by using resources in an efficient and effective manner.

MANAGEMENT SKILLS

A manager's job is complex and multidimensional and, as we shall see throughout this book, requires a range of skills. Although some management theorists propose a long list of skills, the necessary skills for managing a department or an organization can be summarized in three categories: conceptual, human, and technical.[18] As illustrated in Exhibit 1.2, the application of these skills changes as managers move up in the organization. Although the degree of each skill necessary at different levels of an organization may vary, all managers must possess skills in each of these important areas to perform effectively.

Conceptual Skills

Conceptual skill is the cognitive ability to see the organization as a whole and the relationships among its parts. Conceptual skill involves the manager's thinking, information processing, and planning abilities. It involves knowing where one's department fits into the total organization and how the organization fits into the industry, the community, and the broader business and social environment. It means the ability to *think strategically*—to take the broad, long-term view.

Conceptual skills are needed by all managers but are especially important for managers at the top. They must perceive significant elements in a situation and broad, conceptual patterns. For example, recent strategic changes at General Electric reflect the conceptual skills of CEO Jeffrey Immelt. Immelt is remaking GE by thinking on a broad, long-term scale about the types of products and services people around the world are going to need in the future. Immelt is pushing for growth by investing heavily in basic scientific and technological research, looking toward the needs of developing countries, and making structural and cultural changes that focus GE toward creating innovative products and services to meet shifting customer needs.[19]

As managers move up the hierarchy, they must develop conceptual skills or their promotability will be limited. A senior engineering manager who is mired in technical matters rather than thinking strategically will not perform well at the top of the organization. Many of the responsibilities of top managers, such as decision making, resource allocation, and innovation, require a broad view.

Human Skills

Human skill is the manager's ability to work with and through other people and to work effectively as a group member. This skill is demonstrated in the way a manager relates to other people, including the ability to motivate, facilitate, coordinate, lead, communicate, and resolve conflicts. A manager with human skills allows subordinates to express themselves without fear of ridicule and encourages participation.

performance The organization's ability to attain its goals by using resources in an efficient and effective manner.

conceptual skill The cognitive ability to see the organization as a whole and the relationships among its parts.

human skill The ability to work with and through other people and to work effectively as a group member.

EXHIBIT 1.2

Relationship of Conceptual, Human, and Technical Skills to Management

Management Level

Top Managers

Middle Managers

First-Line Managers

Nonmanagers (Individual Contributors)

A manager with human skills likes other people and is liked by them. Heather Coin, the restaurant manager we introduced earlier in this chapter, has exceptional human skills. Coin considers motivating and praising her staff a top priority. "I really try to seek out moments because it's so hard to," she says. "You could definitely go for days without doing it. You have to consciously make that decision [to show appreciation]."[20]

As globalization, workforce diversity, uncertainty, and societal turbulence increase, human skills become even more crucial. In the past, many CEOs could get by without good people skills, but no longer. Today's employees, boards, customers, and communities are demanding that top executives demonstrate an ability to inspire respect, loyalty, and even affection rather than fear. "People are expecting more from the companies they're working for, more from the companies they're doing business with, and more from the companies they're buying from," says Raj Sisodia, a professor of marketing at Bentley College and co-author of a recent book called *Firms of Endearment*.[21] Consider Jeffrey Swartz, CEO of Timberland, who emphasizes the importance of having "real relationships" with employees. As the company has grown larger, Swartz has resisted the temptation to hold huge sales meetings to save time. "You've got to look the other person in the eye. Now that [the company] is 5,000 employees, I've gotta do the meeting ten times."[22] Human skills are important for managers at all levels, and particularly for those who work with employees directly on a daily basis. Organizations frequently lose good employees because of front-line bosses who fail to show respect and concern for workers.[23]

Technical Skills

Technical skill is the understanding of and proficiency in the performance of specific tasks. Technical skill includes mastery of the methods, techniques, and equipment involved in specific functions such as engineering, manufacturing, or finance. Technical skill also includes specialized knowledge, analytical ability, and the competent use of tools and techniques to solve problems in that specific discipline. Technical skills are particularly important at lower organizational levels. Many managers get promoted to their first management jobs by having excellent technical skills. However, technical skills become less important than human and conceptual skills as managers move up the hierarchy. For example, in his seven years as a manufacturing engineer at Boeing, Bruce Moravec developed superb technical skills in his area of operation. But when he was asked to lead the team designing a new fuselage for the Boeing 757, Moravec found that he needed to rely heavily on human skills in order to gain the respect and confidence of people who worked in areas he knew little about.[24]

■ **TAKE A MOMENT**   Complete the experiential exercise on page 31 that pertains to management skills. Reflect on the strength of your preferences among the three skills and the implications for you as a manager.

When Skills Fail

During turbulent times, managers really have to stay on their toes and use all their skills and competencies to benefit the organization and its stakeholders—employees, customers, investors, the community, and so forth. In recent years, numerous, highly publicized examples showed us what happens when managers fail to effectively and ethically apply their skills to meet the demands of an uncertain, rapidly changing world. Companies such as Enron, Tyco, and WorldCom were flying high in the 1990s but came crashing down under the weight of financial scandals. Others, such as Rubbermaid, Kmart, and Xerox, are struggling because of years of management missteps.

technical skill The understanding of and proficiency in the performance of specific tasks.

Although corporate greed and deceit grab the headlines, many more companies falter or fail less spectacularly. Managers fail to listen to customers, misinterpret signals from the marketplace, or can't build a cohesive team and execute a strategic plan. Over the past several years, numerous CEOs, including Carly Fiorina at Hewlett-Packard, Michael Eisner at Disney, and David Pottruck at Charles Schwab Corp., have been ousted due to their failure to implement their strategic plans and improve business results.

Recent examinations of struggling organizations and executives offer a glimpse into the mistakes managers often make in a turbulent environment.[25] Perhaps the biggest blunder is managers' failure to comprehend and adapt to the rapid pace of change in the world around them. For example, even though Xerox's PARC research center practically invented the personal computer, top managers resisted getting into the computer business until it was too late to even get in the game, much less have a chance at winning. A related problem is top managers who create a climate of fear in the organization, so that people are afraid to tell the truth. Thus, bad news gets hidden and important signals from the marketplace are missed.

CONCEPT

C O N N E C T I O N When Google needed a top manager capable of turning the dazzling start-up into a profitable corporation, it knew just where to look. With a computer science Ph.D. from UC Berkeley and work experience at Xerox PARC, Bell Labs, and Sun Microsystems, Eric Schmidt has the **technical skills** to keep Google producing cutting-edge products. As the CEO who engineered a turnaround at Novell, a $1 billion software firm, he has demonstrated the **conceptual skills** a complex, fast-growing company needs. At Google, chairman and CEO Schmidt works with co-founders Sergey Brin and Larry Page to strike the right balance between innovation and discipline. "I keep things focused," he explains.

Other critical management missteps include poor communication skills and failure to listen; treating people only as instruments to be used; suppressing dissenting viewpoints; and the inability to build a management team characterized by mutual trust and respect.[26] The financial scandals of the early twenty-first century, from Enron to mutual fund mismanagement, clearly show what can happen, for instance, when top managers pay more attention to money and Wall Street than they do to their employees and customers. As another example, consider what happened at *The New York Times* when it became publicly known that Jayson Blair, a rising young reporter, had fabricated and plagiarized many of his stories. Only then did top executives acknowledge the pervasive unhappiness that existed in the newsroom. Executive editor Howell Raines, who had created an environment that favored certain editors and reporters, while others were afraid to offer dissenting viewpoints or tell their managers the truth, resigned under pressure following the scandal. The *Times* is still struggling to regain its footing and reclaim its honorable image.[27]

MANAGEMENT TYPES

Managers use conceptual, human, and technical skills to perform the four management functions of planning, organizing, leading, and controlling in all organizations—large and small, manufacturing and service, profit and nonprofit, traditional and Internet-based. But not all managers' jobs are the same. Managers are responsible for different departments, work at different levels in the hierarchy, and meet different requirements for achieving high performance. Twenty-five-year-old Daniel Wheeler is a fist-line manager in his first management job at Del Monte Foods, where he is directly involved in promoting products, approving packaging sleeves, and organizing sampling events.[28] Kevin Kurtz is a middle manager at Lucasfilm, where he works with employees to develop marketing campaigns for some of the entertainment company's hottest films.[29] Domenic Antonellis is CEO of the New England Confectionary Co. (Necco), the company that makes those tiny pastel candy hearts stamped with phrases such as "Be Mine" and "Kiss Me."[30] All three are managers and must contribute to planning, organizing, leading, and controlling their organizations—but in different amounts and ways.

EXHIBIT 1.3

Management Levels in the
Organizational Hierarchy

SOURCE: Adapted from
Thomas V. Bonoma and
Joseph C. Lawler, "Chutes
and Ladders: Growing the
General Manager," *Sloan
Management Review* (Spring
1989), 27–37.

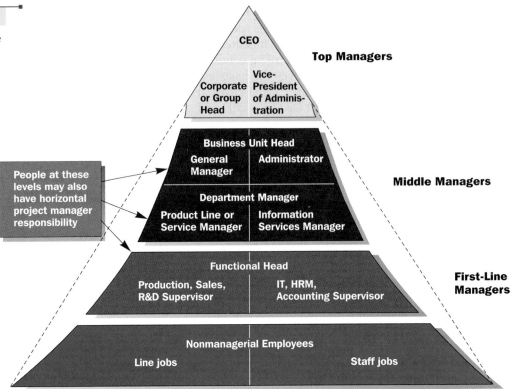

People at these
levels may also
have horizontal
project manager
responsibility

CEO

Top Managers

Corporate or Group Head | Vice-President of Administration

Business Unit Head
General Manager | Administrator

Middle Managers

Department Manager
Product Line or Service Manager | Information Services Manager

Functional Head
Production, Sales, R&D Supervisor | IT, HRM, Accounting Supervisor

First-Line Managers

Nonmanagerial Employees
Line jobs | Staff jobs

Vertical Differences

An important determinant of the manager's job is hierarchical level. Three levels in the hierarchy are illustrated in Exhibit 1.3. **Top managers** are at the top of the hierarchy and are responsible for the entire organization. They have such titles as president, chairperson, executive director, chief executive officer (CEO), and executive vice president. Top managers are responsible for setting organizational goals, defining strategies for achieving them, monitoring and interpreting the external environment, and making decisions that affect the entire organization. They look to the long-term future and concern themselves with general environmental trends and the organization's overall success. Among the most important responsibilities for top managers are communicating a shared vision for the organization, shaping corporate culture, and nurturing an entrepreneurial spirit that can help the company innovate and keep pace with rapid change. Today more than ever before, top managers must engage the unique knowledge, skills, and capabilities of each employee.[31]

Middle managers work at middle levels of the organization and are responsible for business units and major departments. Examples of middle managers are department head, division head, manager of quality control, and director of the research lab. Middle managers typically have two or more management levels beneath them. They are responsible for implementing the overall strategies and policies defined by top managers. Middle managers generally are concerned with the near future rather than with long-range planning.

The middle manager's job has changed dramatically over the past two decades. Many organizations improved efficiency by laying off middle managers and slashing middle management levels. Traditional pyramidal organization charts were flattened to allow information to flow quickly from top to bottom and decisions to be made with greater speed. The shrinking middle management is illustrated in Exhibit 1.3.

Even as middle management levels have been reduced, however, the middle manager's job in many organizations has become much more vital. Rather than managing the flow of information up and down the hierarchy, middle managers create horizontal networks that can help the organization act quickly. Research shows, for example, that middle managers play a critical role in driving innovation

top manager A manager who is at the top of the organizational hierarchy and is responsible for the entire organization.

middle manager A manager who works at the middle levels of the organization and is responsible for major departments.

and enabling organizations to respond to rapid shifts in the environment.[32] As Ralph Stayer, CEO of Johnsonville Sausage said, "Leaders can design wonderful strategies, but the success of the organization resides in the execution of those strategies. The people in the middle are the ones who make it work."[33] People who succeed as middle managers in today's world are those who are constructively critical of the status quo, have a high degree of personal power based on good relationships throughout the organization, are versatile and adaptable, and possess solid interpersonal skills, including the ability to empathize with others and help others grow and excel.[34]

The value of today's middle manager has become evident in organizations that have suffered major crises, where middle managers mobilized employees and successfully executed disaster plans or took it upon themselves to perform amazing acts that helped the organization get up and running again. Consider Jack McCracken, a chief engineer with Norfolk Southern, who put together a team of employees and outside experts to rescue five miles of railroad track that had ripped off a bridge connecting New Orleans and Slidell, Louisiana, during Hurricane Katrina. McCracken knew that without that five miles, his company wouldn't be able to transport goods from the East Coast to western states.[35]

Middle managers' status has also escalated because of the growing use of teams and projects in today's organizations. Strong project managers are in hot demand. A **project manager** is responsible for a temporary work project that involves the participation of people from various functions and levels of the organization, and perhaps from outside the company as well. Minnie Ingersoll works as a project manager for Google, where she coordinates activities between the advertising, finance, and engineering departments.[36] Today's middle manager might work with a variety of projects and teams at the same time, some of which cross geographical and cultural as well as functional boundaries.

Another trend is using *interim managers*, which means hiring temporary management professionals who work on a specific project or provide expertise in a specific area.[37] This approach enables a company to benefit from specialist skills without making a long-term commitment, and it provides flexibility for managers who like the challenge, variety, and learning that comes from working in a wide range of organizations. Even though interim managers are used at all levels, they can be particularly valuable for middle management activities.

First-line managers are directly responsible for the production of goods and services. They are the first or second level of management and have such titles as supervisor, line manager, section chief, and office manager. They are responsible for groups of nonmanagement employees. Their primary concern is the application of rules and procedures to achieve efficient production, provide technical assistance, and motivate subordinates. The time horizon at this level is short, with the emphasis on accomplishing day-to-day goals. For example, Alistair Boot manages the menswear department for a John Lewis department store in Cheadle, England.[38] Boot's duties include monitoring and supervising shop floor employees to make sure sales procedures, safety rules, and customer service policies are followed. This type of managerial job might also involve motivating and guiding young, often inexperienced workers, providing assistance as needed, and ensuring adherence to company policies.

Horizontal Differences

The other major difference in management jobs occurs horizontally across the organization. **Functional managers** are responsible for departments that perform a single functional task and have employees with similar training and skills. Functional departments include advertising, sales, finance, human resources, manufacturing, and accounting. Line managers are responsible for the manufacturing and marketing departments that make or sell the product or service. Staff managers are in charge of departments such as finance and human resources that support line departments.

project manager A manager responsible for a temporary work project that involves the participation of other people from various functions and levels of the organization.

first-line manager A manager who is at the first or second management level and is directly responsible for the production of goods and services.

functional manager A manager who is responsible for a department that performs a single functional task and has employees with similar training and skills.

General managers are responsible for several departments that perform different functions. A general manager is responsible for a self-contained division, such as a Macy's department store or a General Motors assembly plant, and for all the functional departments within it. Project managers also have general management responsibility, because they coordinate people across several departments to accomplish a specific project.

WHAT IS IT LIKE TO BE A MANAGER?

So far we have described how managers at various levels perform four basic functions that help ensure that organizational resources are used to attain high levels of performance. These tasks require conceptual, human, and technical skills, which are today being applied in a turbulent environment for many managers. Unless someone has actually performed managerial work, it is hard to understand exactly what managers do on an hour-by-hour, day-to-day basis. The manager's job is so diverse that a number of studies have been undertaken in an attempt to describe exactly what happens. The question of what managers actually do to plan, organize, lead, and control was answered by Henry Mintzberg, who followed managers around and recorded all their activities.[39] He developed a description of managerial work that included three general characteristics and 10 roles. These characteristics and roles, discussed in the following sections, have been supported in subsequent research.[40]

More recently, research looked at what managers *like* to do. The research found that both male and female managers most enjoy activities such as leading others, networking, and leading innovation. Activities managers like least include, controlling subordinates, handling paperwork, and managing time pressures. Interestingly, managers in five different countries showed substantial agreement among these preferences.[41] Many new managers in particular find the intense time pressures of management, the load of administrative paperwork, and the challenge of directing others to be quite stressful as they adjust to their new roles and responsibilities. Indeed, the initial leap into management can be one of the scariest moments in a person's career.[42]

Making the Leap: Becoming a New Manager

Many people who are promoted into a manager position have little idea what the job actually entails and receive little training about how to handle their new role. It's no wonder that, among managers, the first-line supervisors tend to experience the most job burnout and attrition.[43]

Organizations often promote the star performers—those who demonstrate individual expertise in their area of responsibility and have an ability to work well with others—both to reward the individual and to build new talent into the managerial ranks. But making the shift from individual contributor to manager is often tricky. Dianne Baker, an expert nurse who was promoted to supervisor of an outpatient cardiac rehabilitation center, quickly found herself overwhelmed by the challenge of supervising former peers, keeping up with paperwork, and understanding financial and operational issues.[44] Her experience is duplicated every day as new managers struggle with the transition to their new jobs. One study followed a group of 19 managers over the first year of their managerial careers and found that one key to success is to recognize that becoming a manager involves more than learning a new set of skills. Rather, becoming a manager means a profound transformation in the way people think of themselves, called personal identity, that includes letting go of deeply held attitudes and habits and learning new ways of thinking.[45] Exhibit 1.4 outlines the transformation from individual performer to manager.

general manager A manager who is responsible for several departments that perform different functions.

From Individual Identity ──────⟶ To Manager Identity	
Specialist, performs specific tasks	Generalist, coordinates diverse tasks
Gets things done through own efforts	Gets things done through others
An individual actor	A network builder
Works relatively independently	Works in highly interdependent manner

E X H I B I T   1.4

Making the Leap from Individual Performer to Manager

SOURCE: Based on Exhibit 1.1, "Transformation of Identity," in Linda A. Hill, *Becoming a Manager: Mastery of a New Identity,* 2nd ed. (Boston, MA: Harvard Business School Press, 2003): 6.

The individual performer is a specialist and a "doer." His or her mind is conditioned to think in terms of performing specific tasks and activities as expertly as possible. The manager, on the other hand, has to be a generalist and learn to coordinate a broad range of activities. Whereas the individual performer strongly identifies with his or her specific tasks, the manager has to identify with the broader organization and industry. In addition, the individual performer gets things done mostly through his or her own efforts, and develops the habit of relying on self rather than others. The manager, though, gets things done through other people. Indeed, one of the most common mistakes new managers make is wanting to do all the work themselves rather than delegating to others and developing others' abilities.[46] To be a successful manager means thinking in terms of building teams and networks, becoming a motivator and organizer within a highly interdependent system of people and work. Although the distinctions may sound simple in the abstract, they are anything but. In essence, becoming a manager means becoming a new person and viewing oneself in a completely new way.

Many new managers have to make the transformation in a "trial by fire," learning on the job as they go, but organizations are beginning to be more responsive to the need for new manager training. The cost to organizations of losing good employees who can't make the transition is greater than the cost of providing training to help new managers cope, learn, and grow. In addition, some of today's organizations are using great care in selecting people for managerial positions, including ensuring that each candidate understands what management involves and really wants to be a manager. For example, FedEx offers a training course for aspiring managers called "Is Management for Me?" A career as a manager can be highly rewarding, but it can also be stressful and frustrating. The Manager's Shoptalk box further examines some of the challenges new managers face. After reading the Shoptalk, can you answer "Yes" to the question "Do I really want to be a manager?"

Manager Activities

Most new managers are unprepared for the variety of activities managers routinely perform. One of the most interesting findings about managerial activities is how busy managers are and how hectic the average workday can be. Let's visit our Cheesecake Factory manager, Heather Coin, once more: "I really try to keep the plates spinning," Heather says, comparing her management job to a circus act. "If I see a plate slowing down, I go and give it a spin and move on." She arrives at work about 9:30 A.M. and checks the financials for how the restaurant performed the day before. Next comes a staff meeting and various personnel duties.

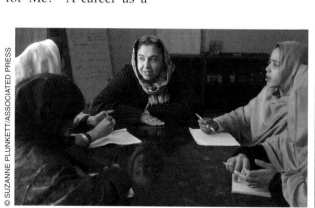

© SUZANNE PLUNKETT/ASSOCIATED PRESS

CONCEPT CONNECTION Supported in part by USAID and published by The Killid Group, a media company headquartered in Kabul, *Mursal*, is the first nationally distributed women's magazine in Afghanistan's history. Aimed at average women, most of whom are illiterate due to the lack of educational opportunities, the publication makes liberal use of photographs to cover a wide range of women's issues. It is the job of **middle managers,** such as the *Mursal* editors shown here talking with board member Palwasha Hassan, to help realize an organization's strategic goals, which are typically defined by top management.

DO YOU REALLY WANT TO BE A MANAGER?

Is management for you? Becoming a manager is considered by most people to be a positive, forward-looking career move and, indeed, life as a manager offers appealing aspects. However, it also holds many challenges, and not every person will be happy and fulfilled in a management position. Here are some of the issues would-be managers should consider before deciding they want to pursue a management career:

:: *The increased workload.* It isn't unusual for managers to work 70–80 hours per week, and some work even longer hours. A manager's job always starts before a shift and ends hours after the shift is over. When Ray Sarnacki was promoted to manager at an aerospace company, he found himself frustrated by the incessant travel, endless paperwork, and crowded meeting schedule. He eventually left the job and found happiness in a position earning about one-fifth of his peak managerial salary.

:: *The challenge of supervising former peers.* This issue can be one of the toughest for new managers. They frequently struggle to find the right approach, with some trying too hard to remain "one of the gang," and others asserting their authority too harshly. In almost all cases, the transition from a peer-to-peer relationship to a manager-to-subordinate one is challenging and stressful.

:: *The headache of responsibility for other people.* A lot of people get into management because they like the idea of having power, but the reality is that many managers feel overwhelmed by the responsibility of hiring, supervising, and disciplining others. Laura Kelso, who today thrives on the fast pace and responsibility of being a manager, says that the first time she had to fire someone, she agonized for weeks over how to

do it. New managers are often astonished at the amount of time it takes to handle "people problems." Kelly Cannell, who quit her job as a manager, puts it this way: "What's the big deal [about managing people]? The big deal is that people are human. . . . To be a good manager, you have to mentor them, listen to their problems, counsel them, and at the end of the day you still have your own work on your plate. . . . Don't take the responsibility lightly, because no matter what you think, managing people is not easy."

:: *Being caught in the middle.* Except for those in the top echelons, managers find themselves acting as a backstop, caught between upper management and the workforce. Even when managers disagree with the decisions of top executives, they are responsible for implementing them.

For some people, the frustrations of management aren't worth it. For others, management is a fulfilling and satisfying career choice and the emotional rewards can be great. One key to being happy as a manager may be carefully evaluating whether you can answer yes to the question, "Do I really want to be a manager?"

SOURCES: Erin White, "Learning to Be the Boss," *The Wall Street Journal* (November 21, 2005): B1; Jared Sandberg, "Down Over Moving Up: Some New Bosses Find They Hate Their Jobs," *The Wall Street Journal* (July 27, 2005): B1; Heath Row, "Is Management for Me? That Is the Question," *Fast Company* (February–March 1998): 50–52; Timothy D. Schellhardt, "Want to Be a Manager? Many People Say No, Calling Job Miserable," *The Wall Street Journal* (April 4, 1997): A1, A4; and Matt Murray, "Managing Your Career—The Midcareer Crisis: Am I in This Business to Become a Manager?" *The Wall Street Journal* (July 25, 2000): B1.

MANAGER'S SHOPTALK

Before and after the lunch shift, she's pitching in with whatever needs to be done—making salads in the kitchen, expediting the food, bussing the tables, or talking with guests. After lunch, from 3:00 P.M. to 4:30 P.M., Heather takes care of administrative duties and paperwork. At 4:30, she holds a shift-change meeting to make sure of a smooth transition from the day crew to the night crew. Throughout the day, Heather also mentors staff members, which she considers the most rewarding part of her job. After the evening rush, she usually heads for home about 10 P.M.[47]

Some top managers are even busier. Jeff Immelt, CEO of General Electric, claims that he has worked 100 hours a week for the past 24 years. He says the most valuable thing he learned in business school was that "there are 24 hours in a day, and you can use all of them."[48]

ADVENTURES IN MULTITASKING

Managerial activity is characterized by variety, fragmentation, and brevity.[49] The widespread and voluminous nature of a manager's involvements leaves little time for quiet reflection. The average time spent on any one activity is less than nine minutes. Managers shift gears quickly. Significant crises are interspersed with trivial events in no predictable sequence. One example of just two typical hours for general manager Janet Howard follows. Note the frequent interruptions and the brevity and variety of tasks.

7:30 A.M.   Janet arrives at work and begins to plan her day.

7:37 A.M.   A subordinate, Morgan Cook, stops in Janet's office to discuss a customer dinner the previous night and to review the cost-benefit analysis for a proposed customer relationship management planning system.

7:45 A.M.   Janet's administrative assistant, Pat, motions for Janet to pick up the telephone. "Janet, they had serious water damage at the downtown office last night. A pipe broke, causing about $50,000 damage. Everything will be back in shape in three days. Thought you should know."

8:00 A.M.   Pat brings in the mail. She also asks instructions for formatting a report Janet gave her yesterday.

8:14 A.M.   Janet gets a phone call from the accounting manager, who is returning a call from the day before. They talk about an accounting problem.

8:25 A.M.   A Mr. Nance is ushered in. Mr. Nance complains that a sales manager mistreats his employees and something must be done. Janet rearranges her schedule to investigate this claim.

9:00 A.M.   Janet returns to the mail. One letter is from an irate customer. Janet types out a helpful, restrained reply. Pat brings in phone messages.

9:15 A.M.   Janet receives an urgent phone call from Larry Baldwin. They discuss lost business, unhappy subordinates, and a potential promotion.[50]

LIFE ON SPEED DIAL

The manager performs a great deal of work at an unrelenting pace.[51] Managers' work is fast paced and requires great energy. The managers observed by Mintzberg processed 36 pieces of mail each day, attended eight meetings, and took a tour through the building or plant. Technology, such as e-mail, instant messaging, cell phones, and laptops, intensifies the pace. It isn't unusual for a manager to receive hundreds of e-mail messages a day. As soon as a manager's daily calendar is set, unexpected disturbances erupt. New meetings are required. During time away from the office, executives catch up on work-related reading, paperwork, and e-mail.

At O'Hare International Airport in Chicago, an unofficial count one Friday found operations manager Hugh Murphy interacting with about 45 airport employees. In addition, he listened to complaints from local residents about airport noise, met with disgruntled executives of a French firm who built the airport's $128 million people-mover system, attempted to soothe a Hispanic city alderman who complained that Mexicana Airlines passengers were being singled out by overzealous tow-truck operators, toured the airport's fire station, and visited the construction site for a new $20 million tower. Murphy's unrelenting pace is typical for managers.[52]

> Are you ready to step into a job as a new manager? Consider the hectic pace and varied activities managers perform. Are you prepared to make a personal transformation from individual performer to accomplishing work by engaging and coordinating other people. Take the New Manager Self-Test to see whether your priorities align with the demands placed on a new manager's job.

■ TAKE A MOMENT

MANAGER ROLE AND REALITY

Rate each of the following items based on what you think is the appropriate emphasis for that task to your success as a new manager of a department. First, read each item and check either High Priority or Low Priority. Second, go through the list again and change answers as needed so that four items are scored as High Priority and four are scored as Low Priority.

	High Priority	Low Priority
1. Spend 50 percent or more of your time in the care and feeding of people.		
2. Make sure people understand that you are in control of the department.		
3. Use lunches to meet and network with peers in other departments.		
4. Implement the changes you believe will improve department performance.		
5. Spend as much time as possible talking with and listening to subordinates.		
6. Make sure jobs get out on time.		
7. Reach out to your boss to discuss his expectations for you and your department.		
8. Make sure you set clear expectations and policies for your department.		

INTERPRETATION: A big surprise for most new managers is that they are much less in control of things than they expected. New managers typically expect to have power, to be in control, and to be personally responsible for departmental outcomes. In fact they are dependent on subordinates more than vice-versa, because they are now evaluated on the work of other people rather than on their own work. They have to let go of their identity as an individual performer and immerse themselves into the dynamics of their department. After a year or so they learn that more than half their time is spent networking and building relationships with other people, especially direct reports. People who fail in their job as new manager typically do so because they had poor working relationships with subordinates, peers, or their boss, or they misjudged management philosophy or cultural values. Developing good relationships in all directions is typically more important than holding on to old work skills, or emphasizing control and task outcomes. Successful outcomes typically will occur if relationships are solid. Bad relationships may undercut the new manager's efforts.

SCORING: All 8 items in the list may be important, but the odd-numbered items are considered more important than the even-numbered items for long-term success as a new manager. If you checked three or four of the odd-numbered items, consider yourself ready for a management position. A successful new manager discovers that a lot of time has to be spent in the care and feeding of people.

SOURCES: Adapted from research findings reported in Linda A. Hill, *Becoming a Manager: How New Managers Master the Challenges of Leadership*, 2nd ed. (Boston, MA: Harvard Business School Press, 2003); and John J. Gabarro, *The Dynamics of Taking Charge* (Boston, MA: Harvard Business School Press, 1987).

Manager Roles

Mintzberg's observations and subsequent research indicate that diverse manager activities can be organized into 10 roles.[53] A **role** is a set of expectations for a manager's behavior. Exhibit 1.5 provides examples of each of the roles. These roles are divided into three conceptual categories: informational (managing by information); interpersonal (managing through people); and decisional (managing through action). Each role represents activities that managers undertake to ultimately accomplish the functions of planning, organizing, leading, and controlling. Although it is necessary to separate the components of the manager's job to understand the different roles and activities of a manager, it is important to remember that the real job of management cannot be practiced as a set of independent parts; all the roles interact in the real world of management. As Mintzberg says, "The manager who only communicates or only conceives never gets anything done, while the manager who only 'does' ends up doing it all alone."[54]

role A set of expectations for one's behavior.

Category	Role	Activity
Informational	**Monitor**	Seek and receive information, scan periodicals and reports, maintain personal contacts.
	Disseminator	Forward information to other organization members; send memos and reports, make phone calls.
	Spokesperson	Transmit information to outsiders through speeches, reports, memos.
Interpersonal	**Figurehead**	Perform ceremonial and symbolic duties such as greeting visitors, signing legal documents.
	Leader	Direct and motivate subordinates; train, counsel, and communicate with subordinates.
	Liaison	Maintain information links both inside and outside organization; use e-mail, phone calls, meetings.
Decisional	**Entrepreneur**	Initiate improvement projects; identify new ideas, delegate idea responsibility to others.
	Disturbance handler	Take corrective action during disputes or crises; resolve conflicts among subordinates; adapt to environmental crises.
	Resource allocator	Decide who gets resources; schedule, budget, set priorities.
	Negotiator	Represent department during negotiation of union contracts, sales, purchases, budgets; represent departmental interests.

E X H I B I T   1.5

Ten Manager Roles

SOURCES: Adapted from Henry Mintzberg, *The Nature of Managerial Work* (New York: Harper & Row, 1973): 92–93; and Henry Mintzberg, "Managerial Work: Analysis from Observation," *Management Science* 18 (1971): B97–B110.

INFORMATIONAL ROLES

Informational roles describe the activities used to maintain and develop an information network. General managers spend about 75 percent of their time talking to other people. The *monitor* role involves seeking current information from many sources. The manager acquires information from others and scans written materials to stay well informed. The *disseminator* and *spokesperson* roles are just the opposite: The manager transmits current information to others, both inside and outside the organization, who can use it. One colorful example of the spokesperson role is Mick Jagger of the Rolling Stones. The rock band is run like a large, multinational organization with Jagger as the CEO. Jagger surrounds himself not only with talented artists, but also with sophisticated and experienced business executives. Yet it is Jagger who typically deals with the media and packages the band's image for a worldwide audience.[55]

INTERPERSONAL ROLES

Interpersonal roles pertain to relationships with others and are related to the human skills described earlier. The *figurehead* role involves handling ceremonial and symbolic activities for the department or organization. The manager represents the organization in his or her formal managerial capacity as the head of the unit. The presentation of employee awards by a division manager at Taco Bell is an example of the figurehead role. The *leader* role encompasses relationships with subordinates, including motivation, communication, and influence. The *liaison* role pertains to the development of information sources both inside and outside the organization. Stephen Baxter, managing director of Scotland's Glasgow Airport, illustrates the liaison role. Baxter led a rapid expansion of the airport by coordinating with executives at other organizations to find ways to woo new airlines to use Glasgow. He recently took on an extra role as president of the Glasgow chamber of commerce, enabling him to develop more sources of information and support.[56]

DECISIONAL ROLES

Decisional roles pertain to those events about which the manager must make a choice and take action. These roles often require conceptual as well as human skills. The *entrepreneur* role involves the initiation of change. Managers are constantly

CONCEPT CONNECTION

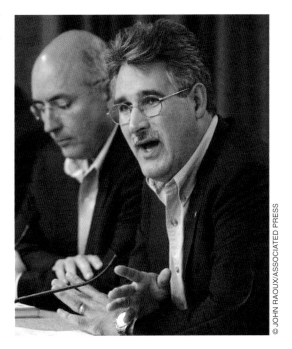

"It became a very easy recommendation for me to say, 'We're good to fly,'" said space shuttle orbiter project manager Steve Poulos shortly before Atlantis's September 2006 lift-off, the first since the 2003 Columbia disaster. In their **decisional role** as managers, Poulos and other NASA executives, including space shuttle program manager N. Wayne Hale Jr. and international space station manager Mike Suffredini, pictured here, gave the go-ahead despite the possibility of a faulty fuel cell. During a careful 48-hour review, they weighed risks against the problems that would be caused by a delay in NASA's already tight schedule for completing the space lab by 2010. After a successful 12-day mission, the craft landed safely.

thinking about the future and how to get there.[57] Managers become aware of problems and search for innovations that will correct them. Oprah Winfrey, head of Harpo Inc., is a master of the entrepreneur role. Although the television talk show *Oprah* is the foundation of Harpo, Winfrey is always looking for innovative projects. She has branched out into movie production, cable television, the Internet, and even launched a hot new magazine.[58] The *disturbance handler* role involves resolving conflicts among subordinates or between the manager's department and other departments. The *resource allocator* role pertains to decisions about how to allocate people, time, equipment, budget, and other resources to attain desired outcomes. The manager must decide which projects receive budget allocations, which of several customer complaints receive priority, and even how to spend his or her own time. The *negotiator* role involves formal negotiations and bargaining to attain outcomes for the manager's unit of responsibility. The manager meets and formally negotiates with others—a supplier about a late delivery, the controller about the need for additional budget resources, or the union about a worker grievance.

The relative emphasis a manager puts on these ten roles depends on a number of factors, such as the manager's position in the hierarchy, natural skills and abilities, type of organization, or departmental goals to be achieved. For example, Exhibit 1.6 illustrates the varying importance of the leader and liaison roles as reported in a survey of top-, middle-, and lower-level managers. Note that the importance of the leader role typically declines while the importance of the liaison role increases as a manager moves up the organizational hierarchy.

Other factors, such as changing environmental conditions, may also determine which roles are more important for a manager at any given time. A top manager may regularly put more emphasis on the roles of spokesperson, figurehead, and

---

EXHIBIT　1.6

Hierarchical Levels and Importance of Leader and Liaison Roles

SOURCE: Based on information from A.I. Kraut, P.R. Pedigo, D.D. McKenna, and M.D. Dunnette, "The Role of The Manager: What's Really Important in Different Management Jobs," *Academy of Management Executive* 3 (1989), 286–293.

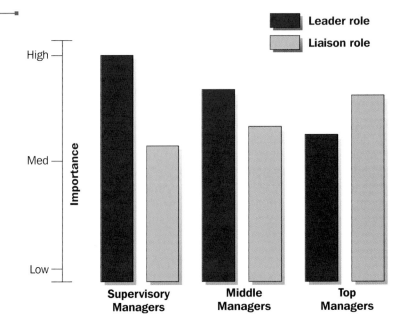

■ Leader role
□ Liaison role

Importance: High — Med — Low

Supervisory Managers　Middle Managers　Top Managers

negotiator. However, the emergence of new competitors may require more attention to the monitor role, or a severe decline in employee morale and direction may mean that the CEO has to put more emphasis on the leader role. A marketing manager may focus on interpersonal roles because of the importance of personal contacts in the marketing process, whereas a financial manager may be more likely to emphasize decisional roles such as resource allocator and negotiator. Despite these differences, all managers carry out informational, interpersonal, and decisional roles to meet the needs of the organization. Managers stay alert to needs both within and outside the organization to determine what roles are most critical at various times.

MANAGING IN SMALL BUSINESSES AND NONPROFIT ORGANIZATIONS

Small businesses are growing in importance. Hundreds of small businesses are opened every month, but the environment for small business today is highly complicated. Globalization, advances in technology, shifting government regulations, and increasing customer demands require that even the smallest of businesses have solid management expertise. Small companies sometimes have difficulty developing the managerial dexterity needed to survive in a turbulent environment. One survey on trends and future developments in small business found that nearly half of respondents saw inadequate management skills as a threat to their companies, as compared to less than 25 percent of larger organizations.[59] Managing in small businesses and entrepreneurial start-ups will be discussed in detail in Chapter 6.

One interesting finding is that managers in small businesses tend to emphasize roles different from those of managers in large corporations. Managers in small companies often see their most important role as that of spokesperson, because they must promote the small, growing company to the outside world. The entrepreneur role is also critical in small businesses, because managers have to be innovative and help their organizations develop new ideas to remain competitive. Small-business managers tend to rate lower on the leader role and on information-processing roles, compared with their counterparts in large corporations.

Nonprofit organizations also represent a major application of management talent. Salvation Army, Nature Conservancy, Parkland Memorial Hospital, Los Angeles County Museum of Art, Girl Scouts, and Cleveland Orchestra all require excellent management. The functions of planning, organizing, leading, and controlling apply to nonprofits just as they do to business organizations, and managers in nonprofit organizations use similar skills and perform similar activities. The primary difference is that managers in businesses direct their activities toward earning money for the company, while managers in nonprofits direct their efforts toward generating some kind of social impact. The unique characteristics and needs of nonprofit organizations created by this distinction present unique challenges for managers.[60]

Financial resources for nonprofit organizations typically come from government appropriations, grants, and donations rather than from the sale of products or services to customers. In businesses, managers focus on improving the organization's products and services to increase sales revenues. In nonprofits, however, services are typically provided to nonpaying clients, and a major problem for many organizations is securing a steady stream of funds to continue operating. Nonprofit managers, committed to serving clients with limited resources, must focus on keeping organizational costs as low as possible.[61] Donors generally want their money to go directly to helping clients rather than for overhead costs. If nonprofit managers can't demonstrate a highly efficient use of resources, they might have a hard time securing additional donations or government appropriations. Although the Sarbanes-Oxley Act (the 2002 corporate governance reform law) doesn't apply to nonprofits, for example, many are adopting its guidelines, striving for greater transparency and accountability to boost credibility with constituents and be more competitive when seeking funding.[62]

In addition, because nonprofit organizations do not have a conventional *bottom line*, managers often struggle with the question of what constitutes results and

Unlocking Innovative Solutions Through **TECHNOLOGY**

CLICK HERE FOR LOWER TAXES

Government agencies are plodding, inefficient bureaucracies. Right? Well, maybe not. The U.S. government is actually on the cutting edge of a movement by governments all over the world. They're using the Internet to provide information and deliver services rapidly and at lower cost to citizens, businesses, and other branches of government.

Consider the U.S. Internal Revenue Service (www.irs.gov), which linked its Web site closely to its mission, organizing the site so that America's citizens can better understand and meet their tax responsibilities. Before the Internet, distributing tax forms was an expensive logistical nightmare for the IRS. Hordes of form pullers, order takers, envelope stuffers, and address labelers processed million of phone and mail requests for various tax publications and forms. The cost of handling a request by hand is about $3.00. Today, more than 100 million tax forms are downloaded directly from the Web site, with each request costing the IRS (and therefore the taxpayer) only a fraction of a cent. E-filing of tax returns save additional time and expense.

Other government agencies have made equally impressive strides in the use of technology. When government first went online, most agencies merely posted static information. Today, their Web pages are increasingly interactive, allowing people to sit down at their computers or whip out their cell phones or PDAs and conduct all manner of business—everything from paying a speeding ticket to applying for a student loan.

In September 2000, the United States took e-government to the next level when it launched its award-winning FirstGov.gov (www.firstgov.gov), the official U.S. portal that links users to more than 26 million federal and state Web sites as well as to local, tribal, and foreign government sites. Visitors can enter the site through citizen, business, federal employee, or government-to-government user gateways and then search by topic, such as "money and taxes," or use an advanced search engine for more complex searches. For instance, a business user can select the topic of "workplace issues" and in just a few clicks find the Labor Department's online employment law guide. An individual planning a trip to Australia can type "entry requirements" and "Australia" into the advanced search engine and be immediately routed to a State Department site with a link to an Australian Web page, where the person can obtain the necessary visa in a matter of seconds rather than weeks.

Customer satisfaction with FirstGov.gov is high—and getting higher. "It's a win-win for the government and consumers," observes Larry Freed of ForeSee Results, a Michigan firm that gauges Web site consumer satisfaction. "Consumers are getting more information, and the government is lowering its cost by making it easier to get information off the Web." Other countries are developing similar comprehensive government Web portals, such as the United Kingdom's Directgov (www.direct.gov.uk) or Singapore's eCitizen (www.ecitizen.gov.sg). The transition to the Internet is helping shatter the image of government workers as paper shufflers and replace it with one of committed people providing real and valuable services to the public.

SOURCES: "About Us," *FirstGov.gov*, www.firstgov.gov; Marc Shapiro, "Survey Examines Trends in Digital Government." *Nation's Cities Weekly* (March 7, 2005) and "Federal Government Offers Expanded E-Gov Websites," (May 23, 2005): www.nlc.org; Valerie Alvord, "It's the Era of Big Government," *USA Today* (August 19, 2004): www.usatoday.com; Caroline E. Mayer, "Federal Web Search Upgraded." *The Washington Post* (February 15, 2006): A19; and Les Gomes, "Fix It and They Will Come; E-commerce Isn't Dead, Just Broken," *The Wall Street Journal* (February 12, 2001): R4.

effectiveness. Whereas it is easy to measure dollars and cents, the metrics of success in nonprofits are much more ambiguous. Managers have to measure intangibles such as "improve public health," "make a difference in the lives of the disenfranchised," or "increase appreciation for the arts." This intangible nature also makes it more difficult to gauge the performance of employees and managers. An added complication is that managers often depend on volunteers and donors, who cannot be supervised and controlled in the same way a business manager deals with employees.

The roles defined by Mintzberg also apply to nonprofit managers, but these may differ somewhat. We might expect managers in nonprofit organizations to place more emphasis on the roles of spokesperson (to "sell" the organization to donors and the public), leader (to build a mission driven community of employees and volunteers), and resource allocator (to distribute government resources or grant funds that are often assigned top-down).

Managers in all organizations—large corporations, small businesses, and nonprofit organizations—carefully integrate and adjust the management functions and roles to meet challenges within their own circumstances and keep their organizations healthy. One way in which many organizations are meeting new challenges is through increased use of the Internet. Some government agencies are using the Web to cut bureaucracy, improve efficiency, and save money, as described in this chapter's Unlocking Innovative Solutions Through Technology box.

MANAGEMENT AND THE NEW WORKPLACE

Over the past decade or so, the central theme being discussed in the field of management has been the pervasiveness of dramatic change. Rapid environmental shifts are causing fundamental transformations that have a dramatic impact on the manager's job. These transformations are reflected in the transition to a new workplace, as illustrated in Exhibit 1.7. The primary characteristic of the new workplace is that it is centered around bits rather than atoms—information and ideas rather than machines and physical assets. Low-cost computing power means that ideas, documents, movies, music, and all sorts of other data can be zapped around the world at the speed of light. The digitization of business has radically altered the nature of work, employees, and the workplace itself.[63] The *old workplace* is characterized by routine, specialized tasks, and standardized control procedures. Employees typically perform their jobs in one specific company facility, such as an automobile factory located in Detroit or an insurance agency located in Des Moines. The organization is coordinated and controlled through the vertical hierarchy, with decision-making authority residing with upper-level managers.

In the *new workplace*, by contrast, work is free-flowing and *flexible*. The shift is most obvious in e-commerce and high-tech organizations, which have to respond to changing markets and competition at a second's notice. However, numerous other organizations, such as McKinsey & Company, can Life, and Nokia, are also incorporating mechanisms to enhance speed and flexibility. *Empowered employees* are expected to seize opportunities and solve problems as they emerge. Structures are flatter, and lower-level employees make decisions based on widespread information and guided by the organization's mission and values.[64] Knowledge is widely shared rather than hoarded by managers, and people throughout the company keep in touch with a broader range of colleagues via advanced technology. The workplace is organized around *networks* rather than rigid hierarchies, and work is often *virtual*, with managers having to supervise and coordinate people who never actually "come to work"

Characteristics	The New Workplace	The Old Workplace
Resources	Bits—information	Atoms—physical assets
Work	Flexible, virtual	Structured, localized
Workers	Empowered employees, free agents	Loyal employees
Forces on Organizations		
Technology	Digital, e-business	Mechanical
Markets	Global, including Internet	Local, domestic
Workforce	Diverse	Homogenous
Values	Change, speed	Stability, efficiency
Events	Turbulent, more frequent crises	Calm, predictable
Management Competencies		
Leadership	Dispersed, empowering	Autocratic
Focus	Connection to customers, employees	Profits
Doing Work	By teams	By individuals
Relationships	Collaboration	Conflict, competition
Design	Experimentation, learning organization	Efficient performance

EXHIBIT 1.7

The Transition to a New Workplace

in the traditional sense. Thanks to modern information and communications technology, employees can perform their jobs from home or another remote location, at any time of the day or night.[65] Flexible hours, telecommuting, and virtual teams are increasingly popular ways of working that require new skills from managers. Using virtual teams allows organizations to use the best people for a particular job, no matter where they are located, thus enabling a fast, innovative response to competitive pressures. Teams may also include outside contractors, suppliers, customers, competitors, and *interim managers* who are not affiliated with a specific organization but work on a project-by-project basis. The valued worker is one who learns quickly, shares knowledge, and is comfortable with risk, change, and ambiguity.

Forces on Organizations

The most striking change affecting organizations and management is *technology*. Consider that computing power has roughly doubled every 18 months over the past 30 years while the cost has declined by half or more every 18 months.[66] In addition, the Internet, which was little more than a curiosity to many managers as recently as a decade ago, has transformed the way business is done. Many organizations use *digital networking* technologies to tie together employees and company partners in far-flung operations. Organizations are increasing shifting significant chunks of what were once considered core functions to outsiders via *outsourcing, joint ventures*, and other complex *alliances*. Companies are becoming interconnected, and managers have to learn how to coordinate relationships with other organizations and influence people who can't be managed and commanded in traditional ways.

The Internet and other new technologies are also tied closely to *globalization*. Global interconnections bring many opportunities, but they also bring new threats, raise new risks, and accelerate complexity and competitiveness. Think about the trend toward outsourcing to low-cost providers in other countries. U.S. companies have been sending manufacturing work to other countries for years to cut costs. Now, high-level knowledge work is also being outsourced to countries such as India, Malaysia, and South Africa. India's Wipro Ltd., for example, writes software, performs consulting work, integrates back-office solutions, performs systems integration, and handles technical support for some of the biggest corporations in the United States—and they do it for 40 percent less than comparable U.S. companies can do the work.[67]

Diversity of the population and the workforce in the United States is another fact of life for all organizations. The general population of the United States, and thus of the workforce, is growing more ethnically and racially diverse. In addition, generational diversity is a powerful force in today's workplace, with employees of all ages working together on teams and projects in a way rarely seen in the past.

The Innovative Response

In the face of these transformations, organizations are learning to value *change, innovation,* and *speed* over stability and efficiency. The fundamental paradigm during much of the twentieth century was a belief that things can be stable. In contrast, the new paradigm recognizes change and chaos as the natural order of things.[68] Events in today's world are *turbulent* and *unpredictable*, with both small and large crises occurring on a more frequent basis.

One way managers are addressing the complexity of today's world is through a renewed emphasis on innovation. With the power of the Internet, for example, companies have lost much of their ability to control information to consumers and the public, so they are forced to innovate with increasingly better products and services to remain competitive. The intense competition brought about by globalization also spurs companies to keep pace with new technologies and innovative management practices.[69] A recent report from a group of leading scientists, executives, and educators points to the growing innovation strength of countries such as China and India, which are poised to usurp America's position as an innovation leader. Between the years of 1991 and 2003, research and development spending in China exceeded that in the United States by billions of dollars.[70]

Over the past few years, though, an explosion of attention to innovation roared through U.S. firms. For example, Motorola, which seemed on the has-been list in the opening years of the twenty-first century, roared back to life with hot new products like the RAZR phone, the ROKR, the first combination cell phone and iPod, and the Q phone and e-mail device, designed to compete with the Blackberry. Motorola CEO Ed Zander is implementing management and cultural changes that support an ongoing process of innovation.[71] His changes reflect a broader movement in U.S. firms, seen in companies from General Electric to IBM to Procter & Gamble, as managers emphasize creativity and innovation to compete in a new era. General Electric CEO Jeff Immelt, for example, shifted from emphasizing growth through acquisition to pushing growth through technological innovation and providing additional resources for GE's scientific research labs. Procter & Gamble collaborates widely with individual entrepreneurs and other firms, even competitors, to crank out innovative products.[72]

New Management Competencies

In the face of these transitions, managers must rethink their approach to organizing, directing, and motivating employees. Today's best managers give up their command-and-control mind-set to focus on coaching and providing guidance, creating organizations that are fast, flexible, innovative, and relationship-oriented. In many of today's best companies, *leadership* is dispersed throughout the organization, and managers empower others to gain the benefit of their ideas and creativity.

■ **TAKE A MOMENT**

Read the ethical dilemma on page 32 that pertains to managing in the new workplace. Think about what you would do and why to begin understanding how you will solve thorny management problems.

Success in the new workplace depends on the strength and quality of collaborative *relationships*. Rather than a single-minded focus on profits, today's managers recognize the critical importance of staying *connected to employees and customers*. New ways of working emphasize collaboration across functions and hierarchical levels as well as with other companies. *Team-building skills* are crucial. Instead of managing a department of employees, many managers act as team leaders of ever-shifting, temporary projects. At SEI Investments, all work is distributed among 140 teams. Some are permanent, such as those that serve major customers or focus on specific markets, but many are designed to work on short-term projects or problems. Computer linkups, called *pythons*, drop from the ceiling. As people change assignments, they just unplug their pythons, move their desks and chairs to a new location, plug into a new python, and get to work on the next project.[73]

An important management challenge in the new workplace is to build a *learning organization* by creating an organizational climate that values experimentation and risk taking, applies current technology, tolerates mistakes and failure, and rewards nontraditional thinking and the sharing of knowledge. Everyone in the organization participates in identifying and solving problems, enabling the organization to continuously experiment, improve, and increase its capability. The role of

© JERRY S. MENDOZA/ASSOCIATED PRESS

CONCEPT CONNECTION

New York Yankees manager Joe Torre knows how to use **new management competencies** to build high performance teams capable of winning American League pennants and World Series titles. His management style is built on paradox. He achieves what's best for the team, always his first priority, by paying close attention to each individual's personality and abilities, routinely setting aside time for one-on-one discussions so he can motivate, correct, and encourage. He succeeds in part because he earns player loyalty by tolerating failure and slumps. "To me, managing is about people," says Torre. "Players look to you more for guidance and calmness than anything else."

managers is not to make decisions, but to create learning capability, where everyone is free to experiment and learn what works best.

> To succeed in the new workplace, you have to learn to network and build collaborative relationships. Expect to manage with little command and control and to master skills such as communication, guiding others, and inspiration.

Turbulent Times: Managing Crises and Unexpected Events

Many managers may dream of working in an organization and a world where life seems relatively calm, orderly, and predictable, but their reality is one of increasing turbulence and disorder. Today's managers and organizations face various levels of crisis every day—everything from the loss of computer data, to charges of racial discrimination, to a factory fire, to workplace violence. However, these organizational crises are compounded by crises on a more global level. Consider a few of the major events that affected U.S. companies within the last few years: the bursting of the dot-com bubble, which led to the failure of thousands of companies and the rapid decline of technology stocks; the crash of Enron due to a complex series of unethical and illegal accounting gimmicks, the subsequent investigations of numerous other corporations, and implementation of new corporate governance laws; terrorist attacks in New York City and Washington, D.C., that destroyed the World Trade Center, seriously damaged the Pentagon, killed thousands of people, and interrupted business around the world; the crash of the space shuttle *Columbia* and ensuing investigation that revealed serious cultural and management problems at NASA; Hurricane Katrina's devastating impact on every organization in New Orleans and the Gulf Coast, as well as numerous companies that do business with them; the removal of spinich from supermarkets because of *e-coli*; and continuing terrorist threats against the United States and its allies. These and other events brought the uncertainty and turbulence of today's world clearly to the forefront of everyone's mind, and made crisis management a critical skill for every manager.

Dealing with the unexpected has always been part of the manager's job, but our world has become so fast, interconnected, and complex that unexpected events happen more frequently and often with greater and more painful consequences. All of the new management skills and competencies we discussed are important to managers in such an environment. In addition, crisis management places further demands on today's managers. Some of the most recent thinking on crisis management suggests the importance of five leadership skills.[74]

1. Stay calm.
2. Be visible.
3. Put people before business.
4. Tell the truth.
5. Know when to get back to business.

STAY CALM

A leader's emotions are contagious, so leaders have to stay calm, focused, and optimistic about the future. Perhaps the most important part of a manager's job in a crisis situation is to absorb people's fears and uncertainties. Although they acknowledge the difficulties, they remain rock-steady and hopeful, which gives comfort, inspiration, and hope to others.

BE VISIBLE

When people's worlds become ambiguous and frightening, they need to feel that someone is in control. After Hurricane Katrina hit New Orleans, Scott Cowen, president of Tulane University, stayed on campus until he was sure everyone was evacuated and everything that could possibly be done to control the damage was in place.[75] Crisis is a time when leadership cannot be delegated. When Russian president Vladimir Putin continued his holiday after the sinking of the submarine Kursk in August 2000, his reputation diminished worldwide.[76]

PUT PEOPLE BEFORE BUSINESS

The companies that weather a crisis best, whether the crisis is large or small, are those in which managers make people and human feelings their top priority. As Ray O'Rourke, managing director for global corporate affairs at Morgan Stanley, put it following September 11, ". . . even though we are a financial services company, we didn't have a financial crisis on our hands; we had a human crisis. After that point, everything was focused on our people."[77]

TELL THE TRUTH

Managers should get as much information from as many diverse sources as they can, do their best to determine the facts, and then be open and straightforward about what's going on. After a 17-year-old patient at Duke University Hospital died following a botched organ transplant, hospital managers compounded the organizational crisis by failing to communicate with the media and community for nine full days after the tragedy was reported in the press.[78]

KNOW WHEN TO GET BACK TO BUSINESS

Although managers should first deal with the physical and emotional needs of people, they also need to get back to business as soon as possible. The company has to keep going, and a natural human tendency makes us want to rebuild and move forward. The rejuvenation of the business is a sign of hope and an inspiration to employees. Moments of crisis also present excellent opportunities for looking forward and using the emotional energy that has emerged to build a better company.

Today is a challenging time to be entering the field of management. Throughout this book, you will learn much more about the new workplace, about the new and dynamic roles managers are playing in the twenty-first century, and about how you can be an effective manager in a complex, ever-changing world.

MANAGER'S SOLUTION

This chapter introduced a number of important concepts and described the changing nature of management. High performance requires the efficient and effective use of organizational resources through the four management functions of planning, organizing, leading, and controlling. To perform the four functions, managers need three skills—conceptual, human, and technical. Conceptual skills are more important at the top of the hierarchy; human skills are important at all levels; and technical skills are most important for first-line managers.

Becoming a manager requires a shift in thinking and can be a challenging transition. New managers often struggle with the challenges of coordinating a broad range of people and activities, delegating to and developing others, and relating to former peers in a new way. Two characteristics of managerial work were explained in the chapter: (1) Managerial activities involve variety, fragmentation, and brevity; and (2) managers perform a great deal of work at an unrelenting pace. Managers are expected to perform activities associated with 10 roles: the informational roles of monitor, disseminator, and spokesperson; the interpersonal roles of figurehead, leader, and liaison; and the decisional roles of entrepreneur, disturbance handler, resource allocator, and negotiator.

These management characteristics apply to small businesses, entrepreneurial start-ups, and nonprofit organizations just as they do in large corporations. In addition, they are being applied in a new workplace and a rapidly changing world. In the new workplace, work is free-flowing and flexible to encourage speed and adaptation, and empowered employees are expected to seize opportunities and solve problems. The workplace is organized around networks rather than vertical hierarchies, and work is often virtual. These changing characteristics result from forces such as advances in technology and e-business, globalization, increased diversity, and a growing emphasis on innovation, change, and speed over stability and efficiency. Managers need new skills and competencies in this new environment. Leadership is dispersed and empowering. Customer relationships are critical, and most work is done by teams that work directly with customers. In the new workplace, managers focus on building relationships, which may include customers, partners, and suppliers. In addition, they strive to build learning capability throughout the organization.

Managers at Mississippi Power, described in the chapter opening, illustrate many of these new management competencies, which enabled the company to execute a swift, ambitious disaster plan and restore power in only 12 days following Hurricane Katrina. Two decades ago, hurricane response was run from the top down, but managers learned that setting priorities from headquarters was ineffective during times of chaos and confusion. Today, decision making has been pushed far down to the level of the substation, and employees are empowered to act within certain guidelines to accomplish a basic mission: "Get the power on." The corporate culture, based on values of unquestionable trust, superior performance, and total commitment, supports individual initiative and management confidence that employees will respond with quick action and on-the-spot innovation. During the disaster recovery, even out-of-state crews working unsupervised were empowered to engineer their own solutions to problems in the field. Networking and team-building skills are also highly valued at Mississippi Power. Middle managers like Melvin Wilson forged networks of relationships throughout the company, with other organizations, and with power company managers in other states, which enabled them to quickly gain access to critical resources and build teams with the right combination of skills. Overall, Mississippi Power reflects the qualities of a learning organization in which employees, from line workers to accountants, are encouraged to experiment, innovate, share knowledge, and solve problems.

Melvin Wilson also illustrates some of the qualities needed for effective crisis management. As director of storm logistics, Wilson suppressed his own emotions to present a calm and focused persona, which kept employees' emotions focused in a positive way on the job to be done. At the same time, he and other managers made sure plans were in place to assist employees whose homes were damaged (fortunately, no employees were killed in the storm). Wilson was a highly visible leader throughout the recovery, working 20 hour days and sleeping on the floor. Top leaders were visible as well, meeting with storm directors every day and helping boost the morale of recovery workers.

Leadership during crises and unexpected events is becoming important for all organizations in today's complex world. Managers in crisis situations should stay calm, be visible, put people before business, tell the truth, and know when to get back to business. Human skills become critical during times of turbulence and crisis.

DISCUSSION QUESTIONS

1. How might the teaching of a management course be designed to prepare future managers to deal with globalization and workforce diversity? What problems and opportunities do you think globalization and diversity present for managers?

2. Why do some organizations seem to have a new CEO every year or two, whereas others have top leaders who stay with the company for many years (e.g., Jack Welch's 20 years as CEO at General Electric)? What factors about the manager or about the company might account for this difference?

3. Discuss some of the ways organizations and jobs changed over the past 10 years. What changes do you anticipate over the next 10 years? How might these changes affect the manager's job and the skills a manager needs to be successful?

4. What is the difference between efficiency and effectiveness? Which is more important for

performance? Can managers improve both simultaneously?

5. If managerial work is characterized by variety, fragmentation, and brevity, how do managers perform basic management functions such as planning, which would seem to require reflection and analysis?

6. Jeff Immelt of GE said that the most valuable thing he learned in business school was that "there are 24 hours in a day, and you can use all of them." Do you agree or disagree? What are some of the advantages to this approach to being a manager? What are some of the drawbacks?

7. A college professor told her students, "The purpose of a management course is to teach students about management, not to teach them to be managers." Do you agree or disagree with this statement? Discuss.

8. Assume you are a project manager at a biotechnology company, working with managers from research, production, and marketing on a major product modification. You notice that every memo you receive from the marketing manager has been copied to senior management. At every company function, she spends time talking to the big shots. You are also aware that sometimes when you and the other project members are slaving away over the project, she is playing golf with senior managers. What is your evaluation of her behavior? As project manager, what do you do?

9. You are a bright, hard-working entry-level manager who fully intends to rise up through the ranks. Your performance evaluation gives you high marks for your technical skills but low marks when it comes to people skills. Do you think people skills can be learned, or do you need to rethink your career path? If people skills can be learned, how would you go about it?

10. How do you feel about having a manager's responsibility in today's world characterized by uncertainty, ambiguity, and sudden changes or threats from the environment? Describe some skills and qualities that are important to managers under these conditions.

MANAGEMENT IN PRACTICE: EXPERIENTIAL EXERCISE

Management Aptitude Questionnaire

Rate each of the following questions according to the following scale:

❶ I am never like this.

❷ I am rarely like this.

❸ I am sometimes like this.

❹ I am often like this.

❺ I am always like this.

1. When I have a number of tasks or homework to do, I set priorities and organize the work around deadlines. ❶ ❷ ❸ ❹ ❺

2. Most people would describe me as a good listener. ❶ ❷ ❸ ❹ ❺

3. When I am deciding on a particular course of action for myself (such as hobbies to pursue, languages to study, which job to take, special projects to be involved in), I typically consider the long-term (three years or more) implications of what I would choose to do. ❶ ❷ ❸ ❹ ❺

4. I prefer technical or quantitative courses rather than those involving literature, psychology, or sociology. ❶ ❷ ❸ ❹ ❺

5. When I have a serious disagreement with someone, I hang in there and talk it out until it is completely resolved. ❶ ❷ ❸ ❹ ❺

6. When I have a project or assignment, I really get into the details rather than the "big picture" issues. ❶ ❷ ❸ ❹ ❺

7. I would rather sit in front of my computer than spend a lot of time with people. ❶ ❷ ❸ ❹ ❺

8. I try to include others in activities or discussions. ❶ ❷ ❸ ❹ ❺

9. When I take a course, I relate what I am learning to other courses I took or concepts I learned elsewhere. ❶ ❷ ❸ ❹ ❺

10. When somebody makes a mistake, I want to correct the person and let her or him know the proper answer or approach. ❶ ❷ ❸ ❹ ❺

11. I think it is better to be efficient with my time when talking with someone, rather than worry about the other person's needs, so that I can get on with my real work. ❶ ❷ ❸ ❹ ❺

12. I know my long-term vision of career, family, and other activities and have thought it over carefully. ❶ ❷ ❸ ❹ ❺

13. When solving problems, I would much rather analyze some data or statistics than meet with a group of people. ❶ ❷ ❸ ❹ ❺

14. When I am working on a group project and someone doesn't pull a fair share of the load, I am more likely to complain to my friends rather than confront the slacker. ① ② ③ ④ ⑤

15. Talking about ideas or concepts can get me really enthused or excited. ① ② ③ ④ ⑤

16. The type of management course for which this book is used is really a waste of time. ① ② ③ ④ ⑤

17. I think it is better to be polite and not to hurt people's feelings. ① ② ③ ④ ⑤

18. Data or things interest me more than people. ① ② ③ ④ ⑤

Scoring and Interpretation

Subtract your scores for questions 6, 10, 14, and 17 from the number 6, and then add the total points for the following sections:

1, 3, 6, 9, 12, 15	Conceptual skills total score _____
2, 5, 8, 10, 14, 17	Human skills total score _____
4, 7, 11, 13, 16, 18	Technical skills total score _____

These skills are three abilities needed to be a good manager. Ideally, a manager should be strong (though not necessarily equal) in all three. Anyone noticeably weaker in any of the skills should take courses and read to build up that skill. For further background on the three skills, please refer to the explanation on pages 11–12.

NOTE: This exercise was contributed by Dorothy Marcic.

MANAGEMENT IN PRACTICE: ETHICAL DILEMMA

Can Management Afford to Look the Other Way?

Harry Rull had been with Shellington Pharmaceuticals for 30 years. After a tour of duty in the various plants and seven years overseas, Harry was back at headquarters, looking forward to his new role as vice president of U.S. marketing.

Two weeks into his new job, Harry received some unsettling news about one of the managers under his supervision. Over casual lunch conversation, the director of human resources mentioned that Harry should expect a phone call about Roger Jacobs, manager of new product development. Jacobs had a history of being "pretty horrible" to his subordinates, she said, and one disgruntled employee asked to speak to someone in senior management. After lunch, Harry did some follow-up work. Jacobs's performance reviews had been stellar, but his personnel file also contained a large number of notes documenting charges of Jacobs's mistreatment of subordinates. The complaints ranged from "inappropriate and derogatory remarks" to subsequently dropped charges of sexual harassment. What was more disturbing was that the amount as well as the severity of complaints had increased with each of Jacobs's 10 years with Shellington.

When Harry questioned the company president about the issue, he was told, "Yeah, he's had some problems, but you can't just replace someone with an eye for new products. You're a bottom-line guy; you

understand why we let these things slide." Not sure how to handle the situation, Harry met briefly with Jacobs and reminded him to "keep the team's morale up." Just after the meeting, Sally Barton from HR called to let him know that the problem she'd mentioned over lunch had been worked out. However, she warned, another employee had now come forward demanding that her complaints be addressed by senior management.

What Would You Do?

1. Ignore the problem. Jacobs's contributions to new product development are too valuable to risk losing him, and the problems over the past 10 years have always worked themselves out anyway. No sense starting something that could make you look bad.

2. Launch a full-scale investigation of employee complaints about Jacobs, and make Jacobs aware that the documented history over the past 10 years has put him on thin ice.

3. Meet with Jacobs and the employee to try to resolve the current issue, then start working with Sally Barton and other senior managers to develop stronger policies regarding sexual harassment and treatment of employees, including clear-cut procedures for handling complaints.

SOURCE: Based on Doug Wallace, "A Talent for Mismanagement: What Would You Do?" *Business Ethics*, 2 (November–December 1992): 3–4.

CASE FOR CRITICAL ANALYSIS

Elektra Products, Inc.

Barbara Russell, a manufacturing vice president, walked into the monthly companywide meeting with a light step and a hopefulness she hadn't felt in a long

time. The company's new, dynamic CEO was going to announce a new era of employee involvement and empowerment at Elektra Products, an 80-year-old, publicly held company that had once been a leading manufacturer and retailer of electrical products and supplies. In recent years, the company experienced a host of problems: market share was declining in the face of increased foreign and domestic competition; new product ideas were few and far between; departments such as manufacturing and sales barely spoke to one another; morale was at an all-time low, and many employees were actively seeking other jobs. Everyone needed a dose of hope.

Martin Griffin, who had been hired to revive the failing company, briskly opened the meeting with a challenge: "As we face increasing competition, we need new ideas, new energy, new spirit to make this company great. And the source for this change is you—each one of you." He then went on to explain that under the new empowerment campaign, employees would be getting more information about how the company was run and would be able to work with their fellow employees in new and creative ways. Martin proclaimed a new era of trust and cooperation at Elektra Products. Barbara felt the excitement stirring within her; but as she looked around the room, she saw many of the other employees, including her friend Simon, rolling their eyes. "Just another pile of corporate crap," Simon said later. "One minute they try downsizing, the next reengineering. Then they dabble in restructuring. Now Martin wants to push empowerment. Garbage like empowerment isn't a substitute for hard work and a little faith in the people who have been with this company for years. We made it great once, and we can do it again. Just get out of our way." Simon had been a manufacturing engineer with Elektra Products for more than 20 years. Barbara knew he was extremely loyal to the company, but he—and a lot of others like him—were going to be an obstacle to the empowerment efforts.

Top management assigned selected managers to several problem-solving teams to come up with ideas for implementing the empowerment campaign. Barbara loved her assignment as team leader of the manufacturing team, working on ideas to improve how retail stores got the merchandise they needed when they needed it. The team thrived, and trust blossomed among the members. They even spent nights and weekends working to complete their report. They were proud of their ideas, which they believed were innovative but easily achievable: permit a manager to follow a product from design through sales to customers; allow salespeople to refund up to $500 worth of merchandise on the spot; make information available to salespeople about future products; and swap sales and manufacturing personnel for short periods to let them get to know one another's jobs.

When the team presented its report to department heads, Martin Griffin was enthusiastic. But shortly into the meeting he had to excuse himself because of a late-breaking deal with a major hardware store chain. With Martin absent, the department heads rapidly formed a wall of resistance. The director of human resources complained that the ideas for personnel changes would destroy the carefully crafted job categories that had just been completed. The finance department argued that allowing salespeople to make $500 refunds would create a gold mine for unethical customers and salespeople. The legal department warned that providing information to salespeople about future products would invite industrial spying.

The team members were stunned. As Barbara mulled over the latest turn of events, she considered her options: keep her mouth shut; take a chance and confront Martin about her sincerity in making empowerment work; push slowly for reform and work for gradual support from the other teams; or look for another job and leave a company she really cared about. Barbara realized there would be no easy choices and no easy answers.

Questions

1. How might top management have done a better job changing Elektra Products into a new kind of organization? What might they do now to get the empowerment process back on track?
2. Can you think of ways Barbara could have avoided the problems her team faced in the meeting with department heads?
3. If you were Barbara Russell, what would you do now? Why?

SOURCE: Based on Lawrence R. Rothstein, "The Empowerment Effort that Came Undone," *Harvard Business Review* (January–February 1995), 20–31.

ENDNOTES

1. Dennis Cauchon, "The Little Company That Could," *USA Today* (October 9, 2005): www.usatoday.com.

2. Daniel Roth, "Catch Us If You Can," *Fortune* (February 9, 2003): 64–74; Ian Austen, "Downloading Again," *The New York Times* (May 3, 2004): C12; Christie Eliezer, "Kazaa Case Grinds on in Australia," *Billboard* (April 17, 2004): 60; and Steve Knopper, "Tower in Trouble," *Rolling Stone* (March 18, 2004): 26.

3. Ian Mitroff and Murat C. Alpaslan, "Preparing for Evil," *Harvard Business Review* (April 2003): 109–115.

4. Darrell Rigby and Barbara Bilodeau, "The Bain 2005 Management Tool Survey," *Strategy & Leadership* 33, no. 4 (2005): 4–12.

5. David Carr, "Media Age Business Tips from U2," *The New York Times,* (November 28, 2005): www.nytimes.com.

6. Susan Spielberg, "The Cheesecake Factory: Heather Coin," *Nation's Restaurant News* (January 26, 2004): 38–39.

7. Geoffrey Colvin, "What Makes GE Great?" *Fortune* (March 6, 2006): 90–96; and Betsy Morris, "The GE Mystique," *Fortune* (March 6, 2006): 98–104.

8. James A. F. Stoner and R. Edward Freeman, *Management*, 4th ed. (Englewood Cliffs, NJ: Prentice Hall, 1989).

9. Peter F. Drucker, *Management Tasks, Responsibilities, Practices* (New York: Harper & Row, 1974).

10. George Anders, "AOL's True Believers," *Fast Company* (July 2002): 96–104.

11. "Scott Livengood, Krispy Kreme" profile in "The Best and Worst Managers of the Year," special report, *BusinessWeek* (January 10, 2005): 55–86; "Krispy Kreme Announces Completion of Special Committee Investigation," *PR Newswire* (August 10, 2005): 1.

12. Stephanie Clifford, "How to Get the Geeks and the Suits to Play Nice," *Business 2.0* (May 2002): 92–93.

13. Jacy L. Youn, "True Calling," *Hawaii Business* (July 1, 2005): 13.

14. Kevin Fedarko, "He Fights Terror with Books," *Parade* (April 6, 2003): 4–6; and David Oliver Relin, "With Your Help, He's Fighting On," *Parade* (February 29, 2004): 12–14.

15. Eryn Brown, "Nine Ways to Win on the Web," *Fortune* (May 24, 1999): 112–125.

16. Louis Uchitelle, "Ready for an Upturn. Not Ready to Spend," *The New York Times* (June 23, 2002): Section 3, 1, 13.

17. Martha Brannigan and Eleena De Lisser, "Cost Cutting at Delta Raises the Stock Price But Lowers the Service," *The Wall Street Journal* (June 20, 1996): A1.

18. Robert L. Katz, "Skills of an Effective Administrator," *Harvard Business Review 52* (September–October 1974): 90–102.

19. Geoffrey Colvin, "The Bionic Manager," *Fortune* (September 19, 2005): 88–100.

20. Spielberg, "The Cheesecake Factory."

21. Quoted in Linda Tischler, "The CEO's New Clothes," *Fast Company* (September 2005): 27–28.

22. Kate Bonamici, "The Shoe-In," *Fortune* (January 23, 2006): 116.

23. Sue Shellenbarger, "From Our Readers: The Bosses That Drove Me to Quit My Job," *The Wall Street Journal* (February 7, 2000): B1.

24. Eric Matson, "Congratulations, You're Promoted. (Now What?)," *Fast Company* (June–July 1997): 116–130.

25. Based on Sydney Finkelstein, "7 Habits of Spectacularly Unsuccessful Executives," *Fast Company* (July 2003): 84–89; Charan and Useem, "Why Companies Fail"; and John W. Slocum Jr., Cass Ragan, and Albert Casey, "On Death and Dying: The Corporate Leadership Capacity of CEOs," *Organizational Dynamics* 30, no. 3 (Spring 2002): 269–281.

26. Ibid.

27. Matthew Rose and Laurie P. Cohen, "Man in the News: Amid Turmoil, Top Editors Resign at New York Times," *The Wall Street Journal* (June 6, 2003): A1, A6; and Jena McGregor, "Gospels of Failure," *Fast Company* (February 2005): 61–67.

28. Eileen Sheridan, "Rise: Best Day, Worst Day," *The Guardian* (September 14, 2002): 3.

29. Heath Row, "Force Play" (Company of Friends column), *Fast Company* (March 2001): 46.

30. Charles Fishman, "Sweet Company," *Fast Company* (February 2001): 136–145.

31. Christopher A. Bartlett and Sumantra Ghoshal, "Changing the Role of Top Management: Beyond Systems to People," *Harvard Business Review* (May–June 1995): 132–142; and Sumantra Ghoshal and Christopher A. Bartlett, "Changing the Role of Top Management: Beyond Structure to Processes," *Harvard Business Review* (January–February 1995): 86–96.

32. Quy Nguyen Huy, "In Praise of Middle Managers," *Harvard Business Review* (September 2003): 72–79; Rosabeth Moss Kanter, *On the Frontiers of Management* (Boston: Harvard Business School Press, 2003).

33. Lisa Haneberg, "Reinventing Middle Management," *Leader to Leader* (Fall 2005): 13–18.

34. Huy, "In Praise of Middle Managers"; Haneberg, "Reinventing Middle Managers"; Jenny C. McCune, "Management's BraveNew World," *Management Review* (October 1997): 10–14; "Middle Managers Are Back—But Now They're 'High Impact Players,'" *The Wall Street Journal* (April 14, 1998): B1; and Geoffrey Colvin, "Revenge of the Nerds," *Fortune* (March 2, 1998): 223–224.

35. Carol Hymowitz, "Middle Managers Are Unsung Heroes on Corporate Stage," *The Wall Street Journal* (September 19, 2005): B1.

36. Dan Tynan, "Jungletalk with . . . Google's Minnie Ingersoll," *MBA Jungle* (October–November 2003): 34–25.

37. Kerr Inkson, Angela Heising, and Denise M. Rousseau, "The Interim Manager: Prototype of the 21st Century Worker," *Human Relations* 54, no. 3 (2001): 259–284.

38. Miles Brignall, "Rise; Launch Pad: The Retailer; Alistair Boot, An Assistant Manager at the John Lewis Store in Cheadle, Talks to Miles Brignall," *The Guardian* (October 4, 2003): 3.

39. Henry Mintzberg, *The Nature of Managerial Work* (New York: Harper & Row, 1973); and Mintzberg, "Rounding Out the Manager's Job," *Sloan Management Review* (Fall 1994): 11–26.

40. Robert E. Kaplan, "Trade Routes: The Manager's Network of Relationships," *Organizational Dynamics* (Spring 1984): 37–52; Rosemary Stewart, "The Nature of Management: A Problem for Management Education," *Journal of Management Studies* 21 (1984): 323–330; John P. Kotter, "What Effective General Managers Really Do," *Harvard Business Review* (November–December 1982): 156–167; and Morgan W. McCall, Jr., Ann M. Morrison, and Robert L. Hannan, "Studies of Managerial Work: Results and Methods" (Technical Report No. 9, Center for Creative Leadership, Greensboro, NC, 1978).

41. Alison M. Konrad, Roger Kashlak, Izumi Yoshioka, Robert Waryszak, and Nina Toren, "What Do Managers *Like* to Do? A Five-Country Study," *Group and Organizational Management* 26, no. 4 (December 2001): 401–433.

42. Mary Ellen Slayter, "New Managers Should Go Slow," *The Ottawa Citizen* (August 17, 2005): F2.

43. For a review of the problems faced by first-time managers, see Loren B. Belker and Gary S. Topchik, *The First-Time Manager: A Practical Guide to the Management of People*, 5th ed. (New York: AMACOM, 2005); J. W. Lorsch and P. F. Mathias, "When Professionals Have to Manage," *Harvard Business Review* (July–August 1987): 78–83; R. A. Webber, *Becoming a Courageous Manager: Overcoming Career Problems of New Managers* (Englewood Cliffs, NJ: Prentice Hall, 1991); D. E. Dougherty, *From Technical Professional to Corporate Manager: A Guide to Career Transition* (New York: Wiley, 1984);

J. Falvey, "The Making of a Manager," *Sales and Marketing Management* (March 1989): 42–83; M. K. Badawy, *Developing Managerial Skills in Engineers and Scientists: Succeeding as a Technical Manager* (New York: Van Nostrand Reinhold, 1982); and M. London, *Developing Managers: A Guide to Motivating and Preparing People for Successful Managerial Careers* (San Francisco: Jossey-Bass, 1985).

44. Erin White, "Learning to Be the Boss; Trial and Error Is the Norm as New Managers Figure Out How to Relate to Former Peers," *The Wall Street Journal* (November 21, 2005): B1.

45. Based on Linda A. Hill, *Becoming a Manager: How New Managers Master the Challenges of Leadership*, 2nd. ed. (Boston, MA: Harvard Business School Press, 2003): 6–8.

46. See also "Boss's First Steps," sidebar in White, "Learning to Be the Boss"; and Belker and Topchik, *The First-Time Manager*.

47. Spielberg, "The Cheesecake Factory."

48. Colvin, "The Bionic Manager."

49. Henry Mintzberg, "Managerial Work: Analysis from Observation," *Management Science* 18 (1971): B97–B110.

50. Based on Carol Saunders and Jack William Jones, "Temporal Sequences in Information Acquisition for Decision Making: A Focus on Source and Medium," *Academy of Management Review* 15 (1990): 29–46; Kotter, "What Effective General Managers Really Do"; and Mintzberg, "Managerial Work."

51. Mintzberg, "Managerial Work."

52. Anita Lienert, "A Day in the Life: Airport Manager Extraordinaire," *Management Review* (January 1995): 57–61.

53. Lance B. Kurke and Howard E. Aldrich, "Mintzberg Was Right!: A Replication and Extension of *The Nature of Managerial Work*," *Management Science* 29 (1983): 975–984; Cynthia M. Pavett and Alan W. Lau, "Managerial Work: The Influence of Hierarchical Level and Functional Specialty," *Academy of Management Journal* 26 (1983): 170–177; and Colin P. Hales, "What Do Managers Do? A Critical Review of the Evidence," *Journal of Management Studies* 23 (1986): 88–115.

54. Mintzberg, "Rounding out the Manager's Job."

55. Andy Serwer, "Inside the Rolling Stones Inc.," *Fortune* (September 30, 2002): 58–72.

56. Valerie Darroch, "High Flyer with Feet on Home Ground; Gorbals-Born Stephen Baxter Combines His Role as Glasgow Airport Boss with Heading the City's Chamber of Commerce," *Sunday Herald* (February 6, 2005): 6.

57. Harry S. Jonas III, Ronald E. Fry, and Suresh Srivastva, "The Office of the CEO: Understanding the Executive Experience," *Academy of Management Executive* 4 (August 1990): 36–48.

58. Patricia Sellers, "The Business of Being Oprah," *Fortune* (April 1, 2002): 50–64.

59. Edward O. Welles, "There Are No Simple Businesses Anymore," *The State of Small Business* (1995): 66–79.

60. This section is based largely on Peter F. Drucker, *Managing the Non-Profit Organization: Principles and Practices* (New York: HarperBusiness, 1992); and Thomas Wolf, *Managing a Nonprofit Organization* (New York: Fireside/Simon & Schuster, 1990).

61. Christine W. Letts, William P. Ryan, and Allen Grossman, *High Performance Nonprofit Organizations* (New York: Wiley & Sons, 1999): 30–35.

62. Carol Hymowitz, "In Sarbanes-Oxley Era, Running a Nonprofit Is Only Getting Harder," *The Wall Street Journal* (June 21, 2005): B1; and Bill Birchard, "Nonprofits by the Numbers," *CFO,* (June 2005): 50–55.

63. The following section is based on Harry G. Barkema, Joel A. C. Baum, and Elizabeth A. Mannix, "Management Challenges in a New Time," *Academy of Management Journal* 45, no. 5 (2002): 916–930; "The New Organization: A Survey of the Company," *The Economist* (January 21, 2006); Michael Harvey and M. Ronald Buckley, "Assessing the 'Conventional Wisdoms' of Management for the 21st Century Organization," *Organizational Dynamics* 30, no. 4 (2002): 368–378; and Toby J. Tetenbaum, "Shifting Paradigms: From Newton to Chaos," *Organizational Dynamics* (Spring 1998): 21–32.

64. Caroline Ellis, "The Flattening Corporation," *MIT Sloan Management Review* (Summer 2003): 5.

65. Edwards, "Wherever You Go, You're on the Job."

66. Barkema, Baum, and Mannix, "Management Challenges in a New Time."

67. Keith H. Hammonds, "Smart, Determined, Ambitious, Cheap: The New Face of Global Competition," *Fast Company* (February 2003): 91–97.

68. Tetenbaum, "Shifting Paradigms: From Newton to Chaos."

69. Jennifer Reingold, "What We Learned in the New Economy," *Fast Company* (March 2004): 57–66.

70. Timothy L. O'Brien, "Not Invented Here: Are U.S. Innovators Losing Their Competitive Edge?" *The New York Times* (November 13, 2005), 1.

71. Kevin Maney, "'Must-Win' Attitude Gets Motorola Back on the Hip Track," *USA Today* (January 18, 2006): B3; and Roger O. Crockett, with Cliff Edwards and Spencer E. Ante, "How Motorola Got Its Groove Back," *BusinessWeek* (August 8, 2005): 68–70.

72. Erick Schonfeld, "GE Sees the Light," *Business 2.0* (July 2004): 80–86; Colvin, "The Bionic Manager," and Colvin, "What Makes GE Great?"; Patricia Sellers, "P&G: Teaching an Old Dog New Tricks," *Fortune* (May 31, 2004): 167–180; and Bettina von Stamm, "Collaboration with Other Firms and Customers: Innovation's Secret Weapon," *Strategy & Leadership* 32, no. 3 (2004): 16–20.

73. Scott Kirsner, "Every Day, It's a New Place," *Fast Company* (April–May 1998): 130–134; Peter Coy, "The Creative Economy," *BusinessWeek* (August 28, 2000): 76–82; and Jeremy Main, "The Shape of the New Corporation," *Working Woman* (October 1998): 60–63.

74. This section is based on Loretta Ucelli, "The CEO's 'How To' Guide to Crisis Communications," *Strategy & Leadership* 30, no. 2 (2002): 21–24; Eric Beaudan, "Leading in Turbulent Times," *Ivey Business Journal* (May–June 2002): 22–26; Christine Pearson, "A Blueprint for Crisis Management," *Ivey Business Journal* (January–February 2002): 68–73; Leslie Wayne and Leslie Kaufman, "Leadership, Put to a New Test," *The New York Times* (September 16, 2001): Section 3, 1, 4; Jerry Useem, "What It Takes," *Fortune* (November 12, 2001): 126–132; and Andy Bowen, "Crisis Procedures That Stand the Test of Time," *Public Relations Tactics* (August 2001): 16.

75. June Kronholz and Stefan Fatsis, "Obstacle Course; After Hurricane, Tulane University Struggles to Survive," *The Wall Street Journal* (September 28, 2005): A1, A8.

76. Beaudan, "Leading in Turbulent Times."

77. Paul Argenti, "Crisis Communication: Lessons from 9/11," *Harvard Business Review* (December 2002): 103–109.

78. Allison Fass, "Duking It Out," *Forbes* (June 9, 2003): 74–76.

CHAPTER 2

CHAPTER OUTLINE

Manager's Challenge

Management and Organization

Classical Perspective

Scientific Management

Bureaucratic Organizations

Administrative Principles

Humanistic Perspective

Human Relations Movement

Human Resources Perspective

Behavioral Sciences Approach

Management Science Perspective

Recent Historical Trends

Systems Theory

Contingency View

Total Quality Management

**Innovative Management Thinking
for Turbulent Times**

The Learning Organization

Managing the Technology-Driven
Workplace

LEARNING OBJECTIVES

After studying this chapter, you should be able to:

1. Understand how historical forces influence the practice of management.

2. Identify and explain major developments in the history of management thought.

3. Describe the major components of the classical and humanistic management perspectives.

4. Discuss the management science perspective and its current use in organizations.

5. Explain the major concepts of systems theory, the contingency view, and total quality management.

6. Describe the learning organization and the changes in structure, empowerment, and information sharing that managers make to support it.

7. Discuss the technology-driven workplace and the role of outsourcing, supply chain management, enterprise resource planning, knowledge management systems, and customer relationship management.

THE EVOLUTION OF MANAGEMENT THINKING

MANAGER'S CHALLENGE

Cementos Mexicanos (Cemex), based in Monterrey, Mexico, has been making and delivering concrete for nearly a century. The company specializes in delivering concrete in developing areas of the world, places where anything can, and usually does, go wrong. Even in Monterrey, for example, Cemex copes with unpredictable weather and traffic conditions, spontaneous labor disruptions, building permit snafus, and arbitrary government inspections of construction sites. In addition, more than half of all orders are changed or cancelled by customers, usually at the last minute. Considering that a load of concrete is never more than 90 minutes from spoiling, these chaotic conditions mean high costs, complex scheduling, and frustration for employees, managers, and customers. As competition in the industry increased, Cemex managers began looking for ways to stand out from the crowd. One idea was a guaranteed delivery time, but despite the efforts of employees, the best Cemex could do was promise delivery within a three-hour window. To make matters worse, the construction business itself was becoming increasingly complex and competitive, leading to even more disruptions and cancellations. Builders were sometimes lucky to get their orders delivered on the right day, let alone at the right hour. Cemex managers began to consider that the company needed a whole new approach to doing business—one that accepted rather than resisted the natural chaos of the marketplace. It would mean massive changes in operations, as well as finding ways to get dispatchers and drivers (who had an average of six years of formal education) to think like entrepreneurs.[1]

> If you were a manager at Cemex, what changes would you implement to help the organization thrive in the face of constant chaos? What advice would you give managers concerning their management approach and the kind of company they might create?

■ **TAKE A MOMENT**

Cemex is faced with a situation similar to many companies. The methods and patterns that kept the organization successful in the past no longer seem enough to keep it thriving in today's turbulent environment. Unexpected market forces or other changes in the environment can devastate a company. Retail chains such as Kmart and Sears are fighting to stay alive in the face of Wal-Mart's growing dominance. Major airlines in the United States are being hammered by new low-cost carriers such as JetBlue. And widespread financial and ethical scandals in the early 2000s affected companies in all industries. Lutheran Health Network, which runs six hospitals in and around Fort Wayne, Indiana, now spends about $250,000 more per year to make sure the organization has documentation to show they are complying with health care regulators and other oversight boards.[2] Confronted by ever-shifting conditions, managers have to make continual changes in their organizations, and sometimes create a new kind of company, as at Cemex, one with which they have little experience or skill.

As discussed in Chapter 1, we are currently shifting to a new kind of workplace and a new approach to management. Managers today face the ultimate paradox: (1) Keep everything running efficiently and profitably, while, at the same time, (2) change everything.[3] It is no longer enough just to learn how to measure and control things. Success accrues to those who learn how to be leaders, to initiate change, and to create organizations with fewer managers and less hierarchy that can shift gears quickly.

Management philosophies and organizational forms change over time to meet new needs. The workplace of today is different from what it was 50 years ago—indeed, from what it was even 10 years ago. Yet some ideas and practices from the past are still highly relevant and applicable to management today. Many students wonder why history matters to managers. A historical perspective provides a broader way of thinking, a way of searching for patterns and determining whether they recur across time periods. For example, certain management techniques that seem modern, such as employee stock-ownership programs, have repeatedly gained and lost popularity since the early twentieth century because of historical forces.[4] William Cooper Procter, grandson of the cofounder of Procter & Gamble, introduced a profit-sharing plan in 1887, and expanded it by tying it to stock ownership a few years later. Sam Walton opened Wal-Mart's financial records, including salaries, to all employees in the 1960s, long before business magazines were touting the value of *open-book management*.[5]

A study of the past contributes to understanding both the present and the future. It is a way of learning from others' mistakes so as not to repeat them; learning from others' successes so as to repeat them in the appropriate situation; and most of all, learning to understand why things happen to improve our organizations in the future. This chapter provides an overview of the ideas, theories, and management philosophies that have contributed to making the workplace what it is today. We examine several management approaches that have been popular and successful throughout the twentieth century. The final section of the chapter looks at recent trends and current approaches that build on this foundation of management understanding. This foundation illustrates that the value of studying management lies not in learning current facts and research but in developing a perspective that will facilitate the broad, long-term view needed for management success.

MANAGEMENT AND ORGANIZATION

A historical perspective on management provides a context or environment in which to interpret current opportunities and problems. However, studying history doesn't mean merely arranging events in chronological order; it means developing an understanding of the impact of societal forces on organizations. Studying history is a way to achieve strategic thinking, see the big picture, and improve conceptual skills. Let's start by examining how social, political, and economic forces have influenced organizations and the practice of management.[6]

Social forces refer to those aspects of a culture that guide and influence relationships among people. What do people value? What do people need? What are the standards of behavior among people? These forces shape what is known as the *social contract*, which refers to the unwritten, common rules and perceptions about relationships among people and between employees and management.

A significant social force today is the changing attitudes, ideas, and values of Generation X and Generation Y employees.[7] Generation X employees, those now in their thirties and forties, have had a profound impact on the workplace, and Generation Y workers (sometimes called Nexters) may have an even greater one. These young workers, the most educated generation in the history of the United States, grew up technologically adept and globally conscious. Unlike many workers of the past, they aren't hesitant to question their superiors and challenge the status quo. They want a work environment that is challenging and supportive, with access to cutting-edge technology, opportunities to learn and further their careers and

social forces The aspects of a culture that guide and influence relationships among people—their values, needs, and standards of behavior.

personal goals, and the power to make substantive decisions and changes in the workplace. In addition, Gen X and Gen Y workers have prompted a growing focus on work/life balance, reflected in trends such as telecommuting, flextime, shared jobs, and organization-sponsored sabbaticals.

Political forces refer to the influence of political and legal institutions on people and organizations. Political forces include basic assumptions underlying the political system, such as the desirability of self-government, property rights, contract rights, the definition of justice, and the determination of innocence or guilt of a crime. The spread of capitalism throughout the world has dramatically altered the business landscape. The dominance of the free-market system and growing interdependencies among the world's countries require organizations to operate differently and managers to think in new ways. At the same time, strong anti-American sentiments in many parts of the world create challenges for U.S. companies and managers.

Economic forces pertain to the availability, production, and distribution of resources in a society. Governments, military agencies, churches, schools, and business organizations in every society require resources to achieve their goals, and economic forces influence the allocation of scarce resources. Less-developed countries are growing in economic power, and the economy of the United States and other developed countries is shifting dramatically, with the sources of wealth, the fundamentals of distribution, and the nature of economic decision making undergoing significant changes.[8] Today's economy is based as much on ideas, information, and knowledge as it is on material resources. Supply chains and distribution of resources have been revolutionized by digital technology. Surplus inventories, which once could trigger recessions, are declining or completely disappearing. Another economic trend is the booming importance of small and midsized businesses, including start-ups, which early in the twenty-first century grew at three times the rate of the national economy. "I call it 'the invisible economy,' yet it is *the* economy," says David Birch of Cognetics Inc., a Cambridge, Massachusetts, firm that tracks business formation.[9]

A massive shift in the economy is not without its upheavals, of course. In the early 2000s, years of seemingly endless growth ground to a halt as stock prices fell, particularly for dot-com and technology companies. Numerous Internet-based companies went out of business, and organizations throughout the United States and Canada began laying off hundreds of thousands of workers. However, this economic downturn may also be a stimulus for even greater technological innovation and small business vitality. Read the Unlocking Innovative Solutions Through Technology box for an interesting angle on the shifting economy of the early twenty-first century.

■ **TAKE A MOMENT**

As a new manager do you appreciate a historical perspective to help you interpret current opportunities and problems? Social, economic, and political forces often repeat themselves, as illustrated in the Unlocking Innovative Solutions Through Technology box on page 40, so your understanding will facilitate a broader view of how organizations adapt and succeed in today's environment.

Management practices and perspectives vary in response to these social, political, and economic forces in the larger society. During difficult times, managers look for ideas to help them cope with environmental turbulence and keep their organizations vital. A management tools survey conducted by Bain & Company, for example, reveals a dramatic increase over the past dozen or so years in the variety of management ideas and techniques used by managers. Challenges such as a tough economy and rocky stock market, environmental and organizational crises, lingering anxieties over war and terrorism, and the public suspicion and skepticism resulting from corporate scandals, leave executives searching for any management tool—new or old—that can help them get the most out of limited resources.[10] This search for guidance is also reflected in a proliferation of books, scholarly articles, and

political forces The influence of political and legal institutions on people and organizations.

economic forces Forces that affect the availability, production, and distribution of a society's resources among competing users.

Unlocking Innovative Solutions Through | T E C H N O L O G Y |

OF RAILROADS AND WEB SITES

About 150 years ago, the railroad revolution transformed the economy. Today, the Internet revolution is doing the same thing. We all know that history doesn't really repeat itself, but historical patterns can help us make sense of the present and predict what the future might be like.

The railroads and the Internet serve the same basic economic function: connecting buyers and sellers. And even though few seem to know how to make the Internet economically profitable, the same thing could have been said about the railroad in its infancy. Yet the railroad's ability to move freight quickly and cheaply changed the world, and the Internet's ability to move information quickly and cheaply promises to do the same thing today. And whereas the railroads created the first national market, the Internet is creating the first truly global one. The railroad made it possible for companies such as Sears Roebuck, Montgomery Ward, and Woolworth to lower their prices and expand their operations nationally through catalog retailing, forcing small local retailers to compete in new ways. Similarly, successful Internet retailers such as Amazon.com are challenging bricks-and-mortar companies to rethink how they interact with suppliers and customers.

But nobody said changing the world was easy, and the early twenty first-century turbulence in the technology sector is clearly an indication. Stock prices took a sharp plunge, many of the thousands of entrepreneurs who rushed in with dreams of getting rich on the Internet fell by the wayside, and numerous dot-com companies went out of business. Over a two-year period (1999–2000), the number of Internet IPOs (initial public offerings) grew at amazing speed, and crashed just as quickly. If the history of the railroad is any indication,

this kind of shake-out is to be expected from such a major economic transformation, and new leaders will step in to revise, strengthen, and perfect the new business models. For example, a few small Web-only retailers, like Blue Nile, which sells jewelry, and eBags, Inc., a luggage retailer, have thrived over the long term, demonstrating that careful management can make the difference in cyberspace just as it does in the physical world.

In the nineteenth century, railroad stocks soared and plunged as practical realities warred with potential profits and the hopes of investors fought with their fears. The railroad vastly overbuilt in the decades after the Civil War, and in the 1880s and 1890s, more than two-thirds of the railroad tracks in the United States passed through receivership and were reorganized by the big Wall Street banks. Savvy entrepreneurs who had stood on the sidelines took advantage of the shake-out in the railroad industry to build stronger companies and make themselves rich. For example, Cornelius (Commodore) Vanderbilt never built a railroad, but rather, bought badly run small, local railway lines, merged them into efficient operations, and managed them expertly, thereby creating the largest fortune of the railroad era. Similarly, the world of Internet commerce may be undergoing consolidation and focusing as today's best e-commerce leaders step in and make changes that will lead to a stronger, more stable future for the companies that survive.

SOURCES: Nick Wingfield, "Internet 2.0: E-tailing Comes of Age," *The Wall Street Journal* (December 8, 2003): B1; John Steele Gordon, "The Golden Spike," *Forbes ASAP* (February 21, 2000): 118–122; and Lee Gomes, "Fix It and They Will Come: E-commerce Isn't Dead. Just Broken," *The Wall Street Journal* (February 12, 2001): R4.

---

conferences dedicated to examining management fashions and trends.[11] Exhibit 2.1 illustrates the evolution of significant management perspectives over time, each of which will be examined in the remainder of this chapter. The timeline reflects the dominant time period for each approach, but elements of each are still used in today's organizations.

CLASSICAL PERSPECTIVE

classical perspective A management perspective that emerged during the nineteenth and early twentieth centuries that emphasized a rational, scientific approach to the study of management and sought to make organizations efficient operating machines.

The practice of management can be traced to 3000 B.C.E. to the first government organizations developed by the Sumerians and Egyptians, but the formal study of management is relatively recent.[12] The early study of management as we know it today began with what is now called the **classical perspective**.

The classical perspective on management emerged during the nineteenth and early twentieth centuries. The factory system that began to appear in the 1800s

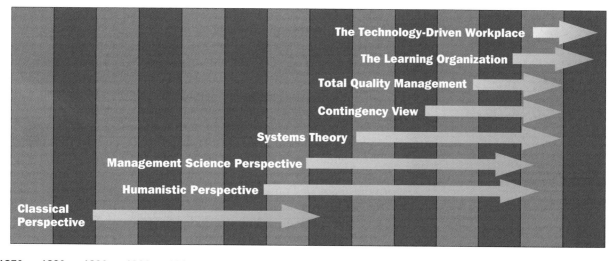

| | 1870 | 1880 | 1890 | 1900 | 1910 | 1920 | 1930 | 1940 | 1950 | 1960 | 1970 | 1980 | 1990 | 2000 | 2010 |

EXHIBIT **2.1**

Management Perspectives over Time

posed challenges that earlier organizations had not encountered. Problems arose in tooling the plants, organizing managerial structure, training employees (many of them non-English-speaking immigrants), scheduling complex manufacturing operations, and dealing with increased labor dissatisfaction and resulting strikes.

These myriad new problems and the development of large, complex organizations demanded a new approach to coordination and control, and a "new subspecies of economic man—the salaried manager"[13]—was born. Between 1880 and 1920, the number of professional managers in the United States grew from 161,000 to more than 1 million.[14] These professional managers began developing and testing solutions to the mounting challenges of organizing, coordinating, and controlling large numbers of people and increasing worker productivity. Thus began the evolution of modern management with the classical perspective.

This perspective contains three subfields, each with a slightly different emphasis: scientific management, bureaucratic organizations, and administrative principles.[15]

CONCEPT CONNECTION

Frederick Winslow Taylor (1856–1915). Taylor's theory that labor productivity could be improved by scientifically determined management practices earned him the status of "father of scientific management."

Scientific Management

Organizations' somewhat limited success in achieving improvements in labor productivity led a young engineer to suggest that the problem lay more in poor management practices than in labor. Frederick Winslow Taylor (1856–1915) insisted that management itself would have to change and, further, that the manner of change could be determined only by scientific study; hence, the label *scientific management* emerged. Taylor suggested that decisions based on rules of thumb and tradition be replaced with precise procedures developed after careful study of individual situations.[16]

Taylor's philosophy is encapsulated in his statement, "In the past the man has been first. In the future, the system must be first."[17] The **scientific management** approach is illustrated by the unloading of iron from rail cars and reloading

scientific management
A subfield of the classical management perspective that emphasized scientifically determined changes in management practices as the solution to improving labor productivity.

CONCEPT
CONNECTION Lillian M. Gilbreth (1878–1972), Frank B. Gilbreth (1868–1924). Shown here using a "motion study" device, this husband-and-wife team contributed to the principles of scientific management. His development of **time and motion studies** and her work in **industrial psychology** pioneered many of today's management and human resource techniques.

COURTESY OF FORD MOTOR COMPANY

CONCEPT
CONNECTION Frederick Taylor's **scientific management** techniques were expanded by automaker Henry Ford, who replaced workers with machines for heavy lifting and moving. One of the first applications of the moving assembly line was the Magneto assembly operation at Ford's Highland Park plant in 1913. Magnetos moved from one worker to the next, reducing production time by one half. The same principle was applied to total-car assembly, improving efficiency and reducing worker-hours required to produce a Model-T Ford to less than two. Under this system, a Ford rolled off the assembly line every 10 seconds.

finished steel for the Bethlehem Steel plant in 1898. Taylor calculated that with correct movements, tools, and sequencing, each man was capable of loading 47.5 tons per day instead of the typical 12.5 tons. He also worked out an incentive system that paid each man $1.85 a day for meeting the new standard, an increase from the previous rate of $1.15. Productivity at Bethlehem Steel shot up overnight.

Although known as the *father of scientific management*, Taylor was not alone in this area. Henry Gantt, an associate of Taylor's, developed the *Gantt chart*—a bar graph that measures planned and completed work along each stage of production by time elapsed. Two other important pioneers in this area were the husband-and-wife team of Frank B. and Lillian M. Gilbreth. Frank B. Gilbreth (1868–1924) pioneered *time and motion study* and arrived at many of his management techniques independently of Taylor. He stressed efficiency and was known for his quest for the one best way to do work. Although Gilbreth is known for his early work with brick-layers, his work had great impact on medical surgery by drastically reducing the time patients spent on the operating table. Surgeons were able to save countless lives through the application of time and motion study. Lillian M. Gilbreth (1878–1972) was more interested in the human aspect of work. When her husband died at the age of 56, she had 12 children ages 2 to 19. The undaunted "first lady of management" went right on with her work. She presented a paper in place of her late husband, continued their seminars and consulting, lectured, and eventually became a professor at Purdue University.[18] She pioneered in the field of industrial psychology and made substantial contributions to human resource management.

The basic ideas of scientific management are shown in Exhibit 2.2. To use this approach, managers should develop standard methods for doing each job, select workers with the appropriate abilities, train workers in the standard methods, support workers and eliminate interruptions, and provide wage incentives.

The ideas of scientific management that began with Taylor dramatically increased productivity across all industries, and they are still important today. Indeed, the concept of arranging work based on careful analysis of tasks for maximum productivity is deeply embedded in our organizations.[19] However, because scientific management ignored the social context and workers' needs, it led to increased conflict and sometimes violent clashes between managers and employees. Under this system, workers often felt exploited—a sharp contrast from the harmony and cooperation that Taylor and his followers had envisioned.

bureaucratic organizations
A subfield of the classical management perspective that emphasized management on an impersonal, rational basis through such elements as clearly defined authority and responsibility, formal record-keeping, and separation of management and ownership.

Bureaucratic Organizations

A systematic approach developed in Europe that looked at the organization as a whole is the **bureaucratic organizations** approach, a subfield within the classical perspective. Max Weber (1864–1920), a German theorist, introduced most of the concepts on bureaucratic organizations.[20]

During the late 1800s, many European organizations were managed on a personal, family-like basis. Employees were loyal to a single individual rather than to the organization or its mission. The dysfunctional consequence of this management

General Approach

- Developed standard method for performing each job.
- Selected workers with appropriate abilities for each job.
- Trained workers in standard methods.
- Supported workers by planning their work and eliminating interruptions.
- Provided wage incentives to workers for increased output.

Contributions

- Demonstrated the importance of compensation for performance.
- Initiated the careful study of tasks and jobs.
- Demonstrated the importance of personnel selection and training.

Criticisms

- Did not appreciate the social context of work and higher needs of workers.
- Did not acknowledge variance among individuals.
- Tended to regard workers as uninformed and ignored their ideas and suggestions.

E X H I B I T   2.2

Characteristics of Scientific Management

practice was that resources were used to realize individual desires rather than organizational goals. Employees in effect owned the organization and used resources for their own gain rather than to serve customers. Weber envisioned organizations that would be managed on an impersonal, rational basis. This form of organization was called a *bureaucracy.* Exhibit 2.3 summarizes the six characteristics of bureaucracy as specified by Weber.

Weber believed that an organization based on rational authority would be more efficient and adaptable to change because continuity is related to formal structure

E X H I B I T   2.3

Characteristics of Weberian Bureaucracy

SOURCE: Adapted from Max Web, *The Theory of Social and Economic Organizations,* ed. and trans. A.M. Henderson and Talcott Parsons (New York: Free Press, 1947), 328–337.

Division of labor, with clear definitions of authority and responsibility

Personnel selected and promoted based on technical qualifications

Positions organized in a hierarchy of authority

THE IDEAL BUREAUCRACY

Administrative acts and decisions recorded in writing

Managers subject to rules and procedures that will ensure reliable, predictable behavior

Management separate from the ownership of the organization

and positions rather than to a particular person, who may leave or die. To Weber, rationality in organizations meant employee selection and advancement based not on who you know, but rather on competence and technical qualifications, which are assessed by examination or according to training and experience. The organization relies on rules and written records for continuity. In addition, rules and procedures are impersonal and applied uniformly to all employees. A clear division of labor arises from distinct definitions of authority and responsibility, legitimized as official duties. Positions are organized in a hierarchy, with each position under the authority of a higher one. The manager depends not on his or her personality for successfully giving orders but on the legal power invested in the managerial position.

■ **TAKE A MOMENT**

Read the ethical dilemma on page 61 that pertains to problems of bureaucracy. What would it be like for you to be a manager in a bureaucratic organization? Would you thrive in that environment?

The term *bureaucracy* has taken on a negative meaning in today's organizations and is associated with endless rules and red tape. We have all been frustrated by waiting in long lines or following seemingly silly procedures. However, rules and other bureaucratic procedures provide a standard way of dealing with employees. Everyone gets equal treatment, and everyone knows what the rules are. This foundation enables many organizations to become extremely efficient. Consider United Parcel Service (UPS), sometimes called *Big Brown*.

United Parcel Service

United Parcel Service took on the U.S. Postal Service at its own game—and won. UPS specializes in the delivery of small packages, delivering more than 13 million every business day. In addition, UPS is gaining market share in air service, logistics, and information services. Television commercials asking, "What can Brown do for you?" signify the company's expanding global information services. Why has Big Brown been so successful? One important factor is the concept of bureaucracy. UPS is bound up in rules and regulations. It teaches drivers an astounding 340 steps for how to correctly deliver a package—such as how to load the truck, how to fasten their seat belts, how to walk, and how to carry their keys. Specific safety rules apply to drivers, loaders, clerks, and managers. Strict dress codes are enforced—clean uniforms (called *browns*), every day, black or brown polished shoes with nonslip soles, no beards, no hair below the collar, and so on. Supervisors conduct three-minute inspections of drivers each day. The company also has rules specifying cleanliness standards for buildings, trucks, and other properties. No eating or drinking is permitted at employee desks. Every manager is given bound copies of policy books and is expected to use them.

UPS has a well-defined division of labor. Each plant consists of specialized drivers, loaders, clerks, washers, sorters, and maintenance personnel. UPS thrives on written records, and has been a leader in using new technology to enhance reliability and efficiency. Drivers use a computerized clipboard to track everything from miles per gallon to data on parcel delivery. All drivers have daily worksheets that specify performance goals and work output.

Technical qualification is the criterion for hiring and promotion. The UPS policy book says the leader is expected to have the knowledge and capacity to justify the position of leadership. Favoritism is forbidden. The bureaucratic model works just fine at UPS, "the tightest ship in the shipping business."[21]

administrative principles
A subfield of the classical management perspective that focuses on the total organization rather than the individual worker, delineating the management functions of planning, organizing, commanding, coordinating, and controlling.

Administrative Principles

Another major subfield within the classical perspective is known as the administrative principles approach. Whereas scientific management focused on the productivity of the individual worker, the **administrative principles** approach focused on the total organization. The contributors to this approach included Henri Fayol, Mary Parker Follett, and Chester I. Barnard.

Henri Fayol (1841–1925) was a French mining engineer who worked his way up to become head of a major mining group known as Comambault. Comambault survives today as part of Le Creusot-Loire, the largest mining and metallurgical group in central France. In his later years, Fayol wrote down his concepts on administration, based largely on his own management experiences.[22]

In his most significant work, *General and Industrial Management*, Fayol discussed 14 general principles of management, several of which are part of management philosophy today. For example:

:: *Unity of command.* Each subordinate receives orders from one—and only one—superior.

:: *Division of work.* Managerial and technical work are amenable to specialization to produce more and better work with the same amount of effort.

:: *Unity of direction.* Similar activities in an organization should be grouped together under one manager.

:: *Scalar chain.* A chain of authority extends from the top to the bottom of the organization and should include every employee.

Fayol felt that these principles could be applied in any organizational setting. He also identified five basic functions or elements of management: *planning, organizing, commanding, coordinating,* and *controlling.* These functions underlie much of the general approach to today's management theory.

Mary Parker Follett (1868–1933) was trained in philosophy and political science at what today is Radcliffe College. She applied herself in many fields, including social psychology and management. She wrote of the importance of common superordinate goals for reducing conflict in organizations.[23] Her work was popular with businesspeople of her day but was often overlooked by management scholars.[24] Follett's ideas served as a contrast to scientific management and are reemerging as applicable for modern managers dealing with rapid changes in today's global environment. Her approach to leadership stressed the importance of people rather than engineering techniques. She offered the pithy admonition, "Don't hug your blueprints," and analyzed the dynamics of management-organization interactions. Follett addressed issues that are timely today, such as ethics, power, and how to lead in a way that encourages employees to give their best. The concepts of *empowerment*, facilitating rather than controlling employees, and allowing employees to act depending on the authority of the situation opened new areas for theoretical study by Chester Barnard and others.[25]

Chester I. Barnard (1886–1961) studied economics at Harvard but failed to receive a degree because he lacked a course in laboratory science. He went to work in the statistical department of AT&T and in 1927 became president of New Jersey Bell. One of Barnard's significant contributions was the concept of the informal organization. The *informal organization* occurs in all formal organizations and includes cliques and naturally occurring social groupings. Barnard argued that organizations are not machines and informal relationships are powerful forces that can help the organization if properly managed. Another significant contribution was the *acceptance theory of authority,* which states that people have free will and can choose whether to follow management orders. People typically follow orders because they perceive positive benefit to themselves, but they do

COURTESY OF RONALD G. GREENWOOD

CONCEPT CONNECTION

Mary Parker Follett (1868–1933). Follett was a major contributor to the **administrative principles** approach to management. Her emphasis on worker participation and shared goals among managers was embraced by many businesspeople of the day and has been recently "rediscovered" by corporate America.

CONCEPT CONNECTION This 1914 photograph shows the initiation of a new arrival at a Nebraska planting camp. This initiation was not part of the formal rules and illustrates the significance of the **informal organization** described by Barnard. Social values and behaviors were powerful forces that could help or hurt the planting organization depending on how they were managed.

FROM NATIONAL ARCHIVES

have a choice. Managers should treat employees properly because their acceptance of authority may be critical to organization success in important situations.[26]

The overall classical perspective as an approach to management was very powerful and gave companies fundamental new skills for establishing high productivity and effective treatment of employees. Indeed, the United States surged ahead of the world in management techniques, and other countries, especially Japan, borrowed heavily from American ideas.

HUMANISTIC PERSPECTIVE

Mary Parker Follett and Chester Barnard were early advocates of a more **humanistic perspective** on management that emphasized the importance of understanding human behaviors, needs, and attitudes in the workplace as well as social interactions and group processes.[27] We will discuss three subfields based on the humanistic perspective: the human relations movement, the human resources perspective, and the behavioral sciences approach.

Human Relations Movement

The United States always espoused the spirit of human equality. However, this spirit did not always translate into practice when it came to power sharing between managers and workers. The human relations school of thought considers that truly effective control comes from within the individual worker rather than from strict, authoritarian control.[28] This school of thought recognized and directly responded to social pressures for enlightened treatment of employees. The early work on industrial psychology and personnel selection received little attention because of the prominence of scientific management. Then a series of studies at a Chicago electric company, which came to be known as the **Hawthorne studies**, changed all that.

Beginning about 1895, a struggle developed between manufacturers of gas and electric lighting fixtures for control of the residential and industrial market.[29] By 1909, electric lighting had begun to win, but the increasingly efficient electric fixtures used less total power. The electric companies began a campaign to convince industrial users that they needed more light to get more productivity. When advertising did not work, the industry began using experimental tests to demonstrate their argument. Managers were skeptical about the results, so the Committee on Industrial Lighting (CIL) was set up to run the tests. To further add to the tests' credibility, Thomas Edison was made honorary chairman of the CIL. In one test location—the Hawthorne plant of the Western Electric Company—some interesting events occurred.

The major part of this work involved four experimental and three control groups. In all, five different tests were conducted. These pointed to the importance of factors *other* than illumination in affecting productivity. To more carefully examine these factors, numerous other experiments were conducted.[30] The results of the most famous study, the first Relay Assembly Test Room (RATR) experiment, were extremely controversial. Under the guidance of two Harvard professors, Elton Mayo and Fritz Roethlisberger, the RATR studies lasted nearly six years (May 10, 1927 to May 4, 1933) and involved 24 separate experimental periods. So many factors were changed and so many unforeseen factors uncontrolled that scholars disagree on the factors that truly contributed to the general increase in performance over that time period. Most early interpretations, however, agreed on one thing: Money was not the cause of the increased output.[31] It was believed that the factor that best explained increased output was *human relations*. Employees performed better when managers treated them in a positive manner. Recent reanalyses of the experiments have revealed that a number of factors were different for the workers involved, and

humanistic perspective A management perspective that emerged near the late nineteenth century and emphasized understanding human behavior, needs, and attitudes in the workplace.

Hawthorne studies A series of experiments on worker productivity begun in 1924 at the Hawthorne plant of Western Electric Company in Illinois; attributed employees' increased output to managers' better treatment of them during the study.

some suggest that money may well have been the single most important factor.[32] An interview with one of the original participants revealed that just getting into the experimental group had meant a huge increase in income.[33]

These new data clearly show that money mattered a great deal at Hawthorne. In addition, worker productivity increased partly as a result of the increased feelings of importance and group pride employees felt by virtue of being selected for this important project.[34] One unintended contribution of the experiments was a rethinking of field research practices. Researchers and scholars realized that the researcher can influence the outcome of an experiment by being too closely involved with research subjects. This phenomenon has come to be known as the *Hawthorne effect* in research methodology. Subjects behaved differently because of the active participation of researchers in the Hawthorne experiments.[35]

From a historical perspective, whether the studies were academically sound is of less importance than the fact that they stimulated an increased interest in looking at employees as more than extensions of production machinery. The interpretation that employees' output increased when managers treated them in a positive manner started a revolution in worker treatment for improving organizational productivity. Despite flawed methodology or inaccurate conclusions, the findings provided the impetus for the **human relations movement**. This approach shaped management theory and practice for well over a quarter-century, and the belief that human relations is the best approach for increasing productivity persists today.

FROM WESTERN ELECTRIC PHOTOGRAPHIC SERVICES

CONCEPT CONNECTION This is the Relay Room of the Western Electric Hawthorne, Illinois, plant in 1927. Six women worked in this relay assembly test room during the controversial experiments on employee productivity. Professors Mayo and Roethlisberger evaluated conditions such as rest breaks and workday length, physical health, amount of sleep, and diet. Experimental changes were fully discussed with the women and were abandoned if they disapproved. Gradually the researchers began to realize they had created a change in supervisory style and **human relations**, which they believed was the true cause of the increased productivity.

Before reading on, take the New Manager Self-Test on page 48. This test will give you feedback about how your personal manager frame of reference relates to the human resources and other perspectives described in this chapter.

■ **TAKE A MOMENT**

Human Resources Perspective

The human relations movement initially espoused a *dairy farm* view of management—contented cows give more milk, so satisfied workers will give more work. Gradually, views with deeper content began to emerge. The **human resources perspective** maintained an interest in worker participation and considerate leadership but shifted the emphasis to consider the daily tasks that people perform. The human resources perspective combines prescriptions for design of job tasks with theories of motivation.[36] In the human resources view, jobs should be designed so that tasks are not perceived as dehumanizing or demeaning but instead allow workers to use their full potential. Two of the best-known contributors to the human resources perspective were Abraham Maslow and Douglas McGregor.

Abraham Maslow (1908–1970), a practicing psychologist, observed that his patients' problems usually stemmed from an inability to satisfy their needs. Thus, he generalized his work and suggested a hierarchy of needs. Maslow's hierarchy started with physiological needs and progressed to safety, belongingness, esteem, and, finally, self-actualization needs. Chapter 16 discusses his ideas in more detail.

Douglas McGregor (1906–1964) had become frustrated with the early simplistic human relations notions while president of Antioch College in Ohio. He challenged both the classical perspective and the early human relations assumptions about

human relations movement A movement in management thinking and practice that emphasizes satisfaction of employees' basic needs as the key to increased worker productivity.

human resources perspective A management perspective that suggests jobs should be designed to meet higher-level needs by allowing workers to use their full potential.

EVOLUTION OF STYLE

This questionnaire asks you to describe yourself. For each item, give the number "4" to the phrase that best describes you, "3" to the item that is next best, and on down to "1" for the item that is least like you.

1. My strongest skills are:

   _____ **a.** Analytical skills

   _____ **b.** Interpersonal skills

   _____ **c.** Political skills

   _____ **d.** Flair for drama

2. The best way to describe me is:

   _____ **a.** Technical expert

   _____ **b.** Good listener

   _____ **c.** Skilled negotiator

   _____ **d.** Inspirational leader

3. What has helped me the most to be successful is my ability to:

   _____ **a.** Make good decisions

   _____ **b.** Coach and develop people

   _____ **c.** Build strong alliances and a power base

   _____ **d.** Inspire and excite others

4. What people are most likely to notice about me is my:

   _____ **a.** Attention to detail

   _____ **b.** Concern for people

   _____ **c.** Ability to succeed in the face of conflict and opposition

   _____ **d.** Charisma

5. My most important leadership trait is:

   _____ **a.** Clear, logical thinking

   _____ **b.** Caring and support for others

   _____ **c.** Toughness and aggressiveness

   _____ **d.** Imagination and creativity

6. I am best described as:

   _____ **a.** An analyst

   _____ **b.** A humanist

   _____ **c.** A politician

   _____ **d.** A visionary

INTERPRETATION: New managers typically view their world through one or more mental frames of reference. (1) The *structural frame* of reference sees the organization as a machine that can be economically efficient and that provides a manager with formal authority to achieve goals. This manager frame became strong during the era of **scientific management** and **bureaucratic administration**. (2) The *human resource frame* sees the organization as people, with manager emphasis given to support, empowerment, and belonging. This manager frame gained importance with the rise of the **humanistic perspective**. (3) The *political frame* sees the organization as a competition for resources to achieve goals, with manager emphasis on negotiation and hallway coalition building. This frame reflects the need within **systems theory** to have all parts working together. (4) The *symbolic frame* of reference sees the organization as theater—a place to achieve dreams—with manager emphasis on symbols, vision, culture, and inspiration. This manager frame is important for **learning organizations**.

Which frame reflects your way of viewing the world? *The first two frames of reference—structural and human resource—are more important for new managers.* These two frames usually are mastered first. As new managers gain experience and move up the organization, they should acquire political skills and also learn to use symbols for communication. It is important for new managers not to be stuck for years in one way of viewing the organization because their progress may be limited. Many new managers evolve through and master each of the four frames as they become more skilled and experienced.

SCORING: Higher score represents your way of viewing the organization and will influence your management style. Compute your scores as follows:

ST = 1a + 2a + 3a + 4a + 5a + 6a = _____

HR = 1b + 2b + 3b + 4b + 5b + 6b = _____

PL = 1c + 2c + 3c + 4c + 5c + 6c = _____

SY = 1d + 2d + 3d + 4d + 5d + 6d = _____

Assumptions of Theory X

- The average human being has an inherent dislike of work and will avoid it if possible.

- Because of the human characteristic of dislike for work, most people must be coerced, controlled, directed, or threatened with punishment to get them to put forth adequate effort toward the achievement of organizational objectives.

- The average human being prefers to be directed, wishes to avoid responsibility, has relatively little ambition, and wants security above all.

Assumptions of Theory Y

- The expenditure of physical and mental effort in work is as natural as play or rest. The average human being does not inherently dislike work.

- External control and the threat of punishment are not the only means for bringing about effort toward organizational objectives. A person will exercise self-direction and self-control in the service of objectives to which he or she is committed.

- The average human being learns, under proper conditions, not only to accept but to seek responsibility.

- The capacity to exercise a relatively high degree of imagination, ingenuity, and creativity in the solution of organizational problems is widely, not narrowly, distributed in the population.

- Under the conditions of modern industrial life, the intellectual potentialities of the average human being are only partially utilized.

E X H I B I T 2.4

Theory X and Theory Y

SOURCE: Douglas McGregor, *The Human Side of Enterprise* (New York: McGraw-Hill, 1960), 33–48.

human behavior. Based on his experiences as a manager and consultant, his training as a psychologist, and the work of Maslow, McGregor formulated his Theory X and Theory Y, which are explained in Exhibit 2.4.[37] McGregor believed that the classical perspective was based on Theory X assumptions about workers. He also felt that a slightly modified version of Theory X fit early human relations ideas. In other words, human relations ideas did not go far enough. McGregor proposed Theory Y as a more realistic view of workers for guiding management thinking.

■ TAKE A MOMENT

Complete the experiential exercise on page 61 that pertains to Theory X and Theory Y. How will your management assumptions about people fit into an organization today?

The point of Theory Y is that organizations can take advantage of the imagination and intellect of all their employees. Employees will exercise self-control and will contribute to organizational goals when given the opportunity. A few companies today still use Theory X management, but many are using Theory Y techniques. Consider how Signet Painting Inc. taps into the full potential of every worker by operating from Theory Y assumptions.

Signet Painting Inc.

A painting contractor might seem an unlikely place to look for modern management techniques, but Signet Painting is on the cutting edge in creating a work environment that affords workers self-esteem and significance as well as a paycheck. Twin brothers Larry and Garry Gehrke first started searching for a new approach to managing workers when the company grew so large they couldn't personally be involved in every project. They began by giving crew leaders the power and authority to make decisions on a job, such as reordering supplies without supervisor approval.

The Gehrkes found a number of ways to involve workers and give them opportunities to share their best knowledge and skills. One approach is a policy committee made up of volunteers who meet to brainstorm solutions to problems they encounter in the field. Managers also strive to incorporate employees' interests and past work experience into their jobs so that each person has the opportunity to make a unique contribution. "Each person wants to feel like they have the knowledge of what they're doing . . . ," says foreman Derrick Borsheim. "I ask my crew questions like, 'What do you think? What should I do?' And I use their ideas."

Chief operating officer Julie Gehrke says that when the management team gave employees in the field more power and authority to make decisions and control their own jobs, it totally changed people's workplace identity. Managers set clear boundaries, rules, and systems, and then trust workers to carry out their responsibilities professionally and reliably. The application of Theory Y assumptions at Signet Painting has given employees a new sense of pride and ownership in their work. Gehrke says, "When I come into the office on Monday morning and hear one of our painters giving an orientation to a new hire and expounding on what a great company this is to work for, I feel triumphant."[38]

Behavioral Sciences Approach

The **behavioral sciences approach** develops theories about human behavior based on scientific methods and study. Behavioral science draws from sociology, psychology, anthropology, economics, and other disciplines to understand employee behavior and interaction in an organizational setting. The approach can be seen in practically every organization. When General Electric conducts research to determine the best set of tests, interviews, and employee profiles to use when selecting new employees, it is using behavioral science techniques. When Circuit City electronics stores train new managers in the techniques of employee motivation, most of the theories and findings are rooted in behavioral science research.

One specific set of management techniques based in the behavioral sciences approach is *organization development* (OD). In the 1970s, organization development evolved as a separate field that applied the behavioral sciences to improve the organization's health and effectiveness through its ability to cope with change, improve internal relationships, and increase problem-solving capabilities.[39] The techniques and concepts of organization development have since been broadened and expanded to address the increasing complexity of organizations and the environment, and OD is still a vital approach for managers. OD will be discussed in detail in Chapter 11. Other concepts that grew out of the behavioral sciences approach include matrix organizations, self-managed teams, ideas about corporate culture, and management by wandering around. Indeed, the behavioral sciences approach has influenced the majority of tools, techniques, and approaches that managers have applied to organizations since the 1970s. In recent years, behavioral sciences and OD techniques have been applied to help managers build learning organizations.

All of the remaining chapters of this book contain research findings and management applications that can be attributed to the behavioral sciences approach. This chapter's Shoptalk box illustrates a number of management innovations that have become popular over the past 50 years. Note the trend of new management concepts from the behavioral sciences, increasing about 1970 and then again from 1980 to the present. The rapid pace of change and the increased pressure of global competition have spurred even greater interest in improved behavioral approaches to management.

MANAGEMENT SCIENCE PERSPECTIVE

World War II caused many management changes. The massive and complicated problems associated with modern global warfare presented managerial decision makers with the need for more sophisticated tools than ever before. The **management science perspective** emerged to address those problems. This view is distinguished for its application of mathematics, statistics, and other quantitative techniques to management decision making and problem solving. During World War II, groups of mathematicians, physicists, and other scientists were formed to solve military problems. Because those problems frequently involved moving massive amounts of materials and large numbers of people quickly and efficiently, the techniques had obvious applications to large-scale business firms.[40]

behavioral sciences approach A subfield of the humanistic management perspective that applies social science in an organizational context, drawing from economics, psychology, sociology, and other disciplines.

management science perspective A management perspective that emerged after World War II and applied mathematics, statistics, and other quantitative techniques to managerial problems.

EBBS AND FLOWS OF MANAGEMENT INNOVATIONS, 1950–2000

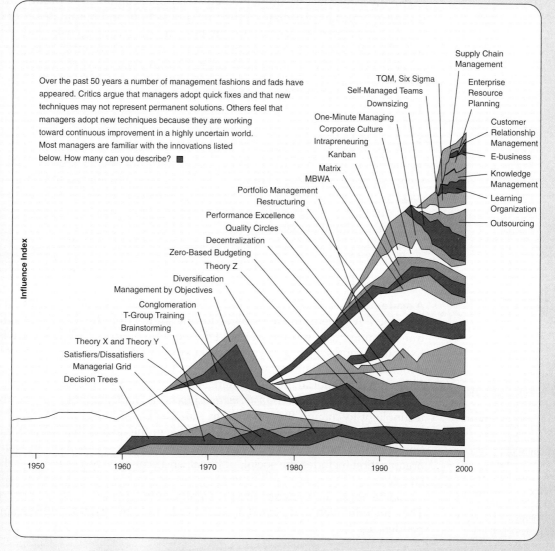

Over the past 50 years a number of management fashions and fads have appeared. Critics argue that managers adopt quick fixes and that new techniques may not represent permanent solutions. Others feel that managers adopt new techniques because they are working toward continuous improvement in a highly uncertain world. Most managers are familiar with the innovations listed below. How many can you describe? ■

SOURCE: Adapted from Fig 1.3, Richard Tanner Pascale, *Managing on the Edge* (New York: Touchstone/Simon & Schuster, 1990), 20. Copyright © 1990 by Richard Pascale.

Operations research grew directly out of the World War II groups (called *operational research teams* in Great Britain and *operations research teams* in the United States).[41] It consists of mathematical model building and other applications of quantitative techniques to managerial problems.

Operations management refers to the field of management that specializes in the physical production of goods or services. Operations management specialists use quantitative techniques to solve manufacturing problems. Some commonly used methods are forecasting, inventory modeling, linear and nonlinear programming, queuing theory, scheduling, simulation, and break-even analysis.

Information technology (IT) is the most recent subfield of the management science perspective, which is often reflected in management information systems. These systems are designed to provide relevant information to managers in a timely and cost-efficient manner. More recently, information technology within organizations evolved to include intranets and extranets, as well as various software programs that help managers estimate costs, plan and track production, manage projects, allocate resources, or schedule employees. When Weyerhaeuser Company's door factory implemented an intranet combined with software to track inventory, calculate estimates, schedule production, and automate order taking, it applied management science to cut both manufacturing costs and production time.[42] Most of today's organizations have departments of information technology specialists who use management science techniques to solve complex organizational problems.

RECENT HISTORICAL TRENDS

Management is, by nature, complex and dynamic. Elements of each of the perspectives discussed here are still in use today. The most prevalent is the humanistic perspective, but even it has undergone change in recent years. Three recent trends that grew out of the humanistic perspective are systems theory, the contingency view, and total quality management.

Systems Theory

A **system** is a set of interrelated parts that function as a whole to achieve a common purpose.[43] A system functions by acquiring inputs from the external environment, transforming them in some way, and discharging outputs back to the environment. Exhibit 2.5 shows the basic **systems theory** of organizations. It consists of five components: inputs, a transformation process, outputs, feedback, and the environment. *Inputs* are the material, human, financial, or information resources used to produce goods and services. The *transformation process* is management's use of production technology to change the inputs into outputs. *Outputs* include the organization's products and services. *Feedback* is knowledge of the results that influence the selection of inputs during the next cycle of the process. The *environment* surrounding the organization includes the social, political, and economic forces noted earlier in this chapter.

Some ideas in systems theory significantly affected management thinking. They include open and closed systems, entropy, synergy, and subsystem interdependencies.[44]

system A set of interrelated parts that function as a whole to achieve a common purpose.

systems theory An extension of the humanistic perspective that describes organizations as open systems characterized by entropy, synergy, and subsystem interdependence.

EXHIBIT 2.5

The Systems View of Organizations

Open systems must interact with the environment to survive; **closed systems** need not. In the classical and management science perspectives, organizations were frequently thought of as closed systems. In the management science perspective, closed system assumptions—the absence of external disturbances—are sometimes used to simplify problems for quantitative analysis. In reality, however, all organizations are open systems, and the cost of ignoring the environment may be failure.

Entropy is a universal property of systems and refers to their tendency to run down and die. If a system does not receive fresh inputs and energy from its environment, it will eventually cease to exist. Organizations must monitor their environments, adjust to changes, and continuously bring in new inputs in order to survive and prosper. Managers try to design the organization/environment interface to reduce entropy.

Synergy means that the whole is greater than the sum of its parts. When an organization is formed, something new comes into the world. Management, coordination, and production that did not exist before are now present. Organizational units working together can accomplish more than those same units working alone. The sales department depends on production, and vice versa.

Subsystems depend on one another as parts of a system. Changes in one part of the organization affect other parts. The organization must be managed as a coordinated whole. Managers who understand subsystem interdependence are reluctant to make changes that do not recognize subsystem impact on the organization as a whole. Consider Toyota's highly successful application of the "just-in-time" inventory control system, which aims to keep inventory at its lowest. Managers knew that the best way to make the system work was to let employees on the factory floor control the flow of materials. Thus the change in production required that the company also make changes in culture and structure. Toyota decentralized decision making so that employees doing the work were empowered to make choices about how to accomplish it. Cultural values were shifted to encourage every employee to think creatively about improving his or her particular piece of the organization and to see problems as opportunities for learning and improving.[45] Major changes in an organization often take quite some time because of the interconnection of the organization's subsystems.

Contingency View

A second contemporary extension to management thinking is the **contingency view**. The classical perspective assumed a *universalist* view. Management concepts were thought to be universal; that is, whatever worked—leader style, bureaucratic structure—in one organization would work in another. In business education, however, an alternative view exists. In this *case* view, each situation is believed to be unique. Principles are not universal, and one learns about management by experiencing a large number of case problem situations. Managers face the task of determining what methods will work in every new situation.

To integrate these views the contingency view emerged, as illustrated in Exhibit 2.6.[46] Here neither of the other views is seen as entirely correct. Instead, certain

open system A system that interacts with the external environment.

closed system A system that does not interact with the external environment.

53

entropy The tendency for a system to run down and die.

synergy The concept that the whole is greater than the sum of its parts.

subsystems Parts of a system that depend on one another for their functioning.

contingency view An extension of the humanistic perspective in which the successful resolution of organizational problems is thought to depend on managers' identification of key variations in the situation at hand.

Chapter 2   THE EVOLUTION OF MANAGEMENT THINKING

EXHIBIT   2.6

Contingency View of Management

Case View — "Every situation is unique."

Universalist View — "There is one best way."

Contingency View
Organizational phenomena exist in logical patterns. Managers devise and apply similar responses to common types of problems.

contingencies, or variables, exist for helping management identify and understand situations. The contingency view means that a manager's response depends on identifying key contingencies in an organizational situation. For example, a consultant might mistakenly recommend the same *management by objectives* (MBO) system for a manufacturing firm that was successful in a school system. The contingency view tells us that what works in one setting might not work in another. Management's job is to search for important contingencies. When managers learn to identify important patterns and characteristics of their organizations, they can then fit solutions to those characteristics.

Important contingencies that managers must understand include industry, technology, the environment, and international cultures. Management practices in a rapidly changing industry, for example, will be very different from those in a stable one.

Total Quality Management

The quality movement in Japan emerged partly as a result of American influence after World War II. The ideas of W. Edwards Deming, known as the "father of the quality movement," were initially scoffed at in the United States, but the Japanese embraced his theories and modified them to help rebuild their industries into world powers.[47] Japanese companies achieved a significant departure from the American model by gradually shifting from an inspection-oriented approach to quality control toward an approach emphasizing employee involvement in the prevention of quality problems.[48]

During the 1980s and into the 1990s, **total quality management (TQM)**, which focuses on managing the total organization to deliver quality to customers, was at the forefront in helping managers deal with global competition. The approach infuses quality values throughout every activity within a company, with front-line workers intimately involved in the process. Four significant elements of quality management are employee involvement, focus on the customer, benchmarking, and continuous improvement.

Employee involvement means that TQM requires companywide participation in quality control. All employees are *focused on the customer;* TQM companies find out what customers want and try to meet their needs and expectations. *Benchmarking* refers to a process whereby companies find out how others do something better than they do and then try to imitate or improve on it. *Continuous improvement* is the implementation of small, incremental improvements in all areas of the organization on an ongoing basis. TQM is not a quick fix, but companies such as General Electric, Texas Instruments, Procter & Gamble, and DuPont achieved astonishing results in efficiency, quality, and customer satisfaction through total quality management.[49] TQM is still an important part of today's organizations, and managers consider benchmarking in particular a highly effective and satisfying management technique.[50]

Some of today's companies pursue highly ambitious quality goals to demonstrate their commitment to improving quality. For example, *Six Sigma*, popularized by Motorola and General Electric, specifies a goal of no more than 3.4 defects per million parts. However, the term also refers to a broad quality control approach that emphasizes a disciplined and relentless pursuit of higher quality and lower costs. TQM will be discussed in detail in Chapter 14.

INNOVATIVE MANAGEMENT THINKING FOR TURBULENT TIMES

All of the ideas and approaches discussed so far in this chapter go into the mix that makes up modern management. A recent book on management thinking indicates dozens of ideas and techniques in current use that can trace their roots to these

total quality management (TQM) A concept that focuses on managing the total organization to deliver quality to customers. Four significant elements of TQM are employee involvement, focus on the customer, benchmarking, and continuous improvement.

historical perspectives.[51] In addition, innovative concepts continue to emerge to address management challenges in today's turbulent world. Organizations experiment with new ways of managing that more adequately respond to the demands of today's environment and customers. Two current innovations in management thinking are the shift to a learning organization and managing the technology-driven workplace.

The Learning Organization

One of the toughest challenges for managers today is to get people focused on adaptive change to meet the demands of a turbulent and rapidly changing environment. Few problems come with ready-made solutions, and they require that people throughout the company think in new ways and learn new values and attitudes.[52] These needs demand a new approach to management and a new kind of organization. Managers began thinking about the concept of the learning organization after the publication of Peter Senge's book, *The Fifth Discipline: The Art and Practice of Learning Organizations*.[53] Senge described the kind of changes managers needed to undergo to help their organizations adapt to an increasingly chaotic world. These ideas gradually evolved to describe characteristics of the organization itself. No single view describes what the learning organization looks like. The learning organization is an attitude or philosophy about what an organization can become.

The **learning organization** can be defined as one in which everyone is engaged in identifying and solving problems, enabling the organization to continuously experiment, change, and improve, thus increasing its capacity to grow, learn, and achieve its purpose. The essential idea is problem solving, in contrast to the traditional organization designed for efficiency. In the learning organization all employees look for problems, such as understanding special customer needs. Employees also solve problems, which means putting things together in unique ways to meet a customer's needs. Many of today's managers are quite aware that sustained competitive advantage can come only by developing the learning capacity of everyone in the organization. This awareness is reflected in a survey conducted by *Strategy + Business*. The magazine asked its online subscribers, along with a group of thinkers, educators, interview subjects, and scholars, to vote for the ideas discussed in *Strategy + Business* over the last 10 years that they consider most likely to remain relevant for at least the next decade. The concept of the learning organization ranked second on the list of top 10 ideas.[54]

To develop a learning organization, managers make changes in all the subsystems of the organization. Three important adjustments to promote continuous learning are shifting to a team-based structure, empowering employees, and sharing information. These three characteristics are illustrated in Exhibit 2.7 and each is described here.

learning organization An organization in which everyone is engaged in identifying and solving problems, enabling the organization to continuously experiment, improve, and increase its capability.

EXHIBIT 2.7

Elements of a Learning Organization

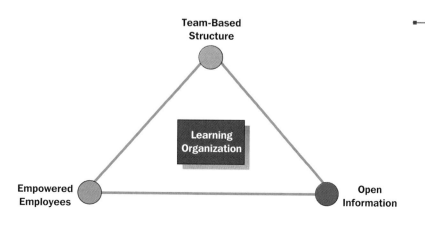

TEAM-BASED STRUCTURE

An important value in a learning organization is collaboration and communication across departmental and hierarchical boundaries. Self-directed teams are the basic building block of the structure. These teams are made up of employees with different skills who share or rotate jobs to produce an entire product or service. Traditional management tasks are pushed down to lower levels of the organization, with teams often taking responsibility for training, safety, scheduling, and decisions about work methods, pay and reward systems, and coordination with other teams. Although team leadership is critical, in learning organizations the traditional boss is practically eliminated. People on the team are given the skills, information, tools, motivation, and authority to make decisions central to the team's performance and to respond creatively and flexibly to new challenges or opportunities that arise.

EMPLOYEE EMPOWERMENT

Empowerment means unleashing the power and creativity of employees by giving them the freedom, resources, information, and skills to make decisions and perform effectively. Traditional management tries to limit employees, while empowerment expands their behavior. Empowerment may be reflected in self-directed work teams, quality circles, job enrichment, and employee participation groups as well as through decision-making authority, training, and information so that people can perform jobs without close supervision.

In learning organizations, people are a manager's primary source of strength, not a cost to be minimized. Companies that adopt this perspective believe in treating employees well by providing competitive wages and good working conditions, as well as by investing time and money in training programs and opportunities for personal and professional development. In addition, they often provide a sense of employee ownership by sharing gains in productivity and profits.[55]

OPEN INFORMATION

A learning organization is flooded with information. To identify needs and solve problems, people have to be aware of what's going on. They must understand the whole organization as well as their part in it. Formal data about budgets, profits, and departmental expenses are available to everyone. "If you really want to respect individuals," says Solectron Corp.'s Winston Chen, "you've got to let them know how they're doing—and let them know soon enough so they can do something about it."[56] Managers know that providing too much information is better than providing too little. In addition, managers encourage people throughout the organization to share information. For example, at Viant Inc., which helps companies build and maintain Web-based businesses, people are rewarded for their willingness to absorb and share knowledge. Rather than encouraging consultants to hoard specialized knowledge, CEO Bob Gett says, "We value you more for how much information you've given to the guy next to you."[57]

Managing the Technology-Driven Workplace

The shift to the learning organization goes hand-in-hand with the current transition to a technology-driven workplace. The physical world that Frederick Taylor and other proponents of scientific management measured determines less and less of what is valued in organizations and society. Our lives and organizations have been engulfed by information technology. Ideas, information, and relationships are becoming more important than production machinery, physical products, and structured jobs.[58] Many employees perform much of their work on computers and may work in virtual teams, connected electronically to colleagues around the world.

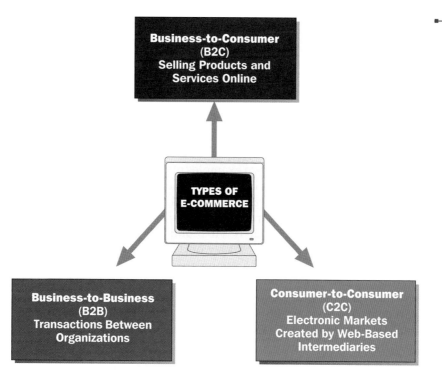

EXHIBIT 2.8

Three Types of
E-Commerce

Even in factories that produce physical goods, machines have taken over much of the routine and uniform work, freeing workers to use more of their minds and abilities. Managers and employees in today's companies focus on opportunities rather than efficiencies, which requires that they be flexible, creative, and unconstrained by rigid rules and structured tasks.

THE SHIFTING WORLD OF E-BUSINESS

Today, much business takes place by digital processes over a computer network rather than in physical space. **E-business** refers to the work an organization does by using electronic linkages (including the Internet) with customers, partners, suppliers, employees, or other key constituents. For example, organizations that use the Internet or other electronic linkages to communicate with employees or customers are engaged in e-business.

E-commerce is a narrower term referring specifically to business exchanges or transactions that occur electronically. E-commerce replaces or enhances the exchange of money and products with the exchange of data and information from one computer to another. Three types of e-commerce—*business-to-consumer, business-to-business,* and *consumer-to-consumer*—are illustrated in Exhibit 2.8. Companies such as Amazon.com, 800-Flowers, Expedia.com, and Progressive are engaged in what is referred to as *business-to-consumer e-commerce (B2C)*, because they sell products and services to consumers over the Internet. Although this type of exchange is probably the most visible expression of e-commerce to the public, the fastest growing area of e-commerce is *business-to-business e-commerce (B2B)*, which refers to electronic transactions between organizations. Today, much B2B e-commerce takes place over the Internet.[59] Large organizations such as Wal-Mart, General Electric, Carrier Corp., General Motors, and Ford Motor Company buy and sell billions of dollars worth of goods and services a year via either public or private Internet linkages.[60] For example, General Motors sells about 300,000 previously owned vehicles a year online through SmartAuction. Ford purchases a large portion of the steel it uses to build cars through e-Steel.[61]

Some companies take e-commerce to high levels to achieve amazing performance through supply chain management. **Supply chain management** refers to managing

57

e-business Work an organization does by using electronic linkages.

e-commerce Business exchanges or transactions that occur electronically.

supply chain management Managing the sequence of suppliers and purchasers, covering all stages of processing from obtaining raw materials to distributing finished goods to final customers.

the sequence of suppliers and purchasers, covering all stages of processing from obtaining raw materials to distributing finished goods to consumers.[62] Dell Computer was a pioneer in the use of end-to-end digital supply-chain networks to keep in touch with customers, take orders, buy components from suppliers, coordinate with manufacturing partners, and ship customized products directly to consumers. This trend is affecting every industry, prompting a group of consultants at a Harvard University conference to conclude that businesses today must either "Dell or be Delled."[63]

The third area of e-commerce, *consumer-to-consumer (C2C)*, is made possible when an Internet-based business acts as an intermediary between and among consumers. One of the best-known examples of C2C e-commerce is Web-based auctions such as those made possible by eBay. Internet auctions create a large electronic marketplace where consumers can buy and sell directly with one another, usually handling practically the entire transaction via the Web. Members of eBay in the United States alone sold approximately $10.6 billion in merchandise during the first six months of 2005. Merchandise sales worldwide in the previous year were approximately $36 billion.[64] Another growing area of C2C commerce is peer-to-peer (P2P) file-sharing networks. Companies such as Kazaa and Grokster provide the technology for swapping music, movies, software, and other files. Online music sharing, in particular, has zoomed in popularity, and although music companies and record retailers are currently engaged in a heated battle with file-sharing services, these companies are likely here to stay.[65]

INNOVATIVE TECHNOLOGY IN THE WORKPLACE

New electronic technologies also shape the organization and how it is managed. A century ago, Frederick Taylor described the kind of worker needed in the iron industry: "Now one of the first requirements for a man who is fit to handle pig iron as a regular occupation is that he shall be so stupid and so phlegmatic that he more nearly resembles in his mental makeup the ox than any other type."[66] The philosophy of scientific management was that managers structured and controlled jobs so carefully that thinking on the part of employees wasn't required—indeed, it was usually discouraged. How different things are today! Many organizations depend on employees' minds more than their physical bodies. In companies where the power of an idea determines success, managers' primary goal is to tap into the creativity and knowledge of every employee.

■ TAKE A MOMENT

As a new manager in today's workplace, how would you develop your employees' abilities to think independently, build relationships, and share knowledge? Be prepared to learn to use technology as a tool to tap into the insight and creativity of each person in the organization.

enterprise resource planning (ERP) Systems that unite a company's major business functions—order processing, product design, purchasing, inventory, and so on.

knowledge management The efforts to systematically find, organize, and make available a company's intellectual capital and to foster a culture of continuous learning and knowledge sharing.

Technology provides the architecture that supports and reinforces this new workplace. One approach to information management is **enterprise resource planning (ERP)** systems, which weave together all of a company's major business functions, such as order processing, product design, purchasing, inventory, manufacturing, distribution, human resources, receipt of payments, and forecasting of future demand.[67] ERP supports a companywide management system in which everyone, from the CEO down to a machine operator on the factory floor, has instant access to critical information. People can see the big picture and act quickly, based on up-to-the-minute information. Thus, ERP also supports management attempts to harness and leverage organizational *knowledge*.

Peter Drucker coined the term *knowledge work* more than 40 years ago,[68] but only in recent years did managers begin to genuinely recognize knowledge as an important organizational resource that should be managed just as they manage cash flow or raw materials. **Knowledge management** refers to the efforts to systematically find, organize, and make available a company's intellectual capital and to foster a culture of continuous learning and knowledge sharing so that a company's activities build on what is already known.[69] One growing segment of knowledge management is the use of sophisticated **customer relationship management (CRM)** systems, which collect and manage large amounts of data about customers and make them available to employees, enabling better decision making and superior customer service. The use of CRM has virtually exploded over the past several years. In Bain and Company's 2005 management tool survey, for example, three out of four companies reported using CRM, up from only 35 percent of companies in 2000, one of the largest and fastest usage increases ever revealed by the survey.[70]

Information technology also contributes to the rapid growth of **outsourcing**, which means contracting out selected functions or activities to other organizations that can do the work more cost-efficiently. Today's companies are outsourcing like crazy to free up cash for investment in long-term research and innovation. Outsourcing—along with other trends such as supply chain management, customer relationship management, telecommuting, and virtual teamwork—requires that managers not only be technologically savvy, but that they also learn to manage a complex web of relationships. These relationships might reach far beyond the boundaries of the physical organization; they are often built through flexible e-links between a company and its employees, suppliers, partners, and customers.[71]

customer relationship management (CRM) Systems that help companies track customers' interaction with the firm and allow employees to call up information on past transactions.

outsourcing Contracting out selected functions or activities of an organization to other organizations that can do the work more cost-efficiently.

MANAGER'S SOLUTION

This chapter examined the historical background leading up to new approaches to managing learning organizations and the technology-driven workplace. An understanding of the evolution of management helps current and future managers understand where we are now and continue to progress toward better management.

The three major perspectives on management evolved since the late 1800s: the classical perspective, the humanistic perspective, and the management science perspective. Each perspective encompasses several specialized subfields. Recent extensions of those perspectives include systems theory, the contingency view, and total quality management. The most recent thinking about organizations was brought about by today's turbulent times and the shift to a new workplace described in Chapter 1. Many managers are redesigning their companies toward the learning organization, which fully engages all employees in identifying and solving problems. The learning organization is characterized by a team-based structure, empowered employees, and open information. The learning organization represents a substantial departure from the traditional management hierarchy.

The shift to a learning organization goes hand-in-hand with today's transition to a technology-driven workplace. Ideas, information, and relationships are becoming more important than production machinery and physical assets, which requires new approaches to management. E-business is burgeoning as more economic activity takes place over digital computer networks rather than in physical space, and supply chain management is a priority. Other management tools used in the digital workplace include enterprise resource planning, knowledge management, customer relationship management, and outsourcing. These approaches require managers to think in new ways about the role of employees, customers, and partners. Today's best managers value employees for their ability to think, build relationships, and share knowledge, which is quite different from the scientific management perspective of a century ago.

One century-old company that is thriving as a technology-driven learning organization is Cementos Mexicanos (Cemex), described at the beginning of the chapter.

To help the organization compete in a turbulent environment, managers looked for both technological and management innovations. A core element of the new approach is the company's complex information technology infrastructure, which includes a global positioning satellite system and on-board computers in all delivery trucks that are continuously fed with streams of day-to-day data on customer orders, production schedules, traffic problems, weather conditions, and so forth. Even more important are changes in how managers and employees think about and do their work. All drivers and dispatchers attended weekly secondary education classes for two years. Regular training in quality, customer service, and computer skills continues, with Cemex devoting at least eight percent of total work time to employee training and development. The company abolished strict and demanding work rules so that workers have more discretion and responsibility for identifying and solving problems.

As a result, Cemex trucks now operate as self-organizing business units, run by well-trained employees who think like businesspeople. The three-hour delivery window has been reduced to 20 minutes, and managers believe a goal of 10 minutes is within reach. According to Francisco Perez, operations manager at Cemex in Guadalajara, "They used to think of themselves as drivers. But anyone can deliver concrete. Now our people know that they're delivering a service that the competition cannot deliver." Cemex transformed the industry by combining extensive networking technology with a new management approach that taps into the mind power of everyone in the company. People at Cemex learn constantly—on the job, in training classes, and through visits to other organizations. As a result, the company achieves a startling capacity to anticipate customer needs, solve problems, and innovate quickly.[72]

DISCUSSION QUESTIONS

1. As organizations become more technology-driven, which do you think will become more important—the management of the human element of the organization or the management of technology? Discuss.

2. To what degree do you think that effective control comes from within the individual worker, or do workers need rules, rewards, and punishments to perform effectively? Explain your reasoning.

3. Which of the three characteristics of learning organizations do you find most appealing? As a manager, which would be hardest for you to adopt? Why?

4. Do you think management theory will ever be as precise as theories in the fields of finance, accounting, or experimental psychology? Why or why not?

5. A management professor once said that for successful management, studying the present was most important, studying the past was next, and studying the future was least important. Do you agree? Why?

6. Identify the major components of systems theory. Is this perspective primarily internal or external to the organization? Explain.

7. Based on your experience at work or school, describe some ways in which the principles of scientific management and bureaucracy are still used in organizations. Do you believe these characteristics will ever cease to be a part of organizational life? Discuss.

8. Why can an event such as the Hawthorne studies be a major turning point in the history of management even if the idea is later shown to be in error? Discuss.

9. How do societal forces influence the practice and theory of management? Do you think new management techniques are a response to these forces?

10. Explain the basic idea underlying the contingency view. How would you go about identifying the key contingencies facing an organization?

11. Why is it important to understand the different perspectives and approaches to management theory that have evolved throughout the history of organizations?

12. Why do you think Mary Parker Follet's ideas tended to be popular with business people of her day, but were ignored by management scholars? Why are her ideas appreciated more today?

Theory X and Theory Y Scale

The following are various types of behavior that a manager may engage in when relating to subordinates. Read each statement carefully and rate each one in terms of the extent to which you would use that behavior, according to the following scale.

❶ Make a great effort to do this

❷ Tend to do this

❸ Tend to avoid doing this

❹ Make a great effort to avoid this

1. Closely supervise my subordinates in order to get better work from them. ❶ ❷ ❸ ❹

2. Set the goals and objectives for my subordinates and sell them on the merits of my plans. ❶ ❷ ❸ ❹

3. Set up controls to assure that my subordinates are getting the job done. ❶ ❷ ❸ ❹

4. Encourage my subordinates to set their own goals and objectives. ❶ ❷ ❸ ❹

5. Make sure that my subordinates' work is planned out for them. ❶ ❷ ❸ ❹

6. Check with my subordinates daily to see if they need any help. ❶ ❷ ❸ ❹

7. Step in as soon as reports indicate that the job is slipping. ❶ ❷ ❸ ❹

8. Push my people to meet schedules if necessary. ❶ ❷ ❸ ❹

9. Have frequent meetings to keep in touch with what is going on. ❶ ❷ ❸ ❹

10. Allow subordinates to make important decisions. ❶ ❷ ❸ ❹

Scoring and Interpretation

Subtract each of your scores for Questions 4 and 10 from the number 5. Then, add the total points and mark your score on the scale below. Refer back to Exhibit 2.4 and review the assumptions related to Theory X and Theory Y. A person who fully subscribes to the assumptions of Theory X would have a score of 10, whereas a person who fully subscribes to the assumptions of Theory Y would have a score of 40. Strong Theory X assumptions are typically considered inappropriate for today's workplace. Where do you fit on the X–Y scale? Does your score reflect your perception of yourself as a current or future manager?

Theory X	10	20	30	40	Theory Y

SOURCE: J. William Pfeiffer and John E. Jones, eds.,"Supervisory Attitudes: The X–Y Scale," *The 1972 Annual Handbook for Group Facilitators* (New York: John Wiley & Sons, 1972): 65–68. This material is used by permission of John Wiley & Sons, Inc. The X–Y scale was adapted from an instrument developed by Robert N. Ford of AT&T for in-house manager training.

The Supervisor

Karen Lowry, manager of a social service agency in a midsized city in Illinois, loved to see her employees learn and grow to their full potential. When a rare opening for a supervising clerk occurred, Karen quickly decided to give Charlotte Hines a shot at the job. Charlotte had been with the agency for 17 years and had shown herself to be a true leader. Charlotte worked hard at being a good supervisor, just as she had always worked hard at being a top-notch clerk. She paid attention to the human aspects of employee problems and introduced modern management techniques that strengthened the entire agency.

However, the Civil Service Board decided that a promotional exam should be given to find a permanent placement for the supervising clerk position. For the sake of fairness, the exam was an open competition—anyone, even a new employee, could sign up and take

it. The board wanted the candidate with the highest score to get the job but allowed Karen, as manager of the agency, to have the final say-so.

Since she had accepted the provisional opening and proven herself on the job, Charlotte was upset that the entire clerical force was deemed qualified to take the test. When the results came back, she was devastated. Charlotte placed twelfth in the field of candidates, while one of her newly hired clerks placed first. The Civil Service Board, impressed by the new clerk's high score, is urging Karen to give her the permanent supervisory job. Karen wonders whether it's fair to base her decision only on the test results.

What Would You Do?

1. Ignore the test. Charlotte has proven herself and deserves the job.

2. Give the job to the candidate with the highest score. You don't need to make enemies on the Civil Service Board, and, after all, it is an objective way to select a permanent placement.

3. Devise a more comprehensive set of selection criteria—including test results as well as supervisory experience, ability to motivate employees, and knowledge of agency procedures—that can be explained and justified to the board and to employees.

SOURCE: Based on Betty Harrigan, "Career Advice," *Working Woman* (July 1986): 22–24.

CASE FOR CRITICAL ANALYSIS

SuperJuice

Luisa de la Cruz sat in her new office thinking about her company's future. After working her way up the corporate ladder for 15 years, she has just been appointed CEO of SuperJuice, a Florida-based company that makes juice and juice drinks that are marketed to high schools and restaurants throughout the Southeast. For nearly two decades, SuperJuice has been the most successful juice drink maker in the region. However, profits haven't risen for four straight years, and several new competitors continue to steal market share. In fact, one of the new companies was started by two former Super-Juice employees who left the company after top management continually rejected their ideas for new exotic drink mixes or new approaches to marketing. It made Luisa cringe to realize that the hottest-selling drink flavors in Florida and several other states had been invented in SuperJuice's own labs but were now being made and sold by a competitor. Competitors were setting up drink carts at outdoor festivals and advertising with jingles and slogans that caught the imaginations of the region's youth. Even Luisa's own 17-year-old son often purchased her competitors' products, saying that "SuperJuice is for kids. This stuff rocks."

SuperJuice management has always prided itself on the company's efficient set of systems, both in the factory and at headquarters. Managers concentrated on making a high-quality product as inexpensively as possible. "SuperJuice is like a well-oiled machine," Luisa told herself with some pride. Most of the company's 200 employees had joined SuperJuice right out of high school or college and liked the way the company operated. They showed up for work on time, performed their jobs efficiently, and rarely complained. The longstanding rules and procedures, combined with an organizational culture that reflected the traditional, family-oriented background of SuperJuice's Cuban-born founder, contributed to a level of politeness and civility in the company that sometimes seemed like a throwback to the 1950s. "SuperJuice is a calm and civilized place to work in the midst of a rapidly changing, chaotic world," Luisa reflected with pleasure.

But her pleasure evaporated as she realized that the company could collapse beneath her if it didn't somehow respond to the changes in the environment. She remembered the scandal that had erupted several years ago when two new employees started "breaking the rules" and pushing for changes in the company. The two worked odd hours, played rock music, and decorated their offices with brightly colored posters, unique photographs, and fanciful "dream catchers" hung from the ceiling. Occasionally, one would tape a note to his door that read, "Gone to the movies to get my creative juices flowing!" Although both workers were highly productive, top management quickly took action to try to bring the two back in line. They worried that this kind of attitude would have a negative impact on the productivity of other employees, who were accustomed to coming to work and putting in their solid eight hours. The previous CEO really blew his stack when the two presented four new drink flavors they had concocted on the sly. He was so angry about the unauthorized use of lab time that he nearly fired both employees on the spot. Luisa remembered finding one of the employees in the lab dejectedly pouring the prototypes down the drain. "You know you can't do anything new in this company," Luisa told her at that time. "It's just not the SuperJuice way." Since that time, SuperJuice has lost a few other young, ambitious employees who have chafed under the tight management control.

Luisa knew she was promoted because she had always followed the rules. But she also realized that continuing to follow the rules could take this company she loved right into bankruptcy. She knows the company has a lot of potential, starting with its loyal, committed workforce. But where should she begin? Can SuperJuice really change itself into a forward-thinking, creative company?

Questions

1. What are some of the social, political, and economic forces affecting SuperJuice and calling for a new approach to management?

2. What do you believe Luisa needs to do first to begin a transformation at SuperJuice?

3. How would you suggest she turn SuperJuice into a learning organization? Think about specific changes she can make to get all employees thinking of new and exciting ways to revitalize the product line and way of doing business.

SOURCE: Based on Suzy Wetlaufer, "What's Stifling the Creativity at CoolBurst?" *Harvard Business Review* (September–October 1997), 36–40.

ENDNOTES

1. Thomas Petzinger, Jr., *The New Pioneers: The Men and Women Who Are Transforming the Workplace and Marketplace* (New York: Simon & Schuster, 1999): 91–93: "In Search of the New World of Work," *Fast Company* (April 1999): 214–220+; and Peter Katel, "Bordering on Chaos," *Wired* (July 1997): 98–107.

2. Jeffrey Zaslow, "Feeling the Shivers of Faraway Scandals in Fort Wayne, Ind.," *The Wall Street Journal* (February 6, 2004): A1, A10.

3. John Huey, "Managing in the Midst of Chaos," *Fortune* (April 5, 1993): 38–48; and Toby J. Tetenbaum, "Shifting Paradigms: From Newton to Chaos," *Organizational Dynamics* (Spring 1998): 21–32.

4. Eric Abrahamson, "Management Fashion," *Academy of Management Review* 21, no. 1 (January 1996): 254–285. Also see "75 Years of Management Ideas and Practice," a supplement to the *Harvard Business Review* (September–October 1997), for a broad overview of historical trends in management thinking.

5. "Of Water Coolers and Coffee Breaks," timeline in Matthew Boyle, "How the Workplace Was Won," *Fortune* (January 22, 2001): 139+.

6. Daniel A. Wren, *The Evolution of Management Thought*, 2d ed. (New York: Wiley, 1979): 6–8. Much of the discussion of these forces comes from Arthur M. Schlesinger, *Political and Social History of the United States, 1829–1925* (New York: Macmillan, 1925); and Homer C. Hockett, *Political and Social History of the United States, 1492–1828* (New York: Macmillan, 1925).

7. Based on Stephanie Armour, "Generation Y: They've Arrived at Work with a New Attitude," *USA Today* (November 6, 2005): www.usatoday.com/money/workplace/2005-11-06-gen-y_x.htm; and Marnie E. Green, "Beware and Prepare: The Government Workforce of the Future," *Public Personnel Management* (Winter 2000): 435+.

8. This section is based heavily on Thomas Petzinger, Jr., "So Long Supply and Demand," *The Wall Street Journal* (January 1, 2000): R31.

9. Petzinger, "So Long Supply and Demand."

10. Darrell Rigby and Barbara Bilodeau, "The Bain 2005 Management Tool Survey," *Strategy & Leadership* 33, no. 4 (2005): 4–12; and Darrell Rigby, "Management Tools Survey 2003: Usage Up as Companies Strive to Make Headway in Tough Times," *Strategy & Leadership* 31, no. 5 (2003): 4–11.

11. See Daniel James Rowley, "Resource Reviews," *Academy of Management Learning and Education* 2, no. 3 (2003): 313–321; Jane Whitney Gibson, Dana V. Tesone, and Charles W. Blackwell, "Management Fads: Here Yesterday, Gone Today?" *SAM Advanced Management Journal* (Autumn 2003): 12–17; David Collins, *Management Fads and Buzzwords: Critical-Practices Perspective*, (London, UK: Routledge, 2000); Timothy Clark, "Management Research on Fashion: A Review and Evaluation," *Human Relations* 54, no. 12 (2001): 1650–1661; Brad Jackson, *Management Gurus and Management Fashions* (London: Routledge, 2001); Patrick Thomas, *Fashions in Management Research: An Empirical Analysis* (Aldershot, UK: Ashgate, 1999).

12. Daniel A. Wren, "Management History: Issues and Ideas for Teaching and Research," *Journal of Management* 13 (1987): 339–350.

13. Business historian Alfred D. Chandler, Jr., quoted in Jerry Useem, "Entrepreneur of the Century," *Inc.* (20th Anniversary Issue, 1999): 159–174.

14. Useem, "Entrepreneur of the Century."

15. The following is based on Wren, *Evolution of Management Thought*, Chapters 4, 5; and Claude S. George, Jr., *The History of Management Thought* (Englewood Cliffs, N.J.: Prentice-Hall, 1968): Chapter 4.

16. Alan Farnham, "The Man Who Changed Work Forever," *Fortune* (July 21, 1997): 114; Charles D. Wrege and Ann Marie Stoka, "Cooke Creates a Classic: The Story Behind F. W. Taylor's Principles of Scientific Management," *Academy of Management Review* (October 1978): 736–749; Robert Kanigel, *The One Best Way: Frederick Winslow Taylor and the Enigma of Efficiency* (New York: Viking, 1997); and "The X and Y Factors: What Goes Around Comes Around," in "The New Organisation: A Survey of the Company," *The Economist* (January 21–27, 2006): special section pp. 17–18.

17. Quoted in Ann Harrington, "The Big Ideas," *Fortune* (November 22, 1999): 152–154.

18. Wren, *Evolution of Management Thought*, 171; and George, *History of Management Thought*, 103–104.

19. Geoffrey Colvin, "Managing in the Info Era," *Fortune* (March 6, 2000): F-5–F-9.

20. Max Weber, *General Economic History*, trans. Frank H. Knight (London: Allen & Unwin, 1927); Max Weber, *The Protestant Ethic and the Spirit of Capitalism*, trans. Talcott Parsons (New York: Scribner, 1930); and Max Weber, *The Theory of Social and Economic Organizations*, ed. and trans. A. M. Henderson and Talcott Parsons (New York: Free Press, 1947).

21. Kelly Barron, "Logistics in Brown," *Forbes* (January 10, 2000): 78–83; Scott Kirsner, "Venture Vérité: United Parcel Service," *Wired* (September 1999): 83–96; "UPS," *The Atlanta Journal and Constitution* (April 26, 1992): H1; and Kathy Goode, Betty Hahn, and Cindy Seibert, "United Parcel Service: The Brown Giant" (unpublished manuscript, Texas A&M University, 1981).

22. Henri Fayol, *Industrial and General Administration*, trans. J. A. Coubrough (Geneva: International Management Institute, 1930); Henri Fayol, *General and Industrial Management*, trans. Constance Storrs (London: Pitman and Sons, 1949); and W. J. Arnold et al., *BusinessWeek, Milestones in Management* (New York: McGraw-Hill, vol. I, 1965; vol. II, 1966).

23. Mary Parker Follett, *The New State: Group Organization: The Solution of Popular Government* (London: Longmans, Green, 1918); and Mary Parker Follett, *Creative Experience* (London: Longmans, Green, 1924).

24. Henry C. Metcalf and Lyndall Urwick, eds., *Dynamic Administration: The Collected Papers of Mary Parker Follett* (New York: Harper & Row, 1940); Arnold, *Milestones in Management*.

25. Follett, *The New State;* Metcalf and Urwick, *Dynamic Administration* (London: Sir Isaac Pitman, 1941).

26. William B. Wolf, *How to Understand Management: An Introduction to Chester I. Barnard* (Los Angeles: Lucas Brothers, 1968); and David D. Van Fleet, "The Need-Hierarchy and Theories of Authority," *Human Relations* 9 (Spring 1982): 111–118.

Chapter 2 THE EVOLUTION OF MANAGEMENT THINKING

27. Gregory M. Bounds, Gregory H. Dobbins, and Oscar S. Fowler, *Management: A Total Quality Perspective* (Cincinnati, OH: South-Western Publishing, 1995): 52–53.

28. Curt Tausky, *Work Organizations: Major Theoretical Perspectives* (Itasca, IL: F. E. Peacock, 1978): 42.

29. Charles D. Wrege, "Solving Mayo's Mystery: The First Complete Account of the Origin of the Hawthorne Studies—The Forgotten Contributions of Charles E. Snow and Homer Hibarger" (paper presented to the Management History Division of the Academy of Management, August 1976).

30. Ronald G. Greenwood, Alfred A. Bolton, and Regina A. Greenwood, "Hawthorne a Half Century Later: Relay Assembly Participants Remember," *Journal of Management* 9 (Fall/Winter 1983): 217–231.

31. F. J. Roethlisberger, W. J. Dickson, and H. A. Wright, *Management and the Worker* (Cambridge, MA: Harvard University Press, 1939).

32. H. M. Parson, "What Happened at Hawthorne?" *Science* 183 (1974): 922–932; John G. Adair, "The Hawthorne Effect: A Reconsideration of the Methodological Artifact," *Journal of Applied Psychology* 69, no. 2 (1984): 334–345; and Gordon Diaper, "The Hawthorne Effect: A Fresh Examination," *Educational Studies* 16, no. 3 (1990): 261–268.

33. R. G. Greenwood, A. A. Bolton, and R. A. Greenwood, "Hawthorne a Half Century Later," 219–221.

34. F. J. Roethlisberger and W. J. Dickson, *Management and the Worker.*

35. Ramon J. Aldag and Timothy M. Stearns, *Management*, 2d ed. (Cincinnati, OH: South-Western Publishing, 1991): 47–48.

36. Tausky, *Work Organizations: Major Theoretical Perspectives*, 55.

37. Douglas McGregor, *The Human Side of Enterprise* (New York: McGraw-Hill, 1960): 16–18.

38. Julie Gehrke, "Power to the Painters," *Painting and Wallcovering Contractor* (September–October 2003): 84.

39. Wendell L. French and Cecil H. Bell Jr., "A History of Organizational Development," in Wendell L. French, Cecil H. Bell Jr., and Robert A. Zawacki, *Organization Development and Transformation: Managing Effective Change* (Burr Ridge, IL: Irwin McGraw-Hill, 2000): 20–42.

40. Mansel G. Blackford and K. Austin Kerr, *Business Enterprise in American History* (Boston: Houghton Mifflin, 1986): Chapters 10, 11; and Alex Groner et al. of *American Heritage and BusinessWeek, The American Heritage History of American Business and Industry* (New York: American Heritage Publishing, 1972): Chapter 9.

41. Larry M. Austin and James R. Burns, *Management Science* (New York: Macmillan, 1985).

42. Marcia Stepanek, "How an Intranet Opened Up the Door to Profits," *BusinessWeek E.Biz* (July 26, 1999): EB32–EB38.

43. Ludwig von Bertalanffy, Carl G. Hempel, Robert E. Bass, and Hans Jonas, "General Systems Theory: A New Approach to Unity of Science," *Human Biology* 23 (December 1951): 302–361; and Kenneth E. Boulding, "General Systems Theory—The Skeleton of Science," *Management Science* 2 (April 1956): 197–208.

44. Fremont E. Kast and James E. Rosenzweig, "General Systems Theory: Applications for Organization and Management," *Academy of Management Journal* (December 1972): 447–465.

45. "Teaming with Bright Ideas," in "The New Organisation: A Survey of the Company," *The Economist* (January 21–27, 2006): special section pp. 4–16.

46. Fred Luthans, "The Contingency Theory of Management: A Path Out of the Jungle," *Business Horizons* 16 (June 1973): 62–72; and Fremont E. Kast and James E. Rosenzweig, *Contingency Views of Organization and Management* (Chicago: Science Research Associates, 1973).

47. Samuel Greengard, "25 Visionaries Who Shaped Today's Workplace," *Workforce* (January 1997): 50–59; and Harrington, "The Big Ideas."

48. Mauro F. Guillen, "The Age of Eclecticism: Current Organizational Trends and the Evolution of Managerial Models," *Sloan Management Review* (Fall 1994): 75–86.

49. Jeremy Main, "How to Steal the Best Ideas Around," *Fortune* (October 19, 1992): 102–106.

50. Rigby and Bilodeau, "The Bain 2005 Management Tool Survey."

51. Thomas H. Davenport and Laurence Prusak, with Jim Wilson, *What's the Big Idea? Creating and Capitalizing on the Best Management Thinking* (Boston, MA: Harvard Business School Press, 2003). Also see Theodore Kinni, "Have We Run Out of Big Ideas?" *Across the Board* (March–April 2003): 16–21.

52. Ronald A. Heifetz and Donald L. Laurie, "The Leader as Teacher: Creating the Learning Organization," *Ivey Business Journal* (January–February 2003): 1–9.

53. Peter Senge, *The Fifth Discipline: The Art and Practice of Learning Organizations* (New York: Doubleday/Currency, 1990).

54. Art Kleiner, "Our 10 Most Enduring Ideas," *Strategy + Business*, no. 41 (December 12, 2005): 36–41.

55. Khoo Hsien Hui and Tan Kay Chuan, "Nine Approaches to Organizational Excellence," *Journal of Organizational Excellence* (Winter 2002): 53–65; Leon Martel, "The Principles of High Performance—And How to Apply Them," *Journal of Organizational Excellence* (Autumn 2002): 49–59; and Jeffrey Pfeffer, "Producing Sustainable Competitive Advantage through the Effective Management of People," *Academy of Management Executive* 9, no. 1 (1995): 55–69.

56. Alex Markels, "The Wisdom of Chairman Ko," *Fast Company* (November 1999): 258–276.

57. Edward O. Welles, "Mind Gains," *Inc.* (December 1999): 112–124.

58. Kevin Kelly, *New Rules for the New Economy: 10 Radical Strategies for a Connected World* (New York: Viking Penguin, 1998).

59. Nick Wingfield, "In the Beginning. . . ," *The Wall Street Journal* (May 21, 2001): R18.

60. Andy Reinhardt, "From Gearhead to Grand High Pooh-Bah," *BusinessWeek* (August 28, 2000): 129–130.

61. Julia Angwin, "Used Car Auctioneers, Dealers Meet Online," *The Wall Street Journal* (November 20, 2003): B1, B13; William J. Holstein and Edward Robinson, "The Re-Education of Jacques Nasser," *Business2.Com* (May 29, 2001): 60–73.

62. Definition based on Steven A. Melnyk and David R. Denzler, *Operations Management: A Value Driven Approach* (Burr Ridge, IL: Richard D. Irwin, 1996): 613.

63. Bernard Wysocki, Jr., "Corporate Caveat: Dell or Be Delled," *The Wall Street Journal* (May 10, 1999): A1.

64. Michelle Singletary, "Beating a Path to the Power Sellers," *Washington Post* (August 7, 2005): F1; and Patricia Sellers, "EBay's Secret," *Fortune* (October 18, 2004): 160–178.

65. Amber Chung, "Music Retailers Face Tough Times as File-Sharing Grows," *Taipei Times* (February 10, 2004): 11; www.taipeitimes.com (accessed on February 10, 2004).

66. Quoted in Colvin, "Managing in the Info Era."

67. Jeffrey Zygmont, "The Ties That Bind," *Inc. Tech* no. 3, (1998): 70–84; and Nancy Ferris, "ERP: Sizzling or Stumbling?" *Government Executive* (July 1999): 99–102.

68. Harrington, "The Big Ideas." Also see Peter Drucker, *Post-Capitalist Society*, (Oxford: Butterworth Heinemann, 1993): 5.

69. Based on Andrew Mayo, "Memory Bankers," *People Management* (January 22, 1998): 34–38; William Miller, "Building the Ultimate Resource," *Management Review* (January 1999): 42–45; and Todd Datz, "How to Speak Geek," *CIO Enterprise*, Section 2 (April 15, 1999): 46–52.

70. Rigby and Bilodeau, "The Bain 2005 Management Tool Survey," and Edward Prewitt, "CRM Gains Ground as Management Tool," *CIO* (September 1, 2005): 28.

71. Reinhardt, "From Gearhead to Grand High Pooh-Bah."

72. Petzinger, *The New Pioneers: The Men and Women Who Are Transforming the Workplace and Marketplace;* "In Search of the New World of Work"; Katel, "Bordering on Chaos"; and Oren Harari, "The Concrete Intangibles," *Management Reviews*, (May 1999): 30–33.

COSTCO WHOLESALE CORPORATION PART ONE
COSTCO: JOIN THE CLUB

If 25 years ago a pair of entrepreneurs aspired to the ranks of Fortune 500 retailers by following unconventional and counterintuitive strategies, investors and colleagues would have likely dismissed the effort or perhaps even advised the idealistic greenhorns to consider other careers. Yet as James Sinegal and Jeffrey Brotman mark their 25th anniversary as co-founders of Costco Wholesale Corporation, the iconoclastic businessmen are the envy of retailers everywhere. By offering a limited selection of merchandise at rock-bottom prices, setting razor-thin profit margins, establishing lofty ethical standards, and rewarding workers with premium wages and healthcare benefits, the enterprising duo defied conventional wisdom and created the No.1 membership warehouse club in the world.

In the years since the co-founders opened their first low-price retail warehouse just miles from its current headquarters in Issaquah, Washington, Costco has grown to over 488 locations serving 48 million enthusiastic cardholders in eight countries. With annual sales of over $50 billion and a workforce of nearly 125,000 highly motivated and famously well-paid employees, Costco is the top warehouse club and fourth-largest retailer in the nation.

The story of Costco's rise from a single Seattle store in 1983 to a multinational chain of enormously profitable warehouses is a tale of exemplary leadership in a rapidly-changing retail world. Under the artful direction of Sinegal and Brotman, Costco Wholesale Corp. developed and perfected the warehouse-club formula pioneered in the 1970s by Sol Price, founder of California retailer Price Club. Initially a protégé to Price, young Jim Sinegal learned his mentor's high-volume low-cost trade secrets, but later left Price Club to launch a competing company—Costco. The two businesses eventually merged in 1993, and Sinegal went on to eclipse Sol Price in the art of getting the right product in the right place for the right price.

The most visible emblem of Sinegal and Brotman's retail strategy is the Costco warehouse itself. With its bare concrete floors, fluorescent lights, and pallets of merchandise piled to the rafters, the colossal 150,000-square-foot theater of retail is worthy of the "big box" appellation. Visitors are immediately struck by the conspicuous absence of signs and displays throughout the massive structures, and the self-checkout lanes and dispersed sales associates betray Costco's barebones, no-frills approach to reducing costs to the absolute minimum.

But if Costco's atmospherics are generic and uninspiring, the company's merchandising mix is anything but. While Wal-Mart stands for low prices and Target is the master of cheap chic, Costco is a treasure hunt. Among the high-end merchandise moving through stores are Waterford crystal, Coach leather goods, Fila jackets, Dom Pérignon Champagne, Apple Video iPods, and Prada sunglasses. Sinegal's quest to offer luxury goods to his characteristically upscale customers has inspired Costco merchandisers to source some unusual surprises: rare Picasso drawings and 10.6-carat yellow-diamond rings priced at $180,000. Yet in a single shopping cart, such pricy merchandise can be found alongside bulk items like 2,250-count Q-Tip packs and vats of mayonnaise—or beside the many products sold under Costco's own Kirkland Signature private label. Of the 4,000 items offered in Costco warehouses, approximately 1,000 are these upscale treasure-hunt goods that come and go at a moment's notice, creating an urgency to buy before it's too late.

Managing warehouses of ever-changing merchandise requires an organization that is flat, fast, and flexible. Sinegal fancies each warehouse a mini-corporation, and each warehouse manager a de facto CEO. These "local CEOs" make rapid, independent merchandising decisions based on knowledge of their customers' wants and needs. Likewise, lower level employees are expected to make decisions guided by the organization's mission and values and based on widely distributed inventory and sales information.

To develop a highly-trained and knowledge-driven workforce, Sinegal and other leaders atop Costco's managerial hierarchy abandon the old command-and-control mindset and emphasize coaching, motivation, and empowerment instead. Sinegal famously spends about 200 days a year visiting his company's warehouses—often dressed in casual attire. During these warehouse tours, Sinegal is at once a monitor, figurehead, leader, and disturbance handler. As the CEO strolls around the "racetrack"—the U-shaped path along the perimeter of the facility—he checks whether stocks are replenished and positioned to sell, discusses sales with warehouse managers, and observes how workers are sharing knowledge and solving problems. This "management-by-walking-around" routine creates a bond of trust and loyalty between Sinegal and his employees.

Costco's benevolent and motivational management approach manifests itself dramatically in wages and benefits paid to workers. The company pays employees an average hourly wage of $17—the highest among discount retailers—while also picking up 92 percent of health-insurance premium costs. The result is high performance and low turnover. Costco's workforce has a reputation for being the most productive and loyal in all of retail.

A winning retail strategy, flexible organization, exemplary leadership, and well-compensated employees—these are the unique qualities that place Costco Wholesale Corporation at the head of its class. As you progress through your course in management, you'll continue to read about the extraordinary leadership of Costco's founders and encounter the innovative planning, organizing, leading, and controlling methods the company uses to outstrip competitors and steer the organization toward future success.

Questions

1. Which of the three management-skill categories do you think Costco CEO James Sinegal draws upon most during his year-round visits to local Costco warehouses? Explain.

2. What aspects of Costco's business model exemplify the transition from "the old workplace" to the "new workplace," and why?

3. How does Costco's high worker-retention rate help the warehouse club maintain low prices?

SOURCES: Matthew Boyle, "Why Costco is So Damn Addictive," *Fortune,* October 30, 2006; Alan B. Goldberg and Bill Ritter, "Costco CEO Finds Pro-Worker Means Profitability," *ABC News,* August 2, 2006, *http://abcnews.go.com,* accessed November 8, 2006; Doug Desjardins, "Bulking Up Sales Through Sales in Bulk," *Retailing Today,* September 25, 2006; Daren Fonda, "Jim Sinegal: Costco's Discount CEO," *Time,* May 8, 2006; Alyce Lomax, "Most Foolish CEO: Jim Sinegal," *The Motley Fool,* September 28, 2006, *http://www.fool.com,* accessed November 6, 2006.

PART 2

THE ENVIRONMENT OF MANAGEMENT

The cultural environment into which a structure is constructed has enormous impact on the final design. Both in terms of the surrounding public culture, as well as any private culture, religious structures reveal the importance of this invisible environment in different physical forms.

The Parthenon in Athens was the ancient temple of Athena. Although only some of the sculptures survived, it is believed the Parthenon was full of images related to Greek ideas, mythology, and gods. Churches and mosques likewise exhibit fundamental elements of theology. Notre Dame Cathedral in Paris, France, uses images of the Virgin Mary and Christian symbols and saints, and the nave is shaped like a cross. The Koutoubia mosque in Marrakech, Morocco, although built at roughly the same time as Notre Dame, features an open courtyard for prayer, a repeating pattern to symbolize the infinity of God, and no human images.

Overall environmental factors are considered when creating and operating a business. Managers must consider both internal and external environments, which are often inter-twined. These elements dictate how the manager will bring firmness, commodity, and delight into harmony. The creative environment is tied to the creative culture. A creative company, Pixar values imagination and expression. As such, paper airplane contests and toy collecting at work are not only acceptable but encouraged because they reinforce the company's culture. A company's culture dictates what is acceptable and what is not acceptable, as different theologies dictate the shape, images, and space in any house of worship.

CHAPTER OUTLINE

Manager's Challenge

The External Environment

General Environment

Task Environment

The Organization–Environment Relationship

Environmental Uncertainty

Adapting to the Environment

The Internal Environment: Corporate Culture

Symbols

Stories

Heroes

Slogans

Ceremonies

Environment and Culture

Adaptive Cultures

Types of Cultures

Shaping Corporate Culture for Innovative Response

Managing the High-Performance Culture

Cultural Leadership

LEARNING OBJECTIVES

After studying this chapter, you should be able to:

1. Describe the general and task environments and the dimensions of each.

2. Explain the strategies managers use to help organizations adapt to an uncertain or turbulent environment.

3. Define corporate culture and give organizational examples.

4. Explain organizational symbols, stories, heroes, slogans, and ceremonies and their relationship to corporate culture.

5. Describe how corporate culture relates to the environment.

6. Define a cultural leader and explain the tools a cultural leader uses to create a high-performance culture.

THE ENVIRONMENT AND CORPORATE CULTURE

MANAGER'S CHALLENGE

Many people think of Microsoft and software as being almost synonymous, the same way folks once thought of Xerox and photocopying. But Xerox learned the hard way that a dominant position is not guaranteed. To avoid the same fate at Microsoft, managers recently warned founder and chairman Bill Gates that his company's PC software business is in danger of becoming "increasingly defunct." It could be a warning that came too late. For years, Microsoft exerted significant control over what appears on the PC desktop and what software programs the majority of customers use, but that control is about to change. Most people, especially home users, set up a new PC by clicking through a series of introductory screens and selecting the software and services they want. Microsoft historically controlled this "first-boot" sequence and the software that comes preinstalled on the computer. Now, though, PC makers are taking back control, selling desktop space to competing software and service providers and giving end users broader choices of software during setup. Google, for example, was negotiating in early 2006 to have its software preinstalled on millions of Dell PCs. Hewlett-Packard is already giving users the option to sign up for a variety of programs and services from companies other than Microsoft. Because Microsoft has long garnered its largest source of revenue and profit from PC software, it's a shift that could spell big trouble.[1]

71

> If you were a manager at Microsoft, how might you have been more prepared for this shift in the way PC makers do business with software companies? What steps would you take to help Microsoft maintain its status in the software industry as it faces new threats from competitors in the environment?

■ TAKE A MOMENT

In high-tech industries, environmental conditions are volatile. Microsoft is currently in a situation similar to the one Xerox faced in the early 1990s. Xerox was dominant in its industry for many years, but managers missed cues from the environment and got blindsided by rivals Canon and Ricoh when they began selling comparable copy machines at lower prices. Moreover, Xerox failed to keep pace with changing methods of document management and had no new products to fill the gaps in the declining copy business. Consequently, the company struggled for more than decade to find its footing in a vastly changed world. Current CEO Anne Mulcahy has used her management skills to mastermind a hot turnaround at Xerox and get the company moving forward again.[2] Similar to Xerox, Microsoft has held a dominant position for nearly 30 years, but the environment is shifting dramatically and Microsoft will have to change significantly to remain competitive.

Yet an organization doesn't have to be high-tech to be devastated by shifts in the environment. Dixon Ticonderoga Company makes pencils and once had a large share of the U.S. market. Today, though, the majority of pencils sold in the United States come from overseas, compared to only 16 percent a decade ago.[3] In the toy industry, Mattel lost 20 percent of its share of the worldwide fashion doll market when rival MGA Entertainment created a hip new line of dolls called Bratz. Mattel failed to recognize that preteen girls are maturing more quickly and want dolls that look like their pop star idols. Mattel eventually came out with a rival line of dolls for preteens called My Scene, but the damage was already done. Barbie, the top fashion doll for over 40 years, fell from her pedestal virtually overnight.[4]

Government actions and red tape can also affect an organization's environment and create problems. The 2002 Sarbanes-Oxley corporate governance law is making life more complicated for managers in all organizations. Scandals in the mutual fund industry prompted the SEC to propose a ban on special incentive payments to brokerage firms. The beef and dairy industries in the United States were hurt by increased rules and restrictions following the discovery of mad cow disease in Washington state. And consider thousands of public schools that use a common land snail called *Helix aspera* as a major unit in their science curricula. The U.S. Department of Agriculture's unexpected ban on the interstate transport of the snails threw school science programs into disarray around the nation.[5]

The environment surprises many managers and leaves them unable to adapt their companies to new competition, shifting consumer interests, or new technologies. The study of management traditionally focused on factors within the organization—a closed systems view—such as leading, motivating, and controlling employees. The classical, behavioral, and management science schools described in Chapter 2 looked at internal aspects of organizations over which managers have direct control. These views are accurate but incomplete. To be effective, managers must monitor and respond to the environment—an open systems view. The events that have the greatest impact on an organization typically originate in the external environment. In addition, globalization and worldwide societal turbulence affect companies in new ways, making the international environment of growing concern to managers everywhere.

This chapter explores in detail components of the external environment and how they affect the organization. We also examine a major part of the organization's internal environment—corporate culture. Corporate culture is shaped by the external environment and is an important part of the context within which managers do their jobs.

THE EXTERNAL ENVIRONMENT

The tremendous and far-reaching changes occurring in today's world can be understood by defining and examining components of the external environment. The external **organizational environment** includes all elements existing outside the boundary of the organization that have the potential to affect the organization.[6] The environment includes competitors, resources, technology, and economic conditions that influence the organization. It does not include those events so far removed from the organization that their impact is not perceived.

The organization's external environment can be further conceptualized as having two layers: general and task environments, as illustrated in Exhibit 3.1.[7] The **general environment** is the outer layer that is widely dispersed and affects organizations indirectly. It includes social, demographic, and economic factors that influence all organizations about equally. Increases in the inflation rate or the percentage of dual-career couples in the workforce are part of the organization's general environment. These events do not directly change day-to-day operations, but they do affect all organizations eventually. The **task environment** is closer to the organization and includes the sectors that conduct day-to-day transactions with the organization and directly influence its basic operations and performance. It is generally considered to include competitors, suppliers, and customers.

The organization also has an **internal environment**, which includes the elements within the organization's boundaries. The internal environment is composed of current employees, management, and especially corporate culture, which defines employee behavior in the internal environment and how well the organization will adapt to the external environment.

organizational environment All elements existing outside the organization's boundaries that have the potential to affect the organization.

general environment The layer of the external environment that affects the organization indirectly.

task environment The layer of the external environment that directly influences the organization's operations and performance.

internal environment The environment that includes the elements within the organization's boundaries.

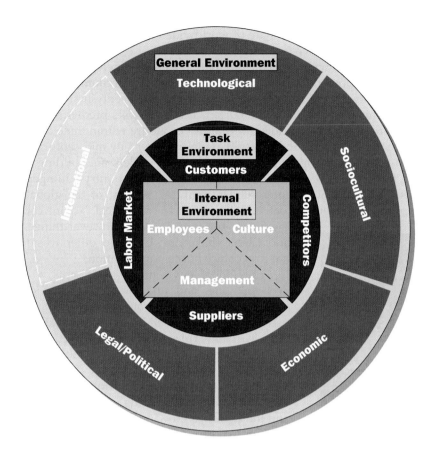

Exhibit 3.1 illustrates the relationship among the general, task, and internal environments. As an open system, the organization draws resources from the external environment and releases goods and services back to it. We will now discuss the two layers of the external environment in more detail. Then we will discuss corporate culture, the key element in the internal environment. Other aspects of the internal environment, such as structure and technology, will be covered in Parts Four and Five of this book.

General Environment

The general environment represents the outer layer of the environment. These dimensions influence the organization over time but often are not involved in day-to-day transactions with it. The dimensions of the general environment include international, technological, sociocultural, economic, and legal-political.

INTERNATIONAL

The **international dimension** of the external environment represents events originating in foreign countries as well as opportunities for U.S. companies in other countries. Note in Exhibit 3.1 that the international dimension represents a context that influences all other aspects of the external environment. The international environment provides new competitors, customers, and suppliers and shapes social, technological, and economic trends, as well.

Today, every company has to compete on a global basis. High-quality, low-priced automobiles from Japan and Korea have permanently changed the American automobile industry. In cell phones and handhelds, U.S.-based companies face stiff competition from Korea's Samsung, Finland's Nokia, and Taiwan's High Tech Computer Corporation (HTC). For many U.S. companies, such as Starbucks and Wal-Mart, domestic markets have become saturated and the only potential for growth lies overseas. E-commerce organizations, too, are making international

73

international dimension
Portion of the external environment that represents events originating in foreign countries as well as opportunities for U.S. companies in other countries.

expansion a priority. The U.S. share of worldwide e-commerce is falling as foreign companies set up their own e-commerce ventures.

The most dramatic change in the international environment in recent years is the shift of economic power to China and India. Together, these countries have the population, brainpower, and dynamism to transform the twenty-first–century global economy. If things continue on the current track, analysts predict that India will overtake Germany as the world's third-largest economy within three decades, and that China would overtake the United States as number 1 by mid-century. In China, per capita income has tripled in a generation, and leaders are building the infrastructure for decades of expansion, as reflected in the country's hunger for raw materials. In 2005, China represented roughly 47 percent of the global cement consumption, 30 percent of coal, and 26 percent of crude steel. No one can predict the future, but it is clear that however things in India and China shake out, U.S. and other western firms have no choice but to pay attention.

The global environment represents a complex, ever-changing, and uneven playing field compared with the domestic environment. Managers who are used to thinking only about the domestic environment must learn new rules to remain competitive. When operating globally, managers have to consider legal, political, sociocultural, and economic factors not only in their home countries but in various other countries as well. For example, the rising consumer class in China and India plays a growing role in setting the standards for high-tech products and services such as cell phones, multimedia gadgets, and wireless Web services.[8]

Chapter 4 describes how today's businesses are operating in an increasingly borderless world and examines in detail how managing in a global environment differs from the management of domestic operations. Perhaps the hardest lesson for managers in the United States to learn is that they do not always know best. U.S. decision makers know little about issues and competition in foreign countries and many pay little attention to cultural factors, which is a sure route to failure. This chapter's Manager's Shoptalk box offers some tips for Western managers doing business in China.

One recent study found that only 28 percent of surveyed executives from the United States think multicultural experience is important.[9] U.S. arrogance is a shortcut to failure. An observer of emerging companies in India issues a wake-up call: "Once they learn to sell at Indian prices with world quality, they can compete anywhere."[10]

© BEN MARGOT/ASSOCIATED PRESS

CONCEPT CONNECTION "The big idea behind fair trade is that you can actually make globalization work for the poor," says Paul Rice, founder and CEO of TransFair USA. TransFair is the only U.S. organization authorized to grant the Fair Trade logo to products made from a growing list of crops, such as coffee, cocoa, and sugar, for which farmers in developing countries have been paid a fair price. The Oakland, California-based nonprofit is influencing the **international dimension** of today's business environment by helping increase the sales of fair trade products around the world. Rice says adhering to TransFair standards is just good business as the global environment grows increasingly important.

TECHNOLOGICAL

The **technological dimension** includes scientific and technological advancements in a specific industry as well as in society at large. In recent years, this dimension created massive changes for organizations in all industries. Twenty years ago, many organizations didn't even use desktop computers. Today, computer networks, Internet access, handheld devices, videoconferencing capabilities, cell phones, fax machines, and laptops are the minimum tools for doing business. A new generation of handhelds allows users to check their corporate e-mail, daily calendars, business contacts, and even customer orders from anywhere there's a wireless network. Cell phones can now switch seamlessly between cellular networks and corporate WiFi connections. Some companies hand out wireless key fobs with continually updated

technological dimension
The dimension of the general environment that includes scientific and technological advancements in the industry and society at large.

MANAGER'S SHOPTALK

THE TIES THAT BIND

With its low labor costs and huge potential market, China is luring thousands of U.S. companies in search of growth opportunities. Yet University of New Haven's Usha C. V. Haley recently found that only one-third of multinationals doing business in China have actually turned a profit. One reason Western businesses fall short of expectations, experts agree, is that they fail to grasp the centuries-old concept of *guanxi* that lies at the heart of Chinese culture.

At its simplest level, guanxi is a supportive, mutually beneficial connection between two people. Eventually, those personal relationships are linked together into a network, and it is through these networks that business gets done. Anyone considering doing business in China should keep in mind the following basic rules:

:: **Business is always personal.** It is impossible to translate "don't take it so personally—it's only business" into Chinese. Western managers tend to believe that if they conclude a successful transaction, a good business relationship will follow. The development of a personal relationship is an added bonus, but not really necessary when it comes to getting things done. In the Chinese business world, though, a personal relationship must be in place before managers even consider entering a business transaction. Western managers doing business in China should cultivate personal relationships—both during and outside of business hours. Accept any and all social invitations—for drinks, a meal, or even a potentially embarrassing visit to a karaoke bar.

:: **Don't skip the small talk.** Getting right down to business and bypassing the small talk during a meeting might feel like an efficient use of time to an American manager. To the Chinese, however, this approach neglects the all-important work of forging an emotional bond. Be aware that the real purpose of your initial meetings with potential business partners is to begin building a relationship, so keep your patience if the deal you're planning to discuss never even comes up.

:: **Remember that relationships are not short-term.** The work of establishing and nurturing guanxi relationships in China is never done. Western managers must put aside their usual focus on short-term results and recognize that it takes a long time for foreigners to be accepted into a guanxi network. Often, foreign companies must prove their trustworthiness and reliability over time. For example, firms that weathered the political instability that culminated in the 1989 student protests in Tiananmen Square found it much easier to do business afterwards.

:: **Make contact frequently.** Some experts recommend hiring ethnic Chinese staff members and then letting them do the heavy lifting of relationship-building. Others emphasize that Westerners themselves should put plenty of time and energy into forging links with Chinese contacts; those efforts will pay off because the contacts can smooth the way by tapping into their own guanxi networks. Whatever the strategy, contact should be frequent and personal. And be sure to keep careful track of the contacts you make. In China, any and all relationships are bound to be important at some point in time.

SOURCES: Michelle Dammon Loyalka, "Doing Business in China," *Business Week Online* (January 6, 2006), www.businessweek.com/smallbiz/; "Guanxi," *Wikipedia*, http://en.wikipedia.org/wiki/Guanxi; Los Angeles Chinese Learning Center, "Chinese Business Culture," http://chinese-school.netfirms.com/guanxi.html; and Beijing British Embassy, "Golden Hints for Doing Business in China," http://chinese-school.netfirms.com/goldenhints.html

security codes that enable employees to log onto their corporate networks and securely view data or write e-mails from any PC with a broadband connection.[11]

Other technological advances will also affect organizations and managers. The decoding of the human genome could lead to revolutionary medical advances. Cloning technology and stem cell research are raising both scientific and ethical concerns. Nanotechnology, which refers to manipulating matter at its tiniest scale, is moving from the research lab to the marketplace. Although only a few products incorporated nanoparticles in 2005, within a few years, nanotechnology could affect every industry. General Electric is researching how nanoceramics can make turbines more efficient. Medical researchers are looking at the potential for portable labs that offer instant analysis for everything from diabetes to HIV. Nanoparticles could someday give us golf balls designed to fly straight, army fatigues that resist chemical weapons, dent-free automobiles, and super-charged fuel cells that could replace fossil-fuel engines. Some 1,200 nanotechnology start-ups have emerged around the world, and smart managers at established organizations such as 3M, Dow Chemical, Samsung, NASA, Intel, Johnson & Johnson, and IBM are investing research dollars in this technological breakthrough.[12]

SOCIOCULTURAL

The **sociocultural dimension** of the general environment represents the demographic characteristics as well as the norms, customs, and values of the general population. Important sociocultural characteristics are geographical distribution and population density, age, and education levels. Today's demographic profiles are the foundation of tomorrow's workforce and consumers. Forecasters see increased globalization of both consumer markets and the labor supply, with increasing diversity both within organizations and consumer markets.[13] Consider the following key demographic trends in the United States:

1. The United States is experiencing the largest influx of immigrants in more than a century. By 2050, non-Hispanic whites will make up only about half of the population, down from 74 percent in 1995 and 69 percent in 2004. Hispanics are expected to make up about a quarter of the U.S. population.[14]

2. People are staying in the workforce longer, and many members of the huge post–World War II baby-boom generation are choosing to work well past traditional retirement age. At the same time, the 76 million or so members of Generation Y, which rivals the baby boom in size, are beginning to flood the job market. For the first time, a significant number of organizations are dealing with four generations working side-by-side.[15]

3. The fastest-growing type of living arrangement is single-father households, which rose 62 percent in 10 years, even though two-parent and single-mother households are still much more numerous.[16]

4. In an unprecedented demographic shift, married couple households have slipped from 80 percent in the 1950s to just over 50 percent in 2003. Couples with kids total just 25 percent, with the number projected to drop to 20 percent by 2010. By that year, it is expected that 30 percent of homes will be inhabited by someone who lives alone.[17]

Demographic trends affect organizations in other countries just as powerfully. Japan, Italy, and Germany are all faced with an aging workforce and customer base due to years of declining birth rates. In both Italy and Japan, the proportion of people over the age of 65 reached 20 percent in 2006.[18]

The sociocultural dimension also includes societal norms and values. The low-carb craze replaced the low-fat craze, spurring restaurants to alter their menus and supermarkets to revise their product mix. Even the Girl Scouts were affected, as sales declined about 10 percent during the 2004 cookie season.[19] Handgun manufacturers in the United States have been tugged back and forth as public acceptance and support of guns in the home fell in the wake of tragic school shootings, then surged following terrorist attacks in the United States.

CONCEPT

C O N N E C T I O N   Want to get the best out of Generation Y employees? Why not let your current Gen Y workers show you how? That's what Monarch Mountain, a ski and snowboard area near Salida, Colorado, does. As millions of GenY employees flood the job market, companies are finding ways to adapt to this shift in the **sociocultural dimension** of the environment. At Monarch, young employees, not managers, talk with prospective hires to answer questions and address their concerns from the perspective of the job seeker. Through the "First Responder" program, the employee provides a realistic picture of what it's like to work at Monarch and often becomes a mentor if the candidate is hired.

sociocultural dimension
The dimension of the general environment representing the demographic characteristics, norms, customs, and values of the population within which the organization operates.

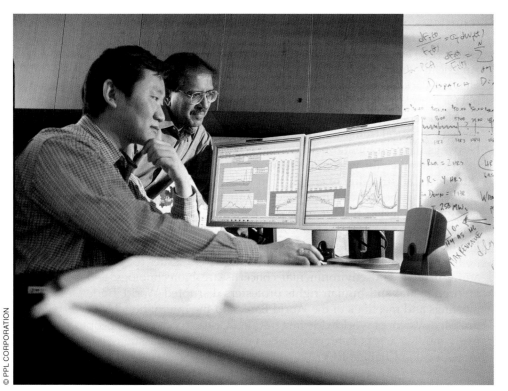

ECONOMIC

The **economic dimension** represents the general economic health of the country or region in which the organization operates. Consumer purchasing power, the unemployment rate, and interest rates are part of an organization's economic environment. Because organizations today are operating in a global environment, the economic dimension has become exceedingly complex and creates enormous uncertainty for managers. The economies of countries are more closely tied together now. For example, the early 2000s economic recession and the decline of consumer confidence in the United States affected economies and organizations around the world. Similarly, economic problems in Asia and Europe had a tremendous impact on companies and the stock market in the United States.

One significant recent trend in the economic environment is the frequency of mergers and acquisitions. Citibank and Travelers merged to form Citigroup, IBM purchased Pricewaterhouse Coopers Consulting, and Cingular acquired AT&T Wireless. In the toy industry, the three largest toy makers—Hasbro, Mattel, and Tyco—gobbled up at least a dozen smaller competitors within a few years. At the same time, however, a tremendous vitality is evident in the small business sector of the economy. Entrepreneurial start-ups are a significant aspect of today's U.S. economy and will be discussed in Chapter 6.

LEGAL-POLITICAL

The **legal-political dimension** includes government regulations at the local, state, and federal levels, as well as political activities designed to influence company behavior. The U.S. political system encourages capitalism, and the government tries not to overregulate business. However, government laws do specify rules of the game. The federal government influences organizations through the Occupational Safety and Health Administration (OSHA), Environmental Protection Agency (EPA), fair trade practices, libel statutes allowing lawsuits against business, consumer protection legislation, product safety requirements, import and export

economic dimension The dimension of the general environment representing the overall economic health of the country or region in which the organization operates.

legal-political dimension The dimension of the general environment that includes federal, state, and local government regulations and political activities designed to influence company behavior.

restrictions, and information and labeling requirements. Many organizations also have to contend with government and legal issues in other countries. The European Union (EU) adopted environmental and consumer protection rules that are costing American companies hundreds of millions of dollars a year. Companies such as Hewlett-Packard, Ford Motor Company, and General Electric have to pick up the bill for recycling the products they sell in the EU, for example.[20]

Managers must also recognize a variety of **pressure groups** that work within the legal-political framework to influence companies to behave in socially responsible ways. Environmental activists have targeted Victoria's Secret, L.L.Bean, and other companies for wasteful catalog-printing practices that the activists say contributes to the stripping of endangered forests.[21] Tobacco companies today are certainly feeling the far-reaching power of antismoking groups. Middle-aged activists who once protested the Vietnam War have gone to battle to keep Wal-Mart from "destroying the quality of small-town life." Some groups also attacked the giant retailer on environmental issues, which likely will be one of the strongest pressure points in coming years.[22] Two of the hottest current issues for pressure groups that are also related to environmental concerns are biotechnology and world trade. Environmental and human rights protesters disrupted World Trade Organization meetings and meetings of the World Bank and the International Monetary Fund to protest a system of worldwide integration that has food, goods, people, and capital freely moving across borders. This current international issue will be discussed in more detail in Chapter 4.

Task Environment

As described earlier, the task environment includes those sectors that have a direct working relationship with the organization, among them customers, competitors, suppliers, and the labor market.

CUSTOMERS

Those people and organizations in the environment who acquire goods or services from the organization are **customers**. As recipients of the organization's output, customers are important because they determine the organization's success. Patients are the customers of hospitals, students the customers of schools, and travelers the customers of airlines. Many companies are searching for ways to reach the coveted teen and youth market by tying marketing messages into online social networks such as MySpace.com, and Facebook.com. With high school and college students representing a $375 billion consumer spending market, it's serious business for managers at companies such as Target, Apple, Coca-Cola, and Walt Disney. Apple sponsors an Apple-lovers group on Facebook.com, giving away iPod Shuffles in weekly contests. Target has sponsored a group on MySpace.com that features a 15-year-old professional snowboarder wearing a Target logo on his helmet.[23]

Customers today have greater power because of the Internet, which presents threats as well as opportunities for managers. Today's customers can directly affect the organization's reputation and sales, for example, through gripe sites such as *walmartsucks.com*, where customers and sales associates cyber-vent about the nation's largest retailer, and *untied.com*, where United Airlines employees and disgruntled fliers rail against the air carrier. "In this new information environment," says Kyle Shannon, CEO of e-commerce consultancy Agency.com, "you've got to assume everyone knows everything."[24]

COMPETITORS

Other organizations in the same industry or type of business that provide goods or services to the same set of customers are referred to as **competitors**. Each industry

pressure group An interest group that works within the legal-political framework to influence companies to behave in socially responsible ways.

customers People and organizations in the environment who acquire goods or services from the organization.

competitors Other organizations in the same industry or type of business that provide goods or services to the same set of customers.

is characterized by specific competitive issues. The recording industry differs from the steel industry and the pharmaceutical industry.

Competitive wars are being waged worldwide in all industries. Coke and Pepsi continue to battle it out for the soft-drink market. UPS and FedEx fight the overnight delivery wars. Home Depot and Lowe's brawl in the retail home improvement market, trying to out-do one another in terms of price, service, and selection.[25] In the travel and tourism industry, Internet companies such as Expedia.com and Hotels.com have hurt the big hotel chains. These chains are fighting back by undercutting the brokers' prices on the hotels' own Web sites. In addition, five of the largest chains banded together to create Travelweb.com, which is aimed directly at the online brokers.[26]

SUPPLIERS

The raw materials the organization uses to produce its output are provided by **suppliers**. A steel mill requires iron ore, machines, and financial resources. A small, private university may utilize hundreds of suppliers for paper, pencils, cafeteria food, computers, trucks, fuel, electricity, and textbooks. Companies from toolmakers to construction firms and auto manufacturers were hurt recently by an unanticipated jump in the price of steel from suppliers. Just as they were starting to see an upturn in their business, the cost of raw materials jumped 30 percent in a two-month period.[27] Consider also that China now produces more than 85 percent of the Vitamin C used by companies in the United States. An agreement among China's four largest producers led to an increase in the price of Vitamin C from $3 a kilogram to as high as $9 a kilogram.[28]

Many companies are using fewer suppliers and trying to build good relationships with them so that they will receive high-quality parts and materials at lower prices. The relationship between manufacturers and suppliers has traditionally been an adversarial one, but managers are finding that cooperation is the key to saving money, maintaining quality, and speeding products to market.

> ■ **TAKE A MOMENT**
>
> As a new manager, you can get a leg up by paying attention to the external environment and international events. Stay in tune with what's going on in the general environment, including social, economic, technological, and political trends. Pay particular attention to the task environment, including your customers, competitors, and suppliers. Be sure to connect the dots among the things you see.

LABOR MARKET

The **labor market** represents people in the environment who can be hired to work for the organization. Every organization needs a supply of trained, qualified personnel. Unions, employee associations, and the availability of certain classes of employees can influence the organization's labor market. Labor market forces affecting organizations right now include (1) the growing need for computer-literate knowledge workers; (2) the necessity for continuous investment in human resources through recruitment, education, and training to meet the competitive demands of the borderless world; and (3) the effects of international trading blocs, automation, outsourcing, and shifting facility location upon labor dislocations, creating unused labor pools in some areas and labor shortages in others.

Changes in these various sectors of the general and task environments can create tremendous challenges, especially for organizations operating in complex, rapidly changing industries. Nortel Networks, a Canadian company with multiple U.S. offices, is an example of an organization operating in a highly complex environment.

suppliers People and organizations who provide the raw materials the organization uses to produce its output.

labor market The people available for hire by the organization.

Nortel Networks

The external environment for Nortel Networks is illustrated in Exhibit 3.2. The Canadian-based company began in 1895 as a manufacturer of telephones and has reinvented itself many times to keep up with changes in the environment. In the late 1990s, the company transformed itself into a major player in wireless technology and equipment for connecting businesses and individuals to the Internet. In 1997, the company was about to be run over by rivals such as Cisco Systems that were focused on Internet gear. Then-CEO John Roth knew he needed to do something bold to respond to changes in the technological environment. A name change to Nortel Networks symbolized and reinforced the company's new goal of providing unified network solutions to customers worldwide.

EXHIBIT 3.2

The External Environment of Nortel

Economic
- Dot-com crash
- Recovering U.S. and Canadian economy
- Worldwide economic slowdown

Legal/Political
- Canadian ownership
- Accounting and regulatory troubles
- Renegotiating with creditors
- Tough EU regulations
- NAFTA
- New tax laws

Competitors
- Lucent, Cisco and 3Com, U.S.
- Siemens, Germany
- Alcatel, France
- Ericsson, Sweden
- NEC, Japan

Customers
- Telephone companies, major corporations for e-business
- Businesses and not-for-profit organizations
- New demand for optical and wireless equipment
- Targeting start-ups with Web products

Technological
- New optical fiber networks
- Expanding wireless technologies (3G)
- Continued need for traditional equipment
- Data and voice networking

Nortel Networks

Sociocultural
- Web surfers
- Opening of new markets worldwide
- Wireless lifestyles
- Risk of terrorism

Suppliers
- Components from subcontractors
- Banks, bondholders provide capital
- Obtain quality parts from suppliers worldwide

Labor Market
- U.S.: Texas, North Carolina, Tennessee, and California
- Treat employees well
- Hire computer-literate college graduates

International
- Headquarters in Brampton, Ontario
- Competes in more than 100 countries
- Deals in China, Brazil, Sweden, Australia, Russia, and Taiwan
- Growing market for telecommunications gear in Japan
- Joint ventures in Spain, Poland, and Israel
- Alliance with Alcatel and Lagardere Group of France
- Forty percent of business outside North America

SOURCES: W. C. Symonds, J. B. Levine, N. Gross, and P. Coy, "High-Tech Star: Northern Telecom Is Challenging Even AT&T," *BusinessWeek* (July 27, 1992): 54–58; I. Austen, "Hooked on the Net," *Canadian Business* (June 26–July 10, 1998): 95–103; J. Weber with A. Reinhardt and P. Burrows, "Racing Ahead at Nortel," *BusinessWeek* (November 8, 1999): 93–99; "Nortel's Waffling Continues: First Job Cuts, Then Product Lines, and Now the CEO," *Telephony* (May 21, 2001): 12; and M. Heinzl, "Nortel's Profits of 499 Million Exceeds Forecast," *The Wall Street Journal* (January 30, 2004): B4.

One response to the competitive environment was to spend billions to acquire data and voice networking companies, including Bay Networks (which makes Internet and data equipment), Cambrian Systems (a hot maker of optical technology), Periphonics (maker of voice-response systems), and Clarify (customer relationship management software). These companies brought Nortel top-notch technology, helping the company snatch customers away from rivals Cisco and Lucent Technologies. In addition, even during rough economic times, Nortel kept spending nearly 20 percent of its revenues on research and development to keep pace with changing technology.

Internationally, Nortel made impressive inroads in Taiwan, China, Brazil, Mexico, Colombia, Japan, and Sweden, among other countries. It also won customers by recognizing the continuing need for traditional equipment and offering hybrid gear that combines old telephone technology with new Internet features, allowing companies to transition from the old to the new. Bold new technologies for Nortel include optical systems that move voice and data at the speed of light and third-generation wireless networks (3G), which zap data and video from phone to phone. Nortel is considered a leader in wireless gear and won contracts from Verizon Communications and Orange SA, a unit of France Telecom, to supply equipment that sends phone calls as packets of digital data like that used over the Internet.

Companies moving in a Net speed environment risk a hard landing, and when the demand for Internet equipment slumped in the early 2000s, Nortel's business was devastated. The company cut more than two-thirds of its workforce and closed dozens of plants and offices. An accounting scandal that led to fraud investigations and senior executive dismissals made things even worse. At one point, Nortel's stock was trading for less than a dollar. By early 2006, though, positive changes in the economic environment, along with a savvy new CEO, put Nortel back on an uphill swing. Analysts predicted that the company would outdo major competitor Lucent in sales growth and other financial metrics. However, as one analyst said, "It's a tough business," and Nortel's managers have to stay on their toes to help the organization cope in an ever-changing, difficult environment.[29]

THE ORGANIZATION–ENVIRONMENT RELATIONSHIP

Why do organizations care so much about factors in the external environment? The reason is that the environment creates uncertainty for organization managers, and they must respond by designing the organization to adapt to the environment.

Environmental Uncertainty

Organizations must manage environmental uncertainty to be effective. *Uncertainty* means that managers do not have sufficient information about environmental factors to understand and predict environmental needs and changes.[30] As indicated in Exhibit 3.3, environmental characteristics that influence uncertainty are the number of factors that affect the organization and the extent to which those factors change. A large multinational like Nortel Networks has thousands of factors in the external environment creating uncertainty for managers. When external factors change rapidly, the organization experiences high uncertainty; examples are telecommunications and aerospace firms, computer and electronics companies, and e-commerce organizations that sell products and services over the Internet. Companies have to make an effort to adapt to the rapid changes in the environment. When an organization deals with only a few external factors and these factors are relatively stable, such as for soft-drink bottlers or food processors, managers experience low uncertainty and can devote less attention to external issues.

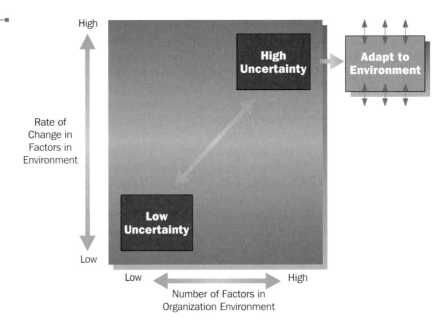

EXHIBIT   3.3

The External Environment
and Uncertainty

■ **TAKE A MOMENT** | Are you ready to become a manager in an organization that operates in a highly uncertain environment? Take the New Manager Self-Test on page 83. Learn whether your new-manager's mind seems ready for environmental uncertainty.

Adapting to the Environment

If an organization faces increased uncertainty with respect to competition, customers, suppliers, or government regulations managers can use several strategies to adapt to these changes, including boundary-spanning roles, interorganizational partnerships, and mergers or joint ventures.

BOUNDARY-SPANNING ROLES

Departments and **boundary-spanning roles** link and coordinate the organization with key elements in the external environment. Boundary spanners serve two purposes for the organization: They detect and process information about changes in the environment, and they represent the organization's interests to the environment.[31] Employees in engineering or research and development scan for new technological developments, innovations, and raw materials. People in departments such as marketing and purchasing span the boundary to work with customers and suppliers, both face-to-face and through market research. Some organizations are staying in touch with customers through the Internet, such as by monitoring gripe sites, communicating with customers on company Web sites, and contracting with market-research firms that use the Web to monitor rapidly changing marketplace trends.[32] Another recent approach to boundary spanning is the use of *business intelligence*, which results from using sophisticated software to search through large amounts of internal and external data to spot patterns, trends, and relationships that might be significant. For example, Verizon uses business intelligence software to actively monitor customer interactions and fix problems almost immediately.[33]

Business intelligence is related to the growing area of boundary spanning known as *competitive intelligence (CI)*, which refers to activities to get as much information as possible about one's rivals. Competitive intelligence specialists use Web sites, commercial databases, financial reports, market activity, news clippings, trade publications, personal contacts, and numerous other sources to scan an

boundary-spanning roles
Roles assumed by people and/or departments that link and coordinate the organization with key elements in the external environment.

MANAGER MIND AND THE ENVIRONMENT

Does your mind fit an uncertain environment? Think back to how you thought or behaved at a time when you were in a formal or informal leadership position. Please answer whether each of the following items was Mostly True or Mostly False for you.

	Mostly True	Mostly False
1. Enjoyed hearing about new ideas even when working toward a deadline.	_____	_____
2. Welcomed unusual viewpoints of others even if we were working under pressure.	_____	_____
3. Made it a point to attend industry trade shows and company events.	_____	_____
4. Specifically encouraged others to express opposing ideas and arguments.	_____	_____
5. Asked "dumb" questions.	_____	_____
6. Always offered comments on the meaning of data or issues.	_____	_____
7. Expressed a controversial opinion to bosses and peers.	_____	_____
8. Suggested ways of improving my and others' ways of doing things.	_____	_____

INTERPRETATION: In an organization in a highly **uncertain environment** everything seems to be changing. In that case, an important quality for a new manager is "mindfulness," which includes the qualities of being open minded and an independent thinker. In a stable environment, a closed minded manager may perform okay because much work can be done in the same old way. In an uncertain environment, even a new manager needs to facilitate new thinking, new ideas, and new ways of working. A high score on the preceding items suggests higher mindfulness and a better fit with an uncertain environment.

SCORING: Give yourself one point for each item you marked as Mostly True. If you scored less than 5 you might want to start your career as a manager in a stable rather than unstable environment. A score of 5 or above suggests a higher level of mindfulness and a better fit for a new manager in an organization with an uncertain environment.

SOURCES: The questions are based on ideas from R. L. Daft and R. M. Lengel, *Fusion Leadership* (San Francisco: Berrett Koehler, 2000): Chapter 4; B. Bass and B. Avolio, *Multifactor Leadership Questionnaire,* 2nd ed. (Mind Garden, Inc); and Karl E. Weick and Kathleen M. Sutcliffe, *Managing the Unexpected: Assuring High Performance in an Age of Complexity* (San Francisco: Jossey-Bass, 2001).

organization's environment and spot potential threats or opportunities.[34] Visa has an employee who searches the Web for two hours each day for insights on MasterCard and other competitors. Harley-Davidson hires an outside research firm to search through massive amounts of data and reveal patterns that help decipher and predict competitors' actions.[35]

Boundary spanning is an increasingly important task in organizations because environmental shifts can happen so quickly in today's world. Managers need good information about their competitors, customers, and other elements of the environment to make good decisions. Thus, the most successful companies involve everyone in boundary-spanning activities. People at the grass-roots often can see and interpret significant changes sooner than managers who are more removed from the day-to-day work.[36] However, top executives, too, need to stay in tune with the environment. Tom Stemberg, CEO of Staples, visits a competitor's store once a week and shares what he learns with others on the management team.[37] Perceiving environmental shifts that could impact the organization isn't always easy. Managers must learn to not only interpret the data right in front of them but also to see weak signals on the periphery and answer the question, "What don't we know that might matter?"[38]

INTERORGANIZATIONAL PARTNERSHIPS

An increasingly popular strategy for adapting to the environment is to reduce boundaries and increase collaboration with other organizations. North American companies have typically worked alone, competing with one another, but an uncertain and interconnected global environment changed that tendency. Companies are joining together to become more effective and to share scarce resources. Sony, Toshiba, and IBM are collaborating to produce a new, tiny computer chip. Supermarket chains Kroger, Albertsons, and Safeway banded together to negotiate with labor unions. General Motors teamed up with German automakers DaimlerChrysler AG and BMW AG to develop a hybrid fuel system to compete with Toyota.[39] Head-to-head competition among independent firms is giving way to networks of alliances that compete for business on a global basis. For example, the aerospace industry is controlled by two networks—those of Boeing and Airbus, each of which is made up of more than 100 partner organizations.[40]

Managers shift from an adversarial orientation to a partnership orientation, as summarized in Exhibit 3.4. The new paradigm is based on trust and the ability of partners to work out equitable solutions to conflicts so that everyone profits from the relationship. Managers work to reduce costs and add value to both sides, rather than trying to get all the benefits for their own company. The new model is also characterized by a high level of information sharing, including e-business linkages for automatic ordering, payments, and other transactions. In addition, person-to-person interaction provides corrective feedback and solves problems. People from other companies may be onsite or participate in virtual teams to enable close coordination. Partners are frequently involved in one another's product design and production, and they are committed for the long term. It is not unusual for business partners to help one another, even outside of what is specified in the contract.[41]

© CAMPBELL'S SOUP COMPANY

|CONCEPT
|C O N C E P T |
|C O N N E C T I O N| A consumer focus group in Mexico evaluates Campbell's soups, reviewing qualities such as packaging, preparation, appearance, and taste. The passage of NAFTA broadened market opportunities in Mexico, where nearly 9 billion servings of soup are consumed each year. Marketing executives act as **boundary spanners** to test reactions and assess whether products meet local needs. Boundary spanning provided competitive intelligence that Mexican consumers like convenient dry-soup varieties as well as condensed and ready-to-serve soups.

MERGERS AND JOINT VENTURES

A step beyond strategic partnerships is for companies to become involved in mergers or joint ventures to reduce environmental uncertainty. A frenzy of merger and acquisition activity both in the United States and internationally in recent years is an attempt by organizations to cope with the tremendous volatility of the environment.[42] A **merger** occurs when two or more organizations combine to become one. For example, Wells Fargo merged with Norwest Corp. to form the nation's fourth largest banking corporation.

A **joint venture** involves a strategic alliance or program by two or more organizations. A joint venture typically occurs when a project is too complex, expensive, or uncertain for one firm to handle alone. Oprah Winfrey's Harpo Inc. formed a joint venture with Hearst Magazines to launch *O, The Oprah Magazine*.[43] Despite her

merger The combining of two or more organizations into one.

joint venture A strategic alliance or program by two or more organizations.

From Adversarial Orientation ⟶ To Partnership Orientation	
• Suspicion, competition, arm's length	• Trust, value added to both sides
• Price, efficiency, own profits	• Equity, fair dealing, everyone profits
• Information and feedback limited	• E-business links to share information and conduct digital transactions
• Lawsuits to resolve conflict	• Close coordination; virtual teams and people onsite
• Minimal involvement and up-front investment	• Involvement in partner's product design and production
• Short-term contracts	• Long-term contracts
• Contracts limit the relationship	• Business assistance goes beyond the contract

EXHIBIT 3.4

The Shift to a Partnership Paradigm

popularity and success with her television show, Winfrey recognized the complexity and uncertainty involved in starting a new magazine. The combined resources and management talents of the partners contributed to the most successful start-up ever in the magazine publishing industry.

Joint ventures are on the rise as companies strive to keep pace with rapid technological change and compete in the global economy. Barnes & Noble formed a joint venture with Germany's Bertelsmann AG to establish Barnesandnoble.com. MTV Networks established joint ventures with companies in Brazil, Australia, and other countries to expand its global presence.[44] Many small businesses are also turning to joint ventures with large firms or with international partners. A larger partner can provide sales staff, distribution channels, financial resources, or a research staff. Small businesses seldom have the expertise to deal internationally, so a company such as Nypro, Inc., a plastic injection-molding manufacturer in Clinton, Massachusetts, joins with overseas experts who are familiar with the local rules. Nypro now does business in four countries.[45]

■ **TAKE A MOMENT**

As a new manager, learning to span the boundary to other units that influence your success is important. As you progress to higher management positions, learn how to use interorganizational partnerships, and even mergers or joint ventures, to help your organization adapt and stay competitive in a shifting environment.

THE INTERNAL ENVIRONMENT: CORPORATE CULTURE

The internal environment within which managers work includes corporate culture, production technology, organization structure, and physical facilities. Of these, corporate culture surfaces as extremely important to competitive advantage. The internal culture must fit the needs of the external environment and company strategy. When this fit occurs, highly committed employees create a high-performance organization that is tough to beat.[46]

Most people don't think about culture; it's just "how we do things around here" or "the way things are here." However, managers have to think about culture, because it typically plays a significant role in organizational success. The concept of culture has been of growing concern to managers since the 1980s, as turbulence in the external environment has grown, often requiring new values and attitudes. Organizational culture has been defined and studied in many and varied ways. For the purposes of this chapter, we define **culture** as the set of key values, beliefs,

culture The set of key values, beliefs, understandings, and norms that members of an organization share.

HONDA/ASSOCIATED PRESS

CONCEPT

CONNECTION Equality stands at the heart of Japanese automaker Honda's **corporate culture,** and visible manifestations of the cultural values are everywhere. For example, at facilities such as this automobile manufacturing plant in Lincoln, Alabama, there are open offices, no assigned parking spaces, and the 4,500 employees, called *associates,* all eat in the same cafeteria and call each other by their first names. Everyone, from the president on down, comes to work, walks into the locker room, and changes into a gleaming white two-piece uniform emblazoned with the Honda insignia. It's no accident that it's hard to tell the managers from the front-line workers.

understandings, and norms shared by members of an organization.[47] The concept of culture helps managers understand the hidden, complex aspects of organizational life. Culture is a pattern of shared values and assumptions about how things are done within the organization. This pattern is learned by members as they cope with external and internal problems and taught to new members as the correct way to perceive, think, and feel.

Culture can be analyzed at three levels, as illustrated in Exhibit 3.5, with each level becoming less obvious.[48] At the surface level are visible artifacts, which include such things as manner of dress, patterns of behavior, physical symbols, organizational ceremonies, and office layout. Visible artifacts are all the things one can see, hear, and observe by watching members of the organization. At a deeper level are the expressed values and beliefs, which are not observable but can be discerned from how people explain and justify what they do. Members of the organization hold these values at a conscious level. They can be interpreted from the stories, language, and symbols organization members use to represent them.

Some values become so deeply embedded in a culture that members are no longer consciously aware of them. These basic, underlying assumptions and beliefs are the essence of culture and subconsciously guide behavior and decisions. In some organizations, a basic assumption might be that people are essentially lazy and will shirk their duties whenever possible; thus, employees are closely supervised and given little freedom, and colleagues are frequently suspicious of one another. More enlightened organizations operate on the basic assumption that people want to do a good job; in these organizations, employees are given more freedom and responsibility, and colleagues trust one another and work cooperatively.

The fundamental values that characterize an organization's culture can be understood through the visible manifestations of symbols, stories, heroes, slogans, and ceremonies.

EXHIBIT   3.5

Levels of Corporate Culture

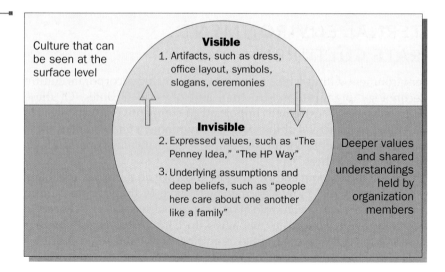

Culture that can be seen at the surface level

Visible
1. Artifacts, such as dress, office layout, symbols, slogans, ceremonies

Invisible
2. Expressed values, such as "The Penney Idea," "The HP Way"

3. Underlying assumptions and deep beliefs, such as "people here care about one another like a family"

Deeper values and shared understandings held by organization members

Symbols

A **symbol** is an object, act, or event that conveys meaning to others. Symbols can be considered a rich, nonverbal language that vibrantly conveys the organization's important values concerning how people relate to one another and interact with the environment.[49] For example, managers at a New York–based start-up that provides Internet solutions to local television broadcasters wanted a way to symbolize the company's unofficial mantra of "drilling down to solve problems." They bought a dented old drill for $2 and dubbed it The Team Drill. Each month, the drill is presented to a different employee in recognition of exceptional work, and the employee personalizes the drill in some way before passing it on to the next winner.[50]

Buildings and office layout can also be symbolic. The headquarters of RadioShack Corp. used to have 22 separate entrances and five parking lots, with employees higher up the hierarchy having more convenient parking and building access. When the company built its new headquarters, top managers asked that it be designed with one parking garage and a single front door for all 2,400 employees. The door spills onto a "main street" corridor that connects all departments. Executives who once took a private elevator to their top floor, marble-clad suite now ride the elevator with everyone else and are located close to rank-and-file employees. The new headquarters symbolizes RadioShack's new cultural values of egalitarianism, horizontal collaboration, teamwork, and innovation.[51]

Stories

A **story** is a narrative based on true events and is repeated frequently and shared among organizational employees. Stories are told to new employees to keep the organization's primary values alive. One of Nordstrom's primary means of emphasizing the importance of customer service is through corporate storytelling. An example is the story about a sales representative who took back a customer's two-year-old blouse with no questions asked.[52] A frequently told story at UPS concerns an employee who, without authorization, ordered an extra Boeing 737 to ensure timely delivery of a load of Christmas packages that had been left behind in the holiday rush. As the story goes, rather than punishing the worker, UPS rewarded his initiative. By telling this story, UPS workers communicate that the company stands behind its commitment to worker autonomy and customer service.[53]

Heroes

A **hero** is a figure who exemplifies the deeds, character, and attributes of a strong culture. Heroes are role models for employees to follow. Sometimes heroes are real, such as the female security supervisor who once challenged IBM's chairman because he wasn't carrying the appropriate clearance identification to enter a security area.[54] Other times they are symbolic, such as the mythical sales representative at Robinson Jewelers who delivered a wedding ring directly to the church because the ring had been ordered late. The deeds of heroes are out of the ordinary, but not so far out as to be unattainable by other employees. Heroes show how to do the right thing in the organization. Companies with strong cultures take advantage of achievements to define heroes who uphold key values.

At 3M Corp., top managers keep alive the heroes who developed projects that were killed by top management. One hero was a vice president who was fired earlier in his career for persisting with a new product even after his boss had told him, "That's a stupid idea. Stop!" After the worker was fired, he would not leave. He stayed in an unused office, working without a salary on the new product

symbol An object, act, or event that conveys meaning to others.

story A narrative based on true events and repeated frequently and shared among organizational employees.

hero A figure who exemplifies the deeds, character, and attributes of a strong corporate culture.

idea. Eventually he was rehired, the idea succeeded, and he was promoted to vice president. The lesson of this hero as a major element in 3M's culture is to persist at what you believe in.[55]

Slogans

A **slogan** is a phrase or sentence that succinctly expresses a key corporate value. Many companies use a slogan or saying to convey special meaning to employees. H. Ross Perot of Electronic Data Systems established the philosophy of hiring the best people he could find and noted how difficult it was to find them. His motto was, "Eagles don't flock. You gather them one at a time." Averitt Express uses the slogan "Our driving force is people" to express its commitment to treating employees and customers well. Cultural values can also be discerned in written public statements, such as corporate mission statements or other formal statements that express the core values of the organization. The mission statement for Hallmark Cards, for example, emphasizes values of excellence, ethical and moral conduct in all relationships, business innovation, and corporate social responsibility.[56]

Ceremonies

A **ceremony** is a planned activity at a special event that is conducted for the benefit of an audience. Managers hold ceremonies to provide dramatic examples of company values. Ceremonies are special occasions that reinforce valued accomplishments, create a bond among people by allowing them to share an important event, and anoint and celebrate heroes.[57] Wal-Mart founder Sam Walton initiated a ceremony in 1962 that thrives to this day and remains the heartbeat of Wal-Mart's culture.

Wal-Mart

On a foggy Saturday morning in Bentonville, Arkansas, nearly 600 people, sometimes including surprise celebrities, politicians, or business luminaries, file into the auditorium at Wal-Mart's home office to participate in a ceremony that's been going on for more than 45 years. At 7:00 A.M. sharp, CEO Lee Scott kicks off the meeting by asking a group of visitors to lead the crowd in the Wal-Mart cheer: "Give me a W! Give me an A! Give me an L! Give me a Squiggly! . . ." and so forth.

After the kick-off, Wal-Mart's Saturday Morning Meeting opens with a review of the previous week's sales numbers and the singling out of certain stores or managers who performed especially well. A series of presentations on merchandising and retail trade tips comes next, often based on ideas that Wal-Mart executives got from managers and employees in stores around the world. Then, special guests are recognized, including store employees who have received recent awards. The meeting ends with a sort of sermon from Scott on the customer-comes-first ethic.

The ceremony of the Saturday Morning Meeting serves as the model for other Wal-Mart ceremonies, all of which begin with the Wal-Mart cheer—the daily shift change meetings in the stores, weekly management operations meetings, and five annual companywide megameetings that each draw more than 10,000 participants. These frequent meetings and ceremonies, part business and part pep rally, are credited with enabling Wal-Mart executives to operate a huge, complex global business on a weekly and sometimes daily basis, moving fast to outflank competitors. But just as importantly, they serve as a way to reinforce and personify the strong corporate culture. As former vice chairman Don Soderquist said, "When your company gets as big as ours, you still need to feel that this is a family, that you're in on things."[58]

slogan A phrase or sentence that succinctly expresses a key corporate value.

ceremony A planned activity at a special event that is conducted for the benefit of an audience.

The Saturday Morning Meeting makes the world's largest company still feel like the small and folksy five-and-dime store that Sam Walton opened in Bentonville, Arkansas, in 1962. This and other company ceremonies became even more important in recent years as Wal-Mart's corporate culture felt the strain of severe public criticism of the company for everything from its size and dominance to how it treats suppliers and employees. Its intensity damaged morale and threatened the almost-evangelical culture. Executives believe the meetings are their most effective tool for weathering Wal-Mart's public relations predicament, reinforcing the basic values that contributed to the company's astounding success, and finding ways to address and correct the inevitable problems of managing this huge, global enterprise.

Many ceremonies include the presentation of a major award. Mary Kay Cosmetics Company holds elaborate awards ceremonies, presenting gold and diamond pins, furs, and luxury cars to high-achieving sales consultants. The setting is typically an auditorium, in front of a large, cheering audience, and everyone dresses in glamorous evening clothes. The most successful consultants are introduced by film clips, like the kind used to present award nominees in the entertainment industry. These ceremonies recognize and celebrate high-performing employees and emphasize the rewards for performance.[59] A company can also bestow an award secretly by mailing it to the employee's home or, if a check, by depositing it in a bank. But such procedures would not make the bestowal of rewards a significant organizational event and would be less meaningful to the employee.

In summary, organizational culture represents the values, norms, understandings, and basic assumptions that employees share, and these values are signified by symbols, stories, heroes, slogans, and ceremonies. Managers help define important symbols, stories, and heroes to shape the culture.

ENVIRONMENT AND CULTURE

A big influence on internal corporate culture is the external environment. Cultures can vary widely across organizations; however, organizations within the same industry often reveal similar cultural characteristics because they are operating in similar environments.[60] The internal culture should embody what it takes to succeed in the environment. If the external environment requires extraordinary customer service, the culture should encourage good service; if it calls for careful technical decision making, cultural values should reinforce managerial decision making.

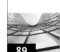

> **TAKE A MOMENT**
>
> As a new manager, pay attention to culture. Recognize the ways in which cultural values can help or hurt your department's performance. Consciously shape adaptive values through the use of symbols, stories, heroes, ceremonies, and slogans.

Adaptive Cultures

Research at Harvard on 207 U.S. firms illustrated the critical relationship between corporate culture and the external environment. The study found that a strong corporate culture alone did not ensure business success unless the culture encouraged healthy adaptation to the external environment. As illustrated in Exhibit 3.6, adaptive corporate cultures have different values and behavior from unadaptive corporate cultures. In adaptive cultures, managers are concerned about customers and those internal people and processes that bring about useful change. In the unadaptive corporate cultures, managers are concerned about themselves, and their values tend to discourage risk taking and change. Thus a strong culture alone is not enough, because an unhealthy culture may encourage the organization to march resolutely in the wrong direction. Healthy cultures help companies adapt to the environment.[61]

EXHIBIT 3.6	Adaptive Corporate Cultures	Unadaptive Corporate Cultures
Visible Behavior	Managers pay close attention to all their constituencies, especially customers, and initiate change when needed to serve their legitimate interests, even if it entails taking some risks.	Managers tend to behave somewhat insularly, politically, and bureaucratically. As a result, they do not change their strategies quickly to adjust to or take advantage of changes in their business environments.
Expressed Values	Managers care deeply about customers, stockholders, and employees. They also strongly value people and processes that can create useful change (e.g., leadership initiatives up and down the management hierarchy).	Managers care mainly about themselves, their immediate work group, or some product (or technology) associated with that work group. They value the orderly and risk-reducing management process much more highly than leadership initiatives.

EXHIBIT 3.6

Environmentally Adaptive versus Unadaptive Corporate Cultures

SOURCE: John P. Kotter and James L. Heskett, *Corporate Culture and Performance* (New York: The Free Press, 1992), 51.

TAKE A MOMENT

Complete the experiential exercise on page 98 that pertains to adaptive cultures. How would you shape adaptive values in a company for which you worked?

Types of Cultures

In considering what cultural values are important for the organization, managers consider the external environment as well as the company's strategy and goals. Studies suggest that the right fit between culture, strategy, and the environment is associated with four categories or types of culture, as illustrated in Exhibit 3.7. These categories are based on two dimensions: (1) the extent to which the external environment requires flexibility or stability; and (2) the extent

EXHIBIT 3.7

Four Types of Corporate Cultures

SOURCES: Based on D. R. Denison and A. K. Mishra, "Toward a Theory of Organizational Culture and Effectiveness," *Organization Science*, 6, no. 2 (March–April 1995): 204–223; R. Hooijberg and F. Petrock, "On Cultural Change: Using the Competing Values Framework to Help Leaders Execute a Transformational Strategy," *Human Resource Management* 32, no. 1 (1993): 29–50; and R. E. Quinn, *Beyond Rational Management: Mastering the Paradoxes and Competing Demands of High Performance* (San Francisco: Jossey-Bass, 1988).

to which a company's strategic focus is internal or external. The four categories associated with these differences are adaptability, achievement, involvement, and consistency.[62]

The **adaptability culture** emerges in an environment that requires fast response and high-risk decision making. Managers encourage values that support the company's ability to rapidly detect, interpret, and translate signals from the environment into new behavior responses. Employees have autonomy to make decisions and act freely to meet new needs, and responsiveness to customers is highly valued. Managers also actively create change by encouraging and rewarding creativity, experimentation, and risk taking. Lush Cosmetics, a fast-growing maker of shampoos, lotions, and bath products made from fresh ingredients such as mangoes and avocados, provides a good example of an adaptability culture. A guiding motto at the company is "We reserve the right to make mistakes." Founder and CEO Mark Constantine is passionately devoted to change and encourages employees to break boundaries, experiment, and take risks. The company kills off a third of its product line every year to offer new and offbeat products.[63] Other companies in the cosmetics industry, as well as those involved in electronics, e-commerce, and fashion, often use an adaptability culture because they must move quickly to respond to rapid changes in the environment.

The **achievement culture** is suited to organizations concerned with serving specific customers in the external environment but without the intense need for flexibility and rapid change. This results-oriented culture values competitiveness, aggressiveness, personal initiative, and willingness to work long and hard to achieve results. An emphasis on winning and achieving specific ambitious goals is the glue that holds the organization together.[64] Siebel Systems, which sells complex software systems, thrives on an achievement culture. Professionalism and aggressiveness are core values. Employees are forbidden to eat at their desks or to decorate with more than one or two personal photographs. People who succeed at Siebel are focused, competitive, and driven to win. Those who perform and meet stringent goals are handsomely rewarded; those who don't are fired.[65]

The **involvement culture** emphasizes an internal focus on the involvement and participation of employees to rapidly adapt to changing needs from the environment. This culture places high value on meeting the needs of employees, and the organization may be characterized by a caring, family-like atmosphere. Managers emphasize values such as cooperation, consideration of both employees and customers, and avoiding status differences. Consider the involvement culture at Valero, which is partly responsible for helping the company become the top oil refinery in the United States.

> When Hurricane Katrina hit New Orleans in late August 2005, companies throughout the region set their disaster plans into action. But few matched the heroic efforts put forth by employees at Valero's St. Charles oil refinery. Just eight days after the storm, the St. Charles facility was up and running, while a competitor's plant across the road was weeks away from getting back online. During the same time period, St. Charles's disaster crew managed to locate every one of the plant's 570 employees.
>
> Part of the credit goes to Valero's family-like, let's-get-it-done-together culture, which has given Valero a distinctive edge during an era of cutthroat global competition in the oil industry. As CEO Bill Greehey transformed Valero, once primarily a natural-gas-pipeline company, into the nation's largest oil refinery business, he also instilled a culture where people care about one another and the company. Many of the refineries Valero bought were old and run-down. After buying a refinery, Greehey's first steps would be to assure people their jobs were secure, bring in new safety equipment, and promise employees that if they worked hard he would put them first, before shareholders and customers. Employees held up their end of the bargain, and so did Greehey.
>
> Greehey maintains a strict no-layoff policy, believing people need to feel secure in their jobs to perform at their best. "I see this cycle with companies where they fire and they hire and they fire and they hire," he says. "Fear does not motivate people." Of course,

adaptability culture A culture characterized by values that support the company's ability to interpret and translate signals from the environment into new behavior responses.

achievement culture A results-oriented culture that values competitiveness, personal initiative, and achievement.

involvement culture A culture that places high value on meeting the needs of employees and values cooperation and equality.

Valero

Chapter 3 THE ENVIRONMENT AND CORPORATE CULTURE

Greehey occasionally has to do some firing of his own—specifically, he'll fire any executive who is condescending or uses profanity when addressing subordinates. Although he's called "Mr. Greehey" by employees, even many at upper management levels, the CEO doesn't put himself above his employees. He'll work side by side with them, chat with them about their jobs and ideas for the company, and listen compassionately as they describe their problems. He set up a Valero SAFE fund, which grants employees up to $10,000 in aid following a disaster.

Putting employees first has engendered amazing loyalty and dedication. When Greehey visited the St. Charles facility after Katrina, he was surprised to be greeted at a giant tent with a standing ovation. Even in the aftermath of a hurricane, employees had held to their tradition of throwing a plant-wide barbecue lunch whenever Greehey visits a plant. "Right now morale is so high in this refinery you can't get at it with a space shuttle," an electrical superintendent at St. Charles said. "Valero has been giving away gas, chain saws, putting up trailers for the employees. They've kept every employee paid. Other refineries shut down and stopped paying. What else can you ask?"[66]

Some managers might think putting employees ahead of customers and share-holders is nice, but not very good for business. But at Valero, a strong involvement culture based on putting employees first has paid off in terms of high employee performance and rising market share, profits, and shareholder value.

The final category of culture, the **consistency culture**, uses an internal focus and a consistency orientation for a stable environment. Following the rules and being thrifty are valued, and the culture supports and rewards a methodical, rational, orderly way of doing things. In today's fast-changing world, few companies operate in a stable environment, and most managers are shifting toward cultures that are more flexible and in tune with changes in the environment. However, one thriving company, Pacific Edge Software, successfully implemented elements of a consistency culture, ensuring that all its projects are on time and on budget. The husband-and-wife team of Lisa Hjorten and Scott Fuller implanted a culture of order, discipline, and control from the moment they founded the company. The emphasis on order and focus means employees can generally go home by 6:00 P.M. rather than working all night to finish an important project. Hjorten insists that the company's culture isn't rigid or uptight, just *careful*. Although sometimes being careful means being slow, so far Pacific Edge has managed to keep pace with the demands of the external environment.[67]

Each of these four categories of culture can be successful. In addition, organizations usually have values that fall into more than one category. The relative emphasis on various cultural values depends on the needs of the environment and the organization's focus. Managers are responsible for instilling the cultural values the organization needs to be successful in its environment.

SHAPING CORPORATE CULTURE FOR INNOVATIVE RESPONSE

Research conducted by a Stanford University professor indicates that the one factor that increases a company's value the most is people and how they are treated.[68] In addition, surveys found that CEOs cite organizational culture as their most important mechanism for attracting, motivating, and retaining talented employees, a capability they consider the single best predictor of overall organizational excellence.[69] In a survey of Canadian senior executives, fully 82 percent believe a direct correlation exists between culture and financial performance.[70]

Corporate culture plays a key role in creating an organizational climate that enables learning and innovative responses to threats from the external environment, challenging new opportunities, or organizational crises. However, managers realize they can't focus all their effort on values; they also need a commitment to solid business performance.

consistency culture A culture that values and rewards a methodical, rational, orderly way of doing things.

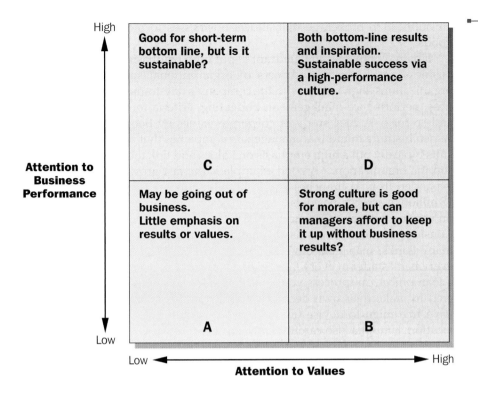

High

Good for short-term bottom line, but is it sustainable? **C**	**Both bottom-line results and inspiration. Sustainable success via a high-performance culture.** **D**
May be going out of business. Little emphasis on results or values. **A**	**Strong culture is good for morale, but can managers afford to keep it up without business results?** **B**

Attention to Business Performance

Low

Low ←————— **Attention to Values** —————→ High

EXHIBIT   3.8

Combining Culture and Performance

SOURCE: Adapted from Jeff Rosenthal and Mary Ann Masarech, "High-Performance Cultures: How Values Can Drive Business Results," *Journal of Organizational Excellence* (Spring 2003): 3–18.

Managing the High-Performance Culture

Companies that succeed in a turbulent world are those that pay careful attention to both cultural values *and* business performance. Cultural values can energize and motivate employees by appealing to higher ideals and unifying people around shared goals. In addition, values boost performance by shaping and guiding employee behavior, so that everyone's actions are aligned with strategic priorities.[71] Exhibit 3.8 illustrates four organizational outcomes based on the relative attention managers pay to cultural values and business performance.[72] A company in Quadrant A pays little attention to either values or business results and is unlikely to survive for long. Managers in Quadrant B organizations are highly focused on creating a strong cohesive culture, but they don't tie organizational values directly to goals and desired business results. When cultural values aren't connected to business performance, they aren't likely to benefit the organization during hard times. For example, Levi Strauss was always highly focused on values, even tying part of managers' pay to how well they toe the values line. The problem is that top executives lost sight of the business performance side of the issue; thus, when Levi jeans began losing market share to new, hip rivals, the company was unable to adapt quickly to the changing environment.[73]

Quadrant C represents organizations that are focused primarily on bottom-line results and pay little attention to organizational values. This approach may be profitable in the short run, but the success is difficult to sustain over the long term because the "glue" that holds the organization together—that is, shared cultural values—is missing. Think about the numerous get-rich-quick goals of dot-com entrepreneurs. Thousands of companies that sprang up in the late 1990s were aimed primarily at fast growth and quick profits, with little effort to build a solid organization based on long-term mission and values. When the crash came, these companies failed. Those that survived were typically companies with strong cultural values that helped them weather the storm. For example, both eBay and Amazon.com managers paid careful attention to organizational culture, as did smaller e-commerce companies like Canada's Mediagrif Interactive Technologies, an online B2B brokerage that allows businesses to meet online and trade their goods.[74]

Finally, companies in Quadrant D put high emphasis on both culture and solid business performance as drivers of organizational success. Managers in these organizations align values with the company's day-to-day operations—hiring practices, performance management, budgeting, criteria for promotions and rewards, and so forth. A 2004 study of corporate values by Booz Allen Hamilton and the Aspen Institute found that managers in companies that report superior financial results typically put a high emphasis on values and link them directly to the way they run the organization.[75] A good example is the fast-growing Umpqua Bank, which expanded from 11 branches and $140 million in assets in 1994 to 92 branches and $5 billion in assets nine years later. At Umpqua, every element of the culture focuses on serving customers, and every aspect of operations reflects the cultural values. Consider training programs. To avoid the "it's not my job" attitude that infects many banks, managers devised the "universal associate" program, which trains every bank staffer in every task, so that a teller can take a mortgage application and a loan officer can process your checking account deposit. Employees are empowered to make their own decisions about how to satisfy customers, and branches have free reign to devise unique ways to coddle the clientele in their particular location. Umpqua also carefully measures and rewards the cultural values it wants to maintain. The bank's executive vice president of cultural enhancement devised a software program that measures how cultural values are connected to performance, which the bank calls "return on quality" (ROQ). The ROQ scores for each branch and department are posted every month, and they serve as the basis for determining incentives and rewards.[76]

Quadrant D organizations represent the **high-performance culture**, a culture that (1) is based on a solid organizational mission or purpose, (2) embodies shared adaptive values that guide decisions and business practices, and (3) encourages individual employee ownership of both bottom-line results and the organization's cultural backbone.[77] This chapter's Unlocking Innovative Solutions Through People box describes the high-performance culture at Semco, where the company's unique cultural values have contributed to amazing business success.

One of the most important things managers do is create and influence organizational culture to meet strategic goals, because culture has a significant impact on performance. In *Corporate Culture and Performance*, Kotter and Heskett provided evidence that companies that intentionally managed cultural values outperformed similar companies that did not. Recent research validated that some elements of corporate culture are positively correlated with higher financial performance.[78] A good example is Caterpillar Inc. Caterpillar developed a Cultural Assessment Process (CAP) to measure and manage how effectively the culture contributes to organizational effectiveness. The assessment gave top executives hard data documenting millions of dollars in savings attributed directly to cultural factors.[79]

■ TAKE A MOMENT

Even as a new manager you can manage for high performance by creating an adaptive culture and tying cultural values to the accomplishment of business results. Act as a cultural leader by communicating the desired values and outcomes and then modeling them in your daily behavior and decisions.

high-performance culture
A culture based on a solid organizational mission or purpose that uses shared adaptive values to guide decisions and business practices and to encourage individual employee ownership of both bottom-line results and the organization's cultural backbone.

Cultural Leadership

A primary way in which managers shape cultural norms and values to build a high-performance culture is through *cultural leadership*. Managers must *overcommunicate* to ensure that employees understand the new culture values, and they signal these values in actions as well as words.

Unlocking Innovative Solutions Through PEOPLE

It's Power (and Responsibility) to the People

Feeling all too burdened by responsibility, 24-year-old Ricardo Semler created a new vision for the culture of his family's business in 1983, while recuperating from a stress-related illness. When Semler had taken over Brazil-based Semco Corp. from his father in 1980 as a freshly minted Harvard MBA (one of the youngest ever to earn the prestigious degree), the company was manufacturing equipment for a Brazilian shipbuilding industry that was in abysmal shape. As Semco's president and majority owner, Semler fired most of the top management and used a series of strategic acquisitions to steer the company into more viable markets. Ironically, as the company's fortunes began to revive, Semler's own health took a nosedive.

As he lay in a hospital bed, Semler had a vision for a new way to manage—by relinquishing control to his employees. Thus began a five-year process of building a radically democratic culture based on open information and employee participation. Semler started modestly—letting employees choose their uniform color, for example—and eventually moved to the creation of egalitarian project teams that had complete responsibility for particular projects, total authority regarding how to perform them, and the opportunity for team members to pocket a substantial percentage of any profits generated. Today, self-directed teams form the basis of the company's loose, flexible organization structure. People typically have a chance to choose what projects they will work on, based on how they think they can best make a contribution.

Semco uses few job titles and only three management levels: counselors (the name Semler now goes by), partners, and associates. The CEO position rotates every six months among the counselors. Workers set their own hours, elect and evaluate supervisors, and have major input into how they are compensated, with some actually setting their own pay rates. All financial information, including salaries, is available to everyone, and any employee is eligible to attend any meeting, including board meetings, where two seats are reserved for employees on a first-come, first-served basis.

The result of applying these rather radical cultural values is that Semco has not only survived but prospered in Brazil's often chaotic economic and political climate. The conglomerate now produces a diverse range of products and services, from manufacturing giant oil pumps to participating in mail processing joint ventures. Its revenues grew from $4 million in 1982 to approximately $240 million today.

"It's about competitive advantage," Semler says. Once you stop trying to control employees, he insists, you release the powerful twin forces of self-discipline and peer pressure. Performance becomes the only criterion for success. At Semco, treating employees like responsible adults is just good business.

SOURCES: Lawrence Fisher, "Ricardo Semler Won't Take Control," *Strategy + Business* (Winter 2005): 78–88; Simon Caulkin, "Who's in Charge Here? No One," *Observer* (April 29, 2003), http://observer.guardian.co.uk; "Ricardo Semler," *Wikipedia*, http://en.wikipedia.org; Nick Easen, "Interview with Ricardo Semler," *CNN.com* (June 14, 2004), http://edition.cnn.com; and Lancourt, Joan and Charles Savage, "Organizational Transformation and the Changing Role of the Human Resource Function," *Compensation & Benefits Management* (Autumn 1995).

A **cultural leader** defines and uses signals and symbols to influence corporate culture. Cultural leaders influence culture in two key areas:

1. *The cultural leader articulates a vision for the organizational culture that employees can believe in.* The leader defines and communicates central values that employees believe in and will rally around. Values are tied to a clear and compelling mission, or core purpose.

2. *The cultural leader heeds the day-to-day activities that reinforce the cultural vision.* The leader makes sure that work procedures and reward systems match and reinforce the values. Actions speak louder than words, so cultural leaders "walk their talk."[80]

Leaders can create a culture that brings people together by ensuring that people have a voice in what the important values should be. Managers at United Stationers built a new, adaptive culture from the ground up by asking all 6,000 globally dispersed employees to help define the values that would be the building blocks of the culture.[81]

cultural leader A manager who uses signals and symbols to influence corporate culture.

Managers widely communicate the cultural values through words and actions. Values statements that aren't reinforced by management behavior are meaningless or even harmful for employees and the organization. Consider Enron, whose values statement included things like communication, respect, and integrity. Managers' actions at the corporation clearly belied those stated values.[82] For values to guide the organization, managers have to model them every day. Canada's WestJet Airlines, which ranked in a survey as having Canada's most admired corporate culture, provides an illustration. WestJet employees (called simply "people" at WestJet) regularly see CEO Clive Beddoe and other top leaders putting the values of equality, teamwork, participation, and customer service into action. At the end of a flight, for example, everyone on hand pitches in to pick up garbage—even the CEO. Top executives spend much of their time chatting informally with employees and customers, and they regularly send notes of thanks to people who have gone above and beyond the call of duty. Top executives have been known to visit the call center on Christmas Day to pitch in and to thank people for working the holiday. Managers don't receive perks over and above anyone else; they get no assigned parking spaces and no club memberships. Every person at WestJet is treated like first-class, exactly the way leaders want employees to treat every passenger on a WestJet flight.[83]

Cultural leaders also uphold their commitment to values during difficult times or crises, as illustrated by the example of Bill Greehey at Valero earlier in this chapter. On *Fortune* magazine's list of 100 Best Companies to Work For, Valero zoomed from Number 23 to Number 3 based on its treatment of employees following the devastating 2005 hurricanes. Despite the costs, Valero kept people on the payroll throughout the crisis, set up special booths to feed volunteers, and donated $1 million to the American Red Cross for hurricane relief efforts.[84] Upholding the cultural values helps organizations weather a crisis and come out stronger on the other side.

Creating and maintaining a high-performance culture is not easy in today's turbulent environment and changing workplace, but through their words—and particularly their actions—cultural leaders let everyone in the organization know what really counts.

MANAGER'S SOLUTION

This chapter discussed several important ideas about internal and external organizational environments. Events in the external environment are considered important influences on organizational behavior and performance. The external environment consists of two layers: the task environment and the general environment. The task environment includes customers, competitors, suppliers, and the labor market. The general environment includes technological, sociocultural, economic, legal-political, and international dimensions. Management techniques for helping the organization adapt to the environment include boundary-spanning roles, interorganizational partnerships, and mergers and joint ventures.

A major internal element for helping organizations adapt to the environment is culture. Corporate culture is an important part of the internal organizational environment and includes the key values, beliefs, understandings, and norms that organization members share. Organizational activities that illustrate corporate culture include symbols, stories, heroes, slogans, and ceremonies. For the organization to be effective, corporate culture should be aligned with organizational strategy and the needs of the external environment. Four types of culture are adaptability, achievement, involvement, and consistency. Strong cultures are effective when they enable an organization to meet strategic goals and adapt to changes in the external environment.

One problem for Microsoft, described in the chapter opening, is that the culture has gotten out of alignment with its environment. Years of success led to complacency and even resistance to changes in key sectors of the environment. The company's adaptability culture did not stay aggressive. The focus on protecting Microsoft's dominance in PC software caused the company to miss two of the hottest technology advances, Internet search and downloading music. Now, its PC software business, which Microsoft still relies on for 80 percent of its sales and 140 percent of its profits, is under attack. Microsoft CEO Steven Ballmer is trying various structural alternatives and management changes to beef up boundary spanning and get employees more focused on customers and new trends in the shifting external environment. Microsoft has more than a dozen new products scheduled for release, which Ballmer believes will keep the company on top. However, most of those products are considered catch-up, while younger, more adaptable companies are already moving to the next level of new products. Microsoft is a large and powerful company, but it may have reached a midlife crisis and likely will need a cultural adjustment to stay in tune with changes in key environmental sectors. Managers can use symbols, stories, heroes, slogans, and cultural leadership to engage adaptable values that will help Microsoft move fast in response to new opportunities.[85]

Culture is important because it can have a significant impact on organizational performance. Managers emphasize both values and business results to create a high-performance culture, enabling the organization to consistently achieve solid business performance through the actions of motivated employees who are aligned with the mission and goals of the company. Managers create and sustain adaptive high-performance cultures through cultural leadership. They define and articulate important values that are tied to a clear and compelling mission, and they widely communicate and uphold the values through their words and particularly their actions. Work procedures, budgeting, decision making, reward systems, and other day-to-day activities are aligned with the cultural values.

DISCUSSION QUESTIONS

1. General Electric is famous for firing the lowest-performing 10 percent of its managers each year. With its strict no-layoff policy, Valero Energy believes people need to feel secure in their jobs to perform their best. Yet both are high-performing companies. How do you account for the success of such opposite philosophies?

2. Contemporary best-selling management books often argue that customers are the most important element in the external environment. Do you agree? In what company situations might this statement be untrue?

3. Both China and India are rising economic powers. How might your approach to doing business with Communist China be different from your approach to doing business with India, the world's most populous democracy? In which country

would you expect to encounter the most rules? The most bureaucracy?

4. Why do you think many managers are surprised by environmental changes and unable to help their organizations adapt? Can a manager ever be prepared for an environmental change as dramatic as that experienced by airlines in the United States following the September 11, 2001, terrorist attacks in New York and Washington?

5. Consider the chairs you have seen in an office. How does the assistant's chair, the manager's chair, and executive's chair differ? What do the differences mean?

6. What do you think are the most important forces in the external environment creating uncertainty for organizations today? Do the forces you identified

typically arise in the task environment or the general environment?

7. Why are symbols important to a corporate culture? Do stories, heroes, slogans, and ceremonies have symbolic value? Discuss.

8. Would the task environment for a cellular phone company contain the same elements as that for a government welfare agency? Discuss.

9. Why are interorganizational partnerships so important for today's companies? What elements in the current environment might contribute to either an increase or a decrease in interorganizational collaboration? Discuss.

10. What can you do now as a student—both inside and outside the classroom—to train yourself to be a more effective manager in an increasingly global business environment?

MANAGEMENT IN PRACTICE: EXPERIENTIAL EXERCISE

Working in an Adaptive Culture

Think of a specific full-time job you have held. Please answer the following questions according to your perception of the *managers above you* in that job. Circle a number on the 1–5 scale based on the extent to which you agree with each statement about the managers above you: ❺ = Strongly agree; ❹ = Agree; ❸ = Neither agree nor disagree; ❷ = Disagree; ❶ = Strongly disagree.

1. Good ideas got serious consideration   ❶ ❷ ❸ ❹ ❺ from management above me.

2. Management above me was interested   ❶ ❷ ❸ ❹ ❺ in ideas and suggestions from people at my level in the organization.

3. When suggestions were made to   ❶ ❷ ❸ ❹ ❺ management above me, they received fair evaluation.

4. Management did not expect me to   ❶ ❷ ❸ ❹ ❺ challenge or change the status quo.

5. Management specifically encouraged   ❶ ❷ ❸ ❹ ❺ me to bring about improvements in my workplace.

6. Management above me took action   ❶ ❷ ❸ ❹ ❺ on recommendations made from people at my level.

7. Management rewarded me for   ❶ ❷ ❸ ❹ ❺ correcting problems.

8. Management clearly expected me to   ❶ ❷ ❸ ❹ ❺ improve work unit procedures and practices.

9. I felt free to make recommendations   ❶ ❷ ❸ ❹ ❺ to management above me to change existing practices.

10. Good ideas did not get communicated   ❶ ❷ ❸ ❹ ❺ upward because management above me was not very approachable.

Scoring and Interpretation

To compute your score: Subtract each of your scores for questions 4 and 10 from 6. Using your adjusted scores, add the numbers for all 10 questions to give you the total score. Divide that number by 10 to get your average score: _____.

An adaptive culture is shaped by the values and actions of top and middle managers. When managers actively encourage and welcome change initiatives from below, the organization will be infused with values for change. These 10 questions measure your management's openness to change. A typical average score for management openness to change is about 3. If your average score was 4 or higher, you worked in an organization that expressed strong cultural values of adaptation. If your average score was 2 or below, the culture was probably unadaptive.

Thinking about your job, is the level of management openness to change correct for the organization? Why? Compare your scores to those of another student, and take turns describing what it was like working for the managers above your jobs. Do you sense a relationship between job satisfaction and your management's openness to change? What specific management characteristics and corporate values explain the openness scores in the two jobs?

SOURCES: S. J. Ashford, N. P. Rothbard, S. K. Piderit, and J. E. Dutton,"Out on a Limb: The Role of Context and Impression Management in Issue Selling,"*Administrative Science Quarterly* 43 (1998): 23–57; and E. W. Morrison and C. C. Phelps,"Taking Charge at Work: Extrarole Efforts to Initiate Workplace Change,"*Academy of Management Journal* 42 (1999): 403–419.

Competitive Intelligence Predicament

Miquel Vasquez was proud of his job as a new product manager for a biotechnology start-up, and he loved the high stakes and tough decisions that went along with the job. But as he sat in his den after a long day, he was troubled, struggling over what had happened earlier that day and the information he now possessed.

Just before lunch, Miquel's boss had handed him a stack of private strategic documents from their closest competitor. It was a competitive intelligence gold mine—product plans, pricing strategies, partnership agreements, and other documents, most clearly marked "proprietary and confidential." When Miquel asked where the documents came from, his boss told him with a touch of pride that he had taken them right off the competing firm's server. "I got into a private section of their intranet and downloaded everything that looked interesting," he said. Later, realizing Miquel was suspicious, the boss would say only that he had obtained "electronic access" via a colleague and had not personally broken any passwords. Maybe not, Miquel thought to himself, but this situation wouldn't pass the *60 Minutes* test. If word of this acquisition of a competitor's confidential data ever got out to the press, the company's reputation would be ruined.

Miquel didn't feel good about using these materials. He spent the afternoon searching for answers to his dilemma, but found no clear company policies or regulations that offered any guidance. His sense of fair play told him that to use the information was unethical, if not downright illegal. What bothered him even more was the knowledge that this kind of thing might happen again. Using this confidential information would certainly give him and his company a competitive advantage, but Miquel wasn't sure he wanted to work for a firm that would stoop to such tactics.

What Would You Do?

1. Go ahead and use the documents to the company's benefit, but make clear to your boss that you don't want him passing confidential information to you in the future. If he threatens to fire you, threaten to leak the news to the press.

2. Confront your boss privately and let him know you're uncomfortable with how the documents were obtained and what possession of them says about the company's culture. In addition to the question of the legality of using the information, point out that it is a public relations nightmare waiting to happen.

3. Talk to the company's legal counsel and contact the Society of Competitive Intelligence Professionals for guidance. Then, with their opinions and facts to back you up, go to your boss.

SOURCE: Adapted from Kent Weber, "Gold Mine or Fool's Gold?" *Business Ethics* (January–February 2001): 18.

CASE FOR CRITICAL ANALYSIS

Society of Equals

Ted Shelby doesn't make very many mistakes, but . . .

"Hey Stanley," says Ted Shelby, leaning in through the door, "you got a minute? I've just restructured my office. Come on and take a look. I've been implementing some great new concepts!"

Stanley is always interested in Ted Shelby's new ideas, for if there is anyone Stanley wants to do as well as, it is Edward W. Shelby IV. Stanley follows Ted back to his office and stops, nonplussed.

Restructured is right! Gone are Ted's size B (junior executive) walnut veneer desk and furniture, and his telephone table. In fact, the room is practically empty save for a large, round, stark white cafeteria table and the half-dozen padded vinyl swivel chairs that surround it.

"Isn't it a beauty! As far as I know, I'm the first executive in the plant to innovate this. The shape is the crucial factor here—no front or rear, no status problems. We can all sit there and communicate more effectively."

We? Communicate? Effectively? Well, it seems that Ted has been attending a series of Executive Development Seminars given by Dr. Faust. The theme of the seminars was—you guessed it—*participative management*. Edward W. Shelby IV has always liked to think of himself as a truly democratic person.

"You see, Stanley," says Ted, managing his best sincere/intense attitude, "the main thing wrong with our culture is that most of the communication is top-down. We in the executive suite send our messages down the line, but we never ask for ideas and suggestions from the rest of the company. Just because we have more status and responsibility doesn't mean that we are necessarily (Stanley duly noted the word *necessarily*) better than the people below us. In fact, with our customers' needs changing so fast these days, we need all the ideas we can get. We've got to shift to a culture of participation and employee involvement if we want to keep up with today's fast pace of business."

"So that's what the cafeteria table is for?" Stanley asks.

"Yes!" says Ted. "We need better two-way communication—up the line as well as down the line. We managers don't have all the answers, and I don't know why I never realized it before that seminar. Why, for example, the folks who run those machines out there. I'll bet any one of them knows a thing or two about how to speed up our manufacturing process that I've never thought of. So I've transformed my office into a full-feedback communication net."

"That certainly is an innovation around here," says Stanley.

A few days later Stanley passed by Ted Shelby's office and was surprised that Ted's desk, furniture, and telephone table were back where they used to be.

Stanley, curious about the unrestructuring, went to Bonnie for enlightenment. "What," he asked, "happened to Shelby's round table?"

"That table we were supposed to sit around and input things?" she said. "All I know is, about two days after he had it put in, Mr. Drake came walking through here. He looked in that office, and then he sort of stopped and went back—and he looked in there for a long time. Then he came over to me, and you know how his face sort of gets red when he's really mad? Well, this time he was so mad that his face was absolutely white. And when he talked to me, I don't think he actually opened his mouth; and I could barely hear him, he was talking so low. And he said, 'Have that removed. Now. Have Mr. Shelby's furniture put back in his office. Have Mr. Shelby see me.'"

My, my. You would think Ted would have known better, wouldn't you? But then, by now you should have a pretty firm idea of just why it is those offices are set up as they are.

Questions

1. How would you characterize the culture in this company? What are the dominant values?

2. Why did Ted Shelby's change experiment fail? To what extent did Ted use the appropriate change tools to increase employee communication and participation?

3. What would you recommend Ted do to change his relationship with subordinates? Is it possible for a manager to change cultural values if the rest of the organization, especially top management, does not agree?

SOURCE: R. Richard Ritti and G. Ray Funkhouser, *The Ropes to Skip & The Ropes to Know,* 3d ed. (New York: Wiley, 1987): 176–177. This material is used by permission of John Wiley & Sons, Inc.

ENDNOTES

1. Robert A. Guth and Kevin J. Delaney, "Default Lines; Pressuring Microsoft, PC Makers Team Up with Software Rivals," *The Wall Street Journal* (February 7, 2006): A1, A25.

2. Betsy Morris, "The Accidental CEO," *Fortune* (June 23, 2003): 58–67; Pamela L. Moore, "She's Here to Fix the Xerox," *BusinessWeek* (August 6, 2001): 47–48; and Ann Harrington and Petra Bartosiewicz, "The 50 Most Powerful Women in Business: Who's Up? Who's Down?" *Fortune* (October 18, 2004): 181–188.

3. Ann Carns, "Point Taken; Hit Hard by Imports, American Pencil Icon Tries to Get a Grip," *The Wall Street Journal* (November 24, 1999): A1, A6.

4. George S. Day and Paul J. H. Schoemaker, "Scanning the Periphery," *Harvard Business Review* (November 2005): 135–148.

5. Christopher Joyce, reporter, transcript of "Analysis: International Panel Says U.S. Department of Agriculture Should Take Further Steps to Protect the U.S. from Mad Cow Disease," *NPR: All Things Considered* (February 5, 2004): 1; Sue Kirchhoff, "Natural Beef Industry Might See Boost from Mad Cow Fears," *USA Today* (January 12, 2004): www.usatoday.com/money/industries/food/2004-01-12-organic_x.htm; June Kronholz, "Kindergarten Crisis: By Federal Order, Snail Races Are Over," *The Wall Street Journal* (February 11, 2004): A1.

6. This section is based on Richard L. Daft, *Organization Theory and Design*, 8th ed. (Cincinnati, OH: South-Western, 2004): 136–140.

7. L. J. Bourgeois, "Strategy and Environment: A Conceptual Integration," *Academy of Management Review* 5 (1980): 25–39.

8. Pete Engardio, "A New World Economy," *BusinessWeek* (August 22–29, 2005): 52–58.

9. Robert Rosen, with Patricia Digh, Marshall Singer, and Carl Phillips, *Global Literacies: Lessons on Business Leadership and National Cultures* (New York: Simon and Schuster, 2000).

10. Engardio, "A New World Economy."

11. Cliff Edwards, "Wherever You Go, You're On the Job," *BusinessWeek* (June 20, 2005): 87–90.

12. Stephen Baker and Adam Astor, "The Business of Nanotech," *BusinessWeek* (February 14, 2005): 64–71.

13. William B. Johnston, "Global Work Force 2000: The New World Labor Market," *Harvard Business Review* (March–April 1991): 115–127.

14. U.S. Census Bureau statistics reported in "Minorities Should Be Very Close to Majority by 2050, Census Projection Says," AP Story in *Johnson City Press* (March 18, 2004): 5A; and Peter Coy, "The Creative Economy," *BusinessWeek* (August 28, 2000): 76–82.

15. Peter Coy, "Old. Smart. Productive," *BusinessWeek* (June 27, 2005): 78–86; Danielle Sacks, "Scenes from the Culture Clash," *Fast Company* (January–February 2006): 73–77; and Ellyn Spragins, "The Talent Pool," *FSB* (October 2005): 93–102.

16. U.S. Census, *www.census.gov/.*

17. Michelle Conlin, "UnMarried America," *BusinessWeek* (October 20, 2003): 106–116.

18. Sebastian Moffett, "Senior Moment: Fast-Aging Japan Keeps Its Elders on the Job Longer," *The Wall Street Journal* (June 15, 2005): A1.

19. Julie Dunn, "Restaurant Chains, Too, Watch Their Carbs," *The New York Times* (January 4, 2004); Brian Grow with Gerry Khermouch, "The Low-Carb Food Fight Ahead," *BusinessWeek* (December 22, 2003): 48; and Laura Crimaldi, "Girl Scout Numbers Drop," *Boston Herald* (March 11, 2005): 7.

20. Samuel Loewenberg, "Europe Gets Tougher on U.S. Companies," *The New York Times* (April 20, 2003): Section 3, 6.

21. Jeremy Caplan, "Paper War," *Time* (January 2006): A11.

22. Linda Himelstein and Laura Zinn, with Maria Mallory, John Carey, Richard S. Dunham, and Joan O. C. Hamilton, "Tobacco: Does It Have a Future?" *BusinessWeek* (July 4, 1994): 24–29; Bob Ortega, "Aging Activists Turn, Turn, Turn Attention to Wal-Mart Protests," *The Wall Street Journal* (October 11, 1994): A1, A8.

23. Jessi Hempel, "The MySpace Generation," *BusinessWeek* (December 12, 2005): 86–94.

24. John Simons, "Stop Moaning About Gripe Sites and Log On," *Fortune* (April 2, 2001): 181–182.

25. Rick Brooks, "Home Depot Turns Copycat in Its Efforts to Stoke New Growth," *The Wall Street Journal* (November 21, 2000): A1; Dan Sewell, "Home Depot, Lowe's Building Up Competition," *Lexington Herald-Leader*: Business Profile supplement (December 8, 1997): 3.

26. Julia Angwin and Motoko Rich, "Inn Fighting: Big Hotel Chains Are Striking Back Against Web Sites," *The Wall Street Journal* (March 14, 2003): A1.

27. Paul Glader, "Steel-Price Rise Crimps Profits, Adds Uncertainty," *The Wall Street Journal* (February 23, 2004): A1.

28. John R. Wilke and Kathy Chen, "Planned Economy; As China's Trade Clout Grows, So Do Price-Fixing Accusations," *The Wall Street Journal* (February 10, 2006): A1.

29. Olga Kharif, "Nortes's New Lease on Life," *BusinessWeek Online* (January 26, 2006); Roger O. Crockett, "Nortel: Desperately Seeking Credibility," *BusinessWeek* (January 17, 2005): 60–61; Bernard Simon, "A Bright New Day for the Telecom Industry, If the Public Will Go Along," *The New York Times* (January 12, 2004): C3; Mark Heinzl, "Nortel's Profit of $499 Million Exceeds Forecast," *The Wall Street Journal* (January 30, 2004): B4; Joseph Weber with Andy Reinhardt and Peter Burrows, "Racing Ahead at Nortel," *BusinessWeek* (November 8, 1999): 93–99; Ian Austen, "Hooked on the Net," *Canadian Business* (June 26–July 10, 1998): 95–103; "Nortel's Waffling Continues; First Job Cuts, Then Product Lines, and Now the CEO. What's Next?" *Telephony* (May 21, 2001): 12.

30. Robert B. Duncan, "Characteristics of Organizational Environment and Perceived Environmental Uncertainty," *Administrative Science Quarterly* 17 (1972): 313–327; and Daft, *Organization Theory and Design.*

31. David B. Jemison, "The Importance of Boundary Spanning Roles in Strategic Decision-Making," *Journal of Management Studies* 21 (1984): 131–152; and Marc J. Dollinger, "Environmental Boundary Spanning and Information Processing Effects on Organizational Performance," *Academy of Management Journal* 27 (1984): 351–368.

32. Sarah Moore, "On Your Markets," *Working Woman* (February 2001): 26; and John Simons, "Stop Moaning about Gripe Sites and Log On," *Fortune* (April 2, 2001): 181–182.

33. Tom Duffy, "Spying the Holy Grail," *Microsoft Executive Circle* (Winter 2004): 38–39.

34. Gary Abramson, "All Along the Watchtower." *CIO Enterprise* (July 15, 1999): 24–34.

35. Girard, "Snooping on a Shoestring," *Business 2.0* (May 2003): 64–66.

36. Edwin M. Epstein, "How to Learn from the Environment about the Environment—A Prerequisite for Organizational Well-Being," *Journal of General Management 29*, no. 1 (Autumn 2003): 68–80.

37. Mark McNeilly, "Gathering Information for Strategic Decisions, Routinely," *Strategy & Leadership* 30, no 5 (2002): 29–34.

38. Day and Schoemaker, "Scanning the Periphery."

39. A discussion of the Sony-Toshiba-IBM alliance was heard by the author on NPR's *Morning Edition*; information on Kroger, Albertson's, and Safeway from an Associated Press story, "Strike Increases Pressure on Safeway CEO," in *Johnson City Press* (February 1, 2004): 7D; Norihiko Shirouzu and Jathon Sapsford, "Power Struggle; As Hybrid Cars Gain Traction, Industry Battles Over Designs," *The Wall Street Journal* (October 19, 2005): A1.

40. Lynn A. Isabella, "Managing an Alliance Is Nothing Like Business as Usual," *Organizational Dynamics* 31, no. 1 (2002): 47–59; Cyrus F. Freidheim, Jr. *The Trillion-Dollar Enterprise: How the Alliance Revolution Will Transform Global Business* (New York: Perseus Books, 1998).

41. Stephan M. Wagner and Roman Boutellier, "Capabilities for Managing a Portfolio of Supplier Relationships," *Business Horizons* (November–December 2002): 79–88; Peter Smith Ring and Andrew H. Van de Ven, "Developmental Processes of Corporate Interorganizational Relationships," *Academy of Management Review* 19 (1994): 90–118; Myron Magnet, "The New Golden Rule of Business," *Fortune* (February 21, 1994): 60–64; and Peter Grittner, "Four Elements of Successful Sourcing Strategies," *Management Review* (October 1996): 41–45.

42. Richard L. Daft, "After the Deal: The Art of Fusing Diverse Corporate Cultures into One," paper presented at the Conference on International Corporate Restructuring,

Institute of Business Research and Education, Korea University, Seoul, Korea (June 16, 1998).

43. Patricia Sellers, "The Business of Being Oprah," *Fortune* (April 1, 2002): 50–64.

44. Warren St. John, "Barnes & Noble's Epiphany," *Wired* (June 1999): 132–144; Ron Grover and Richard Siklos, "When Old Foes Need Each Other," *BusinessWeek* (October 25, 1999): 114, 118.

45. James E. Svatko, "Joint Ventures," *Small Business Reports* (December 1988): 65–70; and Joshua Hyatt, "The Partnership Route," *Inc.* (December 1988): 145–148.

46. Yoash Wiener, "Forms of Value Systems: A Focus on Organizational Effectiveness and Culture Change and Maintenance," *Academy of Management Review* 13 (1988): 534–545; V. Lynne Meek, "Organizational Culture: Origins and Weaknesses," *Organization Studies* 9 (1988): 453–473; John J. Sherwood, "Creating Work Cultures with Competitive Advantage," *Organizational Dynamics* (Winter 1988): 5–27; and Andrew D. Brown and Ken Starkey, "The Effect of Organizational Culture on Communication and Information," *Journal of Management Studies 31*, no. 6 (November 1994): 807–828.

47. Joanne Martin, *Organizational Culture: Mapping the Terrain* (Thousand Oaks, CA: Sage Publications, 2002); Ralph H. Kilmann, Mary J. Saxton, and Roy Serpa, "Issues in Understanding and Changing Culture," *California Management Review* 28 (Winter 1986): 87–94; and Linda Smircich, "Concepts of Culture and Organizational Analysis," *Administrative Science Quarterly* 28 (1983): 339–358.

48. Based on Edgar H. Schein, *Organizational Culture and Leadership*, 2nd ed. (San Francisco: Jossey-Bass, 1992): 3–27.

49. Michael G. Pratt and Anat Rafaeli, "Symbols as a Language of Organizational Relationships," *Research in Organizational Behavior* 23 (2001): 93–132.

50. Christine Canabou, "Here's the Drill," *Fast Company* (February 2001): 58.

51. Alex Frangos, "In Office Mock-Up, Real Workers Put Layout Ideas to Test," *The Wall Street Journal* (December 1, 2004).

52. Patrick M. Lencioni, "Make Your Values Mean Something," *Harvard Business Review* (July 2002): 113–117.

53. Robert E. Quinn and Gretchen M. Spreitzer, "The Road to Empowerment: Seven Questions Every Leader Should Consider," *Organizational Dynamics* (Autumn 1997): 37–49.

54. Martin, *Organizational Culture*: 71–72.

55. Terrence E. Deal and Allan A. Kennedy, *Corporate Cultures: The Rites and Rituals of Corporate Life* (Reading, MA: Addison-Wesley, 1982).

56. Patricia Jones and Larry Kahaner, *Say It and Live It: 50 Corporate Mission Statements That Hit the Mark* (New York: Currency Doubleday, 1995).

57. Harrison M. Trice and Janice M. Beyer, "Studying Organizational Cultures Through Rites and Ceremonials," *Academy of Management Review 9* (1984): 653–669.

58. Brent Schlender, "Wal-Mart's $288 Billion Meeting," *Fortune* (April 18, 2005): 90–106.

59. Alan Farnham, "Mary Kay's Lessons in Leadership," *Fortune* (September 20, 1993): 68–77.

60. Jennifer A. Chatman and Karen A. Jehn, "Assessing the Relationship Between Industry Characteristics and Organizational Culture: How Different Can You Be?" *Academy of Management Journal* 37, no. 3 (1994): 522–553.

61. John P. Kotter and James L. Heskett, *Corporate Culture and Performance* (New York: The Free Press, 1992).

62. This discussion is based on Paul McDonald and Jeffrey Gandz, "Getting Value from Shared Values," *Organizational Dynamics* 21, no. 3 (Winter 1992): 64–76; Daniel R. Denison and Aneil K. Mishra, "Toward a Theory of Organizational Culture and Effectiveness," *Organization Science* 6, no. 2 (March–April 1995): 204–223; and Richard L. Daft, *The Leadership Experience*, 3rd ed. (Cincinnati, OH: South-Western, 2005): 570–573.

63. Lucas Conley, "Rinse and Repeat," *Fast Company* (July 2005): 76–77.

64. Robert Hooijberg and Frank Petrock, "On Cultural Change: Using the Competing Values Framework to Help Leaders Execute a Transformational Strategy," *Human Resource Management* 32, no. 1 (1993): 29–50.

65. Lencioni, "Make Your Values Mean Something"; and Melanie Warner, "Confessions of a Control Freak," *Fortune* (September 4, 2000): 130–140.

66. Janet Guyon, "The Soul of a Moneymaking Machine," *Fortune* (October 3, 2005): 113–120.

67. Rekha Balu, "Pacific Edge Projects Itself," *Fast Company* (October 2000): 371–381.

68. Jeffrey Pfeffer, *The Human Equation: Building Profits by Putting People First* (Boston: Harvard Business School Press, 1998).

69. Jeremy Kahn, "What Makes a Company Great?" *Fortune* (October 26, 1998): 218; James C. Collins and Jerry I. Porras, *Built to Last: Successful Habits of Visionary Companies* (New York: HarperCollins, 1994); and James C. Collins, "Change Is Good—But First Know What Should Never Change," *Fortune* (May 29, 1995): 141.

70. Wahl, "Culture Shock."

71. Jennifer A. Chatman and Sandra Eunyoung Cha, "Leading by Leveraging Culture," *California Management Review* 45, no. 4 (Summer 2003): 20–34.

72. This section is based on Jeff Rosenthal and Mary Ann Masarech, "High Peformance Cultures: How Values Can Drive Business Results," *Journal of Organizational Excellence* (Spring 2003): 3–18.

73. Rosenthal and Masarech, "High-Performance Cultures."

74. Katherine Mieszkowski, "Community Standards," *Fast Company* (September 2000): 368; Rosabeth Moss Kanter, "A More Perfect Union," *Inc.* (February 2001): 92–98; Raizel Robin, "Net Gains" segment of "E-Biz That Works," *Canadian Business* (October 14–October 26, 2003): 107.

75. Reggie Van Lee, Lisa Fabish, and Nancy McGaw, "The Value of Corporate Values: A Booz Allen Hamilton/Aspen Institute Survey," *Strategy + Business*, 39 (Spring 2005): 52–65.

76. Lucas Conley, "Cultural Phenomenon," *Fast Company* (April 2005): 76–77.

77. Rosenthal and Masarech, "High-Performance Cultures."

78. John P. Kotter and James L. Heskett, *Corporate Culture and Performance* (New York: The Free Press, 1992); Eric Flamholtz and Rangapriya Kannan-Narasimhan, "Differential Impact of Cultural Elements on Financial Performance," *European Management Journal* 23, no. 1 (2005): 50–64. Also see J. M. Kouzes and B. Z. Posner, *The Leadership Challenge: How to Keep Getting Extraordinary Things Done in Organizations*, 3rd ed. (San Francisco: Jossey-Bass, 2002).

79. Micah R. Kee, "Corporate Culture Makes a Fiscal Difference," *Industrial Management* (November–December 2003): 16–20.

80. Rosenthal and Masarech, "High-Performance Cultures"; Lencioni, "Make Your Values Mean Something"; and Thomas J. Peters and Robert H. Waterman, Jr., *In Search of Excellence* (New York: Warner, 1988).

81. Jenny C. McCune, "Exporting Corporate Culture," *Management Review* (December 1999): 52–56.

82. Lencioni, "Make Your Values Mean Something."

83. Andrew Wahl, "Culture Shock," *Canadian Business* (October 10–23, 2005): 115–116; and Calvin Leung, Michelle Magnan, and Andrew Wahl, "People Power," *Canadian Business* (October 10–23, 2005): 125–126.

84. Guyon, "The Soul of a Moneymaking Machine" and Geoff Colvin, "The 100 Best Companies to Work For 2006," *Fortune* (January 23, 2006).

85. Buth and Delaney, "Default Lines" Victoria Murphy, "Microsoft's Midlife Crisis," *Forbes* (October 3, 2005): 88; Jonathan Krim, "Microsoft Is Losing Some of Its Elbow Room; As Software King's Growth Slows, Rivals Stake Out Their Own Territory," *The Washington Post* (December 22, 2005): D1; and Jon Birger and David Stires, "The Toughest Jobs in Business: 10 on the Spot," *Fortune* (February 20, 2006): 81–88.

CHAPTER 4

CHAPTER OUTLINE

Manager's Challenge

A Borderless World

Getting Started Internationally

Outsourcing

Exporting

Licensing

Direct Investing

China Inc.

The International Business Environment

The Economic Environment

Economic Development

Infrastructure

Resource and Product Markets

Exchange Rates

The Legal-Political Environment

Political Risk and Instability

Laws and Regulations

The Sociocultural Environment

Social Values

Other Cultural Characteristics

International Trade Alliances

GATT and the World Trade
  Organization

European Union

North American Free Trade
  Agreement (NAFTA)

Other Trade Alliances

The Globalization Backlash

Multinational Corporations

Managing in a Global Environment

Developing Cultural Intelligence

Managing Cross-Culturally

LEARNING OBJECTIVES

After studying this chapter, you should be able to:

1. Describe the emerging borderless world and some issues of particular concern for today's managers.

2. Describe market entry strategies that businesses use to develop foreign markets.

3. Define international management and explain how it differs from the management of domestic business operations.

4. Indicate how dissimilarities in the economic, sociocultural, and legal-political environments throughout the world can affect business operations.

5. Describe how regional trading alliances are reshaping the international business environment.

6. Describe the characteristics of a multinational corporation.

7. Explain cultural intelligence and why it is necessary for managers working in foreign countries.

MANAGING IN A GLOBAL ENVIRONMENT

MANAGER'S CHALLENGE

The year was 1984. Sitting in his Texas college dorm room, Michael Dell had a powerful insight: Why not sell personal computers directly to consumers rather than going through distributors or retailers? Dell Computer Corporation was born, and the computer industry was never the same. Now, Dell is striving to apply its ultra-efficient processes to shake up the Chinese computer industry the same way it did in the United States. But things are off to a shaky start, with the company encountering problems ranging from language barriers and cultural resistance to tough competition from Lenova, a Chinese firm that is quickly becoming a global player in PCs and services. Even the term *direct sales* was a problem for Dell, translating into a Chinese term most often used to describe illegal pyramid marketing schemes. The language glitch was solved, but by sticking to its direct sales model, Dell is losing Chinese customers who typically want to see and touch products before they buy. Lenova, with 4,800 retail outlets, has long been the market leader in China and is now making a global push with the purchase of IBM's PC unit. Dell recently lost its most experienced Asia-Pacific executive when Lenova snared Dell's Asia chief Bill Amelio as its new CEO. Amelio and Lenova chairman Yang Yuanqing vowed that Lenova wouldn't cede the Asia market to Dell. Moreover, Lenova managers are gunning right for Dell in its established markets as well. They invested $60 million to become China's first Olympic sponsor and provider of computers to the 2006 Turin games and the Beijing Summer Olympics in 2008. "It's a coming-out party to say, 'Here's Lenova; we're a global brand and we're here to stay,'" said Amelio.[1]

105

> **TAKE A MOMENT**
>
> Do you believe Dell can duplicate its U.S. success in China? How do you think Lenova will fare as it tries to become a global brand? If you were a manager a Dell, what recommendations would you have for Dell managers as they go head-to-head with Lenova for control of the world's fastest-growing market?

Dell's core U.S. market is saturated, and its biggest potential for growth lies in emerging markets such as China. But managers at Dell are learning, as other companies have, that they may have to adjust how the company operates to succeed in a new country or region. Wal-Mart, for example, has faced significant challenges in Germany, where the giant U.S. firm is still a secondary player after 10 years of effort. The German market is dominated by local retail chains who cater to local tastes and are familiar with tough union rules and labor laws in that country. Wal-Mart also struggled in South America and Japan, partly because of managers' proclivity for doing things the Wal-Mart way without adequately considering local customs.

Other large, successful U.S. businesses, including FedEx and Nike, also found that "the rest of the world is not the United States of America," as one FedEx competitor put it. Yet these companies recognize that international expansion is necessary, despite the risks. Companies such as McDonald's, IBM, Coca-Cola, Kellogg, Texas Instruments, and Gillette rely on international business for a substantial portion of their sales and profits. Internet-based companies headquartered in the United States, such as Amazon, Yahoo!, eBay, and America Online, are also rapidly expanding internationally and finding that, even on the Web, going global is fraught with difficulties. These and other online companies encounter problems ranging from cultural blunders to violations of foreign laws. All organizations face special problems in trying to tailor their products, services, and business management to the unique needs of foreign countries—but if they succeed, the whole world is their marketplace.

How important is international business to the study of management? *If you are not thinking international, you are not thinking business management.* It's that serious. Rapid advances in technology and communications have made the international dimension an increasingly important part of the external environment discussed in Chapter 3. Isolation from international forces is no longer possible. The future of our businesses and our societies will be shaped by global rather than local relationships.[2]

Today's companies can locate different parts of the organization wherever it makes the most business sense—top leadership in one place, technical brainpower and production in other locales. Virtual connections enable close, rapid coordination and communication among people working in different parts of the world, so it is no longer necessary to keep all operations in one place. Samsung, the Korean electronics giant, moved its semiconductor-making facilities to the Silicon Valley to be closer to the best scientific brains in the industry. Canada's Nortel Networks selected a location in the southwest of England as its world manufacturing center for a new fixed-access radio product. Siemens of Germany has moved its electronic ultrasound division to the United States, while the U.S. company DuPont shifted its electronic operations headquarters to Japan.[3] Many of today's organizations also outsource certain functions to contractors in other countries as easily as if the contractor were located right next door.

These examples indicate that the environment for companies is becoming extremely complex and extremely competitive. Less-developed countries are challenging mature countries in a number of industries. China is the world's largest maker of consumer electronics and is rapidly and expertly moving into biotechnology, computer manufacturing, and semiconductors. At least 19 advanced new semiconductor plants are in or nearing operation in China.[4] The pace of innovation in India is startling, in industries as diverse as precision manufacturing, health care, and pharmaceuticals, and some observers see the beginnings of hypercompetitive multinationals in that country.[5]

This chapter introduces basic concepts about the global environment and international management. First, we consider the difficulty managers have operating in an increasingly borderless world. We address challenges—economic, legal-political, and sociocultural—facing companies within the global business environment. Then we discuss multinational corporations and touch on the various types of strategies and techniques needed for entering and succeeding in foreign markets.

A BORDERLESS WORLD

Why do companies such as Dell, FedEx, and eBay want to pursue a global strategy, despite difficulties, failures, and losses? They recognize that business is becoming a unified, global field as trade barriers fall, communication becomes faster and cheaper, and consumer tastes in everything from clothing to cellular phone converge. Thomas Middelhoff of Germany's Bertelsmann AG, which purchased U.S. publisher Random House, put it this way: "There are no German and American companies. There are only successful and unsuccessful companies."[6] In addition, for many companies today, the only potential for significant growth lies overseas. The demand for raw materials such as steel, aluminum, cement, and copper has slowed in the United States but is booming in countries such as China, India, and Brazil.[7] For online companies, too, going global is a key to growth. The number of residential Internet subscribers in China is growing significantly faster than that of the United States. Western Europe and Japan together account for a huge share of the world's e-commerce revenue.[8,9]

Companies that think globally have a competitive edge. Consider the U.S. movie industry, where global markets used to be an afterthought. Not any more. The success of *Crouching Tiger, Hidden Dragon* in both Asian and U.S. markets spurred movie studios to take a broader view. Squeezed at the box office in the United States, studios such as New Line Cinemas, Columbia Pictures, Disney, and Universal are busily striking deals to co-produce foreign language films designed primarily for foreign markets that are experiencing a booming demand. The box-office share for local films in Russia, for example, nearly tripled in 2004.[10] Small companies are finding that thinking globally is the key to survival. Excel Foundry and Machine in Pekin, Illinois, makes parts for machinery used in heavy-construction and mining operations. President Doug Parsons uses a strategy of outsourcing the easily duplicated parts to contractors in China so that Excel can focus more money and energy on making specialty products and innovating for the future.[11]

CONCEPT CONNECTION Today's companies compete in a **borderless world.** Procter & Gamble sales in Southeast Asia make up a rapidly growing percentage of the company's worldwide sales. These shoppers are purchasing P&G's diaper products, Pampers, in Malaysia.

■ **TAKE A MOMENT**

As a new manager, learn to "think globally." Take an interest in international people and issues. Don't hinder your own or your company's success by thinking only in terms of domestic issues, competitors, and markets. Expand your thinking by reading and networking broadly.

The reality of today's borderless companies means consumers can no longer tell from which country they're buying. U.S.-based Ford Motor Company owns Sweden's Volvo, while Chrysler, still considered an American brand, is owned by Germany's DaimlerChrysler and builds its PT Cruiser in Mexico. Toyota is a Japanese company, but it has manufactured more than 10 million vehicles in North American factories. The technology behind Intel's Centrino wireless components was born in a lab in Haifa, Israel, and Chinese researchers designed the microprocessors that control the pitch of the blade on General Electric's giant wind turbines.[12]

Companies can participate in the international arena on a variety of levels. The process of globalization typically passes through four distinct stages, as illustrated in Exhibit 4.1.

EXHIBIT 4.1

Four Stages of Globalization

SOURCE: Based on Nancy J. Adler, *International Dimensions of Organizational Behavior,* 4th ed. (Cincinnati, Ohio: South-Western, 2002), 8–9.

	1. Domestic	2. International	3. Multinational	4. Global
Strategic Orientation	Domestically oriented	Export-oriented, multidomestic	Multinational	Global
Stage of Development	Initial foreign involvement	Competitive positioning	Explosion of international operations	Global
Cultural Sensitivity	Of little importance	Very important	Somewhat important	Critically important
Manager Assumptions	"One best way"	"Many good ways"	"The least-cost way"	"Many good ways"

1. In the *domestic stage*, market potential is limited to the home country, with all production and marketing facilities located at home. Managers may be aware of the global environment and may want to consider foreign involvement.

2. In the *international stage*, exports increase, and the company usually adopts a *multidomestic* approach, meaning that competition is handled for each country independently. Product design, marketing, and advertising are adapted to the specific needs of each country, requiring a high level of sensitivity to local values and interests. Typically, these companies use an international division to deal with the marketing of products in several countries individually.

3. In the *multinational stage*, the company has marketing and production facilities located in many countries, with more than one-third of its sales outside the home country. These companies adopt a *globalization* approach, meaning they focus on delivering a similar product to multiple countries. Product design, marketing, and advertising strategies are standardized throughout the world. A good example of a company at the multinational stage is Coca-Cola.

4. Finally, the *global* (or *stateless*) *stage* of corporate international development transcends any single home country. These corporations operate in true global fashion, making sales and acquiring resources in whatever country offers the best opportunities and lowest cost. At this stage, ownership, control, and top management tend to be dispersed among several nationalities.[13]

Today, the number of global or stateless corporations is increasing and the awareness of national borders decreasing, as reflected in the frequency of foreign participation at the top management level. Schering-Plough tapped Pakistani-born Fred Hassan to rescue the drug giant from a downward spiral following the loss of U.S. patent protection on the allergy drug Claritin. Chiquita Brands CEO Fernando Aquirre was born in Mexico, and Cuban-born Carlos Gutierrez heads the iconic American company Kellogg.[14] Wales-born Howard Stringer was named Sony's first non-Japanese CEO in 2004, and Nancy McKinstry is the first American to head Dutch publisher Wolters Kluwer. Henry McKinnell, CEO of Pfizer, prepared for the job by spending 14 years working for the company in Iran, Japan, and Hong Kong.[15]

For today's managers, international experience is fast becoming a requisite. A survey of the 700 largest U.S. companies by *Chief Executive* and the executive search firm Spencer Stuart found that the percentage of CEOs with international experience jumped from 21 percent in 2002 to 30 percent the following year.[16] Increasingly, managers at lower levels are also expected to know a second or third language and have international experience. Young managers who want their careers to move forward recognize the importance of global experience. According to Harvard Business School professor Christopher Bartlett, author of *Managing Across Borders*, people should try to get global exposure when they are young in order to start building skills and networks that will grow throughout their careers. "If you've lived your whole life in the United States," he says, "you don't have as much sensitivity to all sorts of opportunities."[17]

GETTING STARTED INTERNATIONALLY

Organizations have a couple of ways to become involved internationally. One is to seek cheaper sources of materials or labor offshore, which is called *offshoring* or *global outsourcing*. Another is to develop markets for finished products outside their home countries, which may include exporting, licensing, and direct investing. These **market entry strategies** represent alternative ways to sell products and services in foreign markets. Most firms begin with exporting and work up to direct investment. Exhibit 4.2 shows the strategies companies can use to enter foreign markets.

market entry strategy An organizational strategy for entering a foreign market.

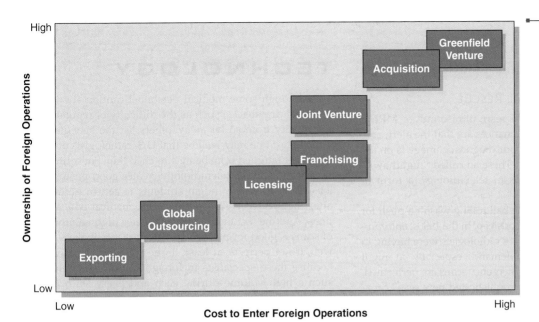

High

Ownership of Foreign Operations

Greenfield
Venture

Acquisition

Joint Venture

Franchising

Licensing

Global
Outsourcing

Exporting

Low

Low   **Cost to Enter Foreign Operations**   High

Outsourcing

Global outsourcing, also called *offshoring*, means engaging in the international division of labor so that work activities can be done in countries with the cheapest sources of labor and supplies. Millions of low-tech jobs such as textile manufacturing have been outsourced to low-wage countries in recent years. The Internet and plunging telecommunications costs are enabling companies to outsource more and higher-level work as well.[18] Netgear, a Santa Clara, California-based company, makes networking equipment that is designed and marketed in the United States, engineered in Taiwan, and manufactured in China, helping the small company take advantage of the efficiencies it can gain in three different countries.[19] Service companies are getting in on the outsourcing trend as well. U.S. data-processing companies use high-speed data lines to ship document images to Mexico and India, where 45,000 workers do everything from processing airline tickets to screening credit card applications. British banks have transferred back-office operations to companies in China and India, as well.[20] Read the Unlocking Innovative Solutions Through Technology box for a description of another growing area of services outsourcing.

A unique variation of global outsourcing is the *maquiladora* industry along the Texas-Mexico border. In the beginning, twin plants were set up, with the U.S. plant manufacturing components with sophisticated machinery and the Mexican plant assembling components using cheap labor. With increasing sophistication in Mexico, new factories with high-tech equipment are being built farther south of the border, with assembled products imported into the United States at highly competitive prices. General Electric, for example, employs more than 30,000 people in appliance factories in Mexico, and is now shifting some of its engineering work to that country, as well as to India, Brazil, and Turkey.

Exporting

With **exporting**, the corporation maintains its production facilities within the home nation and transfers its products for sale in foreign countries.[21] Exporting enables a company to market its products in other countries at modest resource cost and with limited risk. Exporting does entail numerous problems based on physical distances, government regulations, foreign currencies, and cultural differences, but it is less expensive than committing the firm's own capital to building plants in host countries. For example, a high-tech equipment supplier called Gerber Scientific Inc. prefers not to

global outsourcing Engaging in the international division of labor so as to obtain the cheapest sources of labor and supplies regardless of country; also called *global sourcing*.

exporting An entry strategy in which the organization maintains its production facilities within its home country and transfers its products for sale in foreign countries.

Unlocking Innovative Solutions Through | T E C H N O L O G Y |

NIGHTHAWKS TO THE RESCUE

If you need an X-ray, CT scan, ultrasound, or MRI in the middle of the night, chances are that the alert, able physician interpreting your diagnostic image is on the other side of the world. These so-called "nighthawk" radiologists are pioneers in teleradiology, a form of medical outsourcing.

What initially got the ball rolling wasn't a push for lower costs, but a desire for sleep. In the 1990s, entrepreneurs noticed the difficulty radiologists were having in meeting a burgeoning demand, especially at night when almost half of all emergency scans are performed. Stoking the demand are sophisticated new scans capable of quickly and accurately diagnosing everything from appendicitis to blood clots. Limited by the number of U.S. training programs, the supply of radiologists has not kept pace with the need for their services; currently, 20 percent of U.S. radiology vacancies go unfilled.

In response, start-up companies such as Idaho-based NightHawk Radiology Services and India-based Teleradiology Solutions hired U.S.-trained, board-certified, and licensed (though not necessarily American-born) physicians to work in countries many time zones removed. U.S. hospitals send nighttime digital images via broadband to physicians reporting for day shifts in India, Australia, Switzerland, Israel, and Lebanon. They typically shoot back a preliminary diagnosis within 30 minutes. Hospitals are generally pleased with the accuracy of these nighthawks, named for Vietnam-era pilots who flew night missions.

Although some medical personnel caution about potential drawbacks, such as the difficulty of regulating quality from so far away, others list the benefits. The biggest one may well be that U.S. radiologists are no longer fatigued from being stretched thin. For countries such as India, teleradiology creates good-paying jobs likely to entice Indian students to return home after they've received top-notch U.S. medical educations. And the fact that nighthawks see a high volume of scans is good for patients because practice makes—well, if not perfect—at least closer-to-perfect. Finally, because these specialists in foreign countries handle such a high volume during each and every shift, it helps reduce costs for hospitals and patients alike.

Teleradiology is a rapidly growing business. NightHawk Radiology Services revenues, for example, mushroomed from $4.7 million in 2001 to $64.1 million in 2005. Analysts expect the Indian health imaging market to double between 2005 and 2010. And yes, "dayhawk" outsourcing firms are beginning to appear, offering daytime diagnostic services to U.S. medical firms as well.

SOURCES: Lindsey Tanner, "From Altoona to Bangalore," *Associated Press* (December 6, 2004); Sanjay Krishnan, "India to be teleradiology hub!" *Rediff.com* (April 26, 2005): www.rediff.com/money/2005/apr/26inter.htm; NightHawk Radiology Services, "About NightHawk Radiology Services," www.nighthawkrad.net; and George Wiley, "Teleradiologists Venture into Daytime Coverage," *Decisions in Imaging Economics* (2005): www.imagingeconomics.com/library/200510-02.asp.

get involved directly in foreign country operations. Because machinery and machine tools are hot areas of export, executives are happy to ship overseas. Small to midsized U.S. companies are benefiting from increased exporting. Henry Estate, a winery in Umpqua, Oregon, exports quality wines to Canada, Japan, and the United Kingdom and has recently begun exporting to China to tap into the 1.3 billion potential wine drinkers in that country. Multiplex Co., a St. Louis manufacturer of beverage-dispensing equipment for fast-food service, exports about 40 percent of its products.[22]

A form of exporting to less-developed countries is called **countertrade**, which is the barter of products for products rather than the sale of products for currency. Many less-developed countries have products to exchange but have no foreign currency. An estimated 20 percent of world trade is countertrade.

Licensing

The next stage in pursuing international markets is licensing and franchising, which are similar approaches. With **licensing**, a corporation (the licensor) in one country makes certain resources available to companies in another country (the licensee). These resources include technology, managerial skills, and/or patent and trademark rights. They enable the licensee to produce and market a product similar to what the licensor has been producing. This arrangement gives the licensor an opportunity to

countertrade The barter of products for other products rather than their sale for currency.

licensing An entry strategy in which an organization in one country makes certain resources available to companies in another in order to participate in the production and sale of its products abroad.

participate in the production and sale of products outside its home country at relatively low cost. The toy maker Hasbro has used licensing agreements with companies in several Latin American countries and Japan. Hasbro builds brand identity and consumer awareness by contracting with toy companies in other countries to manufacture products locally. Heineken, which has been called the world's first truly global brand of beer, usually begins by exporting to help boost familiarity with its product; if the market looks enticing enough, Heineken then licenses its brands to a local brewer.

Franchising is a special form of licensing that occurs when the franchisee buys a complete package of materials and services, including equipment, products, product ingredients, trademark and trade name rights, managerial advice, and a standardized operating system. Whereas with licensing, a licensee generally keeps its own company name and operating systems, a franchise takes the name and

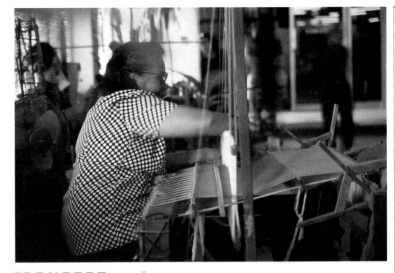

CONCEPT CONNECTION While vacationing in Thailand in 1988, former art student Henry Jacobson was impressed by the luster of the hand-woven silk ties, unlike any he'd seen back home. Soon after returning to the United States, he and Mulberry Neckwear co-founder Katie Smith introduced Thai silk ties to the U.S. market. They caught on. In 2006, the privately held Mulberry, headquartered in Richmond, California, had estimated sales of $60 million. The company uses **global outsourcing,** working with contractors in China, Italy, and Korea to produce ties designed in the United States from Thai and Korean silk. Here, a Thai silk factory worker spins spools of thread.

systems of the franchisor. For example, Anheuser-Busch licenses the right to brew and distribute Budweiser beer to several breweries, including Labatt in Canada and Kirin in Japan, but these breweries retain their own company names, identities, and autonomy. On the other hand, a Burger King franchise anywhere in the world is a Burger King, and managers use standard procedures designed by the franchisor. The fast-food chains are some of the best-known franchisors. KFC, Burger King, Wendy's, and McDonald's outlets are found in almost every large city in the world. The story is often told of the Japanese child visiting Los Angeles who excitedly pointed out to his parents, "They have McDonald's in America."

Licensing and franchising offer a business firm relatively easy access to international markets at low cost, but they limit its participation in and control over the development of those markets.

Direct Investing

A higher level of involvement in international trade is direct investment in facilities in a foreign country. **Direct investing** means that the company is involved in managing the productive assets, which distinguishes it from other entry strategies that permit less managerial control. Home Depot, for example, has stores in 10 Canadian provinces and is planning for stores in China.[23]

Currently, the most popular type of direct investment is to engage in strategic alliances and partnerships. In a **joint venture**, a company shares costs and risks with another firm, typically in the host country, to develop new products, build a manufacturing facility, or set up a sales and distribution network.[24] A partnership is often the fastest, cheapest, and least risky way to get into the global game. Entrepreneurial companies such as Molex, a manufacturer of connectors, and Tacit Networks, which makes software for instant file sharing between networks, have used partnerships to gain overseas access to several countries. Auburn Farms, a Sacramento, California, manufacturer of all-natural snack foods, formed a joint venture with South Africa's Beacon Sweets & Chocolates.[25] Internet companies have also used joint ventures as a way to expand. AOL created a joint venture with Venezuela's Cisneros Group to smooth its entry into Latin America.[26] In addition to joint ventures, the complexity of today's global business environment is causing managers at many companies to

franchising A form of licensing in which an organization provides its foreign franchisees with a complete package of materials and services.

direct investing An entry strategy in which the organization is involved in managing its production facilities in a foreign country.

joint venture A variation of direct investment in which an organization shares costs and risks with another firm to build a manufacturing facility, develop new products, or set up a sales and distribution network.

CONCEPT CONNECTION Wal-Mart's $62.7 billion in international sales for the fiscal year ending January 2006 represented an impressive 11 percent increase over the previous year. The world's largest retailer is not planning to stop there. Faced with slowing domestic growth, the company aims to increase its international division's share of total sales and earnings to 33 percent through a **direct investment** market entry strategy. That strategy includes **joint ventures, acquisitions,** and **greenfield ventures,** such as this Beijing retail store, opened in 2005. Wal-Mart's recent failures in South Korea and Germany taught managers the importance of heeding local customs and culture. It is a lesson they are putting to good use in China.

develop alliance networks, which refers to collections of partnerships with various other firms, often across international boundaries.[27] These alliance networks help companies reduce costs, enhance their competitive position in the international environment, and increase knowledge on a global scale.

The other choice is to have a **wholly owned foreign affiliate**, over which the company has complete control. Direct *acquisition* of an affiliate may provide cost savings over exporting by shortening distribution channels and reducing storage and transportation costs. Local managers also have heightened awareness of economic, cultural, and political conditions. Home Depot purchased the number 2 home-improvement retailer in Mexico, Home Mart, and turned it into today's leading chain, with 50 stores. Philip Morris recently acquired Indonesia's third largest cigarette maker to tap into the lucrative Asian cigarette market.[28]

The most costly and risky direct investment is called a **greenfield venture**, which means a company builds a subsidiary from scratch in a foreign country. The advantage is that the subsidiary is exactly what the company wants and has the potential to be highly profitable. The disadvantage is that the company has to acquire all market knowledge, materials, people, and know-how in a different culture, and mistakes are possible. An example of a greenfield venture is the Nissan plant in Canton, Mississippi. The plant represents the first auto factory ever built in Mississippi, where the Japanese company had to rely on an untested and largely inexperienced workforce. The logistical and cultural hurdles were so enormous and the risks so high that one Nissan executive later said, "We did what nobody thought was possible." The U.S. auto parts maker Delphi is taking a similar leap by building a $40 million, 200,000-square-foot car electronics parts plant in Suzhou, China.[29]

China Inc.

Just as managers at Delphi are looking to China as the wave of the future, many companies today are going straight to China or India as a first step into international business. As we discussed in the previous chapter, business in both countries is booming, and U.S. and European companies are taking advantage of opportunities for all of the tactics we've discussed in this section: outsourcing, exporting, licensing, and direct investment. In 2003, foreign companies invested more in business in China than they spent anywhere else in the world.[30] Multinationals based in the United States and Europe manufacture more and more products in China using design, software, and services from India. This trend prompted one business writer to coin the term "Chindia" to reflect the combined power of the two countries in the international dimension.[31]

Outsourcing is perhaps the most widespread approach to international involvement in China and India. China manufactures an ever-growing percentage of the industrial and consumer products sold in the United States—and in other countries as well. China produces more clothes, shoes, toys, television sets, DVD players, and cell phones than any other country. Manufacturers there are also moving into higher-ticket items such as automobiles, computers, and parts for Boeing 757s. China can manufacture almost any product at a much lower cost than in the West.

wholly owned foreign affiliate A foreign subsidiary over which an organization has complete control.

greenfield venture The most risky type of direct investment, whereby a company builds a subsidiary from scratch in a foreign country.

India, for its part, is a rising power in software design, services, and precision engineering. JPMorgan Chase plans to move 30 percent of its investment bank back-office and support staff functions to India by the end of 2007 to take advantage of the low cost of highly educated workers.[32] Nearly 50 percent of microchip engineering for Conexant Systems, a California company that makes the intricate brains behind Internet access for home computers and satellite-connection set-top boxes for televisions, is done in India.[33]

Many large organizations are also developing joint ventures or building subsidiaries in China and India. Cummins Engine was one of the earliest U.S. firms to open plants in both countries.

> **Cummins Engine**
>
> Cummins Engine forged a joint venture with Tata Motors, Ltd., to build a diesel engine plant in India in 1962, long before the current wave of investment in the country. The Columbus, Indiana, company was also an early mover into China, establishing a joint venture with Dongfeng Motor Company to open a plant there in 1995. For three decades in India and 10 years in China, the company struggled with everything from poor travel conditions to bureaucratic controls on product lines. But the persistence has paid off. In 2005, China and India accounted for $1.9 billion of Cummins' $8.4 billion in sales, and the amount is expected to increase to $5 billion by 2010.
>
> Cummins CEO Theodore M. Solso considers China and India the company's largest growth opportunities. The potential market for big truck engines is shrinking in North America, but growing in China and India. In fact, the booming market in China soaks up all the engines Cummins makes there and even requires the company to bring in more from other plants. The India plant is currently a great base for exporting to other countries, including the United States, Britain, China, and South Africa.
>
> By nurturing partnerships with local companies, Cummins managers were able to reduce their risks, minimize their capital costs, and gain a marketing edge. Whereas some foreign companies want to have clear control of their Chinese or Indian operations, Cummins cherishes its partnerships. In China, where relationships are paramount, the connection with Dongfeng provides invaluable help to Cummins in working through red tape, avoiding cultural blunders, and gaining access to China's markets. Local partners are instrumental in helping Cummins establish research and development centers. In India, 100 highly skilled engineers use 3-D computer modeling and simulated testing of engines and components to help Cummins innovate and cut costs. The research center in China that opened in late 2005 focuses on custom-designing engines for China.[34]

THE INTERNATIONAL BUSINESS ENVIRONMENT

International management is the management of business operations conducted in more than one country. The fundamental tasks of business management, including the financing, production, and distribution of products and services, do not change in any substantive way when a firm is transacting business across international borders. The basic management functions of planning, organizing, leading, and controlling are the same whether a company operates domestically or internationally. However, managers will experience greater difficulties and risks when performing these management functions on an international scale. Consider the following blunders:

:: When U.S. chicken entrepreneur Frank Purdue translated a successful advertising slogan into Spanish, "It takes a tough man to make a tender chicken" came out as "It takes a virile man to make a chicken affectionate."[35]

:: It took McDonald's more than a year to figure out that Hindus in India do not eat beef. The company's sales took off only after McDonald's started making burgers sold in India out of lamb.[36]

:: In Africa, the labels on bottles show pictures of what is inside so illiterate shoppers can know what they're buying. When a baby-food company showed a picture of an infant on its label, the product didn't sell very well.[37]

international management The management of business operations conducted in more than one country.

:: United Airlines discovered that even colors can doom a product. The airline handed out white carnations when it started flying from Hong Kong, only to discover that to many Asians such flowers represent death and bad luck.[38]

Some of these examples might seem humorous, but there's nothing funny about them to managers trying to operate in a highly competitive global environment. What should managers of emerging global companies look for to avoid obvious international mistakes? When they are comparing one country with another, the economic, legal-political, and sociocultural sectors present the greatest difficulties. Key factors to understand in the international environment are summarized in Exhibit 4.3.

CONCEPT CONNECTION   ExxonMobil operates in an **international business environment** with a presence in more than 200 countries and territories. Protecting the safety and health of employees while producing energy and chemical products all over the world is a constant challenge to managers. To reach their goal of no injuries, illnesses, or operational incidents, they developed the Operations Integrity Management System to provide a consistent and disciplined framework across ExxonMobil's diverse operations worldwide. Aboard the tanker Raven in the Mediterranean, two workers inspect equipment to forestall safety and environmental incidents.

THE ECONOMIC ENVIRONMENT

The economic environment represents the economic conditions in the country where the international organization operates. This part of the environment includes such factors as economic development, infrastructure, resource and product markets, and exchange rates, each of which is discussed in the following sections. In addition, factors such as inflation, interest rates, and economic growth are also part of the international economic environment.

EXHIBIT   4.3

Key Factors in the International Environment

Economic Development

Economic development differs widely among the countries and regions of the world. Countries can be categorized as either *developing* or *developed*. Developing countries are referred to as *less-developed countries (LDCs)*. The criterion traditionally used to classify countries as developed or developing is *per capita income*, which is the income generated by the nation's production of goods and services divided by total population. The developing countries have low per capita incomes. LDCs generally are located in Asia, Africa, and South America. Developed countries are generally located in North America, Europe, and Japan. Most international business firms are headquartered in the wealthier, economically advanced countries, but smart managers are investing heavily in Asia, Eastern Europe, Latin America, and Africa.[39] These companies face risks and challenges today, but they stand to reap huge benefits in the future.

Infrastructure

A country's physical facilities that support economic activities make up its **infrastructure**, which includes transportation facilities such as airports, highways, and railroads; energy-producing facilities such as utilities and power plants; and communication facilities such as telephone lines and radio stations. Companies operating in LDCs must contend with lower levels of technology and perplexing logistical, distribution, and communication problems. Undeveloped infrastructures represent opportunities for some firms, such as United Technologies Corporation, based in Hartford, Connecticut, whose businesses include jet engines, air conditioning and heating systems, and elevators. As countries such as China, Russia, and Vietnam open their markets, new buildings need elevators and air and heat systems; opening remote regions for commerce requires more jet engines and helicopters.[40] Cellular telephone companies have found tremendous opportunities in LDCs, where land lines are still limited. China has the world's biggest base of cell phone subscribers at 350 million, and the number is expected to grow to near 600 million by 2009.[41]

infrastructure A country's physical facilities that support economic activities.

Resource and Product Markets

When operating in another country, company managers must evaluate the market demand for their products. If market demand is high, managers may choose to export products to that country. To develop plants, however, resource markets for providing needed raw materials and labor must also be available. For example, the greatest challenge for McDonald's, which sells Big Macs on every continent except Antarctica, is to obtain supplies of everything from potatoes to hamburger buns to plastic straws. At McDonald's in Cracow, the burgers come from a Polish plant, partly owned by Chicago-based OSI Industries; the onions come from Fresno, California; the buns come from a production and distribution center near Moscow; and the potatoes come from a plant in Aldrup, Germany.[42]

AP PHOTO/PAVEL RAHMAN

CONCEPT CONNECTION While working as a New York investment banker, Bangladesh native Iqbal Quadir realized that connectivity equals productivity. He also knew his impoverished homeland was one of the least connected places on earth. That prompted him to collaborate with countryman Muhammad Yunus, Grameen Bank founder and 2006 Nobel Peace Prize winner, to create Village Phone. Entrepreneurs, mostly women, use Grameen Bank microloans to purchase cell phones. "Telephone ladies," such as Monwara Begum pictured here, then earn the money to repay the debt by providing phone service to fellow villagers. Village Phone results in thousands of new small businesses, as well as an improved communication **infrastructure** that makes a wide range of economic development possible.

Exchange Rates

Exchange rate is the rate at which one country's currency is exchanged for another country's. Volatility in exchange rates is a major concern for companies doing business internationally.[43] Changes in the exchange rate can have major implications for the profitability of international operations that exchange millions of dollars into other currencies every day.[44] For example, assume that the U.S. dollar is exchanged for 0.8 euros. If the dollar increases in value to 0.9 euros, U.S. goods will be more expensive in France because it will take more euros to buy a dollar's worth of U.S. goods. It will be more difficult to export U.S. goods to France, and profits will be slim. If the dollar drops to a value of 0.7 euros, by contrast, U.S. goods will be cheaper in France and can be exported at a profit.

THE LEGAL-POLITICAL ENVIRONMENT

Businesses must deal with unfamiliar political systems when they go international, as well as with more government supervision and regulation. Government officials and the general public often view foreign companies as outsiders or even intruders and are suspicious of their impact on economic independence and political sovereignty. Some of the major legal-political concerns affecting international business are political risk, political instability, and laws and regulations.

Political Risk and Instability

A company's **political risk** is defined as its risk of loss of assets, earning power, or managerial control due to politically based events or actions by host governments.[45] An example is Brazil's pressuring of its agencies and citizens to adopt open-source software, which could severely hurt Microsoft and other software companies.[46] Political risk also includes government takeovers of property and acts of violence directed against a firm's properties or employees. In Mexico, business executives and their families are prime targets for gangs of kidnappers, many of which are reportedly led by state and local police. A Japanese tire company, for example, paid a $1 million ransom after its CEO's daughter was kidnapped. Estimates are that big companies in Mexico typically spend between 5 and 15 percent of their annual budgets on security.[47]

Companies operating in other countries also formulate special plans and programs to guard against unexpected losses. Executives at Tricon, which owns KFC and Pizza Hut restaurants, monitor events through an international security service to stay on top of potential hot spots.[48] Some companies buy political risk insurance, and political risk analysis has emerged as a critical component of environmental assessment for multinational organizations.[49] To reduce uncertainty, organizations sometimes also rely on the *Index of Economic Freedom*, which ranks countries according to the impact political intervention has on business decisions, and the *Corruption Perception Index*, which assesses 91 countries according to the level of perceived corruption in government and public administration.[50]

Another frequently cited problem for international companies is **political instability**, which includes riots, revolutions, civil disorders, and frequent changes in government. In recent decades, civil wars and large-scale violence occurred in Haiti, Indonesia, Malaysia, Thailand, Sri Lanka (Ceylon), and Myanmar (Burma). Companies moving into former Soviet republics face continued instability because of changing government personnel and political philosophies. The Middle East is an area of extreme instability as the United States pursues a difficult and protracted reconstruction following the Iraqi war. U.S. firms or companies linked to the United States often are subject to major threats in countries characterized by political instability. For example, on the first Muslim holy day after the U.S. began bombings in Afghanistan, thousands of demonstrators in Pakistan set fire to a KFC restaurant as a symbol of America.[51] Although most companies would prefer to do business in stable countries,

political risk A company's risk of loss of assets, earning power, or managerial control due to politically based events or actions by host governments.

political instability Events such as riots, revolutions, or government upheavals that affect the operations of an international company.

some of the greatest growth opportunities lie in areas characterized by instability.

Laws and Regulations

Government laws and regulations differ from country to country and make doing business a true challenge for international firms. Host governments have myriad laws concerning libel statutes, consumer protection, information and labeling, employment and safety, and wages. International companies must learn these rules and regulations and abide by them. In addition, the Internet increases the impact of foreign laws on U.S. companies because it expands the potential for doing business on a global basis. Lands' End, the Dodgeville, Wisconsin, mail-order retailer, ran afoul of Germany's laws banning lifetime guarantees, rebates, and other forms of sales promotion.[52] First Net Card, started in 1999 to provide credit for online transactions to anyone in the world, found the complication of dealing with international credit and banking laws mind-boggling. After two years and a mountain of legal research, the company was licensed to provide credit only in the United States, Canada, and Britain.[53]

THE SOCIOCULTURAL ENVIRONMENT

A nation's culture includes the shared knowledge, beliefs, and values, as well as the common modes of behavior and ways of thinking, among members of a society. Cultural factors can be more perplexing than political and economic factors when working or living in a foreign country.

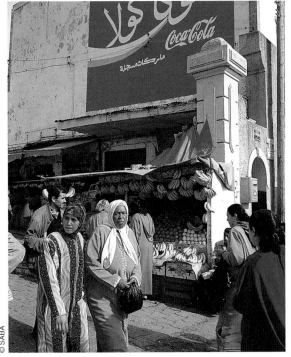

© SABA

CONCEPT CONNECTION Despite the **political risk, political instability,** and the local **laws and regulations** of countries such as Morocco, The Coca-Cola Company earns about 80 percent of its profits from markets outside North America. The soft-drink company suffered in global markets after complaints of tainted products from Belgium bottling plants. Managers are busily trying to rebuild relationships because of the importance of international sales.

Social Values

Culture is intangible, pervasive, and difficult for outsiders to learn. One way managers can comprehend local cultures and deal with them effectively is to understand differences in social values.

HOFSTEDE'S VALUE DIMENSIONS

In research that included 116,000 IBM employees in 40 countries, Geert Hofstede identified four dimensions of national value systems that influence organizational and employee working relationships.[54] Examples of how countries rate on the four dimensions are shown in Exhibit 4.4.

1. *Power distance.* High **power distance** means that people accept inequality in power among institutions, organizations, and people. Low power distance means that people expect equality in power. Countries that value high power distance are Malaysia, the Philippines, and Panama. Countries that value low power distance are Denmark, Austria, and Israel.

2. *Uncertainty avoidance.* High **uncertainty avoidance** means that members of a society feel uncomfortable with uncertainty and ambiguity and thus support beliefs that promise certainty and conformity. Low uncertainty avoidance means that people have high tolerance for the unstructured, the unclear, and the unpredictable. High uncertainty avoidance countries include Greece, Portugal, and Uruguay. Countries with low uncertainty avoidance values are Singapore and Jamaica.

power distance The degree to which people accept inequality in power among institutions, organizations, and people.

uncertainty avoidance A value characterized by people's intolerance for uncertainty and ambiguity and resulting support for beliefs that promise certainty and conformity.

EXHIBIT   4.4

Rank Orderings of Ten Countries along Four Dimensions of National Value Systems

SOURCE: From Dorothy Marcic, *Organizational Behavior and Cases,* 4th ed. (St. Paul, MN: West, 1995). Based on Geert Hofstede, *Culture's Consequences* (London: Sage Publications, 1984); and *Cultures and Organizations: Software of the Mind* (New York: McGraw-Hill, 1991).

Country	Power Distance[a]	Uncertainty Avoidance[b]	Individualism[c]	Masculinity[d]
Australia	7	7	2	5
Costa Rica	8 (tie)	2 (tie)	10	9
France	3	2 (tie)	4	7
West Germany	8 (tie)	5	5	3
India	2	9	6	6
Japan	5	1	7	1
Mexico	1	4	8	2
Sweden	10	10	3	10
Thailand	4	6	9	8
United States	6	8	1	4

[a]1 = highest power distance
10 = lowest power distance
[b]1 = highest uncertainty avoidance
10 = lowest uncertainty avoidance
[c]1 = highest individualism
10 = lowest individualism
[d]1 = highest masculinity
10 = lowest masculinity

individualism A preference for a loosely knit social framework in which individuals are expected to take care of themselves.

collectivism A preference for a tightly knit social framework in which individuals look after one another and organizations protect their members' interests.

masculinity A cultural preference for achievement, heroism, assertiveness, work centrality, and material success.

femininity A cultural preference for relationships, cooperation, group decision making, and quality of life.

long-term orientation A greater concern for the future and high value on thrift and perseverance.

short-term orientation A concern with the past and present and a high value on meeting social obligations.

3. *Individualism and collectivism.* **Individualism** reflects a value for a loosely knit social framework in which individuals are expected to take care of themselves. **Collectivism** means a preference for a tightly knit social framework in which individuals look after one another and organizations protect their members' interests. Countries with individualist values include the United States, Canada, Great Britain, and Australia. Countries with collectivist values are Guatemala, Ecuador, and China.

4. *Masculinity/femininity.* **Masculinity** stands for preference for achievement, heroism, assertiveness, work centrality (with resultant high stress), and material success. **Femininity** reflects the values of relationships, cooperation, group decision making, and quality of life. Societies with strong masculine values are Japan, Austria, Mexico, and Germany. Countries with feminine values are Sweden, Norway, Denmark, and France. Both men and women subscribe to the dominant value in masculine and feminine cultures.

Hofstede and his colleagues later identified a fifth dimension, long-term orientation versus short-term orientation. The **long-term orientation**, found in China and other Asian countries, includes a greater concern for the future and highly values thrift and perseverance. A **short-term orientation**, found in Russia and West Africa, is more concerned with the past and the present and places a high value on tradition and meeting social obligations.[55] Researchers continue to explore and expand on Hofstede's findings. For example, in the last 25 years, more than 1,400 articles and numerous books were published on individualism and collectivism alone.[56]

■ **TAKE A MOMENT**

Read the ethical dilemma on page 133 that pertains to social and cultural differences. As a new manager, would you raise the issue of Zing's management style in a foreign country?

GLOBE PROJECT VALUE DIMENSIONS

Recent research by the GLOBE Project extends Hofstede's assessment and offers a broader understanding for today's managers. The GLOBE (Global Leadership and Organizational Behavior Effectiveness) project used data collected from 18,000 managers in 62 countries to identify nine dimensions that explain cultural differences, including those identified by Hofstede.[57]

1. *Assertiveness.* A high value on assertiveness means a society encourages toughness, assertiveness, and competitiveness. Low assertiveness means that people value tenderness and concern for others over being competitive.

2. *Future orientation.* Similar to Hofstede's time orientation, this dimension refers to the extent to which a society encourages and rewards planning for the future over short-term results and quick gratification.

3. *Uncertainty avoidance.* As with Hofstede's study, this dimension gauges the degree to which members of a society feel uncomfortable with uncertainty and ambiguity.

4. *Gender differentiation.* This dimension refers to the extent to which a society maximizes gender role differences. In countries with low gender differentiation, such as Denmark, women typically have a higher status and stronger role in decision making. Countries with high gender differentiation accord men higher social, political, and economic status.

5. *Power distance.* This dimension is the same as Hofstede's and refers to the degree to which people expect and accept equality or inequality in relationships and institutions.

6. *Societal collectivism.* This term defines the degree to which practices in institutions such as schools, businesses, and other social organizations encourage a tightly knit collectivist society in which people are an important part of a group, or a highly individualistic society.

7. *Individual collectivism.* Rather than looking at how societal organizations favor individualism versus collectivism, this dimension looks at the degree to which individuals take pride in being members of a family, close circle of friends, team, or organization.

8. *Performance orientation.* A society with a high performance orientation places high emphasis on performance and rewards people for performance improvements and excellence. A low performance orientation means people pay less attention to performance and more attention to loyalty, belonging, and background.

9. *Humane orientation.* The final dimension refers to the degree to which a society encourages and rewards people for being fair, altruistic, generous, and caring. A country high on humane orientation places high value on helping others and being kind. A country low on this orientation expects people to take care of themselves. Self-enhancement and gratification are of high importance.

Exhibit 4.5 gives examples of how some countries rank on several of the GLOBE dimensions. These dimensions give managers an added tool for identifying and managing cultural differences. Although Hofstede's dimensions are still valid, the

Dimension	Low	Medium	High
Assertiveness	Sweden Switzerland Japan	Egypt Iceland France	Spain United States Germany (former East)
Future Orientation	Russia Italy Kuwait	Slovenia Australia India	Denmark Canada Singapore
Gender Differentiation	Sweden Denmark Poland	Italy Brazil Netherlands	South Korea Egypt China
Performance Orientation	Russia Greece Venezuela	Israel England Japan	United States Taiwan Hong Kong
Humane Orientation	Germany France Singapore	New Zealand Sweden United States	Indonesia Egypt Iceland

EXHIBIT 4.5

Examples of Country Rankings on Selected GLOBE Value Dimensions

SOURCE: Mansour Javidan and Robert J. House, "Cultural Acumen for the Global Manager: Lessons from Project GLOBE," *Organizational Dynamics* 29, no. 4 (2001), 289–305.

HOW WELL DO YOU PLAY THE CULTURE GAME?

How good are you at understanding cross-cultural differences in communication and etiquette? For fun, see how many of the following questions you can answer correctly. The answers appear at the end.

1. You want to do business with a Greek company, but the representative insists on examining every detail of your proposal for several hours. This time-consuming detail means that the Greek representative:
   a. Doesn't trust the accuracy of your proposal
   b. Is being polite, and really doesn't want to go ahead with the deal
   c. Is signaling you to consider a more reasonable offer, but doesn't want to ask directly
   d. Is uncomfortable with detailed proposals and would prefer a simple handshake
   e. Is showing good manners and respect to you and your proposal

2. Male guests in many Latin American countries often give their visitors an *abrazzo* when greeting them. An *abrazzo* is:
   a. A light kiss on the nose
   b. A special gift, usually wine or food
   c. Clapping hands in the air as the visitor approaches
   d. A strong embrace, or kiss with hand on shoulder
   e. A firm two-handed handshake, lasting almost one minute

3. Japanese clients visit you at your office for a major meeting. Where should the top Japanese official be seated?
   a. Closest to the door
   b. As close to the middle of the room as possible
   c. Anywhere in the room; seating location isn't important to Japanese businesspeople
   d. Somewhere away from the door with a piece of artwork behind him or her
   e. Always beside rather than facing the host

4. One of the most universal gestures is:
   a. A pat on the back (congratulations)
   b. A smile (happiness or politeness)
   c. Scratching your chin (thinking)
   d. Closing your eyes (boredom)
   e. Arm up, shaking back and forth (waving)

5. While visiting a German client, you make a compliment about the client's beautiful pen set. What will probably happen?
   a. The client will insist very strongly that you take it
   b. The client will tell you where to buy such a pen set at a good price
   c. The client will accept the compliment and get on with business
   d. The client will probably get upset that you aren't paying attention to the business at hand
   e. The client will totally ignore the comment

GLOBE research provides a more comprehensive view of cultural similarities and differences.

Social values greatly influence organizational functioning and management styles. Consider the difficulty that managers encountered when implementing self-directed work teams in Mexico. As shown in Exhibit 4.4, Mexico is characterized by very high power distance and a relatively low tolerance for uncertainty, characteristics that often conflict with the American concept of teamwork, which emphasizes shared power and authority, with team members working on a variety of problems without formal guidelines, rules, and structure. Many workers in Mexico, as well as in France and Mediterranean countries, expect organizations to be hierarchical. In Russia, people are good at working in groups and like competing as a team rather than on an individual basis. Organizations in Germany and other central European countries typically strive to be impersonal, well-oiled machines. Effective management styles differ in each country, depending on cultural characteristics.[58]

■ **TAKE A MOMENT** | As a new manager, remember that understanding national culture is as important as paying attention to economic and political matters when working in or with a foreign country. Prepare yourself by studying how the foreign country's social and cultural values compare to your own country. Avoid an ethnocentric attitude and recognize how the ethnocentrism of others may affect your perspective or work attitudes.

6. Managers from which country are least likely to tolerate someone being 5 minutes late for an appointment?
    a. United States
    b. Australia
    c. Brazil
    d. Sweden
    e. Saudi Arabia

7. In which of the following countries are office arrangements NOT usually an indicator of the person's status?
    a. United Kingdom
    b. Germany
    c. Saudi Arabia
    d. China
    e. United States

8. In many Asian cultures, a direct order such as "Get me the Amex report" is most likely to be given by:
    a. Senior management to most subordinates
    b. A junior employee to a peer
    c. Senior management only to very junior employees
    d. Junior employees to outsiders
    e. None of the above

9. In the United States, scratching one's head usually means that the person is confused or skeptical. In Russia, it means:

    a. "You're crazy!"
    b. "I am listening carefully."
    c. "I want to get to know you better."
    d. "I'm confused or skeptical."
    e. None of the above

10. A polite way to give your business card to a Japanese business person is:
    a. Casually, after several hours of getting to know the person
    b. When first meeting, presenting your card with both hands
    c. At the very end of the first meeting
    d. Casually during the meeting, with the information down to show humility
    e. Never; it is considered rude in Japan to give business cards

SOURCES: Steven L. McShane and Mary Ann Von Glinow, *Organizational Behavior: Emerging Realities for the Workplace Revolution*, 3rd ed. (New York: McGraw-Hill/Irwin, 2004). "Cross-Cultural Communication Game" developed by Steven L. McShane, based on material in R. Axtell, *Gestures: The Do's and Taboos of Body Language Around the World* (New York: Wiley, 1991); R. Mead, *Cross-Cultural Management Communication* (Chichester, UK: Wiley, 1990): chapter 7; and J. V. Thill and C. L. Bovée, *Excellence in Business Communication* (New York: McGraw-Hill, 1995): chapter 17.

Answers
1. e; 2. d; 3. d; 4. b; 5. c; 6. d; 7. c; 8. c; 9. d; 10. b

Other Cultural Characteristics

Other cultural characteristics that influence international organizations are language, religion, attitudes, social organization, and education. Some countries, such as India, are characterized by *linguistic pluralism*, meaning that several languages exist there. Other countries rely heavily on spoken versus written language. Religion includes sacred objects, philosophical attitudes toward life, taboos, and rituals. Attitudes toward achievement, work, and people can all affect organizational productivity. For example, one study found that the prevalent American attitude that treats employees as a resource to be used (an *instrumental* attitude toward people) can be a strong impediment to business success in countries where people are valued as an end in themselves rather than as a means to an end (a *humanistic* attitude). U.S. companies sometimes use instrumental human resource policies that conflict with local humanistic values.[59]

Ethnocentrism, which refers to a natural tendency of people to regard their own culture as superior and to downgrade or dismiss other cultural values, can be found in all countries. Strong ethnocentric attitudes within a country make it difficult for foreign firms to operate there. Other factors include social organization, such as status systems, kinship and families, social institutions, and opportunities for social mobility. Education influences the literacy level, the availability of qualified employees, and the predominance of primary or secondary degrees.

American managers are regularly accused of an ethnocentric attitude that assumes the American way is the best way. At an executive training seminar at IMD,

ethnocentrism A cultural attitude marked by the tendency to regard one's own culture as superior to others.

a business school in Lausanne, Switzerland, managers from Europe expressed a mixture of admiration and disdain for U.S. managers. "They admire the financial results," says J. Peter Killing, an IMD professor, "but when they meet managers from the United States they see that even these educated, affluent Americans don't speak any language besides English, don't know how or when to eat and drink properly, and don't know anything about European history, let alone geography."[60] Take the quiz in this chapter's Manager's Shoptalk box to see how much you know about cross-cultural communication and etiquette.

As business grows increasingly global, U.S. managers are learning that cultural differences cannot be ignored if international operations are to succeed. Coke had to withdraw its two-liter bottle from the Spanish market after discovering that compartments of Spanish refrigerators were too small for it. Wal-Mart goofed by stocking footballs in Brazil, a country where soccer rules.[61] Companies can improve their success by paying attention to culture. U.S. companies could take a lesson from South Korean appliance maker LG Electronics, which rules in emerging markets.

LG Electronics

Two decades ago, managers at South Korea's LG Electronics decided to solve a long-time problem for homemakers: how to keep the kimchi from stinking up the fridge. Kimchi, made from fermented cabbage seasoned with garlic and chili, is served with most meals in Korea. Any leftovers in the refrigerator are inevitably going to taint other foods and leave a pungent odor that lingers for weeks. LG built a refrigerator with a special compartment to isolate the smelly kimchi and it quickly became a must-have in Korean homes.

LG managers realized that their understanding of Korean culture led to an amazingly successful new product. So, they reasoned, why not apply that concept to designing products for other markets? LG doesn't just build a standard appliance and expect the whole world to love it. Instead, it taps into local idiosyncrasies in key markets by opening in-country research, manufacturing, and marketing facilities, enabling the company to "speak to consumers individually," as one manager put it. The approach led to products such as the Kebab Microwave in Iran, which includes a microwave-safe skewer rack and a preset for reheating shish kebabs, and the Karaoke phone in Russia that can be programmed with the top 100 Russian songs, whose lyrics scroll across the screen when they're played. The phone was an instant hit in a country where people like to entertain at home during the long winters.

In India, LG has introduced a number of successful products, such as refrigerators with larger vegetable- and water-storage compartments, surge-resistant power supplies, and brightly colored finishes that reflect local preferences. Microwaves are designed with a dark interior to hide masala stains. After learning that many Indians use their televisions to listen to music, LG came out with a model featuring an ultra sound system. These efforts made LG the unprecedented leader in appliance sales in India. Sales were projected to reach $1.8 billion in 2005, and LG's market share in some categories is nearly twice that of the competition.[62]

By making an effort to learn about local tastes and preferences, LG has become the appliance maker to beat in emerging global markets. Managers have now turned their attention to China, where LG is building extensive in-country facilities and learning all it can about local cultural preferences in the world's biggest consumer market.

INTERNATIONAL TRADE ALLIANCES

One of the most visible changes in the international business environment in recent years has been the development of regional trading alliances and international trade agreements. These developments are significantly shaping global trade.

GATT and the World Trade Organization

The General Agreement on Tariffs and Trade (GATT), signed by 23 nations in 1947, started as a set of rules to ensure nondiscrimination, clear procedures, the negotiation of disputes, and the participation of lesser-developed countries in international trade. GATT and its successor, the World Trade Organization (WTO), primarily use tariff concessions as a tool to increase trade. Member countries agree to limit the level of tariffs they will impose on imports from other members. The **most favored nation** clause calls for each member country to grant to every other member country the most favorable treatment it accords to any country with respect to imports and exports.[63]

GATT sponsored eight rounds of international trade negotiations aimed at reducing trade restrictions. The 1986 to 1994 Uruguay Round (the first to be named for a developing country) involved 125 countries and cut more tariffs than ever before. The Round's multilateral trade agreement, which took effect January 1, 1995, was the most comprehensive pact since the original 1947 agreement. It boldly moved the world closer to global free trade by calling for the establishment of the WTO. The WTO represents the maturation of GATT into a permanent global institution that can monitor international trade and has legal authority to arbitrate disputes on some 400 trade issues. As of December 11, 2005, 149 countries were members of the WTO.[64]

The goal of the WTO is to guide—and sometime urge—the nations of the world toward free trade and open markets.[65] The WTO encompasses the GATT and all its agreements, as well as various other agreements related to trade in services and intellectual property issues in world trade. As a permanent membership organization, the WTO is bringing greater trade liberalization in goods, information, technological developments, and services; stronger enforcement of rules and regulations; and greater power to resolve disputes. However, the power of the WTO is partly responsible for a growing backlash against global trade. An increasing number of individuals and public interest groups are protesting that global trade locks poor people into poverty and harms wages, jobs, and the environment.

most favored nation A term describing a GATT clause that calls for member countries to grant other member countries the most favorable treatment they accord any country concerning imports and exports.

European Union

Formed in 1957 to improve economic and social conditions among its members, the European Economic Community, now called the European Union (EU), has grown to the 25-nation alliance illustrated in Exhibit 4.6. The biggest expansion came in 2004,

EXHIBIT 4.6

The Nations of the European Union

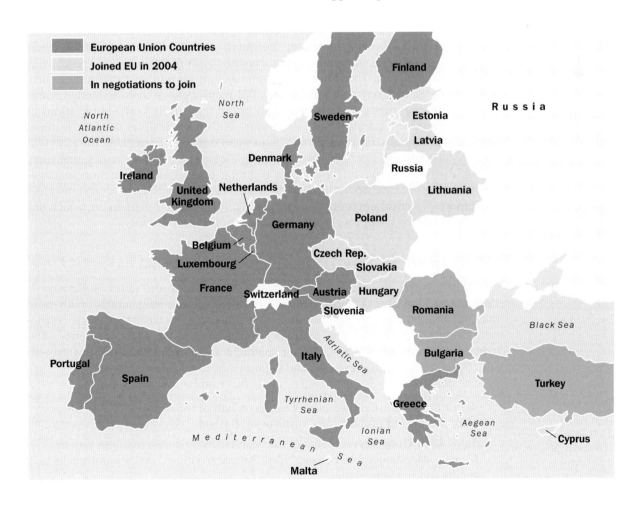

when the EU welcomed 10 new members from southern and eastern Europe: Cyprus, the Czech Republic, Estonia, Hungary, Latvia, Lithuania, Malta, Poland, Slovakia, and Slovenia. In addition, Bulgaria, Romania, and Turkey have opened membership negotiations. A treaty signed in early 2003 formalized new rules and policies to ensure that the EU can continue to function efficiently with 25 or more members.[66]

The EU has its roots in the early 1980s, when Europeans initiated steps to create a powerful single market system called *Europe '92*. The initiative called for the creation of open markets for Europe's millions of consumers, allowing people, goods, and services to move freely. Europe '92 consisted of 282 directives proposing dramatic reform and deregulation in such areas as banking, insurance, health, safety standards, airlines, telecommunications, auto sales, social policy, and monetary union. Common policies for member countries continue to evolve in light of changing social and economic circumstances. For example, the European Union now deals with issues such as citizens' rights, job creation, and how to make globalization work for everyone. In addition, the need to protect the natural environment is a consideration in all EU policies.

Initially opposed and later embraced by European industry, the increased competition and economies of scale within Europe enables companies to grow large and efficient, becoming more competitive in U.S. and other world markets. Some observers fear that the European Union will become a trade barrier, creating a *fortress Europe* that will be difficult to penetrate by companies in other nations. Indeed, an EU directive adopting strict privacy protection laws, which will affect U.S. companies wanting to do international business over the Internet, worries some U.S. officials.[67] The European Union also recently enacted laws that dramatically broaden its power concerning mergers and antitrust issues. For example, officials now have the power to seal off corporate offices for unspecified time periods to search for relevant documents.[68]

Another aspect of significance to countries operating globally is the European Union's monetary revolution and the introduction of the euro. In January 2002, the **euro**, a single European currency, replaced national currencies in 12 member countries and unified a huge marketplace, creating a competitive economy second only to the United States.[69] Belgium, Germany, Greece, France, Spain, Italy, Ireland, the Netherlands, Austria, Finland, Portugal, and Luxembourg traded their deutschemarks, francs, lira, and other currencies to adopt the euro, a currency with a single exchange rate. The United Kingdom has thus far refused to accept the euro, in part because of a sense of nationalism, but many believe that the United Kingdom and new EU members will eventually adopt the currency. The implications of a single European currency are enormous, within as well as outside Europe. Because it potentially replaces up to 25 European domestic currencies, the euro will affect legal contracts, financial management, sales and marketing tactics, manufacturing, distribution, payroll, pensions, training, taxes, and information management systems. Every corporation that does business in or with EU countries will feel the impact.[70] In addition, economic union is likely to speed deregulation, which has already reordered Europe's corporate and competitive landscape.

North American Free Trade Agreement (NAFTA)

The North American Free Trade Agreement, which went into effect on January 1, 1994, merged the United States, Canada, and Mexico into a mega market with more than 421 million consumers. The agreement breaks down tariffs and trade restrictions on most agricultural and manufactured products over a 15-year period. The treaty built on the 1989 U.S.–Canada agreement and was intended to spur growth and investment, increase exports, and expand jobs in all three nations.[71]

The negotiations resulted in agreements in a number of key areas:

:: *Agriculture*. Immediate removal of tariffs on half of U.S. farm exports to Mexico, with phasing out of remaining tariffs over 15 years.

:: *Autos*. Immediate 50 percent cut of Mexican tariffs on autos, reaching zero in 10 years. Mandatory 62.5 percent North American content on cars and trucks to qualify for duty-free status.

euro A single European currency that replaced the currencies of 12 European nations.

:: *Transport.* U.S. trucking of international cargo allowed in Mexican border area by mid-1990s and throughout Mexico by the end of the decade.

:: *Intellectual property.* Mexico's protection for pharmaceutical patents boosted to international standards and North American copyrights safeguarded.

Between 1994 and 2004, U.S. trade with Mexico increased more than threefold, while trade with Canada also rose dramatically.[72] NAFTA spurred the entry of small businesses into the global arena. Jeff Victor, general manager of Treatment Products, Ltd., which makes car cleaners and waxes, credits NAFTA for his surging export volume. Prior to the pact, Mexican tariffs as high as 20 percent made it impossible for the Chicago-based company to expand its presence south of the border.[73]

On the tenth anniversary of the agreement in January 2004, opinions over the benefits of NAFTA appeared to be as divided as they were when talks began, with some people calling it a spectacular success and others referring to it as a dismal failure.[74] Although NAFTA has not lived up to its grand expectations, experts stress that it increased trade, investment, and income and continues to enable companies in all three countries to compete more effectively with rival Asian and European firms.[75]

Other Trade Alliances

The creation of trading blocs is an increasingly important aspect of international business. The Association of Southeast Asian Nations (ASEAN) is a trading alliance of 10 Southeast Asian nations, including Cambodia, Vietnam, Singapore, Malaysia, and the Philippines, as illustrated in Exhibit 4.7. This region will likely be one of the fastest-growing economic regions of the world, and the ASEAN could eventually be as powerful as the European Union and NAFTA. A free trade block known as Mercosur encompasses Argentina, Brazil, Bolivia, Chile, Paraguay, and Uruguay. The Central America Free Trade Agreement (CAFTA), which rolled out in 2006, lowers tariffs and eases regulations between the United States, the Dominican Republic, Guatemala, Honduras, Nicaragua, and El Salvador, with Costa Rica pending.[76] And more than 30 countries in the Americas are negotiating to establish a hemisphere-wide trade agreement, the Free Trade Area of the Americas (FTAA).[77] These agreements entail a new future for international companies, and both corporations and managers will be affected by these important trends.

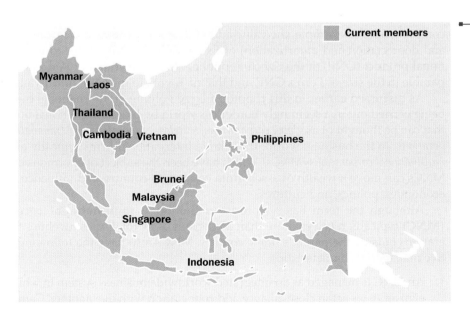

Current members

EXHIBIT 4.7

ASEAN Members

SOURCE: Based on J. McClenahen and T. Clark, "ASEAN at Work," *IW* (May 19, 1997): 42.

The Globalization Backlash

As the world becomes increasingly interconnected, a backlash over globalization is occurring. Perhaps the first highly visible antiglobalization protest occurred at the meeting of the World Trade Organization (WTO) in Seattle, Washington, in the fall of 1999, where business and political leaders were caught off guard by the strong sentiments. Since then, protesters have converged on both the International Monetary Fund (IMF) and the World Bank. These three organizations are sometimes referred to as the *Iron Triangle* of globalization.

A primary concern is the loss of jobs as companies expand their offshoring activities by exporting more and more work to countries with lower wages.[78] Consider, for example, that a 26-year-old engineer in Bangalore, India, designs next-generation mobile phone chips at a Texas Instruments research center for a salary of $10,000 a year. Boeing used aeronautical specialists in Russia to design luggage bins and wing parts for planes. They make about $650 a month, compared to a counterpart in the United States making $6,000. IBM shifted thousands of high-paying programming jobs to cheap-labor sites in China, India, and Brazil.[79] The transfer of jobs such as making shoes, clothing, and toys began two decades ago. Today, services and knowledge work are rapidly moving to developing countries. Outsourcing of white-collar jobs to India jumped 60 percent in 2003 compared to the year before. An analyst at Forrester Research Inc. predicts that at least 3.3 million mostly white-collar jobs and $136 billion in wages will shift from the United States to low-wage countries by 2015.[80]

Activists charge that globalization not only hurts people who lose their jobs in the United States, but also contributes to worldwide environmental destruction and locks poor people in developing nations into a web of poverty and suffering.[81] Political leaders struggle to assure the public of the advantages of globalization and free trade,[82] with President George Bush admonishing those who oppose globalization as "no friends to the poor." Business leaders, meanwhile, insist that the economic benefits flow back to the U.S. economy in the form of lower prices, expanded markets, and increased profits that can fund innovation.[83] Yet the antiglobalization fervor is just getting hotter—and is not likely to dissipate anytime soon. Managers who once saw antiglobalists as a fringe group are starting to pay attention to the growing concerns. In the end, it is not whether globalization is good or bad, but how business and government can work together to ensure that the advantages of a global world are fully and fairly shared.

MULTINATIONAL CORPORATIONS

The size and volume of international businesses are so large that they are hard to comprehend. For example, the value added (the sum of total wages, pretax profits, and depreciation and amortization) of ExxonMobil is comparable to the gross national product (GNP) of the Czech Republic. The value added of Wal-Mart is comparable to the size of Peru's GNP, and that of Toyota to the GNP of Kuwait.[84]

As discussed earlier in this chapter, a large volume of international business is being carried out in a seemingly borderless world by large international businesses that can be thought of as *global corporations, stateless corporations*, or *transnational corporations*. In the business world, these large international firms typically are called *multinational corporations (MNCs)*, which have been the subject of enormous attention. MNCs can move a wealth of assets from country to country and influence national economies, politics, and cultures.

Although the term has no precise definition, a **multinational corporation (MNC)** typically receives more than 25 percent of its total sales revenues from operations outside the parent's home country. MNCs also have the following distinctive managerial characteristics:

1. An MNC is managed as an integrated worldwide business system in which foreign affiliates act in close alliance and cooperation with one another. Capital,

multinational corporation (MNC) An organization that receives more than 25 percent of its total sales revenues from operations outside the parent company's home country; also called *global corporation* or *transnational corporation*.

technology, and people are transferred among country affiliates. The MNC can acquire materials and manufacture parts wherever in the world it is most advantageous to do so.

2. An MNC is ultimately controlled by a single management authority that makes key strategic decisions relating to the parent and all affiliates. Although some headquarters are *binational*, such as the Royal Dutch/Shell Group, some centralization of management is required to maintain worldwide integration and profit maximization for the enterprise as a whole.

3. MNC top managers are presumed to exercise a global perspective. They regard the entire world as one market for strategic decisions, resource acquisition, location of production, advertising, and marketing efficiency.

In a few cases, the MNC management philosophy may differ from that just described. For example, some researchers have distinguished among *ethnocentric companies*, which place emphasis on their home countries, *polycentric companies*, which are oriented toward the markets of individual foreign host countries, and *geocentric companies*, which are truly world oriented and favor no specific country.[85] The truly global companies that transcend national boundaries are growing in number. These companies no longer see themselves as American, Chinese, or German; they operate globally and serve a global market.

MANAGING IN A GLOBAL ENVIRONMENT

Managers working in foreign countries often face tremendous personal difficulties. In addition, they must be sensitive to cultural subtleties and understand that the ways to provide proper leadership, decision making, motivation, and control vary in different cultures. A clue to the complexity of working internationally comes from a study of the factors that contribute to global manager failures. Based on extensive interviews with global managers, researchers found that personal traits, the specific cultural context, or management mistakes made by the organization could all contribute to failure in an international assignment.[86]

■ **TAKE A MOMENT**

Before reading the next section, find out your CQ by answering the questions in the New Manager Self-Test on page 128. Your answers will indicate your level of cultural intelligence and help you relate to the concepts that follow. As a new manager, begin soon to develop cultural intelligence for other countries.

Developing Cultural Intelligence

When managing in a foreign country, the need for personal learning and growth is critical. Managers will be most successful in foreign assignments if they are culturally flexible and able to easily adapt to new situations and ways of doing things. In other words, managers working internationally need cultural intelligence. **Cultural intelligence (CQ)** refers to a person's ability to use reasoning and observation skills to interpret unfamiliar gestures and situations and devise appropriate behavioral responses.[87]

It is important for a manager working in a foreign country to study the language and learn as much as possible about local norms, customs, beliefs, and taboos. However, that information alone cannot prepare the manager for every conceivable situation. Developing a high level of CQ enables a person to interpret unfamiliar situations and adapt quickly. Rather than a list of global "dos and don'ts," CQ is a practical learning approach that enables a person to ferret out clues to a culture's shared understandings and respond to new situations in culturally appropriate ways.

cultural intelligence (CQ)
A person's ability to use reasoning and observation skills to interpret unfamiliar gestures and situations and devise appropriate behavioral responses.

CULTURAL INTELLIGENCE

Most new managers start out with a focus on their local department. The job of a manager demands a lot, and before long your activities will include situations that will test your knowledge and capacity for dealing with people from other national cultures. Are you ready? To find out, think about your experiences in other countries or with people from other countries. To what extent does each of the following statements characterize your behavior? Please answer each of the following items as Mostly True or Mostly False for you.

	Mostly True	Mostly False
1. I plan how I'm going to relate to people from a different culture before I meet them.	_____	_____
2. I understand the religious beliefs of other cultures.	_____	_____
3. When I visit a new culture, I can quickly sense whether something is going well or badly.	_____	_____
4. I seek out opportunities to interact with people from different cultures.	_____	_____
5. I can adapt to living in a different culture with relative ease.	_____	_____
6. I am confident that I can befriend locals in a culture that is unfamiliar to me.	_____	_____
7. I change my speech style (e.g., accent, tone) when a cross-cultural interaction requires it.	_____	_____

	Mostly True	Mostly False
8. I alter my facial expressions and gestures as needed to facilitate a cross-culture interaction.	_____	_____
9. I am quick to change the way I behave when a cross-culture encounter seems to require it.	_____	_____

INTERPRETATION AND SCORING: Each question pertains to some aspect of **cultural intelligence**. The first three Questions 1–3 pertain to the head (**cognitive CQ** subscale), question 4–6 to the heart (**emotional CQ** subscale), and questions 7–9 to the body (**physical CQ** subscale). If you have sufficient international experience and CQ to have answered "Mostly True" to two of three questions for each subscale or six of nine for all the questions, then consider yourself at a high level of CQ for a new manager. If you scored one or fewer "Mostly True" on each subscale or three or fewer for all nine questions, it is time to learn more about other national cultures. Hone your observational skills and learn to pick up on clues about how people from a different country respond to various situations. Be open to new ideas and develop empathy for people who are different from you.

SOURCES: Based on P. Christopher Earley and Elaine Mosakowski,"Cultural Intelligence,"*Harvard Business Review* (October 2004): 139–146; and Lynn Van Dyne and Soon Ang, "Cultural Intelligence: An Essential Capability for Individuals in Contemporary Organizations,"unpublished working paper (June 2005).

Cultural intelligence includes three components that work together: cognitive, emotional, and physical.[88] The cognitive component involves a person's observational and learning skills and the ability to pick up on clues to understanding. The emotional aspect concerns one's self-confidence and self-motivation. A manager has to believe in his or her ability to understand and assimilate into a different culture. Difficulties and setbacks are triggers to work harder, not a cause to give up. Working in a foreign environment is stressful, and most managers in foreign assignments face a period of homesickness, loneliness, and culture shock from being suddenly immersed in a culture with completely different languages, foods, values, beliefs, and ways of doing things. **Culture shock** refers to the frustration and anxiety that result from constantly being subjected to strange and unfamiliar cues about what to

culture shock Feelings of confusion, disorientation, and anxiety that result from being immersed in a foreign culture.

do and how to do it. A person with high CQ is able to move quickly through this initial period of culture shock.

The third component of CQ, the physical, refers to a person's ability to shift his or her speech patterns, expressions, and body language to be in tune with people from a different culture. Most managers aren't equally strong in all three areas, but maximizing cultural intelligence requires that they draw upon all three facets. In a sense, CQ requires that the head, heart, and body work in concert.

High CQ also requires that a manager be open and receptive to new ideas and approaches. One study found that people who adapt to global management most easily are those who have grown up learning how to understand, empathize, and work with others who are different from themselves. For example, Singaporeans consistently hear English and Chinese spoken side by side. The Dutch have to learn English, German, and French, as well as Dutch, to interact and trade with their economically dominant neighbors. English Canadians must not only be well-versed in American culture and politics, but they also have to consider the views and ideas of French Canadians, who, in turn, must learn to think like North Americans, member of a global French community, Canadians, and Quebecois.[89] People in the United States who have grown up without this kind of language and cultural diversity typically have more difficulties with foreign assignments, but willing managers from any country can learn to open their minds and appreciate other viewpoints.

Managing Cross-Culturally

Which two of the following three items go together: a panda, a banana, and a monkey? If you said a monkey and a banana, you answered like a majority of Asians; if you said a panda and a monkey, you answered like a majority of people in Western Europe and the United States. Where Westerners see distinct categories (animals), Asians see relationships (monkeys eat bananas).[90] Although this test is not definitive, it serves to illustrate an important fact for managers. The cultural differences in how people think and see the world affect working relationships. To be effective on an international level, managers need to interpret the culture of the country and organization in which they are working and develop the sensitivity required to avoid making costly cultural blunders.[91]

In addition to developing cultural intelligence, managers can prepare for foreign assignments by understanding how the country differs in terms of the Hofstede and GLOBE social values discussed earlier in this chapter. These values greatly influence how a manager should interact with subordinates and colleagues in the new assignment. For example, the United States scores extremely high on individualism, and a U.S. manager working in a country such as Japan, which scores high on collectivism, will have to modify his or her approach to leading and controlling in order to be successful. The following examples are broad generalizations, but they give some clue to how cultural differences can be significant for expatriate managers.

Complete the experiential exercise on page 132 that pertains to your global management potential. How well do your knowledge and preferences reflect a global perspective?

■ **TAKE A MOMENT**

Leading

In relationship-oriented societies that rank high on collectivism, such as those in Asia, the Arab world, and Latin America, leaders typically use a warm, personalized approach with employees. One of the greatest difficulties U.S. leaders encounter in doing business in China, for example, is failing to recognize that to the Chinese any relationship is a personal relationship.[92] Managers are expected to have periodic social visits with workers, inquiring about morale and health. Leaders should be especially careful about how and in what context they criticize others. To Asians, Africans, Arabs, and Latin Americans, the loss of self-respect brings dishonor to themselves and their families. The principle of *saving face* is highly important in some cultures.

DECISION MAKING

In the United States, mid-level managers may discuss a problem and give the boss a recommendation. On the other hand, managers in Iran, which reflects South Asian cultural values, expect the boss to make a decision and issue specific instructions.[93] In Mexico, employees often don't understand participatory decision making. Mexico ranks extremely high on power distance, and many workers expect managers to exercise their power in making decisions and issuing orders. American managers working in Mexico have been advised to rarely explain a decision, lest workers perceive this as a sign of weakness.[94] In contrast, managers in many Arab and African nations are expected to use consultative decision making in the extreme.

MOTIVATING

Motivation must fit the incentives within the culture. A recent study, for example, confirmed that intrinsic factors such as challenge, recognition, and the work itself are less effective in countries that value high power distance. It may be that workers in these cultures perceive manager recognition and support as manipulative and therefore demotivating.[95] In places such as the United States and the United Kingdom, by contrast, intrinsic factors can be highly motivating. In Japan, which highly values collectivism, employees are motivated to satisfy the company. A financial bonus for star performance would be humiliating to employees from Japan, China, or Ecuador. An American executive in Japan offered a holiday trip to the top salesperson, but employees were not interested. After he realized that Japanese are motivated in groups, he changed the reward to a trip for everyone if together they achieved the sales target. They did. Managers in Latin America, Africa, and the Middle East improve motivation by showing respect for employees as individuals with needs and interests outside of work.[96]

CONTROLLING

When things go wrong, managers in foreign countries often are unable to get rid of employees who do not work out. Consider the following research finding: When asked what to do about an employee whose work had been subpar for a year after 15 years of exemplary performance, 75 percent of Americans and Canadians said fire her; only 20 percent of Singaporeans and Koreans chose that solution.[97] In Europe, Mexico, and Indonesia, as well, to hire and fire based on performance seems unnaturally brutal. In addition, workers in some countries are protected by strong labor laws and union rules.

In foreign cultures, managers also should not control the wrong things. A Sears manager in Hong Kong insisted that employees come to work on time instead of 15 minutes late. The employees did exactly as they were told, but they also left on time instead of working into the evening as they had previously. A lot of work was left unfinished. The manager eventually told the employees to go back to their old ways. His attempt at control had a negative effect.

MANAGER'S SOLUTION

This chapter emphasized the growing importance of an international perspective on management. Successful companies are expanding their business overseas and successfully competing with foreign companies on their home turf. Major alternatives for serving foreign markets are exporting, licensing, franchising, and direct investing through joint ventures or wholly owned subsidiaries. Business in the global arena involves special risks and difficulties because of complicated economic, legal-political, and sociocultural forces. Moreover, the global environment changes rapidly, as illustrated by the emergence of the World Trade Organization, the European Union, the North American Free Trade Agreement, and other emerging trade alliances. The expansion of free-trade policies has sparked a globalization backlash among people who are fearful of losing their jobs and economic security, as well as those who believe economic globalization hurts poor people worldwide.

Much of the growth in international business has been carried out by large businesses called MNCs. These large companies exist in an almost borderless world, encouraging the free flow of ideas, products, manufacturing, and marketing among countries to achieve the greatest efficiencies. Managers in MNCs as well as those in much smaller companies doing business internationally face many challenges and must develop a high level of cultural intelligence (CQ) to be successful. CQ, which involves a cognitive component (head), an emotional component (heart), and a physical component (body), helps managers interpret unfamiliar situations and devise culturally appropriate responses. Social and cultural values differ widely across cultures and influence appropriate patterns of leadership, decision making, motivation, and managerial control.

International markets provide many opportunities but are also fraught with difficulty. Dell Inc., described at the beginning of this chapter, enjoyed significant success translating its direct-sales business model to other countries. However, Dell was unprepared for the difficulties it is facing in China and is outgunned at the moment by Lenova, which has a 20.4 percent market share in Asia and 4,800 retail outlets in China alone. Some observers believe Lenova could eventually challenge Dell's lead on a global basis, which illustrates the growing power of Chinese companies in international business. Behind the scenes, Lenova is scrambling to cut its costs to match Dell's efficiency and has begun dealing with large customers directly rather than through distributors. For its part, Dell has stuck to its direct sales model and is going it alone in China, whereas other computer manufacturers have forged joint ventures with local companies. Dell's strategy has been fairly successful as the company focuses on large business and government customers in major cities. However, observers believe as Dell starts courting consumers and businesses in smaller cities, where demand is growing faster, it will run into more trouble competing with Lenova. Direct sales in China are currently a problem because few Chinese customers use credit cards, for example. Dell is loath to break with its successful model, but somehow establishing "a presence on the street" through kiosks or retailers, or perhaps by partnering with a local company, may be necessary for Dell to compete successfully with the home-town leader in this new market.[98]

DISCUSSION QUESTIONS

1. Compare the advantages associated with the foreign-market entry strategies of exporting, licensing, and wholly owned subsidiaries. What information would you need to collect and what factors would you consider when selecting a strategy?

2. How do you think trade alliances such as NAFTA, the EU, and ASEAN might affect you as a future manager?

3. What steps could a company take to avoid making product design and marketing mistakes when introducing new products into East Germany? How would you go about hiring a plant manager for a facility you are planning to build in East Germany?

4. What is meant by the cultural values of individualism and power distance? How might these

values affect organization design and management processes?

5. What do you think is your strongest component of cultural intelligence? Your weakest? How would you go about shoring up your weaknesses?

6. Two U.S. companies are competing to take over a large factory in the Czech Republic. One delegation tours the facility and asks questions about how the plant might be run more efficiently. The other delegation focuses on ways to improve working conditions and produce a better product. Which delegation do you think is more likely to succeed with the plant? Why? What information would you want to collect to decide whether to acquire the plant for your company?

7. What might be some long-term ramifications of the war in Iraq for U.S. managers and companies operating internationally?

8. What does it mean to say that the world is becoming *borderless?* That large companies are *stateless?*

9. What specifically would the experience of living and working in another country contribute to your skills and effectiveness as a manager in your own country?

10. Should a multinational corporation operate as a tightly integrated, worldwide business system, or would it be more effective to let each national subsidiary operate autonomously?

MANAGEMENT IN PRACTICE: EXPERIENTIAL EXERCISE

Rate Your Global Management Potential

A global environment requires that managers learn to deal effectively with people and ideas from a variety of cultures. How well prepared are you to be a global manager? Read the following statements and circle the number on the response scale that most closely reflects how well the statement describes you.

Good Description ⑩ ❾ ❽ ❼ ❻ ❺ ❹ ❸ ❷ ❶ Poor Description

1. I reach out to people from different cultures.   ⑩❾❽❼❻❺❹❸❷❶

2. I frequently attend seminars and lectures about other cultures or international topics.   ⑩❾❽❼❻❺❹❸❷❶

3. I believe female expatriates can be equally as effective as male expatriates.   ⑩❾❽❼❻❺❹❸❷❶

4. I have a basic knowledge about several countries in addition to my native country.   ⑩❾❽❼❻❺❹❸❷❶

5. I have good listening and empathy skills.   ⑩❾❽❼❻❺❹❸❷❶

6. I have spent more than two weeks traveling or working in another country.   ⑩❾❽❼❻❺❹❸❷❶

7. I easily adapt to the different work ethics of students from other cultures when we are involved in a team project.   ⑩❾❽❼❻❺❹❸❷❶

8. I can speak a foreign language.   ⑩❾❽❼❻❺❹❸❷❶

9. I know which countries tend to cluster into similar sociocultural and economic groupings.   ⑩❾❽❼❻❺❹❸❷❶

10. I feel capable of assessing different cultures on the basis of power distance, uncertainty avoidance, individualism, and masculinity.   ⑩❾❽❼❻❺❹❸❷❶

Total Score: _____

Scoring and Interpretation

Add up the total points for the 10 questions. If you scored 81–100 points, you have a great capacity for developing good global management skills. A score of 61–80 points indicates that you have potential but may lack skills in certain areas, such as language or foreign experience. A score of 60 or less means you need to do some serious work to improve your potential for global management. Regardless of your total score, go back over each item and make a plan of action to increase scores of less than 5 on any question.

SOURCE: Based in part on "How Well Do You Exhibit Good Intercultural Management Skills?" in John W. Newstrom and Keith Davis, *Organizational Behavior: Human Behavior at Work* (Boston, MA: McGraw-Hill Irwin, 2002): 415–416.

AH Biotech

Dr. Abraham Hassan knew he couldn't put off the decision any longer. AH Biotech, the Bound Brook, New Jersey-based company started up by this psychiatrist-turned-entrepreneur, had developed a novel drug that seemed to promise long-term relief from panic attacks. If it gained FDA approval, it would be the company's first product. It was now time for large-scale clinical trials. But where should AH Biotech conduct those tests?

David Berger, who headed up research and development, was certain he already knew the answer to that question: Albania. "Look, doing these trials in Albania will be quicker, easier and a lot cheaper than doing them in the States," he pointed out. "What's not to like?"

Dr. Hassan had to concede Berger's arguments were sound. If they did trials in the United States, AH Biotech would spend considerable time and money advertising for patients and then finding physicians who'd be willing to serve as clinical trial investigators. Rounding up U.S. doctors prepared to take on that job was getting increasingly difficult. They just didn't want to take time out of their busy practices to do the testing, not to mention all the recordkeeping such a study entailed.

In Albania, it was an entirely different story. It was one of the poorest, if not *the* poorest, Eastern European country, with a just barely functioning health care system. Albanian physicians and patients would practically arrive at AH Biotech's doorstep asking to take part. Physicians there could earn much better money as clinical investigators for a U.S. company than they could actually practicing medicine, and patients saw signing up as test subjects as their best chance for receiving any treatment at all, let alone cutting-edge Western medicine. All of these factors meant that the company could count on realizing at least a 25 percent savings, maybe more, by running the tests overseas.

What's not to like? As the Egyptian-born CEO of a start-up biotech company with investors and employees hoping for its first marketable drug, there was absolutely nothing not to like. It was when he thought like a U.S.-trained physician that he felt qualms. If he used U.S. test subjects, he knew they'd likely continue to receive the drug until it was approved. At that point, most would have insurance that cover most of the cost of their prescriptions. But he already knew it wasn't going to make any sense to market the drug in a poor country like Albania, so when the study was over, he'd have to cut off treatment. Sure, he conceded, panic attacks weren't usually fatal. But he knew how debilitating these sudden bouts of feeling completely terrified were—the pounding heart, chest pain, choking sensation, and nausea. The severity and unpredictability of these attacks often made a normal life all but impossible. How could he offer people dramatic relief and then snatch it away?

What Would You Do?

1. Do the clinical trials in Albania. You'll be able to bring the drug to market faster and cheaper, which will be good for AH Biotech's employees and investors and good for the millions of people who suffer from anxiety attacks.

2. Do the clinical trials in the United States. Even though it will certainly be more expensive and time-consuming, you'll feel as if you're living up to the part of the Hippocratic Oath that instructed you to "prescribe regimens for the good of my patients according to my ability and my judgment and never do harm to anyone."

3. Do the clinical trials in Albania, and if the drug is approved, use part of the profits to set up a compassionate use program in Albania, even though setting up a distribution system and training doctors to administer the drug, monitor patients for adverse effects, and track results will entail considerable expense.

SOURCES: Based on Gina Kolata, "Companies Facing Ethical Issue as Drugs Are Tested Overseas," *The New York Times* (March 5, 2004): A1; and Julie Schmit, "Costs, Regulations Move More Drug Tests Outside USA," *USA Today* (June 16, 2005), http://www.usatoday.com/money/industries/health/drugs/2005-05-16-drug-trials-usat_x.htm.

CASE FOR CRITICAL ANALYSIS

Unocal Corporation

Unocal Corporation seemed an unlikely candidate for a high-risk global rampage. Consumers everywhere recognized the ubiquitous 76 logo of this quintessential California oil company. They knew it as a large petroleum retailer, with a prestigious downtown headquarters and important role as a Los Angeles civic booster. Casting aside its reputation as a conservative company with tightly defined domestic markets and focused petroleum interests in California, Unocal spent the 1990s transforming itself into an international company with major investments in some of the world's least-developed economies.

In 1995, immediately after becoming chairman of Unocal, Roger Beach began to sell off domestic retail assets and eliminate exploration and refining activities in the United States. Resources shifted to unlikely places where few other major oil producers had risked operations—places such as Myanmar (formerly known as Burma), Turkmenistan, Uzbekistan, and the strife-ridden Balkans. Beach turned up the heat on company investments in Indonesian oil fields, launched full-service energy subsidiaries through government alliances in Thailand, broadened holdings in Malaysia, and began negotiations for an integrated refining/retailing enterprise in Pakistan. Nearly 40 percent of Unocal's exploration and extraction budget was thrown into these emerging markets, much of it pinpointed for very-high-risk locations in the former Soviet republics and the Persian subcontinent.

Why take these risks? Beach answers that Unocal, unable to compete head-to-head with the oil industry giants for capital markets, decided to create an extremely attractive strategic package of full-service energy production in countries grasping to develop infrastructure. "What every government likes about Unocal's strategy is one-stop shopping; one group able to take the whole project from development to the marketing end," Beach said. "We have become partners in their development and as important to them as they are to us." The Unocal strategy defies normal industry trends based on distributing huge capital investments to tie up oil reserves and mineral rights, then cutting deals for operations. Instead, Unocal comes in the front door with packaged energy services ranging from turning the first spade of dirt on exploration to delivering power to the end user, and that proposal includes oil, gas, or electric power generation.

Beach sees far less risk than industry analysts perceive in the emerging markets. The dangers of war, political upheaval, and currency fluctuations are clear and present, yet the company says it has hedged against these threats by diversifying investments. However, according to Beach, success will depend on creating a globally managed company capable of understanding and participating in foreign market environments. Consequently, in 1996, he initiated a major transformation in Unocal's management systems, beginning by relocating its headquarters from its stately downtown offices to a small, highly efficient suite near the Los Angeles International Airport. Mid-level managers were either repositioned in regional offices, such as Singapore, Istanbul, or Jakarta, or they left the company. The executive core, which had been distinctly Los Angeleno in character, gained a multicultural character, representing Eastern European and Asian group alliances. Subsidiaries in Jakarta, Thailand and Burma took on local names and corporate identities, shedding their American profiles, and Unocal's many foreign alliances have made it part of the communities in which it operates.

In Thailand, Unocal worked on the country's privatization plan to convert its Petroleum Authority of Thailand (PTT) operations into privately owned and operated international oil services. Unocal and the PTT have begun to build pipelines in the Gulf of Thailand linking Unocal's hydrocarbon fields in the nation's rugged peninsula, and a joint venture in Malaysia has begun to open regional energy markets from Myanmar to the Philippines. Surface evaluations have hailed this consortium as a master stroke of strategy; however, related activities have exposed Unocal to strong criticism. Unocal became the largest single U.S. investor in Myanmar as part of the expansion, but Myanmar's military government has languished in political and economic isolation as a result of U.S. legislation aimed at boycotting the country for its unacceptable human-rights practices. Political activists in more than a dozen U.S. states have won passage of legislation barring imports from Myanmar and outlawing private investments there by U.S. firms. Municipal governments in five states have passed boycott laws, as well, and Unocal, together with PepsiCo and several other American companies operating in Myanmar, have become major targets for international pressure groups. PepsiCo bowed to the pressure and moved out of Myanmar, but Unocal has flatly refused to budge.

The company's insistence on remaining in Myanmar, however, is not a vote in support of the country's human-rights record. Indeed, Unocal would find it difficult to withdraw, because it has formed an equity agreement with the giant French petrochemical company Total, which also has substantial pipeline investments with Unocal in the Persian Gulf and southern Asia. Unocal's contracts with Total make it a *de facto* partner of the French government. Moreover, Unocal has invested in public and private interests in Myanmar that spread to five other major Southeast Asian states. But a Unocal representative cites the importance of the company's role in helping the nation's development. "To withdraw and isolate [Myanmar] would have no effect. Questionable human-rights leadership and political practices would continue and perhaps proliferate," she said. "On the other hand, our strength and the fact that we can provide meaningful jobs and ethical international business, encourages changes for the good. Even if every American firm vacated, firms from other nations would welcome the chance to develop [Myanmar] without American competition."

That position doesn't relieve the political or financial risk to Unocal. Ethics and U.S. policies aside, Myanmar lacks a strong track record for keeping its promises. As a closed military state, self-isolated for ideological reasons since the end of World War II, it has few friends anywhere in the world. For years, it was linked to the Soviet Union for aid and military support, and it backed insurgent forces in several neighboring civil conflicts. These situations did not endear the government to potential regional economic allies. However, the country is strategically positioned within the Southeast Asian theater, and it has attracted consideration, with much controversy, for membership in ASEAN.

Unocal holds a rather exposed position in the country, as it does in Uzbekistan, Turkmenistan, and the Balkans. An American company without the legal or political support of its home government can expect little help should the host government decide to freeze its assets, bar currency repatriation, or resort to outright expropriation. Meanwhile, Unocal has tied up several billion dollars in the region while maintaining no safety net at home. Indeed, it faces potentially costly threats from home, and if the company is pushed to the wall by legislation, the chairman says, he will take Unocal out of U.S. control.

Questions

1. What market entry strategies has Unocal used, based on the activities described in the case? Would you classify Unocal as a multinational corporation (MNC)? Why or why not?

2. Identify and discuss the various types of risks faced by Unocal in emerging markets (consider the economic, legal-political, and sociocultural environment). Which risks seem most threatening to the company?

3. What do you think of the Unocal representative's statement that "to withdraw and isolate Myanmar would have no effect" regarding that country's poor human-rights record? Do you believe U.S. companies should stay in such countries in the hope of improving the ethical climate? Discuss.

SOURCE: "Unocal Corporation," from *International Management: Text and Cases*, 143–145, David H. Holt, Copyright © 1998 by Harcourt, Inc. Revised and reprinted by permission of the publisher.

ENDNOTES

1. Evan Ramstad, "Lenova Picks Turin for 'Coming-Out Party': Chinese PC Maker Uses Games to Move Beyond IBM Brand," *The Asian Wall Street Journal* (February 10, 2006): 26; Louise Lee with Peter Burrows and Bruce Einhorn, "Dell May Have to Reboot in China," *BusinessWeek* (November 7, 2005): 46; Evan Ramstad and Gary McWilliams, "Computer Savvy; For Dell, Success in China Tells Tale of Maturing Market," *The Wall Street Journal* (July 5, 2005): A1, A8; and Charles Forelle, "Lenova Taps Dell's Asia Chief as CEO for Next Growth Phase," *The Wall Street Journal* (December 21, 2005): B2.

2. David Kirkpatrick, "One World—For Better or Worse," *Fortune* (November 26, 2001): 74–75.

3. Nilly Ostro-Landau and Hugh D. Menzies, "The New World Economic Order," in *International Business 97/98, Annual Editions*, Fred Maidment, ed. (Guilford, CT: Dushkin Publishing Group, 1997): 24–30; and Murray Weidenbaum, "American Isolationism versus the Global Economy," in *International Business 97/98, Annual Editions*, Fred Maidment, ed. (Guilford CT: Dushkin Publishing Group, 1997): 12–15.

4. Jason Dean, "Upgrade Plan: Long a Low-Tech Player, China Sets Its Sights on Chip Making," *The Wall Street Journal* (February 17, 2004): A1.

5. Pete Engardio, "A New World Economy," *BusinessWeek* (August 22–29, 2005): 52–58.

6. Joseph B. White, "There Are No German or U.S. Companies, Only Successful Ones," *The Wall Street Journal* (May 7, 1998): A1.

7. Ted C. Fishman, "How China Will Change Your Business," *Inc. Magazine* (March 2005): 70–84; and Stephen Baker, "The Bridges Steel Is Building," *BusinessWeek* (June 2, 1997): 39.

8, 9. Figures provided by CXO Media, reported in Steve Ulfelder, "All the Web's a Stage," *CIO* (October 1, 2000): 133–142; and Pete Engardio, "A New World Economy," *BusinessWeek* (August 22–29, 2005): 52–58.

10. Jena McGregor, "A Foreign Affair," *Fast Company* (December 2005): 67–68.

11. Ted C. Fishman, "Half a World Away, An Entrepreneur Grapples With (and Profits from) China's Boom," 79, part of a section titled "How China Will Change Your Business," *Inc Magazine* (March 2005): 70–84.

12. Adam Lashinsky, "Intel Outside," and Patricia Sellers, "Blowing in the Wind," part of a special supplement titled "Fortune 500: The World of Ideas," *Fortune* (July 25, 2005): 127–138.

13. Nancy J. Adler, *International Dimensions of Organizational Behavior,* 4th ed. (Cincinnati, OH: South-Western, 2002): 8–9; William Holstein, Stanley Reed, Jonathan Kapstein, Todd Vogel, and Joseph Weber, "The Stateless Corporation," *BusinessWeek* (May 14, 1990): 98–105; and Richard L. Daft, *Organization Theory and Design* (Cincinnati, OH: South-Western 2005).

14. Dale Buss, "World Class: Non-American CEOs Are Having a Big Impact at Traditional U.S. Companies," *Chief Executive* (April 2004): 44.

15. Phred Dvorak and Merissa Marr, "In Surprise Move, Sony Plans to Hand Reins to a Foreigner," *The Wall Street Journal* (March 7, 2005): A1; Carol Hymowitz, "More American Chiefs Are Taking Top Posts at Overseas Concerns," *The Wall Street Journal* (October 17, 2005): B1; Justin Martin, "The Global CEO: Overseas Experience Is Becoming a Must on Top Executives' Resumes," *Chief Executive* (January–February 2004): 24.

16. Martin, "The Global CEO."

17. Christopher Bartlett, *Managing Across Borders*, 2d ed. (Boston: Harvard Business School Press, 1998); and quote from Buss, "World Class."

18. Daniel W. Drezner, "The Outsourcing Bogeyman," *Foreign Affairs* (May–June 2004).

19. Fishman, "How China Will Change Your Business."

20. Malkin, "Backlash"; Engardio et al., "Is Your Job Next?"

21. Jean Kerr, "Export Strategies," *Small Business Reports* (May 1989): 20–25.

22. Allen P. Roberts Jr., "Localizing the Brand," *Inc.* (October 2005): 54–56; Robert S. Greenberger, "As U.S. Exports Rise, More Workers Benefit," *The Wall Street Journal* (September 10, 1997): A1.

23. Lorrie Grant, "An 'Infinite' Opportunity for Growth," *USA Today* (July 27, 2005); www.usatoday.com.

24. Kathryn Rudie Harrigan, "Managing Joint Ventures," *Management Review* (February 1987): 24–41; and Therese R. Revesz and Mimi Cauley de Da La Sierra, "Competitive Alliances: Forging Ties Abroad," *Management Review* (March 1987): 57–59.

25. Lora Kolodny, "Building a Global Alliance," *Inc.* (September 2005): 48; "Importing Can Help a Firm Expand and Diversify," *Nation's Business* (January 1995): 11.

26. Katz and Malkin, "Battle for the Latin American Net."

27. Anthony Goerzen, "Managing Alliance Networks: Emerging Practices of Multinational Corporations," *Academy of Management Executive* 19, no. 2 (2005): 94–107.

28. Grant, "An 'Infinite' Opportunity for Growth"; Donald Greenlees, "Philip Morris to Buy Indonesian Cigarette Maker," *The New York Times* (March 14, 2005); www.nytimes.com.

29. G. Pascal Zachary, "Dream Factory," *Business 2.0* (June 2005): 96–102; Jothan Sapsford and James T. Areddy, "Why Delphi's Asia Operations Are Booming," *The Wall Street Journal* (October 17, 2005): B1, B4.

30. Fishman, "How China Will Change Your Business."

31. Pete Engardio, "A New World Economy," *BusinessWeek* (August 22–29, 2005): 52–58.

32. David Wighton, "Indian Growth for JPMorgan," *Financial Times* (December 5, 2005): 1, 18.

33. James Flanigan, "Now, High-Tech Work Is Going Abroad," *The New York Times* (November 17, 2005): C6.

34. Pete Engargio and Michael Arndt, "How Cummins Does It," *BusinessWeek* (August 22–29, 2005): 82–84.

35. Cited in Gary Ferraro, *Cultural Anthropology: An Applied Perspective*, 3d ed. (Belmont, CA: West/Wadsworth, 1998): 68.

36. Jim Holt, "Gone Global?" *Management Review* (March 2000): 13.

37. Ibid.

38. "Slogans Often Lose Something in Translation," *The New Mexican* (July 3, 1994): F1, F2.

39. Louis S. Richman, "Global Growth Is on a Tear," in *International Business 97/98, Annual Editions*, Fred Maidment, ed., (Guilford, CT: Dushkin Publishing Group, 1997): 6–11.

40. Amal Kumar Jaj, "United Technologies Looks Far from Home for Growth," *The Wall Street Journal* (May 26, 1994): B4.

41. Engardio, "A New World Economy."

42. Andrew E. Serwer, "McDonald's Conquers the World," *Fortune* (October 17, 1994): 103–116.

43. David W. Conklin, "Analyzing and Managing Country Risks," *Ivey Business Journal* (January–February 2002): 37–41.

44. Bruce Kogut, "Designing Global Strategies: Profiting from Operational Flexibility," *Sloan Management Review* 27 (Fall 1985): 27–38.

45. Ian Bremmer, "Managing Risk in an Unstable World," *Harvard Business Review* (June 2005): 51–60; and Mark Fitzpatrick, "The Definition and Assessment of Political Risk in International Business: A Review of the Literature," *Academy of Management Review* 8 (1983): 249–254.

46. Bremmer, "Managing Risk in an Unstable World."

47. Kevin Sullivan, "Kidnapping Is Growth Industry in Mexico; Businessmen Targeted in Climate of Routine Ransoms, Police Corruption," *The Washington Post* (September 17, 2002): A1.

48. Brian O'Keefe, "Global Brands," *Fortune* (November 26, 2001): 102–110.

49. Conklin, "Analyzing and Managing Country Risks," Nicolas Checa, John Maguire, and Jonathan Barney, "The New World Disorder," *Harvard Business Review* (August 2003): 71–79.

50. See Conklin, "Analyzing and Managing Country Risks."

51. O'Keefe, "Global Brands."

52. Brandon Mitchener, "Border Crossings," *The Wall Street Journal* (November 22, 1999): R41.

53. Barbara Whitaker, "The Web Makes Going Global Easy, Until You Try to Do It," *The New York Times* (September 2000): 20.

54. Geert Hofstede, "The Interaction between National and Organizational Value Systems," *Journal of Management Studies* 22 (1985): 347–357; and Geert Hofstede, "The Cultural Relativity of the Quality of Life Concept," *Academy of Management Review* 9 (1984): 389–398.

55. Geert Hofstede, "Cultural Constraints in Management Theory," *Academy of Management Executive* 7 (1993): 81–94; and G. Hofstede and M. H. Bond, "The Confucian Connection: From Cultural Roots to Economic Growth," *Organizational Dynamics* 16 (1988): 4–21.

56. "Retrospective: *Culture's Consequences*," a collection of articles focusing on Hofstede's work, appeared in *The Academy of Management Executive* 18, no. 1 (February 2004): 72–93. See also Michele J. Gelfand, D. P. S. Bhawuk, Lisa H. Nishii, and David J. Bechtold, "Individualism and Collectivism," in R. J. House, et al., eds., *Culture, Leadership and Organizations: The Globe Study of 62 Societies* (Thousand Oaks, CA: Sage, 2004).

57. Robert J. House, Paul J. Hanges, Mansour Javidan, Peter W. Dorfman, and Vipin Gupta, *Culture, Leadership, and Organizations: The GLOBE Study of 62 Societies* (Thousand Oaks, CA: Sage Publications, 2004); M. Javidan and R. J. House, "Cultural Acumen for the Global Manager: Lessons from Project GLOBE," *Organizational Dynamics* 29, no. 4 (2001): 289–305; and R. J. House, M. Javidan, Paul Hanges, and Peter Dorfman, "Understanding Cultures and Implicit Leadership Theories Across the Globe: An Introduction to Project GLOBE," *Journal of World Business* 37 (2002): 3–10.

58. Chantell E. Nicholls, Henry W. Lane, and Mauricio Brehm Brechu, "Taking Self-Managed Teams to Mexico," *Academy of Management Executive* 13, no. 2 (1999): 15–27; Carl F. Fey and Daniel R. Denison, "Organizational Culture and Effectiveness: Can American Theory Be Applied in Russia?" *Organization Science* 14, no. 6 (November–December 2003): 686–706; Ellen F. Jackofsky, John W. Slocum, Jr., and Sara J. McQuaid, "Cultural Values and the CEO: Alluring Companions?" Academy of Management Executive 2 (1988): 39–49.

59. Terence Jackson, "The Management of People Across Cultures: Valuing People Differently," *Human Resource Management* 41, no. 4 (Winter 2002): 455–475.

60. Carol Hymowitz, "Companies Go Global, But Many Managers Just Don't Travel Well," *The Wall Street Journal* (August 15, 2000): B1.

61. Orla Sheehan, "Managing a Multinational Corporation: Tomorrow's Decision Makers Speak Out," *Fortune* (August 24, 1992): 233; Jonathan Friedland and Louise Lee, "The Wal-Mart Way Sometimes Gets Lost in Translation Overseas," *The Wall Street Journal* (October 8, 1997): A1, A12.

62. Elizabeth Esfahani, "Thinking Locally, Succeeding Globally," *Business 2.0* (December 2005): 96–98.

63. Michael R. Czinkota, Ilkka A. Ronkainen, Michael H. Moffett, and Eugene O. Moynihan, *Global Business* (Fort Worth, TX: The Dryden Press, 1995): 151; and Robert D. Gatewood, Robert R. Taylor, and O. C. Ferrell, *Management* (Burr Ridge, IL: Irwin, 1995): 131–132.

64. "For Richer, for Poorer," *The Economist* (December 1993): 66; Richard Harmsen, "The Uruguay Round: A Boon for the World Economy," *Finance & Development* (March 1995): 24–26; Salil S. Pitroda, "From GATT to WTO: The Institutionalization of World Trade," *Harvard International Review* (Spring 1995): 46–47, 66–67; David H. Holt, *International Management: Text and Cases* (Fort Worth: Dryden, 1998); and www.wto.org (accessed on February 20, 2006).

65. This discussion of WTO is based on William J. Kehoe, "GATT and WTO Facilitating Global Trade," *Journal of Global Business* (Spring 1998): 67–76.

66. "The History of the European Union," www.europa.eu.int/abc/history/index_en.htm (accessed on February 16, 2004).

67. Alan Charles Raul, "World to America: Zip It!" *e-Company Now* (July 2001): 26–29.

68. James Kanter, "EU Watchdog Gets More Teeth: New Powers to Enforce Competition Are Set to Go Into Effect," *The Wall Street Journal* (January 23, 2004): A10.

69. Justin Fox, "Introducing the Euro," *Fortune* (December 19, 2001): 229–236.

70. Lynda Radosevich, "New Money," *CIO Enterprise*, Section 2 (April 15, 1998): 54–58.

71. Barbara Rudolph, "Megamarket," *Time* (August 10, 1992): 43–44.

72. Tapan Munroe, "NAFTA Still a Work in Progress," *Knight Ridder/Tribune News Service* (January 9, 2004); www.contracostatimes.com; and J. S. McClenahan, "NAFTA Works," *IW* (January 10, 2000): 5–6.

73. Amy Barrett, "It's a Small (Business) World," *BusinessWeek* (April 17, 1995): 96–101.

74. Eric Alterman, "A Spectacular Success?" *The Nation* (February 2, 2004): 10; Jeff Faux, "NAFTA at 10: Where Do We Go From Here?" *The Nation* (February 2, 2004): 11; Geri Smith and Cristina Lindblad, "Mexico: Was NAFTA Worth It? A Tale of What Free Trade Can and Cannot Do," *BusinessWeek* (December 22, 2003): 66; Jeffrey Sparshott, "NAFTA Gets Mixed Reviews," *The Washington Times* (December 18, 2003): C10; and Munroe, "NAFTA Is Still Work in Progress."

75. Munroe, "NAFTA Is Still Work In Progress"; Jeffrey Sparshott, "NAFTA Gets Mixed Reviews," *The Washington Times* (December 18, 2003): C10; Amy Borrus, "A Free-Trade Milestone, with Many More Miles to Go," *BusinessWeek* (August 24, 1992): 30–31.

76. Jenalie Moreno, "Treaty Rolls Out; High Hopes Greet CAFTA's Entrance," *Houston Chronicle* (January 1, 2006): 1.

77. C. Sims, "Chile Will Enter a Big South American Free-Trade Bloc," *The New York Times* (June 26, 1996): C2; "NAFTA: Five-Year Anniversary," *Latin Trade* (January 1999): 44–45; and Jorge L. Arrizurieta, "Support for Miami Growing," *South Florida Sun-Sentinel* (January 30, 2006): A23.

78. This review is based on Jyoti Thottam, "Is Your Job Going Abroad?" *Time* (March 1, 2004): 26–36; and Pete Engardio, Aaron Bernstein, and Manjeet Kripalani, "Is Your Job Next?" *BusinessWeek* (February 3, 2003): 50–60.

79. Reported in "IBM Data Give Rare Look at Sensitive 'Offshoring' Plans," *CNNMoney* (January 19, 2004); www.money.cnn.com (accessed on January 19, 2004).

80. Thottam, "Is Your Job Going Abroad?"

81. Jerry Useem, "There's Something Happening Here," *Fortune* (May 15, 2000): Paul Magnusson, "Meet Free Traders' Worst Nightmare," *BusinessWeek* (March 20, 2000): 113–118; Elisabeth Malkin, "Backlash," *BusinessWeek* (April 24, 2000): 38–44.

82. See, for example, Alan Greenspan, "International Trade: Globalization vs. Protectionism," address printed in *Vital Speeches of the Day* (April 15, 2001): 386–388.

83. Michael Schroeder and Timothy Aeppel, "Skilled Workers Sway Politicians with Fervor Against Free Trade," *The Wall Street Journal* (December 10, 2003): A1, A11.

84. World Bank and *Fortune* magazine, as reported in Paul DeGrauwe, University of Leuven and Belgian Senate, and Filip Camerman, Belgian Senate, "How Big Are the Big Multinational Companies?" working paper (2002).

85. Howard V. Perlmutter, "The Tortuous Evolution of the Multinational Corporation," *Columbia Journal of World Business* (January–February 1969): 9–18; and Youram Wind, Susan P. Douglas, and Howard V. Perlmutter, "Guidelines for Developing International Marketing Strategies," *Journal of Marketing* (April 1973): 14–23.

86. Morgan W. McCall Jr. and George P. Hollenbeck, "Global Fatalities: When International Executives Derail," *Ivey Business Journal* (May–June 2002): 75–78.

87. The discussion of cultural intelligence is based on P. Christopher Earley and Elaine Mosakowski, "Cultural Intelligence," *Harvard Business Review* (October 2004): 139; Ilan Alon and James M. Higgins, "Global Leadership Success Through Emotional and Cultural Intelligence," *Business Horizons* 48 (2005): 501–512; P. C. Earley and Soon Ang, *Cultural Intelligence: Individual Actions Across Cultures* (Stanford, CA: Stanford Business Books); and David C. Thomas and Kerr Inkson, *Cultural Intelligence* (San Francisco: Berrett-Koehler, 2004).

88. These components are from Earley and Mosakowski, "Cultural Intelligence."

89. Karl Moore, "Great Global Managers," *Across the Board* (May–June 2003): 40–43.

90. Richard E. Nisbett, *The Geography of Thought: How Asians and Westerners Think Differently . . . and Why* (New York: The Free Press, 2003), reported in Sharon Begley, "East vs. West: One Sees the Big Picture, The Other Is Focused," *The Wall Street Journal* (March 28, 2003): B1.

91. Robert T. Moran and John R. Riesenberger, *The Global Challenge* (London: McGraw-Hill, 1994): 251–262.

92. Valerie Frazee, "Keeping Up on Chinese Culture," *Global Workforce* (October 1996): 16–17; and Jack Scarborough, "Comparing Chinese and Western Cultural Roots: Why 'East Is East and . . . ,'" *Business Horizons* (November–December 1998): 15–24.

93. Mansour Javidan and Ali Dastmalchian, "Culture and Leadership in Iran: The Land of Individual Achievers, Strong Family Ties, and Powerful Elite," *Academy of Management Executive* 17, no. 4 (2003): 127–142.

94. Randall S. Schuler, Susan E. Jackson, Ellen Jackofsky, and John W. Slocum, Jr., "Managing Human Resources in Mexico: A Cultural Understanding," *Business Horizons* (May–June 1996): 55–61.

95. Xu Huang and Evert Van De Vliert, "Where Intrinsic Job Satisfaction Fails to Work: National Moderators of Intrinsic Motivation," *Journal of Organizational Behavior* 24 (2003): 159–179.

96. Shari Caudron, "Lessons from HR Overseas," *Personnel Journal* (February 1995): 88.

97. Reported in Begley, "East vs. West."

98. Lee et al., "Dell May Have to Reboot in China"; and Ramstad and McWilliams, "Computer Savvy."

CHAPTER 5

CHAPTER OUTLINE

Manager's Challenge

What Is Managerial Ethics?

Criteria for Ethical Decision Making

Utilitarian Approach

Individualism Approach

Moral-Rights Approach

Justice Approach

Factors Affecting Ethical Choices

The Manager

The Organization

What Is Social Responsibility?

Organizational Stakeholders

The Ethic of Sustainability and the Natural Environment

Evaluating Corporate Social Responsibility

Economic Responsibilities

Legal Responsibilities

Ethical Responsibilities

Discretionary Responsibilities

Managing Company Ethics and Social Responsibility

Ethical Individuals

Ethical Leadership

Organizational Structures and Systems

Ethical Challenges in Turbulent Times

The Business Case for Ethics and Social Responsibility

Economic Performance

LEARNING OBJECTIVES

After studying this chapter, you should be able to:

1. Define ethics and explain how ethical behavior relates to behavior governed by law and free choice.

2. Explain the utilitarian, individualism, moral-rights, and justice approaches for evaluating ethical behavior.

3. Describe how both individual and organizational factors shape ethical decision making.

4. Define corporate social responsibility and how to evaluate it along economic, legal, ethical, and discretionary criteria.

5. Describe four organizational approaches to environmental responsibility, and explain the philosophy of sustainability.

6. Discuss how ethical organizations are created through ethical leadership and organizational structures and systems.

7. Identify important stakeholders for an organization and discuss how managers balance the interests of various stakeholders.

ETHICS AND SOCIAL RESPONSIBILITY

MANAGER'S CHALLENGE

Eric Corrigan and Thomas Chen have just been called to the boss's office. They're expecting congratulations for a job well done. In the past year, both have received praise and generous bonuses for their work as successful and respected investment bankers at Bank of America. Acting on a tip from a rival banker, Corrigan and Chen contacted Capital One to try to get Bank of America in on a pending merger deal that had yet to be publicly announced. That kind of aggressive move to secure an edge is what made their careers—and helped put Bank of America on the map. The tip came from Thomas Heath, a banker at rival JPMorgan, who recently agreed to take his flourishing practice to Bank of America. In discussions with Corrigan, Heath revealed in strict confidence that JPMorgan was advising a regional bank in its merger talks with Capital One. Corrigan and his colleague Chen had already heard rumors about the deal, and now that they had confirmation from Heath, Chen placed a call to his contact at Capital One. Thus we find the two reaching the executive suite prepared for accolades. A few minutes later, the stunned bankers are hearing that they've been fired. Pressed for clarification, the boss admits they've broken no regulations, and Corrigan and Chen argue that their actions were simply part of the way all bankers do business. Meanwhile, in the executive suite at J.PMorgan, Thomas Heath is also on the hot seat.[1]

139

> **TAKE A MOMENT**
>
> As a potential manager, what do you think Eric Corrigan and Thomas Chen did wrong? If you were Corrigan and Chen's boss, would you reconsider your judgment or stick to your decision to fire them? What would you do about Thomas Heath?

The situation at Bank of America illustrates how difficult ethical issues can be and symbolizes the growing importance of discussing ethics and social responsibility. Managers often face situations in which it is difficult to determine what is right. Thus, ethics has always been a concern for managers. However, recent widespread moral lapses and corporate financial scandals bring the topic to the forefront and pressure managers in both large and small companies to put ethics near the top of their priorities list. Bank of America is not alone in taking a stronger stand against ethical lapses that would once have been considered "the standard way of doing business." Corporations are rushing to adopt stringent codes of ethics, strengthen ethical and legal safeguards, and develop socially responsible policies.

Every decade sees its share of corporate, political, and social villains, but the pervasiveness of ethical lapses in the early 2000s was astounding. Once-respected firms such as Enron, Arthur Andersen, WorldCom, Tyco, and HealthSouth became synonymous with greed, deceit, and financial chicanery. No wonder a public poll found that 79 percent of respondents believe questionable business practices are widespread. Fewer than one-third said they think most CEOs are honest.[2] More-over, more than 20 percent of U.S. employees surveyed report having first-hand knowledge of managers making false or misleading promises to customers, discriminating in hiring or promotions, and violating employees' rights.[3]

However, positive news can be found too. After Hurricane Katrina devastated the Gulf Coast, Kaiser Permanente donated $2 million to the Centers for Disease Control and Prevention Foundation, plus set aside an additional $1 million for long-term recovery efforts. The insurance company St. Paul Travelers works with neighborhood organizations to fund financial literacy programs in low-income areas. And Computer Associates each year pairs 75 employee volunteers with 75 employees from major customers to build playgrounds in needy areas.[4] A number of companies have begun tying managers' pay to ethical factors such as how well they treat employees or how effectively they live up to the stated corporate values.

This chapter expands on the ideas about environment, corporate culture, and the international environment discussed in Chapters 3 and 4. We first focus on the topic of ethical values, which builds on the idea of corporate culture. Then we examine corporate relationships to the external environment as reflected in social responsibility. Ethics and social responsibility are hot topics in corporate America. We will discuss fundamental approaches that help managers think through ethical issues. Understanding ethical approaches helps managers build a solid foundation on which to base future decision making.

WHAT IS MANAGERIAL ETHICS?

Ethics is difficult to define in a precise way. In a general sense, **ethics** is the code of moral principles and values that governs the behaviors of a person or group with respect to what is right or wrong. Ethics sets standards as to what is good or bad in conduct and decision making.[5] Ethics deals with internal values that are a part of corporate culture and shapes decisions concerning social responsibility with respect to the external environment. An ethical issue is present in a situation when the actions of a person or organization may harm or benefit others.[6]

Ethics can be more clearly understood when compared with behaviors governed by laws and by free choice. Exhibit 5.1 illustrates that human behavior falls into three categories. The first is codified law, in which values and standards are written into the legal system and enforceable in the courts. In this area, lawmakers set rules that people and corporations must follow in a certain way, such as obtaining licenses for cars or paying corporate taxes. The courts alleged that Enron executives broke the law, for example, by manipulating financial results, such as using off-balance-sheet partnerships to improperly create income and hide debt.[7] The domain of free choice is at the opposite end of the scale and pertains to behavior about which the law has no say and for which an individual or organization enjoys complete freedom. A manager's choice of where to eat lunch or a music company's choice of the number of CDs to release is an example of free choice.

Between these domains lies the area of ethics. This domain has no specific laws, yet it does have standards of conduct based on shared principles and values about moral conduct that guide an individual or company. Executives at Enron, for example, did not break any specific laws by encouraging employees to buy

ethics The code of moral principles and values that governs the behaviors of a person or group with respect to what is right or wrong.

EXHIBIT   5.1

Three Domains of Human Action

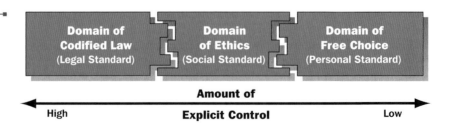

more shares of stock even when they believed the company was in financial trouble and the price of the shares was likely to decline. However, this behavior was a clear violation of the executives' ethical responsibilities to employees.[8] These managers were acting based on their own interests rather than their duties to employees and other stakeholders. In the domain of free choice, obedience is strictly to oneself. In the domain of codified law, obedience is to laws prescribed by the legal system. In the domain of ethical behavior, obedience is to unenforceable norms and standards about which the individual or company is aware. An ethically acceptable decision is both legally and morally acceptable to the larger community.

Many companies and individuals get into trouble with the simplified view that choices are governed by either law or free choice. It leads people to mistakenly assume that if it's not illegal, it must be ethical, as if this third domain didn't exist.[9] A better option is to recognize the domain of ethics and accept moral values as a powerful force for good that can regulate behaviors both inside and outside corporations. As principles of ethics and social responsibility are more widely recognized, companies can use codes of ethics and their corporate cultures to govern behavior, thereby eliminating the need for additional laws and avoiding the problems of unfettered choice.

Because ethical standards are not codified, disagreements and dilemmas about proper behavior often occur. Ethics is always about making decisions, and some issues are difficult to resolve. An **ethical dilemma** arises in a situation concerning right or wrong when values are in conflict.[10] Right and wrong cannot be clearly identified.

The individual who must make an ethical choice in an organization is the *moral agent*.[11] Consider the dilemmas facing a moral agent in the following situations:

:: Your company requires a terrorist watch list screening for all new customers, which takes approximately 24 hours from the time an order is placed. You can close a lucrative deal with a potential long-term customer if you agree to ship the products overnight, even though that means the required watch list screening will have to be done after the fact.[12]

:: As a sales manager for a major pharmaceuticals company, you've been asked to promote a new drug that costs $2,500 per dose. You've read the reports saying the drug is only 1 percent more effective than an alternate drug that costs less than one-fourth as much. Can you in good conscience aggressively promote the $2,500-per-dose drug? If you don't, could lives be lost that might have been saved with that 1 percent increase in effectiveness?

:: Your company is hoping to build a new overseas manufacturing plant. You could save about $5 million by not installing standard pollution control equipment that is required in the United States. The plant will employ many local workers in a poor country where jobs are scarce. Your research shows that pollutants from the factory could potentially damage the local fishing industry. Yet building the factory with the pollution control equipment will likely make the plant too expensive to build.[13]

:: You are the accounting manager of a division that is $15,000 below profit targets. Approximately $20,000 of office supplies were delivered on December 21. The accounting rule is to pay

ethical dilemma A situation that arises when all alternative choices or behaviors are deemed undesirable because of potentially negative consequences, making it difficult to distinguish right from wrong.

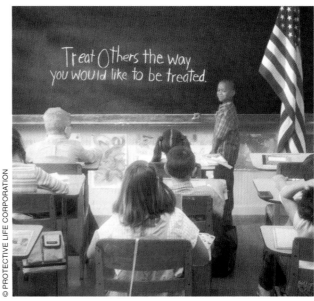

© PROTECTIVE LIFE CORPORATION

CONCEPT CONNECTION Protective Life Corporation shows its commitment to ethics through its corporate strategy: "Offer great products at highly competitive prices and provide the kind of attentive service we'd hope to get from others." Treating others the way you want to be treated is one approach to making ethically-responsible decisions and handling **ethical dilemmas.** However, insurance companies often have to rely on a **utilitarian approach** to ethical decision making that considers how to provide the greatest good to the greatest number of policyholders.

expenses when incurred. The division general manager asks you not to record the invoice until February.

:: You have been collaborating with a fellow manager on an important project. One afternoon, you walk into his office a bit earlier than scheduled and see sexually explicit images on his computer monitor. The company has a zero-tolerance sexual harassment policy, as well as strict guidelines regarding personal use of the Internet. However, your colleague was in his own office and not bothering anyone else.[14]

These kinds of dilemmas and issues fall squarely in the domain of ethics. Now let's turn to approaches to ethical decision making that provide criteria for understanding and resolving these difficult issues.

CRITERIA FOR ETHICAL DECISION MAKING

Most ethical dilemmas involve a conflict between the needs of the part and the whole—the individual versus the organization or the organization versus society as a whole. For example, should a company implement mandatory alcohol and drug testing for employees, which might benefit the organization as a whole but reduce the individual freedom of employees? Or should products that fail to meet tough FDA standards be exported to other countries where government standards are lower, benefiting the company but potentially harming world citizens? Sometimes ethical decisions entail a conflict between two groups. For example, should the potential for local health problems resulting from a company's effluents take precedence over the jobs it creates as the town's leading employer?

Managers faced with these kinds of tough ethical choices often benefit from a normative strategy—one based on norms and values—to guide their decision making. Normative ethics uses several approaches to describe values for guiding ethical decision making. Four of these approaches that are relevant to managers are the utilitarian approach, individualism approach, moral-rights approach, and justice approach.[15]

Utilitarian Approach

The **utilitarian approach**, espoused by the nineteenth-century philosophers Jeremy Bentham and John Stuart Mill, holds that moral behavior produces the greatest good for the greatest number. Under this approach, a decision maker is expected to consider the effect of each decision alternative on all parties and select the one that optimizes the satisfaction for the greatest number of people. Because actual computations can be complex, simplifying them is considered appropriate. For example, a simple economic frame of reference could be used by calculating dollar costs and dollar benefits. Also, a decision could be made that considers only the people who are directly affected by the decision, not those who are indirectly affected. The utilitarian ethic is cited as the basis for the recent trend among companies to monitor employee use of the Internet and police personal habits such as alcohol and tobacco consumption, because such behavior affects the entire workplace.[16] The utilitarian ethic can also be used to explain managers' decision at Northfield Laboratories to continue clinical trials of a product that has showed some troubling results.

utilitarian approach The ethical concept that moral behaviors produce the greatest good for the greatest number.

Northfield Laboratories

During the first clinical trial of a blood substitute called PolyHeme, 10 out of 81 patients who received the product suffered a heart attack within 7 days. Northfield Laboratories quietly shut down the trial, without disclosing the worrisome results. Managers and scientists at Northfield reasoned that the heart attacks were likely the result of doctor inexperience with the product rather than a problem with the product itself. Now, with FDA approval, Northfield is involved in a new clinical trial, testing PolyHeme on hundreds of trauma patients, often without their consent.

Some doctors have expressed concern about the push by Northfield to continue testing, particularly without publicly disclosing the earlier results. Northfield managers, though, argue that the potential benefits of PolyHeme for patients who don't have access to human blood, such as trauma patients in rural areas or soldiers on the battlefield, make the risks worth it. "Our experience suggests the risk-benefit balance is in the patients' favor," said CEO Steven Gould. Indeed, scientists have been searching for a safe, workable blood substitute for more than 50 years. Artificial blood eliminates the need for matching blood types, reduces the risk of hepatitis and HIV infection, and has a far longer shelf life than human blood. Because blood has to be refrigerated, for example, it usually can't be carried into combat. In addition, human blood goes bad in about 42 days, unlike PolyHeme which lasts a year or more. Soldiers who might otherwise die on the battlefield could be saved with an effective blood substitute.[17]

By emphasizing the potential benefits to many over the risks to a few, Northfield managers reflect a decision-making approach based in the utilitarian ethic. The FDA reflects a utilitarian approach as well by allowing experimental treatments on trauma patients who are frequently incapable of giving informed consent. A spokesperson said that without the FDA rule allowing such trials, experiments would be impossible and the larger society wouldn't benefit from advances in trauma care.

Individualism Approach

The **individualism approach** contends that acts are moral when they promote the individual's best long-term interests. Individual self-direction is paramount, and external forces that restrict self-direction should be severely limited.[18] Individuals calculate the best long-term advantage to themselves as a measure of a decision's goodness. The action that is intended to produce a greater ratio of good to bad for the individual compared with other alternatives is the right one to perform. In theory, with everyone pursuing self-direction, the greater good is ultimately served because people learn to accommodate each other in their own long-term interest. *Individualism* is believed to lead to honesty and integrity because that works best in the long run. Lying and cheating for immediate self-interest just causes business associates to lie and cheat in return. Thus, individualism ultimately leads to behavior toward others that fits standards of behavior people want toward themselves.[19] One value of understanding this approach is to recognize short-term variations if they are proposed. People might argue for short-term self-interest based on individualism, but that misses the point. Because individualism is easily misinterpreted to support immediate self-gain, it is not popular in the highly organized and group-oriented society of today. Dozens of disgraced top executives from WorldCom, Enron, Tyco, and other companies demonstrate the flaws of the individualism approach. This approach is closest to the domain of free choice described in Exhibit 5.1.

Moral-Rights Approach

The **moral-rights approach** asserts that human beings have fundamental rights and liberties that cannot be taken away by an individual's decision. Thus, an ethically correct decision is one that best maintains the rights of those affected by it.

Six moral rights should be considered during decision making:

1. *The right of free consent.* Individuals are to be treated only as they knowingly and freely consent to be treated.

2. *The right to privacy.* Individuals can choose to do as they please away from work and have control of information about their private life.

3. *The right of freedom of conscience.* Individuals may refrain from carrying out any order that violates their moral or religious norms.

individualism approach
The ethical concept that acts are moral when they promote the individual's best long-term interests, which ultimately leads to the greater good.

moral-rights approach
The ethical concept that moral decisions are those that best maintain the rights of those people affected by them.

4. *The right of free speech.* Individuals may criticize truthfully the ethics or legality of actions of others.

5. *The right to due process.* Individuals have a right to an impartial hearing and fair treatment.

6. *The right to life and safety.* Individuals have a right to live without endangerment or violation of their health and safety.

To make ethical decisions, managers need to avoid interfering with the fundamental rights of others. Northfield's clinical trials on trauma patients described earlier, for example, might be construed by some people to violate the right to free consent. A decision to eavesdrop on employees violates the right to privacy. Sexual harassment is unethical because it violates the right to freedom of conscience. The right of free speech would support whistle-blowers who call attention to illegal or inappropriate actions within a company.

Justice Approach

The **justice approach** holds that moral decisions must be based on standards of equity, fairness, and impartiality. Three types of justice are of concern to managers. **Distributive justice** requires that different treatment of people not be based on arbitrary characteristics. Individuals who are similar in ways relevant to a decision should be treated similarly. Thus, men and women should not receive different salaries if they are performing the same job. However, people who differ in a substantive way, such as job skills or job responsibility, can be treated differently in proportion to the differences in skills or responsibility among them. This difference should have a clear relationship to organizational goals and tasks.

Procedural justice requires that rules be administered fairly. Rules should be clearly stated and be consistently and impartially enforced.

Compensatory justice argues that individuals should be compensated for the cost of their injuries by the party responsible. Moreover, individuals should not be held responsible for matters over which they have no control.

The justice approach is closest to the thinking underlying the domain of law in Exhibit 5.1, because it assumes that justice is applied through rules and regulations. This theory does not require complex calculations such as those demanded by a utilitarian approach, nor does it justify self-interest as the individualism approach does. Managers are expected to define attributes on which different treatment of employees is acceptable. Questions such as how minority workers should be compensated for past discrimination are extremely difficult. However, this approach does justify the ethical behavior of efforts to correct past wrongs, playing fair under the rules, and insisting on job-relevant differences as the basis for different levels of pay or promotion opportunities. Most of the laws guiding human resource management (Chapter 12) are based on the justice approach.

Understanding these various approaches is only a first step; managers still have to consider how to apply them. The approaches offer general principles that managers can recognize as useful in making ethical decisions.

FACTORS AFFECTING ETHICAL CHOICES

When managers are accused of lying, cheating, or stealing, the blame is usually placed on the individual or on the company situation. Most people believe that individuals make ethical choices because of individual integrity, which is true, but it is not the whole story. Ethical or unethical business practices usually reflect the values, attitudes, beliefs, and behavior patterns of the organizational culture; thus, ethics is as much an organizational as a personal issue.[20] Let's examine how both the manager and the organization shape ethical decision making.[21]

justice approach The ethical concept that moral decisions must be based on standards of equity, fairness, and impartiality.

distributive justice The concept that different treatment of people should not be based on arbitrary characteristics. In the case of substantive differences, people should be treated differently in proportion to the differences among them.

procedural justice The concept that rules should be clearly stated and consistently and impartially enforced.

compensatory justice The concept that individuals should be compensated for the cost of their injuries by the party responsible and also that individuals should not be held responsible for matters over which they have no control.

Many of today's top executives put a renewed emphasis on ethics in light of serious ethical lapses that tarnished the reputations and hurt the performance of previously respected and successful companies. Yet keeping an organization in ethical line is an ongoing challenge, and it requires that people at all levels be willing to stand up for what they think is right. Challenging the boss or other senior leaders on potentially unethical behaviors is particularly unnerving for most people. Here are some tips for talking to the boss about an ethically questionable decision or action. Following these guidelines can increase the odds that you'll be heard and your opinions will be seriously considered.

:: **Do your research.** Marshall any facts and figures that support your position on the issue at hand, and develop an alternative policy or course of action that you can suggest at the appropriate time. Prepare succinct answers to any questions you anticipate being asked about your plan.

:: **Begin the meeting by giving your boss the floor.** Make sure you really do understand what the decision or policy is and the reasons behind it. Ask open-ended questions, and listen actively, showing through both your responses and your body language that you're seriously listening and trying to understand the other person's position. In particular, seek out information about what the senior manager sees as the decision or policy's benefits as well as any potential downsides. It'll give you information you can use later to highlight how your plan can produce similar benefits while avoiding the potential disadvantages.

:: **Pay attention to your word choice and demeanor.** No matter how strongly you feel about the matter, don't rant and rave about it. You're more likely to be heard if you remain calm, objective, and professional. Try to disagree without making it personal. Avoid phrases such as "You're wrong," "You can't," "You should," or

"How could you?" to prevent triggering the other person's automatic defense mechanisms.

:: **Take care how you suggest your alternative solution.** You can introduce your plan with phrases such as "Here's another way to look at this" or "What would you think about . . . ?" Check for your superior's reactions both by explicitly asking for feedback and by being sensitive to body language clues. Point out the potential negative consequences of implementing decisions that might be construed as unethical by customers, shareholders, suppliers, or the public.

:: **Be patient.** Don't demand a resolution on the spot. During your conversation, you may realize that your plan needs some work, or your boss might just need time to digest the information and opinions you've presented. It's often a good idea to ask for a follow-up meeting.

If the decision or action being considered is clearly unethical or potentially illegal, and this meeting doesn't provide a quick resolution, you might need to take your concerns to higher levels, or even blow the whistle to someone outside the organization who can make sure the organization stays in line. However, most managers don't want to take actions that will harm the organization, its people, or the community. In many cases, questionable ethical issues can be resolved by open and honest communication. That, however, requires that people have the courage—and develop the skills—to confront their superiors in a calm and rational way.

SOURCE: Kevin Daley,"How to Disagree: Go Up Against Your Boss or a Senior Executive and Live to Tell the Tale," *T&D* (April 2004); Diane Moore,"How to Disagree with Your Boss—and Keep Your Job," *Toronto Star* (November 12, 2003); "How to Disagree with Your Boss," *WikiHow,* http://wiki.ehow.com/Disagree-With-Your-Boss; and "How to Confront Your Boss Constructively," *The Buzz* (October 23–29, 1996), www.hardatwork.com/Buzz/ten.html.

The Manager

Managers bring specific personality and behavioral traits to the job. Personal needs, family influence, and religious background all shape a manager's value system. Specific personality characteristics, such as ego strength, self-confidence, and a strong sense of independence, may enable managers to make ethical decisions.

One important personal trait is the stage of moral development.[22] A simplified version of one model of personal moral development is shown in Exhibit 5.2. At the *preconventional level*, individuals are concerned with external rewards and

EXHIBIT   5.2

Three Levels of Personal
Moral Development

Level 3: Postconventional

Follows self-chosen principles of justice and right. Aware that people hold different values and seeks creative solutions to ethical dilemmas. Balances concern for individual with concern for common good.

Level 2: Conventional

Lives up to expectations of others. Fulfills duties and obligations of social system. Upholds laws.

Level 1: Preconventional

Follows rules to avoid punishment. Acts in own interest. Obedience for its own sake.

Leadership Style:	Autocratic/coercive	Guiding/encouraging, team oriented	Transforming, or servant leadership
Employee Behavior:	Task accomplishment	Work group collaboration	Empowered employees, full participation

SOURCE: Based on L. Kohlberg, "Moral Stages and Moralization: The Cognitive-Developmental Approach," in Moral Development and Behavior: Theory, Research, and Social Issues, ed. T. Lickona (New York: Holt, Rinehart, and Winston, 1976): 31–53; and Jill W. Graham, "Leadership, Moral Development and Citizenship Behavior," Business Ethics Quarterly 5, no. 1 (January 1995): 43–54.

punishments and obey authority to avoid detrimental personal consequences. In an organizational context, this level may be associated with managers who use an autocratic or coercive leadership style, with employees oriented toward dependable accomplishment of specific tasks.

At level two, called the *conventional level*, people learn to conform to the expectations of good behavior as defined by colleagues, family, friends, and society. Meeting social and interpersonal obligations is important. Work group collaboration is the preferred manner for accomplishment of organizational goals, and managers use a leadership style that encourages interpersonal relationships and cooperation.

At the *postconventional*, or *principled* level, individuals are guided by an internal set of values and standards and will even disobey rules or laws that violate these principles. Internal values become more important than the expectations of significant others. This chapter's Manager's Shoptalk gives some tips for how postconventional managers can effectively challenge their superiors concerning questionable ethical matters. One example of the postconventional or principle approach comes from World War II. When the *USS Indianapolis* sank after being torpedoed, one Navy pilot disobeyed orders and risked his life to save men who were being picked off by sharks. The pilot was operating from the highest level of moral development in attempting the rescue despite a direct order from superiors. When managers operate from this highest level of development, they use transformative or servant leadership, focusing on the needs of followers and encouraging others to think for themselves and to engage in higher levels of moral reasoning. Employees are empowered and given opportunities for constructive participation in governance of the organization.

The great majority of managers operate at level two. A few have not advanced beyond level one. Only about 20 percent of American adults reach the level-three stage of moral development. People at level three are able to act in an independent, ethical manner regardless of expectations from others inside or outside the organization. Managers at level three of moral development will make ethical decisions whatever the organizational consequences for them.

■ **TAKE A MOMENT**

As a new manager, strive for a high level of personal moral development. To get some idea of your own level of manager courage and moral development, complete the items in the New Manager Self-Test on page 148. As you read through this text be sure to practice resolving the ethical dilemmas at the end of each chapter and hone your skills in using the various ethical decision frameworks.

© ROS WURZER/ASSOCIATED PRESS

One interesting study indicates that most researchers fail to account for the different ways in which women view social reality and develop psychologically and have thus consistently classified women as being stuck at lower levels of development. Researcher Carol Gilligan suggested that the moral domain be enlarged to include responsibility and care in relationships. Women may, in general, perceive moral complexities more astutely than men and make moral decisions based not on a set of absolute rights and wrongs but on principles of not causing harm to others.[23]

Globalization makes ethical issues even more complicated for today's managers.[24] For example, although tolerance for bribery is waning, bribes are still considered a normal part of doing business in many foreign countries. Transparency International, an international organization that monitors corruption, publishes an annual report ranking countries according to how many bribes are offered by their international businesses. Exhibit 5.3 shows results of the organization's

A score of 10 represents zero propensity to pay bribes, while a score of 0 reflects very high levels of bribery.

EXHIBIT 5.3

The Transparency International Bribe Payers Index 2002

SOURCE: Transparency International, *www.transparency.org*.

Rank		Score	Rank		Score
1	Australia	8.5	12	France	5.5
2	Sweden	8.4	13	United States	5.3
2 (tie)	Switzerland	8.4	13 (tie)	Japan	5.3
4	Austria	8.2	15	Malaysia	4.3
5	Canada	8.1	15 (tie)	Hong Kong	4.3
6	Netherlands	7.8	17	Italy	4.1
6 (tie)	Belgium	7.8	18	South Korea	3.9
8	United Kingdom	6.9	19	Taiwan	3.8
9	Singapore	6.3	20	People's Republic of China	3.5
9 (tie)	Germany	6.3	21	Russia	3.2
11	Spain	5.8			

MANAGER COURAGE

It probably won't happen right away, but soon enough in your duties as a new manager you will be confronted with a situation that will test the strength of your moral beliefs or your sense of justice. Are your ready? To find out, think about times when you were part of a student or work group. To what extent does each of the following statements characterize your behavior? Please answer each of the following items as Mostly True or Mostly False for you.

	Mostly True	Mostly False
1. I risked substantial personal loss to achieve the vision.	___	___
2. I took personal risks to defend my beliefs.	___	___
3. I would say no to inappropriate things even if I had a lot to lose.	___	___
4. My significant actions were linked to higher values.	___	___
5. I easily acted against the opinions and approval of others.	___	___
6. I quickly told people the truth as I saw it, even when it was negative.	___	___
7. I spoke out against group or organizational injustice.	___	___

	Mostly True	Mostly False
8. I acted according to my conscience even if I would lose stature.	___	___

INTERPRETATION: Each question pertains to some aspect of displaying courage in a group situation, which often reflects a person's level of **moral development.** A person at the **postconventional** level might answer the questions as Mostly True, and someone at a **preconventional** level might answer many as Mostly False. Think about what influences your moral behavior and decisions, such as need for success or approval. Study the behavior of others you consider to be moral individuals. How might you increase your courage as a new manager?

SCORING: Count up the number of checks for Mostly True. If you scored five or more, congratulations! That behavior would enable you to become a courageous manager about moral issues. A score below four indicates that you may avoid difficult issues or have not been in situations that challenged your moral courage. Study the specific questions for which you scored Mostly True and Mostly False to learn more about your specific strengths and weaknesses.

most recent available report. International businesses based in countries such as Russia, China, Taiwan, and South Korea were found to be using bribes "on an exceptional and intolerable scale." However, multinational firms in the United States, Japan, France, and Spain also revealed a relatively high propensity to pay bribes overseas.[25]

American managers working in foreign countries need sensitivity and an openness to other systems, as well as the fortitude to resolve these difficult issues. Companies that don't oil the wheels of contract negotiations in foreign countries can put themselves at a competitive disadvantage, yet managers walk a fine line when doing deals overseas. Although U.S. laws allow certain types of payments, tough federal antibribery laws are also in place. Goldman Sachs got preapproval from the U.S. Justice Department and the Securities and Exchange Commission (SEC) before agreeing to pay a $67 million fee to Beijing power brokers to facilitate a joint venture in China.[26] However, many other companies, including Monsanto, Schering-Plough, and IBM, have gotten into trouble with the SEC for using incentives to facilitate foreign deals.

The Organization

Rarely can ethical or unethical corporate actions be attributed solely to the personal values of a single manager. The values adopted within the organization are highly important, especially when we understand that most people are at the level-two stage of moral development, which means they believe their duty is to fulfill obligations and expectations of others. Consider, for example, how David Myers slid into trouble at WorldCom, which disintegrated in an $11 billion fraud scandal.

WorldCom

WorldCom started out as a small long-distance company and rapidly became a dazzling star during the late 1990s Wall Street telecom boom. Just as rapidly, it all came crashing down as one executive after another was hauled away on conspiracy and securities fraud charges.

For former controller David Myers, now awaiting trial, one small, wrong step put him on a slippery slope to charges of securities fraud and probable jail time. In early 2001, with the telecom industry in a slump, top executives at WorldCom were scrambling to meet Wall Street's expectations for the quarter. CEO Bernard Ebbers and chief financial officer Scott Sullivan asked that Myers reclassify some of the company's biggest expenses—to the tune of about $828 million—that would reduce expenses and boost the company's earnings for the quarter. Myers says now, "I didn't think it was the right thing to do, but I had been asked by Scott to do it." The controller reasoned that he was only doing what his boss asked, and he believed Scott's explanations that the adjustments would straighten out the company's problems.

The problems, though, just got worse. Myers, as well as accountants Buford Yates, Betty Vinson, and Troy Normand, who acted on his orders, all expressed misgivings but continued to make increasingly irregular adjustments over the course of six quarters, clinging to a hope that each would be the last.

Top executives persuaded these managers, who were all known as hardworking, dedicated employees, that their gimmicks would help pull WorldCom out of its troubles and get everything back to normal. The lower-level managers rationalized that if Myers and the chief financial officer thought the transfers and other gimmicks were all right, they didn't have the right to question it. When WorldCom's problems exploded into public view, Myers, Yates, Normand, and Vinson found themselves in the middle of one of the largest financial fraud cases in corporate history. All eventually pled guilty to conspiracy and securities fraud, which will likely result in jail time.[27]

These managers were not unscrupulous people. All had misgivings about what they were doing, but they continued to go along with their superiors' requests. It's a reminder that all of our ethical decisions are made within the context of interactions with other people. The social networks within an organization play an important role in guiding people's actions. For most of us, doing something we know is wrong becomes easier when "everyone else is doing it." In organizations, the norms and values of the team, department, or organization as a whole have a profound influence on ethical behavior. Research verifies that these values strongly influence employee actions and decision making.[28] In particular, corporate culture, as described in Chapter 3, lets employees know what beliefs and behaviors the company supports and those it will not tolerate. If unethical behavior is tolerated or even encouraged, it becomes routine. In many companies, employees believe that if they do not go along, their jobs will be in jeopardy or they will not fit in.[29]

■ TAKE A MOMENT

Complete the experiential exercise on page 166 that pertains to ethical work environments. With what level of ethical climate are you most comfortable? As a manager, how might you improve the ethical climate of a department for which you are responsible?

EXHIBIT   5.4

Questions for Analyzing a
Company's Cultural Impact
on Ethics

SOURCE: Linda Klebe
Treviño, "A Cultural Perspective on Changing and Developing Organizational Ethics,"
in *Research in* Organizational
Change and Development,
ed. R. Woodman and W.
Pasmore (Greenwich, CT: JAI
Press, 1990): 4.

1. Identify the organization's heroes. What values do they represent? Given an ambiguous ethical dilemma, what decision would they make and why?
2. What are some important organizational rituals? How do they encourage or discourage ethical behavior? Who gets the awards, people of integrity or individuals who use unethical methods to attain success?
3. What are the ethical messages sent to new entrants into the organization—must they obey authority at all costs, or is questioning authority acceptable or even desirable?
4. Does analysis of organizational stories and myths reveal individuals who stand up for what's right, or is conformity the valued characteristic? Do people get fired or promoted in these stories?
5. Does language exist for discussing ethical concerns? Is this language routinely incorporated and encouraged in business decision making?
6. What informal socialization processes exist, and what norms for ethical/unethical behavior do they promote?

Culture can be examined to see the kinds of ethical signals given to employees. Exhibit 5.4 lists questions to ask to understand the cultural system. High ethical standards can be affirmed and communicated through public awards and ceremonies. Heroes provide role models that can either support or refute ethical decision making. Culture is not the only aspect of an organization that influences ethics, but it is a major force because it defines company values. Other aspects of the organization, such as explicit rules and policies, the reward system, the extent to which the company cares for its people, the selection system, emphasis on legal and professional standards, and leadership and decision processes, can also affect ethical values and manager decision making.[30]

■ TAKE A MOMENT   As a new manager, be prepared to build or enforce an ethical culture in your area of responsibility. Remember that managers make decisions within the norms of their interactions with others. Make sure your values and the organization's values support and encourage doing the right thing.

WHAT IS SOCIAL RESPONSIBILITY?

Now let's turn to the issue of social responsibility. In one sense, the concept of social responsibility, like ethics, is easy to understand: It means distinguishing right from wrong and doing right. It means being a good corporate citizen. The formal definition of **corporate social responsibility** is management's obligation to make choices and take actions that will contribute to the welfare and interests of society as well as the organization.[31]

As straightforward as this definition seems, social responsibility can be a difficult concept to grasp, because different people have different beliefs as to which actions improve society's welfare.[32] To make matters worse, social responsibility covers a range of issues, many of which are ambiguous with respect to right or wrong. If a bank deposits the money from a trust fund into a low-interest account for 90 days, from which it makes a substantial profit, is it being a responsible corporate citizen? How about two companies engaging in intense competition? Is it socially responsible for the stronger corporation to drive the weaker one into bankruptcy or a forced merger? Or consider companies such as Chiquita, Kmart, or Dana Corporation, all of which declared bankruptcy—which is perfectly legal—to avoid mounting financial obligations to suppliers, labor unions, or competitors. These

corporate social responsibility The obligation of organization management to make decisions and take actions that will enhance the welfare and interests of society as well as the organization.

examples contain moral, legal, and economic considerations that make socially responsible behavior hard to define. A company's impact on the natural environment must also be taken into consideration.

ORGANIZATIONAL STAKEHOLDERS

One reason for the difficulty understanding corporate social responsibility is that managers must confront the question, "Responsibility to whom?" Recall from Chapter 3 that the organization's environment consists of several sectors in both the task and general environment. From a social responsibility perspective, enlightened organizations view the internal and external environment as a variety of stakeholders.

A **stakeholder** is any group within or outside the organization that has a stake in the organization's performance. Each stakeholder has a different criterion of responsiveness, because it has a different interest in the organization.[33] For example, Wal-Mart uses aggressive bargaining tactics with suppliers so that it is able to provide low prices for customers. Some stakeholders see this type of corporate behavior as responsible because it benefits customers and forces suppliers to be more efficient. Others, however, argue that the aggressive tactics are unethical and socially irresponsible because they force U.S. manufacturers to lay off workers, close factories, and outsource from low-wage countries. For instance, Wal-Mart now purchases about 10 percent of all Chinese imports to the United States, and company executives are considering increasing their China purchases significantly over the next five years, which critics charge will hurt American companies and workers even more. One supplier said clothing is being sold so cheaply at Wal-Mart that many U.S. companies could not compete even if they paid their employees nothing.[34]

The organization's performance affects stakeholders, but stakeholders can also have a tremendous effect on the organization's performance and success. Consider the case of Monsanto, a leading competitor in the life sciences industry.

stakeholder Any group within or outside the organization that has a stake in the organization's performance.

Monsanto

> Over the past decade or so, Monsanto has been transformed from a chemicals firm into a biotechnology company. The organization's vast array of stakeholders around the world include customers, investors, suppliers, partners, health and agricultural organizations, regulatory agencies, research institutes, and governments.
>
> Monsanto experienced some big problems in recent years because of its failure to satisfy various stakeholder groups. For example, the company's genetic seed business has been the target of controversy and protest. Small farmers were concerned about new dependencies that might arise for them with using the new seeds. European consumers rebelled against a perceived imposition of unlabeled, genetically modified food ingredients. Research institutes and other organizations took offense at what they perceived as Monsanto's arrogant approach to the new business. Activist groups accused the company of creating "Frankenstein foods." Partly as a result of these public sentiments, investor confidence in the company waned and the stock took a downhill slide. To make matters even worse, in seeking to sell genetically modified seeds in Indonesia, managers allegedly bribed government officials, which got Monsanto into hot water with the U.S. Securities and Exchange Commission.
>
> In light of these stakeholder issues, CEO Hendrik Verfaillie offered an apology to some stakeholders at a *Farm Journal* Conference in Washington, D.C., saying that Monsanto "was so blinded by its enthusiasm for this great new technology that it missed the concerns the technology raised for many people." Verfaillie also announced a five-part pledge that aims to restore positive stakeholder relationships. Each of the five commitments requires an ongoing dialogue between Monsanto managers and various stakeholder constituencies. The company paid $1.5 million to settle the SEC charges and is voluntarily cooperating with regulatory investigators. If Monsanto managers cannot effectively manage critical stakeholder relationships, Monsanto is not likely to survive as a business.[35]

EXHIBIT   5.5

Major Stakeholders
Relevant to Monsanto
Company

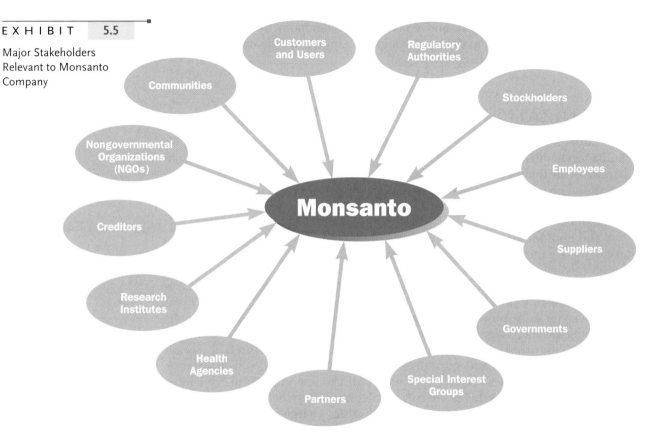

SOURCES: Based on information in D. Wheeler, B. Colbert, and R. E. Freeman, "Focusing on Value: Reconciling Corporate Social Responsibility, Sustainability, and a Stakeholder Approach in a Networked World," *Journal of General Management* 28, no. 3 (Spring 2003): 1–28; and J. E. Post, L. E. Preston, and S. Sachs.

Exhibit 5.5 illustrates important stakeholders for Monsanto. Most organizations are similarly influenced by a variety of stakeholder groups. Investors and shareholders, employees, customers, and suppliers are considered primary stakeholders, without whom the organization cannot survive. Investors, shareholders, and suppliers' interests are served by managerial efficiency—that is, use of resources to achieve profits. Employees expect work satisfaction, pay, and good supervision. Customers are concerned with decisions about the quality, safety, and availability of goods and services. When any primary stakeholder group becomes seriously dissatisfied, the organization's viability is threatened.[36]

Other important stakeholders are the government and the community, which have become increasingly important in recent years. Most corporations exist only under the proper charter and licenses and operate within the limits of safety laws, environmental protection requirements, antitrust regulations, antibribery legislation, and other laws and regulations in the government sector. The community includes local government, the natural and physical environments, and the quality of life provided for residents. Special interest groups, still another stakeholder, may include trade associations, political action committees, professional associations, and consumerists.

Socially responsible organizations consider the effects of their actions on all stakeholder groups and may also invest in a number of philanthropic causes that benefit stakeholders. Cummins Engine, for example, funds the development of schools in China and India, where it has facilities, and has purchased biodiverse forest land in Mexico to demonstrate the company's commitment to the natural environment.[37] Bristol-Myers Squibb provides funding for health clinics in areas of Texas, California, and Florida to hire *promotoras de salud,* or peer health educators, to help fight Type 2 diabetes in the Hispanic population.[38]

Today, special interest groups continue to be one of the largest stakeholder concerns that companies face. Environmental responsibility has become a primary issue as both business and the public acknowledge the damage that has been done to our natural environment.

THE ETHIC OF SUSTAINABILITY AND THE NATURAL ENVIRONMENT

When the first Earth Day celebration was held in 1970, most managers considered environmentalists to be an extremist fringe group and felt little need to respond to environmental concerns.[39] Today environmental issues have become a hot topic among business leaders, and managers and organizations in all industries are jumping on the environmental bandwagon.

One model uses the phrase *shades of green* to evaluate a company's commitment to environmental responsibility.[40] The various shades, which represent a company's approach to addressing environmental concerns, are illustrated in Exhibit 5.6. With a *legal approach,* the organization does just what is necessary to satisfy legal requirements. In general, managers and the company show little concern for environmental issues. For example, Willamette Industries of Portland, Oregon, agreed to install $7.4 million worth of pollution control equipment in its 13 factories to comply with Environmental Protection Agency requirements. The move came only after Willamette was fined a whopping $11.2 million for violating emissions standards.[41] The next shade, the *market approach,* represents a growing awareness of and sensitivity to environmental concerns, primarily to satisfy customers. A company might provide environmentally friendly products because customers want them, for instance, not necessarily because of strong management commitment to the environment.

A further step is to respond to multiple demands from the environment. The *stakeholder approach* means that companies attempt to answer the environmental concerns of various stakeholder groups, such as customers, the local community, business partners, and special interest groups. Ontario Power Generation, Shell, and Alcan Aluminum are among the large companies that are partnering with Environmental Defense to reduce greenhouse gases.[42] The move comes in response to growing concerns among customers, communities where the companies operate,

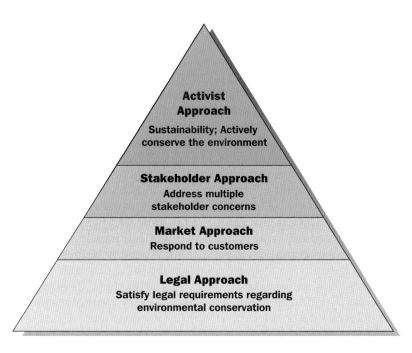

EXHIBIT   5.6

The Shades of Corporate Green

SOURCE: Based on R.E. Freeman, J. Pierce, and R. Dodd, *Shades of Green: Ethics and the Environment* (New York: Oxford University Press, 1995).

Activist Approach

Sustainability; Actively conserve the environment

Stakeholder Approach

Address multiple stakeholder concerns

Market Approach

Respond to customers

Legal Approach

Satisfy legal requirements regarding environmental conservation

CONCEPT

C O N N E C T I O N Bob Smet, an Alcoa Power Generating Inc. (APGI) natural resources specialist, talks to Badin, North Carolina, elementary school students as part of parent company Alcoa Inc.'s "Taking Action" initiative. This annual employee volunteer program represents only one facet of the company's commitment to **sustainable development.** Alcoa's *2020 Strategic Framework for Sustainability* spells out goals for integrating **sustainability principles** into its ongoing operations and establishes specific benchmarks. The World Economic Forum named Alcoa one of the world's most sustainable corporations, and in recognition of its 80 percent reduction of greenhouse gas perfluorocarbon, *Business Week* and The Climate Group cited the world's leading aluminum producer as a top "green" company of the decade.

and environmental groups, as well as recognition that emissions are likely to be regulated by government actions.

Finally, at the highest level of green, organizations take an *activist approach* to environmental issues by actively searching for ways to conserve the Earth's resources. A growing number of companies around the world are embracing a revolutionary idea called *sustainability* or *sustainable development*. **Sustainability** refers to economic development that generates wealth and meets the needs of the current generation while saving the environment so future generations can meet their needs as well.[43] With a philosophy of sustainability, managers weave environmental and social concerns into every strategic decision, revise policies and procedures to support sustainability efforts, and measure their progress toward sustainability goals. The mission of New Leaf Paper Company, for example, is to inspire the paper industry to move toward sustainability. New Leaf developed a paper called EcoBook 100, made from 100 percent post-consumer waste processed without chlorine, which was used for the Canadian printing of *Harry Potter and the Order of the Phoenix*. The small San Francisco-based company is having a big impact on the industry by tying its success closely to its environmental goals. Part of managers' time is devoted to educating printers, designers, paper merchants, and even competing companies on the uses and benefits of environmentally responsible paper. New Leaf generated $4 million in sales in its first year (1999) and expected revenues in 2005 of more than $18 million. Rather than being worried about increased competition from other firms jumping on the green bandwagon, New Leaf managers are delighted because it means the industry is shifting toward sustainability.[44]

Even large U.S. organizations as diverse as DuPont, McDonald's, and UPS are grappling with issues related to sustainability. McDonald's, for example, buys some of its energy from renewable sources, has stopped buying poultry treated with antibiotics, and offers incentives to suppliers that support sustainable practices.[45] The UPS fleet now includes about 2,000 alternative fuel vehicles, which emit 35 percent less pollution than standard diesel engines.[46] DuPont developed biodegradable materials for plastic silverware, a stretchable fabric called Sorona that is made partially from corn, and a housing insulation wrap that saves far more energy than is required to produce it. The company's new vision is to eventually manage a collection of businesses that can go on forever without depleting any natural resources.[47]

Despite these impressive advances, few U.S. firms have fully embraced the principles of sustainability, as reflected in a resistance to adopting ISO 14001 standards.[48] ISO 14001 is an international environmental management system that aims to boost the sustainability agenda. To become ISO 14001 compliant, firms develop policies, procedures, and systems that will continually reduce the organization's impact on the natural environment. Sustainability argues that organizations can find innovative ways to create wealth at the same time they are preserving natural resources. ZipCar, for example, rents cars by the hour, 24 hours a day, with no paperwork. By reducing private car usage, ZipCar contributes to reduced emissions and reduced load on the nation's transit infrastructure.[49]

sustainability Economic development that meets the needs of the current population while preserving the environment for the needs of future generations.

Total Corporate Social Responsibility

Economic Responsibility	Legal Responsibility	Ethical Responsibility	Discretionary Responsibility
Be Profitable	Obey the Law	Be Ethical Do What Is Right Avoid Harm	Contribute to the Community and Quality of Life

EXHIBIT 5.7

Criteria of Corporate Social Performance

SOURCES: Based on Archie B. Carroll, "A Three-Dimensional Conceptual Model of Corporate Perfomance," *Academy of Managemnt Review* 4 (1979), 499; A.B. Carroll, "The Pyramid of Corporate Social Responsibility: Toward the Moral Management of Corporate Stakeholders," *Business Horizons* 34 (July–August 1991), 42; and Mark S. Schwartz and Archie B. Carroll, "Corporate Social Responsibility: A Three-Domain Approach," *Business Ethics Quarterly* 13, no. 4 (2003), 503–530.

EVALUATING CORPORATE SOCIAL RESPONSIBILITY

A model for evaluating corporate social performance is presented in Exhibit 5.7. The model indicates that total corporate social responsibility can be subdivided into four primary criteria: economic, legal, ethical, and discretionary responsibilities.[50] These four criteria fit together to form the whole of a company's social responsiveness. Managers and organizations are typically involved in several issues at the same time, and a company's ethical and discretionary responsibilities are increasingly considered as important as economic and legal issues. Social responsibility has become an important topic on the corporate agenda in the light of corporate scandals, concerns about globalization, and a growing mistrust of business.[51]

Note the similarity between the categories in Exhibit 5.7 and those in Exhibit 5.1. In both cases, ethical issues are located between the areas of legal and freely discretionary responsibilities. Exhibit 5.7 also has an economic category, because profits are a major reason for corporations' existence.

Economic Responsibilities

The first criterion of social responsibility is *economic responsibility.* The business institution is, above all, the basic economic unit of society. Its responsibility is to produce the goods and services that society wants and to maximize profits for its owners and shareholders. Economic responsibility, carried to the extreme, is called the *profit-maximizing view,* advocated by Nobel economist Milton Friedman. This view argues that the corporation should be operated on a profit-oriented basis, with its sole mission to increase its profits as long as it stays within the rules of the game.[52]

T. J. Rodgers, CEO of Cypress Semiconductor, is a strong proponent of the profit-maximizing view. Rodgers believes that businesses should exist for one purpose: to make a profit. He points out, though, that the long-term pursuit of profits necessitates being a good corporate citizen.[53] The purely profit-maximizing view is no longer considered an adequate criterion of performance in Canada, the United States, and Europe. This approach means that economic gain is the only social responsibility and can lead companies into trouble.

© DAVID J. PHILLIP—AP WIDE WORLD PHOTOS

CONCEPT CONNECTION Communities, employees, and other businesses were hurt by the failure of managers at Enron Corporation to honor their **economic, ethical, and legal responsibilities.** Not only did employees such as those in the photo lose their jobs, but some lost most of their 401 (k) retirement savings when the company collapsed. In 2006, top managers including Jeffrey Skilling and Andrew Fastow were found guilty of breaking the law and sent to jail.

Legal Responsibilities

All modern societies lay down ground rules, laws, and regulations that businesses are expected to follow. *Legal responsibility* defines what society deems as important with respect to appropriate corporate behavior.[54] Businesses are expected to fulfill their economic goals within the legal framework. Legal requirements are imposed by local town councils, state legislators, and federal regulatory agencies.

Organizations that knowingly break the law are poor performers in this category. Managers at numerous companies learned in recent years that organizations and managers ultimately pay for ignoring legal responsibilities. Between mid-2002 and mid-2005, the U.S. Justice Department charged more than 900 individuals in more than 400 corporate fraud cases.[55] Other examples of illegal acts by corporations include intentionally selling defective goods, performing unnecessary repairs or procedures, and billing clients for work not done. Tenet Healthcare paid $54 million to settle a federal lawsuit charging that one of their hospitals was cheating Medicare by performing unnecessary cardiac procedures.[56] The press release in Exhibit 5.8 describes the punishment given to another company that broke the law.

Ethical Responsibilities

Ethical responsibility includes behaviors that are not necessarily codified into law and may not serve the corporation's direct economic interests. As described earlier in this chapter, to be *ethical*, organization decision makers should act with equity, fairness, and impartiality, respect the rights of individuals, and provide different treatment of individuals only when relevant to the organization's goals and tasks.[57] *Unethical* behavior occurs when decisions enable an individual or company to gain at the

EXHIBIT 5.8

One Company's
Punishment for
Breaking the Law

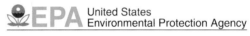

EPA United States
Environmental Protection Agency

Headquarters Press Release
Washington, DC

Date
Published: 07/12/2001

Title: WASHINGTON STATE/ALASKA COMPANY SENTENCED
IN ASBESTOS CASE

FOR RELEASE: THURSDAY, JULY 12, 2001
WASHINGTON STATE/ALASKA COMPANY SENTENCED IN
ASBESTOS CASE

Luke C. Hester 202-564-7818 / hester.luke@epa.gov

On June 27, Great Pacific Seafood, a Washington State corporation operating in Alaska, and its General Manager, Roger D. Stiles, were sentenced for violations of the Clean Air Act. Great Pacific Seafood was sentenced to serve five years probation, pay a $75,000 fine, pay $7,000 in restitution, publish a public apology statement in the local newspaper and adopt an environmental management program. Stiles was sentenced to pay a $5,000 fine, perform 120 hours of community service, and serve two to three years probation. Great Pacific Seafood and Stiles pleaded guilty to having five of its employees directly or indirectly exposed to asbestos fibers without the proper training, equipment or protective clothing. The hazardous nature of abatement was never disclosed to two of the employees. Failure to follow asbestos work practices can expose workers to the inhalation of airborne asbestos fibers which can cause lung cancer, a lung disease known as "asbestosis" and mesothelioma, a cancer of the chest and abdominal cavities. This case was investigated by the EPA Criminal Investigation Division, the FBI and the Alaska State Occupational Safety and Health Administration. Technical assistance was provided by the EPA Office of Air Quality. The case was prosecuted by the U.S. Attorney's Office in Anchorage.

R-105 ###

expense of other people or society as a whole. One firm in the food packaging industry, for example, recently ordered tens of thousands of dollars in goods from a supplier, even though managers knew the company's finances were shaky and it might never pay for them. As another example, a doctor at Louisiana State University Health Sciences Center is in trouble for accepting significant annual payments from a medical device company and heavily promoting its products to his patients.[58]

> Read the ethical dilemma on page 167 that pertains to legal and ethical responsibilities. How important is it to you to protect the natural environment?

■ **TAKE A MOMENT**

Discretionary Responsibilities

Discretionary responsibility is purely voluntary and is guided by a company's desire to make social contributions not mandated by economics, law, or ethics. Discretionary activities include generous philanthropic contributions that offer no payback to the company and are not expected. An example of discretionary behavior occurred when Emigrant Savings deposited $1,000 into the accounts of customers living in areas hit hardest by Hurricane Katrina. CEO Howard Milstein thought only a few hundred customers lived in the area, but he stuck by his decision even when he learned the number of customers was nearly 1,000. The total donation cut straight into the company's bottom line, but Milstein believed it was the right thing to do.[59] Discretionary responsibility is the highest criterion of social responsibility, because it goes beyond societal expectations to contribute to the community's welfare.

discretionary responsibility Organizational responsibility that is voluntary and guided by the organization's desire to make social contributions not mandated by economics, law, or ethics.

MANAGING COMPANY ETHICS AND SOCIAL RESPONSIBILITY

Many managers are concerned with improving the ethical climate and social responsiveness of their companies. As one expert on the topic of ethics said, "Management is responsible for creating and sustaining conditions in which people are likely to behave themselves."[60] Managers can take active steps to ensure that the company stays on an ethical footing. As we discussed earlier in this chapter, ethical business practices depend on individual managers as well as the organization's values, policies, and practices. Exhibit 5.9 illustrates the three pillars that support an ethical organization.[61]

Ethical Individuals

Managers who are essentially ethical individuals make up the first pillar. These individuals possess honesty and integrity, which is reflected in their behavior and decisions. People inside and outside the organization trust them because they can be relied upon to follow the standards of fairness, treat people right, and be ethical in their dealings

⌐**CONCEPT**
⌐**C O N N E C T I O N** The Home Depot, Inc. is dedicated to "creating safe play areas in our communities." The world's largest home improvement retailer demonstrates its commitment to **discretionary responsibility** with its largest nonprofit partner, KaBOOM! Through the KaBOOM! program, Home Depot recently built 52 playgrounds, bringing the total playgrounds built to 152 since 1996.

© THE HOME DEPOT, INC./JAMES HAYES, PHOTOGRAPHER

EXHIBIT 5.9

The Three Pillars of an
Ethical Organization

SOURCE: Adapted from Linda Klebe Treviño, Laura Pincus Hartman, and Michael Brown, "Moral Person and Moral Manager," *California Management Review* 42, no. 4 (Summer 2000), 128–142.

with others. Ethical individuals strive for a high level of moral development, as discussed earlier in the chapter.

However, being a moral person and making ethical decisions is not enough. Ethical managers also encourage the moral development of others.[62] They find ways to focus the entire organization's attention on ethical values and create an organizational environment that encourages, guides, and supports the ethical behavior of all employees. Two additional pillars are needed to provide a strong foundation for an ethical organization: ethical leadership and organizational structures and systems.

Ethical Leadership

In a study of ethics policy and practice in successful ethical companies, no point emerged more clearly than the crucial role of leadership.[63] If people don't hear about ethical values from top leaders, they get the idea that ethics is not important in the organization. Employees are acutely aware of their leaders' ethical lapses, and the company grapevine quickly communicates situations in which top managers choose an expedient action over an ethical one.[64] Lower-level managers and first-line supervisors are perhaps even more important as role models for ethical behavior, because they are the leaders employees see and work with on a daily basis. These managers can strongly influence the ethical climate in the organization by adhering to high ethical standards in their own behavior and decisions. In addition, these leaders articulate the desired ethical values and help others embody and reflect those values.[65]

Using performance reviews and rewards effectively is a powerful way for managers to signal that ethics counts. Managers also take a stand against unethical behavior. Consistently rewarding ethical behavior and disciplining unethical conduct at all levels of the company is a critical component of providing ethical leadership.[66]

Kathryn Reimann, a senior vice president at American Express, recalls the impact one senior executive had on the ethical tone of the organization. The leader heard reports that one of the company's top performers was mistreating subordinates. After he verified the reports, the executive publicly fired the manager and emphasized that no amount of business success could make up for that kind of behavior. The willingness to fire a top performer because of his unethical treatment of employees made a strong statement that ethics was important at American Express.[67]

Organizational Structures and Systems

The third pillar of ethical organizations is the set of tools that managers use to shape values and promote ethical behavior throughout the organization. Three of these tools are codes of ethics, ethical structures, and mechanisms for supporting whistle-blowers.

CODE OF ETHICS

A **code of ethics** is a formal statement of the company's values concerning ethics and social issues; it communicates to employees what the company stands for. Codes of ethics tend to exist in two types: principle-based statements and policy-based statements. *Principle-based statements* are designed to affect corporate culture; they define fundamental values and contain general language about company responsibilities, quality of products, and treatment of employees. General statements of principle are often called *corporate credos*. One good example is Johnson & Johnson's "The Credo."

Go to Johnson & Johnson's Web site at www.jnj.com/home and click on "View Our Credo," which is available in 36 languages. For more than 60 years, the Credo has guided Johnson & Johnson's managers in making decisions that honor the company's responsibilities to employees, customers, the community, and stockholders.

TAKE A MOMENT

Policy-based statements generally outline the procedures to be used in specific ethical situations. These situations include marketing practices, conflicts of interest, observance of laws, proprietary information, political gifts, and equal opportunities. Examples of policy-based statements are Boeing's "Business Conduct Guidelines," Chemical Bank's "Code of Ethics," GTE's "Code of Business Ethics" and "Anti-Trust and Conflict of Interest Guidelines," and Norton's "Norton Policy on Business Ethics."[68]

Codes of ethics state the values or behaviors expected and those that will not be tolerated, backed up by management action. Due to the number of scandals in the financial services industry, a group convened by the American Academy of Arts and Sciences recently suggested that Wall Street needs a broad ethics code similar to the millennia-old Hippocratic oath for doctors. With numerous areas open to ethical abuses and the pressures investment bankers face when millions of dollars are at stake, the group, which includes some of the most respected leaders on Wall Street, believes a code could serve as a guide for managers facing thorny ethical issues.[69] Many financial institutions, of course, have their own individual corporate codes. A survey of *Fortune* 1,000 companies found that 98 percent address issues of ethics and business conduct in formal corporate documents, and 78 percent of those have separate codes of ethics that are widely distributed.[70] When top management supports and enforces these codes, including rewards for compliance and discipline for violation, ethics codes can boost a company's ethical climate.[71] The code of ethics for *The Milwaukee Journal Sentinel* gives employees some guidelines for dealing with ethical questions.

code of ethics A formal statement of the organization's values regarding ethics and social issues.

Milwaukee Journal Sentinel

In recent years, charges of plagiarism and other ethical violations cast a spotlight on newspaper publishers and other media outlets. As a result, many companies put renewed emphasis on journalistic standards of integrity.

Executives at Journal Communications, the parent company of *The Milwaukee Journal Sentinel*, hope the company's clear and comprehensive code of ethics will reinforce the public's trust as well as prevent ethical misconduct. This excerpt from the opening sections of the code outlines some broad provisions for what the company stands for:

> Journal Communications and its subsidiaries operate in a complex and changing society. The actions of the company's employees, officers and directors clearly affect other members of that society. Therefore, every employee has an obligation to conduct the day-to-day business of the company in conformity with the highest ethical standards and in accordance with the various laws and regulations that govern modern business operations. . . .
>
> Journal Communications' ethical standards embrace not only the letter of the law, but also the spirit of the law. To that end, we must apply plain old-fashioned honesty and decency to every aspect of our job. We must never sacrifice ethics for expedience. Broadly put, we should treat others fairly and with respect.
>
> If faced with an ethical question, we should ask:
>
> :: Is this action legal?
>
> :: Does it comply with company policies and/or good business conduct?
>
> :: Is it something I would not want my supervisors, fellow employees, subordinates or family to know about?
>
> :: Is it something I would not want the general public to know about?
>
> We must not condone illegal or unethical behavior . . . by failing to report it, regardless of an employee's level of authority. . . . The company will protect us if we bring unethical activity to its attention.
>
> The *Journal*'s code of ethics also includes statements concerning respect for people, respect for the company, conflicts of interest, unfair competition, relationships with customers, suppliers, and news sources, confidential information, and accepting gifts and favors.[72]

By giving people some guidelines for confronting ethical questions and promising protection from recriminations for people who report wrongdoing, the *Journal*'s code of ethics gives all employees the responsibility and the right to maintain the organization's ethical climate.

ETHICAL STRUCTURES

Ethical structures represent the various systems, positions, and programs a company can undertake to implement ethical behavior. An **ethics committee** is a group of executives appointed to oversee company ethics. The committee provides rulings on questionable ethical issues. The ethics committee assumes responsibility for disciplining wrongdoers, which is essential if the organization is to directly influence employee behavior. For example, Motorola's Ethics Compliance Committee is charged with interpreting, clarifying, and communicating the company's code of ethics and with adjudicating suspected code violations. Many companies, such as Sears, Northrop Grumman, and Columbia/HCA Healthcare, set up ethics offices with full-time staff to ensure that ethical standards are an integral part of company operations. These offices are headed by a **chief ethics officer**, a company executive who oversees all aspects of ethics and legal compliance, including establishing and broadly communicating standards, ethics training, dealing with exceptions or problems, and advising senior managers in the ethical and compliance aspects of decisions.[73] The title of *chief ethics officer* was almost unheard of a decade ago, but highly publicized ethical and legal problems

ethics committee A group of executives assigned to oversee the organization's ethics by ruling on questionable issues and disciplining violators.

chief ethics officer A company executive who oversees ethics and legal compliance.

faced by companies in recent years sparked a growing demand for these ethics specialists. The Ethics and Compliance Officers Association, a trade group, reports that membership soared to more than 1,250 companies, up from about half that number in 2002.[74] Most ethics offices also work as counseling centers to help employees resolve difficult ethical issues. A toll-free confidential hotline allows employees to report questionable behavior as well as seek guidance concerning ethical dilemmas.

Ethics training programs also help employees deal with ethical questions and translate the values stated in a code of ethics into everyday behavior.[75] Training programs are an important supplement to a written code of ethics. General Electric implemented a strong compliance and ethics training program for all 320,000 employees worldwide. Much of the training is conducted online, with employees able to test themselves on how they would handle thorny ethical issues. In addition, small group meetings give people a chance to ask questions and discuss ethical dilemmas or questionable actions. Every quarter, each of GE's business units reports to headquarters the percentage of division employees who completed training sessions and the percentage that have read and signed off on the company's ethics guide, "Spirit and Letter."[76] At McMurray Publishing Company in Phoenix, all employees attend a *weekly* meeting on workplace ethics, where they discuss how to handle ethical dilemmas and how to resolve conflicting values.[77]

A strong ethics program is important, but it is no guarantee against lapses. Enron could boast of a well-developed ethics program, for example, but managers failed to live up to it. Enron's problems sent a warning to other managers and organizations. It is not enough to *have* an impressive ethics program. The ethics program must be merged with day-to-day operations, encouraging ethical decisions throughout the company.

WHISTLE-BLOWING

Employee disclosure of illegal, immoral, or illegitimate practices on the employer's part is called **whistle-blowing**.[78] No organization can rely exclusively on codes of conduct and ethical structures to prevent all unethical behavior. Holding organizations accountable depends to some degree on individuals who are willing to blow the whistle if they detect illegal, dangerous, or unethical activities. Whistle-blowers often report wrongdoing to outsiders, such as regulatory agencies, senators, or newspaper reporters. Some firms have instituted innovative programs and confidential hotlines to encourage and support internal whistle-blowing. For this practice to be an effective ethical safeguard, however, companies must view whistle-blowing as a benefit to the company and make dedicated efforts to protect whistle-blowers.[79]

Without effective protective measures, whistle-blowers suffer. Although whistle-blowing has become widespread in recent years, it is still risky for employees, who can lose their jobs, be ostracized by coworkers, or be transferred to lower-level positions. Consider what happened when Linda Kimble reported that the car rental agency where she worked was pushing the sale of insurance to customers who already had coverage. Within a few weeks after making the complaint to top managers, Kimble was fired. The 2002 Sarbanes-Oxley Act provides some safety for whistle-blowers like Kimble. People fired for reporting wrongdoing can file a complaint under the law and are eligible for back pay, attorney's fees, and a chance to get their old job back, as Kimble did. The impact of the legislation is still unclear, but many whistle-blowers fear that they will suffer even more hostility if they return to the job after winning a case under Sarbanes-Oxley.[80]

Many managers still look upon whistle-blowers as disgruntled employees who aren't good team players. Yet to maintain high ethical standards, organizations need people who are willing to point out wrongdoing. Managers can be trained to view whistle-blowing as a benefit rather than a threat, and systems can be set up to effectively protect employees who report illegal or unethical activities.

ethics training Training programs to help employees deal with ethical questions and values.

whistle-blowing The disclosure by an employee of illegal, immoral, or illegitimate practices by the organization.

Strive to be an ethical leader by adhering to high standards in your personal and business behavior. As a new manager, use tools such as codes of ethics, ethics training programs, and ethics offices to promote ethical behavior in your unit and help people resolve ethical dilemmas. Treasure whistle-blowers who have the courage to point out wrongdoing, and set up organizational systems to nurture and protect them.

ETHICAL CHALLENGES IN TURBULENT TIMES

The problem of lax ethical standards in business is nothing new, but in recent years it seems to have escalated. In addition, public reaction has been swift and unforgiving. Any ethical misstep can cost a company its reputation and hurt its profitability and performance. Within months after Martha Stewart was charged with insider trading, her company's market capitalization plummeted $400 million, although Martha and her company managed to survive the scandal and her stint in jail. Companies such as Nike and Gap have been hurt by accusations of exploitative labor practices in Third World factories. Oil companies have been targeted for allegedly abusing the environment and contributing to a host of social ills in developing nations, while pharmaceutical firms have been accused of hurting the world's poor by pricing drugs out of their reach. Organizational stakeholders, including employees, shareholders, governments, and the general community, are taking a keen interest in how managers run their businesses.

One reason for the proliferation of ethical lapses is the turbulence of our times. Things move so fast that managers who aren't firmly grounded in ethical values can find themselves making poor choices simply because they don't have the time to carefully weigh the situation and exercise considered judgment. When organizations operate in highly competitive industries, rapidly changing markets, and complex cultural and social environments, a strong corporate culture that emphasizes ethical behavior becomes even more important because it guides people to do the right thing even in the face of confusion and change.[81]

The Business Case for Ethics and Social Responsibility

As scandals rocked the corporate world, they prompted new demands from government legislators, stockholders, management experts, and the general public. One consultant argued in a recent *Wall Street Journal* column that the current regulatory climate distracts managers from doing what's good for business.[82] However, the combination of a turbulent domestic environment, the globalization of business, and the increasing public scrutiny convinces many managers that paying attention to ethics and social responsibility is as much of a business issue as paying attention to costs, profits, and growth.

Beyond maintaining high ethical standards, top managers at a growing number of companies recognize how to target their social responsibility efforts in ways that also benefit the business. After Hurricane Katrina, for example, rather than giving a general gift, employees of Papa John's spent weeks in a pizza trailer handing out thousands of free six-inch pies, which benefited local residents and relief workers while also promoting the company's product. Home Depot identified affordable housing for low-income families as its primary social initiative, working collaboratively with Habitat for Humanity. Hundreds of thousands of would-be Home Depot customers participate as volunteers in the housing projects and how-to clinics. Starbucks builds social responsibility into its business model by paying hourly employees above minimum wage, buying fair-trade coffee, and negotiating long-term contracts with coffee growers who farm in environmentally friendly

SOUTH MOUNTAIN PRACTICES COMMUNITY ENTREPRENEURISM

At most companies, managers meet regularly to devise ways of achieving ambitious growth targets. At South Mountain Company, a Massachusetts-based firm that designs, builds, and renovates homes, employees meet every few years to decide whether they want the company to grow modestly—or not at all. That's because they don't believe a business necessarily has to grow to be successful. In fact, South Mountain concluded that, in cofounder John Abrams's words, "Small enterprises, if driven by principled practice as much as profit, can produce workplace satisfaction, support good lives, and shape strong communities."

This sustainable growth philosophy is possible because of a decision Abrams made in 1994. Instead of going public or looking for a buyer, Abrams transformed the 19-year-old firm into an employee-owned cooperative. After a five-year trial period, an employee can buy into ownership; about half the current workers have taken this step. So it is the people actually doing the work, not Wall Street with its penchant for tracking quarterly earnings, who determine the growth rate.

Some of the key principles driving South Mountain include practicing a "business of place" by accepting jobs only on Martha's Vineyard Island, where the company is located, and "thinking like cathedral builders"—in other words, always remembering that the buildings they create will affect the island for years to come. Because the employee-owners work where they live, they take their responsibility to the community seriously. This commitment is reflected in their concern for the natural environment: South Mountain takes care that the houses it crafts blend harmoniously with the landscape, use recycled and salvaged materials whenever possible, and make energy efficiency a high priority.

Employees also routinely find ways to, as Abrams puts it, "bring the community into the company and the company into the community." Many serve on local boards and commissions where they engage in "community entrepreneurism" by bringing business ideas, resources, and problem-solving skills to bear on local issues. One matter South Mountain feels particularly well-positioned to address is the affordable housing crisis, precipitated by the island's relatively recent metamorphosis into an upscale resort. The company funnels a portion of the money it makes on building houses for wealthy clients into developing housing for the not-so-wealthy.

South Mountain's sustainable philosophies certainly haven't hurt the company. It does about $6 million of business annually and is consistently profitable. "Nobody's getting rich," Abrams allows, "but we are living comfortably doing the work we enjoy in the location of our choice."

SOURCES: John Abrams, "Thirty Years in Community Entrepreneurship," *In Business* (September–October 2005): 28; Peter Asmus, "South Mountain Company," *Business Ethics* (Fall 2005): 16–17; John Abrams, "Conscious Growth: Why South Mountain Co. Pursues Deliberate Rather Than Maximum Growth," *OURBiz* (October 3, 2005): www.ourbiz.biz/files/Abrams2.doc; and "Suggested Reading: *The Company We Keep*," Vermont Sustainable Jobs Fund Web Page, www.vsjf.org/resources/suggreading.Abrams.shtml.

ways. These efforts make good business sense at the same time they build the image of these companies as good corporate citizens.[83] One organization in Spain, Unión Fenosa, pioneered the concept of corporate social responsibility as a business issue.

Unión Fenosa is a large Spanish business group that does business in three major industries: energy, consulting services, and telecommunications. The company's approach to corporate social responsibility—called "complicity with the environment"—emerged during the 1980s when Unión Fenosa was building power stations in isolated areas and providing consulting services to other companies moving into developing countries.

Former head engineer José Luis Castro recalls that the company had to essentially build an entire community around a developing power station to serve the personal and social needs of engineers, technicians, local workers, and their families. From the beginning, productivity and progress in business was seen to go hand-in-hand with the well-being of the community. Thus began Unión Fenosa's concept of "complicity with the environment" as a key to business success. The company sees its success as inextricably tied to the well-being of not only shareholders but also workers, suppliers, and the immediate environment in which the company is working.

Unión Fenosa

Although some degree of altruism influences Unión Fenosa's philanthropy, top leaders emphasize that it's really a business issue: The survival of the company is based on its ability to involve itself with the local community in a way that makes money for the company at the same time it makes the community better than it was before.[84]

Unión Fenosa executives believe that a concern with *social sustainability* is essential for a company to remain competitive and successful. Social sustainability refers to interacting with the community in which a company does business in a way that makes money for the company but also improves the long-term well-being of the community. South Mountain Company, a Massachusetts architectural and construction firm, also emphasizes improving the community as a business objective, as described in the Unlocking Innovative Solutions Through People box.

In the United States, varied stakeholders are increasingly pushing new reporting initiatives connected to the sustainability movement that emphasize *the triple bottom line* of economic, social, and environmental performance. Naturally, the relationship of a corporation's ethics and social responsibility to its financial performance concerns both managers and management scholars and has generated a lively debate.[85]

Economic Performance

One concern of managers is whether good citizenship will hurt performance—after all, ethics programs and social responsibility cost money. A number of studies, undertaken to determine whether heightened ethical and social responsiveness increases or decreases financial performance, provided varying results but generally found a small positive relationship between social responsibility and financial performance.[86] For example, a recent study of the financial performance of large U.S. corporations considered "best corporate citizens" found that they enjoy both superior reputations and superior financial performance.[87] Similarly Governance Metrics International, an independent corporate governance ratings agency in New York, found that the stocks of companies run on more selfless principles perform better than those run in a self-serving manner. Top-ranked companies such as Pfizer, Johnson Controls, and Sunoco also outperformed lower-ranking companies in measures such as return on assets, return on investment, and return on capital.[88] Although results from these studies are not proof, they do provide an indication that use of resources for ethics and social responsibility does not hurt companies.[89] Moreover, one survey found that 70 percent of global CEOs believe corporate social responsibility is vital to their companies' profitability.[90]

Companies are also making an effort to measure the nonfinancial factors that create value. Researchers find, for example, that people prefer to work for companies that demonstrate a high level of ethics and social responsibility; these organizations can attract and retain high-quality employees.[91] Customers pay attention too. A study by Walker Research indicates that, price and quality being equal, two-thirds of customers say they would switch brands to do business with a company that is ethical and socially responsible.[92] Enlightened companies realize that integrity and trust are essential elements in sustaining successful and profitable business relationships with an increasingly connected web of employees, customers, suppliers, and partners. Although doing the

© PABLO MARTINEZ MOSIVAIS/ASSOCIATED PRESS

CONCEPT

C O N N E C T I O N It's a Supreme Court case that started with a Birmingham, Alabama, high school coach whose girls' basketball team played in a shabby gym clearly inferior to the one the boys' team used. After Roderick Jackson repeatedly complained to the school system that his team was being denied equal access to facilities, equipment, and funding, he lost his coaching position. Jackson filed suit under Title IX, which prohibits gender discrimination by educational institutions receiving federal funds. Here, Jackson stands flanked by his attorneys in front of the Supreme Court. By a 5-4 decision, the Court expanded the scope of Title IX to not only protect direct victims of discrimination but also shield **whistle-blowers** such as Jackson from retaliation.

right thing might not always be profitable in the short run, many managers believe it can provide a competitive advantage by developing a level of trust that money can't buy.[93]

MANAGER'S SOLUTION

Ethics and social responsibility are hot topics for today's managers. The ethical domain of behavior pertains to values of right and wrong. Ethical decisions and behavior are typically guided by a value system. Four value-based approaches that serve as criteria for ethical decision making are utilitarian, individualism, moral-rights, and justice. For an individual manager, the ability to make correct ethical choices will depend on both individual and organizational characteristics. An important individual characteristic is level of moral development. Corporate culture is an organizational characteristic that influences ethical behavior. Strong ethical cultures become more important in turbulent environments because they help people make the right choices in the face of confusion and rapid change.

Corporate social responsibility concerns a company's values toward society. How can organizations be good corporate citizens? The model for evaluating social performance uses four criteria: economic, legal, ethical, and discretionary. Evaluating corporate social behavior often requires assessing its impact on organizational stakeholders. One issue of growing concern is responsibility to our natural environment. Organizations may take a legal, market, stakeholder, or activist approach to addressing environmental concerns. Sustainability is a growing movement that emphasizes economic development that meets the needs of today while preserving resources for the future.

Ethical organizations are supported by three pillars: ethical individuals, ethical leadership, and organizational structures and systems, including codes of ethics, ethics committees, chief ethics officers, training programs, and mechanisms to protect whistle-blowers. Companies that are ethical and socially responsible perform as well as—and often better than—those that are not socially responsible. Smart managers are finding ways to target their social responsibility efforts in ways that benefit the business. After years of scandal, many managers are recognizing that managing ethics and social responsibility is just as important as paying attention to costs, profits, and growth.

Our management challenge at the beginning of the chapter illustrates how difficult ethical issues can be, especially in today's climate of increased government and public scrutiny, and illustrates why some leaders are calling for a Wall Street code of ethics. Even though Eric Corrigan and Thomas Chen had not broken any government regulations, their boss stuck to his decision to fire them, saying they showed poor judgment and inappropriately used confidential information. Within 15 minutes after being called to the boss's office, the two were cleaning out their desks and turning in their laptops. Bank of America executives are keenly aware of the need to avoid even the appearance of wrongdoing in today's environment. In a statement, a Bank of America spokesperson said, "The environment in the financial sector continues to evolve and in any environment we expect our associates to maintain the highest possible ethical standards in everything they do." Corrigan and Chen, meanwhile, continue to insist that they did nothing wrong, and both are contemplating legal action. The JPMorgan banker, Thomas Heath, was also fired and is no longer welcome to join Bank of America. Heath admits he erred in disclosing information about a deal he was working on to competing parties, but says he thought he could trust Corrigan to keep it in confidence. Heath's actions were clearly unethical, but the wrongdoing of Chen and Corrigan is less clear-cut. However, their dismissal illustrates that "the standard way of doing things" is no longer an acceptable excuse. Current societal norms and values no longer view cutthroat competition as ethical and socially responsible behavior.

1. Do you think a social entrepreneur can run a profitable business with a primary goal of improving society? Discuss.

2. Is it socially responsible for organizations to undertake political activity or join with others in a trade association to influence the government? Discuss.

3. Lincoln Electric considers customers and employees to be more important stakeholders than shareholders. Is it appropriate for management to define some stakeholders as more important than others? Should all stakeholders be considered equal?

4. Imagine yourself in a situation of being encouraged to inflate your expense account. Do you think your choice would be more affected by your individual moral development or by the cultural values of the company for which you worked? Explain.

5. Which do you think would be more effective for shaping long-term ethical behavior in an organization: a written code of ethics combined with ethics training or strong ethical leadership? Which would have more impact on you? Why?

6. Choose two of the dilemmas listed on page 167. First apply the utilitarian approach to ethical decision making in each situation, and then apply the moral-rights approach. Did you reach the same or different conclusions depending on the approach used? Which do you think is generally the better approach for managers to use?

7. Do you believe it is ethical for companies to compile portfolios of personal information about their Web site visitors without informing them? What about organizations monitoring their employees' use of the Web? Discuss.

8. Environmentalists are trying to pass laws for oil spills that would remove all liability limits for the oil companies. This change would punish corporations financially. Is this approach the best way to influence companies to be socially responsible?

9. A noted business executive said, "A company's first obligation is to be profitable. Unprofitable enterprises can't afford to be socially responsible." Do you agree? Discuss.

10. Dr. Martin Luther King, Jr., said, "As long as there is poverty in the world, I can never be rich. . . . As long as diseases are rampant, I can never be healthy. . . . I can never be what I ought to be until you are what you ought to be." Discuss this quote with respect to the material in this chapter. Would this idea be true for corporations, too?

11. Was it ethical during the 1990s for automobile manufacturers to attempt to accommodate an ever-increasing consumer appetite for SUVs with their low fuel efficiency? Was it good business?

MANAGEMENT IN PRACTICE: EXPERIENTIAL EXERCISE ETHICAL WORK CLIMATES

Answer the following questions by circling the number that best describes an organization for which you have worked.

Disagree	❶	❷	❸	❹	❺	Agree

1. What is the best for everyone in the company is the major consideration here. ❶ ❷ ❸ ❹ ❺

2. Our major concern is always what is best for the other person. ❶ ❷ ❸ ❹ ❺

3. People are expected to comply with the law and professional standards over and above other considerations. ❶ ❷ ❸ ❹ ❺

4. In this company, the first consideration is whether a decision violates any law. ❶ ❷ ❸ ❹ ❺

5. It is very important to follow the company's rules and procedures here. ❶ ❷ ❸ ❹ ❺

6. People in this company strictly obey the company policies. ❶ ❷ ❸ ❹ ❺

7. In this company, people are mostly out for themselves. ❶ ❷ ❸ ❹ ❺

8. People are expected to do anything to further the company's interests, regardless of the consequences. ❶ ❷ ❸ ❹ ❺

9. In this company, people are guided by their own personal ethics. ❶ ❷ ❸ ❹ ❺

10. Each person in this company decides for himself or herself what is right and wrong. ❶ ❷ ❸ ❹ ❺

Scoring and Interpretation

Subtract each of your scores for questions 7 and 8 from the number 6. Then, add up your score for all 10 questions: _____. These questions measure the dimensions of an organization's ethical climate. Questions 1 and 2 measure caring for people, questions 3 and 4 measure lawfulness, questions 5 and 6 measure rules adherence, questions 7 and 8 measure emphasis on financial and company performance, and questions 9 and 10 measure individual independence. A total score above 40 indicates a highly positive ethical climate. A score from 30 to 40 indicates above-average ethical climate. A score from 20 to 30 indicates a below-average ethical climate, and a score below 20 indicates a poor ethical climate.

Go back over the questions and think about changes that you could have made to improve the ethical climate in the organization. Discuss with other students what you could do as a manager to improve ethics in future companies you work for.

SOURCE: Based on Bart Victor and John B. Cullen, "The Organizational Bases of Ethical Work Climates," *Administrative Science Quarterly* 33 (1988), 101–125.

MANAGEMENT IN PRACTICE: ETHICAL DILEMMA

Should We Go Beyond the Law?

Nathan Rosillo stared out his office window at the lazy curves and lush, green, flower-lined banks of the Dutch Valley River. He'd grown up near here and he envisioned the day his children would enjoy the river as he had as a child. But now his own company might make that a risky proposition.

Nathan is a key product developer at Chem-Tech Corporation, an industry leader. Despite its competitive position, Chem-Tech experienced several quarters of dismal financial performance. Nathan and his team developed a new lubricant product that the company sees as the turning point in its declining fortunes. Top executives are thrilled that they can produce the new product at a significant cost savings because of recent changes in environmental regulations. Regulatory agencies loosened requirements on reducing and recycling wastes, which means Chem-Tech can now release waste directly into the Dutch Valley River.

Nathan is as eager as anyone to see Chem-Tech survive this economic downturn, but he doesn't think this route is the way to do it. He expressed his opposition regarding the waste dumping to both the plant manager and his direct supervisor, Martin Feldman. Martin has always supported Nathan, but this time was different. The plant manager, too, turned a deaf ear. "We're meeting government standards," he'd said. "It's up to them to protect the water. It's up to us to make a profit and stay in business."

Frustrated and confused, Nathan turned away from the window, his prime office view mocking his inability to protect the river he loved. He knew the manufacturing vice president was visiting the plant next week. Maybe if he talked with her, she would agree that the decision to dump waste materials in the river was ethically and socially irresponsible. But if she didn't, he would be skating on thin ice. His supervisor had already accused him of not being a team player. Maybe he should just be a passive bystander—after all, the company isn't breaking any laws.

What Would You Do?

1. Talk to the manufacturing vice president and emphasize the responsibility Chem-Tech has as an industry leader to set an example. Present her with a recommendation that Chem-Tech participate in voluntary pollution-reduction as a marketing tool, positioning itself as the environmentally friendly choice.

2. Mind your own business and just do your job. The company isn't breaking any laws, and if Chem-Tech's economic situation doesn't improve, a lot of people will be thrown out of work.

3. Call the local environmental advocacy group and get them to stage a protest of the company.

SOURCE: Adapted from Janet Q. Evans, "What Do You Do: What If Polluting Is Legal?" *Business Ethics* (Fall 2002): 20.

CASE FOR CRITICAL ANALYSIS

Massengill's Department Store

Massengill's Department Store had been a fixture in small and mid-sized cities across the Southeast for 75 years. But for the past couple of decades, the Atlanta-based chain had been slowly going downhill. Once a cutting-edge retailer, Massengill's had come to be known primarily for its dilapidated stores and dowdy-looking clothes. Everyone knew the chain was on the verge of bankruptcy. But that was before Marv Heimler.

Heimler had been lured away from his job running a nationwide chain based in Dallas–Fort Worth to rescue Massengill's. And rescue it he had. Massengill's was now the talk of the retail industry, thanks to its soaring sales and accompanying surge in stock price.

Heimler had been offered a generous compensation package that was tied to his performance in leading Massengill's through a rapid turnaround. And, indeed, Heimler realized he had no time to lose if

Massengill's was to survive. He came in with an aggressive plan for change that included remodeling shabby stores, cutting overhead costs, and offering modern, trendy merchandise sold by sophisticated, knowledgeable sales associates. "Link selling," in which shoppers enter the store looking for one item but end up leaving with three or four, was an important part of the new strategy. Unfortunately, the new strategy also meant layoffs were inevitable. Massengill's had long been run by old-fashioned, patriarchal managers who had held fast to their no-layoffs policy. However, to save the company meant aggressively slashing costs and investing the savings in remodeling, new merchandise, and training programs. Closing the in-store snack bars and consolidating distribution centers were the first steps, which eliminated about 500 jobs. In addition, many of the long-time salespeople had neither the abilities required for link selling nor a feel for the chic, sophisticated clothing Massengill's was now offering. Heimler knew he had to cut out the "deadwood" (a term he was careful to never use in public) to make room for a new breed of modern, energized sales associates.

Layoff notices went out to more than 500 floor supervisors and long-time salespeople on Friday before lunch. Heimler believed that would give people time to clean out their desks and say goodbye to their colleagues before the end of the day. And most of the survivors would have a weekend to process what had happened before returning to work.*

Heimler had expected people to be upset about the layoffs, but the severity of the reaction surprised him. Even the new employees he had brought in seemed to be upset. An article in a recent industry magazine had speculated that Massengill's success would be short-lived if morale continued to decline. "There's no trust at Massengill's," the article had said. "People feel like senior management isn't honest with its people. They just want to fix up the company fast and mop up the damage later."

Claire Sparkes, his head of human resources, confirmed that the article was on target. "People are really angry," she told him. "They think you should have held meetings to explain what was happening with the company and give people some warning."

"Everybody knew Massengill's was on the verge of financial collapse," Heimler snapped back. "When a new CEO is brought in to turn things around, everybody knows layoffs are coming. Why rub their noses in it? And if I hadn't moved quickly, nobody here would have a job! The whole chain would have gone down the tubes, and instead of 1,000 or so jobs being lost there would have been 5,000 people out of work! How would people have liked that?"

When Sparkes left his office, Heimler evaluated his situation. Massengill's was clearly soaring again. Customers were flocking in, sales and profits were going up, and Heimler was a hero on Wall Street. His compensation package is already worth more than $1 million, and his contract has just been renewed for two more years, with an increased salary and more stock options. He knew he had transformed Massengill's from an outdated chain that catered to older women to a hip, fun place for affluent young customers. Heimler reviewed last quarter's results and saw that sales and profits were still going up. So why does everyone keep telling him morale is going down?

Questions

1. What approach to ethical decision making (utilitarian, individualism, moral rights, or justice) seems to best describe Marv Heimler's turnaround strategy at Massengill's?

2. At what level of moral development would you place Heimler? Why?

3. How could Heimler have handled the layoffs to avoid the problems he's now facing? If you were in his position, what would you do now?

SOURCE: Based on Suzy Wetlaufer, "After the Layoffs, What Next?" *Harvard Business Review* (September–October 1998), 24–42.

* Note: A new federal regulation now requires that employees be given several weeks' notice of intended layoffs.

ENDNOTES

1. Landon Thomas, Jr. "On Wall Street, A Rise in Dismissals Over Ethics," *The New York Times* (March 29, 2005), www.nytimes.com.

2. Bethany McLean, "Why Enron Went Bust," *Fortune* (December 24, 2001): 58–68; survey results reported in Patricia Wallington, "Honestly?!" *CIO* (March 15, 2003): 41–42.

3. Data from KPMG, reported in Muel Kaptein, "The Diamond of Managerial Integrity," *European Management Journal* 21, no. 1 (2003): 99–108.

4. Katie Hafner and Claudia H. Deutsch, "When Good Will Is Also Good Business," *The New York Times* (September 14, 2005): www.nytimes.com; Peter Asmus, "100 Best Corporate Citizens, 2005," *Business Ethics* (Spring 2005): 20–27; Michelle Conlin and Jessi Hempel, with Joshua Tanzer and David Polek, "Philanthropy 2003: The Corporate Donors," *BusinessWeek* (December 1, 2003): 92–96.

5. Gordon F. Shea, *Practical Ethics* (New York: American Management Association, 1988); and Linda K. Treviño, "Ethical Decision Making in Organizations; A Person-Situation Interactionist Model," *Academy of Management Review* 11 (1986): 601–617.

6. Thomas M. Jones, "Ethical Decision Making by Individuals in Organizations: An Issue-Contingent Model," *Academy of Management Review* 16(1991): 366–395.

7. John R. Emshwiller and Alexei Barrionuevo, "U.S. Prosecutors File Indictment Against Skilling," *The Wall Street Journal* (February 20, 2004): A1, A13.

8. See Clinton W. McLemore, *Street-Smart Ethics: Succeeding in Business Without Selling Your Soul* (Louisville, KY: Westminster John Knox Press, 2003), for a cogent discussion of some ethical and legal issues associated with Enron's collapse.

9. Rushworth M. Kidder, "The Three Great Domains of Human Action," *Christian Science Monitor* (January 30, 1990).

10. Linda K. Treviño and Katherine A. Nelson, *Managing Business Ethics: Straight Talk About How to Do It Right* (New York: John Wiley & Sons, Inc. 1995): 4.

11. Jones, "Ethical Decision Making by Individuals in Organizations."

12. Based on a question from a General Electric employee ethics guide, reported in Kathryn Kranhold, "U.S. Firms Raise Ethics Focus," *The Wall Street Journal* (November 28, 2005): B4.

13. Based on information in Constance E. Bagley, "The Ethical Leader's Decision Tree," *Harvard Business Review* (February 2003): 18–19.

14. Based on information in Vadim Liberman, "Scoring on the Job," *Across the Board* (November–December 2003): 46–50.

15. This discussion is based on Gerald F. Cavanagh, Dennis J. Moberg, and Manuel Velasquez, "The Ethics of Organizational Politics," *Academy of Management Review* 6 (1981): 363–374; Justin G. Longenecker, Joseph A. McKinney, and Carlos W. Moore, "Egoism and Independence: Entrepreneurial Ethics," *Organizational Dynamics* (Winter 1988): 64–72; Carolyn Wiley, "The ABCs of Business Ethics: Definitions, Philosophies, and Implementation," *IM* (February 1995): 22–27; and Mark Mallinger, "Decisive Decision Making: An Exercise Using Ethical Frameworks," *Journal of Management Education* (August 1997): 411–417.

16. Michael J. McCarthy, "Now the Boss Knows Where You're Clicking," and "Virtual Morality: A New Workplace Quandary," *The Wall Street Journal* (October 21, 1999): B1, B4; and Jeffrey L. Seglin, "Who's Snooping on You?" *Business 2.0* (August 8, 2000): 202–203.

17. Thomas M. Burton, "Red Flags; Amid Alarm Bells, A Blood Substitute Keeps Pumping," *The Wall Street Journal* (February 22, 2006): A1, A12.

18. John Kekes, "Self-Direction: The Core of Ethical Individualism," in *Organizations and Ethical Individualism*, ed. Konstanian Kolenda (New York: Praeger, 1988): 1–18.

19. Tad Tulega, *Beyond the Bottom Line* (New York: Penguin Books, 1987).

20. Lynn Sharp Paine, "Managing for Organizational Integrity," *Harvard Business Review* (March–April 1994): 106–117.

21. This discussion is based on Treviño, "Ethical Decision Making in Organizations."

22. L. Kohlberg, "Moral Stages and Moralization: The Cognitive-Developmental Approach," in *Moral Development and Behavior: Theory, Research, and Social Issues,* ed. T. Lickona (New York: Holt, Rinehart & Winston, 1976): 31–83; L. Kohlberg, "Stage and Sequence: The Cognitive-Developmental Approach to Socialization," in *Handbook of Socialization Theory and Research,* ed. D. A. Goslin (Chicago: Rand McNally, 1969); and Jill W. Graham, "Leadership, Moral Development, and Citizenship Behavior," *Business Ethics Quarterly* 5, no. 1 (January 1995): 43–54.

23. Carol Gilligan, *In a Different Voice: Psychological Theory and Women's Development* (Cambridge, MA: Harvard University Press, 1982).

24. See Thomas Donaldson and Thomas W. Dunfee, "When Ethics Travel: The Promise and Peril of Global Business Ethics," *California Management Review* 41, No. 4 (Summer 1999): 45–63.

25. Transparency International, "Transparency International Releases New Bribe Payers Index," www.transparency.org (accessed on February 24, 2004).

26. Paul Burnham Finney, "The Perils of Bribery Meet the Open Palm," *The New York Times* (May 17, 2005): www.nytimes.com.

27. Susan Pulliam, "Crossing the Line; At Center of Fraud, WorldCom Official Sees Life Unravel," *The Wall Street Journal* (March 24, 2005): A1; and S. Pulliam, "Over the Line: A Staffer Ordered to Commit Fraud Balked, Then Caved," *The Wall Street Journal* (June 23, 2003): A1.

28. Duane M. Covrig, "The Organizational Context of Moral Dilemmas: The Role of Moral Leadership in Administration in Making and Breaking Dilemmas," *The Journal of Leadership Studies* 7, no. 1 (2000): 40–59; and James Weber, "Influences Upon Organizational Ethical Subclimates: A Multi-Departmental Analysis of a Single Firm," *Organizational Science* 6, no. 5 (September–October 1995): 509–523.

29. Linda Klebe Treviño, "A Cultural Perspective on Changing and Developing Organizational Ethics," in *Research and Organizational Change and Development,* ed. R. Woodman and W. Pasmore (Greenwich, CT: JAI Press, 1990): 4.

30. *Ibid*; John B. Cullen, Bart Victor, and Carroll Stephens, "An Ethical Weather Report: Assessing the Organization's Ethical Climate," *Organizational Dynamics* (Autumn 1989): 50–62; and Bart Victor and John B. Cullen, "The Organizational Bases of Ethical Work Climates," *Administrative Science Quarterly* 33 (1988): 101–125.

31. Eugene W. Szwajkowski, "The Myths and Realities of Research on Organizational Misconduct," in *Research in Corporate Social Performance and Policy,* ed. James E. Post (Greenwich, CT: JAI Press, 1986): 9:103–122; and Keith Davis, William C. Frederick, and Robert L. Blostrom, *Business and Society: Concepts and Policy Issues* (New York: McGraw-Hill, 1979).

32. Douglas S. Sherwin, "The Ethical Roots of the Business System," *Harvard Business Review* 61 (November–December 1983): 183–192.

33. Nancy C. Roberts and Paula J. King, "The Stakeholder Audit Goes Public," *Organizational Dynamics* (Winter 1989): 63–79; Thomas Donaldson and Lee E. Preston, "The Stakeholder Theory of the Corporation: Concepts, Evidence, and Implications," *Academy of Management Review* 20, no. 1 (1995): 65–91; and Jeffrey S. Harrison and Caron H. St. John, "Managing and Partnering with External Stakeholders," *Academy of Management Executive* 10, no. 2 (1996): 46–60.

34. Clay Chandler, "The Great Wal-Mart of China," *Fortune* (July 25, 2005): 104–116; and Charles Fishman, "The Wal-Mart You Don't Know—Why Low Prices Have a High Cost," *Fast Company* (December 2003): 68–80.

35. David Wheeler, Barry Colbert, and R. Edward Freeman, "Focusing on Value: Reconciling Corporate Social Responsibility, Sustainability, and a Stakeholder Approach in a Networked World," *Journal of General Management* 28, no. 3 (Spring 2003): 1–28; James E. Post, Lee E. Preston, and Sybille Sachs, "Managing the Extended Enterprise: The New Stakeholder View," *California Management Review* 45, no. 1 (Fall 2002): 6–28; and Peter Fritsch and Timothy Mapes, "Seed Money; In Indonesia, A Tangle of Bribes Creates Trouble for Monsanto," *The Wall Street Journal* (April 5, 2005): A1, A6.

36. Max B. E. Clarkson, "A Stakeholder Framework for Analyzing and Evaluating Corporate Social Performance," *Academy of Management Review* 20, no. 1 (1995): 92–117.

37. Asmus, "100 Best Corporate Citizens."

38. "The World We Serve," *Bristol-Myers Squibb 2002 Annual Report,* Bristol-Myers Squibb Company.

39. Mark A. Cohen, "Management and the Environment," *The Owen Manager* 15, no. 1 (1993): 2–6.

40. R. E. Freeman, J. Pierce, and R. Dodd, *Shades of Green: Business Ethics and the Environment* (New York: Oxford University Press, 1995).

41. Greg Toppo, "Company Agrees to Pay Record Pollution Fine," Associated Press, *Johnson City Press* (July 21, 2000): 9.

42. Andrew C. Revkin, "7 Companies Agree to Cut Gas Emissions," *The New York Times* (October 18, 2000): C1, C6.

43. This definition is based on Marc J. Epstein and Marie-Josée Roy, "Improving Sustainability Performance: Specifying, Implementing and Measuring Key Principles," *Journal of General Management* 29, no. 1 (Autumn 2003): 15–31, World Commission on Economic Development, *Our Common Future* (Oxford: Oxford University Press, 1987): and Marc Gunther, "Tree Huggers, Soy Lovers, and Profits," *Fortune* (June 23, 2003): 98–104.

44. Peter Asmus, "17th Annual Business Ethics Awards," *Business Ethics* (Fall 2005): 15–19.

45. Gunther, "Tree Huggers, Soy Lovers, and Profits."

46. Brian Deagon, "New Technology Could Boost Efficiency and Green Image for UPS," *Investor's Business Daily* (December 10, 2003); and Charles Haddad with Christine Tierney, "FedEx and Brown Are Going Green," *BusinessWeek* (August 11, 2003): 60.

47. Gunther, "Tree Huggers, Soy Lovers, and Profits."

48. The discussion of ISO 14001 is based on Pratima Bansal, "The Corporate Challenges of Sustainable Development," *Academy of Management Executive* 16, no. 2 (2002): 122–131.

49. Karina Funk, "Sustainability and Performance," *MIT Sloan Management Review* (Winter 2003): 65–70; and "The Fast 50: Trendsetters," *Fast Company* (March 2002).

50. Mark S. Schwartz and Archie B. Carroll, "Corporate Social Responsibility: A Three-Domain Approach," *Business Ethics Quarterly* 13, no. 4 (2003): 503–530; and Archie B. Carroll, "A Three-Dimensional Conceptual Model of Corporate Performance," *Academy of Management Review* 4 (1979): 497–505. For a discussion of various models for evaluating corporate social performance, also see Diane L. Swanson, "Addressing a Theoretical Problem by Reorienting the Corporate Social Performance Model," *Academy of Management Review* 20, no. 1 (1995): 43–64.

51. N. Craig Smith, "Corporate Social Responsibility: Whether or How?" *California Management Review* 45, no. 4 (Summer 2003): 52–76.

52. Milton Friedman, *Capitalism and Freedom* (Chicago: University of Chicago Press, 1962): 133; and Milton Friedman and Rose Friedman, *Free to Choose* (New York: Harcourt Brace Jovanovich, 1979).

53. Umesh Kher, "Getting Smart at Being Good . . . Are Companies Better Off For It?" *Time* (January 2006): A1–A8.

54. Eugene W. Szwajkowski, "Organizational Illegality: Theoretical Integration and Illustrative Application," *Academy of Management Review* 10 (1985): 558–567.

55. Deborah Solomon and Anne Marie Squeo, "Crackdown Puts Corporations, Executives in New Legal Peril," *The Wall Street Journal Online* (June 20, 2005): http:online.wsj.com.

56. Kurt Eichenwald, "U.S. Awards Tenet Whistle-Blowers $8.1 Million," *The New York Times* (January 8, 2004): www.nytimes.com.

57. David J. Fritzsche and Helmut Becker, "Linking Management Behavior to Ethical Philosophy—An Empirical Investigation," *Academy of Management Journal* 27 (1984): 165–175.

58. Kevin Kelly, "My Slithery Rivals," *FSB* (February 2005): 28–29; Reed Abelson, "Possible Conflicts for Doctors Are Seen on Medical Devices," *The New York Times* (September 22, 2005): www.nytimes.com.

59. Katie Hafner and Claudi H. Deutsch, "When Good Will Is Also Good Business," *The New York Times* (September 14, 2005): www.nytimes.com.

60. Saul W. Gellerman, "Managing Ethics from the Top Down," *Sloan Management Review* (Winter 1989): 73–79.

61. This discussion is based on Linda Klebe Treviño, Laura Pincus Hartman, and Michael Brown, "Moral Person and Moral Manager: How Executives Develop a Reputation for Ethical Leadership," *California Management Review* 42, no. 4 (Summer 2000): 128–142.

62. Muel Kaptein, "The Diamond of Managerial Integrity," *European Management Journal* 21, no. 1 (2003): 99–108.

63. Business Roundtable Institute for Corporate Ethics, www.corporate-ethics.org, and "Corporate Ethics: A Prime Business Asset," (February 1988): *The Business Roundtable,* 200 Park Avenue, Suite 2222, New York, NY 10166.

64. Michael Barrier, "Doing the Right Thing," *Nation's Business* (March 1998): 33–38; Joseph L. Badaracco, Jr., and Allen P. Webb, "Business Ethics: A View from the Trenches," *California Management Review* 37, no. 2 (Winter 1995): 8–28.

65. Gary R. Weaver, Linda Klebe Treviño, and Bradley Agle, "'Somebody I Look Up To:' Ethical Role Models in Organizations," *Organizational Dynamics* 34, no. 4 (2005): 313–330; and L. K. Treviño, G. R. Weaver, David G. Gibson, and Barbara Ley Toffler, "Managing Ethics and Legal Compliance: What Works and What Hurts?" *California Management Review* 41, no. 2 (Winter 1999): 131–151.

66. Treviño, Hartman, and Brown, "Moral Person and Moral Manager."

67. Weaver, Treviño, and Agle, "Somebody I Look Up To."

68. Ibid.

69. Dennis K. Berman, "Does Wall Street Finally Need an Ethics Code?" *The Wall Street Journal* (March 10, 2005): C1.

70. Treviño et al., "Managing Ethics and Legal Compliance."

71. Carolyn Wiley, "The ABC's of Business Ethics: Definitions, Philosophies, and Implementation," *IM* (January–February 1995): 22–27; Badaracco and Webb, "Business Ethics: a View from the Trenches"; and Ronald B. Morgan, "Self- and Co-Worker Perceptions of Ethics and Their Relationships to Leadership and Salary," *Academy of Management Journal* 36, no. 1 (February 1993): 200–214.

72. Journal Communications—Code of Ethics, from Codes of Ethics Online, The Center for the Study of Ethics in the Professions, Illinois Institute of Technology, www.iit.edu/departments/csep/ PublicWWW/codes/index.html.

73. Alan Yuspeh, "Do the Right Thing," *CIO* (August 1, 2000): 56–58.

74. The Ethics and Compliance Officers Association, www.theecoa.org (accessed on February 27, 2006).

75. Beverly Geber, "The Right and Wrong of Ethics Offices," *Training* (October 1995): 102–118.

76. Kranhold, "U.S. Firms Raise Ethics Focus" and "Our Actions: GE 2005 Citizenship Report," General Electric Company, 2005.

77. Amy Zipkin, "Getting Religion on Corporate Ethics," *The New York Times*, (October 18, 2000): C1.

78. Marcia Parmarlee Miceli and Janet P. Near, "The Relationship among Beliefs, Organizational Positions, and Whistle-Blowing Status: A Discriminant Analysis," *Academy of Management Journal* 27 (1984): 687–705.

79. Eugene Garaventa, "*An Enemy of the People* by Henrik Ibsen: The Politics of Whistle-Blowing," *Journal of Management Inquiry* 3, no. 4 (December 1994): 369–374; Marcia P. Miceli and Janet P. Near, "Whistleblowing: Reaping the Benefits," *Academy of Management Executive* 8, no. 3 (1994): 65–74.

80. Jayne O'Donnell, "Blowing the Whistle Can Lead to Harsh Aftermath, Despite Law," *USA Today* (July 31, 2005): www.usatoday.com.

81. Jerry G. Kreuze, Zahida Luqmani, and Mushtaq Luqmani, "Shades of Gray," *Internal Auditor* (April 2001): 48.

82. George Stalk, "Warm and Fuzzy Doesn't Cut It," *The Wall Street Journal* (February 15, 2005): B2.

83. Hafner and Deutsch, "When Good Will Is Also Good Business"; John A. Pearce II and Jonathan P. Doh, "The High Impact of Collaborative Social Initiatives," *MIT Sloan Management Review* (Spring 2005): 30–39; Carol Hymowitz, "Asked to Be Charitable, More CEOs Seek to Aid Their Businesses As Well," *The Wall Street Journal* (February 22, 2005): B1.

84. Cristina Simón, Juan Luis Martínez, and Ana Agüero, "Solidarity Day at Unión Fenosa in Spain," *Business Horizons* 48 (2005): 161–168.

85. Homer H. Johnson, "Does It Pay to Be Good? Social Responsibility and Financial Performance" *Business Horizons* (November–December 2003): 34–40; Jennifer J. Griffin and John F. Mahon, "The Corporate Social Performance and Corporate Financial Performance Debate: Twenty-Five Years of Incomparable Research," *Business and Society* 36, no. 1 (March 1997): 5–31; Bernadette M. Ruf, Krishnamurty Muralidar, Robert M. Brown, Jay J. Janney, and Karen Paul, "An Empirical Investigation of the Relationship between Change in Corporate Social Performance and Financial Performance: A Stakeholder Theory Perspective," *Journal of Business Ethics* 32, no. 2 (July 2001): 143; Philip L. Cochran and Robert A. Wood, "Corporate Social Responsibility and Financial Performance," *Academy of Management Journal* 27 (1984): 42–56.

86. Paul C. Godfrey, "The Relationship Between Corporate Philanthropy and Shareholder Wealth: A Risk Management Perspective," *Academy of Management Review* 30, no. 4 (2005): 777–798; J. A. Pearce II and J. P. Doh, "The High Impact of Collaborative Social Initiatives"; Curtis C. Verschoor and Elizabeth A. Murphy, "The Financial Performance of Large U.S. Firms and Those with Global Prominence: How Do the Best Corporate Citizens Rate?" *Business and Society Review* 107, no. 3 (Fall 2002): 371–381; Johnson, "Does It Pay to Be Good?"; Dale Kurschner, "5 Ways Ethical Business Creates Fatter Profits," *Business Ethics* (March–April 1996): 20–23. Also see studies reported in Lori Ioannou, "Corporate America's Social Conscience," *Fortune* (May 26, 2003): S1–S10.

87. Verschoor and Murphy, "The Financial Performance of Large U.S. Firms."

88. Gretchen Morgenson, "Shares of Corporate Nice Guys Can Finish First," *New York Times* (April 27, 2003): Section 3, 1.

89. Jean B. McGuire, Alison Sundgren, and Thomas Schneeweis, "Corporate Social Responsibility and Firm Financial Performance," *Academy of Management Journal* 31 (1988): 854–872; and Louisa Wah, "Treading the Sacred Ground," *Management Review* (July–August 1998): 18–22.

90. Vogel, "Is There a Market for Virtue?"

91. Daniel W. Greening and Daniel B. Turban, "Corporate Social Performance as a Competitive Advantage in Attracting a Quality Workforce," *Business and Society* 39, no. 3 (September 2000): 254.

92. "The Socially Correct Corporate Business," in Leslie Holstrom and Simon Brady, "The Changing Face of Global Business," *Fortune* (July 24, 2000): S1–S38.

93. Based on survey results from PricewaterhouseCoopers, *2002 Sustainability Survey Report,* reported in Ioannou, "Corporate America's Social Conscience."

CHAPTER OUTLINE

Manager's Challenge

What Is Entrepreneurship?

Entrepreneurship and the Environment

    Entrepreneurship Today

    Definition of Small Business

    Impact of Entrepreneurial
    Companies

Who Are Entrepreneurs?

    Diversity of Entrepreneurs

    Personality Traits

**Social Entrepreneurship:
An Innovative Approach
to Small Business**

**Launching an Entrepreneurial
Start-Up**

    Starting with the Idea

    Writing the Business Plan

    Choosing a Legal Structure

    Getting Financing

    Tactics for Becoming
    a Business Owner

Managing a Growing Business

    Stages of Growth

    Planning

    Organizing

    Leading

    Controlling

LEARNING OBJECTIVES

After studying this chapter, you should be able to:

1. Describe the importance of entrepreneurship to the U.S. economy.

2. Define the personality characteristics of a typical entrepreneur.

3. Explain social entrepreneurship as a vital part of today's small business environment.

4. Outline the planning necessary to launch an entrepreneurial start-up.

5. Describe the five stages of growth for an entrepreneurial company.

6. Explain how the management functions of planning, organizing, leading, and controlling apply to a growing entrepreneurial company.

MANAGING SMALL BUSINESS START-UPS

MANAGER'S CHALLENGE

Stella Ogiale is facing a dilemma. After being out of the workforce for years, she finds herself in need of a job. Ogiale moved to the United States from Nigeria as a teenager to attend college. After earning a masters degree in public administration and finance, she began working in Washington, D.C., where she fell in love, got married, and put her career on hold to have children. Now, years later, after a separation from her husband, Ogiale needs to go back to work. The only problem is, Ogiale doesn't want a regular 9-to-5 job that will interfere with caring for her three young children, especially her son Chester, who was born with autism. In 1996, while working nights part-time at UPS, Ogiale thinks about her determination to keep Chester at home rather than putting him in an institution, and she has an idea. What if she could bring all the amenities of an institution—medical supplies, pharmaceuticals, and specialized physicians and caregivers—to mentally and physically disabled patients at home? Research shows her that starting a home health care business is fraught with challenges. Payments are low, workers are hard to find and keep, and government regulations are overwhelming. Yet Ogiale also sees that the elderly population in the United States is growing and some states are beginning to search for alternatives to costly nursing home care. She borrows $500 from her sister and uses some birthday money to start Chesterfield Health Services, naming it after her son. Then reality sets in. Ogiale knows she has a good idea, but she also knows she's facing tremendous hurdles.[1]

173

> What advice would you give Stella Ogiale about getting her new company started? Do you think one person with a good idea can create a successful company in a high-risk business like home health care?

■ **TAKE A MOMENT**

Many people dream of starting their own business. Some, like Stella Ogiale, decide to start a business because they're inspired by a great idea or want the flexibility that comes from being self-employed. Others decide to go into business for themselves after they get laid off or find their opportunities limited in big companies. Interest in entrepreneurship and small business is at an all-time high. At college campuses across the United States, ambitious courses, programs, and centers teach the fundamentals of starting a small business. Entrepreneurs have access to business incubators, support networks, and online training courses. The enormous growth of franchising gives beginners an escorted route into a new business. In addition, the Internet opens new avenues for small business formation.

Today, the fastest growing segment of small business in both the United States and Canada is in one-owner operations, or *sole proprietorships*.[2] Sole proprietorships in the United States grew about 4 percent in 2002 alone, the most recent year with statistics available, to 17.6 million. Their combined revenues increased 5.5 percent to $770 billion.[3] After the crash of the dot-com boom, many of these entrepreneurs are finding opportunities in low-tech businesses such as landscaping, child care, and janitorial services. Overall, since the 1970s, the number of businesses in the United States economy has been growing faster than the labor force.[4]

However, running a small business is difficult and risky. The Small Business Administration reports that about 34 percent of small businesses fail within two years of opening and 50 percent fold after three years.[5] For high-tech businesses, the failure rate is even higher. Research has found that the chances are only 6 in 1 million that an idea for a high-tech business eventually turns into a successful public company.[6] Businesses that survive the first few years continue to face tremendous challenges, yet despite the risks, people are entering the world of entrepreneurship at an unprecedented rate. In 2004, an estimated 580,900 new businesses were established in the United States, while an estimated 576,200 closed their doors for good.[7] Small business formation is the primary process by which an economy recreates and reinvents itself,[8] and the turbulence in the small business environment is evidence of a shifting but thriving U.S. economy.

WHAT IS ENTREPRENEURSHIP?

Entrepreneurship is the process of initiating a business venture, organizing the necessary resources, and assuming the associated risks and rewards.[9] An **entrepreneur** is someone who engages in entrepreneurship. An entrepreneur recognizes a viable idea for a business product or service and carries it out by finding and assembling the necessary resources—money, people, machinery, location—to undertake the business venture. Entrepreneurs also assume the risks and reap the rewards of the business. They assume the financial and legal risks of ownership and receive the business's profits.

A good example of entrepreneurship is Andra Rush, who quit her nursing job to start a trucking company in 1984. Using her savings and a loan from her parents, Rush bought two used trucks and a new one and maxed out her credit cards to start the business. She couldn't afford a cell phone or an office manager, so she forwarded calls to her grandmother's house while she was out drumming up business. She learned how to do her own truck repairs and made an impression on customers by specializing in emergency shipping, even if she had to get up at 2 A.M. to deliver the load herself. The early days were rough, and Rush made a lot of sacrifices to succeed, but today Rush Trucking has 350 full-time employees and makes 1,400 shipments a day with 1,000 trucks. The company generated $132 million in revenue in 2003. Rush was willing to take the risks and is now reaping the rewards of entrepreneurship.[10]

Successful entrepreneurs have many different motivations, and they measure rewards in different ways. One study classified small business owners in five different categories, as illustrated in Exhibit 6.1. Some people are *idealists*, who like the idea of working on something that is new, creative, or personally meaningful. *Optimizers* are rewarded by the personal satisfaction of being business owners. Entrepreneurs in the *sustainer* category like the chance to balance work

---

entrepreneurship The process of initiating a business venture, organizing the necessary resources, and assuming the associated risks and rewards.

entrepreneur Someone who recognizes a viable idea for a business product or service and carries it out.

EXHIBIT   6.1

Five Types of Small Business Owners

SOURCE: Study conducted by Yankelovich Partners, reported in Mark Henricks, "Type-Cast," *Entrepreneur* (March 2000): 14–16.

Rewarded by chance to work on something new and creative

Thrive on the challenge of building a larger, more profitable business

Enjoy chance to balance work and personal life

Idealists	Optimizers	Hard Workers	Jugglers	Sustainers
24%	21%	20%	20%	15%

Get personal satisfaction from being business owners

High-energy people who enjoy handling every detail of their own businesses and personal life and often don't want the business to grow too large, while *hard workers* enjoy putting in the long hours and dedication to build a larger, more profitable business. The *juggler* category includes entrepreneurs who like the chance a small business gives them to handle everything themselves. These high-energy people thrive on the pressure of paying bills, meeting deadlines, and making payroll.[11]

Compare the motivation of Paula Turpin to that of Greg Littlefield. Turpin borrowed a few thousand dollars to start a hair salon, Truly Blessed Styles, in Shirley, New York. She does all the cutting, styling, and coloring herself, while her mother helps schedule appointments and keeps the books. Turpin likes the flexibility and freedom of working for herself. Although she hopes to expand by adding beauty supplies, she doesn't want the headaches of managing a large business. Greg Littlefield quit his management job and started a cleaning service because he reasoned that it would never lack customers. From the beginning, when he was working two part-time jobs and cleaning buildings by himself at night, Littlefield had plans for expansion. Within a decade, Littlefield's firm, Professional Facilities Management, grew into a 900-employee company providing a range of services including housekeeping, landscaping, minor maintenance, and security services.[12] Greg Littlefield reflects the motivation of a *hard worker*, whereas Paula Turpin's motivation is more that of a *sustainer*.

Sometimes people start new businesses when they lose their jobs due to corporate downsizing. The major layoffs in the early 2000s provided just the push some latent entrepreneurs needed to strike out on their own. Some experts think an economic downturn is actually the best time to start a business. For one thing, a downturn opens up lots of opportunities because people are looking for lower costs and better ways of doing things. The economic climate also enables the new business to hire good people, forces the entrepreneur to keep costs in line, and provides the time needed to build something of lasting value rather than struggling to keep pace with rapid growth.[13]

Many people also regard entrepreneurship as a better use of their time, talent, and energy. Women and minorities, who have sometimes found their opportunities limited in the corporate world, are often seeing entrepreneurship as the only way to go. Hispanic and African American entrepreneurship is on the rise. The National Federation of Women Business Owners reports that Hispanic women are starting companies in the United States at four times the national growth rate. "The [corporate] work environment is not friendly to Latinas," says Alma Morales Fiojas, CEO of Mana, a National Latina Organization. "Sometimes the best avenue . . . is to go into your own business, where there is more flexibility and you can accomplish more."[14]

Are you interested in becoming a new manager by starting your own business? Explore your proclivity for the efforts and benefits of entrepreneurship by completing the items in the New Manager Self-Test on page 176.

■ **TAKE A MOMENT**

ENTREPRENEURSHIP AND THE ENVIRONMENT

Not so long ago, scholars and policy makers were worrying about the potential of small business to survive. The turbulence in the technology sector and the demise of many dot-com start-ups heightened concerns about whether small companies can compete with big business. However, entrepreneurship and small business, including high-tech start-ups, are vital, dynamic, and increasingly important parts of the U.S. economy. Small businesses grew from 19 million in 1992 to 24.7 million in 2004.[15] These firms account for a tremendous portion of the goods and services provided. Entrepreneurship in other countries is also booming. The list of the most entrepreneurial

IMPROVISATION

Do you have what makes an entrepreneur tick? It is not for the faint of heart. An entrepreneur faces many demands. Do you have the proclivity to start and build your own business? To find out, consider the extent to which each of the following statements characterizes your behavior. Please answer each of the following items as Mostly True or Mostly False for you.

	Mostly True	Mostly False
1. Give me a little information and I can come up with a lot of ideas.	___	___
2. I like pressure in order to focus.	___	___
3. I don't easily get frustrated when things don't go my way.	___	___
4. I identify how resources can be recombined to produce novel outcomes.	___	___
5. I enjoy competing against the clock to meet deadlines.	___	___
6. People in my life have to accept that nothing is more important than the achievement of my school, my sport, or my career goals.	___	___
7. I serve as a role model for creativity.	___	___
8. I think "on my feet" when carrying out tasks.	___	___
9. I am determined and action oriented.	___	___

INTERPRETATION AND SCORING: Each question pertains to some aspect of **improvisation**, which is a correlate of entrepreneurial intentions. Entrepreneurial improvisation consists of three elements. Questions 1, 4, and 7 pertain to **creativity/ingenuity**, the ability to produce novel solutions under constrained conditions. Questions 2, 5, and 8 pertain to working under **pressure/stress**, the ability to excel under pressure-filled circumstances. Questions 3, 6, and 9 pertain to **action/persistence**, the determination to achieve goals and solve problems in the moment. If you answered "Mostly True" to at least two of three questions for each subscale or six of nine for all the questions, then consider yourself an entrepreneur in the making with the potential to manage your own business. If you scored one or fewer "Mostly True" on each subscale or three or fewer for all nine questions, you might want to consider becoming a manager by working for someone else.

SOURCES: Based on Keith M. Hmieleski and Andrew C. Corbett,"Proclivity for Improvisation as a Predictor of Entrepreneurial Intentions,"*Journal of Small Business Management* 44, no. 1 (January 2006): 45–63; and "Do You Have an Entrepreneurial Mind?" *Inc.com* (October 19, 2005).

countries, shown in Exhibit 6.2, is intriguing. A project monitoring entrepreneurial activity around the world reports that an estimated 25 percent of adults age 18 to 64 in Venezuela are either starting up or managing new enterprises. The percentage in Thailand is 20.7 percent, and in Jamaica 17 percent. China and New Zealand also show higher rates of entrepreneurial activity than the U.S. rate of 12.4 percent.[16] Japan, which shows a low rate of only 2.2 percent, is attempting to spur entrepreneurial activity with a new law that makes it possible to start a business with capital of just 1 yen.[17] Structural reforms in Russia spurred a jump in small business formation in that country, and one economic study predicts a doubling of small business as a part of Russia's gross domestic product between the years of 2004 and 2009.[18]

Entrepreneurship Today

Small business is such a dynamic part of today's economy for a number of reasons, including economic changes, globalization and increased competition, advancing technology, and new market niches.[19]

Country	Percentage of Individuals Age 18 to 64 Active in Starting or Managing a New Business, 2005
Venezuela	25.00
Thailand	20.70
New Zealand	17.60
Jamaica	17.00
China	13.70
United States	12.40
Brazil	11.30
Chile	11.10
Australia	10.90
Iceland	10.70
Argentina	9.50
Canada	9.30
Singapore	7.20
Latvia	6.60
Croatia	6.10
Average of countries surveyed	8.40

EXHIBIT 6.2

The World's Most Entrepreneurial Countries

SOURCE: Global Entrepreneurship Monitor, "Table 2: Prevalence Rates of Entrepreneurial Activity Across Countries, 2005" *2005 GEM Tables and Figures,* Babson College and the London Business School, (March 14, 2006): www.gemconsortium.org/category_list.asp.

ECONOMIC CHANGES

Today's economy is fertile soil for entrepreneurs. The economy changes constantly, providing opportunities for new businesses. The demand for services is booming, and 97 percent of service firms are small, with fewer than 100 employees. Landscaping, for example, is one of the fastest growing small businesses, spurred by a surge in housing and office construction.[20] The trend toward outsourcing work to companies that can do it cheaper has also given entrepreneurs new openings. Ogio, a small company based in Bluffdale, Utah, engineers and manufactures innovative golf bags for Callaway, helping the smaller firm's sales skyrocket from $8 million to $47 million in five years.[21]

GLOBALIZATION AND INCREASED COMPETITION

Even the largest of companies can no longer dominate their industry in a fast-changing global marketplace. Globaliza-

© OLIVIER ASSELIN/ASSOCIATED PRESS

CONCEPT CONNECTION U2 lead singer Bono is a classic example of an **idealist entrepreneur.** He started a fashion company, Edun (yes, that's *nude* spelled backwards) to reflect his strong commitment to social causes. The for-profit Dublin-based company's high-end apparel is made in locally run African, South American, and Indian factories that use fair labor practices and, whenever possible, out of organic materials. Bono believes fostering increased participation in world trade is the best way to help developing nations. He is shown here talking with Ghanaian women involved in a microfinance program. The microfinance industry gives tiny loans for people in developing nations to start small businesses.

tion demands entrepreneurial behavior and gives an advantage to the flexibility and fast response that small business can offer rather than to huge companies with economies of scale. Rather than being hurt by the globalization of today's business world, many entrepreneurs are finding new opportunities. Stefanie Heiter started a four-person consulting business called HeiterConnect that helps global managers communicate, collaborate, and motivate across borders.[22] Bill Weiller bought a nearly bankrupt company called Purafil, which was then focused exclusively on making air filters for U.S. pulp and paper factories, and transformed it into a global powerhouse. Purafil now sells filters in 11 industries to companies in 50 countries. Sixty percent of Purafil's revenues come from overseas.[23]

Technology

Rapid advances and dropping prices in computer technology spawned whole new industries, as well as entirely new methods of producing goods and delivering services. Unlike technological progress of the past, these advances are within the reach of companies of all sizes. The explosive growth of the Internet created tremendous opportunities for entrepreneurs. For every story of a failed dot-com business, numerous other small companies are successfully using the Web to sell products and services, to improve productivity, communications, and customer service, or to obtain information and market their services. Intranets.com (previously named Intranetics), for example, found new uses for its Web-based data- and document-management systems, such as helping NASA keep track of data after the 2003 Columbia space shuttle explosion.[24] Jeff Fluhr started a company called StubHub Inc., which is a leading Internet player in the burgeoning market of ticket reselling.[25] Thos. Moser Cabinetmakers, a Maine-based business that makes and sells handcrafted furniture, uses the Web as an online catalog, enabling the small company to reach people it could never reach before the advent of the Internet, which leads to lots of new buyers.[26]

Other technological advances also provide opportunities for small business. Biotechnology, aided by recent work in genomics, is a growing field for small businesses. Five Prime Therapeutics, for example, developed a protein-screening process that can accelerate the development of hit drugs for diseases such as cancer, Type 2 diabetes, and rheumatoid arthritis.[27] Research into microelectromechanical systems (MEMS), tiny machines used in numerous applications from biotechnology and telecommunications to the auto industry, is being conducted primarily by small companies.

New Opportunities and Market Niches

Today's entrepreneurs are taking advantage of the opportunity to meet changing needs in the marketplace. Tapping into the growing *sustainability* movement, as discussed in Chapter 5, for example, Ron Warnecke founded NitroCision, a company that mops up radioactive and industrial waste without the use of chemicals.[28] Stampp Corbin spotted an opportunity in the growing need for companies to dispose of outdated equipment such as personal computers, printers, and servers. His company, RetroBox, wipes the machines clean of all data, refurbishes and sells any that are still useful, and makes sure others are disposed of safely. With organizations continually upgrading, Corbin's business grows each year, with revenue climbing to $14 million in 2004.[29] Here's how Barbara Kavovit found a market niche in the home improvement industry.

© ELAINE THOMPSON/ASSOCIATED PRESS

CONCEPT CONNECTION   Team Germany survived fierce competition to become a finalist in Microsoft's 2006 Imagine Cup, an annual student technology competition. Here, two team members, Piotr Wendt and Mark Thomé, demonstrate to Microsoft chairperson Bill Gates their navigation system for the disabled, which is powered by software they developed. Team Germany's invention earned them the right to participate in the Innovation Accelerator, an intensive two-week workshop co-sponsored by Microsoft and BT. The workshop's goal is to give students the business training they need to translate their **technological advances** into commercial ventures.

While watching an episode of *Sex and the City*, Barbara Kavovit had a eureka moment. On the show, Samantha had just moved into a new apartment and didn't know how to put up curtains. Kavovit, who had been running a construction company for seven years, was dismayed that even strong women can be helpless when it comes to handiwork. She knew that women spend $55 billion a year on home improvement, but she also knew from experience in her own neighborhood that many of them had to rely on others to do the work. Kavovit decided to design a line of women-friendly tools that would represent not only a way to get things done but a whole lifestyle of empowerment.

Barbara K! Enterprises was born and was soon selling $5 million a year in stylish, functional kits of drills, hammers, and screwdrivers, each with a how-to book of tips for hanging curtains, fixing a hole in a wall, or hanging a ceiling fan. Everything in the Barbara K! line is designed to be ergonomically, aesthetically, and psychologically in tune with women. Rather than the patronizing color of pink, everything is designed in strong colors of blue and gray. Although the tools are designed for a woman's hand and strength, they're totally capable of the toughest jobs.

It took Kavovit six months of cold calling to get her first tool kit into the first store, JCPenney, but from there on, the business skyrocketed. The idea of "home improvement as self-improvement" hit home with women, and Barbara K! Enterprises soon expanded into a TV show and a book, *Room for Improvement*. Babara K! kits are sold in U.S. stores such as JCPenney, Bed Bath & Beyond, and Fred Meyer, and now also reach women in four European countries. Barbara K!'s total sales were expected to exceed $15 million in 2006.[30]

■ TAKE A MOMENT

As an aspiring entrepreneur, can you see a market niche that is not being met by an existing organization? How do you feel about organizing the necessary resources and taking the risks to start a company to serve that niche?

Definition of Small Business

The full definition of *small business* used by the U.S. Small Business Administration (SBA) is detailed and complex, including 37 different benchmarks that define 1,151 industries and 13 subindustries across the United States. In general, a small business is considered to be "one that is independently owned and operated and which is not dominant in its field of operation."[31] Exhibit 6.3 gives a few examples of how the SBA defines small business for a sample of industries.

However, the definition of small business is currently under revision in response to concerns from small business owners. After nationwide public hearings in 2005, the SBA determined that standards should be changed in light of shifting economic and industry conditions. Redefining small business size standards is a daunting task, but SBA leaders agree that the standards need to be more flexible in today's world. The SBA's definition has been revised a number of times over the years to reflect changing economic conditions.[32]

Exhibit 6.3 also illustrates general categories of businesses most entrepreneurs start: retail, manufacturing, and service. Additional categories of small businesses are construction, hospitality, communications, finance, and real estate.

Impact of Entrepreneurial Companies

The impact of entrepreneurial companies on the U.S. economy is astonishing. According to the Small Business Administration, businesses with fewer than 500 employees represent 99.7 percent of all firms with employees in the United States, employ more than 50 percent of the nation's nonfarm private sector workers, and generate more than 50 percent of the nation's nonfarm gross domestic product (GDP). In addition, small businesses represent 97 percent of America's exporters and produce 26 percent of all export value.[33] In 2000, the status of the SBA

Manufacturing	
Soft-drink manufacturing	Number of employees does not exceed 500
Electronic computer manufacturing	Number of employees does not exceed 1,000
Prerecorded CD, tape, and record producing	Number of employees does not exceed 750

Retail (Store and Nonstore)	
Sporting goods stores	Average annual receipts do not exceed $6.0 million
Electronic auctions	Average annual receipts do not exceed $21.0 million
Vending machine operators	Average annual receipts do not exceed $6.0 million

Miscellaneous Internet Services	
Internet service providers	Average annual receipts do not exceed $21.0 million
Web search portals	Average annual receipts do not exceed $6.0 million
Internet publishing and broadcasting	Number of employees does not exceed 500

E X H I B I T   6.3

Examples of SBA
Definitions of Small
Business

administrator was elevated to a cabinet-level position in recognition of the importance of small business in the U.S. economy.[34]

Inspired by the growth of companies such as eBay, Google, and Amazon.com, entrepreneurs are still flocking to the Internet to start new businesses. In addition, demographic and lifestyle trends create new opportunities in areas such as environmental services, lawn care, computer maintenance, children's markets, fitness, and home health care. Entrepreneurship and small business in the United States is an engine for job creation and innovation.

JOB CREATION

Researchers disagree over what percentage of new jobs is created by small business. Research indicates that the *age* of a company, more than its size, determines the number of jobs it creates. That is, virtually *all* new jobs in recent years have come from new companies, which include not only small companies but also new branches of huge, multinational organizations.[35] However, small companies still are thought to create a large percentage of new jobs in the United States. The SBA reports that small businesses create 65 percent or more of America's new jobs. Jobs created by small businesses give the United States an economic vitality no other country can claim. However, as we discussed earlier, other countries are also finding new ways to encourage entrepreneurial economic activity.

INNOVATION

According to Cognetics, Inc., a research firm run by David Birch that traces the employment and sales records of some 9 million companies, new and smaller firms have been responsible for 55 percent of the innovations in 362 different industries and 95 percent of all radical innovations. In addition, fast-growing businesses, which Birch calls *gazelles*, produce twice as many product innovations per employee as do larger firms. Consulting firm CHI Research, which tracks innovation in both small and large firms, found that among 1,270 "highly innovative" firms, the number of small businesses rose from 33 percent in 2000 to 40 percent in 2002. Small firms that file for patents typically produce 13 to 14 times more patents per employee than large patenting firms.[36]

Among the notable products for which small businesses can be credited are WD-40, the jet engine, and the shopping cart. Virtually every new business represents an innovation of some sort, whether a new product or service, how the product is delivered, or how it is made.[37] Todd Moses started a company called Accentra to make and sell a new kind of desktop stapler.

> A stapler is a stapler, right? Not really much room for innovation there, right? If you're one of the million or so customers who have purchased a PaperPro, you know that's not true. Todd Moses developed the PaperPro out of sheer frustration with standard staplers that can't handle more than a few pages without jamming. He got the idea while trying to staple stacks of documents in preparation for meeting with venture capitalists about a loan to open a chain of wrap restaurants. On the first 19-page copy, the staple went only half-way through. On the next, the stapler jammed completely. In a panic and running late for his meeting, Moses began pulling out the staples to start over, cutting his finger in the process.
>
> The frustration spurred him to put his restaurant plans on hold and think about a new kind of business. Moses wanted to design a desktop version of a high-powered staple gun that Black & Decker sold for construction applications. He tracked down Joel Marks, the mechanical engineer who had designed the spring-loaded shooting mechanism for the Black & Decker product, and sold him on the idea. Typical office staplers require 30 pounds of force to bind a stack of 20 pages. Moses and Marks designed a compact recoil spring for a desktop stapler that can bind 20 pages with only 7 pounds of force.
>
> Moses was astounded by the response he got when he met with potential distributors: 119 out of the first 120 he contacted signed on to carry the PaperPro. By the end of 2004, the new product had sold more than a million units and was the hottest selling new product of the year for some office supply stores. Accentra now distributes the PaperPro in 60 countries and expected sales of more than $50 million in 2005. Next up for Accentra? How to improve the three-hole punch.[38]

Entrepreneurs like Todd Moses and small companies such as Accentra bring fresh new ideas to stale industries. Many of today's new products from giant corporations were originated by small companies. Consider the popular Crest Spin Brush from Procter & Gamble. The product was originally created by a tiny start-up. P&G bought the company and brought in the entrepreneurial leaders to head up the new division.[39] Entrepreneurial innovation often spurs larger companies to try new things. The giant greeting card companies Hallmark and American Greetings, for example, now include lines of cards for nontraditional families, pet owners, and culturally diverse consumers, all of which were first developed and marketed by small greeting card makers.[40] Small business innovation keeps U.S. companies competitive, which is especially important in today's global marketplace.

WHO ARE ENTREPRENEURS?

The heroes of American business—Henry Ford, Steve Jobs, Sam Walton, Bill Gates, Michael Dell, Oprah Winfrey, Larry Page, and Sergey Brin—are almost always entrepreneurs. Entrepreneurs start with a vision. Often they are unhappy with their current jobs and see an opportunity to bring together the resources needed for a new venture. However, the image of entrepreneurs as bold pioneers probably is overly romantic. A survey of the CEOs of the nation's fastest-growing small firms found that these entrepreneurs could be best characterized as hardworking and practical, with great familiarity with their market and industry.[41] For example, Nancy Rodriguez was a veteran R&D manager at Swift Foods before she started

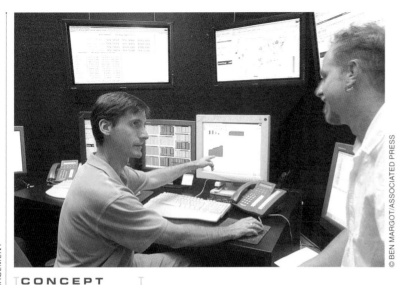

Food Marketing Support Services. Rodriguez started the firm in the mid-1980s when Swift and other big food companies were cutting staff and R&D budgets. Large companies can now take a rough new product idea to Food Marketing, which fully develops the concept, creates prototypes, does taste-testing, and so forth. American Pop Corn, which makes Jolly Time Pop Corn, allocated 100 percent of its new-product development dollars to the 20-person firm, which does about $5 million in business a year.[42]

CONCEPT

C O N N E C T I O N Who hasn't felt trapped in a bad date or an endless meeting? BeVocal, a company that designs voice-activated software for the telecommunications market, used its talent for **innovation** to capitalize on a **new opportunity.** Thanks to BeVocal software, Cingular and Virgin Mobile customers can arrange to be called with a pre-recorded emergency message if they find themselves in a tedious social situation. In the case of Virgin Mobile, it is company founder Richard Branson, feeds excuses the customer can use to make a graceful getaway. Pictured is BeVocal's marketing director Dan Enthoven and interface designer Ryan Bush.

© BEN MARGOT/ASSOCIATED PRESS

Diversity of Entrepreneurs

Entrepreneurs often have backgrounds and demographic characteristics that distinguish them from other people. Entrepreneurs are more likely to be the first-born within their families, and their parents are more likely to have been entrepreneurs. Children of immigrants also are more likely to be entrepreneurs.[43]

Consider Hector Barreto Jr., whose parents were both Mexican immigrants and ran several successful businesses in Kansas City, Missouri, including a restaurant, an import-export business, and a construction firm. After a four-year stint as an area manager for Miller Brewing Company, Hector moved to California and started Barreto Financial Services. Later, he started another firm to provide technical assistance to small businesses. Barreto's next step was into the head office of the Small Business Administration, where he became the first entrepreneur to lead the government agency.[44]

Entrepreneurship offers opportunities for individuals who may feel blocked in established corporations. Women-owned and minority-owned businesses may be the emerging growth companies of the next decade. In 2005, women owned 6.5 million U.S. businesses that generated $950.6 billion in revenues and employed more than 7 million workers. In Canada as well, women entrepreneurs are thriving. Since 1989, the rate of small businesses started by women in Canada grew 60 percent faster than the growth in the number of small businesses started by men.[45] Statistics for minorities in the United States are also impressive, with minorities owning 4.1 million firms that generated $694 billion in revenues and employed 4.8 million people.[46] The number of new firms launched by minorities is growing about 17 percent a year, with African American businesses growing at a rate of about 26 percent a year. African American males between the ages of 25 and 35 start more businesses than any other group in the country. Moreover, the face of entrepreneurship for the future will be increasingly diverse. When Junior Achievement (an organization that educates young people about business) conducted a poll of teenagers ages 13 to 18, it found a much greater interest among minorities than whites in starting a business, as shown in Exhibit 6.4.[47]

The types of businesses launched by minority entrepreneurs are also increasingly sophisticated. The traditional minority-owned mom-and-pop retail store or restaurant is being replaced by firms in industries such as financial services, insurance, and media. For example, Pat Winans, an African American who grew up in a Chicago ghetto, started Magna Securities, a successful institutional brokerage firm in New York City, with just $5,000. Ed Chin, a third-generation Chinese American, founded AIS Corporation to offer small and midsized companies the kind of

	69%
White	

	79%
Hispanic/Latino	

	86%
African American	

	89%
Asian/Pacific Islander	

Percentage of teenagers polled by Junior Achievement who said they want to start their own business

EXHIBIT 6.4

A Glimpse of Tomorrow's Entrepreneurs

SOURCE: Junior Achievement Survey results reported in Cora Daniels,"Minority Rule,"*FSB* (December 2003– January 2004): 65–66.

sophisticated insurance packages usually available only to large companies. Chin originally found a niche by catering to the Asian marketplace, but word-of-mouth has helped his company expand beyond that market.[48]

Personality Traits

A number of studies investigated the personality characteristics of entrepreneurs and how they differ from successful managers in established organizations. Some suggest that entrepreneurs in general want something different from life than do traditional managers. Entrepreneurs seem to place high importance on being free to achieve and maximize their potential. Some 40 traits are identified as associated with entrepreneurship, but 6 have special importance.[49] These characteristics are illustrated in Exhibit 6.5.

INTERNAL LOCUS OF CONTROL

The task of starting and running a new business requires the belief that you can make things come out the way you want. The entrepreneur not only has a vision but also must be able to plan to achieve that vision and believe it will happen. An **internal locus of control** is the belief by individuals that their future is within their control and that external forces have little influence. For entrepreneurs, reaching the future is seen as being in the hands of the individual. Many people, however, feel that the world is highly uncertain and that they are unable to make things come out the way they want. An **external locus of control** is the belief by individuals that their future is not within their control but rather is influenced by external forces. Entrepreneurs are individuals who are convinced they can make the difference between success and failure; hence, they are motivated to take the steps needed to achieve the goal of setting up and running a new business.

internal locus of control The belief by individuals that their future is within their control and that external forces have little influence.

external locus of control The belief by individuals that their future is not within their control but rather is influenced by external forces.

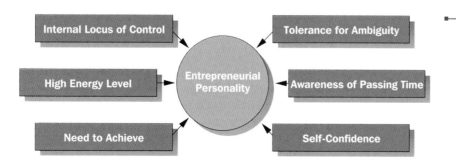

Internal Locus of Control · Tolerance for Ambiguity · High Energy Level · **Entrepreneurial Personality** · Awareness of Passing Time · Need to Achieve · Self-Confidence

EXHIBIT 6.5

Characteristics of Entrepreneurs

SOURCE: Adapted from Charles R. Kuehl and Peggy A. Lambing, *Small Business: Planning and Management* (Ft. Worth: The Dryden Press, 1994): 45.

EXHIBIT 6.6

Reported Hours per Week
Worked by Owners of New
Businesses

SOURCE: National Federa-
tion of Independent Business.
Reported in Mark Robichaux,
"Business First, Family
Second," *The Wall Street
Journal* (May 12, 1989): B1.

HIGH ENERGY LEVEL

A business start-up requires great effort. Most entrepreneurs report struggle and hardship. They persist and work incredibly hard despite traumas and obstacles. A survey of business owners reported that half worked 60 hours or more per week. Another reported that entrepreneurs worked long hours, but that beyond 70 hours little benefit was gained. The data in Exhibit 6.6 show findings from a survey conducted by the National Federation of Independent Business. New business owners work long hours, with only 23 percent working fewer than 50 hours, which is close to a normal workweek for managers in established businesses.

NEED TO ACHIEVE

Another human quality closely linked to entrepreneurship is the **need to achieve**, which means that people are motivated to excel and pick situations in which success is likely.[50] People who have high achievement needs like to set their own goals, which are moderately difficult. Easy goals present no challenge; unrealistically difficult goals cannot be achieved. Intermediate goals are challenging and provide great satisfaction when achieved. High achievers also like to pursue goals for which they can obtain feedback about their success.

SELF-CONFIDENCE

People who start and run a business must act decisively. They need confidence about their ability to master the day-to-day tasks of the business. They must feel sure about their ability to win customers, handle the technical details, and keep the business moving. Entrepreneurs also have a general feeling of confidence that they can deal with anything in the future; complex, unanticipated problems can be handled as they arise.

■ **TAKE A MOMENT**
Go to the experiential exercise on page 199 that pertains to your entrepreneurial potential.

AWARENESS OF PASSING TIME

Entrepreneurs tend to be impatient; they feel a sense of urgency. They want things to progress as if there is no tomorrow. They want things moving immediately and seldom procrastinate. Entrepreneurs seize the moment.

TOLERANCE FOR AMBIGUITY

Many people need work situations characterized by clear structure, specific instructions, and complete information. **Tolerance for ambiguity** is the psychological characteristic that allows a person to be untroubled by disorder and uncertainty. This trait is important, because few situations present more uncertainty than starting a new business. Decisions are made without clear understanding of options or certainty about which option will succeed.

need to achieve A human quality linked to entrepreneurship in which people are motivated to excel and pick situations in which success is likely.

tolerance for ambiguity The psychological characteristic that allows a person to be untroubled by disorder and uncertainty.

These personality traits and the demographic characteristics discussed earlier offer an insightful but imprecise picture of the entrepreneur. Successful entrepreneurs come in all ages, from all backgrounds, and may have a combination of personality traits. No one should be discouraged from starting a business because he or she doesn't fit a specific profile. One review of small business suggests that the three most important traits of successful entrepreneurs in today's turbulent environment are realism, flexibility, and passion. Even the most realistic entrepreneurs tend to underestimate the difficulties of building a business, so they need flexibility and a passion for their idea to survive the hurdles.[51]

SOCIAL ENTREPRENEURSHIP: AN INNOVATIVE APPROACH TO SMALL BUSINESS

In today's shifting business and social environment, a new breed of entrepreneur has emerged—the **social entrepreneur**. Social entrepreneurs are leaders who are committed to both good business and positive social change. They create new business models that meet critical human needs and solve important problems that remain unsolved by current economic and social institutions.[52] Consider John Wood, who quit his job as an executive with Microsoft's Asian operations to start Room to Read, which works collaboratively with villagers in Southeast Asia to build schools and libraries. Earl Martin Phalen founded BELL (Building Educated Leaders for Life) out of his Boston living room in 1992 to provide after-school and summer support services to low-income students in grades K–6. As an African American growing up in the state's foster care system, Bell understood first-hand how the right kind of support can change lives and communities. "To know that [somebody] supported me, and all of a sudden, it took my life from going to jail to going to Yale," he says of his motivation to start BELL. All 20 of the students in BELL's first class went on to college.[53]

Social entrepreneurship combines the creativity, business smarts, passion, and hard work of the traditional entrepreneur with a mission to change the world for the better. One writer referred to this new breed as a cross between Richard Branson, the high-powered CEO of Virgin Airlines, and Mother Teresa, a Catholic nun who dedicated her life to serving the poor.[54] Social entrepreneurs have a primary goal of improving society rather than maximizing profits, but they also emphasize solid business results, high performance standards, and accountability for results. The organizations created by social entrepreneurs may or may not make a profit, but the bottom line for these companies is always social betterment rather than economic return. For entrepreneur Judy Wicks, founder of White Dog Enterprises in Philadelphia, the purpose of business is to make the world a better place. The Unlocking Innovative Solutions Through People box describes how Wicks combines business with social activism.

Social entrepreneurship is not new, but the phenomenon blossomed over the past 20 or so years. Exact figures for the number of social entrepreneurs are difficult to verify, but estimates number in the tens of thousands working around the world. The innovative organizations created by social entrepreneurs are defying the traditional boundaries between business and welfare.[55] One good illustration is Project Impact, founded by David Green. Project Impact helped start a factory in India that makes inexpensive plastic lenses used in cataract surgery. The factory provides lenses, some at no cost, for 200,000 poor Indians a year. It also makes money—30 percent profit margins in 2003—and has captured 10 percent of the global market for intraocular lenses. Green expanded his approach to other parts

social entrepreneur
Entrepreneurial leaders who are committed to both good business and changing the world for the better.

Unlocking Innovative Solutions Through | PEOPLE |

WHITE DOG ENTERPRISES: DOING WELL BY DOING GOOD

Judy Wicks believes the first responsibility of business is to serve the common good. As owner of White Dog Enterprises in Philadelphia, Wicks puts her philosophy into practice every day. "I totally believe that you can do well and do good at the same time," the successful entrepreneur says.

Without question, White Dog is doing well. Begun in 1983 as a small muffin shop, Wicks's restaurant and gift shop now occupy four adjacent Victorian-era brownstones on the edge of the University of Pennsylvania's campus. The 200-seat café is regularly full of both locals as well as out-of-town visitors drawn by its national reputation. They come to lunch on expertly prepared black pepper-seared organic beef salad or dine on herb-roasted free-range chicken. With annual revenues of about $5 million, White Dog has a profit margin of about 7 percent, at least twice the industry average.

Wicks is equally intent on doing good. She believes all business should strive to be humane, sustainable, small, and local. She practices what she preaches by paying entry-level employees a living wage and then creating a sense of community by celebrating their artistic endeavors or partially subsidizing their travels to places such as Cuba or Romania on White Dog cultural exchange trips. White Dog buys all of its produce from nearby organic family farms and its fish from sustainable fisheries. In addition, Wicks insists that the meat and poultry White Dog uses be humanely raised. As another step toward sustainability, the restaurant runs solely on wind-generated electricity. Each year, 20 percent of White Dog's profits go into its own corporate foundation and other nonprofits.

Wicks's commitment to combining business with social activism extends well beyond her restaurant operations. She cheerfully admits using good food to lure customers whom she then attempts to turn into social activists. Her efforts to educate and inspire range from regularly scheduled events such as a three-course dinner followed by a talk on animal rights to a six-day community service trip to hurricane-ravaged New Orleans.

Make no mistake: Wicks is a shrewd businessperson. Her employee policies result in low turnover, her produce is fresher for being locally grown, and those special events she schedules on Monday nights bring in customers on what is typically a slow night in the restaurant business. Still, her refusal to start a White Dog Café chain is a testament to the depth of her conviction that creating a sense of community is just as important as making money. It's her business model, not her brand, that she'd dearly love to spread far and wide.

SOURCES: Justin Martin, "It ain't easy being green, but this Philly institution proves that being good to the earth can be good for the wallet, too," *Fortune Small Business* (June 1, 2003): http://money.cnn.com/magazines/fsb; Lawrence Biemiller, "At Penn, the White Dog Café Feeds Activists' Hunger," *Chronicle of Higher Education* (February 3, 2006): http://chronicle.com; Michael P. Cronin, "Best Work and Life: One Life to Live," *Inc.* (July 1993): 56; www.whitedog.com; and Rebecca Ritzel, "Local Food Fuels Health Economy, Cafe Owner Says," *Intelligencer Journal* (April 21, 2004): 1.

---

of the world, as well as the United States, and is adding hearing aids to the product mix.[56] As another example, ACCIÓN International is a leader in the *microfinance* industry. ACCIÓN developed a network of lending institutions that give tiny loans and business training to poor people to start modest businesses in developing countries. One Bolivian woman used a $100 loan to start a bread-making business using the mud oven in her one-room home. Six years later, she borrowed $2,800 to expand to five mud ovens and a backyard storefront. ACCIÓN now operates in 23 countries and boasts a 97 percent repayment rate on loans of some $7.6 billion.[57]

LAUNCHING AN ENTREPRENEURIAL START-UP

Whether one starts a socially oriented company or a traditional for-profit small business, the first step in pursuing an entrepreneurial dream is to come up with a viable idea and then plan like crazy. Once someone has a new idea in mind, a business plan must be drawn and decisions must be made about legal structure, financing, and basic tactics, such as whether to start the business from scratch and whether to pursue international opportunities from the start.

Starting with the Idea

To some people, the idea for a new business is the easy part. They do not even consider entrepreneurship until they are inspired by an exciting idea. Other people decide they want to run their own business and set about looking for an idea or opportunity. Exhibit 6.7 shows the most important reasons that people start a new business and the source of new business ideas. Note that 37 percent of business founders got their idea from an in-depth understanding of the industry, primarily because of past job experience. Interestingly, almost as many—36 percent—spotted a market niche that wasn't being filled.[58]

The trick for entrepreneurs is to blend their own skills and experience with a need in the marketplace. Acting strictly on one's own skills may produce something no one wants to buy. On the other hand, finding a market niche that one does not have the ability to fill doesn't work either. Both personal skill and market need typically must be present.

Writing the Business Plan

Once an entrepreneur is inspired by a new business idea, careful planning is crucial. A **business plan** is a document specifying the business details prepared by an entrepreneur prior to opening a new business. Planning forces the entrepreneur to carefully think through the issues and problems associated with starting and developing the business. Most entrepreneurs have to borrow money, and a business plan is absolutely critical for persuading lenders and investors to participate in the business. Studies show that small businesses with a carefully thought-out, written business plan are much more likely to succeed than those without one.[59] To attract the interest of venture capitalists or other potential investors, the entrepreneur should keep the plan crisp and compelling.

The details of a business plan may vary, but successful business plans generally share several characteristics:[60]

:: Demonstrate a clear, compelling vision that creates an air of excitement.

:: Provide clear and realistic financial projections.

:: Profile potential customers and the target market.

© CITIZEN SCHOOLS

CONCEPT CONNECTION **Social entrepreneurs** Eric Schwarz and Ned Rimer created Citizen Schools to reach out to middle school children, pictured here, with after-school programs that include hands-on apprenticeships taught by volunteer professionals. The apprentices create actual products, ranging from solar cars to well-managed stock portfolios. The goal is to give students the skills and motivation to do well in their academic and personal lives. One reason the organization is so successful is that it is run on solid business principles, with a well-honed strategy and growth plan that includes concrete objectives and specific performance measures.

business plan A document specifying the business details prepared by an entrepreneur prior to opening a new business.

EXHIBIT 6.7

Sources of Entrepreneurial Motivation and New-Business Ideas

Reasons for Starting a Business

41%	Joined Family Business
36%	To Control My Future
27%	To Be My Own Boss
25%	To Fulfill a Dream
5%	Downsized/Laid Off

Source of New Business Ideas

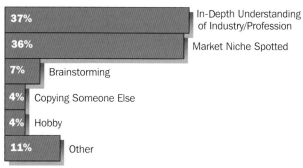

37%	In-Depth Understanding of Industry/Profession
36%	Market Niche Spotted
7%	Brainstorming
4%	Copying Someone Else
4%	Hobby
11%	Other

SOURCES: "The Rewards," *Inc.* (May 29, 2001): 50–51; and Leslie Brokaw, "How to Start an *Inc.* 500 Company," *Inc.* 500 (1994): 51–65.

HELPFUL HINTS FOR WRITING THE BUSINESS PLAN

The Summary

:: Make it no more than three pages.

:: Summarize the what, how, why, where, and so on.

:: Complete this part *after* the finished business plan has been written.

The summary is the most crucial part of your plan because it must capture the reader's interest.

The Business Description Segment

:: List the name of the business.

:: Provide a background of the industry with history of the company (if any).

:: Describe clearly the potential of the new venture.

The Marketing Segment

:: Convince investors that sales projections and competition can be met.

:: Use and disclose market studies.

:: Identify target market, market position, and market share.

:: Evaluate *all* competition and specifically cover why and how you will be better than the competitors.

:: Identify all market sources and assistance used for this segment.

:: Demonstrate pricing strategy; your price must penetrate and maintain a market share to *produce profits*. Thus the lowest price is *not* necessarily the "best" price.

:: Identify your advertising plans with cost estimates to validate the proposed strategy.

The Research, Design, and Development Segment

:: Cover the *extent* of and *costs involved* in needed research, testing, or development.

:: Explain carefully what has been accomplished *already* (prototype, lab testing, early development).

:: Mention any research or technical assistance provided for you.

The Manufacturing Segment

:: Provide the advantages of your location (zoning, tax laws, wage rates).

:: List the production needs in terms of facilities (plant, storage, office space) and equipment (machinery, furnishings, supplies).

:: Describe the access to transportation (for shipping and receiving).

:: Explain proximity to your suppliers.

:: Mention the availability of labor in your location.

:: Provide estimates of manufacturing costs, but be careful because too many entrepreneurs underestimate their costs.

The Management Segment

:: Provide résumés of all key people in the management of the venture.

:: Carefully describe the legal structure of the venture (sole proprietorship, partnership, or corporation).

:: Cover the added assistance (if any) of advisers, consultants, and directors.

:: Provide information on how everyone is to be compensated (how much, also).

The Critical Risks Segment

:: Discuss potential risks *before* investors point them out. Some examples follow:

:: Price cutting by competitors

:: Potentially unfavorable industrywide trends

:: Design or manufacturing costs in excess of estimates

:: Sales projections not achieved

:: Product development schedule not met

:: Difficulties or long lead times encountered in the procurement of parts or raw materials

:: Larger-than-expected innovation and development costs to stay competitive

:: Name alternative courses of action.

The Financial Segment

:: Provide statements.

:: Describe the needed sources for your funds and the uses you intend for the money.

:: Provide a budget.

:: Create stages of financing for the purpose of allowing evaluation by investors at various points.

The Milestone Schedule Segment

:: Provide a timetable or chart to demonstrate when each phase of the venture is to be completed in order to show the relationship of events and provide a deadline for accomplishment.

SOURCE: Donald F. Kuratko, Ray V. Montagno, and Frank J. Sabatine, *The Entrepreneurial Decision* (Muncie, IN: The Midwest Entrepreneurial Education Center, Ball State University, 1997): 45–46. Reprinted with permission.

- :: Include detailed information about the industry and competitors.
- :: Provide evidence of an effective entrepreneurial management team.
- :: Pay attention to good formatting and clear writing.
- :: Keep the plan short—no more than 50 pages.
- :: Highlight critical risks that may threaten business success.
- :: Spell out the sources and uses of start-up funds and operating funds.
- :: Capture the reader's interest with a killer summary.

The business plan should indicate where the product or service fits into the overall industry and should draw on concepts that will be discussed throughout this book. For example, Chapter 8 will describe competitive strategies that entrepreneurs can use. Detailed suggestions for writing a business plan are provided in the Manager's Shoptalk box.

Choosing a Legal Structure

Before entrepreneurs begin a business, and perhaps again as it expands, they must choose an appropriate legal structure for the company. The three basic choices are proprietorship, partnership, or corporation.

SOLE PROPRIETORSHIP

A **sole proprietorship** is defined as an unincorporated business owned by an individual for profit. Proprietorships make up the majority of businesses in the United States. This form is popular because it is easy to start and has few legal requirements. A proprietor has total ownership and control of the company and can make all decisions without consulting anyone. However, this type of organization also has drawbacks. The owner has unlimited liability for the business, meaning that if someone sues, the owner's personal as well as business assets are at risk. Also, financing can be harder to obtain because business success rests on one person's shoulders.

PARTNERSHIP

A **partnership** is an unincorporated business owned by two or more people. Partnerships, like proprietorships, are relatively easy to start. Two friends may reach an agreement to start a graphic arts company. To avoid misunderstandings and to make sure the business is well planned, it is wise to draw up and sign a formal partnership agreement with the help of an attorney. The agreement specifies how partners are to share responsibility and resources and how they will contribute their expertise. The disadvantages of partnerships are the unlimited liability of the partners and the disagreements that almost always occur among strong-minded people. A poll by *Inc.* magazine illustrated the volatility of partnerships. Fifty-nine percent of respondents considered partnerships a bad business move, citing reasons such as partner problems and conflicts. Partnerships often dissolve within five years. Respondents who liked partnerships pointed to the equality of partners (sharing of workload and emotional and financial burdens) as the key to a successful partnership.[61]

CORPORATION

A **corporation** is an artificial entity created by the state and existing apart from its owners. As a separate legal entity, the corporation is liable for its actions and must pay taxes on its income. Unlike other forms of ownership, the corporation has a legal life of its own; it continues to exist regardless of whether the owners live or die. And the corporation, not the owners, is sued in the case of liability. Thus, continuity

CONCEPT CONNECTION Entrepreneurs Roberto Monti and his wife Maria Guerrizio, founders of Milan-based fashion house Piazza Sempione, knew exactly where they wanted the company to go. After getting Piazza Sempione established, they wanted to open more stand-alone stores, expand into handbags and shoes, and go global. But that required an infusion of cash. The partners at L Capital, a private equity firm, were so impressed by the entrepreneurs' solid **business plan** that they acquired a majority stake in the company. That gave Piazza Sempione both the funds and the strategic expertise needed to take it to the next level.

189

Chapter 6 MANAGING SMALL BUSINESS START-UPS

sole proprietorship An unincorporated business owned by an individual for profit.

partnership An unincorporated business owned by two or more people.

corporation An artificial entity created by the state and existing apart from its owners.

and limits on owners' liability are two principal advantages of forming a corporation. For example, a physician can form a corporation so that liability for malpractice will not affect his or her personal assets. The major disadvantage of the corporation is that it is expensive and complex to do the paperwork required to incorporate the business and to keep the records required by law. When proprietorships and partnerships are successful and grow large, they often incorporate to limit liability and to raise funds through the sale of stock to investors.

Getting Financing

Most entrepreneurs are particularly concerned with financing the business. A few types of businesses can still be started with a few thousand dollars, but starting a business usually requires coming up with a significant amount of initial funding. An investment is required to acquire labor and raw materials and perhaps a building and equipment. High-tech businesses, for example, typically need from $50,000 to $500,000 just to get through the first six months, even with the founder drawing no salary.[62] Forrester Research estimates that the total cost to get a business up and running on the Internet ranges from $2 million to $40 million.[63]

Many entrepreneurs rely on their own resources for initial funding, but they often have to mortgage their homes, depend on credit cards, borrow money from a bank, or give part of the business to a venture capitalist.[64] The financing decision initially involves two options—whether to obtain loans that must be repaid (debt financing) or whether to share ownership (equity financing).

DEBT FINANCING

Borrowing money that has to be repaid at a later date in order to start a business is referred to as **debt financing**. One common source of debt financing for a start-up is to borrow from family and friends. Increasingly, entrepreneurs are using their personal credit cards as a form of debt financing. Another common source is a bank loan. Banks provide some 25 percent of all financing for small business. Sometimes entrepreneurs can obtain money from a finance company, wealthy individuals, or potential customers. A typical source of funds for businesses with high potential is through **angel financing**. Angels are wealthy individuals, typically with business experience and contacts, who believe in the idea for the start-up and are willing to invest their personal funds to help the business get started. Significantly, angels also provide advice and assistance as the entrepreneur is developing the company. The entrepreneur wants angels who can make business contacts, help find talented employees, and serve as all-around advisors.

Another form of loan financing is provided by the Small Business Administration (SBA). Staples, which started with one office supply store in Brighton, Massachusetts, in 1986, got its start toward rapid growth with the assistance of SBA financing. Today, Staples is the country's largest operator of office superstores, with more than 1,500 stores and 58,000 employees worldwide.[65] The SBA is especially helpful for people without substantial assets, providing an opportunity for single parents, minority group members, and others with a good idea but who might be considered high-risk by a traditional bank. The percentage of SBA loans to women, Hispanics, African Americans, and Asian Americans increased significantly in recent years.[66]

EQUITY FINANCING

Any money invested by owners or by those who purchase stock in a corporation is considered equity funds. **Equity financing** consists of funds that are invested in exchange for ownership in the company.

A **venture capital firm** is a group of companies or individuals that invests money in new or expanding businesses for ownership and potential profits. This form of capital is a potential for businesses with high earning and growth possibilities.

debt financing Borrowing money that has to be repaid at a later date in order to start a business.

angel financing Financing provided by a wealthy individual who believes in the idea for a start-up and provides personal funds and advice to help the business get started.

equity financing Financing that consists of funds that are invested in exchange for ownership in the company.

venture capital firm A group of companies or individuals that invests money in new or expanding businesses for ownership and potential profits.

Venture capitalists are particularly interested in high-tech businesses such as biotechnology, innovative online ventures, or telecommunications because they have the potential for high rates of return on investment.[67] The venture capital firm Lighthouse Capital Partners, for example, provided some of the early funding for Netflix, the online DVD rental service.[68] Venture capitalists also usually provide assistance, advice, and information to help the entrepreneur prosper. A growing number of minority-owned venture capital firms, such as Provender Capital, founded by African American entrepreneur Fred Terrell, are ensuring that minorities have a fair shot at acquiring equity financing.[69]

Go to the ethical dilemma on page 199 that pertains to raising funds for high-tech start-ups.

TAKE A MOMENT

Tactics for Becoming a Business Owner

Aspiring entrepreneurs can become business owners in several different ways. They can start a new business from scratch, buy an existing business, or start a franchise. Another popular entrepreneurial tactic is to participate in a business incubator.

START A NEW BUSINESS

One of the most common ways to become an entrepreneur is to start a new business from scratch. This approach is exciting because the entrepreneur sees a need for a product or service that has not been filled before and then sees the idea or dream become a reality. Ray Petro invested his $50,000 life savings and took out a $25,000 loan to launch Ray's Mountain Bike Indoor Park after learning from other mountain biking enthusiasts of their frustration with not being able to ride during the winter months. Taryn Rose started her shoe company, Taryn Rose International, after searching for stylish shoes that wouldn't destroy her feet while working long hours as an orthopedic surgeon.[70] The advantage of starting a business is the ability to develop and design the business in the entrepreneur's own way. The entrepreneur is solely responsible for its success. A potential disadvantage is the long time it can take to get the business off the ground and make it profitable. The uphill battle is caused by the lack of established clientele and the many mistakes made by someone new to the business. Moreover, no matter how much planning is done, a start-up is risky, with no guarantee that the new idea will work. Some entrepreneurs, especially in high-risk industries, develop partnerships with established companies that can help the new company get established and grow. Others use the technique of outsourcing—having some activities handled by outside contractors—to minimize the costs and risks of doing everything in-house.[71] For example, Philip Chigos and Mary Domenico are building their children's pajama business from the basement of their two-bedroom apartment, using manufacturers in China and Mexico to produce the goods and partnering with a local firm to receive shipments, handle quality control, and distribute finished products.[72]

© OVERSTOCK.COM/PR NEWSWIRE PHOTO SERVICE (NEWSCOM)

CONCEPT

CONNECTION Finding **financing** can be difficult for entrepreneurs. For example, over 50 **venture capital** firms turned down Patrick Byrne when he was trying to start Overstock.com, a retail liquidation, Web-based business. Motivated in part by his desire to be his own boss, Byrne started the company anyway after liquidating most of his personal assets. Still, the challenges and risks do not stop there. According to the Small Business Administration, only half of all new employer firms survive beyond four years.

BUY AN EXISTING BUSINESS

Because of the long start-up time and the inevitable mistakes, some entrepreneurs prefer to reduce risk by purchasing an existing business. This direction offers the advantage of a shorter time to get started and an existing track record. The entrepreneur may get a bargain price if the owner wishes to retire or has other family considerations. Moreover, a new business may overwhelm an entrepreneur with the amount of work to be done and procedures to be determined. An established business already has filing systems, a payroll tax system, and other operating procedures. Potential disadvantages are the need to pay for goodwill that the owner believes exists and the possible existence of ill will toward the business. In addition, the company may have bad habits and procedures or outdated technology, which may be why the business is for sale.

BUY A FRANCHISE

Franchising is perhaps the most rapidly growing path to entrepreneurship. The International Franchise Association reports that the country's 320,000 franchise outlets account for about $1 trillion in annual sales.[73] According to some estimates, 1 out of every 12 businesses in the United States is franchised, and a franchise opens every eight minutes of every business day.[74] **Franchising** is an arrangement by which the owner of a product or service allows others to purchase the right to distribute the product or service with help from the owner. The franchisee invests his or her money and owns the business but does not have to develop a new product, create a new company, or test the market. Franchises exist for weight-loss clinics, pet-sitting services, sports photography, bakeries, janitorial services, auto repair shops, real estate offices, and numerous other types of businesses, in addition to the traditional fast-food outlets. Exhibit 6.8 lists five franchise concepts that have been popular in recent years, according to *The Wall Street Journal*. The exhibit lists the type of business, the number of franchisees as of late 2003, and the initial costs. Initial franchise fees can range from $1,000 to $250,000, and that doesn't count the other start-up costs the entrepreneur will have to cover. A study by an economics professor several years ago found that the typical franchise costs $94,886 to open.[75] For a casual restaurant such as Buffalo Wild Wings Grill & Bar, listed in the exhibit, the cost is much higher, $969,500 and up, depending on the restaurant location.

The powerful advantage of a franchise is that management help is provided by the owner. For example, Subway, the second fastest growing franchise in the country, does not want a franchisee to fail. Subway has regional development agents who do the research to find good locations for Subway's sandwich outlets. The Subway franchisor also provides two weeks of training at company headquarters and ongoing operational and marketing support.[76] Franchisors provide an established name and national advertising to stimulate demand for the product or service. Potential disadvantages are the lack of control that occurs when franchisors want every business managed in exactly the same way. In some cases, franchisors require

franchising An arrangement by which the owner of a product or service allows others to purchase the right to distribute the product or service with help from the owner.

EXHIBIT 6.8

Five Hot Franchise Concepts for Today

Franchise	Type of Business	Number of Outlets	Initial Costs
Curves for Women	Exercise, weight loss centers	5,646	$30,625, not including real estate
Cruise Planners	Selling ocean cruises	389	$2,095–$18,600
Buffalo Wild Wings Grill & Bar	Sports bar	145	$969,500+
Jani-King	Building cleaning, maintenance	7,843	$11,300–$34,100
Comfort Keepers	Nonmedical home care for seniors	386	$39,700–$65,100

SOURCE: Richard Gibson, "Small Business (A Special Report); Where the Buzz Is: Five of the Hottest Franchise Concepts Out There—and Their Chances of Becoming the Next Big Thing," *The Wall Street Journal* (December 15, 2003): R7.

Questions about the Entrepreneur	Questions about the Franchisor	Before Signing the Dotted Line
1. Will I enjoy the day-to-day work of the business?	1. What assistance does the company provide in terms of selection of location, setup costs, and securing credit; day-to-day technical assistance; marketing; and ongoing training and development?	1. Do I understand the risks associated with this business, and am I willing to assume them?
2. Do my background, experience, and goals make this opportunity a good choice for me?	2. How long does it take the typical franchise owner to start making a profit?	2. Have I had an advisor review the disclosure documents and franchise agreement?
3. Am I willing to work within the rules and guidelines established by the franchisor?	3. How many franchises changed ownership within the past year, and why?	3. Do I understand the contract?

■
E X H I B I T   6.9

Sample Questions for Choosing a Franchise
SOURCES: Based on Thomas Love, "The Perfect Franchisee," Nation's Business (April 1998): 59–65; and Roberta Maynard, "Choosing a Franchise," Nation's Business (October 1996): 56–63.

that franchise owners use certain contractors or suppliers that might cost more than others would. In addition, franchises can be expensive, and the high start-up costs are followed with monthly payments to the franchisor that can run from 2 percent to 15 percent of gross sales.[77]

Entrepreneurs who are considering buying a franchise should investigate the company thoroughly. The prospective franchisee is legally entitled to a copy of franchisor disclosure statements, which include information on 20 topics, including litigation and bankruptcy history, identities of the directors and executive officers, financial information, identification of any products the franchisee is required to buy, and from whom those purchases must be made. The entrepreneur also should talk with as many franchise owners as possible, because they are among the best sources of information about how the company really operates.[78] Exhibit 6.9 lists some specific questions entrepreneurs should ask about themselves and the company when considering buying a franchise. Answering such questions can improve the chances for a successful career as a franchisee.

> As a new manager considering entrepreneurship, think about whether you want to start a business from scratch, buy an existing business, or open a franchise. You will want to evaluate the advantages and disadvantages of each, and talk with other entrepreneurs for advice. Consider joining a business incubator to benefit from the knowledge and expertise of a mentor.

■ **TAKE A MOMENT**

PARTICIPATE IN A BUSINESS INCUBATOR

An attractive option for entrepreneurs who want to start a business from scratch is to join a business incubator. A **business incubator** typically provides shared office space, management support services, and management and legal advice to entrepreneurs. Incubators also give entrepreneurs a chance to share information with one another about local business, financial aid, and market opportunities. A recent innovation is the *virtual incubator*, which does not require that people set up on-site. These virtual organizations connect entrepreneurs with a wide range of experts and mentors and offer lower overhead and cost savings for cash-strapped small business owners. Christie Stone, co-founder of Ticobeans, a coffee distributor in New Orleans, likes the virtual approach because it gives her access to top-notch advice while allowing her to keep her office near her inventory.[79]

The concept of business incubators arose about two decades ago to nurture start-up companies. Business incubators have become a significant segment of the

business incubator An innovation that provides shared office space, management support services, and management advice to entrepreneurs.

small business economy, with approximately 1,100 in operation in the United States in 2005.[80] During the dot-com boom, a tremendous jump in the number of for-profit incubators ended as many of them went out of business when the tech economy crashed.[81] The incubators that are thriving are primarily not-for-profits and those that cater to niches or focus on helping women or minority entrepreneurs. These incubators include those run by government agencies and universities to boost the viability of small business and spur job creation. The great value of an incubator is the expertise of a mentor, who serves as advisor, role model, and cheerleader, and ready access to a team of lawyers, accountants, and other advisors. Incubators also give budding entrepreneurs a chance to network and learn from one another.[82] Incubators are an important part of the international entrepreneurial landscape, as well. For example, Harmony is a global network support system for business incubators. Harmony was started in 1998—with partners in Germany, France, Spain, Finland, Switzerland, Australia, Japan, and the United States—to provide training and support for both new and established incubators worldwide, enabling them to better serve clients and improve the success of small businesses.[83]

MANAGING A GROWING BUSINESS

Once an entrepreneurial business is up and running, how does the owner manage it? Often the traits of self-confidence, creativity, and internal locus of control lead to financial and personal grief as the enterprise grows. A hands-on entrepreneur who gave birth to the organization loves perfecting every detail. But after the start-up, continued growth requires a shift in management style. Those who fail to adjust to a growing business can be the cause of the problems rather than the solution.[84] In this section, we look at the stages through which entrepreneurial companies move and then consider how managers should carry out their planning, organizing, leading, and controlling.

Stages of Growth

Entrepreneurial businesses go through distinct stages of growth, with each stage requiring different management skills. The five stages are illustrated in Exhibit 6.10.

EXHIBIT   6.10

Five Stages of Growth for an Entrepreneurial Company

SOURCE: Based on Neil C. Churchill and Virginia L. Lewis, "The Five Stages of Small Business Growth," *Harvard Business Review* (May–June 1993): 30–50.

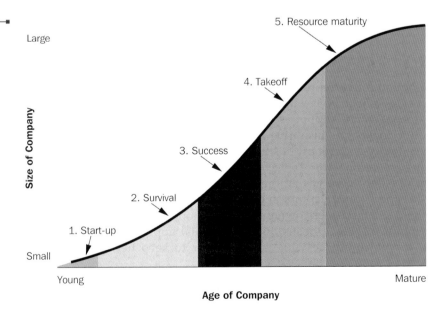

1. *Start-up.* In this stage, the main problems are producing the product or service and obtaining customers. Several key issues facing managers are: Can we get enough customers? Will we survive? Do we have enough money? Burt's Bees was in the start-up stage when Roxanne Quimby was hand-making candles and personal care products from the beeswax of Burt Shavitz's bees and selling them at craft fairs in Maine.

2. *Survival.* At this stage, the business demonstrates that it is a workable business entity. It produces a product or service and has sufficient customers. Concerns here involve with finances—generating sufficient cash flow to run the business and making sure revenues exceed expenses. The organization will grow in size and profitability during this period. Burt's Bees reached $3 million in sales by 1993, and Quimby moved the business from Maine to North Carolina to take advantage of state policies that helped her keep costs in line.

3. *Success.* At this point, the company is solidly based and profitable. Systems and procedures are in place to allow the owner to slow down if desired. The owner can stay involved or consider turning the business over to professional managers. Quimby chose to stay closely involved with Burt's Bees, admitting that she's a bit of a control freak about the business.

4. *Takeoff.* Here the key problem is how to grow rapidly and finance that growth. The owner must learn to delegate, and the company must find sufficient capital to invest in major growth. This period is pivotal in an entrepreneurial company's life. Properly managed, the company can become a big business. However, another problem for companies at this stage is how to maintain the advantages of "smallness" as the company grows. In 2003, Quimby sold 80 percent of Burt's Bees to AEA Investors, a private equity firm, for more than $175 million. She continued as CEO and focuses on continuing to grow the business.

5. *Resource maturity.* At this stage, the company's substantial financial gains may come at the cost of losing its advantages of small size, including flexibility and the entrepreneurial spirit. A company in this stage has the staff and financial resources to begin acting like a mature company with detailed planning and control systems.

As a new manager in an entrepreneurial company, pay attention to the stages of growth, and adapt your planning, organizing, leading, and controlling activities as the company progresses.

■ TAKE A MOMENT

Planning

In the early start-up stage, formal planning tends to be nonexistent except for the business plan described earlier in this chapter. The primary goal is simply to remain alive. As the organization grows, formal planning usually is not instituted until the success stage. Recall from Chapter 1 that planning means defining goals and deciding on the tasks and use of resources needed to attain them. Chapters 7, 8, and 9 will describe how entrepreneurs can define goals and implement strategies and plans to meet them. It is important that entrepreneurs view their original business plan as a living document that evolves as the company grows or the market changes.

One planning concern for today's small businesses is the need to be Web-savvy. For many small companies today, their Web operations are just as critical as traditional warehouse management or customer service operations. The growing importance of e-business means entrepreneurs have to plan and allocate resources for Internet operations from the beginning and grow those plans as the company grows. Of the small companies that have Web sites, more than half say the site has broken even or paid for itself in greater efficiency, improved customer relationships, or increased business.[85]

Organizing

In the first two stages of growth, the organization's structure is typically informal with all employees reporting to the owner. At about stage 3—success—functional managers often are hired to take over duties performed by the owner. A functional organization structure will begin to evolve with managers in charge of finance, manufacturing, and marketing. Another organizational approach is to use outsourcing, as described earlier. Method, a company launched by two 20-something entrepreneurs to develop a line of nontoxic cleaning products in fresh scents and stylish packaging, contracted with an industrial designer for the unique dish soap bottle and uses contract manufacturers in every region of the country to rapidly make products and get them to stores.[86]

During the latter stages of entrepreneurial growth, managers must learn to delegate and decentralize authority. If the business has multiple product lines, the owner may consider creating teams or divisions responsible for each line. The organization must hire competent managers and have sufficient management talent to handle fast growth and eliminate problems caused by increasing size. As an organization grows, it might also be characterized by greater use of rules, procedures, and written job descriptions. For example, Tara Cronbaugh started a small coffeehouse in a college town, but its success quickly led to the opening of three additional houses. With the rapid growth, Cronbaugh found that she needed a way to ensure consistency across operations. She put together an operations manual with detailed rules, procedures, and job descriptions so managers and employees at each coffeehouse would be following the same pattern.[87] Chapters 10 through 13 will discuss organizing in detail.

Leading

The driving force in the early stages of development is the leader's vision. This vision, combined with the leader's personality, shapes corporate culture. The leader can signal cultural values of service, efficiency, quality, or ethics. Often entrepreneurs do not have good people skills but do have excellent task skills in either manufacturing or marketing. By the success stage of growth, the owner must either learn to motivate employees or bring in managers who can. Rapid takeoff is not likely to happen without employee cooperation. Stepping from the self-absorption of the early days of a company to the more active communication necessary for growth can be tricky for entrepreneurs. Stan and Bob Lee built a successful business making spare parts for the corrugated box industry, but as the company grew, the two entrepreneurs had trouble shifting to more active leadership and communication. One consultant joked that the two seemed to fear that sales might actually increase if they listened to their staff.[88] The president of Foreign Candy Company of Hull, Iowa, saw his company grow rapidly when he concentrated more on employee needs and less on financial results. He made an effort to communicate with employees, conducted surveys to

CONCEPT CONNECTION In 2005, Spanish Internet radio broadcaster Batanga.com concluded a merger agreement that propelled it into the **take-off stage of growth.** The Greensboro, North Carolina, company joined forces with Planeta Networks of Miami, a broadband platform supplier, to form Hispanic Media, Inc. "Both companies had turned a corner and we were both looking for ways to expand," explained Batanga co-founder and CEO Troy McConnell, pictured here in Batanga's original offices in the Nussbaum Center for Entrepreneurship **business incubator.** Hispanic Media, Inc. is well positioned to attract more advertising dollars than Batanga could on its own and to appeal to new markets, such as launching a new auto channel that features both text and broadband video.

© LYNN HEY/ASSOCIATED PRESS

learn how they were feeling about the company, and found ways to involve them in decision making. His shift in leadership style allowed the company to enter the takeoff stage with the right corporate culture and employee attitudes to sustain rapid growth.

Leadership also is important because many small firms have a hard time hiring qualified employees. Labor shortages often hurt small firms that grow rapidly. A healthy corporate culture can help attract and retain good people.[89] You will learn more about leadership in Chapters 17 through 21.

Controlling

Financial control is important in each stage of the entrepreneurial firm's growth. In the initial stages, control is exercised by simple accounting records and by personal supervision. By stage 3—success—operational budgets are in place, and the owner should start implementing more structured control systems. During the takeoff stage, the company will need to make greater use of budgets and standard cost systems and use computer systems to provide statistical reports. These control techniques will become more sophisticated during the resource maturity stage.

As Amazon.com grew and expanded internationally, for example, entrepreneur and CEO Jeff Bezos needed increasingly sophisticated control mechanisms. Bezos hired a computer systems expert to develop a system to track and control all of the company's operations.[90] Control will be discussed further in Chapters 14 through 16.

MANAGER'S SOLUTION

This chapter explored entrepreneurship and small business management. Entrepreneurs start new businesses, and entrepreneurship plays an important role in the economy by stimulating job creation, innovation, and opportunities for minorities and women. An entrepreneurial personality includes the traits of internal locus of control, high energy level, need to achieve, tolerance for ambiguity, awareness of passing time, and self-confidence. A new breed of entrepreneur, the *social entrepreneur*, is committed to both good business and positive social change. The organizations started by social entrepreneurs sometimes blur the line between business and social activism.

The U.S. economy is ripe for entrepreneurial ventures, but entrepreneurial activity is also booming in other countries, with some of the highest rates in developing nations. Starting an entrepreneurial firm requires a new-business idea. At that point a comprehensive business plan should be developed and decisions made about legal structure and financing. Tactical decisions for the new venture include whether to start, buy, or franchise, and whether to participate in a business incubator.

Stella Ogiale, described in the chapter opening, is a good example of the diversity of entrepreneurs in the United States today. Ogiale grew up in Nigeria and originally came to the United States to attend college. Ogiale decided to start a new business, Chesterfield Health Services, because she wanted a flexible schedule and she saw a need in her community that wasn't being met. Ogiale wisely chose an idea—home health care—that met an emerging need and also meshed with her experience and skills working for nonprofit organizations. She was prepared for the government regulations and the paperwork that the new business required, but getting the business started was still a challenge. Ogiale describes herself as being "possessed" during the first two years because of the time and effort the new business took. She also describes herself as a social entrepreneur because her motivation for the new business was in part to make a difference in the lives of mentally and physically disabled people, as well as in the lives of the immigrants she provided with jobs. However, the social benefit of her for-profit business is being challenged by employees who claim Chesterfield Health Services doesn't pay them overtime as required by state law. Employees recently voted to join the Service Employees International Union because of their concerns over wages and benefits. All businesses face new challenges as they grow. However, Chesterfield Health Services still has a good reputation with clients and gets about 40 job applications a week from people who believe the company is a good place to work.[91]

After a business is started, it generally proceeds through five stages of growth: start-up, survival, success, takeoff, and resource maturity. The management functions of planning, organizing, leading, and controlling should be tailored to each stage of growth. Chesterfield Health Services reached the resource maturity stage, with about 1,000 employees serving clients out of 11 offices in 19 counties of Washington state. Because its growth means Chesterfield lost some of the advatanges it had as a small company, Ogiale may need to focus more on leadership and set up better control systems to keep the organization functioning smoothly.

DISCUSSION QUESTIONS

1. If you were to start a new business, would you have to search for an idea, or do you already have an idea to try? Explain.

2. Do you think entrepreneurs who launched a new business after deciding to leave a job on their own versus those who have been forced to leave a job as a result of downsizing are likely to have different traits? Which group is more likely to succeed? Why?

3. How would you go about deciding whether you wanted to start a business from scratch, buy an existing business, or buy into a franchise? What information would you collect and analyze?

4. How does starting a high-tech business such as an Internet company differ from starting a small business such as a local auto repair shop or delicatessen? What is the role of alliances and partnerships in online versus traditional small businesses?

5. Consider the six personality characteristics of entrepreneurs. Which two traits do you think are most like those of managers in large companies? Which two are least like those of managers in large companies?

6. What personal skills do you need to keep your financial backers feeling confident in your new business? Which skills are most useful when you're dealing with more informal sources such as family and friends versus receiving funds from stockholders, a bank, or a venture capital firm?

Would these considerations affect your financing strategy?

7. Why would small business ownership have great appeal to immigrants, women, and minorities?

8. Many people who are successful at the start-up stage of a business are not the right people to carry the venture forward. How do you decide whether you're better suited to be a serial entrepreneur (start the business and then move on to start another) or whether you can guide the venture as it grows and matures?

9. Over the past 20 years, entrepreneurship has been the fastest-growing course of study on campuses throughout the country. However, debate continues about whether you can teach someone to be an entrepreneur. Do you think entrepreneurship can be taught? Why or why not?

10. Many entrepreneurs say they did little planning, perhaps scratching notes on a legal pad. How is it possible for them to succeed?

11. Dan McKinnon started an airline with one airplane. To do so required filing more than 10,000 pages of manuals, ordering 50,000 luggage tags, buying more than $500 million in insurance, and spending more than $300,000 to train employees. A single inspection test cost $18,000. Evaluate whether you think this airline is a good entrepreneurial opportunity, and discuss why you think Dan McKinnon undertook it.

What's Your Entrepreneurial IQ?

Rate yourself on the following 15 behaviors and characteristics, according to the following scale.

1 = Strongly disagree

2 = Disagree

3 = Agree

4 = Strongly agree

1. I am able to translate ideas into concrete tasks and outcomes. ① ② ③ ④

2. When I am interested in a project, I tend to need less sleep. ① ② ③ ④

3. I am willing to make sacrifices to gain long-term rewards. ① ② ③ ④

4. Growing up, I was more of a risk-taker than a cautious child. ① ② ③ ④

5. I often see trends, connections, and patterns that are not obvious to others. ① ② ③ ④

6. I have always enjoyed spending much of my time alone. ① ② ③ ④

7. I have a reputation for being stubborn. ① ② ③ ④

8. I prefer working with a difficult but highly competent person to working with someone who is congenial but less competent. ① ② ③ ④

9. As a child, I had a paper route, lemonade stand, or other small enterprise. ① ② ③ ④

10. I usually keep New Year's resolutions. ① ② ③ ④

11. I'm not easily discouraged, and I persist when faced with major obstacles. ① ② ③ ④

12. I recover quickly from emotional setbacks. ① ② ③ ④

13. I would be willing to dip deeply into my "nest egg"—and possibly lose all I had saved—to go it alone. ① ② ③ ④

14. I get tired of the same routine day in and day out. ① ② ③ ④

15. When I want something, I keep the goal clearly in mind. ① ② ③ ④

Scoring and Interpretation

Total your score for the 15 items. If you tallied 50–60 points, you have a strong entrepreneurial IQ. A score of 30–50 indicates good entrepreneurial possibilities. Your chances of starting a successful entrepreneurial business are good if you have the desire and motivation. If you scored below 30, you probably do not have much entrepreneurial potential.

Go back over each question, thinking about changes you might make to become more or less entrepreneurial, depending on your career interests.

Closing the Deal

As the new, heavily recruited CEO of a high-technology start-up backed by several of Silicon Valley's leading venture capitalists, Chuck Campbell is flying high—great job, good salary, stock options, and a chance to be in on the ground floor and build one of the truly great twenty-first–century organizations. Just a few days into the job, Chuck participated in a presentation to a new group of potential investors for funding that could help the company expand marketing, improve its services, and invest in growth. By the end of the meeting, the investors had verbally committed $16 million in funding.

But things turned sour pretty fast. As Chuck was leaving about 9 P.M., the corporate controller, Betty Mars, who just returned from an extended leave, cornered him. He was surprised to find her working so late, but before he could even open his mouth, Betty blurted out her problem: The numbers Chuck had presented to the venture capitalists were flawed. "The assumptions behind the revenue growth plan are absolutely untenable," she said. "Not a chance of ever happening." Chuck was stunned. He told Betty to get on home and he'd stay and take a look at the figures.

At 11 P.M., Chuck was still sitting in his office wondering what to do. His research showed that the numbers were indeed grossly exaggerated, but most of them were at least statistically possible (however remote that possibility was!). However, what really troubled him was that the renewal income figure was just flat-out false—and it was clear that one member of the management team who participated in the presentation knew it was incorrect all along. To make matters worse, it was the renewal income figure that ultimately made the investment so attractive to the venture capital firm. Chuck knew what was at stake—no less than the life or death of the company itself. If he told the truth about the deceptive numbers, the company's valuation would almost certainly be slashed and the $16 million possibly canceled.

What Would You Do?

1. Say nothing about the false numbers. Of course, the company will miss the projections and have to come up with a good explanation, but, after all, isn't that par for the course among fledgling high-tech companies? Chances are the whole thing will blow over without a problem.

2. Go ahead and close the deal, but come clean later. Explain that the controller had been on an extended leave of absence and, because you had been on the job only a few days, you had not had time to personally do an analysis of the numbers.

3. Take swift action to notify the venture capitalists of the truth of the situation—and start cleaning house to get rid of people who would knowingly lie to close a deal.

SOURCE: Adapted from Kent Weber, "The Truth Could Cost You $16 Million," *Business Ethics* (March–April 2001): 18.

CASE FOR CRITICAL ANALYSIS

Radiata Software

The founders of one of the hottest young software companies of the decade were meeting in Rob Larson's den to decide what to do. Radiata Software, founded by the three friends right after they graduated from college, makes financial software targeted to small professional service firms. Radiata had been an instant hit among solo professionals such as accountants and financial planners, as well as among small businesses that did not have the resources and equipment to run big, complex software programs. With a solid customer base, Radiata has been able to expand its product line and add a Web site providing customers with an all-in-one site for small business accounting and finance. One of the most popular features of the site is the electronic bulletin boards where solo professionals trade comments, seek advice, and share their stories of what it's like to be a free agent.

But Radiata's success had also come with some problems. Rapid growth left the founders struggling to keep pace with managing staff, handling development of new products and services, marketing, negotiating contracts, and so forth. Rob, who had come up with the idea for the company, served as CEO, and the other founders each had specific titles and duties, but all three were involved in essentially every aspect of the business. Whenever a major decision had to be made, they made it together, often after hours or days talking with one another to reach an agreement. Eventually, Susan Boyd, a representative from the venture capital firm that was Radiata's biggest source of funds, suggested they needed to bring in professional managers to help run the place. "You'll still have plenty of say in running the business," she said. "But after six years, Radiata is getting too big to manage as an entrepreneurial start-up. You need some professional help to take things to the next level." The founders agreed she was right, and Susan quickly recruited a chief operating officer, a chief information officer, and a chief financial officer to help Radiata through its growing pains. The three brought a tremendous wealth of knowledge and experience to the young company, and everyone seemed sure Radiata would grow even faster and be even more successful with a solid management team behind it.

"So, what went wrong?" Rob asks his co-founders now, after six months of working with the new management team. From the beginning, the three founders and the three new managers had seemed to segregate into two separate camps. The founders had been friends since their freshman year in college, had lived together until the last couple of years, and still partied together on the weekends. It came naturally for them to get together separately from the three newcomers and talk about the business, how the new managers were doing, and so forth. Feeling left out, the three seasoned managers gradually began turning to one another more and more, ignoring the younger trio. Although in the beginning the team of six had vowed to have regular Monday morning meetings, the meetings often got canceled for one reason or another. In addition, over time it became clear to the new managers that the three founders had already met and discussed issues prior to the formal meeting, so the three new managers began doing the same. By now, there were clearly two separate teams trying to run Radiata. Tomorrow, the group will be discussing whether to merge with a larger software company. "They'll swallow us," said Jessie. "Our dream of running our own business will be dead."

"Ha!" barked Thai. "You think it's not already dead? I expect our 'dream team' of senior managers are holed up somewhere right now discussing their strategy. They want this deal to go through, and you know they've got Susan in their back pocket. Who do you think is in charge of this company these days?"

"Look," said Rob. "We have to accept that a lot of this is our fault. It's always been us against them. We never made any effort to really make them a part of the company and share our ideas and vision with them. Almost every day, we find some way to meet without them and make some decision behind their backs—like when we signed that partnership agreement with an accounting services firm without even talking to them about it. It was an innocent mistake, but it clearly didn't sit well. Now they're meeting without us and maybe wanting to take the company in a direction we don't want to go. Also, I heard from our venture capital rep that our CIO is thinking of jumping ship. She's frustrated and miserable here, feels like she's spinning her wheels and wasting her time. If that happens, I don't think Susan and the venture capital team are going to be very happy. If we lose them, we're in serious trouble. Is there any way to get out of this mess?"

Questions

1. What is the underlying cause of the problems at Radiata? Can you think of ways to bring the two sides together and get the company back on the right track?

2. What management functions seem to be needed most at this point—planning, organizing, leading, or controlling? Discuss.

3. What do you think the founders need to do in this situation? What do you think the three new managers should do?

SOURCE: Based on Regina Fazio Maruca, "Entrepreneurs versus Executives at Socaba.com," *Harvard Business Review* (July–August 2000), 30–38.

ENDNOTES

1. Bobbie Gossage, "Stella Ogiale: For Doing Good While Doing Well," profile in "25 Entrepreneurs We Love," *Inc. Magazine* (April 2004): 109–147.

2. Elizabeth Olson, "They May Be Mundane, But Low-Tech Businesses Are Booming," *The New York Times* (April 28, 2005): www.nytimes.com; and "CIBC Report Predicts Canada Will Be Home to One Million Women Entrepreneurs By 2010," *Canada NewsWire* (June 28, 2005): 1.

3. Olson, "They May Be Mundane, But Low-Tech Businesses Are Booming."

4. John Case, "Where We Are Now," *Inc.* (May 29, 2001): 18–19.

5. Reported in Laura Randall, "Lessons Learned the Hardest Way, By Going Belly-Up," *The New York Times* (February 24, 2004): G8.

6. Reported in "Did You Know?" in J. Neil Weintraut, "Told Any Good Stories Lately?" *Business 2.0* (March 2000): 139–140.

7. www.sba.gov.

8. John Case, "Who's Looking at Start-Ups?" *Inc.* (May 29, 2001): 60.

9. Donald F. Kuratko and Richard M. Hodgetts, *Entrepreneurship: A Contemporary Approach*, 4th ed. (Fort Worth: The Dryden Press, 1998): 30.

10. Nadine Heintz, "Andra Rush: For Rolling Up Her Sleeves," *Inc.* (April 2004): 128–129.

11. Study conducted by Yankelovich Partners, reported in Mark Henricks, "Type-Cast," *Entrepreneur* (March 2000): 14–16.

12. Olson, "They May Be Mundane, But Low-Tech Businesses Are Booming."

13. Norm Brodsky, "Street Smarts: Opportunity Knocks," *Inc.* (February 2002): 44–46; and Hilary Stout, "Start Low," *The Wall Street Journal* (May 14, 2001): R8.

14. Kathleen Collins, "¡La Vida Próspera! Latin-Owned Businesses Explode," *Working Woman* (October 2000): 13.

15. Office of Advocacy of the U.S. Small Business Administration, reported in T. Shawn Taylor, "Kitchen Table CEOs," *Essence* (March 2004): 112; and www.sba.gov.

16. Global Entrepreneurship Monitor, "Table 2: Prevalence Rates of Entrepreneurial Activity Across Countries, 200,5" *2005 GEM Tables and Figures*, Babson College and the London Business School, (March 14, 2006): www.gemconsortium.org/category_list.asp.

17. "One-Yen Wonders," *The Economist* (June 28, 2003): 66.

18. Ovetta Wiggins, "Report: Small Business Set to Double By 2009," *The Moscow Times*, as reported on The America's Intelligence Wire, (March 2, 2004): www.themoscowtimes.com.

19. This section based on John Case, "The Wonderland Economy," *The State of Small Business* (1995): 14–29; and Richard L. Daft, *Management*, 3rd ed. (Fort Worth, Texas: The Dryden Press, 1992).

20. "Number of Small Businesses Continues to Grow; Nevada, Georgia Lead the Way," *The Network Journal* (March–April 2005): 54.

21. Susan Greco and Elaine Appleton Grant, "Innovation, Part III: Creation Nation," *Inc.* (October 2002): 72–80.

22. Alessandra Bianchi, "Erasing Borders," in Joshua Hyatt, "Small and Global," *FSB* (June 2004): 44–45.

23. Julia Boorstin, "Exporting Cleaner Air," in Joshua Hyatt, "Small and Global," *FSB* (June 2004): 44–45.

24. Elizabeth Olson, "Dot-Com Survivor Hits on Right Plan," *The New York Times* (February 5, 2004): C6.

25. Steve Stecklow, "StubHut's Ticket to Ride," *The Wall Street Journal* (January 17, 2006): B1.

26. George Mannes, "Don't Give Up on the Web," *Fortune* (March 5, 2001): 184[B]–184[L].

27. Brian Caulfield et al., "12 Hot Startups," *Business 2.0* (January–February 2004): 93–97.

28. Caulfield et al., "12 Hot Startups."

29. Christine Y. Chen, "The E-Recycler," *FSB* (May 2005): 93–94.

30. "How I Did It; Barbara K: With Great Power Tools Comes Great Responsibility," as told to Allen P. Roberts, *Inc.* (May 2005): 112–114.

31. www. sba.gov.

32. Thuy-Doan Le Bee, "How Small Is Small? SBA Holds Hearings to Decide," *The Sacramento Bee* (June 29, 2005): D2.

33. Office of Advocacy, U.S. Small Business Administration, www.sba.gov/advo.

Chapter 6 MANAGING SMALL BUSINESS START-UPS

34. Barbara Benham, "Big Government, Small Business," *Working Woman* (February 2001): 24.

35. Research and statistics reported in "The Job Factory," *Inc.* (May 29, 2001): 40–43.

36. Ian Mount, "The Return of the Lone Inventor," *FSB* (March 2005): 18; Office of Advocacy, U.S. Small Business Administration, www.sba.gov/advo.

37. Kuratko and Hodgetts, *Entrepreneurship: A Contemporary Approach,* 4th ed. (Fort Worth: The Dryden Press, 1998): 11; and "100 Ideas for New Businesses," *Venture* (November 1988): 35–74.

38. Siri Schubert, "Bound to Succeed," *Business 2.0* (April 2005): 50.

39. Robert Berner, "Why P&G's Smile Is So Bright," *BusinessWeek* (August 12, 2002): 58–60.

40. Lorrie Grant, "Little Guys Take On Greeting Card Giants," *USA Today* (June 16, 2005): www.usatoday.com.

41. John Case, "The Origins of Entrepreneurship," *Inc.* (June 1989): 51–53.

42. Greco and Grant, "Innovation, Part III: Creation Nation."

43. Robert D. Hisrich, "Entrepreneurship-Intrapreneurship," *American Psychologist* (February 1990): 209–222.

44. Olson, "From One Business to 23 Million."

45. www.sba.gov; "CIBC Report Predicts Canada Will Be Home to One Million Women Entrepreneurs by 2010," *Canada NewsWire* (June 28, 2005): 1.

46. www.sba.gov.

47. Statistics reported in Cora Daniels, "Minority Rule," *FSB* (December 2003–January 2004): 65–66; Elizabeth Olson, "New Help for the Black Entrepreneur," *The New York Times* (December 23, 2004): C6; and David J. Dent, "The Next Black Power Movement," *FSB* (May 2003): 10–13.

48. Ellyn Spragins, "Pat Winans" profile, and Cora Daniels, "Ed Chin" profile, in "The New Color of Money," *FSB* (December 2003–January 2004): 74–87.

49. This discussion is based on Charles R. Kuehl and Peggy A. Lambing, *Small Business: Planning and Management,* 3rd ed. (Ft. Wort: The Dryden Press, 1994).

50. David C. McClelland, *The Achieving Society* (New York: Van Nostrand, 1961).

51. Paulette Thomas, "Entrepreneurs' Biggest Problems—and How They Solve Them" *The Wall Street Journal* (March 17, 2003): R1.

52. Definition based on Albert R. Hunt, "Social Entrepreneurs: Compassionate and Tough-Minded," *The Wall Street Journal* (July 13, 2000): A27; David Puttnam, "Hearts Before Pockets," *The New Statesman* (February 9, 2004): 26; and Christian Seelos and Johanna Mair, "Social Entrepreneurship: Creating New Business Models to Serve the Poor," *Business Horizons* 48 (2005): 241–246.

53. Cheryl Dahle, "Filling the Void: The 2006 Social Capitalist Award Winners," *Fast Company* (January–February 2006): 50–61.

54. Putnam, "Hearts Before Pockets."

55. Cheryl Dahle, "The Change Masters," *Fast Company* (January 2005): 47–58; David Bornstein, *How to Change the World: Social Entrepreneurs and the Power of New Ideas* (Oxford and New York: Oxford University Press, 2004).

56. Brian Dumaine, "See Me, Hear Me," segment in "Two Ways to Help the Third World," *Fortune* (October 27, 2003): 187–196.

57. Dahle, "Filling the Void"; and Cheryl Dahle, "Social Capitalists: The Top 20 Groups That Are Changing the World," *Fast Company* (January 2004): 45–57.

58. Leslie Brokaw, "How to Start an *Inc.* 500 Company," *Inc. 500* (1994): 51–65.

59. Paul Reynolds, "The Truth about Start-Ups," *Inc.* (February 1995): 23; Brian O'Reilly, "The New Face of Small Businesses," *Fortune* (May 2, 1994) 82–88.

60. Based on Ellyn E. Spragins, "How to Write a Business Plan That Will Get You in the Door," *Small Business Success* (Inc. 2001); Linda Elkins, "Tips for Preparing a Business Plan," *Nation's Business* (June 1996): 60R–61R; Carolyn M. Brown, "The Do's and Don'ts of Writing a Winning Business Plan," *Black Enterprise* (April 1996): 114–116; and Kuratko and Hodgetts, *Entrepreneurship,* 295–397. For a clear, thorough step-by-step guide to writing an effective business plan, see Linda Pinson and Jerry Jinnett, *Anatomy of a Business Plan,* 5th ed. (Virginia Beach, VA: Dearborn, 2001).

61. The INC. FAXPOLL, *Inc.* (February 1992): 24.

62. MacVicar, "Ten Steps to a High-Tech Start-Up."

63. Reported in H. M. Dietel, P. J. Dietel, and K. Steinbuhler, *e-Business and e-Commerce for Managers* (Upper Saddle River, NJ: Prentice Hall, 2001): 58.

64. "Venture Capitalists' Criteria" *Management Review* (November 1985): 7–8.

65. "Staples Makes Big Business from Helping Small Businesses," *SBA Success Stories, www.sba.gov/successstories.html* (accessed on March 12, 2004).

66. Olson, "From One Business to 23 Million."

67. "Where the Venture Money Is Going," *Business 2.0* (January–February 2004): 98.

68. Gary Rivlin, "Does the Kid Stay in the Picture?" *The New York Times* (February 22, 2005): E1, E8.

69. Dent, "The Next Black Power Movement."

70. Kristen Hampshire, "Roll With It," *FSB* (November 2005): 108–112; Jennifer Maxwell profile in Betsy Wiesendanger, "Labors of Love," *Working Woman* (May 1999): 43–56; Jena McGregor, Taryn Rose profile in "25 Top Women Business Builders," *Fast Company* (May 2005): 67–75.

71. Wendy Lea, "Dancing With a Partner," *Fast Company* (March 2000): 159–161.

72. Matt Richtel, "Outsourced All the Way," *The New York Times* (June 21, 2005): www.nytimes.com.

73. Reported in Sheryl Nance-Nash, "More Are Betting the Franchise," *The New York Times* (February 29, 2004): Section 14 LI, 6.

74. Echo Montgomery Garrett, "The Twenty-First-Century Franchise," *Inc.* (January 1995): 79–88; Lisa Benavides, " Linking Up with a Chain," *The Tennessean* (April 6, 1999): 1E.

75. Henry Weil, "Business in a Box," *Working Woman* (September 1999): 59–64.

76. Quinne Bryant, "Who Owns 20+ Subway Franchises?" *The Business Journal of Tri-Cities Tennessee/Virginia* (August 2003): 42–43.

77. For a current discussion of the risks and disadvantages of owning a franchise, see Anne Fisher, "Risk Reward," *FSB* (December 2005–January 2006): 44.

78. Anne Field, "Your Ticket to a New Career? Franchising Can Put Your Skills to Work in Your Own Business," in *Business Week Investor: Small Business* section, *BusinessWeek*

(May 12, 2003): 100+: and Roberta Maynard,"Choosing a Franchise,"*Nation's Business* (October 1996): 56–63.

79. Darren Dahl,"Getting Started: Percolating Profits."*Inc.* (February 2005): 38.

80. Reported in Dahl,"Getting Started: Percolating Profits."

81. Harvard Business School, reported in Kimberly Weisul, "Incubators Lay an Egg,"*BusinessWeek Frontier* (October 9, 2000): F14.

82. Oringel,"Sowing Success."

83. Peter Balan, University of South Australia,"Harmony: A Global Network Support System for Incubators,"and "Harmony: A Network System to Support Innovation Commercialisation,"http://business2.unisa.edu.au/cde/docs/HarmonyOverviewAndBenefits%2025Feb02.pdf.

84. Carrie Dolan,"Entrepreneurs Often Fail as Managers," *The Wall Street Journal* (May 15, 1989): B1.

85. Mannes,"Don't Give Up on the Web."

86. Finn,"Selling Cool in a Bottle."

87. Amanda Walmac,"Full of Beans,"*Working Woman* (February 1999): 38–40.

88. Ron Stodghill,"Boxed Out,"*FSB* (April 2005): 69–72.

89. Udayan Gupta and Jeffery A. Tannenbaum,"Labor Shortages Force Changes at Small Firms,"*The Wall Street Journal* (May 22, 1989): B1, B2;"Harnessing Employee Productivity," *Small Business Report* (November 1987): 46–49; and Molly Kilmas,"How to Recruit a Smart Team,"*Nation's Business* (May 1995): 26–27.

90. Saul Hansell,"Listen Up! It's Time for a Profit: A Front Row Seat as Amazon Gets Serious,"*The New York Times* (May 20, 2001): Section 3, 1.

91. Gossage,"Stella Ogiale"; Marsha King,"Immigrants Build Wealth While Caring For Elderly,"*Seattle Times* (November 10, 2004): A1; Marsha King,"Home-Care Workers Sue Over Pay,"*Seattle Times* (February 16, 2005); and"Home-Care Workers Group Joins Union,"*Seattle Post-Intelligencer* (May 17, 2005): B4.

COSTCO WHOLESALE CORPORATION PART TWO: JAMES SINEGAL, THE CONSCIENCE OF A CORPORATION

Entrepreneurs face enormous challenges in today's complex business world. To succeed in the 21st century, these aspiring business owners must be able to identify global trends, provide ethical leadership, develop effective corporate cultures, and manage the various environments in which they operate. Like jugglers in a circus, entrepreneurs are expected to balance the often-conflicting demands of customers, employees, shareholders, and other stakeholders to whom they are responsible. The ones that rise to the occasion make enormous contributions to society and reap rewards beyond their wildest dreams.

Transforming a startup into a multinational corporation often begins with the vision, drive, and perseverance of a single individual. The entrepreneurial impetus that catapulted Costco Wholesale Corp. from a Seattle warehouse to the nation's top warehouse-club chain originated with James Sinegal, the Pittsburgh native and grandfather-like figure who co-founded Costco and now serves as its chief executive. The son of a steelworker, Sinegal embarked on his retail journey early in life. In 1954, at the age of 18, Sinegal took a job unloading mattresses for Fed-Mart, a new San Diego discount store launched by Sol Price, an early pioneer of the warehouse-club concept. Sinegal worked hard and became Price's protégé, eventually achieving the head manager position at Fed-Mart's flagship store. In the 1970s, Price sold Fed-Mart and launched a new warehouse store, one bearing his name: Price Club. Though Sinegal followed his mentor to the new warehouse establishment, it was only a matter of time before Price's star pupil would venture out on his own. That time came in 1983 when Sinegal founded Costco with business partner and lawyer Jeffrey Brotman, the company's current chairman. Their efforts helped launch an era of "big-box retailers" typified by companies like Wal-Mart, BJ's Wholesale Club, and Target.

From the beginning, Sinegal's vision for Costco was guided by a set of values and priorities now expressed in the company's five-point code of ethics. The Costco Code of Ethics indicates that, to achieve its mission of providing members with quality goods and services at the lowest possible prices, Costco must (1) obey the law, (2) take care of its customers, (3) take care of employees, and (4) respect its suppliers. If the organization follows these four guidelines, it will accomplish its fifth and ultimate goal: reward shareholders.

To ensure that these ethical standards would become the guiding principles for all Costco business operations, Sinegal developed a vibrant corporate culture that embodied and reinforced the co-founders' values and beliefs. One of the most visible and often discussed aspects of Costco's corporate culture is its generous-yet-proportional employee compensation. Convinced that happy workers are productive workers, Sinegal saw to it that his team was lavishly compensated with a livable wage and premium benefits. In 2006, Costco workers made an average hourly wage of $17, an astounding 42 percent higher than rival Sam's Club. Richard Galanti, Costco's executive vice president and chief financial officer, believes the pro-worker wages policy makes good business sense: "It's important to pay people a fair living wage. If you do, and it's better than everybody else, you're going to get better people—and they're going to stick around longer." Despite complaints on Wall Street that Costco's employee-remuneration program functions at the expense of profits and share prices, Sinegal is committed to the long-range benefits of a generous compensation strategy: "On Wall Street, they're in the business of making money between now and next Thursday . . . but we can't take that view. We want to build a company that will still be here 50 and 60 years from now."

Though Costco's employees and first-line managers are the best paid in retail, leaders atop the managerial hierarchy earn a humble living, relative to their peers. Sinegal's salary hovers around $350,000—chump change compared to the greenbacks flooding the wallets of most Fortune 500 bosses. Even with bonuses, Sinegal's annual compensation ranks among the lowest ten percent of chief executives. The worker-centric leader is unapologetic, viewing his company's executive pay policy in terms of distributive justice: "I just think that if you're going to try to run an organization that's very cost-conscious, then you can't have those disparities. Having an individual who is making 100 or 200 or 300 times more than the average person working on the floor is wrong."

The egalitarian-minded CEO reinforces this culture of inclusion and proportionality in other ways, as well. Sinegal dons a Costco Kirkland Signature dress shirt instead of a suit. He wears an ID nametag like other employees, answers his own phones, and spends 200 days each year visiting warehouses and teams. Even his corner office is welcoming: with no door or window, the Costco general's quarters are covered with photographs of family members and store openings. In ways large and small, Sinegal sends the message that employees are the company's most valuable commodity.

Costco's commitment to ethics and social responsibility has not been without challenges, however. In

2006, a stock-options backdating scandal tainted hundreds of businesses, forcing the ouster of dozens of top executives. When an internal investigation at Costco uncovered "imprecisions" in the company's executive options plan, officers proactively cancelled executive bonuses for the year, withholding payouts of up to $200,000. This dramatic act of self-regulation was suggested by the two leaders who had the most to lose: James Sinegal and Richard Galanti. Costco has been accused of other lapses, such as impeding the advancement of female workers to senior-level positions and displaying environmental and cultural insensitivity during its Mexico expansion, but Sinegal & Co. have thus far emerged unscathed.

Despite occasional allegations, Costco has managed to maintain its squeaky-clean reputation. And so long as Jim Sinegal continues serving as the conscience of the corporation, there is every reason to believe it will stay that way.

Questions

1. What are the motivations and personality traits that compel individuals like James Sinegal to strike out on their own, preferring the risks of entrepreneurship to the relative safety of working for others? Does Sinegal qualify as a social entrepreneur? Why or why not?

2. In what way does the carefully crafted order of Costco's five-point Code of Ethics represent a rejection of the profit-maximizing approach to evaluating corporate social performance?

3. Which of the four types of corporate cultures best describes Costco? Identify ways that James Sinegal exhibits cultural leadership to create and maintain a high-performance organization?

SOURCES: Mike Duff, "The Sinegal Factor: Thriving with a Hands-on Approach," *DSN Retailing Today*, December 19, 2005; Doug Desjardins, "Culture of Inclusion: Where Top Executives Lead by Example and Honesty and Frugality Are Valued Virtues," *DSN Retailing Today*, December 19, 2005; Chris Noon, "No Bonuses For You Two," *Forbes*, October 20, 2006; Alyce Lomax, "Most Foolish CEO: Jim Sinegal," *The Motley Fool*, September 28, 2006, *http://www.fool.com*, accessed November 6, 2006; David Pinto, "Costco Named Retailer of the Year, *MMR*, January 9, 2006; Steve Greenhouse, "How Costco Became the Anti-Wal-Mart," *The New York Times*, July 17, 2005; Mike Troy, "A Model Business: Long-term Vision Benefits Customers, Employees," *DSN Retailing Today*, December 19, 2005; Matthew Boyle, "Why Costco is So Damn Addictive," *Fortune*, October 30, 2006; "Code of Ethics," Costco Investor Relations Web site, *http://phx.corporate-ir.net/phoenix.zhtml?c=83830&p=irol-irhome*, accessed November 14, 2006.

PLANNING

Planning does not require perfection, but the better the plan, the more predictable the outcome. In 1935, Frank Lloyd Wright designed "Fallingwater" as a summer house in rural Pennsylvania for Edgar J. Kaufmann, Sr. Although still considered a masterpiece, and currently open as a museum, Fallingwater is also an example of what happens when plans have errors.

As in management, an architectural plan must have a goal and strategy formulation before crews and equipment can be hired and scheduled. In the case of Fallingwater, Wright's goal was to build a house that was a natural retreat and would fit the environment organically. As such, he utilized the natural surroundings, including stones from the original site and used cantilevered balconies to build the house over a running river and waterfall. The results were spectacular and are still considered a masterpiece of architectural design. However, Wright's original plans did not call for enough reinforcement in the balconies. In the execution of the plan, the engineer increased the reinforcement, but even that was not enough to keep the balconies from sagging. Structural repairs were completed in 2002 but would have been unnecessary if the original plan had been correct. However, the flaws were not beyond remedy, and the house is still considered a "master's masterpiece."

Goal setting, planning, strategy formulation and implementation are ongoing for any company, large or small. No company can expect to devise the perfect plan, and while planning doesn't have to be perfect, it does have to be done. Thankfully, even when planning results in unexpected or less than optimal results, usually the only mistake that cannot be rectified is not planning at all.

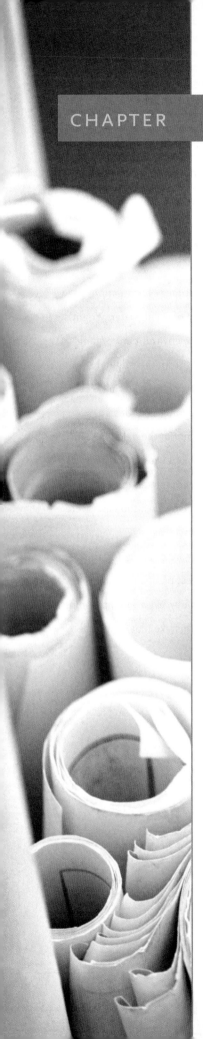

CHAPTER 7

CHAPTER OUTLINE

Manager's Challenge

Overview of Goals and Plans

Purposes of Goals and Plans

Goals in Organizations

    Organizational Mission

    Goals and Plans

    Alignment of Goals

Criteria for Effective Goals

Planning Types

    Management by Objectives

    Single-Use and Standing Plans

    Contingency Plans

Planning in a Turbulent Environment

    Building Scenarios

    Crisis Planning

Planning for High Performance

    Traditional Approaches to Planning

    High-Performance Approaches
    to Planning

LEARNING OBJECTIVES

After studying this chapter, you should be able to:

1. Define goals and plans and explain the relationship between them.

2. Explain the concept of organizational mission and how it influences goal setting and planning.

3. Describe the types of goals an organization should have and why they resemble a hierarchy.

4. Define the characteristics of effective goals.

5. Describe the four essential steps in the MBO process.

6. Explain the difference between single-use plans and standing plans.

7. Describe and explain the importance of the three stages of crisis management planning.

8. Summarize the guidelines for high-performance planning in a fast-changing environment.

MANAGERIAL PLANNING AND GOAL SETTING

MANAGER'S CHALLENGE

Nancy Sorrells isn't easily scared, but the challenges in her new job have her a little worried. Something is definitely wrong at the Marriott hotel just south of the Dallas–Fort Worth International Airport, where Sorrells has recently been hired as general manager. But it's not easy to tell exactly what that *something* is. Winegardner & Hammons Inc. (WHI), the Cincinnati firm that owns the hotel, had warned Sorrells that the hotel was "sneaky-broke." "You walk around and you won't see anything wrong, and there's no reason it should be broken," WHI's senior vice president of human resources, Kent Bruggeman, told her. But broken it was. Despite the fact that the hotel was only four years old and close to the action of a major airport, it had trouble maintaining steady business at premium room rates. The hotel was running nearly $1.5 million behind budget on revenue, and inspections showed numerous deficiencies in all areas. Moreover, employees seemed lackadaisical and unmotivated to improve things. To make matters worse, Sorrells had been hired to replace a manager who was much loved by the staff, and the resentment of employees was palpable. The fact that she had previously managed a Holiday Inn, a lesser brand in the hotel pecking order, didn't help her status either. Sorrells began working through the hotel person-by-person, looking for those who would support her vision for turning the hotel around. Although she gained some cooperation, performance didn't seem to improve. In exasperation, one veteran department head finally blurted, "I'd like to follow you, but I don't know where you're going."[1]

209

> ■ **TAKE A MOMENT**
>
> If you were in Nancy Sorrell's position, what would be your first step to turn things around at the hotel? How would you get everyone moving in the same direction and enable them to achieve high performance?

One of the primary responsibilities of managers is to decide where the organization should go in the future and how to get it there. Without clear goals and plans, employees cannot perform up to their potential and the organization flounders.

In some organizations, typically small ones, planning is informal. In others, managers follow a well-defined planning framework. The company establishes a basic mission and develops formal goals and strategic plans for carrying it out. Companies such as Royal Dutch/Shell, IBM, and United Way undertake a strategic planning exercise each year—reviewing their missions, goals, and plans to meet environmental changes or the expectations of important stakeholders such as the community, owners, or customers. Many of these companies also develop *contingency plans* or *scenarios* for unexpected circumstances and *disaster recovery plans* for what the organization would do in the event of a major disaster such as a hurricane, earthquake, or terrorist attack.

Of the four management functions—planning, organizing, leading, and controlling—described in Chapter 1, planning is considered the most fundamental. Everything else stems from planning. Yet planning also is the most controversial management function. How do managers plan for the future in a constantly changing environment? As we discussed in Chapter 1, most organizations are facing turbulence and uncertainty. The economic, political, and social turmoil of recent years has left many managers wondering how to cope and has sparked a renewed interest in organizational planning, particularly planning for unexpected problems and events. Yet planning cannot read an uncertain future. Planning cannot tame a turbulent environment. A statement by General Colin Powell, former U.S. Secretary of State, offers a warning for managers: "No battle plan survives contact with the enemy."[2]

In this chapter, we will explore the process of planning and consider how managers develop effective plans that can grow and change to meet new conditions. Special attention is given to goal setting, for that is where planning starts. Then, we discuss the various types of plans that managers use to help the organization achieve those goals, including a section on crisis management planning. Finally, we examine new approaches to planning that emphasize the involvement of employees, customers, partners, and other stakeholders in strategic thinking and execution. Chapter 8 will look at strategic planning in depth and examine a number of strategic options managers can use in a competitive environment. In Chapter 9, we look at management decision making. Proper decision-making techniques are crucial to selecting the organization's goals, plans, and strategic options.

OVERVIEW OF GOALS AND PLANS

Goals and plans have become general concepts in our society. A **goal** is a desired future state that the organization attempts to realize.[3] Goals are important because organizations exist for a purpose and goals define and state that purpose. A **plan** is a blueprint for goal achievement and specifies the necessary resource allocations, schedules, tasks, and other actions. Goals specify future ends; plans specify today's means. The word **planning** usually incorporates both ideas; it means determining the organization's goals and defining the means for achieving them.[4]

Exhibit 7.1 illustrates the levels of goals and plans in an organization. The planning process starts with a formal mission that defines the basic purpose of the organization, especially for external audiences. The mission is the basis for the strategic (company) level of goals and plans, which in turn shapes the tactical (divisional)

Part 3 PLANNING

210

EXHIBIT   7.1

Levels of Goals/Plans and Their Importance

DOES GOAL-SETTING FIT YOUR MANAGEMENT STYLE?

How do your work habits fit with making plans and setting goals? Answer the following questions as they apply to your work or study behavior. Please indicate whether each item is Mostly True or Mostly False for you.

	Mostly True	Mostly False
1. I have clear, specific goals in several areas.	_____	_____
2. I have a definite outcome in life I want to achieve.	_____	_____
3. I prefer general to specific goals.	_____	_____
4. I work better without specific deadlines.	_____	_____
5. I set aside time each day or week to plan my work.	_____	_____
6. I am clear about the measures that indicate when I have achieved a goal.	_____	_____

	Mostly True	Mostly False
7. I work better when I set more challenging goals for myself.	_____	_____
8. I help other people clarify and define their goals.	_____	_____

INTERPRETATION: An important part of a new manager's job is setting goals, measuring results, and reviewing progress for their department and their subordinates. Goal setting can be learned. Most organizations have goal setting and review systems that new managers use. The preceding questions indicate the extent to which you have already adopted the disciplined use of goals in your life and work. Not everyone thrives under a disciplined goal-setting system, but as a new manager, setting goals and assessing results are tools that will enhance your impact.

SCORING: Give yourself one point for each item you marked as Mostly True except items 3 and 4. For items 3 and 4 give yourself one point for each one you marked Mostly False. If you scored 4 or less you might want to evaluate and begin to change your goal-setting behavior. Research indicates that setting clear, specific, and challenging goals in key areas will produce better performance. A score of 5 or higher suggests a positive level of goal-setting behavior and better preparation for a new manager role in an organization.

level and the operational (departmental) level.[5] Top managers are typically responsible for establishing *strategic* goals and plans that reflect a commitment to both organizational efficiency and effectiveness, as described in Chapter 1. *Tactical* goals and plans are the responsibility of middle managers, such as the heads of major divisions or functional units. A division manager will formulate tactical plans that focus on the major actions the division must take to fulfill its part in the strategic plan set by top management. *Operational* plans identify the specific procedures or processes needed at lower levels of the organization, such as individual departments and employees. Front-line managers and supervisors develop operational plans that focus on specific tasks and processes and that help to meet tactical and strategic goals. Planning at each level supports the other levels.

> Before reading the rest of this chapter, learn about your personal goal setting behavior by completing the items in the New Manager Self-Test above.

■ **TAKE A MOMENT**

PURPOSES OF GOALS AND PLANS

The complexity of today's environment and uncertainty about the future overwhelm many managers and cause them to focus on operational issues and short-term results rather than long-term goals and plans. However, planning generally positively affects a company's performance.[6] In addition to improving financial and operational performance, developing explicit goals and plans at each level illustrated in Exhibit 7.1 is important because of the external and internal messages they send. These messages go to both external and internal audiences and provide important benefits for the organization:[7]

:: *Legitimacy.* An organization's mission describes what the organization stands for and its reason for existence. It symbolizes legitimacy to external audiences such as investors, customers, suppliers, and the local community. The mission helps them look on the company in a favorable light. Companies have to guard their reputations, as evidenced by recent criticism of Wal-Mart. After years of ignoring critics, who targeted the company for everything from its labor practices to its environmental impact to its tactics with suppliers, managers launched a massive public relations campaign to try to mend relationships. As society's expectations of Wal-Mart change, the company's mission of bringing everyday low prices to average people is being fine-tuned to emphasize a strong commitment to doing business in an ethical and socially responsible way.[8] A strong mission also has an impact on employees, enabling them to become committed to the organization because they identify with its overall purpose and reason for existence. One of the traits often cited by employees in *Fortune* magazine's list of the "100 Best Companies to Work For" is a sense of purpose and meaning.[9] For example, at mutual fund company Vanguard, helping people pay for a happy retirement is a guiding mission for employees.

:: *Source of motivation and commitment.* Goals and plans facilitate employees' identification with the organization and help motivate them by reducing uncertainty and clarifying what they should accomplish. At Boeing, the manufacturing department has a goal of moving a plane, once the wings and landing gear are attached, along the assembly line and out the door in only five days. Managers are revising processes and procedures, mechanics are coming up with innovative machine adjustments, and assembly line workers are trying new techniques to meet this ambitious goal.[10] Lack of a clear goal can damage employee motivation and commitment because people don't understand what they're working toward. Whereas a goal provides the "why" of an organization or subunit's existence, a plan tells the "how." A plan lets employees know what actions to undertake to achieve the goal.

:: *Resource allocation.* Goals help managers decide where they need to allocate resources, such as employees, money, and equipment. For example, DuPont has a goal of generating 25 percent of revenues from renewable resources by 2010. This goal lets managers know they need to use resources to develop renewable and biodegradable materials, acquire businesses that produce products with renewable resources, and buy equipment that reduces waste, emissions, and energy usage. As another example, due to new goals of fighting domestic terrorism, the Federal Bureau of Investigation (FBI) pulled more than 600 agents off their regular beats and reassigned them to terrorist-related cases. The FBI is also allocating resources to rebuild an archaic computer network, open foreign offices, and form terrorism task forces.[11]

:: *Guides to action.* Goals and plans provide a sense of direction. They focus attention on specific targets and direct employee efforts toward important outcomes. Managers at Guitar Center, one of the fastest-growing retailers in the United States, emphasize sales growth. Sales teams at every Guitar Center store are given sales goals each morning, and employees do whatever they need to, short of losing the company money, to meet the targets. The fast-growing retailer's unwritten mantra of "Take the deal" means that salepeople are trained to take any profitable deal, even at razor-thin margins, to meet daily sales targets.[12]

:: *Rationale for decisions.* Through goal setting and planning, managers learn what the organization is trying to accomplish. They can make decisions to ensure that internal policies, roles, performance, structure, products, and expenditures will be made in accordance with desired outcomes. Decisions throughout the organization will be in alignment with the plan.

:: *Standard of performance.* Because goals define desired outcomes for the organization, they also serve as performance criteria. They provide a standard of assessment. If an organization wishes to grow by 15 percent, and actual growth is 17 percent, managers will have exceeded their prescribed standard.

The overall planning process prevents managers from thinking merely in terms of day-to-day activities. When organizations drift away from goals and plans, they typically get into trouble.

GOALS IN ORGANIZATIONS

Setting goals starts with top managers. The overall planning process begins with a mission statement and strategic goals for the organization as a whole.

Organizational Mission

At the top of the goal hierarchy is the **mission**—the organization's reason for existence. The mission describes the organization's values, aspirations, and reason for being. A well-defined mission is the basis for development of all subsequent goals and plans. Without a clear mission, goals and plans may be developed haphazardly and not take the organization in the direction it needs to go.

The formal **mission statement** is a broadly stated definition of purpose that distinguishes the organization from others of a similar type. A well-designed mission statement can enhance employee motivation and organizational performance.[13] The content of a mission statement often focuses on the market and customers and identifies desired fields of endeavor. Some mission statements describe company characteristics such as corporate values, product quality, location of facilities, and attitude toward employees. Mission statements often reveal the company's philosophy as well as purpose. One example is the mission statement for Bristol-Myers Squibb Company, presented in Exhibit 7.2. Such short, straightforward mission statements describe basic business activities and purposes, as well as the values that guide the company. Another example of this type of mission statement is that of State Farm Insurance:

State Farm's mission is to help people manage the risks of everyday life, recover from the unexpected, and realize their dreams.

We are people who make it our business to be like a good neighbor; who built a premier company by selling and keeping promises through our marketing partnership; who bring diverse talents and experiences to our work of serving the State Farm customer.

Our success is built on a foundation of shared values—quality service and relationships, mutual trust, integrity, and financial strength.[14]

Because of mission statements such as those of Bristol-Myers Squibb and State Farm, employees as well as customers, suppliers, and stockholders know the company's stated purpose and values.

CONCEPT CONNECTION A candle-scented office in a cozy yellow house that feels like a retreat from the stresses of life: Does that sound like a trip to the dentist? It's part of what sets the Washington, D.C., practice of Dr. Lynn Locklear apart. Her **mission,** she says, is "to provide a level of services and dental care that significantly enhances the quality of your life." Dr. Locklear takes a holistic approach, viewing dental health as linked to a person's overall physical and emotional well-being. It's a philosophy that helped the 2006 *Black Enterprise* "Business Innovator of the Year" grow revenues from $710,000 in 2003 to $1.2 million in 2005.

mission The organization's reason for existence.

mission statement A broadly stated definition of the organization's basic business scope and operations that distinguishes it from similar types of organizations.

EXHIBIT   7.2

Mission Statement for
Bristol-Myers Squibb

The Bristol-Myers Squibb Pledge

Our company's mission is to extend and enhance human life by providing the highest-quality pharmaceutical and related health care products.

We pledge—to our patients and customers, to our employees and partners, to our shareholders and neighbors, and to the world we serve— to act on our belief that the priceless ingredient of every product is the honor and integrity of its maker.

 Bristol-Myers Squibb Company

Goals and Plans

Broad statements describing where the organization wants to be in the future are called **strategic goals**. They pertain to the organization as a whole rather than to specific divisions or departments. Strategic goals are often called *official goals,* because they are the stated intentions of what the organization wants to achieve. For example, a new strategic goal for the Wm. Wrigley Jr. Co., which for more than 100 years only made gum, is to become a major player in the broader candy market.[15]

Strategic plans define the action steps by which the company intends to attain strategic goals. The strategic plan is the blueprint that defines the organizational activities and resource allocations—in the form of cash, personnel, space, and facilities—required for meeting these targets. Strategic planning tends to be long term and may define organizational action steps from two to five years in the future. The purpose of strategic plans is to turn organizational goals into realities within that time period. Elements of the strategic plan at Wrigley include acquiring candy brands from food companies such as Kraft and investing $45 million in a global innovation center. In 2005, new products accounted for 17 percent of Wrigley's sales, up from less than 6 percent in the late 1990s. As another example, consider the strategic goals and plans at Citigroup.

strategic goals Broad statements of where the organization wants to be in the future; pertain to the organization as a whole rather than to specific divisions or departments.

strategic plans The action steps by which an organization intends to attain strategic goals.

Citigroup

Citigroup is the world's largest financial company, but things haven't been so rosy at the giant firm lately. Since he took over as CEO, Charles O. Prince has dealt with angry government regulators, sagging morale, poor financial results, and a sluggish stock price.

Prince recently announced a new strategic plan to get the company growing again. Strategic goals include (1) restoring Citigroup's bruised reputation; (2) building up the corporate investment bank; (3) reinvigorating the consumer banking business; and (4) dramatically expanding Citigroup's overseas business, where the company has only a low single-digit share in most markets. "Everything we do," says Prince, "should fit under one of those headings."

Strategic plans for meeting these goals include delaying big acquisitions to contain risk and push up the stock price; implementing a five-step ethics plan to mend a wobbly corporate culture and restore public confidence; beefing up staff and adding new services such as electronic and derivatives trading to Citigroup's investment banking options; and reorganizing the consumer banking business to focus more on service rather than just selling products. Prince is investing significant resources in advertising budgets and implementing a more attractive rewards package so consumers can get bigger discounts or perks when they use more Citigroup products and services. To pump up market share internationally, the plan calls for splitting consumer banking into two divisions, separating mature markets such as the United States from fast-growing markets in developing countries; expanding Citigroup's credit card availability overseas; and opening hundreds of new branches in countries such Poland, Turkey, Indonesia, and India.

Regulatory troubles combined with slow growth in consumer banking have hurt Citigroup's earning and stock price, but Prince believes his strategic plans can help Citigroup fix these problems and come out stronger.[16]

In early 2006, Charles Prince was cited by *Fortune* magazine as having one of the top 10 "Toughest Jobs in Business."[17] Wall Street analysts, investors, and consumers are watching to see whether the new strategic goals and plans can alleviate some of the turmoil that entangled Citigroup and get the company back on more solid ground.

After strategic goals are formulated, the next step is defining **tactical goals**, which are the results that major divisions and departments within the organization intend to achieve. These goals apply to middle management and describe what major subunits must do in order for the organization to achieve its overall goals.

Tactical plans are designed to help execute the major strategic plans and to accomplish a specific part of the company's strategy.[18] Tactical plans typically have a shorter time horizon than strategic plans—over the next year or so. The word *tactical* originally comes from the military. In a business or nonprofit organization, tactical plans define what major departments and organizational subunits will do to implement the organization's strategic plan. For example, the overall strategic plan of a large florist might involve becoming the Number 1 telephone and Internet-based purveyor of flowers, which requires high-volume sales during peak seasons such as Valentine's Day and Mother's Day. Human resource managers will develop tactical plans to ensure that the company has the dedicated order takers and customer service representatives it needs during these critical periods. Tactical plans might include cross-training employees so they can switch to different jobs as departmental needs change, allowing order takers to transfer to jobs at headquarters during off-peak times to prevent burnout, and using regular order takers to train and supervise temporary workers during peak seasons.[19] These actions help top managers implement their overall strategic plan. Normally, it is the middle manager's job to take the broad strategic plan and identify specific tactical plans.

The results expected from departments, work groups, and individuals are the **operational goals**. They are precise and measurable. "Process 150 sales applications each week," "achieve 90 percent of deliveries on time," "reduce overtime by 10 percent next month," and "develop two new online courses in accounting" are examples of operational goals. An example of an operational goal at the Internal Revenue Service (IRS) is to give accurate responses to 85 percent of taxpayer questions.[20]

Operational plans are developed at the lower levels of the organization to specify action steps toward achieving operational goals and to support tactical plans. The operational plan is the department manager's tool for daily and weekly operations. Goals are stated in quantitative terms, and the department plan describes how goals will be achieved. Operational planning specifies plans for department managers, supervisors, and individual employees.

Schedules are an important component of operational planning. Schedules define precise time frames for the completion of each operational goal required for the organization's tactical and strategic goals. Operational planning also must be coordinated with the budget, because resources must be allocated for desired activities. For example, Apogee Enterprises, a window and glass fabricator with 150 small divisions, is fanatical about operational planning and budgeting.

tactical goals Goals that define the outcomes that major divisions and departments must achieve in order for the organization to reach its overall goals.

tactical plans Plans designed to help execute major strategic plans and to accomplish a specific part of the company's strategy.

operational goals Specific, measurable results expected from departments, work groups, and individuals within the organization.

operational plans Plans developed at the organization's lower levels that specify action steps toward achieving operational goals and that support tactical planning activities.

**CONCEPT
CONNECTION** In 2001, California fashion house BCBG Max Azria Group was facing possible bankruptcy. Its **strategic goal** was clear: growth. But, its expansion had gone awry. Undeterred, CEO Max Azria hired Ben Malka as president. Together they formulated a new **strategic plan,** obtained $53 million in financing, and got to work. BCBG introduced new lines, concluded licensing agreements, and dramatically increased the number of retail outlets worldwide through acquisitions and by opening new stores. In 2006, BCBG expected to realize $1 billion in sales for the first time. Here Azria and his wife Lubov, who is a BCBG creative designer, acknowledge applause at a New York fashion show.

Committees are set up to review and challenge budgets, profit plans, and proposed expenditures. Assigning the dollars makes the operational plan work for everything from hiring new salespeople to increasing travel expenses.

Alignment of Goals

Effectively designed organizational goals are aligned into a hierarchy; that is, the achievement of goals at low levels permits the attainment of high-level goals, also called a *means-ends chain.* Operational goals lead to the achievement of tactical goals, which, in turn, lead to the attainment of strategic goals. Organizational performance is an outcome of how well these interdependent elements are aligned, so that individuals, teams, departments, and so forth are working in concert to attain specific goals that ultimately help the organization fulfill its mission.[21] Strategic goals are traditionally considered the responsibility of top management, tactical goals that of middle management, and operational goals that of first-line supervisors and workers.

Today, some companies are pushing greater involvement of all employees in goal setting and planning at each level. Microsoft, facing greater competition and new threats from the shifting technological and economic environment, developed a new goal-setting process that emphasizes individual commitments and alignment of goals.

Microsoft

Managers at Microsoft Corporation have long stressed that the achievement of individual goals is what enables the company to achieve high performance. As the company faced new challenges, managers decided to review the goal-setting process to make sure it was contributing to a culture of performance and accountability.

Each year, employees at all levels are asked to develop individual performance goals and discuss them with their managers. One area of concern discovered in the review was that most employee goals were stated as hopes or aspirations rather than as real commitments. Moreover, it was often difficult to see alignment between individual goals and broader team, departmental, divisional, and company goals. Top leaders first changed the terminology they used by asking employees and managers to develop a list of *commitments.* Next, they involved everyone in training to help people establish commitments that were in alignment.

The training was designed so that everyone first got clarity on the mission and commitments (goals) of the corporation. The commitments were then cascaded down to the divisional, departmental, team, and ultimately individual level.[22]

Microsoft executives are currently monitoring the new goal-setting process and providing continuing training and guidance to make sure goals stay in alignment and help the company carry out its mission. An example of a goal hierarchy is illustrated in Exhibit 7.3. Note how the strategic goal of "excellent service to customers" translates into "Open one new sales office" and "Respond to customer inquiries within two hours" at lower management levels.

Mission

Manufacture both standard and custom metal products for various applications in the machine tool industry

EXHIBIT 7.3

Hierarchy of Goals for
a Manufacturing
Organization

Strategic Goals

President
12% return on investment
5% growth
No employee layoffs
Excellent service to customers

Tactical Goals

Finance V.P.
Keep outstanding accounts below $500,000
Keep borrowing below $1,250,000
Provide monthly budget statements for departments
Have delinquent accounts of no more than 2% of total

Production V.P.
Manufacture 1,200,000 products at average cost of $19
Increase manufacturing productivity by 2%
Resolve employee grievances within 3 working days

Marketing V.P.
Sell 1,200,000 units at average price of $27
Introduce 1 new product line
Increase sales by 5% in new market areas
Open 1 new sales office
Attain market share of 19%

Operational Goals

Accounts Receivable Manager
Issue invoices within 5 days of sale
Check new customers' credit within 1 working day
Allow no account to be overdue more than 5 months
Call delinquent accounts weekly

Supervisor—Automatic Machines
Produce 150,000 standard units at average cost of $16
Have machine downtime of less than 7%
Respond to employee grievances within 24 hours

Sales Manager—Region 1
Respond to customer inquiries within 2 hours
Meet sales quota of 120,600 units
Work with salespeople to:
  Visit 1 new customer each day
  Call on each large customer every 4 weeks
  Call on each small customer every 8 weeks

CRITERIA FOR EFFECTIVE GOALS

To ensure goal-setting benefits for the organization, certain characteristics and guidelines should be adopted. The characteristics of both goals and the goal-setting process are listed in Exhibit 7.4. These characteristics pertain to organizational goals at the strategic, tactical, and operational levels:

::   *Specific and measurable.* When possible, goals should be expressed in quantitative terms, such as increasing profits by 2 percent, having zero incomplete sales order forms, decreasing scrap by 1 percent, or increasing average teacher effectiveness ratings from 3.5 to 3.7. Not all goals can be expressed in numerical terms, but vague goals have little motivating power for employees. By necessity, goals are qualitative

Goal Characteristics

- Specific and measurable
- Cover key result areas
- Challenging but realistic
- Defined time period
- Linked to rewards

EXHIBIT 7.4

Characteristics of Effective
Goal Setting

as well as quantitative, especially at the top of the organization. The important point is that the goals be precisely defined and allow for measurable progress.

:: *Cover key result areas.* Goals cannot be set for every aspect of employee behavior or organizational performance; if they were, their sheer number would render them meaningless. Instead, managers establish goals based on the idea of *choice and clarity.* A few carefully chosen, clear, and direct goals can more powerfully focus organizational attention, energy, and resources.[23] Managers should identify a few key result areas—perhaps up to four or five for any organizational department or job. Key result areas are those activities that contribute most to company performance and competitiveness.[24] Most companies use a balanced approach to goal setting. For example, Northern States Power Co. tracks measurements in four key areas: financial performance, customer service and satisfaction, internal processes, and innovation and learning.[25]

:: *Challenging but realistic.* Goals should be challenging but not unreasonably difficult. When goals are unrealistic, they set employees up for failure and lead to a decrease in employee morale. For example, one team at a Texas-based company that was recognized as tops in the organization had its quota raised by 65 percent, an impossible goal to reach, while lesser-performing teams had targets raised by only 15 percent. Members of the high-performing team were so discouraged that most of them began looking for other jobs.[26] However, if goals are too easy, employees may not feel motivated. *Stretch goals* are extremely ambitious but realistic goals that challenge employees to meet high standards. One example comes from 3M, where top managers set a goal that 30 percent of sales must come from products introduced in the past four years; the old standard was 25 percent. Setting ambitious goals helps to keep 3M churning out innovative new products—more than 500 in one recent year alone—and has entrenched the company as a leader in some of today's most dynamic markets.[27] The key to effective stretch goals is ensuring that goals are set within the existing resource base, not beyond departments' time, equipment, or financial resources.

:: *Defined time period.* Goals should specify the time period over which they will be achieved. A time period is a deadline stating the date on which goal attainment will be measured. A goal of implementing a new customer relationship management system, for instance, might have a deadline such as September 1, 2007. If a strategic goal involves a two- to three-year time horizon, specific dates for achieving parts of it can be set up. For example, strategic sales goals could be established on a three-year time horizon, with a $100 million target in year one, a $129 million target in year two, and a $165 million target in year three.

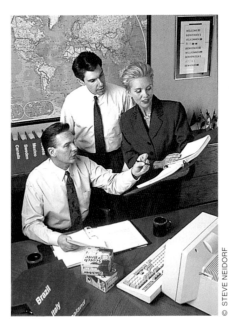

© STEVE NEIDORF

:: *Linked to rewards.* The ultimate impact of goals depends on the extent to which salary increases, promotions, and awards are based on goal achievement. Employees pay attention to what gets noticed and rewarded in the organization, and people who attain goals should be rewarded for doing so. Rewards give meaning and significance to goals and help commit employees to achieving goals. Managers should also remember that failure to attain goals often is due to factors outside employees' control. For example, failure to achieve a financial goal may be associated with a drop in market demand due to industry recession; thus, an employee could not be expected to reach it. A reward might still be appropriate if the employee partially achieved goals under difficult circumstances.[28]

As a new manager, establish operational goals that are in alignment with the tactical and strategic goals set at higher levels in the organization. Make goals specific, measurable, and challenging, but realistic. Remember that a few carefully chosen goals are powerful for directing employee energy and motivation. Reward people when they meet goals.

PLANNING TYPES

Managers use strategic, tactical, and operational goals to direct employees and resources toward achieving specific outcomes that enable the organization to perform efficiently and effectively. Managers use a number of planning approaches. Among the most popular are management by objectives, single-use plans, standing plans, and contingency plans.

Management by Objectives

Management by objectives (MBO) is a method whereby managers and employees define goals for every department, project, and person and use them to monitor subsequent performance.[29] A model of the essential steps of the MBO process is presented in Exhibit 7.5. Four major activities must occur in order for MBO to be successful:[30]

1. *Set goals.* This step is the most difficult in MBO. Setting goals involves employees at all levels and looks beyond day-to-day activities to answer the question "What are we trying to accomplish?" A good goal should be concrete and realistic, provide a specific target and time frame, and assign responsibility. Goals may be quantitative or qualitative. Quantitative goals are described in numerical terms, such as "Salesperson Jones will obtain 16 new accounts in December." Qualitative goals use statements such as "Marketing will reduce complaints by improving customer service next year." Goals should be jointly derived. Mutual agreement between employee and supervisor creates the strongest commitment to achieving goals. In the case of teams, all team members may participate in setting goals.

2. *Develop action plans.* An *action plan* defines the course of action needed to achieve the stated goals. Action plans are made for both individuals and departments.

management by objectives (MBO) A method of management whereby managers and employees define goals for every department, project, and person and use them to monitor subsequent performance.

Step 1: Set Goals

- Corporate Strategic Goals
- Departmental Goals
- Individual Goals

Step 2: Develop Action Plans

Action Plans

Review Progress

Step 3: Review Progress

Take Corrective Action

Appraise Performance

Step 4: Appraise Overall Performance

EXHIBIT 7.5

Model of the MBO Process

3. *Review progress.* A periodic progress review is important to ensure that action plans are working. These reviews can occur informally between managers and subordinates, where the organization may wish to conduct three-, six-, or nine-month reviews during the year. This periodic checkup allows managers and employees to see whether they are on target or whether corrective action is needed. Managers and employees should not be locked into predefined behavior and must be willing to take whatever steps are necessary to produce meaningful results. The point of MBO is to achieve goals. The action plan can be changed whenever goals are not being met.

4. *Appraise overall performance.* The final step in MBO is to carefully evaluate whether annual goals have been achieved for both individuals and departments. Success or failure to achieve goals can become part of the performance appraisal system and the designation of salary increases and other rewards. The appraisal of departmental and overall corporate performance shapes goals for the next year. The MBO cycle repeats itself on an annual basis.

The specific application of MBO must fit the needs of each company. For example, Siemens used MBO to improve its overall financial performance.

Siemens

Siemens of Germany, which makes everything from mobile phones to gas-turbine generators to light bulbs, has always had great engineers bent on producing products of the highest quality. But in recent years, managers have learned that competing with the likes of U.S.-based General Electric and Korea's Samsung takes more than quality—it also requires speed to market, relentless innovation, and ruthless attention to costs. Within two years, Siemens' profits sank by two-thirds and company shares fell even faster. CEO Heinrich von Pierer developed a plan for getting Siemens back on track, with a specific goal (MBO step 1) of strengthening the overall business to be in financial shape for listing on a U.S. stock exchange within three years.

Managers developed an action plan (MBO step 2) that included (1) cutting the time it takes to develop and produce new products; (2) selling or closing poor-performing units and strengthening remaining businesses through acquisitions to achieve world leadership; (3) setting tough profit targets for managers and tying pay to performance; and (4) converting accounting practices to report results according to U.S. accounting standards. Managers of the various business divisions then developed action plans for employees in their own units. Progress was reviewed (MBO step 3) at quarterly meetings where managers from the 14 business units reported on their advancements directly to von Pierer.

Managers were required to explain if benchmarks weren't met and how shortcomings would be corrected. At the end of each year of the turnaround plan, an overall performance appraisal was held for each business and the corporation as a whole (MBO step 4). Managers who met goals were rewarded; those who had consistently failed to meet them were let go, with the poorest performers going first.

Since the plan was implemented, Siemens dramatically improved its speed and overall financial performance. For example, mobile phones that once took a painstaking 13 hours each to produce are now sliding off the assembly line in five minutes. Many of Siemens' businesses have been transformed from money losers to profit drivers, and the stock performance has taken a sharp upturn. Siemens is on track to begin reporting results according to U.S. principles and listing on the U.S. stock exchange. The MBO system helped to energize manager and employee actions companywide toward goals deemed critical by top management.[31]

Many companies, including Intel, Tenneco, Black & Decker, and DuPont, have adopted MBO, and most managers think MBO is an effective management tool.[32] Managers believe they are better oriented toward goal achievement when MBO is used. In recent years, the U.S. Congress required that federal agencies use a type of MBO system to focus government employees on achieving specific outcomes.[33] Like any system, MBO achieves benefits when used properly but results in problems when used improperly. Benefits and problems are summarized in Exhibit 7.6.

Benefits of MBO	Problems with MBO
1. Manager and employee efforts are focused on activities that will lead to goal attainment. 2. Performance can be improved at all company levels. 3. Employees are motivated. 4. Departmental and individual goals are aligned with company goals.	1. Constant change prevents MBO from taking hold. 2. An environment of poor employer-employee relations reduces MBO effectiveness. 3. Strategic goals may be displaced by operational goals. 4. Mechanistic organizations and values that discourage participation can harm the MBO process. 5. Too much paperwork saps MBO energy.

EXHIBIT 7.6

MBO Benefits and Problems

The benefits of the MBO process can be many. Corporate goals are more likely to be achieved when they focus manager and employee efforts. Using a performance measurement system, such as MBO, helps employees see how their jobs and performance contribute to the business, giving them a sense of ownership and commitment.[34] Performance is improved when employees are committed to attaining the goal, are motivated because they help decide what is expected, and are free to be resourceful. Goals at lower levels are aligned with and enable the attainment of goals at top management levels.

Problems with MBO occur when the company faces rapid change. The environment and internal activities must have some stability for performance to be measured and compared against goals. Setting new goals every few months allows no time for action plans and appraisal to take effect. Also, poor employer-employee relations reduce effectiveness because of an element of distrust that may be present between managers and workers. Sometimes goal "displacement" occurs if employees focus exclusively on their operational goals to the detriment of other teams or departments. Overemphasis on operational goals can harm the attainment of overall goals. Another problem arises in mechanistic organizations characterized by rigidly defined tasks and rules that may not be compatible with MBO's emphasis on mutual determination of goals by employee and supervisor. In addition, when participation is discouraged, employees will lack the training and values to jointly set goals with employers. Finally, if MBO becomes a process of filling out annual paperwork rather than energizing employees to achieve goals, it becomes an empty exercise. Once the paperwork is completed, employees forget about the goals, perhaps even resenting the paperwork in the first place.

Single-Use and Standing Plans

Single-use plans are developed to achieve a set of goals that are not likely to be repeated in the future. **Standing plans** are ongoing plans that provide guidance for tasks performed repeatedly within the organization. Exhibit 7.7 outlines the major types of single-use and standing plans. Single-use plans typically include both programs and projects. The primary standing plans are organizational policies, rules, and procedures. Standing plans generally pertain to such matters as employee illness, absences, smoking, discipline, hiring, and dismissal. Many companies are discovering a need to develop standing plans regarding the use of e-mail, as discussed in the Manager's Shoptalk box.

single-use plans Plans that are developed to achieve a set of goals that are unlikely to be repeated in the future.

standing plans Ongoing plans that are used to provide guidance for tasks performed repeatedly within the organization.

Go to the experiential exercise on page 232 that pertains to developing standing plans. ■ **TAKE A MOMENT**

EXHIBIT 7.7

Major Types of Single-Use and Standing Plans

Single-Use Plans	Standing Plans

Program
• Plans for attaining a one-time organizational goal
• Major undertaking that may take several years to complete
• Large in scope; may be associated with several projects
   Examples: Building a new headquarters
              Converting all paper files to digital
 	
Project
• Also a set of plans for attaining a one-time goal
• Smaller in scope and complexity than a program; shorter in horizon
• Often one part of a larger program
   Example: Renovating the office
             Setting up a company intranet
	Policy
	• Broad in scope—general guide to action
	• Based on organization's overall goals/strategic plan
	• Defines boundaries within which to make decisions
	   Examples: Sexual harassment policies
	             Internet and e-mail usage policies
	
	Rule
	• Narrow in scope
	• Describes how a specific action is to be performed
	• May apply to specific setting
	   Examples: No eating rule in areas of company where employees are visible to the public
	
	Procedure
	• Sometimes called a standard operating procedure
	• Defines a precise series of steps to attain certain goals
	   Examples: Procedures for issuing refunds
	             Procedures for handling employee grievances

contingency plans Plans that define company responses to specific situations, such as emergencies, setbacks, or unexpected conditions.

© BENJAMIN LOWRY—CORBIS

CONCEPT CONNECTION A desert flare marks the area where geologists discovered Libya's rich Zilten oilfield in the 1950s. At their peak in 1970, Libyan oil fields operated by Occidental Petroleum were producing 660,000 barrels a day, more than the company's total oil production in 2003. Today, with economic sanctions against Libya lifted by the U.S. government, big oil companies like Occidental, Chevron Texaco, and Exxon Mobil are again ready to do business with Libya's National Oil Corporation. Yet, the current environment of terrorist threats and general uncertainty means managers have to be prepared for whatever might happen. They are busy developing **contingency plans** to define how their companies will respond in case of unexpected setbacks associated with renewed Libyan operations. Companies are willing to take the risks because the potential rewards are huge.

Contingency Plans

When organizations are operating in a highly uncertain environment or dealing with long time horizons, sometimes planning can seem like a waste of time. In fact, strict plans may even hinder rather than help an organization's performance in the face of rapid technological, social, economic, or other environmental change. In these cases, managers can develop multiple future alternatives to help them form more flexible plans.

Contingency plans define company responses to be taken in the case of emergencies, setbacks, or unexpected conditions. To develop contingency plans, managers identify important factors in the environment, such as possible economic downturns, declining markets, increases in cost of supplies, new technological developments, or safety accidents. Managers then forecast a range of alternative responses to the most likely high-impact contingencies, focusing on the worst case.[35] For example, if sales fall 20 percent and prices drop 8 percent, what will the company do? Managers

REGULATING E-MAIL IN THE WORKPLACE

Top executives around the globe are discovering that casual e-mail messages can come back to haunt them—in court. The American Management Association (AMA) surveyed 1,100 companies and found that 14 percent of them had been ordered to disclose e-mail messages. Eight brokerage firms were fined $8 million for not keeping and producing e-mail in accordance with SEC guidelines. Some companies have had to pay millions to settle sexual harassment lawsuits arising from inappropriate e-mail.

As with any powerful tool, e-mail has the potential to be hazardous, backfiring not only on the employee but on the organization as well. One study found that "potentially dangerous or nonproductive" messages account for fully 31 percent of all company e-mail. Experts say a formal written policy is the best way for companies to protect themselves, and they offer some tips for managers on developing effective policies governing the use of e-mail.

:: *Make clear that all e-mail and its contents are the property of the company.* Many experts recommend warning employees that the company reserves the right to read any messages transmitted over its system. "Employees need to understand that a company can access employees' e-mail at any time without advance notice or consent," says lawyer Pam Reeves. This rule helps to discourage frivolous e-mails or those that might be considered crude and offensive.

:: *Tie the policy to the company's sexual harassment policy or other policies governing employee behavior*

on the job. In almost all sexual harassment cases, judges have ruled that the use of e-mail was considered part of the workplace environment.

:: *Establish clear guidelines on matters such as the use of e-mail for jokes and other nonwork-related communications, the sending of confidential messages, and how to handle junk e-mail.* At Prudential Insurance, for example, employees are prohibited from using company e-mail to share jokes, photographs, or any kind of nonbusiness information.

:: *Establish guidelines for deleting or retaining messages.* Retention periods of 30 to 90 days for routine messages are typical. Most organizations also set up a centralized archive for retaining essential e-mail messages.

:: *Consider having policies pop up on users' screens when they log on.* It is especially important to remind employees that e-mail belongs to the employer and may be monitored.

Even deleted e-mails can usually be tracked down by a computer forensics expert. An effective policy is the best step companies can take to manage the potential risks of e-mail abuse.

SOURCES: "E-Mail: The DNA of Office Crimes," *Electric Perspectives* 28, no. 5 (September–October 2003): 4; Marcia Stepanek with Steve Hamm, "When the Devil Is in the E-Mails," *BusinessWeek* (June 8, 1998): 72–74; Joseph McCafferty, "The Phantom Menace," *CFO* (June 1999): 89–91; and "Many Company Internet and E-Mail Policies Are Worth Revising," *The Kiplinger Letter* (February 21, 2003): 1.

can develop contingency plans that might include layoffs, emergency budgets, new sales efforts, or new markets. A real-life example comes from FedEx, which has to cope with some kind of unexpected disruption to its service somewhere in the world on a daily basis. In 2005, for example, managers activated contingency plans related to more than two dozen tropical storms, an air traffic controller strike in France, and a blackout in Los Angeles. The company also has contingency plans in place for events such as labor strikes, social upheavals in foreign countries, or incidents of terrorism.[36]

PLANNING IN A TURBULENT ENVIRONMENT

Today, contingency planning takes on a whole new urgency as increasing turbulence and uncertainty shake the business world. Managers must renew their emphasis on bracing for unexpected—even unimaginable—events. Two recent extensions of contingency planning are *building scenarios* and *crisis planning*.

Building Scenarios

One way managers cope with greater uncertainty is with a forecasting technique known as scenario building. **Scenario building** involves looking at current trends and discontinuities and visualizing future possibilities. Rather than looking only at history and thinking about what has been, managers think about what *could be*. The events that cause the most damage to companies are those that no one even conceived of, such as the collapse of the World Trade Center towers in New York due to terrorist attack. Managers can't predict the future, but they can rehearse a framework within which future events can be managed.[37] With scenario building, a broad base of managers mentally rehearses different scenarios based on anticipating varied changes that could impact the organization. Scenarios are like stories that offer alternative vivid pictures of what the future will be like and how managers will respond. Typically, two to five scenarios are developed for each set of factors, ranging from the most optimistic to the most pessimistic view.[38] Scenario building forces managers to mentally rehearse what they would do if their best-laid plans collapse.

Royal Dutch/Shell has long used scenario building to help managers navigate the turbulence and uncertainty of the oil industry. One scenario Shell managers rehearsed in 1970, for example, focused on an imagined accident in Saudi Arabia that severed an oil pipeline, which in turn decreased supply. The market reacted by increasing oil prices, which allowed OPEC nations to pump less oil and make more money. This story caused managers to reexamine the standard assumptions about oil price and supply and imagine what would happen and how they would respond if OPEC increased prices. Nothing in the exercise told Shell managers to expect an embargo, but by rehearsing this scenario, they were much more prepared than the competition when OPEC announced its first oil embargo in October 1973. This speedy response to a massive shift in the environment enabled Shell to move in two years' from being the world's eighth largest oil company to being number two.[39]

■ **TAKE A MOMENT**   As a new manager, get in the mindset of scenario planning. Go to http://www.shell.com/scenarios, where Shell Oil publishes the outline of its annual scenario planning exercise, and http://www.cia.gov/nic, where the National Intelligence Council pictures possible futures for the year 2020.

Crisis Planning

Some unexpected events are so sudden and devastating that they require immediate response. Consider events such as the November 12, 2001, crash of American Airlines Flight 587 in a New York neighborhood already devastated by terrorist attacks, the 1993 deaths due to e-coli bacteria from Jack-in-the-Box hamburgers, or the 2003 crash of the *Columbia* space shuttle. Companies also face many smaller crises that call for rapid response, such as the conviction of Martha Stewart, chair of Martha Stewart Living Omnimedia, on charges of insider trading; allegations of tainted Coca-Cola in Belgium; or charges that Tyson Foods hired illegal immigrants to work in its processing plants. Crises have become integral features of our organizations.[40] Although crises may vary, a carefully thought-out and coordinated crisis plan can be used to respond to any disaster. In addition, crisis planning reduces the incidence of trouble, much like putting a good lock on a door reduces burglaries.[41]

Exhibit 7.8 outlines the three essential stages of crisis management.[42] The prevention stage involves activities managers undertake to try to prevent crises from occurring and to detect warning signs of potential crises. The preparation stage

scenario building Looking at trends and discontinuities and imagining possible alternative futures to build a framework within which unexpected future events can be managed.

Prevention
- Build relationships.
- Detect signals from environment.

Preparation
- Designate crisis management team and spokesperson.
- Create detailed crisis management plan.
- Set up effective communications system.

Containment
- Rapid response: Activate the crisis management plan.
- Get the awful truth out.
- Meet safety and emotional needs.
- Return to business.

EXHIBIT 7.8

Three Stages of Crisis Management

SOURCE: Based on information in W. Timothy Coombs, *Ongoing Crisis Communication: Planning, Managing, and Responding* (Thousand Oaks, Calif.: Sage Publications, 1999).

includes all the detailed planning to handle a crisis when it occurs. Containment focuses on the organization's response to an actual crisis and any follow-up concerns.

PREVENTION

Although unexpected events and disasters will happen, managers should do everything they can to prevent crises. A critical part of the prevention stage is building trusting relationships with key stakeholders such as employees, customers, suppliers, governments, unions, and the community. By developing favorable relationships, managers can often prevent crises from happening and respond more effectively to those that cannot be avoided. For example, organizations that have open, trusting relationships with employees and unions may avoid crippling labor strikes.

Good communication also helps managers identify problems early so they do not turn into major issues. Coca-Cola suffered a major crisis in Europe because it failed to respond quickly to reports of "foul-smelling" Coke in Belgium. A former CEO observed that every problem the company has faced in recent years "can be traced to a singular cause: We neglected our relationships."[43]

PREPARATION

Three steps in the preparation stage are (1) designating a crisis management team and spokesperson, (2) creating a detailed crisis management plan, and (3) setting up an effective communications system. Some companies are setting up crisis management offices, with high-level leaders who report directly to the CEO.[44] Although these offices are in charge of crisis management, it is important that people throughout the company be involved. The crisis management team, for example, is a cross-functional group of people who are designated to swing into action if a crisis occurs. The organization should also designate a spokesperson

© P. KEVIN MORLEY/RICHMOND TIMES-DISPATCH/ASSOCIATED PRESS

CONCEPT CONNECTION Looks harmless, doesn't it? But three people died and nearly 200 became ill after E. coli-contaminated spinach grown in central California reached consumers throughout the United States. Government and the food industry activated **crisis management plans** to contain the public health menace. Producers voluntarily recalled spinach products, grocers swept shelves clear of bagged spinach, and the FDA worked tirelessly to determine the cause. Various groups also proposed future **prevention** measures. Some advocated more stringent government regulation, while others argued for producers doing more product testing and a better job of tracking produce from field to table.

who will be the voice of the company during the crisis.[45] In many cases, this person is the top leader. However, organizations typically assign more than one spokesperson so that someone else will be prepared if the top leader is not available.

The crisis management plan (CMP) is a detailed, written plan that specifies the steps to be taken, and by whom, if a crisis occurs. The CMP should include the steps for dealing with various types of crises, such as natural disasters like fires or earthquakes, normal accidents like economic crises or industrial accidents, and abnormal events such as product tampering or acts of terrorism.[46] Morgan Stanley Dean Witter, the World Trade Center's largest tenant with 3,700 employees, adopted a crisis management plan for abnormal events after bomb threats during the Persian Gulf War in 1991. Top managers credit its detailed evacuation procedures for saving the lives of all but six employees during the September 11, 2001, attack.[47] A key point is that a crisis management plan should be a living, changing document that is regularly reviewed, practiced, and updated as needed.

CONTAINMENT

Some crises are inevitable no matter how well prepared an organization is. When crisis hits, a rapid response is crucial. Training and practice enable the team to immediately implement the crisis management plan. In addition, the organization should "get the awful truth out" to employees and the public as soon as possible.[48] At this stage, it becomes critical for the organization to speak with one voice so people do not get conflicting stories about what's going on and what the organization is doing about it.

After ensuring people's physical safety, if necessary, during a crisis, the next focus should be on responding to the emotional needs of employees, customers, and the public. Giving facts and statistics to try to downplay the disaster always backfires because it does not meet people's emotional need to feel that someone cares about them and what the disaster has meant to their lives.

Organizations strive to give people a sense of security and hope by getting back to business quickly. Companies that cannot get up and running within 10 days after any major crisis are not likely to stay in business.[49] People want to feel that they are going to have a job and be able to take care of their families. Managers also use a time of crisis to bolster their prevention abilities and be better prepared in the future. Executives at The Home Depot do a postmortem after each catastrophic event to learn how to better prepare for the next one.[50] A crisis is also an important time for companies to strengthen their stakeholder relationships. By being open and honest about the crisis and putting people first, organizations build stronger bonds with employees, customers, and other stakeholders, and gain a reputation as a trustworthy company.

■ **TAKE A MOMENT** Go to the ethical dilemma on page 232 that pertains to crisis management.

PLANNING FOR HIGH PERFORMANCE

The purpose of planning and goal setting is to help the organization achieve high performance. Overall organizational performance depends on achieving outcomes identified by the planning process. The process of planning is changing to be more in tune with a rapidly changing environment. Traditionally, strategy and planning have been the domain of top managers. Today, though, managers involve people throughout the organization, which can spur higher performance because people understand the goals and plans and buy into them. We will first discuss traditional, top-down approaches to planning and then examine some of the newer approaches that emphasize bottom-up planning and the involvement of stakeholders in the planning process.

Traditional Approaches to Planning

Traditionally, corporate planning has been done entirely by top executives, by consulting firms, or, most commonly, by central planning departments. **Central planning departments** are groups of planning specialists who report directly to the CEO or president. This approach was popular during the 1970s. Planning specialists were hired to gather data and develop detailed strategic plans for the corporation as a whole. This planning approach was top down because goals and plans were assigned to major divisions and departments from the planning department after approval by the president. This approach worked well in many applications.

Although traditional approaches to planning still are popular with some companies, formal planning increasingly is being criticized as inappropriate for today's fast-paced environment. Central planning departments may be out of touch with the constantly changing realities faced by front-line managers and employees, which may leave people struggling to follow a plan that no longer fits the environment and customer needs. In addition, formal plans dictated by top managers and central planning departments inhibit innovation and learning because employees have less incentive to think for themselves and come up with new ideas. For example, many divisional managers at Disney chafed under the central planning unit's oversight and argued that the unit has hurt the organization by squashing creativity. As one of his first acts, new Disney CEO Robert A. Iger dismantled the central planning department and gave more authority to the organization's business units, so that managers in areas such as parks and resorts, consumer products, and media will devise many of their own goals and plans to fit their division's situation as they understand it.[51] Other managers are also taking a fresh approach to spur creativity and high performance in a difficult environment.

CONCEPT CONNECTION Not so long ago, only top executives received comprehensive financial information. It came in pages upon pages of spreadsheets filled with hundreds of undigested numbers. Compare that to the easy-to-read Web-based **business performance dashboard,** such as the Celequest version pictured here. A key tool in the **decentralized planning** approach, the dashboard delivers real-time key performance metrics to any employee's desktop. Managers can tailor each display so it delivers exactly the information people need to track their performance and quickly steer a course back towards achieving strategic goals as soon as a problem appears.

High-Performance Approaches to Planning

A new approach to planning is to involve everyone in the organization, and sometimes outside stakeholders as well, in the planning process. The evolution to a new approach began with a shift to **decentralized planning**, which means that planning experts work with managers in major divisions or departments to develop their own goals and plans. This approach enables managers throughout the company to come up with their own creative solutions to problems and become more committed to following through on the plans. As the environment became even more volatile, top executives saw the benefits of pushing decentralized planning even further, by having planning experts work directly with line managers and front-line employees to develop dynamic plans that meet fast-changing needs.

In a complex and competitive business environment, strategic thinking and execution become the expectation of every employee.[52] Planning comes alive when

central planning department A group of planning specialists who develop plans for the organization as a whole and its major divisions and departments and typically report directly to the president or CEO.

decentralized planning Managers work with planning experts to develop their own goals and plans.

employees are involved in setting goals and determining the means to reach them. Here are some guidelines for planning in the new workplace.

START WITH A STRONG MISSION AND VISION

Planning for high performance requires flexibility. Employees may have to adapt plans to meet new needs and respond to changes in the environment. During times of turbulence or uncertainty, a powerful sense of purpose (mission) and direction for the future (vision) become even more important. Without a strong mission and vision to guide employee thinking and behavior, the resources of a fast-moving company can quickly become uncoordinated, with employees pursuing radically different plans and activities. A compelling mission and vision can also increase employee commitment and motivation, which are critical to helping organizations compete in a rapidly shifting environment.[53]

SET STRETCH GOALS FOR EXCELLENCE

Stretch goals are highly ambitious goals that are so clear, compelling, and imaginative that they fire up employees and engender excellence. Stretch goals get people to think in new ways because they are so far beyond the current levels that people don't know how to reach them. At the same time though, as we discussed earlier, the goals must be seen as achievable or employees will be discouraged and demotivated.[54] Stretch goals are extremely important today because things move fast. A company that focuses on gradual, incremental improvements in products, processes, or systems will get left behind. Managers can use stretch goals to compel employees to think in new ways that can lead to bold, innovative breakthroughs. Motorola used stretch goals to achieve *Six Sigma* quality, as described in Chapter 2, which has now become the standard for numerous companies. Managers first set a goal of a tenfold increase in quality over a two-year period. After this goal was met, they set a new stretch goal of a hundredfold improvement over a four-year period.[55]

■ TAKE A MOMENT   As a new manager, involve others in planning and goal setting to enhance commitment and performance. Help people align their individual goals with the organization's mission and vision, and use stretch goals to encourage innovation and excellence.

EMBRACE EVENT-DRIVEN PLANNING

In rapidly shifting environments, managers have to be in tune with what's happening *right now*, rather than focusing only on long-range goals and plans. Long-range strategic planning is not abandoned, but it is accompanied by event-driven planning, which responds to the current reality of what the environment and the marketplace demands.[56] Exhibit 7.9 compares traditional calendar-driven planning

EXHIBIT   7.9

Comparing Two Planning Styles

SOURCE: Chuck Martin, "How to Plan for the Short Term," book excerpt from Chuck Martin, *Managing for the Short Term* (New York: Doubleday, 2002), in *CIO* (September 15, 2002), 90–97.

Calendar-Driven Planning	Event-Driven Planning
Is based on time	Is based on events—small and large
Produces a document	Produces a sequential process
Is declared	Is evolutionary and interactive
Focuses on goals	Focuses on process
Creates obstacles to change once set	Allows for continuous change
Creates strategy implementers	Creates organizationwide strategists

Fighting Fires at Symantec

Vincent Weafer, Symantec Corp.'s senior director of security response, deals with chaos for a living. Day in and day out, he faces down viruses, worms, Trojan horses, and phishers. What he needs is a process, not a plan. He doesn't have time for a plan.

Symantec is currently the leading producer of computer security software, such as the well-known Norton product line. As recently as 1999, the company's Santa Monica, California, security response center was a relatively sleepy place, with a couple dozen employees working 8-hour days. Back then, the team identified perhaps five new viruses a day, determined how to defeat them, and sent out updated software to customers. How things have changed. Today, the California response center has counterparts around the world, with hundreds of investigators working around the clock to crank out as many as 30 security updates a day.

The frenzied pace is necessary to counter the astronomical increase in malicious software designed to invade computers, collectively called *malware*. In 2005, Symantec reported a 143 percent increase in malicious code being transported across the Internet. Attacks are also becoming more sophisticated, more damaging, and harder to detect. Whereas in the past most malware creators were precocious youngsters who launched viruses as a prank, now they're more likely to be criminals crafting contaminating code to steal data for use in identity theft, extortion schemes, money laundering, and other nefarious enterprises.

With its products continually evolving and its markets constantly shifting, planning at Symantec is by necessity fluid and dynamic, allowing managers to shift resources and activities as needed to get the job done. Weafer and his managers hold a weekly planning briefing, with remote locations looped in by speaker phone, to run through the security threats everyone is working on and make sure the various sites are in sync. Mid-course corrections triggered by events are common, such as shifting the work load to reduce the need for staff at one site to pull all-nighters. During one week, the center dealt with three major threats simultaneously, forcing manages to rethink their staffing strategy so that well-trained reserves could step up when analysts on the frontline tired. In between the weekly briefings, managers at the various sites stay in tune with what's happening around the world, so that work in progress, control over activities, and responsibility for new threats shifts smoothly as the day ends on one continent and begins on another.

"There's no question," says Symantec CEO John Thompson, "that you're only as good in this business as your last response to an attack." To stay one step ahead, security center managers take an ongoing, evolutionary approach to planning, continuously working toward an elusive goal: To put in place an entirely predictable process that can help people quickly adapt to the thoroughly unpredictable.

SOURCES: Scott Kirsner, "Sweating in the Hot Zone," *Fast Company* (October 2005): 61–65; Brian Grow, "Coming to Your PC's Back Door: Trojans," *Business Week Online* (January 23, 2006), www.businessweek.com/;/technology/content/jan2006/tc20060123_003410. htm?campaign_id=search; and Luc Hatlestad, "Symantec Warns of '06 Security Threat," *Information Week* (December 7, 2005), www.informationweek.com/showArticle.jhtml;jsessionid=51TW2DTMQKSCAQSND-LOSKHSCJUNN2JVN?articleID=174909533&queryText=Symantec.

to event-driven planning. **Event-driven planning** is a continuous, sequential process rather than a staid planning document. It is evolutionary and interactive, taking advantage of unforeseen events to shift the company as needed to improve performance. Event-driven planning allows for flexibility to adapt to market forces or other shifts in the environment, rather than being tied to a plan that no longer works. For example, Redix International, a software development firm, has a long-term plan for items it wants to incorporate into the software. However, the plan is modified at least four or five times a year. The shifts in direction are based on weekly discussions President and CEO Randall King has with key Redix managers, where they examine what demands from clients indicate about where the marketplace is going.[57] This chapter's Unlocking Innovative Solutions Through Technology box describes Symantec, an organization that lives in a perpetual state of crisis and relies on event-driven planning to respond quickly to new virus threats.

event-driven planning
Evolutionary planning that responds to the current reality of what the environment and the marketplace demand.

USE PERFORMANCE DASHBOARDS

People need a way to see how plans are progressing and gauge their progress toward achieving goals. Companies began using business performance dashboards as a way for executives to keep track of key performance metrics, such as sales in relation to targets, number of products on back order, or percentage of customer service calls resolved within specified time periods. Today, dashboards are evolving into organization-wide systems that help align and track goals across the enterprise. The true power of dashboards comes from deploying them throughout the company, even on the factory floor, so that all employees can track progress toward goals, see when things are falling short, and find innovative ways to get back on course toward reaching the specified targets. At Emergency Medical Associates, a physician-owned medical group that manages emergency rooms for hospitals in New York and New Jersey, dashboards enable the staff to see when performance thresholds related to patient wait times, for example, aren't being met at various hospitals.[58] Some dashboard systems also incorporate software that lets users perform what-if scenarios to evaluate the impact of various alternatives for meeting goals.

ORGANIZE TEMPORARY TASK FORCES

A **planning task force** is a temporary group of managers and employees who take responsibility for developing a strategic plan. Many of today's companies use interdepartmental task forces to help establish goals and make plans for achieving them. The task force often includes outside stakeholders as well, such as customers, suppliers, strategic partners, investors, or even members of the general community. Today's companies are highly focused on satisfying the needs and interests of all stakeholder groups, so they bring these stakeholders into the planning and goal-setting process.[59] LendLease, an Australian real estate and financial services company, for example, involves numerous stakeholders, including community advocates and potential customers, in the planning process for every new project it undertakes.[60]

PLANNING STILL STARTS AND STOPS AT THE TOP

Top managers create a mission and vision worthy of employees' best efforts and that provides a framework for planning and goal setting. Even though planning is decentralized, top managers must show support and commitment to the planning process. Top managers also accept responsibility when planning and goal setting are ineffective, rather than blaming the failure on lower-level managers or employees.

MANAGER'S SOLUTION

This chapter discussed organizational planning, which involves defining goals and developing a plan with which to achieve them. An organization exists for a single, overriding purpose known as its *mission*—the basis for strategic goals and plans. Goals within the organization are aligned in a hierarchical fashion, beginning with strategic goals followed by tactical and operational goals. Plans are defined similarly, with strategic, tactical, and operational plans used to achieve the goals. Other goal concepts include characteristics of effective goals and goal-setting behavior.

Several types of plans were described, including strategic, tactical, operational, single-use, standing, and contingency plans, as well as management by objectives. Two extensions of contingency planning are scenario building and crisis planning. Scenarios are alternative vivid pictures of what the future might be like. They provide

planning task force A group of managers and employees who develop a strategic plan.

a framework for managers to cope with unexpected or unpredictable events. Crisis planning involves the stages of prevention, preparation, and containment.

In the past, planning was almost always done entirely by top managers, by consultants, or by central planning departments. During turbulent times, planning is decentralized and people throughout the organization are involved in establishing dynamic plans that can meet rapidly changing needs in the environment. Some guidelines for planning in a turbulent environment include starting with a powerful mission and vision, setting stretch goals for excellence, embracing event-driven planning, using performance dashboards, and organizing temporary task forces that may include outside stakeholders. Planning is evolutionary and plans are continually adapted to meet new needs and changing markets. However, top managers are still responsible for providing a guiding mission and vision for the future and creating a solid framework for planning and goal setting.

Nancy Sorrells, the general manager at the Dallas–Fort Worth Marriott described in the chapter opening, realized that if people didn't know where they were going, they didn't have any idea how to get there. She needed to get everyone aligned with the hotel's mission before she could expect them to establish and meet high performance goals. Sorrells held meetings with department heads and employees throughout the hotel to talk about the five aspects of the hotel's mission: creating a great experience for guests; creating a great work experience for employees; the profitability of the hotel; quality inside the hotel; and growth of the company. She worked with department heads to set departmental goals and asked them to set clear, measurable goals for employees that fell in line with the five elements of the mission. She reminded everyone that even the slightest ambiguity in the goals could throw people off course. Some department heads resisted and either found other jobs or were let go. Most were inspired by her vision to turn the hotel around and were glad to have a clear focus for what they should be doing. They started with basic employee performance goals such as getting to work on time and taking care of the basics. Each staff meeting, higher goals were set, and guests started noticing and commenting on the improvements. Employees now knew what was expected of them, so they were able to succeed. People began taking more pride in their work, and motivation and performance improved. Sorrells insisted the attention to detail in every department extend to creating a good work experience for employees. She established goals related to employee satisfaction, including the quality of the food, the cleanliness and comfort of the break area and employee restrooms, and so forth. People saw that Sorrells was deeply committed to the mission and to the success of the team. After nine months, basic inspection scores had increased from 59 out of 100 to 95 out of 100. In WHI's annual survey of employee motivation at the company's 31 hotels, the DFW Marriott moved from 25th place to 6th place. The financial picture brightened as well, with sales going from $1.5 million behind budget to $500,000 ahead of budget. By establishing clear, focused, and measurable goals aligned with the mission and vision, Sorrells turned the hotel around and made life better for its employees.[61]

DISCUSSION QUESTIONS

1. Come up with a stretch goal for some aspect of your own life. How do you determine whether it makes sense to pursue a stretch goal?

2. If you were a top manager of a medium-sized real estate sales agency, would you use MBO? If so, give examples of goals you might set for managers and sales agents.

3. In what types of organizations do you think event-based planning would be most useful? What about scenario planning? Why?

4. A new business venture must develop a comprehensive business plan to borrow money to get started. Companies such as FedEx, Nike, and Rolm Corporation say they did not follow the original plan closely. Does that mean that developing the plan was a waste of time for these eventually successful companies?

5. How do you think planning in today's organizations compares to planning 25 years ago? Do you think planning becomes more important or less

important in a world where everything is changing fast and crises are a regular part of organizational life? Why?

6. What strategic plans could the college or university at which you are taking this management course adopt to compete for students in the marketplace? Would these plans depend on the school's goals?

7. Assume Southern University decides to (1) raise its admission standards, and (2) initiate a business fair to which local townspeople will be invited. What types of plans might it use to carry out these two activities?

8. Write a brief mission statement for a local business with which you are familiar. How might having a clear, written mission statement benefit a small organization?

9. When using MBO as a manager, how would you go about achieving mutual agreement between you and your employees to create strong commitment toward achieving the goals? What would you do if a fundamental disagreement between you and your employees arose about goal achievement?

10. Companies such as Wal-Mart and Valero Energy Corp. were days ahead of FEMA in responding to relief operations after Katrina and Rita devastated the Gulf Coast in the fall of 2005. Why do you think they were able to respond more quickly? What types of planning would help federal, state, and local governments prepare for unexpected events?

MANAGEMENT IN PRACTICE: EXPERIENTIAL EXERCISE

Company Crime Wave

Senior managers in your organization are concerned about internal theft. Your department has been assigned the task of writing an ethics policy that defines employee theft and prescribes penalties. Stealing goods is easily classified as theft, but other activities are more ambiguous. Before writing the policy, go through the following list and decide which behaviors should be defined as stealing and whether penalties should apply. Discuss the items with your department members until agreement is reached. Classify each item as an example of (1) theft, (2) acceptable behavior, or (3) in between with respect to written policy. Is it theft when an employee

:: Gets paid for overtime not worked?

:: Takes a longer lunch or coffee break than authorized?

:: Punches a time card for another?

:: Comes in late or leaves early?

:: Fakes injury to receive workers' compensation?

:: Takes care of personal business on company time?

:: Occasionally uses company copying machines or makes long-distance telephone calls for personal purposes?

:: Takes a few stamps, pens, or other supplies for personal use?

:: Takes money from the petty cash drawer?

:: Uses company vehicles or tools for own purposes but returns them?

:: Damages merchandise so a cohort can purchase it at a discount?

:: Accepts a gift from a supplier?

Now consider those items rated "in between." Do these items represent ethical issues as defined in Chapter 5? How should these items be handled in the company's written policy?

MANAGEMENT IN PRACTICE: ETHICAL DILEMMA

Inspire Learning Corp.

When the idea first occurred to her, it seemed like such a win-win situation. Now she wasn't so sure.

Marge Brygay was a hard-working sales rep for Inspire Learning Corporation, a company intent on becoming the top educational software provider in five years. That newly adopted strategic goal translated into an ambitious million-dollar sales target for each of Inspire's sales reps. At the beginning of the fiscal year, her share of the sales department's operational goal seemed entirely reasonable to Marge. She believed in Inspire's products. The company had developed innovative, highly regarded math, language, science, and social studies programs for the K–12 market. What set the software apart was a foundation in truly cutting-edge research. Marge had seen for herself how Inspire programs could engage whole classrooms of normally unmotivated kids; the significant rise in test scores on those increasingly important standardized tests bore out her subjective impressions.

But now, just days before the end of the year, Marge's sales were $1,000 short of her million-dollar goal. The sale that would have put her comfortably over the top fell through due to last-minute cuts in one large school system's budget. At first, she was nearly overwhelmed with frustration, but then it occurred to her that if she contributed $1,000 to Central High, the inner-city high school in her territory probably most in need of what she had for sale, they could purchase the software and put her over the top.

Her scheme would certainly benefit Central High students. Achieving her sales goal would make Inspire happy, and it wouldn't do her any harm, either professionally or financially. Making the goal would earn her a $10,000 bonus check that would come in handy when the time came to write out that first tuition check for her oldest child, who had just been accepted to a well-known, private university.

Initially, it seemed like the perfect solution all the way around. The more she thought about it, though, the more it didn't quite sit well with her conscience. Time was running out. She needed to decide what to do.

What Would You Do?

1. Donate the $1,000 to Central High, and consider the $10,000 bonus a good return on your gift.

2. Accept the fact you didn't quite make your sales goal this year. Figure out ways to work smarter next year to increase the odds of achieving your target.

3. Don't make the donation, but investigate whether any other ways were available to help Central High raise the funds that would allow them to purchase the much-needed educational software.

SOURCE: Based on Shel Horowitz, "Should Mary Buy Her Own Bonus?" *Business Ethics* (Summer 2005): 34.

CASE FOR CRITICAL ANALYSIS

H.I.D.

Dave Collins, president of H.I.D., sat down at the conference table with his management team members Karen Setz, Tony Briggs, Dave King, and Art Johnson. H.I.D. owns 10 Holiday Inns in Georgia, 8 hotels of different types in Canada, and 1 property in the Caribbean. It also owns two Quality Inns in Georgia. Dave Collins and his managers got together to define their mission and goals and to set strategic plans. As they began their strategic planning session, the consultant they had hired suggested that each describe what he or she wanted for the company's domestic operations in the next 10 years—how many hotels it should own, where to locate them, and who the target market was. Another question he asked them to consider was what the driving force of the company should be—that is, the single characteristic that would separate H.I.D. from other companies.

The team members wrote their answers on flip charts, and the consultant summarized the results. Dave Collins's goal included 50 hotels in 10 years, with the number increasing to 26 or 27 in 5 years. All the other members saw no more than 20 hotels in 10 years and a maximum of 15 or 16 within 5 years. Clearly, there was disagreement among the top managers about long-term goals and the desirable growth rate.

With the consultant's direction, the team members began to critique their growth targets. Dave King, director of operations and development, observed,

"We just can't build that many hotels in that time period, certainly not given our current staffing, or any reasonable staffing we could afford. I don't see how we could achieve that goal." Art Johnson, the accountant, agreed. Karen Setz then asked, "Could we build them all in Georgia? You know we've centered on the medium-priced hotel in smaller towns. Do we need to move to bigger towns now, such as Jacksonville, or add another to the one we have in Atlanta?" Dave Collins responded, "We have an opportunity out in California, we may have one in New Jersey, and we are looking at the possibility of going to Jacksonville."

The consultant attempted to refocus the discussion: "Well, how does this all fit with your mission? Where are you willing to locate geographically? Most of your operation is in Georgia. Can you adequately support a national building effort?"

Tony Briggs responded, "Well, you know we have always looked at the smaller-town hotels as being our niche, although we deviated from that for the hotel in Atlanta. But we generally stay in smaller towns where we don't have much competition. Now we are talking about an expensive hotel in California."

Dave Collins suggested, "Maybe it's time we changed our target market, changed our pricing strategy, and went for larger hotels in urban areas across the whole country. Maybe we need to change a lot of factors about our company."

Questions

1. What is H.I.D.'s mission at present? How may this mission change?

2. What do you think H.I.D.'s mission, strategic goals, and strategic plans are likely to be at the end of this planning session? Why?

3. What goal-setting behavior is being used here to reach agreement among H.I.D.'s managers? Do managers typically disagree about the direction of their organization?

SOURCE: This case was provided by James Higgins.

ENDNOTES

1. Rodd Wagner, "Fixing a 'Sneaky-Broke' Hotel," *Gallup Management Journal* (October 13, 2005), http://www.gmj.gallup.com.

2. Quoted in Oren Harari, "Good/Bad News about Strategy," *Management Review* (July 1995): 29–31.

3. Amitai Etzioni, *Modern Organizations* (Englewood Cliffs, NJ: Prentice Hall, 1984): 6.

4. Ibid.

5. Max D. Richards, *Setting Strategic Goals and Objectives,* 2d ed. (St. Paul, MN: West, 1986).

6. C. Chet Miller and Laura B. Cardinal, "Strategic Planning and Firm Performance: A Synthesis of More Than Two Decades of Research," *Academy of Management Journal* 37, no. 6 (1994): 1649–1685.

7. This discussion is based on Richard L. Daft and Richard M. Steers, *Organizations: A Micro/Macro Approach* (Glenview, IL: Scott, Foresman, 1986): 319–321; Herbert A. Simon, "On the Concept of Organizational Goals," *Administrative Science Quarterly* 9 (1964): 1–22; and Charles B. Saunders and Francis D. Tuggel, "Corporate Goals," *Journal of General Management* 5 (1980): 3–13.

8. Carol Hymowitz, "Big Companies Become Big Targets Unless They Guard Images Carefully," *The Wall Street Journal* (December 12, 2005): B1; Robert Berner, "Can Wal-Mart Fit into a White Hat?" *BusinessWeek* (October 3, 2005): 94–96.

9. See "The 100 Best Companies to Work For, 2006," *Fortune* (January 23, 2006): 71–74; "2004 Special Report: The 100 Best Companies to Work For," *Fortune* (January 12, 2004): 56–80; and Kevin E. Joyce, "Lessons for Employers from *Fortune's* 100 Best," *Business Horizons* (March–April 2003): 77–84.

10. J. Lynn Lunsford, "Lean Times: With Airbus on Its Tail, Boeing Is Rethinking How It Builds Planes," *The Wall Street Journal* (September 5, 2001): A1, A16.

11. Marc Gunther, "Tree Huggers, Soy Lovers, and Profits," *Fortune* (June 23, 2003): 98–104; Gary Fields and John R. Wilke, "The Ex-Files: FBI's New Focus Places Big Burden on Local Police," *The Wall Street Journal* (June 30, 2003): A1, A12.

12. Paul Sloan, "The Sales Force That Rocks," *Business 2.0* (July 2005): 102–107.

13. Mary Klemm, Stuart Sanderson, and George Luffman, "Mission Statements: Selling Corporate Values to Employees," *Long-Range Planning* 24, no. 3 (1991): 73–78; John A. Pearce II and Fred David, "Corporate Mission Statements: The Bottom Line," *Academy of Management Executive* (1987): 109–116; Jerome H. Want, "Corporate Mission: The Intangible Contributor to Performance," *Management Review* (August 1986): 46–50; and Forest R. David and Fred R. David, "It's Time to Redraft Your Mission Statement," *Journal of Business Strategy* (January–February 2003): 11–14.

14. "Tennessee News and Notes from State Farm," State Farm Mutual Automobile Insurance Company, 2004.

15. Janet Adamy, "Father, Son, and Gum," *The Wall Street Journal* (March 11–12, 2006): A1, A10.

16. Mara Der Hovanesian, "Chuck Prince's Citi Planning," *BusinessWeek* (September 5, 2005): 88–89.

17. Jon Birger and David Stires, "The Toughest Jobs in Business: 10 on the Spot," *Fortune* (February 20, 2006): 81–88.

18. Paul Meising and Joseph Wolfe, "The Art and Science of Planning at the Business Unit Level," *Management Science* 31 (1985): 773–781.

19. Based in part on information about 1-800-Flowers, in Jenny C. McCune, "On the Train Gang," *Management Review* (October 1994): 57–60.

20. "Study: IRS Employees Often Steer Taxpayers Wrong on Law Questions," *Johnson City Press* (September 4, 2003): 4A.

21. Geary A. Rummler and Kimberly Morrill, "The Results Chain," *TD* (February 2005): 27–35; and John C. Crotts, Duncan R. Dickson, and Robert C. Ford, "Aligning Organizational Processes with Mission: The Case of Service Excellence," *Academy of Management Executive* 19, no. 3 (August 2005): 54–68.

22. Karyll N. Shaw, "Changing the Goal-Setting Process at Microsoft," *Academy of Management Executive* 18, no. 4 (November 2004): 139–142.

23. Sayan Chatterjee, "Core Objectives: Clarity in Designing Strategy," *California Management Review* 47, no. 2 (Winter 2005): 33–49.

24. John O. Alexander, "Toward Real Performance: The Circuit-Breaker Technique," *Supervisory Management* (April 1989): 5–12.

25. Mark J. Fritsch, "Balanced Scorecard Helps Northern States Power's Quality Academy Achieve Extraordinary Performance," *Corporate University Review* (September–October 1997): 22.

26. Carol Hymowitz, "Readers Share Tales of Jobs Where Strategy Became Meeting Target," *The Wall Street Journal* (March 22, 2005): B1; and Joy Riggs, "Empowering Workers by Setting Goals," *Nation's Business* (January 1995): 6.

27. Joel Hoekstra, "3M's Global Grip," *WorldTraveler* (May 2000): 31–34; and Thomas A. Stewart, "3M Fights Back," *Fortune* (February 5, 1996): 94–99.

28. Edwin A. Locke, Gary P. Latham, and Miriam Erez, "The Determinants of Goal Commitment," *Academy of Management Review* 13 (1988): 23–39.

29. George S. Odiorne, "MBO: A Backward Glance," *Business Horizons* 21 (October 1978): 14–24.

30. Jan P. Muczyk and Bernard C. Reimann, "MBO as a Complement to Effective Leadership," *The Academy of Management Executive* 3 (1989): 131–138; and W. Giegold, *Objective Setting and the MBO Process*, vol. 2 (New York: McGraw-Hill, 1978).

31. Jack Ewing, "Siemens Climbs Back," *BusinessWeek* (June 5, 2000): 79–82.

32. John Ivancevich, J. Timothy McMahon, J. William Streidl, and Andrew D. Szilagyi, "Goal Setting: The Tenneco Approach to Personnel Development and Management Effectiveness," *Organizational Dynamics* (Winter 1978): 48–80.

33. Brigitte W. Schay, Mary Ellen Beach, Jacqueline A. Caldwell, and Christelle LaPolice, "Using Standardized Outcome Measures in the Federal Government," *Human Resource Management* 41, no. 3 (Fall 2002): 355–368.

34. Eileen M. Van Aken and Garry D. Coleman, "Building Better Measurement," *Industrial Management* (July–August 2002): 28–33.

35. Curtis W. Roney, "Planning for Strategic Contingencies," *Business Horizons* (March–April 2003): 35–42; and "Corporate Planning: Drafting a Blueprint for Success," *Small Business Report* (August 1987): 40–44.

36. Ellen Florian Kratz, "For FedEx, It Was Time to Deliver," *Fortune* (October 3, 2005): 83–84.

37. Geoffrey Colvin, "An Executive Risk Handbook," *Fortune* (October 3, 2005): 69–70; Syed H. Akhter, "Strategic Planning, Hypercompetition, and Knowledge Management," *Business Horizons* (January–February 2003): 19–24; and Steven Schnaars and Paschalina Ziamou, "The Essentials of Scenario Writing," *Business Horizons* (July–August 2001): 25–31.

38. Schnaars and Ziamou, "The Essentials of Scenario Writing."

39. Colvin, "An Executive Risk Handbook"; and Ian Wylie, "There Is No Alternative To . . . ," *Fast Company* (July 2002): 106–110.

40. Ian Mitroff with Gus Anagnos, *Managing Crises Before They Happen* (New York: AMACOM, 2001).

41. Ian Mitroff and Murat C. Alpaslan, "Preparing for Evil," *Harvard Business Review* (April 2003): 109–115.

42. This discussion is based largely on W. Timothy Coombs, *Ongoing Crisis Communication: Planning, Managing, and Responding* (Thousand Oaks, CA: Sage Publications, 1999).

43. Ian I. Mitroff, "Crisis Leadership," *Executive Excellence* (August 2001): 19; Andy Bowen, "Crisis Procedures that Stand the Test of Time," *Public Relations Tactics* (August 2001): 16.

44. Mitroff and Alpaslan, "Preparing for Evil."

45. Christine Pearson, "A Blueprint for Crisis Management," *Ivey Business Journal* (January–February 2002): 69–73.

46. See Mitroff and Alpaslan, "Preparing for Evil," for a discussion of the "wheel of crises" outlining the many different kinds of crises organizations may face.

47. Grimsley, "Many Firms Lack Plans for Disaster"; "Girding Against New Risks: Global Executives Are Working to Better Protect Their Employees and Businesses from Calamity," *Time* (October 8, 2001): B8+.

48. Mitroff, "Crisis Leadership." Also see Loretta Ucelli, "The CEO's 'How To' Guide to Crisis Communications," *Strategy & Leadership* 30, no. 2 (2002): 21–24; and Paul Argenti, "Crisis Communication: Lessons from 9/11," *Harvard Business Review* (December 2002): 103–109, for tips on crisis communication.

49. "Girding Against New Risks."

50. "After Katrina: New Lessons to Learn," *Fortune* (October 3, 2005): 87–88.

51. Laura M. Holson, "A Different Kind of Chief Executive at Walt Disney," *The New York Times* (March 15, 2005); http://www.nytimes.com; and Laura M. Holson, "Disney Intends to Overhaul Planning Unit," *The New York Times* (March 26, 2005), http://www.nytimes.com.

52. Harari, "Good News/Bad News about Strategy."

53. This discussion of the importance of vision and mission is based on Khoo Hsien Hui and Tan Kay Chuan, "Nine Approaches to Organizational Excellence," *Journal of Organizational Excellence* (Winter 2002): 53–65; Gerald E. Ledford, Jr., Jon R. Wendenhof, and James T. Strahley, "Realizing a Corporate Philosophy," *Organizational Dynamics* (Winter 1995): 5–18; James C. Collins, "Building Companies to Last," *The State of Small Business* (1995): 83–86; James C. Collins and Jerry I. Porras, "Building a Visionary Company," *California Management Review* 37, no. 2 (Winter 1995): 80–100; and James C. Collins and Jerry I. Porras, "The Ultimate Vision," *Across the Board* (January 1995): 19–23.

54. Steven Kerr and Steffan Landauer, "Using Stretch Goals to Promote Organizational Effectiveness and Personal Growth: General Electric and Goldman Sachs," *Academy of Management Executive* 18, no. 4 (November 2004): 134–138.

55. See Kenneth R. Thompson, Wayne A. Hockwarter, and Nicholas J. Mathys, "Stretch Targets: What Makes Them Effective?" *Academy of Management Executive* 11, no. 3 (August 1997): 48.

56. This discussion is based on Chuck Martin, "How to Plan for the Short Term," in Chuck Martin, *Managing for the Short Term* (New York: Doubleday, 2002), as quoted in *CIO* (September 15, 2002): 90–97.

57. Martin, "How to Plan for the Short Term."

58. Doug Bartholomew, "Gauging Success," *CFO-IT* (Summer 2005): 17–19.

59. Jeffrey A. Schmidt, "Corporate Excellence in the New Millennium," *Journal of Business Strategy* (November–December 1999): 39–43.

60. Polly LaBarre, "The Company Without Limits," *Fast Company* (September 1999): 160–186.

61. Wagner, "Fixing a 'Sneaky-Broke' Hotel."

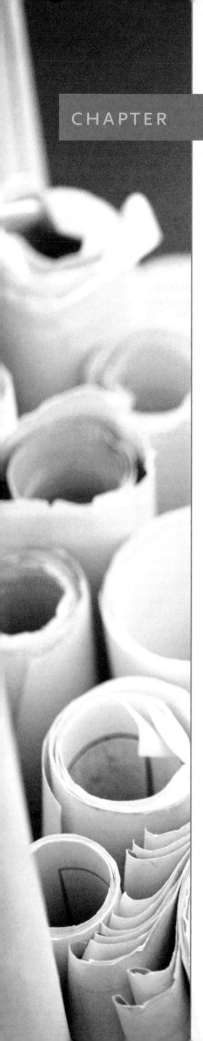

CHAPTER 8

CHAPTER OUTLINE

Manager's Challenge

Thinking Strategically

What Is Strategic Management?

Grand Strategy

Global Strategy

Purpose of Strategy

Levels of Strategy

The Strategic Management Process

Strategy Formulation Versus
Implementation

Situation Analysis

Formulating Corporate-Level Strategy

Portfolio Strategy

The BCG Matrix

Formulating Business-Level Strategy

Porter's Competitive Forces
and Strategies

Partnership Strategies

**Formulating Functional-Level
Strategy**

Strategy Implementation and Control

Leadership

Structural Design

Information and Control Systems

Human Resources

**Implementation During Turbulent
Times**

LEARNING OBJECTIVES

After studying this chapter, you should be able to:

1. Define the components of strategic management.

2. Describe the strategic planning process and SWOT analysis.

3. Understand grand strategies for domestic and international operations.

4. Define corporate-level strategies and explain the portfolio approach.

5. Describe business-level strategies, including Porter's competitive forces and strategies and partnership strategies.

6. Explain the major considerations in formulating functional strategies.

7. Discuss the organizational dimensions used for implementing strategy.

STRATEGY FORMULATION AND IMPLEMENTATION

MANAGER'S CHALLENGE

How did a struggling regional chain of stores overtake the giant of consumer electronics retailing? Circuit City expanded the big-box warehouse concept to consumer electronics in the 1980s and quickly became *the* place to go for televisions and stereos. A strategy of locating stores in lower-priced second-tier shopping areas paid off because customers were willing to drive the extra mile for the wide selection, low prices, and terrific customer service. Circuit City easily sidestepped the competition and grew rapidly. As recently as 1999, the chain was the 800-pound gorilla of the industry. Yet, within only a couple of years, Circuit City had practically been overrun by Best Buy, which raced past the leader to become the nation's Number 1 consumer electronics store in 2001. By early 2005, Best Buy had 608 stores compared to Circuit City's 599 and nearly $25 billion in revenue compared to Circuit City's $9.7 billion. Since then, Best Buy has continued to expand its yellow-tag logo adorning more than 900 spacious stores located in high-traffic areas and stocked with the latest in consumer electronics. Circuit City is now ranked at Number 3, behind Best Buy and Wal-Mart. What went wrong? The differing fates of Circuit City and Best Buy can be attributed to corporate strategy. After struggling to turn things around, longtime CEO Allen McCollough resigned and was recently replaced by Philip Schoonover, who was lured away from competitor Best Buy.[1]

> How did managers at Best Buy formulate and implement strategies that helped the company overtake a large, sophisticated chain like Circuit City? If you were the new CEO of Circuit City, what strategies might you adopt to help the company regain a competitive edge?

■ **TAKE A MOMENT**

The story of Circuit City and Best Buy illustrates the importance of strategic planning. Managers at Best Buy formulated and implemented strategies that made the chain the player to beat in consumer electronics retailing, while Circuit City managers failed to respond to increased competition and changing customer expectations. Top managers are analyzing the situation and considering strategies that can ignite growth and revive the company.

Every company is concerned with strategy. Genentech grew into a biotech powerhouse, with a 42 percent increase in sales and a 72 percent increase in earnings in 2005, based on a strategy of concentrating resources on scientific research that addresses the largest unmet medical needs.[2] McDonald's devised a new strategy of downsizing its menu items and adding healthier products in response to changes in the environment. Supersize french fries and soft drinks were eliminated in favor of fresh salads and low-fat items to counter public accusations that the fast-food icon was responsible for Americans' expanding waistlines and growing health problems. In the auto industry, PSA Peugeot Citroën SA adopted a strategy of being a fierce product innovator, coming out with 25 new models within a three-year period. Strategic blunders can hurt a company. For example, Mattel suffered in recent years by losing sight of its core business and trying to compete as a maker of computer games. Kodak stumbled by failing to plan for the rapid growth of digital photography, assuming sales of film and paper would stay strong for years to come. Between 2001 and 2005, Kodak's earnings dropped about 60 percent as interest in film-photography tanked.[3]

Managers at Mattel, McDonald's, Kodak, and Peugeot are all involved in strategic management. They are finding ways to respond to competitors, cope with difficult environmental changes, meet changing customer needs, and effectively use available resources. Research has shown that strategic thinking and planning positively affects a firm's performance and financial success.[4] Strategic planning has taken on new importance in today's world of globalization, deregulation, advancing technology, and changing demographics and lifestyles. Managers are responsible for positioning their organizations for success in a world that is constantly changing. Today's top companies thrive by changing the rules of an industry to their advantage or by creating entirely new industries.[5] For example, when Lindsay Owens-Jones was running L'Oreal's U.S. division in the early 1980s, he was told by colleagues that European brands such as Lancôme could never compete with established U.S. brands. Owens-Jones refused to accept that, and his strategic decisions changed the whole face of U.S. cosmetics counters. Today, as CEO, Owens-Jones is aggressively promoting L'Oreal's brands globally, gaining huge market share in Asia, Africa, and other parts of the world.[6]

In this chapter, we focus on the topic of strategic management. First we define components of strategic management and then discuss a model of the strategic management process. Next we examine several models of strategy formulation. Finally, we will discuss the tools managers use to implement their strategic plans.

strategic management
The set of decisions and actions used to formulate and implement strategies that will provide a competitively superior fit between the organization and its environment so as to achieve organizational goals.

CONCEPT CONNECTION Rivalry between hotels in Las Vegas is fierce! To compete, Mirage Hotel opened Cravings, a new $12 million buffet restaurant. Gone are the low-priced steam-warmed vats of lasagna; dinner is now $20.50 per person. Food is cooked fresh at individual stations, served up on small, stylish plates, and can be made to order. This restaurant transformation, designed by renowned designer Adam Tihany, is a part of the Mirage's **grand strategy of growth**. In the photo are chefs at the Cravings sweets station. The success of Mirage's plan to attract new customers was reflected recently by comments from two patrons, who drove over an hour to dine at Cravings, "I've eaten in so many buffets but I've never seen anything as beautiful as this."

© CATHERINE GWYNN/GETTY IMAGES

THINKING STRATEGICALLY

Chapter 7 provided an overview of the types of goals and plans that organizations use. In this chapter, we will explore **strategic management**, which is considered one specific type of planning. Strategic planning in for-profit business organizations typically pertains to competitive actions in the marketplace. In nonprofit organizations such as the Red Cross or The Salvation Army, strategic planning pertains to events in the external environment. The final responsibility for strategy rests with top managers and the chief executive. For an organization to succeed, the CEO must be actively involved in making the tough choices and trade-offs that define and support strategy.[7] However, senior executives at such companies as General Electric, 3M, and Johnson & Johnson want middle- and low-level managers to think strategically. Some companies also are finding ways to get front-line workers involved in strategic thinking and planning.

Strategic thinking means to take the long-term view and to see the big picture, including the organization and the competitive environment, and to consider how they fit together. Understanding the strategy concept, the levels of strategy, and strategy formulation versus implementation is an important start toward strategic thinking.

As a potential new manager, practice thinking strategically by studying your department's or your organization's environment, market, and competitors. Think about what the long-term future might hold and how you think the company can best be positioned to stay competitive.

What Is Strategic Management?

Strategic management is the set of decisions and actions used to formulate and implement strategies that will provide a competitively superior fit between the organization and its environment so as to achieve organizational goals.[8] Managers ask questions such as, "What changes and trends are occurring in the competitive environment? Who are our competitors and what are their strengths and weaknesses? Who are our customers? What products or services should we offer, and how can we offer them most efficiently? What does the future hold for our industry, and how can we change the rules of the game?" Answers to these questions help managers make choices about how to position their organizations in the environment with respect to rival companies.[9] Superior organizational performance is not a matter of luck. It is determined by the choices that managers make. Top executives use strategic management to define an overall direction for the organization, which is the firm's grand strategy.

Grand Strategy

Grand strategy is the general plan of major action by which a firm intends to achieve its long-term goals.[10] Grand strategies fall into three general categories: growth, stability, and retrenchment. A separate grand strategy can also be defined for global operations.

grand strategy The general plan of major action by which an organization intends to achieve its long-term goals.

Go to the ethical dilemma on page 265 that pertains to corporate grand strategy.

GROWTH

Growth can be promoted internally by investing in expansion or externally by acquiring additional business divisions. Internal growth can include development of new or changed products, such as Motorola's Razr mobile phone and Toyota's hybrid Camry sedan, or expansion of current products into new markets, such as Avon's selling of products in mall kiosks. External growth typically involves *diversification*, which means the acquisition of businesses that are related to current product lines or that take the corporation into new areas, such as Procter & Gamble's purchase of Iams Company, which makes Iams and Eukanuba pet foods, and Gillette Company, which makes the Mach 3 and Fusion razors.[11] The number of companies choosing to grow through merger and acquisition in recent years has been astounding, as organizations strive to acquire the size and resources to compete on a global scale, to invest

© ASHLEY TWIGGS/*THE CHRISTIAN SCIENCE MONITOR*/GETTY IMAGES

CONCEPT CONNECTION

Former General Electric CEO Jack Welch did not have to go far to find one of his favorite examples of effective **strategic management**. He just dropped in on his neighborhood pizzeria in Boston. Upper Crust Pizza founder Jordan Tobins pursues a **stability strategy**, aiming to grow slowly and in a controlled way by doing one thing better than anyone else. That one thing is his Neopolitan-style pizza, prepared here by Antonio Carlos Filho. As Welch enthused, "You could faint just describing the flavor of the sauce, and the crust puts you over the edge." The free publicity Welch provided boosted sales and attracted investors, enabling the five-year-old chain to open two new restaurants in 2006.

in new technology, and to control distribution channels and guarantee access to markets. For example, Citibank and Travelers merged to form Citigroup, which then acquired Sears' credit card portfolio. Boeing Co. acquired McDonnell Douglas, to move more aggressively into defense contracting, and Hughes Electronics Corp.'s Space & Communications Division to tap into growth opportunities in space travel.[12]

STABILITY

Stability, sometimes called a *pause strategy*, means that the organization wants to remain the same size or grow slowly and in a controlled fashion. The corporation wants to stay in its current business, such as Allied Tire Stores, whose motto is, "We just sell tires." After organizations have undergone a turbulent period of rapid growth, executives often focus on a stability strategy to integrate strategic business units and ensure that the organization is working efficiently. Mattel is currently pursuing a stability strategy to recover from former CEO Jill Barad's years of big acquisitions and new businesses. The current top executive is seeking only modest new ventures to get Mattel on a slower-growth, more stable course.[13]

RETRENCHMENT

Retrenchment means that the organization goes through a period of forced decline by either shrinking current business units or selling off or liquidating entire businesses. The organization may have experienced a precipitous drop in demand for its products or services, prompting managers to order across-the-board cuts in personnel and expenditures. For example, Kodak laid off 12,000 workers when the bottom dropped out of the film photography business. As troubles deepened at General Motors, managers terminated thousands of employees, closed plants to kill off excess capacity, and put the corporation's finance subsidiary up for sale.[14] Managers often use a period of retrenchment to stabilize a company and attempt to restore profitability and competitiveness.

Liquidation means selling off a business unit for the cash value of the assets, thus terminating its existence. An example is the liquidation of Minnie Pearl Fried Chicken. *Divestiture* involves the selling off of businesses that no longer seem central to the corporation. JCPenney sold its Eckerd chain of drugstores to focus on the corporation's core business of department stores and Internet and catalog sales. Studies show that between 33 percent and 50 percent of all acquisitions are later divested. When Figgies International Inc. sold 15 of its 22 business divisions, including crown jewel Rawlings Sporting Goods, and when Italy's Fiat sold its aerospace unit, both corporations were going through periods of retrenchment, also called *downsizing*.[15]

Global Strategy

In addition to the three preceding alternatives—growth, stability, and retrenchment—companies may pursue a separate grand strategy as the focus of global business. In today's global corporations, senior executives try to formulate coherent strategies to provide synergy among worldwide operations for the purpose of fulfilling common goals. A systematic strategic planning process for deciding on the appropriate strategic alternative should be used. The grand strategy of growth is a major motivation for both small and large businesses going international. Each country or region represents a new market with the promise of increased sales and profits.

In the international arena, companies face a strategic dilemma between global integration and national responsiveness. The various global strategies are shown in Exhibit 8.1. Recall from Chapter 4 that the first step toward a greater international presence is when companies begin exporting domestically produced products to selected countries. Because the organization is domestically focused, with only a few exports, managers have little need to pay attention to issues of either local

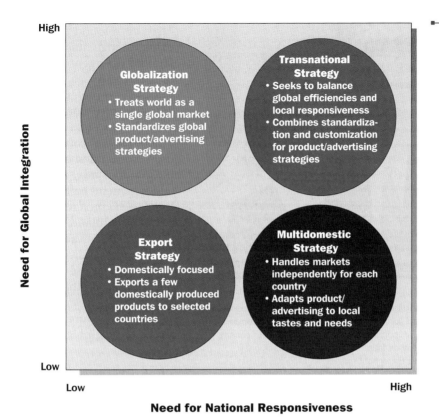

High

Globalization Strategy
- Treats world as a single global market
- Standardizes global product/advertising strategies

Transnational Strategy
- Seeks to balance global efficiencies and local responsiveness
- Combines standardization and customization for product/advertising strategies

Export Strategy
- Domestically focused
- Exports a few domestically produced products to selected countries

Multidomestic Strategy
- Handles markets independently for each country
- Adapts product/advertising to local tastes and needs

Need for Global Integration

Low

Low   **High**

Need for National Responsiveness

E X H I B I T   8.1

Global Corporate Strategies

SOURCES: Based on Michael A. Hitt, R. Duane Ireland, and Robert E. Hoskisson, *Strategic Management: Competitiveness and Globalization* (St. Paul, MN; West, 1995): 239; and Thomas M. Begley and David P. Boyd, "The Need for a Corporate Global Mindset," *MIT Sloan Management Review* (Winter 2003): 25–32.

responsiveness or global integration. Organizations that pursue further international expansion must decide whether they want each global affiliate to act autonomously or whether activities should be standardized and centralized across countries. This choice leads managers to select a basic grand strategy alternative such as globalization versus multidomestic strategy. Some corporations may seek to achieve both global integration and national responsiveness by using a transnational strategy.

GLOBALIZATION

When an organization chooses a strategy of **globalization**, it means that its product design and advertising strategies are standardized throughout the world.[16] This approach is based on the assumption that a single global market exists for many consumer and industrial products. The theory is that people everywhere want to buy the same products and live the same way. People everywhere want to drink Coca-Cola and eat McDonald's hamburgers.[17] A globalization strategy can help an organization reap efficiencies by standardizing product design and manufacturing, using common suppliers, introducing products around the world faster, coordinating prices, and eliminating overlapping facilities. For example, Gillette Company has large production facilities that use common suppliers and processes to manufacture products whose technical specifications are standardized around the world.[18]

Globalization enables marketing departments alone to save millions of dollars. One consumer products company reports that, for every country where the same commercial runs, the company saves $1 million to $2 million in production costs alone. More millions have been saved by standardizing the look and packaging of brands.[19]

MULTIDOMESTIC STRATEGY

When an organization chooses a **multidomestic strategy**, it means that competition in each country is handled independently of industry competition in other countries. Thus, a multinational company is present in many countries, but it encourages marketing, advertising, and product design to be modified and adapted to the specific needs of each country.[20] Many companies reject the idea of a single global market.

globalization The standardization of product design and advertising strategies throughout the world.

multidomestic strategy The modification of product design and advertising strategies to suit the specific needs of individual countries.

AP PHOTO/RON HEFLIN

CONCEPT

CONNECTION Since first going international in 1971, Dallas-based Mary Kay Inc. has expanded to more than 30 markets on five continents. The company uses a **multidomestic strategy** that handles competition independently in each country. In China, for example, Mary Kay is working on lotions that incorporate traditional Chinese herbs, and it sells skin whiteners there, not bronzers. As Mary Kay China President Paul Mak (pictured here) explains, Chinese women prize smooth white skin. Managers' efforts in China have paid off. The company reported 2005 sales of $300 million, accounting for about 8 percent of the Chinese market. Estimates are that by 2015, more Mary Kay product will be sold in China than in the rest of the world combined.

They have found that the French do not drink orange juice for breakfast, that laundry detergent is used to wash dishes in parts of Mexico, and that people in the Middle East prefer toothpaste that tastes spicy. Service companies also have to carefully consider their global strategy. The 7-Eleven convenience store chain uses a multidomestic strategy because the product mix, advertising approach, and payment methods need to be tailored to the preferences, values, and government regulations in different parts of the world. For example, credit card use is rare in Japan and Germany. In Japan, customers like to use convenience stores to pay utility and other bills. 7-Eleven Japan also set up a way for people to pick up and pay for purchases made over the Internet at their local 7-Elevens.[21]

TRANSNATIONAL STRATEGY

A **transnational strategy** seeks to achieve both global integration and national responsiveness.[22] A true transnational strategy is difficult to achieve, because one goal requires close global coordination while the other goal requires local flexibility. However, many industries are finding that, although increased competition means they must achieve global efficiency, growing pressure to meet local needs demands national responsiveness.[23] One company that effectively uses a transnational strategy is Caterpillar, Inc., a heavy equipment manufacturer. Caterpillar achieves global efficiencies by designing its products to use many identical components and centralizing manufacturing of components in a few large-scale facilities. However, assembly plants located in each of Caterpillar's major markets add certain product features tailored to meet local needs.[24]

Although most multinational companies want to achieve some degree of global integration to hold costs down, even global products may require some customization to meet government regulations in various countries or some tailoring to fit consumer preferences. In addition, some products are better suited for standardization than others. Most large multinational corporations with diverse products and services will attempt to use a partial multidomestic strategy for some product or service lines and global strategies for others. Coordinating global integration with a responsiveness to the heterogeneity of international markets is a difficult balancing act for managers, but it is increasingly important in today's global business world.

transnational strategy A strategy that combines global coordination to attain efficiency with flexibility to meet specific needs in various countries.

strategy The plan of action that prescribes resource allocation and other activities for dealing with the environment, achieving a competitive advantage, and attaining organizational goals.

competitive advantage What sets the organization apart from others and provides it with a distinctive edge in the marketplace.

Purpose of Strategy

Within the overall grand strategy of an organization, executives define an explicit **strategy**, which is the plan of action that describes resource allocation and activities for dealing with the environment, achieving a competitive advantage, and attaining the organization's goals. **Competitive advantage** refers to what sets the organization apart from others and provides it with a distinctive edge for meeting customer needs in the marketplace. The essence of formulating strategy is choosing how the organization will be different.[25] Managers make decisions about whether the company will perform different activities or will execute similar activities differently than competitors do. Strategy necessarily changes over time to fit environmental conditions, but to remain competitive, companies develop strategies that focus on core competencies, develop synergy, and create value for customers.

EXPLOIT CORE COMPETENCE

A company's **core competence** is something the organization does especially well in comparison to its competitors. A core competence represents a competitive advantage because the company acquires expertise that competitors do not have. A core competence may be in the area of superior research and development, expert technological know-how, process efficiency, or exceptional customer service.[26] At VF, a large apparel company that owns Vanity Fair, Nautica, Wrangler, and The North Face, strategy focuses on the company's core competencies of operational efficiency and merchandising know-how. When VF bought The North Face, for example, its distribution systems were so poor that stores were getting ski apparel at the end of winter and camping gear at the end of summer. The company's operating profit margin was minus 35 percent. Managers at VF revamped The North Face's sourcing, distribution, and financial systems and within five years doubled sales to $500 million and improved profit margins to a healthy 13 percent. "For VF it was easy, and it's not easy for everybody" said one retail analyst referring to the company's application of its core competencies.[27] Gaylord Hotels, which has large hotel and conference centers in several states as well as the Opryland complex near Nashville, Tennessee, thrives based on a strategy of superior service for large group meetings.[28] Robinson Helicopter succeeds through superior technological know-how for building small, two-seater helicopters used for everything from police patrols in Los Angeles to herding cattle in Australia.[29] In each case, leaders identified what their company does especially well and built strategy around it.

BUILD SYNERGY

When organizational parts interact to produce a joint effect that is greater than the sum of the parts acting alone, **synergy** occurs. The organization may attain a special advantage with respect to cost, market power, technology, or management skill. When properly managed, synergy can create additional value with existing resources, providing a big boost to the bottom line.[30] Synergy was one motivation for the FedEx acquisition of Kinko's Inc. Kinko's document delivery and office services complement FedEx's package delivery and give FedEx a greater presence among small and mid-sized businesses, a market it has long coveted. By providing full-service counters in Kinko's stores, FedEx also has the potential to double its locations over the next few years, particularly overseas, where Kinko's has centers in eight countries.[31]

Synergy can also be obtained by good relations with suppliers or by strong alliances among companies. Yahoo!, for example, uses partnerships, such as a recent deal with Verizon Communications, to help boost its number of paying subscribers to nearly 12 million.[32]

DELIVER VALUE

Delivering value to the customer is at the heart of strategy. Value can be defined as the combination of benefits received and costs paid. Managers help their companies create value by devising strategies that exploit core competencies and attain synergy. To compete with the rising clout of satellite television, for example, cable companies such as Adelphia and Charter Communications are trying to provide better value with *cable value packages* that offer a combination of basic cable, digital premium channels, video on demand, and high-speed Internet for a reduced cost. The Swedish retailer IKEA has become a global cult brand by offering beautiful, functional products at modest cost, thus delivering superior value to customers.[33]

Consider how Save-A-Lot has grown into one of the most successful grocery chains in the United States with a strategy based on exploiting core competencies, building synergy, and providing value to customers.

core competence A business activity that an organization does particularly well in comparison to competitors.

synergy The condition that exists when the organization's parts interact to produce a joint effect that is greater than the sum of the parts acting alone.

Save-A-Lot

When most supermarket executives look at the inner city, they see peeling paint, low-income customers, rampant crime, and low profits. Save-A-Lot looks at the inner city and sees opportunity. Save-A-Lot was started in the late 1970s, when Bill Moran noticed that low-income and rural areas were poorly served by large supermarkets. Moran began opening small stores in low-rent areas and stocking them with a limited number of low-priced staples. Moran hand-wrote price signs and built crude shelves out of particle board. He made his own labels from low-quality paper, which suppliers then slapped on generic products.

Save-A-Lot has thrived ever since by using its core competency of cost efficiency, which enables the stores to sell goods at prices 40 percent lower than major supermarkets. Unlike the typical supermarket, which is about 45,000 square feet, Save-A-Lot stores use a compact 16,000-square-foot no-frills format, targets areas with dirt-cheap rent, and courts households earning less than $35,000 a year. Save-A-Lot stores don't have bakeries, pharmacies, or grocery baggers. Labor costs are kept ultra low. For example, whereas most grocery managers want employees to keep displays well-stocked and tidy, Save-A-Lot managers tell people to let the displays sell down before restocking.

Save-A-Lot has obtained synergy by developing good relationships with a few core suppliers. Most supermarkets charge manufacturers slotting fees to put their products on shelves, but not Save-A-Lot. In addition, the company doesn't ask suppliers to take back damaged goods. It just sticks up a hand-written "Oops" sign and marks prices even lower. Customers love it. Now, even branded food makers want a slice of the Save-A-Lot pie. Procter & Gamble, for example, developed a lower-priced version of Folgers, and the chain also sells a low-priced brand of cheese from Kraft and a cereal from General Mills.

The value customers get from Save-A-Lot is based not just on low prices, but also convenience and the quality. Doc Otis Roper, who makes $8 an hour as a recycling worker, says the Save-A-Lot is a blessing for its combination of low prices and convenience. He used to have to ride the bus to buy groceries or shop at convenience stores where prices were high and quality low. Now, he walks five blocks to Save-A-Lot and gets quality goods at a price even lower than Wal-Mart's.[34]

■ TAKE A MOMENT

As a new manager, can you identify the core competence of your team or department and identify ways that it can contribute to the overall organization's strategy? Who are your team's or department's customers, and how can you deliver value?

Levels of Strategy

Another aspect of strategic management concerns the organizational level to which strategic issues apply. Strategic managers normally think in terms of three levels of strategy—corporate, business, and functional—as illustrated in Exhibit 8.2.[35]

EXHIBIT 8.2

Three Levels of Strategy in Organizations

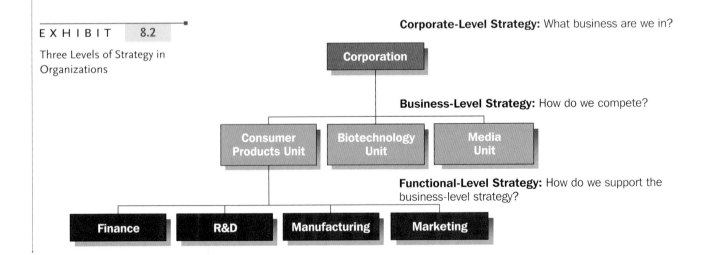

Corporate-Level Strategy: What business are we in?

Corporation

Business-Level Strategy: How do we compete?

Consumer Products Unit   Biotechnology Unit   Media Unit

Functional-Level Strategy: How do we support the business-level strategy?

Finance   R&D   Manufacturing   Marketing

CORPORATE-LEVEL STRATEGY

The question *"What business are we in?"* is the cornerstone of corporate-level strategy. **Corporate-level strategy** pertains to the organization as a whole and the combination of business units and product lines that make up the corporate entity. Strategic actions at this level usually relate to the acquisition of new businesses; additions or divestments of business units, plants, or product lines; and joint ventures with other corporations in new areas. An example of corporate-level strategy is Brunswick, which was once associated primarily with billiard tables and bowling gear. CEO George Buckley is transforming Brunswick into the "Toyota of boating" by selling off unprofitable businesses and buying up companies such as Sea Pro, Hatteras, and Princecraft to give Brunswick a slice of every boating niche. The beefed-up Brunswick Boat Group, combined with the corporation's Mercury Marine engine division and a rapidly growing boat instrumentation business, has given Brunswick a dominant position in the boat industry.[36]

CONCEPT CONNECTION IBM's revolutionary new Cell microprocessor, shown here by semiconductor research and development vice president Lisa Su, is certainly impressive for what it does. A high-speed supercomputer on a chip, it delivers ten times the performance of PC processors. But equally impressive is how the Cell was developed. For five years, IBM engineers worked directly with a team of their Sony and Toshiba counterparts to design exactly the chip they needed for multimedia applications running on networks. The chip reflects IBM's **business-level strategy** that says the company can best compete by letting customers' needs guide its research and new product development.

BUSINESS-LEVEL STRATEGY

The question *"How do we compete?"* is the focus of business-level strategy. **Business-level strategy** pertains to each business unit or product line. It focuses on how the business unit competes within its industry for customers. Many companies have opened e-commerce units as a part of business-level strategy. For example, NutriSystem Inc. was bankrupt a decade ago, but managers reinvented the company as an Internet distributor, shipping customers a month's worth of shelf-stable diet food. People can track their progress online and get virtual counseling when they need a boost. The Internet strategy and a new approach to advertising pushed sales from just $27 million in 2002 to about $150 million in 2005.[37]

Strategic decisions at the business level concern amount of advertising, direction and extent of research and development, product changes, new-product development, equipment and facilities, and expansion or contraction of product and service lines. Here's how managers at the *Los Angeles Times* are trying to revive the struggling paper with a new business-level strategy.

> Newspapers, especially those in large metropolitan areas, are facing some tough times. Overall circulation among U.S. daily newspapers dropped almost 2 percent in a six-month period in 2005. At the *Los Angeles Times*, things were even bleaker, with circulation off 6.5 percent. Advertising volume and revenue sagged as well.
>
> New top managers decided to try a new business-level strategy: focusing on celebrity news and more local coverage. One front-page story, for example, revealed unpublished portions of transcripts of Marilyn Monroe talking to her psychiatrist just days before her 1962 death. The story also referred readers to the company's Web site, where they could find photos and more information. Coverage of Hollywood and the entertainment industry has been bumped up significantly, and stories on serious matters have been scaled back, with managers asking for shorter, to-the-point stories rather than in-depth analyses. The scaled-back national and international coverage also makes room for more local and regional reporting.
>
> The shift to more celebrity coverage is controversial and is creating some tension at the newspaper, which has won numerous Pulitzer Prizes. Editor Dean Baquet admits he's walking a tightrope. He doesn't want to damage the journalistic integrity of the *Times* and insists that the paper will maintain a commitment to tough reporting, but at the same time he has to find ways to draw in more readers and advertisers. Baquet even admitted that the paper might revive the Hollywood gossip column.[38]

corporate-level strategy
The level of strategy concerned with the question "What business are we in?" Pertains to the organization as a whole and the combination of business units and product lines that make it up.

business-level strategy
The level of strategy concerned with the question "How do we compete?" Pertains to each business unit or product line within the organization.

Tribune Company, *Los Angeles Times*

Baquet and other managers believe the new business-level strategy at the *Los Angeles Times* will help them find a profitable niche as the newspaper industry continues to grapple with how to remain relevant in a changing world where people have myriad sources of information and less time for reading in-depth stories in the daily paper.

FUNCTIONAL-LEVEL STRATEGY

The question *"How do we support the business-level competitive strategy?"* is the concern of **functional-level strategy**. It pertains to the major functional departments within the business unit. Functional strategies involve all of the major functions, including finance, research and development, marketing, and manufacturing. The functional-level strategy for NutriSystem's marketing department, for example, is to feature real-life customers in direct-response print and television ads that steer dieters to the company's Web site. Extended pitches for NutriSystem on the QVC shopping channel, for example, drive approximately 11 percent of sales.[39] Another example of functional-level strategy is Procter & Gamble's research and development department, which is taking a new approach to stay competitive in the slow-growing consumer products industry. Instead of developing new products in the lab and then testing them with consumers, researchers are spending hours with customers, watching them do laundry, clean the floor, or apply makeup, looking for nuisances that a new product might solve. Then they go into the lab with a goal of addressing the concerns of real-life customers.[40]

THE STRATEGIC MANAGEMENT PROCESS

The overall strategic management process is illustrated in Exhibit 8.3. It begins when executives evaluate their current position with respect to mission, goals, and strategies. They then scan the organization's internal and external environments and identify strategic factors that might require change. Internal or external events might indicate a need to redefine the mission or goals or to formulate a new strategy at either the corporate, business, or functional level. The final stage in the strategic management process is implementation of the new strategy.

functional-level strategy
The level of strategy concerned with the question "How do we support the business-level strategy?" Pertains to all of the organization's major departments.

EXHIBIT   8.3

The Strategic Management Process

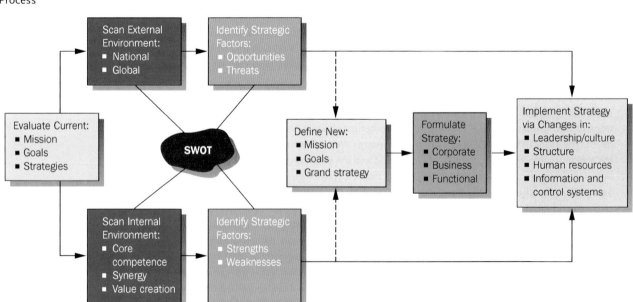

Strategy Formulation Versus Implementation

Strategy formulation includes the planning and decision making that lead to the establishment of the firm's goals and the development of a specific strategic plan.[41] **Strategy formulation** may include assessing the external environment and internal problems and integrating the results into goals and strategy. This process is in contrast to **strategy implementation**, which is the use of managerial and organizational tools to direct resources toward accomplishing strategic results.[42] Strategy implementation is the administration and execution of the strategic plan. Managers may use persuasion, new equipment, changes in organization structure, or a revised reward system to ensure that employees and resources are used to make formulated strategy a reality.

Go to the experiential exercise on page 265 that pertains to strategy formulation and implementation. ■ **TAKE A MOMENT**

Situation Analysis

Formulating strategy often begins with an assessment of the internal and external factors that will affect the organization's competitive situation. **Situation analysis** typically includes a search for SWOT—strengths, weaknesses, opportunities, and threats—that affect organizational performance. Situation analysis is important to all companies but is crucial to those considering globalization because of the diverse environments in which they will operate. External information about opportunities and threats may be obtained from a variety of sources, including customers, government reports, professional journals, suppliers, bankers, friends in other organizations, consultants, or association meetings. Many firms hire special scanning organizations to provide them with newspaper clippings, Internet research, and analyses of relevant domestic and global trends. In addition, many companies are hiring competitive intelligence professionals to scope out competitors, as we discussed in Chapter 3.

Executives acquire information about internal strengths and weaknesses from a variety of reports, including budgets, financial ratios, profit and loss statements, and surveys of employee attitudes and satisfaction. Managers spend 80 percent of their time giving and receiving information. Through frequent face-to-face discussions and meetings with people at all levels of the hierarchy, executives build an understanding of the company's internal strengths and weaknesses.

INTERNAL STRENGTHS AND WEAKNESSES

Strengths are positive internal characteristics that the organization can exploit to achieve its strategic performance goals. *Weaknesses* are internal characteristics that might inhibit or restrict the organization's performance. Some examples of what executives evaluate to interpret strengths and weaknesses are given in Exhibit 8.4. The information sought typically pertains to specific functions such as marketing, finance, production, and R&D. Internal analysis also examines overall organization structure, management competence and quality, and human resource characteristics. Based on their understanding of these areas, managers can determine their strengths or weaknesses compared with other companies.

EXTERNAL OPPORTUNITIES AND THREATS

Threats are characteristics of the external environment that may prevent the organization from achieving its strategic goals. *Opportunities* are characteristics of

strategy formulation The stage of strategic management that involves the planning and decision making that lead to the establishment of the organization's goals and of a specific strategic plan.

strategy implementation The stage of strategic management that involves the use of managerial and organizational tools to direct resources toward achieving strategic outcomes.

situation analysis Analysis of the strengths, weaknesses, opportunities, and threats (SWOT) that affect organizational performance.

EXHIBIT 8.4

Checklist for Analyzing Organizational Strengths and Weaknesses

Management and Organization	Marketing	Human Resources
Management quality	Distribution channels	Employee experience, education
Staff quality	Market share	Union status
Degree of centralization	Advertising efficiency	Turnover, absenteeism
Organization charts	Customer satisfaction	Work satisfaction
Planning, information, control systems	Product quality	Grievances
	Service reputation	
	Sales force turnover	

Finance	Production	Research and Development
Profit margin	Plant location	Basic applied research
Debt-equity ratio	Machinery obsolescence	Laboratory capabilities
Inventory ratio	Purchasing system	Research programs
Return on investment	Quality control	New-product innovations
Credit rating	Productivity/efficiency	Technology innovations

© ATEF HASSAN/CORBIS

CONCEPT

CONNECTION The effects of this oil fire in Iraq were felt thousands of miles away—in the executive suites at companies such as United Airlines, the number 2 air carrier in the United States. Uncertainty about oil costs and supplies is a significant **external threat** to the nation's airlines. Other threats United faces as it struggles to recover from bankruptcy are stiff competition from low-cost carriers and the ever-lingering threat of terrorism.

the external environment that have the potential to help the organization achieve or exceed its strategic goals. Executives evaluate the external environment with information about the nine sectors described in Chapter 3. The task environment sectors are the most relevant to strategic behavior and include the behavior of competitors, customers, suppliers, and the labor supply. The general environment contains those sectors that have an indirect influence on the organization but nevertheless must be understood and incorporated into strategic behavior. The general environment includes technological developments, the economy, legal-political and international events, and sociocultural changes. Additional areas that might reveal opportunities or threats include pressure groups, interest groups, creditors, natural resources, and potentially competitive industries.

Kraft Foods provides an example of how situation analysis can be used to help executives formulate the correct strategy.

Kraft Foods

Kraft has some of the most recognizable brand names in the grocery store, but the giant food company has been facing some difficult challenges in recent years. To get things back on track, managers are evaluating the company by looking at strengths, weaknesses, opportunities, and threats (SWOT).

Kraft's greatest *strengths* are its powerful brands, its positive reputation, its track record as an innovator, and a well-funded R&D budget. Its biggest *weaknesses* include the loss of top management talent in recent years and a sluggish response to environmental changes.

Several major *threats* have been building for a couple of years. The first is that less-expensive, private-label brands are successfully stealing market share from Kraft's core brands such as Kraft Singles cheese slices, Maxwell House coffee, Oscar Mayer cold cuts, and Ritz crackers. At the same time, other major food companies have been quicker to respond to growing consumer demands for less fattening, more healthful food choices. PepsiCo, for example, began cutting trans-fats from Doritos, Tostitos, and Cheetos, and saw sales increase by 28 percent. A third threat to Kraft is that more people are eating ready-made lunches rather than consuming home-prepared lunch foods such as sandwiches made of cheese and cold cuts. Kraft managers recognize *opportunities* in the environment, as well, however. Trends show that Americans are looking for more snack foods and comfort foods, which presents a golden opportunity for Kraft, whose name for many Americans is almost synonymous with comfort food.

What does SWOT analysis suggest for Kraft's future strategy? Kraft managers will try to capitalize on the company's strengths by investing research dollars to develop healthier snack and prepackaged lunch foods, such as lower-fat versions of its popular "Lunchables." To bolster core brands, Kraft has pumped an additional $200 million into its multibillion-dollar marketing and advertising budget. Managers are also exploring new vending opportunities for giant Kraft-branded machines that churn out ready-made food at movie-theaters, shopping malls, and other public venues.[43]

FORMULATING CORPORATE-LEVEL STRATEGY

Portfolio Strategy

Individual investors often wish to diversify in an investment portfolio with some high-risk stocks, some low-risk stocks, some growth stocks, and perhaps a few income bonds. In much the same way, corporations like to have a balanced mix of business divisions called **strategic business units (SBUs)**. An SBU has a unique business mission, product line, competitors, and markets relative to other SBUs in the corporation.[44] Executives in charge of the entire corporation generally define the grand strategy and then bring together a portfolio of strategic business units to carry it out. **Portfolio strategy** pertains to the mix of business units and product lines that fit together in a logical way to provide synergy and competitive advantage for the corporation. Managers don't like to become too dependent on one business. For example, at United Technologies Corp. (UTC), the aerospace-related business units have been struggling through one of the worst slumps in history. However, UTC's Otis Elevator division is keeping the corporation's sales and profits strong. Otis has a commanding share of the worldwide market for new elevators and escalators. In addition, the unit provides a steady revenue stream from elevator maintenance, repair, and upgrade. The elevators in the Waldorf-Astoria, for example, were installed in 1931 and have been steadily upgraded by Otis ever since.[45] One useful way to think about portfolio strategy is the BCG matrix.

The BCG Matrix

The BCG (for Boston Consulting Group) matrix is illustrated in Exhibit 8.5. The **BCG matrix** organizes businesses along two dimensions—business growth rate and market share.[46] *Business growth rate* pertains to how rapidly the entire industry is increasing. *Market share* defines whether a business unit has a larger or smaller share than competitors. The combinations of high and low market share and high and low business growth provide four categories for a corporate portfolio.

The *star* has a large market share in a rapidly growing industry. The star is important because it has additional growth potential, and profits should be plowed into this business as investment for future growth and profits. The star is visible and attractive and will generate profits and a positive cash flow even as the industry matures and market growth slows.

The *cash cow* exists in a mature, slow-growth industry but is a dominant business in the industry, with a large market share. Because heavy investments in

strategic business unit (SBU) A division of the organization that has a unique business mission, product line, competitors, and markets relative to other SBUs in the same corporation.

portfolio strategy The organization's mix of strategic business units and product lines that fit together in such a way as to provide the corporation with synergy and competitive advantage.

BCG matrix A concept developed by the Boston Consulting Group that evaluates strategic business units with respect to the dimensions of business growth rate and market share.

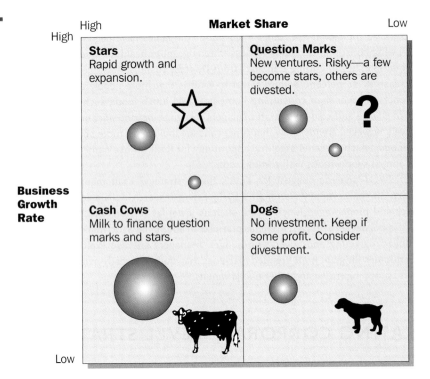

EXHIBIT 8.5

The BCG Matrix

advertising and plant expansion are no longer required, the corporation earns a positive cash flow. It can milk the cash cow to invest in other, riskier businesses.

The *question mark* exists in a new, rapidly growing industry, but has only a small market share. The question mark business is risky: It could become a star, or it could fail. The corporation can invest the cash earned from cash cows in question marks with the goal of nurturing them into future stars.

The *dog* is a poor performer. It has only a small share of a slow-growth market. The dog provides little profit for the corporation and may be targeted for divestment or liquidation if turnaround is not possible.

The circles in Exhibit 8.5 represent the business portfolio for a hypothetical corporation. Circle size represents the relative size of each business in the company's portfolio. Most large organizations, such as General Electric (GE), have businesses in more than one quadrant, thereby representing different market shares and growth rates.

General Electric

Since he took over as General Electric's CEO in 2001, Jeffrey Immelt has been reshuffling the corporation's mix of businesses in a way that he believes will better position GE for the long term. GE is investing heavily in its stars and question marks to ensure that its portfolio will continue to include cash cows in a future that might be very different from today's world.

The most famous cash cows in General Electric's portfolio are the appliance division and lighting, which hold a large share of a stable market and account for a big portion of sales and profits. The GE Security division has star status, and GE is pumping money into development of new products for hot areas such as fire safety, industrial security, and homeland security. GE Healthcare is also a star, and managers are investing research dollars to become a leader in the growing business of biosciences and personalized medicine. Some products under development might not hit the marketplace for a decade but hold the promise of huge returns.

GE's renewable energy business is still a question mark. The company moved into wind and solar power and biogas with acquisitions such as Enron Wind. Managers hope the division can become a star, but the potential demand for renewable energy is uncertain at this point.

GE's consumer finance division is also a question mark. Top executives are currently overhauling the brand image of consumer finance to see whether it will revive the division enough to keep it in the portfolio. If they decide the division is a dog, GE will sell it off as they did the less profitable and slow-growing insurance business.[47]

FORMULATING BUSINESS-LEVEL STRATEGY

Now we turn to strategy formulation within the strategic business unit, in which the concern is how to compete. The same three generic strategies—growth, stability, and retrenchment—apply at the business level, but they are accomplished through competitive actions rather than the acquisition or divestment of business divisions. One model for formulating strategy is Porter's competitive strategies, which provides a framework for business unit competitive action.

Porter's Competitive Forces and Strategies

Michael E. Porter studied a number of business organizations and proposed that business-level strategies are the result of five competitive forces in the company's environment.[48] More recently, Porter examined the impact of the Internet on business-level strategy.[49] New Web-based technology is influencing industries in both positive and negative ways, and understanding this impact is essential for managers to accurately analyze their competitive environments and design appropriate strategic actions.

FIVE COMPETITIVE FORCES

Exhibit 8.6 illustrates the competitive forces that exist in a company's environment and indicates some ways Internet technology is affecting each area. These forces help determine a company's position vis-à-vis competitors in the industry environment.

1. *Potential new entrants.* Capital requirements and economies of scale are examples of two potential barriers to entry that can keep out new competitors. It is far more costly to enter the automobile industry, for instance, than to start a

E X H I B I T   8.6

Porter's Five Forces Affecting Industry Competition

SOURCES: Based on Michael E. Porter, *Competitive Strategy: Techniques for Analyzing Industries and Competitors* (New York: Free Press, 1980); and Michael E. Porter, "Strategy and the Internet," *Harvard Business Review* (March 2001): 63–78.

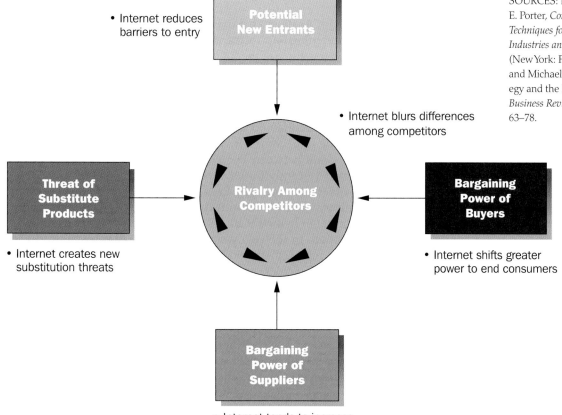

- Internet reduces barriers to entry
- **Potential New Entrants**
- Internet blurs differences among competitors
- **Threat of Substitute Products**
- **Rivalry Among Competitors**
- **Bargaining Power of Buyers**
- Internet creates new substitution threats
- Internet shifts greater power to end consumers
- **Bargaining Power of Suppliers**
- Internet tends to increase bargaining power of suppliers

specialized mail-order business. In general, Internet technology has made it much easier for new companies to enter an industry by curtailing the need for such organizational elements as an established sales force, physical assets such as buildings and machinery, or access to existing supplier and sales channels.

2. *Bargaining power of buyers.* Informed customers become empowered customers. The Internet provides easy access to a wide array of information about products, services, and competitors, thereby greatly increasing the bargaining power of end consumers. For example, a customer shopping for a car can gather extensive information about various options, such as wholesale prices for new cars or average value for used vehicles, detailed specifications, repair records, and even whether a used car has ever been involved in an accident.

3. *Bargaining power of suppliers.* The concentration of suppliers and the availability of substitute suppliers are significant factors in determining supplier power. The sole supplier of engines to a manufacturer of small airplanes will have great power, for example. The impact of the Internet in this area can be both positive and negative. That is, procurement over the Web tends to give a company greater power over suppliers, but the Web also gives suppliers access to a greater number of customers, as well as the ability to reach end users. Overall, the Internet tends to raise the bargaining power of suppliers.

4. *Threat of substitute products.* The power of alternatives and substitutes for a company's product may be affected by changes in cost or in trends such as increased health consciousness that will deflect buyer loyalty. Companies in the sugar industry suffered from the growth of sugar substitutes; manufacturers of aerosol spray cans lost business as environmentally conscious consumers chose other products. The Internet created a greater threat of new substitutes by enabling new approaches to meeting customer needs. For example, offers of low-cost airline tickets over the Internet hurt traditional travel agencies.

5. *Rivalry among competitors.* As illustrated in Exhibit 8.6, rivalry among competitors is influenced by the preceding four forces, as well as by cost and product differentiation. With the leveling force of the Internet and information technology, it has become more difficult for many companies to find ways to distinguish themselves from their competitors, which intensifies rivalry.

Porter referred to the "advertising slugfest" when describing the scrambling and jockeying for position that often occurs among fierce rivals within an industry. Famous examples include the competitive rivalry between Pepsi and Coke, between UPS and FedEx, and between The Home Depot and Lowe's. The rivalry between Gillette Company (recently purchased by Procter & Gamble) and Schick, the No. 2 maker of razors (now owned by Energizer), may soon be just as heated. Although Gillette is still way ahead, the introduction of the Schick Quattro and a massive advertising campaign helped Schick's 2003 sales grow 149 percent, while Gillette's razor sales slipped. In the two years after the Quattro was introduced, Schick's market share for replacement blades jumped 6 percent, while Gillette's declined. In the fall of 2005, Schick brought out a battery-powered version of Quattro, which is aimed directly at stealing market shared from Gillette's M3Power. Gillette took the next shot with its announcement of the new Fusion five-blade razor.[50]

■ **TAKE A MOMENT**   As a new manager, examine the competitive forces that are affecting your organization. What can you do as a lower-level manager to help the firm find or keep its competitive edge through a differentiation, cost-leadership, or focus strategy?

COMPETITIVE STRATEGIES

In finding its competitive edge within these five forces, Porter suggests that a company can adopt one of three strategies: differentiation, cost leadership, or focus. The organizational characteristics typically associated with each strategy are summarized in Exhibit 8.7.

1. *Differentiation.* The **differentiation** strategy involves an attempt to distinguish the firm's products or services from others in the industry. The organization may use advertising, distinctive product features, exceptional service, or new technology to achieve a product perceived as unique. The differentiation strategy can be profitable because customers are loyal and will pay high prices for the product. Examples of products that have benefited from a differentiation strategy include Harley-Davidson motorcycles, Snapper lawn equipment, and Gore-Tex fabrics, all of which are perceived as distinctive in their markets. When lawn equipment maker Simplicity bought Snapper, for example, one of the first things executives did was pull Snapper products out of Wal-Mart. Whereas most manufacturers do whatever they can to sell through the giant retailer, Simplicity's managers recognized that selling mowers at Wal-Mart was incompatible with their strategy, which emphasizes quality, dependability, durability, and cachet rather than high volume and low cost. Customers can buy a lawn mower at Wal-Mart for less than a hundred bucks, but the least expensive Snapper is about $350 and is built to last for decades.[51] Service companies such as Starbucks, Whole Foods Market, and IKEA can also use a differentiation strategy. The Unlocking Innovative Solutions Through People box describes how corporate culture helps the Four Seasons differentiate itself in the hotel industry.

   Companies that pursue a differentiation strategy typically need strong marketing abilities, a creative flair, and a reputation for leadership.[52] A differentiation strategy can reduce rivalry with competitors if buyers are loyal to a company's brand. Successful differentiation can also reduce the bargaining power of large buyers because other products are less attractive, which also helps the firm fight off threats of substitute products. In addition, differentiation erects entry barriers

differentiation A type of competitive strategy with which the organization seeks to distinguish its products or services from that of competitors.

Strategy	Organizational Characteristics
Differentiation	Acts in a flexible, loosely knit way, with strong coordination among departments
	Strong capability in basic rewards
	Creative flair, thinks "out of the box"
	Strong marketing abilities
	Rewards employee innovation
	Corporate reputation for quality or technological leadership
Cost Leadership	Strong central authority; tight cost controls
	Maintains standard operating procedures
	Easy-to-use manufacturing technologies
	Highly efficient procurement and distribution systems
	Close supervision, finite employee empowerment
Focus	Frequent, detailed control reports
	May use combination of above policies directed at particular strategic target
	Values and rewards flexibility and customer intimacy
	Measures cost of providing service and maintaining customer loyalty
	Pushes empowerment to employees with customer contact

E X H I B I T   8.7

Organizational Characteristics of Porter's Competitive Strategies

SOURCES: Based on Michael E. Porter, *Competitive Strategy: Techniques for Analyzing Industries and Competitors* (New York: The Free Press: 1980); Michael Treacy and Fred Wiersema, "How Market Leaders Keep Their Edge," *Fortune* (February 6, 1995): 88–98; and Michael A. Hitt, R. Duane Ireland, and Robert E. Hoskisson, *Strategic Management* (St. Paul, MN: West, 1995): 100–113.

Unlocking Innovative Solutions Through | **PEOPLE** |

FOUR SEASONS HOTELS: MANAGING BY THE GOLDEN RULE

A Four Seasons hotel can be a soaring New York City tower designed by famed architect I. M. Pei or an elegantly restored nineteenth century Art Noveau palace in Budapest. The pricey, spacious rooms and suites—a double can easily run $400 or more a night—might be graced with hand-woven carpets, have a workspace complete with a fax machine, or feature a flat-screen television in a marble bathroom. But these luxurious appointments are only part of what sets the Toronto-based Four Seasons brand apart. The company's impeccable, personalized service has an even bigger impact on its positive worldwide reputation.

At Four Seasons hotels, employees treat guests the way they'd want to be treated themselves. What inspires such exceptional service? Four Seasons discovered that the key is a pro-employee culture. Although offering employees and their families the chance to stay in any hotel for free is a welcome bonus, at the heart of the company's culture is respect for each individual. People feel appreciated, and the company regularly shows up on *Fortune* magazine's list of the 100 best places to work. At Four Seasons, top leaders communicate the lofty standards they expect to be met and then trust managers and staff to come up with the best way to deliver that service. "We want individuals to think and be natural rather than just robotically doing things," explains Christopher Hunsberger, general manager of the Washington, D.C., Four Seasons hotel.

Managers and staff members know that if they pick up on a way to improve service, they can implement the idea on their own initiative. For instance, the Four Seasons restaurant manager in Washington noticed that guests often ate with open laptops at their elbows, and guests without laptops occasionally asked their servers whether they could obtain stock quotes. The alert manager saw a need and responded by acquiring laptops, outfitted with wireless Internet access and a DVD player, so that any guest could have access to a computer and the Internet while dining. The added service was so successful that the restaurant also made portable DVD players and movies available to keep young children entertained, allowing adults a more enjoyable dining experience.

By treating each individual worker with consideration and respect, Four Seasons managers create employees who treat guests the same way, helping Four Seasons move toward its strategic goal of being the undisputed global leader in luxury lodging.

SOURCES: Daniel Roth, "Trading Places: What's It Really Like to Work at a Best Company?" *Fortune* (January 23, 2006), http://money.cnn.com/magazines/fortune/fortune_archive/2006/01/23/8366991/index.htm; "Dining Companion," *Mark Hotels* (January 2003): 48; Four Seasons Hotels and Resorts, http://www.fourseasons.com; "Four Seasons," *Fortune*, http://money.cnn.com/magazines/fortune/bestcompanies/snapshots/ 536.html; and Four Seasons Hotels Inc., "Business of Four Seasons," *Management's Discussion and Analysis* (March 9, 2006): 5.

in the form of customer loyalty that a new entrant into the market would have difficulty overcoming.

2. *Cost leadership.* With a **cost leadership** strategy, the organization aggressively seeks efficient facilities, pursues cost reductions, and uses tight cost controls to produce products more efficiently than competitors. A low-cost position means that the company can undercut competitors' prices and still offer comparable quality and earn a reasonable profit. Comfort Inn and Motel 6 are low-priced alternatives to Four Seasons or Marriott. Enterprise Rent-A-Car is a low-priced alternative to Hertz.

Being a low-cost producer provides a successful strategy to defend against the five competitive forces in Exhibit 8.6. For example, the most efficient, low-cost company is in the best position to succeed in a price war while still making a profit. Likewise, the low-cost producer is protected from powerful customers and suppliers, because customers cannot find lower prices elsewhere, and other buyers would have less slack for price negotiation with suppliers. If substitute products or potential new entrants occur, the low-cost producer is better positioned than higher-cost rivals to prevent loss of market share. The low price acts as a barrier against new entrants and substitute products.[53]

cost leadership A type of competitive strategy with which the organization aggressively seeks efficient facilities, cuts costs, and employs tight cost controls to be more efficient than competitors.

3. *Focus.* With a **focus** strategy, the organization concentrates on a specific regional market or buyer group. The company will use either a differentiation or cost leadership approach, but only for a narrow target market. Save-A-Lot, described earlier, uses a focused cost leadership strategy, putting stores in low-income areas. Another example is low-cost leader Southwest Airlines, which was founded in 1971 to serve only three cities—Dallas, Houston, and San Antonio—and didn't fly outside of Texas for the first eight years of its history. Managers aimed for controlled growth, gradually moving into new geographic areas where Southwest could provide short-haul service from city to city. By using a focus strategy, Southwest was able to grow rapidly and expand to other markets.[54] Edward Jones Investments, a St. Louis-based brokerage house, uses a focused differentiation strategy, building its business in rural and small town America and providing clients with conservative, long-term investment advice. According to management consultant Peter Drucker, the safety-first orientation means Edward Jones delivers a product "that no Wall Street house has ever sold before: peace of mind."[55]

255

COURTESY OF CRISPIN PORTER + BOGUSKY

CONCEPT CONNECTION The MINI's trademarked term "Whiptastic Handling" is one of the ways the company distinguishes itself in the automobile industry. MINI, a division of BMW of North America, is thriving with its **differentiation strategy.** The company trademarked the Whiptastic name to emphasize that driving a MINI Cooper is unlike anything else. Customers seem to agree; sales are zooming.

Managers think carefully about which strategy will provide their company with its competitive advantage. Gibson Guitar Corp., famous in the music world for its innovative, high-quality products, found that switching to a low-cost strategy to compete against Japanese rivals such as Yamaha and Ibanez actually hurt the company. When managers realized people wanted Gibson products because of their reputation, not their price, they went back to a differentiation strategy and invested in new technology and marketing.[56] In his studies, Porter found that some businesses did not consciously adopt one of these three strategies and were stuck with no strategic advantage. Without a strategic advantage, businesses earned below-average profits compared with those that used differentiation, cost leadership, or focus strategies. Similarly, a five-year study of management practices in hundreds of businesses, referred to as the *Evergreen Project,* found that a clear strategic direction was a key factor that distinguished winners from losers.[57]

Because the Internet is having such a profound impact on the competitive environment in all industries, it is more important than ever that companies distinguish themselves through careful strategic positioning in the marketplace.[58] The Internet tends to erode both cost-leadership and differentiation advantages by providing new tools for managing costs and giving consumers greater access to comparison shopping. However, managers can find ways to incorporate the Internet into their strategic approaches in a way that provides unique value to customers in an efficient way. Sears, for example, uses the Web to showcase its line of Kenmore appliances, building the brand's reputation by providing detailed information in a relatively inexpensive way.[59]

Partnership Strategies

So far, we have been discussing strategies that are based on how to compete with other companies. An alternative approach to strategy emphasizes collaboration. In some situations, companies can achieve competitive advantage by cooperating with

focus A type of competitive strategy that emphasizes concentration on a specific regional market or buyer group.

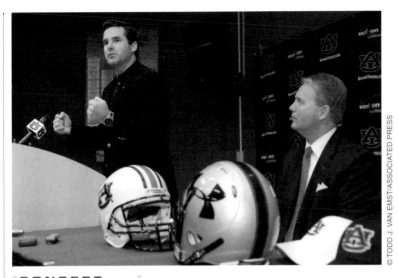

© TODD J. VAN EMST/ASSOCIATED PRESS

CONCEPT
C O N N E C T I O N How do you compete with the likes of Nike? For Under Armour Inc., the phenomenally successful Baltimore company that manufactures high-performance, moisture-wicking athletic apparel, the key is **partnership strategies**. Pictured here are company founder Kevin Plank and Auburn University athletics director Jay Jacob announcing a five-year, $10.6 million **preferred supplier contract**, similar to deals the company has struck with Texas Tech and the University of Maryland. In addition, the upstart company has fueled its soaring sales by using **strategic business partnerships**, such as the one with national retailers such as Dick's Sporting Goods Inc. Dick's now features Under Armour "concept shops" in several stores.

other firms rather than competing. Partnership strategies are becoming increasingly popular as firms in all industries join with other organizations to promote innovation, expand markets, and pursue joint goals. Partnering was once a strategy adopted primarily by small firms that needed greater marketing muscle or international access. Today, however, it has become a way of life for most companies, large and small. The question is no longer whether to collaborate, but rather where, how much, and with whom to collaborate.[60]

Competition and cooperation often exist at the same time. Procter & Gamble and Clorox are fierce rivals in cleaning products and water purification, but both companies profited by collaborating on a new plastic wrap. P&G researchers invented a wrap that seals tightly only where it is pressed, but P&G didn't have a plastic wrap category. Managers negotiated a joint venture with Clorox to market the wrap under the well-established Glad brand name, and Glad Press & Seal became one of the company's most popular products. The two competitors continued the collaboration with the introduction of Glad Force Flex trash bags, which make use of a stretchable plastic invented in P&G's labs.[61]

The Internet is both driving and supporting the move toward partnership thinking. The ability to rapidly and smoothly conduct transactions, communicate information, exchange ideas, and collaborate on complex projects via the Internet means that companies such as Citigroup, Dow Chemical, and Herman Miller have been able to enter entirely new businesses by partnering in business areas that were previously unimaginable.[62] Many companies, including Target, Circuit City, Lands' End, and Golfsmith International, are gaining a stronger online presence by partnering with Amazon.com. Amazon maintains the site and processes orders, while the retailers fill the orders from their own warehouses. The arrangement gives Amazon a new source of revenue and frees the retailers to focus on their bricks-and-mortar business while also gaining new customers online.[63]

Mutual dependencies and partnerships have become a fact of life, but the degree of collaboration varies. Organizations can choose to build cooperative relationships in many ways, such as through preferred suppliers, strategic business partnering, joint ventures, or mergers and acquisitions. Exhibit 8.8 illustrates these major types of strategic business relationships according to the degree of collaboration involved. With preferred supplier relationships, a company such as Wal-Mart, for example, develops a special relationship with a key supplier such as Procter & Gamble that eliminates intermediaries by sharing complete information and reducing the costs of salespeople and distributors. Preferred supplier arrangements provide long-term security for both organizations, but the level of collaboration is relatively low. Strategic business partnering requires a higher level of collaboration. Five of the largest hotel chains—Marriott International, Hilton Hotels Corp., Six Continents, Hyatt Corp., and Starwood Hotels and Resorts Worldwide Inc.—partnered to create their own Web site, Travelweb.com, to combat the growing power of intermediaries such as Expedia and Hotels.com. According to one senior vice president, the hotels felt a need to "take back our room product, and . . . sell it the way we want to sell it and maximize our revenues." At the same time,

E X H I B I T   8.8

A Continuum of Partner-
ship Strategies

SOURCE: Adapted from
Roberta Maynard, "Striking
the Right Match," *Nation's
Business* (May 1996): 18–28.

some chains are striving to build more beneficial partnerships with the third-party brokers.[64]

A still higher degree of collaboration is reflected in joint ventures, which are separate entities created with two or more active firms as sponsors. For example, International Truck and Engine Corporation has a joint venture with Ford Motor Company to build midsized trucks and diesel engine parts.[65] MTV Networks was originally created as a joint venture of Warner Communications and American Express. In a joint venture, organizations share the risks and costs associated with the new venture.

Mergers and acquisitions represent the ultimate step in collaborative relationships. U.S. business has been in the midst of a tremendous merger and acquisition boom. Consider the frenzied deal-making in the telecom industry alone. Sprint acquired Nextel and Verizon Communications purchased MCI. SBC Communications Inc. acquired AT&T and took over the storied brand name, then announced plans to buy BellSouth, making AT&T once again the giant in the telecommunications industry.[66]

Using these various partnership strategies, today's companies simultaneously embrace competition *and* cooperation. Few companies can go it alone under a constant onslaught of international competition, changing technology, and new regulations. Most businesses choose a combination of competitive and partnership strategies that add to their overall sustainable advantage.[67]

FORMULATING FUNCTIONAL-LEVEL STRATEGY

Functional-level strategies are the action plans adopted by major departments to support the execution of business-level strategy. Major organizational functions include marketing, production, finance, human resources, and research and development. Senior managers in these departments adopt strategies that are coordinated with the business-level strategy to achieve the organization's strategic goals.[68]

For example, consider a company that has adopted a differentiation strategy and is introducing new products that are expected to experience rapid growth. The human resources department should adopt a strategy appropriate for growth, which would mean recruiting additional personnel and training middle managers for movement into new positions. The marketing department should undertake test marketing, aggressive advertising campaigns, and consumer product trials. The finance department should adopt plans to borrow money, handle large cash investments, and authorize construction of new production facilities.

A company with mature products or a low-cost strategy will have different functional strategies. The human resources department should develop strategies for retaining and developing a stable work force, including transfers, advancements, and incentives for efficiency and safety. Marketing should stress brand loyalty and the development of established, reliable distribution channels. Production should maintain long production runs, routinization, and cost reduction. Finance should focus on net cash flows and positive cash balances.

■ **TAKE A MOMENT**

As a potential new manager, check out your strategic strengths by completing the New Manager Self-Test on page 259. This assessment will give you a sense of how you can best contribute to your organization's strategy.

STRATEGY IMPLEMENTATION AND CONTROL

The final step in the strategic management process is implementation—how strategy is put into action. Some people argue that strategy implementation is the most difficult and important part of strategic management.[69] No matter how brilliant the formulated strategy, the organization will not benefit if it is not skillfully implemented. Today's competitive environment requires growing recognition of the need for more dynamic approaches to implementing strategies.[70] Strategy is not a static, analytical process; it requires vision, intuition, and employee participation. Effective strategy implementation requires that all aspects of the organization be in congruence with the strategy and that every individual's efforts be coordinated toward accomplishing strategic goals.[71]

Strategy implementation involves using several tools—parts of the firm that can be adjusted to put strategy into action—as illustrated in Exhibit 8.9. Once a new strategy is selected, it is implemented through changes in leadership, structure, information and control systems, and human resources.[72] Implementation involves regularly making difficult decisions about doing things in a way that supports rather than undermines the organization's chosen strategic approach. Remaining chapters of this book examine in detail topics such as leadership, organizational structure, information and control systems, and human resource management. The Manager's Shoptalk box gives some further tips for implementing strategy.

EXHIBIT   8.9

Tools for Putting Strategy into Action

SOURCE: Adapted from Jay R. Galbraith and Robert K. Kazanjian, *Strategy Implementation: Structure, Systems, and Process,* 2d ed. (St. Paul, MN: West, 1986): 115. Used with permission.

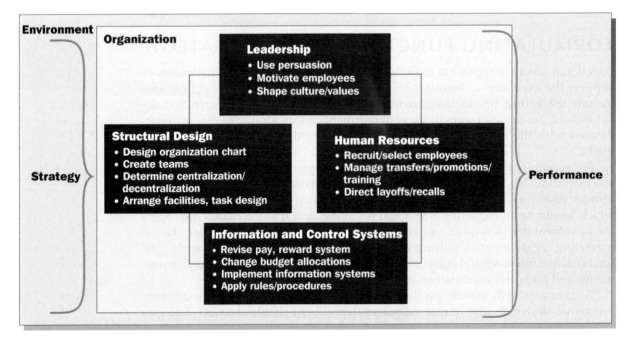

Part 3 PLANNING

258

WHAT IS YOUR STRATEGY STRENGTH?

As a new manager, what are your strengths concerning strategy formulation and implementation? To find out, think about how *you handle challenges and issues* in your school or job. Then mark (a) or (b) for each of the following items, depending on which is more descriptive of your behavior. There are no right or wrong answers. Respond to each item as it best describes how you respond to work situations.

1. When keeping records, I tend to

_____ **a.** be careful about documentation.

_____ **b.** be haphazard about documentation.

2. If I run a group or a project, I

_____ **a.** have the general idea and let others figure out how to do the tasks.

_____ **b.** try to figure out specific goals, timelines, and expected outcomes.

3. My thinking style could be more accurately described as

_____ **a.** linear thinker, going from A to B to C.

_____ **b.** thinking like a grasshopper, hopping from one idea to another.

4. In my office or home things are

_____ **a.** here and there in various piles.

_____ **b.** laid out neatly or at least in reasonable order.

5. I take pride in developing

_____ **a.** ways to overcome a barrier to a solution.

_____ **b.** new hypotheses about the underlying cause of a problem.

6. I can best help strategy by encouraging

_____ **a.** openness to a wide range of assumptions and ideas.

_____ **b.** thoroughness when implementing new ideas.

7. One of my strengths is

_____ **a.** commitment to making things work.

_____ **b.** commitment to a dream for the future.

8. I am most effective when I emphasize

_____ **a.** inventing original solutions.

_____ **b.** making practical improvements.

SCORING AND INTERPRETATION: For *Strategic Formulator* strength, score one point for each (a) answer marked for questions 2, 4, 6, and 8, and for each (b) answer marked for questions 1, 3, 5, and 7. For *Strategic Implementer* strength, score one point for each (b) answer marked for questions 2, 4, 6, and 8, and for each (a) answer marked for questions 1, 3, 5, and 7. Which of your two scores is higher and by how much? The higher score indicates your strategy strength.

Formulator and Implementer are two important ways new managers bring value to strategic management. New managers with implementer strengths tend to work within the situation and improve it by making it more efficient and reliable. Leaders with the formulator strength push toward out-of-the-box strategies and like to seek dramatic breakthroughs. Both styles are essential to strategic management. Strategic formulators often use their skills in creating whole new strategies, and strategic implementers often work with strategic improvements and implementation.

If the difference between your two scores is two or less, you have a balanced formulator/implementer style, and work well in both arenas. If the difference is 4–5, you have a moderately strong style and probably work best in the area of your strength. And if the difference is 7–8, you have a distinctive strength and almost certainly would want to work in the area of your strength rather than in the opposite domain.

SOURCE: Adapted from Dorothy Marcic and Joe Seltzer, *Organizational Behavior: Experiences and Cases* (Cincinnati, OH: South-Western, 1998): 284–287, and William Miller, *Innovation Styles* (Global Creativity Corporation, 1997).

Leadership

The primary key to successful strategy implementation is leadership. *Leadership* is the ability to influence people to adopt the new behaviors needed for strategy implementation. An important part of implementing strategy is building consensus. People throughout the organization must believe in the new strategy and have a strong commitment to achieving the vision and goals. Leadership means using persuasion, motivating employees, and shaping culture and values to support the new strategy. Managers can make speeches to employees, build coalitions

TIPS FOR EFFECTIVE STRATEGY IMPLEMENTATION

In a recent survey, only 57 percent of responding firms reported that managers successfully implemented the new strategies they had devised. Strategy gives a company a competitive edge only if it is skillfully executed through the decisions and actions of front-line managers and employees. Here are a few clues for creating an environment and process conducive to effective implementation.

1. *Build commitment to the strategy.* People throughout the organization have to buy into the new strategy. Managers make a deliberate and concentrated effort to bring front-line employees into the loop so they understand the new direction and have a chance to participate in decisions about how it will be implemented. When Saab managers wanted to shift their strategy, they met with front-line employees and dealers to explain the new direction and ask for suggestions and recommendations on how to put it into action. Clear, measurable goals and rewards that are tied to implementation efforts are also important for gaining commitment.

2. *Devise a clear implementation plan.* Too often, managers put forth great effort to formulate a strategy and next to none crafting a game plan for its implementation. Without such a plan, managers and staff are likely to lose sight of the new strategy when they return to the everyday demands of their jobs. For successful execution, translate the strategy into a simple, streamlined plan that breaks the implementation process into a series of short-term actions, with a timetable for each step. Make sure the plan spells out who is responsible for what part of the implementation, how success will be measured and tracked, and what resources will be required and how they will be allocated.

3. *Pay attention to culture.* Culture drives strategy, and without the appropriate cultural values, employees' behavior will be out of sync with the company's desired positioning in the marketplaces. For example, Air Canada's CEO made a sincere commitment to making the airline the country's customer service leader.

However, employee behavior didn't change because the old culture values supported doing things the way they had always been done.

4. *Take advantage of employees' knowledge and skills.* Managers need to get to know their employees on a personal basis so they understand how people can contribute to implementing the strategy. Most people want to be recognized and want to be valuable members of the organization. People throughout the organization have unused talents and skills that might be crucial for the success of a new strategy. In addition, managers can be sure people get training so they are capable of furthering the organization's new direction.

5. *Communicate, communicate, communicate.* Top managers have to continually communicate, through words and actions, their firm commitment to the strategy. In addition, managers have to keep tabs on how things are going, identify problems, and keep people informed about the organization's progress. Managers should break down barriers to effective communication across functional and hierarchical boundaries, often bringing customers into the communication loop as well. Information systems should provide accurate and timely information to the people who need it for decision making.

Implementing strategy is a complex job that requires everyone in the company to be aligned with the new direction and working to make it happen. These tips, combined with the information in the text, can help managers meet the challenge of putting strategy into action.

SOURCES: Brooke Dobni, "Creating a Strategy Implementation Environment," *Business Horizons* (March–April 2003): 43–46; Michael K. Allio, "A Short Practical Guide to Implementing Strategy," *Journal of Business Strategy* (August 2005): 12–21; "Strategy Execution: Achieving Operational Excellence," *Economist Intelligence Unit* (November 2004); and Thomas W. Porter and Stephen C. Harper, "Tactical Implementation: The Devil Is in the Details," *Business Horizons* (January–February 2003): 53–60.

of people who support the new strategic direction, and persuade middle managers to go along with their vision for the company. At IBM, for example, CEO Sam Palmisano is using leadership to get people throughout the organization aligned with a new strategy focused on getting IBM intimately involved in revamping and even running customers' business operations. To implement the new approach, Palmisano dismantled the executive committee that previously presided over strategic initiatives and replaced it with committees made up of people from all over the company. He's investing tons of money to teach managers at all levels how to lead rather than control their staff. And he is talking to people all over the company, appealing to their sense of pride and uniting them behind this new vision and strategy.[73] With a clear sense of direction and a shared purpose, employees feel motivated, challenged, and empowered to pursue new strategic goals. Another way leaders build consensus and commitment is through broad participation. When people participate in strategy formulation, implementation is easier because managers and employees already understand the reasons for the new strategy and feel more committed to it.

Structural Design

Structural design typically begins with the organization chart. It pertains to managers' responsibilities, their degree of authority, and the consolidation of facilities, departments, and divisions. Structure also pertains to such matters as centralization versus decentralization, the design of job tasks, and the organization's production technology. Structure will be discussed in detail in Chapter 10.

In many cases, implementing a new strategy requires making changes in organizational structure, such as adding or changing positions, reorganizing to teams, redesigning jobs, or shifting managers' responsibility and accountability. At IBM, the company is being reorganized into teams that will work directly with customers; Palmisano believes that breaking down functional and hierarchical boundaries is the only way IBM can find out what customers want and deliver it fast. As the company moves into new businesses such as insurance claims processing and supply-chain optimization, IBM assigns SWAT teams to work with a handful of initial clients, for example. Practically every job in the giant corporation is being redefined to support the new strategy.[74]

Information and Control Systems

Information and control systems include reward systems, pay incentives, budgets for allocating resources, information technology systems, and the organization's rules, policies, and procedures. Changes in these systems represent major tools for putting strategy into action. For example, managers can reassign resources from research and development to marketing if a new strategy requires increased advertising but no product innovations. Managers and employees must also be rewarded for adhering to the new strategy and making it a success.[75]

At General Electric, described earlier in the chapter, CEO Jeff Immelt is tying manager's compensation to their ability to come up with new ideas, demonstrate improved customer service, generate growth, and boost sales. For example, 20 percent of division managers' bonuses is based on how well the business is improving its ability to meet customer needs.[76] Executives at ConAgra, maker of Healthy Choice and Banquet brands, instituted top-down cost controls in the corporation's operating units and developed new systems for pooling resources to reduce purchasing, warehousing, and transportation costs.[77] Retailers such as Wal-Mart and Dollar General made masterful use of sophisticated information technology to support a low-cost strategy by accelerating checkout, managing inventory, and controlling distribution. Kmart, by contrast, performed poorly on implementation because of weak information and control systems that leave unpopular merchandise languishing on store shelves and hot items frequently out of stock.[78] New information technology can also be used to support differentiation strategies, such as by enabling collaborative design of new products or customizing products and services to exact customer specification.

Human Resources

The organization's *human resources* are its employees. The human resource function recruits, selects, trains, transfers, promotes, and lays off employees to achieve strategic goals. Training employees can help them understand the purpose and importance of a new strategy or help them develop the necessary skills and behaviors.

New strategies involve change, which naturally generates some resistance. Sometimes employees may have to be let go and replaced. One newspaper shifted its strategy from an evening to a morning paper to compete with a large newspaper from a nearby city. The new strategy required a change from working days to working from 1 P.M. to about midnight or so, fostering resentment and resistance among department heads. In order to implement it, 80 percent of the department heads had to be let go because they refused to cooperate. New people were recruited and placed in those positions, and the morning newspaper strategy was a resounding success.[79] At IBM, employees in administration and computer repair are being let go by the thousands, replaced by people skilled in business operations as well as technology.[80]

IMPLEMENTATION DURING TURBULENT TIMES

The challenges of implementing strategy continue to escalate with the increased complexity and turbulence in today's business environment. Many managers feel confident that they have found the right strategy to provide a competitive advantage, but they are less optimistic about their ability to implement it. Three issues that are particularly critical for implementing strategy during turbulent times are a global mind-set, paying close attention to corporate culture, and embracing the Internet and other information technologies.

Global Mind-Set

To implement strategies on a global scale, managers need to adopt a global mind-set and be aware of varying implementation issues. Flexibility and openness emerge as mandatory leadership skills. Structural issues are more complex, as managers struggle to find the right mix to achieve the desired level of global integration and local responsiveness, as we discussed earlier. Information, control, and reward systems have to fit the values and incentives within the local cultures. Finally, the recruitment, training, transfer, promotion, and layoff of international human resources create an array of problems not confronted in North America. To be effective internationally, managers have to apply a global perspective to strategy implementation. For example, one well-respected multinational formed a task force of U.S. employees to review and revise workforce policies in connection with a new strategy. Employees from different levels and functional areas met for months and sent out employee surveys to all U.S.-based facilities to get wider input. The final draft was reviewed and approved by top executives. They were surprised when the streamlined workforce manual, which reduced the number of policies from 120 to 10 core ones, was met with resistance and even hostility by the overseas units. Managers' lack of a global mind-set led them to assume incorrectly that the international units would accept whatever was handed down from U.S. headquarters. Another multinational that used a worldwide task force for a similar process had much greater success with implementation.[81]

Corporate Culture

At the same time managers need a global mind-set, they also have to create and maintain a cohesive corporate culture that supports strategy. *Culture* is the link between strategy and performance outcomes, and different culture styles are better suited to different strategic directions.[82] Recall our discussion of different types of culture and the high-performance culture from Chapter 3. A study of the world's most admired companies, as reported annually in *Fortune* magazine, found that managers in these organizations pay close attention to culture and to the values that contribute to strategic success.[83] Managers want to develop a culture that is oriented toward performance—that encourages in everyone the behaviors and attitudes needed to meet the company's strategic goals and holds everyone responsible for success.[84] One example comes from Ansys, a developer of engineering simulation products used to predict product design behavior in manufacturing operations. Ansys has more than two dozen sales offices on three continents and a network of partners in 40 countries. Serving diverse customers around the world with superior technology requires both a commitment to a global mind-set as well as a culture of intense customer focus. Ansys managers built a family-like high-performance culture that embraces customers as well as employees. Employees are committed to the vision of meeting customers' emerging technology needs. Because people feel appreciated and cared about, they feel safe taking risks that lead to better products and better service. One key aspect is, as one executive put it, "giving people enough leeway, enough rope, but not letting them hang themselves." Employees are empowered with decision making authority, but the company has in place systems that prevent people from possibly taking a hard fall.[85]

Information Technology

A final concern for managers implementing strategy during turbulent times is to incorporate the Internet and other information technology. Dell pioneered the use of an online system to let customers configure computers to their exact specifications and submit the order over the Web, saving the cost of salespeople. Online mass customization is now used by many firms to decrease costs while enhancing their product mix and building their brand reputation.[86] Another company that successfully uses the Internet to implement strategy is independent toy retailer Kazoo & Company. Owner Diane Nelson competes with giant retailers such as Wal-Mart by using a differentiation strategy, focusing primarily on selling educational, nonviolent toys. She considered franchising as a way to grow the business, but decided that expanding via a Web site would better enable the company to maintain its distinctiveness. Kazoo.com quickly became a go-to site for people seeking specialty toys, and Nelson negotiated deals with some vendors who will send products directly to customers who order online. About 40 percent of Kazoo's business is now online, and at least a quarter of that comes from overseas.[87]

MANAGER'S SOLUTION

This chapter described important concepts of strategic management. Strategic management begins with an evaluation of the organization's current mission, goals, and strategy. This evaluation is followed by situation analysis (called SWOT analysis), which examines opportunities and threats in the external environment as well as strengths and weaknesses within the organization. Situation analysis leads to the formulation of explicit strategies, which indicate how the company intends to achieve a competitive advantage. Managers formulate strategies that focus on core competencies, develop synergy, and create value.

Strategy formulation takes place at three levels: corporate, business, and functional. Corporate grand strategies include growth, stability, retrenchment, and global. One framework for accomplishing them is the BCG matrix. An approach to business-level strategy is Porter's competitive forces and strategies. The Internet is having a profound impact on the competitive environment, and managers should consider its influence when analyzing the five competitive forces and formulating business strategies. An alternative approach to strategic thought emphasizes cooperation rather than competition. Partnership strategies include preferred supplier arrangements, strategic business partnering, joint ventures, and mergers and acquisitions. Most of today's companies choose a mix of competitive and partnership strategies. Once business strategies have been formulated, functional strategies for supporting them can be developed.

Even the most creative strategies have no value if they cannot be translated into action. Implementation is the most important and most difficult part of strategy. Managers implement strategy by aligning all parts of the organization to be in congruence with the new strategy. Four areas that managers focus on for strategy implementation are leadership, structural design, information and control systems, and human resources. Three additional issues for managers in today's turbulent and complex environment are adopting a global mind-set, paying close attention to corporate culture, and embracing use of the Internet in implementation.

The opening discussion of Circuit City indicated that it got distracted from its core business. How? By expanding into unrelated businesses such as a bank and private label credit card, a used car dealership, and a pay-per-view DVD business. Best Buy, on the other hand, used superior strategy formulation and implementation to overtake the former leader in consumer electronics retailing. It stayed focused on just being the best consumer electronics store, and managers implemented a carefully thought out customer-focused strategy. For example, rapid expansion began when top managers did away with commission-based selling and put salespeople on straight salary. Customers liked the no-pressure atmosphere at Best Buy, while Circuit City stuck with commission-based compensation to please suppliers who wanted salespeople to push high-ticket items. Circuit City also stayed with its strategy of locating stores in second-tier shopping centers, but customers were no longer willing to drive the extra mile. Why should they, when Best Buy stores were located right near Wal-Mart or other high-traffic areas?

Circuit City's new CEO, Philip Schoonover, sold off noncore businesses to refocus all the firm's energies and resources on the consumer electronics business. The company is closing some stores and relocating to more high-traffic areas. Managers are also striving to implement a customer-centric business-level strategy based on delivering a personalized experience to each individual customer. Commission-based pay is a thing of the past. Schoonover is requiring that managers at all levels spend time talking with customers and store employees, and he's revised evaluation and bonus systems to be sure they know he's serious. Another important part of implementation is a new information technology system that gives people real-time access to information about customers, promotions, inventory, and store performance, enabling managers to make better decisions and giving store level employees the information they need to provide personalized service. Whereas technology spending was about $37 million in 2004, it jumped to $112 million in 2005, reflecting the drive to have IT systems that support the new strategy. Business results at Circuit City have improved since managers refocused on the core business and began taking careful steps to strategy implementation. However, it remains to be seen whether the company can regain a competitive edge and hold its own against Best Buy, which continues to change the rules of the game in consumer electronics retailing. Best Buy CEO Brad Anderson says leaders have to "think about the next 15 years, not the next five."[88]

DISCUSSION QUESTIONS

1. In 2004, Kmart emerged from bankruptcy and acquired Sears. Based on your experience in the two stores, how would you define the core competencies of the two retailers? Do you think the store changes so far show evidence of the synergy the dealmakers hoped for?

2. How might a corporate management team go about determining whether it should formulate a growth strategy or a stability strategy? What

factors should they take into consideration? What kinds of information should they collect?

3. You are a middle manager helping to implement a new corporate cost-cutting strategy, and you're meeting skepticism, resistance, and in some cases, outright hostility from your subordinates. In what ways might you or the company have been able to avoid this situation? Where do you go from here?

4. Perform a situation (SWOT) analysis for the school or university you attend. Do you think university administrators consider the same factors when devising their strategy?

5. Do you think the movement toward corporate collaborations, alliances, and partnership rather than competition is a passing phenomenon or here to stay? What skills would make a good manager in a strategic alliance with another company? What skills would make a good manager operating in competition with another company?

6. Using Porter's competitive strategies, how would you describe the strategies of Wal-Mart, Bloomingdale's, and Target? Do any of these companies also use partnership strategies? Discuss.

7. Walt Disney Company has four major strategic business units: movies (including Miramax and Touchstone), theme parks, consumer products, and television (ABC and cable). Place each of these SBUs on the BCG matrix based on your knowledge of them.

8. As an administrator for a medium-sized hospital, you and the board of directors have decided to change to a drug dependency hospital from a short-term, acute-care facility. How would you go about implementing this strategy?

9. If you are the CEO of a global company, how might you determine whether a globalization, a transnational, or a multidomestic strategy would work best for your enterprise? What factors would influence your decision? How would your choice reflect the products or services your company is offering?

10. Describe how the Internet increases the bargaining power of consumers, one of Porter's five competitive forces. Have you felt increased power as a consumer because of the Internet? Explain.

MANAGEMENT IN PRACTICE: EXPERIENTIAL EXERCISE

Developing Strategy for a Small Business

Instructions: Your instructor may ask you to do this exercise individually or as part of a group. Select a local business with which you (or group members) are familiar. Complete the following activities.

Activity 1 Perform a SWOT analysis for the business.

Strengths:

Weaknesses:

Opportunities:

Threats:

Activity 2 Write a statement of the business's current strategy.

Activity 3 Decide on a goal you would like the business to achieve in two years, and write a statement of proposed strategy for achieving that goal.

Activity 4 Write a statement describing how the proposed strategy will be implemented.

Activity 5 What have you learned from this exercise?

MANAGEMENT IN PRACTICE: ETHICAL DILEMMA

The Spitzer Group

Irving Silberstein, marketing director for The Spitzer Group, a growing regional marketing and corporate communications firm, was hard at work on an exciting project. He was designing Spitzer's first word-of-mouth campaign for an important client, a manufacturer of beauty products.

In a matter of just a few years, word-of-mouth advertising campaigns morphed from a small fringe specialty to a mainstream marketing technique embraced by no less than consumer product giant Procter & Gamble (P&G). The basic idea was simple, really. You harnessed the power of existing social networks to sell your products and services. The place to start, Irving knew, was to take a close look at how P&G's in-house unit, Vocalpoint, conducted its highly successful campaigns, both for its own products and those of its clients.

Because women were key purchasers of P&G consumer products, Vocalpoint focused on recruiting mothers with extensive social networks, participants known internally by the somewhat awkward term, *connectors.* The Vocalpoint Web page took care to emphasize that participants were members of an "exclusive" community of moms who exerted significant influence on P&G and other major companies. Vocalpoint not only sent the women new product samples and solicited their opinions, but it also carefully tailored its pitch to the group's interests and preoccupations so the women would want to tell their friends about a product. For example, it described a new dishwashing foam that was so much fun to use, kids would actually volunteer to clean up the kitchen, music to any mother's ears. P&G then furnished the mothers with coupons to hand out if they wished. It's all voluntary, P&G pointed out. According to a company press release issued shortly before Vocalpoint went national in early 2006, members "are never obligated to do or say anything."

One of the things Vocalpoint members weren't obligated to say, Irving knew, was that the women were essentially unpaid participants in a P&G-sponsored marketing program. When asked about the policy, Vocalpoint CEO Steve Reed replied, "We have a deeply held belief you don't tell the consumer what to say." However, skeptical observers speculated that what the company really feared was that the women's credibility might be adversely affected if their Vocalpoint affiliation were known. Nondisclosure really amounted to lying for financial gain, Vocalpoint's critics argued, and furthermore the whole campaign shamelessly exploited personal relationships for commercial purposes. Others thought the critics were making mountains out of molehills. P&G wasn't forbidding participants from disclosing their ties to Vocalpoint and P&G. And the fact that they weren't paid meant the women had no vested interest in endorsing the products.

So as Irving designs the word-of-mouth campaign for his agency's client, just how far should he emulate the company that even its detractors acknowledge as a master of the technique?

What Would You Do?

1. Don't require Spitzer "connectors" to reveal their affiliation with the corporate word-of-mouth marketing campaign. They don't have to recommend a product they don't believe in.

2. Require that Spitzer participants reveal their ties to the corporate marketing program right up front before they make a recommendation.

3. Instruct Spitzer participants to reveal their participation in the corporate marketing program only if directly asked by the person they are talking to about the client's products.

SOURCES: Robert Berner, "I Sold It Through the Grapevine," *BusinessWeek* (May 29, 2006): 32–34; "Savvy Moms Share Maternal Instincts; Vocalpoint Offers Online Moms the Opportunity to be a Valuable Resource to Their Communities," *Business Wire* (December 6, 2005); and "Word of Mouth Marketing: To Tell or Not To Tell," *AdRants.com* (May 2006), www.adrants.com/2006/05/word-of-mouth-marketing-to-tell-or-not-to.php.

CASE FOR CRITICAL ANALYSIS

Edmunds Corrugated Parts & Services

Larry Edmunds grimaces as he tossed his company's latest quarterly earnings onto his desk. When Virginia-based Edmunds Corrugated Parts & Service Co.'s sales surged past the $10 million mark awhile back, he was certain the company was well-positioned for steady growth. Today the company, which provided precision machine parts and service to the domestic corrugated box industry, still enjoys a dominant market share and is showing a profit, though not quite the profit seen in years past. However, it is no longer possible to ignore the fact that revenues were beginning to show clear signs of stagnation.

More than two decades ago, Larry's grandfather loaned him the money to start the business and then handed over the barn on what had been the family's Shenandoah Valley farm to serve as his first factory. Today, he operates from a 50,000 square-foot factory located near I-81 just a few miles from that old barn. The business allowed him to realize what had once seemed an almost impossible goal: He was making a good living without having to leave his close-knit extended family and rural roots. He also felt a sense of satisfaction at employing about 100 people, many of them neighbors. They were among the most hard-working, loyal workers you'd find anywhere. However, many of his original employees were now nearing retirement. Replacing those skilled workers was going to be difficult, he realized from experience. The area's brightest and best young people were much more likely to move away in search of employment than their parents had been. Those who remained behind just didn't seem to have the work ethic Larry had come to expect in his employees.

He didn't feel pressured by the emergence of any new direct competitors. After slipping slightly a couple years ago, Edmunds's formidable market share—based on its reputation for reliability and exceptional, personalized service—was holding steady at 75 percent. He did feel plagued, however, by higher raw material costs resulting from the steep increase in steel prices. But the main source of concern stemmed from changes in the box industry itself. The industry had never been particularly recession resistant, with demand fluctuating with manufacturing output. Now alternative shipping products were beginning to make their appearance, mostly flexible plastic films and reusable plastic containers. It remained to be seen how much of a dent they'd make in the demand for boxes.

More worrying, consolidation in the paper industry had wiped out hundreds of the U.S. plants that Edmunds once served, with many of the survivors either opening overseas facilities or entering into joint ventures abroad. The surviving manufacturers were investing in higher quality machines that broke down less frequently, thus requiring fewer of Edmunds's parts. Still, he had to admit that although the highly fragmented U.S. corrugated box industry certainly qualified as a mature one, no one seriously expected U.S. manufacturers to be dislodged from their position as major producers for both the domestic and export markets.

Edmunds was clearly at a crossroads. If Larry wanted that steady growth he'd assumed he could count on not so long ago, he suspect that business as usual wasn't going to work. But if he wanted the company to grow, what was the best way to achieve that goal? Should he look into developing new products and services, possibly serving industries other than the box market? Should he investigate the possibility of going the mergers and acquisitions route or look for a partnership opportunity? He thought about the company's rudimentary Web page, one that did little beside give a basic description of the company, and wondered whether he could find ways of making better use of the Internet? Was it feasible for Edmunds to find new markets by exporting its parts globally?

All he knew for sure was that once he decided where to take the company from here, he would sleep better.

Questions

1. What would the SWOT analysis look like for this company?
2. What role do you expect the Internet to play in the corrugated box industry? What are some ways that Edmunds could better use the Internet to foster growth?
3. Which of Porter's competitive strategies would you recommend that Edmunds follow? Why? Which of the strategies do you think would be least likely to succeed?

SOURCES: Based on Ron Stodghill, "Boxed Out," *FSB* (April 2005): 69–72; "SIC 2653 Corrugated and Solid Fiber Boxes," *Encyclopedia of American Industries,* www.referenceforbusiness.com/industries/Paper-Allied/Corrugated-Solid-Fiber-Boxes.html; "Paper and Allied Products," *U.S. Trade and Industry Outlook 2000,* 10-12 to 10-15; and "Smurfit-Stone Container: Market Summary," *BusinessWeek Online* (May 4, 2006), research.businessweek.com/business_summary.asp?Symbol=SSCC.

ENDNOTES

1. Meridith Levinson, "Change Management; Circuit City Rewires," *CIO* (July 1, 2005): http://www.cio.com; and Matthew Boyle, "Best Buy's Giant Gamble," *Fortune* (April 3, 2006): 69–75.

2. Suzanne Woolley, ed., "Best Leaders," *BusinessWeek* (December 19, 2005): 60–64.

3. Christopher Palmeri, "Mattel: Up the Hill Minus Jill," *BusinessWeek* (April 9, 2001): 53–54; William M. Bulkeley, "SofterView; Kodak Sharpens Digital Focus on Its Best Customers: Women," *The Wall Street Journal* (July 6, 2005): A1.

4. Chet Miller and Laura B. Cardinal, "Strategic Planning and Firm Performance: A Synthesis of More than Two Decades of Research," *Academy of Management Journal* 37, no. 6 (1994): 1649–1665.

5. Gary Hamel, "Killer Strategies," *Fortune* (June 23, 1997): 70–84; and Costantinos Markides, "Strategic Innovation," *Sloan Management Review* (Spring 1997): 9–23.

6. Richard Tomlinson, "L'Oreal's Global Makeover," *Fortune* (September 30, 2002): 141–146.

7. Keith H. Hammonds, "Michael Porter's Big Ideas," *Fast Company* (March 2001): 150–156.

8. John E. Prescott, "Environments as Moderators of the Relationship between Strategy and Performance," *Academy of Management Journal* 29 (1986): 329–346; John A. Pearce II and Richard B. Robinson, Jr., *Strategic Management: Strategy, Formulation, and Implementation,* 2d ed. (Homewood, IL: Irwin, 1985); and David J. Teece, "Economic Analysis and Strategic Management," *California Management Review* 26 (Spring 1984): 87–110.

9. Jack Welch, "It's All in the Sauce," excerpt from his book, *Winning,* in *Fortune* (April 18, 2005): 138–144; and Markides, "Strategic Innovation."

10. Kotha Suresh and Daniel Orna, "Generic Manufacturing Strategies: A Conceptual Synthesis," *Strategic Management Journal* 10 (1989): 211–231; and John A. Pearce II, "Selecting Among Alternative Grand Strategies," *California Management Review* (Spring 1982): 23–31.

11. Diane Brady, "Pets Are People Too, You Know," *BusinessWeek* (November 28, 2005): 114; Sarah Ellison and Charles Forelle, "Gilette's Smooth Bet: Men Will Pay More for Five-Blade Razor," *The Wall Street Journal* (September 25, 2005): B1.

12. "Citigroup Buys Sears Credit Card Portfolio," *New York Times News Service;* Stanley Holmes, "Boeing: What Really Happened?" *BusinessWeek* (December 15, 2003): 33–38.

13. Palmeri, "Mattel: Up the Hill Minus Jill."

14. Bulkeley, "SofterView: Kodak Sharpens Digital Focus"; Carol J. Loomis, "The Tragedy of General Motors," *Fortune* (February 20, 2006): 58–75.

15. Zachary Schiller, "Figgies Turns Over a New Leaf," *BusinessWeek* (February 27, 1995): 94–96; and Gail Edmondson, "Fiat's Last Stand," *BusinessWeek* (April 21, 2003): 79–80.

16. Kenichi Ohmae, "Managing in a Borderless World," *Harvard Business Review* (May–June 1990): 152–161.

17. Theodore Levitt, "The Globalization of Markets," *Harvard Business Review* (May–June 1983): 92–102.

18. Mainardi, Salva, and Sanderson, "Label of Origin."

19. Joanne Lipman, "Marketers Turn Sour on Global Sales Pitch Harvard Guru Makes," *The Wall Street Journal* (May 12, 1988): 1, 8.

20. Michael E. Porter, "Changing Patterns of International Competition," *California Management Review* 28 (Winter 1986): 40.

21. Mohanbir Sawhney and Sumant Mandal, "What Kind of Global Organization Should You Build?" *Business 2.0* (May 2000): 213.

22. Based on Michael A. Hitt, R. Duane Ireland, and Robert E. Hoskisson, *Strategic Management: Competitiveness and Globalization* (St. Paul, MN: West, 1995): 238.

23. Anil K. Gupta and Vijay Govindarajan, "Converting Global Presence into Global Competitive Advantage," *Academy of Management Executive* 15, no. 2 (2001): 45–56.

24. Thomas S. Bateman and Carl P. Zeithaml, *Management: Function and Strategy,* 2d ed. (Homewood, IL: Irwin, 1993): 231.

25. Michael E. Porter, "What Is Strategy?" *Harvard Business Review* (November–December 1996): 61–78.

26. Arthur A. Thompson, Jr., and A. J. Strickland III, *Strategic Management: Concepts and Cases,* 6th ed. (Homewood, IL: Irwin, 1992); and Briance Mascarenhas, Alok Baveja, and Mamnoon Jamil, "Dynamics of Core Competencies in Leading Multinational Companies," *California Management Review* 40, no. 4 (Summer 1998): 117–132.

27. Michael V. Copeland, "Stitching Together an Apparel Powerhouse," *Business 2.0* (April 2005): 52–54.

28. "Gaylord Says Hotels Prosper by Becoming Destinations," *The Tennessean* (July 24, 2005): http://www.tennessean.com.

29. Chris Woodyard, "Big Dreams for Small Choppers Paid Off," *USA Today* (September 11, 2005), http://www.usatoday.com.

30. Michael Goold and Andrew Campbell, "Desperately Seeking Synergy," *Harvard Business Review* (September–October 1998): 131–143.

31. Chris Woodyard, "FedEx Ponies Up $2.4B for Kinko's," *USA Today* (December 30, 2003): http://www.usatoday.com/money/industries/2003-12-30-fdx-kinkos_x.htm (accessed January 2, 2004); and Claudia H. Deutsch, "FedEx Moves to Expand with Purchase of Kinko's," *The New York Times* (December 31, 2003): C1.

32. Woolley, "Best Leaders."

33. Kerry Capell, "IKEA: How the Swedish Retailer Became a Global Cult Brand," *BusinessWeek* (November 14, 2005): 96–106.

34. Janet Adamy, "Bare Essentials; To Find Growth, No-Frills Grocer Goes Where Other Chains Won't," *The Wall Street Journal* (August 30, 2005): A1, A8.

35. Milton Leontiades, *Strategies for Diversification and Change* (Boston: Little, Brown, 1980): 63; and Dan E. Schendel and Charles W. Hofer, eds., *Strategic Management: A New View of Business Policy and Planning* (Boston: Little, Brown, 1979): 11–14.

36. Georgia Flight, "Powerboating's New Powerhouse," *Business 2.0* (November 2005): 62–67.

37. Christopher Palmeri, "How NutriSystem Got Fat and Happy," *BusinessWeek* (September 19, 2005): 82–84.

38. Joseph T. Hallinan, "Los Angeles Paper Bets on Softer News, Shorter Stories," *The Wall Street Journal* (October 3, 2005): B1, B6.

39. Palmeri, "How NutriSystem Got Fat and Happy."

40. Sarah Ellison, "Focus Group; P&G Chief's Turnaround Recipe: Find Out What Women Want," *The Wall Street Journal* (June 1, 2005): A1, A16.

41. Milton Leontiades, "The Confusing Words of Business Policy," *Academy of Management Review* 7 (1982): 45–48.

42. Lawrence G. Hrebiniak and William F. Joyce, *Implementing Strategy* (New York: Macmillan, 1984).

43. Pallavi Gogoi, "The Heat in Kraft's Kitchen; Cheap Rivals and Demands for Leaner Fare Close In," *BusinessWeek* (August 4, 2003): 82; and Shelly Branch, "Critical Curds; At Kraft, Making Cheese 'Fun' Is Serious Business," *The Wall Street Journal* (May 31, 2002): A1, A6.

44. Frederick W. Gluck, "A Fresh Look at Strategic Management," *Journal of Business Strategy* 6 (Fall 1985): 4–19.

45. J. Lynn Lunsford, "Going Up; United Technologies' Formula: A Powerful Lift from Elevators," *The Wall Street Journal* (July 2, 2003): A1, A6.

46. Thompson and Strickland, *Strategic Management*; and William L. Shanklin and John K. Ryans, Jr., "Is the International Cash Cow Really a Prize Heifer?" *Business Horizons* 24 (1981): 10–16.

47. Diane Brady, "The Immelt Revolution," *BusinessWeek* (March 28, 2005): 64–73.

48. Michael E. Porter, *Competitive Strategy* (New York: Free Press, 1980): 36–46; Danny Miller, "Relating Porter's Business Strategies to Environment and Structure: Analysis and Performance Implementations," *Academy of Management Journal* 31 (1988): 280–308; and Michael E. Porter, "From Competitive Advantage to Corporate Strategy," *Harvard Business Review* (May–June 1987): 43–59.

49. Michael E. Porter, "Strategy and the Internet," *Harvard Business Review* (March 2001): 63–78.

50. William C. Symonds, "Can Gillette Regain Its Edge?" *BusinessWeek* (January 26, 2004): 46.

51. Charles Fishman, "The Man Who Said No to Wal-Mart," *Fast Company* (January–February 2006): 66–71, excerpted from *The Wal-Mart Effect*, published by Penguin Press.

52. Thomas L. Wheelen and J. David Hunger, *Strategic Management and Business Policy* (Reading, MA: Addison-Wesley, 1989).

53. Andrew Park and Peter Burrows, "Dell, the Conqueror," *BusinessWeek* (September 24, 2001): 92–102; and Thompson and Strickland, *Strategic Management*.

54. "We Weren't Just Airborne Yesterday; A Brief History of Southwest Airlines," http://www.southwest.com/about_swa/airborne.html (accessed March 29, 2004); Micheline Maynard, "Are Peanuts No Longer Enough?" *The New York Times* (March 7, 2004): Section 3, 1; and Wendy Zellner with Michael Arndt, "Holding Steady," *BusinessWeek* (February 3, 2003): 66–68.

55. Richard Teitelbaum, "The Wal-Mart of Wall Street," *Fortune* (October 13, 1997): 128–130.

56. Joshua Rosenbaum, "Guitar Maker Looks for a New Key," *The Wall Street Journal* (February 11, 1998): B1, B5.

57. Nitin Nohria, William Joyce, and Bruce Roberson, "What Really Works," *Harvard Business Review* (July 2003): 43–52.

58. Porter, "Strategy and the Internet"; Hammonds, "Michael Porter's Big Ideas"; and G. T. Lumpkin, Scott B. Droege, and Gregory G. Dess, "E-Commerce Strategies: Achieving Sustainable Competitive Advantage and Avoiding Pitfalls," *Organizational Dynamics* 30, no 4 (2002): 325–340.

59. Lumpkin et al., "E-Commerce Strategies."

60. Based on John Burton, "Composite Strategy: The Combination of Collaboration and Competition," *Journal of General Management* 21, No. 1 (Autumn 1995): 1–23; and Roberta Maynard, "Striking the Right Match," *Nation's Business* (May 1996): 18–28.

61. Alice Dragoon, "A Travel Guide to Collaboration," *CIO* (November 15, 2004): 68–75.

62. Don Tapscott, "Rethinking Strategy in a Networked World," *Strategy & Business,* no. 24 (Third Quarter 2001): 34–41.

63. Nick Wingfield, "New Chapter; A Web Giant Tries to Boost Profits by Taking on Tenants," *The Wall Street Journal* (September 24, 2003): A1, A10; and Nick Wingfield, "Amazon's eBay Challenge," *The Wall Street Journal* (June 3, 2004): B1, B2.

64. Julia Angwin and Motoka Rich, "Inn Fighting; Big Hotel Chains Are Striking Back Against Web Sites," *The Wall Street Journal* (March 14, 2003): A1, A7.

65. Tonya Vinas, "It Starts with Parts," *Industry Week* (September 2003): 40–43.

66. Dionne Searcey, Almar Latour, and Dennis K. Berman, "Wedding Bells; A Reborn AT&T to Buy BellSouth," *The Wall Street Journal* (March 6, 2006): A1, A13.

67. Burton, "Composite Strategy: The Combination of Collaboration and Competition."

68. Harold W. Fox, "A Framework for Functional Coordination," *Atlanta Economic Review* (now *Business Magazine*) (November–December 1973).

69. Eric M. Olson, Stanley F. Slater, and G. Tomas M. Hult, "The Importance of Structure and Process to Strategy Implementation," *Business Horizons* 48 (2005): 47–54; L. J. Bourgeois III and David R. Brodwin, "Strategic Implementation: Five Approaches to an Elusive Phenomenon," *Strategic Management Journal* 5 (1984): 241–264; Anil K. Gupta and V. Govindarajan, "Business Unit Strategy, Managerial Characteristics, and Business Unit Effectiveness at Strategy Implementation," *Academy of Management Journal* (1984): 25–41; and Jeffrey G. Covin, Dennis P. Slevin, and Randall L. Schultz, "Implementing Strategic Missions: Effective Strategic, Structural, and Tactical Choices," *Journal of Management Studies* 31, no. 4 (1994): 481–505.

70. Rainer Feurer and Kazem Chaharbaghi, "Dynamic Strategy Formulation and Alignment," *Journal of General Management* 20, no. 3 (Spring 1995): 76–90; and Henry Mintzberg, *The Rise and Fall of Strategic Planning* (Toronto: Maxwell Macmillan Canada, 1994).

71. Olson, Slater, and Hult, "The Importance of Structure and Process to Strategy Implementation."

72. Jay R. Galbraith and Robert K. Kazanjian, *Strategy Implementation: Structure, Systems and Process,* 2d ed. (St. Paul, MN.: West, 1986); and Paul C. Nutt, "Selecting Tactics to Implement Strategic Plans," *Strategic Management Journal* 10 (1989): 145–161.

73. Spencer E. Ante, "The New Blue," *BusinessWeek* (March 17, 2003): 80–88.

74. Steve Hamm, "Beyond Blue," *BusinessWeek* (April 18, 2005): 68–76.

75. Gupta and Govindarajan, "Business Unit Strategy"; and Bourgeois and Brodwin, "Strategic Implementation."

76. Brady, "The Immelt Revolution."

77. Greg Burns, "How a New Boss Got ConAgra Cooking Again," *BusinessWeek* (July 25, 1994): 72–73.

78. Nohria et al., "What Really Works."

79. James E. Skivington and Richard L. Daft, "A Study of Organizational 'Framework' and 'Process' Modalities for the Implementation of Business-Level Strategies" (unpublished manuscript, Texas A&M University, 1987).

80. Hamm, "Beyond Blue."

81. Thomas M. Begley and David P. Boyd, "The Need for a Corporate Global Mind-Set," *MIT Sloan Management Review* (Winter 2003): 25–32.

82. Abby Ghobadian and Nicholas O'Regan, "The Link Between Culture, Strategy, and Performance in Manufacturing SMEs," *Journal of General Management* 28, no. 1 (Autumn 2002): 16–34.

83. Melvyn J. Stark, "Five Years of Insight Into the World's Most Admired Companies," *Journal of Organizational Excellence* (Winter 2002): 3–12.

84. Nitin Nohria, William Joyce, and Bruce Roberson, "What Really Works," *Harvard Business Review* (July 2003): 43–52; and Jeff Rosenthal and Mary Ann Masarech, "High Performance Cultures: How Values Can Drive Business Results," *Journal of Organizational Excellence* (Spring 2003): 3–18.

85. James E. Cashman, "Strategy Sustains Success," *Industrial Management* (September–October 2005): 15–19.

86. Lumpkin et al. "E-Commerce Strategies."

87. Paulette Thomas, "Fighting the Giants with a Savvy Mix," *The Wall Street Journal* (November 29, 2005): B12.

88. Levinson, "Change Management: Circuit City Rewires"; and Boyle, "Best Buy's Giant Gamble."

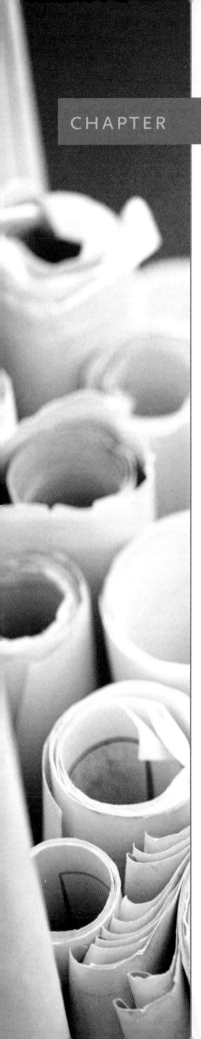

CHAPTER OUTLINE

Manager's Challenge

Types of Decisions and Problems

Programmed and Nonprogrammed Decisions

Certainty, Risk, Uncertainty, and Ambiguity

Decision-Making Models

Classical Model

Administrative Model

Political Model

Decision-Making Steps

Recognition of Decision Requirement

Diagnosis and Analysis of Causes

Development of Alternatives

Selection of Desired Alternative

Implementation of Chosen Alternative

Evaluation and Feedback

Personal Decision Framework

Increasing Participation in Decision Making

The Vroom-Jago Model

New Decision Approaches for Turbulent Times

LEARNING OBJECTIVES

After studying this chapter, you should be able to:

1. Explain why decision making is an important component of good management.

2. Explain the difference between programmed and nonprogrammed decisions and the decision characteristics of risk, uncertainty, and ambiguity.

3. Describe the classical, administrative, and political models of decision making and their applications.

4. Identify the six steps used in managerial decision making.

5. Explain four personal decision styles used by managers.

6. Discuss the advantages and disadvantages of participative decision making.

7. Identify techniques for improving decision making in today's turbulent environment.

MANAGERIAL
DECISION MAKING

MANAGER'S CHALLENGE

Marjorie Yang is contemplating the biggest decision of her career—perhaps the biggest decision in her company's history. As chairperson and CEO of Esquel Group, a textile manufacturer in Hong Kong that makes clothes for J. Crew, Tommy Hilfiger, Brooks Brothers, and other top brands, Yang has the ultimate say in whether the company invests $150 million in a brand-new fabric mill that will be the best mill in China and could make Esquel the top shirt maker in the world. Like most textile manufacturers, Esquel is going through a rough period. With the end of U.S. textile quotas in early 2005, world capacity is going up, prices are going down, and profit margins are squeezed in the middle. Esquel's strategy for years has been to go for top quality, first aiming to achieve Japanese quality in the 1980s and now shooting to reach Italian quality, the best in the world. Esquel grows its own high-quality cotton in western China, and Yang figures the new factory can help them make the most of it. With the end of quotas, she reasons that more competitors will be investing in the low-quality end of the market; thus, if Esquel can be the first company in China to reach the pinnacle of quality, it will have a huge advantage with higher profit margins and less competition. Yet doing the deal now is risky. At least half of the money will have to be borrowed, and profits are sure to suffer in the short run. Although most of Esquel's top executives agree that the idea is good, at least half of them believe building the factory now is too risky and that Yang should wait a couple of years until the industry settles down and trends are clearer.[1]

> If you were Marjorie Yang, how would you decide whether to wait or move ahead now with the $150 million factory? What decision would you make and why?

■ **TAKE A MOMENT**

271

Every organization grows, prospers, or fails as a result of decisions by its managers, and top executives like Marjorie Yang make difficult decisions every day. Managers often are referred to as *decision makers*. Although many of their important decisions are strategic, such as Yang's decision whether to build a new factory. Managers also make decisions about every other aspect of an organization, including structure, control systems, responses to the environment, and human resources. Managers scout for problems, make decisions for solving them, and monitor the consequences to see whether additional decisions are required. Good decision making is a vital part of good management, because decisions determine how the organization solves its problems, allocates resources, and accomplishes its goals.

The business world is full of evidence of both good and bad decisions. For example, CEO Robert Iger is revamping Disney's "Old Media" image with his decision to make popular television programs from ABC and other Disney channels available free of charge on the Web, a first in the industry.[2] Cadillac managers ditched stuffy golf and yachting sponsorships and instead tied in with top Hollywood movies, a decision that boosted sales by 43 percent.[3] On the other hand, Maytag's decision to introduce the Neptune Drying Center was a complete flop. The new $1,200 product was hyped as a breakthrough in laundry, but the six-foot tall Drying Center wouldn't fit into most people's existing laundry rooms. Or, consider the decision of Timex managers to replace the classic tag line, "It takes a licking and keeps on ticking," with the bland "Life is ticking." The desire to modernize their company's image led Timex managers to ditch one of the most recognizable advertising slogans in the world in favor of a lame and rather depressing new one.[4] Decision making is not easy. It must be done amid ever-changing factors, unclear information, and conflicting points of view.

Chapters 7 and 8 described strategic planning. This chapter explores the decision process that underlies strategic planning. Plans and strategies are arrived at through decision making; the better the decision making, the better the strategic planning. First we examine decision characteristics. Then we look at decision-making models and the steps executives should take when making important decisions. The chapter also examines participative decision making and discusses techniques for improving decision making in today's organizations.

TYPES OF DECISIONS AND PROBLEMS

A **decision** is a choice made from available alternatives. For example, an accounting manager's selection among Colin, Tasha, and Carlos for the position of junior auditor is a decision. Many people assume that making a choice is the major part of decision making, but it is only a part.

Decision making is the process of identifying problems and opportunities and then resolving them. Decision making involves effort both before and after the actual choice. Thus, the decision as to whether to select Colin, Tasha, or Carlos requires the accounting manager to ascertain whether a new junior auditor is needed, determine the availability of potential job candidates, interview candidates to acquire necessary information, select one candidate, and follow up with the socialization of the new employee into the organization to ensure the decision's success.

Programmed and Nonprogrammed Decisions

Management decisions typically fall into one of two categories: programmed and nonprogrammed. **Programmed decisions** involve situations that have occurred often enough to enable decision rules to be developed and applied in the future.[5] Programmed decisions are made in response to recurring organizational problems. The decision to reorder paper and other office supplies when inventories drop to a certain level is a programmed decision. Other programmed decisions concern the types of skills required to fill certain jobs, the reorder point for manufacturing inventory, exception reporting for expenditures 10 percent or more over budget, and selection of freight routes for product deliveries. Once managers formulate decision rules, subordinates and others can make the decision, freeing managers for other tasks.

Nonprogrammed decisions are made in response to situations that are unique, are poorly defined and largely unstructured, and have important consequences for the organization. Many nonprogrammed decisions involve strategic planning, because uncertainty is great and decisions are complex. Decisions to build a new factory, develop a new product or service, enter a new geographical market, or relocate headquarters to another city are all nonprogrammed decisions. One good example of a nonprogrammed decision is Exxon Mobil's decision to form a consortium to drill for oil in Siberia. One of the largest foreign investments in Russia, the consortium committed $4.5 billion before pumping the first barrel and expects a total capital cost of $12 billion-plus. The venture could produce 250,000 barrels a day, about 10 percent of Exxon Mobil's global production. But if things go wrong,

decision A choice made from available alternatives.

decision making The process of identifying problems and opportunities and then resolving them.

programmed decision A decision made in response to a situation that has occurred often enough to enable decision rules to be developed and applied in the future.

nonprogrammed decision A decision made in response to a situation that is unique, is poorly defined and largely unstructured, and has important consequences for the organization.

the oil giant, which has already invested some $4 billion, will take a crippling hit. At General Motors, top executives are facing multiple, enormously complex nonprogrammed decisions. The company has been rapidly losing market share, and 2005 losses totaled $10.6 billion. The giant corporation is also subject to six Securities and Exchange Commission probes, is entangled in the impending bankruptcy of its largest supplier, Delphi, and is burdened by massive health care and unionized labor costs. Top GM executives have to analyze complex problems, evaluate alternatives, and make decisions about the best way to reverse GM's sagging fortunes and keep the company out of bankruptcy.[6]

Go to the ethical dilemma on page 297 that pertains to making nonprogrammed decisions.

■ **TAKE A MOMENT**

Certainty, Risk, Uncertainty, and Ambiguity

One primary difference between programmed and nonprogrammed decisions relates to the degree of certainty or uncertainty that managers deal with in making the decision. In a perfect world, managers would have all the information necessary for making decisions. In reality, however, some things are unknowable; thus, some decisions will fail to solve the problem or attain the desired outcome. Managers try to obtain information about decision alternatives that will reduce decision uncertainty. Every decision situation can be organized on a scale according to the availability of information and the possibility of failure. The four positions on the scale are certainty, risk, uncertainty, and ambiguity, as illustrated in Exhibit 9.1. Whereas programmed decisions can be made in situations involving certainty, many situations that managers deal with every day involve at least some degree of uncertainty and require nonprogrammed decision making.

CERTAINTY

Certainty means that all the information the decision maker needs is fully available.[7] Managers have information on operating conditions, resource costs or constraints, and each course of action and possible outcome. For example, if a company considers a $10,000 investment in new equipment that it knows for certain will yield $4,000 in cost savings per year over the next five years, managers can calculate a before-tax

certainty The situation in which all the information the decision maker needs is fully available.

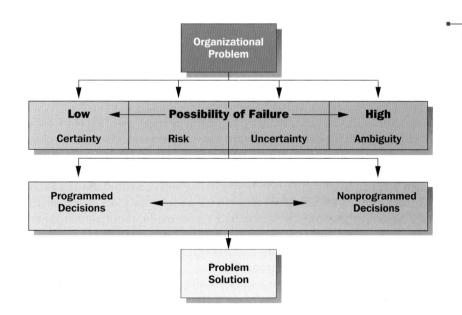

E X H I B I T   9.1

Conditions That Affect the Possibility of Decision Failure

© GREGORY BULL/ASSOCIATED PRESS

CONCEPT
CONNECTION "Why in God's name would you ever put that guy on the air?" That's the question Sirius Satellite System's board chairperson Joseph Clayton remembers his neighbors asking. They were reacting to Sirius's five-year, $500 million deal with shock jock Howard Stern. It was one of a series of controversial moves designed to develop programming the company hopes will enable it to overtake competitor XM Satellite Radio. Managers felt comfortable with the degree of **risk** involved in the **nonprogrammed decision.** Clayton calculated that if Stern persuaded just one million of his estimated 12 million "terrestrial" listeners to subscribe to Sirius, the gamble would pay off.

rate of return of about 40 percent. If managers compare this investment with one that will yield only $3,000 per year in cost savings, they can confidently select the 40 percent return. However, few decisions are certain in the real world. Most contain risk or uncertainty.

RISK

Risk means that a decision has clear-cut goals and that good information is available, but the future outcomes associated with each alternative are subject to chance. However, enough information is available to allow the probability of a successful outcome for each alternative to be estimated.[8] Statistical analysis might be used to calculate the probabilities of success or failure. The measure of risk captures the possibility that future events will render the alternative unsuccessful. For example, to make restaurant location decisions, McDonald's can analyze potential customer demographics, traffic patterns, supply logistics, and the local competition and come up with reasonably good forecasts of how successful a restaurant will be in each possible location.[9]

UNCERTAINTY

Uncertainty means that managers know which goals they wish to achieve, but information about alternatives and future events is incomplete. Managers do not have enough information to be clear about alternatives or to estimate their risk. Factors that may affect a decision, such as price, production costs, volume, or future interest rates are difficult to analyze and predict. Managers may have to make assumptions from which to forge the decision even though it will be wrong if the assumptions are incorrect. Managers may have to come up with creative approaches to alternatives and use personal judgment to determine which alternative is best.

Managers at Wolters Kluwer, a leader in online information services based in The Netherlands, faced uncertainty as they considered ways to spark growth. The company had historically grown through acquisition, but that strategy had reached its limit. CEO Nancy McKinstry and other top managers talked with customers, analyzed the industry and Wolters Kluwer's market position and capabilities, and decided to shift the company toward growing through internal development of new products and services. Wolters Kluwer didn't have a track record in internal growth, and analysts were skeptical. Decisions about how to finance the internal development were complex and unclear, involving such considerations as staff reductions, restructuring of departments and divisions, and shifting operations to lower-cost facilities. Furthermore, decisions had to be made about which new and existing products to fund and at what levels.[10] These decisions and others like them have no clear-cut solutions and require that managers rely on creativity, judgment, intuition, and experience to craft a response.

Many decisions made under uncertainty do not produce the desired results, but managers face uncertainty every day. They find creative ways to cope with uncertainty in order to make more effective decisions.

risk A situation in which a decision has clear-cut goals and good information is available, but the future outcomes associated with each alternative are subject to chance.

uncertainty The situation that occurs when managers know which goals they wish to achieve, but information about alternatives and future events is incomplete.

AMBIGUITY

Ambiguity is by far the most difficult decision situation. Ambiguity means that the goals to be achieved or the problem to be solved is unclear, alternatives are difficult to define, and information about outcomes is unavailable.[11] Ambiguity is what students would feel if an instructor created student groups, told each group to complete a project, but gave the groups no topic, direction, or guidelines whatsoever. Ambiguity has been called a *wicked decision problem*. Managers have a difficult time coming to grips with the issues. Wicked problems are associated with manager conflicts over goals and decision alternatives, rapidly changing circumstances, fuzzy information, and unclear linkages among decision elements.[12] Sometimes managers will come up with a "solution" only to realize that they hadn't clearly defined the real problem to begin with.[13] One example of a wicked decision problem was when managers at Ford Motor Company and Firestone confronted the problem of tires used on the Ford Explorer coming apart on the road, causing deadly blowouts and rollovers. Just defining the problem and whether the tire itself or the design of the Explorer was at fault was the first hurdle. Information was fuzzy and fast-changing, and managers were in conflict over how to handle the problem. Neither side dealt effectively with this decision situation and the reputations of both companies suffered as a result. Fortunately, most decisions are not characterized by ambiguity. But when they are, managers must conjure up goals and develop reasonable scenarios for decision alternatives in the absence of information.

> As a new manager, consider the degree of risk, uncertainty, or ambiguity in a specific decision you face. Develop decision rules for programmed decisions and let other people handle the decisions. Save your time and energy for coping with complex, nonprogrammed decisions.

■ TAKE A MOMENT

DECISION-MAKING MODELS

The approach managers use to make decisions usually falls into one of three types—the classical model, the administrative model, or the political model. The choice of model depends on the manager's personal preference, whether the decision is programmed or nonprogrammed, and the extent to which the decision is characterized by risk, uncertainty, or ambiguity.

Classical Model

The **classical model** of decision making is based on economic assumptions. This model has arisen within the management literature because managers are expected to make decisions that are economically sensible and in the organization's best economic interests. The four assumptions underlying this model are as follows:

1. The decision maker operates to accomplish goals that are known and agreed upon. Problems are precisely formulated and defined.

2. The decision maker strives for conditions of certainty, gathering complete information. All alternatives and the potential results of each are calculated.

3. Criteria for evaluating alternatives are known. The decision maker selects the alternative that will maximize the economic return to the organization.

4. The decision maker is rational and uses logic to assign values, order preferences, evaluate alternatives, and make the decision that will maximize the attainment of organizational goals.

The classical model of decision making is considered to be **normative**, which means it defines how a decision maker *should* make decisions. It does not describe how managers actually make decisions so much as it provides guidelines on how to

275

Chapter 9 MANAGERIAL DECISION MAKING

ambiguity A condition in which the goals to be achieved or the problem to be solved is unclear, alternatives are difficult to define, and information about outcomes is unavailable.

classical model A decision-making model based on the assumption that managers should make logical decisions that will be in the organization's best economic interests.

normative An approach that defines how a decision maker should make decisions and provides guidelines for reaching an ideal outcome for the organization.

reach an ideal outcome for the organization. The value of the classical model has been its ability to help decision makers be more rational. Many managers rely solely on intuition and personal preferences for making decisions.[14] For example, during this era of rising medical costs, decisions in hospitals and medical centers about who gets scarce resources such as expensive procedures and drugs are usually made on an ad hoc basis. Administrators at the University of Texas Medical Branch, however, are using the classical model to provide some clear guidelines and rules that can be consistently applied. A committee of administrators, doctors, and mid-level staffers codified a top-to-bottom system for allocating medical services. Patients without insurance must pay up front to see a doctor. Strict rules bar expensive drugs being given to patients who can't pay for them. Screeners see patients as soon as they come in and follow clear, rational procedures for determining who is eligible for what services. A special fund can pay for drugs that are off-limits to poor patients, but approval has to come from the chief medical director, who often uses cost-benefit analysis to make her decisions. The hospital's rationing system is controversial. However, top managers argue that it helps the institution impartially care for the poor at the same time it adheres to rational budget restrictions needed to keep the institution financially solid.[15]

In many respects, the classical model represents an "ideal" model of decision making that is often unattainable by real people in real organizations. It is most valuable when applied to programmed decisions and to decisions characterized by certainty or risk, because relevant information is available and probabilities can be calculated. For example, new analytical software programs automate many programmed decisions, such as freezing the account of a customer who has failed to make payments, determining the cellular phone service plan that is most appropriate for a particular customer, or sorting insurance claims so that cases are handled most efficiently.[16] Airlines use automated systems to optimize seat pricing, flight scheduling, and crew assignment decisions. GE Energy Rentals uses a system that captures financial and organizational information about customers to help managers evaluate risks and make credit decisions. The system has enabled the division to reduce costs, increase processing time, and improve cash flow. In the retail industry, software programs analyze current and historical sales data to help companies such as The Home Depot and Gap decide when, where, and how much to mark down prices.[17] This chapter's Unlocking Innovative Solutions Through Technology box describes how Southwest Airlines uses quantitative models to help keep costs low and retain its position as the low-cost leader.

The growth of quantitative decision techniques that use computers has expanded the use of the classical approach. Quantitative techniques include such things as decision trees, payoff matrices, break-even analysis, linear programming, forecasting, and operations research models. The NBC television network uses a computer-based system to create optimum advertising schedules.

NBC

For television viewers, news and entertainment is the primary function of the NBC network. But for NBC managers, one of the biggest concerns is optimizing the advertising schedule. Each year, managers have to develop a detailed advertising plan and a schedule that meets advertisers' desires in terms of cost, target audience, program mix, and other factors. At the same time, the schedule has to get the most revenues for the available amount of inventory (advertising slots).

Creating an advertising plan and schedule can be extremely complex, with numerous decision constraints and variables, such as product conflict restraints, airtime availability restraints, client requirements, or management restrictions. NBC offices use a computerized system that quickly and efficiently makes optimal use of advertising slots. When an advertiser makes a request, planners enter all the information into the system, including the budgeted amount the customer is willing to pay for a total package of commercials, the number of people the advertiser wants to reach, the targeted demographic characteristics, how the budget is to be distributed over four quarters of the year, the number of weeks in the program year, the unit lengths of commercials, the specific shows the advertiser is interested in, and so forth. Management ranks the shows and weeks of the year by their

SOUTHWEST USES TECHNOLOGY TO KEEP A HAWK'S EYE ON COSTS

Could things get any worse for the large U.S. air carriers? Already riding out the worst slump in the industry's history and fighting a host of new low-cost competitors, airlines were devastated by a spike in jet fuel prices following the Gulf Coast hurricanes to well over $100 a barrel. In 2005, the industry posted a net loss of $5.7 billion, and both Delta and Northwest were finally pushed into bankruptcy. Yet Southwest Airlines rode out the turbulent times in style. In 2005, Southwest saw net profits of $548 million, up sharply from $313 million in 2004. Southwest's wacky, people-oriented culture has often been cited as a key factor in the company's success. But managers point out that keeping a hawk's eye on costs is just as much a part of the culture as silliness and fun.

One way managers keep a lid on costs is by applying technology to support decision making. Consider the use of a new breed of simulation software to help make decisions about the airline's freight operations. BiosGroup, a joint venture between Santa Fe Institute biologist Stuart Kauffman and the consulting firm Cap Gemini Ernst & Young, uses adaptive, agent-based computer modeling to help companies like Southwest and Procter & Gamble solve complex business problems. For the Southwest project, the computer simulation model represented individual baggage handlers and other employees; the model was created to see how thousands of individual day-to-day decisions and interactions determined the behavior of the airline's overall freight operation.

A BiosGroup team spent many hours interviewing all the employees whose jobs related to freight handling. Then, they programmed the computer to simulate the people in the freight house who accepted a customer's package, those who figured out which flight the package should go on, those on the ramp who were loading the planes, and so forth. When the computer ran a simulation of a week's worth of freight operations, various aspects of operations were measured—such as how many times employees had to load and unload cargo or how often freight had to be stored overnight. The simulation indicated that, rather than unloading cargo from incoming flights and putting it on the next direct flight to its destination, Southwest would be better off to just let the freight take the long way around. Paradoxically, this approach turned out to usually get the freight to its destination faster and saved the time and cost of unloading and reloading.

Southwest managers lost no time in implementing the decision to change the freight handling system. By applying technology to find a more efficient way of doing things, Southwest is saving an estimated $10 million over 5 years. Now that's one way to become the most profitable airline in the country.

SOURCES: Mitchell Waldrop, "Chaos, Inc.," *Red Herring* (January 2003): 38–40; Andy Serwer, "Southwest Airlines: The Hottest Thing in the Sky," *Fortune* (March 8, 2004): 86–106; Perry Flint, "The Darkest Hour," *Air Transport World* (December 2005): 52–53; *Southwest Airlines 2005 Annual Report,* www.southwest.com/investor_relations/swaar05.pdf; and John Heimlich, "State of the Industry Q&A," Air Transport Association of America, Inc. (April 11, 2006), www.airlines.org/econ/d.aspx?nid=9630.

importance, and these data are also entered into the system, along with the availability of advertising slots during each week and other constraints. The system formulates an advertising plan that uses the least amount of premium inventory subject to meeting client requirements.

By using the classical approach, NBC generates optimal plans that meet the advertiser's needs while at the same time saving millions of dollars of premium inventory, which can be used to lure new advertisers who will pay high fees to advertise on the hottest shows.[18]

Administrative Model

The **administrative model** of decision making describes how managers actually make decisions in difficult situations, such as those characterized by nonprogrammed decisions, uncertainty, and ambiguity. Many management decisions are not sufficiently programmable to lend themselves to any degree of quantification. Managers are unable to make economically rational decisions even if they want to.[19]

administrative model A decision-making model that describes how managers actually make decisions in situations characterized by nonprogrammed decisions, uncertainty, and ambiguity.

BOUNDED RATIONALITY AND SATISFICING

The administrative model of decision making is based on the work of Herbert A. Simon. Simon proposed two concepts that were instrumental in shaping the administrative model: bounded rationality and satisficing. **Bounded rationality** means that people have limits, or boundaries, on how rational they can be. The organization is incredibly complex, and managers have the time and ability to process only a limited amount of information with which to make decisions.[20] Because managers do not have the time or cognitive ability to process complete information about complex decisions, they must satisfice. **Satisficing** means that decision makers choose the first solution alternative that satisfies minimal decision criteria. Rather than pursuing all alternatives to identify the single solution that will maximize economic returns, managers will opt for the first solution that appears to solve the problem, even if better solutions are presumed to exist. The decision maker cannot justify the time and expense of obtaining complete information.[21]

An example of both bounded rationality and satisficing occurs when a manager on a business trip spills coffee on her blouse just before an important meeting. She will run to a nearby clothing store and buy the first satisfactory replacement she finds. Having neither the time nor the opportunity to explore all the blouses in town, she satisfices by choosing a blouse that will solve the immediate problem. In a similar fashion, managers sometimes generate alternatives for complex problems only until they find one they believe will work. For example, several years ago, then-CEO William Smithburg of Quaker attempted to thwart takeover attempts but had limited options. He satisficed with a quick decision to acquire Snapple, thinking he could use the debt acquired in the deal to discourage a takeover. The acquisition had the potential to solve the problem at hand; thus, Smithburg looked no further for possibly better alternatives.[22]

The administrative model relies on assumptions different from those of the classical model and focuses on organizational factors that influence individual decisions. It is more realistic than the classical model for complex, nonprogrammed decisions. According to the administrative model:

1. Decision goals often are vague, conflicting, and lack consensus among managers. Managers often are unaware of problems or opportunities that exist in the organization.

2. Rational procedures are not always used, and, when they are, they are confined to a simplistic view of the problem that does not capture the complexity of real organizational events.

3. Managers' searches for alternatives are limited because of human, information, and resource constraints.

4. Most managers settle for a satisficing rather than a maximizing solution, partly because they have limited information and partly because they have only vague criteria for what constitutes a maximizing solution.

The administrative model is considered to be **descriptive**, meaning that it describes how managers actually make decisions in complex situations rather than dictating how they *should* make decisions according to a theoretical ideal. The administrative model recognizes the human and environmental limitations that affect the degree to which managers can pursue a rational decision-making process.

bounded rationality The concept that people have the time and cognitive ability to process only a limited amount of information on which to base decisions.

satisficing To choose the first solution alternative that satisfies minimal decision criteria, regardless of whether better solutions are presumed to exist.

descriptive An approach that describes how managers actually make decisions rather than how they should.

■ TAKE A MOMENT

As a new manager, choose the right decision approach. Use the classical model when problems are clear-cut, goals are agreed upon, and clear information is available. For the classical model, use analytical procedures, including new software programs, to calculate the potential results of each alternative. When goals are vague or conflicting, decision time is limited, and information is unclear, use bounded rationality, satisficing, and intuition for decision making.

INTUITION

Another aspect of administrative decision making is intuition. **Intuition** represents a quick apprehension of a decision situation based on past experience but without conscious thought.[23] Intuitive decision making is not arbitrary or irrational, because it is based on years of practice and hands-on experience that enable managers to quickly identify solutions without going through painstaking computations. In today's fast-paced, turbulent business environment, intuition plays an increasingly important role in decision making. A survey of managers conducted by Christian and Timbers found that nearly half of executives say they rely more on intuition than on rational analysis to run their companies.[24]

Cognitive psychologist Gary Klein studied how people make good decisions using their intuition under extreme time pressure and uncertainty.[25] Klein found that intuition begins with *recognition*. When people build a depth of experience and knowledge in a particular area, the right decision often comes quickly and effortlessly as a recognition of information that has been largely forgotten by the conscious mind. For example, firefighters make decisions by recognizing what is typical or abnormal about a fire, based on their experience. Similarly, in the business world, managers continuously perceive and process information that they may not consciously be aware of, and their base of knowledge and experience helps them make decisions that may be characterized by uncertainty and ambiguity.

Research by a growing number of psychologists and neuroscientists affirms the power of our unconscious minds in making decisions. Studies of intuition indicate that the unconscious mind has cognitive abilities that sometimes surpass those of the conscious mind.[26] Howard Shultz turned Starbucks into a household name by following his intuition that the leisurely *caffe* model he observed in Italy would work in the United States. Jerry Jones based his decision to buy the losing Dallas Cowboys on intuition, then made a series of further intuitive decisions that turned the team back into a winner.[27] Another example comes from the Fox television network, where prime time ratings were dismal until Steven Chao came up with *America's Most Wanted* and *Cops*. Initially, everyone hated the idea of these raw, crime-oriented shows, but Chao and his boss Barry Diller stuck with their gut feelings and pushed the projects.[28]

However, many other examples show intuitive decisions that failed, and recent scholarly studies emphasize that managers should take a cautious approach, applying intuition under the right circumstances and in the right way rather than considering it a magical way to make important decisions.[29] Managers may walk a fine line between two extremes: on the one hand, making arbitrary decisions without careful study, and on the other, relying obsessively on rational analysis. One is not better than the other, and managers need to take a balanced approach by considering both rationality and intuition as important components of effective decision making.[30]

intuition The immediate comprehension of a decision situation based on past experience but without conscious thought.

Political Model

The third model of decision making is useful for making nonprogrammed decisions when conditions are uncertain, information is limited, and managers may disagree about what goals to pursue or what course of action to take. Most organizational decisions involve many

© STAN GODLEWSKI PHOTOGRAPHY

CONCEPT CONNECTION "Lots of people hear what I'm doing and think, 'That's a crazy idea!'" says Russell Simmons. The successful entrepreneur, who heads the New York-based media firm, Rush Communications Inc., has relied on his **intuition** to build a half-billion dollar empire on one profitable "crazy idea" after another. It all began with his belief that he could go mainstream with the vibrant rap music he heard in African American neighborhoods. In 1983, he started the pioneering hip-hop Def Jam record label, launching the careers of Beastie Boys, LL Cool J, and Run-DMC, among others. He's since moved on to successful ventures in fashion, media, consumer products, and finance.

managers who are pursuing different goals, and they have to talk with one another to share information and reach an agreement. Managers often engage in coalition building for making complex organizational decisions. A **coalition** is an informal alliance among managers who support a specific goal. *Coalition building* is the process of forming alliances among managers. In other words, a manager who supports a specific alternative, such as increasing the corporation's growth by acquiring another company, talks informally to other executives and tries to persuade them to support the decision. When the outcomes are not predictable, managers gain support through discussion, negotiation, and bargaining. Without a coalition, a powerful individual or group could derail the decision-making process. Coalition building gives several managers an opportunity to contribute to decision making, enhancing their commitment to the alternative that is ultimately adopted.[31]

The political model closely resembles the real environment in which most managers and decision makers operate. For example, interviews with CEOs in high-tech industries found that they strived to use some type of rational process in making decisions, but the way they actually decided things was through a complex interaction with other managers, subordinates, environmental factors, and organizational events.[32] Decisions are complex and involve many people, information is often ambiguous, and disagreement and conflict over problems and solutions are normal. The political model begins with four basic assumptions:

1. Organizations are made up of groups with diverse interests, goals, and values. Managers disagree about problem priorities and may not understand or share the goals and interests of other managers.

2. Information is ambiguous and incomplete. The attempt to be rational is limited by the complexity of many problems as well as personal and organizational constraints.

3. Managers do not have the time, resources, or mental capacity to identify all dimensions of the problem and process all relevant information. Managers talk to each other and exchange viewpoints to gather information and reduce ambiguity.

4. Managers engage in the push and pull of debate to decide goals and discuss alternatives. Decisions are the result of bargaining and discussion among coalition members.

An example of the political model was when AOL chief executive Jonathan Miller built a coalition to support the development of a Yahoo-like free Web site. Opposition to offering AOL's rich content for free was strong, but Miller talked with other executives and formed a coalition that supported the move as the best way to rejuvenate the declining AOL in the shifting Internet service business. The decision proved to be a turning point, making AOL once more a relevant force on the Web and enticing tech titans such as Google and Microsoft as potential partners.[33]

The inability of leaders to build coalitions often makes it difficult or impossible for managers to get their decisions implemented. Hershell Ezrin resigned as CEO of Canada's Speedy Muffler King because he was unable to build a coalition of managers who supported his decisions for change at the troubled company. Many senior-level executives resented Ezrin's appointment and refused to go along with his ideas for reviving the company.[34] Similarly, former U.S. Treasury Secretary Lawrence Summers took the job as president of Harvard University in 2001 with plans for shaking up many of the university's longtime ways of doing things. However, his inability to build a coalition to support his changes led Summers to resign five years later with the campus in turmoil and few of his desired changes effectively implemented.[35]

The key dimensions of the classical, administrative, and political models are listed in Exhibit 9.2. Recent research into decision-making procedures found rational, classical procedures to be associated with high performance for organizations in stable environments. However, administrative and political decision-making

coalition An informal alliance among managers who support a specific goal.

Classical Model	Administrative Model	Political Model
Clear-cut problem and goals	Vague problem and goals	Pluralistic; conflicting goals
Condition of certainty	Condition of uncertainty	Condition of uncertainty/ambiguity
Full information about alternatives and their outcomes	Limited information about alternatives and their outcomes	Inconsistent viewpoints; ambiguous information
Rational choice by individual for maximizing outcomes	Satisficing choice for resolving problem using intuition	Bargaining and discussion among coalition members

E X H I B I T   **9.2**

Characteristics of Classical, Administrative, and Political Decision-Making Models

procedures and intuition have been associated with high performance in unstable environments in which decisions must be made rapidly and under more difficult conditions.[36]

TAKE A MOMENT

As a new manager, use your political skills to reach a decision in the midst of disagreement about goals or problem solutions. Talk with other managers or employees and negotiate to gain support for the goal or solution you favor. Learn to compromise and to support others when appropriate.

DECISION-MAKING STEPS

Whether a decision is programmed or nonprogrammed and regardless of managers' choice of the classical, administrative, or political model of decision making, six steps typically are associated with effective decision processes. These steps are summarized in Exhibit 9.3.

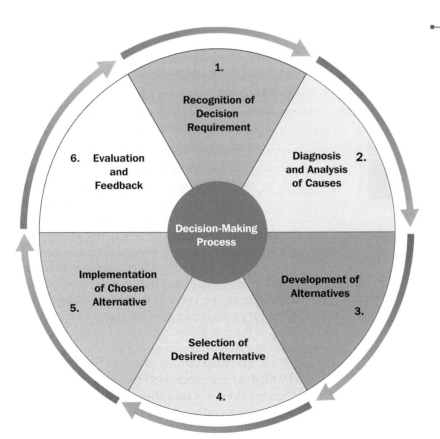

E X H I B I T   **9.3**

Six Steps in the Managerial Decision-Making Process

Recognition of Decision Requirement

Managers confront a decision requirement in the form of either a problem or an opportunity. A **problem** occurs when organizational accomplishment is less than established goals. Some aspect of performance is unsatisfactory. An **opportunity** exists when managers see potential accomplishment that exceeds specified current goals. Managers see the possibility of enhancing performance beyond current levels.

Awareness of a problem or opportunity is the first step in the decision sequence and requires surveillance of the internal and external environment for issues that merit executive attention.[37] This process resembles the military concept of gathering intelligence. Managers scan the world around them to determine whether the organization is satisfactorily progressing toward its goals.

Some information comes from periodic financial reports, performance reports, and other sources that are designed to discover problems before they become too serious. Managers also take advantage of informal sources. They talk to other managers, gather opinions on how things are going, and seek advice on which problems should be tackled or which opportunities embraced.[38] Recognizing decision requirements is difficult, because it often means integrating bits and pieces of information in novel ways. For example, the failure of U.S. intelligence leaders to recognize the imminent threat of Al Qaeda prior to September 11, 2001, terrorist attacks has been attributed partly to the lack of systems that could help leaders put together myriad snippets of information that pointed to the problem.[39]

problem A situation in which organizational accomplishments have failed to meet established goals.

opportunity A situation in which managers see potential organizational accomplishments that exceed current goals.

diagnosis The step in the decision-making process in which managers analyze underlying causal factors associated with the decision situation.

© DON MURRAY/GETTY IMAGES

CONCEPT CONNECTION Jon Bon Jovi is a rock star and entrepreneur, who co-owns the Philadelphia Soul, an expansion team of the Arena Football League (AFL). Bon Jovi and his partner, businessman Craig Spencer, spotted an **opportunity** to capitalize on Bon Jovi's personality and fame, as well as his savvy marketing skills, by acquiring the franchise. Bon Jovi personally made decisions such as naming the team the Soul (because "anybody can have soul," he says) and creating a mascot (the Soul Man), and he is actively involved in decisions regarding everything from advertising budgets to where to place the autograph tables after a game. Today, the Soul leads the AFL in ticket sales, advertising sales, and merchandising revenue.

Diagnosis and Analysis of Causes

Once a problem or opportunity comes to a manager's attention, the understanding of the situation should be refined. **Diagnosis** is the step in the decision-making process in which managers analyze underlying causal factors associated with the decision situation. Managers make a mistake here if they jump right into generating alternatives without first exploring the cause of the problem more deeply.

Kepner and Tregoe, who conducted extensive studies of manager decision making, recommend that managers ask a series of questions to specify underlying causes, including the following:

:: What is the state of disequilibrium affecting us?

:: When did it occur?

:: Where did it occur?

:: How did it occur?

:: To whom did it occur?

:: What is the urgency of the problem?

:: What is the interconnectedness of events?

:: What result came from which activity?[40]

Such questions help specify what actually happened and why. Managers at General Motors are struggling to diagnose the underlying factors in the company's recent troubles. The problem is an urgent one, with sales, profits, market share, and the stock price all plummeting and the giant corporation on the verge of bankruptcy. Managers are examining the multitude of problems facing GM, tracing the pattern of the decline, and looking at the interconnectedness of issues such as changing consumer tastes in vehicles, surging gas prices that make trucks and SUVs less appealing, the rising burden of retiree benefits promised to workers in more profitable times, increased competition and the growth of auto manufacturing in low-cost countries such as China, excess factory capacity and high costs, poor headquarters planning, and weak control systems that allowed the company to drift further and further into crisis.[41]

Development of Alternatives

Once the problem or opportunity has been recognized and analyzed, decision makers begin to consider taking action. The next stage is to generate possible alternative solutions that will respond to the needs of the situation and correct the underlying causes. Studies find that limiting the search for alternatives is a primary cause of decision failure in organizations.[42]

For a programmed decision, feasible alternatives are easy to identify and in fact usually are already available within the organization's rules and procedures. Non-programmed decisions, however, require developing new courses of action that will meet the company's needs. For decisions made under conditions of high uncertainty, managers may develop only one or two custom solutions that will satisfice for handling the problem.

Decision alternatives can be thought of as the tools for reducing the difference between the organization's current and desired performance. For example, to improve sales at fast-food giant McDonald's, executives considered alternatives such as using mystery shoppers and unannounced inspections to improve quality and service, motivating demoralized franchisees to get them to invest in new equipment and programs, taking R&D out of the test kitchen and encouraging franchisees to help come up with successful new menu items, and closing some stores to avoid cannibalizing its own sales.[43]

Selection of Desired Alternative

Once feasible alternatives are developed, one must be selected. The decision choice is the selection of the most promising of several alternative courses of action. The best alternative is one in which the solution best fits the overall goals and values of the organization and achieves the desired results using the fewest resources.[44] The manager tries to select the choice with the least amount of risk and uncertainty. Because some risk is inherent for most nonprogrammed decisions, managers try to gauge prospects for success. Under conditions of uncertainty, they might rely on their intuition and experience to estimate whether a given course of action is likely to succeed. Basing choices on overall goals and values can also effectively guide selection of alternatives. Recall from Chapter 3 Valero Energy's decision to keep everyone on the payroll after Hurricane Katrina hit the Gulf Coast, while other refineries shut down and laid off workers. For Valero managers, the choice was easy based on values of putting employees first. Valero's values-based decision making helped the company zoom from Number 23 to Number 3 on *Fortune* magazine's list of best companies to work for—and enabled Valero to get back to business weeks faster than competitors.[45]

Choosing among alternatives also depends on managers' personality factors and willingness to accept risk and uncertainty. For example, **risk propensity** is the willingness to undertake risk with the opportunity of gaining an increased payoff. The level of risk a manager is willing to accept will influence the analysis of cost and benefits to be derived from any decision. Consider the situations in Exhibit 9.4.

risk propensity The willingness to undertake risk with the opportunity of gaining an increased payoff.

EXHIBIT 9.4

Decision Alternatives with Different Levels of Risk

For each of the following decisions, which alternative would you choose?

1. In the final seconds of a game with the college's traditional rival, the coach of a college football team may choose a play that has a 95 percent chance of producing a tie score or one with a 30 percent chance of leading to victory or to sure defeat if it fails.

2. The president of a Canadian company must decide whether to build a new plant within Canada that has a 90 percent chance of producing a modest return on investment or to build it in a foreign country with an unstable political history. The latter alternative has a 40 percent chance of failing, but the returns would be enormous if it succeeded.

3. A college senior with considerable acting talent must choose a career. She has the opportunity to go on to medical school and become a physician, a career in which she is 80 percent likely to succeed. She would rather be an actress but realizes that the opportunity for success is only 20 percent.

DECISION BIASES TO AVOID

At a time when decision making is so important, many managers do not know how to make a good choice among alternatives. They might rely on computer analysis or personal intuition without realizing that their own cognitive biases affect their judgment. Many errors in judgment originate in the human mind's limited capacity and in the natural biases most managers display during decision making. Awareness of the following six biases can help managers make more enlightened choices:

1. *Being influenced by initial impressions.* When considering decisions, the mind often gives disproportionate weight to the first information it receives. These initial impressions, statistics, or estimates act as an anchor to our subsequent thoughts and judgments. Anchors can be as simple as a random comment by a colleague or a statistic read in a newspaper. Past events and trends also act as anchors. For example, in business, managers frequently look at the previous year's sales when estimating sales for the coming year. Giving too much weight to the past can lead to poor forecasts and misguided decisions.

2. *Justifying past decisions.* Many people fall into the trap of making choices that justify their past decisions, even if those decisions no longer seem valid. Consider that many managers invest tremendous time and energy into improving the performance of a problem employee whom they now realize should never have been hired in the first place. Another example is when a manager continues to pour money into a failing project, hoping to turn things around. People don't like to make mistakes, so they continue to make flawed decisions in an effort to correct the past.

3. *Seeing what you want to see.* People frequently look for information that supports their existing instinct or point of view and avoid information that contradicts it. This bias affects where managers look for information, as well as how they interpret the information they find. People tend to give too much weight to supporting information and too little to information that conflicts with their established viewpoints. It is important for managers to be honest with themselves about their motives and to examine all the evidence with equal rigor. Having a devil's advocate to argue against a decision can also help avoid this decision trap.

4. *Perpetuating the status quo.* Managers may base decisions on what has worked in the past and fail to explore new options, dig for additional information, or investigate new technologies. For example, DuPont clung to its cash cow, nylon, despite growing evidence in the scientific community that a new product, polyester, was superior for tire cords. Celanese, a relatively small competitor, blew DuPont out of the water by exploiting this new evidence, quickly capturing 75 percent of the tire market.

5. *Being influenced by problem framing.* The decision response of a manager can be influenced by the mere wording of a problem. For example, consider a manager faced with a decision about salvaging the cargo of three barges that sank off the coast of Alaska. If managers are given the option of approving plan (A) that has a 100 percent chance of saving the cargo of one of the three barges, worth $200,000, or plan (B) that has a one-third chance of saving the cargo of all three barges, worth $600,000 and a two-thirds chance of saving nothing, most managers choose option A. The same problem with a negative frame would give managers a choice of selecting plan (C) that has a 100 percent chance of losing two of the three cargoes, worth $400,000, or plan (D) that has a two-thirds chance of losing all three cargoes but a one-third chance of losing no cargo. With this framing, most managers choose option (D). Because both problems are identical, the decision choice depends strictly on how the problem is framed.

6. *Overconfidence.* Most people overestimate their ability to predict uncertain outcomes. Before making a decision, managers have unrealistic expectations of their ability to understand the risk and make the right choice. Overconfidence is greatest when answering questions of moderate to extreme difficulty. For example, when people are asked to define quantities about which they have little direct knowledge ("What was Wal-Mart's 2005 revenue?" "What was the market value of Google as of March 14, 2006?"), they overestimate their accuracy. Evidence of overconfidence is illustrated in cases in which subjects were so certain of an answer that they assigned odds of 1,000 to 1 of being correct but in fact were correct only about 85 percent of the time. When uncertainty is high, managers may unrealistically expect that they can successfully predict outcomes and hence select the wrong alternative.

SOURCES: Based on John Hammond, Ralph L. Keeney, and Howard Raiffa, "The Hidden Traps in Decision Making," *Harvard Business Review* (September–October 1998): 47–58; Oren Harari, "The Thomas Lawson Syndrome," *Management Review* (February 1994): 58–61; Dan Ariely, "Q&A: Why Good CIOs Make Bad Decisions," *CIO* (May 1, 2003): 83–87; Leigh Buchanan, "How to Take Risks in a Time of Anxiety," *Inc.* (May 2003): 76–81; and Max H. Bazerman, *Judgment in Managerial Decision Making,* 5th ed. (New York: John Wiley & Sons, 2002).

In each situation, which alternative would you choose? A person with a low risk propensity would tend to take assured moderate returns by going for a tie score, building a domestic plant, or pursuing a career as a physician. A risk taker would go for the victory, build a plant in a foreign country, or embark on an acting career. This chapter's Manager's Shoptalk box describes biases to avoid when selecting the desired alternative.

Implementation of Chosen Alternative

The **implementation** stage involves the use of managerial, administrative, and persuasive abilities to ensure that the chosen alternative is carried out. This step is similar to the idea of strategic implementation described in Chapter 8. The ultimate success of the chosen alternative depends on whether it can be translated into action.[46] Sometimes an alternative never becomes reality because managers lack the resources or energy needed to make things happen. Implementation may require discussion with people affected by the decision. Communication, motivation, and leadership skills must be used to see that the decision is carried out. When employees see that managers follow up on their decisions by tracking implementation success, they are more committed to positive action.[47]

At Boeing Commercial Airplanes, CEO Alan R. Mulally engineered a remarkable turnaround by skillfully implementing decisions that reduced waste, streamlined production lines, and moved Boeing into breakthrough technologies for new planes.[48] If managers lack the ability or desire to implement decisions, the chosen alternative cannot be carried out to benefit the organization.

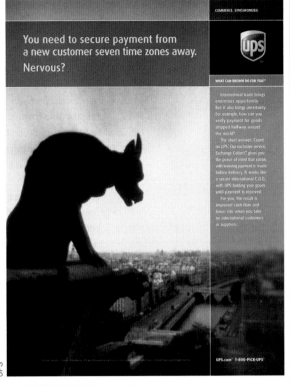

UPS

CONCEPT CONNECTION UPS knows many businesses have a low **risk propensity** when it comes to matters affecting their cash flow, so it spotted a business opportunity. The company's UPS Capital Insurance division reduces customers' risk of delayed payments through a variety of trade insurance policies. This advertisement for Exchange Collect promises peace of mind for companies dealing with international customers or suppliers. The service works like a secure international C.O.D., with UPS securing payment on behalf of the customer before delivering goods. For UPS customers, the results is improved cash flow and less risk.

Evaluation and Feedback

In the evaluation stage of the decision process, decision makers gather information that tells them how well the decision was implemented and whether it was effective in achieving its goals. For example, Tandy executives evaluated their decision to open computer centers for businesses and feedback revealed poor sales performance. Feedback indicated that implementation was unsuccessful, and computer centers were closed so Tandy could focus on its successful Radio Shack retail stores.

Feedback is important because decision making is a continuous, never-ending process. Decision making is not completed when an executive or board of directors votes yes or no. Feedback provides decision makers with information that can precipitate a new decision cycle. The decision may fail, thus generating a new analysis of the problem, evaluation of alternatives, and selection of a new alternative. Many big problems are solved by trying several alternatives in sequence, each providing modest improvement. Feedback is the part of monitoring that assesses whether a new decision needs to be made.

To illustrate the overall decision-making process, including evaluation and feedback, we can look at the decision to introduce a new deodorant at Tom's of Maine.

implementation The step in the decision-making process that involves using managerial, administrative, and persuasive abilities to translate the chosen alternative into action.

Tom's of Maine

Tom's of Maine, known for its all-natural personal hygiene products, saw an opportunity to expand its line with a new natural deodorant. However, the opportunity quickly became a problem when the deodorant worked only half of the time with half of the customers who used it, and its all-recyclable plastic dials were prone to breakage.

The problem of the failed deodorant led founder Tom Chappell and other managers to analyze and diagnose what went wrong. They finally determined that the company's product development process had run amok. The same group of merry product developers was responsible from conception to launch of the product. They were so attached to the product that they failed to test it properly or consider potential problems, becoming instead "a mutual admiration society." Managers considered several alternatives for solving the problem. The decision to publicly admit the problem and recall the deodorant was an easy one for Chappell, who runs his company on principles of fairness and honesty. Not only did the company apologize to its customers, but it also listened to their complaints and suggestions. Chappell himself helped answer calls and letters. Even though the recall cost the company $400,000 and led to a stream of negative publicity, it ultimately helped improve relationships with customers.

Evaluation and feedback also led Tom's of Maine to set up *acorn groups*, from which it hopes mighty oaks of successful products will grow. Acorn groups are cross-departmental teams that will shepherd new products from beginning to end. The cross-functional teams are a mechanism for catching problems—and new opportunities—that ordinarily would be missed. They pass on their ideas and findings to senior managers and the product-development team.

Tom's was able to turn a problem into an opportunity, thanks to evaluation and feedback. Not only did the disaster ultimately help the company solidify relationships with customers, but it also led to a formal mechanism for learning and sharing ideas—something the company did not have before.[49]

Tom's of Maine's decision illustrates all the decision steps, and the process ultimately ended in success. Strategic decisions always contain some risk, but feedback and follow-up decisions can help get companies back on track. By learning from their decision mistakes, managers and companies can turn problems into opportunities.

■ **TAKE A MOMENT**

Did you know that decision behavior differs markedly between new managers and successful senior executives? To understand how, complete the New Manager Self-Test on page 287.

PERSONAL DECISION FRAMEWORK

Imagine you were a manager at Tom's of Maine, Boeing Commercial Airplanes, a local movie theater, or the public library. How would you go about making important decisions that might shape the future of your department or company? So far we have discussed a number of factors that affect how managers make decisions. For example, decisions may be programmed or nonprogrammed, situations are characterized by various levels of uncertainty, and managers may use the classical, administrative, or political model of decision making. In addition, the decision-making process follows six recognized steps.

However, not all managers go about making decisions in the same way. In fact, significant differences distinguish the ways in which individual managers may approach problems and make decisions concerning them. These differences can be explained by the concept of personal **decision styles**. Exhibit 9.5 illustrates the role of personal style in the decision-making process. Personal decision style refers to distinctions among people with respect to how they perceive problems and make decisions. Research identified four major decision styles: directive, analytical, conceptual, and behavioral.[50]

1. The *directive style* is used by people who prefer simple, clear-cut solutions to problems. Managers who use this style often make decisions quickly because

decision styles Differences among people with respect to how they perceive problems and make decisions.

YOUR DECISION-MAKING BEHAVIOR

How do you make decisions? You probably make decisions automatically and without realizing that people have diverse decision-making behaviors, which they bring to management positions. Think back to how you make decisions in your personal, student, or work life, especially where other people are involved. Please answer whether each of the following items is Mostly True or Mostly False for you.

	Mostly True	Mostly False
1. I like to decide quickly and move on to the next thing.	____	____
2. I would use my authority to make the decision if certain I was right.	____	____
3. I appreciate decisiveness.	____	____
4. There is usually one correct solution to a problem.	____	____
5. I identify everyone who needs to be involved in the decision.	____	____
6. I explicitly seek conflicting perspectives.	____	____
7. I use discussion strategies to reach a solution.	____	____

	Mostly True	Mostly False
8. I look for different meanings when faced with a great deal of data.	____	____
9. I take time to reason things through and use systematic logic.	____	____

INTERPRETATION: New managers typically use a different decision behavior than seasoned executives. The decision behavior of a successful CEO may be almost the opposite of a first-level supervisor. The difference is due partly to the types of decisions and partly to learning what works at each level. New managers typically start out with a more directive, decisive, command-oriented behavior and gradually move toward more openness, diversity of viewpoints, and interactions with others as they move up the hierarchy.

SCORING: All 9 items in the list reflect appropriate decision-making behavior, but items 1–4 are more typical of new managers. Items 5–8 are typical of successful senior manager decision making. Item 9 is considered part of good decision making at all levels. If you checked Mostly True for three or four of items 1–4 and 9, consider yourself typical of a new manager. If you checked Mostly True for three or four of items 5–8 and 9, you are using behavior consistent with top managers. If you checked a similar number of both sets of items, your behavior is probably flexible and balanced.

EXHIBIT 9.5

Personal Decision Framework

Situation	Personal Decision Style	Decision Choice
• Programmed/nonprogrammed • Classical, administrative, political • Decision steps	• Directive • Analytical • Conceptual • Behavioral	• Best solution to problem

they do not like to deal with a lot of information and may consider only one or two alternatives. People who prefer the directive style generally are efficient and rational and prefer to rely on existing rules or procedures for making decisions.

2. Managers with an *analytical style* like to consider complex solutions based on as much data as they can gather. These individuals carefully consider alternatives and often base their decisions on objective, rational data from management control systems and other sources. They search for the best possible decision based on the information available.

3. People who tend toward a *conceptual style* also like to consider a broad amount of information. However, they are more socially oriented than those with an analytical style and like to talk to others about the problem and possible alternatives for solving it. Managers using a conceptual style consider many broad alternatives, rely on information from both people and systems, and like to solve problems creatively.

4. The *behavioral style* is often the style adopted by managers having a deep concern for others as individuals. Managers using this style like to talk to people one-on-one and understand their feelings about the problem and the effect of a given decision upon them. People with a behavioral style usually are concerned with the personal development of others and may make decisions that help others achieve their goals.

■ **TAKE A MOMENT** | To learn more about how you rate on these four styles, go to the experiential exercise on page 296 that evaluates your personal decision style. How does your decision style score relate to your score on the New Manager Self-Test?

Many managers have a dominant decision style. One example is Jeff Zucker at NBC Entertainment. Zucker uses a primarily conceptual style, which makes him well suited to the television industry. He consults with dozens of programmers about possible new shows and likes to consider many broad alternatives before making decisions.[51] However, managers frequently use several different styles or a combination of styles in making the varied decisions they confront daily. A manager might use a directive style for deciding on which printing company to use for new business cards, yet shift to a more conceptual style when handling an interdepartmental conflict. The most effective managers are able to shift among styles as needed to meet the situation. Being aware of one's dominant decision style can help a manager avoid making critical mistakes when his or her usual style may be inappropriate to the problem at hand.

INCREASING PARTICIPATION IN DECISION MAKING

Managers do make some decisions as individuals, but decision makers more often are part of a group. Indeed, major decisions in the business world rarely are made entirely by an individual. Effective decision making often depends on whether managers involve the right people in the right ways in helping to solve problems. One model that provides guidance for practicing managers was originally developed by Victor Vroom and Arthur Jago.[52]

The Vroom-Jago Model

The **Vroom-Jago model** helps a manager gauge the appropriate amount of participation by subordinates in making a specific decision. The model has three major components: leader participation styles, a set of diagnostic questions with which to analyze a decision situation, and a series of decision rules.

LEADER PARTICIPATION STYLES

Vroom-Jago model A model designed to help managers gauge the amount of subordinate participation in decision making.

The model employs five levels of subordinate participation in decision making, ranging from highly autocratic (leader decides alone) to highly democratic (leader delegates to group), as illustrated in Exhibit 9.6.[53] The exhibit shows five decision styles, starting with the leader making the decision alone (Decide); presenting the problem to subordinates individually for their suggestions and then making the

Area of Influence by Leader			Area of Freedom for Group	
Decide	**Consult Individually**	**Consult Group**	**Facilitate**	**Delegate**
You make the decision alone and either announce or sell it to the group. You may use your expertise in collecting information that you deem relevant to the problem from the group or others.	You present the problem to the group members individually, get their suggestions, and make the decision.	You present the problem to the group members in a meeting, get their suggestions, and then make the decision.	You present the problem to the group in a meeting. You act as facilitator, defining the problem to be solved and the boundaries within which the decision must be made. Your objective is to get concurrence on a decision. Above all, you take care to show that your ideas are not given any greater weight than those of others simply because of your position.	You permit the group to make the decision within prescribed limits. The group undertakes the identification and diagnosis of the problem, developing alternative procedures for solving it and deciding on one or more alternative solutions. While you play no direct role in the group's deliberations unless explicitly asked, your role is an important one behind the scenes, providing needed resources and encouragement.

decision (Consult Individually); presenting the problem to subordinates as a group, collectively obtaining their ideas and suggestions, then making the decision (Consult Group); sharing the problem with subordinates as a group and acting as a facilitator to help the group arrive at a decision (Facilitate); or delegating the problem and permitting the group to make the decision within prescribed limits (Delegate).

DIAGNOSTIC QUESTIONS

How does a manager decide which of the five decision styles to use? The appropriate degree of decision participation depends on a number of situational factors, such as the required level of decision quality, the level of leader or subordinate expertise, and the importance of having subordinates commit to the decision. Leaders can analyze the appropriate degree of participation by answering seven diagnostic questions.

1. *Decision significance: How significant is this decision for the project or organization?* If the quality of the decision is highly important to the success of the project or organization, the leader has to be actively involved.

2. *Importance of commitment: How important is subordinate commitment to carrying out the decision?* If implementation requires a high level of commitment to the decision, leaders should involve subordinates in the decision process.

3. *Leader expertise: What is the level of the leader's expertise in relation to the problem?* If the leader does not have a high amount of information, knowledge, or expertise, the leader should involve subordinates to obtain it.

4. *Likelihood of commitment: If the leader were to make the decision alone, would subordinates have high or low commitment to the decision?* If subordinates typically go along with whatever the leader decides, their involvement in the decision-making process will be less important.

5. *Group support for goals: What is the degree of subordinate support for the team's or organization's objectives at stake in this decision?* If subordinates have low support for the goals of the organization, the leader should not allow the group to make the decision alone.

EXHIBIT   9.6

Five Leader Participation Styles

SOURCE: Victor H. Vroom, "Leadership and the Decision-Making Process," *Organizational Dynamics* 28 no. 4 (Spring 2000): 82–94. This exhibit is Vroom's adaptation of Tannenbaum and Schmidt's Taxonomy. Used with permission.

6. *Group expertise: What is the level of group members' knowledge and expertise in relation to the problem?* If subordinates have a high level of expertise in relation to the problem, more responsibility for the decision can be delegated to them.

7. *Team competence: How skilled and committed are group members to working together as a team to solve problems?* When subordinates have high skills and high desire to work together cooperatively to solve problems, more responsibility for decision making can be delegated to them.

These questions seem detailed, but considering these seven situational factors can quickly narrow the options and point to the appropriate level of group participation in decision making.

SELECTING A DECISION STYLE

The decision matrix in Exhibit 9.7 allows a manager to adopt a participation style by answering the diagnostic questions in sequence. The manager enters the matrix at the left-hand side, at Problem Statement, and considers the seven situational questions in sequence from left to right, answering high (H) or low (L) to each one and avoiding crossing any horizontal lines. The first question would be: *How significant is this decision for the project or organization?* If the answer is High, the leader proceeds to importance of commitment: *How important is subordinate commitment to carrying out the decision?* An answer of High leads to a question about leader expertise: *What is the level of the leader's expertise in relation to the problem?* If

EXHIBIT 9.7

Vroom-Jago Decision Model for Determining an Appropriate Decision-Making Style—Group Problems

SOURCE: Victor H. Vroom "Leadership and the Decision-Making Process," *Organizational Dynamics* 28, no. 4 (Spring 2000): 82–94. Used with permission.

Instructions: The matrix operates like a funnel. You start at the left with a specific decision problem in mind. The column headings denote situational factors that may or may not be present in that problem. You progress by selecting High or Low (H or L) for each relevant situational factor. Proceed down the funnel, judging only those situational factors for which a judgment is required, until you reach the recommended process.

Decision Significance?	Importance of Commitment?	Leader Expertise?	Likelihood of Commitment?	Group Support?	Group Expertise?	Team Competence?	
			H	–	–	–	Decide
		H				H	Delegate
			L	H	H	L	
					L	–	Consult (Group)
				L	–	–	
	H					H	Facilitate
			H	H	H	L	
					L	–	Consult (Individually)
H		L		L	–	–	
			L		H	H	Facilitate
				H		L	
					L	–	Consult (Group)
				L	–	–	
		H	–	–	–	–	Decide
	L				H	H	Facilitate
		L	–	H		L	
					L	–	Consult (Individually)
				L	–	–	
	H	–	H	–	–	–	Decide
L						H	Delegate
			L	–	–	L	Facilitate
	L	–	–	–	–	–	Decide

the leader's knowledge and expertise is High, the leader next considers likelihood of commitment: *If the leader were to make the decision alone, how likely is it that subordinates would be committed to the decision?* A high likelihood that subordinates would be committed means the decision matrix leads directly to the Decide style of decision making, in which the leader makes the decision alone and presents it to the group.

The Vroom-Jago model has been criticized as being less than perfect,[54] but it is useful to managers, and the body of supportive research is growing.[55] Managers can use the model to make timely, high-quality decisions. Consider the application of the model to the following hypothetical problem.

> When Madison Manufacturing won a coveted contract from a large auto manufacturer to produce an engine to power their flagship sports car, Dave Robbins was thrilled to be selected as project manager. This project dramatically enhanced the reputation of Madison, and Robbins and his team of engineers took great pride in their work. However, their enthusiasm was dashed by a recent report of serious engine problems in cars delivered to customers. Taking quick action, the auto manufacturer suspended sales of the sports car, halted current production, and notified owners of the current model not to drive the car. Everyone involved knows this situation is a disaster. Unless the engine problem is solved quickly, Madison Manufacturing could be exposed to extended litigation. In addition, Madison's valued relationship with one of the world's largest auto manufacturers would likely be lost forever.
>
> As the project manager, Robbins spent two weeks in the field inspecting the seized engines and the auto plant where they were installed. Based on this extensive research, Robbins has some pretty good ideas about what is causing the problem, but he knows members of his team who may have stronger expertise for solving it. In addition, while he was in the field, other team members were carefully evaluating the operations and practices in Madison's plant where the engine is manufactured. Therefore, Robbins chooses to get the team together and discuss the problem before making his final decision. The group meets for several hours, discussing the problem in detail and sharing their varied perspectives, including the information Robbins and team members gathered. Following the group session, Robbins makes his decision, which will be presented at the team meeting the following morning, after which testing and correction of the engine problem will begin.[56]

Madison Manufacturing

The Vroom-Jago model in Exhibit 9.7 shows that Robbins used the correct decision style. Moving from left to right in Exhibit 9.7, the questions and answers are as follows: *How significant is the decision?* Definitely high. The company's future might be at stake. *How important is subordinate commitment to the decision?* Also high. The team members must support and implement Robbins's solution. *What is the level of Robbins's information and expertise?* Probably low. Even though he has spent several weeks researching the seized engines, other team members have additional information and expertise that needs to be considered. *If Robbins makes the decision on his own, would team members have high or low commitment to it?* The answer to this question is probably also low. Even though team members respect Robbins, they take pride in their work as a team and know Robbins does not have complete information. This leads to the question, *What is the degree of subordinate support for the team's or organization's objectives at stake in this decision?* Definitely high. This leads to the question, *What is the level of group members' knowledge and expertise in relation to the problem?* The answer to this question is low, which leads to the Consult Group decision style, as described earlier in Exhibit 9.6. Thus, Robbins used the style that would be recommended by the Vroom-Jago model.

In many situations, several decision styles might be equally acceptable. However, smart managers are encouraging greater employee participation in solving problems whenever possible. The use of new knowledge management technologies allows for accessing the ideas and knowledge of a much broader group of people, both inside and outside the organization.[57] Broad participation often leads to better decisions. Involving others in decision making also contributes to individual and organizational learning, which is critical for rapid decision making in a turbulent environment.

New Decision Approaches for Turbulent Times

The ability to make fast, widely supported, high-quality decisions on a frequent basis is a critical skill in today's fast-moving organizations.[58] In many industries, the rate of competitive and technological change is so extreme that opportunities are fleeting, clear and complete information is seldom available, and the cost of a slow decision means lost business or even company failure. Do these factors mean managers should make the majority of decisions on their own? No. The rapid pace of the business environment calls for just the opposite—that is, for people throughout the organization to be involved in decision making and have the information, skills, and freedom they need to respond immediately to problems and questions. Business is taking a lesson from today's military. For example, the U.S. Army, once considered the ultimate example of a rigid, top-down organization, is pushing information and decision making to junior officers in the field. Fighting a fluid, fast-moving, and fast-changing terrorist network means that people who are knowledgeable about the local situation have to make quick decisions, learning through trial and error and sometimes departing from standard Army procedures. Junior leaders rely on a strong set of core values and a clear understanding of the mission to craft creative solutions to problems that the Army might never have encountered before.[59]

Similarly, in today's fast-moving businesses, people often have to act first and analyze later.[60] Top managers do not have the time to evaluate options for every decision, conduct research, develop alternatives, and tell people what to do and how to do it. When speed matters, a slow decision may be as ineffective as the wrong decision, and companies can learn to make decisions fast. Effective decision making under turbulent conditions relies on the following guidelines.

START WITH BRAINSTORMING

One of the best-known techniques for rapidly generating creative alternatives is **brainstorming**. Brainstorming uses a face-to-face interactive group to spontaneously suggest a wide range of alternatives for decision making. The keys to effective brainstorming are that people can build on one another's ideas; all ideas are acceptable, no matter how crazy they seem; and criticism and evaluation are not allowed. The goal is to generate as many ideas as possible. Brainstorming has been found to be highly effective for quickly generating a wide range of alternate solutions to a problem, but it does have some drawbacks. For one thing, people in a group often want to conform to what others are saying, a problem sometimes referred to as *groupthink*. Others may be concerned about pleasing the boss or impressing colleagues. In addition, many creative people simply have social inhibitions that limit their participation in a group session or make it difficult to come up with ideas in a group setting. In fact, one study found that when four people are asked to "brainstorm" individually, they typically come up with twice as many ideas as a group of four brainstorming together.

One recent approach, electronic brainstorming, takes advantage of the group approach while overcoming some disadvantages. **Electronic brainstorming**, sometimes called *brainwriting*, brings people together in an interactive group over a computer network.[61] One member writes an idea, another reads it and adds other ideas, and so on. Studies show that electronic brainstorming generates about 40 percent more ideas than individuals brainstorming alone, and 25 to 200 percent more ideas than regular brainstorming groups, depending on group size.[62] Why? Because the process is anonymous, the sky's the limit in terms of what people feel free to say. People can write down their ideas immediately, avoiding the possibility that a good idea might slip away while the person is waiting for a chance to speak in a face-to-face group. Social inhibitions and concerns are avoided, which typically allows for a broader range of participation. Another advantage is that electronic brainstorming can potentially be done with groups made up of employees from around the world, further increasing the diversity of alternatives.

brainstorming A technique that uses a face-to-face group to spontaneously suggest a broad range of alternatives for decision making.

electronic brainstorming Bringing people together in an interactive group over a computer network to suggest alternatives; sometimes called *brainwriting*.

LEARN, DON'T PUNISH

Decisions made under conditions of uncertainty and time pressure produce many errors, but smart managers are willing to take the risk in the spirit of trial and error. If a chosen decision alternative fails, the organization can learn from it and try another alternative that better fits the situation. Each failure provides new information and learning. People throughout the organization are encouraged to engage in *experimentation*, which means taking risks and learning from their mistakes. Good managers know that every time a person makes a decision, whether it turns out to have positive or negative consequences, it helps the employee learn and be a better decision maker the next time around. By making mistakes, people gain valuable experience and knowledge to perform more effectively in the future. PSS World Medical of Jacksonville, Florida, encourages people to take initiative and try new things with a policy of never firing anyone for an honest mistake. In addition, PSS promises to find another, more appropriate job in the company for any employee who is failing in his or her current position. This "soft landing" policy fosters a climate in which mistakes and failure are viewed as opportunities to learn and improve.[63]

When people are afraid to make mistakes, the company is stuck. For example, when Robert Crandall led American Airlines, he built a culture in which any problem that caused a flight delay was followed by finding someone to blame. People became so scared of making a mistake that whenever something went wrong, no one was willing to jump in and try to fix the problem. In contrast, Southwest Airlines uses what it calls *team delay*, which means a flight delay is everyone's problem. This puts the emphasis on fixing the problem rather than on finding an individual to blame.[64] In a turbulent environment, managers do not use mistakes and failure to create a climate of fear. Instead, they encourage people to take risks and move ahead with the decision process, despite the potential for errors.

CONCEPT CONNECTION The decisions Whole Foods Market chairman John Mackey likes best are the ones he doesn't have to make. The philosophy at Whole Foods, the Austin, Texas-based natural foods grocer, is that, whenever possible, decisions should be made by those closest to where they're carried out. Ideally, that means in the stores themselves by a team of employees, who decide everything from who gets hired to what products to carry. Curtis Hellman, pictured here, is part of a team that serves beer and barbeque at the chain's flagship store in Austin. Whole Foods' emphasis on **group decision making** reflects new decision-making processes for today's turbulent times.

KNOW WHEN TO BAIL

Even though managers encourage risk taking and learning from mistakes, they also aren't hesitant to pull the plug on something that is not working. Research found that organizations often continue to invest time and money in a solution despite strong evidence that it is not appropriate. This tendency is referred to as **escalating commitment**. Managers might block or distort negative information because they don't want to be responsible for a bad decision, or they might simply refuse to accept that their solution is wrong. A recent study in Europe verified that even highly successful managers often miss or ignore warning signals because they become committed to a decision and believe if they persevere it will pay off.[65] As companies face increasing competition, complexity, and change, it is important that managers don't get so attached to their own ideas that they're unwilling to recognize when to move on. According to Stanford University professor Robert Sutton, the key to successful creative decision making is to "fail early, fail often, and pull the plug early."[66]

escalating commitment
Continuing to invest time and resources in a failing decision.

CONCEPT

C O N N E C T I O N The current scores for the worldwide market share of video games are Sony's PlayStation 2: 69%, Nintendo's GameCube: 16%, and Microsoft's Xbox: 15%. Microsoft plans to change all that by getting a big jump on the competition. Managers have made a series of decisions that shaved a full year off development time for the next version of Xbox. That means the company can bring out hot new games ahead of Sony and Nintendo—a tremendous advantage in a business where content is king. Microsoft operates in a highly turbulent industry and managers have to make difficult decisions incredibly fast. Top leaders encourage experimentation and risk-taking to improve decision making that keeps Microsoft on the cutting edge. Some decisions fail, but Microsoft learns from the failure and tries a new alternative, in line with the **learn, don't punish** philosophy.

devil's advocate A decision-making technique in which an individual is assigned the role of challenging the assumptions and assertions made by the group to prevent premature consensus.

point-counterpoint A decision-making technique in which people are assigned to express competing points of view.

PRACTICE THE FIVE WHYS

One way to encourage good decision making under high uncertainty is to get people to think more broadly and deeply about problems rather than going with a superficial understanding and a first response. However, this approach doesn't mean people have to spend hours analyzing a problem and gathering research. One simple procedure adopted by a number of leading companies is known as the five whys.[67] For every problem, employees learn to ask "Why?" not just once, but five times. The first *why* generally produces a superficial explanation for the problem, and each subsequent *why* probes deeper into the causes of the problem and potential solutions. The point of the *five whys* is to improve how people think about problems and generate alternatives for solving them.

ENGAGE IN RIGOROUS DEBATE

An important key to better decision making under conditions of uncertainty is to encourage a rigorous debate of the issue at hand.[68] Good managers recognize that constructive conflict based on divergent points of view can bring a problem into focus, clarify people's ideas, stimulate creative thinking, create a broader understanding of issues and alternatives, and improve decision quality.[69] Chuck Knight, the former CEO of Emerson Electric, always sparked heated debates during strategic planning meetings. Knight believed rigorous debate gave people a clearer picture of the competitive landscape and forced managers to look at all sides of an issue, helping them reach better decisions.[70]

Stimulating rigorous debate can be done in several ways. One way is by ensuring that the group is diverse in terms of age and gender, functional area of expertise, hierarchical level, and experience with the business. Some groups assign a **devil's advocate**, who has the role of challenging the assumptions and assertions made by the group.[71] The devil's advocate may force the group to rethink its approach to the problem and avoid reaching premature conclusions. Jeffrey McKeever, CEO of MicroAge, often plays the devil's advocate, changing his position in the middle of a debate to ensure that other executives don't just go along with his opinions.[72] Another approach is to have group members develop as many alternatives as they can as quickly as they can.[73] It allows the team to work with multiple alternatives and encourages people to advocate ideas they might not prefer simply to encourage debate. Still another way to encourage constructive conflict is to use a technique called **point-counterpoint**, which breaks a decision-making group into two subgroups and assigns them different, often competing responsibilities.[74] The groups then develop and exchange proposals and discuss and debate the various options until they arrive at a common set of understandings and recommendations.

Decision making in today's high-speed, complex environment is one of the most important—and most challenging—responsibilities for managers. By using brainstorming, learning from mistakes rather than assigning blame, knowing when to bail, practicing the *five whys*, and engaging in rigorous debate, managers can improve the quality and effectiveness of their organizational decisions.

This chapter made several important points about the process of organizational decision making. The study of decision making is important because it describes how managers make successful strategic and operational decisions. Managers must confront many types of decisions, including programmed and nonprogrammed, and these decisions differ according to the amount of risk, uncertainty, and ambiguity in the environment.

Three decision-making approaches were described: the classical model, the administrative model, and the political model. The classical model explains how managers should make decisions so as to maximize economic efficiency. The administrative model describes how managers actually make nonprogrammed, uncertain decisions with skills that include intuition. The political model relates to making nonprogrammed decisions when conditions are uncertain, information is limited and ambiguous, and managers are in conflict about what goals to pursue or what course of action to take. Managers have to engage in discussion and coalition building to reach agreement for decisions.

Decision making should involve six basic steps: problem recognition, diagnosis of causes, development of alternatives, choice of an alternative, implementation of the alternative, and feedback and evaluation. Another factor affecting decision making is the manager's personal decision style. The four major decision styles are directive, analytical, conceptual, and behavioral.

Marjorie Yang, described in the chapter opening, uses a primarily conceptual style of decision making. She likes to talk to other managers about a problem or opportunity and get different perspectives on alternatives for action. However, she ultimately makes the decision on her own, based both on her analysis of the organization and its industry and her gut feelings about the decision. Concerning the nonprogrammed decision of whether to build a new factory, Yang's intuition told her to pursue this golden opportunity, even though the managers were split about 50-50 on whether to move ahead with the factory. She ran the numbers and was willing to take the risks for the potential rewards of becoming the first company in China to achieve top quality. Yang believes the new factory can help Esquel double its sales by 2008 to become a billion-dollar company. Implementation of the decision occurred when Esquel broke ground on the factory in mid-2004, with the factory scheduled for completion in 2006. As the factory gets up and running, top managers will gather feedback and evaluate whether the decision was effective in helping Esquel achieve its quality and sales goals.[75]

This chapter also explained the Vroom-Jago model, which managers can use to determine when a decision calls for group participation. Involving others in decision making contributes to individual and organizational learning, which is critical during turbulent times and in high-tech industries. Decisions often have to be made quickly and with limited information. Managers can use the following guidelines: start with brainstorming; learn, don't punish; know when to bail; practice the five whys; and engage in rigorous debate. These techniques improve the quality and effectiveness of decision making in today's turbulent business environment.

DISCUSSION QUESTIONS

1. You are a busy partner in a legal firm, and an experienced secretary complains of continued headaches, drowsiness, dry throat, and occasional spells of fatigue and flu. She tells you she believes air quality in the building is bad and would like something to be done. How would you respond?

2. Why do you think decision making is considered a fundamental part of management effectiveness?

3. Explain the difference between risk and ambiguity. How might decision making differ for a risky versus ambiguous situation?

4. Analyze three decisions you made over the past six months. Which of these were programmed and which were nonprogrammed? Which model—the classical, administrative, or political—best describes the approach you took to make each decision?

5. What opportunities and potential problems are posed by the formation of more than one coalition within an organization, each one advocating a different direction or alternatives? What steps can you take as a manager to make sure that dueling coalitions result in construction discussion rather than dissension?

6. The Vroom-Jago model for group decision making has been criticized as being less than perfect. What do you think are the major criticisms of the model?

7. As a new, entry-level manager, how important is it to find ways to compensate for your relative lack of experience when trying to determine which alternative before you is most likely to succeed? What are some ways you can meet this challenge?

8. List some possible advantages and disadvantages to using computer technology for managerial decision making.

9. Do you think intuition is a valid approach to making decisions in an organization? Why or why not? How might intuition be combined with a rational decision approach?

10. Do you see a conflict between today's emphasis on risk taking and learning and the six steps in Exhibit 9.3 that are associated with effective decision making? Discuss.

11. What do you think is your dominant decision style? Which style are you most comfortable using? Which style feels least comfortable? What are the implications for the type of job you might want to seek?

12. What do you see as the advantages and disadvantages of electronic brainstorming versus face-to-face brainstorming?

MANAGEMENT IN PRACTICE: EXPERIENTIAL EXERCISE

What's Your Personal Decision Style?

Read each of the following questions and circle the answer that best describes you. Think about how you typically act in a work or school situation and mark the answer that first comes to mind. There are no right or wrong answers.

1. In performing my job or class work, I look for:
   a. practical results
   b. the best solution
   c. creative approaches or ideas
   d. good working conditions

2. I enjoy jobs that:
   a. are technical and well-defined
   b. have a lot of variety
   c. allow me to be independent and creative
   d. involve working closely with others

3. The people I most enjoy working with are:
   a. energetic and ambitious
   b. capable and organized
   c. open to new ideas
   d. agreeable and trusting

4. When I have a problem, I usually:
   a. rely on what has worked in the past
   b. apply careful analysis
   c. consider a variety of creative approaches
   d. seek consensus with others

5. I am especially good at:
   a. remembering dates and facts
   b. solving complex problems
   c. seeing many possible solutions
   d. getting along with others

6. When I don't have much time, I:
   a. make decisions and act quickly
   b. follow established plans or priorities
   c. take my time and refuse to be pressured
   d. ask others for guidance and support

7. In social situations, I generally:
   a. talk to others
   b. think about what's being discussed
   c. observe
   d. listen to the conversation

8. Other people consider me:
   a. aggressive
   b. disciplined
   c. creative
   d. supportive

9. What I dislike most is:
   a. not being in control
   b. doing boring work
   c. following rules
   d. being rejected by others

10. **The decisions I make are usually:**
    a. direct and practical
    b. systematic or abstract
    c. broad and flexible
    d. sensitive to others' needs

Scoring and Interpretation

These questions rate your personal decision style, as described in the text and listed in Exhibit 9.5.

Count the number of *a* answers. They provide your *directive* score.

Count the number of *b* answers for your *analytical* score.

The number of *c* answers is your *conceptual* score.

The number of *d* answers is your *behavioral* score.

What is your dominant decision style? Are you surprised, or does this result reflect the style you thought you used most often?

SOURCE: Adapted from Alan J. Rowe and Richard O. Mason, *Managing with Style: A Guide to Understanding, Assessing, and Improving Decision Making* (San Francisco: Jossey-Bass, 1987): 40–41.

MANAGEMENT IN PRACTICE: ETHICAL DILEMMA

The No-Show Consultant

Jeffrey Moses was facing one of the toughest decisions of his short career as a manager with International Consulting. Andrew Carpenter, one of his best consultants, was clearly in trouble, and his problems were affecting his work. International Consulting designs, installs, and implements complex back-office software systems for companies all over the world. About half the consultants work out of the main office, while the rest, including Carpenter, work primarily from home.

This Monday morning, Moses had gotten an irate call from a major New York client saying Carpenter never showed up at the company's headquarters, where the client had been expecting his new computer system to go live for the first time. In calling around to other customers on the East Coast trying to locate the missing consultant, Moses heard other stories. Carpenter had also missed a few other appointments—all on Monday mornings—but no one had felt the need to report it because he had called to reschedule. In addition, he practically came to blows with an employee who challenged him about the capabilities of the new system, and he inexplicably walked out of one customer's office in the middle of the day without a word to anyone. Another client reported that the last time he saw Carpenter he appeared to have a serious hangover. Most of the clients liked Carpenter, but they were concerned that his behavior was increasingly erratic. One client suggested that she would prefer to work with someone else. As for the major New York customer, he preferred that Andrew rather than a new consultant finish the project, but they were also demanding that International eat half the $250,000 consultant's fee.

After Moses finally located Carpenter by calling his next-door neighbor, Andrew confessed that he'd had a "lost weekend" and been too drunk to get on the plane. He then told Moses that his wife had left and taken their two-year-old son with her. He admitted that he had been drinking a little more than usual lately, but insisted that

he was getting himself under control and promised no more problems. "I'm really not an alcoholic or anything," he said. "I've just been upset about Brenda leaving, and I let it get out of hand this weekend." Moses told Carpenter that if he would get to New York and complete the project, all would be forgiven.

Now, however, he wondered whether he should really just let things slide. Moses talked to Carpenter's team leader about the situation and was told that the leader was aware of his recent problems but thought everything would smooth itself over. "Consultants with his knowledge, level of skill, and willingness to travel are hard to find. He's well-liked among all the customers; he'll get his act together." However, when Moses discussed the problem with Carolyn Walter, vice president of operations, she argued that Carpenter should be dismissed. "You're under no obligation to keep him just because you said you would," she pointed out. "This was a major screw-up, and it's perfectly legal to fire someone for absenteeism. Your calls to customers should make it clear that this situation was not a one-time thing. Get rid of him now before things get worse. If you think eating half that $250,000 fee hurts now, just think what could happen if this behavior continues."

What Would You Do?

1. Give him a month's notice and terminate. He's known as a good consultant, so he probably won't have any trouble finding a new job, and you'll avoid any further problems associated with his emotional difficulties and his possible alcohol problem.

2. Let it slide. Missing the New York appointment is Carpenter's first big mistake. He says he is getting things under control and you believe he should be given a chance to get himself back on track.

3. Let Carpenter know that you care about what he's going through, but insist that he take a short paid leave and get counseling to deal with his emotional

difficulties and evaluate the seriousness of his problems with alcohol. If the alcohol abuse continues, require him to attend a treatment program or find another job.

SOURCES: Based on information in Jeffrey L. Seglin, "The Savior Complex," *Inc.* (February 1999): 67–69; and Nora Johnson, "'He's Been Beating Me,' She Confided," *Business Ethics* (Summer 2001): 21.

CASE FOR CRITICAL ANALYSIS

Pinnacle Machine Tool Co.

Don Anglos had to decide whether to trust his gut or his head, and he had to make that decision by next week's board meeting. Either way, he knew he was bound to make at least a member or two of his senior management team unhappy.

The question at hand was whether Pinnacle Co., the small, publicly held Indiana-based machine tool company he led as CEO, should attempt to acquire Hoilman Inc. Hoilman was a company known for the cutting-edge sensor technology and communications software it had developed to monitor robotics equipment. Anglos had just heard a credible rumor that one of Pinnacle's chief competitors was planning a hostile takeover of the company. Coincidentally, Don Anglos knew Hoilman well because he had recently held exploratory talks about the possibility of a joint venture designed to develop similar technology capable of monitoring a broad range of manufacturing equipment. The joint venture did not work out. But now, by acquiring Hoilman, Pinnacle could develop software that transmitted real-time information on its customers' equipment, enabling it to set itself apart by providing top-notch service far more sophisticated than its current standard maintenance and service contracts.

Don, a hard-charging 48-year-old, firmly believed that bigger was better. It was a premise that had served his Greek immigrant father well as he built a multimillion-dollar business from nothing by acquiring one commercial laundry after another. The CEO had to admit, though, that getting bigger in the machine tool industry, currently a slow-growing sector facing increasing competition from low-priced foreign manufacturers, was going to be a challenge. Still, he had been convinced to sign on as Pinnacle's CEO four years ago not only because the company had relatively healthy earnings, but also because his sixth sense told him the company had growth potential. He hadn't been entirely sure where that potential lay, but he was a problem-solver with a proven track record of successfully spotting new market opportunities. In the past, he acted on hunches, which had paid off handsomely.

So far, Anglos had managed to modestly nudge Pinnacle's revenue growth and increase its market share through aggressive pricing that successfully kept customers from switching to several potential

foreign rivals. But those moves inevitably chipped away at the company's healthy profit margins. In any case, he recognized he'd taken the company down that road as far as he could. It was time for a real change in strategy. Instead of concentrating on manufacturing, he wanted to transform Pinnacle into a high-tech service company. Such a drastic metamorphosis was going to require a new, service-oriented corporate culture, he admitted, but it was the only way he could see achieving the growth and profitability he envisioned. Acquiring Hoilman looked like a good place to start, but this option would be gone if Hoilman sold out to another firm.

Jennifer Banks, services division head, was enthusiastic about both the acquisition and the new strategy. "Acquiring Hoilman is the chance of a lifetime," she crowed. Not all the senior managers agreed. In particular, CFO Sam Lodge advanced arguments against the acquisition that were hard to dismiss. The timing was wrong, he insisted. Pinnacle's recent drop in profitability hadn't escaped Wall Street's attention, and the further negative impact on earnings that would result from the Hoilman acquisition wasn't likely to make already wary investors feel any better. But then Sam shocked Don by offering an even more fundamental critique. "Getting into the service business is a mistake, Don. It's what everybody's doing right now. Just look at the number of our competitors who've already taken steps to break into the services market. What makes you think we'll come out on top? And when I look at our customers, I just don't see any evidence that even if they wanted to, they could afford to buy any add-on services any time soon."

With such a big decision, Don's head had to agree with Lodge's position that was based on his usual CFO thoroughness with number-crunching. But his gut wasn't so sure. Sometimes, he thought, you just have to go with your instincts. And his instincts were champing at the bit to go after Hoilman.

Questions

1. What steps in the decision-making process have Don Anglos and Pinnacle taken? Which ones have they not completed?

2. Which decision-making style best describes Don's approach: directive, analytical, conceptual, or

behavioral? Which style best describes Sam Lodge's approach?

3. What leadership style is Anglos employing? Is it the participation style you'd recommend based on a Vroom-Jago analysis of the situation? Why or why not?

4. Would you recommend that Pinnacle attempt to acquire Hoilman? If so, why? If not, what alternatives would you suggest?

SOURCE: Based on Paul Hemp, "Growing for Broke," Harvard Business Review (September 2002): 27–37.

ENDNOTES

1. Cait Murphy, "Building a New Factory," interview with Marjorie Yang in "The Path to Power," *Fortune* (November 14, 2005): 145–156.

2. Brooks Barnes, "Disney Will Offer Many TV Shows Free on the Web; ABC's Prime-Time Hits and Zap-Proof Commercials Are Pillars of Bold Strategy," *The Wall Street Journal* (April 10, 2006): A1, A10.

3. Michael V. Copeland and Owen Thomas, "Hits (& Misses)," *Business 2.0* (January–February 2004): 126.

4. Michael V. Copeland, "Stuck in the Spin Cycle" *Business 2.0* (May 2005): 74–75; Adam Horowitz, Mark Athitakis, Mark Lasswell, and Owen Thomas, "101 Dumbest Moments in Business," *Business 2.0* (January–February 2004):72–81.

5. Herbert A. Simon, *The New Science of Management Decision* (Englewood Cliffs, NJ: Prentice Hall, 1977): 47.

6. Monica Langley, Lee Hawkins Jr., and Dennis Berman, "GM Board Seeks Probe of Mistakes in Bookkeeping," *The Wall Street Journal* (March 18–19, 2006): A1, A6; and Carol J. Loomis, "The Tragedy of General Motors," *Fortune* (February 20, 2005): 58–75.

7. Samuel Eilon, "Structuring Unstructured Decisions," *Omega 13* (1985): 369–377; and Max H. Bazerman, *Judgment in Managerial Decision Making* (New York: Wiley, 1986).

8. James G. March and Zur Shapira, "Managerial Perspectives on Risk and Risk Taking," *Management Science* 33 (1987): 1404–1418; and Inga Skromme Baird and Howard Thomas, "Toward a Contingency Model of Strategic Risk Taking," *Academy of Management Review* 10 (1985): 230–243.

9. Hugh Courtney, "Decision-Driven Scenarios for Assessing Four Levels of Uncertainty," *Strategy & Leadership* 31, no. 1 (2003): 14–22.

10. Janet Guyon, "Changing Direction," interview with Nancy McKinstry in "The Path to Power," *Fortune* (November 14, 2005): 145–156.

11. Michael Masuch and Perry LaPotin, "Beyond Garbage Cans: An AI Model of Organizational Choice," *Administrative Science Quarterly* 34 (1989): 38–67; and Richard L. Daft and Robert H. Lengel, "Organizational Information Requirements, Media Richness and Structural Design," *Management Science* 32 (1986): 554–571.

12. David M. Schweiger, William R. Sandberg, and James W. Ragan, "Group Approaches for Improving Strategic Decision Making: A Comparative Analysis of Dialectical Inquiry, Devil's Advocacy, and Consensus," *Academy of Management Journal* 29 (1986): 51–71; and Richard O. Mason and Ian I. Mitroff, *Challenging Strategic Planning Assumptions* (New York: Wiley Interscience, 1981).

13. Michael Pacanowsky, "Team Tools for Wicked Problems," *Organizational Dynamics* 23, no. 3 (Winter 1995): 36–51.

14. Boris Blai, Jr., "Eight Steps to Successful Problem Solving," *Supervisory Management* (January 1986): 7–9; and Earnest R. Archer, "How to Make a Business Decision: An Analysis of Theory and Practice," *Management Review* 69 (February 1980): 54–61.

15. Bernard Wysocki Jr., "The Rules: At One Hospital, a Stark Solution for Allocating Care," *The Wall Street Journal* (September 23, 2003): A1, A21.

16. Thomas H. Davenport and Jeanne G. Harris, "Automated Decision Making Comes of Age," *MIT Sloan Management Review* (Summer 2005): 83–89; and Stacie McCullough, "On the Front Lines," *CIO*, (October 15, 1999): 78–81.

17. Srinivas Bollapragada, Prasanthi Ganti, Mark Osborn, James Quaile, and Kannan Ramanathan, "GE's Energy Rentals Business Automates Its Credit Assessment Process," *Interfaces* 33, no. 5 (September–October 2003): 45–56; Julie Schlosser, "Markdown Lowdown," *Fortune* (January 12, 2004): 40.

18. Srinivas Bollapragada, Hong Cheng, Mary Phillips, Marc Garbinas, Michael Scholes, Tim Gibbs, and Mark Humphreville, "NBC's Optimization Systems Increase Revenues and Productivity," *Interfaces* 32, no. 1 (January–February 2002): 47–60.

19. Herbert A. Simon, *The New Science of Management Decision* (New York: Harper & Row, 1960): 5–6; and Amitai Etzioni, "Humble Decision Making," *Harvard Business Review* (July–August 1989): 122–126.

20. James G. March and Herbert A. Simon, *Organizations* (New York: Wiley, 1958).

21. Herbert A. Simon, *Models of Man* (New York: Wiley, 1957): 196–205; and Herbert A. Simon, *Administrative Behavior*, 2d ed. (New York: Free Press, 1957).

22. Paul C. Nutt, "Expanding the Search for Alternatives During Strategic Decision Making," *Academy of Management Executive* 18, no. 4 (2004): 13–28.

23. Weston H. Agor, "The Logic of Intuition: How Top Executives Make Important Decisions," *Organizational Dynamics* 14 (Winter 1986): 5–18; and Herbert A. Simon, "Making Management Decisions: The Role of Intuition and Emotion," *Academy of Management Executive* 1 (1987): 57–64.

24. Study reported in C. Chet Miller and R. Duane Ireland, "Intuition in Strategic Decision Making: Friend or Foe in the Fast-Paced 21st Century?" *Academy of Management Executive* 19, no. 1 (2005): 19–30.

25. Gary Klein, *Intuition at Work: Why Developing Your Gut Instincts Will Make You Better at What You Do* (New York: Doubleday, 2002).

26. Malcolm Gladwell, *Blink: The Power of Thinking Without Thinking* (New York: Little Brown 2005); Sharon Begley,

"Follow Your Intuition: The Unconscious You May Be the Wiser Half," *The Wall Street Journal* (August 30, 2002): B1.

27. Thomas Stewart, "How to Think With Your Gut," *Business 2.0* (November 2002): http://www.business2.com; Thomas George, "Head Cowboy Gets Off His High Horse," *The New York Times* (December 21, 2003): Section 8, 1.

28. Chris Smith, "Chao, Baby," *New York* (October 18, 1993): 66–75; and "Chao in Charge," *Cablevision* (November 29, 1999): 24.

29. Miller and Ireland, "Intuition in Strategic Decision Making," and Eric Bonabeau, "Don't Trust Your Gut," *Harvard Business Review* (May 2003): 116ff.

30. Eugene Sadler-Smith and Erella Shefy, "The Intuitive Executive: Understanding and Applying 'Gut Feel' in Decision Making," *Academy of Management Executive* 18, no. 4 (2004): 76–91; and Ann Langley, "Between 'Paralysis by Analysis' and 'Extinction by Instinct,'" *Sloan Management Review* (Spring 1995): 63–76.

31. William B. Stevenson, Jon L. Pierce, and Lyman W. Porter, "The Concept of 'Coalition' in Organization Theory and Research," *Academy of Management Review* 10 (1985): 256–268.

32. George T. Doran and Jack Gunn, "Decision Making in High-Tech Firms: Perspectives of Three Executives," *Business Horizons* (November–December 2002): 7–16.

33. Stephanie N. Mehta and Fred Vogelstein, "AOL: The Relaunch," *Fortune* (November 14, 2005): 78–84.

34. Jonathan Harris, "Why Speedy Got Stuck in Reverse," *Canadian Business* (September 26, 1997): 87–88.

35. Daniel Golden and Steve Stecklow, "Crimson Tide; Facing War with His Faculty, Harvard's Summers Resigns," *The Wall Street Journal* (February 22, 2006): A1, A13.

36. James W. Fredrickson, "Effects of Decision Motive and Organizational Performance Level on Strategic Decision Processes," *Academy of Management Journal* 28 (1985): 821–843; James W. Fredrickson, "The Comprehensiveness of Strategic Decision Processes: Extension, Observations, Future Directions," *Academy of Management Journal* 27 (1984): 445–466; James W. Dean, Jr., and Mark P. Sharfman, "Procedural Rationality in the Strategic Decision-Making Process," *Journal of Management Studies* 30, no. 4 (July 1993): 587–610; Nandini Rajagopalan, Abdul M. A. Rasheed, and Deepak K. Datta, "Strategic Decision Processes: Critical Review and Future Directions," *Journal of Management* 19, no. 2 (1993): 349–384; and Paul J. H. Schoemaker, "Strategic Decisions in Organizations: Rational and Behavioral Views," *Journal of Management Studies* 30, no. 1 (January 1993): 107–129.

37. Marjorie A. Lyles and Howard Thomas, "Strategic Problem Formulation: Biases and Assumptions Embedded in Alternative Decision-Making Models," *Journal of Management Studies* 25 (1988): 131–145; and Susan E. Jackson and Jane E. Dutton, "Discerning Threats and Opportunities," *Administrative Science Quarterly* 33 (1988): 370–387.

38. Richard L. Daft, Juhani Sormunen, and Don Parks, "Chief Executive Scanning, Environmental Characteristics, and Company Performance: An Empirical Study" (unpublished manuscript, Texas A&M University, 1988).

39. Jena McGregor, "Gospels of Failure," *Fast Company* (February 2005): 62–67.

40. C. Kepner and B. Tregoe, *The Rational Manager* (New York: McGraw-Hill, 1965).

41. Joseph B. White and Lee Hawkins Jr., "Harried Driver; At General Motors, Troubles Mount for Man Behind the Wheel," *The Wall Street Journal* (November 11, 2005): A1; and Loomis, "The Tragedy of General Motors."

42. Paul C. Nutt, "Expanding the Search for Alternatives During Strategic Decision Making," *Academy of Management Executive* 18, no. 4 (2004): 13–28; and P. C. Nutt, "Surprising But True: Half the Decisions in Organizations Fail," *Academy of Management Executive* 13, no. 4 (1999): 75–90.

43. Gogoi and Arndt, "Hamburger Hell."

44. Peter Mayer, "A Surprisingly Simple Way to Make Better Decisions," *Executive Female* (March–April 1995): 13–14; and Ralph L. Keeney, "Creativity in Decision Making with Value-Focused Thinking," *Sloan Management Review* (Summer 1994): 33–41.

45. Janet Guyon, "The Soul of a Moneymaking Machine," *Fortune* (October 3, 2005): 113–120; Robert Levering and Milton Moskowitz, "And the Winners Are . . ." (The 100 Best Companies to Work For), *Fortune* (January 23, 2006): 89–108.

46. Mark McNeilly, "Gathering Information for Strategic Decisions, Routinely," *Strategy & Leadership* 30, no. 5 (2002): 29–34.

47. Ibid.

48. Woolley, "Best Leaders."

49. Jenny C. McCune, "Making Lemonade," *Management Review* (June 1997): 49–53, 51.

50. Based on A. J. Rowe, J. D. Boulgaides, and M. R. McGrath, *Managerial Decision Making* (Chicago: Science Research Associates, 1984); and Alan J. Rowe and Richard O. Mason, *Managing with Style: A Guide to Understanding, Assessing, and Improving Your Decision Making* (San Francisco: Jossey-Bass, 1987).

51. Gunther, "Jeff Zucker Faces Life Without *Friends*."

52. V. H. Vroom and Arthur G. Jago, *The New Leadership: Managing Participation in Organizations* (Englewood Cliffs, NJ: Prentice Hall, 1988).

53. Victor H. Vroom, "Leadership and the Decision-Making Process," *Organizational Dynamics* 28, no. 4 (Spring 2000): 82–94.

54. R. H. G. Field, "A Test of the Vroom-Yetton Normative Model of Leadership," *Journal of Applied Psychology* (October 1982): 523–532; and R. H. G. Field, "A Critique of the Vroom-Yetton Contingency Model of Leadership Behavior," *Academy of Management Review* 4 (1979): 249–257.

55. Vroom, "Leadership and the Decision Making Process"; Jennifer T. Ettling and Arthur G. Jago, "Participation under Conditions of Conflict: More on the Validity of the Vroom-Yetton Model," *Journal of Management Studies* 25 (1988): 73–83; Madeline E. Heilman, Harvey A. Hornstein, Jack H. Cage, and Judith K. Herschlag, "Reactions to Prescribed Leader Behavior as a Function of Role Perspective: The Case of the Vroom-Yetton Model," *Journal of Applied Psychology* (February 1984): 50–60; and Arthur G. Jago and Victor H. Vroom, "Some Differences in the Incidence and Evaluation of Participative Leader Behavior," *Journal of Applied Psychology* (December 1982): 776–783.

56. Based on a decision problem presented in Victor H. Vroom, "Leadership and the Decision-Making Process," *Organizational Dynamics* 28, no. 4 (Spring 2000): 82–94.

57. Nathaniel Foote, Eric Matson, Leigh Weiss, and Etienne Wenger, "Leveraging Group Knowledge for High-Performance Decision Making," *Organizational Dynamics* 31, no. 3 (2002): 280–295.

58. Kathleen M. Eisenhardt, "Strategy as Strategic Decision Making," *Sloan Management Review* (Spring 1999): 65–72.

59. Major Chip Daniels, "Making Values-Based, Mission-Focused Decisions," *Leader to Leader* Special Supplement (May 2005): 48–59; Greg Jaffe, "Trial by Fire; On Ground in Iraq, Capt. Ayers Writes His Own Playbook," *The Wall Street Journal* (September 22, 2004): A1.

60. See Katharine Mieskowski, "Digital Competition," *Fast Company* (December 1999): 155–162; Thomas A. Stewart, "Three Rules for Managing in the Real-Time Economy," *Fortune* (May 1, 2000): 333–334; and Geoffrey Colvin, "How to Be a Great eCEO," *Fortune* (May 24, 1999): 104–110.

61. R. B. Gallupe, W. H. Cooper, M. L. Grise, and L. M. Bastianutti, "Blocking Electronic Brainstorms," *Journal of Applied Psychology* 79 (1994): 77–86; R. B. Gallupe and W. H. Cooper, "Brainstorming Electronically," *Sloan Management Review* (Fall 1993): 27–36; and Alison Stein Wellner, "A Perfect Brainstorm," *Inc.* (October 2003): 31–35.

62. Wellner, "A Perfect Brainstorm"; Gallupe and Cooker, "Brainstorming Electronically."

63. Charles O'Reilly III and Jeffrey Pfeffer, *Hidden Value: How Great Companies Achieve Extraordinary Performance with Ordinary People* (Boston: Harvard Business School Press, 2000).

64. Michael V. Copeland, "Mistakes Happen," *Red Herring* (May 2000): 346–354.

65. Hans Wissema, "Driving Through Red Lights; How Warning Signals Are Missed or Ignored," *Long Range Planning* 35 (2002): 521–539.

66. Ibid.

67. Joshua Klayman, Richard P. Larrick, and Chip Heath, "Organizational Repairs," *Across the Board* (February 2000): 26–31.

68. Michael A. Roberto, "Making Difficult Decisions in Turbulent Times," *Ivey Business Journal* (May–June 2003): 1–7.

69. Eisenhardt, "Strategy as Strategic Decision Making"; and David A. Garvin and Michael A. Roberto, "What You Don't Know About Making Decisions," *Harvard Business Review* (September 2001): 108–116.

70. Roberto, "Making Difficult Decisions in Turbulent Times."

71. David M. Schweiger and William R. Sandberg, "The Utilization of Individual Capabilities in Group Approaches to Strategic Decision Making," *Strategic Management Journal* 10 (1989): 31–43; and "The Devil's Advocate," *Small Business Report* (December 1987): 38–41.

72. Doran and Gunn, "Decision Making in High-Tech Firms."

73. Eisenhardt, "Strategy as Strategic Decision Making."

74. Garvin and Roberto, "What You Don't Know About Making Decisions."

75. Murphy, "Building a New Factory."

Costco Wholesale Corporation Part Three: Costco Turns 500

November 22, 2006, marks a major milestone in the history of Costco Wholesale Corporation. On that date, in the city of La Quinta, California, the world's top warehouse-club operator opened its 500th location since pioneering the discount warehouse concept in the 1970s and '80s.

Throngs of customers, city planners, and interested observers gathered in the Southern California suburb to celebrate the store's grand opening, days before the onset of the 2006 holiday shopping season. At 8 A.M., the boxy 148,000 square-foot facility threw open its doors, welcoming hundreds of enthusiastic bargain hunters giddy at the prospect of buying the year's hottest merchandise at rock-bottom prices. As the morning hours passed, Xbox 360s, Panasonic plasma TVs, and AG brand jeans began beeping briskly through the checkouts—a sure sign that holiday stockings across the Greater Palm Springs area would soon be filled with gift-giving cheer.

The landmark opening of Costco's 500th warehouse was not only a sign of good things to come for local residents or for La Quinta officials anticipating a one-million-dollar boost to the city's annual tax revenues; for Costco CEO James Sinegal and his team of strategic planners, breaking the 500 barrier was confirmation that Costco's long-term growth plan was working. In the 25 years since Sinegal and Costco co-founder Jeffrey Brotman broke ground on their first archetypal no-frills warehouse in Seattle, Washington, Costco has consistently executed its mission to build warehouse clubs that provide quality goods and services at the lowest possible prices. The general merchandise retailer has grown at an average of 20 warehouses per year and now ranks No.1 among discount warehouse chains.

For some businesses, reaching the top might seem like a time for self-congratulation. But for Sinegal & Co., success is handled with a kind of "business-as-usual" modesty. Far from causing Costco's top brass to rest on their laurels, hitting the 500 marker has emboldened management to set even more aggressive expansion goals. During an August 2006 conference call, CFO Richard Galanti announced plans for 35 to 40 new stores, with a target of 700 U.S. locations—a sizable increase over previous goals.

Launching new storefronts is central to any major retailer's grand strategy. First and foremost, adding locations is about increasing revenues and profits. A typical Costco warehouse averages $128 million in annual sales. By raising expansion projections for 2007, the Issaquah, Washington-based retailer has set itself on track for double-digit percentage revenue growth beyond its record $60 billion achieved in 2006.

Costco doesn't throw warehouses up just anywhere, however. Sinegal's strategic planning effort involves the careful identification of sites that provide a good fit between the organization and its environment. A majority of Costco store openings target suburban commercial districts, where suburban customers like their bulk-packaged soup, toilet paper, and peanut butter under a single roof with computers, copiers, hot tubs, and grand pianos. But in Costco's urban outlets, such as the tower-complex location in the heart of downtown Vancouver, Canada, merchandise caters to downtown demographics. The club's urban-tailored product mix features upscale Louis Vuitton fashion goods and a hearty deli selection of home-ready meals—a nod to Vancouver's many downtown condo dwellers. "It is the most unique Costco in the world," says Regional Marketing Director Robin Ross, reflecting on the store's uncommon placement within big-city surroundings. "This is a place where you can buy tires *and* a two carat diamond ring for $19,699."

Though revenue generation and demographic fit are primary goals for all Costco locations, certain warehouses also serve as testing labs for new ventures. One such idea incubator is Costco's 205,000 square-foot superstore in Hillsboro, Oregon, near Portland. The store's footprint was designed 40% larger than typical stores to test out a mini-version of Costco Home, the retailer's high-end home furnishings chain store. "It gives us lots of extra space where we can test some things and it's close enough where we can keep an eye on it," said Galanti.

Management's strategy of designating certain locations for test marketing purposes has proven successful, especially in light of the fact that most of Costco's present ancillary businesses began in such warehouses before being rolled out nationwide. The company's $2 billion-in-sales pharmacy division began as an experiment in a Portland store in 1986. More recently, in 2006, Costco's drive-through Car Wash business made its test-market debut at the famous Fourth Avenue store in south Seattle.

But as Costco implements expansion plans in locations ranging from Manhattan and Mexico to Taiwan, the discounter's big box concept faces challenges from numerous forces in the external environment. Various stakeholders—including unions, local governments, and anti-globalization groups—are engaged in a contentious dispute over the rapid growth of big boxes. Though city developers and state officials typically view superstores as a preferred means of filling government coffers with millions in tax revenues, labor and anti-growth forces see the price-slashing mega-stores as detrimental to their interests. The debate is growing particularly acrimonious in California, where arguments rage over whether superstore retailers belong in a neighborhood and legislative bills threaten a severe restriction of big box expansion.

Keen to the threat from outside forces, and dedicated to his team's plan for growth, Sinegal sets course and asserts his rock-steady leadership. To Costco's seasoned founder and chief, the company's growth from one single Seattle store into a 500-warehouse retail chain is a powerful motivator for future performance. "We still take pictures of that original building and show it at our manager's meetings and then show the contrast to what our businesses look like today," Sinegal says. "If we are going to continue to prosper as a company, we had better be as creative in the next twenty years as we have been in the past twenty years. It is an imperative that you continue to be creative and build your business."

Questions

1. What strategy formulation tools might top management at Costco use to assess opportunities and threats to the company's future expansion?

2. Explain how Costco's select test-market warehouses demonstrate cooperation and connectedness between the different levels of planning and strategy throughout an organization.

3. How does James Sinegal's recounting of Costco's history using early warehouse photographs at manager's meetings illustrate the role of corporate culture in supporting an organization's strategy and performance?

SOURCES: Marcel Honore, "Valley's Second Costco Lands in La Quinta," *The Desert Sun*, November 21, 2006; Will Fifield, "500 and Counting," *The Costco Connection*, November 2006; Doug Desjardins, "Bulking Up Sales Through Sales in Bulk," *Retailing Today*, September 25, 2006; Gillian Shaw, "Costco Opens Yaletown Warehouse Store," *Vancouver Sun*, November 10, 2006; John Howard, "Big Box Debate," *Capitol Weekly*, November 16, 2006; "Ancillary Businesses Continue to Drive Through Sales," *Retailing Today*, September 25, 2006; Doug Desjardins, "Retailer's Largest Store a Learning Lab," *Retailing Today*, November 6, 2006; Mac Greer, "Is Costco Giving Away the Store?," *The Motley Fool*, November 22, 2006, *http://www.fool.com*.

PART 4

ORGANIZING

When approaching a building project, an architect organizes at two levels. First, the architect organizes the design of the structure in electronic blueprints. These blueprints are the architect's instructions for how the structure is to be built and tracks any changes that are made to the original design. The architect is also interested in the organization of the final structure, which must be clearly integrated in the structure's function.

Organization must do more than simply accommodate function. Organization is inherent in function and when properly implemented leads to fitness and form. When an architect designs a structure, organization underlies how the pieces fit together and give meaning to the form, fit, and function of that structure. How a structure is organized will dictate how people or objects flow through that structure and a good design will inherently accommodate the most natural movement from place to place. A museum must be designed to gently lead visitors through the exhibits, guiding their way at a subconscious level. A restaurant can be elegant or cozy, but the staff must be able to flow easily through the dining area, bringing diners their meals without fear of accidents or collisions.

Managers must organize people, technology, and institutional knowledge to achieve goals as well. Sometimes that means organizing a company's internal structures, but it can also mean reorganizing a department, region, or entire company in the face of advancing technology, changing markets, or a changing workforce. The manufacturing process is the most obvious application of organizing: moving physical objects from point A to point B and performing certain tasks in a certain order. And while abstract yet just as real, managers must also organize ideas, information, and technology whjch requires innovation and imagination. And finally the manager must be prepared to alter that organization again as needed to accommodate the ever changing world.

CHAPTER OUTLINE

Manager's Challenge

Organizing the Vertical Structure

Work Specialization

Chain of Command

Span of Management

Centralization and Decentralization

Departmentalization

Vertical Functional Approach

Divisional Approach

Matrix Approach

Team Approach

The Virtual Network Approach

Advantages and Disadvantages
of Each Structure

**Organizing for Horizontal
Coordination**

The Need for Coordination

Task Forces, Teams, and Project
Management

Reengineering

Factors Shaping Structure

Structure Follows Strategy

Structure Reflects the Environment

Structure Fits the Technology

LEARNING OBJECTIVES

After studying this chapter, you should be able to:

1. Discuss the fundamental characteristics of organizing, including such concepts as work specialization, chain of command, span of management, and centralization versus decentralization.

2. Describe functional and divisional approaches to structure.

3. Explain the matrix approach to structure and its application to both domestic and international organizations.

4. Describe the contemporary team and virtual network structures and why they are being adopted by organizations.

5. Explain why organizations need coordination across departments and hierarchical levels, and describe mechanisms for achieving coordination.

6. Identify how structure can be used to achieve an organization's strategic goals.

7. Illustrate how organization structure can be designed to fit environmental uncertainty.

8. Define production technology (manufacturing, service, and digital) and explain how it influences organization structure.

DESIGNING ADAPTIVE ORGANIZATIONS

MANAGER'S CHALLENGE

The call to Carlos Ghosn came on a blustery March day. Louis Schweitzer, CEO of Renault, was asking Ghosn to take on the biggest challenge of his management career—to lead a turnaround of Japan's Nissan. Renault and Nissan had just agreed to an important strategic alliance, but its success depended on transforming Nissan into a profitable business. Ghosn had succeeded before as a turnaround artist, but Nissan was a whole different story. The once-thriving company had been struggling to turn a profit for eight years. Purchasing and manufacturing costs were high and profit margins notoriously low. The company's debt, even after the Renault investment, amounted to a staggering $11 billion. Product innovation was at a standstill, and the company was trying to compete with aging and outdated car models. When Ghosn got to Nissan, he found deeper problems, including a culture of blame where no one was willing to accept responsibility for mistakes. One reason, he discovered, was that most Nissan managers did not have clearly defined areas of responsibility and authority. Another impediment was the lack of trust, communication, and collaboration across departments. When something went wrong, sales blamed product planning, product planning blamed engineering, engineering blamed sales, sales blamed finance, and on and on—and nothing ever got solved. Ghosn knew he was facing a do-or-die situation: Either fix these fundamental problems, or Nissan would die.[1]

> What advice would you give Carlos Ghosn about using structural design to help turn Nissan around? What structural changes might solve Nissan's problems with poor coordination and shatter the pervasive culture of blame?

TAKE A MOMENT

The problem confronting Carlos Ghosn at Nissan is largely one of structural design. Ghosn wants to use elements of structure to define authority and responsibility for managers, promote accountability, and improve coordination so that Nissan can bring out new products and regain a competitive edge. Every firm wrestles with the problem of how to organize. Reorganization often is necessary to reflect a new strategy, changing market conditions, or innovative technology. In recent years, many companies, including American Express, IBM, Microsoft, Hewlett-Packard, and Ford Motor Co., have realigned departmental groupings, chains of command, and horizontal coordination mechanisms to attain new strategic goals. Structure is a powerful tool for reaching strategic goals, and a strategy's success often is determined by its fit with organization structure.

Many companies have found a need to make structural changes that are compatible with use of the Internet for e-business, which requires stronger horizontal coordination. Brady Corporation, a Milwaukee-based manufacturer of identification and safety products, reorganized to increase cross-functional collaboration in connection with the rollout of a new system that links customers, distributors, and suppliers over the Internet.[2] Ford Motor Company used a horizontal team approach to design and build the Escape Hybrid, bringing the first hybrid SUV to market in record time.[3]

Companies are increasingly using outsourcing as a structural option, as the Internet has expanded the types of activities firms can farm out to subcontractors. WuXi Pharmatech in Shanghai, China, for example, not only manufactures drugs but does laboratory and drug development work for most of the large pharmaceuticals firms in the United States and Europe. Drug makers such as Roche Holding of Switzerland, GlaxoSmithKline of Britain, and Eli Lilly of the United States are also outsourcing clinical trial work to low-wage countries such as India, a practice that is raising both economic and ethical concerns.[4] Some of today's companies operate as virtual network organizations, limiting themselves to a few core activities and letting outside specialists handle everything else. Each of these organizations is using fundamental concepts of organizing. **Organizing** is the deployment of organizational resources to achieve strategic goals. The deployment of resources is reflected in the organization's division of labor into specific departments and jobs, formal lines of authority, and mechanisms for coordinating diverse organization tasks.

Organizing is important because it follows from strategy—the topic of Part 3. Strategy defines *what* to do; organizing defines *how* to do it. Organization structure is a tool that managers use to harness resources for getting things done. Part 4 explains the variety of organizing principles and concepts used by managers. This chapter covers fundamental concepts that apply to all organizations and departments, including organizing the vertical structure and using mechanisms for horizontal coordination. The chapter also examines how managers tailor the various elements of structural design to the organization's situation. Chapter 11 discusses how organizations can be structured to facilitate innovation and change. Chapters 12 and 13 consider how to utilize human resources to the best advantage within the organization's structure.

ORGANIZING THE VERTICAL STRUCTURE

The organizing process leads to the creation of organization structure, which defines how tasks are divided and resources deployed. **Organization structure** is defined as (1) the set of formal tasks assigned to individuals and departments; (2) formal reporting relationships, including lines of authority, decision responsibility, number of hierarchical levels, and span of managers' control; and (3) the design of systems to ensure effective coordination of employees across departments.[5]

The set of formal tasks and formal reporting relationships provides a framework for vertical control of the organization. The characteristics of vertical structure are portrayed in the **organization chart**, which is the visual representation of an organization's structure.

A sample organization chart for a water bottling plant is illustrated in Exhibit 10.1. The plant has four major departments—accounting, human resources, production, and marketing. The organization chart delineates the chain of command, indicates departmental tasks and how they fit together, and provides order and logic for the organization. Every employee has an appointed task, line of authority, and decision responsibility. The following sections discuss several important features of vertical structure in more detail.

organizing The deployment of organizational resources to achieve strategic goals.

organization structure The framework in which the organization defines how tasks are divided, resources are deployed, and departments are coordinated.

organization chart The visual representation of an organization's structure.

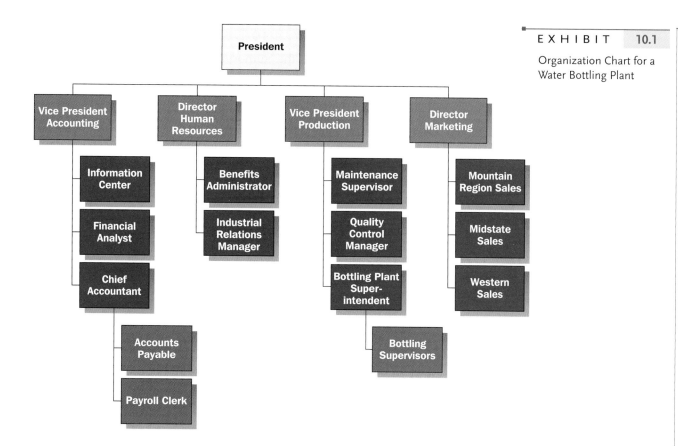

EXHIBIT 10.1

Organization Chart for a
Water Bottling Plant

Work Specialization

Organizations perform a wide variety of tasks. A fundamental principle is that work can be performed more efficiently if employees are allowed to specialize.[6] **Work specialization**, sometimes called *division of labor*, is the degree to which organizational tasks are subdivided into separate jobs. Work specialization in Exhibit 10.1 is illustrated by the separation of production tasks into bottling, quality control, and maintenance. Employees within each department perform only the tasks relevant to their specialized function. When work specialization is extensive, employees specialize in a single task. Jobs tend to be small, but they can be performed efficiently. Work specialization is readily visible on an automobile assembly line where each employee performs the same task over and over again. It would not be efficient to have a single employee build the entire automobile, or even perform a large number of unrelated jobs.

Despite the apparent advantages of specialization, many organizations are moving away from this principle. With too much specialization, employees are isolated and do only a single, boring job. Many companies are enlarging jobs to provide greater challenges or assigning teams so that employees can rotate among the several jobs performed by the team.

Chain of Command

The **chain of command** is an unbroken line of authority that links all persons in an organization and shows who reports to whom. It is associated with two underlying principles. *Unity of command* means that each employee is held accountable to only one supervisor. The *scalar principle* refers to a clearly defined line of authority in the organization that includes all employees. Authority and responsibility for different tasks should be distinct. All persons in the organization should know to whom they report as well as the successive management levels all the way to the top. In Exhibit 10.1, the payroll clerk reports to the chief accountant, who in turn reports to the vice president, who in turn reports to the company president.

work specialization The degree to which organizational tasks are subdivided into individual jobs; also called division of labor.

chain of command An unbroken line of authority that links all individuals in the organization and specifies who reports to whom.

AUTHORITY, RESPONSIBILITY, AND DELEGATION

The chain of command illustrates the authority structure of the organization. **Authority** is the formal and legitimate right of a manager to make decisions, issue orders, and allocate resources to achieve organizationally desired outcomes. Authority is distinguished by three characteristics:[7]

1. *Authority is vested in organizational positions, not people.* Managers have authority because of the positions they hold, and other people in the same positions would have the same authority.

2. *Authority is accepted by subordinates.* Although authority flows top-down through the organization's hierarchy, subordinates comply because they believe that managers have a legitimate right to issue orders. The *acceptance theory of authority* argues that a manager has authority only if subordinates choose to accept his or her commands. If subordinates refuse to obey because the order is outside their zone of acceptance, a manager's authority disappears.[8]

3. *Authority flows down the vertical hierarchy.* Positions at the top of the hierarchy are vested with more formal authority than are positions at the bottom.

Responsibility is the flip side of the authority coin. **Responsibility** is the duty to perform the task or activity as assigned. Typically, managers are assigned authority commensurate with responsibility. When managers have responsibility for task outcomes but little authority, the job is possible but difficult. They rely on persuasion and luck. When managers have authority exceeding responsibility, they may become tyrants, using authority toward frivolous outcomes.[9]

authority The formal and legitimate right of a manager to make decisions, issue orders, and allocate resources to achieve organizationally desired outcomes.

responsibility The duty to perform the task or activity an employee has been assigned.

accountability The fact that the people with authority and responsibility are subject to reporting and justifying task outcomes to those above them in the chain of command.

■ **TAKE A MOMENT**

Go to the ethical dilemma on page 341 that pertains to issues of authority, responsibility, and delegation.

Accountability is the mechanism through which authority and responsibility are brought into alignment. **Accountability** means that the people with authority and responsibility are subject to reporting and justifying task outcomes to those above them in the chain of command.[10] For organizations to function well, everyone needs to know what they are accountable for and accept the responsibility and authority for performing it. Accountability can be built into the organization structure. For example, at Whirlpool, incentive programs tailored to different hierarchical levels provide strict accountability. Performance of all managers is monitored, and bonus payments are tied to successful outcomes. Another example comes from Caterpillar Inc., which got hammered by new competition in the mid-1980s and reorganized to build in accountability.

Caterpillar Inc.

Caterpillar, which makes large construction equipment, engines, and power systems, had almost total control of its markets until the mid-1980s, when a combination of global recession and runaway inflation opened the door to a host of new competitors, including Japan's Komatsu. The unanticipated surge of competition almost put Cat under, and the company was losing $1 million a day seven days a week in 1983 and 1984.

When George Schaefer took over as CEO, he and other top managers decided to undertake a major transformation to make sure Cat wasn't caught flat-footed again. They started with structure. One major problem Schaefer saw was that the organization didn't have clear accountability. Schaefer pushed authority, responsibility, and accountability dramatically downward by reorganizing Caterpillar into several new business divisions that would be judged on divisional profitability. Business units could now design their own products, develop their own manufacturing processes, and set their own prices rather than getting permission or directives from headquarters. The division managers were strictly accountable for how they used their new decision-making authority. Each division was judged on profitability and return on assets (ROA), and any division that couldn't demonstrate 15 percent ROA was subject to elimination. The CEO held regular meetings with each division president and kept notes of what they said they would achieve. Then at the next meeting, he would review each manager's performance compared to his or her commitments. The compensation plan was also overhauled to base individual managers' bonuses on meeting divisional plan targets.

Previously, if things went wrong, division managers would blame headquarters. The clear accountability of the new structure forced people to find solutions to their problems rather than assigning blame.[11]

Some top managers at Caterpillar had trouble letting go of authority and responsibility in the new structure because they were used to calling all the shots. Another important concept related to authority is delegation.[12] **Delegation** is the process managers use to transfer authority and responsibility to positions below them in the hierarchy. Most organizations today encourage managers to delegate authority to the lowest possible level to provide maximum flexibility to meet customer needs and adapt to the environment. However, as at Caterpillar, many managers find delegation difficult. Microsoft's chief financial officer John Conners nearly resigned because of CEO Steven Ballmer's inability to delegate. By taking it upon himself to make financial decisions, Ballmer undermined the role of Conners and his team. Ballmer is learning to give up some control and delegate more so that people can do their jobs more effectively.[13] Techniques for effective delegation are discussed in the Manager's Shoptalk box.

> As a new manager, delegate authority and responsibility to employees so they can quickly respond to customer needs and other shifts in the environment. Don't hoard control and limit the effectiveness and creativity of others.

■ TAKE A MOMENT

LINE AND STAFF AUTHORITY

An important distinction in many organizations is between line authority and staff authority, reflecting whether managers work in line or staff departments in the organization's structure. *Line departments* perform tasks that reflect the organization's primary goal and mission. In a software company, line departments make and sell the product. In an Internet-based company, line departments would be those that develop and manage online offerings and sales. *Staff departments* include all those that provide specialized skills in support of line departments. Staff departments have an advisory relationship with line departments and typically include marketing, labor relations, research, accounting, and human resources.

Line authority means that people in management positions have formal authority to direct and control immediate subordinates. **Staff authority** is narrower and includes the right to advise, recommend, and counsel in the staff specialists' area of expertise. Staff authority is a communication relationship; staff specialists advise managers in technical areas. For example, the finance department of a manufacturing firm would have staff authority to coordinate with line departments about which accounting forms to use to facilitate equipment purchases and standardize payroll services.

Span of Management

The **span of management** is the number of employees reporting to a supervisor. Sometimes called the *span of control*, this characteristic of structure determines how closely a supervisor can monitor subordinates. Traditional views of organization design recommended a span of management of about seven subordinates per manager. However, many lean organizations today have spans of management as high as 30, 40, and even higher. For example, at Consolidated Diesel's team-based engine assembly plant, the span of management is 100.[14] Research over the past 40 or so years shows that span of management varies widely and that several factors influence the span.[15] Generally, when supervisors must be closely involved with

delegation The process managers use to transfer authority and responsibility to positions below them in the hierarchy.

line authority A form of authority in which individuals in management positions have the formal power to direct and control immediate subordinates.

staff authority A form of authority granted to staff specialists in their area of expertise.

span of management The number of employees reporting to a supervisor; also called *span of control*.

HOW TO DELEGATE

The attempt by top management to decentralize decision making often gets bogged down because middle managers are unable to delegate. Managers may cling tightly to their decision making and task responsibilities. Failure to delegate occurs for a number of reasons: Managers are most comfortable making familiar decisions; they feel they will lose personal status by delegating tasks; they believe they can do a better job themselves; or they have an aversion to risk—they will not take a chance on delegating because performance responsibility ultimately rests with them.

Yet decentralization offers an organization many advantages. Decisions are made at the right level, lower-level employees are motivated, and employees have the opportunity to develop decision-making skills. Overcoming barriers to delegation in order to gain these advantages is a major challenge. The following approach can help each manager delegate more effectively:

1. *Delegate the whole task.* A manager should delegate an entire task to one person rather than dividing it among several people. This type of delegation gives the individual complete responsibility and increases his or her initiative while giving the manager some control over the results.

2. *Select the right person.* Not all employees have the same capabilities and degree of motivation. Managers must match talent to task if delegation is to be effective. They should identify subordinates who made independent decisions in the past and show a desire for more responsibility.

3. *Ensure that authority equals responsibility.* Merely assigning a task is not effective delegation. Managers often load subordinates with increased responsibility but do not extend their decision-making range. In addition to having responsibility for completing a task, the worker must be given the authority to make decisions about how best to do the job.

4. *Give thorough instruction.* Successful delegation includes information on what, when, why, where, who, and how. The subordinate must clearly understand the task and the expected results. It is a good idea to write down all

provisions discussed, including required resources and when and how the results will be reported.

5. *Maintain feedback.* Feedback means keeping open lines of communication with the subordinate to answer questions and provide advice, but without exerting too much control. Open lines of communication make it easier to trust subordinates. Feedback keeps the subordinate on the right track.

6. *Evaluate and reward performance.* Once the task is completed, the manager should evaluate results, not methods. When results do not meet expectations, the manager must assess the consequences. When they do meet expectations, the manager should reward employees for a job well done with praise, financial rewards when appropriate, and delegation of future assignments.

ARE YOU A POSITIVE DELEGATOR?

Positive delegation is the way an organization implements decentralization. Do you help or hinder the decentralization process? If you answer yes to more than three of the following questions, you may have a problem delegating:

:: I tend to be a perfectionist.

:: My boss expects me to know all the details of my job.

:: I don't have the time to explain clearly and concisely how a task should be accomplished.

:: I often end up doing tasks myself.

:: My subordinates typically are not as committed as I am.

:: I get upset when other people don't do the task right.

:: I really enjoy doing the details of my job to the best of my ability.

:: I like to be in control of task outcomes.

SOURCES: Thomas R. Horton "Delegation and Team Building: No Solo Acts Please," *Management Review* (September 1992): 58–61; Andrew E. Schwartz, "The Why, What, and to Whom of Delegation," *Management Solutions* (June 1987): 31–38; "Delegation," *Small Business Report* (June 1986): 38–43; and Russell Wild, "Clone Yourself," *Working Woman* (May 2000): 79–80.

subordinates, the span should be small, and when supervisors need little involvement with subordinates, it can be large. The following factors are associated with less supervisor involvement and thus larger spans of control:

1. Work performed by subordinates is stable and routine.

2. Subordinates perform similar work tasks.

3. Subordinates are concentrated in a single location.

4. Subordinates are highly trained and need little direction in performing tasks.

5. Rules and procedures defining task activities are available.

6. Support systems and personnel are available for the manager.

7. Little time is required in nonsupervisory activities such as coordination with other departments or planning.

8. Managers' personal preferences and styles favor a large span.

The average span of control used in an organization determines whether the structure is tall or flat. A **tall structure** has an overall narrow span and more hierarchical levels. A **flat structure** has a wide span, is horizontally dispersed, and has fewer hierarchical levels.

Having too many hierarchical levels and narrow spans of control is a common structural problem for organizations. The result may be routine decisions that are made too high in the organization, which pulls higher-level executives away from important long-range strategic issues, and it limits the creativity and innovativeness of lower-level managers in solving problems.[16] The trend in recent years has been toward wider spans of control as a way to facilitate delegation.[17] One study of 300 large U.S. corporations found that the average number of division heads reporting directly to the CEO tripled between the years of 1986 and 1999.[18] Exhibit 10.2 illustrates how an international metals company was reorganized. The multilevel set of managers shown in panel *a* was replaced with 10 operating managers and nine staff specialists reporting directly to the CEO, as shown in panel *b*. The CEO welcomed this wide span of 19 management subordinates because it fit his style, his management team was top quality and needed little supervision, and they were all located on the same floor of an office building.

Centralization and Decentralization

Centralization and decentralization pertain to the hierarchical level at which decisions are made. **Centralization** means that decision authority is located near the top of the organization. With **decentralization**, decision authority is pushed downward to lower organization levels. Organizations may have to experiment to find the correct hierarchical level at which to make decisions.

In the United States and Canada, the trend over the past 30 years has been toward greater decentralization of organizations. Decentralization is believed to relieve the burden on top managers, make greater use of employees' skills and

tall structure A management structure characterized by an overall narrow span of management and a relatively large number of hierarchical levels.

flat structure A management structure characterized by an overall broad span of control and relatively few hierarchical levels.

centralization The location of decision authority near top organizational levels.

decentralization The location of decision authority near lower organizational levels.

EXHIBIT 10.2

Reorganization to Increase Span of Management for President of an International Metals Company

a. Old, Tall Structure

President

Executive Vice President — Staff Specialists (6)

Executive Vice President — Operating Managers (5) — Staff Specialists (3)

Executive Vice President — Operating Managers (4) — Staff Specialists (5)

Vice President — Operating Managers (10) — Staff Specialists (5)

b. New, Flat Structure

President

Operating Managers (10)   Staff Specialists (9)

© UNITED STATES NAVY

CONCEPT

C O N N E C T I O N Prior to the early 1990s, there were seven management layers at Electric Boat Corporation's Quonset Point facility in Rhode Island, which fabricates and assembles U.S. Navy nuclear submarines. This **tall structure** resulted in high costs and a lengthy chain of command that slowed decision making. After the General Dynamics Corporation subsidiary re-engineered itself into a **flat structure** with only three layers, overhead and indirect labor costs were cut by 50 percent, and communications, efficiency, and productivity all improved. The Best Manufacturing Practice (BPM) Center of Excellence ranks Electric Boat's practices as among the best. BPM is a partnership of the Office of Naval Research, the Commerce Department, and the University of Maryland.

abilities, ensure that decisions are made close to the action by well-informed people, and permit more rapid response to external changes.

However, this trend does not mean that every organization should decentralize all decisions. Managers should diagnose the organizational situation and select the decision-making level that will best meet the organization's needs. Factors that typically influence centralization versus decentralization are as follows:

1. *Greater change and uncertainty in the environment are usually associated with decentralization.* A good example of how decentralization can help cope with rapid change and uncertainty occurred following Hurricane Katrina. Recall from the Chapter 1 opening example how Mississippi Power restored power in just 12 days thanks largely to a decentralized management system that empowered people at the electrical substations to make rapid on-the-spot decisions. Similarly, decentralized decision making at UPS enabled trucks to keep running on time in New York after the September 2001 terrorist attacks.[19]

2. *The amount of centralization or decentralization should fit the firm's strategy.* For example, Johnson & Johnson gives almost complete authority to its 180 operating companies to develop and market their own products. Decentralization fits the corporate strategy of empowerment that gets each division close to customers so it can speedily adapt to their needs.[20] Taking the opposite approach, Procter & Gamble recentralized some of its operations to take a more focused approach and leverage the giant company's capabilities across business units.[21]

3. *In times of crisis or risk of company failure, authority may be centralized at the top.* When Honda could not get agreement among divisions about new car models, President Nobuhiko Kawamoto made the decision himself.[22]

DEPARTMENTALIZATION

departmentalization The basis on which individuals are grouped into departments and departments into the total organization.

Another fundamental characteristic of organization structure is **departmentalization**, which is the basis for grouping positions into departments and departments into the total organization. Managers make choices about how to use the chain of command to group people together to perform their work. Five approaches to structural design reflect different uses of the chain of command in departmentalization, as illustrated in Exhibit 10.3. The functional, divisional, and matrix are traditional approaches that rely on the chain of command to define departmental groupings and reporting relationships along the hierarchy. Two innovative approaches are the use of teams and virtual networks, which have emerged to meet changing organizational needs in a turbulent global environment.

The basic difference among structures illustrated in Exhibit 10.3 is the way in which employees are departmentalized and to whom they report.[23] Each structural approach is described in detail in the following sections.

1. Vertical Functional

Human Resources   Manufacturing   Accounting

2. Divisional

Product Division 1

Human Resources   Manufacturing   Accounting

Product Division 2

Human Resources   Manufacturing   Accounting

3. Matrix

Human Resources   Manufacturing   Accounting

Product Division 1

Product Division 2

4. Team-Based

5. Network

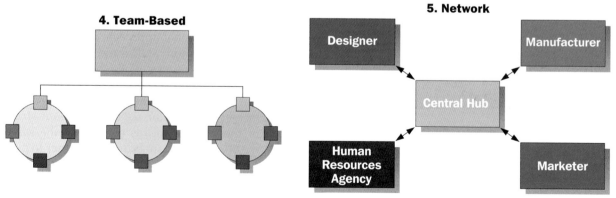

Designer   Manufacturer

Central Hub

Human Resources Agency   Marketer

EXHIBIT 10.3

Five Approaches to Structural Design

Vertical Functional Approach

WHAT IT IS

Functional structure is the grouping of positions into departments based on similar skills, expertise, work activities, and resource use. A functional structure can be thought of as departmentalization by organizational resources, because each type of functional activity—accounting, human resources, engineering, manufacturing—represents specific resources for performing the organization's task. People, facilities, and other resources representing a common function are grouped into a single department. One example is Blue Bell Creameries, which relies on in-depth expertise in its various functional departments to produce high-quality ice creams for a limited regional market. The quality control department, for example, tests all incoming ingredients and ensures that only the best go into Blue Bell's ice cream. Quality inspectors also test outgoing products and because of their years of experience can detect the slightest deviation from expected quality. Blue Bell also has functional departments such as sales, production, maintenance, distribution, research and development, and finance.[24]

functional structure The grouping of positions into departments based on similar skills, expertise, and resource use.

divisional structure An organization structure in which departments are grouped based on similar organizational outputs.

HOW IT WORKS

Refer back to Exhibit 10.1 on page 309 for an example of a functional structure. The major departments under the president are groupings of similar expertise and resources, such as accounting, human resources, production, and marketing. Each of the functional departments is concerned with the organization as a whole. The marketing department is responsible for all sales and marketing, for example, and the accounting department handles financial issues for the entire company.

The functional structure is a strong vertical design. Information flows up and down the vertical hierarchy, and the chain of command converges at the top of the organization. In a functional structure, people within a department communicate primarily with others in the same department to coordinate work and accomplish tasks or implement decisions that are passed down the hierarchy. Managers and employees are compatible because of similar training and expertise. Typically, rules and procedures govern the duties and responsibilities of each employee, and employees at lower hierarchical levels accept the right of those higher in the hierarchy to make decisions and issue orders.

© COURTESY OF AVERY DENNISON CORP.

CONCEPT CONNECTION These members of the Avery Hi-Liter® EverBold™ marker team, part of the North American consumer products division at Avery Dennison Corporation, collaborated as a **cross-functional team** to launch a new pen-style highlighter product. Avery Dennison is a company committed to using the team-based approach to maintain and grow their market leadership. The company empowers multi-functional teams of employees to develop and launch new consumer products.

Divisional Approach

WHAT IT IS

In contrast to the functional approach, in which people are grouped by common skills and resources, the **divisional structure** occurs when departments are grouped together based on organizational outputs. The divisional structure is sometimes called a *product structure, program structure*, or *self-contained unit structure*. Each of these terms means essentially the same thing: Diverse departments are brought together to produce a single organizational output, whether it be a product, a program, or a service to a single customer.

Most large corporations have separate divisions that perform different tasks, use different technologies, or serve different customers. When a huge organization produces products for different markets, the divisional structure works because each division is an autonomous business. Microsoft has reorganized into three business divisions: Platform Products & Services (which includes Windows and MSN); Business (including Office and Business Solutions products); and Entertainment & Devices (Xbox games, Windows mobile, and Microsoft TV). Each unit is headed by a president who is accountable for the performance of the division, and each contains the functions of a stand-alone company, doing its own product development, sales, marketing, and finance. Facing new competitive threats from Google and makers of the free Linux operating system, top executives initiated the restructuring to help Microsoft be more flexible and nimble in developing and delivering new products. The structure groups together products and services that depend on similar technologies at the same time it will enable more rapid decision making and less red tape at the giant corporation.[25]

How It Works

Functional and divisional structures are illustrated in Exhibit 10.4. In the divisional structure, divisions are created as self-contained units with separate functional departments for each division. For example, in Exhibit 10.4, each functional department resource needed to produce the product is assigned to each division. Whereas in a functional structure, all engineers are grouped together and work on all products, in a divisional structure separate engineering departments are created within each division. Each department is smaller and focuses on a single product line or customer segment. Departments are duplicated across product lines.

The primary difference between divisional and functional structures is that the chain of command from each function converges lower in the hierarchy. In a divisional structure, differences of opinion among research and development, marketing, manufacturing, and finance would be resolved at the divisional level rather than by the president. Thus, the divisional structure encourages decentralization. Decision making is pushed down at least one level in the hierarchy, freeing the president and other top managers for strategic planning.

Geographic- or Customer-Based Divisions

An alternative for assigning divisional responsibility is to group company activities by geographic region or customer group. For example, the Internal Revenue Service shifted to a structure focused on four distinct taxpayer (customer) groups: individuals, small businesses, corporations, and nonprofit or government agencies.[26]

EXHIBIT 10.4

Functional Versus Divisional Structures

a. Functional Structure

President

R&D | Finance | Manufacturing | Marketing

b. Divisional Structure

President

Division 1 (Electronics) | Division 2 (Biotechnology) | Division 3 (Consumer Products)

R&D | Manufacturing | R&D | Manufacturing | R&D | Manufacturing

Finance | Marketing | Finance | Marketing | Finance | Marketing

A global geographic structure is illustrated in Exhibit 10.5. In this structure, all functions in a specific country or region report to the same division manager. The structure focuses company activities on local market conditions. Competitive advantage may come from the production or sale of a product or service adapted to a given country or region. Colgate-Palmolive Company is organized into regional divisions in North America, Europe, Latin America, the Far East, and the South Pacific.[27] The structure works for Colgate because personal care products often need to be tailored to cultural values and local customs.

Large nonprofit organizations such as the United Way, National Council of YMCAs, Habitat for Humanity International, and the Girl Scouts of the USA also frequently use a type of geographical structure, with a central headquarters and semi-autonomous local units. The national organization provides brand recognition, coordinates fund-raising services, and handles some shared administrative functions, while day-to-day control and decision making is decentralized to local or regional units.[28]

Matrix Approach

WHAT IT IS

The **matrix approach** combines aspects of both functional and divisional structures simultaneously in the same part of the organization. The matrix structure evolved as a way to improve horizontal coordination and information sharing.[29] One unique feature of the matrix is that it has dual lines of authority. In Exhibit 10.6, the functional hierarchy of authority runs vertically, and the divisional hierarchy of authority runs horizontally. The vertical structure provides traditional control within functional departments, and the horizontal structure provides coordination across departments. The matrix structure therefore supports a formal chain of command for both functional (vertical) and divisional (horizontal) relationships. As a result of this dual structure, some employees actually report to two supervisors simultaneously.

HOW IT WORKS

The dual lines of authority make the matrix unique. To see how the matrix works, consider the global matrix structure illustrated in Exhibit 10.7. The two lines of authority are geographic and product. The geographic boss in Germany coordinates all subsidiaries in Germany, and the plastics products boss coordinates the manufacturing and sale of plastics products around the world. Managers of local subsidiary companies in Germany would report to two superiors, both the country boss and the product boss. The dual authority structure violates the unity-of-command concept described earlier in this chapter but is necessary to give equal emphasis to both

matrix approach An organization structure that utilizes functional and divisional chains of command simultaneously in the same part of the organization.

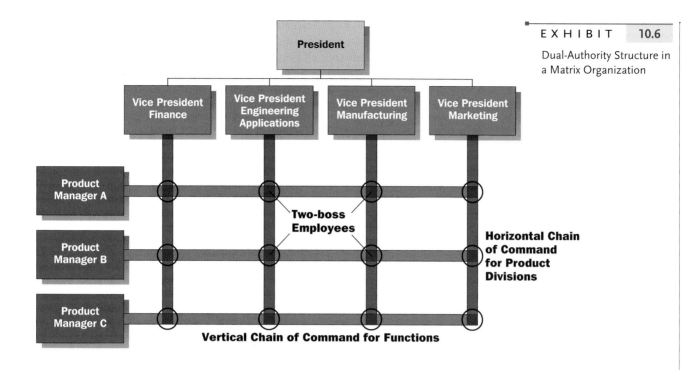

EXHIBIT 10.6

Dual-Authority Structure in a Matrix Organization

EXHIBIT 10.7

Global Matrix Structure

319

Chapter 10 DESIGNING ADAPTIVE ORGANIZATIONS

functional and divisional lines of authority. Dual lines of authority can be confusing, but after managers learn to use this structure, the matrix provides excellent coordination simultaneously for each geographic region and each product line.

The success of the matrix structure depends on the abilities of people in key matrix roles. **Two-boss employees**, those who report to two supervisors simultaneously, must resolve conflicting demands from the matrix bosses. They must confront senior managers and reach joint decisions. They need excellent human relations skills with which to confront managers and resolve conflicts. The **matrix boss** is the product or functional boss, who is responsible for one side of the matrix. The **top leader** is responsible for the entire matrix. The **top leader** oversees both the product and functional chains of command. His or her responsibility is to maintain a power balance between the two sides of the matrix. If disputes arise between them, the problem will be kicked upstairs to the top leader.[30]

At General Motors' Information Systems and Services, CIO Ralph Szygenda created a matrix that helped the unit cut costs and increase effectiveness.

two-boss employees Employees who report to two supervisors simultaneously.

matrix boss The product or functional boss, responsible for one side of the matrix.

top leader The overseer of both the product and functional chains of command, responsible for the entire matrix.

General Motors Information Systems and Services

When General Motors hired Ralph Szygenda as its first chief information officer in 1996, the company didn't even *have* an information office. Because the entire information technology (IT) function had been spun off to EDS in the early 1990s, GM had no IT staff of its own. Szygenda started with a clean slate and decided to create something unique among corporate IT units—a matrix structure. Szygenda believed the matrix was the best way to cope with the massive IT problems associated with a huge enterprise like GM with several highly autonomous divisions.

Szygenda hired five divisional CIOs to be in charge of information systems and services for the various GM divisions: North America, Europe, Asia-Pacific, Latin America/Africa/Middle East, and GM Finance. At the same time, he put in place five process information officers (PIOs) to work horizontally in different processes that crossed divisional lines: product development, supply chain management, production, customer experience, and business services. Many Information Systems and Services employees thus report to both a divisional chief information officer and a process information officer (matrix bosses). Szygenda serves as the top leader, in charge of the entire matrix.

Implementing the matrix structure was not without its problems, but employees learned to balance their overlapping responsibilities. Szygenda credits the matrix with helping to cut $1 billion out of GM's IT budget over a seven-year period. General Motors' CEO Rick Waggoner was so impressed by the success of the matrix that he set up global process leaders in other parts of the business, hoping it could help the company reap gains in productivity and manufacturing efficiency.[31]

Team Approach

WHAT IT IS

Probably the most widespread trend in departmentalization in recent years has been the implementation of team concepts. The vertical chain of command is a powerful means of control, but passing all decisions up the hierarchy takes too long and keeps responsibility at the top. The team approach gives managers a way to delegate authority, push responsibility to lower levels, and be more flexible and responsive in the competitive global environment. Chapter 21 will discuss teams in detail.

HOW IT WORKS

One approach to using teams in organizations is through **cross-functional teams**, which consist of employees from various functional departments who are responsible to meet as a team and resolve mutual problems. Team members typically still report to their functional departments, but they also report to the team, one member of whom may be the leader. Cross-functional teams are used to provide needed horizontal coordination to complement an existing divisional or functional structure. A frequent use of cross-functional teams is for change projects, such as new product or service innovation. A cross-functional team of mechanics, flight attendants, reservations agents, ramp workers, luggage attendants, and aircraft cleaners, for example, collaborated to plan and design a new low-fare airline for US Airways.[32]

The second approach is to use **permanent teams**, groups of employees who are brought together in a way similar to a formal department. Each team brings together employees from all functional areas focused on a specific task or project, such as parts supply and logistics for an automobile plant. Emphasis is on horizontal communication and information sharing because representatives from all functions are coordinating their work and skills to complete a specific organizational task. Authority is pushed down to lower levels, and front-line employees are often given the freedom to make decisions and take action on their own. Team members may share or rotate team leadership. With a **team-based structure**, the entire organization is made up of horizontal teams that coordinate their work and work directly with customers to accomplish the organization's goals. Imagination Ltd., Britain's largest design firm, is based entirely on teamwork. Imagination puts together a diverse

cross-functional teams A group of employees from various functional departments that meet as a team to resolve mutual problems.

permanent teams A group of participants from several functions who are permanently assigned to solve ongoing problems of common interest.

team-based structure Structure in which the entire organization is made up of horizontal teams that coordinate their activities and work directly with customers to accomplish the organization's goals.

Unlocking Innovative Solutions Through PEOPLE

TEAMS WORK AT IMAGINATION LTD.

The essence of teamwork is that people contribute selflessly, putting the good of the whole above their own individual interests. It doesn't always work that way, but London-based Imagination Ltd., Europe's largest independent design and communications agency, seems to have found the secret ingredient to seamless teamwork. According to Adrian Caddy, Imagination's creative director: "The culture at Imagination is this: You can articulate your ideas without fear."

Imagination Ltd. has made a name for itself by producing award-winning, often highly theatrical programs. For example, in February 2006, it staged a launch event for the *Harry Potter and the Prisoner of Azkaban* DVD and video by inviting 800 guests to an historic London building where it had recreated four movie sets, among them the Great Hall at the Hogwarts School of Witchcraft and Wizardry. Accomplishing such feats are teams of designers, architects, lighting experts, writers, theater people, film directors, and artists, in addition to IT specialists, marketing experts, and other functional specialties. By having employees with a wide range of skills, the company is able to put together a diverse team to provide each client with a new approach to its design problems. Imagination is deliberately nonhierarchical; only four people have formal titles, and on most project teams, no one is really in charge. Teams meet weekly, and everyone participates in every meeting from the very beginning, so

there is no perception that any particular talent is primary—or secondary. Information technology specialists, production people, and client-contact personnel are just as much a part of the team as the creative types. In addition, each person is expected to come up with ideas outside his or her area of expertise. The philosophy is that people at Imagination must be willing to *make* all kinds of suggestions and also to *take* all kinds of suggestions. So many ideas get batted around, revised, and adapted at the weekly meetings that no one can claim ownership of a particular element of the project. The team also works closely with the client as a source of ideas and inspiration.

Talent and respect help to make the system work. Imagination hires its people carefully, based not only on the quality of their work but also on their open-mindedness and curiosity about the world beyond their functional area of expertise. Then, the company makes sure everyone's work is so closely integrated that people gain an understanding and respect for what others do. "The integrated approach breeds respect for one another," says writer Chris White. "When you work alone, or in isolation within your discipline, you can get an overblown sense of your own importance to a project."

SOURCES: Charles Fishman, "Total Teamwork: Imagination Ltd.," *Fast Company* (April 2000): 156–168; and Kelly Wardle, "Confetti: Imagination Creates One Enchanted Evening," *Special Events* (February 1, 2006), http://specialevents.com/corporate.

---

team at the beginning of each new project it undertakes, whether it be creating the lighting for Disney cruise ships or redesigning the packaging for Ericsson's cell phone products. The team then works closely with the client throughout the project.[33] Imagination Ltd. has managed to make every project a smooth, seamless experience by building a culture that supports teamwork, as described in this chapter's Unlocking Innovative Solutions Through People box.

The Virtual Network Approach

WHAT IT IS

The most recent approach to departmentalization extends the idea of horizontal coordination and collaboration beyond the boundaries of the organization. In a variety of industries, vertically integrated, hierarchical organizations are giving way to loosely interconnected groups of companies with permeable boundaries.[34] *Outsourcing*, which means farming out certain activities, such as manufacturing or credit processing, has become a significant trend. In addition, partnerships, alliances, and other complex collaborative forms are now a leading approach to accomplishing strategic goals. In the music industry, firms such as Vivendi Universal and Sony have formed networks of alliances with Internet service providers, digital

EXHIBIT 10.8

Network Approach to
Departmentalization

retailers, software firms, and other companies to bring music to customers in new ways.[35] Some organizations take this networking approach to the extreme to create an innovative structure. The **virtual network structure** means that the firm subcontracts most of its major functions to separate companies and coordinates their activities from a small headquarters organization.[36] Indian telecom company Bharti Tele-Ventures Ltd., for example, outsources everything except marketing and customer management.[37]

How It Works

The organization may be viewed as a central hub surrounded by a network of outside specialists, as illustrated in Exhibit 10.8. Rather than being housed under one roof, services such as accounting, design, manufacturing, and distribution are outsourced to separate organizations that are connected electronically to the central office.[38] Networked computer systems, collaborative software, and the Internet enable organizations to exchange data and information so rapidly and smoothly that a loosely connected network of suppliers, manufacturers, assemblers, and distributors can look and act like one seamless company.

The idea behind networks is that a company can concentrate on what it does best and contract out other activities to companies with distinctive competence in those specific areas, which enables a company to do more with less.[39] The Birmingham, England-based company, Strida, provides an example of the virtual network approach.

virtual network structure
An organization structure that disaggregates major functions to separate companies that are brokered by a small headquarters organization.

Strida

How do two people run an entire company that sells thousands of high-tech folding bicycles all over the world? Steedman Bass and Bill Bennet do it with a virtual network approach that outsources design, manufacturing, customer service, logistics, accounting, and just about everything else to other organizations.

Bass, an avid cyclist, got into the bicycle business when he and his partner Bennet bought the struggling British company Strida, which was having trouble making enough quality bicycles to meet even minimum orders. The partners soon realized why Strida was struggling. The design for the folding bicycle was a clever engineering idea, but it was a manufacturing nightmare. Bass and Bennet immediately turned over production engineering and new product development to an American bicycle designer, still with intentions of building the bikes at the Birmingham factory. However, a large order from Italy sent them looking for other options. Eventually, they transferred all manufacturing to Ming Cycle Company of Taiwan, which builds the bikes with parts sourced from parts manufacturers in Taiwan and mainland China.

Finally, the last piece of the puzzle was to contract with a company in Birmingham that would take over everything else—from marketing to distribution. Bass and Bennet concentrate their energies on managing the partnerships that make the network function smoothly.[40]

With a network structure such as that used at Strida, it is difficult to answer the question, "Where is the organization?" in traditional terms. The different organizational parts may be spread all over the world. They are drawn together contractually and coordinated electronically, creating a new form of organization. Much like building blocks, parts of the network can be added or taken away to meet changing needs.[41]

A similar approach to networking is called the **modular approach**, in which a manufacturing company uses outside suppliers to provide entire chunks of a product, which are then assembled into a final product by a handful of workers. The Canadian firm Bombardier's new Continental business jet is made up of about a dozen huge modular components from all over the world: the engines from the United States; the nose and cockpit from Canada; the mid-fuselage from Northern Ireland; the tail from Taiwan; the wings from Japan; and so forth.[42] Automobile plants, including General Motors, Ford, Volkswagen, and DaimlerChrysler, are leaders in using the modular approach. The modular approach hands off responsibility for engineering and production of entire sections of an automobile, such as the chassis or interior, to outside suppliers. Suppliers design a module, making some of the parts themselves and subcontracting others. These modules are delivered right to the assembly line, where a handful of employees bolt them together into a finished vehicle.[43]

Advantages and Disadvantages of Each Structure

Each of these approaches to departmentalization—functional, divisional, matrix, team, and network—has strengths and weaknesses. The major advantages and disadvantages of each are listed in Exhibit 10.9.

FUNCTIONAL APPROACH

Grouping employees by common task permits economies of scale and efficient resource use. For example, at American Airlines, all information technology (IT) people work in the same, large department. They have the expertise and skills to

modular approach The process by which a manufacturing company uses outside suppliers to provide large components of the product, which are then assembled into a final product by a few workers.

EXHIBIT 10.9

Structural Advantages and Disadvantages

Structural Approach	Advantages	Disadvantages
Functional	Efficient use of resources; economies of scale In-depth skill specialization and development Top manager direction and control	Poor communication across functional departments Slow response to external changes; lagging innovation Decisions concentrated at top of hierarchy, creating delay
Divisional	Fast response, flexibility in unstable environment Fosters concern for customer needs Excellent coordination across functional departments	Duplication of resources across divisions Less technical depth and specialization Poor coordination across divisions
Matrix	More efficient use of resources than single hierarchy Flexibility, adaptability to changing environment Interdisciplinary cooperation, expertise available to all divisions	Frustration and confusion from dual chain of command High conflict between two sides of the matrix Many meetings, more discussion than action
Team	Reduced barriers among departments, increased compromise Shorter response time, quicker decisions Better morale, enthusiasm from employee involvement	Dual loyalties and conflict Time and resources spent on meetings Unplanned decentralization
Virtual Network	Can draw on expertise worldwide Highly flexible and responsive Reduced overhead costs	Lack of control; weak boundaries Greater demands on managers Employee loyalty weakened

handle almost any IT problem for the organization. Large, functionally based departments enhance the development of in-depth skills because people work on a variety of related problems and are associated with other experts within their own department. Because the chain of command converges at the top, the functional structure also provides a way to centralize decision making and provide unified direction from top managers. The primary disadvantages reflect barriers that exist across departments. Because people are separated into distinct departments, communication and coordination across functions are often poor, causing a slow response to environmental changes. Innovation and change require involvement of several departments. Another problem is that decisions involving more than one department may pile up at the top of the organization and be delayed.

DIVISIONAL APPROACH

By dividing employees and resources along divisional lines, the organization will be flexible and responsive to change because each unit is small and tuned in to its environment. By having employees working on a single product line, the concern for customers' needs is high. Coordination across functional departments is better because employees are grouped together in a single location and committed to one product line. Great coordination exists within divisions; however, coordination *across* divisions is often poor. Problems occurred at Hewlett-Packard, for example, when autonomous divisions went in opposite directions. The software produced in one division did not fit the hardware produced in another. Thus, the divisional structure was realigned to establish adequate coordination across divisions. Another major disadvantage is duplication of resources and the high cost of running separate divisions. Instead of a single research department in which all research people use a single facility, each division may have its own research facility. The organization loses efficiency and economies of scale. In addition, the small size of departments within each division may result in a lack of technical specialization, expertise, and training.

MATRIX APPROACH

The matrix structure is controversial because of the dual chain of command. However, the matrix can be highly effective in a complex, rapidly changing environment in which the organization needs to be flexible and adaptable.[44] The conflict and frequent meetings generated by the matrix allow new issues to be raised and resolved. The matrix structure makes efficient use of human resources because specialists can be transferred from one division to another. The major problem is the confusion and frustration caused by the dual chain of command. Matrix bosses and two-boss employees have difficulty with the dual reporting relationships. The matrix structure also can generate high conflict because it pits divisional against functional goals in a domestic structure, or product line versus country goals in a global structure. Rivalry between the two sides of the matrix can be exceedingly difficult for two-boss employees to manage. This problem leads to the third disadvantage: time lost to meetings and discussions devoted to resolving this conflict. Often the matrix structure leads to more discussion than action because different goals and points of view are being addressed. Managers may spend a great deal of time coordinating meetings and assignments, which takes time away from core work activities.[45]

■ TAKE A MOMENT   As a new manager, understand the advantages and disadvantages of each approach to departmentalization. Recognize how each structure can provide benefits but might not be appropriate for every organization and situation.

TEAM APPROACH

The team concept breaks down barriers across departments and improves cooperation. Team members know one another's problems and compromise rather than blindly pursue their own goals. The team concept also enables the organization to more quickly adapt to customer requests and environmental changes and speeds decision making because decisions need not go to the top of the hierarchy for approval. Another big advantage is the morale boost. Employees are enthusiastic about their involvement in bigger projects rather than narrow departmental tasks. At video games company Ubisoft, for example, each studio is set up so that teams of employees and managers work collaboratively to develop new games. Employees don't make a lot of money, but they're motivated by the freedom they have to propose new ideas and put them into action.[46]

However, the team approach has disadvantages as well. Employees may be enthusiastic about team participation, but they may also experience conflicts and dual loyalties. A cross-functional team may make different demands on members than do their department managers, and members who participate in more than one team must resolve these conflicts. A large amount of time is devoted to meetings, thus increasing coordination time. Unless the organization truly needs teams to coordinate complex projects and adapt to the environment, it will lose production efficiency with them. Finally, the team approach may cause too much decentralization. Senior department managers who traditionally made decisions might feel left out when a team moves ahead on its own. Team members often do not see the big picture of the corporation and may make decisions that are good for their group but bad for the organization as a whole.

VIRTUAL NETWORK APPROACH

The biggest advantages to a virtual network approach are flexibility and competitiveness on a global scale. The extreme flexibility of a network approach is illustrated by today's "war on terrorism." Most experts agree that the primary reason the insurgency is so difficult to fight is that it is a far-flung collection of groups that share a specific mission but are free to act on their own. "Attack any single part of it, and the rest carries on largely untouched," wrote one journalist after talking with U.S. and Iraqi officials. "It cannot be decapitated, because the insurgency, for the most part, has no head."[47] One response is for the United States and its allies to organize into networks to quickly change course, put new people in place as needed, and respond to situations and challenges as they emerge.[48]

Today's business organizations can also benefit from a flexible network approach that lets them shift resources and respond quickly. A network organization can draw on resources and expertise worldwide to achieve the best quality and price and can sell its products and services worldwide. Flexibility comes from the ability to hire whatever services are needed, and to change a few months later without constraints from owning plant, equipment, and facilities. The organization can continually redefine itself to fit new product and market opportunities. This structure is perhaps the leanest of all organization forms because little supervision is required. Large teams of staff specialists and administrators are not needed. A network organization may have only two or three levels of hierarchy, compared with ten or more in traditional organizations.[49]

One of the major disadvantages is lack of hands-on control. Managers do not have all operations under one roof and must rely on contracts, coordination, negotiation, and electronic linkages to hold things together. Each partner in the network necessarily acts in its own self-interest. The weak and ambiguous boundaries create higher uncertainty and greater demands on managers for defining shared goals, coordinating activities, managing relationships, and keeping people focused and motivated.[50] Finally, in this type of organization, employee loyalty can weaken. Employees might feel they can be replaced by contract services. A cohesive corporate culture is less likely to develop, and turnover tends to be higher because emotional commitment between organization and employee is weak.

ORGANIZING FOR HORIZONTAL COORDINATION

One reason for the growing use of teams and networks is that many companies are recognizing the limits of traditional vertical organization structures in today's fast-shifting environment. In general, the trend is toward breaking down barriers between departments, and many companies are moving toward horizontal structures based on work processes rather than departmental functions.[51] However, regardless of the type of structure, every organization needs mechanisms for horizontal integration and coordination. The structure of an organization is not complete without designing the horizontal as well as the vertical dimensions of structure.[52]

The Need for Coordination

As organizations grow and evolve, two things happen. First, new positions and departments are added to deal with factors in the external environment or with new strategic needs. For example, in recent years most colleges and universities established in-house legal departments to cope with increasing government regulations and a greater threat of lawsuits in today's society. Whereas small schools once relied on outside law firms, legal counsel is now considered crucial to the everyday operation of a college or university.[53] Many organizations establish information technology departments to manage the proliferation of new information systems. As companies add positions and departments to meet changing needs, they grow more complex, with hundreds of positions and departments performing incredibly diverse activities.

Second, senior managers have to find a way to tie all of these departments together. The formal chain of command and the supervision it provides is effective, but it is not enough. The organization needs systems to process information and enable communication among people in different departments and at different levels. **Coordination** refers to the quality of collaboration across departments. Without coordination, a company's left hand will not act in concert with the right hand, causing problems and conflicts. Coordination is required regardless of whether the organization has a functional, divisional, or team structure. Employees identify with their immediate department or team, taking its interest to heart, and may not want to compromise with other units for the good of the organization as a whole.

Without a major effort at coordination, an organization may be like Chrysler Corporation in the 1980s when Lee Iacocca took over:

> What I found at Chrysler were 35 vice presidents, each with his own turf. . . . I couldn't believe, for example, that the guy running engineering departments wasn't in constant touch with his counterpart in manufacturing. But that's how it was. Everybody worked independently. I took one look at that system and I almost threw up. That's when I knew I was in really deep trouble.
>
> I'd call in a guy from engineering, and he'd stand there dumbfounded when I'd explain to him that we had a design problem or some other hitch in the engineering-manufacturing relationship. He might have the ability to invent a brilliant piece of engineering that would save us a lot of money. He might come up with a terrific new design. There was only one problem: He didn't know that the manufacturing people couldn't build it. Why? Because he had never talked to them about it. Nobody at Chrysler seemed to understand that interaction among the different functions in a company is absolutely critical. People in engineering and manufacturing almost have to be sleeping together. These guys weren't even flirting![54]

coordination The quality of collaboration across departments.

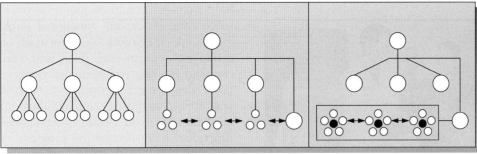

EXHIBIT   10.10

Evolution of Organization
Structures

**Traditional Vertical
Structure**

**Cross-Functional Teams and
Project Managers**

**Reengineering to
Horizontal Teams**

If one thing changed at Chrysler (now DaimlerChrysler) in the years before Iacocca retired, it was improved coordination. Cooperation among engineering, marketing, and manufacturing enabled the rapid design and production of the Chrysler
PT Cruiser, for example.

The problem of coordination is amplified in the international arena, because
organizational units are differentiated not only by goals and work activities but
by geographical distance, time differences, cultural values, and perhaps language
as well. How can managers ensure that needed coordination will take place in
their company, both domestically and globally? Coordination is the outcome of
information and cooperation. Managers can design systems and structures to
promote horizontal coordination. For example, to support its global strategy,
Whirlpool decentralized its operations, giving more authority and responsibility
to teams of designers and engineers in developing countries like Brazil, and
established outsourcing relationships with manufacturers in China and India.[55]
Exhibit 10.10 illustrates the evolution of organizational structures, with a growing
emphasis on horizontal coordination. Although the vertical functional structure is
effective in stable environments, it does not provide the horizontal coordination
needed in times of rapid change. Innovations such as cross-functional teams, task
forces, and project managers work within the vertical structure but provide a
means to increase horizontal communication and cooperation. The next stage
involves reengineering to structure the organization into teams working on horizontal processes. The vertical hierarchy is flattened, with perhaps only a few
senior executives in traditional support functions such as finance and human
resources.

Task Forces, Teams, and Project Management

A **task force** is a temporary team or committee designed to solve a short-term
problem involving several departments.[56] Task force members represent their
departments and share information that enables coordination. For example, the
Shawmut National Corporation created a task force in human resources to consolidate all employment services into a single area. The task force looked at job banks,
referral programs, employment procedures, and applicant tracking systems; found
ways to perform these functions for all Shawmut's divisions in one human
resource department; and then disbanded.[57] In addition to creating task forces,
companies also set up *cross-functional teams*, as described earlier. A cross-functional
team furthers horizontal coordination because participants from several departments meet regularly to solve ongoing problems of common interest.[58] This team is
similar to a task force except that it works with continuing rather than temporary
problems and might exist for several years. Team members think in terms of working together for the good of the whole rather than just for their own department.
For example, top executives at one large consumer products company had to

task force A temporary
team or committee formed to
solve a specific short-term
problem involving several
departments.

PEPSICO

**CONCEPT
CONNECTION** Frito-Lay, a subsidiary of PepsiCo Inc., introduced Lay's Cool Guacamole potato chips and Doritos Guacamole tortilla chips in 2003. A **task force** that included members of Adelante, the Frito-Lay network for Hispanic employees, helped develop both products. In the photo, Frito-Lay researchers and Adelante members check the quality of the new guacamole chips.

hold frequent marathon meetings to resolve conflicts among functional units. Functional managers were focused on achieving departmental goals and were engaged in little communication across units. Resolving the conflicts that arose was time-consuming and arduous for everyone involved. Establishing a cross-functional team solved the problem by ensuring regular horizontal communication and cooperation regarding common issues and problems.[59]

Companies also use project managers to increase coordination between functional departments. A **project manager** is a person who is responsible for coordinating the activities of several departments for the completion of a specific project.[60] Project managers are critical today because many organizations are continually reinventing themselves, creating flexible structures, and working on projects with an ever-changing assortment of people and organizations.[61] Project managers might work on several different projects at one time and might have to move in and out of new projects at a moment's notice.

The distinctive feature of the project manager position is that the person is not a member of one of the departments being coordinated. Project managers are located outside of the departments and have responsibility for coordinating several departments to achieve desired project outcomes. For example, General Mills, Procter & Gamble, and General Foods all use product managers to coordinate their product lines. A manager is assigned to each line, such as Cheerios, Bisquick, and Hamburger Helper. Product managers set budget goals, marketing targets, and strategies and obtain the cooperation from advertising, production, and sales personnel needed for implementing product strategy.

■ **TAKE A MOMENT** As a new manager, be a team or task force member who reaches out to facilitate horizontal coordination. Don't limit yourself to your own function. Share information across departmental boundaries to improve horizontal communication and understanding. Build your people skills to influence and persuade as an effective project manager.

project manager A person responsible for coordinating the activities of several departments on a full-time basis for the completion of a specific project.

In some organizations, project managers are included on the organization chart, as illustrated in Exhibit 10.11. The project manager is drawn to one side of the chart to indicate authority over the project but not over the people assigned to it. Dashed lines to the project manager indicate responsibility for coordination and communication with assigned team members, but department managers retain line authority over functional employees.

Project managers might also have titles such as product manager, integrator, program manager, or process owner. Project managers need excellent people skills. They use expertise and persuasion to achieve coordination among various departments, and their jobs involve getting people together, listening, building trust, confronting problems, and resolving conflicts and disputes in the best interest of the project and the organization. Consider the role of Hugh Hoffman at American Standard Companies.

Hugh J. Hoffman began working at American Standard as a ceramic engineer in 1970. Today, he works as a full-time project manager in the company's chinaware business, which makes toilets and bidets. Hoffman, whose official title is process owner, chinaware order fulfillment, coordinates all the activities that ensure that American Standard's factories turn out the products customers order and deliver them on time. Hoffman's job requires that he think about everything that happens between the time an order comes in and the time it gets paid for, including design, manufacturing, painting, sales, shipping and receiving, and numerous other tasks. Project managers such as Hoffman have to act as if they are running their own business, setting goals and developing strategies for achieving them. It is not always easy because Hoffman works outside the boundaries and authority structure of traditional departments. His years of experience and good people skills help him motivate others and coordinate the work of many departments and geographically dispersed factories. "I move behind the scenes," Hoffman says. "I understand the workings of the company and know how to get things done."[62]

American Standard Companies

Using project managers has helped American Standard do things faster, better, and cheaper than competitors. Many organizations move to a stronger horizontal approach such as the use of permanent teams, project managers, or process owners after going through a redesign procedure called reengineering.

Reengineering

Reengineering, sometimes called *business process reengineering*, is the radical redesign of business processes to achieve dramatic improvements in cost, quality, service, and speed.[63] Because the focus of reengineering is on process rather than function, reengineering generally leads to a shift away from a strong vertical structure to one emphasizing stronger horizontal coordination and greater flexibility in responding to changes in the environment.

Reengineering changes the way managers think about how work is done in their organizations. Rather than focusing on narrow jobs structured into distinct, functional departments, they emphasize core processes that cut horizontally across the company and involve teams of employees working to provide value directly to customers.[64] A **process** is an organized group of related tasks and activities that work together to transform inputs into outputs and create value. Common examples of processes include new product development, order fulfillment, and customer service.[65]

Reengineering frequently involves a shift to a horizontal team-based structure, as described earlier in this chapter. All the people who work on a particular process have easy access to one another so they can easily communicate and coordinate their efforts, share knowledge, and provide value directly to customers.[66]

reengineering The radical redesign of business processes to achieve dramatic improvements in cost, quality, service, and speed.

process An organized group of related tasks and activities that work together to transform inputs into outputs and create value.

For example, reengineering at Texas Instruments led to the formation of product development teams that became the fundamental organizational unit. Each team is made up of people drawn from engineering, marketing, and other departments, and takes full responsibility for a product from conception through launch.[67]

Reengineering can also squeeze out the dead space and time lags in work flows, as illustrated by reengineering of the travel system at the U.S. Department of Defense.

U.S. Department of Defense

The Pentagon can act quickly to move thousands of tons of humanitarian aid material or hundreds of thousands of troops, but until recently, sending employees on routine travel has been a different story. Before Pentagon travelers could even board a bus, they had to secure numerous approvals and fill out reams of paperwork. Coming home wasn't any easier—the average traveler spent six hours preparing vouchers for reimbursement following a trip.

The Department of Defense set up a task force to reengineer the cumbersome travel system, aiming to make it cheaper, more efficient, and more customer friendly. The reengineered system reduces the steps in the pretravel process from an astounding 11 to only 4, as shown in Exhibit 10.12. Travel budgets and authority to approve travel requests and vouchers, which traditionally rested in the budget channels of the various service commands, were transferred to local supervisors. Travelers make all their arrangements through a commercial travel office, which prepares a "should-cost" estimate for each trip. This document is all a traveler needs before, during, and after a trip: With a supervisor's signature, it becomes a travel authorization; during travel, it serves as an itinerary; after amendments to reflect variations from plans, it becomes an expense report. Other travel expenses and needed cash or travelers' checks can be charged to a government-issued travel card, with payment made directly to the travel card company through electronic funds transfer.[68]

As illustrated by this example, reengineering can lead to stunning results, but, like all business ideas, it has its drawbacks. Simply defining the organization's key business processes can be mind-boggling. AT&T's Network Systems division started with a list of 130 processes and then began working to pare them down to 13 core ones.[69] Organizations often have difficulty realigning power relationships and management processes to support work redesign, and thus do not reap the intended benefits of reengineering. According to some estimates, 70 percent of reengineering efforts fail to reach their intended goals.[70] Because reengineering is expensive, time consuming, and usually painful, it seems best suited to companies that are facing serious competitive threats.

E X H I B I T   10.12

Reengineering the Travel System—U.S. Department of Defense

SOURCE: Richard Koonce, "Reengineering the Travel Game," *Government Executive* (May 1995), 28–34, 69–70.

AUTHORITY ROLE MODELS

An organization's structure is based on authority. Beliefs about authority for a new manager are often based on experiences in your first authority figures and role models—Mom and Dad. To understand your authority role models, please answer each of the following items as Mostly True or Mostly False for you. Think in terms about each statement as it applies to the parent or parents who made primary decisions about raising you.

	Mostly True	Mostly False
1. My parent(s) believed that children should get their way in the family as often as the parents do.	⎯⎯	⎯⎯
2. When a family policy was established, my parent(s) discussed the reasoning behind it with the children.	⎯⎯	⎯⎯
3. My parent(s) believed it was for my own good if I was made to conform to what they thought was right.	⎯⎯	⎯⎯
4. My parents felt the children should make up our own minds about what we wanted to do even if we did not agree with them.	⎯⎯	⎯⎯
5. My parent(s) directed my activities through reasoning and discussion.	⎯⎯	⎯⎯
6. My parent(s) was clear about who was the boss in the family.	⎯⎯	⎯⎯
7. My parent(s) allowed me to decide most things for myself without a lot of direction.	⎯⎯	⎯⎯

	Mostly True	Mostly False
8. My parent(s) took the children's opinions into consideration when making family decisions.	⎯⎯	⎯⎯
9. If I didn't meet parental rules and expectations, I could expect to be punished.	⎯⎯	⎯⎯

INTERPRETATION AND SCORING: Each question pertains to one of three subscales of **parental authority**. Questions 1, 4, and 7 reflect *permissive* parental authority, questions 2, 5, and 8 indicate *flexible* authority, and questions 3, 6, and 9 indicate *authoritarian* parental authority. The subscale for which you checked more items Mostly True may reveal personal beliefs from your early role models that shape your comfort with authority as a new manager. *Authoritarian* beliefs typically would fit in a traditional vertical hierarchy. *Flexible* authority beliefs typically would fit with horizontal organizing, such as managing teams, projects, and reengineering. Because most organizations thrive on structure, *permissive* beliefs may be insufficient to enforce accountability under any structure. How do you think your childhood role models affect your authority beliefs? Remember, this questionnaire is just a guide because your current beliefs about authority may not directly reflect your childhood experiences.

SOURCE: Adapted from John R. Buri, "Parental Authority Questionnaire," *Journal of Personality and Social Assessment* 57 (1991): 110–119.

As a potential new manager, check out your authority role models by completing the New Manager Self-Test above. Your score will give you a sense of the type of structure in which you may fit best as a new manager.

▪ **TAKE A MOMENT**

FACTORS SHAPING STRUCTURE

Despite the trend toward horizontal design, vertical hierarchies continue to thrive because they often provide important benefits for organizations.[71] How do managers know whether to design a structure that emphasizes the formal, vertical hierarchy or one with an emphasis on horizontal communication and collaboration? The answer lies in the contingency factors that influence organization structure.

EXHIBIT 10.13

Contingency Factors That
Influence Organization
Structure

Research on organization design shows that structure depends on a variety of *contingencies*, as defined in Chapter 2. The right structure is designed to "fit" the contingency factors of strategy, environment, and production technology, as illustrated in Exhibit 10.13. These three areas are changing quite dramatically for most organizations, creating a need for stronger horizontal coordination.

Structure Follows Strategy

In Chapter 8, we discussed several strategies that business firms can adopt. Two strategies proposed by Porter are differentiation and cost leadership.[72] With a differentiation strategy, the organization attempts to develop innovative products unique to the market. With a cost leadership strategy, the organization strives for internal efficiency. The strategies of cost leadership versus differentiation typically require different structural approaches. A recent study demonstrated that business performance is strongly influenced by how well the company's structure is aligned with its strategic intent, so managers strive to pick strategies and structures that are congruent.[73]

Exhibit 10.14 shows a simplified continuum that illustrates how structural approaches are associated with strategic goals. The pure functional structure is appropriate for achieving internal efficiency goals. The vertical functional structure uses task specialization and a strict chain of command to gain efficient use of scarce resources, but it does not enable the organization to be flexible or innovative. In contrast, horizontal teams are appropriate when the primary goal is innovation and flexibility. Each team is small, is able to be responsive, and has the people and resources necessary for performing its task. The flexible horizontal structure enables organizations to differentiate themselves and respond quickly to the demands of a shifting environment but at the expense of efficient resource use. New strategies also shape structure in government organizations. Under financial pressure to cut costs and political pressure to keep customers happy, Departments of Motor Vehicles are farming out DMV business whenever possible by building strong

EXHIBIT 10.14

Relationship of Strategic
Goals to Structural
Approach

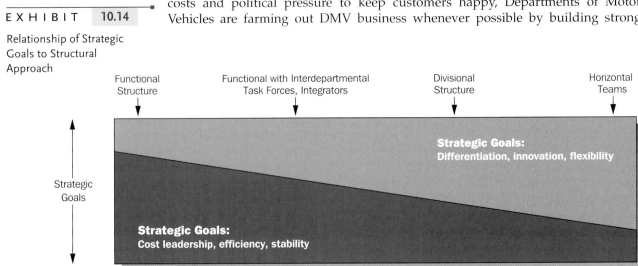

partnerships with other companies. For example, in most states, auto dealers register new cars on site when they are sold.[74]

Exhibit 10.14 also illustrates how other forms of structure represent intermediate steps on the organization's path to efficiency or innovation. The functional structure with cross-functional teams and project managers provides greater coordination and flexibility than the pure functional structure. The divisional structure promotes differentiation because each division can focus on specific products and customers, although divisions tend to be larger and less flexible than small teams. Exhibit 10.14 does not include all possible structures, but it illustrates how structures can be used to facilitate the strategic goals of cost leadership or differentiation.

Structure Reflects the Environment

In Chapter 3, we discussed the nature of environmental uncertainty. Environmental uncertainty means that decision makers have difficulty acquiring good information and predicting external changes. Uncertainty occurs when the external environment is rapidly changing and complex. An uncertain environment causes three things to happen within an organization.

1. *Increased differences occur among departments.* In an uncertain environment, each major department—marketing, manufacturing, research and development— focuses on the task and environmental sectors for which it is responsible and hence distinguishes itself from the others with respect to goals, task orientation, and time horizon.[75] Departments work autonomously. These factors create barriers among departments.

2. *The organization needs increased coordination to keep departments working together.* Additional differences require more emphasis on horizontal coordination to link departments and overcome differences in departmental goals and orientations.

3. *The organization must adapt to change.* The organization must maintain a flexible, responsive posture toward the environment. Changes in products and technology require cooperation among departments, which means additional emphasis on coordination through the use of teams, project managers, and horizontal information processing.[76]

The terms *mechanistic* and *organic* can be used to explain structural responses to the external environment.[77] When the environment is stable, the organization uses a mechanistic system. It typically has a rigid, vertical, centralized structure, with most decisions made at the top. The organization is highly specialized and characterized by rules, procedures, and a clear hierarchy of authority. In rapidly changing environments, however, the organization tends to be much looser, free-flowing, and adaptive, using an organic system. The structure is more horizontal and decision-making authority is decentralized. People at lower levels have more

© AIRMAN PETER CARNICELLI/UNITED STATES NAVY

333

CONCEPT CONNECTION There is nothing like the approach of a fighter jet with a landing speed of 150 miles per hour to shake up an organization—especially if you're standing on a small, moving flight deck, such as that of the *USS Dwight D. Eisenhower.* Here, crew members on the nuclear aircraft supercarrier practice a waveoff, signaling to an FA-18 Hornet pilot that he or she should take another pass before touching down. The crew adapts to the high-stakes, **uncertain environment** surrounding the orchestrated take-offs and landings of high-speed planes by shifting from a **mechanistic** to an **organic** system that allows for flexibility and rapid response.

STRUCTURE

	Vertical	Horizontal
Uncertain (Unstable)	**Incorrect Fit:** Vertical structure in uncertain environment — Mechanistic structure too tight	**Correct Fit:** Horizontal structure in uncertain environment
Certain (Stable)	**Correct Fit:** Vertical structure in certain environment	**Incorrect Fit:** Horizontal structure in certain environment — Organic structure too loose

ENVIRONMENT (row label)

EXHIBIT 10.15

Relationship Between Environment and Structure

responsibility and authority for solving problems, enabling the organization to be more fluid and adaptable to changes in the environment.[78]

TAKE A MOMENT Go to the experiential exercise on page 340 that pertains to organic versus mechanistic structure.

The contingency relationship between environmental uncertainty and structural approach is illustrated in Exhibit 10.15. When the external environment is stable, the organization can succeed with a mechanistic structure that emphasizes vertical control. With little need for change, flexibility, or intense coordination, the structure can emphasize specialization and centralized decision making. When environmental uncertainty is high, however, a flexible organic structure that emphasizes lateral relationships such as teams and horizontal projects is appropriate. Vertical structure characteristics such as specialization and centralization should be downplayed. In an uncertain environment, the organization figures things out as it goes along, departments must cooperate, and decisions should be decentralized to the teams and task forces working on specific problems. The flight deck of the *USS Dwight D. Eisenhower*, a nuclear-powered aircraft carrier, provides an excellent example of the relationship between structure and the environment.

USS Dwight D. Eisenhower

Launching or landing a plane from the oil-slicked deck of a nuclear-powered aircraft carrier, such as the *USS Dwight D. Eisenhower*, is a tricky, finely balanced procedure. A sudden wind shift, a mechanical breakdown, or the slightest of miscommunications could spell disaster. Yet, surprisingly, flight deck operations generally run as smooth as silk, and accidents are quite rare. The reason has a lot to do with organizational structure.

At first glance, a nuclear aircraft carrier is structured in a rigid, hierarchical way—the captain issues orders to commanders, who direct lieutenants, who pass orders on to ensigns, and on down the hierarchy. Within a strict chain of command, people are expected to follow orders promptly and without question. Manuals detail standard operating procedures for everything. But an interesting thing happens in times of high demand, such as the launching and recovery of planes during real or simulated wartime. In this different environment, the hierarchy dissolves and a loosely organized, collaborative structure in which sailors and officers work together as colleagues takes its place. People discuss and negotiate the best procedure to use, and everyone typically follows the lead of whoever has the most experience and knowledge in a particular area, no matter the person's rank or job title.

During this time, no one is thinking about job descriptions, authority, or chain of command; they are just thinking about getting the job done safely. Planes landing every 60 seconds leave no time to send messages up the chain of command and wait for decisions to come down from the top. Anyone who notices a problem is expected to respond quickly, and each member of the crew has the power—and the obligation—to shut down flight operations immediately if the circumstances warrant it.[79]

Researchers studied this ability to glide smoothly from a rigid, hierarchical structure to a loosely structured, horizontal one, not only on aircraft carriers but in other organizations that need to be exceptionally responsive to environmental changes—for example, air-traffic controllers or workers at nuclear power plants. The hierarchical side helps keep discipline and ensure adherence to rules that have been developed and tested over many years to cope with expected and well-understood problems and situations. However, during times of complexity and high uncertainty, the most effective structure is one that loosens the lines of command and enables people to work across departmental and hierarchical lines to anticipate and avoid problems.[80]

Not all organizations have to be as super-responsive to the environment as the *USS Dwight D. Eisenhower*, but using the correct structure for the environment is important for businesses as well. When managers use the wrong structure for the environment, reduced performance results. A rigid, vertical structure in an uncertain environment prevents the organization from adapting to change. Likewise, a loose, horizontal structure in a stable environment is inefficient. Too many resources are devoted to meetings and discussions when employees could be more productive focusing on specialized tasks.

Structure Fits the Technology

Technology includes the knowledge, tools, techniques, and activities used to transform organizational inputs into outputs.[81] Technology includes machinery, employee skills, and work procedures. A useful way to think about technology is as production activities. The production activities may be to produce steel castings, television programs, or computer software. Technologies vary between manufacturing and service organizations. In addition, new digital technology has an impact on structure.

WOODWARD'S MANUFACTURING TECHNOLOGY

The most influential research into the relationship between manufacturing technology and organization structure was conducted by Joan Woodward, a British industrial sociologist.[82] She gathered data from 100 British firms to determine whether basic structural characteristics, such as administrative overhead, span of control, and centralization were different across firms. She found that manufacturing firms could be categorized according to three basic types of production technology:

1. *Small-batch and unit production.* **Small-batch production** firms produce goods in batches of one or a few products designed to customer specification. Each customer orders a unique product. This technology also is used to make large, one-of-a-kind products, such as computer-controlled machines. Small-batch manufacturing is close to traditional skilled-craft work, because human beings are a large part of the process. Examples of items produced through small-batch manufacturing include custom clothing, special-order machine tools, space capsules, satellites, and submarines.

2. *Large-batch and mass production.* **Mass production** technology is distinguished by standardized production runs. A large volume of products is produced, and all customers receive the same product. Standard products go into inventory for sale as customers need them. This technology makes greater use of machines than does small-batch production. Machines are designed to do most of the physical work, and employees complement the machinery. Examples of mass production are automobile assembly lines and the large-batch techniques used to produce tobacco products and textiles.

3. *Continuous process production.* In **continuous process production**, the entire work flow is mechanized in a sophisticated and complex form of production technology. Because the process runs continuously, it has no starting and stopping.

small-batch production A type of technology that involves the production of goods in batches of one or a few products designed to customer specification.

mass production A type of technology characterized by the production of a large volume of products with the same specifications.

continuous process production A type of technology involving mechanization of the entire work flow and nonstop production.

CONCEPT

CONNECTION Employees at ConocoPhillips' Los Angeles, California, petroleum refinery at Wilmington use **continuous process production** to supply refined products to markets in California, Nevada, and Arizona. This sophisticated type of technology is typically associated with a small span of control, a high degree of horizontal communication, and a **flexible structure** to handle the complexities that arise. The ConocoPhillips global refining network has a crude oil processing capacity of 2.6 million barrels per day, including 2.2 million in the United States.

Human operators are not part of actual production because machinery does all of the work. Human operators simply read dials, fix machines that break down, and manage the production process. Examples of continuous process technologies are chemical plants, distilleries, petroleum refineries, and nuclear power plants.

The difference among the three manufacturing technologies is called **technical complexity**. Technical complexity is the degree to which machinery is involved in the production to the exclusion of people. With a complex technology, employees are hardly needed except to monitor the machines.

The structural characteristics associated with each type of manufacturing technology are illustrated in Exhibit 10.16. Note that centralization is high for mass production technology and low for continuous process. Unlike small-batch and continuous process production, standardized mass-production machinery requires centralized decision making and well-defined rules and procedures. The administrative ratio and the percentage of indirect labor required also increase with technological complexity. Because the production process is nonroutine, closer supervision is needed. More indirect labor in the form of maintenance people is required because of the machinery's complexity; thus, the indirect/direct labor ratio is high. Span of control for first-line supervisors is greatest for mass production. On an assembly line, jobs are so routinized that a supervisor can handle an average of 48 employees. The number of employees per supervisor in small-batch and continuous process production is lower because closer supervision is needed. Overall, small-batch and continuous process firms have somewhat loose, flexible structures (organic), and mass production firms have tight vertical structures (mechanistic).

technical complexity The degree to which complex machinery is involved in the production process to the exclusion of people.

EXHIBIT 10.16

Relationship Between Manufacturing Technology and Organization Structure

SOURCE: Based on Joan Woodward, *Industrial Organizations: Theory and Practice* (London: Oxford University Press, 1965).

	Manufacturing Technology		
	Small Batch	Mass Production	Continuous Process
Technical Complexity of Production Technology:	Low	Medium	High
Organization Structure:			
Centralization	Low	High	Low
Top administrator ratio	Low	Medium	High
Indirect/direct labor ratio	1/9	1/4	1/1
Supervisor span of control	23	48	15
Communication:			
Written (vertical)	Low	High	Low
Verbal (horizontal)	High	Low	High
Overall structure	Organic	Mechanistic	Organic

The important conclusion about manufacturing technology was described by Woodward as follows: "Different technologies impose different kinds of demands on individuals and organizations, and these demands have to be met through an appropriate structure."[83] Woodward found that the relationship between structure and technology was directly related to company performance. Low-performing firms tended to deviate from the preferred structural form, often adopting a structure appropriate for another type of technology. High-performing organizations had characteristics similar to those listed in Exhibit 10.16.

SERVICE TECHNOLOGY

Service organizations are increasingly important in North America. For the past two decades, more people have been employed in service organizations than in manufacturing firms. Examples of service organizations include consulting companies, law firms, brokerage houses, airlines, hotels, advertising companies, amusement parks, and educational organizations. In addition, service technology characterizes many departments in large corporations, even manufacturing firms. In a manufacturing company such as Ford Motor Company, the legal, human resources, finance, and market research departments all provide service. Thus, the structure and design of these departments reflect their own service technology rather than the manufacturing plant's technology. **Service technology** can be defined as follows:

1. *Intangible output.* The output of a service firm is intangible. Services are perishable and, unlike physical products, cannot be stored in inventory. The service is either consumed immediately or lost forever. Manufactured products are produced at one point in time and can be stored until sold at another time.

2. *Direct contact with customers.* Employees and customers interact directly to provide and purchase the service. Production and consumption are simultaneous. Service firm employees have direct contact with customers. In a manufacturing firm, technical employees are separated from customers, and hence no direct interactions occur.[84]

One distinct feature of service technology that directly influences structure is the need for employees to be close to the customer.[85] Structural characteristics are similar to those for continuous manufacturing technology, shown in Exhibit 10.16. Service firms tend to be flexible, informal, and decentralized. Horizontal communication is high because employees must share information and resources to serve customers and solve problems. Services also are dispersed; hence each unit is often small and located geographically close to customers. For example, banks, hotels, fast-food franchises, and doctors' offices disperse their facilities into regional and local offices to provide faster and better service to customers.

Some services can be broken down into explicit steps, so that employees can follow set rules and procedures. For example, McDonald's has standard procedures for serving customers and Marriott has standard procedures for cleaning hotel rooms. When services can be standardized, a tight centralized structure can be effective, but service firms in general tend to be more organic, flexible, and decentralized.

As a new manager, recognize how structure fits the contingency factors of strategy, environment, and technology. Design the right mix of structural characteristics to fit the contingency factors.

TAKE A MOMENT

DIGITAL TECHNOLOGY

Digital technology is characterized by use of the Internet and other digital processes to conduct or support business online. E-commerce organizations such as Amazon.com, which sells books and other products to consumers over the Internet; eBay, an online auction site; Google, an Internet search engine; and Priceline.com,

service technology Technology characterized by intangible outputs and direct contact between employees and customers.

digital technology Technology characterized by use of the Internet and other digital processes to conduct or support business operations.

which allows consumers to name their own prices and then negotiates electronically with its partner organizations on behalf of the consumer, are all examples of firms based on digital technology. In addition, large companies such as General Electric, Dell Inc., and Ford Motor Company are involved in business-to-business commerce, using digital technology to conduct transactions with suppliers and partners.

Like service firms, organizations based on digital technology tend to be flexible and decentralized. Horizontal communication and collaboration are typically high, and these companies may frequently be involved in virtual network arrangements. Digital technology is driving the move toward horizontal forms that link customers, suppliers, and partners into the organizational network, with everyone working together as if they were one organization. People may use electronic connections to link themselves together into teams. For example, an employee may send an e-mail to people both within and outside the organization who can help with a particular customer problem and quickly form a virtual team to develop a solution.[86] In other words, digital technology encourages *boundarylessness*, where information and work activities flow freely among various organizational participants. Centralization is low, and employees are empowered to work in teams to meet fast-changing needs. Verbal and electronic communication is high, both up and down as well as across the organization, because up-to-the minute information is essential. In the digital world, advantage comes from seeing first and moving fastest, which requires extraordinary openness and flexibility.[87]

MANAGER'S SOLUTION

This chapter introduced a number of important organizing concepts. Fundamental characteristics of organization structure include work specialization, chain of command, authority and responsibility, span of management, and centralization and decentralization. These dimensions represent the vertical hierarchy and define how authority and responsibility are distributed.

Another major concept is departmentalization, which describes how organization employees are grouped. Three traditional approaches are functional, divisional, and matrix; contemporary approaches are team and virtual network structures. The functional approach groups employees by common skills and tasks. The opposite structure is divisional, which groups people by organizational output such that each division has a mix of functional skills and tasks. The matrix structure uses two chains of command simultaneously, and some employees have two bosses. The team approach uses permanent teams and cross-functional teams to achieve better coordination and employee commitment than is possible with a pure functional structure. The network approach means that a firm concentrates on what it does best and subcontracts other functions to separate organizations that are connected to the headquarters electronically. Each organization form has advantages and disadvantages and can be used by managers to meet the needs of the competitive situation. In addition, managers adjust elements of the vertical structure, such as the degree of centralization or decentralization, to meet changing needs.

As organizations grow, they add new departments, functions, and hierarchical levels. A major problem for management is how to tie the whole organization together. Horizontal coordination mechanisms provide coordination across departments and include reengineering, task forces, project managers, and horizontal teams.

Contingency factors of strategy, environment, and production technology influence the correct structural approach. When a firm's strategy is to differentiate its products or services, an organic flexible structure using teams, decentralization, and empowered employees is appropriate. A mechanistic structure is appropriate for a low-cost strategy. Similarly, the structure needs to be looser and more flexible when environmental uncertainty is high. For manufacturing firms, small batch, continuous process, and flexible manufacturing technologies tend to be structured loosely, whereas a tighter vertical structure is appropriate for mass production. Service technologies are people oriented, and firms are located geographically close to dispersed customers. In general, services have more flexible, horizontal structures, with decentralized decision making. Similarly, organizations based on new digital technology are typically horizontally structured and highly decentralized.

Returning to the opening example, Carlos Ghosn used structural changes to help revive Nissan and restore its competitive position in the auto industry. Today, Nissan is on a roll, with hot new car and truck models that customers want. The company has the highest profit margins of any major automaker, and racked up record earnings of $4.8 billion in 2004, a year when most other auto manufacturers were reeling from losses. One of Ghosn's first steps was to clarify managers' areas of responsibility and authority and implement mechanisms to ensure accountability. Positions were redesigned so that managers who previously acted as advisors had direct line authority and a clear understanding of how they were expected to contribute to the organization. The compensation and advancement systems were also revised. The major structural change Ghosn made was to create nine cross-functional management teams that would determine a detailed turnaround plan for the organization. Ghosn believed the team approach was the best way to get managers to see beyond the functional and regional boundaries that were hampering collaboration and new product development. Each team was made up of managers from various functional areas. For example, the purchasing team consisted of members from purchasing, engineering, manufacturing, and finance. Within three months, the teams had created a detailed blueprint for Nissan's turnaround. Within three years, implementation of various aspects of the plan had returned Nissan to profitability. The cross-functional teams continue as an integral part of Nissan's management structure, helping ensure continued horizontal communication and collaboration to help the company compete in the turbulent auto industry.[88]

DISCUSSION QUESTIONS

1. Sandra Holt, manager of Electronics Assembly, asked Hector Cruz, her senior technician, to handle things in the department while Sandra worked on the budget. She needed peace and quiet for at least a week to complete her figures. After 10 days, Sandra discovered that Hector had hired a senior secretary, not realizing that Sandra had promised interviews to two other people. Evaluate Sandra's approach to delegation.

2. Many experts note that organizations have been making greater use of teams in recent years. What factors might account for this trend?

3. An organizational consultant was heard to say, "Some aspect of functional structure appears in every organization." Do you agree? Explain.

4. The divisional structure is often considered almost the opposite of a functional structure. Do you agree? Briefly explain the major differences in these two approaches to departmentalization.

5. Some people argue that the matrix structure should be adopted only as a last resort because the dual chains of command can create more problems than they solve. Discuss. Do you agree or disagree? Why?

6. What is the virtual network approach to structure? Is the use of authority and responsibility different compared with other forms of departmentalization? Explain.

7. The Hay Group published a report that some managers have personalities suited to horizontal relationships such as project management that achieve results with little formal authority. Other managers are more suited to operating roles with much formal authority in a vertical structure. In what type of structure—functional, matrix, team, or virtual network—would you feel most comfortable managing? Which structure would be the most challenging for you? Give your reasons.

8. Experts say that organizations are becoming increasingly decentralized, with authority, decision-making responsibility, and accountability being pushed farther down into the organization. How will this trend affect what will be asked of you as a new manager? The chapter suggested that structure should be designed to fit strategy. Some theorists argue that strategy should be designed to fit the organization's structure. With which theory do you agree? Explain.

9. Carnival Cruise Lines provides pleasure cruises to the masses. Carnival has several ships and works on high volume/low price rather than offering luxury cruises. What would you predict about the organization structure of a Carnival Cruise ship compared with a company that had smaller ships for wealthy customers? Discuss why an organization in an uncertain environment requires more horizontal relationships than one in a certain environment.

10. What is the difference between manufacturing and service technology? How would you classify a university, a local discount store, a nursery school? How would you expect the structure of a service organization to differ from that of a manufacturing organization?

11. What impact does the growing use of digital technology have on organizational structure? Would you expect the structure of an Internet-based organization such as eBay, which operates almost entirely online, to be different from a bricks-and-mortar company such as General Electric that uses the Internet for business-to-business transactions with vendors? Why or why not?

MANAGEMENT IN PRACTICE: EXPERIENTIAL EXERCISE

Organic Versus Mechanistic Organization Structure

Interview an employee at your university, such as a department head or secretary. Have the employee answer the following 13 questions about his or her job and organizational conditions. Then, answer the same set of questions for a job you have held.

Disagree Strongly	❶	❷	❸	❹	❺	Agree Strongly

1. Your work would be considered routine. ❶ ❷ ❸ ❹ ❺

2. A clearly known way is established to do the major tasks you encounter. ❶ ❷ ❸ ❹ ❺

3. Your work has high variety and frequent exceptions. ❶ ❷ ❸ ❹ ❺

4. Communications from above consist of information and advice rather than instructions and directions. ❶ ❷ ❸ ❹ ❺

5. You have the support of peers and your supervisor to do your job well. ❶ ❷ ❸ ❹ ❺

6. You seldom exchange ideas or information with people doing other kinds of jobs. ❶ ❷ ❸ ❹ ❺

7. Decisions relevant to your work are made above you and passed down. ❶ ❷ ❸ ❹ ❺

8. People at your level frequently have to figure out for themselves what their jobs are for the day. ❶ ❷ ❸ ❹ ❺

9. Lines of authority are clear and precisely defined. ❶ ❷ ❸ ❹ ❺

10. Leadership tends to be democratic rather than autocratic in style. ❶ ❷ ❸ ❹ ❺

11. Job descriptions are written and up-to-date for each job. ❶ ❷ ❸ ❹ ❺

12. People understand each other's jobs and often do different tasks. ❶ ❷ ❸ ❹ ❺

13. A manual of policies and procedures is available to use when a problem arises. ❶ ❷ ❸ ❹ ❺

Scoring and Interpretation

To obtain the total score, subtract the scores for questions 1, 2, 6, 7, 9, 11, and 13 from the number 6 and total the adjusted scores.

Total Score, Employee: _____

Total Score, You: _____

Compare the total score for a place you have worked to the score of the university employee you interviewed. A total score of 52 or above suggests that you or the other respondent is working in an organic organization. The score reflects a loose, flexible structure that is often associated with uncertain environments and small-batch or service technology. People working in this structure feel empowered. Many organizations today are moving in the direction of flexible structures and empowerment.

A score of 26 or below suggests a mechanistic structure. This structure utilizes traditional control and functional specialization, which often occurs in a certain environment, a stable organization, and routine or mass-production technology. People in this structure may feel controlled and constrained.

Discuss the pros and cons of organic versus mechanistic structure. Does the structure of the employee you interviewed fit the nature of the organization's environment, strategic goals, and technology? How about the structure for your own workplace? How might you redesign the structure to make the work organization more effective?

A Matter of Delegation

Tom Harrington loved his job as an assistant quality-control officer for Rockingham Toys. After six months of unemployment, he was anxious to make a good impression on his boss, Frank Golopolus. One of his new responsibilities was ensuring that new product lines met federal safety guidelines. Rockingham had made several manufacturing changes over the past year. Golopolus and the rest of the quality-control team had been working 60-hour weeks to troubleshoot the new production process.

Harrington was aware of numerous changes in product safety guidelines that he knew would impact the new Rockingham toys. Golopolus was also aware of the guidelines, but he was taking no action to implement them. Harrington wasn't sure whether his boss expected him to implement the new procedures. The ultimate responsibility was his boss's, and Harrington was concerned about moving ahead on his own. To cover for his boss, he continued to avoid the questions he received from the factory floor, but he was beginning to wonder whether Rockingham would have time to make changes with the Christmas season rapidly approaching.

Harrington felt loyalty to Golopolus for giving him a job and didn't want to alienate him by interfering. However, he was beginning to worry what might happen if he didn't act. Rockingham had a fine product safety reputation and was rarely challenged on matters of quality. Should he question Golopolus about implementing the new safety guidelines?

What Would You Do?

1. Prepare a memo to Golopolus, summarizing the new safety guidelines that affect the Rockingham product line and requesting his authorization for implementation.

2. Mind your own business. Golopolus hasn't said anything about the new guidelines and you don't want to overstep your authority. You've been unemployed and need this job.

3. Send copies of the reports anonymously to the operations manager, who is Golopolus's boss.

SOURCE: Based on Doug Wallace, "The Man Who Knew Too Much," *Business Ethics*, 2 (March–April 1993): 7–8.

CASES FOR CRITICAL ANALYSIS

FMB&T

Marshall Pinkard, president and CEO of FMB&T, a growing California-based regional commercial and consumer retail bank, clicked on an e-mail from Ayishia Coles. Ayishia was the bright, hard-working, self-confident woman who'd recently come onboard as the bank's executive vice president and chief information officer. The fact that the person in Coles's position in the company's traditional vertical organization now reported directly to him and was a full-fledged member of the executive committee reflected FMB&T's recognition of just how important information technology was to all aspects of its increasingly competitive business. The successful, leading-edge banks were the ones using information technology not only to operate efficiently, but also to help them focus more effectively on customer needs. Marshall settled back to read what he expected would be a report on how she was settling in. He was sadly mistaken.

After a few months on the job, Ayishia Coles was frustrated. What she needed from him, she wrote, was a clear statement of her responsibilities and authority. The way Ayishia saw it, the relationship between information technology and the bank's other business units was muddled, often causing considerable confusion, friction, and inefficiency. Typically someone from retail banking or marketing, for example, came to her department with a poorly defined problem, such as how to link up checking account records with investment records, and they always expected a solution the same day. What made the situation even more vexing was that more often than not, the problem crossed organizational lines. She found that generally the more work units the problem affected, the less likely it was that any single unit took responsibility for defining exactly what they wanted IT to do. Who exactly was supposed to be getting all these units together and coordinating requests? When she tried to step into the breach and act as a facilitator, unit managers usually didn't welcome her efforts.

Despite the vagueness of their requests, the work units still expected IT to come up with a solution—and come up with it quickly. All of these expectations seemed almost calculated to drive the methodical IT folks mad. Before taking on a problem, they wanted to make sure they thoroughly understood all of its dimensions so that the solution would fit seamlessly into the existing systems. This coordination took time that other parts of the bank weren't willing to give IT.

In addition, Ayishia knew the IT staff was increasingly feeling underutilized. The staff wanted to identify opportunities for dazzling new IT developments to contribute to business strategies, but it found itself limited to applications work. Ayishia's greatest concern was the president of a large regional branch who was actively campaigning to locate decentralized IT departments in each large branch under branch authority so that work would be completed faster to meet branch needs. He said it would be better to let work-units coordinate their own IT departments rather than run everything though corporate IT. Under that scenario, Ayishia Coles' department could end up one-half its current size.

Marshall leaned back in his high-backed executive chair and sighed. At the very least, he needed to clarify Ayishia's authority and responsibilities as she had asked him to do. But he recognized that the new vice president was talking about a much larger can of worms. Was it time to rethink the bank's entire organizational structure?

Questions

1. What are the main organizational causes of the frustration that Ayishia Coles feels?

2. If you were Marshall Pinkard, how would you address both Ayishia's request for clarification about her authority and responsibilities and the underlying problems her e-mail brings to his attention? Can the problems be addressed with minor adjustments, or would you need to consider a drastic overhaul of the bank's organizational structure? What environmental and technological factors would influence your decision?

3. Sketch a general chart for the type of organization that you think would work best for IT at FMB&T.

SOURCES: Based on Perry Glasser, "In CIOs We Trust," *CIO Enterprise,* (June 15, 1999): 34–44; Stephanie Overby, "What Really Matters: Staying in the Game," *CIO Magazine* (October 1, 2004), www.cio.com/archive/100104/role.html; and Alenka Grealish, "Banking Trends in 2005 That Will Make A Difference," *Bank Systems & Technology* (December 14, 2004): www.banktech.com/news/showarticle.jhtml?articleid=55301770.

ENDNOTES

1. Carlos Ghosn, "Saving the Business without Losing the Company," *Harvard Business Review* (January 2002): 37–45.

2. Karen Chan, "From Top to Bottom," *The Wall Street Journal* (May 21, 2001): R12.

3. Chuck Salter, "Ford's Escape Route," *Fast Company* (October 2004): 106–110; and Bernard Simon, "Ford Aims to Build on Hybrid's Success," *National Post* (January 26, 2005): FP–10.

4. Andrew Pollack, "Medical Companies Join Offshore Trend," *The New York Times* (February 24, 2005), http://www.nytimes.com; Saritha Rai, "Drug Companies Cut Costs With Foreign Clinical Trials," *The New York Times* (February 24, 2004), http://www.nytimes.com.

5. John Child, *Organization: A Guide to Problems and Practice,* 2d ed. (London: Harper & Row, 1984).

6. Adam Smith, *The Wealth of Nations* (New York: Modern Library, 1937).

7. This discussion is based on Richard L. Daft, *Organization Theory and Design,* 4th ed. (St. Paul, MN: West, 1992): 387–388.

8. C. I. Barnard, *The Functions of the Executive* (Cambridge, MA: Harvard University Press, 1938).

9. Thomas A. Stewart, "CEOs See Clout Shifting," *Fortune* (November 6, 1989): 66.

10. Michael G. O'Loughlin, "What Is Bureaucratic Accountability and How Can We Measure It?" *Administration & Society* 22, no. 3 (November 1990): 275–302; and Brian Dive, "When Is an Organization Too Flat?" *Across the Board* (July–August 2003): 20–23.

11. Gary L. Neilson and Bruce A. Pasternack, "The Cat That Came Back," *Strategy + Business*, no. 40 (August 17, 2005): 32–45.

12. Carrie R. Leana, "Predictors and Consequences of Delegation," *Academy of Management Journal* 29 (1986): 754–774.

13. Robert A. Guth, "Midlife Correction: Inside Microsoft, Financial Managers Win New Clout," *The Wall Street Journal* (July 23, 2003): A1, A6.

14. Curtis Sittenfeld, "Powered by the People," *Fast Company* (July–August 1999): 178–189.

15. Barbara Davison, "Management Span of Control: How Wide Is Too Wide?" *Journal of Business Strategy* 24, no. 4 (2003): 22–29; Paul D. Collins and Frank Hull, "Technology and Span of Control: Woodward Revisited," *Journal of Management Studies* 23 (March 1986): 143–164; David D. Van Fleet and Arthur G. Bedeian, "A History of the Span of Management," *Academy of Management Review* 2 (1977): 356–372; and C. W. Barkdull, "Span of Control—A Method of Evaluation," *Michigan Business Review* 15 (May 1963): 25–32.

16. Gary Neilson, Bruce A. Pasternack, and Decio Mendes, "The Four Bases of Organizational DNA," *Strategy + Business*, Issue 33 (December 10, 2003): 48–57.

17. Barbara Davison, "Management Span of Control"; Brian Dive, "When Is an Organization Too Flat?"; and Brian

Dumaine, "What the Leaders of Tomorrow See," *Fortune* (July 3, 1989): 48–62.

18. Raghuram G. Rajan and Julie Wulf, "The Flattening Firm: Evidence from Panel Data on the Changing Nature of Corporate Hierarchies," working paper, reported in Caroline Ellis, "The Flattening Corporation," *MIT Sloan Management Review* (Summer 2003): 5.

19. Dennis Cauchon, "The Little Company That Could," *USA Today* (October 9, 2005), http://www.usatoday.com; Charles Haddad, "How UPS Delivered Through the Disaster," *BusinessWeek* (October 1, 2001): 66.

20. Brian O'Reilly, "J&J Is on a Roll," *Fortune* (December 26, 1994): 178–191; and Joseph Weber, "A Big Company That Works," *BusinessWeek* (May 4, 1992): 124–132.

21. Steffan M. Lauster and J. Neely, "The Core's Competence," *Strategy + Business*, Issue 38 (April 15, 2005): 40–49.

22. Clay Chandler and Paul Ingrassia, "Just as U.S. Firms Try Japanese Management, Honda Is Centralizing," *The Wall Street Journal* (April 11, 1991): A1, A10.

23. The following discussion of structural alternatives draws heavily from Jay R. Galbraith, *Designing Complex Organizations* (Reading, MA: Addison-Wesley, 1973); Jay R. Galbraith, *Organization Design* (Reading, MA: Addison-Wesley, 1977); Jay R. Galbraith, *Designing Dynamic Organizations* (New York: AMACOM, 2002); Robert Duncan, "What Is the Right Organization Structure?" *Organizational Dynamics* (Winter 1979): 59–80; and J. McCann and Jay R. Galbraith, "Interdepartmental Relations," in *Handbook of Organizational Design*, ed. P. Nystrom and W. Starbuck (New York: Oxford University Press, 1981): 60–84.

24. Based on the story of Blue Bell Creameries in Richard L. Daft, *Organization Theory and Design*, 9th ed. (Mason, OH: South-Western, 2007): 103.

25. Jay Greene, "Less Could Be More at Microsoft," *BusinessWeek* (October 3, 2005): 40; and Robert A. Guth, "Code Red; Battling Google, Microsoft Changes How It Builds Software," *The Wall Street Journal* (September 23, 2005): A1, A14.

26. Eliza Newlin Carney, "Calm in the Storm," *Government Executive* (October 2003): 57–63; and http://www.irs. gov (accessed on April 20, 2004).

27. Robert J. Kramer, *Organizing for Global Competitiveness: The Geographic Design* (New York: The Conference Board, 1993): 29–31.

28. Maisie O'Flanagan and Lynn K. Taliento, "Nonprofits: Ensuring That Bigger Is Better," *McKinsey Quarterly*, no. 2 (2004): 112ff.

29. Lawton R. Burns, "Matrix Management in Hospitals: Testing Theories of Matrix Structure and Development," *Administrative Science Quarterly* 34 (1989): 349–368; Carol Hymowitz, "Managers Suddenly Have to Answer to a Crowd of Bosses," *The Wall Street Journal* (August 12, 2003): B1.

30. Stanley M. Davis and Paul R. Lawrence, *Matrix* (Reading, MA: Addison-Wesley, 1977).

31. Edward Prewitt, "GM's Matrix Reloads," *CIO* (September 2003): 90–92.

32. Susan Carey, "US Air 'Peon' Team Pilots Start-Up of Low-Fare Airline," *The Wall Street Journal* (March 24, 1998): B1.

33. Charles Fishman, "Total Teamwork: Imagination Ltd.," *Fast Company* (April 2000): 156–168.

34. Melissa A. Schilling and H. Kevin Steensma, "The Use of Modular Organizational Forms: An Industry-Level Analysis," *Academy of Management Journal*, 44, no. 6 (December 2001): 1149–1169.

35. Susan G. Cohen and Don Mankin, "Complex Collaborations for the New Global Economy," *Organizational Dynamics* 31, no. 2 (2002): 117–133; David Lei and John W. Slocum Jr., "Organizational Designs to Renew Competitive Advantage," *Organizational Dynamics* 31, no. 1 (2002): 1–18.

36. Raymond E. Miles and Charles C. Snow, "The New Network Firm: A Spherical Structure Built on a Human Investment Philosophy," *Organizational Dynamics* (Spring 1995): 5–18; and Raymond E. Miles, Charles C. Snow, John A. Matthews, Grant Miles, and Henry J. Coleman, Jr., "Organizing in the Knowledge Age: Anticipating the Cellular Form," *Academy of Management Executive* 11, no. 4 (1997): 7–24.

37. Jena McGregor, with Michael Arndt, Robert Berner, Ian Rowley, Kenji Hall, Gail Edmondson, Steve Hamm, Moon Ihlwan, and Andy Reinhardt, "The World's Most Innovative Companies," *BusinessWeek* (April 24, 2006), http://www.businessweek.com.

38. Raymond E. Miles and Charles C. Snow, "Organizations: New Concepts for New Forms," *California Management Review* 28 (Spring 1986): 62–73; and "Now, The Post-Industrial Corporation," *BusinessWeek* (March 3, 1986): 64–74.

39. N. Anand, "Modular, Virtual, and Hollow Forms of Organization Design," working paper, London Business School (2000); Don Tapscott, "Rethinking Strategy in a Networked World," *Strategy & Business*, Issue 24 (Third Quarter 2001): 34–41.

40. Malcolm Wheatley, "Cycle Company with a Virtual Spin," *MT* (September 2003): 78–81.

41. Gregory G. Dess, Abdul M. A. Rasheed, Kevin J. McLaughlin, and Richard L. Priem, "The New Corporate Architecture," *Academy of Management Executive* 9, no. 3 (1995): 7–20.

42. Philip Siekman, "The Snap-Together Business Jet," *Fortune* (January 21, 2002): 104[A]–104[H].

43. Kathleen Kerwin, "GM: Modular Plants Won't Be a Snap," *BusinessWeek* (November 9, 1998): 168, 172.

44. Robert C. Ford and W. Alan Randolph, "Cross-Functional Structures: A Review and Integration of Matrix Organization and Project Management," *Journal of Management* 18, no. 2 (1992): 267–294; and Paula Dwyer with Pete Engardio, Zachary Schiller, and Stanley Reed, "Tearing Up Today's Organization Chart," *BusinessWeek/Twenty-First Century Capitalism*, 80–90.

45. These disadvantages are based on Michael Goold and Andrew Campbell, "Making Matrix Structures Work: Creating Clarity on Unit Roles and Responsibilities," *European Management Journal* 21, no. 3 (June 2003): 351–363; Hymowitz, "Managers Suddenly Have to Answer to a Crowd of Bosses"; and Dwyer et al., "Tearing Up Today's Organization Chart."

46. Geoff Keighley, "Massively Multinational Player," *Business 2.0* (September 2005): 64–66.

47. Dexter Filkins, "Profusion of Rebel Groups Helps Them Survive in Iraq," *The New York Times* (December 2, 2005), http://www.nytimes.com.

48. Scott Shane and Neil A. Lewis, "At Sept. 11 Trial, Tale of Missteps and Mismanagement," *The New York Times* (March 31, 2006), http://www.nytimes.com.

49. Raymond E. Miles, "Adapting to Technology and Competition: A New Industrial Relations System for the Twenty-First

Century," *California Management Review* (Winter 1989): 9–28; and Miles and Snow, "The New Network Firm."

50. Dess et al., "The New Corporate Architecture"; Henry W. Chesbrough and David J. Teece, "Organizing for Innovation: When Is Virtual Virtuous?" *The Innovative Entrepreneur* (August 2002): 127–134; N. Anand, "Modular, Virtual, and Hollow Forms," and M. Lynne Markus, Brook Manville, and Carole E. Agres, "What Makes a Virtual Organization Work?" *Sloan Management Review* (Fall 2000): 13–26.

51. Laurie P. O'Leary, "Curing the Monday Blues: A U.S. Navy Guide for Structuring Cross-Functional Teams," *National Productivity Review* (Spring 1996): 43–51; and Alan Hurwitz, "Organizational Structures for the 'New World Order,'" *Business Horizons* (May–June 1996): 5–14.

52. Jay Galbraith, Diane Downey, and Amy Kates, *Designing Dynamic Organizations*, Chapter 4: Processes and Lateral Capability (New York: AMACOM, 2002).

53. Sara Lipka, "The Lawyer Is In," *The Chronicle of Higher Education* (July 1, 2005): A19, A21.

54. Lee Iacocca with William Novak, *Iacocca: An Autobiography* (New York: Phantom Books, 1984): 152–153.

55. Miriam Jordan and Jonathan Karp, "Machines for the Masses," *The Wall Street Journal* (December 9, 2003): A1, A20.

56. William J. Altier, "Task Forces: An Effective Management Tool," *Management Review* (February 1987): 52–57.

57. "Task Forces Tackle Consolidation of Employment Services," *Shawmut News*, Shawmut National Corp. (May 3, 1989): 2.

58. Henry Mintzberg, *The Structure of Organizations* (Englewood Cliffs, NJ: Prentice Hall, 1979).

59. Gary Neilson, Bruce A. Pasternack, and Decio Mendes, "The Four Bases of Organizational DNA," *Strategy + Business* Issue 33 (December 10, 2003): 48–57.

60. Paul R. Lawrence and Jay W. Lorsch, "New Managerial Job: The Integrator," *Harvard Business Review* (November–December 1967): 142–151.

61. Ronald N. Ashkenas and Suzanne C. Francis, "Integration Managers: Special Leaders for Special Times," *Harvard Business Review* (November–December 2000): 108–116.

62. Jeffrey A. Tannenbaum, "Why Are Companies Paying Close Attention to This Toilet Maker?" *The Wall Street Journal* (August 20, 1999): B1.

63. This discussion is based on Michael Hammer and Steven Stanton, "How Process Enterprises *Really* Work," *Harvard Business Review* (November–December 1999): 108–118; Richard L. Daft, *Organization Theory and Design*, 5th ed. (Minneapolis, MN: West Publishing Company, 1995): 238; Raymond L. Manganelli and Mark M. Klein, "A Framework for Reengineering," *Management Review* (June 1994): 9–16; and Barbara Ettorre, "Reengineering Tales from the Front," *Management Review* (January 1995): 13–18.

64. Hammer and Stanton, "How Process Enterprises *Really* Work."

65. Michael Hammer, definition quoted in "The Process Starts Here," *CIO* (March 1, 2000): 144–156; and David A. Garvin, "The Processes of Organization and Management," *Sloan Management Review* (Summer 1998): 33–50.

66. Frank Ostroff, *The Horizontal Organization: What the Organization of the Future Looks Like and How It Delivers Value to Customers* (New York: Oxford University Press, 1999).

67. Hammer and Stanton, "How Process Enterprises *Really* Work."

68. Richard Koonce, "Reengineering the Travel Game," *Government Executive* (May 1995): 28–34, 69–70.

69. John A. Byrne, "The Horizontal Corporation," *BusinessWeek* (December 20, 1993): 76–81.

70. Erik Brynjolfsson, Amy Austin Renshaw, and Marshall Van Alstyne, "The Matrix of Change," *Sloan Management Review* (Winter 1997): 37–54.

71. See Harold J. Leavitt, "Why Hierarchies Thrive," *Harvard Business Review* (March 2003): 96–102, for a discussion of the benefits and problems of hierarchies.

72. Michael E. Porter, *Competitive Strategy* (New York: Free Press, 1980): 36–46.

73. Eric M. Olson, Stanley F. Slater, and G. Tomas M. Hult, "The Importance of Structure and Process to Strategy Implementation," *Business Horizons* 48 (2005): 47–54.

74. Pam Black, "Finally, Human Rights for Motorists," *BusinessWeek* (May 1, 1995): 45.

75. Paul R. Lawrence and Jay W. Lorsch, *Organization and Environment* (Homewood, IL: Irwin, 1969).

76. Robert B. Duncan, "Characteristics of Organizational Environments and Perceived Environmental Uncertainty," *Administrative Science Quarterly* 17 (1972): 313–327; W. Alan Randolph and Gregory G. Dess, "The Congruence Perspective of Organization Design: A Conceptual Model and Multivariate Research Approach," *Academy of Management Review* 9 (1984): 114–127; and Masoud Yasai-Ardekani, "Structural Adaptations to Environments," *Academy of Management Review* 11 (1986): 9–21.

77. Tom Burns and G. M. Stalker, *The Management of Innovation* (London: Tavistock, 1961).

78. John A. Coutright, Gail T. Fairhurst, and L. Edna Rogers, "Interaction Patterns in Organic and Mechanistic Systems," *Academy of Management Journal* 32 (1989): 773–802.

79. Robert Pool, "In the Zero Luck Zone," *Forbes ASAP* (November 27, 2000): 85+.

80. Ibid.

81. Denise M. Rousseau and Robert A. Cooke, "Technology and Structure: The Concrete, Abstract, and Activity Systems of Organizations," *Journal of Management* 10 (1984): 345–361; Charles Perrow, "A Framework for the Comparative Analysis of Organizations," *American Sociological Review* 32 (1967): 194–208; and Denise M. Rousseau, "Assessment of Technology in Organizations: Closed versus Open Systems Approaches," *Academy of Management Review* 4 (1979): 531–542.

82. Joan Woodward, *Industrial Organizations: Theory and Practice* (London: Oxford University Press, 1965); and Joan Woodward, Management and Technology (London: Her Majesty's Stationery Office, 1958).

83. Woodward, *Industrial Organizations*, vi.

84. Peter K. Mills and Thomas Kurk, "A Preliminary Investigation into the Influence of Customer-Firm Interface on Information Processing and Task Activity in Service Organizations," *Journal of Management* 12 (1986): 91–104; Peter K. Mills and Dennis J. Moberg, "Perspectives on the Technology of Service Operations," *Academy of Management Review* 7 (1982): 467–478; and Roger W. Schmenner, "How Can Service Businesses Survive and Prosper?" *Sloan Management Review* 27 (Spring 1986): 21–32.

85. Richard B. Chase and David A. Tansik, "The Customer Contact Model for Organization Design," *Management Science* 29

(1983): 1037–1050; and Gregory B. Northcraft and Richard B. Chase, "Managing Service Demand at the Point of Delivery," *Academy of Management Review* 10 (1985): 66–75.

86. Michael Hammer in "The Process Starts Here"; and Emelie Rutherford, "End Game," (an interview with David Weinberger, coauthor of *The Cluetrain Manifesto*), CIO (April 1, 2000): 98–104.

87. Thomas A. Stewart, "Three Rules for Managing in the Real-Time Economy," *Fortune* (May 1, 2000): 333–334.

88. Ghosn, "Saving the Business"; and G. Pascal Zachary, "Dream Factory," *Business 2.0* (June 1005): 96–102.

CHAPTER 11

CHAPTER OUTLINE

Manager's Challenge

Turbulent Times and the Changing Workplace

Changing Things: New Products and Technologies

Exploration

Cooperation

Entrepreneurship

Changing People and Culture

Training and Development

Organization Development

Model of Planned Organizational Change

Forces for Change

Need for Change

Implementing Change

Resistance to Change

Force-Field Analysis

Implementation Tactics

LEARNING OBJECTIVES

After studying this chapter, you should be able to:

1. Define organizational change and explain the forces driving innovation and change in today's organizations.

2. Identify the three innovation strategies managers implement for changing products and technologies.

3. Explain the value of creativity, idea incubators, horizontal linkages, open innovation, idea champions, and new-venture teams for innovation.

4. Discuss why changes in people and culture are critical to any change process.

5. Define organization development (OD) and large group interventions.

6. Explain the OD stages of unfreezing, changing, and refreezing.

7. Describe the sequence of change activities that must be performed in order for change to be successful.

8. Identify sources of resistance to change.

9. Explain force-field analysis and other implementation tactics that can be used to overcome resistance.

MANAGING CHANGE AND INNOVATION

MANAGER'S CHALLENGE

Samsung Electronics began selling black and white televisions in Korea in the early 1970s and soon expanded its product line and extended its markets around the world. But when Samsung chairman Kun-Hee Lee visited a Los Angeles retailer two decades later, he had a painful experience. While customers inspected and admired the cutting edge equipment from companies such as Sony, Nokia, and Motorola, Samsung's products sat gathering dust on back shelves, ignored even by the sales clerks. It was a wake-up call to Lee, who realized that U.S. consumers had come to regard Samsung products as cheap, low-quality knockoffs, suitable only for the bargain bin. Back home in Korea, things weren't looking so bright either. To celebrate the growing success of Samsung Group, the electronics firm's parent company, Lee had given Samsung mobile phones to friends and colleagues. Within days he began receiving complaints that the phones were defective. Humiliated, Lee issued an order that $50 million worth of inventory from the company's Gumi factory be piled in a heap in the courtyard and destroyed. Top managers and employees watched as workers smashed phones, fax machines, and other products under a banner proclaiming that Samsung would become known as a world-class innovator. "We must change no matter what," the chairman proclaimed. But managers know it won't be easy. Samsung's culture is focused on imitation, not innovation, and its strong traditions make it ultra-resistant to change.[1]

> If you were a manager at Samsung, what steps would you take to encourage creativity and get designers and engineers to come up with innovative products rather than crank out cheap imitations? What techniques would you use to overcome resistance and implement the desired changes?

■ **TAKE A MOMENT**

The Samsung managers struggling with change are not alone in their predicament. Every organization sometimes faces the need to change quickly and dramatically to survive in a changing environment. Many firms in the United States, Europe, and Japan recognize the need for greater product and service innovation to keep pace with technological and societal advances and compete with the growing power of companies in China and other developing countries. Rather than focusing on ways to improve efficiency and cut costs, today's companies are rewiring their organizations for creativity and innovation. Some observers of business trends suggest that the *knowledge economy* of the late 1900s and early 2000s is rapidly being transformed into the *creativity economy*. As more high-level knowledge work is outsourced to less-developed countries, companies in the United States, Europe, and Japan are evolving to the next level—generating economic value from creativity, imagination, and innovation.[2]

TURBULENT TIMES AND THE CHANGING WORKPLACE

Today's organizations face an almost continual need for change. Sometimes, changes are brought about by forces outside the organization, such as when a powerful retailer such as Wal-Mart demands annual price cuts or when a key supplier goes out of business. Many U.S. companies revised their procedures to comply with provisions of the Sarbanes-Oxley corporate governance reform law. In China, organizations feel pressure from the government to increase wages to help workers cope with rising food costs. At the same time, costs of steel and other raw materials are skyrocketing for Chinese companies seeking to expand their businesses.[3] These outside forces compel managers to look for greater efficiencies in operations and other changes to keep their organizations profitable. Other times managers within the company want to initiate major changes, such as forming employee-participation teams, introducing new products, or instituting new training systems, but they don't know how to make the change successful. Organizations must embrace many types of change. Businesses must develop improved production technologies, create new products and services desired in the marketplace, implement new administrative systems, and upgrade employees' skills. Companies such as Samsung, Apple, Toyota, and General Electric implement all of these changes and more.

How important is organizational change? Consider this: The parents of today's college students grew up without e-mail, digital cameras, video on demand, laptop computers, iPods, laser checkout systems, and online shopping. As companies that produce the new products and services prosper, many companies are caught with outdated products and failed technologies. Today's successful companies are constantly innovating. For example, Johnson & Johnson Pharmaceuticals uses biosimulation software from Entelos that compiles all known information about a disease such as diabetes or asthma and runs extensive virtual tests of new drug candidates. With a new-drug failure rate of 50 percent even at the last stage of clinical trials, the process helps scientists cut the time and expense of early testing and focus their efforts on the most promising prospects. Telephone companies such as AT&T are investing in technology to push deeper into the television and broadband markets. Automakers DaimlerChrysler, General Motors, and Toyota are perfecting fuel-cell power systems that could make today's internal combustion engine as obsolete as the steam locomotive.[4] Computer companies are developing computers that are smart enough to configure themselves, balance huge workloads, and know how to anticipate and fix problems before they happen.[5] Organizations that change successfully are both profitable and admired.

Organizational change is defined as the adoption of a new idea or behavior by an organization.[6] In this chapter, we look at how organizations can be designed to respond to the environment through internal change and development. First we look at two key aspects of change in organizations: introducing new products and technologies, and changing people and culture. Then we examine the basic forces for change and present a model for planned organizational change. Finally, we discuss how managers implement change, including overcoming resistance.

CHANGING THINGS: NEW PRODUCTS AND TECHNOLOGIES

Competition is more intense than ever before, and companies are driven by a new innovation imperative. The past decade's attention to efficiency in operations is no longer enough to keep organizations successful in a new, hypercompetitive

© PAUL HAWTHORNE/STARBUCKS ASSOCIATED PRESS

CONCEPT CONNECTION   Starbucks leaders realize that the Seattle-based chain's current business model won't continue to meet their goals for growth, so they're searching for ways to reinvent the company. This **internal force for change** has led the company to branch into entertainment, such as by experimenting with self-service CD burners in test stores, like the one pictured here. Starbucks has also released music compilation CDs, marketed audiobooks, produced a feature-length film, and reached an agreement with Apple that allows customers to purchase a variety of Starbucks' titles from the iTunes store.

organizational change
The adoption of a new idea or behavior by an organization.

Exploration	Cooperation	Entrepreneurship
• Creativity • Experimentation • Idea incubators	• Horizontal coordination mechanisms • Customers, partners • Open innovation	• Idea champions • New venture teams • Skunkworks • New venture fund

SOURCE: Based on Patrick Reinmoeller and Nicole van Baardwijk, "The Link Between Diversity and Resilience," *MIT Sloan Management Review* (Summer 2005), 61–65.

environment. To thrive, companies must innovate more—and more quickly—than ever. One vital area for innovation is introducing new products and technologies.

A **product change** is a change in the organization's product or service outputs. Product and service innovation is the primary way in which organizations adapt to changes in markets, technology, and competition.[7] Examples of new products include Apple's iPod Shuffle and the iPod Hi-Fi, Glad Force Flex trash bags, the Motorola Q cell phone, and Subaru's B9Tribeca. The introduction of *e-file*, which allows online filing of tax returns, by the U.S. Internal Revenue Service (IRS) is an example of a new service innovation. Product changes are related to changes in the technology of the organization. A **technology change** is a change in the organization's production process—how the organization does its work. Technology changes are designed to make the production of a product or service more efficient. The adoption of automatic mail sorting machines by the U.S. Postal Service is one example of a technology change.

Three critical innovation strategies for changing products and technologies are illustrated in Exhibit 11.1.[8] The first strategy, *exploration*, involves designing the organization to encourage creativity and the initiation of new ideas. The strategy of *cooperation* refers to creating conditions and systems to facilitate internal and external coordination and knowledge sharing. Finally, *entrepreneurship* means that managers put in place processes and structures to ensure that new ideas are carried forward for acceptance and implementation.

© SPPEDO/PRNEWSFOTO (NEWSCOM)

CONCEPT CONNECTION For a swimmer, a split second can mean the difference between a medal and going home empty-handed. That's why Speedo recruited fabric and garment engineers, marine biologists, biomechanists, physiologists, and aerospace engineers to design a swimsuit with improved drag-reducing properties. As part of its **new product development** process, Speedo used sophisticated computer programs to study water flow around a virtual swimmer's body and collaborated with London's Natural History Museum to study how sharks swim. The result was the innovative Fastskin, a ribbed synthetic material that cuts water resistance by mimicking a shark's scales, as seen in the swimsuits pictured here.

Exploration

Exploration is the stage where ideas for new products and technologies are born. Managers design the organization for exploration by establishing conditions that encourage creativity and allow new ideas to spring forth. **Creativity**, which refers to the generation of novel ideas that might meet perceived needs or respond to opportunities for the organization, is the essential first step in innovation.[9] People noted for their creativity include Edwin Land, who invented the Polaroid camera; Richard Tait and Whit Alexander, who came up with the idea for the mega-hit board game Cranium; and Swiss engineer George de Mestral, who created Velcro after noticing the tiny hooks on the burrs caught on his wool socks. Each of these people saw unique and creative opportunities in a familiar situation.

Characteristics of highly creative people are illustrated in the left-hand column of Exhibit 11.2. Creative people often are known for originality, open-mindedness, curiosity, a focused approach to problem solving, persistence, a relaxed and playful

product change A change in the organization's product or service outputs.

technology change A change that pertains to the organization's production process.

creativity The generation of novel ideas that might meet perceived needs or offer opportunities for the organization.

EXHIBIT 11.2	The Creative Individual	The Creative Organization or Department
Characteristics of Creative People and Organizations	1. Conceptual fluency Open-mindedness	1. Open channels of communication Contact with outside sources Overlapping territories; cross-polination of ideas across disciplines Suggestion systems, brainstorming, freewheeling discussions
	2. Originality	2. Assigning nonspecialists to problems Eccentricity allowed Hiring outside your comfort zone
	3. Less authority Independence Self-confidence	3. Decentralization, loosely defined positions, loose control Acceptance of mistakes; rewarding risk-taking People encouraged to challenge their bosses
	4. Playfulness Undisciplined exploration Curiosity	4. Freedom to choose and pursue problems Not a tight ship, playful culture, doing the impractical Freedom to discuss ideas; long time horizon
	5. Persistence Commitment Focused approach	5. Resources allocated to creative personnel and projects without immediate payoff Reward system encourages innovation Absolution of peripheral responsibilities

SOURCES: Based on Gary A. Steiner, ed., *The Creative Organization* (Chicago: University of Chicago Press, 1965): 16–18; Rosabeth Moss Kanter, "The Middle Manager as Innovator," *Harvard Business Review* (July–August 1982): 104–105; James Brian Quinn, "Managing Innovation: Controlled Chaos," *Harvard Business Review* (May–June 1985): 73–84; Robert I. Sutton, "The Weird Rules of Creativity," *Harvard Business Review* (September 2001): 94–103; and Bridget Finn, "Playbook: Brainstorming for Better Brainstorming," *Business 2.0* (April 2005), 109–114.

attitude, and receptivity to new ideas.[10] Creativity can also be designed into organizations. Companies or departments within companies can be organized to be creative and initiate ideas for change. Most companies want more highly creative employees and often seek to hire creative individuals. However, the individual is only part of the story, and each of us has some potential for creativity. Managers are responsible for creating a work environment that allows creativity to flourish.[11]

The characteristics of creative organizations correspond to those of individuals, as illustrated in the right-hand column of Exhibit 11.2. Creative organizations are loosely structured. People find themselves in a situation of ambiguity, assignments are vague, territories overlap, tasks are poorly defined, and much work is done through teams. Managers strive to involve employees in a varied range of projects, so that people are not stuck in the rhythm of routine jobs, and they drive out the fear of making mistakes that can inhibit creative thinking.[12] Creative organizations have an internal culture of playfulness, freedom, challenge, and grass-roots participation.[13] They harness all potential sources of new ideas.

■ **TAKE A MOMENT**

As a new manager, you can inspire people to be more creative by giving them opportunities to explore ideas outside their regular jobs and encouraging them to experiment and take risks. Be open-minded and willing to listen to "crazy ideas," and let people know it's okay to make mistakes.

Advertising agency Leo Burnett holds a regular "Inspire Me" day, when one team takes the rest of the department out to do something totally unrelated to advertising. One team took the group to a Mexican wrestling match, where team members showed up in costumes and masks like some of the more ardent wrestling fans. One idea that grew out of the experience was a new slogan for The Score, a sports network: "The Score: Home for the Hardcore."[14] To keep creativity alive at

Google, managers let people spend 20 percent of their time working on any project they choose, even if the project doesn't tie in with the company's central mission. Many Google managers hold open office hours two or three times a week, when anyone can come by to bat around ideas.[15]

The most creative companies embrace risk and encourage employees to experiment and make mistakes. At software company Intuit, managers in the various divisions hold free-association sessions at least once a week, where people can propose all sorts of seemingly kooky ideas without embarrassment or fear.[16] One manager at Intel used to throw a dinner party every month for the "failure of the month," demonstrating to people that failure was an inevitable and accepted part of risk-taking.[17] Jim Read, president of the Read Corporation, says, "When my employees make mistakes trying to improve something, I give them a round of applause. No mistakes mean no new products. If they ever become afraid to make one, my company is doomed."[18]

Another popular way to encourage new ideas within the organization is the **idea incubator**. An idea incubator provides a safe harbor where ideas from employees throughout the company can be developed without interference from company bureaucracy or politics.[19] The great value of an internal incubator is that an employee with a good idea has specific place to go to develop it, rather than having to shop the idea all over the company and hope someone pays attention. Companies as diverse as Boeing, Adobe Systems, Ball Aerospace, United Parcel Service, and Ziff Davis are using incubators to quickly produce products and services related to the company's core business.[20]

Go to the experiential exercise on page 372 that pertains to creativity in organizations.

■ **TAKE A MOMENT**

Cooperation

Another important aspect of innovation is providing mechanisms for both internal and external coordination. Ideas for product and technology innovations typically originate at lower levels of the organization and need to flow horizontally across departments. Implementation of an innovation typically requires changes in behavior across several departments. In addition, people and organizations outside the firm can be rich sources of innovative ideas. Lack of innovation is widely recognized as one of the biggest problems facing today's businesses. Consider that 72 percent of top executives surveyed by *BusinessWeek* and the Boston Consulting Group reported that innovation is a top priority, yet almost half said they are dissatisfied with their results in that area.[21] Thus, many companies are undergoing a transformation in the way they find and use new ideas, focusing on improving both internal and external coordination.

INTERNAL COORDINATION

Successful innovation requires expertise from several departments simultaneously, and failed innovation is often the result of failed cooperation.[22] Companies that successfully innovate usually have the following characteristics:

1. People in marketing have a good understanding of customer needs.

2. Technical specialists are aware of recent technological developments and make effective use of new technology.

3. Members from key departments—research, manufacturing, marketing—cooperate in the development of the new product.[23]

One approach to successful innovation is called the **horizontal linkage model**, which is illustrated in the center circle of Exhibit 11.3.[24] The model shows that the research, manufacturing, and sales and marketing departments within an organization must simultaneously contribute to new products and technologies. People from

idea incubator An in-house program that provides a safe harbor where ideas from employees throughout the organization can be developed without interference from company bureaucracy or politics.

horizontal linkage model An approach to product change that emphasizes shared development of innovations among several departments.

EXHIBIT   11.3

Coordination Model for Innovation

New Technologies

Open Innovation Mechanisms

Organization

Manufacturing Department

Research Department

Marketing Department

Horizontal Linkages

Formal Innovation Partners

Customers, Market Needs

these departments meet frequently in teams and task forces to share ideas and solve problems. For example, research people inform marketing of new technical developments to learn whether they will be useful to customers. Marketing people pass customer complaints to research to use in the design of new products and to manufacturing people to develop new ideas for improving production speed and quality. Manufacturing informs other departments whether a product idea can be manufactured within cost limits.

The appliance maker Electrolux was struggling with spiraling costs and shrinking market share until CEO Hans Straberg introduced a new approach to product development that has designers, engineers, marketers, and production people working side-by-side to come up with hot new products such as the Pronto cordless stick vacuum, which gained a 50 percent market share in Europe within two years. "We never used to create new products together," says engineer Giuseppe Frucco. "The designers would come up with something and then tell us to build it." The new horizontal approach saves both time and money at Electrolux by avoiding the technical glitches that crop up as a new design moves through the development process.[25]

The horizontal linkage model is increasingly important in today's high-pressure business environment that requires developing and commercializing products and services incredibly fast. Sprinting to market with a new product requires a *parallel approach*, or *simultaneous linkage* among departments. This kind of teamwork is similar to a rugby match wherein players run together, passing the ball back and forth as they move downfield.[26] Speed is emerging as a pivotal strategic weapon in the global marketplace for a wide variety of industries.[27] Stockholm's H&M (Hennes & Mauritz) has become one of the hottest fashion retailers around because it can spot trends and rush items into stores in as little as three weeks. Nissan cut the time it takes to get a new car to market from 21 months to about 10.[28] Some companies use fast-cycle teams to deliver products and services faster than competitors, giving them a significant strategic advantage. A **fast-cycle team** is a multifunctional, and sometimes multinational, team that

© MARSH STARKS/ASSOCIATED PRESS

CONCEPT CONNECTION   How does eBay keep coming up with new approaches to business and new sources of income? By tapping into the collective intelligence of customers, employees, and outsiders. "It is far better to have an army of a million than a command and control system," said eBay CEO Meg Whitman, referring to eBay's approach of letting buyers and sellers largely determine how the company operates. eBay has thrived on this process of **open innovation,** reflected in the slogan "The power of all of us," which adorned the stage at the 2006 eBay Live convention in Las Vegas, shown here. The convention drew around 15,000 eBayers from around the world.

fast-cycle team A multifunctional team that is provided with high levels of resources and empowerment to accomplish an accelerated product development project.

works under stringent timelines and is provided with high levels of resources and empowerment to accomplish an accelerated product development project.[29]

■ TAKE A MOMENT

Even as a new manager, you can make sure people are communicating and cooperating across organizational boundaries. Implement mechanisms to help your team or department members stay in touch with what's happening in other departments and in the marketplace.

EXTERNAL COORDINATION

Exhibit 11.3 also illustrates that organizations look outside their boundaries to find and develop new ideas. Engineers and researchers stay aware of new technological developments. Marketing personnel pay attention to shifting market conditions and customer needs. Some organizations build formal strategic partnerships such as alliances and joint ventures to improve innovation success. Outsourcing partnerships can help companies get things done incredibly fast. Some leading cell phone makers, for example, work with outsourcing partner Cellon Inc. to take a new phone model from design to market in five months. Cellon, with operations in China, keeps a half-dozen basic designs that it can quickly customize for a particular client. Then, the company works with local manufacturers to rapidly move designs into production. People want hot new phones, and the life cycle of a cell phone model is about 9 months. Companies can't afford the 12 to 18 months it typically takes to develop a new model from scratch.[30]

Today's most successful companies are including customers, strategic partners, suppliers, and other outsiders directly in the product and service development process. One of the hottest trends is *open innovation*.[31] Think of Google, which opened its mapping technology to the public, allowing programmers to combine Google's maps with anything from real estate listings to local poker game sites.[32] At online game designer Linden Lab's Second Life, players have the freedom to create just about everything, from new characters to buildings to whole new games.[33]

In the past, most businesses generated their own ideas in house and then developed, manufactured, marketed, and distributed them, a closed innovation approach. Today, though, forward-looking companies are trying a different method. **Open innovation** means extending the search for and commercializing new ideas beyond the boundaries of the organization and even beyond the boundaries of the industry. Smart companies find and use ideas from anywhere within and outside the organization.[34] Procter & Gamble, not so long ago a stodgy consumer products company, has become one of the country's hottest innovators and a role model for the open innovation process.

open innovation Extending the search for and commercialization of new ideas beyond the boundaries of the organization.

Procter & Gamble (P&G)

Swiffer Wet Jet. Crest Whitestrips. Mr. Clean Magic Reach. Downy Wrinkle Releaser. Iams Dental Defense. Olay Regenerist. They're some of Procter & Gamble's best-selling products—and all of them were developed in whole or in part by someone outside of P&G. The technology that helps P&G's Swiffer products pick up so much dust and debris came from a competitor in Japan. The Crest Spin Brush was invented by a small entrepreneurial firm in Cleveland.

Procter & Gamble CEO A. G. Lafley set a goal to get 50 percent of the company's innovation from outside the organization, up from about 35 percent in 2004 and only 10 percent in 2000. P&G developed a detailed, well-organized process for open innovation with its Connect + Develop (C + D) initiative, which taps into networks of inventors, scientists, academics, partners, and suppliers to embrace the collective brains of the world. "Inventors are evenly distributed in the population," says Lafley, "and we're as likely to find invention in a garage as in our labs." One technique is to contract with external "innovation sourcing" firms such as NineSigma Inc. and InnoCentive, which link companies with outside inventors, problem solvers, academic researchers, and small entrepreneurial companies. When P&G was looking for an antiwrinkling spray that consumers could use on cotton clothing, NineSigma used the Web to blast out queries to about 6,000 people, eventually signing two of them to contracts. InnoCentive's 80,000 independent inventors provided solutions to more than one-third of the two dozen requests P&G submitted. But P&G doesn't just look for extensions of its current product categories. An important part of its open innovation process is networking with external scientists in totally new areas that could lead to totally new businesses.

Between 2002 and 2004, P&G raised its new product success rate from 70 percent to 90 percent, thanks largely to the Connect + Develop initiative. At the same time, R&D spending as a percentage of sales decreased because of the more efficient and effective innovation process.[35]

Connecting with customers is also a critical aspect of open innovation. At companies such as P&G and Electrolux, rather than relying on focus groups, researchers now spend time with people in their homes, watching how they wash their dishes or clean their floors, and asking questions about their habits and frustrations with household chores. P&G's CEO makes 10 to 15 visits a year to watch women applying their beauty products or doing their laundry.[36]

In line with the new way of thinking we discussed in Chapter 1, which sees partnership and collaboration as more important than independence and competition, the boundaries between an organization and its environment are becoming porous, so that ideas flow back and forth among different people and companies that engage in partnerships, joint ventures, licensing agreements, and other alliances. Japanese high-tech firms such as Fujitsu, for example, are achieving rapid innovation by building strategic innovation communities that link managers from all levels with partners, customers, and other outsiders for developing new products. Similarly, in the United States, external collaboration and innovation networking were key to IBM's reemergence as a technology powerhouse.[37]

Entrepreneurship

The third aspect of product and technology innovation is creating mechanisms to make sure new ideas are carried forward, accepted, and implemented. Here is where idea champions come in. The formal definition of an **idea champion** is a person who sees the need for and champions productive change within the organization. Wendy Black of Best Western International championed the idea of coordinating the corporate mailings to the company's 2,800 hoteliers into a single packet every two weeks. Some hotels were receiving three special mailings a day from different departments. Her idea saved $600,000 a year in postage alone.[38]

Remember: Change does not occur by itself. Personal energy and effort are required to successfully promote a new idea. Often a new idea is rejected by management. Champions are passionately committed to a new product or idea despite rejection by others. Robert Vincent was fired twice by two different division managers at a semiconductor company. Both times, he convinced the president and chairman of the board to reinstate him to continue working on his idea for an airbag sensor that measures acceleration and deceleration. He couldn't get approval for research funding, so Vincent pushed to complete another project in half the time and used the savings to support the new product development.[39] At Kyocera Wireless, lead engineer Gary Koerper was a champion for the Smartphone. When he couldn't get his company's testing department to validate the new product, he had an outside firm do the testing for him—at a cost of about $30,000—without approval from Kyocera management. Once the Smartphone was approved and went into production, demand was so great the company could barely keep up.[40]

Championing an idea successfully requires roles in organizations, as illustrated in Exhibit 11.4. Sometimes a single person may play two or more of these roles, but successful innovation in most companies involves an interplay of different people, each adopting one role. The *inventor* comes up with a new idea and understands its technical value but has neither the ability nor the interest to promote it for acceptance within the organization. The *champion* believes in the idea, confronts the organizational realities of costs and benefits, and gains the political and financial

idea champion A person who sees the need for and champions productive change within the organization.

Inventor	**Champion**	**Sponsor**	**Critic**
Develops and understands technical aspects of idea	Believes in idea	High-level manager who removes organizational barriers	Provides reality test
Does not know how to win support for the idea or make a business of it	Visualizes benefits	Approves and protects idea within organization	Looks for shortcomings
	Confronts organizational realities of cost, benefits		Defines hard-nosed criteria that idea must pass
	Obtains financial and political support		
	Overcomes obstacles		

SOURCES: Based on Harold L. Angle and Andrew H. Van de Ven, "Suggestions for Managing the Innovation Journey," in *Research in the Management of Innovation: The Minnesota Studies*, ed. A.H. Van de Ven, H.L. Angle, and Marshall Scott Poole (Cambridge, MA: Ballinger/Harper & Row, 1989); and Jay R. Galbraith, "Designing the Innovating Organization," *Organizational Dynamics* (Winter 1982): 5–25.

EXHIBIT 11.4

Four Roles in Organizational Change

support needed to bring it to reality. The *sponsor* is a high-level manager who approves the idea, protects the idea, and removes major organizational barriers to acceptance. The *critic* counterbalances the zeal of the champion by challenging the concept and providing a reality test against hard-nosed criteria. The critic prevents people in the other roles from adopting a bad idea.[41]

Managers can directly influence whether champions will flourish. When Texas Instruments studied 50 of its new-product introductions, a surprising fact emerged: Without exception, every new product that failed lacked a zealous champion. In contrast, most of the new products that succeeded had a champion. Managers made an immediate decision: No new product would be approved unless someone championed it. Research confirms that successful new ideas are generally those that are backed by someone who believes in the idea wholeheartedly and is determined to convince others of its value.[42]

TAKE A MOMENT

As a new manager, have the courage to promote useful change. Are you an idea champion for changes or new ideas you believe in? To find out, complete the New Manager Self Test on page 356.

Another way to facilitate entrepreneurship is through a **new-venture team**. A new-venture team is a unit separate from the rest of the organization that is responsible for developing and initiating a major innovation.[43] Motorola's successful Razr cell phone was developed in an innovation lab 50 miles from employees' regular offices in the company's traditional research and development facility. Team members were free from the distractions of their everyday routines and were given the autonomy to implement product ideas without the usual process of running things past regional managers.[44] Whenever BMW Group begins developing a new car, the project's team members—from engineering, design, production, marketing, purchasing, and finance—are relocated to a separate Research and Innovation Center, where they work collaboratively to speed the new product to market.[45] New-venture teams give free rein to members' creativity because their separate facilities and location unleash people from the restrictions imposed by organizational rules and procedures. These teams typically are small, loosely structured, and flexible, reflecting the characteristics of creative organizations described in Exhibit 11.2.

One variation of a new-venture team is called a **skunkworks**.[46] A skunkworks is a separate small, informal, highly autonomous, and often secretive group that focuses on breakthrough ideas for the business. The original skunkworks, which still exists, was created by Lockheed Martin more than 50 years ago. The essence of a skunkworks is that highly talented people are given the time and freedom to let

new-venture team A unit separate from the mainstream of the organization that is responsible for developing and initiating innovations.

skunkworks A separate small, informal, highly autonomous, and often secretive group that focuses on breakthrough ideas for the business.

TAKING CHARGE OF CHANGE

As a new manager, do you have what it takes to be an idea champion? Will you initiate change? Think of a job you held for a period of time. Answer the following questions according to your behaviors and perspective on that job. Please answer whether each item is Mostly True or Mostly False for you.

	Mostly True	Mostly False
1. I often tried to adopt improved procedures for doing my job.		
2. I felt a personal sense of responsibility to bring about change in my workplace.		
3. I often tried to institute new work methods that were more effective for the company.		
4. I often tried to change organizational rules or policies that were nonproductive or counterproductive.		
5. It was up to me to bring about improvement in my workplace.		
6. I often made constructive suggestions for improving how things operated.		
7. I often tried to implement new ideas for pressing organizational problems.		

	Mostly True	Mostly False
8. I often tried to introduce new structures, technologies, or approaches to improve efficiency.		

SCORING AND INTERPRETATION: An important part of a new manager's job is to facilitate improvements through innovation and change. Will you be a champion for change? Your answers to the questions may indicate the extent to which you have a natural inclination toward taking charge of change. Not everyone thrives in a position of initiating change, but as a new manager, initiating change within the first six months will enhance your impact.

Give yourself one point for each item you marked as Mostly True. If you scored 4 or less you may not have been flexing your change muscles on the job. You may need to become more active at taking charge of change. Moreover, you may need to be in a more favorable change situation. Research indicates that a job with open-minded management and a job where change is believed likely to succeed and be rewarded, increase a person's initiative. So the organization in which you are a new manager plus your own inclination will influence your initiation of change. A score of 5 or more suggests a positive level of previous change initiation behavior and solid preparation for a new manager role as an idea champion.

SOURCE: Based on Elizabeth W. Morrison and Corey C. Phelps, "Taking charge at work: Extrarole efforts to initiate workplace change," *Academy of Management Journal* 42 (1999): 403–419.

creativity reign.[47] The laser printer was invented by a Xerox researcher who was transferred to a skunkworks, the Xerox Palo Alto Research Center (PARC), after his ideas about using lasers were stifled within the company for being "too impractical and expensive."[48] IBM is launching entirely new businesses by using the skunkworks concept. Managers identify "emerging business opportunities," or EBOs, that have the potential to become profitable businesses in the next five to seven years, then put a senior leader in charge of building the business, often with only a few hand-picked colleagues. A digital media EBO, which helps companies manage video, audio, and still images, has grown into a $1.7 billion business in only three years.[49]

A related idea is the **new-venture fund**, which provides resources from which individuals and groups can draw to develop new ideas, products, or businesses. At 3M, scientists can apply for Genesis Grants to work on innovative project ideas. 3M awards from 12 to 20 of these grants each year, ranging from $50,000 to $100,000 each, for researchers to hire supplemental staff, acquire equipment, or whatever is

new-venture fund A fund providing resources from which individuals and groups can draw to develop new ideas, products, or businesses.

needed to develop the new idea. Intel has been highly successful with Intel Capital, which provides new-venture funds to both employees and outside organizations to develop promising ideas. An Intel employee came up with the idea for liquid crystal on silicon, a technology that lowers the cost of big-screen TV projection. "We took an individual who had an idea, gave him money to pursue it, and turned it into a business," said Intel CEO Craig Barrett.[50]

Go to the ethical dilemma on page 373 that pertains to structural change.   ■ **TAKE A MOMENT**

CHANGING PEOPLE AND CULTURE

All successful changes involve changes in people and culture as well. For example, getting products to market fast requires that people learn to work collaboratively. Changes in people and culture pertain to how employees think—changes in mindset. **People change** pertains to just a few employees, such as sending a handful of middle managers to a training course to improve their leadership skills. **Culture change** pertains to the organization as a whole, such as when the IRS shifted its basic mind-set from an organization focused on collection and compliance to one dedicated to informing, educating, and serving customers (taxpayers).[51] In the business world, Jeff Immelt at General Electric strives to replace GE's famous obsession with bottom-line results with a new culture of risk-taking, bold thinking, and creative energy.

> **General Electric**
>
> General Electric, long revered as a hard-driving company focused on cost-cutting and process efficiency, evaluated and rewarded its managers based on the continual improvement of operations and their ability to achieve bottom-line results. Since he took over as CEO, however, Jeff Immelt has been on a mission to change that efficiency and productivity-oriented culture to one wired for creativity, risk-taking, and innovation.
>
> In today's environment, Immelt knows that efficiency is not enough. To shift the culture toward one of bold thinking and creative energy, Immelt tossed out some of GE's long-standing traditions and began evaluating top executives on innovation-oriented traits such as "external focus" and "imagination and courage." Bonuses are now linked to a manager's ability to generate new ideas, improve customer satisfaction, and boost sales. In a gathering called the Commercial Council, top executives hold monthly phone meetings and meet in person each quarter to talk about new ideas and new markets. Division heads are expected to submit at least three "Imagination Breakthrough" proposals a year that go before the council for evaluation and possible funding. Immelt already committed at least $5 billion to breakthrough projects that take GE into a new line of business, geographic region, or customer base. He also spent big bucks to beef up GE's research facilities and create other structural mechanisms that foster a culture of creativity and imagination. Some executives hold "idea jams," where people from various divisions brainstorm ideas. A "virtual idea box" allows people to brainstorm and submit ideas over the Internet.
>
> Immelt knows this massive cultural shift is difficult for most of GE's managers and employees. "These guys just aren't dreamer types," said one consultant about GE's workforce. "It almost seems painful to them, like a waste of time." Immelt, though, believes the culture change is essential to keep GE relevant and thriving in the changing world of the twenty-first century.[52]

Culture change of the magnitude at GE is not easy. Indeed, executives routinely report that improving people and corporate culture is their most difficult job.[53] Two specific tools for changing people and culture are training and development programs and organizational development (OD).

Training and Development

Training is one of the most frequently used approaches to changing people's mindsets. A company might offer training programs to large blocks of employees on

people change A change in the attitudes and behaviors of a few employees in the organization.

culture change A major shift in the norms, values, attitudes, and mindset of the entire organization.

CONCEPT
C O N N E C T I O N   Innovative companies such as Intuit want everyone to continually be coming up with new ideas. Founder Scott Cook and CEO Steve Bennett, shown here, encourage **creativity** during the **exploration phase** by embracing failure as readily as they do success. "I've had my share of really bad ideas," Cook admits. Yet failure can have hidden possibilities. Sticky notes, such as those shown here on Intuit's board, were invented at 3M Corporation based on a failed product—a not-very-sticky adhesive that resulted from a chemist's attempts to create a superglue. Post-it Notes became one of the best-selling office products ever.

subjects such as teamwork, diversity, emotional intelligence, quality circles, communication skills, or participative management. General Electric, for example, initiated new courses in marketing and idea generation to help shift attitudes and values. Training and development programs aimed at changing individual behavior and interpersonal skills are a big business for consultants, universities, and training firms.

Some companies particularly emphasize training and development for managers, with the idea that the behavior and attitudes of managers will influence people throughout the organization and lead to culture change. A number of Silicon Valley companies, including Intel, Advanced Micro Devices (AMD), and Sun Microsystems, regularly send managers to the Growth and Leadership Center (GLC), where they learn to use emotional intelligence to build better relationships. Nick Kepler, director of technology development at AMD, was surprised to learn how his emotionless approach to work was intimidating people and destroying the rapport needed to shift to a culture based on collaborative teamwork.[54]

Leading companies also want to provide training and development opportunities for everyone. An excellent example of training is First Data Corp., which uses a multifaceted, team-based approach first initiated by CFO Kim Patmore to boost morale among finance personnel.[55] First Data's "Extreme Teams" bring together employees from all hierarchical levels to organize departmental training and development programs for each of First Data's six regional finance units. One team is charged with organizing a mentoring program that pairs less-experienced personnel with seasoned managers who support and encourage them to make changes needed to further their own and the organization's well-being. Another team focuses on a program called *Fast Tracks*, an annual two-day seminar that brings people from all areas and levels of the company together to learn skills such as communication or conflict resolution.

Organization Development

Organization development (OD) is a planned, systematic process of change that uses behavioral science knowledge and techniques to improve an organization's health and effectiveness through its ability to adapt to the environment, improve internal relationships, and increase learning and problem-solving capabilities.[56] OD focuses on the human and social aspects of the organization and works to change attitudes and relationships among employees, helping to strengthen the organization's capacity for adaptation and renewal.[57]

OD can help managers address at least three types of current problems:[58]

organization development (OD) The application of behavioral science techniques to improve an organization's health and effectiveness through its ability to cope with environmental changes, improve internal relationships, and increase learning and problem-solving capabilities.

1. *Mergers/acquisitions.* The disappointing financial results of many mergers and acquisitions are caused by the failure of executives to determine whether the administrative style and corporate culture of the two companies fit. Executives may concentrate on potential synergies in technology, products, marketing, and control systems but fail to recognize that two firms may have widely different values, beliefs, and practices. These differences create stress and anxiety for employees, and these negative emotions affect future performance. Cultural

differences should be evaluated during the acquisition process, and OD experts can be used to smooth the integration of two firms.

2. *Organizational decline/revitalization.* Organizations undergoing a period of decline and revitalization experience a variety of problems, including a low level of trust, lack of innovation, high turnover, and high levels of conflict and stress. The period of transition requires opposite behaviors, including confronting stress, creating open communication, and fostering creative innovation to emerge with high levels of productivity. OD techniques can contribute greatly to cultural revitalization by managing conflicts, fostering commitment, and facilitating communication.

3. *Conflict management.* Conflict can occur at any time and place within a healthy organization. For example, a product team for the introduction of a new software package was formed at a computer company. Made up of strong-willed individuals, the team made little progress because members could not agree on project goals. At a manufacturing firm, salespeople promised delivery dates to customers that were in conflict with shop supervisor priorities for assembling customer orders. In a publishing company, two managers disliked each other intensely. They argued at meetings, lobbied politically against each other, and hurt the achievement of both departments. Organization development efforts can help resolve these kinds of conflicts, as well as conflicts that are related to growing diversity and the global nature of today's organizations.

© DANIEL LEVIN/GETTY IMAGES

CONCEPT CONNECTION **Organization development** specialists have long recognized that fun can be a powerful tool in the serious business of **team building.** Here, Target Corporation store employees engage in some group problem solving. While holding hands, each member must wriggle through two hula hoops without breaking the human chain. Such noncompetitive games not only break the ice but also give team members practice in working cooperatively to achieve a common goal.

Organization development can be used to solve the types of problems just described and many others. However, to be truly valuable to companies and employees, organization development practitioners go beyond looking at ways to settle specific problems. Instead, they become involved in broader issues that contribute to improving organizational life, such as encouraging a sense of community, pushing for an organizational climate of openness and trust, and making sure the company provides employees with opportunities for personal growth and development.[59] At Great Britain's General Communications Headquarters, OD specialists helped managers transform a rigid, insular culture into a flexible and collaborative one designed for the twenty-first century, as described in the Unlocking Innovative Solutions Through People box. Specialized techniques have been developed to help meet OD goals.

OD Activities

A number of OD activities have emerged in recent years. Three of the most popular and effective are the following:

1. *Team-building activities.* **Team building** enhances the cohesiveness and success of organizational groups and teams. For example, a series of OD exercises can be used with members of cross-departmental teams to help them learn to act and function as a team. An OD expert can work with team members to increase their communication skills, facilitate their ability to confront one another, and help them accept common goals.

2. *Survey-feedback activities.* **Survey feedback** begins with a questionnaire distributed to employees on values, climate, participation, leadership, and group

team building A type of OD intervention that enhances the cohesiveness of departments by helping members learn to function as a team.

survey feedback A type of OD intervention in which questionnaires on organizational climate and other factors are distributed among employees and their results reported back to them by a change agent.

Unlocking Innovative Solutions Through │ **PEOPLE** │

THE SPIES WHO CAME IN FROM THE COLD

Transforming the secretive culture of Great Britain's General Communications Headquarters (GCHQ) wasn't easy. It took the concerted efforts of computer experts, organization development (OD) specialists, and the architects and builders responsible for the "Doughnut," the GCHQ's award-winning headquarters in Cheltenham.

The U.S. National Security Agency's counterpart, GCHQ produces intelligence obtained largely by intercepting phone calls, e-mail, and other electronic signals originating throughout the world. It's also charged with keeping government communication and information systems safe from cybercriminals, terrorists, and other saboteurs. Up until the late 1990s, staff members worked in a structured, compartmentalized hierarchy. Employees not only didn't talk to outsiders about their work, they didn't even share information with coworkers who didn't have a clear "need to know."

It made sense during the Cold War, but the Cold War has been over for nearly a decade. GCHQ now faces global threats, especially from decentralized terrorist networks, as well as the challenge of monitoring and securing communication systems revolutionized by digital technology. Recognizing that GCHQ had to become more agile, top executives consolidated its technological infrastructure, but soon realized that a flexible, responsive infrastructure meant little without an equally flexible, responsive culture. They needed to create cross-functional, multidisciplinary teams engaged in collaborative learning and knowledge-sharing.

In 1998, GCHQ called on outside OD consultants to help create and implement *Lead 21*, a project designed to promote a new collaborative, flexible culture and give people practice in the new ways of working. Initially, consultants and GCHQ executives believed training senior managers in the desired behaviors was enough, because those behaviors would trickle down through the organization. They quickly saw a need to

expand the project, first to middle managers in 1999 and then to the remaining 3,000 staff members the following year.

Top leaders also realized early on that the physical environment—50 buildings located several miles apart—was hindering the shift to a collaborative culture, so they began planning for a new headquarters. The result is the Doughnut, a $615 million, million-square-foot, ring-shaped building completed in 2003. Architects designed the facility to encourage interaction and collaboration. For example, all three main entrances empty onto a circular "street," a common corridor surrounding an interior garden. The corridor provides access to the open-plan workstations, occupied by almost everyone—including senior managers—so that employees are likely to bump into colleagues from all levels and departments. Employees not only don't have conventional offices, they don't even have their own desks. They simply log onto a workstation wherever it makes the most sense for the task at hand, and their computer files and phone calls automatically find them.

Has this cultural retooling produced the desired results? The spy organization offers outsiders only limited information. But it will say that in contrast to September 2001, when it took a full three months to install a response team, it took only 24 hours to get a team up and running when terrorist-planted explosions ripped through London in 2005.

SOURCES: GCHQ Corporate Development and Corporate Communications Teams, "GCHQ: The Change Journey" (July 2003), http://www.gchq.gov.uk/press/publications.html; Steve Crabb, "Out in the Open," *People Management* (October 13, 2005); Chartered Institute of Personnel and Development, "Removing Barriers and Encouraging Collaborative Learning at GCHQ," http://www.cipd.co.uk/helpingpeoplelearn/researchinpractice_3.asp#section7; Dave Barista, "Spy Central," *Building Design & Construction* (August 2004): 34ff; and Richard Norton-Taylor, "The Doughnut, the Less Secretive Weapon in the Fight Against International Terrorism," *The Guardian* (June 10, 2003).

---

large-group intervention
An approach that brings together participants from all parts of the organization (and may include key outside stakeholders as well) to discuss problems or opportunities and plan for major change.

cohesion within their organization. After the survey is completed, an OD consultant meets with groups of employees to provide feedback about their responses and the problems identified. Employees are engaged in problem solving based on the data.

3. *Large-group interventions.* In recent years, the need for bringing about fundamental organizational change in today's complex, fast-changing world prompted a growing interest in applications of OD techniques to large group settings.[60] The **large-group intervention** approach brings together participants from all parts of the organization—often including key stakeholders from outside the

	Traditional Organization Development Model	Large-Group Intervention Model
Focus for action:	Specific problem or group	Entire system
Information Source:	Organization	Organization and environment
Distribution:	Limited	Widely shared
Time frame:	Gradual	Fast
Learning:	Individual, small group	Whole organization

Change process:	Incremental change	Rapid transformation

EXHIBIT 11.5

OD Approaches to Culture Change

SOURCE: Adapted from Barbara Benedict Bunker and Billie T. Alban, "Conclusion: What Makes Large Group Interventions Effective," *Journal of Applied Behavioral Science* 28, no. 4 (December 1992): 579–591.

organization as well—to discuss problems or opportunities and plan for change. A large-group intervention might involve 50 to 500 people and last several days. The idea is to include everyone who has a stake in the change, gather perspectives from all parts of the system, and enable people to create a collective future through sustained, guided dialogue.

Large-group interventions reflect a significant shift in the approach to organizational change from earlier OD concepts and approaches. Exhibit 11.5 lists the primary differences between the traditional OD model and the large-scale intervention model of organizational change.[61] In the newer approach, the focus is on the entire system, which takes into account the organization's interaction with its environment. The source of information for discussion is expanded to include customers, suppliers, community members, even competitors, and this information is shared widely so that everyone has the same picture of the organization and its environment. The acceleration of change when the entire system is involved can be remarkable. In addition, learning occurs across all parts of the organization simultaneously, rather than in individuals, small groups, or business units. The result is that the large-group approach offers greater possibilities for fundamental, radical transformation of the entire culture, whereas the traditional approach creates incremental change in a few individuals or small groups at a time. General Electric's Work-Out Program provides an excellent example of the large-group intervention approach.

GE's Work-Out began in large-scale off-site meetings facilitated by a combination of top leaders, outside consultants, and human resources specialists. In each business unit, the basic pattern was the same. Hourly and salaried workers came together from many different parts of the organization in an informal three-day meeting to discuss and solve problems. Gradually, the Work-Out events began to include external stakeholders such as suppliers and customers as well as employees. Today, Work-Out is not an event, but a process of how work is done and problems are solved at GE.

The format for Work-Out includes seven steps:

1. Choose a work process or problem for discussion.
2. Select an appropriate cross-functional team, to include external stakeholders.
3. Assign a "champion" to follow through on recommendations.
4. Meet for several days and come up with recommendations to improve processes or solve problems.
5. Meet with leaders, who are asked to respond to recommendations on the spot.
6. Hold additional meetings as needed to implement the recommendations.
7. Start the process all over again with a new process or problem.

GE's Work-Out process forces a rapid analysis of ideas, the creation of solutions, and the development of a plan for implementation. Over time, this large-group process creates an organizational culture where ideas are rapidly translated into action and positive business results.[62]

General Electric's Work-Out

Large-group interventions represent a significant shift in the way leaders think about change and reflect an increasing awareness of the importance of dealing with the entire system, including external stakeholders, in any significant change effort.

■ **TAKE A MOMENT**

> As a new manager, look for and implement training opportunities that can help people shift their attitudes, beliefs, and behaviors toward what is needed for team, department, and organization success. Use organization development consultants and techniques such as team building, survey feedback, and large-group intervention for widespread change.

OD Steps

Organization development experts acknowledge that changes in corporate culture and human behavior are tough to accomplish and require major effort. The theory underlying OD proposes three distinct stages for achieving behavioral and attitudinal change: (1) unfreezing, (2) changing, and (3) refreezing.[63]

The first stage, **unfreezing**, means that people throughout the organization are made aware of problems and the need for change. This stage creates the motivation for people to change their attitudes and behaviors. Unfreezing may begin when managers present information that shows discrepancies between desired behaviors or performance and the current state of affairs. In addition, managers need to establish a sense of urgency to unfreeze people and create an openness and willingness to change. The unfreezing stage is often associated with *diagnosis*, which uses an outside expert called a *change agent*. The **change agent** is an OD specialist who performs a systematic diagnosis of the organization and identifies work-related problems. He or she gathers and analyzes data through personal interviews, questionnaires, and observations of meetings. The diagnosis helps determine the extent of organizational problems and helps unfreeze managers by making them aware of problems in their behavior.

The second stage, **changing**, occurs when individuals experiment with new behavior and learn new skills to be used in the workplace. This process is sometimes known as intervention, during which the change agent implements a specific plan for training managers and employees. The changing stage might involve a number of specific steps.[64] For example, managers put together a coalition of people with the will and power to guide the change, create a vision for change that everyone can believe in, and widely communicate the vision and plans for change throughout the company. In addition, successful change involves using emotion as well as logic to persuade people and empowering employees to act on the plan and accomplish the desired changes.

The third stage, **refreezing**, occurs when individuals acquire new attitudes or values and are rewarded for them by the organization. The impact of new behaviors is evaluated and reinforced. The change agent supplies new data that show positive changes in performance. Managers may provide updated data to employees that demonstrate positive changes in individual and organizational performance. Top executives celebrate successes and reward positive behavioral changes. At this stage, changes are institutionalized in the organizational culture, so that employees begin to view the changes as a normal, integral part of how the organization operates. Employees may also participate in refresher courses to maintain and reinforce the new behaviors.

MODEL OF PLANNED ORGANIZATIONAL CHANGE

Change does not happen easily, but change can be managed. By observing external trends, patterns, and needs, managers use planned change to help the organization adapt to external problems and opportunities.[65] When organizations are caught flat-footed, failing to anticipate or respond to new needs, management is at fault.

unfreezing The stage of organization development in which participants are made aware of problems in order to increase their willingness to change their behavior.

change agent An OD specialist who contracts with an organization to facilitate change.

changing The intervention stage of organization development in which individuals experiment with new workplace behavior.

refreezing The reinforcement stage of organization development in which individuals acquire a desired new skill or attitude and are rewarded for it by the organization.

EXHIBIT 11.6

Model of Change
Sequence of Events

An overall model for planned change is presented in Exhibit 11.6. Three events make up the change sequence: (1) internal and external forces for change exist; (2) organization managers monitor these forces and become aware of a need for change; and (3) the required change is implemented. How each of these activities is handled depends on the organization and managers' styles.

We now turn to a brief discussion of the specific activities associated with the first two events—forces for change and the perceived need for the organization to respond. Later, we will discuss change implementation.

Forces for Change

Forces for organizational change exist both in the external environment and within the organization.

ENVIRONMENTAL FORCES

As described in Chapters 3 and 4, external forces originate in all environmental sectors, including customers, competitors, technology, economic forces, and the international arena. For example, shifts in customer tastes led McDonald's, the giant purveyor of burgers and fries, to begin offering salads, fruit, whole grain muffins, and grilled chicken sandwiches that are perceived as healthier.[66] Changes in technology and the health care needs of customers caused Medtronic to shift how it views medical devices, from simply providing therapy to monitoring a patient's health condition. The company's cardioverter-defibrillators, for example, can now send information to a secure server, allowing medical personnel to review the patient's condition in real time and identify any problems.[67] Increased competition spurred Microsoft to change how it designs and builds software. With competitors such as Google rapidly introducing innovative software products over the Internet, Microsoft had to find a faster, more flexible way to bring out a new version of Windows onto which new features can be added one by one over time.[68]

INTERNAL FORCES

Internal forces for change arise from internal activities and decisions. If top managers select a goal of rapid company growth, internal actions will have to be changed to meet that growth. New departments or technologies will be created and additional people hired to pursue growth opportunities. To support growth goals at 3M, CEO James McNerney revved up the company's product innovation with a new approach to research and development.

> How could it be? 3M, a century-old icon of American innovation, was looking a little tired when James McNerney took over as CEO. Sales and profits were stalled. What's worse, though, was that scientists seemed to be so focused on their current markets that the

3M

company was no longer creating breakthrough products. Scotchgard and Post-it Notes were all well and good—but where were the pioneering products that could keep 3M growing?

McNerney asked Larry Wendling, the vice president in charge of 3M's central research and development (R&D) lab, to shake things up. He did it by stripping "technologies of the present" from R&D's priorities and reorganizing scientists around fast-growth "technologies of the future." The company's R&D system, with 12 separate research units, each focused on specific target markets, worked fine for launching families of new products from existing product lines, but it gave researchers little incentive to look beyond them. Wendling reorganized R&D so that the majority of 3M scientists were assigned to the major business units. A core group at central R&D was charged specifically with working on breakthrough research.

Today, the products that are driving 3M's growth are coming primarily from nanotechnology, an area that has proven the hardest for many companies to get out of the research lab. Scotchgard and Post-it Notes are still big sellers, but 3M is now pulling in $500 million a year in sales of nanotech-based products such as natural-looking dental fillings, superconductive power cables, ultra-bright cell phone displays, and filters that prevent nosy onlookers from seeing your laptop screen. 3M is currently the world's biggest manufacturer of nanotech materials, controlling more than a third of the global market.[69]

By changing the company's approach to R&D, McNerney and Wendling got 3M's sales and profits growing again. New business strategies, shifts in the labor pool, demands from unions, and production inefficiencies all can generate a force to which management must respond with change. Production inefficiencies at DaimlerChrysler's U.S. factories, for example, prompted managers to initiate a total overhaul of the assembly process, resulting in a new, flexible assembly system that makes extensive use of robots and allows for building more than one type of vehicle on a single assembly line. The flexibility can keep Chrysler's plants running at full capacity, enabling the company to increase profits.[70]

Need for Change

As indicated in Exhibit 11.6, external or internal forces translate into a perceived need for change within the organization. Many people are not willing to change unless they perceive a problem or a crisis. Managers at Humana Inc., for example, changed how the company sells health insurance after losing more than 100,000 private health insurance members in 2005 due to a rapid decrease in the number of small and midsized companies providing benefits to their employees.[71] In many cases, however, it is not a crisis that prompts change. Most problems are subtle, so managers have to recognize and then make others aware of the need for change.[72]

One way managers sense a need for change is through the appearance of a **performance gap**—a disparity between existing and desired performance levels. They then try to create a sense of urgency so that others in the organization will recognize and understand the need for change. For example, the chief component-purchasing manager at Nokia noticed that order numbers for some of the computer chips it purchased from Philips Electronics weren't adding up, and he discovered that a fire at Philips' Albuquerque, New Mexico, plant had delayed production. The manager moved quickly to alert top managers, engineers, and others throughout the company that Nokia could be caught short of chips unless it took action. Within weeks, a crisis team had redesigned chips, found new suppliers, and restored the chip supply line. In contrast, managers at a competing firm that also purchased chips from Philips, had the same information but failed to recognize or create a sense of crisis for change, which left the company millions of chips short of what it needed to produce a key product.[73]

Recall from Chapter 8 the discussion of SWOT analysis. Managers are responsible for monitoring threats and opportunities in the external environment as well as strengths and weaknesses within the organization to determine whether a need for

performance gap A disparity between existing and desired performance levels.

change exists. Managers in every company must be alert to problems and opportunities, because the perceived need for change is what sets the stage for subsequent actions that create a new product or technology. Big problems are easy to spot. Sensitive monitoring systems are needed to detect gradual changes that can fool managers into thinking their company is doing fine. An organization may be in greater danger when the environment changes slowly, because managers may fail to trigger an organizational response. Failing to use planned change to meet small needs can place the organization in hot water, as illustrated in the following passage:

> When frogs are placed in a boiling pail of water, they jump out—they don't want to boil to death. However, when frogs are placed in a cold pail of water, and the pail is placed on a stove with the heat turned very low, over time the frogs will boil to death.[74]

IMPLEMENTING CHANGE

The final step to be managed in the change process is *implementation*. A new, creative idea will not benefit the organization until it is in place and being fully used. One frustration for managers is that employees often seem to resist change for no apparent reason. To effectively manage the implementation process, managers should be aware of the reasons people resist change and use techniques to enlist employee cooperation. Major, corporate-wide changes can be particularly challenging, as discussed in the Manager's Shoptalk box.

Resistance to Change

Idea champions often discover that other employees are unenthusiastic about their new ideas. Members of a new-venture group may be surprised when managers in the regular organization do not support or approve their innovations. Managers and employees not involved in an innovation often seem to prefer the status quo. Employees appear to resist change for several reasons, and understanding them can help managers implement change more effectively.

SELF-INTEREST

People typically resist a change they believe will take away something of value. A proposed change in job design, structure, or technology may lead to a real or perceived loss of power, prestige, pay, or company benefits. The fear of personal loss is perhaps the biggest obstacle to organizational change.[75] For example, when FedEx first expanded into ground transportation to be more competitive with UPS, the company's express air service employees felt threatened. Managers smoothly implemented the change by being aware of this possibility and taking steps to alleviate the concerns. Similarly, the acquisition of Kinko's required FedEx managers to recognize that the self-interest of Kinko's employees could trigger some resistance to changes in the organization.[76]

LACK OF UNDERSTANDING AND TRUST

Employees often distrust the intentions behind a change or do not understand the intended purpose of a change. If previous working relationships with an idea champion have been negative, resistance may occur. One manager had a habit of initiating a change in the financial reporting system about every 12 months and then losing interest and not following through. After the third time, employees no longer went along with the change because they did not trust the manager's intention to follow through to their benefit.

Employees are not always receptive to change. A combination of factors can lead to rejection of, or even outright rebellion against, management's "new and better ideas."

Lands' End Inc. of Dodgeville, Wisconsin, began as a small mail-order business specializing in sailing gear. Employees enjoyed the family-like atmosphere and uncomplicated work environment. By the mid-1990s, the company had blossomed into a $1 billion company with several overseas outlets, passing giant L.L.Bean as number one in specialty catalog sales in the United States.

Such success encouraged founder and chairman Gary Comer to embark on a dramatic management experiment incorporating many of today's trends—teams, 401(k) plans, peer reviews, and the elimination of guards and time clocks. Comer brought in top talent, including former L.L.Bean executive William T. End as CEO, to implement the changes.

But employees balked. Weekly production meetings became a nuisance. "We spent so much time in meetings that we were getting away from the basic stuff of taking care of business," says one employee. Even a much-ballyhooed new mission statement seemed "pushy." One long-time employee complained that "we don't need anything hanging over our heads telling us to do something we're already doing."

Confusion and frustration reigned at Lands' End and was reflected in an earnings drop of 17 percent. Eventually, End left the company, and a new CEO initiated a return to the familiar "Lands' End Way" of doing things. Teams were disbanded, and many of the once-promising initiatives were shelved as workers embraced what was familiar and uncomplicated.

The inability of people to adapt to change is not new. Neither is the failure of management to sufficiently lay the groundwork to prepare employees for change. Harvard professor John P. Kotter established an eight-step plan for implementing change that can provide a greater potential for successful transformation of a company:

1. Establish a sense of urgency through careful examination of the market and identification of opportunities and potential crises.
2. Form a powerful coalition of managers able to lead the change.
3. Create a vision to direct the change and the strategies for achieving that vision.
4. Communicate the vision throughout the organization.
5. Empower others to act on the vision by removing barriers, changing systems, and encouraging risk taking.
6. Plan for and celebrate visible, short-term performance improvements.
7. Consolidate improvements, reassess changes, and make necessary adjustments in the new programs.
8. Articulate the relationship between new behaviors and organizational success.

Major change efforts can be messy and full of surprises, but following these guidelines can break down resistance and mean the difference between success and failure.

SOURCES: Gregory A. Patterson, "Lands' End Kicks Out Modern New Managers, Rejecting a Makeover," *The Wall Street Journal* (April 3, 1995): A1, A6; and John P. Kotter, "Leading Changes: Why Transformation Efforts Fail," *Harvard Business Review* (March–April 1995): 59–67.

UNCERTAINTY

Uncertainty is the lack of information about future events. It represents a fear of the unknown. Uncertainty is especially threatening for employees who have a low tolerance for change and fear anything out of the ordinary. They do not know how a change will affect them and worry about whether they will be able to meet the demands of a new procedure or technology.[77] For example, union leaders at an American auto manufacturer resisted the introduction of employee participation programs. They were uncertain about how the program would affect their status and thus initially opposed it.

DIFFERENT ASSESSMENTS AND GOALS

Another reason for resistance to change is that people who will be affected by an innovation may assess the situation differently from an idea champion or new-venture group. Critics frequently voice legitimate disagreements over the proposed benefits of a change. Managers in each department pursue different goals, and an innovation may detract from performance and goal achievement for some departments. For example, if marketing gets the new product it wants for customers, the cost of manufacturing may increase, and the manufacturing superintendent thus will resist. Resistance may call attention to problems with the innovation. At a consumer products company in Racine, Wisconsin, middle managers resisted the introduction of a new employee program that turned out to be a bad idea. The managers truly believed that the program would do more harm than good.[78]

These reasons for resistance are legitimate in the eyes of employees affected by the change. The best procedure for managers is not to ignore resistance but to diagnose the reasons and design strategies to gain acceptance by users.[79] Strategies for overcoming resistance to change typically involve two approaches: the analysis of resistance through the force-field technique and the use of selective implementation tactics to overcome resistance.

Force-Field Analysis

Force-field analysis grew from the work of Kurt Lewin, who proposed that change was a result of the competition between *driving* and *restraining forces*.[80] Driving forces can be thought of as problems or opportunities that provide motivation for change within the organization. Restraining forces are the various barriers to change, such as a lack of resources, resistance from middle managers, or inadequate employee skills. When a change is introduced, management should analyze both the forces that drive change (problems and opportunities) as well as the forces that resist it (barriers to change). By selectively removing forces that restrain change, the driving forces will be strong enough to enable implementation, as illustrated by the move from A to B in Exhibit 11.7. As barriers are reduced or removed, behavior will shift to incorporate the desired changes.

Just-in-time (JIT) inventory control systems schedule materials to arrive at a company just as they are needed on the production line. In an Ohio manufacturing company, management's analysis showed that the driving forces (opportunities) associated with the implementation of JIT were (1) the large cost savings from reduced inventories, (2) savings from needing fewer workers to handle the inventory, and (3) a quicker, more competitive market response for the company. Restraining forces (barriers) discovered by managers were (1) a freight system that was too slow to deliver inventory on time, (2) a facility layout that emphasized inventory maintenance over new deliveries, (3) worker skills inappropriate for handling rapid inventory deployment, and (4) union resistance to loss of jobs. The driving forces were not sufficient to overcome the restraining forces.

force-field analysis The process of determining which forces drive and which resist a proposed change.

EXHIBIT 11.7

Using Force-Field Analysis to Change from Traditional to Just-in-Time Inventory System

Driving Forces (Need for Change)
- Inventory cost savings
- Fewer workers
- More competitive market response

Restraining Forces (Barriers to Change)
- Freight system
- Facilities layout
- Worker skills
- Union resistance to job loss

A. Traditional Inventory System

Desired Movement

Driving Forces
- Inventory cost savings
- Fewer workers
- More competitive market response

Reduced Restraining Forces
- Use of trucks
- Addition of docks
- Training program
- Reassignment

B. Just-in-Time Inventory System

To shift the behavior to JIT, managers attacked the barriers. An analysis of the freight system showed that delivery by truck provided the flexibility and quickness needed to schedule inventory arrival at a specific time each day. The problem with facility layout was met by adding four new loading docks. Inappropriate worker skills were attacked with a training program to instruct workers in JIT methods and in assembling products with uninspected parts. Union resistance was overcome by agreeing to reassign workers no longer needed for maintaining inventory to jobs in another plant. With the restraining forces reduced, the driving forces were sufficient to allow the JIT system to be implemented.

■ **TAKE A MOMENT**

> As a new manager, recognize that people often have legitimate and rational reasons for resisting change. Don't try to bulldoze a change through a wall of resistance. Use force-field analysis to evaluate the forces that are driving a change and those that are restraining it. Try communication and education, participation, and negotiation to melt resistance, and be sure to enlist the support of top-level managers. Use coercion to implement a change only when absolutely necessary.

Implementation Tactics

The other approach to managing implementation is to adopt specific tactics to overcome employee resistance. For example, resistance to change may be overcome by educating employees or inviting them to participate in implementing the change. Researchers have studied various methods for dealing with resistance to change. The following five tactics, summarized in Exhibit 11.8, have proven successful.[81]

COMMUNICATION AND EDUCATION

Communication and *education* are used when solid information about the change is needed by users and others who may resist implementation. Education is especially important when the change involves new technical knowledge or users are unfamiliar with the idea. Canadian Airlines International spent a year and a half preparing and training employees before changing its entire reservations, airport, cargo, and financial systems as part of a new "Service Quality" strategy. Smooth

EXHIBIT 11.8

Tactics for Overcoming Resistance to Change

SOURCE: Based on J.P. Kotter and L.A. Schlesinger, "Choosing Strategies for Change," *Harvard Business Review* 57 (March–April 1979): 106–114.

Approach	When to Use
Communication, education	• Change is technical. • Users need accurate information and analysis to understand change.
Participation	• Users need to feel involved. • Design requires information from others. • Users have power to resist.
Negotiation	• Group has power over implementation. • Group will lose out in the change.
Coercion	• A crisis exists. • Initiators clearly have power. • Other implementation techniques have failed.
Top management support	• Change involves multiple departments or reallocation of resources. • Users doubt legitimacy of change.

implementation resulted from this intensive training and communications effort, which involved 50,000 tasks, 12,000 people, and 26 classrooms around the world.[82] Managers should also remember that implementing change requires speaking to people's hearts (touching their feelings) as well as to their minds (communicating facts). Emotion is a key component in persuading and influencing others. People are much more likely to change their behavior when they both understand the rational reasons for doing so and see a picture of change that influences their feelings.[83]

PARTICIPATION

Participation involves users and potential resisters in designing the change. This approach is time consuming, but it pays off because users understand and become committed to the change. Participation also helps managers determine potential problems and understand the differences in perceptions of change among employees.[84] When General Motors tried to implement a new management appraisal system for supervisors in its Adrian, Michigan, plant, it met with immediate resistance. Rebuffed by the lack of cooperation, top managers proceeded more slowly, involving supervisors in the design of the new appraisal system. Through participation in system design, managers understood what the new approach was all about and dropped their resistance to it.

NEGOTIATION

Negotiation is a more formal means of achieving cooperation. *Negotiation* uses formal bargaining to win acceptance and approval of a desired change. For example, if the marketing department fears losing power if a new management structure is implemented, top managers may negotiate with marketing to reach a resolution. Companies that have strong unions frequently must formally negotiate change with the unions. The change may become part of the union contract reflecting the agreement of both parties.

COERCION

Coercion means that managers use formal power to force employees to change. Resisters are told to accept the change or lose rewards or even their jobs. In most cases, this approach should not be used because employees feel like victims, are angry at change managers, and may even sabotage the changes. However, coercion may be necessary in crisis situations when a rapid response is urgent. For example, a number of top managers at Coca-Cola had to be reassigned or let go after they refused to go along with a new CEO's changes for revitalizing the sluggish corporation.[85]

TOP MANAGEMENT SUPPORT

The visible support of top management also helps overcome resistance to change. *Top management support* symbolizes to all employees that the change is important for the organization. Top management support is especially important when a change involves multiple departments or when resources are being reallocated among departments. Fred Smith, the founder of FedEx, got personally involved in communicating about the addition of ground shipping services. By giving talks on the corporate television network, going on road trips, and communicating via e-mail and newsletters, Smith signaled that the change was important to the company's future success. Without top management support, changes can get bogged down in squabbling among departments. Moreover, when change agents fail to enlist the support of top executives, these leaders can inadvertently undercut the change project by issuing contradictory orders.

CONCEPT CONNECTION

Implementing change, especially when workers are unionized, often requires **negotiation.** For instance, managers at Goodyear Tire & Rubber Co. concluded that the company needed to pull out of some of its private label business to compete with low-cost foreign producers, but this would lead to plant closings. After having made major concessions several years earlier to help the ailing tire manufacturer get back on track, the United Steelworkers union was adamantly opposed to further job losses. Despite months of talks, the two sides failed to reach an agreement and 15,000 USW members went on strike in October 2006.

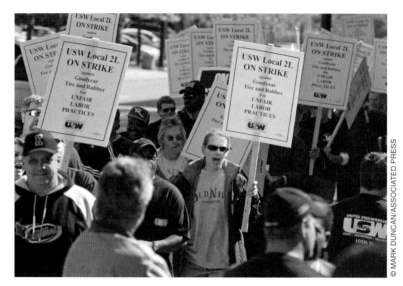

The following example illustrates how smart implementation techniques can smooth the change process.

Remploy Ltd.

Remploy, the United Kingdom's top employer of disabled people, owns 82 manufacturing sites making a diverse range of products, including car headrests, school furniture, and protective clothing for military and civil use. Top managers set some audacious growth goals—to increase staff from 12,500 to 25,000 and triple output within four years, but they knew meeting the goals would require massive changes in how work was done. To ensure success, Remploy used a team of internal consultants to identify the weakest link in a production process, fix it, and then move on to whatever emerged as the next weakest link.

The entire change process was at first frightening and confusing to Remploy's workers, 90 percent of whom have some sort of disability. However, by communicating with employees, providing training, and closely involving them in the change process, the implementation occurred smoothly. For example, at Remploy's Stirling site, top executives made sure factory manager Margaret Harrison understood the program and could communicate its importance to the plant workers. Harrison and the consultants trained people on the factory floor to look for ways to improve day-to-day work processes. "The more we involved the shopfloor people, the more they bought into it, because they were part of the decision-making process," Harrison said. As people saw their ideas implemented, they proposed even more solutions. One worker, for example, suggested sticking colored tape on the machinists' tables to ensure absolute accuracy while speeding up the process. Another group repositioned a huge overhanging machine so that shopfloor workers could see one another, communicate more easily, and pitch in to overcome any workflow slowdowns.

These changes helped Remploy achieve a 5 percent increase in its profit margin and the first growth in business in more than a decade. "If you think, 'I can do this a different way,' you approach the team leaders and tell them," machinist Helen Galloway said. "It's all teamwork. Change is frightening but, because we all have a say, we feel more confident making those changes."[86]

Communication and participation were the key to smooth implementation of significant changes at Remploy's factories. When managers use appropriate implementation techniques, resistance to change softens and the change process proceeds more quickly and smoothly.

Change is inevitable in organizations. This chapter discussed the techniques available for managing the change process. Two key aspects of change in organizations are changing products and technologies and changing people and culture. Three essential innovation strategies for changing products and technologies are exploration, cooperation, and entrepreneurship. Exploration involves designing the organization to promote creativity, imagination, and idea generation. Cooperation requires mechanisms for internal coordination, such as horizontal linkages across departments, and mechanisms for connecting with external parties. One popular approach is open innovation, which extends the search for and commercialization of ideas beyond the boundaries of the organization. Entrepreneurship includes encouraging idea champions and establishing new-venture teams, skunkworks, and new-venture funds.

People and culture changes pertain to the skills, behaviors, and attitudes of employees. Training and organization development are important approaches to changing people's mind-sets and corporate culture. The OD process entails three steps—unfreezing (diagnosis of the problem), the actual change (intervention), and refreezing (reinforcement of new attitudes and behaviors). Popular OD techniques include team building, survey feedback, and large-group interventions.

Managers should think of change as having three elements—the forces for change, the perceived need for change, and the implementation of change. Forces for change can originate either within or outside the firm, and managers are responsible for monitoring events that may require a planned organizational response. The final step is implementation. Managers should be prepared to encounter resistance to change. Some typical reasons for resistance include self-interest, lack of trust, uncertainty, and conflicting goals. Force field analysis is one technique for diagnosing barriers, which often can be removed. Managers can also draw on the implementation tactics of communication, participation, negotiation, coercion, or top management support.

Samsung Electronics, described in the chapter opening, has become a hotbed of technology and product change and is the global leader in eight consumer electronics categories. The consulting firm Interbrand calculates that in 2006 Samsung was the world's most valuable electronics brand. Between the years of 2000 and 2005, the company won more awards from the Industrial Design Society of America than any other firm on the planet. One step executives took to create a new mind-set that values creativity, cooperation, and innovation over imitation and internal competition was to set up the Innovative Design Lab (IDS), where designers, engineers, marketers, and managers from various disciplines took a year-long series of courses aimed at fostering a collaborative environment. The courses also gave people the skills and confidence to risk thinking differently. At the IDS, designers are trained in how to better champion their ideas. Cross-discipline teams study consumers and create what-if scenarios about the world's future buying patterns. Samsung stimulates creativity with the Global Design Workshop, which sends employees to the world's great art and design centers. Designers get Wednesday afternoons off to explore for ideas outside the office. Although managers admit it seemed like slow-going at first, over time these efforts transformed the culture at Samsung. The company also reflects the horizontal model. In the Value Innovation Program (VIP) Center, cross-functional product teams work on problems and cutting-edge ideas without the interruption of phone calls, annoying administrative tasks, or other day-to-day matters that distract people from the project. In a major shift from the past, Samsung is also involved in collaborative relationships with other organizations, such as a partnership with XM Satellite Radio to produce the first portable satellite radio combined with a digital music player. "We cannot live without change," says Samsung Vice Chairman Jong-Yong Yun. "The race for survival in this world is not to the strongest, but to the most adaptive."[87]

DISCUSSION QUESTIONS

1. Times of shared crisis, such as the September 11, 2001, terrorist attack on the World Trade Center or the Gulf Coast hurricanes in 2005, can induce many companies that have been bitter rivals to put their competitive spirit aside and focus on cooperation and courtesy. Do you believe this type of change will be a lasting one? Discuss.

2. A manager of an international chemical company said that few new products in her company were successful. What would you advise the manager to do to help increase the company's success rate?

3. What is meant by the terms *internal* and *external forces for change*? Which forces do you think are causes of change in a university? In a pharmaceuticals firm?

4. As a manager, how would you deal with resistance to change when you suspect employee fears of job loss are well-founded?

5. How might businesses use the Internet to identify untapped customer needs through open innovation? What do you see as the major advantages and disadvantages of the open innovation approach?

6. Why do organizations experience resistance to change? What techniques can managers use to overcome resistance?

7. Explain force-field analysis. Use examples from your own experience to analyze the driving and restraining forces for a change.

8. Which role or roles—the inventor, champion, sponsor, or critic—would you most like to play in the innovation process? Which roles would you be least comfortable playing? Why do you think idea champions are so essential to the initiation of change?

9. You are a manager, and you believe the expense reimbursement system for salespeople is far too slow, taking weeks instead of days. How would you go about convincing other managers that this problem needs to be addressed?

10. Do the underlying values of organization development differ from assumptions associated with other types of change? Discuss.

11. How do large-group interventions differ from OD techniques such as team building and survey feedback?

MANAGEMENT IN PRACTICE: EXPERIENTIAL EXERCISE

Is Your Company Creative?

An effective way to assess the creative climate of an organization for which you have worked is to fill out the following questionnaire. Answer each question based on your work experience in that firm. Discuss the results with members of your group, and talk about whether changing the firm along the dimensions in the questions would make it more creative.

Instructions: Answer each of the following questions using the five-point scale (*Note:* No rating of 4 is used):

⓪ We never do this.
① We rarely do this.
② We sometimes do this.
③ We frequently do this.
⑤ We always do this.

1. We are encouraged to seek help anywhere inside or outside the organization with new ideas for our work unit.   ⓪ ① ② ③ ⑤

2. Assistance is provided to develop ideas into proposals for management review.   ⓪ ① ② ③ ⑤

3. Our performance reviews encourage risky, creative efforts, ideas, and actions.   ⓪ ① ② ③ ⑤

4. We are encouraged to fill our minds with new information by attending professional meetings and trade fairs, visiting customers, and so on.   ⓪ ① ② ③ ⑤

5. Our meetings are designed to allow people to free-wheel, brainstorm, and generate ideas.   ⓪ ① ② ③ ⑤

6. All members contribute ideas during meetings.   ⓪ ① ② ③ ⑤

7. Meetings often involve much spontaneity and humor.   ⓪ ① ② ③ ⑤

8. We discuss how company structure and our actions help or spoil creativity within our work unit.   ⓪ ① ② ③ ⑤

9. During meetings, the chair is rotated among members.   ⓪ ① ② ③ ⑤

10. Everyone in the work unit receives training in creativity techniques and maintaining a creative climate.   ⓪ ① ② ③ ⑤

Scoring and Interpretation

Add your total score for all 10 questions: _____

To measure how effectively your organization fosters creativity, use the following scale:

Highly effective: 35–50
Moderately effective: 20–34

Moderately ineffective: 10–19
Ineffective: 0–9

SOURCE: Adapted from Edward Glassman, *Creativity Handbook: Idea Triggers and Sparks That Work* (Chapel Hill, NC: LCS Press, 1990). Used by permission.

MANAGEMENT IN PRACTICE: ETHICAL DILEMMA

Crowdsourcing

Last year, when Ai-Lan Nguyen told her friend, Greg Barnwell, that Asheville, North Carolina-based Off the Hook Tees, was going to experiment with crowdsourcing, he warned her she wouldn't like the results. Now, as she was about to walk into a meeting called to decide whether to adopt this new business model, she was afraid her friend had been right.

Crowdsourcing uses the Internet to invite anyone, professionals and amateurs alike, to perform tasks such as product design that employees usually perform. In exchange, contributors receive recognition—but little or no pay. Ai-Lan, as vice president of operations for Off the Hook, a company specializing in witty T-shirts aimed at young adults, upheld the values of founder Chris Woodhouse, who like Ai-Lan was a graphic artist. Before he sold the company, the founder always insisted that T-shirts be well-designed by top-notch graphic artists to make sure each screen print was a work of art. Those graphic artists reported to Ai-Lan.

During the past 18 months, Off the Hook's sales stagnated for the first time in its history. The crowdsourcing experiment was the latest in a series of attempts to jump-start sales growth. Last spring, Off the Hook issued its first open call for T-shirt designs and then posted the entries on the Web so people could vote for their favorites. The top five vote-getters were handed over to the in-house designers, who tweaked the submissions until they met the company's usual quality standards.

When CEO Rob Taylor first announced the company's foray into crowdsourcing, Ai-Lan found herself reassuring the designers that their positions were not in jeopardy. Now Ai-Lan was all but certain she would have to go back on her word. Not only had the crowdsourced tees sold well, but Rob had put a handful of winning designs directly into production, bypassing the design department altogether. Customers didn't notice the difference.

Ai-Lan concluded that Rob was ready to adopt some form of the Web-based crowdsourcing because it made T-shirt design more responsive to consumer desires. Practically speaking, it reduced the uncertainty that surrounded new designs, and it dramatically lowered costs. The people who won the competitions were delighted with the exposure it gave them.

However, when Ai-Lan looked at the crowdsourced shirts with her graphic artist's eye, she felt that the designs were competent, but none achieved the aesthetic standards attained by her in-house designers. Crowdsourcing essentially replaced training and expertise with public opinion. That made the artist in her uncomfortable.

More distressing, it was beginning to look as if Greg had been right when he'd told her that his working definition of crowdsourcing was "a billion amateurs want your job." It was easy to see that if Off the Hook adopted crowdsourcing, she would be handing out pink slips to most of her design people, long-time employees whose work she admired. "Sure, crowdsourcing costs the company less, but what about the human cost?" Greg asked.

What future course should Ai-Lan argue for at the meeting? And what personal decisions did she face if Off the Hook decided to put the crowd completely in charge when it came to T-shirt design?

What Would You Do?

1. Go to the meeting and argue for abandoning crowdsourcing for now in favor of maintaining the artistic integrity and values that Off the Hook has always stood for.

2. Accept the reality that because Off the Hook's CEO Rob Taylor strongly favors crowdsourcing, it's a fait accompli. Be a team player and help work out the details of the new design approach. Prepare to lay off graphic designers as needed.

3. Accept the fact that converting Off the Hook to a crowdsourcing business model is inevitable, but because it violates your own personal values, start looking for a new job elsewhere.

SOURCES: Based on Paul Boutin, "Crowdsourcing: Consumers as Creators," *BusinessWeek Online* (July 13, 2006), www.businessweek.com/innovate/content/jul2006/id20060713_55844.htm?campaign_id=search; Jeff Howe, "The Rise of Crowdsourcing," *Wired* (June 2006), www.wired.com/wired/archive/14.06/crowds.html; and Jeff Howe, Crowdsourcing Blog, www.crowdsourcing.com.

Southern Discomfort

Jim Malesckowski remembers the call of two weeks ago as if he just put down the telephone receiver. "I just read your analysis and I want you to get down to Mexico right away," Jack Ripon, his boss and chief executive officer, had blurted in his ear. "You know we can't make the plant in Oconomo work anymore—the costs are just too high. So go down there, check out what our operational costs would be if we move, and report back to me in a week."

At that moment, Jim felt as if a shiv had been stuck in his side, just below the rib cage. As president of the Wisconsin Specialty Products Division of Lamprey, Inc., he knew quite well the challenge of dealing with high-cost labor in a third-generation, unionized U.S. manufacturing plant. And although he had done the analysis that led to his boss's knee-jerk response, the call still stunned him. There were 520 people who made a living at Lamprey's Oconomo facility, and if it closed, most of them wouldn't have a journeyman's prayer of finding another job in the town of 9,000 people.

Instead of the $16-per-hour average wage paid at the Oconomo plant, the wages paid to the Mexican workers—who lived in a town without sanitation and with an unbelievably toxic effluent from industrial pollution—would amount to about $1.60 an hour on average. That's a savings of nearly $15 million a year for Lamprey, to be offset in part by increased costs for training, transportation, and other matters.

After two days of talking with Mexican government representatives and managers of other companies in the town, Jim had enough information to develop a set of comparative figures of production and shipping costs. On the way home, he started to outline the report, knowing full well that unless some miracle occurred, he would be ushering in a blizzard of pink slips for people he had come to appreciate.

The plant in Oconomo had been in operation since 1921, making special apparel for persons suffering injuries and other medical conditions. Jim had often talked with employees who would recount stories about their fathers or grandfathers working in the same Lamprey company plant—the last of the original manufacturing operations in town.

But friendship aside, competitors had already edged past Lamprey in terms of price and were dangerously close to overtaking it in product quality. Although both Jim and the plant manager had tried to convince the union to accept lower wages, union leaders resisted. In fact, on one occasion when Jim and the plant manager tried to discuss a cell manufacturing approach, which would cross-train employees to perform up to three different jobs, local union leaders could barely restrain their anger. Yet probing beyond the fray, Jim sensed the fear that lurked under the union reps' gruff exterior. He sensed their vulnerability, but could not break through the reactionary bark that protected it.

A week has passed and Jim just submitted his report to his boss. Although he didn't specifically bring up the point, it was apparent that Lamprey could put its investment dollars in a bank and receive a better return than what its Oconomo operation is currently producing.

Tomorrow, he'll discuss the report with the CEO. Jim doesn't want to be responsible for the plant's dismantling, an act he personally believes would be wrong as long as there's a chance its costs can be lowered. "But Ripon's right," he says to himself. "The costs are too high, the union's unwilling to cooperate, and the company needs to make a better return on its investment if it's to continue at all. It sounds right but feels wrong. What should I do?"

Questions

1. What forces for change are evident at the Oconomo plant?

2. What is the primary type of change needed—changing "things" or changing the "people and culture?" Can the Wisconsin plant be saved by changing things alone, by changing people and culture, or must both be changed? Explain your answer.

3. What do you think is the major underlying cause of the union leaders' resistance to change? If you were Jim Malesckowski, what implementation tactics would you use to try to convince union members to change in order to save the Wisconsin plant?

SOURCE: Doug Wallace, "What Would You Do?" *Business Ethics* (March/April 1996), 52–53. Reprinted with permission.

ENDNOTES

1. Bill Breen, "The Seoul of Design," *Fast Company* (December 2005): 90–99; and Peter Lewis, "A Perpetual Crisis Machine," *Fortune* (September 19, 2005): 58–76.

2. Bruce Nussbaum, with Robert Berner and Diane Brady, "Get Creative," *BusinessWeek* (August 1, 2005): 60–68;

Jena McGregor, Michael Arndt, Robert Berner, Ian Rowley, Kenji Hall, Gail Edmondson, Steve Hamm, Moon Ihlwan, and Andy Reinhardt, "The World's Most Innovative Companies," *BusinessWeek* (April 24, 2006), http://www.businessweek.com.

3. Keith Bracsher, "Newest Export Out of China: Inflation Fears," *The New York Times* (April 16, 2004), http://www.nytimes.com.

4. Scott Kirsner, "5 Technologies That Will Change the World," *Fast Company* (September 2003): 93–98; Peter Grant and Amy Schatz, "Battle Lines; For Cable Giants, AT&T Deal Is One More Reason to Worry," *The Wall Street Journal* (March 7, 2006): A1; Stuart F. Brown, "The Automaker's Big-Time Bet on Fuel Cells," *Fortune* (March 30, 1998): 122(B)–122(D); Alex Taylor III, "Billion-Dollar Bets," *Fortune* (June 27, 2005): 138–154.

5. Kirsner, "5 Technologies That Will Change the World."

6. Richard L. Daft, "Bureaucratic vs. Nonbureaucratic Structure in the Process of Innovation and Change," in *Perspectives in Organizational Sociology: Theory and Research*, ed. Samuel B. Bacharach (Greenwich, CT: JAI Press, 1982): 129–166.

7. Glenn Rifkin, "Competing Through Innovation: The Case of Broderbund," *Strategy + Business* 11 (Second Quarter 1998): 48–58; and Deborah Dougherty and Cynthia Hardy, "Sustained Product Innovation in Large, Mature Organizations: Overcoming Innovation-to-Organization Problems," *Academy of Management Journal* 39, no. 5 (1996): 1120–1153.

8. Adapted from Patrick Reinmoeller and Nicole van Baardwijk, "The Link Between Diversity and Resilience," *MIT Sloan Management Review* (Summer 2005): 61–65.

9. Teresa M. Amabile, "Motivating Creativity in Organizations: On Doing What You Love and Loving What You Do," *California Management Review* 40, no. 1 (Fall 1997): 39–58; Brian Leavy, "Creativity: The New Imperative," *Journal of General Management* 28, no. 1 (Autumn 2002): 70–85; and Timothy A. Matherly and Ronald E. Goldsmith, "The Two Faces of Creativity," *Business Horizons* (September–October 1985): 8.

10. Gordon Vessels, "The Creative Process: An Open-Systems Conceptualization," *Journal of Creative Behavior* 16 (1982): 185–196.

11. Robert J. Sternberg, Linda A. O'Hara, and Todd I. Lubart, "Creativity as Investment," *California Management Review* 40, no. 1 (Fall 1997): 8–21; Teresa M. Amabile, "Motivating Creativity in Organizations"; Leavy, "Creativity: The New Imperative"; and Ken Lizotte, "A Creative State of Mind," *Management Review* (May 1998): 15–17.

12. James Brian Quinn, "Managing Innovation: Controlled Chaos," *Harvard Business Review* 63 (May–June 1985): 73–84; Howard H. Stevenson and David E. Gumpert, "The Heart of Entrepreneurship," *Harvard Business Review* 63 (March–April 1985): 85–94; Marsha Sinetar, "Entrepreneurs, Chaos, and Creativity—Can Creative People Really Survive Large Company Structure?" *Sloan Management Review* 6 (Winter 1985): 57–62; and Constantine Andriopoulos, "Six Paradoxes in Managing Creativity: An Embracing Act," *Long Range Planning* 36 (2003): 375–388.

13. Cynthia Browne, "Jest for Success," *Moonbeams* (August 1989): 3–5; and Rosabeth Moss Kanter, *The Change Masters* (New York: Simon and Schuster, 1983).

14. Micheal A. Prospero, "Fast Talk: Creative to the Core," *Fast Company* (December 2005): 25–32.

15. Joann S. Lublin, "Nurturing Innovation," *The Wall Street Journal* (March 20, 2006): B1; and Ben Elgin, "Managing Google's Idea Factory," *BusinessWeek* (October 3, 2005): 88–90.

16. David Kirkpatrick, "Throw It at the Wall and See If It Sticks," *Fortune* (December 12, 2005): 142–150.

17. Harold J. Leavitt, "Why Hierarchies Thrive," *Harvard Business Review* (March 2003): 96–102.

18. "Hands On: A Manager's Notebook," *Inc.* (January 1989): 106.

19. Eng, "Hatching Schemes."

20. Ibid.

21. McGregor et al., "The World's Most Innovative Companies," *BusinessWeek* (April 24, 2006), http://www.businessweek.com.

22. Barry Jaruzelski, Kevin Dehoff, and Rakesh Bordia, "Money Isn't Everything," *Strategy + Business*, no. 41 (December 5, 2005): 54–67; William L. Shanklin and John K. Ryans, Jr., "Organizing for High-Tech Marketing," *Harvard Business Review* 62 (November–December 1984): 164–171; and Arnold O. Putnam, "A Redesign for Engineering," *Harvard Business Review* 63 (May–June 1985): 139–144.

23. Andrew H. Van de Ven, "Central Problems in the Management of Innovation," *Management Science* 32 (1986): 590–607; Daft, *Organization Theory*; and Science Policy Research Unit, University of Sussex, *Success and Failure in Industrial Innovation* (London: Centre for the Study of Industrial Innovation, 1972).

24. Daft, *Organization Theory*.

25. Ariane Sains and Stanley Reed, with Michael Arndt, "Electrolux Cleans Up," *BusinessWeek* (February 27, 2006): 42–43.

26. Brian Dumaine, "How Managers Can Succeed Through Speed," *Fortune* (February 13, 1989): 54–59; and George Stalk, Jr., "Time—The Next Source of Competitive Advantage," *Harvard Business Review* (July–August 1988): 41–51.

27. Steve Hamm, with Ian Rowley, "Speed Demons," *BusinessWeek* (March 27, 2006): 68–76; and John A. Pearce II, "Speed Merchants," *Organizational Dynamics* 30, no. 3 (2002): 191–205.

28. Hamm, "Speed Demons."

29. V. K. Narayanan, Frank L. Douglas, Brock Guernsey, and John Charnes, "How Top Management Steers Fast Cycle Teams to Success," *Strategy & Leadership* 30, no. 3 (2002): 19–27.

30. Hamm, "Speed Demons."

31. Timothy L. O'Brien, "Not Invented Here; Are U.S. Innovators Losing Their Edge?" *The New York Times* (November 13, 2005), http://www.nytimes.com; Darrell Rigby and Barbara Bilodeau, "The Bain 2005 Management Tool Survey," *Strategy & Leadership* 33, no. 4 (2005): 4–12; Ian Mount, "The Return of the Lone Inventor," *FSB (Fortune Small Business)* (March 2005): 18; McGregor et al., "The World's Most Innovative Companies;" Henry Chesbrough, "The Logic of Open Innovation: Managing Intellectual Property," *California Management Review* 45, no. 3 (Spring 2003): 33–58.

32. McGregor et al., "The World's Most Innovative Companies."

33. Robert D. Hof, "The Power of Us," *BusinessWeek* (June 20, 2005): 74–82.

34. Henry Chesbrough, "The Era of Open Innovation," *MIT Sloan Management Review* (Spring 2003): 35–41; Amy Muller and Liisa Välikangas, "Extending the Boundary of Corporate Innovation," *Strategy & Leadership* 30, no. 3 (2002): 4–9; and Navi Radjou, "Networked Innovation Drives Profits," *Industrial Management* (January–February 2005): 14–21.

35. G. Gil Cloyd, "P&G's Secret: Innovating Innovation," *Industry Week* (December 2004): 26–34; McGregor et al., "The World's

Most Innovative Companies"; Bettina von Stamm, "Collaboration with Other Firms and Customers: Innovation's Secret Weapon," *Strategy & Leadership* 32, no. 3 (2004): 16–20; Robert Berner, "Why P&G's Smile Is So Bright," *BusinessWeek* (August 12, 2002): 58–60; Robert D. Hof, "Building an Idea Factory," *BusinessWeek* (October 11, 2004): 194–200; Patricia Sellers, "P&G: Teaching an Old Dog New Tricks," *Fortune* (May 31, 2004): 167–180; Ian Mount, "The Return of the Lone Inventor," *FSB* (March 2005): 18; and Hof, "The Power of Us."

36. Sarah Ellison, "Focus Group; P&G Chief's Turnaround Recipe: Find Out What Women Want," *The Wall Street Journal* (June 1, 2005): A1, A16.

37. Mitsuru Kodama, "Case Study; How Two Japanese High-Tech Companies Achieved Rapid Innovation Via Strategic Community Networks," *Strategy & Leadership* 33, no. 6 (2005): 39–47; Radjou, "Networked Innovation Drives Profits."

38. Katy Koontz, "How to Stand Out from the Crowd," *Working Woman* (January 1988): 74–76.

39. Jane M. Howell, "The Right Stuff: Identifying and Developing Effective Champions of Innovation," *Academy of Management Executive* 19, no. 2 (2005): 108–119.

40. George Anders, "Hard Cell," *Fast Company* (May 2001): 108–122.

41. Harold L. Angle and Andrew H. Van de Ven, "Suggestions for Managing the Innovation Journey," in *Research in the Management of Innovation: The Minnesota Studies,* ed. A. H. Van de Ven, H. L. Angle, and Marshall Scott Poole (Cambridge, MA: Ballinger/Harper & Row, 1989).

42. Robert I. Sutton, "The Weird Rules of Creativity," *Harvard Business Review* (September 2001): 94–103.

43. C. K. Bart, "New Venture Units: Use Them Wisely to Manage Innovation," *Sloan Management Review* (Summer 1988): 35–43; Michael Tushman and David Nadler, "Organizing for Innovation," *California Management Review* 28 (Spring 1986): 74–92; Peter F. Drucker, *Innovation and Entrepreneurship* (New York: Harper & Row, 1985); and Henry W. Chesbrough, "Making Sense of Corporate Venture Capital, *Harvard Business Review* (March 2002), http://www.hbsp.harvard.edu.

44. Joseph Weber, with Stanley Holmes and Christopher Palmeri, "'Most Pits' of Creativity," *BusinessWeek* (November 7, 2005): 98–100.

45. McGregor et al., "The World's Most Innovative Companies."

46. Christopher Hoenig, "Skunk Works Secrets," *CIO* (July 1, 2000): 74–76; and Tom Peters and Nancy Austin, *A Passion for Excellence: The Leadership Difference* (New York: Random House, 1985).

47. Hoenig, "Skunk Works Secrets."

48. Sutton, "The Weird Rules of Creativity."

49. Alan Deutschman, "Building a Better Skunkworks," *Fast Company* (March 2005): 69–73.

50. McGregor et al., "The World's Most Innovative Companies"; Interview with Craig Barrett in Ellen Florian, "CEO Voices: 'I Have a Cast-Iron Stomach,'" *Fortune* (March 8, 2004); and Sherry Eng, "Hatching Schemes," *The Industry Standard* (November 27–December 4, 2000): 174–175.

51. E. H. Schein, "Organizational Culture," *American Psychologist* 45 (February 1990): 109–119; Eliza Newlin Carey, "Calm in the Storm."

52. Diane Brady, "The Immelt Revolution," *BusinessWeek* (March 28, 2005): 64.

53. Rosabeth Moss Kanter, "Execution: The Un-Idea," sidebar in Art Kleiner, "Our 10 Most Enduring Ideas," *Strategy + Business,* no. 41 (December 12, 2005): 36–41.

54. Michelle Conlin, "Tough Love for Techie Souls," *BusinessWeek* (November 29, 1999): 164–170.

55. Alix Nyberg, "Kim Patmore," profile in "The Class of 2000," *CFO* (October 2000): 81–82.

56. M. Sashkin and W. W. Burke, "Organization Development in the 1980s," *General Management* 13 (1987): 393–417; and Richard Beckhard, "What Is Organization Development?" in *Organization Development and Transformation: Managing Effective Change,* Wendell L. French, Cecil H. Bell, Jr., and Robert A. Zawacki, eds. (Burr Ridge, IL: Irwin McGraw-Hill, 2000): 16–19.

57. Wendell L. French and Cecil H. Bell, Jr., "A History of Organization Development," in French, Bell, and Zawacki, *Organization Development and Transformation,* 20–42; and Christopher G. Worley and Ann E. Feyerherm, "Reflections on the Future of Organization Development," *The Journal of Applied Behavioral Science* 39, no. 1 (March 2003): 97–115.

58. Paul F. Buller, "For Successful Strategic Change: Blend OD Practices with Strategic Management," *Organizational Dynamics* (Winter 1988): 42–55; Robert M. Fulmer and Roderick Gilkey, "Blending Corporate Families: Management and Organization Development in a Postmerger Environment," *The Academy of Management Executive* 2 (1988): 275–283; and Worley and Feyerherm, "Reflections on the Future of Organization Development."

59. W. Warner Burke, "The New Agenda for Organization Development," *Organizational Dynamics* (Summer 1997): 7–19.

60. This discussion is based on Kathleen D. Dannemiller and Robert W. Jacobs, "Changing the Way Organizations Change: A Revolution of Common Sense," *The Journal of Applied Behavioral Science* 28, no. 4 (December 1992): 480–498; and Barbara Benedict Bunker and Billie T. Alban, "Conclusion: What Makes Large Group Interventions Effective?" *The Journal of Applied Behavioral Science* 28, no. 4 (December 1992): 570–591.

61. Bunker and Alban, "What Makes Large Group Interventions Effective?"

62. Dave Ulrich, Steve Kerr, and Ron Ashkenas, with Debbie Burke and Patrice Murphy, *The GE Work-Out: How to Implement GE's Revolutionary Method for Busting Bureaucracy and Attacking Organizational Problems—Fast!* (New York: McGraw-Hill, 2002); J. Quinn, "What a Work-Out!" *Performance* (November 1994): 58–63; and B. B. Bunker and B. T. Alban, "Conclusion: What Makes Large Group Interventions Effective?" *Journal of Applied Behavioral Science* 28, no. 4 (December 1992): 572–591.

63. Kurt Lewin, "Frontiers in Group Dynamics: Concepts, Method, and Reality in Social Science," *Human Relations* 1 (1947): 5–41; and E. F. Huse and T. G. Cummings, *Organization Development and Change*, 3rd ed. (St. Paul, MN: West, 1985).

64. Based on John Kotter's eight-step model of planned change, which is described in John Kotter, *Leading Change* (Boston: Harvard Business School Press, 1996): 20–25, and "Leading Change: Why Transformation Efforts Fail," *Harvard Business Review* (March–April, 1995): 59–67.

65. Andre L. Delbecq and Peter K. Mills, "Managerial Practices that Enhance Innovation," *Organizational Dynamics* 14 (Summer 1985): 24–34.

66. Steven Gray, "Beyond Burgers; McDonald's Menu Upgrade Boosts Meal Prices and Results," *The Wall Street Journal* (February 18–19, 2006): A1, A7.

67. Interview with Art Collins in Ellen Florian, "CEO Voices: 'I Have a Cast-Iron Stomach,'" *Fortune* (March 8, 2004).

68. Robert A. Guth, "Code Red; Battling Google, Microsoft Changes How It Builds Software," *The Wall Street Journal* (September 23, 2005): A1, A14.

69. Daniel Del Re, "Pushing Past Post-Its," *Business 2.0* (November 2005): 54–56.

70. Neal E. Boudette, "Shifting Gears; Chrysler Gains Edge by Giving New Flexibility to Its Factories," *The Wall Street Journal* (April 11, 2006): A1, A15.

71. Vanessa Fuhrmans, "Bedside Manner; An Insurer Tries a New Strategy: Listen to Patients," *The Wall Street Journal* (April 11, 2006): A1.

72. John P. Kotter, *Leading Change* (Boston: Harvard University Press, 1996): 20–25; and "Leading Change: Why Transformation Efforts Fail," *Harvard Business Review* (March–April, 1995): 59–67.

73. Almar Latour, "Trial by Fire: A Blaze in Albuquerque Sets Off Major Crisis for Cell-Phone Giants," *The Wall Street Journal* (January 29, 2001): A1, A8.

74. Attributed to Gregory Bateson in Andrew H. Van de Ven, "Central Problems in the Management of Innovation," *Management Science* 32 (1986): 595.

75. J. P. Kotter and L. A. Schlesinger, "Choosing Strategies for Change," *Harvard Business Review* 57 (March–April 1979): 106–114.

76. Interview with Fred Smith in Ellen Florian, "CEO Voices."

77. G. Zaltman and Robert B. Duncan, *Strategies for Planned Change* (New York: Wiley Interscience, 1977).

78. Leonard M. Apcar, "Middle Managers and Supervisors Resist Moves to More Participatory Management," *The Wall Street Journal* (September 16, 1985): 25.

79. Dorothy Leonard-Barton and Isabelle Deschamps, "Managerial Influence in the Implementation of New Technology," *Management Science* 34 (1988): 1252–1265.

80. Kurt Lewin, *Field Theory in Social Science: Selected Theoretical Papers* (New York: Harper & Brothers, 1951).

81. Paul C. Nutt, "Tactics of Implementation," *Academy of Management Journal* 29 (1986): 230–261; Kotter and Schlesinger, "Choosing Strategies"; R. L. Daft and S. Becker, *Innovation in Organizations: Innovation Adoption in School Organizations* (New York: Elsevier, 1978); and R. Beckhard, *Organization Development: Strategies and Models* (Reading, MA: Addison-Wesley, 1969).

82. Rob Muller, "Training for Change," *Canadian Business Review* (Spring 1995): 16–19.

83. Gerard H. Seijts and Grace O'Farrell, "Engage the Heart: Appealing to the Emotions Facilitates Change," *Ivey Business Journal* (January–February 2003): 1–5; John P. Kotter and Dan S. Cohen, *The Heart of Change: Real-Life Stories of How People Change Their Organizations* (Boston: Harvard Business School Press, 2002); and Shaul Fox and Yair Amichai-Hamburger, "The Power of Emotional Appeals in Promoting Organizational Change Programs," *Academy of Management Executive* 15, no. 4 (2001): 84–95.

84. Taggart F. Frost, "Creating a Teamwork-Based Culture within a Manufacturing Setting," *IM* (May–June 1994): 17–20.

85. Dean Foust with Gerry Khermouch, "Repairing the Coke Machine," *BusinessWeek* (March 19, 2001): 86–88.

86. Joy Persaud, "Strongest Links," *People Management* (May 29, 2003): 40–41.

87. Breen, "The Seoul of Design"; Lewis, "A Perpetual Crisis Machine"; Hamm, "Speed Demons"; and Martin Fackler, "Electronics Company Aims to Create Break-Out Product," *The New York Times* (April 25, 2006): C1.

CHAPTER   12

CHAPTER OUTLINE

Manager's Challenge

The Strategic Role of Human
Resource Management

Environmental Influences on HRM

Competitive Strategy

Federal Legislation

The Changing Nature of Careers

The Changing Social Contract

HR Issues in the New Workplace

Attracting an Effective Workforce

Human Resource Planning

Recruiting

Selecting

Developing an Effective Workforce

Training and Development

Performance Appraisal

Maintaining an Effective Workforce

Compensation

Benefits

Termination

LEARNING OBJECTIVES

After studying this chapter, you should be able to:

1. Explain the role of human resource manage-
    ment in organizational strategic planning.

2. Describe federal legislation and societal
    trends that influence human resource
    management.

3. Explain what the changing social contract
    between organizations and employees
    means for workers and human resource
    managers.

4. Show how organizations determine their
    future staffing needs through human
    resource planning.

5. Describe the tools managers use to recruit
    and select employees.

6. Describe how organizations develop an
    effective workforce through training and
    performance appraisal.

7. Explain how organizations maintain a
    workforce through the administration
    of wages and salaries, benefits, and
    terminations.

HUMAN RESOURCE MANAGEMENT

MANAGER'S CHALLENGE

Every hour or so throughout the night, big brown trucks back into the bays at UPS's distribution center in Buffalo, New York, where part-time workers load, unload, and sort packages at a rate of 1,200 boxes an hour. A typical employee handles a box every three seconds. The packages don't stop until the shift is over, which allows little time for friendly banter and chitchat, even if you could hear over the din of the belts and ramps that carry packages through the cavernous 270,000-square-foot warehouse. It's not the easiest job in the world, and many people don't stick around for long. When Jennifer Shroeger arrived in Buffalo as the new district manager, the attrition rate of part-time workers, who account for half of Buffalo's workforce, was 50 percent a year. With people deserting at that rate, hiring and training costs were through the roof, not to mention the slowdown in operations caused by continually training new workers. Something had to be done to bring in the right employees and make them want to stay longer than a few weeks.[1]

> How would you address this enormous human resources challenge? What changes in recruiting, hiring, training, and other human resource practices can help to solve Jennifer Shroeger's problem in Buffalo?

■ **TAKE A MOMENT**

The situation at UPS's Buffalo distribution center provides a dramatic example of the challenges managers face every day. Hiring and retaining quality employees is one of the most urgent concerns of today's managers.[2] The people who make up an organization give the company its primary source of competitive advantage, and human resource management plays a key role in finding and developing the organization's people as human resources that contribute to and directly affect company success. The term **human resource management (HRM)** refers to the design and application of formal systems in an organization to ensure the effective and efficient use of human talent to accomplish organizational goals.[3] This system includes activities undertaken to attract, develop, and maintain an effective workforce.

Managers at Electronic Arts, the world's largest maker of computer games, include a commitment to human resources as one of the company's four worldwide goals. They have to, in a company where the creativity and mind power of artists, designers, model makers, mathematicians, and filmmakers determines strategic success, and the competition for talent is intense.[4] HRM is equally important for government and nonprofit organizations. For example, public schools in the United States are facing a severe teacher shortage, with HRM directors struggling with how to fill an estimated 2.2 million teacher vacancies over the next decade. Many are trying innovative programs such as recruiting in foreign countries, establishing relationships with leaders at top universities, and having their most motivated and enthusiastic teachers work with university students considering teaching careers.[5]

Over the past decade, human resource management has shed its old "personnel" image and gained recognition as a vital player in corporate strategy.[6] Increasingly,

human resource management (HRM) Activities undertaken to attract, develop, and maintain an effective workforce within an organization.

CONCEPT
C O N N E C T I O N With a booming economy, the Republic of Ireland had employers looking for workers. Poland, on the other hand, had plenty of workers looking for jobs. The result was the Warsaw job fair pictured here, an example of how **globalization** affects **human resource management.** Because both countries are European Union members, Irish construction companies were free to come to the Polish capital in search of the engineers, project managers, and skilled carpenters they needed. Polish applicants flocked to the job fair from all over the country, seeking to escape high unemployment and a job market where the take-home pay for even an experienced engineer is roughly $800 a month.

large corporations are outsourcing routine HR administrative activities, freeing HRM staff from time-consuming paperwork and enabling them to take on more strategic responsibilities. In 2003, human resources topped Gartner Inc.'s list of most commonly outsourced business activities.[7] Today's best human resources departments not only support the organization's strategic objective but actively pursue an ongoing, integrated plan for furthering the organization's performance.[8] Human resource managers are key players on the executive team. Research has found that effective human resource management has a positive impact on strategic performance, including higher employee productivity and stronger financial results.[9]

Today, all managers need to be skilled in the basics of human resource management. Flatter organizations often require that managers throughout the organization play an active role in recruiting and selecting the right personnel, developing effective training programs, or creating appropriate performance appraisal systems. HRM professionals act to guide and assist line managers in managing their human resources to achieve the organization's strategic goals.

THE STRATEGIC ROLE OF HUMAN RESOURCE MANAGEMENT

The strategic approach to human resource management recognizes three key elements. First, as we just discussed, all managers are human resource managers. For example, at IBM every manager is expected to pay attention to the development and satisfaction of subordinates. Line managers use surveys, career planning, performance appraisal, and compensation to encourage commitment to IBM.[10] Second, employees are viewed as assets. Employees, not buildings and machinery, give a company its competitive advantage. How a company manages its workforce may be the single most important factor in sustained competitive success.[11] Third, human resource management is a matching process, integrating the organization's strategy and goals with the correct approach to managing the firm's human capital.[12] Current strategic issues of particular concern to managers include the following:

:: Becoming more competitive on a global basis

:: Improving quality, innovation, and customer service

:: Managing mergers and acquisitions

:: Applying new information technology for e-business

All of these strategic decisions determine a company's need for skills and employees.

■ **TAKE A MOMENT** Go to the experiential exercise on page 409 that pertains to your potential for strategic human resource management.

This chapter examines the three primary goals of HRM as illustrated in Exhibit 12.1. HRM activities and goals do not take place inside a vacuum but within

EXHIBIT 12.1

Strategic Human Resource
Management

Company Strategy

Attract an Effective Workforce
HRM planning
Job analysis
Forecasting
Recruiting
Selecting

HRM Environment
Legislation
Trends in society
International events
Changing technology

Maintain an Effective Workforce
Wages and salary
Benefits
Labor relations
Terminations

Develop an Effective Workforce
Training
Development
Appraisal

the context of issues and factors affecting the entire organization, such as globalization, changing technology and the shift to knowledge work, a growing need for rapid innovation, quick shifts in markets and the external environment, societal trends, government regulations, and changes in the organization's culture, structure, strategy, and goals.

The three broad HRM activities outlined in Exhibit 12.1 are to attract an effective workforce, develop the workforce to its potential, and maintain the workforce over the long term.[13] Achieving these goals requires skills in planning, recruiting, training, performance appraisal, wage and salary administration, benefit programs, and even termination. Each of the activities in Exhibit 12.1 will be discussed in this chapter.

ENVIRONMENTAL INFLUENCES ON HRM

"Our strength is the quality of our people."

"Our people are our most important resource."

These often-repeated statements by executives emphasize the importance of HRM. Human resource managers must find, recruit, train, nurture, and retain the best people.[14] Without the right people, the brightest idea or management trend—whether virtual teams, e-business, or flexible compensation—is doomed to failure. In addition, when employees don't feel valued, usually they are not willing to give their best to the company and often leave to find a more supportive work environment. For these reasons, it is important that human resource executives be involved in competitive strategy. Human resource managers also interpret federal legislation and respond to the changing nature of careers and work relationships.

Competitive Strategy

HRM contributes directly to the bottom line, because it is the organization's human assets—its people—that meet or fail to meet strategic goals. To keep companies competitive, HRM is changing in three primary ways: focusing on building human capital, developing global HR strategies, and using information technology.

BUILDING HUMAN CAPITAL

Today, more than ever, strategic decisions are related to human resource considerations. In many companies, especially those that rely more on employee information, creativity, knowledge, and service rather than on production machinery, success depends on the ability to manage *human capital*.[15] **Human capital** refers to the economic value of the combined knowledge, experience, skills, and capabilities of employees.[16] To build human capital, HRM develops strategies for finding the best talent, enhancing their skills and knowledge with training programs and opportunities for personal and professional development, and providing compensation and benefits that enhance the sharing of knowledge and appropriately reward people for their contributions to the organization. One organization that recognizes the strategic role of HRM in getting employees mobilized to meet goals is The Home Depot, the nation's largest home improvement retail chain.

The Home Depot

One of Bob Nardelli's first moves as new CEO of The Home Depot was to hire a highly visible, experienced human resources executive to immediately dive into leading major strategy and change initiatives. As executive vice president of human resources, Dennis Donavan reports directly to the CEO, has the second-highest salary in the company, and holds one of the most powerful positions in the giant corporation. It's a reflection of the importance Nardelli puts on building human capital.

The Home Depot relies on the quality of its employees' interactions with customers to stay on top in its business. More than 325,000 employees interact with customers at a rate of 3 billion times a year, often at a personal level, helping them select bathroom fixtures or discussing how to repair a garbage disposal. When Nardelli took over as CEO, those human interactions were beginning to show signs of strain due to rapid growth. Donovan and his HR team came up with 300 different strategic change projects to initiate over a three-year period, many of them designed to strengthen management and leadership skills. Because store managers are so critical to achieving corporate goals, for example, the HR department created a learning forum for district and store-level managers and within only a few months had put nearly 1,800 store managers through a weeklong intensive leadership program. Today, thanks to Donovan, every Home Depot store has its own HR manager who works directly with the store manager to facilitate hiring and developing store-level employees, including creating staff education seminars and e-learning kiosks.

The Home Depot is on the cutting edge in involving HRM managers in all areas of business decision making, whether it be ongoing operational concerns, changes in the market, or long-term strategic initiatives. In fact, many of the company's most important strategic initiatives have been initiated and led by the human resources department.[17]

Home Depot's HRM team often uses data-driven research to develop human capital initiatives. For example, data showed that senior workers had fewer absences and stayed with their jobs longer, so the company signed a recruiting partnership with the American Association of Retired Persons (AARP). Surveys revealed that employees prefer semiannual bonuses to annual ones, so the HRM department made the switch.[18] These types of initiatives, combined with opportunities for personal and professional development, help create an environment that gives highly talented people compelling reasons to stay.

Another concern related to human capital for HRM managers is building *social capital,* which refers to the quality of interactions among employees and whether they share a common perspective.[19] In organizations with a high degree of social capital, for example, relationships are based on honesty, trust, and respect, and people cooperate smoothly to achieve shared goals and outcomes.

human capital The economic value of the knowledge, experience, skills, and capabilities of employees.

■ **TAKE A MOMENT**

As a new manager, recognize that human capital is the organization's most valuable asset. If you are involved in hiring decisions, look for the best people you can find, and then treat them like gold, with opportunities to learn, grow, and develop new skills and earn appropriate compensation and benefits. Strive to build a high level of social capital for your team or department so that people work together smoothly and relationships are based on trust, respect, and cooperation.

GLOBALIZATION

An issue of significant concern for today's organizations is competing on a global basis, which brings tremendous new challenges for human resource management. Most companies are still in the early stages of developing effective HRM policies, structures, and services that respond to the current reality of globalization.[20] In a study of more than 200 global companies, including Eli Lilly, PPG Industries, and UPS, managers reported that the biggest challenge for HRM is leadership development and training for the international arena. In addition, HRM is responsible for recruitment, training, and performance management of employees who might have to work across geographical, technical, and cultural boundaries to help the organization achieve its goals. The success of global business strategies is closely tied to the effectiveness of the organization's global HR strategies.[21]

A subfield known as **international human resource management (IHRM)** specifically addresses the added complexity that results from coordinating and managing diverse people on a global scale.[22] Research in IHRM has revealed that, as the world becomes increasingly interconnected, some HR practices and trends are converging. However, IHRM managers need a high degree of cultural sensitivity and the ability to tailor and communicate policies and practices for different cultures.[23] What works in one country may not translate well to another. Consider the human resources department at the U.K. division of Electronic Arts. In the United States, talented young people are eager to work for companies such as Electronic Arts, but bright college graduates in the United Kingdom often don't see designing computer games as a worthwhile career. Thus, the U.K. division's HR director has to take a different approach to recruiting, developing close relationships with specific universities and finding other innovative ways to promote the company.[24] Exhibit 12.2 lists some interesting trends related to selection, compensation, performance appraisal, and training in different countries.

INFORMATION TECHNOLOGY

Information technology is transforming human resource management and helping to meet the challenges of today's global environment. A study of the transition from traditional HR to e-HR found that the Internet and information technology significantly affects every area of human resource management, from recruiting, to training and career development, to retention strategies.[25] A **human resource information system** is an integrated computer system designed to provide data and information used in HR planning and decision making. The most basic use is the automation of administrative duties such as handling pay, benefits, and retirement plans, which is convenient for employees and can lead to significant cost savings for the organization.

international human resource management (IHRM) A subfield of human resource management that addresses the complexity that results from recruiting, selecting, developing, and maintaining a diverse workforce on a global scale.

human resource information system An integrated computer system designed to provide data and information used in HR planning and decision making.

EXHIBIT   12.2

Some Trends in International Human Resource Management

Selection	• In Japan, HR managers focus on a job applicant's potential and his or her ability to get along with others. Less emphasis is placed on job-related skills and experience. • Employment tests are considered a crucial part of the selection process in Korea, whereas in Taiwan, the job interview is considered the most important criterion for selection.
Compensation	• Seniority-based pay is used to a greater extent in Asian and Latin countries. • China and Taiwan have surprisingly high use of pay incentives, and are moving toward more incentives based on individual rather than group performance.
Performance Appraisal	• Across ten countries surveyed, managers consider recognizing subordinates' accomplishments, evaluating their goal achievement, planning their development, and improving their performance to be the most important reasons for performance appraisals.
Training	• In Mexico, managers consider training and development a reward to employees for good performance. • HR managers in Korea incorporate team-building into nearly all training and development practices.

SOURCE: Mary Ann Von Glinow, Ellen A. Drost, and Mary B. Teagarden, "Converging on IHRM Best Practices: Lessons Learned from a Globally Distributed Consortium on Theory and Practice," *Human Resource Management* 41, no. 1 (Spring 2002): 123–140.

Some organizations are coming close to a paperless HRM system, which not only saves time and money but also frees staff from mundane chores so they can focus on important strategic issues, such as how to effectively evaluate and compensate virtual workers or how to meet the challenge of a coming skilled labor shortage.[26] Consider that annual labor force growth is expected to slow to 0.2 percent by 2020 and stay there for decades.[27] By simplifying the task of analyzing vast amounts of data, human resource information systems can dramatically improve the effectiveness of long-term planning to meet this and other HR challenges.

Federal Legislation

Over the past 40 years, a number of federal laws have been passed to ensure equal employment opportunity (EEO). Some of the most significant legislation and executive orders are summarized in Exhibit 12.3. The point of the laws is to stop

EXHIBIT 12.3

Major Federal Laws Related to Human Resource Management

Federal Law	Year	Provisions
Equal Opportunity/Discrimination Laws		
Civil Rights Act	1991	Provides for possible compensatory and punitive damages plus traditional back pay for cases of intentional discrimination brought under title VII of the 1964 Civil Rights Act. Shifts the burden of proof to the employer.
Americans with Disabilities Act	1990	Prohibits discrimination against qualified individuals by employers on the basis of disability and demands that "reasonable accommodations" be provided for the disabled to allow performance of duties.
Vocational Rehabilitation Act	1973	Prohibits discrimination based on physical or mental disability and requires that employees be informed about affirmative action plans.
Age Discrimination in Employment Act (ADEA)	1967 (amended 1978, 1986)	Prohibits age discrimination and restricts mandatory retirement.
Civil Rights Act, Title VII	1964	Prohibits discrimination in employment on the basis of race, religion, color, sex, or national origin.
Compensation/Benefits Laws		
Health Insurance Portability and Accountability Act (HIPPA)	1996	Allows employees to switch health insurance plans when changing jobs and get the new coverage regardless of preexisting health conditions; prohibits group plans from dropping a sick employee.
Family and Medical Leave Act	1993	Requires employers to provide up to 12 weeks unpaid leave for childbirth, adoption, or family emergencies.
Equal Pay Act	1963	Prohibits sex differences in pay for substantially equal work.
Health/Safety Laws		
Consolidated Omnibus Budget Reconciliation Act (COBRA)	1985	Requires continued health insurance coverage (paid by employee) following termination.
Occupational Safety and Health Act (OSHA)	1970	Establishes mandatory safety and health standards in organizations.

discriminatory practices that are unfair to specific groups and to define enforcement agencies for these laws. EEO legislation attempts to balance the pay given to men and women; provide employment opportunities without regard to race, religion, national origin, and gender; ensure fair treatment for employees of all ages; and avoid discrimination against disabled individuals.

The Equal Employment Opportunity Commission (EEOC) created by the Civil Rights Act of 1964 initiates investigations in response to complaints concerning discrimination. The EEOC is the major agency involved with employment discrimination. **Discrimination** occurs when some applicants are hired or promoted based on criteria that are not job relevant. For example, refusing to hire a black applicant for a job he is qualified to fill or paying a woman a lower wage than a man for the same work are discriminatory acts. When discrimination is found, remedies include providing back pay and taking affirmative action. **Affirmative action** requires that an employer take positive steps to guarantee equal employment opportunities for people within protected groups. An affirmative action plan is a formal document that can be reviewed by employees and enforcement agencies. The goal of organizational affirmative action is to reduce or eliminate internal inequities among affected employee groups.

Failure to comply with equal employment opportunity legislation can result in substantial fines and penalties for employers. Suits for discriminatory practices can cover a broad range of employee complaints. One issue of growing concern is *sexual harassment*, which is also a violation of Title VII of the Civil Rights Act. The EEOC guidelines specify that behavior such as unwelcome advances, requests for sexual favors, and other verbal and physical conduct of a sexual nature becomes sexual harassment when submission to the conduct is tied to continued employment or advancement or when the behavior creates an intimidating, hostile, or offensive work environment.[28] Sexual harassment will be discussed in more detail in Chapter 13.

Exhibit 12.3 also lists the major federal laws related to compensation and benefits and health and safety issues. The scope of human resource legislation is increasing at federal, state, and municipal levels. The working rights and conditions of women, minorities, older employees, and the disabled will likely receive increasing legislative attention in the future.

THE CHANGING NATURE OF CAREERS

Another current issue is the changing nature of careers. HRM can benefit employees and organizations by responding to recent changes in the relationship between employers and employees and new ways of working such as telecommuting, job sharing, outsourcing, and virtual teams.

The Changing Social Contract

In the old social contract between organization and employee, the employee could contribute ability, education, loyalty, and commitment and expect in return that the company would provide wages and benefits, work, advancement, and training throughout the employee's working life. But volatile changes in the environment have disrupted this contract. As many organizations downsized, significant numbers of employees were eliminated. Employees who are left may feel little stability. In a fast-moving company, a person is hired and assigned to a project. The project changes over time, as do the person's tasks. Then the person is assigned to another project and then to still another. These new projects require working with different groups and leaders and schedules, and people may be working in a virtual environment, where they rarely see their colleagues face to face.[29] Careers no longer progress up a vertical hierarchy but move across jobs horizontally. In many of today's companies, everyone is expected to be a self-motivated worker, with excellent interpersonal relationships, who is continuously acquiring new skills.

discrimination The hiring or promoting of applicants based on criteria that are not job relevant.

affirmative action A policy requiring employers to take positive steps to guarantee equal employment opportunities for people within protected groups.

EXHIBIT   12.4

The Changing Social
Contract

	New Contract	Old Contract
Employee	• Employability, personal responsibility • Partner in business improvement • Learning	• Job security • A cog in the machine • Knowing

Employer	• Continuous learning, lateral career
	  movement, incentive compensation
	• Creative development opportunities
	• Challenging assignments
	• Information and resources
		• Traditional compensation
		  package
		• Standard training programs
		• Routine jobs
		• Limited information

SOURCES: Based on Louisa Wah,"The New Workplace Paradox,"*Management Review* (January 1998): 7;
and Douglas T. Hall and Jonathan E. Moss,"The New Protean Career Contract: Helping Organizations and
Employees Adapt,"*Organizational Dynamics* (Winter 1998): 22–37.

Exhibit 12.4 lists some elements of the new social contract. The new contract is
based on the concept of employability rather than lifetime employment. Individuals manage their own careers; the organization no longer takes care of them or
guarantees employment. Companies agree to pay somewhat higher wages and invest in creative training and development opportunities so that people will be more
employable when the company no longer needs their services. Employees take
more responsibility and control in their jobs, becoming partners in business improvement rather than cogs in a machine. In return, the organization provides challenging work assignments as well as information and resources to enable people to
continually learn new skills. The new contract can provide many opportunities for
employees to be more involved and express new aspects of themselves.

However, many employees are not prepared for new levels of cooperation or responsibility on the job. In addition, some companies take the new approach as an
excuse to treat employees as economic factors to be used when needed and then let
go. This attitude leads to a decline in morale and commitment in organizations, as
well as a decline in performance. Studies in the United States and China found
lower employee and firm performance and decreased commitment in companies
where the interaction between employer and employee is treated as a contract-like
economic exchange rather than a genuine human and social relationship.[30] In general, it is harder than it was in the past to gain an employee's full commitment and
enthusiasm. One study found that even though most workers feel they are contributing to their companies' success, they are increasingly skeptical that their hard
work is being fully recognized and appreciated.[31] Some companies find it hard to
keep good workers because of diminished employee trust. An important challenge
for HRM is revising performance evaluation, training, compensation, and reward
practices to be compatible with the new social contract. In addition, smart organizations contribute to employees' long-term success by offering extensive professional training and development opportunities, career information and assessment,
and career coaching.[32] These programs help to preserve trust and enhance the organization's social capital. Even when employees are let go or voluntarily leave, they
often maintain feelings of goodwill toward the company.

■ **TAKE A MOMENT**

As a new manager, appreciate the opportunities that are offered by the new social contract. Allow people to make genuine contributions of their talents to the
organization, and provide them with challenging work and opportunities to
learn new skills they can transfer to other jobs in the future.

HR Issues in the New Workplace

The rapid change and turbulence in today's business environment bring significant
new challenges for human resource management. Some important current issues
are becoming an employer of choice, responding to the increasing use of teams and

project management, addressing the needs of temporary employees and virtual workers, acknowledging growing employee demands for work/life balance, and humanely managing downsizing.

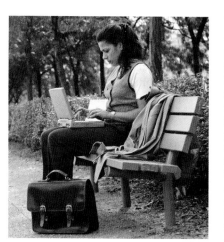

BECOMING AN EMPLOYER OF CHOICE

The old social contract may be broken for good, but today's best companies recognize the importance of treating people right and thinking for the long term rather than looking for quick fixes based on an economic exchange relationship with employees. An *employer of choice* is a company that is highly attractive to potential employees because of human resources practices that focus not just on tangible benefits such as pay and profit sharing, but also on intangibles (such as work/life balance, a trust-based work climate, and a healthy corporate culture), and that embraces a long-term view to solving immediate problems.[33] To engage people and spur high commitment and performance, an employer of choice chooses a carefully balanced set of HR strategies, policies, and practices that are tailored to the organization's own unique goals and needs. Motek Software, for example, has a strict 9 A.M. to 5 P.M. policy and gives employees a full month of vacation each year. Founder and CEO Ann Price wants the best and brightest IT workers, and she doesn't want them to burn out and leave after a couple of years. The consulting and training firm, IHS Help Desk, on the other hand, doesn't expect people to stay more than a couple of years. People work long hours, but IHS keeps them motivated and builds social capital by offering plenty of training and career development opportunities.[34]

TEAMS AND PROJECTS

The advent of *teams* and *project management* is a major trend in today's workplace. People who used to work alone on the shop floor, in the advertising department, or in middle management are now thrown into teams and succeed as part of a group. Each member of the team acts like a manager, becoming responsible for quality standards, scheduling, and even hiring and firing other team members. With the emphasis on projects, the distinctions between job categories and descriptions are collapsing. Many of today's workers straddle functional and departmental boundaries and handle multiple tasks and responsibilities.[35]

TEMPORARY EMPLOYEES

In the opening years of the twenty-first century, the largest employer in the United States was a temporary employment agency, Manpower Inc.[36] Temporary agencies grew rapidly during the 1990s, and early 2000s, and millions of employees today are in temporary firm placements. People in these temporary jobs do everything from data entry, to project management, to becoming the interim CEO. Although in the past, most temporary workers were in clerical and manufacturing positions, in recent years demand has grown for professionals, particularly financial analysts, interim managers, information technology specialists, accountants, product managers, and operations experts.[37] **Contingent workers** are people who work for an organization, but not on a permanent or full-time basis. These workers include temporary placements, contracted professionals, leased employees, or part-time workers. One estimate is that contingent workers make up at least 25 percent of the U.S. workforce.[38] The use of contingent workers means reduced payroll and benefit costs, as well as increased flexibility for both employers and employees.

CONCEPT CONNECTION

It is technology—such as laptops, home computers, and broadband—that makes **telecommuting** possible. But it's social and cultural trends that make its continuing growth probable. For example, many employees believe telecommuting makes it easier to achieve **work-life balance,** whereas employers find the new arrangement expands their labor pool and cuts overhead expenses. The federal government has encouraged the practice as well because fewer commuters means improved air quality and reduced energy consumption. So managers will continue to find themselves dealing with the issues telecommuting raises: just how do you select, train, monitor, and reward employees you very rarely see?

contingent workers People who work for an organization, but not on a permanent or full-time basis, including temporary placements, contracted professionals, or leased employees.

TECHNOLOGY

Related trends are virtual teams and telecommuting. Some **virtual teams** are made up entirely of people who are hired on a project-by-project basis. Team members are geographically or organizationally dispersed and rarely meet face to face, doing their work instead through advanced information technologies and collaborative software. **Telecommuting** means using computers and telecommunications equipment to do work without going to an office. TeleService Resources has more than 25 telephone agents who work entirely from home, using state-of-the-art call-center technology that provides seamless interaction with TSR's Dallas–Fort Worth call center.[39] Millions of people in the United States and Europe telecommute on a regular or occasional basis.[40] Wireless Internet devices, laptops, cell phones, and fax machines make it possible for people to work just about anywhere. A growing aspect of this phenomenon is called *extreme telecommuting,* which means that people live and work in countries far away from the organization's physical location. For example, Paolo Concini works from his home in Bali, Indonesia, even though his company's offices are located in China and Europe.[41]

WORK/LIFE BALANCE

Telecommuting is one way organizations are helping employees lead more balanced lives. By working part of the time from home, for example, parents can avoid some of the conflicts they often feel in coordinating their work and family responsibilities. *Flexible scheduling* for regular employees is also important in today's workplace. Approximately 27 percent of the U.S. workforce has flexible hours. When and where an employee does the job is becoming less important. In addition, broad work/life balance initiatives play a critical role in retention strategy, partly in response to the shift in expectations among young employees.[42] Generation Y workers are a fast-growing segment of the workforce. Typically, Gen Y employees work smart and work hard on the job, but they refuse to let work be their whole life. Unlike their parents, who placed a high priority on career, Gen Y workers expect the job to accommodate their personal lives.[43]

Many managers recognize that individuals may have personal needs that require special attention. Some HR responses include benefits such as on-site gym facilities and childcare, assistance with arranging child- and eldercare, and paid leaves or sabbaticals.

DOWNSIZING

In some cases, organizations have more people than they need and have to let some employees go. **Downsizing**, which refers to an intentional, planned reduction in the size of a company's workforce, is a reality for many of today's companies. In the first three years of the twenty-first century, for example, employers cut some 2.7 million jobs.[44] Some researchers found that massive downsizing often failed to achieve the intended benefits and in some cases significantly harmed the organization.[45] Unless HRM departments effectively and humanely manage the downsizing process, layoffs can lead to decreased morale and performance. Managers can smooth the downsizing process by regularly communicating with employees and providing them with as much information as possible, providing assistance to workers who will lose their jobs, and using training and development to help address the emotional needs of remaining employees and enable them to cope with new or additional responsibilities.[46]

virtual team A team made up of members who are geographically or organizationally dispersed, rarely meet face to face, and do their work using advanced information technologies.

telecommuting Using computers and telecommunications equipment to perform work from home or another remote location.

downsizing Intentional, planned reduction in the size of a company's workforce.

INC. MAGAZINE, AUGUST 2004, P83

CONCEPT CONNECTION This employee is working in the wiring room at Cobalt Boats, whose high-performance craft are widely admired as the Steinways of the runabout class. Cobalt builds its boat in Neodesha, Kansas, a town of 2,800 in the middle of the prairie, about as far from a lapping tide as one can get in America. But the location has a tremendous advantage—it enables Cobalt to **attract an effective workforce,** mostly second- and third-generation farmers who can no longer make a living from farming alone. These farm-toughened employees have a can-do attitude and an owner's mindset that matches perfectly with Cobalt's emphasis on individual initiative, ingenuity, and responsibility. Cobalt truly values its employees as "the finest boat builders in the world."

These various issues present many challenges for organizations and human resource management, such as new ways of recruiting and compensation that address the interests and needs of contingent and virtual workers, new training methods that help people work cross-functionally, or new ways to retain valuable employees. All of these concerns are taken into consideration as human resource managers work toward the three primary HR goals described earlier: attracting, developing, and maintaining an effective workforce.

ATTRACTING AN EFFECTIVE WORKFORCE

The first goal of HRM is to attract individuals who show signs of becoming valued, productive, and satisfied employees. The first step in attracting an effective workforce involves human resource planning, in which managers or HRM professionals predict the need for new employees based on the types of vacancies that exist, as illustrated in Exhibit 12.5. The second step is to use recruiting procedures to communicate with potential applicants. The third step is to select from the applicants those persons believed to be the best potential contributors to the organization. Finally, the new employee is welcomed into the organization.

Underlying the organization's effort to attract employees is a matching model. With the **matching model**, the organization and the individual attempt to match the needs, interests, and values that they offer each other.[47] HRM professionals attempt to identify a correct match. For example, a small software developer might require long hours from creative, technically skilled employees. In return, it can offer freedom from bureaucracy, tolerance of idiosyncrasies, and potentially high pay. A large manufacturer can offer employment security and stability, but it might have more rules and regulations and require greater skills for "getting approval from the higher-ups." The individual who would thrive working for the software developer might feel stymied and unhappy working for a large manufacturer. Both the company and the employee are interested in finding a good match. A new approach, called *job sculpting*, attempts to match people to jobs that enable them to fulfill deeply embedded life interests.[48] This matching effort often requires that HR managers play detective to find out what really makes a person happy. The idea is that people can fulfill deep-seated needs and interests on the job, which will induce them to stay with the organization.

matching model An employee selection approach in which the organization and the applicant attempt to match each other's needs, interests, and values.

389

Chapter 12 HUMAN RESOURCE MANAGEMENT

EXHIBIT 12.5

Attracting an Effective Workforce

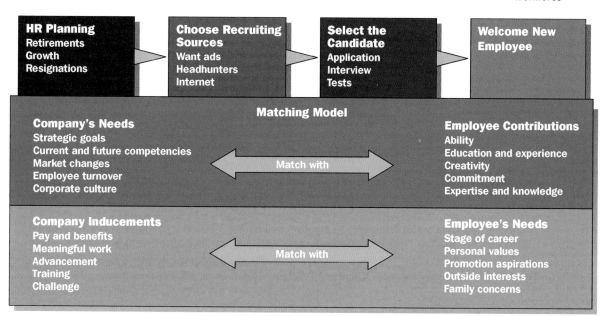

Human Resource Planning

Human resource planning is the forecasting of human resource needs and the projected matching of individuals with expected vacancies. Human resource planning begins with several questions:

:: What new technologies are emerging, and how will these affect the work system?

:: What is the volume of the business likely to be in the next 5–10 years?

:: What is the turnover rate, and how much, if any, is avoidable?

The responses to these questions are used to formulate specific questions pertaining to HR activities, such as the following:

:: How many senior managers will we need during this time period?

:: What types of engineers will we need, and how many?

:: Are persons with adequate computer skills available for meeting our projected needs?

:: How many administrative personnel—technicians, IT specialists—will we need to support the additional managers and engineers?

:: Can we use temporary, contingent, or virtual workers to handle some tasks?[49]

Answers to these questions help define the direction for the organization's HRM strategy. For example, if forecasting suggests a strong upcoming need for more technically trained individuals, the organization can (1) define the jobs and skills needed in some detail, (2) hire and train recruiters to look for the specified skills, and (3) provide new training for existing employees. By anticipating future human resource needs, the organization can prepare itself to meet competitive challenges more effectively than organizations that react to problems only as they arise.

One of the most successful applications of human resource planning is the Tennessee Valley Authority's development of an eight-step system.

human resource planning
The forecasting of human resource needs and the projected matching of individuals with expected job vacancies.

Tennessee Valley Authority (TVA)

In the confusion and uncertainty following a period of reorganization and downsizing, a crucial role for HRM is balancing the need for future workforce planning with the creation of a climate of stability for the remaining workers. TVA created an eight-step plan that assesses future HR needs and formulates actions to meet those needs. The first step is laying the groundwork for later implementation of the program by creating planning and oversight teams within each business unit. Step two involves assessing processes and functions that can be benchmarked. Step three involves projecting the skills and employee numbers (demand data) that will be necessary to reach goals within each business unit. Once these numbers are in place, step four involves projecting the current employee numbers (supply data) over the planning horizon without new hires and taking into consideration the normal attrition of staff through death, retirement, resignation, and so forth. Comparison of the difference between supply and demand (step five) gives the future gap, or surplus situation. This knowledge enables HR to develop strategies and operational plans (step six). Step seven involves communicating the action plan to employees. The final step is to periodically evaluate and update the plan as the organization's needs change.

In a small organization, developing demand and supply data could be handled with a pad and a calculator. However, TVA uses a sophisticated automated system to update and revise the plan as needed to meet new competitive situations. Determining skills-gap and surplus information (step five) helped TVA develop a workforce plan to implement cross-organizational placement and retraining as alternatives to further employee cutbacks in the individual business units, thereby providing a greater sense of stability for workers. If needs change and TVA faces a demand for additional employees, this process will enable the company to recruit workers with the skills needed to help meet organizational goals.[50]

Other organizations use similar human resource planning approaches. IBM looks at trends in information technology to try to gauge what its clients' needs might be in the future, then builds a plan for finding people with the right skills to meet those needs. Recently, for example, the company has built up its roster of people with skills in areas such as open software standards, grid computing, and autonomic computing.[51]

Recruiting

Recruiting is defined as "activities or practices that define the characteristics of applicants to whom selection procedures are ultimately applied."[52] Today, recruiting is sometimes referred to as *talent acquisition* to reflect the importance of the human factor in the organization's success.[53] Although we frequently think of campus recruiting as a typical recruiting activity, many organizations use *internal recruiting*, or *promote-from-within* policies, to fill their high-level positions.[54] At oil field services company Schlumberger, Ltd., for example, current employees are given preference when a position opens. Eighty percent of top managers have been moved up the ranks based on the promote-from-within philosophy; many of them started fresh out of school as field engineers.[55] Internal recruiting has several advantages: It is less costly than an external search, and it generates higher employee commitment, development, and satisfaction because it offers opportunities for career advancement to employees rather than outsiders.

Frequently, however, *external recruiting*—recruiting newcomers from outside the organization—is advantageous. Applicants are provided by a variety of outside sources including advertising, state employment services, online recruiting services, private employment agencies *(headhunters),* job fairs, and employee referrals.

ASSESSING ORGANIZATIONAL NEEDS

An important step in recruiting is to get a clear picture of what kinds of people the organization needs. Basic building blocks of human resource management include job analysis, job descriptions, and job specifications. **Job analysis** is a systematic process of gathering and interpreting information about the essential duties, tasks, and responsibilities of a job, as well as about the context within which the job is performed.[56] To perform job analysis, managers or specialists ask about work activities and work flow, the degree of supervision given and received in the job, knowledge and skills needed, performance standards, working conditions, and so forth. The manager then prepares a written **job description**, which is a clear and concise summary of the specific tasks, duties, and responsibilities, and **job specification**, which outlines the knowledge, skills, education, physical abilities, and other characteristics needed to adequately perform the job.

Job analysis helps organizations recruit the right kind of people and match them to appropriate jobs. For example, to enhance internal recruiting, Sara Lee Corporation identified six functional areas and 24 significant skills that it wants its finance executives to develop, as illustrated in Exhibit 12.6. Managers are tracked on their development and moved into other positions to help them acquire the needed skills.[57] New software programs and Web-based, on-demand subscription services are aiding today's companies in more efficiently and effectively recruiting and matching the right candidates with the right jobs.

REALISTIC JOB PREVIEWS

Job analysis also helps enhance recruiting effectiveness by enabling the creation of **realistic job previews**. A realistic job preview (RJP) gives applicants all pertinent and realistic information—positive and negative—about the job and the organization.[58] RJPs enhance employee satisfaction and reduce turnover, because they facilitate matching individuals, jobs, and organizations. Individuals have a better

recruiting The activities or practices that define the desired characteristics of applicants for specific jobs.

job analysis The systematic process of gathering and interpreting information about the essential duties, tasks, and responsibilities of a job.

job description A concise summary of the specific tasks and responsibilities of a particular job.

job specification An outline of the knowledge, skills, education, and physical abilities needed to adequately perform a job.

realistic job preview A recruiting approach that gives applicants all pertinent and realistic information about the job and the organization.

CONCEPT

C O N C E P T I O N This ad from Black Enterprise magazine enhances **external recruiting** by giving potential applicants a **realistic job preview.** The applicant must possess critical skills such as speaking a foreign language, have a four-year college degree plus three years of professional work experience, be willing to live anywhere on assignment, be between the ages of 23 and 36, and be able to pass "a rigorous physical fitness test." If you possess these requirements, you can even apply online at http://www.fbijobs.com.

basis on which to determine their suitability to the organization and "self-select" into or out of positions based on full information.

LEGAL CONSIDERATIONS

Organizations must ensure that their recruiting practices conform to the law. As discussed earlier in this chapter, equal employment opportunity (EEO) laws stipulate that recruiting and hiring decisions cannot discriminate on the basis of race, national origin, religion, or gender. The Americans with Disabilities Act underscored the need for well-written job descriptions and specifications that accurately reflect the mental and physical dimensions of jobs, so that people with disabilities will not be discriminated against. *Affirmative action* refers to the use of goals, timetables, or other methods in recruiting to promote the hiring, development, and retention of *protected groups*—persons historically underrepresented in the workplace. For example, a city might establish a goal of recruiting one black firefighter for every white firefighter until the proportion of black firefighters is commensurate with the black population in the community.

Most large companies try to comply with affirmative action and EEO guidelines. Prudential Insurance Company's policy is presented in Exhibit 12.7. Prudential actively recruits employees and takes affirmative action steps to recruit individuals from all walks of life.

E-CRUITING

One of the fastest-growing approaches to recruiting is use of the Internet for recruiting, or *e-cruiting*.[59] Recruiting job applicants online dramatically extends

EXHIBIT 12.7

An Equal Opportunity Employer

Prudential recruits, hires, trains, promotes, and compensates individuals without regard to race, color, religion or creed, age, sex, marital status, national origin, ancestry, liability for service in the armed forces of the United States, status as a special disabled veteran or veteran of the Vietnam era, or physical or mental handicap.

This is official company policy because: • we believe it is right
  • it makes good business sense
  • it is the law

We are also committed to an ongoing program of affirmative action in which members of under-represented groups are actively sought out and employed for opportunities in all parts and at all levels of the company. In employing people from all walks of life, Prudential gains access to the full experience of our diverse society.

the organization's recruiting reach, offering access to a wider pool of applicants and saving time and money. Besides posting job openings on company Web sites, many organizations use commercial recruiting sites such as Monster.com, where job seekers can post their résumés and companies can search for qualified applicants. In addition, as competition for high-quality employees heats up, new online companies, such as Jobster and JobThread, emerge to help companies search for "passive candidates," people who aren't looking for jobs but might be the best fit for a company's opening. Expedia calls it "anti-in-box recruiting." Instead of waiting until it has job openings, it uses Jobster to build up a ready supply of passive prospects who have the skills and experience the company might need.[60] This chapter's Unlocking Innovative Solutions Through Technology box describes a unique new approach to finding passive candidates, and one that enables organizations to tap into a global pool of first-rate technical talent.

Companies as diverse as Deloitte Touche Tohmatsu, Cisco Systems, and Atkinsson Congregational Church use the Web for recruiting. Organizations have not given up their traditional recruiting strategies, but the Internet gives HR managers new tools for searching the world to find the best available talent.

OTHER RECENT APPROACHES TO RECRUITING

Organizations are finding other ways to enhance their recruiting success. One highly effective approach is getting referrals from current employees. A company's employees often know of someone who would be qualified for a position and fit in with the organization's culture. Many organizations offer cash awards to employees who submit names of people who subsequently accept employment, because referral by current employees is one of the cheapest and most reliable methods of external recruiting.[61] NewsMarket, a New York-city based company that distributes broadcast-standard video clips over the Internet, shelled out $10,000 in cash awards to employees who referred candidates in 2005. Referrals generate about 40 percent of the new hires at NewsMarket.[62] At many of today's top companies, managers emphasize that recruiting is part of everyone's job. Here's how the Container Store finds quality employees.

Kip Tindell and Garrett Boone opened the first Container Store in Dallas in 1978, and the company has quietly expanded into a 33-store nationwide chain. Annual sales growth has topped 20 percent in all of the company's 23 years of business.

Part of that success is due to the popular storage items and knick-knacks the Container Store sells for neat freaks and people with more stuff than they know what to do with. But another, perhaps even greater, element is the Container Store's approach to recruiting, which turns the company's best customers into loyal, top-performing employees. With retail industry turnover averaging more than 70 percent, the Container Store enjoys a low 10 percent turnover for full-time employees and around 30 to 35 percent for part-timers.

Whether you're a store manager or a stocker, at the Container Store recruiting is an important part of your job. All employees carry recruiting cards, and can earn awards of $500

Container Store

Unlocking Innovative Solutions Through TECHNOLOGY

TOPCODER TO THE RESCUE

For some college students, logging onto a TopCoder online contest is their idea of a good time. Trying to solve challenging computer programming problems as rapidly as possible, they compete with hundreds of others throughout the world for glory, the adrenalin rush, and a chance at prize money. Although it might not be uppermost in their minds as their fingers fly over the keyboard, they're all actually auditioning for a job.

That's because Glastonbury, Connecticut-based software developer TopCoder uses member registrations to create an ever-growing database of tens of thousands of developers in more than 200 countries. Many of those members are students or young people in places such as Taiwan or Belarus—the kind of people who rarely respond to formal job postings.

TopCoder founder and chairperson Jack Hughes and his brother, president and chief operating officer Rob Hughes, first staged a worldwide online computer tournament in 2001 to see whether it could help flush out first-rate programmers for an industry having difficulty tracking them down. It was so successful that companies such as Sun Microsystems, Intel, Yahoo!, and Google were soon asking TopCoder to run more contests under their sponsorship. Today, TopCoder earns revenues in excess of $10 million in part by organizing several Web-based competitions each month for technology clients.

Clients meet with TopCoder's developers to identify their needs and requirements. The developers break the project into components and post them online, where TopCoder's thousands of members can view them and decide whether to enter the competition. Each submission is scored by both the client and a TopCoder review panel. Experts rank regular contestants for speed and accuracy in these competitions, which essentially function as assessment tools. TopCoder posts detailed statistics for top performers in each category, along with information such as their

rank, home country, and score history. Often, these summaries are personalized by a photo and the contestant's favorite quote. TopCoder also holds special events to which it invites top-ranked contestants, such as the 64 finalists who competed for $150,000 in prize money at the TopCoder Open, sponsored in 2006 by Advanced Micro Devices and held in Las Vegas. For Google, TopCoder organized the India Code Jam, a contest that drew some 14,000 registrants from all over South and Southeast Asia for the first round. First prize was nearly $7,000 and a job offer. Although the winner, Singapore undergraduate student Ardian Poernomo, didn't commit to a job, the India Code Jam gave Google a new pool of passive job candidates from which to choose.

For a fee, companies of any size can tap into TopCoder's vast global talent pool, one that includes developers in Russia, Poland, China, and Canada, currently among the nations with the highest average ratings on TopCoder contests. The company also posts notices for contract programming jobs or permanent positions on its Web site. It's all appreciated by technology companies looking for the best talent around the world. Phil Fillippelli, who heads the tech efforts for Gentiva Health Services, the Melville, New York-based national home health services giant, notes that if Gentiva were left to its own devices, "there's no way we could recruit or retain people of this caliber."

SOURCES: Darren Dahl, "Put a Hacker to Work," *Inc.* (January 2006): 39, 42; Tom Krazit, "Coding for Fame, and Dollars," *CNET News.com* (May 3, 2006), http://news.com.com/Coding+for+fame%2C+and+dollars/2100-1007_3-6067549.html; Marianne Kolbasuk McGee, "Winning Design Ways," *InformationWeek* (October 31, 2005): http://www.informationweek.com/story/showarticle.jhtml?articleID=172901456; Lee Gomes, "Programming Contest Pits World's Top Geeks in Battles over Coding," *The Wall Street Journal* (February 8, 2006), B1: and http://www.topcoder.com.

for every full-time and $200 for every part-time hire. Employees get to know their customers on a personal level and they learn which ones have the right attitude and personality to fit the store. As they chat up customers in the aisles, workers offer recruiting cards to people they think would make good employees.

The in-store head-hunting approach has been so successful that approximately a third of the company's 2,500 workers come from employee referrals. In an industry where most companies are running classified ads every week or two for new staff, the Container Store often goes six to eight months without placing a single help-wanted ad.[63]

Having employees assist with recruiting has the added bonus of providing potential candidates with a realistic job preview. At the Container Store, employees share with customers what it's like to work for the company. They want people to know the positive and potentially negative aspects of the job, because it's important to get people who will fit in.

Some companies turn to nontraditional sources to find dedicated employees, particularly in a tight labor market. For example, when Walker Harris couldn't find workers for his ice company on the west side of Chicago, Harris Ice, he began hiring former prison inmates, many of whom have turned out to be reliable, loyal employees.[64] Manufacturer Dee Zee, which makes aluminum truck accessories in a factory in Des Moines, Iowa, found a source of hard-working employees among refugees from Bosnia, Vietnam, and Kosovo.[65] Since 1998, Bank of America has hired and trained more than 3,000 former welfare recipients in positions that offer the potential for promotions and long-term careers. Numerous companies recruit older workers, who typically have lower turnover rates, especially for part-time jobs. The Home Depot offers "snowbird specials"—winter work in Florida and summers in Maine. Border's Bookstores entices retired teachers with book discounts and reading and discussion groups.[66] Recruiting on a global basis is on the rise, as well. Public schools are recruiting teachers from overseas. High-tech companies are looking for qualified workers in foreign countries because they cannot find people with the right skills in the United States.[67]

TAKE A MOMENT

Test your own preparation as a new manager for recruiting and selecting the right people on your team. Go to the New Manager Self-Test on page 396.

Selecting

The next step for managers is to select desired employees from the pool of recruited applicants. In the **selection** process, employers assess applicants' characteristics in an attempt to determine the "fit" between the job and applicant characteristics. Several selection devices are used for assessing applicant qualifications. The most frequently used are the application form, interview, employment test, and assessment center. Studies indicate that the greater the skill requirements and work demands of an open position, the greater the number and variety of selection tools the organization will use.[68] Human resource professionals may use a combination of devices to obtain a valid prediction of employee job performance. **Validity** refers to the relationship between one's score on a selection device and one's future job performance. A valid selection procedure will provide high scores that correspond to subsequent high job performance.

APPLICATION FORM

The **application form** is used to collect information about the applicant's education, previous job experience, and other background characteristics. Research in the life insurance industry shows that biographical information inventories can validly predict future job success.[69]

One pitfall to be avoided is the inclusion of questions that are irrelevant to job success. In line with affirmative action, the application form should not ask questions that will create an adverse impact on protected groups unless the questions are clearly related to the job.[70] For example, employers should not ask whether the applicant rents or owns his or her own home because (1) an applicant's response might adversely affect his or her chances at the job, (2) minorities and women may be less likely to own a home, and (3) home ownership is probably unrelated to job performance. By contrast, the CPA exam is relevant to job performance in a CPA firm; thus, it is appropriate to ask whether an applicant for employment has passed the CPA exam, even if only one-half of all female or minority applicants have done so versus nine-tenths of male applicants.

selection The process of determining the skills, abilities, and other attributes a person needs to perform a particular job.

validity The relationship between an applicant's score on a selection device and his or her future job performance.

application form A device for collecting information about an applicant's education, previous job experience, and other background characteristics.

PEOPLE ON THE BUS

As a new manager, how much emphasis will you give to getting the right people on your team? How much emphasis on people is needed? Find out by answering the following questions based on your expectations and beliefs for handling the people part of your management job. Please answer whether each item is Mostly True or Mostly False for you.

	Mostly True	Mostly False
1. Will readily fire someone who isn't working out for the interests of the organization.	____	____
2. Selecting the right people for a winning business team is as important to me as it is to a winning sports team.	____	____
3. I expect to spend 40 percent to 60 percent of my management time on issues such as recruiting, developing, and placing people.	____	____
4. I will paint a realistic picture of negative job aspects that will help scare off the wrong people for the job.	____	____
5. My priority as a manager is first to hire the right people, second to put people in the right positions, and third to then decide strategy and vision.	____	____
6. With the right people on my team, problems of motivation and supervision will largely go away.	____	____

	Mostly True	Mostly False
7. I expect that hiring the right people is a lengthy and arduous process.	____	____
8. I view firing someone as helping them find the place where they belong to find fulfillment.	____	____

SCORING AND INTERPRETATION: Most new managers are shocked at the large amount of time, effort, and skill required to recruit, place, and retain the right people. In recent years, the importance of "getting the right people on the bus" has been described in popular business books such as *Good to Great* and *Execution*. The right people can make an organization great; the wrong people can be catastrophic. Many of the questions are based on the ideas expressed in recent popular books.

Give yourself one point for each item you marked as Mostly True. If you scored 4 or less you may be in for a shock as a new manager. People issues will take up most of your time, and if you don't handle people correctly, your effectiveness will suffer. You should learn how to get the right people on the bus, and how to get the wrong people off the bus. The faster you learn these lessons, the better new manager you will be. A score of 5 or more suggests you have the right understanding and expectations for becoming a manager and dealing with people on the bus.

SOURCES: Based on ideas presented in Jim Collins, *Good to Great: Why Some Companies Make the Leap . . . and Others Don't* (New York: Harper Business, 2001); and other publications.

INTERVIEW

The *interview* serves as a two-way communication channel that allows both the organization and the applicant to collect information that would otherwise be difficult to obtain. This selection technique is used in almost every job category in nearly every organization. It is another area where the organization can get into legal trouble if the interviewer asks questions that violate EEO guidelines. Exhibit 12.8 lists some examples of appropriate and inappropriate interview questions.

Although widely used, the interview is not generally a valid predictor of job performance. Studies of interviewing suggest that people tend to make snap judgments of others within the first few seconds of meeting them and only rarely change their opinions based on anything that occurs in the interview.[71] However, the interview as a selection tool has high *face validity*. That is, it seems valid to employers, and managers prefer to hire someone only after they have been through some form of interview, preferably face-to-face. The Manager's Shoptalk offers some tips for effective interviewing and provides a humorous look at some interview blunders.

Category	Okay to Ask	Inappropriate or Illegal to Ask
National origin	• The applicant's name • If applicant has ever worked under a different name	• The origin of applicant's name • Applicant's ancestry/ethnicity
Race	• Nothing	• Race or color of skin
Disabilities	• Whether applicant has any disabilities that might inhibit performance of job	• If applicant has any physical or mental defects • If applicant has ever filed workers' compensation claim
Age	• If applicant is over 18	• Applicant's age • When applicant graduated from high school
Religion	• Nothing	• Applicant's religious affiliation • What religious holidays applicant observes
Criminal record	• If applicant has ever been convicted of a crime	• If applicant has ever been arrested
Marital/family status	• Nothing	• Marital status, number of children or planned children • Childcare arrangements
Education and experience	• Where applicant went to school • Prior work experience	• When applicant graduated • Hobbies
Citizenship	• If applicant has a legal right to work in the United States	• If applicant is a citizen of another country

SOURCES: Based on "Appropriate and Inappropriate Interview Questions," in George Bohlander, Scott Snell, and Arthur Sherman, *Managing Human Resources*, 12th ed. (Cincinnati, OH: South-Western, 2001): 207; and "Guidelines to Lawful and Unlawful Preemployment Inquiries," Appendix E, in Robert L. Mathis and John H. Jackson, *Human Resource Management*, 2nd ed. (Cincinnati, OH: South-Western, 2002), 189–190.

EXHIBIT 12.8

Employment Applications and Interviews: What Can You Ask?

Today's organizations are trying different approaches to overcome the limitations of the interview. Some put candidates through a series of interviews, each one conducted by a different person and each one probing a different aspect of the candidate. At Microsoft, for example, interviewers include HRM professionals, managers of the appropriate functional department, peers, and people outside the department who are well grounded in the corporate culture.[72] Other companies, including Virginia Power and Philip Morris USA, use *panel interviews*, in which the candidate meets with several interviewers who take turns asking questions, to increase interview validity.[73] The Container Store, described earlier, uses group interviews, in which as many as 10 candidates are asked to make a pitch for a product that solves a particular organization challenge. This approach gives managers a chance to see how people function as part of a team.[74]

Some organizations also supplement traditional interviewing information with *computer-based interviews*. This type of interview typically requires a candidate to answer a series of multiple-choice questions tailored to the specific job. The answers are compared to an ideal profile or to a profile developed on the basis of other candidates. Companies such as Pinkerton Security, Coopers & Lybrand, and Pic n' Pay Shoe Stores found computer-based interviews to be valuable for searching out information regarding the applicant's honesty, work attitude, drug history, candor, dependability, and self-motivation.[75]

■ **TAKE A MOMENT**

As a new manager, get the right people in the right jobs by assessing your team's or department's needs, offering realistic job previews, using a variety of recruiting methods, and striving to match the needs and interests of the individual to those of the organization. It is typically wise to use a variety of selection tools. For lower-skilled jobs, an application and brief interview might be enough, but higher-skilled jobs call for a combination of interviews, aptitude and skills tests, and assessment exercises.

THE RIGHT WAY TO INTERVIEW A JOB APPLICANT

A so-so interview usually nets a so-so employee. Many hiring mistakes can be prevented during the interview. The following techniques will ensure a successful interview:

1. *Know what you want.* Before the interview, prepare questions based on your knowledge of the job to be filled.

2. *Prepare a road map.* Develop questions that will reveal whether the candidate has the correct background and qualifications. The questions should focus on previous experiences that are relevant to the current job.

3. *Use open-ended questions in which the right answer is not obvious.* Ask the applicant to give specific examples of previous work experiences. For example, don't ask, "Are you a hard worker?" or "Tell me about yourself." Instead ask, "Can you give me examples from your previous work history that reflect your level of motivation?" or "How did you go about getting your current job?"

4. *Do not ask questions that are irrelevant to the job.* This caution is particularly important when the irrelevant questions might adversely affect minorities or women.

5. *Listen; don't talk.* You should spend most of the interview listening. If you talk too much, the focus will shift to you, and you might miss important cues. One expert actually recommends stating all your questions right at the beginning of the interview. This approach forces you to sit back and listen and also gives you a chance to watch a candidate's behavior and body language.

6. *Allow enough time so that the interview will not be rushed.* Leave time for the candidate to ask questions about the job. The types of questions the candidate asks can be an important clue to his or her interest in the job.

7. *Avoid reliance on your memory.* Request the applicant's permission to take notes; then do so unobtrusively during the interview or immediately after.

Even a well-planned interview may be disrupted by the unexpected. Here are some of the unusual things that have happened during job interviews, based on surveys of vice presidents and human resource directors at major U.S. corporations:

:: The applicant announced she hadn't had lunch and proceeded to eat a hamburger and french fries in the interviewer's office.

:: When asked if he had any questions about the job, the candidate answered, "Can I get an advance on my paycheck?"

:: The applicant chewed bubble gum and constantly blew bubbles.

:: The job candidate said the main thing he was looking for in a job was a quiet place where no one would bother him.

:: The job applicant challenged the interviewer to arm wrestle.

:: The applicant dozed off and started snoring during the interview.

:: When asked how she would handle a difficult situation, the candidate replied, "I'd let you do it."

SOURCES: James M. Jenks and Brian L. P. Zevnik, "ABCs of Job Interviewing," *Harvard Business Review* (July–August 1989): 38–42; Dr. Pierre Mornell, "Zero Defect Hiring," *Inc.* (March 1998): 75–83; Martha H. Peak, "What Color Is Your Bumbershoot?" *Management Review* (October 1989): 63; and Meridith Levinson, "How to Hire So You Don't Have to Fire," *CIO* (March 1, 2004): 72–80.

EMPLOYMENT TEST

employment test A written or computer-based test designed to measure a particular attribute such as intelligence or aptitude.

assessment center A technique for selecting individuals with high managerial potential based on their performance on a series of simulated managerial tasks.

Employment tests may include intelligence tests, aptitude and ability tests, and personality inventories, particularly those shown to be valid predictors. Many companies today are particularly interested in personality inventories that measure such characteristics as openness to learning, initiative, responsibility, creativity, and emotional stability. Brian Kautz of Arnold Logistics uses a Web-based personality assessment called the Predictive Index (PI) to hire good employees for Arnold's IT department. The PI, originally developed in the 1950s, provides information about the working conditions that are most rewarding to an applicant and that make the person the most motivated and productive. The test is based on the notion that different types of jobs require different personality characteristics and behaviors.[76]

ASSESSMENT CENTER

First developed by psychologists at AT&T, assessment centers are used to select individuals with high potential for managerial careers by such organizations as IBM, General Electric, and JCPenney.[77] **Assessment centers** present a series of managerial situations to groups of applicants over, say, a two- or three-day period. One technique is the *in-basket simulation,* which requires the applicant to play the role of a manager who must decide how to respond to 10 memos in his or her in-basket within a two-hour period. Panels of two or three trained judges observe the applicant's decisions and assess the extent to which they reflect interpersonal, communication, and problem-solving skills.

Assessment centers have proven to be valid predictors of managerial success, and some organizations now use them for hiring front-line workers as well. Mercury Communications in England uses an assessment center to select customer assistants. Applicants participate in simulated exercises with customers and in various other exercises designed to assess their listening skills, customer sensitivity, and ability to cope under pressure.[78]

DEVELOPING AN EFFECTIVE WORKFORCE

Following selection, the next goal of HRM is to develop employees into an effective workforce. Development includes training and performance appraisal.

Training and Development

Training and development represent a planned effort by an organization to facilitate employees' learning of job-related skills and behaviors.[79] Organizations spent some $51.1 billion for training in 2005. The training budget of IBM alone in that year was $750 million.[80] The most common method of training is on-the-job training. In **on-the-job training (OJT)**, an experienced employee is asked to take a new employee "under his or her wing" and show the newcomer how to perform job duties. OJT has many advantages, such as few out-of-pocket costs for training facilities, materials, or instructor fees and easy transfer of learning back to the job. When implemented well, OJT is considered the fastest and most effective means of facilitating learning in the workplace.[81] One type of on-the-job training involves moving people to various types of jobs within the organization, where they work with experienced employees to learn different tasks. This *cross-training* may place an employee in a new position for as short a time as a few hours or for as long as a year, enabling the employee to develop new skills and giving the organization greater flexibility.

Another type of on-the-job training is *mentoring,* which means a more experienced employee is paired with a newcomer or a less-experienced worker to provide guidance, support, and learning opportunities. Other frequently used training methods include the following:

:: *Orientation training*, in which newcomers are introduced to the organization's culture, standards, and goals

:: *Classroom training,* including lectures, films, audiovisual techniques, and simulations—makes up approximately 70 percent of all formal corporate training.[82]

:: *Self-directed learning,* also called programmed instruction, which involves the use of books, manuals, or computers to provide subject matter in highly organized and logical sequences that require employees to answer a series of questions about the material.

:: *Computer-based training,* sometimes called *e-training,* including computer-assisted instruction, Web-based training, and teletraining. As with self-directed learning, the employee works at his or her own pace and instruction is individualized, but the training program is interactive and more complex, nonstructured information can be communicated. E-training has soared in recent years because it offers cost savings to organizations and allows people to learn at their own pace.[83]

Exhibit 12.9 shows the most frequently used types and methods of training in today's organizations.

on-the-job training (OJT)
A type of training in which an experienced employee "adopts" a new employee to teach him or her how to perform job duties.

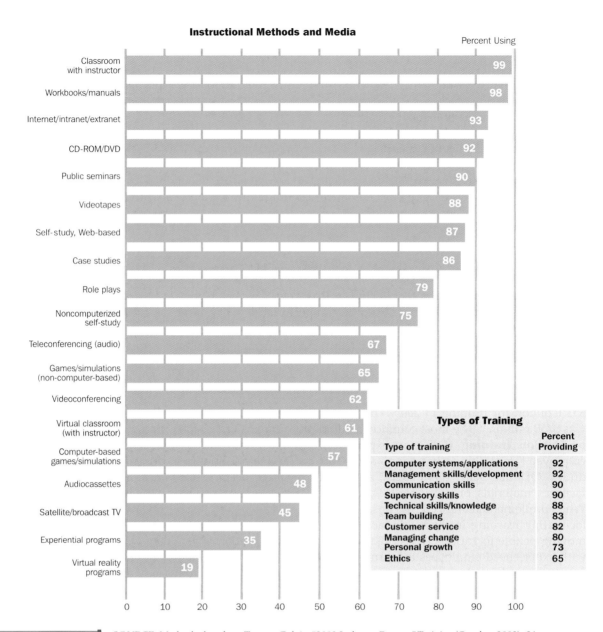

Instructional Methods and Media

Percent Using

Method	Percent
Classroom with instructor	99
Workbooks/manuals	98
Internet/intranet/extranet	93
CD-ROM/DVD	92
Public seminars	90
Videotapes	88
Self-study, Web-based	87
Case studies	86
Role plays	79
Noncomputerized self-study	75
Teleconferencing (audio)	67
Games/simulations (non-computer-based)	65
Videoconferencing	62
Virtual classroom (with instructor)	61
Computer-based games/simulations	57
Audiocassettes	48
Satellite/broadcast TV	45
Experiential programs	35
Virtual reality programs	19

Types of Training

Type of training	Percent Providing
Computer systems/applications	92
Management skills/development	92
Communication skills	90
Supervisory skills	90
Technical skills/knowledge	88
Team building	83
Customer service	82
Managing change	80
Personal growth	73
Ethics	65

EXHIBIT 12.9

Types and Methods of Training

SOURCE: Methods data from Tammy Galvin, "2003 Industry Report," *Training* (October 2003): 21+. Reprinted with permission from the October 2003 issue of *Training* magazine, Copyright 2003, Bill Communications, Minneapolis, Minn. All rights reserved. Not for resales. Types data from Holly Dolezalek, "2005 Industry Report," *Training* (December 2005): 14–28.

CORPORATE UNIVERSITIES

A recent popular approach to training and development is the corporate university. A **corporate university** is an in-house training and education facility that offers broad-based learning opportunities for employees—and frequently for customers, suppliers, and strategic partners as well—throughout their careers.[84] One well-known corporate university is Hamburger University, McDonald's worldwide training center, which has been in existence for more than 40 years. Numerous other companies, including IBM, FedEx, General Electric, Intel, Harley-Davidson, and Capital One, pump millions of dollars into corporate universities to continually build human capital.[85] Employees at Caterpillar attend courses at Caterpillar University, which combines e-training, classroom session, and hands-on training activities. The U.S. Department of Defense runs Defense Acquisition University to provide ongoing training to 129,000 military and civilian workers in acquisitions, technology,

corporate university
An in-house training and education facility that offers broad-based learning opportunities for employees.

and logistics.[86] Although corporate universities have extended their reach with new technology that enables distance learning via videoconferencing and on-line education, most emphasize the importance of classroom interaction.[87]

PROMOTION FROM WITHIN

Another way to further employee development is through promotion from within, which helps companies retain valuable people. This provides challenging assignments, prescribes new responsibilities, and helps employees grow by expanding and developing their abilities. The Peebles Hydro Hotel in Scotland is passionate about promoting from within as a way to retain good people and give them opportunities for growth. A maid has been promoted to head housekeeper, a wine waitress to restaurant head, and a student worker to deputy manager. The hotel also provides constant training in all areas. These techniques, combined with a commitment to job flexibility,

CONCEPT

CONNECTION "We don't do training," says Equifax senior vice president and chief learning officer Lynn Slavenski. "We do change." Slavenski oversaw the establishment of Equifax University for the consumer credit reporting company. What distinguishes **corporate universities** from most old-style training programs is that the courses—from classes teaching a specific technical skill to corporate-run MBA programs—are intentionally designed to foster the changes needed to achieve the organization's strategy. It's clearly an idea whose time has come. In 1993, there were just 400 in-house corporate universities. By 2005, that number increased fivefold, and observers predict it will reach 3,700 by 2010.

have helped the hotel retain high-quality workers at a time when others in the tourism and hospitality industry are suffering from a shortage of skilled labor. Staff members with 10, 15, or even 20 years of service aren't uncommon at Hydro.[88]

WORKFORCE OPTIMIZATION

A related approach is **workforce optimization**, which can be defined as putting the right person in the right place at the right time.[89] With today's emphasis on managing and building human capital, HR professionals are pursuing a range of strategies that help organizations make the best use of the talent they have and effectively develop that talent for the future. New software programs and information technology can help identify people with the right mix of skills to tackle a new project, for example, as well as pinpoint where to move staff internally to ensure they have opportunities for growth and development. IBM is a leader in workforce optimization with a technology-based staff-deployment tool it calls the Workforce Management Initiative. One use of the system is a sort of in-house recruiting tool that lets managers search for employees with the precise skills needed for particular projects. However, the system's greatest impact is that it helps HR professionals and managers analyze what skills employees have, see how those talents match up with current and anticipated needs in the business and technology environment, and devise job transfers and other training to help close skills-gaps.[90]

Performance Appraisal

Performance appraisal comprises the steps of observing and assessing employee performance, recording the assessment, and providing feedback to the employee. During performance appraisal, skillful managers give feedback and praise concerning the acceptable elements of the employee's performance. They also describe performance areas that need improvement. Employees can use this information to change their job performance.

Performance appraisal can also reward high performers with merit pay, recognition, and other rewards. However, the most recent thinking is that linking

workforce optimization
Implementing strategies to put the right people in the right jobs, make the best use of employee talent and skills, and develop human capital for the future.

performance appraisal
The process of observing and evaluating an employee's performance, recording the assessment, and providing feedback to the employee.

performance appraisal to rewards has unintended consequences. The idea is that performance appraisal should be ongoing, not something that is done once a year as part of a consideration of raises. At go2call.com, a provider of VOIP (voice over Internet protocol) phone services, people are reviewed every two weeks. Founders John Nix and Larry Speer were ranked among the 15 "2005 Best Bosses" by *Fortune Small Business* magazine and Winning Workplaces, partly because of innovative practices that let their mostly young workers know how they're doing and how they can get better.[91]

Generally, HRM professionals concentrate on two things to make performance appraisal a positive force in their organizations: (1) the accurate assessment of performance through the development and application of assessment systems such as rating scales, and (2) training managers to effectively use the performance appraisal interview, so managers can provide feedback that will reinforce good performance and motivate employee development.

ASSESSING PERFORMANCE ACCURATELY

To obtain an accurate performance rating, managers acknowledge that jobs are multidimensional and performance thus may be multidimensional as well. For example, a sports broadcaster might perform well on the job-knowledge dimension; that is, she or he might be able to report facts and figures about the players and describe which rule applies when there is a questionable play on the field. But the same broadcaster might not perform as well on another dimension, such as communication. The person might be unable to express the information in a colorful way that interests the audience or might interrupt the other broadcasters.

For performance to be rated accurately, the appraisal system should require the rater to assess each relevant performance dimension. A multidimensional form increases the usefulness of the performance appraisal and facilitates employee growth and development.

A recent trend in performance appraisal is called **360-degree feedback**, a process that uses multiple raters, including self-rating, as a way to increase awareness of strengths and weaknesses and guide employee development. Members of the appraisal group may include supervisors, coworkers, and customers, as well as the individual, thus providing appraisal of the employee from a variety of perspectives.[92] One study found that 26 percent of companies used some type of multirater performance appraisal.[93]

Another alternative performance-evaluation method is the *performance review ranking system*.[94] This method grew quite popular over the past several years, with as many as one third of U.S. corporations using some type of forced ranking system.[95] However, because these systems essentially evaluate employees by pitting them against one another, the method is increasingly coming under fire. As most commonly used, a manager evaluates his or her direct reports relative to one another and categorizes each on a scale, such as A = outstanding performance, B = high-middle performance, or C = in need of improvement. Most companies routinely fire those managers falling in the bottom 10 percent of the ranking. Proponents say the technique provides an effective way to assess performance and offer guidance for employee development. But critics of these systems, sometimes called *rank and yank,* argue that they are based on subjective judgments, produce skewed results, and discriminate against employees who are "different" from the mainstream. A class-action lawsuit charges that Ford's ranking system discriminates against older managers. Use of the system has also triggered employee lawsuits at Conoco and Microsoft, and employment lawyers warn that other suits will follow.[96]

In addition, critics warn that ranking systems significantly hinder collaboration and risk taking, which are increasingly important for today's companies striving for innovation. One recent study found that forced rankings that include firing the bottom 5 or 10 percent can lead to a dramatic improvement in organizational performance in the short term, but the benefits dissipate over several years as people

360-degree feedback A process that uses multiple raters, including self-rating, to appraise employee performance and guide development.

become focused on competing with one another rather than improving the business.[97] Many companies, including General Electric, the most famous advocate of forced rankings in recent years, are building more flexibility into the performance review ranking system, and some are abandoning it altogether.[98]

Despite these concerns, the appropriate use of performance ranking has been useful for many companies, especially as a short-term way to improve performance. A forced ranking system instituted by new HR director Priscilla Vacassin, for instance, has been one key to helping the British banking firm Abbey recover from years of sluggish performance.[99] A variation of the system is helping U.S. restaurant chain Applebee's retain quality workers in the high-turnover restaurant business.

Most people working in fast-food and casual dining restaurants don't stay long. Turnover of hourly employees is a perpetual problem, averaging more than 200 percent a year in the casual dining sector for the past 30 years. Applebee's managers wanted to reduce their turnover rate, but they also wanted to focus their retention efforts on the best people.

A key aspect of the new retention strategy was the Applebee's Performance Management system, called ApplePM. ApplePM took performance appraisal to the Web, making it easier for managers to complete the evaluations and—more importantly—put the results to good use. Twice a year each hourly employee conducts a self-evaluation that covers nine areas: appearance, reliability, fun (including the ability to tolerate frustration), ability, guest service, willingness to be a team player, initiative, stamina, and cooperation. The store manager does the same for each employee; then they meet, compare results, and discuss areas for improvement. But the feedback loop doesn't end there. With a few mouse clicks the manager looks at how each employee ranks with respect to all others in the restaurant, separating employees into the top 20 percent, the middle 60 percent, and the bottom 20 percent.

The system is not the basis for firing low-ranking employees, but they usually leave soon enough anyway. Its value lies in helping managers focus their retention efforts on the top 20 percent, who have management potential, and provide training and development opportunities to the middle 60 percent, who have the potential to move up the ranking. Concentrating on certain employees is paying off for Applebee's. The turnover rate dropped almost 50 percentage points within less than two years.[100]

Applebee's

PERFORMANCE EVALUATION ERRORS

Although we would like to believe that every manager assesses employees' performance in a careful and bias-free manner, researchers have identified several rating problems.[101] One of the most dangerous is **stereotyping**, which occurs when a rater places an employee into a class or category based on one or a few traits or characteristics—for example, stereotyping an older worker as slower and more difficult to train. Another rating error is the **halo effect**, in which a manager gives an employee the same rating on all dimensions even if his or her performance is good on some dimensions and poor on others.

One approach to overcome performance evaluation errors is to use a behavior-based rating technique, such as the behaviorally anchored rating scale. The **behaviorally anchored rating scale (BARS)** is developed from critical incidents pertaining to job performance. Each job performance scale is anchored with specific behavioral statements that describe varying degrees of performance. By relating employee performance to specific incidents, raters can more accurately evaluate an employee's performance.[102]

Exhibit 12.10 illustrates the BARS method for evaluating a production line supervisor. The production supervisor's job can be broken down into several dimensions, such as equipment maintenance, employee training, or work scheduling. A behaviorally anchored rating scale should be developed for each dimension. The dimension in Exhibit 12.10 is work scheduling. Good performance is represented by a 4 or 5 on the scale and unacceptable performance as a 1 or 2. If a production supervisor's job has eight dimensions, the total performance evaluation will be the sum of the scores for each of eight scales.

stereotyping Placing an employee into a class or category based on one or a few traits or characteristics.

halo effect A type of rating error that occurs when an employee receives the same rating on all dimensions regardless of his or her performance on individual ones.

behaviorally anchored rating scale (BARS) A rating technique that relates an employee's performance to specific job-related incidents.

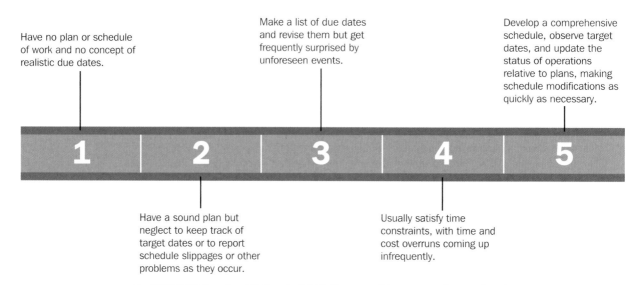

Job: Production Line Supervisor
Work Dimension: Work Scheduling

Have no plan or schedule of work and no concept of realistic due dates.

Make a list of due dates and revise them but get frequently surprised by unforeseen events.

Develop a comprehensive schedule, observe target dates, and update the status of operations relative to plans, making schedule modifications as quickly as necessary.

1   2   3   4   5

Have a sound plan but neglect to keep track of target dates or to report schedule slippages or other problems as they occur.

Usually satisfy time constraints, with time and cost overruns coming up infrequently.

EXHIBIT   12.10

Example of a Behaviorally Anchored Rating Scale

SOURCES: Based on J.P. Campbell, M.D. Dunnette, R.D. Arvey, and L.V. Hellervik, "The Development and Evaluation of Behaviorally Based Rating Scales," *Journal of Applied Psychology* 57 (1973), 15–22; and Francine Alexander, "Performance Appraisals," *Small Business Reports* (March 1989), 20–29.

■ **TAKE A MOMENT**

As a new manager evaluating subordinates, beware of the halo effect, which is a tendency to give a person the same rating on all dimensions of the job. Remember that jobs are multidimensional and people need to be evaluated separately on each relevant dimension so they can be rewarded appropriately and improve their performance where needed. Be aware of your own prejudices so you can avoid stereotyping people during evaluations.

MAINTAINING AN EFFECTIVE WORKFORCE

Now we turn to the topic of how managers and HRM professionals maintain a workforce that has been recruited and developed. Maintenance of the current workforce involves compensation, wage and salary systems, benefits, and occasional terminations.

Compensation

The term **compensation** refers to (1) all monetary payments and (2) all goods or commodities used in lieu of money to reward employees.[103] An organization's compensation structure includes wages and/or salaries and benefits such as health insurance, paid vacations, or employee fitness centers. Developing an effective compensation system is an important part of human resource management because it helps to attract and retain talented workers. In addition, a company's compensation system has an impact on strategic performance.[104] Human resource managers design the pay and benefits systems to fit company strategy and to provide compensation equity.

WAGE AND SALARY SYSTEMS

Ideally, management's strategy for the organization should be a critical determinant of the features and operations of the pay system.[105] For example, managers may have the goal of maintaining or improving profitability or market share by

compensation Monetary payments (wages, salaries) and nonmonetary goods/commodities (benefits, vacations) used to reward employees.

Part 4 ORGANIZING

404

stimulating employee performance. Thus, they should design and use a merit pay system rather than a system based on other criteria such as seniority.

The most common approach to employee compensation is *job-based pay*, which means linking compensation to the specific tasks an employee performs. However, these systems present several problems. For one thing, job-based pay may fail to reward the type of learning behavior needed for the organization to adapt and survive in today's environment. In addition, these systems reinforce an emphasis on organizational hierarchy and centralized decision making and control, which are inconsistent with the growing emphasis on employee participation and increased responsibility.[106]

Skill-based pay systems are becoming increasingly popular in both large and small companies, including Sherwin-Williams, au Bon Pain, and Quaker Oats. Employees with higher skill levels receive higher pay than those with lower skill levels. At Quaker Oats pet food plant in Topeka, Kansas, for example, employees might start at something like $8.75 per hour but reach a top hourly rate of $14.50 when they master a series of skills.[107] Also called *competency-based pay*, skill-based pay systems encourage employees to develop their skills and competencies, thus making them more valuable to the organization as well as more employable if they leave their current jobs.

COMPENSATION EQUITY

Whether the organization uses job-based pay or skill-based pay, good managers strive to maintain a sense of fairness and equity within the pay structure and thereby fortify employee morale. **Job evaluation** refers to the process of determining the value or worth of jobs within an organization through an examination of job content. Job evaluation techniques enable managers to compare similar and dissimilar jobs and to determine internally equitable pay rates—that is, pay rates that employees believe are fair compared with those for other jobs in the organization.

Organizations also want to make sure their pay rates are fair compared to other companies. HRM managers may obtain **wage and salary surveys** that show what other organizations pay incumbents in jobs that match a sample of "key" jobs selected by the organization. These surveys are available from a number of sources, including the U.S. Bureau of Labor Statistics National Compensation Survey.

PAY-FOR-PERFORMANCE

Many of today's organizations develop compensation plans based on a *pay-for-performance standard* to raise productivity and cut labor costs in a competitive global environment. **Pay-for-performance**, also called *incentive pay*, means tying at least part of compensation to employee effort and performance, whether it be through merit-based pay, bonuses, team incentives, or various gainsharing or profit-sharing plans. Data show that, while growth in base wages is slowing in many industries, the use of pay-for-performance has steadily increased since the early 1990s, with approximately 70 percent of companies now offering some form of incentive pay.[108] The U.S. Congress and President Bush recently called for implementing performance-based pay in agencies of the federal government. The seniority-based pay system used by most federal agencies has come under intense scrutiny in recent years, with critics arguing that it creates an environment where poor performers tend to stay and the best and brightest leave out of frustration. A survey conducted by the Office of Personnel Management found that only one in four federal employees believe adequate steps are taken to deal with poor performers, and only two in five think strong performers are appropriately recognized and rewarded.[109]

With pay-for-performance, incentives are aligned with the behaviors needed to help the organization achieve its strategic goals. Employees have an incentive to make the company more efficient and profitable because if goals are not met, no bonuses are paid.

job evaluation The process of determining the value of jobs within an organization through an examination of job content.

wage and salary surveys Surveys that show what other organizations pay incumbents in jobs that match a sample of "key" jobs selected by the organization.

pay-for-performance Incentive pay that ties at least part of compensation to employee effort and performance.

Benefits

The best human resource managers know that a compensation package requires more than money. Although wage/salary is an important component, it is only a part. Equally important are the benefits offered by the organization. Benefits make up 40 percent of labor costs in the United States.[110]

Some benefits are required by law, such as Social Security, unemployment compensation, and workers' compensation. In addition, companies with 50 or more employees are required by the Family and Medical Leave Act to give up to 12 weeks of unpaid leave for such things as the birth or adoption of a child, the serious illness of a spouse or family member, or an employee's serious illness. Other types of benefits, such as health insurance, vacations, and such things as on-site daycare or fitness centers are not required by law but are provided by organizations to maintain an effective workforce. At Aegis Living, a chain of assisted living centers based in Redmond, Washington, CEO Dwayne Clark uses benefits to keep turnover of low-paid patient care staff to a low 34 percent (the average annual turnover rate in assisted living is 93 percent). Clark offers Appreciation Days for employees to take days off and negotiates with suppliers and prospective vendors to provide perks such as discounted massages and haircuts, special mortgage interest rates, and prepared meals from community kitchens.[111]

One reason benefits make up such a large portion of the compensation package is that health care costs continue to increase. Many organizations are requiring that employees absorb a greater share of the cost of medical benefits, such as through higher co-payments and deductibles. Microsoft, for example, recently sliced health care benefits by requiring a higher co-pay on prescription drugs.[112]

Computerization cuts the time and expense of administering benefits programs tremendously. At many companies, such as Wells Fargo and LG&E Energy, employees access their benefits package through an intranet, creating a "self-service" benefits administration.[113] This access also enables employees to change their benefits selections easily. Today's organizations realize that the "one-size-fits-all" benefits package is no longer appropriate, so they frequently offer *cafeteria-plan benefits packages* that allow employees to select the benefits of greatest value to them.[114] Other companies use surveys to determine which combination of fixed benefits is most desirable. The benefits packages provided by large companies attempt to meet the needs of all employees.

Termination

Despite the best efforts of line managers and HRM professionals, the organization will lose employees. Some will retire, others will depart voluntarily for other jobs, and still others will be forced out through mergers and cutbacks or for poor performance.

■ **TAKE A MOMENT**

Even as a new manager, play a role in how people are compensated. Consider skill-based pay systems and incentive pay to encourage high performers. Don't be dismayed if some people have to be let go. If people have to be laid off or fired, do it humanely. Go to the ethical dilemma on page 409 that pertains to termination of employees for poor performance.

The value of termination for maintaining an effective workforce is twofold. First, employees who are poor performers can be dismissed. Productive employees often resent disruptive, low-performing employees who are allowed to stay with the company and receive pay and benefits comparable to theirs. Second, employers can use exit interviews as a valuable HR tool, regardless of whether the employee leaves voluntarily or is forced out. An **exit interview** is an interview conducted with departing employees to determine why they are leaving. The value of the exit

exit interview An interview conducted with departing employees to determine the reasons for their termination.

interview is to provide an inexpensive way to learn about pockets of dissatisfaction within the organization and hence reduce future turnover. The oil services giant Schlumberger includes an exit interview as part of a full-scale investigation of every departure, with the results posted online so managers all around the company can get insight into problems.[115] However, in many cases, employees who leave voluntarily are reluctant to air uncomfortable complaints or discuss their real reasons for leaving. Companies such as T-Mobile, Campbell Soup, and Conair found that having people complete an online exit questionnaire yields more open and honest information. When people have negative things to say about managers or the company, the online format is a chance to speak their mind without having to do it in a face-to-face meeting.[116]

For companies experiencing downsizing through mergers or because of global competition or a shifting economy, often a large number of managers and workers are terminated at the same time. In these cases, enlightened companies try to find a smooth transition for departing employees. For example, General Electric laid off employees in three gradual steps. It also set up a reemployment center to assist employees in finding new jobs or in learning new skills. It provided counseling in how to write a résumé and conduct a job search. Additionally, GE placed an advertisement in local newspapers saying that these employees were available.[117] By showing genuine concern in helping laid-off employees, a company communicates the value of human resources and helps maintain a positive corporate culture.

MANAGER'S SOLUTION

This chapter described several important points about human resource management in organizations. All managers are responsible for human resources, and most organizations have a human resource department that works with line managers to ensure a productive workforce. Human resource management plays a key strategic role in today's organizations. HRM is changing in three ways to keep today's organizations competitive—focusing on human and social capital; globalizing HR systems, policies, and structures; and using information technology to help achieve strategic HR goals. The HR department must also implement procedures to reflect federal and state legislation and respond to changes in working relationships and career directions. The old social contract of the employee being loyal to the company and the company taking care of the employee until retirement no longer holds. Employees are responsible for managing their own careers. Although many people still follow a traditional management career path, others look for new opportunities as contingent workers, telecommuters, project managers, and virtual employees. Other current issues of concern to HRM are becoming an employer of choice, implementing work/life balance initiatives, and humanely managing downsizing.

The first goal of HRM is to attract an effective workforce through human resource planning, recruiting, and employee selection. The second is to develop an effective workforce. Newcomers are introduced to the organization and to their jobs through orientation and training programs. Moreover, employees are evaluated through performance appraisal programs. The third goal is to maintain an effective workforce through wage and salary systems, benefits packages, and termination procedures. In many organizations, information technology is being used to more effectively meet all three of these important HR goals.

At UPS, described in the opening example, new district manager Jennifer Shroeger worked with the HR department to solve the problem of high turnover at the Buffalo distribution center, dramatically cutting the attrition rate to a low 6 percent. Managers realized that retaining employees had a lot to do with how those people were selected in the first place. Previously, UPS basically hired the first applicant who walked in and was capable of handling heavy packages. Shroeger decided they needed to start asking what the applicant was looking for in the job. Many of those hired as part-timers were really looking for full-time jobs, which rarely opened up. After a few months, these people realized their chances of full-time work were slim, so they'd move on. UPS started giving realistic job previews, emphasizing not only the hard, intimidating environment of the warehouse, but also the fact that these positions were part-time jobs and short shifts that were never going to be anything else. The upside to this aspect of the job is that it is perfect for students, mothers, and other people who genuinely *want* to work only part-time. But hiring those people meant UPS needed to build in flexibility. Students and mothers, for example, tend to need more occasional days off or frequent changes in their schedule. Instead of just saying "we can't do that," HRM started looking for ways the company could do it. Other changes involved improved training and mentoring for new employees, handled by part-time shift supervisors who understood the problems of the work environment. The supervisors themselves also got upgraded training in communication skills, motivation, and flexibility to meet the needs of diverse workers. A final, important aspect of the new strategy was to accept that most people they hired wouldn't want to load and unload boxes for their entire careers. "Instead of worrying about them leaving, we should be taking an interest in their future," Shroeger says. "I'd like for all of those part-time workers to graduate from college and start their own businesses—and become UPS customers."[118]

DISCUSSION QUESTIONS

1. It is the year 2018. In your company, central planning has given way to frontline decision making, and bureaucracy has given way to teamwork. Shop floor workers use handheld computers and robots. A labor shortage currently affects many job openings, and the few applicants you do attract lack skills to work in teams, make their own production decisions, or use sophisticated technology. As vice president of human resource management since 2006, what should you have done to prepare for this situation?

2. If you were asked to advise a private company about its equal employment opportunity responsibilities, what two points would you emphasize as most important?

3. How might the human resource activities of recruiting, performance appraisal, and compensation be related to corporate strategy?

4. Think back to your own job experience. What human resource management activities described in this chapter were performed for the job you filled? Which ones were absent?

5. How "valid" do you think the information obtained from a personal interview versus an employment test versus an assessment center would be for predicting effective job performance for a college professor? For an assembly-line worker in a manufacturing plant? Discuss.

6. How do you think the growing use of telecommuters, contingent workers, and virtual teams affect human resource management? How can managers improve recruiting and retention of these new kinds of employees?

7. If you are in charge of training and development, which training option or options—such as on-the-job training, cross-training, classroom, self-directed, or computer-based—would you be likely to choose for your company's production line manager? A customer service representative? An entry-level accountant?

8. If you were to draw up a telecommuting contract with an employee, what would it look like? Include considerations such as job description, compensation and benefits, performance measures, training, and grounds for dismissal.

9. How would you go about deciding whether to use a job-based, skills-based, or pay-for-performance compensation plan for employees in a textile manufacturing plant? For wait staff in a restaurant? For salespeople in an insurance company?

10. What purpose do exit interviews serve for human resource management?

Do You Want to Be an HR Manager?

The following questions are based on a Human Resources Capability Model developed by the Australian Public Service (APS) for HR managers who work in government agencies. People who work with HR managers complete a 72-item questionnaire assessing a range of expectations for the HR manager. The results are given to the manager, who then works to improve low scores. The following questions give a glimpse of the expectations for APS HR managers. Please think about how other people would rate you as a potential HR manager and then respond to each statement by rating yourself on how well you think you would fulfill each expectation.

❶ = not well at all; ❷ = not very well; ❸ = moderately well; ❹ = very well; ❺ = extremely well

Bringing HR to the Business

1. Has a detailed knowledge of current HR approaches, tools, and technology.   ❶ ❷ ❸ ❹ ❺

2. Understands the human behavior triggers that affect or improve organizational performance.   ❶ ❷ ❸ ❹ ❺

Connecting HR with the Business

3. Maintains knowledge of the business through frequent interaction with people in the workplace.   ❶ ❷ ❸ ❹ ❺

4. Presents strong business cases for HR initiatives.   ❶ ❷ ❸ ❹ ❺

Partnering with the Business

5. Establishes and maintains good relationships across the organization.   ❶ ❷ ❸ ❹ ❺

6. Guides the top executive and line managers in actively managing people issues.   ❶ ❷ ❸ ❹ ❺

Achieving High-Quality Business Results

7. Applies business acumen to HR decisions.   ❶ ❷ ❸ ❹ ❺

8. Continuously monitors HR initiatives to maintain consistency with business outcomes.   ❶ ❷ ❸ ❹ ❺

Bringing Ideas to the Business

9. Continually looks for ways to enhance or create new HR methods to achieve business outcomes.   ❶ ❷ ❸ ❹ ❺

10. Critically evaluates and explores alternatives to the way things are done.   ❶ ❷ ❸ ❹ ❺

Scoring and Interpretation

Correct answers are not the point of the preceding questions. The subscales (Bringing HR to the Business, Partnering with Business, etc.), represent elements of the HR Capability Model that APS HR managers are expected to master. Any questions for which you receive a 4 or 5 would be strong areas for you. If you aspire to become an HR manager it would be good to study the entire model at the following Web site: *http://www.apsc.gov.au/publications01/hrmodel.htm.*

SOURCE: Based on "Human Resources Capability Model," Australian Public Service Commission, Australian Government, as reported at *http://www.apsc.gov.au/publications01/hrmodel.htm.*

A Conflict of Responsibilities

As director of human resources, Tess Danville was asked to negotiate a severance deal with Terry Winston, the Midwest regional sales manager for Cyn-Com Systems. Winston's problems with drugs and alcohol had become severe enough to precipitate his dismissal. His customers were devoted to him, but top management was reluctant to continue gambling on his reliability. Lives depended on his work as the salesperson and installer of Cyn-Com's respiratory diagnostic technology. Winston had been warned twice to clean up his act, but had never succeeded. Only his unique blend of technical knowledge and high-powered sales ability had saved him before.

Now the vice president of sales asked Danville to offer Winston the option of resigning rather than being fired if he would sign a noncompete agreement and agree to go into rehabilitation. Cyn-Com would also extend a guarantee of confidentiality on the abuse issue and a good work reference as thanks for the millions of dollars of business that Winston had brought to Cyn-Com. Winston agreed to take the deal. After his departure, a series of near disasters was uncovered as a result of Winston's mismanagement. Some of his maneuvers to cover up his mistakes bordered on fraud.

Today, Danville received a message to call the human resource director at a cardiopulmonary technology company to give a personal reference on Terry Winston. From the area code, Danville could see that he was not in violation of the noncompete agreement. She had also heard that Winston had completed a 30-day treatment program as promised. Danville knew she was expected to honor the confidentiality agreement, but she also knew that if his shady dealings had been discovered before his departure, he would have been fired without any agreement. Now she was being asked to give Winston a reference for another medical sales position.

What Would You Do?

1. Honor the agreement, trusting Winston's rehabilitation is complete on all levels and that he is now ready for a responsible position. Give a good recommendation.

2. Contact the vice president of sales and ask him to release you from the agreement or to give the reference himself. After all, he made the agreement. You don't want to lie.

3. Without mentioning specifics, give Winston such an unenthusiastic reference that you hope the other human resources director can read between the lines and believe that Winston will be a poor choice.

CASE FOR CRITICAL ANALYSIS

Waterway Industries

Lee Carter and her husband, Jack Schiffer, became two of Waterway Industries most valuable managers almost by accident. But now, if the snatch of conversation CEO Cyrus Maher just overheard on his way to get coffee meant what he thought it did, he was in danger of losing the very people who'd contributed most to Waterway's recent growth surge.

Cyrus had met Lee and Jack, both paddling enthusiasts, when he was advisor to a university outing club. Lee had been majoring in marketing at the time, while Jack was studying engineering. He took a liking to the young couple and offered them part-time work at Waterways, then a small manufacturer of high-quality canoes in upstate New York. After graduation, the newlyweds decided to stay on full-time and take a breather before launching their demanding professional careers. That was 10 years ago.

When Lee and Jack joined Waterway, they found a laid-back atmosphere. Even as Waterway had grown steadily over the years, it continued to attract shop-floor employees who loved water sports and enjoyed making quality products they themselves used in their off-hours. Workers spent time good-naturedly horsing around with each other, but they got their work done on time. In fact, on nice days, they often completed their tasks early so they could leave by midafternoon and get some canoeing in before dark.

In late 2003, Lee took a hard look at the slowing demand for canoes and the rapidly growing kayak market. "Cyrus," she asked, "have you ever thought about making kayaks?" Intrigued, Cyrus gave Lee and Jack the go-ahead to see what they could do. Jack responded by designing a compact, inexpensive, lightweight kayak that immediately found favor among baby boomers looking for a way to have some fun. Lee established a formal marketing department to drive sales. That's when things really took off. Many Waterway canoe customers placed sizable kayak orders, and a number of private labels asked Cyrus to make kayaks for their companies.

Energized by their success, Cyrus, Lee, Jack (who'd recently been named design department head), and other Waterway managers developed a long-range strategic plan that called for aggressive growth, new product designs, and nationwide marketing and distribution by 2008. These ambitious plans resulted in an increased workload and a faster-paced work environment. Waterway managers provided employees across-the-board pay raises.

In Cyrus's opinion, the pay increases were more than reasonable, but lately he has heard complaints, both from the shop floor and from managers. He is dealing with compensation issues the way he always has—on a case-by-case basis. When a plant manager suggested top hourly performers receive additional wage increases, Cyrus turned it down, contending that Waterway's wages were in line with other manufacturers in rural New York. Shortly afterwards, a new automotive parts plant offering a slightly higher wage lured away three of Waterway's best workers.

When the company's CFO threatened to leave unless his compensation package included profit-sharing, Cyrus appeased him with a pay increase and extra vacation. But Lee and Jack have been more insistent. What they feel they deserve, in view of their contribution to the company's growth, is a share in the profits. He turned them down, and now, if he heard correctly, they are considering a lucrative job offer from a competing company.

What should the CEO do? He sees Lee and Jack's point of view, but would the other managers understand if he granted the couple the part ownership in the company he'd denied the others? And how would the hourly workers react?

Questions

1. Does Waterway's current compensation system seem to fit the company's strategy of aggressive growth and product innovation? How might it be changed to achieve a better fit?

2. Specifically, how would you gather the data and design a competitive compensation system for Waterway? Would your approach be different for hourly workers versus managers? Would you treat all managers equally?

3. How might nonfinancial incentives play a role in helping Waterway retain hourly shop workers? How can they help keep aggressive and ambitious professionals such as Lee and Jack?

SOURCES: Based on Robert D. Nicoson, "Growing Pains," *Harvard Business Review* (July–August 1996): 20–36.

ENDNOTES

1. Keith H. Hammonds, "Handle with Care," *Fast Company* (August 2002): 103–107; and Leigh Branham, "Planning to Become an Employer of Choice," *Journal of Organizational Excellence* (Summer 2005): 57–68.

2. Results of a McKinsey Consulting survey, reported in Branham, "Planning to Become an Employer of Choice."

3. Robert L. Mathis and John H. Jackson, *Human Resource Management: Essential Perspectives*, 2nd ed. (Cincinnati, OH: South-Western Publishing, 2002): 1.

4. Joy Persaud, "Game On," *People Management* (September 25, 2003): 40–41.

5. Jonathan Poet, "Schools Looking Overseas for Teachers," *Johnson City Press* (April 20, 2001): 6; and Jill Rosenfeld, "How's This for a Tough Assignment?" *Fast Company* (November 1999): 104–106.

6. See James C. Wimbush, "Spotlight on Human Resource Management," *Business Horizons* 48 (2005): 463–467; Jonathan Tompkins, "Strategic Human Resources Management in Government: Unresolved Issues," *Public Personnel Management* (Spring 2002): 95–110; Noel M. Tichy, Charles J. Fombrun, and Mary Anne Devanna, "Strategic Human Resource Management," *Sloan Management Review* 23 (Winter 1982): 47–61; Cynthia A. Lengnick-Hall and Mark L. Lengnick-Hall, "Strategic Human Resources Management: A Review of the Literature and a Proposed Typology," *Academy of Management Review* 13 (July 1988): 454–470; Eugene B. McGregor, *Strategic Management of Human Knowledge, Skills, and Abilities*, (San Francisco: Jossey-Bass, 1991).

7. Edward E. Lawler III, "HR on Top," *Strategy + Business,* no. 35 (Second Quarter 2004): 21–25.

8. Tompkins, "Strategic Human Resource Management in Government: Unresolved Issues"; and Wimbush, "Spotlight on Human Resource Management."

9. Mark A. Huselid, Susan E. Jackson, and Randall S. Schuler, "Technical and Strategic Human Resource Management Effectiveness as Determinants of Firm Performance," *Academy of Management Journal* 40, no. 1 (1997): 171–188; and John T. Delaney and Mark A. Huselid, "The Impact of Human Resource Management Practices on Perceptions of Organizational Performance," *Academy of Management Journal* 39, no. 4 (1996): 949–969.

10. D. Kneale, "Working at IBM: Intense Loyalty in a Rigid Culture," *The Wall Street Journal* (April 7, 1986): 17.

11. Jeffrey Pfeffer, "Producing Sustainable Competitive Advantage Through the Effective Management of People," *Academy of Management Executive* 9, no. 1 (1995): 55–72; and Harry Scarbrough, "Recipe for Success," *People Management* (January 23, 2003): 32–25.

12. James N. Baron and David M. Kreps, "Consistent Human Resource Practices," *California Management Review* 41, no. 3 (Spring 1999): 29–53.

13. Cynthia D. Fisher, "Current and Recurrent Challenges in HRM," *Journal of Management* 15 (1989): 157–180.

14. See Dave Ulrich, "A New Mandate for Human Resources," *Harvard Business Review* (January–February 1998): 124–134; Philip H. Mirvis, "Human Resource Management: Leaders, Laggards, and Followers," *Academy of Management Executive* 11, no. 2 (1997): 43–56; Richard McBain, "Attracting,

Retaining, and Motivating Capable People," *Manager Update* (Winter 1999): 25–36; and Oren Harari, "Attracting the Best Minds," *Management Review* (April 1998): 23–26.

15. Floyd Kemske, "HR 2008: A Forecast Based on Our Exclusive Study," *Workforce* (January 1998): 46–60.

16. This definition and discussion is based on George Bollander, Scott Snell, and Arthur Sherman, *Managing Human Resources,* 12th ed. (Cincinnati, OH: South-Western, 2001): 13–15; and Scarbrough, "Recipe for Success."

17. Victoria Griffith, "Winning Hearts and Minds at Home Depot" *Strategy + Business*, Issue 38 (First Quarter 2005): 61–71; and Lawler, "HR on Top."

18. Griffith, "Winning Hearts and Minds."

19. Mark C. Bolino, William H. Turnley, and James M. Bloodgood, "Citizenship Behavior and the Creation of Social Capital in Organizations," *Academy of Management Review* 27, no. 5 (2002): 505–522.

20. Rich Wellins and Sheila Rioux, "The Growing Pains of Globalizing HR," *Training and Development* (May 2000): 79–85.

21. Ibid.

22. Helen DeCieri, Julie Wolfram Cox, and Marilyn S. Fenwick, "Think Global, Act Local: From Naive Comparison to Critical Participation in the Teaching of Strategic International Human Resource Management," *Tamara: Journal of Critical Postmodern Organization Science* 1, no. 1 (2001): 68+; S. Taylor, S. Beecher, and N. Napier, "Towards an Integrative Model of Strategic Human Resource Management," *Academy of Management Review* 21 (1996): 959–985; Mary Ann Von Glinow, Ellen A. Drost, and Mary B. Teagarden, "Converging on IHRM Best Practices: Lessons Learned from a Globally Distributed Consortium on Theory and Practice," *Human Resource Management* 41, no. 1 (Spring 2002): 123–140.

23. Von Glinow, Drost, and Teagarden, "Converging on IHRM Best Practices"; and Jennifer J. Laabs, "Must-Have Global HR Competencies," *Workforce* 4, no. 2 (1999): 30–32.

24. Joy Persaud, "Game On."

25. Ellen A. Ensher, Troy R. Nielson, and Elisa Grant-Vallone, "Tales from the Hiring Line: Effects of the Internet and Technology on HR Processes," *Organizational Dynamics* 31, no. 3 (2002): 224–244.

26. Krass, "Precious Resources?"; Alison Stein Wellner, "Click Here for HR," *BusinessWeek Frontier* (April 24, 2000): F24–F26; and Esther Shein, "Requiem for a Paperweight," *eCFO* (Winter 2000): 81–83.

27. Aaron Bernstein, "Too Many Workers? Not For Long," *BusinessWeek* (May 20, 2002): 126–130.

28. Section 1604.1 of the EEOC Guidelines based on the Civil Rights Act of 1964, Title VII.

29. Charles F. Falk and Kathleen A. Carlson, "Newer Patterns in Management for the Post–Social Contract Era," *Midwest Management Society Proceedings* (1995): 45–52.

30. A. S. Tsui, J. L. Pearce, L. W. Porter, and A. M. Tripoli, "Alternative Approaches to the Employee-Organization Relationship: Does Investment in Employees Pay Off?" *Academy of Management Journal* 40 (1997): 1089–1121; D. Wang, A. S. Tsui, Y. Zhang, and L. Ma, "Employment Relationships and Firm Performance: Evidence from an Emerging Economy," *Journal of Organizational Behavior* 24 (2003): 511–535.

31. Richard Pascale, "The False Security of 'Employability,'" *Fast Company* (April–May 1996): 62, 64; and Louisa Wah, "The New Workplace Paradox," *Management Review* (January 1998): 7.

32. Douglas T. Hall and Jonathan E. Moss, "The New Protean Career Contract: Helping Organizations and Employees Adapt," *Organizational Dynamics* (Winter 1998): 22–37.

33. Based on Branham, "Planning to Become an Employer of Choice."

34. Ibid.

35. Sean Donahue, "New Jobs for the New Economy," *Business 2.0* (July 1999): 102–109.

36. The discussion of temporary employment agencies is based on David Wessel, "Capital: Temp Workers Have a Lasting Effect," *The Wall Street Journal* (February 1, 2001): A1.

37. Brenda Paik Sunoo, "Temp Firms Turn Up the Heat on Hiring," *Workforce* (April 1999): 50–54; H. Lancaster, "Some Veteran Bosses Find More Excitement in Doing Temp Work," *The Wall Street Journal* (November 17, 1998): B1; and J. Thottam,, "When Execs Go Temp," *Time* (April 26, 2004): 40–41.

38. Jaclyn Fierman, "The Contingency Workforce," *Fortune* (January 24, 1994): 30–31.

39. Nancy B. Kurland and Diane E. Bailey, "Telework: The Advantages and Challenges of Working Here, There, Anywhere, Anytime," *Organizational Dynamics* (Autumn 1999): 53–68.

40. Kevin Voigt, "For 'Extreme Telecommuters,' Remote Work Means Really Remote," *The Wall Street Journal* (January 31, 2001): B1.

41. Ibid.

42. John Challenger, "There Is No Future for the Workplace," *Public Management* (February 1999): 20–23; Susan Caminiti, "Work-Life," *Fortune* (September 19, 2005): S1–S17.

43. Stephanie Armour, "Generation Y: They've Arrived at Work With a New Attitude," *USA Today* (November 6, 2005), http://www.usatoday.com; Ellyn Spragins, "The Talent Pool," *FSB* (October 2005): 92–101; and Caminiti, "Work-Life."

44. B. Nussbaum, "Where Are the Jobs?" *BusinessWeek* (March 22, 2004): 36–37.

45. James R. Morris, Wayne F. Cascio, and Clifford Young, "Downsizing After All These Years: Questions and Answers About Who Did It, How Many Did It, and Who Benefited From It," *Organizational Dynamics* (Winter 1999): 78–86; William McKinley, Carol M. Sanchez, and Allen G. Schick, "Organizational Downsizing: Constraining, Cloning, Learning," *Academy of Management Executive* 9, no. 3 (1995): 32–42; and Brett C. Luthans and Steven M. Sommer, "The Impact of Downsizing on Workplace Attitudes," *Group and Organization Management* 2, no. 1 (1999): 46–70.

46. Effective downsizing techniques are discussed in detail in Bob Nelson, "The Care of the Un-Downsized," *Training and Development* (April 1997): 40–43; Shari Caudron, "Teaching Downsizing Survivors How to Thrive," *Personnel Journal* (January 1996): 38; Joel Brockner, "Managing the Effects of Layoffs on Survivors," *California Management Review* (Winter 1992): 9–28; and Kim S. Cameron, "Strategies for Successful Organizational Downsizing," *Human Resource Management* 33, no. 2 (Summer 1994): 189–211.

47. James G. March and Herbert A. Simon, *Organizations* (New York: Wiley, 1958).

48. Richard McBain, "Attracting, Retaining, and Motivating Capable People: A Key to Competitive Advantage," *Manager Update* (Winter 1999): 25–36.

49. Dennis J. Kravetz, *The Human Resources Revolution* (San Francisco: Jossey-Bass, 1989).

50. David E. Ripley, "How to Determine Future Workforce Needs," *Personnel Journal* (January 1995): 83–89.

51. Ted Hoff, interviewed by Ryan Underwood, in "Fast Talk: Now Hiring," *Fast Company* (May 2004): 57–64.

52. J. W. Boudreau and S. L. Rynes, "Role of Recruitment in Staffing Utility Analysis," *Journal of Applied Psychology* 70 (1985): 354–366.

53. Megan Santosus, "The Human Capital Factor," *CFO-IT* (Fall 2005): 26–27.

54. Brian Dumaine, "The New Art of Hiring Smart," *Fortune* (August 17, 1987): 78–81.

55. Nanette Byrnes, "Star Search," *BusinessWeek* (October 10, 2005): 68–78.

56. This discussion is based on Mathis and Jackson, *Human Resource Management,* Chapter 4, 49–60.

57. Victoria Griffith, "When Only Internal Expertise Will Do," *CFO* (October 1998): 95–96, 102.

58. J. P. Wanous, *Organizational Entry* (Reading, MA: Addison-Wesley, 1980).

59. Samuel Greengard, "Technology Finally Advances HR," *Workforce* (January 2000): 38–41; and Scott Hays, "Hiring on the Web," *Workforce* (August 1999): 77–84.

60. Jessica Mintz, "Online Tools Aid Job Recruiters in Search of 'Passise' Prospects," *The Wall Street Journal* (July 12, 2005): B6.

61. Kathryn Tyler, "Employees Can Help Recruit New Talent," *HR Magazine* (September 1996): 57–60.

62. Scott Westcott, "Scenes from the Talent Wars," *Inc.* (January 2006): 29–31.

63. Vicki Powers, "Finding Workers Who Fit," *Business 2.0* (November 2004): 74.

64. Ron Stodghill, "Soul on Ice," *FSB* (October 2005): 129–134.

65. Ann Harrington, "Anybody Here Want a Job?" *Fortune* (May 15, 2000): 489–498.

66. Milt Freudenheim, "More Help Wanted: Older Workers Please Apply," *The New York Times* (March 23, 2005), http://www.nytimes.com.

67. "Bank of America to Hire 850 Ex-Welfare Recipients," *Johnson City Press* (January 14, 2001): 29; E. Blacharczyk, "Recruiters Challenged by Economy, Shortages, Unskilled," *HR News* (February 1990): B1; Victoria Rivkin, "Visa Relief," *Working Woman* (January 2001): 15.

68. Wimbush, "Spotlight on Human Resource Management."

69. P. W. Thayer, "Somethings Old, Somethings New," *Personnel Psychology* 30 (1977): 513–524.

70. J. Ledvinka, *Federal Regulation of Personnel and Human Resource Management* (Boston: Kent, 1982); and Civil Rights Act, Title VII, 42 U.S.C. Section 2000e et seq. (1964).

71. Studies reported in William Poundstone, "Impossible Questions," *Across the Board* (September–October 2003): 44–48.

72. Anne S. Tsui and Joshua B. Wu, "The New Employment Relationship Versus the Mutual Investment Approach: Implications for Human Resource Management," *Human Resource Management* 44, no. 2 (Summer 2005): 115–121.

73. Bohlander, Snell, and Sherman, *Managing Human Resources,* 202.

74. Powers, "Finding Workers Who Fit."

75. Bohlander, Snell, and Sherman, *Managing Human Resources.*

76. Meridith Levinson, "How to Hire So You Don't Have to Fire," *CIO* (March 1, 2004): 72–80.

77. "Assessment Centers: Identifying Leadership through Testing," *Small Business Report* (June 1987): 22–24; and W. C. Byham, "Assessment Centers for Spotting Future Managers," *Harvard Business Review* (July–August 1970): 150–167.

78. Mike Thatcher, "'Front-line' Staff Selected by Assessment Center," *Personnel Management* (November 1993): 83.

79. Bernard Keys and Joseph Wolfe, "Management Education and Development: Current Issues and Emerging Trends," *Journal of Management* 14 (1988): 205–229.

80. "2005 Industry Report," *Training* (December 2005): 14–28; "Pinpointing Inside Up-and-Comers," sidebar in Nanette Byrnes, "Star Search," *BusinessWeek* (October 10, 2005): 68–78.

81. William J. Rothwell and H. C. Kazanas, *Improving On-the-Job Training: How to Establish and Operate a Comprehensive OJT Program* (San Francisco: Jossey-Bass, 1994).

82. "2005 Industry Report."

83. Doug Bartholomew, "Taking the E-Train," *Industry Week* (June 2005): 34–37.

84. Jeanne C. Meister, "The Brave New World of Corporate Education" *The Chronicle of Higher Education* (February 9, 2001): B10; and Meryl Davids Landau, "Corporate Universities Crack Open Their Doors," *The Journal of Business Strategy* (May–June 2000): 18–23.

85. Meister, "The Brave New World of Corporate Education"; Edward E. Gordon, "Bridging the Gap," *Training* (September 2003): 30; and John Byrne, "The Search for the Young and Gifted," *BusinessWeek* (October 4, 1999): 108–116.

86. Bartholomew, "Taking the E-Train"; Joel Schettler, "Defense Acquisition University: Weapons of Mass Instruction," *Training* (February 2003): 20–27.

87. Gordon, "Bridging the Gap."

88. Jim Dow, "Spa Attraction," *People Management* (May 29, 2003): 34–35.

89. Scott Leibs, "Building a Better Workforce," *CFO-IT* (Fall 2005): 20–27; and Charles Forelle, "IBM Tool Dispatches Employees Efficiently," *The Wall Street Journal* (July 14, 2005).

90. "Pinpointing Inside Up-and-Comers"; and Forelle, "IBM Tool Dispatches Employees Efficiently."

91. Spragins, "The Talent Pool."

92. Walter W. Tornow, "Editor's Note: Introduction to Special Issue on 360-Degree Feedback," *Human Resource Management* 32, no. 2–3 (Summer–Fall 1993): 211–219; and Brian O'Reilly, "360 Feedback Can Change Your Life," *Fortune* (October 17, 1994): 93–100.

93. Kris Frieswick, "Truth & Consequences," *CFO* (June 2001): 56–63.

94. This discussion is based on Dick Grote, "Forced Ranking: Behind the Scenes," *Across the Board* (November–December 2002): 40–45; Matthew Boyle, "Performance Reviews: Perilous Curves Ahead," *Fortune* (May 28, 2001): 187–188; Carol Hymowitz, "Ranking Systems Gain Popularity But Have Many Staffers Riled," *The Wall Street Journal* (May 15, 2001): B1; and Frieswick, "Truth & Consequences."

95. Dick Grote, *Forced Ranking: Making Performance Management Work* (Boston: Harvard Business School Press, 2005); Jena McGregor, "The Struggle to Measure Performance," *BusinessWeek* (January 9, 2006): 26–28.

96. Hymowitz, "Ranking Systems Gain Popularity"; and Boyle, "Performance Reviews."

97. Reported in McGregor, "The Struggle to Measure Performance."

98. Ibid.

99. Catherine Edwards, "Called to Account," *People Management* (July 2004): 33–34.

100. Lou Kaucic, "Finding Your Stars," *Microsoft Executive Circle* (Summer 2003): 14.

101. V. R. Buzzotta, "Improve Your Performance Appraisals," *Management Review* (August 1988): 40–43; and H. J. Bernardin and R. W. Beatty, *Performance Appraisal: Assessing Human Behavior at Work* (Boston: Kent, 1984).

102. Ibid.

103. Richard I. Henderson, *Compensation Management: Rewarding Performance*, 4th ed. (Reston, VA: Reston, 1985).

104. L. R. Gomez-Mejia, "Structure and Process Diversification, Compensation Strategy, and Firm Performance," *Strategic Management Journal* 13 (1992): 381–397; and E. Montemayor, "Congruence Between Pay Policy and Competitive Strategy in High-Performing Firms," *Journal of Management* 22, no. 6 (1996): 889–908.

105. Renée F. Broderick and George T. Milkovich, "Pay Planning, Organization Strategy, Structure and 'Fit': A Prescriptive Model of Pay," paper presented at the 45th Annual Meeting of the Academy of Management, San Diego (August 1985).

106. E. F. Lawler, III, *Strategic Pay: Aligning Organizational Strategies and Pay Systems* (San Francisco: Jossey-Bass, 1990); and R. J. Greene, "Person-Focused Pay: Should It Replace Job-Based Pay?" *Compensation and Benefits Management* 9, no. 4 (1993): 46–55.

107. L. Wiener, "No New Skills? No Raise," *U.S. News and World Report* (October 26, 1992): 78.

108. Data from Hewitt Associates, Bureau of Labor Statistics, reported in Michelle Conlin and Peter Coy, with Ann Therese Palmer, and Gabrielle Saveri, "The Wild New Workforce," *BusinessWeek* (December 6, 1999): 39–44.

109. Brian Friel, "The Rating Game," *Government Executive* (August 2003): 46–52.

110. *Employee Benefits*, (Washington, DC: U. S. Chamber of Commerce, 1997): 7.

111. Danielle Sacks, "Not the Retiring Sort," *Fast Company* 94 (May 2005): 28.

112. Jay Greene, "Troubling Exits at Microsoft," *BusinessWeek* (September 26, 2005): 98–108.

113. Frank E. Kuzmits, "Communicating Benefits: A Double-Click Away," *Compensation and Benefits Review* 30, no. 5 (September–October 1998): 60–64; and Lynn Asinof, "Click and Shift: Workers Control Their Benefits Online," *The Wall Street Journal* (November 27, 1997): C1.

114. Robert S. Catapano-Friedman, "Cafeteria Plans: New Menu for the '90s," *Management Review* (November 1991): 25–29.

115. Byrnes, "Star Search."

116. Mike Brewster, "No Exit," *Fast Company* (April 2005): 93.

117. Yvette Debow, "GE: Easing the Pain of Layoffs," *Management Review* (September 1997): 15–18.

118. Hammonds, "Handle with Care"; and Branham, "Becoming an Employer of Choice."

CHAPTER 13

CHAPTER OUTLINE

Manager's Challenge

Valuing Diversity

Dimensions of Diversity

Attitudes Toward Diversity

The Changing Workplace

Challenges Minorities Face

Management Challenges

Current Debates About Affirmative Action

The Glass Ceiling

The Opt-Out Trend

The Female Advantage

Current Responses to Diversity

Changing the Corporate Culture

Changing Structures and Policies

Diversity Training

Defining New Relationships in Organizations

Emotional Intimacy

Sexual Harassment

Global Diversity

Selection and Training

Communication Differences

Diversity in a Turbulent World

Multicultural Teams

Employee Network Groups

LEARNING OBJECTIVES

After studying this chapter, you should be able to:

1. Explain the dimensions of employee diversity and why ethnorelativism is the appropriate attitude for today's organizations.

2. Discuss the changing workplace and how to effectively manage a culturally diverse workforce.

3. Understand the challenges minority employees face daily.

4. Explain affirmative action and why factors such as the glass ceiling have kept it from being more successful.

5. Describe how to change corporate culture, structure, and policies and how to use diversity training to foster an inclusive work environment.

6. Explain the importance of addressing sexual harassment in the workplace.

7. Define the importance of multicultural teams and employee network groups for today's globally diverse organizations.

MEETING THE CHALLENGE OF DIVERSITY

MANAGER'S CHALLENGE

Hungry travelers on America's highways are often thrilled to see the rustic brown and yellow sign of a Cracker Barrel just ahead. Based in Lebanon, Tennessee, and with more than 530 restaurants in 41 states, Cracker Barrel is an icon of Southern comfort food, serving up favorites such as biscuits and gravy, meatloaf, fried chicken, and hash brown casserole. In recent years, however, Cracker Barrel has become an icon of something far more sinister: corporate racism and discrimination. A series of racial discrimination lawsuits involving more than 100 plaintiffs charge that the company segregated black customers in the smoking section and ignored them. Furthermore, some black employees say they were denied promotions, pay raises, and training that were offered to white workers. Cracker Barrel recently settled the series of lawsuits for $8.7 million and hired the former executive director of 100 Black Men of Middle Tennessee as director of community outreach. The company has also begun making financial contributions to historically black colleges and scholarship funds for minorities. Yet the troubles continue. One lawsuit still pending in Illinois charges the company with both racial and sexual harassment in three restaurants. The attorney for the Illinois Equal Employment Opportunity Commission says the financial commitment Cracker Barrel has made to diversity efforts is so small that it "almost borders on an insult." Managers are struggling with how to mend Cracker Barrel's damaged reputation and prove the company's commitment to treating all customers and employees fairly and respectfully.[1]

> If you were a top manager at Cracker Barrel, what steps would you take to solve this problem? What changes can make Cracker Barrel a restaurant chain where everyone feels valued and respected?

TAKE A MOMENT

Cracker Barrel isn't the only company that has faced difficulties with issues of diversity. In recent years, high-profile racial or sexual discrimination lawsuits have been filed against Texaco, Wal-Mart, Coca-Cola, and Boeing.[2] Mitsubishi is still reeling from a sexual harassment lawsuit charging that managers ignored complaints that women were regularly groped on the factory floor and made to endure crude jokes and lewd photographs.[3]

In the United States, diversity in the population, the workforce, and the marketplace is a fact of life no manager can afford to ignore. In addition, diversity issues are growing more complex than they were 30 years ago. Among the groups now seeking full inclusion in the workplace are many not even considered back then, including the disabled, the obese, and nonheterosexuals. Managing diversity today entails recruiting, training, valuing, and maximizing the potential of people who reflect the broad spectrum of society in all areas—gender, race, age, disability, ethnicity, religion, sexual orientation, education, and economic level. Managers in other countries are struggling with similar diversity issues. Japanese companies, for example, face mounting criticism about the scarcity of women in management positions. In Japan,

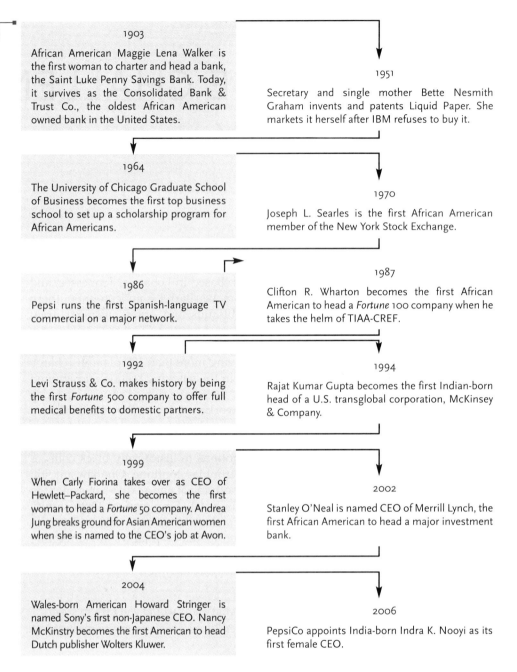

EXHIBIT 13.1

Some Milestones in the History of Corporate Diversity in the United States

SOURCE: "Spotlight on Diversity," special advertising section, *MBA Jungle* (March–April 2003): 58–61.

1903
African American Maggie Lena Walker is the first woman to charter and head a bank, the Saint Luke Penny Savings Bank. Today, it survives as the Consolidated Bank & Trust Co., the oldest African American owned bank in the United States.

1951
Secretary and single mother Bette Nesmith Graham invents and patents Liquid Paper. She markets it herself after IBM refuses to buy it.

1964
The University of Chicago Graduate School of Business becomes the first top business school to set up a scholarship program for African Americans.

1970
Joseph L. Searles is the first African American member of the New York Stock Exchange.

1986
Pepsi runs the first Spanish-language TV commercial on a major network.

1987
Clifton R. Wharton becomes the first African American to head a *Fortune* 100 company when he takes the helm of TIAA-CREF.

1992
Levi Strauss & Co. makes history by being the first *Fortune* 500 company to offer full medical benefits to domestic partners.

1994
Rajat Kumar Gupta becomes the first Indian-born head of a U.S. transglobal corporation, McKinsey & Company.

1999
When Carly Fiorina takes over as CEO of Hewlett–Packard, she becomes the first woman to head a *Fortune* 50 company. Andrea Jung breaks ground for Asian American women when she is named to the CEO's job at Avon.

2002
Stanley O'Neal is named CEO of Merrill Lynch, the first African American to head a major investment bank.

2004
Wales-born American Howard Stringer is named Sony's first non-Japanese CEO. Nancy McKinstry becomes the first American to head Dutch publisher Wolters Kluwer.

2006
PepsiCo appoints India-born Indra K. Nooyi as its first female CEO.

women make up 41 percent of the workforce but occupy less than 3 percent of high-level management positions.[4]

Many managers are finding innovative ways to integrate diversity initiatives into their organizations. These initiatives teach current employees to value differences, direct corporate recruiting efforts, influence supplier decisions, and provide development training for women and minorities. Smart managers value diversity and enforce the value in day-to-day decision making.

In the United States, today's companies reflect the country's image as a melting pot, but with a difference. In the past, the United States was a place where people of different national origins, ethnicities, races, and religions came together and blended to resemble one another. Opportunities for advancement were limited to those workers who easily fit into the mainstream of the larger culture. Some immigrants chose desperate measures to fit in, such as abandoning their native languages, changing their last names, and sacrificing their own unique cultures. In essence, everyone in workplace organizations was encouraged to share similar beliefs, values, and lifestyles despite differences in gender, race, and ethnicity.[5]

Now organizations recognize that everyone is not the same and that the differences people bring to the workplace are valuable.[6] Rather than expecting all employees to adopt similar attitudes and values, managers are learning that these differences enable their companies to compete globally and to tap into rich sources of new talent. Although diversity in North America has been a reality for some time, genuine efforts to accept and *manage* diverse people began only in recent years. Exhibit 13.1 lists some interesting milestones in the history of corporate diversity.

This chapter introduces the topic of diversity, its causes, and its consequences. We look at some of the challenges minorities face, ways managers deal with workforce diversity, and organizational responses to create an environment that welcomes and values diverse employees. The chapter also considers issues of sexual harassment, global diversity, and new approaches to managing diversity in today's workplace.

VALUING DIVERSITY

Top managers say their companies value diversity for a number of reasons, such as to give the organization access to a broader range of opinions and viewpoints, to spur greater creativity and innovation, to reflect an increasingly diverse customer base, to obtain the best talent in a competitive environment, and to more effectively compete in a global marketplace.[7] A recent study of diversity management in the United Kingdom, Scandinavia, and Continental Europe found managers reporting similar motives, as well as a desire to enhance the company's image and to improve employee satisfaction.[8] Indeed, a survey commissioned by *The New York Times* found that 91 percent of job seekers think diversity programs make a company a better place to work, and nearly all minority job seekers said they would prefer to work in a diverse workplace.[9] In a survey by the Society for Human Resource Management and *Fortune* magazine, more than 70 percent of human resources executives indicated that diversity has enhanced their organizations' recruitment efforts and improved the overall corporate culture.[10]

However, many managers are ill-prepared to handle diversity issues. Many Americans grew up in racially unmixed neighborhoods and had little exposure to people substantially different from themselves.[11] The challenge is particularly great when working with people from other countries and cultures. One recent challenge at IBM involved a new immigrant, a Muslim woman who was required to have a photo taken for a company identification badge. She protested that her religious beliefs required that, as a married woman, she wear a veil and not expose her face to men in public. A typical American manager, schooled in traditional management training, might insist that she have the photo taken or hit the door. Fortunately, IBM has a well-developed diversity program and managers worked out a satisfactory compromise.[12] Consider some other mistakes that American managers could easily make:[13]

:: To reward a Vietnamese employee's high performance, her manager promoted her, placing her at the same level as her husband, who also worked at the factory. Rather than being pleased, the worker became upset and declined the promotion because Vietnamese husbands are expected to have a higher status than their wives.

:: A manager, having learned that a friendly pat on the arm or back would make workers feel good, took every chance to touch his subordinates. His Asian employees hated being touched and thus started avoiding him, and several asked for transfers.

:: A manager declined a gift offered by a new employee, an immigrant who wanted to show gratitude for her job. He was concerned about ethics and explained the company's policy about not accepting gifts. The employee was so insulted she quit.

These issues related to cultural diversity are difficult and real. Similar complicated issues occur for managers in other countries. For example, the United Kingdom and other European countries are facing a growing diversity challenge because of a recent influx of immigrants. A scan of the classifieds in any major newspaper in the United Kingdom finds numerous advertisements for skilled diversity management leaders.[14] Before discussing how companies handle the challenges of diversity, let's define *diversity* and explore people's attitudes toward it.

CONCEPT CONNECTION Many people are opting to stay in the workforce long past retirement age, giving managers opportunities to enhance **workforce diversity** by incorporating older employees. When CPI Aerostructures in Edgewood, New York, earned new contracts to provide spare parts to the U.S. government, CEO Edward J. Fred needed skilled mechanics ready to work. He was flooded with inquiries from retired mechanics, many well past the age of 65. Fred hired two seniors as parttime workers, and two as full-time employees. The decision gave CPI flexibility in scheduling, experienced workers to serve as teachers to younger colleagues, and a workplace culture that increased pride in the work for employees of all ages.

Dimensions of Diversity

Workforce diversity means a workforce made up of people with different human qualities or who belong to various cultural groups. From the perspective of individuals, diversity means including people different from themselves along dimensions such as race, age, ethnicity, gender, or social background. It is important to remember that diversity includes everyone, not just racial and ethnic minorities.

Key dimensions of diversity are illustrated in Exhibit 13.2. The inner circle represents primary dimensions of diversity, which include inborn differences or differences that have an impact throughout one's life.[15] Primary dimensions are core elements through which people shape their self-image and world view. These dimensions include age, race, ethnicity, gender, mental or physical abilities, and sexual orientation.

Secondary dimensions, shown in the outer ring of Exhibit 13.2, can be acquired or changed throughout one's lifetime. These dimensions tend to have less impact than those of the core but nevertheless affect a person's self-definition and world view and have an impact on how

EXHIBIT 13.2

Primary and Secondary Dimensions of Diversity

SOURCE: Adapted from Marilyn Loden and Judy B. Rosener, *Workforce America!* (Homewood, IL: Business One Irwin, 1991): 20. Used with permission.

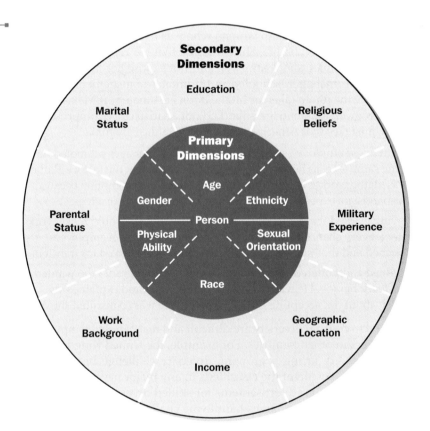

workforce diversity Hiring people with different human qualities or who belong to various cultural groups.

the person is viewed by others. For example, an employee living in a public housing project will certainly be perceived differently from one who lives in an affluent part of town. Married people and people with children may be perceived differently and have different attitudes from those who are single and childless. Likewise, a person's military experience, religion, native language, socioeconomic status, and educational and work background add dimensions to the way that person defines himself or herself and is defined by others. Secondary dimensions such as work style, communication style, and educational or skill level are particularly relevant in the organizational setting.[16] One interesting finding is that today's CEOs in the United States, while still mostly white and male, come from a wider variety of economic and educational backgrounds than they did in the past, with growing numbers of top leaders coming from humble backgrounds and fewer having attended Ivy League colleges. The number of top executives in the United Kingdom who graduated from exclusive colleges such as Oxford and Cambridge is also declining.[17]

Attitudes Toward Diversity

Valuing diversity by recognizing, welcoming, and cultivating differences among people so they can develop their unique talents and be effective organizational members is difficult to achieve. **Ethnocentrism** is the belief that one's own group and subculture are inherently superior to other groups and cultures. Ethnocentrism makes it difficult to value diversity. Viewing one's own culture as the best culture is a natural tendency among most people. Moreover, the business world still tends to reflect the values, behaviors, and assumptions based on the experiences of a rather homogeneous, white, middle-class, male workforce. Indeed, most theories of management presume that workers share similar values, beliefs, motivations, and attitudes about work and life in general. These theories presume one set of behaviors best helps an organization to be productive and effective and therefore should be adopted by all employees.[18]

> Go to the experiential exercise on page 441 that pertains to attitudes toward diversity.

■ **TAKE A MOMENT**

Ethnocentric viewpoints and a standard set of cultural practices produce a **monoculture**, a culture that accepts only one way of doing things and one set of values and beliefs, which can cause problems for minority employees. People of color, women, gay people, the disabled, the elderly, and other diverse employees may feel undue pressure to conform, may be victims of stereotyping attitudes, and may be presumed deficient because they are different. White, heterosexual men, many of whom themselves do not fit the notion of the "ideal" employee, may also feel uncomfortable with the monoculture and resent stereotypes that label white males as racists and sexists. Valuing diversity means ensuring that *all* people are given equal opportunities in the workplace.[19]

The goal for organizations seeking cultural diversity is pluralism rather than a monoculture and ethnorelativism rather than ethnocentrism. **Ethnorelativism** is the belief that groups and subcultures are inherently equal. **Pluralism** means that an organization accommodates several subcultures. Movement toward pluralism seeks to fully integrate into the organization the employees who otherwise would feel isolated and ignored.

Most of today's organizations are applying conscious efforts to shift from a monoculture perspective to one of pluralism. Consider a recent report from the National Bureau of Economic Research, entitled "Are Greg and Emily More Employable than Lakisha and Jamal?" which shows that employers often unconsciously discriminate against job applicants based solely on the Afrocentric or black-sounding names on their resume. In interviews prior to the research, most human resource managers surveyed said they expected only a small gap and some

ethnocentrism The belief that one's own group or subculture is inherently superior to other groups or cultures.

monoculture A culture that accepts only one way of doing things and one set of values and beliefs.

ethnorelativism The belief that groups and subcultures are inherently equal.

pluralism An environment in which the organization accommodates several subcultures, including employees who would otherwise feel isolated and ignored.

expected to find a pattern of reverse discrimination. The results showed instead that white-sounding names got 50 percent more callbacks than black-sounding names, even when skills and experience were equal.[20]

This type of discrimination is often not intentional but is based on deep-seated personal biases and deep-rooted organizational assumptions. Many managers are not even aware of their own "culture" and don't see that they are specifically failing to hire, develop, and promote minorities, women, or others who are different from themselves.[21] In addition, employees in a monoculture may not be aware of their biases and the negative stereotypes they apply toward people who represent diverse groups. Through effective training, people can be helped to accept different ways of thinking and behaving, the first step away from narrow, ethnocentric thinking. Ultimately, employees are able to integrate diverse cultures, which means that judgments of appropriateness, goodness, badness, and morality are no longer applied to racial or cultural differences. These differences are experienced as essential, natural, and joyful, enabling an organization to enjoy true pluralism and take advantage of diverse human resources.[22]

One organization that is making a firm commitment to break out of monoculture thinking is Hyatt hotels, which has a diversity council made up of employees and managers from different parts of the company and representing different cultural and ethnic backgrounds. The council meets three times a year to review how well the company is recognizing, developing, and promoting minorities. For managers at Hyatt, 15 percent of their bonus is dependent on meeting specific diversity goals.[23]

■ **TAKE A MOMENT** | As a new manager, adopt a viewpoint that accepts all groups and subcultures as inherently equal. Appreciate the differences that people bring to the workplace and consciously work toward hiring, developing, and promoting diverse people.

THE CHANGING WORKPLACE

Diversity is no longer just the right thing to do; it has become a business imperative and perhaps the single most important factor of the twenty-first century for organization performance.[24] One reason is the dramatic change taking place in the workplace, in our society, and in the economic environment. These changes include globalization and the changing workforce and customer base.[25] Earlier chapters described the impact of global competition on business in North America. Competition is intense. At least 70 percent of all U.S. businesses are engaged directly in competition with companies overseas. Companies that ignore diversity have a hard time competing in today's multicultural global environment. As Ted Childs, director of diversity at IBM, puts it, "Diversity is the bridge between the workplace and the marketplace."[26]

Companies that succeed in this environment adopt radical new ways of doing business, with sensitivity toward the needs of different cultural practices. Consider the consulting firm McKinsey & Co. In the 1970s, most consultants were American, but by the turn of the century, McKinsey's chief partner was a foreign national (Rajat Gupta from India), only 40 percent of consultants were American, and the firm's foreign-born consultants came from 40 different countries.[27] Many other companies based in the United States reflect a similar mix of native and foreign-born managers. This chapter's Manager's Shoptalk lists some interesting tips for foreign managers working in the United States to help them understand and relate to Americans. Do you agree that these statements provide a good introduction to American culture for a non-native?

The other dominant trend is the changing composition of the workforce and the customer base. The average worker is older now, and many more women, people of color, and immigrants are seeking job and advancement opportunities. The demographics of the U.S. population are shifting dramatically. The people who used to be

A GUIDE FOR EXPATRIATE MANAGERS IN AMERICA

Although each person is different, individuals from a specific country typically share certain values and attitudes. Managers planning to move to a foreign country can learn about these broad value patterns to help them adjust to working and living abroad. The following characteristics are some that are often used to help foreign managers understand what Americans are like.

1. Americans are informal. They tend to treat everyone alike, even when individuals differ significantly in age or social status.

2. Americans are direct and decisive. To some foreigners, this behavior may seem abrupt or even rude. Typically, Americans don't "beat around the bush," which means they don't talk around things but get right to the point. They quickly define a problem and decide on the course of action they believe is most likely to get the desired results.

3. Americans love facts. They value statistics, data, and information in any form.

4. Americans are competitive. They like to keep score, whether at work or play. Americans like to win, and they don't tolerate failure well. Some foreigners might think Americans are aggressive or overbearing. For example, Americans are not at all shy about selling themselves. In fact, it's expected.

5. Americans believe in work. For many, commitment to work and career comes first. In general, Americans rarely take time off, even if a family member is ill. They don't believe in long vacations—even corporation presidents often take only two weeks, if that.

6. Americans are independent and individualistic. They place a high value on freedom and believe that people can control their own destinies.

7. Americans are questioners. They ask a lot of questions, even of someone they have just met. Some of these questions may seem pointless ("How ya' doin'?") or personal ("What kind of work do you do?").

8. Americans dislike silence. They would rather talk about the weather than deal with silence in a conversation.

9. Americans value punctuality. They keep appointment calendars and live according to schedules and clocks.

10. Americans pay close attention to appearances. They take note of designer clothing and good grooming. They may in fact seem obsessed with bathing, eliminating body odors, and wearing clean clothes.

How many of these statements do you agree with? Discuss them with your friends and classmates, including people from different countries and members of different subcultural groups from the United States.

SOURCES: Winston Fletcher, "The American Way of Work," *Management Today* (August 1, 2005): 46; "What Are Americans Like?" Exhibit 4-6 in Stephen P. Robbins and Mary Coulter, *Management*, 8th ed. (Upper Saddle River, NJ: Pearson Prentice Hall, 2005), as adapted from M. Ernest, ed., *Predeparture Orientation Handbook: For Foreign Students and Scholars Planning to Study in the United States* (Washington, DC: U.S. Information Agency, Bureau of Cultural Affairs, 1984): 103–105; Amanda Bennett, "American Culture Is Often a Puzzle for Foreign Managers in the U.S.," *The Wall Street Journal* (February 12, 1986): 29; "Don't Think Our Way's the Only Way," *The Pryor Report* (February 1988): 9; and B. Wattenberg, "The Attitudes Behind American Exceptionalism," *U.S. News and World Report* (August 7, 1989): 25.

called minorities now make up a majority of the U.S. population. Nonwhite residents are the majority in 48 of the nation's 100 largest cities, as they are in New Mexico, Hawaii, the District of Columbia, and California—the largest consumer market in the country. Hispanics, African Americans, and Asian Americans together represent $1.5 trillion in annual purchasing power.[28] During the 1990s, the foreign-born population of the United States nearly doubled, and immigrants now number more than 34 million, meaning that almost one in eight people living in the United States was born in another country, the highest percentage since the 1920s.[29] The U.S. Bureau of Labor Statistics indicates that by 2008, women and minorities are expected to make up fully 70 percent new entrants into the workforce.[30] So far, the ability of organizations to manage diversity has not kept pace with these demographic trends, thus creating a number of significant challenges for minority workers and managers.

Challenges Minorities Face

A one-best-way approach leads to a mind-set that views difference as deficiency or dysfunction. For many career women and minorities, their experience suggests that no matter how many college degrees they earn, how many hours they work, how they dress, or how much effort and enthusiasm they invest, they are never perceived as "having the right stuff." If the standard of quality were based, for instance, on being white and male, anything else would be seen as deficient. This dilemma often is difficult for white men to understand because most of them are not intentionally racist and sexist. As one observer points out, you would need to be nonwhite to understand what it is like to have people assume a subordinate is your superior simply because he is white, or to lose a sale after the customer sees you in person and finds out you're not Caucasian.[31]

Although blatant discrimination is not as widespread as in the past, bias in the workplace often shows up in subtle ways: a lack of choice assignments, the disregard by a subordinate of a minority manager's directions, or the ignoring of comments made by women and minorities at meetings. A survey by Korn Ferry International found that 59 percent of minority managers surveyed had observed a racially motivated double standard in the delegation of assignments.[32] Their perceptions are supported by a study that showed minority managers spend more time in the "bullpen" waiting for their chance and then have to prove themselves over and over again with each new assignment. Another recent study found that white managers gave more negative performance ratings to black leaders and white subordinates and more positive ratings to white leaders and black subordinates, affirming the widespread acceptance of these employees in their stereotypical roles.[33] Minority employees typically feel that they have to put in longer hours and extra effort to achieve the same status as their white colleagues. "It's not enough to be as good as the next person," says Bruce Gordon, president of Bell Atlantic's enterprise group. "We have to be better."[34]

Another problem is that many minority workers feel they have to become bicultural in order to succeed. **Biculturalism** can be defined as the sociocultural skills and attitudes used by racial minorities as they move back and forth between the dominant culture and their own ethnic or racial culture.[35] Research on differences between whites and blacks has focused on issues of biculturalism and how it affects employees' access to information, level of respect and appreciation, and relation to superiors and subordinates. In general, African Americans feel less accepted in their organizations, perceive themselves to have less discretion on their jobs, receive lower ratings on job performance, experience lower levels of job satisfaction, and reach career plateaus earlier than whites. They find themselves striving to adopt behaviors and attitudes that will help them be successful in the white-dominated corporate world while at the same time maintaining their ties to the black community and culture.

Other minority groups struggle with biculturalism as well. For example, Asian Americans who aspire to management positions are often frustrated by the stereotype that they are hardworking but not executive material because they are too quiet and deferential. Assertiveness and pressing your views in a group is seen as a characteristic of leadership in American culture, but Asians typically view this behavior as inappropriate and immature.[36] Some Asian Americans feel they have a chance for career advancement only by becoming bicultural or abandoning their native cultures altogether.

Management Challenges

What do these factors mean for managers who are responsible for creating a workplace that offers fulfilling work, opportunities for professional development and career advancement, and respect for all individuals? Inappropriate behavior by

biculturalism The sociocultural skills and attitudes used by racial minorities as they move back and forth between the dominant culture and their own ethnic or racial culture.

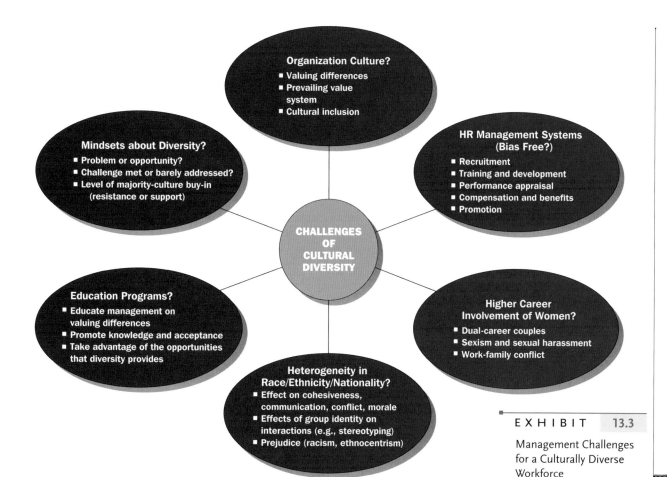

Organization Culture?
- Valuing differences
- Prevailing value system
- Cultural inclusion

Mindsets about Diversity?
- Problem or opportunity?
- Challenge met or barely addressed?
- Level of majority-culture buy-in (resistance or support)

HR Management Systems (Bias Free?)
- Recruitment
- Training and development
- Performance appraisal
- Compensation and benefits
- Promotion

CHALLENGES OF CULTURAL DIVERSITY

Education Programs?
- Educate management on valuing differences
- Promote knowledge and acceptance
- Take advantage of the opportunities that diversity provides

Higher Career Involvement of Women?
- Dual-career couples
- Sexism and sexual harassment
- Work-family conflict

Heterogeneity in Race/Ethnicity/Nationality?
- Effect on cohesiveness, communication, conflict, morale
- Effects of group identity on interactions (e.g., stereotyping)
- Prejudice (racism, ethnocentrism)

E X H I B I T   13.3

Management Challenges for a Culturally Diverse Workforce

SOURCE: Taylor H. Cox and Stacy Blake, "Managing Cultural Diversity: Implications for Organizational Competitiveness," *Academy of Management Executive* 5, no. 3 (1991): 45–56.

employees lands squarely at the door of the organization's top executives. Managers can look at different areas of the organization to see how well they are doing in creating a workplace that values and supports all people. Exhibit 13.3 illustrates some of the key areas of management challenge for dealing with a diverse workforce. Managers focus on these issues to see how well they are addressing the needs and concerns of diverse employees. One step is to ensure that their organizations' human resources systems are designed to be bias-free, dropping the perception of the middle-aged white male as the ideal employee. Consider how the FBI expanded its recruiting efforts.

How does the FBI gain credibility and obtain the information it needs to investigate and solve crimes? One way is by looking and thinking like the people in the communities where it seeks information. Not so long ago, if you were a woman or member of a minority group, you didn't stand a chance of becoming an FBI agent. Today, though, the agency's goal is to reflect the diversity of U.S. society. Each of the FBI's 56 field offices gets a report card on how well they've done in terms of making their offices reflective of the community. Each office is responsible for bringing minorities on board and providing them with advancement opportunities.

In addition, the FBI's national recruitment office was launched specifically to develop programs for recruiting women and minorities. One innovative initiative was the EdVenture Partners Collegiate Marketing Program, which worked with two historically black universities. The program gave students college credit and funding to devise and implement a local marketing plan for the FBI. As a result of the program, the agency received 360 minority applications. "In many cases, the students' perceptions about the FBI were totally changed," says Gwen Hubbard, acting chief of the national recruitment office. "Initially, we were not viewed as an employer of choice by the diverse student populations." The EdVenture

Federal Bureau of Investigation (FBI)

Partners program is being expanded to eight colleges and universities. Another initiative is a minority summer intern program, which started with 21 full-time student interns and is being expanded to at least 40.

These programs on the national level, along with emphasis in the field offices on reflecting the local communities, ensure that the Federal Bureau of Investigation recruits diverse candidates. Today, the FBI has thousands of female and minority agents. Top leaders are also focusing on ways to make sure those people have full opportunity to move up the ranks so that there is diversity at leadership levels as well.[37]

Recruiting and career development are only one part of the human resources challenge. For example, the increased career involvement of women represents an enormous opportunity to organizations, but it also means managers must deal with issues such as work-family conflicts, dual-career couples, and sexual harassment. Providing reasonable accommodation for disabled employees requires more than putting in a handicap access ramp. Demands for equal opportunities for the physically and mentally disabled are growing, and most companies have done little to respond. "When it comes to dealing with the disabled, we are about where we were with race in the 1970s," says David Thomas, a professor of organizational behavior and human resource management at Harvard Business School.[38] In fact, employment rates for disabled people dropped 30 percent between 1990 and 2004. And for the most part, the workers who do find jobs are tracked into low-skill, low-pay jobs rather than being allowed to fully participate in training and educational programs available to other employees.[39] One company bucking that trend is Habitat International, a manufacturer of carpet and turf based in Chattanooga, Tennessee. David Morris, Habitat's owner and CEO, admits that giving disabled workers a chance originally "had to be forced down my throat." Today, though, nearly every employee at the company, including some managers, has a physical or mental disability. Performance and quality have gone up at Habitat and turnover and absenteeism have gone down since Morris began hiring people with disabilities. The plant's defect rate, for example is less than one-half of 1 percent, and every order is delivered on time.[40]

The growing immigrant population presents other challenges. Whereas in previous generations most foreign-born immigrants came from Western Europe, 84 percent of recent immigrants come from Asia and Latin America.[41] These immigrants come to the United States with a wide range of backgrounds, often without adequate skills in using English. Organizations must face not only the issues of dealing with race, ethnicity, and nationality to provide a prejudice-free workplace, but also develop sufficient educational programs to help immigrants acquire the technical and customer service skills required in a service economy.

CURRENT DEBATES
ABOUT AFFIRMATIVE ACTION

Affirmative action refers to government-mandated programs that focus on providing opportunities to women and members of minority groups who previously faced discrimination. It is not the same thing as diversity, but affirmative action has facilitated greater recruitment, retention, and promotion of minorities and women. Affirmative action has made workplaces much more fair and equitable. However, research shows that full integration of women and racial minorities into organizations is still nearly a decade away.[42] Despite affirmative action's successes, salaries and promotion opportunities for women and minorities continue to lag behind those of white males.

Affirmative action was developed in response to conditions 40 years ago. Adult white males dominated the workforce, and economic conditions were stable and improving. Because of widespread prejudice and discrimination, legal and social coercion were necessary to allow women, people of color, immigrants, and other minorities to become part of the economic system.[43]

affirmative action
Government-mandated programs that focus on providing opportunities to women and members of minority groups who previously experienced discrimination.

Affirmative action is highly controversial today. The economic and social environment has changed tremendously since the 1960s. "Minority" groups have become the majority in large U.S. cities. More than half the U.S. workforce consists of women and minorities, and the economic climate changes rapidly as a result of globalization. Some members of nonprotected groups argue that affirmative action is no longer needed and that it leads to *reverse discrimination*. Even the intended beneficiaries of affirmative action programs often disagree as to their value, and some believe these programs do more harm than good. One reason may be the *stigma of incompetence* that often is associated with affirmative action hires. One study found that both working managers and students consistently rated people portrayed as affirmative action hires as less competent and recommended lower salary increases than for those not associated with affirmative action.[44] In addition, people who perceive that they were hired because of affirmative action requirements may demonstrate negative self-perceptions and negative views of the organization, which leads to lower performance and reinforces the opinions of others that they are less competent.[45]

Recent court decisions weakened affirmative action's clout while still upholding its value. For example, the Supreme Court preserved affirmative action policies as a means of achieving diversity in universities, but barred the use of point systems that might favor minority candidates.[46] Other court decisions have also limited the use of certain affirmative action practices for hiring and college admissions. In general, though, the courts support the continued use of affirmative action as a means of giving women and minority groups equal access to opportunities. In addition, according to a Gallup poll conducted to coincide with the 50th anniversary of the *Brown v. Board of Education* ruling that declared school segregation unconstitutional, 57 percent of Americans support the continued use of affirmative action.[47]

THE GLASS CEILING

The **glass ceiling** is an invisible barrier that separates women and minorities from top management positions. They can look up through the ceiling and see top management, but prevailing attitudes and stereotypes are invisible obstacles to their own advancement.

In addition, women and minorities are often excluded from informal manager networks and often don't get access to the type of general and line management experience that is required for moving to the top.[48] Research suggests the existence of *glass walls* that serve as invisible barriers to important lateral movement within the organization. Glass walls, like exclusion from manager networks, bar experience in areas such as line supervision that would enable women and minorities to advance vertically.[49]

Go to the ethical dilemma on page 442 that pertains to the glass ceiling. ■ **TAKE A MOMENT**

Evidence that the glass ceiling persists is the distribution of women and minorities, who are clustered at the bottom levels of the corporate hierarchy. Among minority groups, women have made the biggest strides in recent years, but they still represent only 15.7 percent of corporate officers in America's 500 largest companies, up from 12.5 percent in 2000 and 8.7 percent in 1995.[50] In 2006, only eight *Fortune* 500 companies had female CEOs. And both male and female African Americans and Hispanics continue to hold only a small percentage of all management positions in the United States.[51]

Women and minorities also make less money. As shown in Exhibit 13.4, black men earn about 22 percent less, white women 24 percent less, and Hispanic men 37 percent less than white males. Minority women fare even worse, with black women earning 35 percent less and Hispanic women 46 percent less than white males.[52]

Another sensitive issue related to the glass ceiling is homosexuals in the workplace. Many gay men and lesbians believe they will not be accepted as they are and

glass ceiling Invisible barrier that separates women and minorities from top management positions.

EXHIBIT   13.4

The Wage Gap

SOURCE: U.S. Census
Bureau, Current Population
Survey, 2004 Annual Social
and Economic Supplement,
reported in "2000 Median
Annual Earnings by Race and
Sex," http://www.infoplease.
com/ipa/A0197814.html.

■ Male
▨ Female

Black

$32,241

$26,965

Hispanic

$26,083

$22,363

White

$41,211

$31,169

© AP/STUART RAMSON

CONCEPT

CONNECTION As Indian-born Indra Nooyi, pictured here, once observed, "If you are a woman, and especially a person-of-color woman, there are two strikes against you. Immigrant, person of color, and woman—three strikes against you." She has certainly overcome the odds. *Fortune* named Nooyi its 2006 most powerful woman in business shortly after she became PepsiCo's CEO. How did she break through the **glass ceiling?** There's her considerable talent and powerful work ethic, of course. But she also benefited from PepsiCo's supportive culture and commitment to diversity. Under her predecessor, Steve Reinemund, half of all new hires were women or ethnic minorities, a policy spurred by the company's desire to have its workforce reflect its increasingly global customers.

risk losing their jobs or their chances for advancement. Gay employees of color are particularly hesitant to disclose their sexual orientation at work because by doing so they risk a double dose of discrimination.[53] Although some examples of openly gay corporate leaders can be found, such as David Geffen, co-founder of DreamWorks SKG, and Ford Vice Chairman Allan D. Gilmour, most managers still believe staying in the closet is the only way they can succeed at work. Thus, gays and lesbians often fabricate heterosexual identities to keep their jobs or avoid running into the glass ceiling they see other employees encounter.

The Opt-Out Trend

Many women are never hitting the glass ceiling because they choose to get off the fast track long before it comes into view. In recent years, an ongoing discussion concerns something referred to as the *opt-out trend*. In a recent survey of nearly 2,500 women and 653 men, 37 percent of highly qualified women report that they voluntarily left the workforce at some point in their careers, compared to only 24 percent of similarly qualified men.[54]

Quite a debate rages over the reasons for the larger number of women who drop out of mainstream careers. Opt-out proponents say women are deciding that corporate success isn't worth the price in terms of reduced family and personal time, greater stress, and negative health effects.[55] Women don't want corporate power and status in the same way that men do, and clawing one's way up the corporate ladder has become less appealing. For example, Marge Magner left her job as CEO of Citigroup's Consumer Group after suffering both the death of her mother and a personal life-changing accident in the same year. In evaluating her reasons, Magner said she realized that "life is about everything, not just the work." For many women today, the high-pressure climb to the top is just not worth it. Some are opting out to be stay-at-home moms, while others want to continue working but just not in the kind of fast-paced, competitive, aggressive environment that exists in most corporations. Some researchers who study the opt-out trend say that most women just don't want to work as hard and competitively as most men want to work.[56]

Critics, however, argue that this view is just another way to blame women themselves for the dearth of female managers at higher levels.[57] Vanessa Castagna, for example, left JCPenney after decades with the company not because she wanted more family or personal time but because she kept getting passed over for top jobs.[58] Although some women are voluntarily leaving the fast track, many more genuinely want to move up the corporate ladder but find their paths blocked. Fifty-five percent of executive women surveyed by Catalyst said they aspire to senior leadership levels.[59] In addition, a survey of 103 women voluntarily leaving executive jobs in *Fortune* 1000 companies found that corporate culture was cited as the number 1 reason for leaving.[60] The greatest disadvantages of women leaders stem largely from prejudicial attitudes and a heavily male-oriented corporate culture.[61] Some years ago, when Procter & Gamble asked the female executives it considered "regretted losses" (that is, high performers the company wanted to retain) why they left their jobs, the most common answer was that they didn't feel valued by the company.[62] Top-level corporate culture evolves around white, heterosexual, American males, who tend to hire and promote people who look, act, and think like them. Compatibility in thought and behavior plays an important role at higher levels of organizations. For example, among women who managed to break through the glass ceiling, fully 96 percent said adapting to a predominantly white male culture was necessary for their success.[63]

The Female Advantage

Some people think women might actually be better managers, partly because of a more collaborative, less hierarchical, relationship-oriented approach that is in tune with today's global and multicultural environment.[64] As attitudes and values change with changing generations, the qualities women seem to naturally possess may lead to a gradual role reversal in organizations. For example, a stunning gender reversal is taking place in U.S. education, with girls taking over almost every leadership role from kindergarten to graduate school. In addition, women of all races and ethnic groups are outpacing men in earning bachelor's and master's degrees. In 2005, women made up 57 percent of undergraduate college students. The gender gap in some states is even wider, with Maine reporting the greatest gap, with 154 women for every 100 men in the state's colleges and universities.[65] Among 25- to 29-year-olds, 32 percent of women have college degrees, compared to 27 percent of men. Women are rapidly closing the M.D. and Ph.D. gap, and they make up about half of all U.S. law students, half of all undergraduate business majors, and about 30 percent of MBA candidates. Overall, women's participation in both the labor force and civic affairs steadily increased since the mid-1950s, while men's participation has slowly but steadily declined.[66]

According to James Gabarino, an author and professor of human development at Cornell University, women are "better able to deliver in terms of what modern society requires of people—paying attention, abiding by rules, being verbally competent, and dealing with interpersonal relationships in offices."[67] His observation is supported by the fact that female managers are typically rated higher by subordinates on interpersonal skills as well as on factors such as task behavior, communication, ability to motivate others, and goal accomplishment.[68] Recent research found a correlation between balanced gender composition in companies (that is, roughly equal male and female representation) and higher organizational performance. Moreover, a study by Catalyst indicates that organizations with the highest percentage of women in top management financially outperform, by about 35 percent, those with the lowest percentage of women in higher-level jobs.[69] It seems that women should be marching right to the top of the corporate hierarchy, but prevailing attitudes, values, and perceptions in organizations create barriers and a glass ceiling.

CURRENT RESPONSES TO DIVERSITY

Today's companies are searching for inclusive practices that go well beyond affirmative action to confront the obstacles that prevent women and minorities from advancing to senior management positions. Procter & Gamble, for example, dramatically improved its retention of women and increased the number who moved into senior level positions by offering time management training and greater flexibility that enabled more women to accept career-oriented line management jobs.[70] When the Boston-based law firm Mintz Levin Cohn Ferris Glovsky & Popeo decided to build an employment law practice in Washington, the partners determined to create a diverse, inclusive environment by hiring many minority lawyers for senior positions from the start. The goal is to create a "critical mass" of people who can serve as role models and mentors for younger minority lawyers who typically find it difficult to move up the ranks and become partners in large law firms.[71]

To prepare for and respond to an increasingly diverse business climate, managers in most companies are also expanding the organization's emphasis on diversity beyond race and gender to consider such factors as ethnicity, age, physical ability, religion, and sexual orientation. Generational diversity is a key concern for managers in many of today's companies, with four generations working side-by-side, each with a different mind-set and different expectations. "In my career, I was trained not to start a meeting without an agenda," says 55-year-old manager J. Robert Carr. "Gen Yers make up the agenda as they go along."[72]

Once managers create and define a vision for a diverse workplace, they can analyze and assess the current culture and systems within the organization. Actions to develop an inclusive workplace that values and respects all people include three major steps: (1) building a corporate culture that values diversity; (2) changing structures, policies, and systems to support diversity; and (3) providing diversity awareness training.

Changing the Corporate Culture

When the underlying culture of an organization does not change, all the other efforts to support diversity fail, as managers at Mitsubishi learned. Even though the company settled a sexual harassment suit filed by women at the Normal, Illinois, plant, established a zero tolerance policy, and fired workers who were guilty of blatant harassment, workers complained that the work environment remained deeply hostile to women and minorities. Although the incidents of harassment decreased, women and minority workers still felt threatened and powerless because the culture and environment that allowed the harassment to occur had not changed. Mitsubishi managers are still struggling with these difficult issues.[73]

Chapters 3 and 11 described approaches for changing corporate culture. Managers can start by actively using symbols for the new values, such as encouraging and celebrating the promotion of minorities and disciplining employees who display behavior that does not fit a diverse workplace. At Baxter Healthcare, CEO Harry Jansen Kraemer symbolizes the importance of balance by writing a newsletter column about his family. For executives juggling a career and family, this action sends a clear signal that personal and family issues are important and do not limit career advancement. Culture change starts at the top, and most organizations recognized as diversity leaders have CEOs and other top executives who demonstrate a strong commitment to making diversity part of the organizational mission.[74]

Managers throughout the company can be educated to help transform the culture. For one thing, they can examine the unwritten rules and assumptions. What are the myths about minorities? What are the values that exemplify the existing culture? Are unwritten rules communicated from one person to another in a way that excludes women and minorities? For example, many men may not discuss unwritten rules with women and minorities because they assume everyone is aware of them and they do not want to seem patronizing.[75]

SUBTLE BIASES

As a new manager, your day-to-day behavior will send signals about your biases and values. Some personal biases are active and well known to yourself and others. Other biases are more subtle, and the following questions may provide some hints about where you are biased and don't know it. Please answer whether each item is Mostly True or Mostly False for you.

	Mostly True	Mostly False
1. I prefer to be in work teams with people who think like me.	_____	_____
2. I have avoided talking about culture differences with people I met from different cultures because I didn't want to say the wrong thing.	_____	_____
3. My mind has jumped to a conclusion without first hearing all sides of a story.	_____	_____
4. The first thing I notice about people is the physical characteristics that make them different from the norm.	_____	_____
5. Before I hire someone, I have a picture in mind of what they should look like.	_____	_____
6. I typically ignore movies, magazines, and TV programs that are targeted toward groups and values that are different from mine.	_____	_____

	Mostly True	Mostly False
7. When someone makes a bigoted remark or joke, I don't confront them about it.	_____	_____
8. I prefer to not discuss sensitive topics such as race, age, gender, sexuality, or religion at work.	_____	_____
9. There are people I like but would feel uncomfortable inviting to be with my family or close friends.	_____	_____

SCORING AND INTERPRETATION: Give yourself one point for each item you marked as Mostly True. The ideal score is zero, but few people reach the ideal. Each question reflects an element of "passive bias," which can cause people different from you to feel ignored or disrespected by you. Passive bias may be more insidious than active discrimination because it excludes people from opportunities for expression and interaction. If you scored 5 or more, you should take a careful look at how you think and act toward people different from yourself. The sooner you learn to actively include diverse views and people, the better new manager you will be.

SOURCE: Based on Lawrence Otis Graham, *Proversity: Getting Past Face Values and Finding the Soul of People* (New York: John Wiley & Sons, 1997).

As a new manager, you may have the courage to take an active stand against prejudice and inappropriate, disrespectful behavior. But will you inadvertently exclude people who are different from the mainstream? Find out by taking the New Manager Self-Test above.

■ **TAKE A MOMENT**

Companies are addressing the issue of changing culture in a variety of ways. Some are using surveys, interviews, and focus groups to identify how the cultural values affect minorities and women. Others have set up structured networks of people of color, women, and other minority groups to explore the issues they face in the workplace and to recommend changes to senior management. R. Roosevelt Thomas, founder of the American Institute for Managing Diversity, consults with many CEOs about diversity issues and often recommends a "cultural audit" to help top executives understand the hidden values, norms, and assumptions

Denny's Restaurants, which was hit with a series of discrimination lawsuits in the early 1990s, has been **changing structures and policies** to promote and support diversity. The company responded to the discrimination charges with aggressive minority hiring and supplier-diversity efforts. In July 2006, *Black Enterprise* magazine ranked Denny's at the top of its list of "Best 40 Companies for Diversity." Around 51 percent of Denny's employees, 43 percent of franchisees, and 36 percent of managers are members of minority groups.

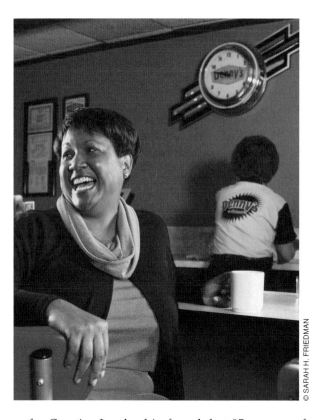

© SARAH H. FRIEDMAN

that might be getting in the way of building a truly inclusive workplace.[76] Although Thomas sees diversity as the most valuable element for competitive advantage in the twenty-first century, he believes cultural factors prevent most organizations from leveraging the power of a diverse workforce.[77]

Changing Structures and Policies

Many policies within organizations originally were designed to fit the stereotypical male employee. Now leading companies are changing structures and policies to facilitate and support diversity. A survey of *Fortune* 1,000 companies conducted by the Center for Creative Leadership found that 85 percent of companies surveyed have formal policies against racism and gender discrimination, and 76 percent have structured grievance procedures and complaint review processes.[78] Companies are also developing policies to support the recruitment and career advancement of diverse employees. At least half of *Fortune* 1,000 companies have staff dedicated exclusively to encouraging diversity. Increasingly, organizations such as Procter & Gamble, Ernst & Young, and Allstate Insurance are tying managers' bonuses and promotions to how well they diversify the workforce. Exhibit 13.5 illustrates some of the most common diversity initiatives.

RECRUITMENT

A good way to revitalize the recruiting process is for the company to examine employee demographics, the composition of the labor pool in the area, and the composition of the customer base. Managers then can work toward a workforce composition

EXHIBIT 13.5

The Most Common Diversity Initiatives: Percentage of *Fortune* 1,000 Respondents

SOURCE: Data reported in "Impact of Diversity Initiatives on the Bottom Line: A SHRM Survey of the *Fortune* 1000," pp. S12–S14, in *Fortune,* special advertising section, "Keeping Your Edge: Managing a Diverse Corporate Culture," produced in association with the Society for Human Resource Management, http://www.fortune.com/sections.

75% — Diversity-Focused Recruiting

66% — Training and Education

61% — Community Outreach

that reflects the labor pool and the customer base. Kodak, for example, set a goal of matching the multicultural makeup of the company's workforce to that of the available labor pool by the end of 2006.[79]

For many organizations, a new approach to recruitment means making better use of formal recruiting strategies, offering internship programs to give people opportunities, and developing creative ways to draw upon previously unused labor markets. Nationwide's Scholars Program brings in Hispanic and African American college students for a three-year program that includes summer internships and year-long mentoring.[80] Marathon Ashland Petroleum created a six-point recruiting strategy to increase diversity, including (1) recruiting corporate-wide and cross-functionally; (2) building relationships with first- and second-tiered schools to recruit minority students; (3) offering internships for racial and ethnic minorities; (4) offering minority scholarships; (5) establishing informal mentoring programs; and (6) forming affiliations with minority organizations.[81]

CAREER ADVANCEMENT

The successful advancement of diverse group members means that organizations must find ways to eliminate the glass ceiling. One of the most successful structures to accomplish this goal is the mentoring relationship. A **mentor** is a higher-ranking organizational member who is committed to providing upward mobility and support to a protégé's professional career.[82] Mentoring provides minorities and women with direct training and inside information on the norms and expectations of the organization. A mentor also acts as a friend or counselor, enabling the employee to feel more confident and capable. Joseph Cleveland has made a point of helping young African Americans navigate the corporate maze in his career at General Electric and Lockheed Martin. For Pamela Blow-Mitchell, Cleveland's mentoring changed the course of her career and enabled her to seize opportunities she might otherwise have missed. "He kind of dunked down deep in the organization to initiate a conversation with someone that he saw potential in," said Mitchell. "At the time, I could not see the range of opportunities, but I trusted his advice."[83]

One researcher who studied the career progress of high-potential minorities found that those who advance the furthest all share one characteristic—a strong mentor or network of mentors who nurtured their professional development.[84] However, research also indicates that minorities, as well as women, are much less likely than men to develop mentoring relationships.[85] Women and minorities might not seek mentors because they feel that job competency should be enough to succeed, or they might feel uncomfortable seeking out a mentor when most of the senior executives are white males. Women might fear that initiating a mentoring relationship could be misunderstood as a romantic overture, whereas male mentors may think of women as mothers, wives, or sisters rather than as executive material. Cross-race mentoring relationships sometimes leave both parties uncomfortable, but the mentoring of minority employees must often be across race because of the low number of minorities in upper-level positions. The few minorities and women who have reached the upper ranks often are overwhelmed with mentoring requests from people like themselves, and they may feel uncomfortable in highly visible minority-minority or female-female mentoring relationships, which isolate them from the white male status quo.

mentor A higher-ranking, senior organizational member who is committed to providing upward mobility and support to a protégé's professional career.

█ **TAKE A MOMENT**

Even as a new manager, you may have an opportunity to act as a mentor to a younger or less experienced minority employee. Use your interpersonal skills to build the person's confidence and help him or her develop valuable contacts. Assist the employee in navigating the office politics and learning the unwritten rules about how things are done in the organization.

The solution is for organizations to overcome some of the barriers to mentor relationships between white males and minorities. When organizations can institutionalize the value of white males actively seeking women and minority protégés, the benefits will mean that women and minorities will be steered into pivotal jobs and positions critical to advancement. Mentoring programs also are consistent with the Civil Rights Act of 1991 that requires the diversification of middle and upper management.

ACCOMMODATING SPECIAL NEEDS

Many people have special needs of which top managers are unaware. For example, if numerous people entering the organization at the lower level are single parents, the company can reassess job scheduling and opportunities for child care. If a substantial labor pool is non-English–speaking, training materials and information packets can be provided in another language, or the organization can provide English language classes.

In many families today, both parents work, which means that the company can provide structures to deal with child care, maternity or paternity leave, flexible work schedules, home-based employment, and perhaps part-time employment or seasonal hours that reflect the school year. The key to attracting and keeping elderly or disabled workers may include long-term care insurance and special health or life insurance benefits. Alternative work scheduling also may be important for these groups of workers. Organizations struggling with generational diversity must find ways to meet the needs of workers at different ages and place in the life cycle.[86] Pitney Bowes created the Life Balance Resources program to help employees in different generations cope with life cycle issues, such as helping Generation Y workers find their first apartments or cars, assisting Generation X employees in locating child care or getting home loans, helping baby boomers plan for retirement, and aiding older workers in researching insurance and long-term care options.[87]

Another issue for U.S. companies is that racial/ethnic minorities and immigrants often had fewer educational opportunities than other groups. Some companies work with high schools to provide fundamental skills in literacy and math, or they provide these programs within the company to upgrade employees to appropriate educational levels. The movement toward providing educational services for employees can be expected to increase for immigrants and the economically disadvantaged in the years to come.

Changing organizational structures and policies is important because it demonstrates a concrete commitment to supporting diversity. If managers talk about the value of a diverse workforce but do not do anything to ensure that diverse workers have opportunities and support in the workplace, employees are not likely to trust that the company truly values diversity.

Diversity Training

Most of today's organizations provide special training, called **diversity training**, to help people identify their own cultural boundaries, prejudices, and stereotypes and develop the skills for managing and working in a diverse workplace. By some estimates, about $80 billion has been invested in corporate diversity programs over the past 10 years, much of it spent on training.[88] Working or living within a multicultural context requires a person to use interaction skills that transcend the skills typically effective when dealing with others from one's own in-group.[89]

The first step is typically *diversity awareness training* to make employees aware of the assumptions they make and to increase people's sensitivity and openness to those who are different from themselves. Exhibit 13.6 shows a model of six stages of diversity awareness. The continuum ranges from a total lack of awareness to a complete understanding and acceptance of people's differences. This model is

diversity training Special training designed to educate employees about the importance of diversity, make people aware of their own biases, and teach them skills for communicating and working in a diverse workplace.

Highest Level of Awareness

Integration
- Multicultural attitude—enables one to integrate differences and adapt both cognitively and behaviorally

Adaptation
- Able to empathize with those of other cultures
- Able to shift from one cultural perspective to another

Acceptance
- Accepts behavioral differences and underlying differences in values
- Recognizes validity of other ways of thinking and perceiving the world

Minimizing Differences
- Hides or trivializes cultural differences
- Focuses on similarities among all peoples

Defense
- Perceives threat against one's comfortable worldview
- Uses negative stereotyping
- Assumes own culture superior

Denial
- Parochial view of the world
- No awareness of cultural differences
- In extreme cases, may claim other cultures are subhuman

Lowest Level of Awareness

EXHIBIT 13.6

Stages of Diversity Awareness

SOURCE: Based on M. Bennett, "A Developmental Approach to Training for Intercultural Sensitivity," *International Journal of Intercultural Relations* 10 (1986): 179–196.

useful in helping diversity awareness trainers assess participants' openness to change. People at different stages might require different kinds of training. A basic aim of awareness training is to help people recognize that hidden and overt biases direct their thinking about specific individuals and groups. If people can come away from a training session recognizing that they prejudge people and that this tendency needs to be consciously addressed in communications with and treatment of others, an important goal of diversity awareness training has been reached.

The next step is *diversity skills training* to help people learn how to communicate and work effectively in a diverse environment. Rather than just attempting to increase employees' understanding and sensitivity, this training gives people concrete skills they can use in everyday situations, such as how to handle conflict in a constructive manner or how to modify nonverbal communication such as body language and facial expression.[90] Verizon Communications uses an online training tool where managers can tap into various diversity scenarios that might occur in the workplace and see how they can manage them in an appropriate way.[91] In addition to online training, companies may also use classroom sessions, experiential exercises, videotapes or DVDs, and outside consulting firms that help organizations with diversity management issues.

DEFINING NEW RELATIONSHIPS IN ORGANIZATIONS

One outcome of diversity is an increased incidence of close personal relationships in the workplace, which can have both positive and negative results for employees as well as the organization. Two issues of concern are emotional intimacy and sexual harassment.

Emotional Intimacy

Close emotional relationships, particularly between men and women, often have been discouraged in companies for fear that they would disrupt the balance of power and threaten organizational stability.[92] This opinion grew out of the assumption that organizations are designed for rationality and efficiency, which were best achieved in a nonemotional environment.

However, a recent study of friendships in organizations sheds interesting light on this issue.[93] Managers and workers responded to a survey about emotionally intimate relationships with both male and female coworkers. Many men and women reported having close relationships with an opposite-sex coworker. Called *nonromantic love relationships*, the friendships resulted in trust, respect, constructive feedback, and support in achieving work goals. Intimate friendships did not necessarily become romantic, and they affected each person's job and career in a positive way. Rather than causing problems, nonromantic love relationships, according to the study, affected work teams in a positive manner because conflict was reduced. Indeed, men reported somewhat greater benefit than women from these relationships, perhaps because the men had fewer close relationships outside the workplace upon which to depend.

However, when such relationships *do* become romantic or sexual in nature, real problems can result. Romances that require the most attention from managers are those that arise between a supervisor and a subordinate. These relationships often lead to morale problems among other staff members, complaints of favoritism, and questions about the supervisor's intentions or judgment. Harry Stonecipher was ousted as CEO of Boeing Corporation in 2005 after the board learned of an extramarital affair with a female executive. However, office romances in general are tolerated far more today than in the past. Some companies, including Xerox and IBM, have formal policies that allow romantic relationships between employees as long as neither party directly reports to the other. Surveys show that approximately 25 percent of sexual harassment policies now include guidelines about office relationships, and 70 percent of companies surveyed have policies prohibiting romantic relationships between a superior and a subordinate.[94]

Sexual Harassment

Although psychological closeness between men and women in the workplace may be a positive experience, sexual harassment is not. Sexual harassment is illegal. As a form of sexual discrimination, sexual harassment in the workplace is a violation of Title VII of the 1964 Civil Rights Act. Sexual harassment in the classroom is a violation of Title VIII of the Education Amendment of 1972. The following list categorizes various forms of sexual harassment as defined by one university:

:: *Generalized.* This form involves sexual remarks and actions that are not intended to lead to sexual activity but that are directed toward a coworker based solely on gender and reflect on the entire group.

:: *Inappropriate/offensive.* Though not sexually threatening, it causes discomfort in a coworker, whose reaction in avoiding the harasser may limit his or her freedom and ability to function in the workplace.

:: *Solicitation with promise of reward.* This action treads a fine line as an attempt to "purchase" sex, with the potential for criminal prosecution.

:: *Coercion with threat of punishment.* The harasser coerces a coworker into sexual activity by using the threat of power (through recommendations, grades, promotions, and so on) to jeopardize the victim's career.

:: *Sexual crimes and misdemeanors.* The highest level of sexual harassment, these acts would, if reported to the police, be considered felony crimes and misdemeanors.[95]

Statistics in Canada indicate that between 40 and 70 percent of women and about 5 percent of men have been sexually harassed at work.[96] The situation in the United States is just as dire. Over a recent 10-year period, the Equal Employment Opportunity Commission shows a 150 percent increase in the number of sexual harassment cases filed annually.[97] About 10 percent of those were filed by males. The Supreme Court held that same-sex harassment as well as harassment of men by female coworkers is just as illegal as the harassment of women by men. In the suit that prompted the Court's decision, a male oil-rig worker claimed he was singled out by other members of the all-male crew for crude sex play, unwanted touching, and threats of rape.[98] A growing number of men are urging recognition that sexual harassment is not just a woman's problem.[99]

Because the corporate world is dominated by a male culture, however, sexual harassment affects women to a much greater extent. Companies such as Dow Chemical, Xerox, and *The New York Times* have been swift to fire employees for circulating pornographic images, surfing pornographic Web sites, or sending offensive e-mails.[100]

■ **TAKE A MOMENT**

As a new manager, be careful about a romantic involvement in the workplace. In particular, steer clear of such relationships with superiors or subordinates, which is a slippery ethical area. Know what sexual harassment means, and make sure everyone in your team or department understands that sexual harassment is disrespectful and against the law.

GLOBAL DIVERSITY

Globalization is a reality for today's companies. As stated in a report from the Hudson Institute, *Workforce 2020,* "The rest of the world matters to a degree that it never did in the past."[101] For example, Google, which employs about 4,000 people worldwide, has seen a tremendous increase in the number of immigrants working in its U.S. headquarters. This realization prompted leaders to take a new approach to the company cafeteria, as described in this chapter's Unlocking Innovative Solutions Through People box.

Even small companies that do not do business in other countries are affected by global diversity issues. However, large multinational companies that hire employees in many countries face tremendous challenges because they apply diversity management across a broader stage than North America. Citigroup has

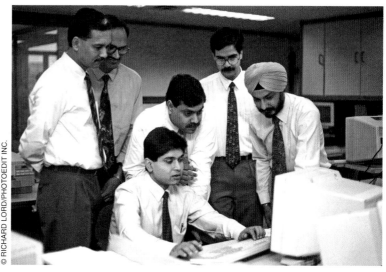

© RICHARD LORD/PHOTOEDIT INC.

CONCEPT

CONNECTION With roughly half of its 66,000 employees working outside the United States, it's not surprising that American Express is an acknowledged leader in managing **global diversity.** These East Indian staff members are shown in the company's Delhi offices. American Express developed a training module, "Valuing Diversity and Practicing Inclusion," for managers throughout the world, but executives let local facilitators customize the tool to fit their cultures. "We always allow them a period of time to be able to adapt, modify, and customize . . . so that it resonates well with employees," explains Henry Hernandez, vice president and chief diversity officer.

Google Chow

As Google's first food guru, chef Charlie Ayers had plenty of opportunity to indulge his penchant for varied, eclectic flavors. When hired in 1999, Ayers oversaw food services for only about 50 employees. By the time he departed in 2005, he left behind 100 chefs serving more than 2,000 meals a day at the Googleplex, Google's Mountain View, California, headquarters. Google offers expertly prepared meals, free of charge, to all its employees.

Today, those employees arrive from all corners of the world, and the cafeteria offerings reflect that diversity. Ayers's eclectic tastes and the needs of an increasingly diverse workforce meshed nicely. He created his own dishes, searched all types of restaurants for new recipes, and often got some of his best ideas from foreign-born employees. For example, a Filipino accountant offered a recipe for chicken *adobo,* a popular dish from her native country. Scattered around the Googleplex are cafes specializing in Southwestern, Italian, California-Mediterranean, and vegetarian cuisines. And because more and more Googlers originally hail from Asia, employees can find sushi at the Japanese-themed Pacific Café or Thai red curry beef at the East Meets West Café.

Google cafeteria fare has such a sterling reputation it's rumored that Yahoo! employees working nearby sneak onto campus just to grab a bite. Whether that rumor is true or not, the company indisputably stands at the forefront of organizations that believe in paying careful attention to their corporate cafeteria offerings.

For Google, the company's $6 million plus annual food budget is an investment in productivity.

Why? First of all, by offering appetizing cuisine on campus, the company saves people the time and trouble of driving to an eatery, as well as provides a place for them to mingle informally. In addition, serving all employees the kind of tasty food usually reserved for swank executive dining rooms sends a clear message that Google values its human capital. Even more fundamentally, Google managers believe that what you eat literally affects your work. Indeed, the company requires that its chefs not only keep people well fed but also provide healthy foods that leave them feeling energized when they get up from the table.

Last, but not least, along with companies such as REI and Nintendo, Google believes food can be a tool for supporting an inclusive workplace. The diversity of options gives people a chance to try new things and learn more about their coworkers. And when people just need a little comfort and familiarity? Nothing takes the edge off of working in a foreign country, Google knows, like eating food that reminds you of home.

SOURCES: Jim Carlton, "Dig In," *The Wall Street Journal* (November 14, 2005): R9; Tony DiRomualdo, "Is Google's Cafeteria a Competitive Weapon?" *Wisconsin Technology Network* (August 30, 2005): http://wistechnology.com/article.php?id=2190; Marc Ramirez, "Tray Chic: At Work, Cool Cafeterias, Imaginative Menus," *The Seattle Times* (November 21, 2005): http://seattletimes. nwsource.com/html/living/2002634266_cafes21.html?pageid= display-in-the-news.module&pageregion=itn-body.

---

more than 260,000 employees in more than 100 countries, creating a tremendous multicultural management challenge. Managers must develop new skills and awareness to handle the unique challenges of global diversity: cross-cultural understanding, the ability to build networks, and the understanding of geopolitical forces. Two significant aspects of global diversity programs involve employee selection and training and the understanding of the communication context.

Selection and Training

Expatriates are employees who live and work in a country other than their own. Careful screening, selection, and training of employees to serve overseas increase the potential for corporate global success. Human resource managers consider global skills in the selection process. In addition, expatriates receive cross-cultural training that develops language skills and provides cultural and historical orientation.[102]

Equally important is honest self-analysis by overseas candidates and their families. Before seeking or accepting an assignment in another country, a candidate should ask himself or herself such questions as the following:

expatriates Employees who live and work in a country other than their own.

:: Is your spouse interrupting his or her own career path to support your career? Is that acceptable to both of you?

:: Is family separation for long periods involved?

:: Can you initiate social contacts in a foreign culture?

:: Can you adjust well to different environments and changes in personal comfort or quality of living, such as the lack of television, limited hot water, varied cuisine, and national phone strikes?

:: Can you manage your future reentry into the job market by networking and maintaining contacts in your home country?[103]

Employees working overseas must adjust to all of these conditions. Managers going global might find that their management styles need adjustment to succeed in a foreign country. One aspect of this adjustment is understanding differences in social and cultural values as identified by the Hofstede research and the GLOBE project described in Chapter 4 of this text. Another important consideration is understanding the communication context of a foreign location.

Communication Differences

People from some cultures tend to pay more attention to the social context (social setting, nonverbal behavior, social status) of their verbal communication than Americans do. For example, American managers working in China have discovered that social context is considerably more important in that culture, and they can learn to suppress their impatience and devote the time needed to establish personal and social relationships.

Exhibit 13.7 indicates how the emphasis on social context varies among countries. In a **high-context culture**, people are sensitive to circumstances surrounding social exchanges. People use communication primarily to build personal social relationships; meaning is derived from context—setting, status, nonverbal behavior—more than from explicit words; relationships and trust are more important than business; and the welfare and harmony of the group are valued. In a **low-context culture**, people use communication primarily to exchange facts and information; meaning is derived primarily from words; business transactions are more important than building relationships and trust; and individual welfare and achievement are more important than the group.[104]

To understand how differences in cultural context affect communications, consider the U.S. expression, "The squeaky wheel gets the oil." It means that the loudest person will get the most attention, and attention is assumed to be favorable. Equivalent sayings in China and Japan are "Quacking ducks get shot," and "The nail that sticks up gets hammered down," respectively. Standing out as an individual in these cultures clearly merits unfavorable attention.

High-context cultures include Asian and Arab countries. Low-context cultures tend to be American and Northern European. Even within North America, cultural subgroups vary in the extent to which context counts, explaining why differences among groups can hinder successful communication. White females, Native Americans, and African Americans all tend to prefer higher context communication than do white males. A high-context interaction requires more time because a

High
Context

Chinese
Korean
Japanese
Vietnamese
Arab
Greek
Spanish
Italian
English
North American
Scandinavian
Swiss
German

Low
Context

EXHIBIT 13.7

Arrangement of High- and Low-Context Cultures

SOURCES: Edward T. Hall, *Beyond Culture* (Garden City, NY: Anchor Press/Doubleday, 1976); and J. Kennedy and A. Everest, "Put Diversity in Context," *Personnel Journal* (September 1991): 50–54.

high-context culture A culture in which communication is used to enhance personal relationships.

low-context culture A culture in which communication is used to exchange facts and information.

relationship has to be developed, and trust and friendship must be established. Furthermore, most male managers and most people doing the hiring in organizations are from low-context cultures, which conflicts with people entering the organization from a background in a higher context culture. Overcoming these differences in communication is a major goal of diversity skills training. For Lenova Corp., which was created when Chinese computer giant Lenova bought IBM's personal-computer business, this training is crucial to the company's survival.

Lenova Corp.

Lenova's chairman, Yang Yuanquing, is Chinese; its CEO, Stephen Ward, is American; and its chief marketing officer, Deepak Advani, is Indian. A little more than 50 percent of the company's 20,000 or so employees work in China, with the rest scattered around the world, mostly in the United States. About half of them speak only English and no Mandarin, while the other half speak Chinese and little English.

With such a culturally, geographically, and linguistically diverse workforce, Lenova has no choice but to implement some serious diversity training. And managers are rising to the challenge, initiating a wide-ranging worldwide strategy designed to educate Lenova's far-flung employees on the cultures, customs, and languages of their overseas colleagues. Programs include Mandarin lessons for U.S. executives and English lessons for managers in China, training sessions on the predominant cultural values of the various countries where Lenova operates, and weekly lunchtime cultural understanding seminars exploring issues such as how different cultures regard silence in conversations. A "knowledge exchange" program sends employees on short-term overseas assignments so people can learn different perspectives. Lenova even has a cross-cultural children's pen-pal program, called "Culture Kids," for the children of employees to help them learn about one another.

Top executives at Lenova consider the diversity of the company to be its biggest competitive advantage. However, they know that to realize Lenova's full potential, they must find ways to smooth the tensions and stress that diversity can bring and take advantage of differences to create a stronger company.[105]

DIVERSITY IN A TURBULENT WORLD

Ninety-one percent of companies responding to a survey by the Society for Human Resource Management believe that diversity initiatives help maintain a competitive advantage. Some specific benefits include improving employee morale, decreasing interpersonal conflict, facilitating progress in new markets, and increasing the organization's creativity.[106] In addition to the ideas already discussed, two new approaches to diversity management—multicultural teams and employee networks—have arisen in response to the rapid change and complexity of the twenty-first–century organization.

Multicultural Teams

Companies have long known that putting together teams made up of members from different functional areas results in better problem solving and decision making. Now, they are recognizing that **multicultural teams**—teams made up of members from diverse national, racial, ethnic, and cultural backgrounds—provide even greater potential for enhanced creativity, innovation, and value in today's global marketplace.[107] Research indicates that diverse teams generate more and better alternatives to problems and produce more creative solutions than homogeneous teams.[108] A team made up of people with different perspectives, backgrounds, and cultural values creates a healthy mix of ideas and leads to greater creativity and better decisions.

Some organizations, such as RhonePoulenc Rorer (RPR), based in Collegeville, Pennsylvania, are committed to mixing people from diverse countries and cultures, from the top to the bottom of the organization. Fifteen nationalities are represented in RPR's top management teams, including a French CEO, an Austrian head of operations, an American general counsel, an Egyptian head of human resources, and an Italian director of corporate communications.[109]

multicultural teams Teams made up of members from diverse national, racial, ethnic, and cultural backgrounds.

Multicultural teams are becoming common in both U.S. and Canadian organizations. One consultant notes that the workforce of many Canadian organizations is often jokingly referred to as the *United Nations* because companies have so many different nationalities working together on project teams.[110]

Despite their many advantages,[111] multicultural teams are more difficult to manage because of the increased potential for miscommunication and misunderstanding. Multicultural teams typically have more difficulty learning to communicate and work well together, but with effective cross-cultural training and good management, the problems seem to dissipate over time.[112] One management team videotaped its meetings so members could see how their body language reflects cultural differences. An American manager remarked, "I couldn't believe how even my physical movements dominated the table, while Ron [a Filipino American] . . . actually worked his way off-camera within the first five minutes."[113]

Employee Network Groups

Employee network groups are based on social identity, such as gender or race, and are organized by employees to focus on concerns of employees from that group.[114] For example, when Marita Golden was teaching at George Mason University, she often heard other African American women at the university talk about how they felt isolated and needed to get together. So, Golden started a networking group that has grown and expanded, incorporating women from other local colleges and universities as well, who get together and share their research interests, talk about career and personal development issues, and explore both positive and negative experiences of their work lives.[115] At Visteon Corporation, a global automotive systems producer, the women's network group develops the leadership and technical skills of female employees, designs strategies for how members can contribute to Visteon's business and diversity goals, and works to keep top managers informed of members' contributions, concerns, and needs.[116] Whereas multicultural teams help bind diverse people together for the accomplishment of shared goals, network groups provide people with comfort and support in an often-crazy world. The idea behind network groups is that minority employees can join together across traditional organizational boundaries for mutual support and to extend member influence in the organization.

Network groups pursue a variety of activities, such as meetings to educate top managers, mentoring programs, networking events, training sessions and skills seminars, minority intern programs, and community volunteer activities. These activities give people a chance to meet, interact with, and develop social and professional ties to others throughout the organization, which may include key decision makers. Network groups are a powerful way to reduce social isolation for women and minorities, help these employees be more effective, and enable members to achieve greater career advancement. A recent study confirms that network groups can be an important tool for helping organization's retain managerial-level minority employees.[117]

An important characteristic of network groups is that they are created informally by employees, not the organization, and membership is voluntary. However, successful organizations support and encourage network groups. Even managers who once thought of minority networks as "gripe groups" are now seeing them as essential to organizational success because they help to retain minority employees, enhance diversity efforts, and spark new ideas that can benefit the organization.[118] Although at first glance the proliferation of employee network groups seems to be in direct opposition to the trend toward multicultural teams, the two mechanisms actually work quite well together. At Kraft Foods, networks are considered critical to the success of multicultural teams because they build awareness and acceptance of cultural differences and help people feel more comfortable working together.[119]

Employee networks for minorities who have faced barriers to advancement in organizations, including African Americans, Hispanics, American Indians, Asian

employee network groups Groups based on social identity, such as gender or race, and organized by employees to focus on concerns of employees from that group.

Americans, women, gays and lesbians, and disabled employees, show tremendous growth. In general, female and minority employees who participate in a network group feel more pride about their work and are more optimistic about their careers than those who do not have the support of a network.[120]

MANAGER'S SOLUTION

Several important ideas pertain to workforce diversity, which is the inclusion of people with different human qualities and from different cultural groups. Dimensions of diversity are both primary, such as age, gender, and race; and secondary, such as education, marital status, and income. Ethnocentric attitudes generally produce a monoculture that accepts only one way of doing things and one set of values and beliefs, thereby excluding nontraditional employees from full participation. Minority employees face several significant challenges in the workplace.

Acceptance of diversity is becoming especially important because of globalization, sociocultural changes, and the changing workforce. Diversity in the workplace reflects diversity in the larger environment. Managers at Cracker Barrel, described in the chapter opening, have been through the wringer over diversity issues, beginning with public outrage over the company's policy of firing homosexuals, a policy Cracker Barrel ended in 2002, and continuing more recently with racial discrimination lawsuits. Managers have taken a number of steps to try to solve these problems. Cracker Barrel is now a top contributor to the Multicultural Foodservice and Hospitality Alliance, a national group that promotes diversity in the restaurant industry. Managers volunteer their time to supplier groups and other companies that want to learn from Cracker Barrel's experiences, as well as to organizations working to place minority job candidates. Derek Young, an African American who now serves as director of community outreach, has been instrumental in helping set up leadership classes for minority high school students in collaboration with 100 Black Men of America. Some observers believe the company is making a sincere move toward thinking and acting like an inclusive organization, but others think it has yet to prove its commitment to diversity and racial harmony. Managers say they will continue searching for new initiatives that go beyond affirmative action and work to shift the culture toward valuing diversity.[121]

Affirmative action programs have been successful in gaining employment for women and minorities, but the glass ceiling has kept many from obtaining top management positions. Some women are opting to get off the corporate ladder, although studies indicate that women have characteristics that may make them better managers than men in today's diverse organizations. Breaking the glass ceiling ultimately means changing the corporate culture within organizations; changing internal structures and policies toward employees, including accommodating special needs; and providing diversity training to help people become aware of their own cultural boundaries and prejudices and teach them skills for effectively working with people different from themselves.

Another result of increased diversity in organizations is the opportunity for emotional intimacy and friendships between men and women that are beneficial to all parties. However, even though emotional connections are a positive outcome, sexual harassment has become a serious problem for today's managers. Increasing diversity also means that organizations must develop programs to deal with global as well as domestic diversity and with potential conflicts that arise.

Two recent approaches to supporting and leveraging the power of diversity in organizations are multicultural teams and employee network groups. Multicultural teams provide a broader and deeper base of experience and ideas for enhanced problem solving, creativity, and innovation. Organizations that value diversity also encourage and support network groups to enable minority organization members to reduce their social isolation, be more effective in their jobs, have a greater impact on the organization, and achieve greater opportunities for career advancement.

1. If you were a senior manager at a company such as Mitsubishi, Allstate Insurance, or Wal-Mart, how would you address the challenges faced by minority employees?

2. Some people argue that social class is a major source of cultural differences, yet social class is not listed as a primary or secondary dimension in Exhibit 13.2. Discuss reasons it is not there.

3. Evaluate your own experiences so far with people from other backgrounds. How well do you think those experiences prepared you to understand the unique needs and dilemmas of a diverse workforce?

4. What is the glass ceiling, and why do you think it has proven to be such a barrier to women and minorities?

5. How might employee network groups contribute to the advancement of women and minorities to higher-level positions in an organization?

6. In preparing an organization to accept diversity, do you think it is more important to change the corporate culture or to change structures and policies? Explain.

7. If a North American corporation could choose either high-context or low-context communications, which do you think would be best for the company's long-term health? Discuss.

8. Why do you think a large number of women are *opting out* of corporate management? Discuss whether this trend is likely to continue over the next 10 years.

9. As a manager, how would you accommodate the special needs of different groups (e.g., single parents, older workers, or employees with poor English language skills or religious restrictions) without appearing to show favoritism or offending other groups?

10. How can organizations strike a balance between respecting and meeting the needs of a diverse workforce and shaping a high-performance corporate culture where shared values contribute to the accomplishment of strategic goals?

11. You are a manager at an organization that has decided it needs a more diverse workforce. What steps or techniques will you use to accomplish this goal? What steps will you take to retain diverse employees once you have successfully recruited them?

MANAGEMENT IN PRACTICE: EXPERIENTIAL EXERCISE

How Tolerant Are You?

For each of the following questions, circle the answer that best describes you.

1. Most of your friends
   a. are very similar to you
   b. are very different from you and from each other
   c. are like you in some respects but different in others

2. When someone does something you disapprove of, you
   a. break off the relationship
   b. tell how you feel but keep in touch
   c. tell yourself it matters little and behave as you always have

3. Which virtue is most important to you?
   a. kindness
   b. objectivity
   c. obedience

4. When it comes to beliefs, you
   a. do all you can to make others see things the same way you do
   b. actively advance your point of view but stop short of argument
   c. keep your feelings to yourself

5. Would you hire a person who has had emotional problems?
   a. no
   b. yes, provided the person shows evidence of complete recovery
   c. yes, if the person is suitable for the job

6. Do you voluntarily read material that supports views different from your own?
   a. never
   b. sometimes
   c. often

7. You react to old people with
   a. patience
   b. annoyance
   c. sometimes a, sometimes b

8. Do you agree with the statement, "What is right and wrong depends upon the time, place, and circumstance"?
   a. strongly agree
   b. agree to a point
   c. strongly disagree

9. Would you marry someone from a different race?
   a. yes
   b. no
   c. probably not

10. If someone in your family were homosexual, you would
   a. view this as a problem and try to change the person to a heterosexual orientation
   b. accept the person as a homosexual with no change in feelings or treatment
   c. avoid or reject the person

11. You react to little children with
   a. patience
   b. annoyance
   c. sometimes a, sometimes b

12. Other people's personal habits annoy you
   a. often
   b. not at all
   c. only if extreme

13. If you stay in a household run differently from yours (cleanliness, manners, meals, and other customs), you
   a. adapt readily
   b. quickly become uncomfortable and irritated
   c. adjust for a while, but not for long

14. Which statement do you agree with most?
   a. We should avoid judging others because no one can fully understand the motives of another person.
   b. People are responsible for their actions and have to accept the consequences.
   c. Both motives and actions are important when considering questions of right and wrong.

Scoring and Interpretation

Circle your score for each of the answers and total the scores:

1. a = 4; b = 0; c = 2
2. a = 4; b = 2; c = 0
3. a = 0; b = 2; c = 4
4. a = 4; b = 2; c = 0
5. a = 4; b = 2; c = 0
6. a = 4; b = 2; c = 0
7. a = 0; b = 4; c = 2
8. a = 0; b = 2; c = 4
9. a = 0; b = 4; c = 2
10. a = 2; b = 0; c = 4
11. a = 0; b = 4; c = 2
12. a = 4; b = 0; c = 2
13. a = 0; b = 4; c = 2
14. a = 0; b = 4; c = 2

Total Score

0–14: If you score 14 or below, you are a very tolerant person and dealing with diversity comes easily to you.

15–28: You are basically a tolerant person and others think of you as tolerant. In general, diversity presents few problems for you; you may be broad-minded in some areas and have less tolerant ideas in other areas of life, such as attitudes toward older people or male-female social roles.

29–42: You are less tolerant than most people and should work on developing greater tolerance of people different from you. Your low tolerance level could affect your business or personal relationships.

43–56: You have a very low tolerance for diversity. The only people you are likely to respect are those with beliefs similar to your own. You reflect a level of intolerance that could cause difficulties in today's multicultural business environment.

SOURCE: Adapted from the Tolerance Scale by Maria Heiselman, Naomi Miller, and Bob Schlorman, Northern Kentucky University, 1982. In George Manning, Kent Curtis, and Steve McMillen, *Building Community: The Human Side of Work,* (Cincinnati, OH: Thomson Executive Press, 1996): 272–277.

MANAGEMENT IN PRACTICE: ETHICAL DILEMMA

Sunset Prayers

Frank Piechowski, plant manager for a Minnesota North Woods Appliance Corp. refrigerator plant, just received his instructions from the vice president for manufacturing. He was to hire 40 more temporary workers through Twin Cities Staffing, the local labor agency North Woods used. Frank already knew from past experience that most, if not all, of the new hires available to work the assembly line would be Muslim Somali refugees, people who had immigrated to Minnesota from their war-torn native country en masse over the past 15 years.

North Woods, like all appliance manufacturers, was trying to survive in a highly competitive, mature industry. Appliance companies were competing mainly on price. The entrance of large chains such as Best Buy and Home Depot only intensified the price wars, not to mention that consumers could easily do comparison shopping before leaving home by logging onto the Internet. The pressure to keep production costs low was considerable.

That's where the Somali workers came in. In an effort to keep labor costs low, North Woods was relying more and more on temporary workers rather than increasing the ranks of permanent employees. Frank was quite pleased with the Somalis already at work on the assembly line. Although few in number, they were responsible, hard-working, and willing to work for the wages he could afford to pay.

It was the first time this son of Polish immigrants had ever come into contact with Muslims, but so far, it had gone well. Frank had established a good working relationship with the Somalis' spokesperson, Halima Adan, who explained that unlike most Western faiths, Islamic religious practices were inextricably woven into everyday life. So together, they worked out ways to accommodate Muslim customs. Frank authorized changes in the plant's cafeteria menu so the Somali workers had more options that conformed to their dietary restrictions, and he allowed women to wear traditional clothing as long as they weren't violating safety standards.

After learning that the Somalis would need to perform at least some of the ceremonial washing and prayers they were required to do five times a day during work hours, the plant manager set aside a quiet, clean room where they could observe their 15-minute rituals during their breaks and at sunset. The Maghrib sunset prayers second shift workers had to perform were disruptive to a smooth workflow. Compared to their midday and afternoon rituals, the Muslim faithful had considerably less leeway as to when they said the sunset prayers, and of course, the sun set at a slightly different time each day. But so far, they'd all coped.

But what was he going to do about the sunset prayers with an influx of 40 Somali workers that would dramatically increase the number of people who would need to leave the line to pray? Was it time to modify his policy? He knew that Title VII of the Civil Right Act required that he make "reasonable" accommodations to his employees' religious practices unless doing so would impose an "undue hardship" on the employer. Had he reached the point where the accommodations Halima Adan would probably request crossed the line from reasonable to unreasonable? But if he changed his policy, did he risk alienating his workforce?

What Would You Do?

1. Continue the current policy that leaves it up to the Muslim workers as to when they leave the assembly line to perform their sunset rituals.

2. Try to hire the fewest possible Muslim workers so the work line will be efficient on second shift.

3. Ask the Muslim workers to delay their sunset prayers until a regularly scheduled break occurs, pointing out that North Woods is primarily a place of business, not a house of worship.

SOURCES: Based on Rob Johnson, "30 Muslim Workers Fired for Praying on Job at Dell," *The Tennessean,* (March 10, 2005): http://tennessean.com/local/archives/05/03/66733769.shtml?Element_ID=66733769; Anayat Durrani, "Religious Accommodation for Muslim Employees," *Workforce.com,* www.workforce.com/archive/feature/22/26/98/index.php?ht=muslim%20muslim; U.S. Equal Employment Opportunity Commission, "Questions and Answers about Employer Responsibilities Concerning the Employment of Muslims, Arabs, South Asians, and Sikhs," www.eeoc.gov/facts/backlash-employer.html; and U.S. Department of Commerce, Office of Health and Consumer Goods, "2005 Appliance Industry Outlook," *Trade.gov,* www.ita.doc.gov/td/ocg/outlook05_appliances.pdf.

CASE FOR CRITICAL ANALYSIS

Draper Manufacturing

"You see what I'm up against?" asked Ralph Draper wearily as he escorted Ted Hanrahan, a diversity consultant, into his modest office on a rainy October day. Ralph was the new CEO of Draper Manufacturing, a small mattress manufacturer. He'd recently moved back to Portland, Oregon, his hometown, to take over the reins of the family-owned company from his ailing father. Ralph and Ted had just come from a contentious meeting of Draper's top managers that vividly illustrated the festering racial tensions Ralph wanted Ted to help alleviate.

It hadn't taken long for sales manager Brent Myers to confront shipping and receiving department head Adam Fox, an African American and the only non-white manager. "Why can't your boys get orders shipped out on time?" Brent demanded. "Isn't there some way you can get them to pay a little less attention to their bling and a little more to their responsibilities?" Adam Fox shot back angrily, "If you tightwads actually hired enough people to get the job done, there wouldn't be any problem." The other managers sat by silently, looking acutely uncomfortable, until the quality control head worked in a joke about his wife. Most laughed loudly, and Ralph took the opportunity to steer the conversation to other agenda topics.

The main challenge Draper faces is the price of oil, which had passed $60 per barrel mark that summer. In addition to powering its operations and shipping, petroleum is an essential raw material for many mattress components, from polyester and thread to foam. Then the Gulf hurricanes caused severe shortages of TDI, the chemical used to make polyurethane foam, a key component. So far, the company had passed its cost increases on to the consumer, but with increased competition from low-priced Asian imports, no one knew how long that strategy would work. To survive in mattress manufacturing, Draper needs to find ways to lower costs and increase productivity. Ralph completely understands why Brent is pressuring Adam to ship orders out more quickly.

The current workforce reflects Draper's determination to keep labor costs low. It employs 90 people full-time, the majority of whom are Asian and Hispanic immigrants and African Americans. Although women make up 75 percent of the workforce, nearly all of the shipping department employees are young African American men. Instead of adding to its permanent workforce, the company hires part-time workers from time to time, mostly Hispanic females. It tends to engage Asians as mechanics and machine operators because human resources head Teresa Burns believes they have superior technical skills. The result is a diverse but polarized workforce. "This is a time everyone needs to pull together," said Ralph. "But what's happening is that each minority group sticks to itself. The blacks and Asians rarely mix, and most of the Mexicans stay to themselves and speak only in Spanish."

When two of the older white shipping employees retired last year, Ralph didn't replace them, hoping to improve efficiency by cutting salary costs. "It seems to me that some of our workers are just downright lazy sometimes." said Ralph. "I myself have talked to Adam about pushing his kids to develop a work ethic. But he insists on blaming the company for the department's problems. You can see why we want your help."

Questions

1. Based on the information in the case, at what stage of diversity awareness do managers at Draper Manufacturing seem to be? Discuss.

2. If you were the shipping and receiving or human resources manager, how do you think you would feel about working at Draper? What are some of the challenges you might face at this company?

3. If you were Ted Hanrahan, what suggestions would you make to Draper's managers to help them move toward successfully managing diversity issues?

SOURCES: Based on "Northern Industries," a case prepared by Rae Andre of Northeastern University; "Interesting Times Indeed. Let's Review, Shall We?" *BedTimes* (December 2005): www.sleepproducts.org/Content/ContentGroups/BEDtimes1/20052/December6/Interesting_times_indeed.htm; and Jacqueline A. Gilbert, Norma Carr-Rufino, John M. Ivancevich and Millicent Lownes-Jackson, "An Empirical Examination of Inter-Ethnic Stereotypes: Comparing Asian American and African American Employees," *Public Personnel Management* (Summer 2003): 251–266.

ENDNOTES

1. Naomi Snyder, "Cracker Barrel Is Striving to Shed Shadow of Bias Cases," *The Tennessean* (December 1, 2005): 1E, 3E.

2. Kenneth Labich, "No More Crude at Texaco," *Fortune* (September 6, 1999): 205–212; Wendy Zellner, "No Way to Treat a Lady," *BusinessWeek* (March 3, 2003): 63; Aaron Bernstein with Michael Arndt, "Racism in the Workplace," *BusinessWeek* (July 30, 2001); and "Boeing Will Pay $72.5 Million to Settle Sex-Discrimination Suit," *The Wall Street Journal* (November 12, 2005), http://www.wsj.com.

3. Reed Abelson, "Can Respect Be Mandated? Maybe Not Here," *The New York Times* (September 10, 2000), http://www.nytimes.com.

4. Ginny Parker Woods, "Japan's Diversity Problem," *The Wall Street Journal* (October 24, 2005): B1, B4.

5. M. Fine, F. Johnson, and M. S. Ryan, "Cultural Diversity in the Workforce," *Public Personnel Management* 19 (1990): 305–319.

6. Taylor H. Cox, "Managing Cultural Diversity: Implications for Organizational Competitiveness," *Academy of Management Executive* 5, no. 3 (1991): 45–56; and Faye Rice, "How to Make Diversity Pay," *Fortune* (August 8, 1994): 78–86.

7. Roy Harris, "The Illusion of Inclusion," *CFO* (May 2001): 42–50; C. J. Prince, "Doing Diversity: The Question Isn't Why to Do It—But How," *Chief Executive* (April, 2005): 46; and results of a study conducted by the Society for Human Resource Management and *Fortune* magazine, reported in "Diversity Hiring in 2005: Are You in the Minority?" *Fortune* (January 24, 2005): 57–58.

8. Val Singh and Sébastien Point, "Strategic Responses by European Companies to the Diversity Challenge: An Online Comparison," *Long Range Planning* 37 (2004): 295–318.

9. Survey results reported in "Diversity Initiatives Shown to Be Critical to Job Seekers," *The New York Times Magazine* (September 14, 2003): 100.

10. Results reported in "Diversity Hiring in 2005."

11. Lennie Copeland "Valuing Diversity, Part I: Making the Most of Cultural Differences at the Workplace," *Personnel* (June 1988): 52–60.

12. Lee Smith, "The Business Case for Diversity" in "The Diversity Factor," *Fortune* (October 13, 2003): S1–S12.

13. Lennie Copeland, "Learning to Manage a Multicultural Workforce," *Training* (May 25, 1988): 48–56; and D. Farid Elashmawi, "Culture Clashes: Barriers to Business," *Managing Diversity* 2, no. 11 (August 1993): 1–3.

14. Singh and Point, "Strategic Responses by European Companies to the Diversity Challenge."

15. Marilyn Loden and Judy B. Rosener, *Workforce America!* (Homewood, IL: Business One Irwin, 1991); and Marilyn Loden, *Implementing Diversity* (Homewood, IL: Irwin, 1996).

16. Frances J. Milliken and Luis I. Martins, "Searching for Common Threads: Understanding the Multiple Effects of Diversity in Organizational Groups," *Academy of Management Review* 21, no. 2 (1996): 402–433.

17. David Leonhardt, "Who's in the Corner Office?" *The New York Times* (November 27, 2005), http://www.nytimes.com.

18. Robert Doktor, Rosalie Tung, and Mary Ann von Glinow, "Future Directions for Management Theory Development," *Academy of Management Review* 16 (1991): 362–365; and Mary Munter, "Cross-Cultural Communication for Managers," *Business Horizons* (May–June 1993): 69–78.

19. Renee Blank and Sandra Slipp, "The White Male: An Endangered Species?" *Management Review* (September 1994): 27–32; Michael S. Kimmel, "What Do Men Want?" *Harvard Business Review* (November–December 1993): 50–63; and Sharon Nelton, "Nurturing Diversity," *Nation's Business* (June 1995): 25–27.

20. Marianne Bertrand and Sendhil Mullainathan, *Are Emily and Greg More Employable than Lakisha and Jamal?* National Bureau of Economic Research report, as reported in L. A. Johnson, "What's in a Name: When Emily Gets the Job Over Lakisha," *The Tennessean* (January 4, 2004): 14A.

21. N. Songer, "Workforce Diversity," *B&E Review* (April–June 1991): 3–6; Lee Smith, "Closing the Gap," *Fortune* (November 14, 2005): 211–218; Prince, "Doing Diversity."

22. M. Bennett, "A Developmental Approach to Training for Intercultural Sensitivity," *International Journal of Intercultural Relations* 10 (1986): 179–196.

23. Prince, "Doing Diversity."

24. Michael L. Wheeler, "Diversity: The Performance Factor," *Harvard Business Review* (March 2005): S1–S7.

25. Jason Forsythe, "Winning with Diversity," *The New York Times Magazine* (March 28, 2004): 65–72; Amy Aronson, "Getting Results: Corporate Diversity, Integration, and Market Penetration," special advertising section, *BusinessWeek* (October 20, 2003): 140–144; and Nixon and West, "America Addresses Work Force Diversity,"

26. Wheeler, "Diversity: The Performance Factor."

27. G. Pascal Zachary, "Mighty Is the Mongrel," *Fast Company* (July 2000): 270–284.

28. Kimberly L. Allers with Nadira A. Hira, "The Diversity List," *Fortune* (August 22, 2005); Elizabeth Wasserman, "A Race for Profits," *MBA Jungle* (March–April 2003): 40–41; Amy Aronson, "Getting Results."

29. Immigrant statistics from the U.S. Census Bureau reported in Chris Woodyard, "Multilingual Staff Can Drive Up Auto Sales," *USA Today* (February 21, 2005), http://www.usatoday.com.

30. Bureau of Labor Statistics data reported in Prince, "Doing Diversity."

31. Stephanie N. Mehta, "What Minority Employees Really Want," *Fortune* (June 10, 2000): 181–186.

32. Harris, "The Illusion of Inclusion."

33. Jennifer L. Knight, Michelle R. Hebl, Jessica B. Foster, and Laura M. Mannix, "Out of Role? Out of Luck: The Influence of Race and Leadership Status on Performance Appraisals," *The Journal of Leadership and Organizational Studies* 9, no. 3 (2003): 85–93.

34. Mehta, "What Minority Employees Really Want."

35. Robert Hooijberg and Nancy DiTomaso, "Leadership In and Of Demographically Diverse Organizations," *Leadership Quarterly* 7, no. 1 (1996): 1–19.

36. Harris, "The Illusion of Inclusion"; and Smith, "Closing the Gap."

37. "Diversity in the Federal Government," report of a roundtable discussion on "Addressing Diversity Issues in the Government," July 10, 2003, moderated by Omar Wasow, executive director of BlackPlanet.com, reported in *The New York Times Magazine* (September 14, 2003): 95–99.

38. Quoted in Lee Smith, "The Business Case for Diversity."

39. Bryan Gingrich, "Individual and Organizational Accountabilities: Reducing Stereotypes and Prejudice within the Workplace," *Diversity Factor* 8, no. 2 (Winter 2000): 14–20.

40. Alison Stein Wellner, "The Disability Advantage," *Inc. Magazine* (October 2005): 29–31.

41. Copeland, "Valuing Diversity, Part I: Making the Most of Cultural Differences at the Workplace"; Judy and D'Amico, *Workforce 2020*; and S. Hutchins, Jr., "Preparing for Diversity: The Year 2000," *Quality Process* 22, no. 10 (1989): 66–68.

42. Fred L. Fry and Jennifer R. D. Burgess, "The End of the Need for Affirmative Action: Are We There Yet?" *Business Horizons* (November–December 2003): 7–16.

43. Roosevelt Thomas, Jr., "From Affirmative Action to Affirming Diversity," *Harvard Business Review* (March–April 1990): 107–117; Nicholas Lemann, "Taking Affirmative Action Apart," *The New York Times Magazine* (July 11, 1995): 36–43; and Terry H. Anderson, *The Pursuit of Fairness: A History of Affirmative Action* (New York: Oxford University Press, 2004).

44. Robert J. Grossman, "Behavior at Work," *HR Magazine* 46, no. 3 (March 2001): 50+; Madeline E. Heilman, Caryn J. Block, and Peter Stathatos, "The Affirmative Action Stigma of Incompetence: Effects of Performance Information Ambiguity," *Academy of Management Journal* 40, no. 1 (1997): 603–625.

45. Fry and Burgess, "The End of the Need for Affirmative Action"; and Erika H. James, Arthur P. Brief, Joerg Dietz, and Robin R. Cohen, "Prejudice Matters: Understanding the Reactions of Whites to Affirmative Action Programs Targeted to Benefit Blacks," *Journal of Applied Psychology* 86, no. 6 (December 2001): 1120+.

46. Greg Winter, "After Ruling, 3 Universities Maintain Diversity in Admissions," *The New York Times* (April 13, 2004): A22.

47. "Race Relations Better But Bias Persists, Poll Finds," *Jet* (May 3, 2004): 10.

48. Sheila Wellington, Marcia Brumit Kropf, and Paulette R. Gerkovich, "What's Holding Women Back?" *Harvard Business Review* (June 2003): 18–19.

49. Julie Amparano Lopez, "Study Says Women Face Glass Walls as Well as Ceilings," *The Wall Street Journal* (March 3, 1992): B1, B2; Ida L. Castro, "Q: Should Women Be Worried About the Glass Ceiling in the Workplace?" *Insight* (February 10, 1997): 24–27; Debra E. Meyerson and Joyce K. Fletcher, "A Modest Manifesto for Shattering the Glass Ceiling," *Harvard Business Review* (January–February 2000): 127–136; and Wellington, Brumit Kropf, and Gerkovich, "What's Holding Women Back?"; Finnegan, "Different Strokes."

50. Catalyst survey results reported in Forsythe, "Winning with Diversity."

51. Jory Des Jardins, "I Am Woman (I Think)," *Fast Company* (May 2005): 25–26; Lisa Belkin, "The Opt-Out Revolution," *The New York Times Magazine* (October 26, 2003): 43–47, 58; Annie Finnigan, "Different Strokes," *Working Woman* (April 2001): 42–48; and Meyerson and Fletcher, "A Modest Manifesto for Shattering the Glass Ceiling."

52. Statistics from the U.S. Census Bureau, Current Population Survey, 2004 Annual Social and Economic Supplement, as reported in "2003 Median Annual Earnings by Race and Sex," http://www.infoplease.com/ipa/A0197814.html; and "The Economics of Gender and Race: Examining the Wage Gap in

the United States,"The Feminist Majority Foundation Choices Campus Campaign, http://www.feministcampus.org.

53. Cliff Edwards, "Coming Out in Corporate America," *BusinessWeek* (December 15, 2003): 64–72; Belle Rose Ragins, John M. Cornwell, and Janice S. Miller, "Heterosexism in the Workplace: Do Race and Gender Matter?" *Group & Organization Management 28*, no. 1 (March 2003): 45–74.

54. Sylvia Ann Hewlett and Carolyn Buck Luce, "Off-Ramps and On-Ramps; Keeping Talented Women on the Road to Success," *Harvard Business Review* (March 2005): 43–54.

55. Belkin, "The Opt-Out Revolution."

56. John Byrne, "The Price of Balance," *Fast Company* (February 2004); Tischler, "Where Are the Women?" *Fast Company* (February 2004): 52–60; Patricia Sellers, "Power: Do Women Really Want It?" *Fortune* (October 13, 2003): 80–100.

57. C. J. Prince, "Media Myths: The Truth About the Opt-Out Hype," *NAFE Magazine* (Second Quarter 2004): 14–18; Sellers, "Power: Do Women Really Want It?"

58. Jia Lynn Yang, "Goodbye to All That," *Fortune* (November 14, 2005): 169–170.

59. Welllington et al., "What's Holding Women Back?"

60. The Leader's Edge/Executive Women Research 2002 survey, reported in "Why Women Leave," *Executive Female* (Summer 2003): 4.

61. Barbara Reinhold, "Smashing Glass Ceilings: Why Women *Still* Find It Tough to Advance to the Executive Suite," *Journal of Organizational Excellence* (Summer 2005): 43–55; Des Jardins, "I Am Woman (I Think)"; and Alice H. Eagly and Linda L. Carli, "The Female Leadership Advantage: An Evaluation of the Evidence," *The Leadership Quarterly* 14 (2003): 807–834.

62. Claudia H. Deutsch, "Behind the Exodus of Executive Women: Boredom," *USA Today* (May 2, 2005).

63. C. Soloman, "Careers under Glass," *Personnel Journal* 69, no. 4 (1990): 96–105; and Belle Rose Ragins, Bickley Townsend, and Mary Mattis, "Gender Gap in the Executive Suite: CEOs and Female Executives Report on Breaking the Glass Ceiling," *Academy of Management Executive* 12, no. 1 (1998): 28–42.

64. Eagly and Carli, "The Female Leadership Advantage: An Evaluation of the Evidence"; Reinhold, "Smashing Glass Ceilings"; Sally Helgesen, *The Female Advantage: Women's Ways of Leadership* (New York: Doubleday Currency, 1990); Rochelle Sharpe, "As Leaders, Women Rule: New Studies Find that Female Managers Outshine Their Male Counterparts in Almost Every Measure," *BusinessWeek* (November 20, 2000): 5+; and Del Jones, "2003: Year of the Woman Among the Fortune 500?" (December 30, 2003): 1B.

65. Reported in Mary Beth Marklein, "College Gender Gap Widens: 57% Are Women," *USA Today* (October 19, 2005), http://www.usatoday.com.

66. Michelle Conlin, "The New Gender Gap," *BusinessWeek* (May 26, 2003): 74–82; and "A Better Education Equals Higher Pay."

67. Quoted in Conlin, "The New Gender Gap."

68. Kathryn M. Bartol, David C. Martin, and Julie A. Kromkowski, "Leadership and the Glass Ceiling: Gender and Ethnic Group Influences on Leader Behaviors at Middle and Executive Managerial Levels," *The Journal of Leadership and Organizational Studies* 9, no. 3 (2003): 8–19; Bernard M. Bass and Bruce J. Avolio, "Shatter the Glass Ceiling: Women May Make Better Managers," *Human Resource Management* 33, no. 4 (Winter 1994): 549–560; and Rochelle Sharpe, "As Leaders, Women Rule," *BusinessWeek* (November 20, 2002): 75–84.

69. Dwight D. Frink, Robert K. Robinson, Brian Reithel, Michelle M. Arthur, Anthony P. Ammeter, Gerald R. Ferris, David M. Kaplan, and Hubert S. Morrisette, "Gender Demography and Organization Performance: A Two-Study Investigation with Convergence," *Group & Organization Management* 28, no. 1 (March 2003): 127–147; Catalyst research project cited in Reinhold, "Smashing Glass Ceilings."

70. Deutsch, "Behind the Exodus of Executive Women."

71. Jonathan D. Glater, "In Washington, Taking the Express Lane to Diversity," *The New York Times* (July 22, 2005), http://www.nytimes.com.

72. Smith, "Closing the Gap."

73. Abelson, "Can Respect Be Mandated?"

74. Jacqueline A. Gilbert and John M. Ivancevich, "Valuing Diversity: A Tale of Two Organizations," *Academy of Management Executive* 14, no. 1 (2000): 93–105; and Vanessa Weaver, "What These CEOs and Their Companies Know About Diversity," in "Winning with Diversity," *BusinessWeek*, (September 10, 2001).

75. Copeland, "Learning to Manage a Multicultural Workforce."

76. Amy Chozick, "Beyond the Numbers," *The Wall Street Journal* (November 14, 2005): R4.

77. R. Roosevelt Thomas, *Building on the Promise of Diversity: How We Can Move to the Next Level in Our Workplaces, Our Communities, and Our Society* (New York: AMACOM, 2006).

78. Reported in "Strength Through Diversity for Bottom-Line Success," *Working Woman* (March 1999).

79. Prince, "Doing Diversity."

80. Finnigan, "Different Strokes."

81. "Diversity in an Affiliated Company," in Vanessa J. Weaver, "Winning with Diversity," *BusinessWeek* (September 10, 2001).

82. Melanie Trottman, "A Helping Hand," *The Wall Street Journal* (November 14, 2005) R5, R9; B. Ragins, "Barriers to Mentoring: The Female Manager's Dilemma," *Human Relations* 42, no. 1 (1989): 1–22; and Ragins et al., "Gender Gap in the Executive Suite."

83. Trottman, "A Helping Hand."

84. David A. Thomas, "The Truth About Mentoring Minorities—Race Matters," *Harvard Business Review* (April 2001): 99–107.

85. Mary Zey, "A Mentor for All," *Personnel Journal* (January 1988): 46–51.

86. Joanne Sujansky, "Lead a Multi-Generational Workforce," *The Business Journal of Tri-Cities, Tennessee–Virginia* (February 2004): 21–23.

87. "Keeping Your Edge: Managing a Diverse Corporate Culture," *Fortune* (June 3, 2001).

88. Kimberly L. Allers, "Won't It Be Grand When We Don't Need Diversity Lists?" *Fortune* (August 22, 2005): 101.

89. J. Black and M. Mendenhall, "Cross-Cultural Training Effectiveness: A Review and a Theoretical Framework for Future Research," *Academy of Management Review* 15 (1990): 113–136.

90. Laura Egodigwe, "Back to Class," *The Wall Street Journal* (November 14, 2005): R4.

91. Smith, "Closing the Gap."

92. E. G. Collins, "Managers and Lovers," *Harvard Business Review* 61 (1983): 142–153.

93. Sharon A. Lobel, Robert E. Quinn, Lynda St. Clair, and Andrea Warfield, "Love Without Sex: The Impact of Psychological Intimacy Between Men and Women at Work," *Organizational Dynamics* (Summer 1994): 5–16.

94. Carol Hymowitz and Joann S. Lublin, "Many Companies Look the Other Way at Employee Affairs," *The Wall Street Journal* (March 8, 2005): B1; William C. Symonds with Steve Hamm and Gail DeGeorge, "Sex on the Job," *BusinessWeek* (February 16, 1998): 30–31.

95. "Sexual Harassment: Vanderbilt University Policy" (Nashville: Vanderbilt University, 1993).

96. Rachel Thompson, "Sexual Harassment: It Doesn't Go with the Territory," *Horizons* 15, no. 3 (Winter 2002): 22–26.

97. Statistics reported in Jim Mulligan and Norman Foy, "Not in My Company: Preventing Sexual Harassment," *Industrial Management* (September/October 2003): 26–29; also see *EEOC Charge Complaints,* http://www.eeoc.gov.

98. Jack Corcoran, "Of Nice and Men," *Success* (June 1998): 65–67.

99. Barbara Carton, "At Jenny Craig, Men Are Ones Who Claim Sex Discrimination," *The Wall Street Journal* (November 29, 1994): A1, A11.

100. Thompson, "Sexual Harassment: It Doesn't Go with the Territory."

101. Richard W. Judy and Carol D'Amico, *Workforce 2020: Work and Workers in the 21st Century* (Indianapolis, IN: Hudson Institute, 1997).

102. Joann S. Lublin, "Companies Use Cross-Cultural Training to Help Their Employees Adjust Abroad," *The Wall Street Journal* (August 4, 1992): B1, B9.

103. Gilbert Fuchsberg, "As Costs of Overseas Assignments Climb, Firms Select Expatriates More Carefully," *The Wall Street Journal* (January 9, 1992): B3, B4.

104. J. Kennedy and A. Everest, "Put Diversity in Context," *Personnel Journal* (September 1991): 50–54.

105. Egodigwe, "Back to Class."

106. "Impact of Diversity Initiatives on the Bottom Line: A SHRM Survey of the Fortune 1000," (pp. S12–S14), in *Fortune,* "Keeping Your Edge: Managing a Diverse Corporate Culture," produced in association with the Society for Human Resource Management, (June 3, 2001) http://www.fortune.com/sections.

107. Joseph J. Distefano and Martha L. Maznevski, "Creating Value with Diverse Teams in Global Management,"

Organizational Dynamics 29, no. 1 (Summer 2000): 45–63; and Finnigan, "Different Strokes."

108. W. E. Watson, K. Kumar, and L. K. Michaelsen, "Cultural Diversity's Impact on Interaction Process and Performance: Comparing Homogeneous and Diverse Task Groups," *Academy of Management Journal* 36 (1993): 590–602; G. Robinson and K. Dechant, "Building a Business Case for Diversity," *Academy of Management Executive* 11, no. 3 (1997): 21–31; and D. A. Thomas and R. J. Ely, "Making Differences Matter: A New Paradigm for Managing Diversity," *Harvard Business Review* (September–October 1996): 79–90.

109. Marc Hequet, Chris Lee, Michele Picard, and David Stamps, "Teams Get Global," *Training* (December 1996): 16–17.

110. Lionel Laroche, "Teaming Up," *CMA Management* (April 2001): 22–25.

111. See Distefano and Maznevski, "Creating Value with Diverse Teams" for a discussion of the advantages of multicultural teams.

112. Watson, Kumar, and Michaelsen, "Cultural Diversity's Impact on Interaction Process and Performance."

113. Distefano and Maznevski, "Creating Value with Diverse Teams."

114. This definition and discussion is based on Raymond A. Friedman, "Employee Network Groups: Self-Help Strategy for Women and Minorities," *Performance Improvement Quarterly* 12, no. 1 (1999): 148–163.

115. Ann C. Logue, "Girl Gangs: They Got It Goin' On," *Training & Development* (January 2001): 24–28.

116. "Leveraging Diversity: Opportunities in the New Market," Part III of "Diversity: The Bottom Line," *Forbes* (November 13, 2000).

117. Raymond A. Friedman and Brooks Holtom, "The Effects of Network Groups on Minority Employee Turnover Intentions," *Human Resource Management* 41, no. 4 (Winter 2002): 405–421.

118. Wassserman, "A Race for Profits."

119. Finnigan, "Different Strokes."

120. Raymond A. Friedman, Melinda Kane, and Daniel B. Cornfield, "Social Support and Career Optimism: Examining the Effectiveness of Network Groups Among Black Managers," *Human Relations* 51, no. 9 (1998): 1155–1177; "Diversity in the New Millennium," *Working Woman* (March 2000).

121. Snyder, "Cracker Barrel Is Striving to Shed Shadow of Bias Cases."

COSTCO WHOLESALE CORPORATION PART FOUR: COSTCO'S GENEROUS PAY YIELDS GENEROUS PROFITS

Attracting and retaining a loyal and productive workforce is essential to the success of any business. But in retailing, where employee turnover can nearly outpace rapidly churning inventories, a stable and satisfied workforce can be of critical importance. When it comes to cultivating human capital, Costco Wholesale Corp. stands heads and shoulders above its discount-retailing peers. The No. 1 membership warehouse chain boasts the highest-paid, most dependable workforce in the industry. This distinction stands in sharp contrast to prevalent labor trends, where many businesses have abandoned the lifetime-employee concept and are engaged in a lower-wages race to the bottom. When viewed against this backdrop, Costco's strategy for developing a loyal and empowered labor force is at once the most innovative and most controversial in retailing today.

Costco's unconventional approach to human resource management is immediately apparent in the recruitment of its warehouse workers. In keeping with the company's bare-bones, cost-cutting ethic that eliminates overhead and passes the savings to its customers, the big-box discounter doesn't retain outside recruiters, and the human resource staff doesn't participate in hiring. When a new warehouse is being built in a location, regional and local managers pitch office tents onsite to take applications and place help-wanted ads in area newspapers. After conducting interviews with job candidates, managers select hires and schedule training sessions, where the recruits are assigned a mentor. For their first assignment, trainees go on a scavenger hunt for information about their new company, gathering facts and reporting their discoveries to managers within the month. Once acclimated to the Costco way, the new workers finish their orientation and prepare for the store's grand opening. The entire process is carried out on a shoestring budget, in keeping with Costco's no-frills, low-budget operations philosophy.

Bolstering Costco's recruitment effort is one of the most generous compensation packages in retail. Costco's workers earn an average of $17 per hour—42 percent more than employees at rival Sam's Club and high above U.S. retail industry averages. Employees at this pay level are eligible for bonuses of between $2,000 and $3,000, and, after four years, full-time hourly employees earn $40,000 annually. Equally alluring are Costco's premium health benefits that are the envy of many American workers. Costco employees, whether part- or full-time, pay only 8 percent of healthcare costs, compared to the retail average of 25 percent. Topping it off is Costco's 401(k) program for new hires that eventually matches up to 9 percent of workers' annual pay.

The expense on such lavish compensation adds up: Costco's labor and benefit costs make up about 70 percent of its operating expenses, a lofty number that troubles some analysts who say the $60-billion-a-year retailer is showering benefits at the shareholders' expense. But CEO James Sinegal maintains that his company's investment in human capital is good business, not corporate altruism. "It absolutely makes good business sense," Sinegal states. "Most people agree that we're the lowest-cost provider. Yet we pay the highest wages. So it must mean we get better productivity . . . you get what you pay for." Costco financial chief Richard Galanti sees things in a similar light: "One of the things Wall Street chided us on is that we're too good to our employees . . . we don't think that's possible."

The numbers speak for themselves—Costco's workers stay longer and produce more than workers of competing retailers. After the first year, only 6 percent of Costco employees leave, compared with 21 percent at Sam's. With recruitment and training costs estimated at around $2,500 per trainee, a sizable retention rate means sizable savings. Moreover, Costco workers generate $918 in per square foot of retail space annually, outstripping worker productivity at other major retailers. Sam's Club employees yield $552 in sales per foot of space, and Wal-Mart and Target staffs produce $438 and $307 per foot, respectively.

Costco displays the same pro-worker mindset with the recruitment of top management. Sinegal has claimed that up to 98 percent of managerial positions are filled from within the company—in fact, most upper-level managers worked their way up the ladder starting at the warehouse floor. This official policy of promoting from within fosters loyalty and helps to develop warehouse managers, buyers, and executives who have thorough knowledge of the company. When sourcing such talent, recruiters look for leaders with people skills, smarts, and an entrepreneurial love of merchandising. The company has been accused of lacking diversity among top management, however. Sinegal admits that having 17 percent of management jobs occupied by women is low: "We don't let ourselves off the hook on that," he says. "We think we can do better. We know we can do better."

Costco's success proves that low prices for customers don't have to come at the expense of wages and benefits for workers. Sinegal chooses to save money elsewhere in the business while generating ample revenues through membership fees and high-volume sales. Reflecting Sinegal's labor-oriented values, Costco's top brass views people as a competitive advantage, not another expense to be reduced to the minimum. "Some companies control these expenses by figuring out how little they must pay their employees and how much of the health care cost they can pass on to their employees," Galanti remarks. "While we agree with the idea of cost efficiency, we believe the rest of that stuff is mostly about sacrificing the well-being of your employees in order to increase profits; we don't buy that. We believe you can do both."

Questions

1. What sacrifices does Costco make so that it may pay employees higher wages?

2. What are the benefits of promoting from within? What might be possible drawbacks to having a high internal promotion rate?

3. What steps could Costco take to foster greater diversity among its management, particularly as it relates to the promotion of women?

SOURCES: Michelle V. Rafter, "Welcome to the Club–Parts 1 & 2; Costco Employees Enjoy Some of the Most Generous Wages and Benefits Among U.S. Retailers" *Workforce Management,* April 1, 2005; Matthew Boyle, "Why Costco is So Damn Addictive," *Fortune,* October 30, 2006; S. Holmes and W. Zellner, "The Costco Way: Higher Wages Mean Higher Profits. But Try Telling Wall Street," *Business Week,* April 12, 2004; Steven Greenhouse, "How Costco Became the Anti-Wal-Mart," *The New York Times,* July 17, 2005; Nina Shapiro, "Company For the People," *Seattle Weekly,* December 15, 2004; Jim Underwood, *What's Your Corporate IQ?: How the Smartest Companies Learn, Transform, Lead,* Chicago, Ill.: Dearborn Trade, 2004, quoted in Cecil Johnson, "Treating Employees Well Is One Key to Firm's Success, Professor Writes," *Fort Worth Star-Telegram,* October 7, 2004.

CONTROLLING

Castles, fortresses, and fortifications were designed both to project power and for defense. The need to project power and control areas of interest leads to innovative designs in such structures. Sometimes changing technology can overcome what was once innovative. Or a line of defense that seems impenetrable is found to have an unexpected weakness. Two examples include Edinburgh Castle in Scotland and the Maginot Line in France.

Since the 7th century, some form of stronghold has been on the site of present-day Edinburgh Castle. The modern castle is the result of centuries of both expansion and destruction. In 1386, a tower was build to serve as the main entrance to what was then the castle. Called David's Tower after David II of Scotland who commissioned it, the tower was roughly 3 stories tall and enormous by the current standards. But in 1573, rebels loyal to the ousted Queen Mary of Scotland seized the castle. The legitimate Scot rulers called on Elizabeth I of England to assist them, and she sent heavy guns. The nearly 200 year old tower was no match for the modern armament and collapsed, forcing the rebels to surrender.

The Maginot Line was built during the peace (or paranoia, depending on your perspective) following World War I along the border between France and Germany as an attempt to prevent another frontal German invasion. It is a hallmark of architecture and engineering. Connected by underground tunnels, most of the fortresses that comprise the Maginot Line are not even visible from the surface but blend with the surrounding countryside. The fortresses themselves run three or four stories below ground. The line was designed to turn back a frontal German assault and there is little doubt it would have succeeded if that is what the Germans had tried. But when the time came, Germany simply went around the line, through occupied Holland and Belgium.

Managers must project power and maintain standards, but even the best control mechanism will prove useless if can be easily circumvented. Quality controls make certain that goals are still being met, products are being made to specification, customers are getting the desired service, and employees are upholding company ethics and standards. But changing technology requires innovation and imagination both in applying to technology to solve problems as well as addressing new problems that come along with the new technology. So along with the efficiencies gained by the computer age, managers must also address concerns such as inappropriate emails or employees misusing access to the Internet.

CHAPTER 14

CHAPTER OUTLINE

Manager's Challenge

The Meaning of Control

Organizational Control Focus

Feedforward Control

Concurrent Control

Feedback Control

Feedback Control Model

Steps of Feedback Control

Application to Budgeting

Financial Control

Financial Statements

Financial Analysis: Interpreting
the Numbers

The Changing Philosophy of Control

Total Quality Management

TQM Techniques

TQM Success Factors

**Trends in Quality and Financial
Control**

International Quality Standards

New Financial Control Systems

**Innovative Control Systems
for Turbulent Times**

Open-Book Management

The Balanced Scorecard

New Workplace Concerns

LEARNING OBJECTIVES

After studying this chapter, you should be able to:

1. Define organizational control and explain why it is a key management function.

2. Describe differences in control focus, including feedforward, concurrent, and feedback control.

3. Explain the four steps in the control process.

4. Discuss the use of financial statements, financial analysis, and budgeting as management controls.

5. Contrast the bureaucratic and decentralized control approaches.

6. Describe the concept of total quality management and major TQM techniques.

7. Identify current trends in financial control and discuss their impact on organizations.

8. Explain the value of open-book management and the balanced scorecard approaches to control in a turbulent environment.

MANAGERIAL AND QUALITY CONTROL

MANAGER'S CHALLENGE

Rude, insensitive, or condescending doctors have been around for as long as the medical profession, and the Rochester Independent Practice Association, like other medical groups, has its fair share. But medical director Dr. Howard Beckman fears that uncaring physicians are becoming more common as cost pressures put greater demands on doctors to see more patients. With less time to spend on each client, some doctors rely more on technology than on human interaction. Patients are rarely comfortable confronting a doctor when they feel they've been treated with indifference or disrespect. Those who are sufficiently offended or embarrassed simply never return, which hurts the doctor, the association, and the patient. With growing demands from patients, health insurers, and employers who purchase health plans for better customer service as well as increased efficiency, Dr. Beckman knows something must be done to boost doctors' communication skills and improve the overall quality of patient care.[1]

> What advice would you give Dr. Beckman and other administrators about using control systems and strategies to improve the quality of the doctor-patient interaction? What is the first step you would recommend they take?

Control is an important issue facing every manager in every organization. At Rochester Independent Practice Association, administrators have implemented new systems for cutting costs and increasing efficiency, but they also need to find new ways to maintain the quality of care, including the quality of the doctor-patient relationship. Other organizations face similar challenges, such as improving product quality, minimizing the time needed to resupply merchandise in retail stores, decreasing the number of steps needed to process an online merchandise order, or improving the tracking procedures for overnight package delivery. Control, including quality control, also involves office productivity, such as elimination of bottlenecks and reduction in paperwork mistakes. In addition, every organization needs basic systems for allocating financial resources, developing human resources, analyzing financial performance, and evaluating overall profitability.

This chapter introduces basic mechanisms for controlling the organization. We begin by summarizing the basic structure and objectives of the control process. Then we discuss controlling financial performance, including the use of budgets and financial statements. The next sections examine the changing philosophy of control, today's approach to total quality management, and recent trends such as ISO certification, economic value-added and market value-added systems, and activity-based costing. The chapter concludes with a discussion of control systems for a turbulent environment, including the use of open-book management and the balanced scorecard, and looks at some special control problems in today's workplace.

THE MEANING OF CONTROL

It seemed like a perfect fit. In the chaotic aftermath of 2005's Hurricane Katrina, the American Red Cross needed private-sector help to respond to the hundreds of thousands of people seeking emergency aid. Spherion Corp., a staffing company based in Fort Lauderdale, Florida, had the expertise to hire and train temporary workers fast, and the company had a good track record working with the Red Cross. Yet Red Cross officials soon noticed that an unusually large number of Katrina victim money orders, authorized by employees at the Spherion-staffed call center, were being cashed near the call center itself—in Bakersfield, California. A federal investigation found that some call-center employees were issuing money orders to fake hurricane victims and cashing them for themselves. Fortunately, the fraud was discovered quickly, but the weak control systems that allowed the scam to occur got both the Red Cross and Spherion into a public relations and political mess.[2]

A lack of effective control can seriously damage an organization's health, hurt its reputation, and threaten its future. Consider Enron, which was held up as a model of modern management in the late 1990s but came crashing down a couple of years later.[3] Numerous factors contributed to Enron's shocking collapse, including unethical managers and an arrogant, free-wheeling culture. But it ultimately comes down to a lack of control. No one was keeping track to make sure managers stayed within acceptable ethical and financial boundaries. Although former chairman and CEO Kenneth Lay claimed he didn't know the financial shenanigans were going on at the company, a Houston jury disagreed and found him guilty, along with former CEO Jeffrey Skilling, of conspiracy and fraud.[4] Some still believe that Lay—who died of a heart attack less than six weeks after the verdict—was telling the truth. However, at a minimum, he and other top leaders neglected their responsibilities by failing to set up and maintain adequate controls on the giant corporation. Since Enron, numerous organizations have established more clear-cut standards for ethical conduct and more stringent control systems regarding financial activities.

COURTESY OF HONEYWELL, INC.

CONCEPT

CONNECTION A new philosophy about **organizational control** involves lower-level workers in management and control decisions. At the Honeywell Industrial Automation and Control facility in Phoenix, employees' quality-control decisions cut defect rates by 70 percent, inventory by 46 percent, and customer lead times by an average of 75 percent.

Organizational control refers to the systematic process of regulating organizational activities to make them consistent with the expectations established in plans, targets, and standards of performance. In a classic article on the control function, Douglas S. Sherwin summarizes the concept as follows: "The essence of control is action which adjusts operations to predetermined standards, and its basis is information in the hands of managers."[5] Thus, effectively controlling an organization requires information about performance standards and actual performance, as well as actions taken to correct any deviations from the standards. To effectively control an organization, managers need to decide what information is essential, how they will obtain that information (and share it with employees), and how they can and should respond to it. Having the correct data is essential. Managers decide which standards, measurements, and metrics are needed to effectively monitor and control the organization and set up systems for obtaining that information. For example, an important metric for a pro football or basketball team might be the number of season tickets, which reduces the organization's dependence on more labor-intensive box-office sales.[6]

organizational control The systematic process through which managers regulate organizational activities to make them consistent with expectations established in plans, targets, and standards of performance.

ORGANIZATIONAL CONTROL FOCUS

Control can focus on events before, during, or after a process. For example, a local automobile dealer can focus on activities before, during, or after sales of new cars. Careful inspection of new cars and cautious selection of sales employees are ways to ensure high quality or profitable sales even before those sales take place. Monitoring how salespeople act with customers would be considered control during the sales task. Counting the number of new cars sold during the month or telephoning buyers about their satisfaction with sales transactions would constitute control after sales have occurred. These three types of control are formally called *feedforward*, *concurrent*, and *feedback,* and are illustrated in Exhibit 14.1.

Feedforward Control

Control that attempts to identify and prevent deviations before they occur is called **feedforward control**. Sometimes called *preliminary* or *preventive control*, it focuses on human, material, and financial resources that flow into the organization. Its purpose is to ensure that input quality is high enough to prevent problems when the organization performs its tasks.

Feedforward controls are evident in the selection and hiring of new employees. Organizations attempt to improve the likelihood that employees will perform up to standards by identifying the necessary skills, using tests and other screening devices to hire people who have those skills, and providing necessary training to upgrade important skills. The problems at Spherion and the Red Cross, referred to earlier, resulted primarily from weak feedforward controls. Severe time pressure and a sincere desire to get aid to the storm victims as quickly as possible caused Spherion to put new people in the call center before it completed all of its usual background checks and other tests. Numerous nursing homes and assisted living centers have come under fire in recent years due to lax feedforward controls, such as failing to ensure that workers have the appropriate skills or providing them with the training needed to adequately care for residents. Brookside Gables, an assisted living center in the Panhandle region of Florida, eventually closed after a

feedforward control Control that focuses on human, material, and financial resources flowing into the organization; also called *preliminary* or *preventive* control.

EXHIBIT 14.1

Organizational Control Focus

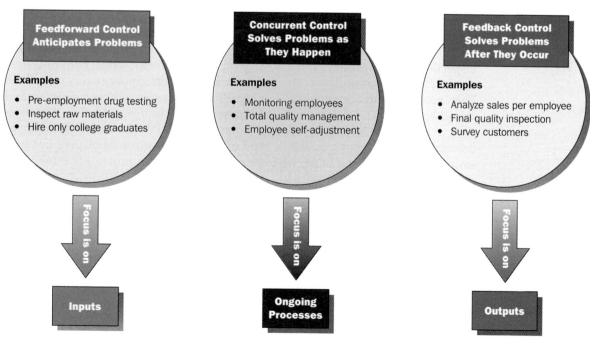

resident died because caregivers didn't have basic skills in first aid and emergency procedures.[7]

Another type of feedforward control is forecasting trends in the environment and managing risk. In tough economic times, for example, consulting companies such as A. T. Kearney stay in close touch with clients to monitor how much business and money will be coming in. The fashion company Liz Claiborne gathers information about consumer fads to determine what supplies to purchase and inventory to stock. Banks typically require extensive documentation before approving major loans to identify and manage risks.[8]

Concurrent Control

Control that monitors ongoing employee activities to ensure they are consistent with performance standards is called **concurrent control**. Concurrent control assesses current work activities, relies on performance standards, and includes rules and regulations for guiding employee tasks and behaviors.

Many manufacturing operations include devices that measure whether the items being produced meet quality standards. Employees monitor the measurements; if they see that standards are not met in some area, they make a correction themselves or signal the appropriate person that a problem is occurring. Technology advancements are adding to the possibilities for concurrent control in services as well. For example, retail stores such as Beall's, Sunglass Hut, and Saks use cash-register-management software to monitor cashiers' activities in real time and help prevent employee theft. Trucking companies like Schneider National and Covenant use computers to track the position of their trucks and monitor the status of deliveries.[9] This chapter's Shoptalk describes the widespread practice of monitoring employees' e-mail and Web use as a means of concurrent control.

Other concurrent controls involve the ways in which organizations influence employees. An organization's cultural norms and values influence employee behavior, as do the norms of an employee's peers or work group. Concurrent control also includes self-control, through which individuals impose concurrent controls on their own behavior because of personal values and attitudes.

Feedback Control

Sometimes called *postaction* or *output control*, **feedback control** focuses on the organization's outputs—in particular, the quality of an end product or service. An example of feedback control in a manufacturing department is an intensive final inspection of a refrigerator at an assembly plant. In Kentucky, school administrators conduct feedback control by evaluating each school's performance every other year. They review reports of students' test scores as well as the school's dropout and attendance rates. The state rewards schools with rising scores and brings in consultants to work with schools whose scores have fallen.[10] Performance evaluation, as described in Chapter 12, is also a type of feedback control. Managers evaluate employees' work output to see whether people are meeting previously established standards of performance.

Besides producing high-quality products and services and meeting other goals, businesses need to earn a profit, and even nonprofit organizations need to operate efficiently to carry out their missions. Therefore, many feedback controls focus on financial measurements. Budgeting, for example, is a form of feedback control because managers monitor whether they have operated within their budget targets and make adjustments accordingly. Most organizations also have outside audits of their financial records. The U.S. government set up a special office to investigate the reconstruction effort in Iraq, which includes auditing how funds are being spent.

concurrent control Control that consists of monitoring ongoing activities to ensure that they are consistent with standards.

feedback control Control that focuses on the organization's outputs; also called *postaction* or *output control*.

CYBERSLACKERS BEWARE: THE BOSS IS WATCHING

When employees have access to the Internet's vast resources, and the ability to communicate quickly via e-mail and instant messaging with anyone in the world, that's got to be good for productivity, right?

Not necessarily, as many organizations are discovering. Many companies are experiencing a growing problem with "cyberslackers," people who spend part of their workday sending personal e-mails, shopping, or downloading music and videos that hog available bandwidth and sometimes introduce viruses. In addition, it takes just a few bad apples engaging in harmful and possibly illegal activities, such as harassing other employees over the Web, to cause serious problems for their employers. So it's not surprising that since 2001, the use of increasingly sophisticated software to both block employees' access to certain sites and monitor their Internet and e-mail use has grown exponentially.

A certain degree of vigilance is clearly warranted. However, enlightened managers strive for a balanced approach that protects the organization's interests while at the same time maintaining a positive, respectful work environment. Surveillance overkill can sometimes cost more than it saves, and it can also have a distinctly negative impact on employee morale. At the very least, employees may feel as though they're not being treated as trustworthy, responsible adults.

Here are some guidelines for creating an effective but fair "acceptable use policy" for workplace Internet use.

:: *Make sure employees understand that they have no legal right to privacy in the workplace.* The courts so far have upheld an organization's right to monitor any and all employee activities on computers purchased by an employer for work purposes.

:: *Create a written Internet policy.* Make sure you clearly state what qualifies as a policy violation by giving clear, concrete guidelines for acceptable use of e-mail, the Internet, and any other employer-provided hardware or software. For example, spell out the types of Web sites that

are never to be visited while at work and what constitutes acceptable e-mail content. Are employees ever permitted to use the Web for personal use? If so, specify what they can do, for how long, and whether they need to confine their personal use to lunchtime or breaks. List the devices you'll be checking and tell them the filtering and monitoring procedures you have in place. Get employees to sign a statement saying they've read and understand the policy.

:: *Describe the disciplinary process.* Give people a clear understanding of the consequences of violating the organization's Internet and electronic use policy. Make sure they know the organization will cooperate if a criminal investigation arises.

:: *Review the policy at regular intervals.* You'll need to modify your guidelines as new technologies and devices appear.

Managers should remember that monitoring e-mail and Internet use doesn't have to be an all-or-nothing process. Some organizations use continuous surveillance; others only screen when they believe a problem exists, or they disseminate a policy and leave enforcement to the honor system. Look carefully at your workforce and the work they're doing, and assess your potential liability and security needs. Then come up with a policy and monitoring plan that makes sense for your organization.

SOURCES: Lorraine Cosgrove Ware, "People Watching," www.cio.com (August 15, 2005): 24; Art Lambert, "Technology in the Workplace: A Recipe for Legal Trouble," *Workforce.com* (February 14, 2005): www.workforce.com/archive/article/23/95/08.php?ht=lambert%20lambert; Technical Resource Group, "Employee E-mail and Internet Usage Monitoring: Issues and Concerns," www.picktrg.com/pubs/EmployeeMonitoring_WP062804.pdf; Pui-Wing Tam, Erin White, Nick Wingfield, and Kris Maher, "Snooping E-Mail by Software Is Now a Workplace Norm," *The Wall Street Journal* (March 9, 2005): B1; and Ann Sherman, "Firms Address Worries over Workplace Web Surfing," *Broward Daily Business Review* (May 17, 2006): 11.

As the inspector general in charge of probing U.S. rebuilding efforts in Iraq, Stuart Bowen oversees a staff of about 100 lawyers, investigators, and auditors divided between Baghdad and Arlington, Virginia.

Some of the feedback from Bowen's office has been troubling. For example, in an audit of the American office in charge of distributing reconstruction funds in Hillah, Iraq, Bowen found that one contractor had been paid twice for the same work. Of the $119.9 million allocated for regional projects, $89.4 million was disbursed without contracts or other documentation. An additional $7.2 million couldn't be found at all. In another investigation,

Coalition Provisional Authority (CPA) Inspector General

Bowen concluded that an American occupation authority failed to keep track of $9 billion that it transferred to Iraqi government ministries, which did not have their own financial controls and internal safeguards to prevent misuse of funds.

Paul Bremer, former head of the Coalition Provisional Authority (CPA), has harshly criticized Bowen's office for "misconceptions and inaccuracies" and for expecting the CPA to follow overly strict accounting standards amid postwar chaos. Bowen acknowledges that the organization is operating under difficult and dangerous conditions, yet he insists that the U.S. government should have established more effective control systems for oversight. He hopes his feedback can help the government do a better job as it continues the rebuilding effort. "My job is to help promote success in Iraq by identifying inefficiencies and helping correct them," Bowen says. "I want to be part of the solution."[11]

Bowen's statement reflects the purpose of feedback control—that is, to help the organization improve. Feedback from the CPA Inspector General's office indicates that U.S. officials need to establish stronger feedforward and concurrent controls as the reconstruction effort moves forward.

FEEDBACK CONTROL MODEL

All well-designed control systems involve the use of feedback to determine whether performance meets established standards. In this section, we will examine the key steps in the feedback control model and then look at how the model applies to organizational budgeting.

Steps of Feedback Control

Managers set up control systems that consist of the four key steps illustrated in Exhibit 14.2: establish standards, measure performance, compare performance to standards, and make corrections as necessary.

ESTABLISH STANDARDS OF PERFORMANCE

Within the organization's overall strategic plan, managers define goals for organizational departments in specific, operational terms that include a *standard of performance* against which to compare organizational activities. A standard of performance could include "reducing the reject rate from 15 to 3 percent," "increasing the corporation's return on investment to 7 percent," or "reducing the number of accidents to one per each 100,000 hours of labor." Managers should carefully assess what they will measure and how they will define it. For example, at pharmaceutical companies such as Wyeth, getting more productivity from research and development has become a top priority, so Wyeth's R&D chief Robert Ruffolo set firm targets for how many compounds must move forward at each stage of the drug

EXHIBIT 14.2

Feedback Control Model

development process. The clear standards have helped Wyeth boost the number of potentially hot products in its drug pipeline.[12]

Tracking such matters as customer service, employee involvement, and turnover is an important supplement to traditional financial and operational performance measurement, but many companies have a hard time identifying and defining nonfinancial measurements.[13] To effectively evaluate and reward employees for the achievement of standards, managers need clear standards that reflect activities that contribute to the organization's overall strategy in a significant way. Standards should be defined clearly and precisely so employees know what they need to do and can determine whether their activities are on target.[14]

MEASURE ACTUAL PERFORMANCE

Most organizations prepare formal reports of quantitative performance measurements that managers review daily, weekly, or monthly. These measurements should be related to the standards set in the first step of the control process. For example, if sales growth is a target, the organization should have a means of gathering and reporting sales data. If the organization has identified appropriate measurements, regular review of these reports helps managers stay aware of whether the organization is doing what it should.

In most companies, managers do not rely exclusively on quantitative measures. They get out into the organization to see how things are going, especially for such goals as increasing employee participation or improving customer satisfaction. Managers have to observe for themselves whether employees are participating in decision making and have opportunities to add to and share their knowledge. Interaction with customers is necessary for managers to really understand whether activities are meeting customer needs.

COMPARE PERFORMANCE TO STANDARDS

The third step in the control process is comparing actual activities to performance standards. When managers read computer reports or walk through the plant, they identify whether actual performance meets, exceeds, or falls short of standards. Typically, performance reports simplify such comparisons by placing the performance standards for the reporting period alongside the actual performance for the same period and by computing the variance—that is, the difference between each actual amount and the associated standard. To correct the problems that most require attention, managers focus on variances.

When performance deviates from a standard, managers must interpret the deviation. They are expected to dig beneath the surface and find the cause of the problem. If the sales goal is to increase the number of sales calls by 10 percent and a salesperson achieved an increase of 8 percent, where did she fail to achieve her goal? Perhaps several businesses on her route closed, additional salespeople were assigned to her area by competitors, or she needs training in making cold sales calls more effectively. Managers should take an inquiring approach to deviations in order to gain a broad understanding of factors that influence performance. Effective management control involves subjective judgment and employee discussions, as well as objective analysis of performance data.

EVAN KAFKA

CONCEPT CONNECTION Is it possible to make scientific discovery efficient? Managers at pharmaceuticals company Wyeth think so. They devised a streamlined research and development system driven by ambitious, quantifiable **standards of performance.** Managers routinely **compare performance to standards** and issue automated scorecards for each individual. Wyeth ties compensation to accomplishment of these all-or-nothing targets. "If the goal was to discover 12 drugs, 11 drugs are worth no points," says Wyeth Research President Robert Ruffolo Jr., who oversaw the reengineering effort. So far, the approach has yielded impressive results. With no additional investment, Wyeth has seen the number of new drugs that emerge from the early discovery phase increase fourfold.

As a new manager, apply the feedback control model to determine whether your team is functioning well or if changes are needed. Define clear standards of performance, measure outcomes regularly, and work with team members to take corrective actions when necessary.

TAKE CORRECTIVE ACTION

Managers also determine what changes, if any, are needed. In a traditional top-down approach to control, managers exercise their formal authority to make necessary changes. Managers may encourage employees to work harder, redesign the production process, or fire employees. In contrast, managers using a participative control approach collaborate with employees to determine the corrective action necessary.

In some cases, managers may take corrective action to change performance standards. They may realize that standards are too high or too low if departments continually fail to meet or routinely exceed standards. If contingency factors that influence organizational performance change, performance standards may need to be altered to make them realistic and to provide continued motivation for employees.

Managers may wish to provide positive reinforcement when performance meets or exceeds targets. For example, they may reward a department that has exceeded its planned goals or congratulate employees for a job well done. Managers should not ignore high-performing departments at the expense of taking corrective actions elsewhere. The online auction company eBay provides a good illustration of the feedback control model.

eBay

One of Meg Whitman's guiding rules is: "If you can't measure it, you can't control it." As CEO of eBay, Whitman runs a company that is obsessed with performance measurement. She personally monitors a slew of performance metrics, including standard measurements such as site visitors, new users, and time spent on the site, as well as the ratio of eBay's revenues to the value of goods traded.

Managers and employees throughout the company also monitor performance almost obsessively. Category managers, for example, have clear standards of performance for their auction categories (such as sports memorabilia; jewelry and watches; health and beauty; fashion, etc.). They are constantly measuring, tweaking, and promoting their categories to meet or outperform the targets.

Whitman believes getting a firm grip on performance measurement is essential for a company to know where to spend money, where to assign more personnel, and which projects to promote or abandon. But performance measurement isn't just about numbers. At eBay, "it's all about the customer," and gauging customer (user) satisfaction requires a mix of methods, such as surveys, monitoring eBay's discussion boards, and personal contact. Whitman gets her chance to really connect with users at the annual eBay Live conference. There, she wanders the convention-hall floor talking with anyone and everyone about their eBay experiences.

By defining standards, using a combination of measurement approaches, and comparing performance to standards, eBay managers are able to identify trouble spots and move quickly to take corrective action when and where it's needed.[15]

Application to Budgeting

Budgetary control, one of the most commonly used methods of managerial control, is the process of setting targets for an organization's expenditures, monitoring results and comparing them to the budget, and making changes as needed. As a control device, budgets are reports that list planned and actual expenditures for cash, assets, raw materials, salaries, and other resources. In addition, budget reports usually list the variance between the budgeted and actual amounts for each item.

I   Go to the experiential exercise on page 481 that pertains to budgetary control.   I

A budget is created for every division or department within an organization, no matter how small, as long as it performs a distinct project, program, or function. The fundamental unit of analysis for a budget control system is called a responsibility center. A **responsibility center** is defined as any organizational department or unit under the supervision of a single person who is responsible for its activity.[16] A three-person appliance sales office in Watertown, New York, is a responsibility center, as is a quality control department, a marketing department, and an entire refrigerator manufacturing plant. The manager of each unit has budget responsibility. Top managers use budgets for the company as a whole, and middle managers traditionally focus on the budget performance of their department or division. Budgets that managers typically use include expense budgets, revenue budgets, cash budgets, and capital budgets.

EXPENSE BUDGET

An **expense budget** includes anticipated and actual expenses for each responsibility center and for the total organization. An expense budget may show all types of expenses or may focus on a particular category, such as materials or research and development expenses. When actual expenses exceed budgeted amounts, the difference signals the need for managers to identify whether a problem exists and take corrective action if needed. The difference may arise from inefficiency, or expenses may be higher because the organization's sales are growing faster than anticipated. Conversely, expenses below budget may signal exceptional efficiency or possibly the failure to meet some other standards, such as a desired level of sales or quality of service. Either way, expense budgets help identify the need for further investigation but do not substitute for it.

REVENUE BUDGET

A **revenue budget** lists forecasted and actual revenues of the organization. In general, revenues below the budgeted amount signal a need to investigate the problem to see whether the organization can improve revenues. In contrast, revenues above budget would require determining whether the organization can obtain the necessary resources to meet the higher-than-expected demand for its products or services. Managers then formulate action plans to correct the budget variance.

CASH BUDGET

The **cash budget** estimates receipts and expenditures of money on a daily or weekly basis to ensure that an organization has sufficient cash to meet its obligations. The cash budget shows the level of funds flowing through the organization and the nature of cash disbursements. If the cash budget shows that the firm has more cash than necessary to meet short-term needs, the company can arrange to invest the excess to earn interest income. In contrast, if the cash budget shows a payroll expenditure of $20,000 coming at the end of the week but only $10,000 in the bank, the organization must borrow cash to meet the payroll.

CAPITAL BUDGET

The **capital budget** lists planned investments in major assets such as buildings, heavy machinery, or complex information technology systems, often involving expenditures over more than a year. Capital expenditures not only have a large impact on future expenses, they are investments designed to enhance profits. Therefore, a capital budget is necessary to plan the impact of these expenditures on cash flow and profitability. Controlling involves not only monitoring the amount of capital

responsibility center An organizational unit under the supervision of a single person who is responsible for its activity.

expense budget A budget that outlines the anticipated and actual expenses for a responsibility center.

revenue budget A budget that identifies the forecasted and actual revenues of the organization.

cash budget A budget that estimates and reports cash flows on a daily or weekly basis to ensure that the company has sufficient cash to meet its obligations.

capital budget A budget that plans and reports investments in major assets to be depreciated over several years.

expenditures but evaluating whether the assumptions made about the return on the investments are holding true. Managers can evaluate whether continuing investment in particular projects is advisable, as well as whether their procedures for making capital expenditure decisions are adequate. Some companies, including Boeing, Merck, Shell, United Technologies, and Whirlpool, evaluate capital projects at several stages to determine whether they are still in line with the company's strategy.[17]

Budgeting is an important part of organizational planning and control. Many traditional companies use **top-down budgeting**, which means that the budgeted amounts for the coming year are literally imposed on middle- and lower-level managers.[18] These managers set departmental budget targets in accordance with overall company revenues and expenditures specified by top executives. Although the top-down process provides some advantages, the movement toward employee empowerment, participation, and learning means that many organizations are adopting **bottom-up budgeting**, a process in which lower-level managers anticipate their departments' resource needs and pass them up to top management for approval.[19] Companies of all kinds are increasingly involving line managers in the budgeting process. At the San Diego Zoo, scientists, animal keepers, and other line managers use software and templates to plan their department's budget needs because, as CFO Paula Brock says, "Nobody knows that side of the business better than they do."[20] Each of the 145 zoo departments also does a monthly budget close and reforecast so that resources can be redirected as needed to achieve goals within budget constraints. Thanks to the bottom-up process, for example, the Zoo was able to quickly redirect resources to protect its valuable exotic bird collection from an outbreak of a highly infectious bird disease, without significantly damaging the rest of the organization's budget.[21]

FINANCIAL CONTROL

In every organization, managers need to watch how well the organization is performing financially. Not only do financial controls tell whether the organization is on sound financial footing, but they can be useful indicators of other kinds of performance problems. For example, a sales decline may signal problems with products, customer service, or sales force effectiveness.

Financial Statements

Financial statements provide the basic information used for financial control of an organization. Two major financial statements—the balance sheet and the income statement—are the starting points for financial control.

The **balance sheet** shows the firm's financial position with respect to assets and liabilities at a specific point in time. An example of a balance sheet is presented in Exhibit 14.3. The balance sheet provides three types of information: assets, liabilities, and owners' equity. *Assets* are what the company owns, and they include *current assets* (those that can be converted into cash in a short time period) and *fixed assets* (such as buildings and equipment that are long term in nature). *Liabilities* are the firm's debts, including both *current debt* (obligations that will be paid by the company in the near future) and *long-term debt* (obligations payable over a long period). *Owners' equity* is the difference between assets and liabilities and is the company's net worth in stock and retained earnings.

The **income statement**, sometimes called a profit-and-loss statement or P&L for short, summarizes the firm's financial performance for a given time interval, usually one year. A sample income statement is shown in Exhibit 14.4. Some organizations calculate the income statement at three-month intervals during the year to see whether they are on target for sales and profits. The income statement shows revenues coming into the organization from all sources and subtracts all expenses,

top-down budgeting A budgeting process in which middle- and lower-level managers set departmental budget targets in accordance with overall company revenues and expenditures specified by top management.

bottom-up budgeting A budgeting process in which lower-level managers budget their departments' resource needs and pass them up to top management for approval.

balance sheet A financial statement that shows the firm's financial position with respect to assets and liabilities at a specific point in time.

income statement A financial statement that summarizes the firm's financial performance for a given time interval; sometimes called a profit-and-loss statement.

New Creations Landscaping
Consolidated Balance Sheet
December 31, 2007

Assets			Liabilities and Owners' Equity		
Current assets:			Current liabilities:		
Cash	$ 25,000		Accounts payable	$200,000	
Accounts receivable	75,000		Accrued expenses	20,000	
Inventory	500,000		Income taxes payable	30,000	
Total current assets		$ 600,000	Total current liabilities		$ 250,000
Fixed assets:			Long-term liabilities:		
Land	250,000		Mortgages payable	350,000	
Buildings and fixtures	1,000,000		Bonds outstanding	250,000	
Less depreciation	200,000		Total long-term liabilities		$ 600,000
Total fixed assets		1,050,000	Owners' equity:		
			Common stock	540,000	
			Retained earnings	260,000	
			Total owners' equity		800,000
Total assets		$1,650,000	Total liabilities and net worth		$1,650,000

EXHIBIT 14.3

Balance Sheet

including cost of goods sold, interest, taxes, and depreciation. The *bottom line* indicates the net income—profit or loss—for the given time period.

The owner of Aahs!, a specialty retailing chain in California, used the income statement to detect that sales and profits were dropping significantly during the summer months.[22] He immediately evaluated company activities and closed two money-losing stores. He also began a training program to teach employees how to increase sales and cut costs to improve net income. This use of the income statement follows the control model described in the previous section, beginning with setting targets, measuring actual performance, and then taking corrective action to improve performance to meet targets.

Financial Analysis: Interpreting the Numbers

A manager needs to be able to evaluate financial reports that compare the organization's performance with earlier data or industry norms. These comparisons enable

New Creations Landscaping
Statement of Income
For the Year Ended December 31, 2007

EXHIBIT 14.4

Income Statement

Gross sales	$3,100,000	
Less sales returns	200,000	
Net sales		$2,900,000
Less expenses and cost of goods sold:		
Cost of goods sold	2,110,000	
Depreciation	60,000	
Sales expenses	200,000	
Administrative expenses	90,000	2,460,000
Operating profit		440,000
Other income		20,000
Gross income		460,000
Less interest expense	80,000	
Income before taxes		380,000
Less taxes	165,000	
Net income		$ 215,000

EXHIBIT 14.5

Common Financial Ratios

Liquidity Ratios	
Current ratio	Current assets/Current liabilities

Activity Ratios	
Inventory turnover	Total sales/Average inventory
Conversion ratio	Purchase orders/Customer inquiries

Profitability Ratios	
Profit margin on sales	Net income/Sales
Gross margin	Gross income/Sales
Return on assets (ROA)	Net income/Total assets

Leverage Ratios	
Debt ratio	Total debt/Total assets

the manager to see whether the organization is improving and whether it is competitive with others in the industry. The most common financial analysis focuses on ratios, statistics that express the relationships between performance indicators such as profits and assets, sales, and inventory. Ratios are stated as a fraction or proportion; Exhibit 14.5 summarizes some financial ratios, which are measures of an organization's liquidity, activity, profitability, and leverage. These ratios are among the most common, but many measures are used. Managers decide which ratios reveal the most important relationships for their business.

LIQUIDITY RATIOS

A **liquidity ratio** indicates an organization's ability to meet its current debt obligations. For example, the *current ratio* (current assets divided by current liabilities) tells whether the company has sufficient assets to convert into cash to pay off its debts, if needed. If a hypothetical company, Oceanographics, Inc., has current assets of $600,000 and current liabilities of $250,000, the current ratio is 2.4, meaning it has sufficient funds to pay off immediate debts 2.4 times. This level for the current ratio is normally considered a satisfactory margin of safety.

ACTIVITY RATIOS

An **activity ratio** measures internal performance with respect to key activities defined by management. For example, *inventory turnover* is calculated by dividing total sales by average inventory. This ratio tells how many times the inventory is used up to meet the total sales figure. If inventory sits too long, money is wasted. Dell Inc. has achieved a strategic advantage by minimizing its inventory costs. Dividing Dell's annual sales by its small inventory generates an inventory turnover rate of 35.7, up from 14 in 1997.[23] Another type of activity ratio, the *conversion ratio*, is purchase orders divided by customer inquiries. This ratio is an indicator of a company's effectiveness in converting inquiries into sales. For example, if Cisco Systems moves from 26.5 to 28.2 percent conversion ratio, more of its inquiries are turned into sales, indicating better sales activity.

PROFITABILITY RATIOS

Managers analyze a company's profits by studying **profitability ratios**, which state profits relative to a source of profits, such as sales or assets. One important profitability ratio is the *profit margin on sales*, which is calculated as net income divided by sales. Similarly, *gross margin* is the gross (before-tax) profit divided by total sales. Managers at Tesco.com, the online grocery service of Britain's top supermarket chain, pay close attention to the profit margin. Tesco.com managers implemented strict financial controls from the beginning. The online division was

liquidity ratio A financial ratio that indicates the organization's ability to meet its current debt obligations.

activity ratio A financial ratio that measures the organization's internal performance with respect to key activities defined by management.

profitability ratio A financial ratio that describes the firm's profits in terms of a source of profits (for example, sales or total assets).

immediately profitable, earning about \$6 on the average online sale, whereas U.S.-based Webvan, which eventually failed, lost about \$100 per sale because of its huge start-up costs and high operating expenses.[24]

Another profitability measure is *return on total assets (ROA)*, which is a percentage representing what a company earned from its assets, computed as net income divided by total assets. ROA is a valuable yardstick for comparing a company's ability to generate earnings with other investment opportunities. In basic terms, the company should be able to earn more by using its assets to operate the business than it could by putting the same investment in the bank. Caterpillar Inc., which produces construction and mining equipment, uses return on assets as its main measure of performance. It sets ROA standards for each area of the business and uses variances from the standards to identify whether the company is fully using its assets and improving operational efficiency. Since it began using ROA standards, Caterpillar has enjoyed double-digit returns.[25]

LEVERAGE RATIOS

Leverage refers to funding activities with borrowed money. A company can use leverage to make its assets produce more than they could on their own. However, too much borrowing can put the organization at risk such that it will be unable to keep up with repayment of its debt. Managers therefore track their *debt ratio*, or total debt divided by total assets, to make sure it does not exceed a level they consider acceptable. Lenders may consider a company with a debt ratio above 1.0 to be a poor credit risk.

bureaucratic control The use of rules, policies, hierarchy of authority, reward systems, and other formal devices to influence employee behavior and assess performance.

THE CHANGING PHILOSOPHY OF CONTROL

Managers' approach to control is changing in many of today's organizations. In connection with the shift to employee participation and empowerment, many companies are adopting a *decentralized* rather than a *bureaucratic* control process. Bureaucratic control and decentralized control represent different philosophies of corporate culture, which was discussed in Chapter 3. Most organizations display some aspects of both bureaucratic and decentralized control, but managers generally emphasize one or the other, depending on the organizational culture and their own beliefs about control.

Bureaucratic control involves monitoring and influencing employee behavior through extensive use of rules, policies, hierarchy of authority, written documentation, reward systems, and other formal mechanisms.[26] In contrast, decentralized control relies on cultural values, traditions, shared beliefs, and trust to foster compliance with organizational goals. Managers operate on the assumption that employees are trustworthy and willing to perform effectively without extensive rules and close supervision.

Exhibit 14.6 contrasts the use of bureaucratic and decentralized methods of control. Bureaucratic methods define explicit rules, policies, and procedures for employee behavior. Control relies on centralized authority, the formal hierarchy, and close personal supervision. Responsibility for quality control rests with quality control inspectors and supervisors rather than with employees. Job descriptions generally are specific and task related, and managers define minimal standards for acceptable employee performance. In exchange for meeting the standards, individual employees are given extrinsic rewards such

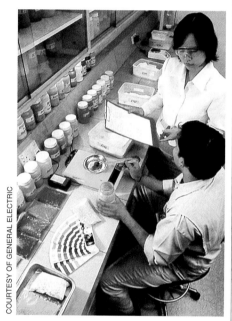

COURTESY OF GENERAL ELECTRIC

CONCEPT CONNECTION For more than a decade, managers at General Electric have been dedicated to **decentralized control** through a program called "Work Out." Work Out is an ongoing effort to achieve what former CEO Jack Welch called boundaryless behavior—behavior that "ends all barriers of rank, function, geography, and bureaucracy in an endless pursuit of the best idea." With boundaries diminished, GE launched **Six Sigma**, a disciplined methodology that focuses on quality for every process that affects the GE customer. Cindy Lee and S. Mani were part of a Six Sigma team at the color lab of the GE Plastics plant in Singapore. The team reduced the lead time for matching colors of GE resins to customer requirements by 85 percent, providing a distinct competitive advantage in the fast-paced global market for plastics.

EXHIBIT 14.6

Bureaucratic and Decentralized Methods of Control

SOURCES: Based on Ricahrd E. Walton, "From Control to Commitment in the Workplace," *Harvard Business Review* (March–April 1985), 76–84; and Don Hellriegel, Susan E. Jackson, and John W. Slocum, Jr., *Management,* 8th ed. (Cincinnati, Ohio: South-Western, 1999), 663.

Bureaucratic Control	Decentralized Control
Uses detailed rules and procedures; formal control systems	Limited use of rules; relies on values, group and self-control, selection and socialization
Top-down authority, formal hierarchy, position power, quality control inspectors	Flexible authority, flat structure, expert power, everyone monitors quality
Task-related job descriptions; measurable standards define minimum performance	Results-based job descriptions; emphasis on goals to be achieved
Emphasis on extrinsic rewards (pay, benefits, status)	Extrinsic and intrinsic rewards (meaningful work, opportunities for growth)
Rewards given for meeting individual performance standards	Rewards individual and team; emphasis on equity across employees
Limited, formalized employee participation (e.g., grievance procedures)	Broad employee participation, including quality control, system design, and organizational governance
Rigid organizational culture; distrust of cultural norms as means of control	Adaptive culture; culture recognized as means for uniting individual, team, and organizational goals for overall control

as wages, benefits, and possibly promotions up the hierarchy. Employees rarely participate in the control process, with any participation being formalized through mechanisms such as grievance procedures. With bureaucratic control, the organizational culture is somewhat rigid, and managers do not consider culture a useful means of controlling employees and the organization. Technology often is used to control the flow and pace of work or to monitor employees, such as by measuring how long employees spend on phone calls or how many keystrokes they make at the computer.

Bureaucratic control techniques can enhance organizational efficiency and effectiveness. Many employees appreciate a system that clarifies what is expected of them, and they may be motivated by challenging, but achievable, goals.[27] However, although many managers effectively use bureaucratic control, too much control can backfire. Employees resent being watched too closely, and they may try to sabotage the control system. One veteran truck driver expressed his unhappiness with electronic monitoring to a *Wall Street Journal* reporter investigating the use of devices that monitor truck locations. According to the driver, "It's getting worse and worse all the time. Pretty soon they'll want to put a chip in the drivers' ears and make them robots." He added that he occasionally escapes the relentless monitoring by parking under an overpass to take a needed nap out of the range of the surveillance satellites.[28]

In addition, some managers take bureaucratic control to an extreme, hovering over employees and micromanaging every detail, which is inefficient as well as damaging to morale and motivation.[29] The Qwest call center in Idaho Falls was about to go under partly as a result of overcontrolling front-line supervisors, until a new manager arrived with a different philosophy, as described in the Unlocking Innovative Solutions Through People box.

Decentralized control is based on values and assumptions that are almost opposite to those of bureaucratic control. Rules and procedures are used only when necessary. Managers rely instead on shared goals and values to control employee behavior. The organization places great emphasis on the selection and socialization of employees to ensure that workers have the appropriate values needed to

decentralized control The use of organizational culture, group norms, and a focus on goals, rather than rules and procedures, to foster compliance with organizational goals.

Unlocking Innovative Solutions Through | **PEOPLE** |

CONTROLLING WITH LOVE, NOT FEAR

"I would think of any reason not to go to work," says Chyanne Smith about her job at Qwest Communication's Idaho Falls call center. "I would think, 'Somebody hit me with a truck. I do not want to go to work today.'" Smith wasn't alone in her feelings. The environment at the call center, one of eleven Qwest Communications centers around the United States, was bleak. Doors slamming. People crying on the phone to their friends. Rumors that the center would soon close.

When Larry Walters, a 13-year Qwest veteran, took on the daunting challenge of pulling the Idaho Falls operation back from the brink of extinction, he realized the center was clear proof that control through fear and intimidation just doesn't work. One of Walters's first moves was to bring in the six so-called "coaches," front-line managers who supervised teams of 10–12 telephone representatives. Walters made it clear that these supervisors had to live up to the title of coach by helping people be their best. Four of the managers simply refused to go along with the new approach and were fired, sending a clear signal to the reps that it was a new day in Idaho Falls.

An important aspect of Walters's transformation was focusing people on clear performance standards, being consistent and direct about what he wanted, and letting people know how they were doing. Within the first week, Walters posted the call center's results on the walls for all to see, showing how the center ranked for sales, customer service, and attrition compared to other Qwest centers. "I wanted to start building that sense of pride in our center . . .," Walters says. "I was actually showing people, 'Do you realize we're last in sales right now? Does that bother you?'"

This focus on results could have landed flat, except for Walters's genuine concern for rank-and-file employees. His first question to an employee in the morning wouldn't be "How are your numbers?" but "How was your son's Little League game?" or "Did you have a fun weekend?" Walters got out on the floor and got to know people by name. He listened to their frustrations and made changes to alleviate them where he could. He dressed up in silly costumes. He stood on a desk in the middle of the building and told people he loved them and believed they could accomplish great things.

Before long, people were accomplishing great things. The center buzzed with activity and enthusiasm as figures for sales and customer service consistently went up. Sales productivity skyrocketed 68 percent. Within less than two years, the Idaho Falls center not only exceeded its sales target but ranked Number 1. Senior executives were so impressed that they decided to expand the center. Walters cried along with other managers and employees as the announcement was made.

Down to just 65 people and with the lights out in half of the building when Walters arrived in April 2003, the Idaho Falls center employed about 400 in two buildings by early 2005 and was the largest Qwest call center in the country. And what about Chyanne Smith? "I'm proud to come to work," she says, "and I'm proud to say I'm a Qwest employee."

SOURCE: Rodd Wagner, "Becoming the Best at Qwest," *Gallup Management Journal* (January 13, 2005): http://gmj.gallup.com/content/default.aspx?ci=14593&pg=3.

influence behavior toward meeting company goals. No organization can control employees 100 percent of the time, and self-discipline and self-control are what keep workers performing their jobs up to standard. Empowerment of employees, effective socialization, and training all can contribute to internal standards that provide self-control.

With decentralized control, power is more dispersed and is based on knowledge and experience as much as position. The organizational structure is flat and horizontal, as discussed in Chapter 10, with flexible authority and teams of workers solving problems and making improvements. Everyone is involved in quality control on an ongoing basis. Job descriptions generally are results-based, with an emphasis more on the outcomes to be achieved than on the specific tasks to be performed. Managers use not only extrinsic rewards such as pay, but the intrinsic rewards of meaningful work and the opportunity to learn and grow. Technology is used to empower employees by giving them the information they need to make effective decisions, work together, and solve problems. People are rewarded for team and organizational success as well as their individual performance, and the emphasis is on equity among employees. Employees participate in a wide range of areas, including setting goals, determining standards of performance, governing quality, and designing control systems.

With decentralized control, the culture is adaptive, and managers recognize the importance of organizational culture for uniting individual, team, and organizational goals for greater overall control. Ideally, with decentralized control, employees will pool their areas of expertise to arrive at procedures that are better than managers could come up with working alone.

■ **TAKE A MOMENT**

> What is your philosophy of control? As a new manager will you tend to watch things closely or give others freedom to perform? Complete the New Manager Self-Test on page 469 to get some feedback on your own beliefs about control.

TOTAL QUALITY MANAGEMENT

One popular approach based on a decentralized control philosophy is **total quality management (TQM)**, an organization-wide effort to infuse quality into every activity in a company through continuous improvement. Managing quality is a concern for every organization. The Yugo was the lowest-priced car on the market when it was introduced in the United States in 1985, yet four years later, the division went bankrupt, largely as a result of quality problems in both products and services.[30] In contrast, Toyota has steadily gained market share over the past several decades and will likely soon overtake General Motors as the world's top-selling auto maker.[31] The difference comes down to quality. Toyota is a model of what happens when a company makes a strong commitment to total quality management.

TQM became attractive to U.S. managers in the 1980s because it had been successfully implemented by Japanese companies, such as Toyota, Canon, and Honda, which were gaining market share and an international reputation for high quality. The Japanese system was based on the work of such U.S. researchers and consultants as Deming, Juran, and Feigenbaum, whose ideas attracted U.S. executives after the methods were tested overseas.[32] The TQM philosophy focuses on teamwork, increasing customer satisfaction, and lowering costs. Organizations implement TQM by encouraging managers and employees to collaborate across functions and departments, as well as with customers and suppliers, to identify areas for improvement, no matter how small. Each quality improvement is a step toward perfection and meeting a goal of zero defects. Quality control becomes part of the day-to-day business of every employee, rather than being assigned to specialized departments.

The implementation of total quality management is similar to that of other decentralized control methods. Feedforward controls include training employees to think in terms of prevention, not detection, of problems and giving them the responsibility and power to correct errors, expose problems, and contribute to solutions. Concurrent controls include an organizational culture and employee commitment that favor total quality and employee participation. Feedback controls include targets for employee involvement and for zero defects.

total quality management (TQM) An organization-wide commitment to infusing quality into every activity through continuous improvement.

TQM Techniques

The implementation of total quality management involves the use of many techniques, including quality circles, benchmarking, Six Sigma principles, reduced cycle time, and continuous improvement.

FREEDOM VERSUS REGULATION

What is your attitude toward organizational regulation and control? Organizations have to control people to survive, yet control should be the right amount and type. Companies are often less democratic than the society of which they are a part. Think honestly about your beliefs toward the regulation of other people and answer each item that follows as Mostly True or Mostly False.

	Mostly True	Mostly False
1. I believe people should be guided more by feelings and less by rules.	_____	_____
2. I think employees should be on time to work and to meetings.	_____	_____
3. I believe efficiency and speed are not as important as letting everyone have their say when making a decision.	_____	_____
4. I think employees should conform to company policies.	_____	_____

	Mostly True	Mostly False
5. I let my significant other make the decision and have his/her way most of the time.	_____	_____
6. I like to tell other people what to do.	_____	_____
7. I am more patient with the least capable people.	_____	_____
8. I like to have things running "just so."	_____	_____

SCORING AND INTERPRETATION: Give yourself 1 point for each Mostly True answer for the odd-numbered questions and 1 point for each Mostly False answer to the even-numbered questions. A score of 6 or above suggests you prefer decentralized control for other people in organizations. A score of three or less suggests a preference for more control and bureaucracy in a company. Enthusiastic new managers may exercise too much of their new control and get a negative backlash. However, too little control may mean less output. The challenge for new managers is to strike the right balance for the job and people at hand.

SOURCE: Adapted from J. J. Ray, "Do Authoritarians Hold Authoritarian Attitudes?" *Human Relations* 29 (1976): 307–325.

QUALITY CIRCLES

One technique for implementing the decentralized approach of TQM is to use quality circles. A **quality circle** is a group of 6 to 12 volunteer employees who meet regularly to discuss and solve problems affecting the quality of their work.[33] At a set time during the workweek, the members of the quality circle meet, identify problems, and try to find solutions. Circle members are free to collect data and take surveys. Many companies train people in team building, problem solving, and statistical quality control. The reason for using quality circles is to push decision making to an organization level at which recommendations can be made by the people who do the job and know it better than anyone else.

BENCHMARKING

Introduced by Xerox in 1979, benchmarking is now a major TQM component. **Benchmarking** is defined as "the continuous process of measuring products, services, and practices against the toughest competitors or those companies recognized as industry leaders to identify areas for improvement."[34] The key to successful benchmarking lies in analysis. Starting with its own mission statement, a company should honestly analyze its current procedures and determine areas for improvement. As a second step, a company *carefully* selects competitors worthy of

quality circle A group of 6 to 12 volunteer employees who meet regularly to discuss and solve problems affecting the quality of their work.

benchmarking The continuous process of measuring products, services, and practices against major competitors or industry leaders.

copying. For example, Xerox studied the order fulfillment techniques of L.L.Bean, the Freeport, Maine, mail-order firm, and learned ways to reduce warehouse costs by 10 percent. Companies can emulate internal processes and procedures of competitors, but must take care to select companies whose methods are compatible. Once a strong, compatible program is found and analyzed, the benchmarking company can then devise a strategy for implementing a new program.

SIX SIGMA

Six Sigma quality principles were first introduced by Motorola in the 1980s and were later popularized by General Electric, where former CEO Jack Welch praised Six Sigma for quality and efficiency gains that saved the company billions of dollars. Based on the Greek letter *sigma*, which statisticians use to measure how far something deviates from perfection, **Six Sigma** is a highly ambitious quality standard that specifies a goal of no more than 3.4 defects per million parts. That essentially means being defect-free 99.9997 percent of the time.[35] However, Six Sigma has deviated from its precise definition to become a generic term for a quality-control approach that takes nothing for granted and emphasizes a disciplined and relentless pursuit of higher quality and lower costs. The discipline is based on a five-step methodology referred to as *DMAIC* (Define, Measure, Analyze, Improve, and Control, pronounced "de-May-ick" for short), which provides a structured way for organizations to approach and solve problems.[36]

Effectively implementing Six Sigma requires a major commitment from top management, because Six Sigma involves widespread change throughout the organization. Hundreds of organizations have adopted some form of Six Sigma program in recent years. Highly committed companies, including ITT Industries, Motorola, General Electric, Allied Signal, ABB Ltd., and DuPont & Co., send managers to weeks of training to become qualified as Six Sigma "black belts." These black belts lead projects aimed at improving targeted areas of the business.[37] Although originally applied to manufacturing, Six Sigma has evolved to a process used in all industries and affecting every aspect of company operations, from human resources to customer service. Exhibit 14.7 lists some statistics that illustrate why Six Sigma is important for both manufacturing and service organizations. Cox Communications, Inc., based in Atlanta, Georgia, used Six Sigma to improve the "time to answer" metric for the company's help desk. According to Tom Guthrie, vice president of operations, the process enabled Cox to reduce staffing by 20 percent, saving big bucks, while also cutting the abandon rate (the number of calls abandoned before being answered) by 40 percent.[38]

REDUCED CYCLE TIME

Cycle time has become a critical quality issue in today's fast-paced world. **Cycle time** refers to the steps taken to complete a company process, such as teaching a class, publishing a textbook, or designing a new car. The simplification of work cycles,

Six Sigma A quality control approach that emphasizes a relentless pursuit of higher quality and lower costs.

cycle time The steps taken to complete a company process.

EXHIBIT   14.7

The Importance of Quality Improvement Programs

SOURCE: Based on data from *Statistical Abstract of the United States*, U.S. Postal Service, as reported in Tracy Mayor, "Six Sigma Comes to IT: Targeting Perfection," *CIO* (December 1, 2003): 62–70.

99 Percent Amounts to:	Six Sigma Amounts to:
117,000 pieces of lost first-class mail per hour	1 piece of lost first-class mail every two hours
800,000 mishandled personal checks each day	3 mishandled checks each day
23,087 defective computers shipped each month	8 defective computers shipped each month
7.2 hours per month without electricity	9 seconds per month without electricity

including dropping barriers between work steps and among departments and removing worthless steps in the process, enables a TQM program to succeed. Even if an organization decides not to use quality circles or other techniques, substantial improvement is possible by focusing on improved responsiveness and acceleration of activities into a shorter time. Reduction in cycle time improves overall company performance as well as quality.[39]

L.L.Bean is a recognized leader in cycle time control. Workers used flowcharts to track their movements, pinpoint wasted motions, and completely redesign the order-fulfillment process. Today, a computerized system breaks down an order based on the geographic area of the warehouse in which items are stored. Items are placed on conveyor belts, where electronic sensors re-sort the items for individual orders. After orders are packed, they are sent to a FedEx facility on site. Improvements such as these have enabled L.L.Bean to process most orders within two hours after the order is received.[40]

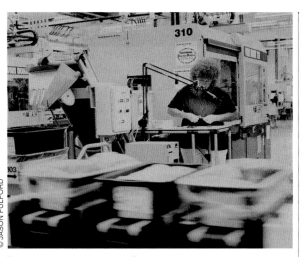

© JASON FULFORD

CONCEPT

CONNECTION Delphi Automotive Systems' injection-molding plant in Cortland, Ohio, produces a billion plastic housings a year for electrical connectors used in motor vehicles and telecom equipment. Delphi spent $14 million to renovate the building and another $30 million for production equipment, computers and software, and a network linking the factory floor with suppliers and customers. This investment in automation and e-business systems has greatly improved the plant's **cycle time**, enabling Delphi to churn out products faster than ever before. Even from his PC at home, plant superintendent John Stefanko can see what part a machine is currently making, whether it's taking 15, 18, or 20 seconds to do so, and how many parts it has made in the last 15 minutes.

CONTINUOUS IMPROVEMENT

In North America, crash programs and designs have traditionally been the preferred method of innovation. Managers measure the expected benefits of a change and favor the ideas with the biggest payoffs. In contrast, Japanese companies have realized extraordinary success from making a series of mostly small improvements. This approach, called **continuous improvement**, or *kaizen*, is the implementation of a large number of small, incremental improvements in all areas of the organization on an ongoing basis. In a successful TQM program, all employees learn that they are expected to contribute by initiating changes in their own job activities. The basic philosophy is that improving things a little bit at a time, all the time, has the highest probability of success. Innovations can start simple, and employees can build on their success in this unending process. Here's how one auto parts plant benefits from a TQM and continuous improvement philosophy.

continuous improvement
The implementation of a large number of small, incremental improvements in all areas of the organization on an ongoing basis.

The Dana Corporation's Perfect Circle Products Franklin Steel Products Plant in Franklin, Kentucky, manufactures as many as 3,500 different part numbers, primarily for automakers Ford, General Motors, and DaimlerChrysler, as well as thousands of after-market products. In one recent year, the company churned out about 60 million oil-ring expanders, for example.

Despite the high-volume, high-mix environment, Dana Franklin has maintained a 99 percent on-time delivery rate to customers since 2001. For the first six months of 2004, customer complaints were zero per million products sold, and the customer reject rate was zero parts per million. The plant has been named one of *Industry Week* magazine's 10 Best North American Manufacturing Facilities a record-setting six times. These results are amazing accomplishments for the plant's small workforce (just 44 production and management personnel), especially considering that some of the equipment they use is more than 50 years old. Yet the philosophy here is that with each unit produced, with each hour, with each day and each week, the plant gets just a little bit better. As plant manager Tim Parys says: "We've sort of adopted the Japanese philosophy in that the worst that the equipment ever runs is the day that you put it on the floor."

In addition to continuous improvement on the plant floor, typically two or three active Six Sigma initiatives are underway at any time in the plant. Almost everyone in the plant is a Six Sigma green belt or black belt. Dana Franklin holds regular four-day *kaizen* events, in which team members selected from the entire workforce focus on eliminating wasteful materials, activities, and processes. Production technician Ronnie Steenbergen is convinced that *kaizen* works and can enable the factory to squeeze out even more improvements from its "old machines."[41]

Dana Corp. Perfect Circle Products Franklin Steel Products Plant

EXHIBIT 14.8

Quality Program Success
Factors

Positive Factors	Negative Factors
• Tasks make high skill demands on employees.	• Management expectations are unrealistically high.
• TQM serves to enrich jobs and motivate employees.	• Middle managers are dissatisfied about loss of authority.
• Problem-solving skills are improved for all employees.	• Workers are dissatisfied with other aspects of organizational life.
• Participation and teamwork are used to tackle significant problems.	• Union leaders are left out of QC discussions.
• Continuous improvement is a way of life.	• Managers wait for big, dramatic innovations.

STEVE JONES

CONCEPT CONNECTION University of Miami public safety officers used to take a hit-or-miss approach to auto theft. The result: cars continued to disappear. To upgrade their tactics, a **continuous improvement** team collected data, analyzed it, and pinpointed exactly where and when thieves were most likely to strike. Now a marked patrol car and security guards on bicycles, similar to the ones being assembled by Smith & Wesson employees here, patrol known campus "hot spots." Car thefts dropped by approximately 75 percent. The continuous improvement effort continues because "ten auto thefts may seem like a small number, but it is ten more than we want."

Unfortunately, despite the effectiveness of the Franklin plant and the quality of its parts and service, the parent company, 102-year-old Dana Corp., filed for Chapter 11 bankruptcy protection in March of 2006. Production cutbacks by U.S. automakers, along with pressure from the automakers for ever-lower prices even as the cost of raw materials was skyrocketing pushed Dana into bankruptcy. The company is now struggling to restructure and survive in an increasingly tough industry.[42]

TQM Success Factors

Despite its promise, total quality management does not always work. A few firms have had disappointing results. In particular, Six Sigma principles might not be appropriate for all organizational problems, and some companies have expended tremendous energy and resources for little payoff.[43] Many contingency factors (listed in Exhibit 14.8) can influence the success of a TQM program. For example, quality circles are most beneficial when employees have challenging jobs; participation in a quality circle can contribute to productivity because it enables employees to pool their knowledge and solve interesting problems. TQM also tends to be most successful when it enriches jobs and improves employee motivation. In addition, when participating in the quality program improves workers' problem-solving skills, productivity is likely to increase. Finally, a quality program has the greatest chance of success in a corporate culture that values quality and stresses continuous improvement as a way of life, as at the Dana Franklin plant just described.

TRENDS IN QUALITY AND FINANCIAL CONTROL

Many companies are responding to changing economic realities and global competition by reassessing organizational management and processes—including control mechanisms. Some of the major trends in quality and financial control include international quality standards, economic value-added and market value-added systems, and activity-based costing.

International Quality Standards

One impetus for total quality management in the United States is the increasing significance of the global economy. Many countries have adopted a universal benchmark for quality assurance, **ISO certification**, which is based on a set of international standards for quality established by the International Standards Organization in Geneva, Switzerland.[44] Hundreds of thousands of organizations in 150 countries, including the United States, have been certified to demonstrate their commitment to quality. Europe continues to lead in the total number of certifications, but the greatest number of new certifications in recent years has been in the United States. One of the more interesting organizations to recently become ISO certified was the Phoenix, Arizona, Police Department's Records and Information Bureau. In today's environment, where the credibility of law enforcement agencies has been called into question, the Bureau wanted to make a clear statement about its commitment to quality and accuracy of information provided to law enforcement personnel and the public.[45] ISO certification has become the recognized standard for evaluating and comparing companies on a global basis, and more U.S. companies are feeling the pressure to participate in order to remain competitive in international markets. In addition, many countries and companies require ISO certification before they will do business with an organization.

> As a new manager, be aware of current trends in financial and quality control. Learn quality principles, new financial control systems, and open-book management and apply what works for you.

■ TAKE A MOMENT

New Financial Control Systems

In addition to traditional financial tools, managers in many of today's organizations are using systems such as economic value-added, market value-added, and activity-based costing to provide effective financial control.

ECONOMIC VALUE-ADDED (EVA)

Hundreds of companies, including AT&T, Quaker Oats, the Coca-Cola Company, and Philips Petroleum Company, have set up **economic value-added (EVA)** measurement systems as a new way to gauge financial performance. EVA can be defined as a company's net (after-tax) operating profit minus the cost of capital invested in the company's tangible assets.[46] Measuring performance in terms of EVA is intended to capture all the things a company can do to add value from its activities, such as run the business more efficiently, satisfy customers, and reward shareholders. Each job, department, process, or project in the organization is measured by the value added. EVA can also help managers make more cost-effective decisions. At Boise Cascade, the vice president of IT used EVA to measure the cost of replacing the company's existing storage devices against keeping the existing storage assets that had higher maintenance costs. Using EVA demonstrated that buying new storage devices would lower annual maintenance costs significantly and easily make up for the capital expenditure.[47]

MARKET VALUE-ADDED (MVA)

Market value-added (MVA) adds another dimension because it measures the stock market's estimate of the value of a company's past and projected capital investment projects. For example, when a company's market value (the value of all

ISO certification Certification based on a set of international standards for quality management, setting uniform guidelines for processes to ensure that products conform to customer requirements.

economic value-added (EVA) A control system that measures performance in terms of after-tax profits minus the cost of capital invested in tangible assets.

market value-added (MVA) A control system that measures the stock market's estimate of the value of a company's past and expected capital investment projects.

outstanding stock plus the company's debt) is greater than all the capital invested in it from shareholders, bondholders, and retained earnings, the company has a positive MVA, an indication that it has increased the value of capital entrusted to it and thus created shareholder wealth. A positive MVA usually, though not always, goes hand-in-hand with a high overall EVA measurement.[48] For example, in one study, General Electric had both the highest MVA and the highest EVA in its category (companies were categorized by size). Microsoft was ranked second in MVA but had a lower EVA rating than GE and many other companies. This comparison indicates that the stock market believes Microsoft has greater opportunities for further growth, which will, in turn, increase its EVA.[49]

Activity-Based Costing (ABC)

activity-based costing (ABC) A control system that identifies the various activities needed to provide a product and allocates costs accordingly.

Managers measure the cost of producing goods and services so they can be sure they are selling those products for more than the cost to produce them. Traditional methods of costing assign costs to various departments or functions, such as purchasing, manufacturing, human resources, and so on. With a shift to more horizontal, flexible organizations has come a new approach called **activity-based costing (ABC)**, which allocates costs across business processes. ABC attempts to identify all the various activities needed to provide a product or service and allocate costs accordingly. For example, an activity-based costing system might list the costs associated with processing orders for a particular product, scheduling production for that product, producing it, shipping it, and resolving problems with it. Because ABC allocates costs across business processes, it provides a more accurate picture of the cost of various products and services.[50] In addition, it enables managers to evaluate whether more costs go to activities that add value (meeting customer deadlines, achieving high quality) or to activities that do not add value (such as processing internal paperwork). They can then focus on reducing costs associated with non–value-added activities.

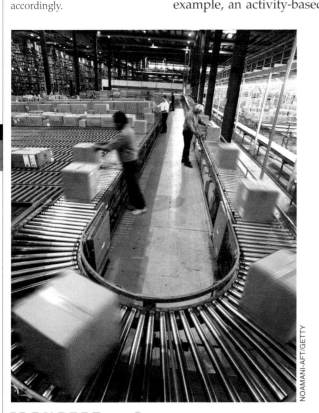

NOAMANI-AFT/GETTY

CONCEPT CONNECTION "Our goal was to build a company of business-literate associates," explains Chris Doyle of Dallas-based Cisco-Eagle, which assembles and services material handling systems such as the conveyor belt shown here. The employee-owned company practices a form of **open-book management** that shares all financials except for salaries. Each month, President Steve Strifler leads "huddles" via video and teleconference that allow people to review the previous month's performance. Inspired in part by their participation in an incentive system tied to the bottom line, employees take corrective actions, which often don't require managerial approval. The result is a highly motivated workforce about whom one observer marveled, "I don't think they ever tell their customers 'No.'"

INNOVATIVE CONTROL SYSTEMS FOR TURBULENT TIMES

As we have discussed throughout this text, globalization, increased competition, rapid change, and uncertainty have resulted in new organizational structures and management methods that emphasize information sharing, employee participation, learning, and teamwork. These shifts have, in turn, led to some new approaches to control. Two additional aspects of control in today's organizations are open-book management and use of the balanced scorecard.

Open-Book Management

In an organizational environment that promotes information sharing, teamwork, and the role of managers as facilitators, executives cannot hoard information and financial data. They admit employees throughout the organization into the loop of financial control and responsibility to encourage active participation and commitment to goals. A growing number of managers are opting for full disclosure in the form of open-book management. **Open-book management** allows employees to see for themselves—through charts, computer printouts, meetings, and so forth—the financial condition of the company. Second, open-book management shows the individual employee how his or her job fits into the big picture and affects the financial future of the organization. Finally, open-book management ties employee rewards to the company's overall success. With training in interpreting the financial data, employees can see the interdependence and importance of each function. If they are rewarded according to performance, they become motivated to take responsibility for their entire team or function, rather than merely their individual jobs.[51] Cross-functional communication and cooperation are also enhanced.

The goal of open-book management is to get every employee thinking and acting like a business owner. To get employees to think like owners, management provides them with the same information owners have: what money is coming in and where it is going. Open-book management helps employees appreciate why efficiency is important to the organization's success as well as their own. Open-book management turns traditional control on its head. Development Counsellors International, a New York City public relations firm, found an innovative way to involve employees in the financial aspects of the organization.

> When Andrew Levine took over as president of Development Counsellors International (DCI), the public relations firm founded by his father in 1960, he was eager to try open-book management. His first step was to add a financial segment to the monthly staff meeting, but employees just seemed bored. Most of them had no interest or skills in finance, statistics, and ratios.
>
> Rather than providing standard training, Levine had an idea: Why not appoint a different staffer each month to be CFO for the day. That person would be required to figure out the financials and then present the financial reports at the monthly staff meeting. His first appointment was the receptionist, Sergio Barrios, who met with Levine and the company's chief financial officer to go over the figures, look at any unusual increases or decreases in revenue or expenses, and talk about ideas to spark discussion. Levine was astounded by the reaction of staffers at the monthly meeting. Unlike Levine or another manager, Barrios was new to accounting and consequently explained things in a way that any layperson could understand. In addition, employees wanted to support Barrios as "one of their own," so they paid more attention and asked more questions.
>
> At each monthly meeting, the CFO of the day goes through a breakdown of the company's sales and expenses, points out irregularities and trends in the numbers, takes questions from other staff members, and sparks discussion of current financial issues. At the end of the report, the person reveals the bottom line, indicating whether the company met its profit goal for the month. Each time DCI's accumulated profit hits another $100,000 increment during the course of the year, 30 percent is distributed to employees.[52]

Development Counsellors International

DCI has been profitable ever since Levine began the CFO-of-the-day program. In addition, employees are happier with their jobs, so turnover has decreased. Clients tend to stick around longer too, because employees put more effort into building relationships. "Nobody wants to see a zero next to their client in the income column," Levine says.[53]

Managers in some countries have more trouble running an open-book company because prevailing attitudes and standards encourage confidentiality and even secrecy concerning financial results. Many businesspeople in countries such as China, Russia, and Indonesia, for example, are not accustomed to publicly disclosing financial details, which can present problems for multinational companies operating there.[54] Exhibit 14.9 lists a portion of a recent *Opacity Index*, which offers some indication of the degree to which various countries are open regarding economic matters. The higher the rating, the more opaque, or hidden, the economy of

open-book management
Sharing financial information and results with all employees in the organization.

EXHIBIT 14.9

International Opacity
Index: Which Countries
Have the Most Secretive
Economies?

SOURCE: Joel Kurtzman,
Glenn Yago, and Triphon
Phumiwasana, "The Opacity
Index, 2004," published by
*MIT Sloan Management
Review* (October 2004),
http://www.opacityindex.com
accessed on July 7, 2006.

Country	Opacity Rating
Indonesia	59
Venezuela	51
China	50
India	48
Russia	46
Mexico	44
Turkey	43
Korea	37
Thailand	35
Taiwan	34
Japan	28
Singapore	24
Canada	23
United States	21
Hong Kong	20
United Kingdom	19
Finland	13

The higher the opacity rating, the more secretive the national economy, meaning that prevailing attitudes and standards discourage openness regarding financial results and other data.

that country. In the partial index in Exhibit 14.9, Indonesia has the highest opacity rating at 59, and Finland the lowest at 13. The United States has an opacity rating of 21, which is fairly low on the index of countries. In countries with higher ratings, financial figures are typically closely guarded and managers may be discouraged from sharing information with employees and the public. Globalization is beginning to have an impact on economic opacity in various countries by encouraging a convergence toward global accounting standards that support more accurate collection, recording, and reporting of financial information.

The Balanced Scorecard

Another recent innovation is to integrate the various dimensions of control, combining internal financial measurements and statistical reports with a concern for markets and customers as well as employees.[55] Whereas many managers once focused primarily on measuring and controlling financial performance, they are increasingly recognizing the need to measure other, intangible aspects of performance to assess the value-creating activities of the contemporary organization.[56] Many of today's companies compete primarily on the basis of ideas and relationships, which requires that managers find ways to measure intangible as well as tangible assets.

One fresh approach is the balanced scorecard. The **balanced scorecard** is a comprehensive management control system that balances traditional financial measures with operational measures relating to a company's critical success factors.[57] A balanced scorecard contains four major perspectives, as illustrated in Exhibit 19.10: financial performance, customer service, internal business processes, and the organization's capacity for learning and growth.[58] Within these four areas, managers identify key performance metrics the organization will track. The *financial performance* perspective reflects a concern that the organization's activities contribute to improving short- and long-term financial performance. It includes traditional measures such as net income and return on investment. *Customer service* indicators measure such things as how customers view the organization, as well as customer retention and satisfaction. *Business process* indicators focus on production and operating statistics, such as order fulfillment or cost per order. The final component looks at the organization's *potential for learning and growth*, focusing on how well resources and human capital are being managed for the company's future. Metrics

balanced scorecard A comprehensive management control system that balances traditional financial measures with measures of customer service, internal business processes, and the organization's capacity for learning and growth.

Financial

Do actions contribute to improving financial performance?

Targets	Measures	Outcomes	Initiatives

Customers

How well do we serve our customers?

Targets	Measures	Outcomes	Initiatives

Mission and Goals

Internal Business Processes

Do internal activities and processes add value for customers and shareholders?

Targets	Measures	Outcomes	Initiatives

Learning and Growth

Are we learning, changing, and improving?

Targets	Measures	Outcomes	Initiatives

EXHIBIT 14.10

The Balanced Scorecard

SOURCES: Based on Robert S. Kaplan and David P. Norton, "Using the Balanced Scorecard as a Strategic Management System," *Harvard Business Review* (January–February 1996): 75–85; and Chee W. Chow, Kamal M. Haddad, and James E. Williamson, "Applying the Balanced Scorecard to Small Companies," *Management Accounting* 79, no. 2 (August 1997): 21–27.

may include such things as employee retention and the introduction of new products. The components of the scorecard are designed in an integrative manner, as illustrated in Exhibit 14.10.

Managers record, analyze, and discuss these various metrics to determine how well the organization is achieving its strategic goals. The balanced scorecard is an effective tool for managing and improving performance only if it is clearly linked to a well-defined organizational strategy and goals.[59] At its best, use of the scorecard cascades down from the top levels of the organization, so that everyone becomes involved in thinking about and discussing strategy.[60] The scorecard has become the core management control system for many organizations, including well-known organizations such as Bell Emergis (a division of Bell Canada), ExxonMobil, Cigna Insurance, British Airways, Hilton Hotels Corp., and even some units of the U.S. federal government.[61] British Airways clearly ties its use of the balanced scorecard to the feedback control model we discussed early in this chapter. Scorecards are used as the agenda for monthly management meetings. Managers focus on the various elements of the scorecard to set targets, evaluate performance, and guide discussion about what further actions need to be taken.[62] As with all management systems, the balanced scorecard is not right for every organization in every situation. The simplicity of the system causes some managers to underestimate the time and commitment that is needed for the approach to become a truly useful management control system. If managers implement the balanced scorecard using a *performance measurement* orientation rather than a *performance management* approach that links targets and measurements to corporate

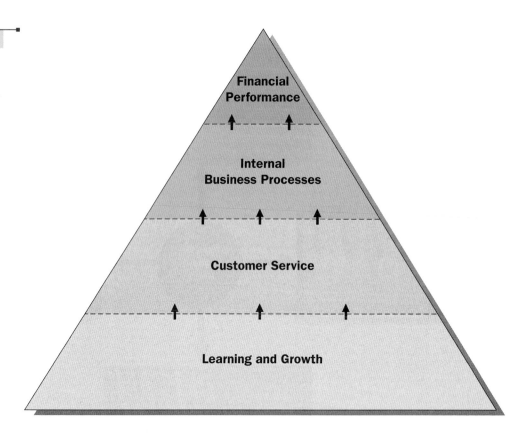

strategy, use of the scorecard can actually hinder or even decrease organizational performance.[63]

In addition, the scorecard has evolved from a system that places equal emphasis on the four categories of performance management illustrated in Exhibit 14.10 into a cause-effect relationship that calls attention to how organizations achieve higher performance. This adapted approach to the scorecard, illustrated in Exhibit 14.11, indicates that financial results are the final outcome of other processes within the company. The foundation of high financial performance is learning and growth, which reflects that it is an organization's people and culture that cause excellent business processes. Excellent business processes in turn cause customers to be satisfied. And happy customers lead to financial success. Thus, the components of the scorecard can be organized into a pyramid, indicating that each level shown in Exhibit 14.11 reinforces the level above it. Thus, high financial performance is an outgrowth of success in other areas, starting with a firm commitment to developing human capital and internal business processes.

New Workplace Concerns

Managers in today's organizations face some difficult control issues. The matter of control has come to the forefront in light of the failure of top executives and corporate directors to provide adequate oversight and control at companies such as Enron, HealthSouth, Adelphia, and WorldCom. Thus, many organizations are moving toward increased control, particularly in terms of **corporate governance**, which refers to the system of governing an organization so that the interests of corporate owners are protected. The financial reporting systems and the roles of boards of directors are being scrutinized in organizations around the world. At the same time, top leaders are also keeping a closer eye on the activities of lower-level managers and employees.

In a fast-moving environment, *undercontrol* can be a problem because managers can't keep personal tabs on everything in a large, global organization. Consider, for

corporate governance The system of governing an organization so the interests of corporate owners are protected.

example, that many of the CEOs who have been indicted in connection with financial misdeeds have claimed that they were unaware that the misconduct was going on. In some cases, these claims might be true, but they reflect a significant breakdown in control. In response, the U.S. government enacted the Sarbanes-Oxley Act of 2002, often referred to as SOX, which requires several types of reforms, including better internal monitoring to reduce the risk of fraud, certification of financial reports by top leaders; improved measures for external auditing; and enhanced public financial disclosure. SOX has been unpopular with many business leaders, largely because of the expense of complying with the act. In addition, some critics argue that SOX is creating a culture of overcontrol that is stifling innovation and growth. Even among those who agree that government regulation is needed, calls for a more balanced regulatory scheme that requires transparency and objectivity without restraining innovation are growing.[64]

■ TAKE A MOMENT

As a new manager, keep in mind that overcontrol can be just as detrimental to your team's performance as undercontrol. People resent being watched too closely. To keep a contemporary team working smoothly, find a balance between oversight and control on the one hand and mutual trust and respect on the other. Go to the ethical dilemma on page 481 that pertains to new workplace control issues.

Overcontrol of employees can be damaging to an organization as well. Managers might feel justified in monitoring e-mail and Internet use, as described earlier in the Manager's Shoptalk, for example, to ensure that employees are directing their behavior toward work rather than personal outcomes, and to alleviate concerns about potential racial or sexual harassment. Yet employees often resent and feel demeaned by close monitoring that limits their personal freedom and makes them feel as if they are constantly being watched. Excessive control of employees can lead to demotivation, low morale, lack of trust, and even hostility among workers. Managers have to find an appropriate balance, as well as develop and communicate clear policies regarding workplace monitoring. Although oversight and control are important, good organizations also depend on mutual trust and respect among managers and employees.

MANAGER'S SOLUTION

This chapter introduced a number of important concepts about organizational control. Organizational control is the systematic process through which managers regulate organizational activities to meet planned goals and standards of performance. The focus of the control system may include feedforward control to prevent problems, concurrent control to monitor ongoing activities, and feedback control to evaluate past performance. Well-designed control systems include four key steps: establish standards, measure performance, compare performance to standards, and make corrections as necessary.

At the Rochester Independent Practice Association, described in the chapter opening, Dr. Howard Beckman realized that, for doctors to improve the quality of their interaction with patients, they needed objective feedback about how they were doing. Beckman tapped into a growing trend among medical groups to use scientific methods to survey patient satisfaction and rate doctors on how well they're communicating. Many doctors were surprised by their low scores. To take corrective action, Beckman taught doctors communication skills, such as how to be a better listener and get patients to tell their complete story rather than immediately jumping in to suggest tests or medication. One doctor was skeptical but called

Beckman later and enthusiastically reported, "I can't believe how different it is. I hear things I don't usually hear." By giving doctors feedback, the Rochester Association is enabling them to provide better service, and most of them are happier with their patient interactions.[65]

The feedback control model also applies to budgeting, which is one of the most commonly used forms of managerial control. Managers might use expense budgets, revenue budgets, cash budgets, and capital budgets, for example. Other financial controls include use of the balance sheet, income statement, and financial analysis of these documents. Besides monitoring financial results, organizations control the quality of their goods and services. The application of total quality management (TQM) includes techniques such as quality circles, benchmarking, Six Sigma, reduced cycle time, and continuous improvement.

The philosophy of controlling has shifted to reflect changes in leadership methods. Traditional bureaucratic controls emphasize establishing rules and procedures, then monitoring employee behavior to make sure the rules and procedures are followed. With decentralized control, employees assume responsibility for monitoring their own performance.

Recent trends in control include the use of international quality standards, economic value-added (EVA) and market value-added (MVA) systems, and activity-based costing (ABC). Other important aspects of control in today's turbulent environment are open-book management and use of the balanced scorecard. In addition, concerns such as corporate governance and employee monitoring are significant issues for today's managers.

DISCUSSION QUESTIONS

1. You're a manager who employs a participative control approach. You've concluded that corrective action is necessary to improve customer satisfaction, but first you need to convince your employees that the problem exists. What kind of evidence do you think employees will find more compelling: quantitative measurements or anecdotes from your interactions with customers? Explain your answer.

2. How might a public school system use feedforward control to identify the best candidates for its teaching positions?

3. What are some examples of feedback control that might be used in a family-style restaurant? In a large hospital?

4. Think of a class you've taken in the past. What standards of performance did your professor establish? How was your actual performance measured? How was your performance compared to the standards? Do you think the standards and methods of measurement were fair? Were they appropriate to your assigned work? Why or why not?

5. Some critics argue that Six Sigma is a collection of superficial changes that often result in doing a superb job of building the wrong product or offering the wrong service. Do you agree or disagree? Explain.

6. In what ways could a university benefit from bureaucratic control? In what ways might it benefit from decentralized control? Overall, which approach do you think would be best at your college or university? Why?

7. What types of analysis can managers perform to help them diagnose a company's financial condition? How might a review of financial statements help managers diagnose other kinds of performance problems as well?

8. Why is benchmarking an important component of total quality management (TQM) programs? Do you believe a company could have a successful TQM program without using benchmarking?

9. How might activity-based costing provide better financial control tools for managers of a company such as Kellogg that produces numerous food products?

10. Why do you think today's managers would want to use the balanced scorecard to measure and control organizational performance? Think of two different kinds of organizations. Do you think the balanced scorecard approach is equally suitable for them both? Why or why not?

Is Your Budget in Control?

By the time you are in college, you are in charge of at least some of your own finances. How well you manage your personal budget may indicate how well you will manage your company's budget on the job. Respond to the following statements to evaluate your own budgeting habits. If the statement doesn't apply directly to you, respond the way you think you would behave in a similar situation.

1. I spend all my money as soon as I get it. Yes No

2. At the beginning of each week (or month, or term), I write down all my fixed expenses. Yes No

3. I never seem to have any money left over at the end of the week (or month). Yes No

4. I pay all my expenses, but I never seem to have any money left over for fun. Yes No

5. I am not putting any money away in savings right now; I'll wait until after I graduate from college. Yes No

6. I can't pay all my bills. Yes No

7. I have a credit card, but I pay the balance in full each month. Yes No

8. I take cash advances on my credit card. Yes No

9. I know how much I can spend on eating out, movies, and other entertainment each week. Yes No

10. I pay cash for everything. Yes No

11. When I buy something, I look for value and determine the best buy. Yes No

12. I lend money to friends whenever they ask, even if it leaves me short of cash. Yes No

13. I never borrow money from friends. Yes No

14. I am putting aside money each month to save for something that I really need. Yes No

Scoring and Interpretation

Yes responses to statements 2, 9, 10, 13, and 14 point to the most disciplined budgeting habits; *yes* responses to 4, 5, 7, and 11 reveal adequate budgeting habits; yes responses to 1, 3, 6, 8, and 12 indicate the poorest budgeting habits. If you have answered honestly, chances are you'll have a combination of all three. Look to see where you can improve your budgeting.

The Wages of Sin?

Chris Dykstra, responsible for loss prevention at Westwind Electronics, took a deep breath before he launched into making his case for the changes he was proposing in the company's shoplifting policy. He knew convincing Ross Chenoweth was going to be a hard sell. Ross, the president and CEO, was the son of the founder of the local, still family-owned consumer electronics chain based in Phoenix, Arizona. He'd inherited not only the company but also his father's strict moral code.

"I think it's time to follow the lead of other stores," Chris began. He pointed out that most other retailers didn't bother calling the police and pressing charges unless the thief had shoplifted merchandise worth more than $50 to $100. In contrast, Westwind currently had the zero-tolerance policy toward theft that Ross's father had put in place when he started the business. Chris wanted to replace that policy with one that only prosecuted individuals between 18 and 65, had stolen more than $20 worth of goods, and had no previous history of theft at Westwind. In the case of first-time culprits under 18 or over 65, he argued for letting them off with a strict warning regardless of the value of their ill-gotten goods. Repeat offenders would be arrested.

"Frankly, the local police are getting pretty tired of having to come to our stores every time a teenager sticks a CD in his jacket pocket," Chris pointed out. "And besides, we just can't afford the costs associated with prosecuting everyone." Every time he pressed charges against a shoplifter who'd made off with a $10 item, Westwind lost money. The company had to engage a lawyer and pay employees overtime for their court appearances. In addition, Chris was looking at hiring more security guards to keep up with the workload. Westwind was already in a battle it was losing at the moment with the mass retailers who were competing all too successfully on price, so passing on the costs of its zero-tolerance policy to customers wasn't really an option. "Let's concentrate on catching dishonest employees and those organized theft rings. They're the ones who are really hurting us," Chris concluded.

There was a long pause after Chris finished his carefully prepared speech. Ross thought about his recently deceased father, both an astute businessman and a person for whom honesty was a key guiding principle. If he were sitting here today, he'd no doubt say that theft was theft, that setting a minimum was tantamount to saying that stealing was acceptable just as long as you don't steal too much. He looked at

Chris. "You know, we've both got teenagers. Is this really a message you want to send out, especially to kids? You know as well as I do that there's nothing they like better than testing limits. It's almost an invitation to see if you can beat the system." But then Ross faltered as he found himself glancing at the latest financial figures on his desk—another in a string of quarterly losses. If Westwind went under, a lot of employees would be looking for another way to make a living. In his heart, he believed in his father's high moral standards, but he had to ask himself: Just how moral could Westwind afford to be?

What Would You Do?

1. Continue Westwind's zero-tolerance policy toward shoplifting. It's the right thing to do—and it will pay off in the end in higher profitability because the chain's reputation for being tough on crime will reduce overall losses from theft.

2. Adopt Chris Dykstra's proposed changes and show more leniency to first-time offenders. It is a more cost-effective approach to the problem than the current policy, plus it stays close to your father's original intent.

3. Adopt Chris Dykstra's proposed changes with an even higher limit of $50 or $100, which is still less than the cost of prosecution. In addition, make sure the policy isn't publicized. That way you'll reduce costs even more and still benefit from your reputation for prosecuting all shoplifters.

SOURCE: Based on Michael Barbaro, "Some Leeway for the Small Shoplifter," *The New York Times* (July 13, 2006): section C, 1.

CASE FOR CRITICAL ANALYSIS

Lincoln Electric

Imagine having a management system that is so successful people refer to it with capital letters—the Lincoln Management System—and other businesses benchmark their own systems by it. That is the situation of Ohio-based Lincoln Electric. For a number of years, other companies have tried to figure out Lincoln Electric's secret—how management coaxes maximum productivity and quality from its workers, even during difficult financial times. Lately, however, Lincoln Electric has been trying to solve a mystery of its own: Why is the company having such difficulty exporting a management system abroad that has worked so well at home?

Lincoln Electric is a leading manufacturer of welding products, welding equipment, and electric motors, with more than $1 billion in sales and 6,000 workers worldwide. The company's products are used for cutting, manufacturing, and repairing other metal products. Although it is now a publicly traded company, members of the Lincoln family still own more than 60 percent of the stock.

Lincoln uses a diverse control approach. Tasks are precisely defined, and individual employees must exceed strict performance goals in order to achieve top pay. The incentive and control system is powerful. Production workers are paid on a piece-rate basis, plus merit pay based on performance. Employees also are eligible for annual bonuses, which fluctuate according to the company's profits, and they participate in stock purchase plans. A worker's bonus is based on four factors: work productivity, work quality, dependability, and cooperation with others. Some factory workers at Lincoln have earned more than $100,000 a year.

However, the Lincoln system succeeds largely because of an organizational culture based on openness and trust, shared control, and an egalitarian spirit. To begin with, the company has earned employee trust with its no layoff policy. In fact, the last time it laid off anyone was in 1951. Although the line between managers and workers at Lincoln is firmly drawn, managers respect the expertise of production workers and value their contributions to many aspects of the business. The company has an open-door policy for all top executives, middle managers, and production workers, and regular face-to-face communication is encouraged. Workers are expected to challenge management if they believe practices or compensation rates are unfair. Most workers are hired right out of high school, then trained and cross-trained to perform different jobs. Some eventually are promoted to executive positions, because Lincoln believes in promoting from within. Many Lincoln workers stay with the company for life.

One of Lincoln's founders felt that organizations should be based on certain values, including honesty, trustworthiness, openness, self-management, loyalty, accountability, and cooperativeness. These values continue to form the core of Lincoln's culture, and management regularly rewards employees who manifest them. Because Lincoln so effectively socializes employees, they exercise a great degree of self-control on the job. Each supervisor oversees 100 workers, and less tangible rewards complement the piece-rate incentive system. Pride of workmanship and feelings of involvement, contribution, and esprit de corps are intrinsic rewards that flourish at Lincoln Electric. Cross-functional teams, empowered to make decisions, take responsibility for product planning, development, and marketing. Information about the company's operations and financial performance is openly shared with workers throughout the company.

Lincoln emphasizes anticipating and solving customer problems. Sales representatives are given the technical training they need to understand customer needs, help customers understand and use Lincoln's products, and solve problems. This customer focus is backed by attention to the production process through the use of strict accountability standards and formal measurements for productivity, quality, and innovation for all employees. In addition, a software program called Rhythm helps streamline the flow of goods and materials in the production process.

Lincoln's system worked so well in the United States that senior executives decided to extend it overseas. Lincoln built or purchased eleven plants in Japan, South America, and Europe, with plans to run the plants from the United States using Lincoln's expertise with management control systems. Managers saw the opportunity to beat local competition by applying manufacturing control incentive systems to reduce costs and raise production in plants around the world. The results were abysmal and nearly sunk the company. Managers at international plants failed to meet their production and financial goals every year—they exaggerated the goals sent to Lincoln's managers in order to receive more resources, especially during the recession in Europe and South America. Many overseas managers had no innate desire to increase sales, and workers were found sleeping on benches because not enough work was available. The European labor culture was hostile to the piecework and bonus control system. The huge losses in the international plants, which couldn't seem to adopt Lincoln's vaunted control systems, meant the company would have to borrow money to pay U.S. workers' bonuses, or forgo bonuses for the first time in Lincoln's history. Top managers began to wonder. Had they simply done a poor job of applying the Lincoln Management System to other cultures, or was it possible that it simply wasn't going to work abroad?

Questions

1. What types of control described in the chapter—feedforward, concurrent, or feedback—are illustrated in this case? Would you characterize Lincoln's control approach as primarily bureaucratic or decentralized? Explain your answers.

2. Based on what you've just read, what do you think makes the Lincoln System so successful in the United States?

3. What is the problem with transporting Lincoln's control systems to other national cultures? What suggestions would you make to Lincoln's managers to make future international manufacturing plants more successful?

4. Should Lincoln borrow money and pay bonuses to avoid breaking trust with its U.S. workers? Why or why not?

SOURCES: Based on Herb Greenberg, "Why Investors May Do Well with Firms That Avoid Layoffs," *The Wall Street Journal* (September 9, 2006): B4; Mark Gottlieb, "Feeding the Dragon," *Industry Week* 251, no. 1 (February 2002): 54–55; Donald Hastings, "Lincoln Electric's Harsh Lessons from International Expansion," *Harvard Business Review* (May–June, 1999): 3–11; and Joseph Maciariello, "A Pattern of Success: Can This Company Be Duplicated?" *Drucker Management* 1, no. 1 (Spring 1997): 7–11.

ENDNOTES

1. Gina Kolata, "When the Doctor Is In, But You Wish He Wasn't," *The New York Times* (November 30, 2005): www.nytimes.com.

2. Yochi J. Dreazen, "More Katrina Woes: Incidents of Fraud at Red Cross Centers," *The Wall Street Journal* (October 19, 2005): B1, B2.

3. John A. Byrne with Mike France and Wendy Zellner, "The Environment Was Ripe for Abuse," *BusinessWeek* (February 25, 2002): 118–120.

4. Bethany McLean and Peter Elkind, "The Enron Verdict: The Guiltiest Guys in the Room," *Fortune* (June 12, 2006): 26–28.

5. Douglas S. Sherwin, "The Meaning of Control," *Dunn's Business Review* (January 1956).

6. Russ Banham, "Nothin' But Net Gain," *eCFO* (Fall 2001): 32–33.

7. Kevin McCoy and Julie Appleby, "Problems with Staffing, Training Can Cost Lives," *USA Today* (May 26, 2004): www.usatoday.com

8. Carol Hymowitz, "As Economy Slows, Executives Learn Ways to Make Predictions," *The Wall Street Journal* (August 21, 2001): B1.

9. Jennifer S. Lee, "Tracking Sales and the Cashiers," *The New York Times* (July 11, 2001): C1, C6; Anna Wilde Mathews, "New Gadgets Track Truckers' Every Move," *The Wall Street Journal* (July 14, 1997): B1, B10.

10. Steve Stecklow, "Kentucky's Teachers Get Bonuses, But Some Are Caught Cheating," *The Wall Street Journal* (September 2, 1997): A1, A5.

11. Yochi J. Dreazen, "Digging In; Former Bush Aide Turns Tough Critic As Iraq Inspector," *The Wall Street Journal* (July 26, 2005): A1, A5.

12. Amy Barrett, "Cracking the Whip at Wyeth," *BusinessWeek* (February 6, 2006): 70–71.

13. Richard E. Crandall, "Keys to Better Performance Measurement," *Industrial Management* (January–February 2002): 19–24; Christopher D. Ittner and David F. Larcker, "Coming Up Short on Nonfinancial Performance Measurement," *Harvard Business Review* (November 2003): 88–95.

14. Crandall, "Keys to Better Performance Measurement."

15. Adam Lashinsky, "Meg and the Machine," *Fortune* (September 1, 2003): 68–78.

16. Sumantra Ghoshal, *Strategic Control* (St. Paul, MN: West, 1986): Chapter 4; and Robert N. Anthony, John Dearden, and Norton M. Bedford, *Management Control Systems*, 5th ed. (Homewood, IL: Irwin, 1984).

17. John A. Boquist, Todd T. Milbourn, and Anjan V. Thakor, "How Do You Win the Capital Allocation Game?" *Sloan Management Review* (Winter 1998): 59–71.

18. Anthony, Dearden, and Bedford, *Management Control Systems*.

19. Participation in budget setting is described in a number of studies, including Neil C. Churchill, "Budget Choice: Planning versus Control," *Harvard Business Review* (July–August 1984): 150–164; Peter Brownell, "Leadership Style, Budgetary Participation, and Managerial Behavior," *Accounting Organizations and Society* 8 (1983): 307–321; and Paul J. Carruth and Thurrell O. McClandon, "How Supervisors React to 'Meeting the Budget' Pressure," Management Accounting 66 (November 1984): 50–54.

20. Tim Reason, "Budgeting in the Real World," *CFO* (July 2005): 43–48.

21. Ibid.

22. Bruce G. Posner, "How to Stop Worrying and Love the Next Recession," *Inc.* (April 1986): 89–95.

23. Lawrence M. Fisher, "Inside Dell Computer Corporation," *Strategy and Business* 10, (First Quarter 1998): 68–75; and Randy Myers, "Cash Crop: The 2000 Working Capital Survey," *CFO* (August 2000): 59–69.

24. Andy Reinhardt, "Tesco Bets Small—And Wins Big," *BusinessWeek e.biz* (October 1, 2001): EB26–EB32.

25. Robin Goldwyn Blumenthal, "'Tis the Gift to Be Simple," *CFO* (January 1998): 61–63.

26. William G. Ouchi, "Markets, Bureaucracies, and Clans," *Administrative Science Quarterly* 25 (1980): 129–141; and B. R. Baligia and Alfred M. Jaeger, "Multinational Corporations: Control Systems and Delegation Issues," *Journal of International Business Studies* (Fall 1984): 25–40.

27. Sherwin, "The Meaning of Control."

28. Mathews, "New Gadgets Track Truckers' Every Move," B10.

29. Jared Sandberg, "Overcontrolling Bosses Aren't Just Annoying; They're Also Inefficient," *The Wall Street Journal* (March 30, 2005): B1.

30. John A. Parnell, C. W. Von Bergen, and Barlow Soper, "Profiting from Past Triumphs and Failures: Harnessing History for Future Success," *SAM Advanced Management Journal* (Spring 2005): 36–59.

31. Stephen Power and Guy Chazan, "Politics & Economics: Europe Auto Relations Get Testy; Car Makers' Friction with Workers Rises Over Plans to Relocate Jobs," *The Wall Street Journal* (June 15, 2006): A8.

32. A. V. Feigenbaum, *Total Quality Control: Engineering and Management* (New York: McGraw-Hill, 1961); John Lorinc, "Dr. Deming's Traveling Quality Show," *Canadian Business* (September 1990): 38–42; Mary Walton, *The Deming Management Method* (New York: Dodd-Meade & Co., 1986); and J. M. Juran and Frank M. Gryna, eds., *Juran's Quality Control Handbook,* 4th ed. (New York: McGraw-Hill, 1988).

33. Edward E. Lawler III and Susan A. Mohrman, "Quality Circles after the Fad," *Harvard Business Review* (January–February 1985): 65–71; and Philip C. Thompson, *Quality Circles: How to Make Them Work in America* (New York: AMACOM, 1982).

34. D. J. Ford, "Benchmarking HRD," *Training and Development* (July 1993): 37–41.

35. Tracy Mayor, "Six Sigma Comes to IT: Targeting Perfection," *CIO* (December 1, 2003): 62–70; Hal Plotkin, "Six Sigma: What It Is and How to Use It," *Harvard Management Update* (June 1999): 3–4; Tom Rancour and Mike McCracken, "Applying 6 Sigma Methods for Breakthrough Safety Performance," *Professional Safety* 45, no. 10 (October 2000): 29–32; G. Hasek, "Merger Marries Quality Efforts," *Industry Week* (August 21, 2000): 89–92; and Lee Clifford, "Why You Can Safely Ignore Six Sigma," *Fortune* (January 22, 2001): 140.

36. Dick Smith and Jerry Blakeslee "The New Strategic Six Sigma," *Training & Development* (September 2002): 45–52; Michael Hammer and Jeff Goding, "Putting Six Sigma in Perspective," *Quality* (October 2001): 58–62; and Mayor, "Six Sigma Comes to IT."

37. Plotkin, "Six Sigma: What It Is"; Timothy Aeppel, "Nicknamed 'Nag,' She's Just Doing Her Job," *The Wall Street Journal* (May 14, 2002): B1, B12; John S. McClenahen, "ITT's Value Champion," *IndustryWeek* (May 2002): 44–49.

38. M. Elisebeth Tyler, "Magic Number," *Microsoft Executive Circle* (Spring 2004): 31–32.

39. Philip R. Thomas, Larry J. Gallace, and Kenneth R. Martin, *Quality Alone Is Not Enough* (New York: American Management Association, August 1992).

40. Kate Kane, "L.L.Bean Delivers the Goods," *Fast Company* (August–September 1997): 104–113.

41. George Taninecz, "Change for the Better," *Industry Week* (October 2004): 49–50; and "Dana Corporation Earns Record Sixth Industry Week 10 Best Plants Award," *PR Newswire* (September 27, 2004): 1.

42. Sholnn Freeman, "Auto Parts Maker Files Chapter 11; Rising Costs, Cuts in Detroit Prompt Move by Dana Corp.," *The Washington Post* (March 4, 2006): D1; and Doron Levin, "Dana's Bankruptcy Is Payback to Ford, Other Automakers," *Pittsburgh Post-Gazette* (March 9, 2006): E8.

43. Clifford, "Why You Can Safely Ignore Six Sigma"; and Hammer and Goding, "Putting Six Sigma in Perspective."

44. Syed Hasan Jaffrey, "ISO 9001 Made Easy," *Quality Progress* 37, no. 5 (May 2004): 104; Frank C. Barnes, "ISO 9000 Myth and Reality: A Reasonable Approach to ISO 9000," *SAM Advanced Management Journal* (Spring 1998): 23–30; and Thomas H. Stevenson and Frank C. Barnes, "Fourteen Years of ISO 9000: Impact, Criticisms, Costs, and Benefits," *Business Horizons* (May–June 2001): 45–51.

45. David Amari, Don James, and Cathy Marley, "ISO 9001 Takes On a New Role—Crime Fighter," *Quality Progress* 37, no. 5 (May 2004): 57+.

46. Don L. Bohl, Fred Luthans, John W. Slocum Jr., and Richard M. Hodgetts, "Ideas That Will Shape the Future of Management Practice," *Organizational Dynamics* (Summer 1996): 7–14.

47. John Berry, "How to Apply EVA to I.T.," *CIO* (January 15, 2003): 94–98.

48. Stephen Taub, "MVPs of MVA," *CFO* (July 2003): 59–66; and K. Lehn and A. K. Makhija, "EVA and MVA as Performance Measures and Signals for Strategic Change," *Strategy & Leadership* (May–June 1996): 34–38.

49. Taub, "MVPs of MVA."

50. Sidney J. Baxendale, "Activity-Based Costing for the Small Business: A Primer," *Business Horizons* (January–February 2001): 61–68; Terence C. Pare, "A New Tool for Managing Costs," *Fortune* (June 14, 1993): 124–129; and Don L. Bohl, Fred Luthans, John W. Slocum Jr., and Richard M. Hodgetts,

"Ideas That Will Shape the Future of Management Practice," *Organizational Dynamics* (Summer 1996): 7–14.

51. Perry Pascarella, "Open the Books to Unleash Your People," *Management Review* (May 1998): 58–60.

52. Nadine Heintz, "Everyone's a CFO," *Inc.* (September 2005): 42, 45.

53. Ibid.

54. Mel Mandell, "Accounting Challenges Overseas," *World Trade* (December 1, 2001).

55. This discussion is based on a review of the balanced scorecard in Richard L. Daft, *Organization Theory and Design*, 7th ed. (Cincinnati, OH: South-Western, 2001): 300–301.

56. "On Balance," a *CFO* Interview with Robert Kaplan and David Norton, *CFO* (February 2001): 73–78; and Bill Birchard, "Intangible Assets + Hard Numbers = Soft Finance," *Fast Company* (October 1999): 316–336.

57. Robert Kaplan and David Norton, "The Balanced Scorecard: Measures That Drive Performance," *Harvard Business Review* (January–February 1992): 71–79; and Chee W. Chow, Kamal M. Haddad, and James E. Williamson, "Applying the Balanced Scorecard to Small Companies," *Management Accounting* 79, no. 2 (August 1997): 21–27.

58. Based on Kaplan and Norton, "The Balanced Scorecard"; Chow, Haddad, and Williamson, "Applying the Balanced Scorecard"; and Cathy Lazere, "All Together Now," *CFO* (February 1998): 28–36.

59. Geert J. M. Braam and Edwin J. Nijssen, "Performance Effects of Using the Balanced Scorecard: A Note on the Dutch Experience," *Long Range Planning* 37 (2004): 335–349; Kaplan and Norton, "The Balanced Scorecard"; and Cam Scholey, "Strategy Maps: A Step-by-Step Guide to Measuring, Managing, and Communicating the Plan," *Journal of Business Strategy* 26, no. 3 (2005): 12–19.

60. Nils-Göran Olve, Carl-Johan Petri, Jan Roy, and Sofie Roy, "Twelve Years Later: Understanding and Realizing the Value of Balanced Scorecards," *Ivey Business Journal* (May–June 2004); Eric M. Olson and Stanley F. Slater, "The Balanced Scorecard, Competitive Strategy, and Performance," *Business Horizons* (May–June 2002): 11–16; and Eric Berkman, "How to Use the Balanced Scorecard," *CIO* (May 15, 2002): 93–100.

61. Ibid.; and Brigitte W. Schay, Mary Ellen Beach, Jacqueline A. Caldwell, and Christelle LaPolice, "Using Standardized Outcome Measures in the Federal Government," *Human Resource Management* 41, no. 3 (Fall 2002): 355–368.

62. Olve et al., "Twelve Years Later: Understanding and Realizing the Value of Balanced Scorecards."

63. Braam and Nijssen, "Performance Effects of Using the Balanced Scorecard."

64. "Business: The Trial of Sarbanes-Oxley; Regulating Business," *The Economist* (April 22, 2006): 69; and Maurice R. Greenberg, "Regulation, Yes; Stangulation, No," *The Wall Street Journal* (August 21, 2006): A10.

65. Kolata, "When the Doctor Is In, But You Wish He Wasn't."

CHAPTER 15

CHAPTER OUTLINE

Manager's Challenge

Information Technology Has
Changed Everything

Boundaries Dissolve; Collaboration
Reigns

People Do Better Work

Things Are More Efficient

Employees Are Engaged

People Can Suffer from Information
Overload

The Evolving World of Information
Technology

A New Generation of IT

Applying New IT Within
Organizations

Types of Information Systems

Data Versus Information

Operations Information Systems

Management Information Systems

The Internet and E-Business

E-Business Strategies

E-Marketplaces

Enterprise Resource Planning
Systems

Customer Relationship
Management

Turning Data and Information
into Knowledge

LEARNING OBJECTIVES

After studying this chapter, you should be able to:

1. Explain the importance of information technology for organizations and discuss specific ways in which IT has changed the manager's job.

2. Describe new developments in information technology and identify the different types of IT systems used in organizations.

3. Tell how information systems support daily operations and decision making.

4. Summarize the key components of e-business and explain e-business strategies.

5. Describe enterprise resource planning and customer relationship management systems.

6. Explain the importance of knowledge management and business intelligence in today's organizations.

INFORMATION TECHNOLOGY AND E-BUSINESS

MANAGER'S CHALLENGE

As the public relations firm for Wal-Mart, Edelman is facing a tough challenge. The giant corporation has been under steady assault, with critics accusing the retailer of all manner of evil, from driving local retailers out of business, to paying workers pitiful wages, to squeezing suppliers to death. Protestors carrying signs outside stores started the criticism decades ago, but the Internet has intensified the damage. A single Wal-Mart detractor can go from zero to global in just a few minutes, using Web sites and blogs to spread negative opinions, rumors, or company mistakes. Bloggers had a field day after the group Wal-Mart Watch leaked an internal draft memo about health benefits to *The New York Times*, then posted excerpts on its Web site. In the memo, Wal-Mart's executive vice president for benefits indicated that the company's health plan requires such high out-of-pocket payments that employees hit by a costly illness "almost certainly end up declaring personal bankruptcy." The memo also proposed that the company rewrite job descriptions to involve more physical activity to "dissuade unhealthy people from coming to work at Wal-Mart." These revelations added fuel to the already raging storm in the blogosphere over the company's alleged poor treatment of its workers. Considering how fast bad publicity spreads on the Internet, some of Edelman's PR staff began wondering how the company might use the Internet to more quickly tell its side of the story.[1]

TAKE A MOMENT

If you were a PR consultant to Wal-Mart, what would you suggest the company do to rapidly respond to new charges of wrongdoing and get its side of the story out to the public? Do you think Wal-Mart can use the power of the Internet to improve its battered image?

The Internet, little more than a curiosity to many managers just a decade ago, now influences their lives and jobs in myriad ways. Managers at Arch Coal use the Internet and GPS networking to monitor and manage major mining equipment. Trinchero Family Estates, producer of Sutter Hill wines, uses an online system to track the processing of grapes from harvesting to bottling to selling. And the American Society for the Prevention of Cruelty to Animals used the Web to quickly recruit volunteers after Hurricane Katrina—even though the organization had never before recruited volunteers in its 130-year history.[2] Some companies, such as Wal-Mart, are profiting by using Web sites to sell more products, but also discovering that the Internet has drawbacks.

Almost every company uses the Internet to some extent as part of its information technology system. The strategic use of information technology is one of the defining aspects of organizational success in today's world. Indeed, Wal-Mart is a classic example of the effective use of information technology to improve operational efficiency and manage every aspect of the business. Managers use information systems that rely on a massive data warehouse to make decisions about what to stock, how to price and promote it, and when to reorder or discontinue items.

Handheld scanners enable managers to keep close tabs on inventory and monitor sales; at the end of each workday, orders for new merchandise are sent by computer to headquarters, where they are automatically organized and sent to regional distribution centers, which have electronic linkages with key suppliers for reordering. A recent innovation is using tiny chips with identification numbers on shipments of products (called radio-frequency identification, or RFID), which enables close tracking of inventory all through the supply chain. Back at headquarters, top Wal-Mart executives analyze buying patterns and other information, enabling them to spot problems or opportunities and convey the information to stores.[3] Numerous other companies, in industries from manufacturing to entertainment, as well as not-for-profit and government organizations, are using information technology to get closer to customers, enter new markets, and streamline business processes.

Information technology and e-business have changed the way people and organizations work and thus present new challenges for managers. The Internet continues to disrupt and transform the traditional ways of business as well as convulse entire industries by giving advantages to nimble upstarts. Yet existing businesses are using e-business to cut costs, increase efficiency, improve customer service, speed up innovation, and improve productivity.[4] This chapter explores the management of information technology and e-business. We begin by looking at the management implications of using advanced information technology. Next, we examine some recent technology trends and the types of information systems frequently used in organizations. Then, the chapter looks at the growing use of the Internet and e-business, including a discussion of fundamental e-business strategies, business-to-business marketplaces, use of information technology in business operations, and the importance of knowledge management.

INFORMATION TECHNOLOGY HAS CHANGED EVERYTHING

An organization's **information technology (IT)** consists of the hardware, software, telecommunications, database management, and other technologies it uses to store data and make them available in the form of information for organizational decision making. IT, including use of the Internet for e-business, can enable managers to be better connected with employees, the environment, and each other. In general, information technology has positive implications for the practice of management, although it can also present problems. Some specific implications of information technology for managers, as shown in Exhibit 15.1, include enhanced collaboration, improved employee effectiveness, increased efficiency, empowered employees, and potential information overload.

Boundaries Dissolve; Collaboration Reigns

Walk into the video conference room at Infosys Technologies, a leader in India's outsourcing and software industry, and the first thing you'll see is a wall-size flat-screen television. On that screen, Infosys can hold virtual meetings of the key players from its entire global supply chain for any project at any time of the day or night. For example, American designers could be onscreen talking to their Indian software writers and their Asian manufacturers all at once.[5] Time, distance, and other boundaries between individuals, departments, and organizations are irrelevant in today's business world. Collaboration is what it's all about.

One of the most significant advantages of using advanced information technology is that it enhances collaboration both within the organization and with customers, suppliers, and partners. As historian Thomas L. Friedman puts it, "Wherever you look today . . . hierarchies are being flattened and value is being created less and less within vertical silos and more and more through horizontal collaboration within

information technology (IT) The hardware, software, telecommunications, database management, and other technologies used to store, process, and distribute information.

EXHIBIT 15.1

Implications of Information Technology for Managers

companies, between companies, and among individuals."[6] Information technology can connect employees around the world for the sharing and exchange of information and ideas. The emphasis on using information technology rather than personal travel for collaboration is a response to reduced travel budgets and rising airfares, concern over incidents such as international terrorism, and the need for speed in today's global marketplace.[7]

People Do Better Work

Information technology can provide employees with all kinds of information about their customers, competitors, markets, and service, as well as enable them to instantly share information and insights with colleagues. In addition, with time and geographic boundaries dissolving, a team can work throughout the day on a project in Switzerland and, while they sleep, a team in the United States can continue where the Swiss team left off.

In general, information technology enables managers to design jobs to provide people with more intellectual engagement and more challenging work. The availability of information technology does not guarantee increased job performance, but when implemented and used appropriately, it can have a dramatic influence on employee effectiveness. For example, an Internet system at Continental Airlines alerts the company when planes arrive late and assesses passengers' needs, enabling employees to delay the departure of other flights or send carts to make connections easier for passengers. Continental's various systems for analyzing data to improve customer service helped the company move into the top ranks in terms of customer satisfaction, after being dead last in the industry during the 1990s.[8]

Things Are More Efficient

Information technology can significantly speed work processes, cut costs, and increase efficiency. McDonald's is experimenting with a system that allows workers at a call center in Santa Maria, California, to remotely take drive-through orders from 40 restaurants scattered around the United States, in places such as Honolulu,

Hawaii; Gulfport, Mississippi; and Gillette, Wyoming. The orders are zapped back to the restaurant via the Internet to be filled, and most customers have no idea their order has just traveled hundreds or thousands of miles. The system saves just a few seconds per order, but over the course of time at a busy drive-through, that adds up to significant cost savings and increased sales.[9]

Sweeping away administrative paperwork, automating mundane tasks, and standardizing services are other advantages of information technology. For example, at IBM, automating customer service helped reduce the number of call center employees and saved $750 million in one year alone. Intermountain Health Care, based in Salt Lake City, Utah, automated its pharmacies in the 1990s and is now applying information technology to standardize medical care, resulting in fewer mistakes, greater consistency in applying the latest medical advances, and lower costs.

Intermountain Health Care

Modern Healthcare has five times named Intermountain Health Care as the best-run of the nation's 582 integrated health systems. Intermountain's CEO, Bill Nelson, and Brent James, vice president for medical research, believe the success is largely due to the judicious application of information technology.

James is in charge of a project that uses data and networks to standardize care across Intermountain's 21 hospitals and 90 clinics. In essence, the system pores over data on different ways of treating a disease, such as diabetes or pneumonia, finds the approach that works the best, and gets every doctor to use that approach. Standardization of medical care is somewhat controversial, but it is growing in popularity as results show it typically results in better care and greater efficiency.

At Intermountain, teams of doctors use electronic records of every patient to periodically review, revise, and approve the approaches Intermountain's hospitals and clinics take to treat a particular disease. The dozen or so care-process models have had some significant positive results on patient care and the bottom line. For example, changes in how oxygen is administered to critical care patients reduced fatalities by preventing pneumonia, and saved millions of dollars a year. A study in one hospital found that adverse drug events were reduced from 570 a year to 230. A protocol preventing early birth inductions unless medically necessary saves Intermountain about $500,000 a year, and keeps about 5 percent of the babies who would arrive early from a stay in neonatal intensive care. Overall, Intermountain's inpatient hospital costs are 27 percent below the national average, and its operating margins are near the top of the hospital industry.[10]

Applying information technology at Intermountain has both improved the quality of care and resulted in greater efficiency. With health care and insurance costs spiraling out of control in the United States, other hospital systems are also looking at innovative IT applications as a way to streamline operations.

Employees Are Engaged

Information technology is profoundly affecting the way organizations are structured. With IT, managers can change the locus of knowledge by providing information to people who would not otherwise receive it. Lower-level employees are increasingly challenged with more information and more interesting jobs. Nurses, bellhops, truck drivers, utility repair workers, and warehouse staffers all need easy access to information to do their jobs well in today's fast-paced environment.[11]

IT enables decisions to be made by the employees who are in the best position to implement them and monitor their effects. For example, the U.S. Army is using new technology that pushes information about battlefield conditions, the latest intelligence on the enemy, and so forth, down the line to the lower troops. Armed with better data and trained to see patterns in the barrage of information, lieutenants in the field are making more of the decisions once made by commanders.[12] Avnet, a computer systems, component, and embedded subsystems manufacturer, uses an IT system that pushes data on orders, shipment schedules, and dates by which the company will cease manufacturing certain products directly to front-line sales teams, who use this information to modify their work practices and improve customer service.[13]

BRAIN HEMISPHERIC DOMINANCE

The questions that follow ask you to describe your behavior. For each question, check the answer that best describes you.

1. I am usually running late for class or other appointments:

   _____ **a.** Yes

   _____ **b.** No

2. When taking a test I prefer:

   _____ **a.** Subjective questions (discussion or essay)

   _____ **b.** Objective questions (multiple choice)

3. When making decisions, I typically:

   _____ **a.** Go with my gut—what feels right

   _____ **b.** Carefully weigh each option

4. When solving a problem, I would more likely:

   _____ **a.** Take a walk, mull things over, then discuss

   _____ **b.** Write down alternatives, prioritize them, then pick the best

5. I consider time spent daydreaming as:

   _____ **a.** A viable tool for planning my future

   _____ **b.** A waste of time

6. To remember directions, I typically:

   _____ **a.** Visualize the information

   _____ **b.** Make notes

7. My work style is mostly:

   _____ **a.** Juggle several things at once

   _____ **b.** Concentrate on one task at a time until complete

8. My desk, work area, or laundry area are typically:

   _____ **a.** Cluttered

   _____ **b.** Neat and organized

INTERPRETATION AND SCORING: People have two thinking processes—one visual and intuitive in the right half of the brain, and the other verbal and analytical in the left half of the brain. As a new manager, the thinking process you prefer predisposes you to certain types of knowledge and information—visual dashboards vs. written reports, tacit suggestions vs. quantitative data—as effective input to your thinking and decision making.

Count the number of checked "a" items and "b" items. Each "a" represents right-brain processing, and each "b" represents left-brain processing. If you scored 6 or higher on either, you have a distinct processing style. If you checked less than 6 for either, you probably have a balanced style. New managers typically need left-brain processing to handle data and to justify decisions. At middle and upper management levels, right-brain processing enables visionary thinking and strategic insights.

SOURCE: Adapted from Carolyn Hopper, *Practicing Management Skills* (New York: Houghton Mifflin, 2003); and Jacquelyn Wonder and Priscilla Donovan, "Mind Openers," *Self* (March 1984).

As a new manager, does your mind prefer explicit data or visual presentation? Are you drawn to IT trends, such as business intelligence and performance dashboards? Take the New Manager Self-Test above to learn about your orientation toward IT-based knowledge.

■ **TAKE A MOMENT**

People Can Suffer from Information Overload

Getting data and information to people who need it and can use it to improve their performance and decision-making is important, but it's possible to have too much of a good thing. One major problem associated with advances in technology is that the company can become a quagmire of information, with employees so overwhelmed by the sheer volume that they are unable to sort out the valuable from the useless.[14]

In many cases, the ability to produce data and information is outstripping employees' ability to process it. One British psychologist claims to have identified a new mental disorder caused by too much information; he has termed it *information fatigue syndrome*.[15] Information technology is a primary culprit in contributing to this new "disease." However, managers have the ability to alleviate the problem and improve information quality. The first step is to ensure that suppliers of information technology and CIOs work closely with employees to identify the kinds of questions they must answer and the kinds of data and information they really need. Specialists often are enamored with the volume of data a system can produce and overlook the need to provide small amounts of quality information in a timely and useful manner for decision making. Top executives should be actively involved in setting limits by focusing the organization on key strategies and on the critical questions that must be answered to pursue those strategies.[16]

THE EVOLVING WORLD OF INFORMATION TECHNOLOGY

Information technology changes rapidly, and organizations that want to stay competitive are adopting new technologies and approaches to improve their operations. However, most organizations merge new IT applications with existing operational and management information systems.

A New Generation of IT

The force that is fueling growth on the Internet today isn't a bunch of dot-com start-ups, or even long-established companies making waves in the online world. Instead, power has shifted to the individual, with blogs and social networking becoming the most explosive outbreaks in the world of information technology since the emergence of the Internet itself.[17] A **blog** is a running Web log that allows an individual to post opinions and ideas about anything from the weather and dating relationships to a company's products, management, or business practices. There were an estimated 60 million bloggers in mid-2006, and the number was growing.[18] Smart managers are paying attention to the phenomenon. For example, before announcing a major investment in energy efficient technology, managers at General Electric engaged with environmental bloggers to build support. Companies such as Microsoft and Cingular Wireless have enlisted the aid of bloggers to spread the word about new products or services.[19] An entire industry is springing up to help companies navigate the new world of blogs, such as monitoring what is being said about the company, implementing damage control strategies, and tracking what the majority of the world is thinking, minute by minute, to help the organization respond to emerging trends and opportunities.[20]

Social networking, also referred to as *social media* or *user generated content*, is an extension of blogs.[21] Sites such as MySpace, Facebook, and Friendster provide an unprecedented peer-to-peer communication channel, where people interact in an online community, sharing personal information and photos, producing and sharing all sorts of information and opinions, or unifying activists and raising funds. MySpace, now owned by News Corp., had 72 million members within only two years, with an estimated quarter of a million more signing up every day. A new social networking site, TagWorld, which is being referred to as the "MySpace killer" by bloggers, could grow even bigger. TagWorld offers an expanded range of services, including not only blogging but a multipage site, a gigabyte of storage, a music player, classifieds, and photo- and video-sharing capabilities. In addition, TagWorld gathers and provides real-time information, such as letting a musician who posts his music online to see exactly who is listening and where. This real-time information and automated feedback makes TagWorld especially valuable to businesses for spotting trends, marketing products and services, and other activities.

Single-use social networks, such as YouTube (video), Craiglist (classified ads), and Wikipedia (encyclopedia articles) are also growing in popularity. On YouTube's Web site, for example, individual users post more than 60,000 video clips a day, many of them home-shot, and consumers all over the world are viewing them at a

blog Web log that allows individuals to post opinions and ideas.

social networking Online interaction in a community format where people share personal information and photos, produce and share all sorts of information and opinions, or unify activists and raise funds.

rate of 70 million times a day.[22] NBC Universal, which originally demanded that YouTube take down clips of its programming, decided to join the trend rather than fight it, announcing that it would make promotional clips of popular shows available on the site and holding contests for users to submit their own promotional videos for certain shows.[23]

Blogs and social networking sites have the potential to shake up every business, government, and nonprofit organization in the world, for good or ill. Smart managers and organizations are searching for ways to use the power of these innovations to their advantage and minimize the damage or disruptions they might bring.

Applying New IT Within Organizations

Many companies are tapping the power of new IT applications as collaboration tools within organizations, using alternatives such as group blogs, editable Web sites called *wikis*, peer-to-peer file sharing, and group project management services. Internal blogs can serve as superb horizontal and bottom-up communication and collaboration tools. The simplicity and informality of blogs make them an easy and comfortable medium for people to communicate and share ideas. Some companies extend the approach to external blogs, which provide a way to communicate with customers, market products, and monitor public opinion about the organization. Similar to a blog, a **wiki** uses software to create a Web site that allows anyone with access, inside or outside the organization, to create, share, and edit content through a simple, browser-based user interface. Rather than simply sharing opinions and ideas as with a blog, wikis are free-form, allowing people to edit what they find on the site and add content.[24]

Peer-to-peer file sharing, such as that pioneered by Napster for sharing music online, enables PCs to communicate directly with one another over the Internet, bypassing central databases, servers, control points, and Web pages.[25] Peer-to-peer software lets any individual's computer "talk" directly to another PC without an intermediary, enhancing the opportunities for information sharing and collaboration. Peer-to-peer technology improves efficiency by eliminating the need for setting up and managing huge central storage systems. GlaxoSmithKline uses P2P technology to let its employees and researchers outside the company share their drug test data digitally and work collaboratively on new projects. Law firm Baker & McKenzie uses it to allow major clients to tap directly into its attorneys' files stored on computers worldwide. For example, clients closing a merger can monitor the progress of the deal without attorneys having to keep files in one place or send lengthy electronic documents, improving organizational speed and efficiency.[26] Group project management services, provided by software and services firms such as Basecamp, based in Chicago, lets groups of people use a password to post messages, files, or queries, create to-do lists, and set milestones for a project on simple, no-frills Web pages.

TYPES OF INFORMATION SYSTEMS

Organizations typically incorporate new and emerging tools into their existing IT systems. Most managers appreciate the value of making information readily available and easily shared with those who need it in some kind of formal, computer-based information system. Such a system combines hardware, software, and human resources to support organizational information and communication needs. One way to distinguish among the many types of information systems is to focus on the functions they perform and the people they serve in an organization. Two broad categories of information systems widely used today are shown in Exhibit 15.2. **Operations information systems** support information-processing needs of a business's day-to-day operations, as well as low-level operations management functions. Management information systems typically support the strategic decision-making needs of higher-level managers.

wiki Web site that allows anyone with access, inside or outside the organization, to create, share, and edit content through a simple, browser-based user interface.

peer-to-peer file sharing File sharing that allows PCs to communicate directly with one another over the Internet, bypassing central databases, servers, control points, and Web pages.

operations information system A computer-based information system that supports a company's day-to-day operations.

EXHIBIT   15.2

Types of Information
Systems

CONCEPT
C O N N E C T I O N Just how completely will the Internet and **information technology** revolutionize banking? Start-ups such as everbank.com believe there's a place for branchless, Internet-only "click banks." Everbank.com offers full banking and brokerage services 24 hours a day, and without the expense of building and staffing offices, it can offer customers higher interest rates than its brick-and-mortar competitors. To be sure, everbank does have to overcome security concerns, compensate for the lack of ATM machines, and compete against improved online services at traditional banks. Still, managers such as CEO Frank Trotter, pictured here, think the new Web bank can prosper by targeting affluent, computer-savvy professionals who value its time-saving convenience.

Data Versus Information

A central purpose of both operations information systems and management information systems is to translate *data* into *information*. **Data** are raw facts and figures that in and of themselves may not be useful. To be useful, data must be processed into finished **information**—that is, data that have been converted into a meaningful and useful context for specific users. New software and systems can help managers effectively identify and access useful information. For example, American Greetings Corporation, which sells greeting cards, might gather *data* about demographics in various parts of the country. These data are then translated into *information*; for example, stores in Florida require an enormous assortment of greeting cards directed at grandson, granddaughter, niece, and nephew, while stores in some other parts of the country might need a larger percentage of slightly irreverent, youth-oriented products.[27]

data Raw, unsummarized, and unanalyzed facts and figures.

information Data that have been converted into a meaningful and useful context for the receiver.

Operations Information Systems

A variety of tools referred to as operations information systems support the information-processing needs related to a business's day-to-day operations. Types of operations information systems include transaction-processing systems, process control systems, and office automation systems. Each of these supports daily operations and decisions that typically are made by nonmanagement employees or lower-level managers.

Transaction-processing systems (TPSs) record and process data resulting from business operations, including such data as sales to customers, purchases from suppliers, inventory changes, and wages to employees. A TPS collects data from these transactions and stores them in a database. Employees use the database to produce reports and other information, such as customer statements and employee paychecks. Most of an organization's reports are generated from these databases. Transaction-processing systems identify, collect, and organize the fundamental information from which an organization operates.

While a transaction-processing system keeps track of the size, type, and financial consequences of the organization's transactions, companies also need information about the quantity and quality of their production activities. Therefore, they may use process control systems to monitor and control ongoing physical processes. For example, petroleum refineries, pulp and paper mills, food manufacturing plants, and electric power plants use **process control systems** with special sensing devices that monitor and record physical phenomena such as temperature or pressure changes. The system relays the measurements or sensor-detected data to a computer for processing; employees and operations managers can check the data to look for problems requiring action.

Office automation systems combine modern hardware and software such as word processors, desktop publishers, e-mail, and teleconferencing to handle the tasks of publishing and distributing information. Office automation systems can also use data from other operations systems to transform manual accounting procedures to electronic media or to automatically make programmed decisions, as described in Chapter 9. Some banks, for example, use automated systems to make credit decisions. Cellular phone companies use automation to determine the best service package for a particular customer.[28] Merrill Lynch uses office automation to electronically manage consultants' travel and entertainment expenses, cutting the time it takes to process a report and issue reimbursement from six weeks to four days and slashing the average cost of processing a report from $25 to only a few bucks.[29] These systems enable businesses to streamline office tasks, reduce errors, and improve customer service. In this way, office automation systems support the other kinds of information systems.

Operations information systems aid organizational decision makers in many ways and across various settings. For example, Enterprise Rent-A-Car's Automated Rental Management System (ARMS) provides front-line employees with up-to-the-minute information that enables them to provide exceptional service to each customer. ARMS helps Enterprise keep track of the millions of transactions the company logs every hour. If a customer visits a branch office and requests a certain kind of car, the agent can immediately determine whether one is available anywhere in the city. Insurance companies such as Geico can also link their claims systems directly to Enterprise's automated rental system, book a reservation, and send payments electronically, eliminating the need for paper invoices and checks.[30]

Management Information Systems

A **management information system (MIS)** is a computer-based system that provides information and support for effective managerial decision making. The basic elements of a management information system are illustrated in Exhibit 15.3. The MIS is supported by the organization's operations information systems and by organizational databases (and frequently databases of external data as well). Management information systems typically include reporting systems, decision support systems, executive information systems, and groupware, each of which will be explained in this section.

MISs typically support strategic decision-making needs of mid-level and top management. However, as technology becomes more widely accessible, more employees

transaction-processing system (TPS) A type of operations information system that records and processes data resulting from routine business transactions such as sales, purchases, and payroll.

process control system A computer system that monitors and controls ongoing physical processes, such as temperature or pressure changes.

office automation systems Systems that combine modern hardware and software to handle the tasks of publishing and distributing information.

management information system (MIS) A computer-based system that provides information and support for effective managerial decision making.

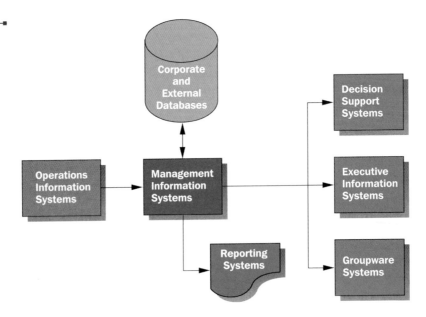

E X H I B I T   15.3

Basic Elements of Management Information Systems

SOURCE: Adapted from Ralph M. Stair and George W. Reynolds, *Principles of Information Systems: A Managerial Approach*, 4th ed. (Cambridge, MA: Course Technology, 1999): 391.

are wired into networks, and organizations push decision making downward in the hierarchy, these kinds of systems are seeing use at all levels of the organization.

■ **TAKE A MOMENT**

> As a new manager, incorporate new IT tools to extend the power of your organization's operational and management information systems. Recognize that people need different tools, depending on their work as well as how they like to process and use information. Go to the experiential exercise on page 511 that pertains to how you use information for decision making.

When a production manager needs to make a decision about production scheduling, he or she may need data on the anticipated number of orders in the coming month, inventory levels, and availability of computers and personnel. The MIS can provide these data. **Information reporting systems**, the most common form of MIS, provide managers and decision makers with reports that support day-to-day decision-making needs. At Harrah's casinos, an information reporting system uses quantitative models to predict each customer's potential long-term value and enables managers to create customized marketing and rewards programs that address individual players' unique preferences. "Almost everything we do in marketing and decision making is influenced by technology," says Harrah's CEO Gary Loveman. The approach helped Harrah's achieve 16 straight quarters of same-store sales growth, as well as the highest profit growth in the industry.[31]

Decision support systems (DSSs) are interactive, computer-based information systems that rely on decision models and specialized databases to support decision makers. With electronic spreadsheets and other decision support software, users can pose a series of what-if questions to test alternatives they are considering. Based on the assumptions used in the software or specified by the user, managers can explore various alternatives and receive tentative information to help them choose the alternative with the best outcome. Big retailers such as The Home Depot, Bloomingdale's, and Gap use decision support systems to help them gauge when to mark down prices and what items to discount, for example.[32]

Executive information systems (EISs) are management information systems to facilitate strategic decision making at the highest level of management. These systems are typically based on software that provides easy access to large amounts of complex data and can analyze and present the data in a timely fashion. EISs provide top management with quick access to relevant internal and external information and, if designed properly, can help them diagnose problems as well as develop solutions. Wake County, North Carolina, set up an executive information system that local social service agencies use to track each homeless person across the breadth of services they draw on, enabling them to improve strategic planning as

information reporting system A system that organizes information in the form of prespecified reports that managers use in day-to-day decision making.

decision support system (DSS) An interactive, computer-based system that uses decision models and specialized databases to support organization decision makers.

executive information system (EIS) A management information system designed to facilitate strategic decision making at the highest levels of management by providing executives with easy access to timely and relevant information.

PUTTING PERFORMANCE DASHBOARDS TO WORK

It's first thing in the morning. You sit down at your computer, coffee cup in hand, and click on an icon. Attractively arrayed on the screen is current information organized under various headings—for example, "Calendar," "Tasks," "Key Performance Indicators," "Sales by Manager," and those always eye-catching "Alerts." Critical information about your business is presented in colorful tables, pie charts, graphs, and other visual displays. With just a glance, you're up-to-date on everything you need to know before you start your day. If you're puzzled by a particular figure or alarmed by an alert, you just click on the item and start "drilling down" into the data until you get a better picture of exactly what is going on. Welcome to the world of business performance dashboards.

Estimates are that nearly half of the 2,000 largest companies already use Web-based business performance dashboards. And observers expect dashboards to become even more ubiquitous. In addition, organizations are increasingly sharing this new tool—originally designed to help top executives steer their organizations toward strategic goals—with lower-level managers and employees to help them be more effective and in control. However, as impressive as the technology is, it's the way organizations design and use these tools that determines whether they turn out to be a boon or a distracting bane. Here are some tips.

:: **Don't contribute to information overload.** Because dashboards collate information from many databases and programs, it's all too easy to construct a Web page that delivers too much information. To make dashboards useful, carefully choose what data will be tracked and what information will be displayed. Make sure it's what employees need to know to do their jobs better.

:: **Let line managers and employees drive the development.** Always remember that designing a dashboard is primarily a strategic project, not a technical one. The IT department can help implement the dashboard, but it is the responsibility of managers to determine its content. One way to make sure people get the right information is to solicit input from end users during the design process.

:: **Carefully assess who needs a dashboard.** At General Electric, business unit chiefs use dashboards, but CEO Jeffrey Immelt rarely does. Immelt doesn't want to get so mired in the details that he loses sight of the big picture. On the other hand, using dashboards to push information farther down into the organization can help employees at all levels see from day to day in concrete terms exactly how their actions contribute to an organization's success or failure in achieving its goals.

:: **Don't forget the human touch.** Having all the latest facts and figures at your fingertips is certainly valuable, but it's only part of what managers need to know to run an effective organization. Getting out and talking to employees and customers is still just as important.

SOURCES: Spencer E. Ante, "Giving the Boss the Big Picture," *BusinessWeek* (February 13, 2006): 48–51; Tad Leahy, "Warming Up to Performance Dashboards," *Business Finance Mag.com* (June 2006): www.businessfinancemag.com/magazine/archives/article.html?articleID=14638&Print=Y; and Doug Bartholomew, "Gauging Success," *CFO-IT* (Summer 2005): 17–19.

© MINDJET/PRNEWSFOTO (NEWSCOM)

well as provide better informed, targeted services to the homeless population.[33] Many companies use executive information systems that enable top managers to view a *dashboard* of key performance indicators on their PCs or laptops. A **business performance dashboard** uses software to present key business information (e.g., sales data, fill rates for orders, or profits per product line) in graphical, easy-to-interpret form, and can alert managers to any deviations or unusual patterns in the data. Dashboards pull data from a variety of organizational systems and databases; gauge the data against key performance metrics; and pull out the right nuggets of information to deliver to top managers for analysis and action.[34] The effective use of business performance dashboards is further discussed in this chapter's Shoptalk.

Modern information technology systems also recognize that many organizational and managerial activities involve groups of people working together to solve problems and meet customer needs. **Groupware** is software that works on a computer network or via the Internet to link people or workgroups across a room or around the globe. The software enables managers or team members to communicate, share information, and work simultaneously on the same document, chart, or diagram and see changes and comments as they are made by others. Sometimes called *collaborative work systems*, groupware systems allow people to interact with one another in an electronic meeting space and at the same time take advantage of computer-based support data. Groupware supports virtual and global teamwork by facilitating efficient and accurate sharing of ideas and simultaneous task execution. Team members in different geographical areas with varied expertise can work together almost as easily as if they were in the same room.

THE INTERNET AND E-BUSINESS

In recent years, most organizations have incorporated the Internet as part of their information technology strategy.[35] The **Internet** is a global collection of computer networks linked together for the exchange of data and information. The Internet became accessible as a public information and communications tool after Tim Berners-Lee, a researcher at CERN (Centre Européan pour la Recherche Nucléaire) in Geneva, Switzerland, designed software for the original **World Wide Web (WWW)**, a user-friendly interface that today allows people to easily communicate with each other and with the Internet via a set of central servers.[36]

Both business and nonprofit organizations quickly realized the potential of the Internet for expanding their operations globally, improving business processes, reaching new customers, and making the most of their resources. Exhibit 15.4 shows the opening Web page for IKEA, a Swedish furniture retailer with more than 200 stores around the world and a thriving catalog and Internet business. E-business began to boom. **E-business** can be defined as any business that takes place by digital processes over a computer network rather than in physical space. Most commonly today, it refers to electronic linkages over the Internet with customers, partners, suppliers, employees, or other key constituents. **E-commerce** is a more limited term that refers specifically to business exchanges or transactions that occur electronically.

Some organizations are set up as e-businesses that are run completely over the Internet, such as eBay, Amazon.com, Expedia, and Yahoo! These companies would not exist without the Internet. However, most

© NEWSWEEK/PRNEWSFOTO (NEWSCOM)

CONCEPT CONNECTION

The next stop in the **evolving world of information technology** is Web 2.0, a term that's been coined to refer to Web-based services such as social networking and wikis. This *Newsweek* cover from spring 2006 reflects Web 2.0's basic philosophy of putting the "*we*" in *Web* with sites such as social networking site MySpace and video-sharing service YouTube. Entrepreneurs all over the world are tapping into the Web's ability to help people in far-flung locations share, collaborate, socialize, and form communities. They're setting up new Web businesses staffed by only a handful of people, inviting users to create and organize the site's content.

Part 5 CONTROLLING

498

EXHIBIT   15.4

Opening Page of the Web
Site for IKEA.

traditional, established organizations, including General Electric, the City of Madison, Wisconsin, Target stores, and the U.S. Postal Service, also make extensive use of the Internet, and we will focus on these types of organizations in the remainder of this section. The goal of e-business for established organizations is to digitalize as much of the business as possible to make the organization more efficient and effective. Companies are using the Internet and the Web for everything from filing expense reports and calculating daily sales to connecting directly with suppliers for the exchange of information and ordering of parts.[37]

Exhibit 15.5 illustrates the key components of e-business for two organizations, a manufacturing company and a retail chain. First, each organization operates an **intranet**, an internal communications system that uses the technology and standards

intranet An internal communications system that uses the technology and standards of the Internet but is accessible only to people within the organization.

EXHIBIT   15.5

The Key Components of E-Business for Two Traditional Organizations

SOURCE: Based on Jim Turcotte, Bob Silveri, and Tom Jobson, "Are You Ready for the E-Supply Chain?" *APICS—The Performance Advantage* (August 1998): 56–59.

of the Internet but is accessible only to people within the company. The next component is a system that allows the separate companies to share data and information. Two options are an electronic data interchange network or an extranet. **Electronic data interchange (EDI)** networks link the computer systems of buyers and sellers to allow the transmission of structured data primarily for ordering, distribution, and payables and receivables.[38] An **extranet** is an external communications system that uses the Internet and is shared by two or more organizations. With an extranet, each organization moves certain data outside of its private intranet, but makes the data available only to the other companies sharing the extranet. The final piece of the overall system is the Internet, which is accessible to the general public. Organizations make some information available to the public through their Web sites, which may include products or services offered for sale. For example, at the Web site of IKEA, consumers can chat with an automated online assistant, use room planning tools for interior design, and order furniture and other products.

E-Business Strategies

The first step toward a successful e-business is for managers to determine why they need such a business to begin with.[39] Failure to align the e-business initiative with corporate strategy can lead to e-business failure. Two basic strategic approaches for traditional organizations setting up an Internet operation are illustrated in Exhibit 15.6. Some companies embrace e-business primarily to expand into new markets and reach new customers. Others use e-business as a route to increased productivity and cost efficiency. As shown in the exhibit, these strategies are implemented either by setting up an in-house Internet division or by partnering with other organizations to handle online activities.

MARKET EXPANSION

An Internet division allows a company to establish direct links to customers and expand into new markets. The organization can provide access around the clock to a worldwide market and thus reach new customers. ESPN.com, for example, is the biggest Internet draw for sports, attracting a devoted audience of 18- to 34-year-old men, an audience that is less and less interested in traditional television. The site's ESPN360, a customizable high-speed service, offers super-sharp video clips of everything from *SportsCenter* to poker tournaments, as well as behind-the-scenes coverage. To reach young viewers, other television networks, including Comedy Central, E. W. Scripps Networks, which owns HGTV and the Food Network, CBS Broadcasting, and NBC Universal, are also launching high-speed broadband

electronic data interchange (EDI) A network that links the computer systems of buyers and sellers to allow the transmission of structured data primarily for ordering, distribution, and payables and receivables.

extranet An external communications system that uses the Internet and is shared by two or more organizations.

EXHIBIT 15.6

Strategies for Engaging
Clicks with Bricks

E-Business Strategy:	Market expansion and revenue growth	Increased productivity and cost efficiency
Benefits:	• Add new markets • Integrate bricks and clicks • Increase market size	• Immediate short-term effects • Measurable productivity impact • Driven by internal processes
Implementation:	In-house division or partnership	In-house division or partnership

Competitive Business Environment

channels to deliver short videos, pilots of new shows, or abbreviated and behind-the-scenes looks.[40] Print media organizations use Web sites to reach new customers, as well. *Radar* magazine is taking an innovative approach by launching a Web site to build a market *before* publishing the magazine itself.

> In the summer of 2006, an intriguing new Web site turned up on the Internet. A click on www.radarmagazine.com revealed an above-ground stone crypt, from which protrudes a hand holding a copy of *Radar* magazine. *Radar* was first introduced in 2003 but ran out of cash and closed after only two issues. But the Web site says it all: "Hard to Kill. Radar Rises Again. Online This Summer—On Newsstands 2007."
>
> With an infusion of cash from publishing and real estate mogul Mortimer B. Zuckerman and financier Jeffrey Epstein, managers are reviving *Radar* as an irreverent, fun, urban-oriented publication aimed at 25- to-39-year-olds. But this time around, they decided to take a fresh approach by introducing a Web page long before the first issue is published. Maer Roshan, *Radar*'s editor, and Elinore Carmody, senior vice president and chief marketing and sales officer, say easing into the marketplace with a Web site will help promote the magazine to its target audience, as well as take some pressure off the first print issue. "We don't want to be a one-hit wonder," Carmody says. "Slower is better when you launch." Managers and editors hope the Web site will build buzz and lure advertisers, who are increasingly diverting money from print media to the Web.
>
> *Radar*'s Web site will continue after the magazine emerges in print form, showcasing a series of features and offering fresh takes daily on news, gossip, and social or cultural events. With all the resources and energy going into the Web site, some question why *Radar* wants to publish a traditional magazine at all. Yet *Radar* believes there's still a place for magazines that allow for in-depth stories. "And," Roshan says, "there is just something tactilely great about the way paper feels and the way pictures look" in a magazine. Time will tell whether the marketplace agrees.[41]

Radar

Go to the ethical dilemma on page 512 that pertains to using the Internet for market expansion.

■ **TAKE A MOMENT**

It remains to be seen whether *Radar* will succeed in any form—print or online. Efforts have just begun to build a market for the new publication. For established firms, the market expansion strategy is competitively sustainable because the e-business division works in conjunction with a conventional bricks-and-mortar company. For example, The Finish Line, a retailer of athletic clothing, footwear, and accessories, sells products online but also uses the Web site as a way to drive more traffic into its stores.[42]

PRODUCTIVITY AND EFFICIENCY

With this approach, the e-business initiative is seen primarily as a way to improve the bottom line by increasing productivity and cutting costs. An automaker, for example, might use e-business to reduce the cost of ordering and tracking parts and supplies and to implement just-in-time manufacturing. GM has implemented wireless Internet technology to increase productivity in 90 of its plants, where Wi-Fi devices are mounted on forklifts and used by assembly workers to track the movement of engine parts and car seats tagged with tiny chips that emit electronic signals.[43] At Nibco, a manufacturer of piping products, 12 plants and distribution centers automatically share data on inventory and orders, resulting in about 70 percent or orders being automated. The technology has enabled Nibco to trim its inventory by 13 percent, as well as respond more quickly to changes in orders from customers.[44]

Several studies attest to real and significant gains in productivity from e-business, and productivity gains from U.S. businesses were projected to reach $450 billion by 2005.[45] Even the smallest companies can realize gains. Rather than purchasing parts from a local supplier at premium rates, a small firm can access a worldwide market and find the best price, or negotiate better terms with the local supplier.[46] Service firms and government agencies can benefit too. New York City became the first city to use the Internet to settle personal injury claims more efficiently. Using NYC Comptroller's Cybersettle Service, lawyers submit blind offers until a match is hit. If an agreement can't be reached, the parties go back to face-to-face negotiations. The city saved $17 million in less than two years by settling 1,137 out of 7,000 claims online, and reduced settlement times from four years to 9 months.[47]

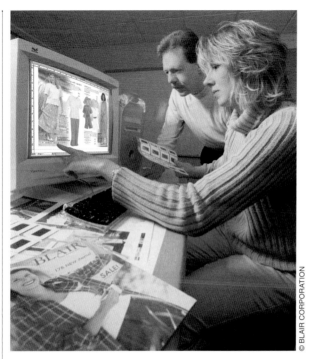

© BLAIR CORPORATION

CONCEPT
C O N N E C T I O N Blair Corporation is a multichannel direct marketer of apparel and home merchandise for value-conscious customers. In 2003, Blair launched an Internet division aimed at **market expansion**. Using a variety of tools and techniques, including virtual catalogs, Blair.com added 170,000 new-to-file customers in its first year, with an average age nearly 15 years younger than their traditional core customers: "proof of the power of this new channel."

IMPLEMENTING E-BUSINESS STRATEGIES

When traditional organizations such as Nibco, CBS Broadcasting, or General Motors Corporation want to establish an Internet division, managers have to decide how best to integrate bricks and clicks—that is, how to blend their traditional operations with an Internet initiative.[48] One approach is to set up an *in-house division*. This approach offers tight integration between the online business and the organization's traditional operation. Managers create a separate department or unit within the company that functions within the structure and guidance of the traditional organization. This approach gives the new division several advantages by piggybacking on the established company, including brand recognition, purchasing leverage with suppliers, shared customer information, and marketing opportunities. Office Depot, for example, launched an online unit for market expansion as a tightly integrated in-house part of its overall operation. Managers and employees within the company are assigned to the unit to handle Web site maintenance, product offerings, order fulfillment, customer service, and other aspects of the online business.[49]

A second approach is through *partnerships*, such as joint ventures or alliances. Safeway partnered with the British supermarket chain Tesco, described in the previous chapter, to establish its online grocery business in the United States. Safeway first tried to go it alone, but found that it needed the expertise of an established online player with a proven business model.[50] In many cases, a traditional company will partner with an established Internet firm to reach a broader customer base or to handle activities such as customer service, order fulfillment, and Web site maintenance. Companies such as Linens 'n Things, Timberland, and Reebok partner with GSI Commerce, which stores goods, takes orders, and then picks, packs, and ships orders directly to customers. The bricks-and-mortar companies get the expertise and services of a world-class Internet business without having to hire more people with IT expertise and build the capabilities themselves.[51]

GOING INTERNATIONAL

When businesses were first rushing to set up Web sites, managers envisioned easily doing business all over the world. Soon, though, they awakened to the reality that national boundaries matter just as much as they ever did. The global e-market can't be approached as if it were one homogeneous piece.[52] Organizations that want to succeed with international e-business are tailoring their Web sites to address differences in language, regulations, payment systems, and consumer preferences in different parts of the world. For example, Yahoo!, Amazon, Dell, Walt Disney, and the National Football League have all set up country-specific sites in the local language. Washingtonpost.com gives its news a broader global flavor during the overnight hours when international readers frequent the site. EBay is struggling with currency issues, as it has alienated many potential users in other countries by quoting prices only in U.S. dollars. And companies with online stores are finding that they may need to offer a different product mix and discounts tailored to local preferences. The Internet is a powerful way to reach customers and partners around the world, and managers are learning to address the cross-national challenges that come with serving a worldwide market.

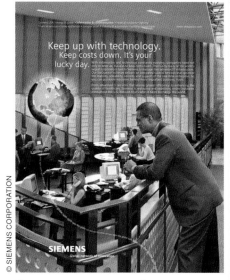

© SIEMENS CORPORATION

CONCEPT CONNECTION Many of the world's largest corporations depend on Siemens Business Services to manage their advanced information technology infrastructures. Turning to outside experts such as Siemens helps companies keep up with constantly-evolving technology as they keep their IT costs down. This advertisement promotes Siemens' SieQuence solution, which provides an integrated suite of services, from managing networks and **knowledge management systems**, to integrated **enterprise resource planning** and real-time management of the entire IT infrastructure. Within a year of its introduction in the United States, SieQuence was making up 30% of the company's total U.S. revenue, prompting a global launch in 2004.

E-Marketplaces

The biggest boom in e-commerce has been in business-to-business (B2B) transactions, or buying and selling between companies. Business-to-business transactions are at $2.4 trillion and growing, according to Forrester Research Inc.[53] One significant trend is the development of **B2B marketplaces**, in which an intermediary sets up an electronic marketplace where buyers and sellers meet, acting as a hub for B2B commerce. Exhibit 15.7 illustrates a B2B marketplace, where many different sellers offer products and services to many different buyers through a *hub*, or online portal. Conducting business through a Web marketplace can mean lower transaction costs, more favorable negotiations, and productivity gains for both buyers and sellers. For example, defense contractor United Technologies buys around $450 million worth of metals, motors, and other products annually via an e-marketplace and gets prices about 15 percent less than what it once paid.[54] Whirlpool uses Rearden Commerce, an online marketplace that is the world's largest hub for services, to book travel arrangements, make restaurant reservations for managers, schedule shipping, and arrange other services. Within the first two months of using the system, shipping department employees saved 10 percent and cut the time spent arranging for shipping by 52 percent.[55]

Ebay, which started out as a marketplace primarily for consumers, has also expanded into B2B commerce. Reliable Tools, Inc., a machine tool shop, tried listing a few items on eBay in late 1998, including items such as a $7,000, 2,300-pound milling machine. The items "sold like ice cream in August," and sales on eBay now make up about 75 percent of Reliable's overall business. Pioneers such as Reliable spurred eBay to set up an industrial products marketplace, which is now on track to

B2B marketplace An electronic marketplace set up by an intermediary where buyers and sellers meet.

EXHIBIT   15.7

B2B Marketplace Model

Sellers

Many sellers offer products and services through an intermediary to many buyers.

Online portal or "hub" for B2B marketplace (intermediary)

Buyers

top $500 million in annual gross sales.[56] The success of eBay has created an entirely new kind of marketplace, where both individuals and businesses are buying and selling billions of dollars worth of goods a year. A Canadian organization, Mediagrif Interactive Technologies, is giving eBay a run for its money in the B2B marketplace. Mediagrif focuses its efforts entirely on business-to-business exchanges in markets such as used computer parts, routers and switches, automotive parts, medical equipment, and other areas.[57]

In addition to open, public B2B marketplaces such as eBay, Mediagrif, and AutoTradeCenter, where dealers buy about 100,000 used cars a year, some companies set up private marketplaces to link with a specially invited group of suppliers and partners.[58] For example, General Motors spends billions a year on public marketplaces, but it also operates its own private marketplace, GMSupplyPower, to share proprietary information with thousands of its parts suppliers. E-marketplaces can bring efficiencies to many operations, but some companies find that they don't offer the personal touch their type of business needs, as described in this chapter's Unlocking Innovative Solutions Through People box.

Enterprise Resource Planning Systems

A key e-business component for many companies is an approach to information management called enterprise resource planning. **Enterprise resource planning (ERP) systems** integrate and optimize all the various business processes across the entire firm.[59] The massive computing power required to run complex ERP systems once prohibited many smaller companies from using ERP. However, the top ERP vendors today host the applications themselves and offer their products through Internet portals; customers access the applications with standard browsers.

An enterprise resource planning system can become the backbone of an organization's operations. It collects, processes, and provides information about an organization's entire enterprise, including orders, product design, production, purchasing, inventory, distribution, human resources, receipt of payments, and forecasting of future demand. Such a system links these areas of activity into a network, as illustrated in Exhibit 15.8. When a salesperson takes an order, the ERP system checks to see how the order affects inventory levels, scheduling, human resources, purchasing, and distribution. The system replicates organizational processes in software, guides employees through the processes step by step, and automates as many of them as possible. For example, the software can automatically cut an accounts

enterprise resource planning (ERP) system A networked information system that collects, processes, and provides information about an organization's entire enterprise, from identification of customer needs and receipt of orders to distribution of products and receipt of payments.

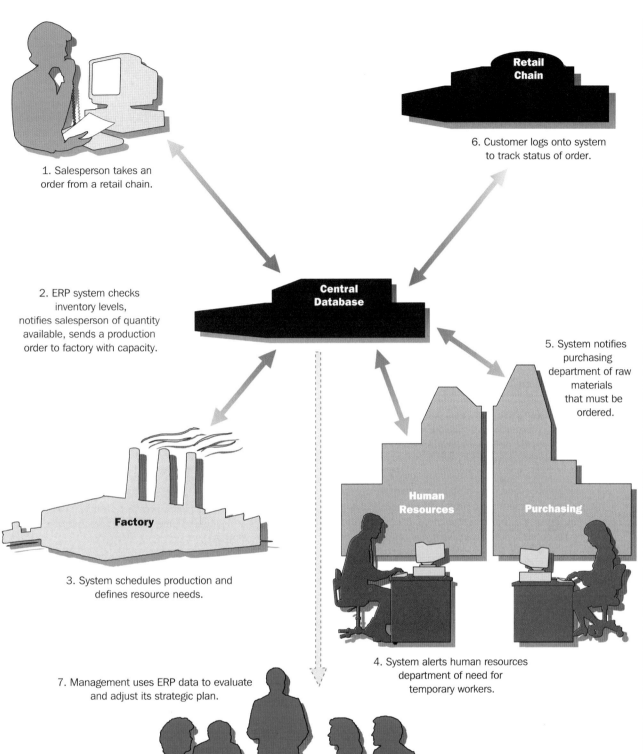

1. Salesperson takes an order from a retail chain.

2. ERP system checks inventory levels, notifies salesperson of quantity available, sends a production order to factory with capacity.

3. System schedules production and defines resource needs.

7. Management uses ERP data to evaluate and adjust its strategic plan.

Retail Chain

6. Customer logs onto system to track status of order.

Central Database

5. System notifies purchasing department of raw materials that must be ordered.

Human Resources

Purchasing

4. System alerts human resources department of need for temporary workers.

Factory

Strategic Planning Group

EXHIBIT 15.8

Example of ERP Applications

SOURCE: Adapted from Gail Edmondson, "Silicon Valley on the Rhine," *BusinessWeek* (November 2, 1997): 162–166.

Unlocking Innovative Solutions Through | P E O P L E |

GRANT J. HUNT CO. LIKES THE PERSONAL TOUCH

For five generations, family-owned Grant J. Hunt Co. has reached out for new technology to speed up its food distribution business. So, when sales crews began pitching the concept of an online produce marketplace, 47-year-old Grant Hunt listened. One executive from a B2B marketplace start-up assured Hunt he could lay off half his sales staff because of the efficiencies gained. Others pointed out the potential for gaining new customers all over the world and getting higher prices by advertising produce to the highest bidder.

Yet today, Hunt's salespeople are working the way they have for years, buying and selling produce using the telephone and the fax machine. Although the B2B marketplaces put Hunt in touch with a host of potential new customers, most of them were marginal operations with shaky credit histories. In addition, Hunt was a little leery about the public nature of the exchanges, which meant that all sorts of confidential information could get out to customers and competitors. However, the biggest drawback was that the online marketplace could not provide personal attention to customers or to constantly shifting marketplace conditions. "No B-to-B site can say to a buyer at a supermarket, 'How about a special this weekend on tomatoes, because we are coming into a lot of them right now,'" Hunt points out.

The Hunt Co. has always tried to develop close, personalized relationships with its suppliers and customers, negotiating deals on an individual basis. Hunt prides himself on the fact that customers trust him to provide accurate and honest information. He or his salespeople make daily visits to large growers and the local produce markets, shaking hands and talking small talk. The rest of the time they spend glued to the telephone, matching farmers' crops with buyers such as regional supermarket chains, wholesalers, and restaurant supply outfits, often varying their prices as needed with each customer to close a deal. "The Internet is very good at taking one message and sending it out to the whole world," he says. "That's not how our world works."

Hunt found that the relationships he had developed and the processes he had in place were so efficient that he had little to gain from joining the B2B marketplace craze. In fact, over time, many of the start-ups have also realized that the produce business doesn't fit well with the online marketplace concept. BuyProduce.com, for example, has shifted its emphasis from its exchange business to helping produce companies such as Hunt improve their own in-house systems. Hunt is careful to point out that he is not anti-technology. "If they provided something that would be of real value, I would use it in a heartbeat."

SOURCE: Lee Gomes, "How Lower-Tech Gear Beat Web 'Exchanges' at Their Own Game," *The Wall Street Journal* (March 16, 2001): A11.

payable check as soon as a clerk confirms that goods have been received in inventory, send an online purchase order immediately after a manager has authorized a purchase, or schedule production at the most appropriate plant after an order is received.[60] In addition, because the system integrates data about all aspects of operations, managers and employees at all levels can see how decisions and actions in one part of the organization affect other parts, using this information to make better decisions. Customers and suppliers are typically linked into the information exchange as well.

When carefully implemented, ERP can cut costs, shorten cycle time, enhance productivity, and improve relationships with customers and suppliers. One organization that is reaping benefits from an ERP system is Medecins du Monde (Doctors of the World).

Medecins du Monde

When Catherine Duffau joined Medecins du Monde as chief information officer, the international aid organization had disparate systems for purchasing, finance, accounting, and communication. Trying to keep people connected and get them the information and supplies they needed to provide medical services to victims of war, famine, and drought in 59 countries was overwhelming the staff and its limited resources.

Duffau believed an ERP system would solve the problem by helping integrate functions as well as collect precise data on doctors' needs and expenses in the field. She selected a small ERP system provided by French software maker Qualiac, which was known for its ease of use, thus making it more manageable for Medecins du Monde's many volunteers.

So far, the accounting, purchasing, stock, and investment records are set up and running on the system, and tests in the field have begun. When a rebellion in the Ivory Coast left thousands dead and more than a million homeless, doctors and volunteers could log onto the system and quickly see how much had already been spent and how much they had left to expand treatment when needed. Volunteers enter information into the ERP system so offices back in France can keep track of expenses, supplies, and needs.

Duffau's ultimate goal for the ERP system is information in real time. "Then we would know immediately when we had enough money to expand our missions," she says. The integration provided by ERP answers the urgent problem of connecting people who have to rely on their brains, commitment, and limited resources to solve huge human problems around the world.[61]

Customer Relationship Management

In addition to better internal information management and information sharing with suppliers and other organizations, companies are using e-business solutions to build stronger customer relationships. One approach is **customer relationship management (CRM) systems** that help companies track potential customers, follow customers' interactions with the firm, and allow employees to call up a customer's past sales and service records, outstanding orders, or unresolved problems.[62] According to a 2005 study by Gartner Group, 60 percent of midsized businesses had plans to adopt or expand their CRM usage, while only 2 percent of surveyed companies had no plans for using this technology.[63]

Today, CRM tools are evolving to provide "collaborative customer experiences."[64] Whereas the traditional CRM model gives the organization insight into customers, the new approach will provide for a two-way relationship that also gives customers transparency into company thinking. This means that, rather than having employees provide what they *think* customers want and need, employees and customers will jointly craft the customer experience, with the customer, rather than the company, defining what value means.

Increasingly, what distinguishes an organization from its competitors are its knowledge resources, such as product ideas and the ability to identify and find solutions to customers' problems. Exhibit 15.9 lists examples of how CRM and other information technology can shorten the distance between customers and the organization, contributing to organizational success through customer loyalty, superior service, better information gathering, and organizational learning.

© BMW FINANCIAL SERVICES NA, LLC/PRNEWSFOTO (NEWSCOM)

CONCEPT CONNECTION The BMW subsidiary MINI offers customers a voice in everything from personalizing their credit cards to designing their cars. BMW Financial Services's MINI Platinum Visa cardholders can customize the MINI image that graces their card by accessing the Web page, shown here. There they can choose from four body styles, 36 different wheels, 21 body colors, and 24 roof options. Similar software allows individuals to customize their actual MINI vehicles. "No two MINIs are exactly alike," the MINI Web site proclaims. This type of collaborative customer experience is the next step in **customer relationship management (CRM)**, as companies court Internet-savvy Gen X and Gen Y consumers.

customer relationship management (CRM) systems Systems that help companies track customers' interactions with the firm and allow employees to call up information on past transactions.

Competitive Advantage	Example
• **Increase in customer loyalty**	Full information about customer profile and previous requests or preferences is instantly available to sales and service representatives when a customer calls.
• **Superior service**	Customer representatives can provide personalized service, offer new products and services based on customer's purchasing history.
• **Superior information gathering and knowledge sharing**	The system is updated each time a customer contacts the organization, whether the contact is in person, by phone, or via the Web. Sales, marketing, service, and technical support have access to shared database.
• **Organizational learning**	Managers can analyze patterns to solve problems and anticipate new ones.

EXHIBIT 15.9

Competitive Advantages Gained from Customer Relationship Management (CRM) Systems

Turning Data and Information into Knowledge

The Internet also plays a key role in the recent emphasis managers are putting on **knowledge management**, the efforts to systematically gather knowledge, make it widely available throughout the organization, and foster a culture of learning. Some researchers believe that intellectual capital will soon be the primary way in which businesses measure their value.[65] Therefore, managers see knowledge as an important resource to manage, just as they manage cash flow, raw materials, and other resources. An effective knowledge management system may incorporate a variety of technologies, supported by leadership that values learning, an organizational structure that supports communication and information sharing, and processes for managing change.[66] Two specific technologies that facilitate knowledge management are business intelligence software and corporate intranets or networks. The use of new business intelligence software helps organizations make sense out of huge amounts of data. These programs combine related pieces of information to create knowledge. Knowledge that can be codified, written down, and contained in databases is referred to as *explicit knowledge*. However, much organizational knowledge is unstructured and resides in people's heads. This *tacit knowledge* cannot be captured in a database, making it difficult to formalize and transmit. Intranets and knowledge sharing networks can support the spread of tacit knowledge.

BUSINESS INTELLIGENCE

Today's organizations can collect and store tremendous amounts of data. Some companies use **data warehousing**, which refers to the use of a huge database that combines all of a company's data and allows business users to access the data directly, create reports, and obtain answers to what-if questions. Others have data stored in multiple sources. In addition, companies have access to numerous sources of outside data. How do managers make sense of it all? They do so through the use of business intelligence.

Business intelligence (BI) is an umbrella term that refers to a variety of software applications that analyze a company's data and extract useful insights to help managers make better strategic decisions.[67] Business intelligence includes activities such as *data mining*, which searches out and analyzes data from multiple sources across the enterprise, and sometimes from outside sources, to identify patterns and relationships that might be significant, as well as online statistical analysis, querying, and reporting. Many managers like getting BI information via a business performance dashboard, as described earlier in the chapter, because it provides a user-friendly way to view and navigate through information.[68]

Business intelligence tools are the hottest area of software right now, with companies spending billions on powerful new tools that can manipulate trillions of pieces of data and provide managers with targeted information to help them improve efficiency, increase customer satisfaction and loyalty, and pump up sales and profits.[69] Managers can, for example, identify sets of products that particular market segments purchase, patterns of transactions that signal possible fraud, or patterns of product performance that may indicate defects. The application of business intelligence helped managers at Staples, the office-supply chain, create a more profitable product mix in its stores. Managers had thought that devoting a large part of their floor space to desks, file cabinets, and other big-ticket items made sense. However, the BI system indicated that the overall profitability of the furniture category was actually less than that for smaller goods such as paper and pens. Staples now devotes more of its floor space to such items as paper clips, highlighters, mailing labels, post-it notes, and yellow pads, helping to keep the chain's net income growing at a 12 percent compounded rate for five straight years.[70]

In addition, BI is being applied to improve day-to-day operations. Unlike early BI applications that often produced reports too late for managers to make needed

knowledge management The process of systematically gathering knowledge, making it widely available throughout the organization, and fostering a culture of learning.

data warehousing The use of a huge database that combines all of a company's data and allows users to access the data directly, create reports, and obtain answers to what-if questions.

business intelligence (BI) The high-tech analysis of data from multiple sources to identify patterns and relationships that might be significant.

changes, newer versions connect with other IT systems to let managers or others throughout the organization keep track of business intelligence in real-time. Cendant Hotel Group, for example, can know immediately when a huge surge of interest in triple rooms in San Diego or Phoenix happens, enabling the company to add inventory or adjust offerings on its Web site or those of partners such as Expedia and Travelocity. The following example illustrates how Anheuser-Busch makes profitable use of business intelligence.

Anheuser Busch

Only a few years ago, Anheuser Busch beer distributors and sales reps were turning their information in on stacks of paper invoices and sales orders. Keeping track of what products were selling and what marketing campaigns were effective was an arduous and time-consuming process. If a certain product wasn't going over well in a particular market, managers wouldn't even know it for months.

But all that changed at Anheuser-Busch with the introduction of BudNet, a corporate data network through which distributors and sales reps report in excruciating detail on everything from new orders and level of sales to competitors' shelf stock and current promotional efforts. Sales reps use handheld PDAs and laptops to enter data that are compiled and transmitted nightly to Anheuser corporate headquarters. Then, business intelligence software goes to work, helping brand managers find out what beer drinkers are buying, as well as when, where, and why. Managers use the intelligence to constantly alter marketing strategies, design promotions to target the ethnic makeup of various markets, and get an early warning when rivals may be gaining an edge. For example, by cross-analyzing company data with U.S. Census figures on the ethnic and economic makeup of neighborhoods, Anheuser can tailor marketing campaigns with local precision. It knows that Tequiza goes over well in San Antonio, but not in Peoria; that the Fourth of July is a big beer sales holiday in Atlanta but St. Patrick's Day isn't; and that beer drinkers in blue-collar neighborhoods prefer cans over bottles.

Every morning, distributors log on to BudNet to access the latest intelligence and get their new marching orders for what products to promote, what displays to use, and what discounts to offer in what neighborhoods. "They're drilling down to the level of the individual store," says Joe Thompson, president of Independent Beverage Group. "They can pinpoint if customers are gay, Latino, 30-year-old college-educated conservatives."[71]

Store-level data have become the lifeblood of Anheuser-Busch's business. Since it began collecting the right data and using business intelligence to analyze it and spot trends and patterns, Anheuser-Busch has greatly expanded its market share compared to competitors. Independent wholesalers are benefiting too. The operating income for the average Anheuser wholesaler is five times greater than the average for Miller or Coors distributors. As one independent distributor's representative said about the competition, "It's no extra work to get the competitive info. . . . I think I know more about these guys' business than they do."[72]

INTRANETS

Many companies are building knowledge management portals on the corporate intranet to give employees an easier way to access and share information. A **knowledge management portal** is a single, personalized point of access for employees to multiple sources of information on the corporate intranet. Intranets can give people access to explicit knowledge that may be stored in databases, but the greatest value of intranets for knowledge management is increasing the transfer of tacit knowledge. For example, Xerox tried to codify the knowledge of its service technicians and embed it in an expert decision system that was installed in the copiers. The idea was that technicians could be guided by the system and complete repairs more quickly, sometimes even off-site. However, the project failed because it did not take into account the tacit knowledge—the nuances and details—that could not be codified. After a study found that service techs shared their knowledge primarily by telling

knowledge management portal A single point of access for employees to multiple sources of information that provides personalized access on the corporate intranet.

"war stories," Xerox developed an intranet system called *Eureka* to link 25,000 field service representatives. Eureka, which enables technicians to electronically share war stories and tips for repairing copiers, has cut average repair time by 50 percent.[73]

Organizations typically combine several technologies to facilitate the sharing and transfer of both tacit and explicit knowledge. For example, to spur sharing of explicit knowledge, a leading steel company set up a centralized data warehouse containing the financial and operational performance data and standards for each business unit. Managers can use business intelligence and other decision tools to identify performance gaps and make changes as needed. The company also enables tacit knowledge transfer through an intranet-based document management system, combined with Web conferencing systems, where worldwide experts can exchange ideas.[74] Similarly, when employees of Barclays Global Investors are working on proposals from large customers who require answers to hundreds of complex questions, they can access the knowledge network to reuse answers from previous similar proposals. In addition, employees set up online workspaces to tap into subject experts who can collaborate to help answer new kinds of queries and complete proposals faster.[75]

Overall, information technology, including e-business and knowledge management systems, can enable managers to be better connected with employees, customers, partners, and each other.

MANAGER'S SOLUTION

Information technology and e-business are changing the way people and organizations work. Specific implications of IT include enhanced collaboration, more effective employees, increased efficiency, empowered employees, and potential information overload.

New IT tools include blogs, wikis, social networking, peer-to-peer file sharing, and group project management services. These new tools are used in conjunction with information systems that gather huge amounts of data and transform them into useful information for decision makers. Operations information systems, including transaction-processing systems, process control systems, and office automation systems, support daily business operations and the needs of low-level managers. Management information systems, including information reporting systems, decision support systems, and executive information systems, typically support the decision-making needs of middle and upper-level managers. Collaborative work systems allow groups of managers or employees to share information, collaborate electronically, and have access to computer-based support data for group decision making and problem solving.

Most organizations have incorporated the Internet and e-business as part of their information technology strategy. Traditional organizations use an online division primarily for market expansion or to increase productivity and reduce costs. Two primary ways e-business strategies are implemented are through an in-house dot-com division or by partnering with other organizations for the Internet business. Companies are also benefiting from participation in electronic marketplaces, where many different sellers offer products and services to many different buyers through an online hub.

Important e-business solutions for improving business operations and customer relationships include enterprise resource planning (ERP) and customer relationship management (CRM) systems. Knowledge management is also an important application for new technology. Key technologies for knowledge management are business intelligence software and knowledge management portals on the corporate intranet.

In the opening example, Wal-Mart learned how quickly bad news can spread on the Internet. Marshall Manson, a senior account supervisor at Edelman, the company's PR firm, decided to turn the power of blogs to Wal-Mart's advantage. Manson e-mailed a number of bloggers who were known to support Wal-Mart and asked if they would like to receive regular communications from the company. Edelman then began feeding these bloggers exclusive nuggets of news, suggesting topics for postings, and promoting positive aspects of the company. Many organizations have used blogs to help shape public opinion, but Wal-Mart was the first major company to use blogging as a general PR tool. Some bloggers and observers are incensed by the approach, saying a blog should be about the blogger's own voice, not someone else's. Others, though, say Wal-Mart's blogging initiative is no different from a company sending a press release to a newspaper. The tactic could backfire, but Wal-Mart and Edelman believe it's a valid approach to telling the retailer's side of the story. "As more and more Americans go to the Internet to get information from varied, credible, trusted sources," a Wal-Mart spokeswoman said, "Wal-Mart is committed to participating in that online conversation."[76]

DISCUSSION QUESTIONS

1. Business writer Nicholas Carr argued that because computers and software have become so available and affordable, it's getting harder to achieve a competitive edge by being a technology leader. Do you agree or disagree? Explain your answer.

2. What types of information technology do you as a student use on a regular basis? How might your life be different if this technology were not available to you?

3. Has the growth of increasingly sophisticated management information systems (MIS) changed the importance of personal experience and intuition in decision making? In other words, does MIS make decision making more of a science than an art?

4. How might the organizers of an upcoming Olympics use an extranet to get all the elements of the event up and running on schedule?

5. You are a manager assigned the task of deciding how to blend your organization's traditional operations with a new Internet initiative for both purchasing and sales. What are the main factors you would consider? What information would you collect?

6. If you were a manager in charge of new product marketing, what are some ways you might harness the power of blogs and social networking sites to help market your latest products?

7. The openness of wikis is both their strength and their weakness. As a business owner, how would you take advantage of this new technology but guard against its potential problems, such as their vulnerability to mistakes, pranks, inaccurate and self-serving posts, and cybervandalism?

8. Define the difference between explicit knowledge and tacit knowledge and give an example of each from your own experience. How can knowledge management systems be designed to promote the sharing of both explicit and tacit knowledge?

9. Do you believe information overload is a problem for today's students? For managers or employees in an organization where you have worked? How might people deal with information overload?

10. How is e-business affecting the way organizations are structured and the way jobs are designed?

11. Have you ever used peer-to-peer file-sharing technology? Discuss your experiences—positive and negative—with P2P.

MANAGEMENT IN PRACTICE: EXPERIENTIAL EXERCISE

What Is Your MIS Style?

For each of the following 14 statements, circle the number that indicates how much you agree that each statement is characteristic of you. The questions refer to how you use information and make decisions.

Disagree Strongly ❶ ❷ ❸ ❹ ❺ Strongly Agree

1. I like to wait until all relevant information is examined before deciding something. ❶ ❷ ❸ ❹ ❺

2. I prefer information that can be interpreted in several ways and leads to different but acceptable solutions. ❶ ❷ ❸ ❹ ❺

3. I like to keep gathering data until an excellent solution emerges. ❶ ❷ ❸ ❹ ❺

4. To make decisions, I often use information that means different things to different people. ❶ ❷ ❸ ❹ ❺

5. I want just enough data to make a decision quickly. ❶ ❷ ❸ ❹ ❺

6. I act on logical analysis of the situation rather than on my "gut feelings" about the best alternative. ① ② ③ ④ ⑤

7. I seek information sources or people that will provide me with many ideas and details. ① ② ③ ④ ⑤

8. I try to generate more than one satisfactory solution for the problem faced. ① ② ③ ④ ⑤

9. When reading something, I confine my thoughts to what is written rather than search for additional understanding. ① ② ③ ④ ⑤

10. When working on a project, I try to narrow, not broaden, the scope so it is clearly defined. ① ② ③ ④ ⑤

11. I typically acquire all possible information before making a final decision. ① ② ③ ④ ⑤

12. I like to work on something I've done before rather than take on a complicated problem. ① ② ③ ④ ⑤

13. I prefer clear, precise data. ① ② ③ ④ ⑤

14. When working on a project, I like to explore various options rather than maintain a narrow focus. ① ② ③ ④ ⑤

Scoring and Interpretation

Your information-processing style determines the extent to which you will benefit from computer-based information systems. First, subtract each of your scores for questions 5, 6, 9, 10, 12, and 13 from the number 6 and indicate the adjusted score next to each question. Use the adjusted scores to calculate your totals as follows:

The odd-numbered questions pertain to the "amount of information" you like to use. Your total score for odd-numbered questions: _____. A score of 28 or more suggests you prefer a large amount of information. A score of 14 or less indicates you like a small amount.

The even-numbered questions pertain to the "focus of information" you prefer. Your total score for even-numbered questions: _____. A score of 28 or more suggests you are comfortable with ambiguous, multifocused information, while a score of 14 or less suggests you like clear, unifocused data.

If you are a person who likes a large amount of information and clear, focused data, you will tend to make effective use of management information systems. You could be expected to benefit greatly from an EIS or MIS in your company. If you are a person who prefers a small amount of information and data that are multifocused, you would probably not get the information you need to make decisions through formal information systems. You probably won't utilize EIS or MIS to a great extent, preferring instead to get decision data from other convenient sources, including face-to-face discussions.

SOURCES: This questionnaire is adapted from Richard L. Daft and Norman B. Macintosh, "A Tentative Exploration into the Amount and Equivocality of Information Processing in Organizational Work Units," *Administrative Science Quarterly* 26 (1981): 207–224; and Dorothy Marcic, *Organizational Behavior: Experiences and Cases,* 4th ed. (St. Paul, MN: West, 1995).

MANAGEMENT IN PRACTICE: ETHICAL DILEMMA

Manipulative or Not?

As head of the marketing department for Butter Crisp Snack Foods, 55-year-old Frank Bellows has been forced to learn a lot about the Internet in recent years. Although he initially resisted the new technology, Frank has gradually come to appreciate the potential of the Internet for serving existing customers and reaching potential new ones. In fact, he has been one of the biggest supporters of the company's increasing use of the Internet to stay in touch with customers.

However, something about this new plan just doesn't feel right. At this morning's meeting, Keith Deakins, Butter Crisp's CEO, announced that the company would soon be launching a Web site geared specifically to children. Although Deakins has the authority to approve the site on his own, he has asked all department heads to review the site and give their approval for its launch. He then turned the meeting over to the Information Technology team that developed the new site, which will offer games and interactive educational activities. The team pointed out that although it will be clear that Butter Crisp is the sponsor of the site, the site will not include advertising of Butter Crisp products. So far, so good, Frank thinks. However, he knows that two of the young hot-shot employees in his department have been helping to develop the site and that they provided a list of questions that children will be asked to answer online. Just to enter the Web site, for example, a user must provide name, address, gender, e-mail address, and favorite TV show. In return, users receive "Crisp Cash," a form of virtual money that they can turn in for toys, games, Butter Crisp samples, and other prizes. After they enter the site, children can earn more Crisp Cash by providing other information about themselves and their families.

Frank watched the demonstration and agreed that the Web site does indeed have solid educational content. However, he is concerned about the tactics for gathering information from children when that information will almost certainly be used for marketing purposes. So far, it seems that the other department heads are solidly in favor of launching the Web site. Frank is wondering whether he can sign his approval with a clear conscience. He also knows that several groups, including the national PTA and the Center for Media Education, are calling for stricter governmental controls regarding collecting information from children via the Internet.

What Would You Do?

1. Stop worrying about it. There's nothing illegal about what Butter Crisp is proposing to do, and any personal information gathered will be closely guarded by the company. Children can't be harmed in any way by using the new Web site.

2. Begin talking with other managers and try to build a coalition in support of some stricter controls, such as requiring parental permission to enter areas of the site that offer Crisp Cash in exchange for personal information.

3. Contact the Center for Media Education and tell them you suspect Butter Crisp intends to use the Web site to conduct marketing research. The Center might be able to apply pressure that would make it uncomfortable enough for Deakins to pull the plug on the new kid's Web site.

SOURCE: Based on Denise Gellene,"Internet Marketing to Kids Is Seen as a Web of Deceit," *Los Angeles Times* (March 29, 1996): A1, A20.

CASE FOR CRITICAL ANALYSIS

Tri-Angle Equipment and Leasing

Joe Jett, president of Tri-Angle Equipment and Leasing, which owns several agricultural equipment dealerships in the midwestern United States, tried computers 15 years ago. He didn't like them, and he didn't think he needed information technology to run his business.

But as the company grew, Jett realized he had taken on more debt than he was comfortable with, so he hired a chief financial officer named Dan Fraley. Jett also got back into the information technology game, investing $150,000 in a proprietary inventory and accounting system. When Jett and Fraley approached Citigroup's Global Equipment Finance Division seeking better financing for the company, Jett was surprised that Citigroup seemed to be more interested in Tri-Angle's information technology capacity than it was in how many million-dollar machines the company had sold. As a Citigroup representative explained, "The theory goes that if you can trust the computer systems, you can trust the company's numbers."

Tri-Angle wanted to borrow a significant amount of money, so Citigroup sent information technology consultants to evaluate the company's systems and make sure they were capable of generating the sort of accurate monthly financial reports required by the firm for such a sizable loan. Tri-Angle was already on the right track with the new inventory and accounting system, so the necessary data were in the database. However, the consultants soon learned that it was difficult to translate the data into quality information. For instance, if someone wanted a list of accounts receivable that were past due, the database would spit out 500 pages of indecipherable codes and numbers. "None of the answers just popped out of the computer," recalls Fraley.

Fraley began using a software program called Monarch (ironically, already installed on the computer) to turn the data into useful information printed on neat, readable spreadsheets. In the process, Tri-Angle not only qualified for a $5 million loan, but also discovered some of its own poor business practices. For example, Jett and Fraley found more than $100,000 worth of outdated, unused parts that could be returned to manufacturers. As Tri-Angle's ability to turn data into quality information has increased, the leaders are able to see at a moment's notice how the company is performing. They can see immediately which pieces of equipment are being sold or leased and which are not—and on which sales lots. In addition, salespeople, who now carry laptops, can enter sales figures directly into a customer's file using contract management software. When a salesperson gives a customer a quote, it is automatically e-mailed to Jett. As soon as Jett opens the e-mail, the quote is deposited in the central database for later reference.

With the success of Monarch and other management information systems, Jett is now thinking about moving into the world of e-business. He has read about extranets, Web pages, customer relationship management software, and the like, and he wonders how these new technologies might help his business.

Questions

1. With its newfound reliance on information technology, do you think Tri-Angle might fall into a trap of poor information quality or information overload? Why or why not?

2. How does information technology contribute to Tri-Angle's knowledge management? What other strategic advantages does MIS provide?

3. What would you recommend to Tri-Angle as a first step into e-business? Why?

SOURCES: Based on Joshua Macht,"The Accidental Automator," *Inc. Tech,* no. 2 (1997): 66–71.

Part 5 CONTROLLING

514

1. Michael Barbaro, "Wal-Mart Enlists Bloggers in P.R. Campaign," *The New York Times* (March 7, 2006): www.nytimes.com; Daniel McGinn, "Wal-Mart Hits the Wall," *Newsweek* (November 14, 2005): 42; Reed Abelson, "One Giant's Struggle Is Corporate America's, Too; Rewriting the Social Contract— The Wal-Mart Challenge," *The New York Times* (October 29, 2005): C1; www.walmartwatch.com; and Jerry Useem, "Should We Admire Wal-Mart?" *Fortune* (March 8, 2004): 118ff.

2. "The Web Smart 50," *BusinessWeek* (November 21, 2005): 82–112.

3. Christopher Palmeri, "Believe in Yourself, Believe in the Merchandise," *Continental* (December 1997): 49–51; Timothy J. Mullaney with Heather Green, Michael Arndt, Robert D. Hof, and Linda Himelstein, "The E-Biz Surprise," *Business Week,* (May 12, 2003): 60–68.

4. "The Web Smart 50"; Timothy J. Mullaney, "E-Biz Strikes Again," *BusinessWeek* (May 10, 2004): 80–82; and Mullaney et al., "The E-Biz Surprise."

5. Thomas L. Friedman, "It's a Flat World, After All," *The New York Times Magazine* (April 3, 2005): www.nytimes.com/2005/04/03/magazine.

6. Ibid.

7. Michael A. Fontaine, Salvatore Parise, and David Miller, "Collaborative Environments: An Effective Tool for Transforming Business Processes," *Ivey Business Journal* (May–June 2004).

8. "The Web Smart 50."

9. Matt Richtel, "The Long-Distance Journey of a Fast-Food Order," *The New York Times* (April 11, 2006): www.nytimes.com.

10. Timothy J. Mullaney, "Doctors Wielding Data" (pp. 94–98), in "The Web Smart 50," *BusinessWeek* (November 21, 2005): 82–112.

11. Liz Thach and Richard W. Woodman, "Organizational Change and Information Technology: Managing on the Edge of Cyberspace," *Organizational Dynamics* (Summer 1994): 30–46; and Elizabeth Horwitt, "Going Deep: Empowering Employees," *Microsoft Executive Circle* (Summer 2003): 24–26.

12. Greg Jaffe, "Tug of War: In the New Military, Technology May Alter Chain of Command," *The Wall Street Journal* (March 30, 2001): A3, A6.

13. Meridith Levinson, "Business Intelligence: Not Just for Bosses Anymore," *CIO* (January 15, 2006): 82–86.

14. Tonya Vinas, "Surviving Information Overload," *Industry Week* (April 2003): 24–29.

15. Joseph McCafferty, "Coping with Infoglut," *CFO* (September 1998): 101–102.

16. Leonard M. Fuld, "The Danger of Data Slam," *CIO Enterprise* (September 15, 1998): 28–33.

17. Anya Kamenetz, "The Network Unbound," *Fast Company* (June 2006): 68ff; and Stephen Baker and Heather Green, "Blogs Will Change Your Business," *BusinessWeek* (May 2, 2005): 56–67.

18. Kamenetz, "The Network Unbound."

19. Barbaro, "Wal-Mart Enlists Bloggers in P.R. Campaign."

20. Baker and Green, "Blogs Will Change Your Business."

21. This discussion of social networks is based on Kamenetz, "The Network Unbound."

22. Kevin J. Delaney, "Garage Brand; With NBC Pact, YouTube Site Tries to Build a Lasting Business," *The Wall Street Journal* (June 27, 2006): A1, A13.

23. Ibid.

24. Cindy Waxer, "Workers of the World—Collaborate," *FSB* (April 2005): 57–58.

25. Spencer E. Ante et al., "In Search of the Net's Next Big Thing" *BusinessWeek* (March 26, 2001): 140–141; Amy Cortese, "Peer to Peer: P2P Taps the Power of Distant Computers in a Way That Could Transform Whole Industries," *The BusinessWeek 50,* Supplement to *BusinessWeek* (Spring 2001): 194–196.

26. Mark Roberti, "Peer-to-Peer Isn't Dead," *The Industry Standard* (April 23, 2001): 58–59.

27. Derek Slater, "Chain Commanders," *CIO Enterprise* (August 15, 1998): 29–30+.

28. Thomas H. Davenport and Jeanne G. Harris, "Automated Decision Making Comes of Age," *MIT Sloan Management Review* (Summer 2005): 83–89.

29. John P. Mello Jr., "Fly Me to the Web," *CFO* (March 2000): 79–84.

30. Heather Harreld, "Pick-Up Artists," *CIO* (November 1, 2000): 148–154; and Carol J. Loomis, "The Big Surprise Is Enterprise," *Fortune* (July 24, 2006): 140–150.

31. Gary Loveman, "Diamonds in the Data Mine," *Harvard Business Review* (May 2003): 109–113; and Meridith Levinson, "Harrah's Knows What You Did Last Night," *Darwin Magazine* (May 2001): 61–68.

32. Julie Schlosser, "Markdown Lowdown," *Fortune* (January 12, 2004): 40.

33. Ben Worthen, "Down But Not Out in North Carolina," *CIO* (December 1, 2005): 84–94.

34. Spencer E. Ante, "Giving the Boss the Big Picture," *BusinessWeek* (February 13, 2006): 48–51; Doug Bartholomew, "Gauging Success," *CFO-IT* (Summer 2005): 17–19; Russ Banham, "Seeing the Big Picture: New Data Tools Are Enabling CEOs to Get a Better Handle on Performance Across Their Organizations," *Chief Executive* (November 2003): 46.

35. Jim Turcotte, Bob Silveri, and Tom Jobson, "Are You Ready for the E-Supply Chain?" *APICS–The Performance Advantage* (August 1998): 56–59.

36. "History of the Internet: Origin of World Wide Web," (Chapter 6 Excerpt), The Moschovitis Group, www.historyoftheinternet.com/chap6.html.

37. Steve Hamm with David Welch, Wendy Zellner, Faith Keenan, and Peter Engardio, "E-Biz: Down But Hardly Out," *BusinessWeek* (March 26, 2001): 126–130.

38. David Drickhamer, "EDI Is Dead! Long Live EDI!" *Industry Week* (April 2003): 31–38; Ian Mount, "Why EDI Won't Die," *Business 2.0* (August 2003): 68–69; and Marie-Claude Boudreau, Karen D. Loch, Daniel Robey, and Detmar Straud, "Going Global: Using Information Technology to Advance the Competitiveness of the Virtual Transnational Organization," *Academy of Management Executive* 12, no. 4 (1998): 120–128.

39. This discussion is based on Long W. Lam and L. Jean Harrison-Walker, "Toward an Objective-Based Typology

of E-Business Models," *Business Horizons* (November–December 2003): 17–26; and Detmar Straub and Richard Klein, "E-Competitive Transformations," *Business Horizons* (May–June 2001): 3–12.

40. Tom Lowry, "In the Zone," *BusinessWeek* (October 17, 2005): 66–78; Tom Lowry, "TV's New Parallel Universe," *BusinessWeek* (November 14, 2005): 72–74.

41. Katharine Q. Seelye, "Reviving a Magazine with Ballast of a Web Site First," *The New York Times* (April 11, 2005): www.nytimes.com; and www.radarmagazine.com.

42. Russ Banham, "Old Dogs, New Clicks," *CFO-IT* (Summer 2005): 21–26.

43. Mullaney et al., "The E-Biz Surprise."

44. "The Web Smart 50."

45. Jonathan L. Willis, "What Impact Will E-Commerce Have on the U.S. Economy?" *Economic Review—Federal Reserve Bank of Kansas City* 89, no. 2 (Second Quarter 2004): 53ff; 2005 productivity gains reported in Mullaney et al., "The E-Biz Surprise."

46. Straub and Klein, "E-Competitive Transformations."

47. "The Web Smart 50."

48. This discussion of implementation approaches is based on Ranjay Gulati and Jason Garino, "Get the Right Mix of Bricks and Clicks," *Harvard Business Review* (May–June 2000): 107–114.

49. Ibid.

50. "Business: Surfing USA," *The Economist* (June 30, 2001): 58; and James R. Hagerty and James Hall, "British Supermarket Giant Cooks Up Plans to Go Global—Tesco's Move to Duplicate High Growth at Home Comes with Big Risks," *The Wall Street Journal* (July 5, 2001): A9.

51. Banham, "Old Dogs, New Clicks."

52. This discussion is based on Mauro F. Guillén, "What Is the Best Global Strategy for the Internet?" *Business Horizons* (May–June 2002): 39–46; and Bob Tedeschi, "American Web Sites Speak the Language of Overseas Users," *The New York Times* (January 12, 2004): www.nytimes.com.

53. Statistic reported in Mullaney et al., "The E-Biz Surprise." This discussion is based on Pamela Barnes-Vieyra and Cindy Claycomb, "Business-to-Business E-Commerce: Models and Managerial Decisions," *Business Horizons* (May–June 2001): 13–20.

54. Reported in Hamm et al., "E-Biz: Down But Hardly Out."

55. "The Web Smart 50."

56. Robert D. Hof, "The eBay Economy," *BusinessWeek* (August 25, 2003): 124+.

57. Raizel Robin, "Net Gains," *Canadian Business* (October 14–October 26, 2003): 107.

58. Eric Young, "Web Marketplaces That Really Work," *Fortune/CNET Tech Review* (Winter 2001): 78–86.

59. F. C. "Ted" Weston, Jr., "ERP II: The Extended Enterprise System," *Business Horizons* (November–December 2003): 49–55; and Vincent A. Mabert, Ashok Soni, and M. A. Venkataramanan, "Enterprise Resource Planning: Common Myths Versus Evolving Reality," *Business Horizons* (May–June 2001): 69–76.

60. Derek Slater, "What Is ERP?" *CIO Enterprise* (May 15, 1999): 86.

61. Susannah Patton, "Doctors' Group Profits From ERP," *CIO* (September 1, 2003): 32.

62. Brian Caulfield, "Facing Up to CRM," *Business 2.0* (August–September 2001): 149–150; and "Customer Relationship Management: The Good. The Bad. The Future." *BusinessWeek* (April 28, 2003): 53–64.

63. Ellen Neuborne, "A Second Act for CRM," *Inc.* (March 2005): 40.

64. The discussion of collaborative customer experiences is based on Paul Greenberg, "Applied Insight: Move Over, Baby Boomers," *CIO* (March 1, 2006), http://www.cio.com.

65. Reported in Eric Seubert, Y. Balaji, and Mahesh Makhija, "The Knowledge Imperative," *CIO Advertising Supplement* (March 15, 2001): S1–S4.

66. Ryan K. Lahti and Michael M. Beyerlein, "Knowledge Transfer and Management Consulting: A Look at 'The Firm,'" *Business Horizons* (January–February 2000): 65–74.

67. Meridith Levinson, "Business Intelligence: Not Just for Bosses Anymore," *CIO* (January 15, 2006): 82–88; and Alice Dragoon, "Business Intelligence Gets Smart," *CIO* (September 15, 2003): 84–91.

68. John Edwards, "Picture This," *CFO* (November 2005): 80–83.

69. Julie Schlosser, "Looking for Intelligence in Ice Cream," *Fortune* (March 17, 2003): 114–120.

70. Reported in Schlosser, "Looking for Intelligence in Ice Cream."

71. Kevin Kelleher, "66,207,896 Bottles of Beer on the Wall," *Business 2.0* (January–February 2004): 47–49.

72. Ibid.

73. Morten T. Hansen, Nitin Nohria, and Thomas Tierney, "What's Your Strategy for Managing Knowledge?" *Harvard Business Review* (March–April 1999): 106–116; Louisa Wah, "Behind the Buzz," *Management Review* (April 1999): 17–26; and Jenny C. McCune, "Thirst for Knowledge," *Management Review* (April, 1999): 10–12.

74. Seubert, Balaji, and Makhija, "The Knowledge Imperative."

75. Tony Kontzer with Melanie Turek, "Learning to Share," *Information Week* (May 5, 2003): 29–37.

76. Barbaro, "Wal-Mart Enlists Bloggers in P.R. Campaign"; and David Watkins, "Media: How Big Business Barged In on the Bloggers: Companies Once Saw Them as a Nuisance," *The Guardian* (March 20, 2006): 6.

CHAPTER 16

CHAPTER OUTLINE

Manager's Challenge

The Organizations as a Value Chain

  Manufacturing and Service Operations

  Operations Management and Competitive Strategy

  The Integrated Enterprise

Designing Operations Management Systems

  Product and Service Design

  Procurement

  Facilities Layout

  Technology Automation

  Facility Location

  Capacity Planning

Inventory Management

  The Importance of Inventory

  Economic Order Quantity

  Material Requirements Planning

  Just-in-Time Inventory

  Logistics and Distribution Management

Lean Manufacturing and Productivity

  Lean Manufacturing

  Measuring Productivity

  Improving Productivity

LEARNING OBJECTIVES

After studying this chapter, you should be able to:

1. Define *operations management* and describe its application within manufacturing and service organizations.

2. Discuss the role of operations management strategy in the company's overall competitive strategy.

3. Explain the role of e-business in today's partnership approach to supply chain management.

4. Summarize considerations in designing an operations system, including product and service design, facilities layout, and capacity planning.

5. Explain why small inventories are preferred by most organizations.

6. Discuss major techniques for the management of materials and inventory.

7. Describe what is meant by lean manufacturing.

8. Define *productivity* and explain why and how managers seek to improve it.

OPERATIONS AND VALUE CHAIN MANAGEMENT

MANAGER'S CHALLENGE

After nearly 30 years in business, West Marine is thriving. Randy Repass started the company from his garage in Sunnyvale, California, selling nylon rope by mail order, and gradually expanded into a robust wholesale business and opening of retail stores on both coasts, offering everything from foul weather gear and boat safety equipment to electronics. Now, West has acquired one of its oldest and most respected competitors, E&B Marine. Whereas West's target customer has always been a sailor with a large, coastal boat, E&B has served primarily powerboaters with small craft. The merger gives West 150 stores across the country, making it nearly 300 percent larger than its closest competitor and a one-stop shopping destination for everything to do with boating except the boat itself. But managers wonder whether business has been a little too good. Distribution has become chaotic, and stores are having trouble keeping items in stock, with out-of-stock levels during peak season climbing to more than 12 percent. As the business has expanded, getting the right orders from suppliers at the right time has also become a nightmare. The on-time fill rate for vendor orders at West's distribution centers has dropped to about 35 percent. Sales have started to decline because the stores don't have the right equipment and supplies when customers want them.[1]

> If you were a manager at West Marine, how would you help the retail stores get the equipment and supplies they need when they need them? How can West's managers get suppliers to do a better job of delivering the right products to distribution centers on time, and then make sure products get from the centers into the stores where they're needed?

■ **TAKE A MOMENT**

Like West Marine, many companies with successful products and services find themselves with out-of-date, inefficient operations systems that contribute to performance problems. Strategic success depends on efficient operations. The importance of operational efficiency is illustrated by the chaos that surrounds many relief efforts following major disasters. Aid groups are typically deluged with donated supplies but have a hard time getting them to where they're needed. The global cargo industry, including companies such as express shipper DHL and the giant logistics company TNT, has embarked on an innovative volunteer effort to help governments and private aid groups improve their operations to respond faster and more effectively to major disasters. As a repository of knowledge on how to move huge loads to remote places fast, these companies can help in areas such as improving air-traffic logistics after a disaster, keeping track of supplies, and effectively and rationally distributing aid.[2]

For all organizations, operational concerns such as obtaining parts and supplies, updating production technology, and implementing efficient delivery systems take on extreme importance in today's competitive, global environment. Production costs are a major expense for organizations, especially for manufacturers, but service organizations such as West Marine have to be concerned with productivity and efficiency too. Organizations therefore try to limit costs and increase quality by improving how they obtain materials, set up production facilities, and produce goods and services. Likewise, companies are seeking a strategic advantage in the ways they deliver products and services to consumers. In the manufacturing sector, the efficiency of Toyota's automobile production is legendary. Wal-Mart is a leader in operations excellence in the service sector, with executives using sophisticated technology to manage a supremely efficient supply and distribution network that enables the company to keep costs and prices at rock bottom. Manufacturing and service operations such Wal-Mart, Toyota, and West Marine are important because they signify the company's basic purpose—indeed, its reason for existence. Without the ability to produce products and services that are competitive in the global marketplace, companies cannot expect to succeed.

This chapter describes techniques for the planning and control of manufacturing and service operations. Whereas the two preceding chapters described overall control concepts, including management information systems, this chapter will focus on the management and control of production operations. First we define operations management. Then we look at how some companies bring operations into strategic decision making and provide an overview of the integrated enterprise, in which managers use electronic linkages to manage interrelated operations activities. Next, we consider specific operational design issues, such as product and service design, procurement, location planning and facilities layout, production technology, and capacity planning. We give special attention to inventory management, including a discussion of just-in-time inventory systems and logistics. Finally, we look at how managers measure and improve productivity.

THE ORGANIZATION AS A VALUE CHAIN

In Chapter 1, the organization was described as a system used for transforming inputs into outputs. At the center of this transformation process is the **technical core**, which is the heart of the organization's production of its product or service.[3] In an automobile company, the technical core includes the plants that manufacture automobiles. In a university, the technical core includes the academic activities of teaching and research.

As illustrated in Exhibit 16.1, the organization can be thought of as a *value chain* that receives inputs from the environment, such as raw materials and other resources, and adds value by transforming them into products and services for

technical core The heart of the organization's production of its product or service.

EXHIBIT   16.1

The Organization as a
Value Chain

customers. Inputs into the technical core typically include materials and equipment, human resources, land and buildings, and information. Outputs from the technical core are the goods and services produced by the organization and sold or provided to customers and clients. Operations strategy and control feedback shape the quality of outputs and the efficiency of operations within the technical core.

The topic of operations management pertains to the day-to-day management of the technical core, as illustrated in Exhibit 16.1, including acquiring inputs, transforming them, and distributing outputs. **Operations management** is formally defined as the field of management that specializes in the production of goods and services and uses special tools and techniques for solving production problems. In essence, operations managers are concerned with all the activities involved in converting inputs into outputs, including decisions about matters such as how and where to obtain raw materials, where to locate facilities and what equipment to install in them, and how to get products or services to customers. For example, PepsiCo has gotten into the farming business in order to get the raw materials it needs to build its snack foods business in emerging markets. Sales of Western-style snack foods are growing fast in China and other developing countries, and Pepsi wants to be the global leader. However, getting the tens of millions of potatoes needed to serve the Chinese market alone turned out to be a major problem. Today, Pepsi is the largest private potato grower in China and also has potato programs in Russia, South Africa, and Poland.[4] Pepsi's operations managers also have to consider the best location to manufacture snack foods for global markets, how to get raw materials to manufacturing facilities, and how to efficiently produce products and get them onto store shelves.

As with all areas of management, operations management also requires the ability to lead people. For example, Toyota's operations are admired worldwide as a model of quality and efficiency, but this success is not merely a result of using the right machines or setting the right standards. U.S. automakers have had difficulty duplicating Toyota's success with *lean manufacturing* because they have focused primarily on the technical elements of the system and failed to implement the necessary cultural and leadership changes.[5] Toyota's system combines techniques, systems, and philosophy, such as commitment to employee empowerment and a creative culture. Besides installing the methodology for running an efficient assembly line, such as *just-in-time* shipments of supplies, managers must instill the necessary attitudes, such as concern for quality and a desire to innovate.

Manufacturing and Service Operations

Although terms such as *production* and *operations* seem to imply manufacturing organizations, operations management applies to all organizations. The service sector has increased three times as fast as the manufacturing sector in the North American economy. Today, more than half of all businesses are service organizations and two-thirds of the U.S. workforce is employed in services, such as hospitals, hotels and resorts, retail, financial services, or telecommunications firms. Operations management tools and techniques apply to services as well as manufacturing. Exhibit 16.2 shows differences between manufacturing and service organizations.

Manufacturing organizations are those that produce physical goods, such as cars, books, computers, or tennis balls. In contrast, **service organizations** produce nonphysical outputs, such as medical, educational, communication, or transportation services provided for customers. Doctors, consultants, online auction companies, and the local barber all provide services. Services also include the sale of merchandise. Although merchandise is a physical good, the service company does not manufacture it but merely sells it as a service to the customer.

Services differ from manufactured products in two ways. First, the service customer is involved in the actual production process.[6] The patient actually visits the doctor to receive the service, and it's difficult to imagine a hairstylist providing services without direct customer contact. The same is true for airlines, restaurants,

operations management The field of management that focuses on the physical production of goods or services and uses specialized techniques for solving manufacturing problems.

manufacturing organization An organization that produces physical goods.

service organization An organization that produces nonphysical outputs that require customer involvement and cannot be stored in inventory.

EXHIBIT   16.2

Differences Between
Manufacturing and Service
Organizations

SOURCES: Based on Richard
L. Daft, *Organization Theory
and Design* (Cincinnati, OH:
South-Western, 2005): 256;
and Byron J. Finch and
Richard L. Luebbe, *Operations
Management* (Fort Worth, TX:
The Dryden Press, 1995): 50.

Manufacturing Organizations	Service Organizations
Produce physical goods	Produce nonphysical outputs
Goods inventoried for later consumption	Simultaneous production and consumption
Quality measured directly	Quality perceived and difficult to measure
Standardized output	Customized output
Production process removed from consumer	Consumer participates in production process
Facilities site moderately important to business success	Facilities site crucial to success of firm
Capital intensive	Labor intensive
Examples:	*Examples:*
Automobile manufacturers	Airlines
Steel companies	Hotels
Soft-drink companies	Law firms

and banks. Second, manufactured goods can be placed in inventory, whereas service outputs, being intangible, cannot be stored. Manufactured products such as clothes, food, cars, or iPods all can be put in warehouses and sold at a later date. However, a hairstylist cannot wash, cut, and style hair in advance and leave it on the shelf for the customer's arrival, nor can a doctor place examinations in inventory. The service must be created and provided for the customer exactly when he or she wants it.

Despite the differences between manufacturing and service firms, they face similar operational problems. First, each kind of organization needs to be concerned with scheduling. A medical clinic must schedule appointments so that doctors' and patients' time will be used efficiently. Second, both manufacturing and service organizations must obtain materials and supplies. Third, both types of organizations should be concerned with quality and productivity. Because many operational problems are similar, operations management tools and techniques can and should be applied to service organizations as readily as they are to manufacturing operations.

■ TAKE A MOMENT

As a new manager, think about your team as part of a value chain that receives inputs, adds value, and provides outputs to customers or clients. Help your team implement operating techniques to achieve superior customer responsiveness, innovation, quality, and efficiency.

Operations Management and Competitive Strategy

Many operations managers are involved in day-to-day problem solving and lose sight of the fact that the best way to control operations is through strategic planning. When operations managers become enmeshed in operational details, they are less likely to see the big picture with respect to inventory buildups, parts shortages, and seasonal fluctuations. To manage operations effectively, managers understand the importance of competitive strategy.

operations strategy means that operations managers are directly involved in the organization's strategic planning by developing plans and tactics that increase operational effectiveness and help the company attain its strategic goals. Superior operations effectiveness can support existing strategy, as well as contribute to new strategic directions that can be difficult for competitors to copy.[7] When an organization's operations effectiveness is based on capabilities that are ingrained in its employees, its culture, and its operating processes, the company can be tough to beat.[8]

operations strategy The recognition of the importance of operations to the firm's success and the involvement of operations managers in the organization's strategic planning.

Managers focus on four major outcomes to build a highly effective operations system:[9]

:: *Achieving superior customer responsiveness.* The operations system should be designed so that the organization can satisfy customer needs, giving customers what they want, when they want it, at an acceptable price. Companies that are more responsive to customers and provide good value are more competitive. Enterprise became the largest and most profitable rental car company in the United States based largely on an intense focus on customers, especially those who have lost the use of their automobile due to a traffic accident. The idea of picking customers up at their homes was a stroke of genius.[10]

:: *Achieving superior innovation with speed and flexibility.* Innovation leads to new and better products and services as well as better ways of producing them and delivering them to customers. Innovation is a top priority for many organizations today, including big, established companies like John Deere. Deere is building tractors with computer systems that enable farmers to analyze fertilizer, soil composition, and yields in each section of their fields, and producing forestry equipment that allows operators to select and cut trees in a way that fosters regrowth.[11] As discussed in Chapter 11, successful innovation, including the ability to introduce new or improved products fast, means a company can differentiate itself from rivals and attract more customers.

:: *Achieving superior quality.* Quality means producing products or services that are highly reliable and have features or characteristics that customers desire. Offering high-quality products builds brand-name reputation, which means the company can typically charge higher prices for its products or services. For example, Hyundai Motor Company's high-volume, low-cost Hyundai brand jumped from eleventh place to third place, behind Porsche and Toyota, in the 2006 J. D. Power & Associates Initial Quality Study. Hyundai's reputation for quality is growing rapidly, nearly approaching that of Toyota, enabling the company to increase prices and profits.[12] Today's organizations are using a variety of techniques, such as quality circles, Six Sigma principles, and benchmarking, as described in Chapter 15, to improve quality in products, service, and processes.

:: *Achieving superior efficiency.* As discussed in Chapter 1, efficiency refers to the amount of resources used to achieve organizational goals. As applied to the operations system, efficiency measures the amount of inputs used to produce a given amount of outputs, as illustrated in Exhibit 16.1. An organization that uses fewer inputs for a given level of outputs is more efficient, meaning its costs will be lower and it can provide outputs to customers at a more competitive price and still make money. Enterprise improved efficiency with an innovative computer system called ARMS (automated rental management system), as described in Chapter 15. ARMS, which links all of the car rental's locations and connects Enterprise to major auto insurers, saves employees an average of 8 to 9 phone calls per rental, which adds up to time and money for Enterprise.[13]

The Integrated Enterprise

To adopt a strategic approach, operations managers appreciate that their operations are not independent of other activities. To operate efficiently, innovate, and produce high-quality items that meet customers' needs, the organization must have reliable deliveries of high-quality, reasonably priced supplies and materials. It also requires an

© BECKFORD ENTERPRISES/PRNEWSFOTO (NEWSCOM)

CONCEPT CONNECTION A doctor's office is a classic example of a **service operation**, but Dr. Rita Beckford doesn't limit her practice of medicine to the clinic. Her mission is to empower people everywhere to take control of their own health. Beckford didn't need anyone to tell her that her post-pregnancy weight of 210 pounds put her at risk for the diabetes that killed her grandmother. So she shed more than 80 pounds, became a certified fitness instructor, and offered her services to medical clinics, community centers, and churches. Beckford's popular exercise routines became the core of a DVD, *Home with Dr. B.*, and she also offers her services as a motivational speaker.

EXHIBIT 16.3

Dell Computer's Integrated Supply Chain

SOURCE: Jason Dedrick and Kenneth L. Kraemer, "The Impacts of IT on Firm and Industry Structure: The Personal Computer Industry," *California Management Review* 47, no. 3 (Spring 2005); 132. Used with permission.

Dell Computer's Integrated Supply Chain: Contract manufacturers, Original design manufacturers — Logistics Companies — System Integrators — Component Suppliers — Dell — Customer — Hardware and Software Suppliers — Distributors — Repair and Support Companies.

Legend: —— Physical Flows   – – – Information Flows

supply chain management
Managing the sequence of suppliers and purchasers, covering all stages of processing from obtaining raw materials to distributing finished goods to final consumers.

efficient and reliable system for distributing finished products, making them readily accessible to customers. Operations managers with a strategic focus therefore recognize that they need to manage the entire supply chain. **Supply chain management** is the term for managing the sequence of suppliers and purchasers covering all stages of processing from obtaining raw materials to distributing finished goods to final consumers.[14]

The most recent advances in supply chain management involve using Internet technologies to achieve the right balance of low inventory levels and customer responsiveness. An e-supply chain creates a seamless, integrated link that stretches from customers to suppliers, by establishing electronic linkages between the organization and these external partners for the sharing and exchange of data.[15] Dell's integrated supply chain, illustrated in Exhibit 16.3 provides an excellent example.

Dell Inc.

Even Dell Inc.'s rivals admit that the most efficient way to make, sell, and deliver personal computers is the way Dell does it. Dell's PCs are made to order and delivered directly to customers. Each customer gets exactly what he or she wants—and gets it faster and cheaper than the competition could provide it.

Dell is electronically connected to suppliers, contract manufacturers, and distributors, as shown in the exhibit, so that everyone along the supply chain has almost completely transparent information about sales, orders, shipments, and other data. That means, for instance, that suppliers have data about orders and production levels and know what parts Dell's factories are going to need and when they'll need them. Distributors know when computers will be ready for shipment and where they'll be going. At the end of the supply chain, Dell develops close connections to customers through a range of channels, including online sales and services, call centers, and a direct sales force and technical personnel serving larger customers.

Dell's role in the supply chain is to manage the electronic information flows and physical connections among suppliers, partners, and customers. As one Dell executive says, "Information systems driven by direct sales make it possible. We get rich market signals from customers and pass them to suppliers [and partners] to coordinate our whole network."[16]

AMR Research recently ranked Dell as the best-performing supply chain in the world, based on ratings from a panel of experts and on the company's return on assets, sales, and rate of growth. Wal-Mart was ranked at No. 5, Toyota Motor Co. at No. 6, and the British supermarket chain Tesco at No. 9.[17]

Enterprise integration through the use of electronic linkages is creating a level of cooperation not previously imaginable for many organizations. Supplier relationships used to be based on an *arm's-length* approach, in which an organization spreads purchases among many suppliers and encourages them to compete with one another. With integration, more companies, like Dell, are opting for a *partnership* approach, which involves cultivating intimate relationships with a few carefully selected suppliers and collaborating closely to coordinate tasks that benefit both parties. Ford Motor Company plans to cut in half the number of suppliers it uses, which will benefit both the suppliers, by giving them larger, longer-term deals, and Ford, by enabling it to obtain supplies at lower cost.[18]

Electronic linkages also contribute to more rapid response to end consumers by reducing the time it takes to move critical data through the information pipeline. Manufacturers have immediate access to sales data and can deliver new products as needed. In addition, electronic linkages enable the rapid manufacture of all types of customized products. Ford Motor Company has been undergoing a supply-chain makeover intended to enable the company to manufacture cars on a reasonable build-to-order basis, so that customers no longer have to wait months for delivery of the car of their dreams.[19]

By integrating everyone along the entire supply chain, the idea is that every organization involved can move in lock-step to meet the customer's product and time demands.

TAKE A MOMENT

Managing a supply chain requires interpersonal influence and political skills because of the lack of direct control over outside suppliers. Take the New Manager Self-Test on page 524 to learn about your political skills.

DESIGNING OPERATIONS MANAGEMENT SYSTEMS

Every organization must design its production system. This process starts with the design of the product or service to be produced. A restaurant designs the food items on the menu. An automobile manufacturer designs the cars it produces. A management consulting firm designs the various types of services it will offer to clients. Other considerations in designing the production system include purchasing raw materials, layout of facilities, designing production technology, facilities location, and capacity planning.

Product and Service Design

The way a product or service is designed affects its appeal for customers; it also affects how easy or expensive operations will be. Design has become a critical aspect of product development for many companies, even old-line manufacturers of products such as appliances and tools. Whirlpool's Duet line of washers and dryers, with soft curves and splashes of color, captured 19 percent of the front-loading washer market in only two years.[20] Solo Cup's sales of disposable plates began growing at a double-digit pace after a design company observed people picnicking and suggested adding deep wells and indented hand grips to make the plates easier to manage with one hand.[21]

However, some product designs are difficult to execute properly. When Volant began making an unconventional type of skis from steel, skiers began snapping them up, delighted with their flexibility and tight grip of the snow. However,

POLITICAL SKILLS

How good are you at influencing people horizontally across an organization? To learn something about your skills, answer the questions that follow. Please answer whether each item that follows is Mostly True or Mostly False for you.

	Mostly True	Mostly False
1. I am able to communicate easily and effectively with others.	____	____
2. I spend a lot of time at work developing connections with people outside my area.	____	____
3. I instinctively know the right thing to say or do to influence others.	____	____
4. I am good at using my connections outside my area to get things done at work.	____	____
5. When communicating with others I am absolutely genuine in what I say and do.	____	____
6. It is easy for me to reach out to new people.	____	____

	Mostly True	Mostly False
7. I make strangers feel comfortable and at ease around me.	____	____
8. I am good at sensing the motivations and hidden agendas of others.	____	____

INTERPRETATION: Having some basic political skill helps a new manager gain broad influence. Managing a supply chain will mean asserting influence and gaining cooperation without having formal authority. Political skills help a new manager build personal and organizational relationships that enhance your team's outcomes. New managers often learn task and people skills first. Political skills tend to be subtle and are typically mastered after gaining management experience.

SCORING: Give yourself 1 point for each item marked as Mostly True. A score of 6 or higher suggests active political skills and a good start for your career as a new manager. If you scored 3 or less, you may want to focus more on building horizontal relationships as you progress in your career as a manager.

SOURCE: Adapted from Gerald R. Ferris, Darren C. Treadway, Robert W. Kolodinsky, Wayne A. Hochwarter, Charles J. Kacmer, Ceasar Douglas, and Dwight D. Frink, "Development and Validation of the Political Skill Inventory, *Journal of Management* 31 (February 2005): 126–152.

producing the skis turned out to be a nightmare, and many pairs had to be scrapped or reworked. Expenses mounted, and the company failed to meet promised delivery dates. Eventually, Volant hired Mark Soderberg, an engineer with experience at Boeing. Soderberg made a small design change that allowed more generous manufacturing tolerances (variances from the design specifications). After the tooling was adjusted to accommodate the design change, Volant began producing the modified skis—and forecast its first year of operating in the black.

To prevent such problems in the first place, a growing number of businesses are using *design for manufacturability and assembly* (DFMA). In the past, many engineering designers fashioned products with disdain for how they would be produced. Elegant designs nearly always had too many parts. The watchword today is simplicity, making the product easy and inexpensive to manufacture. At Seagate, the largest and most efficient maker of hard drives in the world, with its drives used in computers and cameras, MP3 players and cell phones, and Xboxes and Tivos, all products have at least 75 percent of their parts and machinery in common with one another. It wasn't always that way. When then-manufacturing chief William Watkins (he's now CEO) first asked engineers how many parts could be shared in more than one drive, the answer was 2 percent. Watkins threw a bunch of parts on the conference table and told his engineers to start over, beginning with the simplest of parts such as screws and working their way up to more intricate components.[22]

Using DFMA is extremely inexpensive, but it does require a shift in how design work is done. DFMA often requires restructuring operations, creating teams of designers, manufacturers, and assemblers to work together. They collaborate on achieving four objectives of product design:

1. *Producibility.* The degree to which a product or service can actually be produced for the customer within the firm's existing operational capacity.

2. *Cost.* The sum of the materials, labor, design, transportation, and overhead expense associated with a product or service. Striving for simplicity and few parts keeps product and service designs within reasonable costs.

3. *Quality.* The excellence of the product or service—the serviceability and value that customers gain by purchasing the product. Companies are taking the time to ask questions such as "How do people use this product?" and "How can we make this product more user friendly?"

4. *Reliability.* The degree to which the customer can count on the product or service to fulfill its intended function. The product should function as designed for a reasonable length of time. Highly complex products often have lower reliability because more things can go wrong.

Go to the ethical dilemma on page 543 that pertains to product design.   ■ **TAKE A MOMENT**

The design of services also should reflect producibility, cost, quality, and reliability. However, services have one additional design requirement: timing. *Timing* is the degree to which the provision of a service meets the customer's delivery requirements. Recall that a service cannot be stored in inventory and must be provided when the customer is present. Self-service checkout, banking by machine, and pumping your own gas are all ways that organizations provide timely service, which is important in today's time-pressured world. In recent years, the idea of improving the timing of service delivery has spread to the medical profession. A number of programs are springing up around the country to help doctors and medical clinics redesign their practices to overcome problems such as long waiting times for patients and weeks-long delays in getting appointments. Family physician L. Gordon Moore of Rochester, New York, for example, now relies heavily on electronic health records and practice-management software for handling administrative tasks, which increases efficiency and allows more time for attending to patients. One patient says she switched to Dr. Moore because the wait time at her previous physician was usually an hour and a half, with only 5 minutes for the actual appointment.[23]

Procurement

The purchasing of supplies, services, and raw materials for use in the production process, known as **procurement**, has increased in importance as an operations issue. On average, a manufacturing company spends 50 to 60 percent of its revenues to buy materials and supplies. For example, auto manufacturers spend about 60 percent of revenues on material purchases, food processors about 70 percent, and oil refineries about 80 percent, and the percentages keep going up.[24] Expenses for materials, supplies, and services also represent a huge expense for service companies. Having the right materials of the correct design and quality is essential to the smooth functioning of the production process.

The Internet and business-to-business (B2B) commerce are having a tremendous impact on procurement. Purchasing department employees can now use the Internet to search for new sources of materials, place orders, request bids via B2B marketplaces, and participate in online auctions. Employees have quick access to more information about availability and cost. They can often submit purchase orders online and track the status of orders over the Web, cutting down on operating costs and speeding up the procurement lead time.[25] For example, by

procurement Purchasing supplies, services, and raw materials for use in the production process.

eliminating purchase orders and moving procurement online where employees ordered from suppliers that offered the company a discount, DuPont cut procurement costs by $200 million in one recent year. In addition, the typical order is now processed in one day instead of five.[26] Verizon Wireless hopes to shave 5 to 10 percent off the $150 million it spends on procurement of temporary contract workers each year by using competitive bidding and contract management over the Internet.[27] Whether they're looking for paper clips, jet engines, or consultants, more and more companies are using the Internet to control and streamline the procurement process.

Burlington Northern Santa Fe Railway set up an online procurement system for supplies as a first step toward a fully Web-enabled supply chain. Employees are required to make all purchases—from pencils to computers—over the Web, where they can be easily tracked. The goal, according to vice president and chief sourcing officer for BNSF, Jeff Campbell, was to eliminate *maverick spends*—random purchases made by employees at local office supply stores. The maverick spend makes it practically impossible for procurement departments to track costs or budget and forecast accurately. Purchase orders are now submitted online, with automated approval based on certain criteria, eliminating the time-sapping manual approval process. Campbell estimates that online procurement saves 3 percent to 8 percent on all the various purchases made, because of the opportunity to negotiate discounts by purchasing in volume from a few suppliers.[28]

Facilities Layout

Once a product or service has been designed and systems set up for procurement of materials, the next consideration is planning for the actual production through facilities layout. The four most common types of layout are process, product, cellular, and fixed-position, shown in Exhibit 16.4.

PROCESS LAYOUT

As illustrated in Exhibit 16.4(a), a **process layout** is one in which all machines that perform a similar function or task are grouped together. In a machine shop, the lathes perform a similar function and are located together in one section. The grinders are in another section of the shop. Service organizations also use process layouts. In a bank, the loan officers are in one area, the tellers in another, and the managers in a third.

The advantage of the process layout is that it has the potential for economies of scale and reduced costs. For example, having all painting done in one spray-painting area means that fewer machines and people are required to paint all products for the organization. In a bank, having all tellers located in one controlled area provides increased security. Placing all operating rooms together in a hospital makes it possible to control the environment for all rooms simultaneously.

The drawback to the process layout, as illustrated in Exhibit 16.4(a), is that the actual path a product or service takes can be long and complicated. A product may need several different processes performed on it and thus must travel through many different areas before production is complete.

PRODUCT LAYOUT

Exhibit 16.4(b) illustrates a **product layout**—one in which machines and tasks are arranged according to the progressive steps in producing a single product. The automobile assembly line is a classic example, because it produces a single product starting from the raw materials to the finished output. Many fast-food restaurants use the product layout, with activities arranged in sequence to produce hamburgers or fried chicken, depending on the products available.

process layout A facilities layout in which machines that perform the same function are grouped together in one location.

product layout A facilities layout in which machines and tasks are arranged according to the sequence of steps in the production of a single product.

(a) Process Layout

(b) Product Layout

(c) Cellular Layout

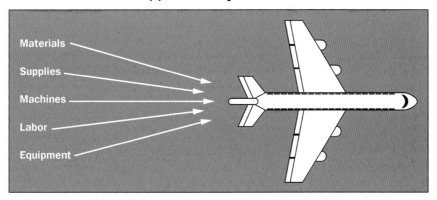

(d) Fixed-Position Layout

EXHIBIT 16.4

Basic Production Layouts
SOURCES: Based on J. T. Black, "Cellular Manufacturing Systems Reduce Setup Time, Make Small Lot Production Economical," *Industrial Engineering* (November 1983): 36–48; and Richard J. Schonberger, "Plant Layout Becomes Product-Oriented with Cellular, Just-in-Time Production Concepts," *Industrial Engineering* (November 1983): 66–77.

The product layout is efficient when the organization produces huge volumes of identical products. Note in Exhibit 16.4(b) that two lines have paint areas. This duplication of functions can be economical only if the volume is high enough to keep each paint area busy working on specialized products.

CELLULAR LAYOUT

Illustrated in Exhibit 16.4(c) is an innovative layout, called **cellular layout**, based on group-technology principles. In a manufacturing plant, all machines dedicated to sequences of operations are grouped into cells, as shown in the exhibit. In a

cellular layout A facilities layout in which machines dedicated to sequences of production are grouped into cells in accordance with group-technology principles.

A GERMAN FACTORY SHOWS HOW TO BE FAST AND FLEXIBLE

Many students might think a factory that makes polymer bearings and power-supply chains is not the best place to get a view of the factory of the future, but they'd be wrong. Cologne, Germany's igus Inc. manufacturing plant represents a highly innovative approach to facilities design. The plant's flexible design enables the factory to shrink or expand at a moment's notice, keeping pace with an unpredictable market. Almost nothing is bolted down on the plant floor, so that machines, modules, and entire departments can be rearranged. Other design features, such as exposed overhead wiring and few support columns, mean the company can redesign itself as needed with little disruption to the 24-7 production flow. Over the past five years, igus has made at least 50 significant changes to the factory's configuration to accommodate strategic shifts, facilitate fast growth, or meet new customer needs.

Fast, agile organizations do not occur on their own. Managers have to make decisions that include considering the physical as well as the human environment. Frank Blase, president of igus, offers the following tips for building a nimble organization:

1. *Create a flexible environment.* A plant's space, facilities design, and layout should accommodate the business, not the other way around.

2. *Recruit carefully.* Not everyone is comfortable working in a highly flexible, fast-changing

environment. Human resource managers should screen job candidates carefully and make sure they understand the nature of the workplace. At igus, candidates are given a *schnuppertag*, or sniffing-around day, to explore, observe, and ask questions.

3. *Practice being fast.* Every aspect of the company should be designed to encourage speed and agility. All igus employees are equipped with mobile phones and get around on shiny, motorized scooters. An open physical environment encourages collaboration and information transparency. Department teams conduct quick daily huddles to review what went well and what didn't the day before.

4. *Inspire your staff.* This last tip may be the most important of all. Flexibility hinges on innovation and creativity, Blase says, which depends on employees who are inspired to think differently and express their ideas and opinions. "We're trying to be a different kind of company," he adds, "and our building helps us tremendously in doing that. It creates a holistic system for how to behave."

SOURCE: Chuck Salter, "This Is One Fast Factory," *Fast Company* (August 2001): 32–33.

MANAGER'S SHOPTALK

service organization, all the people who work on a process, such as insurance claims processing, are organized into cells where they can see and easily communicate with one another. Work flows from one station to another, similar to materials movement in the manufacturing plant.[29] Grouping technology into cells provides some of the efficiencies of both process and product layouts. Even more important, the U-shaped cells in Exhibit 16.4(c) provide efficiencies in material and tool handling and inventory movement. Employees work in clusters that facilitate teamwork and joint problem solving. Staffing flexibility is enhanced because people are cross-trained so that each worker can perform all the tasks, assisting coworkers as needed.

FIXED-POSITION LAYOUT

As shown in Exhibit 16.4(d), the **fixed-position layout** is one in which the product remains in one location, and employees and equipment are brought to it. The fixed-position layout is used to create a product or service that is either large or one of a kind, such as aircraft, ships, and buildings. The product cannot be moved from function to function or along an assembly line; rather, the people, materials, and machines all come to the fixed-position site for assembly and processing. This layout is not good for high volume, but it is often necessary for large, bulky products and custom orders. However, the fixed position layout is being adapted by many of today's companies to speed up production. Boeing now builds many of its planes on a type of moving assembly line, which cut in half the time it takes to assemble a

fixed-position layout A facilities layout in which the product remains in one location and the required tasks and equipment are brought to it.

single-aisle 737. Airbus uses assembly stations, moving the plane only from one major work station to the next, with the idea that a glitch in one plane won't slow a whole production line.[30]

As the need for speed and responsiveness increased, many organizations designed facilities layout to allow for a high level of flexibility. This chapter's Shoptalk offers some tips from a German factory that is on the cutting edge of a new way of working.

Technology Automation

One goal of many operations managers is to implement more sophisticated technologies for producing goods and services. Extremely advanced systems that can work almost unaided by employees are being designed.

Service Technology

Services have seen tremendous growth in automation technologies in recent years. Restaurant kitchen managers can use computer programs to calculate the exact cost and ingredient needs for each menu item, from building a cheeseburger to

CONCEPT CONNECTION Because its manufactured goods are too large and cumbersome to move along a traditional assembly line, Boeing Corporation typically uses a **fixed-position layout**. Products remain in one location, and employees, components, and equipment are brought to them for assembly. However, to increase speed and flexibility, Boeing has begun implementing a hybrid system. After the wings and landing gear have been attached, a plane such as the 737 (shown here) is dragged toward the door at two inches a minute, with workers moving along it on a float-like apparatus. Boeing's **productivity goal** is to push a 737 out the door in only five days. A similar slow-moving assembly line for the 777 is set for completion by 2008.

putting together a seafood buffet, instead of having to perform arduous and time-consuming manual calculations. Many gas stations now have pay-at-pump systems where customers insert a credit or debit card to pay for their gas without having to go inside the station. In the banking industry, ATMs (automatic teller machines) and telephone and online banking allow customers to obtain a wide range of banking services at any time of day or night. Some banks, including Bank of America, are now using pop-up solicitations, based on split-second analysis of a customer's online activity, to invite customers to chat with a live representative about bank services.[31]

More complex technologies are also revolutionizing the service industry. The rage in retailing is *radio-frequency identification (RFID)*, a sort of high-tech barcode that is tucked inside a sticker on boxes of merchandise or individual products. The RFID tags emit signals that can be read remotely by electronic readers and provide precise, real-time information about the location of merchandise as it moves through the supply chain.[32] The biggest names in retail, including Wal-Mart, The Home Depot, Carrefour, and Tesco, are already taking advantage of this new technology. One study showed that Wal-Mart stores using RFID technology were able to restock shelves at three times the speed of stores that relied on traditional methods to locate stock.[33] The potential of RFID for streamlining inventory management and cutting costs for retailers is enormous.

Other service firms use RFID as well. New York's E-Z Pass and California's FasTrak both use RFID to speed cars through toll booths, for example.[34] The U.S. Department of Defense has begun requiring suppliers to use RFID on shipping pallets and cases, enabling the military to easily track shipments of combat-support goods and other items.[35] FedEx is using RFID to prevent problems drivers face in the event of key loss. The company is permanently replacing ordinary locks with locks that are activated by RFID wristbands.[36]

New technology systems are continuously being integrated into today's service organizations to improve operations efficiency. For example, many pharmacies

Unlocking Innovative Solutions Through TECHNOLOGY

AT PRAIRIESTONE PHARMACY, SMALLER IS BETTER

Does the world need another drugstore? The founders of PrairieStone Pharmacy think it does—but not the kind where you have to wait half an hour for a prepackaged antibiotic, or fight for a few minutes of a stressed-out pharmacist's time to answer your questions. Lewis Zeidner, Marvin Richardson, and John Brady wanted to build a different kind of drugstore, one that uses sophisticated integrated technology to achieve maximum efficiency, improve customer service, reduce prescription errors, and free pharmacists from mundane chores such as counting pills or checking technicians' work. "You pay $100,000 for a well-trained pharmacist to spend six years in school studying how best to educate people about use of chemicals, and you have them counting by five?" Zeidner asks incredulously.

At PrairieStone, a Plymouth, Minnesota-based start-up, you won't see many people counting pills. That task is handled by automated devices that dispense the most-frequently prescribed drugs, combined with a rigid bar-code scanning system that assures pharmacists of accuracy. That means the pharmacist can actually come out from behind the counter and talk to customers about their health care issues and drug concerns. It's the dream of what every pharmacist wants to practice, says Deborah Fawcette, director of pharmacy operations for the National Association of Chain Drug Stores Foundation.

In addition to providing employees with more satisfying jobs and giving customers better service,

the technology has other operational benefits for PrairieStone. For example, it means stores need only 400 square feet, whereas most pharmacies occupy at least 1,000. That saves money, and it means PrairieStone can squeeze into small spaces in supermarkets and other retail outlets. PrairieStone stocks about 2,000 drugs, more than in an average pharmacy, but most inventory is stored in a vertical 14-foot-high carousel that reaches up into the ceiling. Push a button and, with the aid of bar coding, the desired item descends to eye level. The storage system works in conjunction with other technologies, such as a dispensing device that quickly and accurately counts and sorts tablets for up to 400 prescriptions a day, and workflow management software that increases overall efficiency. Each prescription goes through numerous checks for accuracy.

"The bottom line is that customer service is where we need to separate ourselves from the group and do things better than our competitors," notes PrairieStone operations director Jim Cox. Judging by the fledgling pharmacy's rapid growth—with 28 pharmacies in Minnesota and Michigan and prescription sales growing at four to five times the national average—PrairieStone's sophisticated use of technology is doing the job.

SOURCES: Jena McGregor,"The Starbucks of Pharmacies?" *Fast Company* (April 2005): 62–63; Sandra Levy, "PrairieStone Pharmacy: Drug Topics' Chain of the Year," *Drug Topics* (April 18, 2005): www.drugtopics.com/drugtopics/article/articleDetail.jsp?id=1564 90; www.prairiestonerx.com; and "PrairieStone Pharmacy Makes Its Debut," *Chain Drug Review* (May 2, 2005): 69.

have added some elements of automation. None, though, have yet applied technology in the integrated, efficient, and customer-responsive way used by PrairieStone Pharmacy, as described in the Unlocking Innovative Solutions Through Technology box.

FLEXIBLE MANUFACTURING SYSTEMS

Advanced technology is also revolutionizing manufacturing. The use of automated production lines that can be quickly adapted to produce more than one kind of product is called a **flexible manufacturing system**.[37] The machinery uses sophisticated computer technology to coordinate and integrate the machines. Automated functions include loading, unloading, storing parts, changing tools, and machining. The computer can instruct the machines to change parts, machining, and tools when a new product must be produced. Human operators made adjustments to the computer, not the production machinery itself, dramatically cutting the time and expense of making changes. This approach is a breakthrough compared with the product layout, in which a single line is restricted to a single product. With a flexible manufacturing system, a single production line can be readily adapted to small batches of different products based on computer instructions. At the Nissan factory in Canton,

flexible manufacturing system A small or medium-sized automated production line that can be adapted to produce more than one product line.

Mississippi, for example, minivans, pickup trucks, and sport utility vehicles can all be sent down the same assembly line. Robotic arms on machines are programmed to weld in the spots needed for different vehicles. Highly automated painting machines are programmed to paint all kinds of vehicles one after another, with no down time for reconfiguration.[38] Other automakers are playing catch-up with Japan's Nissan, Honda, and Toyota, which were early movers in equipping factories to build more than one model on a single line. U.S. automakers produce fewer than half of their models on flexible lines, while the lowest level among the three big Japanese firms is Honda at 69 percent.[39]

© AMERICAN HONDA MOTOR CO., INC./PRNEWSFOTO (NEWSCOM)

CONCEPT
CONNECTION Frustrated by the five months it took Honda to retool a Japanese plant to produce the popular CR-Vs, industrial engineer Masaki Iwai asked himself, "Why not standardize production so Honda has a single manufacturing system worldwide?" Why not, indeed? The insight gave Honda a global **flexible manufacturing system** that can produce multiple models in any given factory. More importantly, any factory can switch over to producing a new model overnight, a process that typically takes U.S. automakers weeks. It's allowed Honda to rapidly increase North American production of its fuel-efficient Civic, shown here, as consumer demand swells along with rising gas prices.

CAD/CAM

Operations management in most businesses today employs computers for the design of products, and often for their manufacture as well. **CAD** (computer-aided design) enables engineers to develop new-product designs in about half the time required with traditional methods. Computers provide a visual display for the engineer and illustrate the implications of any design change.

CAM (computer-aided manufacturing) uses computers to direct manufacturing processes, as in flexible manufacturing systems. Typically, the CAM system is linked to CAD, so that the product specifications drive the manufacturing specifications. The computer system thus guides and controls the manufacturing process. For example, a sportswear manufacturer can use computers to mechanize the entire sequence of manufacturing operations—pattern scaling, layout, and printing. Computer-controlled cutting tables are installed. Once the computer has mathematically defined the geometry, it guides the cutting blade, eliminating the need for paper patterns. Computer programs also can direct fabric requisitions, production orders for cutting and sewing operations, and sewing line work.

The most advanced factories are using **product life-cycle management (PLM)** software, which manages a product from creation through development, manufacturing, testing, and even maintenance in the field. PLM can coordinate people and facilities around the world for the design, development, and manufacture of products as small as the roller skates produced by GID of Yorba Linda, California, or as large as Boeing's new 787 Dreamliner passenger jet. PLM connects design and development of new products to the design of tools, assembly lines, and even entire factories. In addition, it links employees to a digital repository of project data so that ideas and parts can be accessed and used efficiently.[40] The software can link well-known older programs, such as CAD/CAM, with newer tools that perform tasks such as simulating an assembly line or an entire factory. The most efficient manufacturing layout can be created even as the product is being designed.

Pratt & Whitney Canada has been using PLM software since 2002 and estimates that it saves $500,000 to $1 million on each new engine design. In addition, PLM has helped the company reduce scrap by 86 percent and cut rework by nearly 10 percent. Inventory turns jumped from 4 per year to 14 per year. One application of PLM at Pratt & Whitney Canada uses a visual computer-imaged manikin equipped with digital bones, joints, and ligaments to reach inside a 3-D computer image of an aircraft engine. Nicknamed George, the manikin tests to see whether a human repair

CAD A production technology in which computers perform new-product design.

CAM A production technology in which computers help guide and control the manufacturing system.

product life-cycle management (PLM) Manufacturing software that manages a product from creation through development, manufacturing, testing, and even maintenance in the field.

person would encounter any obstructions in accessing parts of a real-life engine. If George cannot reach a part, his arm turns red, letting designers know that a change needs to be made. The 3-D design and development is also linked to manufacturing, so that manufacturing processes and machining are automatically programmed, telling production floor machines the right paths to take as they cut engine parts. PLM software is relatively new, and few factories have mastered the technology. Those that have, though, typically report profits that are 73 percent higher than other leading manufacturers.[41]

Facility Location

At some point, almost every organization must decide on the location of facilities. Commerce Bank needs to open a new branch office in central Ohio, Subway needs to find locations for new restaurants, or Intel needs to find locations somewhere in the world for a new research facility and a new chip assembly and testing plant. When these decisions are made unwisely, they are expensive and troublesome for the organization.

The most common approach to selecting a site for a new location is to do a cost-benefit analysis. For example, managers at bank headquarters may identify four possible locations. The costs associated with each location are the land (purchase or lease); moving from the current facility; and construction, including zoning laws, building codes, land features, and size of the parking lot. Taxes, utilities, rents, and maintenance are other cost factors to be considered in advance. Each possible bank location also will have certain benefits. Benefits to be evaluated are accessibility of customers, location of major competitors, general quality of working conditions, and nearness to restaurants and shops, which would be desirable for both employees and customers. Once the bank managers have evaluated the worth of each benefit, they can divide total benefits by total costs for each location, then select the location with the highest ratio.

New location scouting software is helping managers turn facilities location from guesswork into a science. These programs use sophisticated number crunching tools, for example, to help fast-food chains determine the best areas for expansion. However, most companies don't rely on technology alone, but also use human location scouts, who combine heaps of research with an eye for details and a honed instinct about where the business will succeed. Barbara Vinson is the top scout for Arby's Restaurant Group, Inc.

Arby's Restaurant Group, Inc.

Whenever a new franchisee for Arby's needs to locate a site, Barbara Vinson is likely to get a call. She's the top location scout for Arby's and travels about 15 days a month looking for locations.

Vinson uses mapping software, demographic analysis, and personal observation to pick good new locations. When scouting for a new store, Vinson drives thousands of miles crisscrossing the same streets, watching traffic patterns, chatting up people in McDonald's and other competitors, and seeing where people spend their time during weekdays and weekends. She likes to locate near booming retail areas, especially Wal-Mart, because it generates traffic. However, for Arby's, which is trying to position itself as more upscale and healthier than competing fast-food chains, finding the right *type* of neighborhood is important, too. Once, Vinson thought the mapping technology had pinpointed a good piece of real estate near a Sam's Club—until personal investigation revealed an all-you-can-eat pizza place nearby. Further investigation confirmed Vinson's hunch that the neighborhood was too poor for the type of area Arby's wants. Similarly, if one glance at the parking lot of a mall reveals a lot of Jaguars, Vinson moves on. "Too high end," she says. "I'm not going in."

Although Vinson appreciates the support of new analytical tools, she believes personal investigation and "gut instinct" play a big part in location selection as well. So far, her instincts are right on in picking good locations for restaurants. She picked hot spots for drive-in burger chain Sonic for years before being lured away by Arby's.[42]

Particularly for global corporations, selecting facility location is an important and complex consideration. When locating facilities in other countries, managers must take into account cost-based variables such as transportation, exchange rates, and cost of labor. In addition, the skill levels of potential workers, the development of regional infrastructure, a good quality of life, and a favorable business climate are important considerations in selecting a location overseas. For high-tech firms, proximity to world-class research institutions and access to venture capital are also essential criteria.[43]

Capacity Planning

Capacity planning is the determination and adjustment of an organization's ability to produce products or services to match demand. For example, if an automaker anticipates a 15 percent increase in sales over the next year, capacity planning is the procedure whereby it will ensure that it has sufficient capacity to service that demand.

Organizations can do several things to increase capacity. One is to create additional shifts and hire people to work on them. A second is to ask existing people to work overtime to add to capacity. A third is to outsource or subcontract extra work to other firms. A fourth is to expand a plant and add more equipment. Each of these techniques will increase the organization's ability to meet demand without risk of major excess capacity.

The biggest problem for most organizations, however, is excess capacity. When misjudgments occur, transporta-

CONCEPT CONNECTION Harley-Davidson Motor Company is using **capacity planning** to keep pace with the growing, worldwide demand for its high-quality motorcycles. As the only major American-based motorcycle, Harley-Davidson has brand names that are among the best known in the industry. All three of the company's manufacturing facilities have been extensively redesigned and reconfigured to improve productivity, workflow, product quality, and the environment. Facilities such as this touring motorcycle assembly line in York, Pennsylvania, have put Harley-Davidson a full year ahead in its production schedule, and the company plans to have the capacity to produce 115,000 units a year.

tion companies have oil tankers sitting empty in the harbor, oil companies have refineries sitting idle, semiconductor companies have plants shuttered, developers have office buildings half full, and the service industry may have hotels or amusement parks operating at partial capacity. Consider movie theater chains, which have grossly overbuilt in recent years, more than doubling the number of screens in the United States in a 20-year period. Some theaters show films to only one or two people at a time because of excess capacity.[44] The challenge is for managers to add capacity as needed without excess. For many companies, the solution is contracting work out to other organizations. Outsourcing and new organizational forms such as the virtual network organization described in Chapter 10 enable companies to quickly ramp up production to increase capacity and dissolve partnerships when extra help is no longer needed.

INVENTORY MANAGEMENT

A large portion of the operations manager's job consists of inventory management. **Inventory** is the goods the organization keeps on hand for use in the production process. Most organizations have three types of inventory: finished goods prior to shipment, work in process, and raw materials.

Finished-goods inventory includes items that have passed through the entire production process but have not been sold. This inventory is highly visible. The new cars parked in the storage lot of an automobile factory are finished-goods

capacity planning The determination and adjustment of the organization's ability to produce products and services to match customer demand.

inventory The goods that the organization keeps on hand for use in the production process up to the point of selling the final products to customers.

finished-goods inventory Inventory consisting of items that have passed through the complete production process but have yet to be sold.

EXHIBIT 16.5

Large Inventories Hide
Operations Management
Problems

SOURCE: R. J. Schonberger,
*Japanese Manufacturing Tech-
niques: Nine Hidden Lessons
in Simplicity* (New York: The
Free Press, 1982).

inventory, as are the hamburgers and french fries stacked under the heat lamps at a
McDonald's restaurant. Finished-goods inventory is expensive, because the organization has invested labor and other costs to make the finished product.

Work-in-process inventory includes the materials moving through the stages
of the production process that are not completed products. Work-in-process inventory in an automobile plant includes engines, wheel and tire assemblies, and dashboards waiting to be installed. In a fast-food restaurant, the french fries in the fryer
and hamburgers on the grill are work-in-process inventory.

Raw materials inventory includes the basic inputs to the organization's production process. This inventory is cheapest, because the organization has not yet invested labor in it. Steel, wire, glass, and paint are raw materials inventory for an
auto plant. Meat patties, buns, and raw potatoes are the raw materials inventory in
a fast-food restaurant.

The Importance of Inventory

Inventory management is vitally important to organizations, because inventory
sitting idly on the shop floor or in the warehouse costs money. Many years ago, a
firm's wealth was measured by its inventory. Today inventory is recognized as an
unproductive asset in cost-conscious firms. Dollars not tied up in inventory can be
used in other productive ventures. Keeping inventory low is especially important
for high-tech firms, because so many of their products lose value quickly, as they are
replaced by more innovative and lower-cost models. For example, the value of a
completed personal computer falls rapidly; even if shelf space for PCs were free, a
company would lose money on its PC inventory.[45]

Services are concerned with inventory too. Managers at retail giants such as
Wal-Mart, Toys"R"Us, The Home Depot, and Best Buy understand that efficient inventory management is essential to their ability to keep prices low and attract more
customers. State-of-the-art, integrated e-business systems, including the use of new
wireless RFID technology as described earlier, allow tight inventory control and enable the retailers to eliminate excess inventory. Their suppliers have refined their
delivery systems so that the stores receive only the products needed to meet customer purchases.

The Japanese analogy of rocks and water describes the current thinking about
the importance of inventory.[46] As illustrated in Exhibit 16.5, the water is the
inventory in the organization. The higher the water, the less managers have to
worry about the rocks, which represent problems. In operations management, these
problems apply to scheduling, facilities layout, product or service design, and quality. When the water level goes down, managers see the rocks and must deal with
them. When inventories are reduced, the problems of a poorly designed and managed operations process also are revealed. The problems then must be solved. When
inventory can be kept at an absolute minimum, operations management is considered excellent.

We now consider specific techniques for inventory management. Four important concepts are economic order quantity, material requirements planning, just-in-
time inventory systems, and distribution management.

**work-in-process inven-
tory** Inventory composed of
the materials that still are
moving through the stages of
the production process.

raw materials inventory
Inventory consisting of the
basic inputs to the organization's production process.

Economic Order Quantity

Two basic decisions that can help minimize inventory are how many raw materials to order and when to order from outside suppliers. Ordering the minimum amounts at the right time keeps the raw materials, work-in-process, and finished-goods inventories at low levels. One popular technique is **economic order quantity (EOQ)**, which is designed to minimize the total of ordering costs and holding costs for inventory items. *Ordering costs* are the costs associated with actually placing the order, such as postage, receiving, and inspection. *Holding costs* are costs associated with keeping the item on hand, such as storage space charges, finance charges, and materials-handling expenses.

The EOQ calculation indicates the order quantity size that will minimize holding and ordering costs based on the organization's use of inventory. The EOQ formula includes ordering costs *(C)*, holding costs *(H)*, and annual demand *(D)*. For example, consider a hospital's need to order surgical dressings. Based on hospital records, the ordering costs for surgical dressings are $15, the annual holding cost is $6, and the annual demand for dressings is 605. The following is the formula for the economic order quantity:

$$\text{EOQ} = \sqrt{\frac{2DC}{H}} = \sqrt{\frac{2(605)(15)}{6}} = 55$$

The EOQ formula tells us that the best quantity to order is 55.

The next question is when to make the order. For this decision, a different formula, called **reorder point (ROP)**, is used. ROP is calculated by the following formula, where *D* is the annual demand for dressings, *T* is the time period (365 days in the year), and *L* is the lead time, or number of days between ordering and receiving the product. In this example, we assume that it takes three days to receive the order after the hospital has placed it:

$$\text{ROP} = \frac{D}{T}(L) = \frac{605}{365}(3) = 4.97, \text{ or } 5$$

The reorder point tells us that because it takes three days to receive the order, at least 5 dressings should be on hand when the order is placed. As nurses use surgical dressings, operations managers will know that when the level reaches the point of 5, the new order should be placed for a quantity of 55.

This relationship is illustrated in Exhibit 16.6. Whenever the reorder point of 5 dressings is reached, the new order is initiated, and the 55 arrive just as the inventory

economic order quantity (EOQ) An inventory management technique designed to minimize the total of ordering and holding costs for inventory items.

reorder point (ROP) The most economical level at which an inventory item should be reordered.

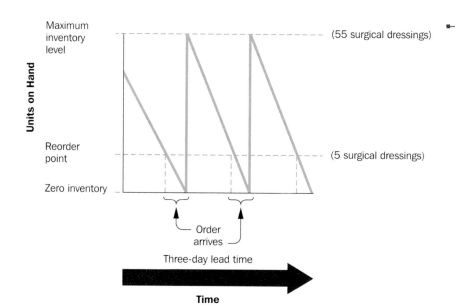

EXHIBIT 16.6

Inventory Control of Surgical Dressings by EOQ

is depleted. In a typical hospital, however, some variability in lead time and use of surgical dressings will occur. Thus, a few extra items of inventory, called safety stock, are used to ensure that the hospital does not run out of surgical dressings. In general, companies keep more safety stock when demand for items is highly variable. When demand is easy to predict, the safety stock may be lower. However, a careful inventory manager may take into account other criteria as well. A sizable price cut or volume discount might make a large purchase economically more attractive, especially in the case of a product the company is almost certain to need in the future.[47]

Material Requirements Planning

The EOQ formula works well when inventory items are not dependent on one another. For example, in a restaurant the demand for hamburgers is independent of the demand for milkshakes; thus, an economic order quantity is calculated for each item. A more complicated inventory problem occurs with **dependent demand inventory**, meaning that item demand is related to the demand for other inventory items. For example, if Ford Motor Company decides to make 100,000 cars, it will also need 400,000 tires, 400,000 rims, and 400,000 hubcaps. The demand for tires is dependent on the demand for cars.

The most common inventory control system used for handling dependent demand inventory is **material requirements planning (MRP)**. MRP is a dependent demand inventory planning and control system that schedules the exact amount of all materials required to support the desired end product. MRP is computer based and requires sophisticated calculations to coordinate information on production scheduling, inventory location, forecasting, and ordering. Unlike with EOQ, inventory levels are not based on past consumption; rather, they are based on precise estimates of future needs for production. MRP can dramatically reduce inventory costs. With MRP, managers can better control the quantity and timing of deliveries of raw materials, ensuring that the right materials arrive at approximately the right time they are needed in the production process. The computerized MRP system can slow or accelerate the inflow of materials in response to changes in the production schedule. These controls result in lower labor, materials, and overhead costs.[48]

As competitive pressures increased, MRP gradually evolved into the broader enterprise resource planning (ERP) systems described in Chapter 15.[49] MRP is focused only on manufacturing and inventory, while ERP incorporates computerized links to other business functions, such as human resources, finance, and sales, enabling managers to evaluate trade-offs such as the balance between workload and the human resources and manufacturing capacity.[50] ERP systems can integrate, track, and optimize functions across the entire organization. MRP systems are a valuable subset of ERP, enabling managers to have greater insight into operations so they can optimize the use of human and material resources.

dependent demand inventory Inventory in which item demand is related to the demand for other inventory items.

material requirements planning (MRP) A dependent demand inventory planning and control system that schedules the precise amount of all materials required to support the production of desired end products.

just-in-time (JIT) inventory system An inventory control system that schedules materials to arrive precisely when they are needed on a production line.

■ **TAKE A MOMENT**

As a new manager, recognize the financial importance of inventory management. Use economic order quantity and material requirements planning to minimize inventory levels. Consider a just-in-time inventory system for your organization.

Just-in-Time Inventory

Just-in-time (JIT) inventory systems are designed to reduce the level of an organization's inventory and its associated costs, aiming to push to zero the amount of time that raw materials and finished products are sitting in the factory, being inspected, or in transit.[51] Sometimes these systems are referred to as *stockless systems*, *zero inventory systems*, or *kanban systems*. Each system centers on the concept that suppliers deliver materials only at the exact moment needed, thereby reducing raw material inventories to zero. Moreover, work-in-process inventories are kept to a minimum because goods are produced only as needed to service the next stage of production. Finished-goods inventories are minimized by matching them exactly to sales demand. Just-in-time systems have tremendous advantages. In particular, the reduced inventory level frees productive capital for other company uses.

Recall the analogy of the rocks and the water. To reduce inventory levels to zero means that all management and coordination problems will surface and must be resolved. Scheduling must be scrupulously precise and logistics tightly coordinated. For example, follow the movement of a shipment of odometers and speedometers from a supplier in Winchester, Virginia, to the Nissan plant in Canton, Mississippi.

Thursday, 9 A.M.	A truck arrives at the supplier. As workers load the parts, drivers check on-board computers for destination, route, and estimated time of arrival (ETA) data.
Friday, 3 A.M.	The truck arrives at Canton, Mississippi, and approaches a switching yard two miles from the Nissan plant, parking in a computer-assigned spot. The driver downloads a key-shaped floppy disk from the on-board computer into the trucking company's mainframe, which relays the performance report directly to Nissan.
Friday, 12:50 P.M.	The trailer leaves the switching yard at a designated time and arrives at a predetermined receiving dock at the Nissan plant, where workers unload the parts and send them to the production line just in time.[52]

The coordination required by JIT demands that information be shared among everyone in the supply chain. Communication between only adjoining links in the supply chain is too slow. Rather, coordination requires a kind of information web in which members of the supply chain share information simultaneously with all other participants, often using Internet technologies and perhaps RFID.[53] For example, Dell's factory near Round Rock, Texas, uses online information exchange so effectively that it can order only the materials needed to keep production running for the next two hours. In addition, Web hookups to shipping companies mean that finished inventory can often be loaded onto trucks less than 15 hours after a customer submits an order.[54]

Just-in-time inventory systems also require excellent employee motivation and cooperation. Workers are expected to perform at their best because they are entrusted with the responsibility and authority to make the zero inventory system work. Employees must help one another when they fall behind and must be capable of doing different jobs. Workers experience the satisfaction of being in charge of the system and making useful improvements in the company's operations.[55]

© BARNES & NOBLE/FEATURE PHOTO SERVICE (NEWSCOM)

CONCEPT CONNECTION

The 2005 publication of J.K. Rowling's eagerly-awaited *Harry Potter and the Half-Blood Prince* placed massive demands on the **distribution** and **order fulfillment** systems of everyone involved. First of all, they handled a huge volume of product: Scholastic, the novel's American publisher, had an initial print run of 10.8 million copies. On top of that, Scholastic—together with retailers, wholesale distributors, and delivery companies—had to put stringent security measures in place so that, in accordance with Rowling's wishes, no customers got their hands on the book a moment before 12:01 a.m. on July 16. Here Barnes & Noble employees inspect the shipment brought to a company warehouse by a caravan of 124 tractor-trailers.

Logistics and Distribution Management

A critical aspect of managing inventory is efficiently moving raw materials into the facility and moving finished products out to customers. Some companies develop the necessary logistics expertise in house. **Logistics** refers to managing the movement of materials within the facility, the shipment of incoming materials from suppliers, and the shipment of outgoing products to customers. For example, Wal-Mart uses regional distribution centers, such as the one in New Braunfels, Texas, which has more than 1 million square feet of floor space, 96 dock doors for loading and unloading trailers, and 5.62 miles of conveyors for moving merchandise.[56] These regional centers receive incoming shipments from suppliers, receive orders from the retail stores, make up the orders, and load and ship merchandise orders to stores throughout the region. Distribution center employees coordinate the entire system and schedule inbound trucks from suppliers and company-owned trucks outbound to the retail stores. Using computers, the system can be so precisely coordinated that the stores don't need warehouses; orders of merchandise go directly from the trucks to the shelves, usually within 48 hours.

Moving finished products out to customers is usually referred to as **distribution** or *order fulfillment*. The faster and more accurately a company can fill customer orders, the lower the costs for the organization and the greater the likelihood that the customer will return. Many firms are shifting some of their warehouses and distribution facilities to China so that imported goods can go straight to retailers and manufacturers, bypassing a stop at a U.S. warehouse and saving time and money. UPS had about 50 warehouses in China in 2005 with plans to add 10 more by the end of 2006.[57]

Organizations are finding ways to deliver products faster and less expensively by using the Internet. In the latest advance, some companies share transportation information and resources with unrelated companies, even competitors, so they can share truck space and avoid hauling an empty trailer on a return trip. Subaru of America is talking with a rival automaker about the possibility of sharing rail and truck space so cars will get to dealers faster. Nabisco uses electronic linkages to share warehouses and trucks with companies such as Dole and Lea & Perrins, and coordinate order shipments to retailers, enabling stores to more closely match orders to consumer needs.[58]

LEAN MANUFACTURING AND PRODUCTIVITY

Productivity is significant because it influences the well-being of the entire society as well as of individual companies. The only way to increase the output of goods and services to society is to increase organizational productivity.

Lean Manufacturing

Many of the concepts we have discussed, including just-in-time inventory and an emphasis on quality, are central to the philosophy of lean manufacturing. Today's organizations are trying to become more efficient, and implementing the lean manufacturing philosophy is one popular approach to doing so. **Lean manufacturing**, sometimes called *lean production*, uses highly trained employees at every stage of the production process who take a painstaking approach to details and problem solving to cut waste and improve quality and productivity. Lean manufacturing was pioneered by Toyota and the concept has spread around the world to both manufacturing and service organizations.

The heart of lean manufacturing is not machines or technology, but employee involvement. Employees are trained to "think lean," and empowered to make changes to attack waste and strive for continuous improvement in all areas.[59] The system combines techniques such as just-in-time inventory, continuous-flow production, quick changeover of assembly lines, continuous improvement, and

logistics The activities required to physically move materials into the company's operations facility and to move finished products to customers.

distribution Moving finished products to customers; also called *order fulfillment*.

lean manufacturing Manufacturing process using highly trained employees at every stage of the production process to cut waste and improve quality.

preventive maintenance with a management system that encourages employee involvement and problem solving. Any employee can stop the production line at any time to solve a problem. In addition, equipment is often designed to stop automatically so that a defect can be fixed.[60] Thomas Betts Corp., which makes electrical outlet conduit boxes and other electrical parts, applied classic lean production techniques to achieve world-class performance.

"We're a 40-year-old plant . . . and a mature workforce, yet we can compete with anybody around. We can compete with China. We can compete with India," says Darrell Dumont, manufacturing engineering manager at Thomas Betts Corporation's Athens, Tennessee, factory. Only a few years ago, managers couldn't say that. What has made the difference is a serious commitment to lean manufacturing.

The improvement effort began by carefully analyzing, or mapping, every aspect of production operations to reveal areas of wasted time, material, and effort and then identify actions to remove that waste. For example, the plant had two months' worth of raw materials and work-in-progress inventory, as well as about three months' of finished goods inventory. Forecasting of future demand was horribly off, and response time to actual customer demand was sometimes as long as 60 days.

Since beginning the improvement project, Thomas Betts has involved employees in 37 or more *kaizen*, or continuous improvement projects. The plant cut the number of suppliers from 300 to about 100 and maintains close, collaborative relationships with them. More than 80 percent of raw materials inventory is now managed by suppliers and delivered just as it is needed. Small carts move through the plant every 20 minutes delivering components to the various work stations.

Adopting the lean philosophy made Thomas Betts much more competitive on a global basis. The dollar value of finished goods inventory dropped 32 percent, raw materials and work-in-progress inventory decreased 74 percent, and manufacturing floor space reduced 29 percent. Moreover, customer complaints were cut in half, and sales volume increased by 23 percent.

"Change has been the only constant for the last four years," says one manager. That's likely to be the case from here on. With lean manufacturing, continually striving for perfection is what it's all about.[61]

Three years after embarking on its lean manufacturing endeavor, the Athens plant was named by Thomas Betts as both "Plant of the Year" and "Most Important Plant." Lean production is also increasingly being applied in service industries.[62]

productivity The organization's output of products and services divided by its inputs.

Measuring Productivity

One important question when considering productivity improvements is: What is productivity, and how do managers measure it? In simple terms, **productivity** is the organization's output of goods and services divided by its inputs. This means that productivity can be improved by either increasing the amount of output using the same level of inputs or reducing the number of inputs required to produce the output. Sometimes a company can even do both. Ruggieri & Sons, for example, invested in mapping software to help it plan deliveries of heating fuel. The software plans the most efficient routes based on the locations of customers and fuel reloading terminals, as well as the amount of fuel each customer needs. When Ruggieri switched from planning routes by hand to using the software, its drivers began driving fewer miles but making 7 percent more stops each day—in others words, burning less fuel in order to sell more fuel.[63]

© DREW DONAVAN FORTUNE

CONCEPT
CONNECTION For Anadarko, **productivity** is measured by the amount of oil and natural gas it can locate and extract from deep inside the earth. To measure the company's productivity, the cost of inputs (which includes exploration and drilling costs) must be measured against the value of the outputs (the oil and natural gas it can produce). Recent productivity has been very high for Anadarko, due mainly to its use of cutting-edge technology and exploration techniques. For instance, while exploring in a part of Algeria that bigger competitors had given up on, these Anadarko workers used an unorthodox imaging technique to discover a three-billion barrel field of oil.

The accurate measure of productivity can be complex. Two approaches for measuring productivity are total factor productivity and partial productivity. **Total factor productivity** is the ratio of total outputs to the inputs from labor, capital, materials, and energy:

$$Total\ factor\ productivity = \frac{Output}{Labor + Capital + Materials + Energy}$$

Total factor productivity represents the best measure of how the organization is doing. Often, however, managers need to know about productivity with respect to certain inputs. **Partial productivity** is the ratio of total outputs to a major category of inputs. For example, many organizations are interested in labor productivity, which would be measured as follows:

$$Labor\ productivity = \frac{Output}{Labor\ dollars}$$

Calculating this formula for labor, capital, or materials provides information on whether improvements in each element are occurring. However, managers often are criticized for relying too heavily on partial productivity measures, especially direct labor.[64] Measuring direct labor misses the valuable improvements in materials, work processes, and quality. Labor productivity is easily measured, but may show an increase as a result of capital improvements. Thus, managers will misinterpret the reason for productivity increases.

Improving Productivity

When an organization decides that improving productivity is important, managers can look at two critical areas, employee productivity and managerial productivity.

■ **TAKE A MOMENT** As a new manager, take personal responsibility for improving productivity. Go to the experiential exercise on page 543 that pertains to your personal orientation toward productivity improvements.

EMPLOYEE PRODUCTIVITY

Increased *employee productivity* means having workers produce more output in the same time period. Companies can improve employee productivity by establishing the means for existing employees to do more, such as by acquiring more efficient technology, by improving work processes, or by training employees to work more efficiently. Employees may simply need more knowledge, better technology, or improved task or workplace design. The company may also decide to hire employees with greater expertise or to outsource certain operations to a firm with expertise in that area. NationsBank, for example, arranged for Pitney Bowes Management Services (PBMS) to handle its mail services, in part because PBMS has the computer applications and technological know-how to more efficiently handle the task.[65]

Improving employee productivity has sometimes been a real challenge for American companies, because too often workers have an antagonistic relationship with management. Thus, increasing employee productivity often requires improving the worker-management relationship. Many of the leadership and management approaches described in this book can enhance worker productivity by motivating and inspiring employees.

MANAGERIAL PRODUCTIVITY

Increased managerial productivity simply means that managers do a better job of running the business. Leading experts in productivity and quality often have stated that the real reason for productivity problems in the United States is poor

total factor productivity The ratio of total outputs to the inputs from labor, capital, materials, and energy.

partial productivity The ratio of total outputs to the inputs from a single major input category.

1. Create constancy of purpose toward improvement of product and service, with the aim to become competitive and to stay in business, and to provide jobs.

2. Adopt the new philosophy. We are in a new economic age. Western management must awaken to the challenge, must learn its responsibilities, and take on leadership for change.

3. Cease dependence on inspection to achieve quality. Eliminate the need for inspection on a mass basis by building quality into the product in the first place.

4. End the practice of awarding business on the basis of price tag. Instead, minimize total cost. Move toward a single supplier for any one item, on a long-term relationship of loyalty and trust.

5. Improve constantly and forever the system of production and service, to improve quality and productivity, and thus constantly decrease costs.

6. Institute training on the job.

7. Institute leadership (see Point 11). The aim of supervision should be to help people and machines and gadgets do a better job. Supervision of management is in need of overhaul as well as supervision of production workers.

8. Drive out fear, so that everyone may work effectively for the company.

9. Break down barriers between departments. People in research, design, sales, and production must work as a team, to foresee problems of production and in use that may be encountered with the product or service.

10. Eliminate slogans, exhortations, and targets for the workforce asking for zero defects and new levels of productivity. Such exhortations only create adversarial relationships, as the bulk of the causes of low quality and low productivity belong to the system and thus lie beyond the power of the workforce.

11. a. Eliminate work standards (quotas) on the factory floor. Substitute leadership.

    b. Eliminate management by objective. Eliminate management by numbers, numerical goals. Substitute leadership.

12. a. Remove barriers that rob hourly workers of their right to pride of workmanship. The responsibility of supervisors must be changed from sheer numbers to quality.

    b. Remove barriers that rob people in management and in engineering of their right to pride of workmanship. This means, *inter alia*, abolishment of the annual merit rating and of management by objective.

13. Institute a vigorous program of education and self-improvement.

14. Put everybody in the company to work to accomplish the transformation. The transformation is everybody's job.

EXHIBIT 16.7

Condensation of the
14 Points for Management

management.[66] One of these authorities, W. Edwards Deming, proposed specific points for telling management how to improve productivity. These points are listed in Exhibit 16.7.

Managerial productivity improves when managers emphasize quality over quantity, break down barriers and empower their employees, and do not overmanage using numbers. Managers can learn to use reward systems, employee involvement, teamwork, and other management techniques that have been described throughout this book. However, it is important for managers to consider the linkage between these techniques and the company's strategy—not just to blindly insert a technique into the organization's activities. For example, although many managers have encouraged their employees to share knowledge, their efforts often fail because employees see no benefits and they lose interest. In contrast, knowledge management efforts succeed when managers establish a strategy-related focus for what information is to be shared, then measure the results. At General Electric, for example, employees focused on learning about how to improve response time. Management determined that improvements in this area would significantly improve the company's performance. When GE instituted its knowledge management system, managers looked for—and found—improvements in such performance measures as sales per employee.[67] In this example, as in many others throughout this chapter, the difference can be attributed to better management, not to specific techniques.

MANAGER'S SOLUTION

This chapter described several points about operations management. Operations management pertains to the tools and techniques used to manage the organization's core production process. These techniques apply to both manufacturing and service organizations. Operations management has a great impact when it influences competitive strategy, applying strategic tools such as supply chain management. Areas of operations management described in the chapter include product and service design, procurement, location of facilities, facilities layout, capacity planning, and the use of new technologies.

At West Marine, described in the chapter opening, managers applied new technology to integrate the supply chain, dramatically improving effectiveness and efficiency. West undertook a three-year project that linked its distribution centers with store-level replenishment systems, so that the centers had real-time data about what products were sold and when store levels were getting low. The stores and centers were also linked electronically to suppliers. By quickly sharing sales data with a limited number of key suppliers, on-time fill rates for vendor orders improved from 35 percent to 80 percent. Stores have been able to maintain peak season in-stock levels at 96 percent or better because of the enhanced coordination.[68]

The chapter also discussed inventory management. Three types of inventory are raw materials, work in process, and finished goods. Economic order quantity, material requirements planning, and just-in-time inventory are techniques for minimizing inventory levels. Logistics is an important part of inventory management because it manages the movement of materials within the facility, the shipment of incoming materials from suppliers, and the shipment of outgoing products to customers.

Another important concept is that operations management can enhance organizational productivity. Many organizations are striving to become more productive and efficient through lean manufacturing. Total factor productivity is the best measurement of organizational productivity. Managers can focus on improving productivity in three areas: technological productivity, worker productivity, and managerial productivity.

DISCUSSION QUESTIONS

1. What are the major differences between manufacturing and service organizations? Give examples of each type.

2. To what extent is each of the four major outcomes of a highly effective operations system—superior customer responsiveness, innovation, quality, and efficiency—equally important? Does it make a difference if you are considering a manufacturing versus a service organization?

3. In today's fast-changing environment, manufacturers need their supply chains to be flexible, speedy, and lower the cost of producing a product. Yet sometimes, in an effort to cut costs, organizations outsource to distant locations such as China or India, perhaps sacrificing some degree of flexibility and speed in the process. Do you think outsourcing to distant countries is a worthwhile tradeoff? Why or why not?

4. Why is procurement considered such an important part of operations management? What are some of the major changes in the procurement process in recent years?

5. What type of production layout do you think would work best in a car dealership? What type would work best for a company that produces handmade pottery? Discuss reasons for your answers.

6. If you were asked to identify a location for a new resort catering to retirees, what steps would you take? How would you plan for the new resort's capacity?

7. What are the three types of inventory? Which type is most likely to be affected by the just-in-time inventory system? Explain.

8. Some companies are using both lean manufacturing and Six Sigma methods simultaneously to improve their operations. How do you think the two approaches might complement or conflict with each other? Explain.

9. Discuss the importance of logistics and distribution in managing inventory. Why do you think many of today's companies outsource this function?

10. If you were a consultant to a local manufacturing plant that wants to improve productivity, what advice would you give managers?

11. Critics argue that *radio-frequency identifications* (RFIDs) can potentially jeopardize consumer privacy by making it possible to link purchases to individuals. Should this concern prevent companies from adopting RFIDs? Explain.

MANAGEMENT IN PRACTICE: EXPERIENTIAL EXERCISE

What Is Your Attitude Toward Productivity?

Complete the following questions based on how you think and act in a typical work situation. For each item, circle the number that best describes you.

Disagree Strongly   ❶   ❷   ❸   ❹   ❺   Agree Strongly

1. I spend time developing new ways of approaching old problems.   ❶ ❷ ❸ ❹ ❺

2. As long as things are done correctly and efficiently, I prefer not to take on the hassle of changing them.   ❶ ❷ ❸ ❹ ❺

3. I always believe the effort to improve something should be rewarded, even if the final improvement is disappointing.   ❶ ❷ ❸ ❹ ❺

4. A single change that improves things 30 percent is much better than 30 improvements of 1 percent each.   ❶ ❷ ❸ ❹ ❺

5. I frequently compliment others on changes they have made.   ❶ ❷ ❸ ❹ ❺

6. I let people know in a variety of ways that I like to be left alone to do my job efficiently.   ❶ ❷ ❸ ❹ ❺

7. I am personally involved in several improvement projects at one time.   ❶ ❷ ❸ ❹ ❺

8. I try to be a good listener and be patient with what people say, except when it is a stupid idea.   ❶ ❷ ❸ ❹ ❺

9. I am always proposing unconventional techniques and ideas.   ❶ ❷ ❸ ❹ ❺

10. I usually do not take risks that would create a problem for me if the idea failed.   ❶ ❷ ❸ ❹ ❺

Scoring and Interpretation

Subtract each of your scores for questions 2, 4, 6, 8, and 10 from the number 6. Then, using the adjusted scores, add the scores from all 10 items for your total score.

This scale indicates the extent to which your orientation toward productivity is based on *efficiency* or *continuous improvement*. Efficiency sometimes can be maximized by eliminating change. This approach may be appropriate in a stable organizational environment. Continuous improvement is an attitude that productivity can always get better and you take personal responsibility to improve it. This attitude is appropriate for a quality-conscious company experiencing frequent change.

A score of 40 or higher indicates that you take personal responsibility for improving productivity and frequently initiate change. A score of 20 or less indicates you make contributions through efficient work in a stable environment. Discuss the pros and cons of the efficiency versus continuous improvement orientations for organizations and employees.

MANAGEMENT IN PRACTICE: ETHICAL DILEMMA

A Friend for Life?

Priscilla Dennis has always loved her job as president of Smallworld, a small company that produces and markets toys for young children. As a mother, Priscilla appreciates the care that goes into producing safe, high-quality toys. Late last year, Smallworld's designer invented a small, cuddly talking bear. Called the Binky-Bear, the toy was made of soft brown simulated fur and had a digital chip inside that played 50 messages. To see what kind of appeal the Binky-Bear might have, Smallworld produced 50 of the toys and placed them in kindergartens and nurseries.

Results were better than managers had hoped, with many of the kindergartens reporting that the toy quickly became the most popular in the school.

Based on these results, Smallworld decided to produce 1,000 of the bears, and they developed a catchy marketing slogan: "A Friend for Life." The bear was marketed as a toy that children could play with for years and years, and perhaps still have around as a keepsake when they had long outgrown toys. The first batch sold out within a week, so the company scheduled another production run of 25,000. However, during the run, the production manager discovered a problem. In the excitement over the new product, the designer and managers had failed to look carefully at manufacturing considerations. It turned out that the process needed to make Binky-Bear's soft fur was much more expensive than anticipated. Using the original fur will cost the company $4.98 per bear, but the manufacturing department can produce a substitute that will cut the cost to only $2.25 per bear. However, as compared with the original fur, which should last approximately eight years, the alternate, less-expensive fur will last for only eight months.

Market research indicates that a price increase to cover the greater expense of the original fur would significantly hurt sales; the Binky-Bear is already considered rather costly for a stuffed animal toy. In an emergency meeting to discuss the problem, Smallworld's managers are considering two options: absorb the extra cost, or use the cheaper substitute fur that will not last nearly as long. Many of the managers emphasize that children aren't interested in playing with toys for more than a few months—or even weeks—anyway, so substituting the less-expensive fur shouldn't be a problem. Others, including the production manager, believe the company's reputation for quality will be severely damaged. "We're going to have complaints within eight months, and we will rue the day we agreed to a cheaper substitute," the production manager said. The vice president for manufacturing agreed, asking, "What are we going to do about our slogan—change it to "A Friend for

Eight Months"? The marketing and sales managers forcefully argued the opposite viewpoint, pointing out that Smallworld already had a fortune tied up in the bear. "If you stop production now or continue with the expensive fur, we'll lose our shirts," the sales manager said. "The bear looks the same. I say we substitute the cheaper fur and no one will ever know the difference."

The final decision about how to handle the problem rests with Priscilla Dennis. She knows Smallworld can't afford to absorb the extra production costs, but can it afford to lose its reputation for quality? Also, she wonders whether she can look her young daughter in the eye if she goes along with what the sales manager is suggesting.

What Would You Do?

1. Substitute the less expensive fur but insist on a revised marketing campaign and advise buyers about the change in the production process.

2. Substitute the less expensive fur and wait to see what happens. The company would not be doing anything illegal, and most customers probably will never notice that the fur wears out so quickly.

3. Absorb the extra production costs. It's the right thing to do, and besides, the company's reputation for quality is too important to risk.

SOURCE: Based on "A Friend for Life," in Donald F. Kuratko and Richard M. Hodgetts, *Entrepreneurship: A Contemporary Approach*, 4th ed. (Fort Worth, TX: The Dryden Press, 1998): 172–173.

CASE FOR CRITICAL ANALYSIS

SunBright Outdoor Furniture, Inc.

James Cowart started making and selling outdoor furniture in 1984. He built up the business to 300 employees and $28 million in sales in 2003. SunBright operates a single factory in northern Florida, where it fabricates and assembles a wide range of outdoor furniture, including tables, chairs, umbrellas, and matching accessories. SunBright's major production tasks include extruding the aluminum furniture parts, bending and shaping the extruded parts, finishing and painting the parts, and then assembling the parts into completed furniture. Cloth and leather upholstery, glass for tabletops, wood finishing, and hardware such as screws and bolts are purchased from outside vendors.

Running this business was an almost 24-hour-a-day job for Cowart, because manufacturing or sales problems arose constantly. Cowart seemed to be the only person who could solve them. In 2003, Cowart decided to hire a general manager to run the manufacturing and sales department so he could have more time for other interests, including his grandchildren.

To his good fortune, he was approached by Eva Rucker, who offered to invest in the business and grow it from a regional manufacturer to one that sold to major national retailers. Rucker had excellent experience in sales and understood manufacturing. After a few months of getting to know each other, Cowart sold Rucker 25 percent of the business and installed her as general manager. Cowart retained for himself the position of president. Although he would not be at work full time, he would retain final authority on major decisions.

After just two months, Rucker started adding salespeople, with the goal of doubling the sales force in one year in order to reach new regional and national retail accounts. As sales began to increase, she also hired additional support staff, including a purchasing agent, two furniture designers, and an accountant. By the end of Rucker's first year, SunBright was carried by three national retail chains on a trial basis. However, new problems started to surface. SunBright was missing the delivery dates promised by sales reps and a few orders had been returned for not meeting quality standards. With the consolidation of retail stores into fewer chains, the national retailers had the power to demand high quality, low prices, and rapid delivery from SunBright or they would order outdoor furniture from other suppliers.

At the end of her first year, Rucker was struggling to improve operations to meet the demands of national retailers, but with little success. She invited a consultant to evaluate SunBright's operations. The consultant's report contained the following elements.

1. Cooperation among departments is minimal or nonexistent. For example, the purchasing manager changed to a new supplier for paint because it saved a few cents per gallon. But the paint had to be applied in a thicker coat to wear as long in outdoor use. The additional labor and paint actually cost more than the few cents saved in purchasing, and no one in the manufacturing department had been consulted.

2. Salespeople frequently run promotions and promise sales delivery dates that are impossible for manufacturing to meet. The department head of manufacturing emphasizes that it takes time to work out the bugs when introducing new products or increasing production levels.

3. The furniture designers have added features that are difficult and expensive to produce. On the new "Monarch" line, for example, the table legs required a new die that cost $26,000. The designers could have designed a table leg that would be produced on one of the existing dies.

4. The accounting department reports that productivity for the plant is low. Equipment utilization is too low. The operation is not lean enough to make acceptable profits.

5. The comptroller reports that inventory is too high. Too much capital is tied up in raw materials. Too much capital is also tied up in excessive in-process inventory waiting at machines to be finished and processed for delivery to customers.

6. Salespeople want to use the Internet to publicize SunBright product information and to make routine sales, freeing them to call on new customers. This approach would entail hiring people who could design and manage a sophisticated SunBright Web page.

Eva Rucker discussed these six issues with the consultant and agreed with the report's findings. She met with Jim Cowart to report the findings and ask for his support and financial resources to make corrections. Cowart listened to the presentation and then said he had some other things to attend to. "I don't think it's as serious as you say," he told Rucker, "but you can have a meeting with the department heads if you want to discuss it with them. Remember that our production problems are no worse than our competitors' issues. You don't have to fix everything overnight. Things worked pretty well before we started to grow so fast, and I'm sure they'll work well again."

Questions

1. At what stage of operations strategy is SunBright? Explain.

2. Which of the problems outlined by the consultant do you consider the highest priority? Second priority? Why? What steps would you take to solve them?

3. If you were James Cowart, how would you have responded to the report from Eva Rucker? If you were Rucker, what would you do now?

SOURCE: Adapted from "Taracare, Inc.," in Jack R. Meredith and Scott M. Shafer, *Operations Management for MBAs* (New York: John Wiley, 2002): 17–18.

ENDNOTES

1. Susannah Patton, "The Perfect Order," *CIO* (August 1, 2005): 38–44; and West Marine Company History: A Lesson in Navigation, www.westmarine.com.

2. Glenn R. Simpson, "Just in Time: In Year of Disasters, Experts Bring Order to Chaos of Relief," *The Wall Street Journal* (November 22, 2005): A1, A12; and Ellen Florian Kratz, "For FedEx, It Was Time to Deliver," *Fortune* (October 3, 2005): 83–84.

3. James D. Thompson, *Organizations in Action* (New York: McGraw-Hill, 1967).

4. Chad Terhune, "Growing Pains; To Bag China's Snack Market, Pepsi Takes Up Potato Farming," *The Wall Street Journal* (December 19, 2005): A1, A6.

5. Brian Heymans, "Leading the Lean Enterprise," *Industrial Management* (September–October 2002): 28–33; and Norihiko Shirouzu, "Gadget Inspector: Why Toyota Wins Such High Marks on Quality Surveys," *The Wall Street Journal* (March 15, 2001): A1, A11.

6. Gregory B. Northcraft and Richard B. Chase, "Managing Service Demand at the Point of Delivery," *Academy of Management Review* 10 (1985): 66–75; and Richard B. Chase and David A. Tanski, "The Customer Contact Model for Organization Design," *Management Science* 29 (1983): 1037–1050.

7. Robert H. Lowson, "Strategic Operations Management—The New Competitive Advantage?" *Journal of General Management* 28, no. 1 (Autumn 2002): 36–56; and Everett E. Adam Jr. and Paul M. Swamidass, "Assessing Operations Management from a Strategic Perspective," *Journal of Management* 15 (1989): 181–203.

8. Robert H. Hayes and David M. Upton, "Operations-Based Strategy," *California Management Review* 40, no. 4 (Summer 1998): 8–25.

9. This section is based on Charles W. L. Hill and Gareth R. Jones, *Strategic Management: An Integrated Approach*, 6th ed. (Boston: Houghton Mifflin, 2004): Chapter 4.

10. Carol J. Loomis, "The Big Surprise Is Enterprise," *Fortune* (July 24, 2006): 140–150.

11. Carol Hymowitz, "For Now, the Focus Is More on Innovation Than on Budget Cuts," *The Wall Street Journal* (July 17, 2006): B1.

12. Terry Kosdrosky, "Porsche Jumps to No.1 in Auto-Quality Survey," *The Wall Street Journal (Europe)*, (June 8, 2006): 6.

13. Heather Harreld, "Pick-Up Artists," *CIO* (November 1, 2000): 148–154; Cheryl Rosen, "Online Repair Updates with a Click," *InformationWeek* (July 30, 2001): 67; and Loomis, "The Big Surprise Is Enterprise."

14. Definition based on Steven A. Melnyk and David R. Denzler, *Operations Management: A Value-Driven Approach* (Burr Ridge, IL: Richard D. Irwin, 1996): 613.

15. Based on Jim Turcotte, Bob Silveri, and Tom Jobson, "Are You Ready for the E-Supply Chain?" *APICS–The Performance Advantage* (August 1998): 56–59.

16. Jason Dedrick and Kenneth L. Kraemer, "The Impacts of IT on Firm and Industry Structure: The Personal Computer Industry," *California Management Review* 47, no. 3 (Spring 2005): 122–142; Kathryn Jones, "The Dell Way," *Business 2.0* (February 2003): 61–66; and Stewart Deck, "Fine Line," *CIO* (February 1, 2000): 88–92.

17. AMR Research rankings reported in Patton, "The Perfect Order."

18. Jeffrey McCracken, "Ford Seeks Big Savings by Overhauling Supply System" *The Wall Street Journal* (September 29, 2005): A1, A11.

19. Russ Banham, "Caught in the Middle," *CFO* (May 2001): 69–74.

20. Jason Tanz, "From Drab to Fab," *Fortune* (December 8, 2003): 178–184.

21. David Goldenberg, "Fresh Breath, Fresher Packaging," *Business 2.0* (December 2005): 74–76

22. Erika Brown, "Drive Fast, Drive Hard," *Forbes* (January 9, 2006): 92.

23. Laura Landro, "The Informed Patient: Cutting Waits at the Doctor's Office—New Programs Reorganize Practices to Be More Efficient," *The Wall Street Journal* (April 19, 2006): D1.

24. Christopher Koch, "The Big Payoff," *CIO* (October 1, 2000): 101–112; Norman Gaither and Greg Frazier, *Operations Management*, 9th ed. (Cincinnati, OH: South-Western Publishing, 2002): 428–429.

25. Gaither and Frazier, *Operations Management*, 429.

26. David Rocks, "The Net as a Lifeline," *BusinessWeek e.biz* (October 29, 2001): EB16–EB28.

27. Scott Leibs, "First Pencils, Now People," *CFO* (November 2001): 91–94.

28. Christopher Koch, "Four Strategies," *CIO* (October 1, 2000): 116–128.

29. Nancy Lea Hyer and Karen A. Brown, "Work Cells with Staying Power: Lessons for Process–Complete Operations," *California Management Review* 46, no. 1 (Fall 2003): 27–52.

30. Daniel Michaels and J. Lynn Lunsford, "Streamlined Plane Making," *The Wall Street Journal* (April 1, 2005): B1, B2.

31. Valerie Bauerlein, "Online Banking Strives for the Human Touch," *The Wall Street Journal* (July 6, 2006): D1.

32. Dean Elmuti and Michael Abebe, "RFID Reshapes the Global Supply Chain," *Industrial Management* (March–April 2005): 27–31; John Teresko, "Plant Strategies: Winning with Wireless," *Industry Week* (June 2003): 60–66; and Meridith Levinson, "The RFID Imperative," *CIO* (December 1, 2003): 78–91.

33. Barnaby J. Feder, "Military to Urge Suppliers to Adopt Radio ID Tags," *The New York Times* (November 12, 2005): www.nytimes.com.

34. Maryanne Murray Buechner, "Cracking the Code," *FSB: Fortune Small Business* (March 2004): 72–73.

35. Feder, "Military to Urge Suppliers to Adopt Radio ID Tags."

36. Elmuti and Abebe, "RFID Reshapes the Global Supply Chain."

37. Sumer C. Aggarwal, "MRP, JIT, OPT, FMS?" *Harvard Business Review* 63 (September–October 1985): 8–16; and Paul Ranky, *The Design and Operation of Flexible Manufacturing Systems* (New York: Elsevier, 1983).

38. David Welch, "How Nissan Laps Detroit," *BusinessWeek* (December 22, 2003): 58–60.

39. Neal E. Boudette, "Shifting Gears: Chrysler Gains Edge by Giving New Flexibility to Its Factories. Some Can Build One Vehicle, Then Switch to Another, A Skill Japanese Pioneered," *The Wall Street Journal* (April 11, 2006): A1.

40. This discussion of product life-cycle management software is based on Gene Bylinsky, "Not Your Grandfather's Assembly Line," *Fortune* special section, "Industrial Management and Technology (June 28, 2004): www.fortune.com.

41. Ibid.

42. Shirley Leung, "Where's the Beef? A Glutted Market Leaves Food Chains Hungry for Sites," *The Wall Street Journal* (October 1, 2003): A1, A12.

43. Alan David MacCormack, Lawrence James Newman III, and Donald B. Rosenfield, "The New Dynamics of Global Manufacturing Site Location," *Sloan Management Review* (Summer 1994): 69–80; and Chen May Yee, "Let's Make a Deal," *The Wall Street Journal* (September 25, 2000): R10.

44. Claudia Eller and James Bates, "Not All Projections Bad for Overgrown Theater Chains," *Los Angeles Times* (September 8, 2000).

45. Evan Ramstad, "Compaq Stumbles Amid New Pressures on PCs," *The Wall Street Journal* (March 9, 1998): B1, B8.

46. R. J. Schonberger, *Japanese Manufacturing Techniques: Nine Hidden Lessons in Simplicity* (New York: Free Press, 1982).

47. Cathy Lazere, "Taking Stock of Inventory: Beyond Mean and Lean," *CFO* (November 1997): 95–97.

48. Gaither and Frazier, *Operations Management*, 587.

49. F. C. "Ted" Watson, Jr., "ERP II: The Extended Enterprise System," *Business Horizons* (November–December 2003): 49–55.

50. Vincent A. Mabert, Ashok Soni, and M. A. Venkataramanan, "Enterprise Resource Planning: Common Myths Versus Evolving Reality," *Business Horizons* (May–June 2001): 69–76.

51. Luciana Beard and Stephen A. Butler, "Introducing JIT Manufacturing: It's Easier Than You Think," *Business Horizons* (September–October 2000): 61–64.

52. Based on Ronald Henkoff, "Delivering the Goods," *Fortune* (November 28, 1994): 64–78.

53. Noel P. Greis and John D. Kasarda, "Enterprise Logistics in the Information Era," *California Management Review* 39, no. 4 (Summer 1997): 55–78.

54. David Rocks, "Dell's Second Web Revolution," *BusinessWeek e.biz* (September 18, 2000): EB62–EB63.

55. "Kanban: The Just-in-Time Japanese Inventory System," *Small Business Report* (February 1984): 69–71; and Richard C. Walleigh, "What's Your Excuse for Not Using JIT?" *Harvard Business Review* 64 (March–April 1986): 38–54.

56. Gaither and Frazier, *Operations Management*, 150–151.

57. Andrew Ward, Dan Roberts, and Alexandra Harney, "U.S. Groups Shift Their Warehouses to China," *Financial Times* (November 17, 2005): www.ft.com.

58. Faith Keenan, "Logistics Gets a Little Respect," and "One Smart Cookie," *BusinessWeek e.biz* (November 20, 2000): EB120.

59. Art Kleiner, "Leaning Toward Utopia," *Strategy + Business*, no. 39 (Second Quarter 2005): 76–87; Fara Warner, "Think Lean," *Fast Company* (February 2002): 40, 42; and James P. Womack and Daniel T. Jones, *The Machine That Changed the World: The Story of Lean Production* (New York: HarperCollins, 1991).

60. Peter Strozniak, "Toyota Alters Face of Production," *Industry Week* (August 13, 2001): 46–48.

61. George Tanninecz, "Even Better," pp. 60–62 in Jill Jusko, "Successful by Design: *IndustryWeek*'s 2005 Best Plants Excel by Intent, Not by Accident," *IndustryWeek* (October 2005): 34–68.

62. Kleiner, "Leaning Toward Utopia."

63. Emily Esterson, "First-Class Delivery," *Inc. Technology* (September 15, 1998): 89.

64. W. Bouce Chew, "No-Nonsense Guide to Measuring Productivity," *Harvard Business Review* (January–February 1988): 110–118.

65. The Outsourcing Institute, "Outsourcing: The New Midas Touch," *BusinessWeek* (December 15, 1997): special advertising section.

66. W. E. Deming, *Quality, Productivity, and Competitive Position* (Cambridge, MA: Center for Advanced Engineering Study, MIT, 1982); and P. B. Crosby, *Quality Is Free* (New York: McGraw-Hill, 1979).

67. Charles E. Lucier and Janet D. Torsilieri, "Why Knowledge Programs Fail: A C.E.O.'s Guide to Managing Learning," *Strategy + Business* (Fourth Quarter 1997): 14–16, 21–27.

68. Patton, "The Perfect Order."

COSTCO WHOLESALE CORPORATION
PART SIX: COSTCO'S WHOPPER OF A FISH TALE

Continuous improvement isn't a mere buzzword at Costco Wholesale: it's a *modus operandi*. To offer high-quality products at rock-bottom prices, the $60-billion-a-year warehouse club must manage its daily operations and supply chain with ever-increasing efficiency and innovation. Without this commitment, selling stacks of AG dark-rinse jeans and Canon high-performance digital cameras at deep discounts would be a losing business proposition.

When illustrating Costco's ongoing quest for an ever-higher standard of quality and efficiency, senior executives recount an old fish tale—fortunately, this is not about the one that got away. The story begins with a salmon fillet that Costco's seafood department once sold for $5.99 per pound. At the time, shoppers saw nothing unusual or impressive about the fish—the pinkish-orange tender fillets lined the seafood aisle, complete with skin, bones, fins, and belly fat. One day, merchandisers began looking for a way to boost the fish's $200,000-per-week sales. Their objective was to improve the product while lowering its price. In a breakthrough procurement effort, staffers located a salmon-jerky manufacturer in Japan that could deliver the fish trimmed and stripped of bones, after retaining the belly fat for its jerky product. The new leaner salmon fillet sold for $5.29 per pound, producing a 20 to 30 percent rise in sales. After additional improvements, Costco offered a fully trimmed, skinless and boneless fillet for $4.99 per pound. At this price point, sales of the salmon jumped from about $850,000 per week to $1.4 million. The higher volume sales now enabled Costco's buyers to source the product directly from salmon farms in Canada and Chile, creating even greater cost savings. The final result of Costco's fishing expedition: a $3.99-per-pound salmon delicacy generating over $2 million in weekly revenues.

This salmon story has come to symbolize Costco's unique operating philosophy—so much so that it is now tightly woven throughout the company's corporate culture. The oft-recounted tale has given rise to the Salmon Awards, the company's annual achievement program that recognizes the merchant or vendor who does the most to improve a product's quality while lowering its cost. In addition, Costco's Issaquah, Washington headquarters prominently displays a statue of spawning salmon—a shrine dedicated to the cherished Pacific Northwest fish and to Costco's value-driven merchandising.

Establishing cost-saving partnerships with suppliers requires the resourcefulness of Costco's dedicated managers, but maintaining these relationships on a day-to-day basis is made possible through cutting-edge technology. For example, coordinating the order, transport, and replenishment of inventories would be nearly impossible without computerized information systems like the Costco Collaborative Retail Exchange (CRX), a high-tech program that creates an electronic link between Costco and its vendors. The program gives manufacturers, suppliers, and other partners constant visibility of Costco's warehouse management to effectively reduce out-of-stocks, increase new product introduction success, and manage item performance. With Costco CRX, vendors gain direct, interactive access to Costco's warehouse-specific, item-level data—in real time. "The CRX program is our approach to providing our vendor community with standard, secure access to current and detailed information about their business at Costco Wholesale," said Ed Maron, executive vice president at Costco. Maron added that CRX transforms Costco's point-of-sale information into actionable business insights for retail partners.

Other Costco business operations depend on technology as well. As a result of having many retail partners, Costco must manage thousands of communications in and out of the company each day. The warehouse club operator can't afford to get bogged down in delayed responses to purchase orders, debit memos, or invoices. To streamline processing of the nearly 30,000 documents exchanged between Costco and its suppliers daily—6.7 million each year—the company employs a document imaging system that scans documents for digital storage and retrieval. The system facilitates fast, effective communication between Costco and outside firms, resulting in improved service to warehouse, depot, and vendor customers.

Though high-tech coordination with suppliers has played a vital role in Costco's past, it also holds the key to Costco's future. Nowhere is this more evident than with Costco.com, the company's e-commerce division. Costco.com offers about 4,000 items for sale online, and nearly 70 percent of products ordered through the site are shipped directly from external suppliers to the customer. By connecting outside vendors and manufacturers to its e-supply chain, Costco saves millions of dollars in warehousing, inventory, and shipping expenses. The retailer's Internet-based strategy is paying off: in 2005, Costco.com ranked 27 among online retailers, boasting sales of $534 million. Looking ahead, the e-business division is projected to generate over $1 billion annually.

Whether the objective is to offer customers the best salmon product at the lowest possible price or to implement state-of-the-art technologies that streamline daily business processes, Costco Wholesale is dedicated to keeping continuous improvement at the center of its business. After more than 25 years of retailing success, the No.1 warehouse club is as determined as ever to lead the way to the future with ever-increasing efficiency, profitability, and success.

Questions

1. How does Costco's famous and oft-recounted salmon story help management create a culture of performance and quality?

2. What role does the Salmon Awards program play in Costco's system of control?

3. How does Costco reduce its operating expenses by investing in technologies that enable outside suppliers to manage inventories and ship orders directly to customers?

SOURCES: Tim Craig, "Impressed by Costco? Join the Club," *DSN Retailing Today,* December 19, 2005; Mike Duff, "Innovation Has Its Own Reward," *DSN Retailing Today,* December 19, 2005; "Salmon Tells the Costco Story," *MMR,* August 23, 2004; "Costco Makes It Easier for Suppliers," *MMR,* December 12, 2005; "Costco Keeps Prices Low with Document Imaging," *Transform,* December 2004; Mya Frazier, "What Long Tail," *Advertising Age,* August 21, 2006.

LEADING

Architects lead the construction process: They determine the size and shape of a building, how it will be built, where it will be built, and other salient choices. These choices often have a subtle impact in how that structure will embody and even influence the culture. Architecture has always been used as a means of cultural leadership, leading by the embodiment of foundational ideas.

The first permanent structures ever built were temples, shrines to ancient gods. Religion was the central rule of ancient life and the ancient temples embodied how those people saw themselves and the world around them. The people lived in temporary structures that were not expected to outlast the occupants, but the temples were built of stone, intended to survive for ages, which in fact, many of them did.

Many times architects are keenly aware of the culture into which a structure is being built, and that structure is designed specifically to either reinforce the current culture or to lead the culture in a new direction, to express new ideas. Roman and Greek architecture is similar, particularly since Rome borrowed heavily from Greek thought and architecture, but the ideas embodied differ vastly. Greek architecture displayed the Greek ideas of democracy, piety and independence; Roman architecture, however, valued authority and practicality. So where Greek architecture was largely concerned with temples, Roman architecture expanded to secular structures—law courts, theaters, and houses—exemplifying and reinforcing centralized Roman thinking and authority. Ironically, when the Byzantine Empire emerged from the ashes of the Roman Empire, around 500 a.d., the Christian churches were constructed in the same style as the surrounding buildings; instead of standing out, the early Byzantium churches blended in, a startling departure from Greek and Roman concepts of worship and deity.

Although a manager's job includes issuing directives, leadership is not simply ordering people: go here, do that. A leader must also guide the culture and spirit of a company or business. A manager must lead with ideas and be an embodiment of those ideas—a cultural leader.

CHAPTER 17

CHAPTER OUTLINE

Manager's Challenge

Organizational Behavior

Attitudes

Components of Attitudes

High-Performance Work Attitudes

Conflicts Among Attitudes

Perception

Perceptual Selectivity

Perceptual Distortions

Attributions

Personality and Behavior

Personality Traits

Emotional Intelligence

Attitudes and Behaviors Influenced
by Personality

Person–Job Fit

Learning

The Learning Process

Learning Styles

Continuous Learning

Stress and Stress Management

Type A and Type B Behavior

Causes of Work Stress

Innovative Responses to Stress
Management

LEARNING OBJECTIVES

After studying this chapter, you should be able to:

1. Define attitudes, including their major components, and explain their relationship to personality, perception, and behavior.

2. Discuss the importance of work-related attitudes.

3. Identify major personality traits and describe how personality can influence workplace attitudes and behaviors.

4. Define the four components of emotional intelligence and explain why they are important for today's managers.

5. Explain how people learn in general and in terms of individual learning styles.

6. Discuss the effects of stress and identify ways individuals and organizations can manage stress to improve employee health, satisfaction, and productivity

DYNAMICS OF BEHAVIOR IN ORGANIZATIONS

MANAGER'S CHALLENGE

Since the day Kevin Kelly left a full-time journalism career to run his family's California company, Emerald Packaging—a maker of plastic bags for the food industry—he's successfully solved many management problems. But suddenly Kelly feels out of his league. Kelly has been accustomed to thinking of himself as on top of his game, chief architect of the company's growing sales and profits. But lately he's noticed a disturbing situation. Managers at the company seem to have lost the drive to push through new ideas and proposals that can keep Emerald thriving, and Kelly catches himself complaining about his subordinates without taking steps to improve things. Realizing that everyone is under stress from several years of rapid growth, Kelly hires a pack of new, young managers to reinforce his exhausted troops. Surprisingly, though, things just seem to get worse, with the new managers feeling adrift and the old-timers seeming even less focused than before. Then Kelly has a revelation that both unnerves and excites him. Rather than complain about his managers' shortcomings, Kelly realizes that he has to remake himself, change his own attitude. Kelly wants to become a mentor who shapes positive attitudes in others and to knit the newcomers and long-time employees into a cohesive and productive team.[1]

If you were Kevin Kelly, how would you gain a better understanding of yourself and the personal changes you need to make to help people feel more satisfied and committed to Emerald Packaging? Do you believe the personality and attitudes of a small company's CEO will affect economic performance?

TAKE A MOMENT

The situation at Emerald Packaging illustrates the importance of understanding organizational behavior. Managers' attitudes, and their ability to understand and shape the attitudes of employees, can profoundly affect the workplace and influence employee motivation, morale, and job performance. People differ in many ways. Some are quiet and shy while others are gregarious; some are thoughtful and serious while others are impulsive and fun-loving. Employees—and managers—bring their individual differences to work each day. Differences in attitudes, values, personality, and behavior influence how people interpret an assignment, whether they like to be told what to do, how they handle challenges, and how they interact with others. People are an organization's most valuable resource—and the source of some of managers' most difficult problems. Three basic leadership skills are at the core of identifying and solving people problems: (1) diagnosing, or gaining insight into the situation a manager is trying to influence; (2) adapting individual behavior and resources to meet the needs of the situation; and (3) communicating in a way that others can understand and accept. Thus, managers need insight about individual differences to understand what a behavioral situation is now and what it may be in the future.

To handle this responsibility, managers need to understand the principles of organizational behavior—that is, the ways individuals and groups tend to act in organizations. By increasing their knowledge of individual differences in the areas of attitudes, personality, perception, learning, and stress management, managers can understand and lead employees and colleagues through many workplace challenges. This chapter introduces basic principles of organizational behavior in each of these areas.

ORGANIZATIONAL BEHAVIOR

Organizational behavior, commonly called OB, is an interdisciplinary field dedicated to the study of human attitudes, behavior, and performance in organizations. OB draws concepts from many disciplines, including psychology, sociology, cultural anthropology, industrial engineering, economics, ethics, and vocational counseling, as well as the discipline of management. The concepts and principles of organizational behavior are important to managers because in every organization human beings ultimately make the decisions that control how the organization acquires and uses resources. Those people may cooperate with, compete with, support, or undermine one another. Their beliefs and feelings about themselves, their coworkers, and the organization shape what they do and how well they do it. People can distract the organization from its strategy by engaging in conflict and misunderstandings, or they can pool their diverse talents and perspectives to accomplish much more as a group than they could ever do as individuals.

By understanding what causes people to behave as they do, managers can exercise leadership to achieve positive outcomes. By creating a positive environment, for example, managers can foster **organizational citizenship**, which refers to the tendency of people to help one another and put in extra effort that goes beyond job requirements to contribute to the organization's success. An employee demonstrates organizational citizenship by being helpful to coworkers and customers, doing extra work when necessary, and looking for ways to improve products and procedures. These behaviors enhance the organization's performance and help to build *social capital*, as described in Chapter 12.[2] Organizational citizenship contributes to positive relationships both within the organization and with customers, leading to a high level of social capital and smooth organizational functioning. Managers can encourage organizational citizenship by applying their knowledge of human behavior, such as selecting people with positive attitudes and personalities, helping them see how they can contribute, and enabling them to learn from and cope with workplace challenges.

ATTITUDES

Most students have probably heard the expression that someone "has an attitude problem," which means some consistent quality about the person affects his or her behavior in a negative way. An employee with an attitude problem might be hard to get along with, might constantly gripe and cause problems, and might persistently resist new ideas. We all seem to know intuitively what an attitude is, but we do not consciously think about how strongly attitudes affect our behavior. Defined formally, an **attitude** is an evaluation—either positive or negative—that predisposes a person to act in a certain way. Understanding employee attitudes is important to managers because attitudes determine how people perceive the work environment, interact with others, and behave on the job. Emerging research is revealing the importance of positive attitudes to both individual and organizational success. For example, studies have found that the characteristic most common to top executives is an optimistic attitude. People rise to the top because they have the ability to see opportunities where others see problems and can instill in others a sense of hope and possibility for the future.[3]

Good managers strive to develop and reinforce positive attitudes among all employees, because happy, positive people are healthier, more effective, and more productive.[4] A person who has the attitude "I love my work; it's challenging and fun" will typically tackle work-related problems cheerfully, while one who comes to

organizational behavior
An interdisciplinary field dedicated to the study of how individuals and groups tend to act in organizations.

organizational citizenship
Work behavior that goes beyond job requirements and contributes as needed to the organization's success.

attitude A cognitive and affective evaluation that predisposes a person to act in a certain way.

work with the attitude "I hate my job" is not likely to show much enthusiasm or commitment to solving problems. Some companies, such as David's Bridal, the nation's largest bridal-store chain, are applying scientific research to improve employee attitudes—and sales performance.

Planning a wedding can be one of the most joyful experiences in a woman's life—and one of the most nerve-wracking. The salespeople at David's Bridal, a 267-store chain owned by Federated Department Stores, bear the brunt of these intense emotions. For many, dealing with those emotions can be overwhelming and exhausting, translating into negative attitudes and impatience with already-stressed customers.

Managers turned to new research on happiness to help employees cope and develop more positive attitudes. Adaptiv Learning Systems, based in King of Prussia, Pennsylvania, conducted a pilot training program in four stores based on the work of psychologist Martin Seligman. Salespeople were taught how to feel more cheerful with techniques such as "emotion regulation," "impulse control," and "learned optimism." They learned coping techniques to use when dealing with a harried, indecisive bride-to-be, such as making a mental list of the top five things that bring them joy. These techniques enable salespeople to be more calm and centered, which helps customers stay calm and centered as well. That attitude/behavior translates into better sales, meaning employees make better commissions, which in turn contributes to more positive attitudes toward the job.

The success of the pilot project spurred David's Bridal to consider various training options, such as online training, to expand the strategies to all of the company's 3,000 employees.[5]

As the example at David's Bridal shows, sometimes negative attitudes can result from characteristics of the job, such as a high stress level, but managers can find ways to help people have more positive attitudes. Managers should pay attention to negative attitudes because they can be both the result of underlying problems in the workplace as well as a contributor to forthcoming problems.[6]

Components of Attitudes

One important step for managers is recognizing and understanding the *components* of attitudes, which is particularly important when attempting to change attitudes.

Behavioral scientists consider attitudes to have three components: cognitions (thoughts), affect (feelings), and behavior.[7] The cognitive component of an attitude includes the beliefs, opinions, and information the person has about the object of the attitude, such as knowledge of what a job entails and opinions about personal abilities. The affective component is the person's emotions or feelings about the object of the attitude, such as enjoying or hating a job. The behavioral component of an attitude is the person's intention to behave toward the object of the attitude in a certain way. Exhibit 17.1 illustrates the three

© ERNEST WASHINGTON

EXHIBIT   17.1

Components of an Attitude

Cognitive...thoughts...

"My job is interesting."

Affective...feelings...
"I love my job."

Behavioral...intention to act...
"I'm going to get to work early with a smile on my face."

Attitude: Job Satisfaction

components of a positive attitude toward one's job. The cognitive element is the conscious thought that "my job is interesting and challenging." The affective element is the feeling that "I love this job." These elements, in turn, are related to the behavioral component—an employee might arrive at work early because he or she is happy with the job.

Often, when we think about attitudes, we focus on the cognitive component. However, it is important for managers to remember the other components as well. The emotional (affective) component is often the stronger factor in affecting behavior. When people feel strongly about something, the affective component may influence them to act in a certain way no matter what someone does to change their thoughts or opinions. Recall the discussion of idea champions in Chapter 11. When someone is passionate about a new idea, he or she may go to great lengths to implement it, even when colleagues and superiors say the idea is stupid. Another example is an employee who is furious about being asked to work overtime on his birthday. The supervisor might present clear, rational reasons for the need to put in extra hours, but the employee might still act based on his anger—by failing to cooperate, lashing out at coworkers, or even quitting. In cases such as these, effective leadership includes addressing the emotions associated with the attitude. Are employees so excited that their judgment may be clouded, or so discouraged that they have given up trying? If nothing else, the manager probably needs to be aware of situations that involve strong emotions and give employees a chance to vent their feelings appropriately.

As a general rule, changing just one component—cognitions, affect, or behavior— can contribute to an overall change in attitude. Suppose a manager concludes that some employees have the attitude that the manager should make all the decisions affecting the department, but the manager prefers that employees assume more decision-making responsibility. To change the underlying attitude, the manager would consider whether to educate employees about the areas in which they can make good decisions (changing the cognitive component), build enthusiasm with pep talks about the satisfaction of employee empowerment (changing the affective component), or simply insist that employees make their own decisions (behavioral component) with the expectation that, once they experience the advantages of decision-making authority, they will begin to like it.

■ **TAKE A MOMENT**

As a new manager, be mindful of your own attitude and how it affects people who work for you. A positive attitude can go a long way toward helping others feel good about themselves and their work responsibilities. If you want to change employees' attitudes, don't underestimate the strength of the emotions.

High-Performance Work Attitudes

The attitudes of most interest to managers are those related to work, especially attitudes that influence how well employees perform. To lead employees effectively, managers logically seek to cultivate the kinds of attitudes that are associated with high performance. Two attitudes that might relate to high performance are satisfaction with one's job and commitment to the organization.

JOB SATISFACTION

A positive attitude toward one's job is called **job satisfaction**. In general, people experience this attitude when their work matches their needs and interests, when working conditions and rewards (such as pay) are satisfactory, when they like their coworkers, and when they have positive relationships with supervisors. You can take the quiz in Exhibit 17.2 to better understand some of the factors that contribute to job satisfaction.

Many managers believe job satisfaction is important because they think satisfied employees will do better work. In fact, research shows that the link between satisfaction and performance is generally small and is influenced by other factors.[8] For example, the importance of satisfaction varies according to the amount of control the employee has;

MARCIO JOSE SANCHEZ/ASSOCIATED PRESS

[CONCEPT
⌐CONNECTION⌐ "To shake the hand of someone who was nearly dead—there's no feeling like that in the world." That's how one physician assistant (PA) explained why he finds the profession so fulfilling. **Job satisfaction** is extraordinarily high for PAs, such as Jim Johnson, shown here helping patients in a makeshift medical tent after Hurricane Katrina hit Gulfport, Mississippi. A recent survey reported that 90 percent would make the same career choice all over again. In addition to good pay and flexible working conditions, PAs relish the autonomy of the job, a chance to help others, the challenge of diagnosing and treating a variety of ailments, and working as part of a team.

an employee doing routine tasks may produce about the same output no matter how he or she feels about the job. However, one internal study at Sears found a clear link between employee satisfaction, customer satisfaction, and revenue. In particular, employees' attitudes about whether their workloads were manageable and well-organized ranked among the top 10 indicators of company performance.[9]

Managers of today's knowledge workers often rely on job satisfaction to keep motivation and enthusiasm for the organization high. Organizations don't want to lose talented, highly skilled workers. In addition, most managers care about their employees and simply want them to feel good about their work—and almost everyone prefers being around people who have positive attitudes. Regrettably, a survey by International Survey Research found that Gen X employees, those who are carrying the weight of much of today's knowledge work, are the least satisfied of all demographic groups.[10] Managers play an important role in whether employees have positive or negative attitudes toward their jobs.[11] The CEO of

job satisfaction A positive attitude toward one's job.

Think of a job—either a current or previous job—that was important to you, and then answer the following questions with respect to how satisfied you were with that job. Please answer the six questions with a number 1–5 that reflects the extent of your satisfaction.

1 = Very dissatisfied   3 = Neutral   5 = Very satisfied
2 = Dissatisfied   4 = Satisfied

	1	2	3	4	5
1. Overall, how satisfied are you with your job?	1	2	3	4	5
2. How satisfied are you with the opportunities to learn new things?	1	2	3	4	5
3. How satisfied are you with your boss?	1	2	3	4	5
4. How satisfied are you with the people in your work group?	1	2	3	4	5
5. How satisfied are you with the amount of pay you receive?	1	2	3	4	5
6. How satisfied are you with the advancement you are making in the organization?	1	2	3	4	5

Scoring and Interpretation: Add up your responses to the six questions to obtain your total score: _____. The questions represent various aspects of satisfaction that an employee may experience on a job. If your score is 24 or above, you probably feel satisfied with the job. If your score is 12 or below, you probably do not feel satisfied. What is your level of performance in your job, and is your performance related to your level of satisfaction?

SOURCES: These questions were adapted from Daniel R. Denison, *Corporate Culture and Organizational Effectiveness* (New York: John Wiley, 1990); and John D. Cook, Susan J. Hepworth, Toby D. Wall, and Peter B. Warr, *The Experience of Work: A Compendium and Review of 249 Measures and their Use* (San Diego, CA: Academic Press, 1981).

General Mills recognizes that managers have to pay attention to their own attitudes and behaviors to influence the attitudes and performance of others.

General Mills

As Steve Sanger, CEO of General Mills, was reviewing his 360-degree feedback, he discovered that many managers thought he needed to do a better job of coaching his direct reports. Rather than becoming defensive, Sanger adopted the attitude that he needed to improve himself in order to help others grow and improve.

When the top leader of a company displays arrogance and simply tells everyone else how they need to improve, that attitude and behavior filters down to every level of management. An "us-versus-them" mind-set often develops between employees and managers and job satisfaction, motivation, and performance decline.

Steve Sanger, though, had an insight. By being open with people and admitting his own weaknesses and efforts to improve, he set an example for others to do the same. Sanger is noted for his enlightened attitudes about how to help employees be successful both at work and in their personal lives. The first step, he knows, is for a leader to be aware of how his attitudes and behaviors influence others and create either a positive or a negative organizational environment.[12]

By creating a positive environment, leaders such as Steve Sanger contribute to higher job satisfaction for employees. A related attitude is organizational commitment.

ORGANIZATIONAL COMMITMENT

Organizational commitment refers to an employee's loyalty to and engagement with the organization. An employee with a high degree of organizational commitment is likely to say *we* when talking about the company. Such a person likes being a part of the organization and tries to contribute to its success. This attitude is illustrated by an incident at the A. W. Chesterton Company, a Massachusetts manufacturer of mechanical seals and pumps. When two Chesterton pumps that supply water on Navy ship *USS John F. Kennedy* failed on a Saturday night just before the ship's scheduled departure, Todd Robinson, the leader of the team that produces the seals, swung into action. He and his fiancèe, who also works for Chesterton, worked through the night to make new seals and deliver them to be installed before the ship left port.[13]

organizational commitment Loyalty to and heavy involvement in one's organization.

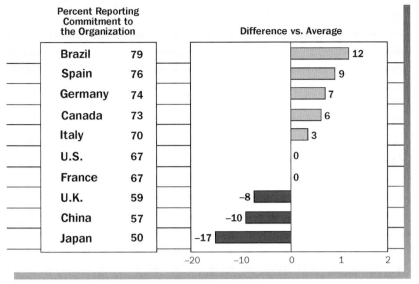

Percent Reporting Commitment to the Organization		Difference vs. Average
Brazil	79	12
Spain	76	9
Germany	74	7
Canada	73	6
Italy	70	3
U.S.	67	0
France	67	0
U.K.	59	−8
China	57	−10
Japan	50	−17

Shaded difference bar denotes a statistically significant difference.

EXHIBIT 17.3

Variations in Organizational Commitment: The World's 10 Largest Economies

Most managers want to enjoy the benefits of loyal, committed employees, including low turnover and willingness to do more than the job's basic requirements. In addition, results of a survey of more than 650,000 employees in global organizations suggest that companies with committed employees perform better. The study found that companies with highly committed employees outperformed the industry average over a 12-month period by 6 percent, while those with low levels of commitment underperformed the average by 9 percent.[14] Alarmingly, levels of commitment in the United States are significantly lower than those in half of the world's other large economies, as illustrated in Exhibit 17.3. U.S. employees are less committed than those in Brazil, Spain, Germany, Canada, and Italy. This low level of organizational commitment puts U.S. firms at a serious disadvantage in the global marketplace.[15]

The high motivation and engagement that comes with organizational commitment is essential to the success of organizations that depend on employees' ideas and creativity. Trust in management's decisions and integrity is an important component of organizational commitment.[16] Unfortunately, in recent years, many employees have lost that trust, resulting in a decline in commitment. Just 28 percent of employees surveyed by *Fast Company* magazine said they think the CEO of their company has integrity. Another recent survey by Ajilon Professional Staffing found that only 29 percent of employees believe their boss truly cares about them and looks out for their interests.[17]

Managers can promote organizational commitment by keeping employees informed, giving them a say in decisions, providing the necessary training and other resources that enable them to succeed, treating them fairly, and offering rewards they value. For example, recent studies suggest that employee commitment in today's workplace is strongly correlated with initiatives and benefits that help people balance their work and personal lives.[18]

Conflicts Among Attitudes

Sometimes a person may discover that his or her attitudes conflict with one another or are not reflected in behavior. For example, a person's high level of organizational commitment might conflict with a commitment to family members. If employees routinely work evenings and weekends, their long hours and dedication to the job might conflict with their belief that family ties are important. This conflict can create a state of **cognitive dissonance**, a psychological discomfort that occurs when individuals recognize inconsistencies in their own attitudes and behaviors.[19] The theory of cognitive dissonance, developed by social psychologist Leon Festinger in the 1950s, says that people want to behave in accordance with their attitudes

cognitive dissonance A condition in which two attitudes or a behavior and an attitude conflict.

and usually will take corrective action to alleviate the dissonance and achieve balance.

In the case of working overtime, people who can control their hours might restructure responsibilities so that they have time for both work and family. In contrast, those who are unable to restructure workloads might develop an unfavorable attitude toward the employer, reducing their organizational commitment. They might resolve their dissonance by saying they would like to spend more time with their kids but their unreasonable employer demands that they work too many hours.

PERCEPTION

Another critical aspect of understanding behavior is perception. **Perception** is the cognitive process people use to make sense out of the environment by selecting, organizing, and interpreting information from the environment. Attitudes affect perceptions, and vice versa. For example, a person might have developed the attitude that managers are insensitive and arrogant, based on a pattern of perceiving arrogant and insensitive behavior from managers over a period of time. If the person moves to a new job, this attitude will continue to affect the way he or she perceives superiors in the new environment, even though managers in the new workplace might take great pains to understand and respond to employees' needs.

Because of individual differences in attitudes, personality, values, interests, and so forth, people often "see" the same thing in different ways. A class that is boring to one student might be fascinating to another. One student might perceive an assignment to be challenging and stimulating, whereas another might find it a silly waste of time. Referring back to the topic of diversity discussed in Chapter 13, many African Americans perceive that blacks are regularly discriminated against, whereas many white employees perceive that blacks are given special opportunities in the workplace.[20] Similarly, in a survey of financial profession executives, 40 percent of women perceive that women face a "glass ceiling" that keeps them from reaching top management levels, while only 10 percent of men share that perception.[21]

We can think of perception as a step-by-step process, as shown in Exhibit 17.4. First, we observe information (sensory data) from the environment through our senses: taste, smell, hearing, sight, and touch. Next, our mind screens the data and will select only the items we will process further. Third, we organize the selected data into meaningful patterns for interpretation and response. Most differences in perception among people at work are related to how they select and organize sensory data. You can experience differences in perceptual organization by looking at the visuals in Exhibit 17.5. What do you see in part *a* of Exhibit 17.5? Most people see this as a dog, but others see only a series of unrelated ink blots. Some people will see the figure in part *b* as a beautiful young woman while others will see an old one. Now look at part *c*. How many blocks do you see—six or seven? Some people have to turn the figure upside down before they can see seven blocks. These visuals illustrate how complex perception is.

Perceptual Selectivity

We all are aware of our environment, but not everything in it is equally important to our perception of it. We tune in to some data (e.g., a familiar voice off in the distance) and tune out other data (e.g., paper shuffling next to us). People are bombarded by so much sensory data that it is impossible to process it all. The brain's solution is to run the data through a perceptual filter that retains some parts and eliminates others.

perception The cognitive process people use to make sense out of the environment by selecting, organizing, and interpreting information.

EXHIBIT   17.4

The Perception Process

a. Do you see the dog?   **b.** Old woman or young woman?   **c.** How many blocks?

Perceptual selectivity is the process by which individuals screen and select the various objects and stimuli that vie for their attention. Certain stimuli catch their attention, and others do not.

People typically focus on stimuli that satisfy their needs and that are consistent with their attitudes, values, and personality. For example, employees who need positive feedback to feel good about themselves might pick up on positive statements made by a supervisor but tune out most negative comments. A supervisor could use this understanding to tailor feedback in a positive way to help the employee improve work performance. The influence of needs on perception has been studied in laboratory experiments and found to have a strong impact on what people perceive.[22]

Characteristics of the stimuli themselves also affect perceptual selectivity. People tend to notice stimuli that stand out against other stimuli or that are more intense than surrounding stimuli. Examples would be a loud noise in a quiet room or a bright red dress at a party where most women are wearing basic black. People also tend to notice things that are familiar to them, such as a familiar voice in a crowd, as well as things that are new or different from their previous experiences. In addition, *primacy* and *recency* are important to perceptual selectivity. People pay relatively greater attention to sensory data that occur toward the beginning of an event or toward the end. Primacy supports the old truism that first impressions really do count, whether it be on a job interview, meeting a date's parents, or participating in a new social group. Recency reflects the reality that the last impression might be a lasting impression. For example, Malaysian Airlines discovered its value in building customer loyalty. A woman traveling with a nine-month-old might find the flight itself an exhausting blur, but one such traveler enthusiastically told people for years how Malaysian Airlines flight attendants helped her with baggage collection and ground transportation.[23]

As these examples show, perceptual selectivity is a complex filtering process. Managers can use an understanding of perceptual selectivity to obtain clues about why one person sees things differently from others, and they can apply the principles to their own communications and actions, especially when they want to attract or focus attention.

Perceptual Distortions

Once people select the sensory data to be perceived, they begin grouping the data into recognizable patterns. Perceptual organization is the process by which people organize or categorize stimuli according to their own frame of reference. Of particular concern in the work environment are **perceptual distortions**, errors in perceptual judgment that arise from inaccuracies in any part of the perceptual process.

Some types of errors are so common that managers should become familiar with them. These include stereotyping, the halo effect, projection, and perceptual defense. Managers who recognize these perceptual distortions can better adjust their perceptions to more closely match objective reality.

Stereotyping is the tendency to assign an individual to a group or broad category (e.g., female, black, elderly; or male, white, disabled) and then to attribute

perceptual selectivity The process by which individuals screen and select the various stimuli that vie for their attention.

perceptual distortions Errors in perceptual judgment that arise from inaccuracies in any part of the perceptual process.

stereotyping The tendency to assign an individual to a group or broad category and then attribute generalizations about the group to the individual.

widely held generalizations about the group to the individual. Thus, someone meets a new colleague, sees he is in a wheelchair, assigns him to the category "physically disabled," and attributes to this colleague generalizations she believes about people with disabilities, which may include a belief that he is less able than other coworkers. However, the person's inability to walk should not be seen as indicative of lesser abilities in other areas. Indeed, the assumption of limitations may not only offend him, it also prevents the person making the stereotypical judgment from benefiting from the many ways in which this person can contribute. Stereotyping prevents people from truly knowing those they classify in this way. In addition, negative stereotypes prevent talented people from advancing in an organization and fully contributing their talents to the organization's success.

The **halo effect** occurs when the perceiver develops an overall impression of a person or situation based on one characteristic, either favorable or unfavorable. In other words, a halo blinds the perceiver to other characteristics that should be used in generating a more complete assessment. The halo effect can play a significant role in performance appraisal, as we discussed in Chapter 12. For example, a person with an outstanding attendance record may be assessed as responsible, industrious, and highly productive; another person with less-than-average attendance may be assessed as a poor performer. Either assessment may be true, but it is the manager's job to be sure the assessment is based on complete information about all job-related characteristics and not just his or her preferences for good attendance.

Projection is the tendency of perceivers to see their own personal traits in other people; that is, they project their own needs, feelings, values, and attitudes into their judgment of others. A manager who is achievement oriented might assume that subordinates are as well. This assumption might cause the manager to restructure jobs to be less routine and more challenging, without regard for employees' actual satisfaction. The best guards against errors based on projection are self-awareness and empathy.

Perceptual defense is the tendency of perceivers to protect themselves against ideas, objects, or people that are threatening. People perceive things that are satisfying and pleasant but tend to disregard things that are disturbing and unpleasant. In essence, people develop blind spots in the perceptual process so that negative sensory data do not hurt them. For example, the director of a nonprofit educational organization in Tennessee hated dealing with conflict because he had grown up with parents who constantly argued and often put him in the middle of their arguments. The director consistently overlooked discord among staff members until things would reach a boiling point. When the blowup occurred, the director would be shocked and dismayed, because he had truly perceived that everything was going smoothly among the staff. Recognizing perceptual blind spots can help people develop a clearer picture of reality.

Attributions

As people organize what they perceive, they often draw conclusions, such as about an object or a person. Among the judgments people make as part of the perceptual process are attributions. **Attributions** are judgments about what caused a person's behavior—something about the person or something about the situation. An *internal attribution* says characteristics of the person led to the behavior ("My boss yelled at me because he's impatient and doesn't listen"). An *external attribution* says something about the situation caused the person's behavior ("My boss yelled at me because I missed the deadline and the customer is upset"). Attributions are important because they help people decide how to handle a situation. In the case of the boss yelling, a person who blames the yelling on the boss's personality will view the boss as the problem and might cope by avoiding the boss. In contrast, someone who blames the yelling on the situation might try to help prevent such situations in the future.

Social scientists have studied the attributions people make and identified three factors that influence whether an attribution will be external or internal.[24] These three factors are illustrated in Exhibit 17.6.

halo effect An overall impression of a person or situation based on one characteristic, either favorable or unfavorable.

projection The tendency to see one's own personal traits in other people.

perceptual defense The tendency of perceivers to protect themselves by disregarding ideas, objects, or people that are threatening to them.

attributions Judgments about what caused a person's behavior—either characteristics of the person or of the situation.

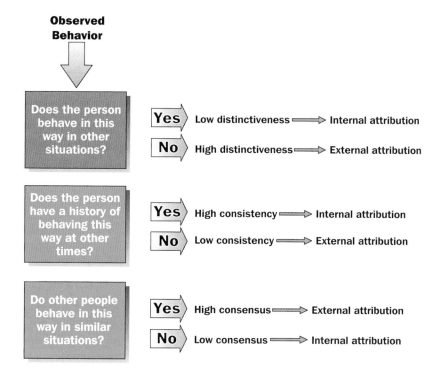

Observed Behavior

Does the person behave in this way in other situations?

Yes Low distinctiveness ⟹ Internal attribution

No High distinctiveness ⟹ External attribution

Does the person have a history of behaving this way at other times?

Yes High consistency ⟹ Internal attribution

No Low consistency ⟹ External attribution

Do other people behave in this way in similar situations?

Yes High consensus ⟹ External attribution

No Low consensus ⟹ Internal attribution

1. *Distinctiveness.* Whether the behavior is unusual for that person (in contrast to a person displaying the same kind of behavior in many situations). If the behavior is distinctive, the perceiver probably will make an *external* attribution.

2. *Consistency.* Whether the person being observed has a history of behaving in the same way. People generally make *internal* attributions about consistent behavior.

3. *Consensus.* Whether other people tend to respond to similar situations in the same way. A person who has observed others handle similar situations in the same way will likely make an *external* attribution; that is, it will seem that the situation produces the type of behavior observed.

In addition to these general rules, people tend to have biases that they apply when making attributions. When evaluating others, we tend to underestimate the influence of external factors and overestimate the influence of internal factors. This tendency is called the **fundamental attribution error**. Consider the case of someone being promoted to CEO. Employees, outsiders, and the media generally focus on the characteristics of the person that allowed him or her to achieve the promotion. In reality, however, the selection of that person might have been heavily influenced by external factors, such as business conditions creating a need for someone with a strong financial or marketing background at that particular time.

Another bias that distorts attributions involves attributions we make about our own behavior. People tend to overestimate the contribution of internal factors to their successes and overestimate the contribution of external factors to their failures. This tendency, called the **self-serving bias**, means people give themselves too much credit for what they do well and give external forces too much blame when they fail. Thus, if your manager says you don't communicate well enough, and you think your manager doesn't listen well enough, the truth may actually lie somewhere in between.

PERSONALITY AND BEHAVIOR

Another area of particular interest to organizational behavior is personality. In recent years, many employers showed heightened interest in matching people's personalities to the needs of the job and the organization.

In the workplace, we find people whose behavior is consistently pleasant or aggressive or stubborn in a variety of situations. An individual's **personality** is the set

fundamental attribution error The tendency to underestimate the influence of external factors on another's behavior and to overestimate the influence of internal factors.

self-serving bias The tendency to overestimate the contribution of internal factors to one's successes and the contribution of external factors to one's failures.

personality The set of characteristics that underlie a relatively stable pattern of behavior in response to ideas, objects, or people in the environment.

of characteristics that underlie a relatively stable pattern of behavior in response to ideas, objects, or people in the environment. Understanding personality can help managers predict how a person might act in a particular situation. Managers who appreciate the ways their employees' personalities differ have insight into what kinds of leadership behavior will be most influential.

Personality Traits

In common usage, people think of personality in terms of traits, the fairly consistent characteristics a person exhibits. Researchers investigated whether any traits stand up to scientific scrutiny. Although investigators examined thousands of traits over the years, their findings fit into five general dimensions that describe personality. These dimensions, often called the "Big Five" personality factors, are illustrated in Exhibit 17.7.[25] Each factor may contain a wide range of specific traits. The **Big Five personality factors** describe an individual's extroversion, agreeableness, conscientiousness, emotional stability, and openness to experience:

1. *Extroversion.* The degree to which a person is outgoing, sociable, assertive, and comfortable with interpersonal relationships.

2. *Agreeableness.* The degree to which a person is able to get along with others by being good-natured, likable, cooperative, forgiving, understanding, and trusting.

3. *Conscientiousness.* The degree to which a person is focused on a few goals, thus behaving in ways that are responsible, dependable, persistent, and achievement oriented.

4. *Emotional stability.* The degree to which a person is calm, enthusiastic, and self-confident, rather than tense, depressed, moody, or insecure.

5. *Openness to experience.* The degree to which a person has a broad range of interests and is imaginative, creative, artistically sensitive, and willing to consider new ideas.

As illustrated in the exhibit, these factors represent a continuum. That is, a person may have a low, moderate, or high degree of each quality. Answer the questions in

Big Five personality factors Dimensions that describe an individual's extroversion, agreeableness, conscientiousness, emotional stability, and openness to experience.

EXHIBIT 17.7

The Big Five Personality Traits

Each individual's collection of personality traits is different; it is what makes us unique. But, although each *collection* of traits varies, we all share many common traits. The following phrases describe various traits and behaviors. Rate how accurately each statement describes you, based on a scale of 1 to 5, with 1 being very inaccurate and 5 very accurate. Describe yourself as you are now, not as you wish to be. There are no right or wrong answers.

	1	2	3	4	5
	Very Inaccurate			Very Accurate	

Extroversion

	1	2	3	4	5
I am usually the life of the party.	1	2	3	4	5
I feel comfortable around people.	1	2	3	4	5
I am talkative.	1	2	3	4	5

Neuroticism (Low Emotional Stability)

	1	2	3	4	5
I often feel critical of myself.	1	2	3	4	5
I often envy others.	1	2	3	4	5
I am temperamental.	1	2	3	4	5

Agreeableness

	1	2	3	4	5
I am kind and sympathetic.	1	2	3	4	5
I have a good word for everyone.	1	2	3	4	5
I never insult people.	1	2	3	4	5

Openness to New Experiences

	1	2	3	4	5
I am imaginative.	1	2	3	4	5
I prefer to vote for liberal political candidates.	1	2	3	4	5
I really like art.	1	2	3	4	5

Conscientiousness

	1	2	3	4	5
I am systematic and efficient.	1	2	3	4	5
I pay attention to details.	1	2	3	4	5
I am always prepared for class.	1	2	3	4	5

Which are your most prominent traits? For fun and discussion, compare your responses with those of classmates.

Exhibit 17.7 to see where you fall on the Big Five scale for each of the factors. Having a moderate-to-high degree of each of the Big Five personality factors is considered desirable for a wide range of employees, but this isn't always a key to success. For example, having an outgoing, sociable personality (extroversion) is considered desirable for managers, but many successful top leaders, including Bill Gates, Charles Schwab, and Steven Spielberg, are introverts, people who become drained by social encounters and need time alone to reflect and recharge their batteries. One study found that 4 in 10 top executives test out to be introverts.[26] Thus, the quality of extroversion is not as significant as is often presumed. Traits of agreeableness, on the other hand, seem to be particularly important in today's collaborative organizations. The days are over when a hard-driving manager can run roughshod over others to earn a promotion. Companies want managers who work smoothly with others and get help from lots of people inside and outside the organization. Today's successful CEOs are not the tough guys of the past but those men and women who know how to get people to like and trust them. Philip Purcell was forced out as CEO of Morgan Stanley largely because he was a remote, autocratic leader who treated many employees with contempt and failed to build positive relationships with clients. Purcell had little goodwill to back him up when things started going against him. Many people just didn't like him. In contrast, Procter & Gamble, CEO A. G. Lafley stresses good relationships with employees, suppliers, partners, and customers as a key to effective management.[27]

One recent book argues that the secret to success in work and in life is *likability*. We all know we're more willing to do something for someone we like than for someone we don't, whether it be a teammate, a neighbor, a professor, or a supervisor. Managers can increase their likeability by developing traits of agreeableness, including being friendly and cooperative, understanding other people in a genuine way, and striving to make people feel positive about themselves.[28]

Many companies, including JCPenney, DuPont, Toys"R"Us, and the Union Pacific Railroad, use personality testing to hire, evaluate, or promote employees. Surveys show that at least 30 percent of organizations use some kind of personality testing for hiring.[29] American MultiCinema (AMC), one of the largest theater chains in the United States, looks for front-line workers with high conscientiousness and high emotional stability.[30] Marriott Hotels looks for people who score high on conscientiousness and agreeableness because they believe these individuals will provide better service to guests.[31] Companies also use personality testing for managers. Hewlett-Packard, Dell Computer, and General Electric all put candidates for top positions through testing, interviews with psychologists, or both to see whether they have the "right stuff" for the job.[32] Executives at franchises such as Little Gym International and Yum Brands, which owns Pizza Hut, KFC, and Taco Bell, are using personality testing to make sure potential franchisees can fit into their system and be successful.[33] As described in the Unlocking Innovative Solutions Through Technology box, a growing number of entrepreneurs are using sophisticated personality testing to match singles through online dating services. EHarmony, for example, claims to have facilitated 30,000 marriages by matching people based on their compatible personalities.

Despite growing use of personality tests, little hard evidence shows them to be valid predictors of job or relationship success. The long-term tracking of data of romantic matchmaking sites has been referred to as "the early days of a social experiment of unprecedented proportions, involving millions of couples and possibly extending over the course of generations."[34] Similarly, scientific evidence for the valid use of personality testing for job success is still years away.

Emotional Intelligence

In recent years, new insights into personality are emerging through research in the area of *emotional intelligence*. Emotional intelligence (EQ) includes four basic components:[35]

1. *Self-awareness.* The basis for all the other components; being aware of what you are feeling. People who are in touch with their feelings are better able to guide their own lives and actions. A high degree of self-awareness means you can

Unlocking Innovative Solutions Through TECHNOLOGY

Can Success Be Guaranteed in Affairs of the Heart?

"Experience for yourself the magic and joy of true compatibility," Dr. Neil Clark Warren urges television viewers in his commercials for eHarmony.com, an on-line dating service with a mission to create happy, lasting marriages. Millions of people think that sounds like a good idea, and according to eHarmony, more than 30,000 marriages have resulted from the service.

The online dating industry has grown into a half-a-billion dollar industry in just over 10 years. In recent years, personality tests have been central to some of these organizations' strategies. Companies such as eHarmony, Chemistry.com, and PerfectMatch.com use them to pursue so-called serious daters, people whose search for lasting relationships means they're more likely to become subscribers. Increasingly, companies enlist social scientists to help devise personality tests they hope will make the quest for a soul mate more efficient and successful.

After administering a test and determining an individual's personality traits, the companies use the results, along with other information, to match the member up with compatible prospective partners, saving subscribers the time and trouble of wading through volumes of online personal ads. Each company bases its assessment tools and matching process on their varying theories of what makes successful relationships tick. Sociologist Pepper Schwartz helped PerfectMatch.com develop its Duet Total Compatibility System, with its relatively brief 48-question test. The survey focuses on eight specific personality traits, such as romantic impulsivity, personal energy, and decision making, and then takes both a couple's similarities and differences into account during the matching process. Over at Chemistry.com, a Match.com offshoot, anthropologist Helen Fisher helped translate her theory that all personalities are literally chemical in nature

into a 146-question test that categorizes people into four personality types. For example, Directors are testosterone-driven whereas Negotiators tend to run on estrogen. Builders are ruled by their serotonin, and Explorers by their dopamine. Each of these ruling chemicals, according to Fisher's theory, generates specific personality characteristics. "My hypothesis is that we're unconsciously drawn to chemical personalities that complement our type," she says.

And finally, eHarmony's Compatibility Matching System employs an exhaustive 436-question instrument. The personality survey is based on founder Neil Clark Warren's past professional experience and his company's own research into long-lived marriages. Warren, who holds both divinity and clinical psychology degrees, believes the unions most likely to succeed are those between people who share at least 10 of the 29 personality traits eHarmony measures.

Does the approach work? So far, the only company to track relationships it's helped create is eHarmony. Claiming to have helped bring about 16,000 marriages in 2005 alone, the company conducted an in-house study it says showed eHarmony couples enjoyed higher levels of marital satisfaction than those who had met through other channels. But most observers say it's too soon to tell whether using personality tests really will increase your odds of finding your one true love.

SOURCES: Lori Gottlieb, "How Do I Love Thee?" *The Atlantic Monthly* (March 2006): 58–70; Rachel Lehmann-Haupt, "Is the Right Chemistry a Click Nearer?" *The New York Times* (February 12, 2006): Sec. 9, 2; Christopher Palmeri "Dr. Warren's Lonely Hearts Club," *BusinessWeek Online* (February 20, 2006): www.businessweek.com/magazine/content/06_08/b3972111.htm?campaign_id=search; and Alex Salkever, "Finding Love Online, Version 2.0," *BusinessWeek Online* (June 10, 2003): www.businessweek.com/technology/content/jun2003/tc20030610_4294_tc104.htm?campaign_id=search.

accurately assess your own strengths and limitations and have a healthy sense of self-confidence.

2. *Self-management.* The ability to control disruptive or harmful emotions and balance one's moods so that worry, anxiety, fear, or anger do not cloud thinking and get in the way of what needs to be done. People who are skilled at self-management remain optimistic and hopeful despite setbacks and obstacles. This ability is crucial for pursuing long-term goals. For example, MetLife found that applicants who failed the regular sales aptitude test but scored high on optimism made 21 percent more sales in their first year and 57 percent more in their second year than those who passed the sales test but scored high on pessimism.[36]

3. *Social awareness.* The ability to understand others and practice *empathy*, which means being able to put yourself in someone else's shoes, to recognize what others are feeling without them needing to tell you. People with social awareness are capable of understanding divergent points of view and interacting effectively with many different types of people.

4. *Relationship awareness.* The ability to connect to others, build positive relationships, respond to the emotions of others, and influence others. People with relationship awareness know how to listen and communicate clearly and they treat others with compassion and respect.

Studies find a positive relationship between job performance and high degrees of emotional intelligence in a variety of jobs. Numerous organizations, including the U.S. Air Force and Canada Life, use EQ tests to measure such things as self-awareness, ability to empathize, and capacity to build positive relationships.[37] EQ seems to be particularly important for jobs that require a high degree of social interaction, which includes managers, who are responsible for influencing others and building positive attitudes and relationships in the organization. Managers with low emotional intelligence can undermine employee morale and harm the organization.

© KEITH BROFSKY/PHOTODISC/GETTY IMAGES

CONCEPT CONNECTION Managers at One Georgia Bank routinely refer to their personality test results to gauge their progress toward improving the skills or personal characteristics that need work. CEO Willard Lewis firmly believes in the value of **personality testing** to help him gauge whether job applicants have the optimal traits for the position and to aid employees in their personal development. He's not alone. A 2005 Society for Human Resource Management survey revealed that more than a third of the respondents were already using behavioral or personality assessments, with more organizations planning to incorporate such tests in the near future.

As a new manager, one thing that influences your EQ, agreeableness, and other behavior is self-confidence—an important foundation for a good manager. Take the New Manager Self-Test on page 568 to see how your level of self-confidence may affect your behavior as a new manager.

■ **TAKE A MOMENT**

At times of great change or crisis, managers rely on a high EQ level to help employees cope with the anxiety and stress they may be experiencing. In the United States, fears of terrorism, devastating natural disasters such as Hurricane Katrina, anxiety and sorrow over the war in Iraq, and continuing economic hardship for many people all make meeting the psychological and emotional needs of employees a new role for managers. This chapter's Shoptalk outlines some elements of emotional intelligence that are particularly important in times of crisis and turmoil. It is important to remember that emotional intelligence is not an in-born personality characteristic, but something that can be learned and developed.[38]

Attitudes and Behaviors Influenced by Personality

An individual's personality influences a wide variety of work-related attitudes and behaviors. Four that are of particular interest to managers are locus of control, authoritarianism, Machiavellianism, and problem-solving styles.

LOCUS OF CONTROL

People differ in terms of what they tend to accredit as the cause of their success or failure. Their **locus of control** defines whether they place the primary responsibility within themselves or on outside forces.[39] Some people believe that their own actions strongly influence what happens to them. They feel in control of their own fate. These individuals have a high *internal* locus of control. Other people believe

locus of control The tendency to place the primary responsibility for one's success or failure either within oneself (internally) or on outside forces (externally).

SELF-CONFIDENCE

Self-confidence is the foundation for many behaviors of a new manager. To learn something about your level of self-confidence, answer the following questions. Please answer whether each item is Mostly True or Mostly False for you.

	Mostly True	Mostly False
1. I have lots of confidence in my decisions.	___	___
2. I would like to change some things about myself.	___	___
3. I am satisfied with my appearance and personality.	___	___
4. I would be nervous about meeting important people.	___	___
5. I come across as a positive person.	___	___
6. I sometimes think of myself as a failure.	___	___
7. I am able to do things as well as most people.	___	___
8. I find it difficult to believe nice things someone says about me.	___	___

SCORING AND INTERPRETATION: Many good things come from self-confidence. If a new manager lacks self-confidence, he or she is more likely to avoid difficult decisions and confrontations, and may tend to overcontrol subordinates, which is called micromanaging. A lack of self-confidence also leads to less sharing of information and less time hiring and developing capable people. Self-confident managers, by contrast, can more easily delegate responsibility, take risks, give credit to others, confront problems, and assert themselves for the good of their team.

Give yourself one point for each *odd-numbered* item above marked as Mostly True and one point for each *even-numbered* item marked Mostly False. If you scored three or less, your self-confidence may not be very high. You might want to practice new behavior in problematic areas to develop greater confidence. A score of 6 or above suggests a higher level of self-confidence and a solid foundation on which to begin your career as a new manager.

that events in their lives occur because of chance, luck, or outside people and events. They feel more like pawns of their fate. These individuals have a high *external* locus of control. Many top leaders of e-commerce and high-tech organizations possess a high internal locus of control. These managers have to cope with rapid change and uncertainty associated with Internet business. They must believe that they and their employees can counter the negative impact of outside forces and events. John Chambers, CEO of Cisco Systems, is a good example. Despite a tough economy and a drastically diminished stock price in the early 2000s, Chambers maintained his belief that Cisco can defeat any challenge thrown its way.[40] A person with a high external locus of control would likely feel overwhelmed trying to make the rapid decisions and changes needed to keep pace with the industry, particularly when environmental conditions are unstable.

Research on locus of control shows real differences in behavior across a wide range of settings. People with an internal locus of control are easier to motivate because they believe the rewards are the result of their behavior. They are better able to handle complex information and problem solving, are more achievement oriented, but are also more independent and therefore more difficult to manage. By contrast, people with an external locus of control are harder to motivate, less involved in their jobs, more likely to blame others when faced with a poor performance evaluation, but more compliant and conforming and, therefore, easier to manage.[41]

Do you believe luck plays an important role in your life, or do you feel that you control your own fate? To find out more about your locus of control, read the instructions and complete the questionnaire in Exhibit 17.8.

MANAGER'S SHOPTALK

WHAT'S YOUR CRISIS EQ?

Threats of terrorist attacks. Downsizing. The SARS virus. Company failures. Anthrax in the mail. Stock market crashes. Rapid technological changes. Information overload. The turbulence of today's world has left lingering psychological and emotional damage in workplaces all across the United States, as well as in the rest of the world. When even a minor crisis hits an organization, uncertainty and fear are high. Today's managers need the skills to help people deal with their emotions and return to a more normal work routine. Although managers cannot take the place of professional counselors, they can use patience, flexibility, and understanding to assist people through a crisis. Here are some important elements of crisis EQ for managers:

:: Be visible and provide as much up-to-date, accurate information as possible about what's going on in the company and the industry. Rumor control is critical.

:: Find simple ways to get employees together. Order pizza for the entire staff. Invite telecommuters to come in to the office so they can connect with others and have a chance to share their emotions.

:: Give employees room to be human. It is natural for people to feel anger and other strong emotions, so allow those feelings to be expressed as long as they aren't directed at other employees.

:: Publicize the company's charitable endeavors and make employees aware of the various opportunities both within and outside the organization to volunteer and donate to charity.

:: Thank employees in person and with handwritten notes when they go above and beyond the call of duty during a difficult time.

:: Recognize that routine, structured work can help people heal. Postpone major, long-term projects and decisions to the extent possible, and break work into shorter, more manageable tasks. Listen to employees and determine what they need to help them return to a normal work life.

:: Provide professional counseling services for people who need it. Those with a history of alcohol abuse, trouble at home, or previous mental or emotional problems are especially at risk, but anyone who has trouble gradually returning to his or her previous level of work may need outside counseling.

SOURCES: Based on Matthew Boyle,"Nothing Really Matters,"*Fortune* (October 15, 2001): 261–264; and Sue Shellenbarger, "Readers Face Dilemma Over How Far to Alter Post-Attack Workplace," *The Wall Street Journal* (October 31, 2001): B1.

AUTHORITARIANISM

Authoritarianism is the belief that power and status differences should exist within the organization.[42] Individuals high in authoritarianism tend to be concerned with power and toughness, obey recognized authority above them, stick to conventional values, critically judge others, and oppose the use of subjective feelings. The degree to which managers possess authoritarianism will influence how they wield and share power. The degree to which employees possess authoritarianism will influence how they react to their managers. If a manager and employees differ in their degree of authoritarianism, the manager may have difficulty leading effectively. The trend toward empowerment and shifts in expectations among younger employees for more equitable relationships contribute to a decline in strict authoritarianism in many organizations.

MACHIAVELLIANISM

Another personality dimension that is helpful in understanding work behavior is **Machiavellianism**, which is characterized by the acquisition of power and the manipulation of other people for purely personal gain. Machiavellianism is named after Niccolo Machiavelli, a sixteenth-century author who wrote *The Prince*, a book for noblemen of the day on how to acquire and use power.[43] Psychologists developed instruments to measure a person's Machiavellianism (Mach) orientation.[44] Research shows that high Machs are predisposed to being pragmatic, capable of

authoritarianism The belief that power and status differences should exist within the organization.

Machiavellianism The tendency to direct much of one's behavior toward the acquisition of power and the manipulation of other people for personal gain.

EXHIBIT 17.8

Measuring Locus of
Control

Your Locus of Control

This questionnaire is designed to measure locus-of-control beliefs. Researchers using this questionnaire in a study of college students found a mean of 51.8 for men and 52.2 for women, with a standard deviation of 6 for each. The higher your score on this questionnaire, the more you tend to believe that you are generally responsible for what happens to you; in other words, higher scores are associated with internal locus of control. Low scores are associated with external locus of control. Scoring low indicates that you tend to believe that forces beyond your control, such as powerful other people, fate, or chance, are responsible for what happens to you.

For each of these 10 questions, indicate the extent to which you agree or disagree using the following scale:

1 = strongly disagree	4 = neither disagree nor agree	7 = strongly agree
2 = disagree	5 = slightly agree	
3 = slightly disagree	6 = agree	

1. When I get what I want, it is usually because I worked hard for it. 1 2 3 4 5 6 7

2. When I make plans, I am almost certain to make them work. 1 2 3 4 5 6 7

3. I prefer games involving some luck over games requiring pure skill. 1 2 3 4 5 6 7

4. I can learn almost anything if I set my mind to it. 1 2 3 4 5 6 7

5. My major accomplishments are entirely due to my hard work and ability. 1 2 3 4 5 6 7

6. I usually don't set goals, because I have a hard time following through on them. 1 2 3 4 5 6 7

7. Competition discourages excellence. 1 2 3 4 5 6 7

8. Often people get ahead just by being lucky. 1 2 3 4 5 6 7

9. On any sort of exam or competition, I like to know how well I do relative to everyone else. 1 2 3 4 5 6 7

10. It's pointless to keep working on something that's too difficult for me. 1 2 3 4 5 6 7

Scoring and Interpretation

To determine your score, reverse the values you selected for questions 3, 6, 7, 8, and 10 (1 = 7, 2 = 6, 3 = 5, 4 = 4, 5 = 3, 6 = 2, 7 = 1). For example, if you strongly disagree with the statement in question 3, you would have given it a value of 1. Change this value to a 7. Reverse the scores in a similar manner for questions 6, 7, 8, and 10. Now add the point values for all 10 questions together.

Your score _____

SOURCES: Adapted from J. M. Burger, *Personality: Theory and Research* (Belmont, CA: Wadsworth, 1986): 400–401, cited in D. Hellriegel, J. W. Slocum, Jr., and R. W. Woodman, *Organizational Behavior*, 6th ed. (St. Paul, MN: West, 1992): 97–100. Original source: D. L. Paulhus, "Sphere-Specific Measures of Perceived Control," *Journal of Personality and Social Psychology*, 44, 1253–1265.

lying to achieve personal goals, more likely to win in win-lose situations, and more likely to persuade than be persuaded.[45]

Different situations may require people who demonstrate one or the other type of behavior. In loosely structured situations, high Machs actively take control, while low Machs accept the direction given by others. Low Machs thrive in highly structured situations, while high Machs perform in a detached, disinterested way. High Machs are particularly good in jobs that require bargaining skills or that involve substantial rewards for winning.[46]

PROBLEM-SOLVING STYLES AND THE MYERS–BRIGGS TYPE INDICATOR

Managers also need to understand that individuals differ in the way they solve problems and make decisions. One approach to understanding problem-solving styles grew out of the work of psychologist Carl Jung. Jung believed differences resulted from our preferences in how we go about gathering and evaluating information.[47] According to Jung, gathering information and evaluating information are separate activities. People gather information either by *sensation* or *intuition*, but not by both

Personal Style	Action Tendencies	Likely Occupations
Sensation-Thinking	• Emphasizes details, facts, certainty • Is a decisive, applied thinker • Focuses on short-term, realistic goals • Develops rules and regulations for judging performance	• Accounting • Production • Computer programming • Market research • Engineering
Intuitive-Thinking	• Prefers dealing with theoretical or technical problems • Is a creative, progressive, perceptive thinker • Focuses on possibilities using impersonal analysis • Is able to consider a number of options and problems simultaneously	• Systems design • Systems analysis • Law • Middle/top management • Teaching business, economics
Sensation-Feeling	• Shows concern for current, real-life human problems • Is pragmatic, analytical, methodical, and conscientious • Emphasizes detailed facts about people rather than tasks • Focuses on structuring organizations for the benefit of people	• Directing supervisor • Counseling • Negotiating • Selling • Interviewing
Intuitive-Feeling	• Avoids specifics • Is charismatic, participative, people oriented, and helpful • Focuses on general views, broad themes, and feelings • Decentralizes decision making, develops few rules and regulations	• Public relations • Advertising • Human Resources • Politics • Customer service

EXHIBIT 17.9

Four Problem-Solving Styles

simultaneously. Sensation-type people would rather work with known facts and hard data and prefer routine and order in gathering information. Intuitive-type people would rather look for possibilities than work with facts and prefer solving new problems and using abstract concepts.

Evaluating information involves making judgments about the information a person has gathered. People evaluate information by *thinking* or *feeling*. These represent the extremes in orientation. Thinking-type individuals base their judgments on impersonal analysis, using reason and logic rather than personal values or emotional aspects of the situation. Feeling-type individuals base their judgments more on personal feelings such as harmony and tend to make decisions that result in approval from others.

According to Jung, only one of the four functions—sensation, intuition, thinking, or feeling—is dominant in an individual. However, the dominant function usually is backed up by one of the functions from the other set of paired opposites. Exhibit 17.9 shows the four problem-solving styles that result from these matchups, as well as occupations that people with each style tend to prefer.

Two additional sets of paired opposites not directly related to problem solving are *introversion–extroversion* and *judging–perceiving*. Introverts gain energy by focusing on personal thoughts and feelings, whereas extroverts gain energy from being around others and interacting with others. On the judging versus perceiving dimension, people with a judging preference like certainty and closure and tend to make decisions quickly based on available data. Perceiving people, on the other hand, enjoy ambiguity, dislike deadlines, and may change their minds several times as they gather large amounts of data and information to make decisions.

A widely used personality test that measures how people differ on all four of Jung's sets of paired opposites is the **Myers–Briggs Type Indicator (MBTI)**. The MBTI measures a person's preferences for introversion versus extroversion, sensation versus intuition, thinking versus feeling, and judging versus perceiving. The various combinations of these four preferences result in 16 unique personality types.

Myers–Briggs Type Indicator (MBTI) Personality test that measures a person's preference for introversion vs. extroversion, sensation vs. intuition, thinking vs. feeling, and judging vs. perceiving.

> Go to the experiential exercise on page 581 that pertains to evaluating your Myers–Briggs personality type.

■ TAKE A MOMENT

Each of the 16 different personality types can have positive and negative consequences for behavior. Based on the limited research that has been done, the two preferences that seem to be most strongly associated with effective management in a variety of organizations and industries are thinking and judging.[48] However, people with other preferences can also be good managers. One advantage of understanding your natural preferences is to maximize your innate strengths and abilities. Dow Chemical manager Kurt Swogger believes the MBTI can help put people in the right jobs—where they will be happiest and make the strongest contribution to the organization.

When Kurt Swogger arrived at Dow Chemical's plastics business in 1991, it took anywhere from 6 to 15 years to launch a new product—and the unit hadn't launched a single one for 3 years. Today, a new product launch takes just 2 to 4 years, and Swogger's R&D team has launched 13 product hits over the past decade.

How did Swogger lead such an amazing transformation? By making sure people were doing the jobs they were best suited for. The simple fact, Swogger says, "is that some [people] do development better than others. The biggest obstacle to launching great new products was not having the right people in the right jobs." Swogger began reassigning people based on his intuition and insight, distinguishing pure inventors from those who could add value later in the game and still others who were best at marketing the new products. Swogger says he was right-on about 60 percent of the time. If someone didn't work out after six months, he'd put them in another assignment.

Seeking a better way to determine people's strengths, Swogger turned to a former Dow employee, Greg Stevens, who now owns a consulting firm. Stevens and Swogger used the Myers–Briggs Type Indicator (MBTI), predicting which types would be best suited to each stage of the product development and launch cycles. After administering the test to current and former Dow plastics employees, they found some startling results. In 1991, when Swogger came on board, the match between the right personality type and the right role was only 29 percent. By 2001, thanks to Swogger's great instincts, the rate had jumped to 93 percent.

Swogger's next step is to administer the MBTI to new hires, so the job match is right to begin with. He believes the MBTI can help him assign people to jobs that match their natural thinking and problem-solving styles, leading to happier employees and higher organizational performance.[49]

Other organizations also use the MBTI, with 89 of the *Fortune* 100 companies recently reporting that they use the test in hiring and promotion decisions.[50] Matching the right people to the right jobs is an important responsibility for managers, whether they do it based on intuition and experience or by using personality tests such as the MBTI. Managers strive to create a good fit between the person and the job he or she is asked to do.

Person–Job Fit

Given the wide variation among personalities and among jobs, an important responsibility of managers is to try to match employee and job characteristics so that work is done by people who are well suited to do it. This goal requires that managers be clear about what they expect employees to do and have a sense of the kinds of people who would succeed at various types of assignments. The extent to which a person's ability and personality match the requirements of a job is called **person–job fit**. When managers achieve person–job fit, employees are more likely to contribute and have higher levels of job satisfaction and commitment.[51] The importance of person–job fit became especially apparent during the dot-com heyday of the late 1990s. People who rushed to Internet companies in hopes of finding a new challenge—or making a quick buck—found themselves floundering in jobs for which they were unsuited. One manager recruited by a leading executive search firm lasted less than two hours at his new job. The search firm, a division of Russell Reynolds Associates, later developed a "Web Factor" diagnostic to help determine whether people have the right personality for the Internet, including such things as a tolerance for risk and uncertainty, an obsession

person–job fit The extent to which a person's ability and personality match the requirements of a job.

with learning, and a willingness to do whatever needs doing, regardless of job title.[52]

A related concern is *person–environment fit*, which looks not only at whether the person and job are suited to one another but also at how well the individual will fit in the overall organizational environment. An employee who is by nature strongly authoritarian, for example, would have a hard time in an organization such as W. L. Gore and Associates, which has few rules, no hierarchy, no fixed or assigned authority, and no bosses. Many of today's organizations pay attention to person–environment fit from the beginning of the recruitment process. Texas Instruments' Web page includes an area called Fit Check that evaluates personality types anonymously and gives prospective job candidates a chance to evaluate for themselves whether they would be a good match with the company.[53]

© DAVID FOSTER

CONCEPT CONNECTION Andrew Field, who owns a $10.3 million printing services company, PrintingForLess.com., uses dogs to help him create the person–environment fit when hiring new employees. Every day for five years, Jessie (far left), Field's Border collie and black Labrador mix, has accompanied him to work. The idea caught on and as many as eight dogs frequent the company offices. With rules such as owner accountability, a dog review board, and a dog-approval process, employees find that the dogs are a great release for stress. Field says that the dog policy helps him make good hires; candidates who respond favorably to the canine rule are likely to fit in with the office culture.

LEARNING

Years of schooling condition many of us to think that learning is something students do in response to teachers in a classroom. With this view, in the managerial world of time deadlines and concrete action, learning seems remote—even irrelevant. However, successful managers need specific knowledge and skills as well as the ability to adapt to changes in the world around them. Managers have to learn.

Learning is a change in behavior or performance that occurs as the result of experience. Experience may take the form of observing others, reading or listening to sources of information, or experiencing the consequences of one's own behavior. This important way of adapting to events is linked to individual differences in attitudes, perception, and personality.

learning A change in behavior or performance that occurs as the result of experience.

Two individuals who undergo similar experiences—for example, a business transfer to a foreign country—probably will differ in how they adapt their behaviors to (that is, learn from) the experience. In other words, each person learns in a different way.

The Learning Process

One model of the learning process, shown in Exhibit 17.10, depicts learning as a four-stage cycle.[54] First, a person encounters a concrete experience. This event is followed by thinking and reflective observation, which lead to abstract conceptualization and, in turn, to active experimentation. The results of the experimentation generate new experiences, and the cycle repeats.

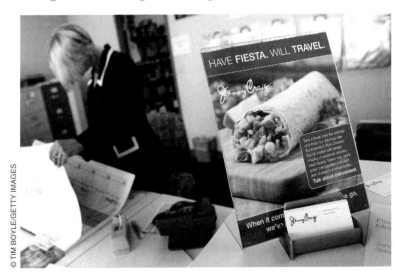

© TIM BOYLE/GETTY IMAGES

CONCEPT CONNECTION Jenny Craig, the pioneering weight-loss company, believes in **continuous learning** for both employees and clients. Its program combines Web-based tools with more traditional methods, including videos and sessions led by instructors, such as trainer Jeri Dawn Martel, shown here. Employees undergo an extensive orientation, as well as several days of training each time they assume new responsibilities. In addition, headquarters provides over 600 centers with product and services updates for their semimonthly staff meetings and in-depth training materials for quarterly continuing education courses.

The Best Buy chain of consumer electronics superstores owes its birth to the learning process of its founder, Richard M. Schulze. In the 1960s, Schulze built a stereo store called Sound of Music into a chain of nine stores in and near St. Paul, Minnesota. However, a tornado destroyed his largest and most profitable store, so he held a massive clearance sale in the parking lot. So many shoppers descended on the lot that they caused traffic to back up for two miles. Reflecting on this experience, Schulze saw great demand for a store featuring large selection and low prices, backed by heavy advertising. He tried out his idea by launching his first Best Buy superstore. Today Best Buy has nearly 800 retail stores in the United States and Canada, as well as a thriving online division.[55]

The arrows in the model of the learning process in Exhibit 17.10 indicate that this process is a recurring cycle. People continually test their conceptualizations and adapt them as a result of their personal reflections and observations about their experiences.

Learning Styles

Individuals develop personal learning styles that vary in terms of how much they emphasize each stage of the learning cycle. These differences occur because the learning process is directed by individual needs and goals. For example, an engineer might place greater emphasis on abstract concepts, while a salesperson might emphasize concrete experiences. Because of these preferences, personal learning styles typically have strong and weak points.

Questionnaires can assess a person's strong and weak points as a learner by measuring the relative emphasis the person places on each of the four learning stages shown in Exhibit 17.10: concrete experience, reflective observation, abstract conceptualization, and active experimentation. Some people have a tendency to overemphasize one stage of the learning process, or to avoid some aspects of learning. Not many people have totally balanced profiles, but the key to effective learning is competence in each of the four stages when it is needed.

Researchers identified four fundamental learning styles that combine elements of the four stages of the learning cycle.[56] Exhibit 17.11 summarizes the characteristics and dominant learning abilities of these four styles, labeled Diverger, Assimilator, Converger, and Accommodator. The exhibit also lists occupations that frequently attract individuals with each of the learning styles. For example, people whose dominant style is Accommodator are often drawn to sales and marketing. A good example is Gertrude Boyle, who took over Columbia Sportswear after the death of her husband. She and her son, Tim, propelled the company from sales of

EXHIBIT   17.11

Learning Style Types

Learning Style Type	Dominant Learning Abilities	Learning Characteristics	Likely Occupations
Diverger	• Concrete experience • Reflective observation	• Is good at generating ideas, seeing a situation from multiple perspectives, and being aware of meaning and value • Tends to be interested in people, culture, and the arts	• Human resource management • Counseling • Organization development specialist
Assimilator	• Abstract conceptualization • Reflective observation	• Is good at inductive reasoning, creating theoretical models, and combining disparate observations into an integrated explanation • Tends to be less concerned with people than ideas and abstract concepts.	• Research • Strategic planning
Converger	• Abstract conceptualization • Active experimentation	• Is good at decisiveness, practical application of ideas, and hypothetical deductive reasoning • Prefers dealing with technical tasks rather than interpersonal issues	• Engineering
Accommodator	• Concrete experience • Active experimentation	• Is good at implementing decisions, carrying out plans, and getting involved in new experiences • Tends to be at ease with people but may be seen as impatient or pushy	• Marketing • Sales

$13 million to $358 million over a 13-year period by observing what competitors were doing and actively experimenting to find a novel sales approach. The 74-year-old Gert Boyle decided to star in her own "Tough Mother" ads as a way to distinguish the company from competitors who advertised their products worn by fit, young models. Boyle believes in constantly pushing herself and her company, questioning everything, and trying new ideas.[57] Exhibit 17.11 lists other likely occupations for Divergers, Assimilators, Convergers, and Accommodators.

> As a new manager, determine your natural learning style to understand how you approach problems, recognize your learning strengths, and better relate to people who have different learning styles. As you grow in your management responsibilities, strive for a balance among the four learning stages shown in Exhibit 17.10.

■ TAKE A MOMENT

Continuous Learning

To thrive in today's turbulent business climate, individuals and organizations must be continuous learners. For individuals, continuous learning entails looking for opportunities to learn from classes, reading, and talking to others, as well as looking for the lessons in life's experiences. One manager who embodies the spirit of continuous learning is Larry Ricciardi, senior vice president and corporate counsel at IBM. Ricciardi is an avid traveler and voracious reader who likes to study art, literature, and history. In addition, Ricciardi likes to add supermarket tabloids to his daily fare of *The Wall Street Journal*. On business trips, he scouts out side trips to exotic or interesting sites so he can learn something new.[58] Ricciardi never knows when he might be able to apply a new idea or understanding to improve his life, his job, or his organization.

For organizations, continuous learning involves the processes and systems through which the organization enables its people to learn, share their growing knowledge, and apply it to their work. In an organization in which continuous learning is taking place, employees actively apply comments from customers, news about competitors, training programs, and more to increase their knowledge and improve the organization's practices. For example, at the Mayo Clinic, doctors are expected to consult with doctors in other departments, with the patient, and with anyone else inside or outside the clinic who might help with any aspect of the patient's problem.[59] The emphasis on teamwork, openness, and collaboration keeps learning strong at Mayo.

Managers can foster continuous learning by consciously stopping from time to time and asking, "What can we learn from this experience?" They can allow employees time to attend training and reflect on their experiences. Recognizing that experience can be the best teacher, managers should focus on how they and their employees can learn from mistakes, rather than fostering a climate in which employees hide mistakes because they fear being punished for them. Managers also encourage organizational learning by establishing information systems that enable people to share knowledge and learn in new ways. Information technology was discussed in detail in Chapter 15. As individuals, managers can help themselves and set an example for their employees by being continuous learners, listening to others, reading widely, and reflecting on what they observe.

STRESS AND STRESS MANAGEMENT

Just as organizations can support or discourage learning, organizational characteristics also interact with individual differences to influence other behaviors. In every organization, these characteristics include sources of stress. Formally defined, **stress** is an individual's physiological and emotional response to external stimuli that place physical or psychological demands on the individual and create uncertainty and lack of personal control when important outcomes are at stake.[60] These stimuli, called *stressors*, produce some combination of frustration (the inability to achieve a goal, such as the inability to meet a deadline because of inadequate resources) and anxiety (such as the fear of being disciplined for not meeting deadlines).

People's responses to stressors vary according to their personalities, the resources available to help them cope, and the context in which the stress occurs. Thus, a looming deadline will feel different depending on the degree to which the individual enjoys a challenge, the willingness of coworkers to team up and help each other succeed, and family members' understanding of an employee's need to work extra hours, among other factors.

■ **TAKE A MOMENT**   Go to the ethical dilemma on page 584 that pertains to organizational sources of stress.

When the level of stress is low relative to a person's coping resources, stress can be a positive force, stimulating desirable change and achievement. However, too much stress is associated with many negative consequences, including sleep disturbances, drug and alcohol abuse, headaches, ulcers, high blood pressure, and heart disease. People who are experiencing the ill effects of too much stress may become irritable or withdraw from interactions with their coworkers, take excess time off, and have more health problems. For example, a recent study of manufacturing workers in Bangladesh found a significant connection between job stress and absenteeism. Another study of 46,000 workers in the United States found that health care costs are 147 percent higher for individuals who are stressed or depressed.[61] People suffering from stress are less productive and may leave the organization. Clearly, too much stress is harmful to employees as well as to companies.

Type A and Type B Behavior

Researchers observed that some people seem to be more vulnerable than others to the ill effects of stress. From studies of stress-related heart disease, they categorized people as having behavior patterns called Type A and Type B.[62] The **Type A behavior**

stress A physiological and emotional response to stimuli that place physical or psychological demands on an individual.

Type A behavior Behavior pattern characterized by extreme competitiveness, impatience, aggressiveness, and devotion to work.

pattern includes extreme competitiveness, impatience, aggressiveness, and devotion to work. In contrast, people with a **Type B behavior** pattern exhibit less of these behaviors. They consequently experience less conflict with other people and a more balanced, relaxed lifestyle. Type A people tend to experience more stress-related illness than Type B people.

Most Type A individuals are high-energy people and may seek positions of power and responsibility. One example is John Haughom, senior vice president for health care improvement at PeaceHealth, a network of private hospitals in the Pacific Northwest. When Haughom was in charge of establishing an information network of community-wide medical records to support patient care, he typically began his day at 6 A.M. and worked until 11 P.M. His days were a blur of conference calls, meetings, and e-mail exchanges. "I could move mountains if I put my mind to it," he says. "That's what good executives do."[63]

By pacing themselves and learning control and intelligent use of their natural high-energy tendencies, Type A individuals can be powerful forces for innovation and leadership within their organizations, as John Haughom has been at Peace-Health. However, many Type A personalities cause stress-related problems for themselves, and sometimes for those around them. Haughom eventually reached burnout. He couldn't sleep, he began snapping at colleagues, and he finally took a sabbatical and learned to lead a more balanced life.[64] Type B individuals typically live with less stress unless they are in high-stress situations. A number of factors can cause stress in the workplace, even for people who are not naturally prone to high stress.

Causes of Work Stress

Workplace stress is skyrocketing worldwide. A recent World Congress on Health and Safety at Work presented studies suggesting that job-related stress may be as big a danger to the world's people as chemical and biological hazards.[65] In the United States, the number of people who say they are overworked has risen from 28 percent in 2001 to 44 percent in 2005, and one third of Americans between the ages of 25 and 39 say they feel burned out by their jobs. The United Kingdom's Health and Safety Executive says that half a million people in the U.K. are ill because of workplace stress, and stress-related illnesses are second only to back pain as a cause of work absences. In India, growing numbers of young software professionals and call-center workers are falling prey to depression, anxiety, and other mental illnesses because of increasing workplace stress.[66]

Most people have a general idea of what a stressful job is like: difficult, uncomfortable, exhausting, even frightening. Managers can better cope with their own stress and establish ways for the organization to help employees cope if they define the conditions that tend to produce work stress. One way to identify work stressors is to think about stress caused by the demands of job tasks and stress caused by interpersonal pressures and conflicts.

- *Task demands* are stressors arising from the tasks required of a person holding a particular job. Some kinds of decisions are inherently stressful: those made under time pressure, those that have serious consequences, and those that must be made with incomplete information. For example, emergency room doctors are under tremendous stress as a result of the task demands of their jobs. They regularly have to make quick decisions, based on limited information, that may determine whether a patient lives or dies. Almost all jobs, especially those of managers, have some level of stress associated with task demands. Task demands also sometimes cause stress because of **role ambiguity**, which means that people are unclear about what task behaviors are expected of them.

Type B behavior Behavior pattern that lacks Type A characteristics and includes a more balanced, relaxed lifestyle.

role ambiguity Uncertainty about what behaviors are expected of a person in a particular role.

© EVAN SKLAR

CONCEPT CONNECTION Sylvia Weinstock is founder of Sylvia Weinstock Cakes in New York City, known for celebrity wedding cakes, including those for Catherine Zeta-Jones, Liam Neeson, and Donald Trump. Weinstock, named "New York's reigning cake diva" by *InStyle* magazine, loves her job but feels the stress of **task demands.** "This is an obsessive business because of the intensity and personal value that everyone places on their occasion," she says. "And I honor that. I fret. I worry. And unless I heard that the cake arrived happy, I'm checking that phone all the time."

- *Interpersonal demands* are stressors associated with relationships in the organization. Although in some cases interpersonal relationships can alleviate stress, they also can be a source of stress when the group puts pressure on an individual or when conflicts arise between individuals. Managers can resolve many conflicts using techniques that will be discussed in Chapter 21. **Role conflict** occurs when an individual perceives incompatible demands from others. Managers often feel role conflict because the demands of their superiors conflict with those of the employees in their department. They may be expected to support employees and provide them with opportunities to experiment and be creative, while at the same time top executives are demanding a consistent level of output that leaves little time for creativity and experimentation.

Almost everyone experiences some degree of job stress associated with these factors. For example, consider the stress caused by task demands on Verizon's call center representatives.

Verizon Communications

Roland G. Collins Jr. loves his job as a call center representative for Verizon Communications. He enjoys connecting with customers; he makes good money and has good benefits. But he admits that it's not the job for everyone. About a third of the 100 or so calls a representative handles each day are stressful. Besides dealing with irate customers and handling calls regarding billing or other problems, representatives have to be able to rattle off Verizon's string of products and services, including terms and rates, and try to sell them to each and every call. It doesn't matter how angry or rude the customer on the other end of the line—pushing new services is a key requirement of the job.

What makes matters worse is that representatives often have to do these tasks under observation. Managers routinely sit next to a representative or listen in on a call to check whether the rep has hit on nearly 80 different points required in every customer contact. Call center reps must meet precise performance specifications, and managers defend the observation practice as a way to ensure consistency and better customer service. However, employees almost always find the experience adds to their stress level. For some employees, particularly inexperienced ones, an observation can create a panic situation, causing heart pounding and profuse sweating, which, in turn, creates even greater stress.[67]

The situation for call center representatives in other countries, who are handling calls for U.S.-based companies such as American Express, Citibank, Sprint, and IBM, can be even more stressful. There, the high stress caused by task demands is compounded by interpersonal issues, primarily "hate calls" from American customers angry over the loss of U.S. jobs. A survey by the Indian magazine *Dataquest* found that most call center employees find these calls "psychologically disturbing" and identify them as a major cause of job stress.[68]

■ **TAKE A MOMENT**

> As a new manager, learn to recognize the conditions that cause stress in the workplace and then change what you can to alleviate unnecessary or excessive stress for employees. Remember that not all stress is negative, but try to help people manage stress in a healthy way.

Innovative Responses to Stress Management

Organizations that want to challenge their employees and stay competitive in a fast-changing environment will never be stress-free. But because many consequences of stress are negative, managers need to make stress management a priority. In Britain, lawmakers implemented a new requirement that employers meet certain conditions that help to manage workplace stress, such as ensuring that employees are not exposed to a poor physical work environment, have the necessary skills and training to meet their job requirements, and are given a chance to offer input into the way their work is done.[69]

A variety of techniques can help individuals manage stress. Among the most basic strategies are those that help people stay healthy: exercising regularly, getting plenty of rest, and eating a healthful diet.

role conflict Incompatible demands of different roles.

Although individuals can pursue stress management strategies on their own, today's enlightened companies support healthy habits to help people manage stress and be more productive. Stress costs businesses billions of dollars a year in absenteeism, lower productivity, staff turnover, accidents, and higher health insurance and workers' compensation costs.[70] In today's workplace, taking care of employees has become a business as well as an ethical priority.

Supporting employees can be as simple as encouraging people to take regular breaks and vacations. Consider that more than a third of U.S. employees surveyed by the Families and Work Institute currently don't take their full allotment of vacation time.[71] Some companies, including BellSouth, First Union, and Tribble Creative Group, also have designated *quiet rooms* or meditation centers where employees can take short, calming breaks at any time they feel the need.[72] The time off is a valuable investment when it allows employees to approach their work with renewed energy and a fresh perspective.

Companies develop other programs aimed at helping employees reduce stress and lead healthier, more balanced lives. Some have wellness programs that provide access to nutrition counseling and exercise facilities. A worldwide study of wellness programs conducted by the Canadian government found that for each dollar spent, the company gets from $1.95 to $3.75 return payback from benefits.[73] Other organizations create broad work–life balance initiatives that may include flexible work options such as telecommuting and flexible hours, as well as benefits such as onsite daycare, fitness centers, and personal services such as pickup and delivery of dry cleaning. *Daily flextime* is considered by many employees to be the most effective work–life practice, which means giving employees the freedom to vary their hours as needed, such as leaving early to take an elderly parent shopping or taking time off to attend a child's school play.[74]

The study of organizational behavior reminds managers that employees are *human* resources with human needs. By acknowledging the personal aspects of employees' lives, work–life practices communicate that managers and the organization care about employees. In addition, managers' attitudes make a tremendous difference in whether employees are stressed out and unhappy or relaxed, energetic, and productive.

MANAGER'S SOLUTION

The principles of organizational behavior describe how people as individuals and groups behave and affect the performance of the organization as a whole. Desirable work-related attitudes include job satisfaction and organizational commitment. Employees' and managers' attitudes can strongly influence employee motivation, performance, and productivity. Three components of attitudes are cognitions, emotions, and behavior.

Attitudes affect people's perceptions, and vice versa. Individuals often "see" things in different ways. The perceptual process includes perceptual selectivity and perceptual organization. Perceptual distortions, such as stereotyping, the halo effect, projection, and perceptual defense, are errors in judgment that can arise from inaccuracies in the perception process. Attributions are judgments that individuals make about whether a person's behavior was caused by internal or external factors.

Another area of interest is personality, the set of characteristics that underlie a relatively stable pattern of behavior. One way to think about personality is the Big Five personality traits of extroversion, agreeableness, conscientiousness, emotional stability, and openness to experience. Some important work-related attitudes and behaviors influenced by personality are locus of control, authoritarianism, Machiavellianism, and problem-solving styles. A widely used personality test is the Myers–Briggs Type Indicator. Managers want to find a good person–job fit by ensuring that a person's personality, attitudes, skills, abilities, and problem-solving styles match the requirements of the job and the organizational environment.

New insight into personality has been gained through research in the area of emotional intelligence (EQ). Emotional intelligence includes the components of self-awareness, self-management, social awareness, and relationship management.

Even though people's personalities may be relatively stable, individuals can learn new behaviors. Learning refers to a change in behavior or performance that occurs as a result of experience. The learning process goes through a four-stage cycle, and individual learning styles differ. Four learning styles are Diverger, Assimilator, Converger, and Accommodator. Rapid changes in today's marketplace create a need for ongoing learning. They may also create greater stress for many of today's workers. The causes of work stress include task demands and interpersonal demands. Individuals and organizations can alleviate the negative effects of stress by engaging in a variety of techniques for stress management.

Returning to our opening example, Kevin Kelly at Emerald Packaging realized that he had developed some negative attitudes that were affecting his managers' attitudes and performance. Rather than continuing to complain about the shortcomings of others, Kelly adopted a new attitude that it was his responsibility as a leader to meld everyone into a cohesive, high-performing team. He eagerly began looking for classes he could take to learn new people skills and boost his emotional intelligence. Kelly realized that the infusion of new, young managers into the organization had left some of the long-time executives feeling insecure about whether they were about to be replaced by the "new kids." Kelly addressed the emotional component of managers' negative attitudes toward the new hires by reassuring them that they were valued and that their jobs were safe. He also met regularly with the new hires, rather than expecting other managers to do all the work of integrating them into the team. The long-time managers seemed reinvigorated and became more receptive to new ideas and more responsive to the new executives. The newcomers, in turn, developed more positive attitudes about the veteran managers, seeing them as teammates who were eager to implement new ideas and improve the organization. By shifting his own attitude and acting as a mentor and coach, Kelly successfully united the two groups into a cohesive team in which each person appreciated the values and strengths of the others.[75]

DISCUSSION QUESTIONS

1. If you were trying to change a subordinate's attitude, which approach do you think would be more effective: changing cognition, affect, or behavior? Why? Why is it important for managers to have an understanding of organizational behavior? Do you think a knowledge of OB might be more important at some managerial levels than at others? Discuss.

2. In what ways might the cognitive and affective components of attitude influence the behavior of employees who are faced with learning an entirely new set of computer-related skills in order to retain their jobs at a manufacturing facility?

3. Suggest a way that a manager might be able to use his or her understanding of perceptual selectivity and organization to communicate more effectively with subordinates. What steps might managers at a company that is about to merge with another company take to promote organizational commitment among employees?

4. In the Big Five personality factors, extroversion is considered a "good" quality to have. Why might introversion be an equally positive quality?

5. Why do you think surveys show that Generation X employees (those born between 1961 and 1981) experience the least job satisfaction of all demographic groups? Do you expect this finding to be true throughout their careers?

6. What is meant by perceptual selectivity? Explain some characteristics of the perceiver and of the stimuli that might affect perception?

7. Which of the four components of emotional intelligence do you consider most important to an effective manager in today's world? Why?

8. How might understanding whether an employee has an internal or an external locus of control help a manager better communicate with, motivate, and lead the employee?

9. You are a manager, and you realize that one of your employees repeatedly teases coworkers born in

India that they come from a backward country with pagan beliefs. How would you decide whether it's necessary to respond to the situation? If you decide to intervene, what would your response be? Why is it important for managers to achieve person-job fit when they are hiring employees?

10. Review Exhibit 17.11. Which learning style best characterizes you? How can you use this understanding to improve your learning ability? To improve your management skills?

11. Describe a time when you experienced role ambiguity or role conflict. What stress management techniques did you use to cope with the stress this situation created?

12. Why do you think workplace stress seems to be skyrocketing? Do you think it is a trend that will continue? Explain the reasons for your answer. Do you think it is the responsibility of managers and organizations to help employees manage stress? Why or why not?

MANAGEMENT IN PRACTICE: EXPERIENTIAL EXERCISE

Personality Assessment: Jung's Typology and the Myers-Briggs Type Indicator

For each of the following items, circle either a or b. In some cases, both a and b may apply to you. You should decide which is more like you, even if it is only slightly more true.

1. I would rather
   a. Solve a new and complicated problem
   b. Work on something that I have done before

2. I like to
   a. Work alone in a quiet place
   b. Be where "the action" is

3. I want a boss who
   a. Establishes and applies criteria in decisions
   b. Considers individual needs and makes exceptions

4. When I work on a project, I
   a. Like to finish it and get some closure
   b. Often leave it open for possible change

5. When making a decision, the most important considerations are
   a. Rational thoughts, ideas, and data
   b. People's feelings and values

6. On a project, I tend to
   a. Think it over and over before deciding how to proceed
   b. Start working on it right away, thinking about it as I go along

7. When working on a project, I prefer to
   a. Maintain as much control as possible
   b. Explore various options

8. In my work, I prefer to
   a. Work on several projects at a time, and learn as much as possible about each one
   b. Have one project that is challenging and keeps me busy

9. I often
   a. Make lists and plans whenever I start something and may hate to seriously alter my plans
   b. Avoid plans and just let things progress as I work on them

10. When discussing a problem with colleagues, it is easy for me
    a. To see "the big picture"
    b. To grasp the specifics of the situation

11. When the phone rings in my office or at home, I usually
    a. Consider it an interruption
    b. Don't mind answering it

12. The word that describes me better is
    a. Analytical
    b. Empathetic

13. When I am working on an assignment, I tend to
    a. Work steadily and consistently
    b. Work in bursts of energy with "downtime" in between

14. When I listen to someone talk on a subject, I usually try to
    a. Relate it to my own experience and see whether it fits
    b. Assess and analyze the message

15. When I come up with new ideas, I generally
    a. "Go for it"
    b. Like to contemplate the ideas some more

16. When working on a project, I prefer to
    a. Narrow the scope so it is clearly defined
    b. Broaden the scope to include related aspects

17. When I read something, I usually
    a. Confine my thoughts to what is written there
    b. Read between the lines and relate the words to other ideas

18. When I have to make a decision in a hurry, I often
    a. Feel uncomfortable and wish I had more information
    b. Am able to do so with available data

19. In a meeting, I tend to
    a. Continue formulating my ideas as I talk about them
    b. Speak out only after I have carefully thought the issue through

20. In work, I prefer spending a great deal of time on issues of
    a. Ideas
    b. People

21. In meetings, I am most often annoyed with people who
    a. Come up with many sketchy ideas
    b. Lengthen the meeting with many practical details

22. I tend to be
    a. A morning person
    b. A night owl

23. My style in preparing for a meeting is
    a. To be willing to go in and be responsive
    b. To be fully prepared and sketch an outline of the meeting

24. In meetings, I would prefer for people to
    a. Display a fuller range of emotions
    b. Be more task-oriented

25. I would rather work for an organization where
    a. My job was intellectually stimulating
    b. I was committed to its goals and mission

26. On weekends, I tend to
    a. Plan what I will do
    b. Just see what happens and decide as I go along

27. I am more
    a. Outgoing
    b. Contemplative

28. I would rather work for a boss who is
    a. Full of new ideas
    b. Practical

In the following, choose the word in each pair that appeals to you more:

29. a. Social   b. Theoretical

30. a. Ingenuity   b. Practicality

31. a. Organized   b. Adaptable

32. a. Active   b. Concentration

Scoring and Interpretation

Count one point for each of the following items that you circled in the inventory.

Score for I (Introversion)	Score for E (Extroversion)	Score for S (Sensing)	Score for N (Intuition)
2a	2b	1b	1a
6a	6b	10b	10a
11a	11b	13a	13b
15b	15a	16a	16b
19b	19a	17a	17b
22a	22b	21a	21b
27b	27a	28b	28a
32b	32a	30b	30a
Totals ____	____	____	____

Circle the one with more points:
I or E
(If tied on I/E, don't count #11)

Circle the one with more points:
S or N
(If tied on S/N, don't count #16)

Score for T (Thinking)	Score for F (Feeling)	Score for J (Judging)	Score for P (Perceiving)
3a	3b	4a	4b
5a	5b	7a	7b
12a	12b	8b	8a
14b	14a	9a	9b
20a	20b	18b	18a
24b	24a	23b	23a
25a	25b	26a	26b
29b	29a	31a	31b
Totals ____	____	____	____

Circle the one with more points:
T or F
(If tied on T/F, don't count #24)

Circle the one with more points:
J or P
(If tied on J/P, don't count #23)

Your Score Is: I or E _____ S or N _____ T or F _____ J or P _____

Your MBTI type is _____ (example: INTJ; ESFP; etc.)

Characteristics Frequently Associated with Each Myers-Briggs Type

Sensing Types

Intuitive Types

Introverts

ISTJ

Quiet, serious, earn success by thoroughness and dependability. Practical, matter-of-fact, realistic, and responsible. Decide logically what should be done and work toward it steadily, regardless of distractions. Take pleasure in making everything orderly and organized—their work, their home, their life. Value traditions and loyalty.

ISFJ

Quiet, friendly, responsible, and conscientious. Committed and steady in meeting their obligations. Thorough, painstaking, and accurate. Loyal, considerate, notice and remember specifics about people who are important to them, concerned with how others feel. Strive to create an orderly and harmonious environment at work and at home.

INFJ

Seek meaning and connection in ideas, relationships, and material possessions. Want to understand what motivates people and are insightful about others. Conscientious and committed to their firm values. Develop a clear vision about how best to serve the common good. Organized and decisive in implementing their vision.

INTJ

Have original minds and great drive for implementing their ideas and achieving their goals. Quickly see patterns in external events and develop long-range explanatory perspectives. When committed, organize a job and carry it through. Skeptical and independent, have high standards of competence and performance—for themselves and others.

ISTP

Tolerant and flexible, quiet observers until a problem appears, then act quickly to find workable solutions. Analyze what makes things work and readily get through large amounts of data to isolate the core of practical problems. Interested in cause and effect, organize facts using logical principles, value efficiency.

ISFP

Quiet, friendly, sensitive, and kind. Enjoy the present moment, what's going on around them. Like to have their own space and to work within their own time frame. Loyal and committed to their values and to people who are important to them. Dislike disagreements and conflicts, do not force their opinions or values on others.

INFP

Idealistic, loyal to their values and to people who are important to them. Want an external life that is congruent with their values. Curious, quick to see possibilities, can be catalysts for implementing ideas. Seek to understand people and to help them fulfill their potential. Adaptable, flexible, and accepting unless a value is threatened.

INTP

Seek to develop logical explanations for everything that interests them. Theoretical and abstract, interested more in ideas than in social interaction. Quiet, contained, flexible, and adaptable. Have unusual ability to focus in depth to solve problems in their area of interest. Skeptical, sometimes critical, always analytical.

Extraverts

ESTP

Flexible and tolerant, they take a pragmatic approach focused on immediate results. Theories and conceptual explanations bore them—they want to act energetically to solve the problem. Focus on the here-and-now, spontaneous, enjoy each moment that they can be active with others. Enjoy material comforts and style. Learn best through doing.

ESFP

Outgoing, friendly, and accepting. Exuberant lovers of life, people, and material comforts. Enjoy working with others to make things happen. Bring common sense and a realistic approach to their work, and make work fun. Flexible and spontaneous, adapt readily to new people and environments. Learn best by trying a new skill with other people.

ENFP

Warmly enthusiastic and imaginative. See life as full of possibilities. Make connections between events and information very quickly, and confidently proceed based on the patterns they see. Want a lot of affirmation from others, and readily give appreciation and support. Spontaneous and flexible, often rely on their ability to improvise and their verbal fluency.

ENTP

Quick, ingenious, stimulating, alert, and outspoken. Resourceful in solving new and challenging problems. Adept at generating conceptual possibilities and then analyzing them strategically. Good at reading other people. Bored by routine, will seldom do the same thing the same way, apt to turn to one new interest after another.

ESTJ

Practical, realistic, matter-of-fact. Decisive, quickly move to implement decisions. Organize projects and people to get things done, focus on getting results in the most efficient way possible. Take care of routine details. Have a clear set of logical standards, systematically follow them and want others to also. Forceful in implementing their plans.

ESFJ

Warmhearted, conscientious, and cooperative. Want harmony in their environment, work with determination to establish it. Like to work with others to complete tasks accurately and on time. Loyal, follow through even in small matters. Notice what others need in their day-by-day lives and try to provide it. Want to be appreciated for who they are and for what they contribute.

ENFJ

Warm, empathetic, responsive, and responsible. Highly attuned to the emotions, needs, and motivations of others. Find potential in everyone, want to help others fulfill their potential. May act as catalysts for individual and group growth. Loyal, responsive to praise and criticism. Sociable, facilitate others in a group, and provide inspiring leadership.

ENTJ

Frank, decisive, assume leadership readily. Quickly see illogical and inefficient procedures and policies, develop and implement comprehensive systems to solve organizational problems. Enjoy long-term planning and goal setting. Usually well informed, well read, enjoy expanding their knowledge and passing it on to others. Forceful in presenting their ideas.

The Myers-Briggs Type Indicator (MBTI), based on the work of psychologist Carl Jung, is the most widely used personality assessment instrument in the world. The MBTI, which was described in the chapter text, identifies 16 different "types," shown with their dominant characteristics in the chart above. Remember that no one is a pure type; however, each individual has preferences for introversion versus extroversion, sensing versus intuition, thinking versus feeling, and judging versus perceiving. Read the description of your type as determined by your scores in the survey. Do you believe the description fits your personality?

SOURCE: From *Organizational Behavior: Experience and Cases*, 4th ed. by Dorothy Marcic. © 1995. Reprinted with permission of South-Western, a division of Thomson Learning: http://www.thomsonrights.com.

MANAGEMENT IN PRACTICE: ETHICAL DILEMMA

Should I Fudge the Numbers?

Sara MacIntosh recently joined MicroPhone, a large telecommunications company, to take over the implementation of a massive customer service training project. The program was created by Kristin Cole, head of human resources and Sara's new boss. According to the grapevine, Kristin was hoping this project alone would give her the "star quality" she needed to earn a coveted promotion. Industry competition was heating up, and MicroPhone's strategy called for being the best at customer service, which meant having the most highly trained people in the industry, especially those who worked directly with customers. Kristin's new training program called for an average of one full week of intense customer service training for each of 3,000 people and had a price tag of about $40 million.

Kristin put together a team of overworked staffers to develop the training program, but now she needed someone well qualified and dedicated to manage and implement the project. Sara, with eight years of experience, a long list of accomplishments, and advanced degrees in finance and organizational behavior, seemed perfect for the job. However, during a thorough review of the proposal, Sara discovered some assumptions built into the formulas that raised red flags. She approached Dan Sotal, the team's coordinator, about her concerns, but the more Dan tried to explain how the financial projections were derived, the more Sara realized that Kristin's proposal was seriously flawed. No matter how she tried to work them out, the most that could be squeezed out of the $40 million budget was 20 hours of training per person, not the 40 hours everyone expected for such a high price tag.

Sara knew that, although the proposal had been largely developed before she came on board, it would bear her signature. As she carefully described the problems with the proposal to Kristin and outlined the potentially devastating consequences, Kristin impatiently tapped her pencil. Finally, she stood up, leaned forward, and interrupted Sara, quietly saying, "Sara, make the numbers work so that it adds up to 40 hours and stays within the $40 million budget." Sara glanced up and replied, "I don't think it can be done unless we either change the number of employees who are to be trained or the cost figure. . . ." Kristin's smile froze on her face and her eyes began to snap as she again interrupted. "I don't think you understand what I'm saying. We have too much at stake here. *Make the previous numbers work.*" Stunned, Sara belatedly began to realize that Kristin was ordering her to fudge the numbers. She felt an anxiety attack coming on as she wondered what she should do.

What Would You Do?

1. Make the previous numbers work. Kristin and the entire team have put massive amounts of time into the project and they all expect you to be a team player. You don't want to let them down. Besides, this project is a great opportunity for you in a highly visible position.

2. Stick to your principles and refuse to fudge the numbers. Tell Kristin you will work overtime to help develop an alternate proposal that stays within the budget by providing more training to employees who work directly with customers and fewer training hours for those who don't have direct customer contact.

3. Go to the team and tell them what you've been asked to do. If they refuse to support you, threaten to reveal the true numbers to the CEO and board members.

SOURCE: Adapted from Doug Wallace, "Fudge the Numbers or Leave," *Business Ethics* (May–June 1996): 58–59. Adapted with permission.

CASE FOR CRITICAL ANALYSIS

Reflex Systems

As the plane took off from the L.A. airport for Chicago and home, Henry Rankin tried to unwind, something that didn't come naturally to the Reflex Systems software engineer. He needed time to think, and the flight from Los Angeles was a welcome relief. He went to L.A. to help two members of his project team solve technical glitches in software. Rankin had been pushing himself and his team hard for three months now, and he didn't know when they would get a break. Rankin was responsible for the technical implementation of the new customer relationship management

software being installed for western and eastern sales offices in L.A. and Chicago. The software was badly needed to improve follow-up sales for his company, Reflex Systems. Reflex sold exercise equipment to high schools and colleges through a national force of 310 salespeople. Reflex also sold products to small and medium-sized businesses for recreation centers.

Rankin knew CEO Mike Frazer saw the new CRM software as the answer to one of the exercise equipment manufacturer's most persistent problems. Even though Reflex's low prices generated healthy sales, follow-up service was spotty. Consequently, getting repeat business from customers—high schools, colleges, and corporate recreation centers—was an uphill battle. Excited by the prospect of finally removing this major roadblock, Frazer ordered the CRM software installed in just 10 weeks, a goal Rankin privately thought was unrealistic. He also felt the project budget wasn't adequate. Rankin thought about meeting the next day with his three Chicago team members, and about the status update he would give his boss, Nicole Dyer, the senior vice president for Information Technology. Rankin remembered that Dyer had scheduled 10 weeks for the CRM project. He had always been a top performer by driving himself hard, and had been in his management position three years now. He was good with technology, but was frustrated when members of his five-person team didn't seem as committed. Dyer told him last week that she didn't feel a sense of urgency from his team. How could she think that? Rankin requested that team members work evenings and weekends because the budget was too tight to fill a vacant position. They agreed to put in the hours, although they didn't seem enthusiastic.

Still, Frazer was the boss, so if he wanted the job done in 10 weeks, Rankin would do everything in his power to deliver, even if it meant the entire team worked nights and weekends. He wasn't asking any more of his subordinates than he was asking of himself, as he frequently reminded them when they came to him with bloodshot eyes and complained about the hours. Rankin thought back to a flight one month ago when he returned to Chicago from L.A. Sally Phillips sat next to him. Phillips was on one of five members on Rankin's team and told him she had an offer from a well-known competitor. The money was less, but she was interested in the quality of life aspect of the company. Phillips asked for feedback on how she was doing and about her career prospects at Reflex. Rankin said he didn't want her to leave, but what more could he say? She got along well with people but she wasn't as technically gifted as some on the team. Rankin needed her help to finish the project and he told her so. Two weeks later she turned in her letter of resignation, and now the team was shorthanded. Rankin was also aware that his own possible promotion in two years, when Nicole Dyer was eligible for retirement, depended on his success with this project.

He would just take up the slack himself. He loved studying, analyzing, and solving technical problems when he could get time alone.

Henry Rankin knew that Nicole Dyer had noticed a lack of commitment on the part of the team members. He wondered whether she had discussed the team's performance with Frazer as well. Rankin hadn't noticed any other problems, but he recalled his partner on the project, Sam Matheny, saying that two Chicago team members, Bob Finley and Lynne Johnston, were avoiding each other. How did Sam know that? Matheny was in charge of nontechnical sales implementation of the CRM project, which meant training salespeople, redesigning sales procedures, updating customer records, and so forth. Rankin called Finley and Johnston to his office and said he expected them to get along for the good of the project. Finley said he had overreacted to Johnston from lack of sleep, and wondered when the project would be over. Rankin wasn't certain because of all the problems with both software and hardware, but he said the project shouldn't last more than another month.

As the plane taxied to the gate, an exhausted Rankin couldn't quell his growing fears that as the deadline fast approached, the project team was crumbling. How could he meet that deadline? As the plane taxied to the gate at Chicago, Rankin wondered about the project's success. Was there more to managing this team than working hard and pushing others hard? Even he was tired. Maybe he would ask his wife when he got home. He hadn't seen her or the kids for a week, but they had not complained.

Questions

1. What personality and behavior characteristics does Henry Rankin exhibit? Do you think these traits contribute to a good person-job fit for him? If you were an executive coach hired to help Rankin be a better manager, what would you say to him? Why?

2. Does Rankin display type A or type B behavior? What are the causes of stress for his team?

3. If you were Rankin, how would you have handled your team members (Sally Phillips, Bob Finley, and Lynne Johnston)? Be specific. What insights or behaviors would make Rankin a better manager?

ENDNOTES

1. Kevin Kelly, "Branching Out," *FSB* (December 2005–January 2006): 39.

2. See Michael West, "Hope Springs," *People Management* (October 2005): 38ff ; and Mark C. Bolino, William H. Turnley, and James M. Bloodgood, "Citizenship Behaviors and the Creation of Social Capital in Organizations," *Academy of Management Review 27*, no. 4 (2002): 505–522.

3. Reported in Del Jones, "Optimism Puts Rose-Colored Tint in Glasses of Top Execs," *USA Today* (December 15, 2005), http://www.usatoday.com.

4. Jerry Krueger and Emily Killham, "At Work, Feeling Good Matters," *Gallup Management Journal* (December 8, 2005).

5. Jeffrey Zaslow, "Pursuits: Happiness, Inc.," *The Wall Street Journal* (March 18, 2006): P-1.

6. John W. Newstrom and Keith Davis, *Organizational Behavior: Human Behavior at Work*, 11th ed. (Burr Ridge, IL: McGraw-Hill Irwin, 2002): Chapter 9.

7. S. J. Breckler, "Empirical Validation of Affect, Behavior, and Cognition as Distinct Components of Attitude," *Journal of Personality and Social Psychology* (May 1984): 1191–1205; and J. M. Olson and M. P. Zanna, "Attitudes and Attitude Change," *Annual Review of Psychology* 44 (1993): 117–154.

8. M. T. Iaffaldano and P. M. Muchinsky, "Job Satisfaction and Job Performance: A Meta-Analysis," *Psychological Bulletin* (March 1985): 251–273; C. Ostroff, "The Relationship Between Satisfaction, Attitudes, and Performance: An Organizational Level Analysis," *Journal of Applied Psychology* (December 1992): 963–974; and M. M. Petty, G. W. McGee, and J. W. Cavender, "A Meta-Analysis of the Relationship Between Individual Job Satisfaction and Individual Performance," *Academy of Management Review* (October 1984): 712–721.

9. Sue Shellenbarger, "Companies Are Finding Real Payoffs in Aiding Employee Satisfaction," *The Wall Street Journal* (October 11, 2000): B1.

10. "Worried at Work: Generation Gap in Workplace Woes," International Survey Research, http://www.isrsurveys.com (accessed May 19, 2004).

11. Tony Schwartz, "The Greatest Sources of Satisfaction in the Workplace Are Internal and Emotional," *Fast Company* (November 2000): 398–402.

12. Marshall Goldsmith, "To Help Others Develop, Start with Yourself," *Fast Company* (March, 2004): 100; and Bonnie Miller Rubin and Sharman Stein, "Think Outside the [Cereal] Box," *Working Mother* (October 2002): 60.

13. William C. Symonds, "Where Paternalism Equals Good Business," *BusinessWeek* (July 20, 1998): 16E4, 16E6.

14. "The People Factor: Global Survey Shows That an Engaged Workforce Measurably Improves the Bottom Line—and How," International Survey Research, http://www.isrsurveys.com (accessed May 19, 2004).

15. "Employee Commitment; U.S.: Leader or Follower?" International Survey Research, http://www.isrsurveys.com (accessed May 19, 2004).

16. W. Chan Kin and Renée Mauborgne, "Fair Process: Managing in the Knowledge Economy," *Harvard Business Review* (January 2003): 127–136.

17. Survey results reported in Jones, "Optimism Puts Rose-Colored Tint in Glasses of Top Execs."

18. Jennifer Laabs, "They Want More Support—Inside and Outside of Work," *Workforce* (November 1998): 54–56.

19. For a discussion of cognitive dissonance theory, see Leon A. Festinger, *Theory of Cognitive Dissonance* (Stanford, CA: Stanford University Press, 1957).

20. D. A. Kravitz and S. L. Klineberg, "Reactions to Two Versions of Affirmative Action Among Whites, Blacks, and Hispanics," *Journal of Applied Psychology* 85 (2000): 597–611; and Robert J. Grossman, "Race in the Workplace" *HR Magazine* (March 2000): 41–45.

21. Jaclyne Badal, "Surveying the Field: Cracking the Glass Ceiling," *The Wall Street Journal* (June 19, 2006): B3.

22. J. A. Deutsch, W. G. Young, and T. J. Kalogeris, "The Stomach Signals Satiety," *Science* (April 1978): 22–33.

23. Richard B. Chase and Sriram Dasu, "Want to Perfect Your Company's Service? Use Behavioral Science," *Harvard Business Review* (June 2001): 79–84.

24. H. H. Kelley, "Attribution in Social Interaction," in E. Jones et al. (eds.), *Attribution: Perceiving the Causes of Behavior* (Morristown, NJ: General Learning Press, 1972).

25. See J. M. Digman, "Personality Structure: Emergence of the Five-Factor Model," *Annual Review of Psychology* 41 (1990): 417–440; M. R. Barrick and M. K. Mount, "Autonomy as a Moderator of the Relationships Between the Big Five Personality Dimensions and Job Performance," *Journal of Applied Psychology* (February 1993): 111–118; and J. S. Wiggins and A. L. Pincus, "Personality: Structure and Assessment," *Annual Review of Psychology* 43 (1992): 473–504.

26. Del Jones, "Not All Successful CEOs Are Extroverts," *USA Today* (June 6, 2006), http://www.usatoday.com.

27. Joseph Nocera, "In Business, Tough Guys Finish Last," *The New York Times* (June 18, 2005): C1; Carol Hymowitz, "Rewarding Competitors Over Collaborators No Longer Makes Sense," *The Wall Street Journal* (February 13, 2006): B1.

28. Tim Sanders, *The Likeability Factor: How to Boost Your L-Factor and Achieve the Life of Your Dreams* (New York: Crown, 2005).

29. Lisa Takeuchi Cullen, "SATs for J-O-B-S," *Time* (April 3, 2006): 89.

30. Michelle Leder, "Is That Your Final Answer?" *Working Woman* (December–January 2001): 18; "Can You Pass the Job Test?" *Newsweek* (May 5, 1986): 46–51.

31. Alan Farnham, "Are You Smart Enough to Keep Your Job?" *Fortune* (January 15, 1996): 34–47.

32. Cora Daniels, "Does This Man Need a Shrink?" *Fortune* (February 5, 2001): 205–208.

33. Julie Bennett, "Franchising: Do You Have What It Takes?" *The Wall Street Journal* (September 19, 2005): R11.

34. Lori Gottlieb, "How Do I Love Thee?" *The Atlantic Monthly* (March 2006): 58–70.

35. Daniel Goleman, "Leadership That Gets Results," *Harvard Business Review* (March–April 2000): 79–90; Richard E. Boyatzis and Daniel Goleman, *The Emotional Competence Inventory–University Edition*, The Hay Group, 2001; and Daniel Goleman, *Emotional Intelligence: Why It Can Matter More than IQ* (New York: Bantam Books, 1995).

36. Farnham, "Are You Smart Enough to Keep Your Job?"

37. Hendrie Weisinger, *Emotional Intelligence at Work* (San Francisco: Jossey–Bass, 2000); D. C. McClelland, "Identifying Competencies with Behavioral-Event Interviews," *Psychological Science* (Spring 1999): 331–339; Daniel Goleman, "Leadership That Gets Results," *Harvard Business Review* (March–April 2000): 78–90; D. Goleman, *Working with Emotional Intelligence* (New York: Bantam Books, 1999); and Lorie Parch, "Testing . . . 1, 2, 3," *Working Woman* (October 1997): 74–78.

38. Goleman, "Leadership That Gets Results."

39. J. B. Rotter, "Generalized Expectancies for Internal versus External Control of Reinforcement," *Psychological Monographs* 80, no. 609 (1966).

40. Andy Serwer, "There's Something about Cisco," *Fortune* (May 15, 2000); Stephanie N. Mehta, "Cisco Fractures Its Own Fairy Tale," *Fortune* (May 14, 2001): 104–112.

41. See P. E. Spector, "Behavior in Organizations as a Function of Employee's Locus of Control," *Psychological Bulletin* (May 1982): 482–497.

42. T. W. Adorno, E. Frenkel-Brunswick, D. J. Levinson, and R. N. Sanford, *The Authoritarian Personality* (New York: Harper & Row, 1950).

43. Niccolo Machiavelli, *The Prince*, trans. George Bull (Middlesex: Penguin, 1961).

44. Richard Christie and Florence Geis, *Studies in Machiavellianism* (New York: Academic Press, 1970).

45. R. G. Vleeming, "Machiavellianism: A Preliminary Review," *Psychological Reports* (February 1979): 295–310.

46. Christie and Geis, *Studies in Machiavellianism.*

47. Carl Jung, *Psychological Types* (London: Routledge and Kegan Paul, 1923).

48. Mary H. McCaulley, "Research on the MBTI and Leadership: Taking the Critical First Step," keynote address, The Myers–Briggs Type Indicator and Leadership: An International Research Conference, January 12–14, 1994.

49. Alison Overhold, "Are You a Polyolefin Optimizer? Take This Quiz!" *Fast Company* (April 2004): 37.

50. Reported in Cullen, "SATs for J-O-B-S."

51. Charles A. O'Reilly III, Jennifer Chatman, and David F. Caldwell, "People and Organizational Culture: A Profile Comparison Approach to Assessing Person-Organization Fit," *Academy of Management Journal* 34, no. 3 (1991): 487–516.

52. Anna Muoio, "Should I Go .Com?" *Fast Company* (July 2000): 164–172.

53. Leder, "Is That Your Final Answer?"

54. David A. Kolb, "Management and the Learning Process," *California Management Review* 18, no. 3 (Spring 1976): 21–31.

55. De'Ann Weimer, "The Houdini of Consumer Electronics," *BusinessWeek* (June 22, 1998): 88, 92; and http://www.bestbuy.com (accessed June 19, 2006).

56. See David. A. Kolb, I. M. Rubin, and J. M. McIntyre, *Organizational Psychology: An Experimental Approach*, 3rd ed. (Englewood Cliffs, NJ: Prentice Hall, 1984): 27–54.

57. Stephanie Gruner, "Our Company, Ourselves," *Inc.* (April 1998): 127–128.

58. Ira Sager, "Big Blue's Blunt Bohemian," *BusinessWeek* (June 14, 1999): 107–112.

59. Paul Roberts, "The Best Interest of the Patient Is the Only Interest to be Considered," *Fast Company* (April 1999): 149–162.

60. T. A. Beehr and R. S. Bhagat, *Human Stress and Cognition in Organizations: An Integrated Perspective* (New York: Wiley, 1985); and Bruce Cryer, Rollin McCraty, and Doc Childre, "Pull the Plug on Stress," *Harvard Business Review* (July 2003): 102–107.

61. Ekramul Hoque and Mayenul Islam, "Contribution of Some Behavioural Factors to Absenteeism of Manufacturing Workers in Bangladesh," *Pakistan Journal of Psychological Research* 18, no. 3–4 (Winter 2003): 81–96; U.S. research study conducted by HERO, a not-for-profit coalition of organizations with common interests in health promotion, disease management, and health-related productivity research, and reported in Bruce Cryer, Rollin McCraty, and Doc Childre, "Pull the Plug on Stress," *Harvard Business Review* (July 2003): 102–107.

62. M. Friedman and R. Rosenman, *Type A Behavior and Your Heart* (New York: Knopf, 1974).

63. John L. Haughom, "How to Pass the Stress Test," *CIO* (May 1, 2003): 50–52; Quote from Cora Daniels, "The Last Taboo," *Fortune* (October 28, 2002): 137–144.

64. Haughom, "How to Pass the Stress Test."

65. Reported in "Work Stress Is Costly," *Morning Call* (October 18, 2005): E1.

66. Families and Work Institute survey, reported in "Reworking Work," *Time* (July 25, 2005): 50–55; Spherion survey, reported in Donna Callea, "Workers Feeling the Burn: Employee Burnout a New Challenge to Productivity, Morale, Experts Say," *News Journal* (March 27, 2006): A11; "Workplace Stress Now Causing Huge Loss of Working Days," *Birmingham Post* (April 19, 2006): 23; Vani Doraisamy, "Young Techies Swell the Ranks of the Depressed," *The Hindu* (October 11, 2005): 1.

67. Kris Maher, "At Verizon Call Center, Stress Is Seldom on Hold," *The Wall Street Journal* (January 16, 2001): B1, B12.

68. Rama Lakshmi, "India Call Centers Suffer Storm of 4-Letter Words; Executives Blame American Anger Over Outsourcing," *The Washington Post* (February 27, 2005): A22.

69. Donalee Moulton, "Buckling Under the Pressure," *OH & S Canada* 19, no. 8 (December 2003): 36.

70. Claire Sykes, "Say Yes to Less Stress," *Office Solutions* (July–August 2003): 26; and Andrea Higbie, "Quick Lessons in the Fine Old Art of Unwinding," *The New York Times* (February 25, 2001): BU–10.

71. Rosabeth Moss Kanter, "Balancing Work and Life," *Knight-Ridder Tribune News Service* (April 8, 2005): 1.

72. Leslie Gross Klass, "Quiet Time at Work Helps Employee Stress," *Johnson City Press* (January 28, 2001): 30.

73. Moulton, "Buckling Under the Pressure."

74. David T. Gordon, "Balancing Act," *CIO* (October 15, 2001): 58–62.

75. Kelly, "Branching Out."

CHAPTER OUTLINE

Manager's Challenge

The Nature of Leadership

Leadership for Contemporary Times

Level 5 Leadership

Women's Ways of Leading

Leadership Versus Management

Leadership Traits

Behavioral Approaches

Ohio State Studies

Michigan Studies

The Leadership Grid

Contingency Approaches

Hersey and Blanchard's Situational
Theory

Fiedler's Contingency Theory

Matching Leader Style
to the Situation

Path–Goal Theory

Substitutes for Leadership

Leading Change

Charismatic and Visionary
Leadership

Transformational Leaders

Power and Influence

Position Power

Personal Power

Interpersonal Influence Tactics

Enduring Leadership Approaches

Servant Leadership

Moral Leadership

LEARNING OBJECTIVES

After studying this chapter, you should be able to:

1. Define leadership and explain its importance for organizations.

2. Describe how leadership is changing in today's organizations.

3. Identify personal characteristics associated with effective leaders.

4. Define task-oriented behavior and people-oriented behavior and explain how these categories are used to evaluate and adapt leadership style.

5. Describe Hersey and Blanchard's situational theory and its application to subordinate participation.

6. Explain the path–goal model of leadership.

7. Discuss how leadership fits the organizational situation and how organizational characteristics can substitute for leadership behaviors.

8. Describe transformational leadership and when it should be used.

9. Identify the five sources of leader power and the tactics leaders use to influence others.

10. Explain servant leadership and moral leadership and their importance in contemporary organizations.

LEADERSHIP

MANAGER'S CHALLENGE

Building a motivated, satisfied, and committed workforce for low-skill, low-wage jobs such as food service, hospital cleaning, and lawn mowing can be a nightmare. Aramark Corporation is involved in all those businesses and more as a leader in managed services for corporations, universities, hospitals, parks and resorts, and other organizations. Roy Pelaez loves working for Aramark, and he takes great pride in his new job as head of a service operation that cleans airplanes for Delta and Southwest in several northeastern cities. Yet, he had no idea how hard it would be to keep 400 mostly non–English-speaking immigrants motivated and inspired to give their best to a minimum wage job. Morale is dismal, and turnover exceeds 100 percent a year. People don't seem to take any pride in their work. Moreover, wallets or other valuables that passengers leave on planes have a funny way of disappearing. Pelaez is determined to turn the operation around by creating an environment where employees feel committed to the company, their fellow workers, and customers. But how is he to do it? He's always believed that managers shouldn't get involved in the personal problems of their subordinates, but Pelaez thinks he might need a different approach to tap into the energy and enthusiasm of his employees.[1]

> If you were in Roy Pelaez's position, what leadership approach would you take? Do you think it is possible for a leader to improve job satisfaction and organizational commitment for low-skilled, low-paid employees such as those Pelaez is supervising?

■ **TAKE A MOMENT**

589

In the previous chapter, we explored differences in attitudes and personality that affect behavior. The attitudes and behaviors of leaders play an important role in shaping employee attitudes, such as their job satisfaction and organizational commitment. Yet there are as many variations among leaders as there are among other individuals, and many different styles of leadership can be effective.

Different leaders behave in different ways depending on their individual differences as well as their followers' needs and the organizational situation. For example, contrast the styles of Pat McGovern, founder and chair of International Data Group, a technology publishing and research firm that owns magazines such as *CIO*, *PC World*, and *Computerworld*, with that of Tom Siebel, CEO of software company Siebel Systems. McGovern treats each employee to lunch at the Ritz on his or her tenth anniversary with IDG to tell them how important they are to the success of the company. He personally thanks almost every person in every business unit once a year, which takes about a month of his time. Managers provide him with a list of accomplishments for all their direct reports, which McGovern memorizes the night before his visit so he can congratulate people on specific accomplishments. In addition to appreciating and caring about employees, McGovern also shows that he believes in them by decentralizing decision making so that people have the autonomy to make their own decisions about how best to accomplish organizational goals. Tom Siebel, in contrast, is known as a disciplined and dispassionate manager who remains somewhat aloof from his employees and likes to maintain strict control over every aspect of the business. He enforces a dress code, sets tough goals and standards, and holds people strictly accountable. "We go to work to realize our professional ambitions, not to have a good time," Siebel says.[2] Both Siebel and McGovern have been successful as leaders, although their styles are quite different.

This chapter explores one of the most widely discussed and researched topics in management—leadership. Here we define leadership and explore the differences between leadership and management. We look at some important leadership approaches for contemporary organizations, as well as examine trait, behavioral, and contingency theories of leadership effectiveness, discuss charismatic and transformational leadership, and consider how leaders use power and influence to get things done. The final section of the chapter discusses servant leadership and moral leadership, two enduring approaches that have received renewed emphasis in recent years. Chapters 19 through 21 will look in detail at many of the functions of leadership, including employee motivation, communication, and encouraging teamwork.

THE NATURE OF LEADERSHIP

No topic is probably more important to organizational success today than leadership. Leadership matters. In most situations, a team, military unit, or volunteer organization is only as good as its leader. Consider the situation in Iraq, as U.S. military advisors strive to build Iraqi forces that can take over security duties without support from coalition troops. Many trainers say they encounter excellent individual soldiers and junior leaders but that many of the senior commanders are stuck in old authoritarian patterns that undermine their units. Whether an Iraqi unit succeeds or fails often comes down to one person—its commander—so advisors are putting emphasis on finding and strengthening good leaders.[3] Top leaders make a difference in business organizations as well. Baron Partners Fund, which picks stocks based largely on an evaluation of companies' senior executives, was the best-performing diversified stock fund of 2004, with a return of 42 percent. Manager Ron Baron says top leaders who are smart, honorable, and treat their employees right typically lead their companies to greater financial success and greater shareholder returns.[4]

The concept of leadership continues to evolve as the needs of organizations change. Among all the ideas and writings about leadership, three aspects stand out—people, influence, and goals. Leadership occurs among people, involves the use of influence, and is used to attain goals.[5] *Influence* means that the relationship among people is not passive. Moreover, influence is designed to achieve some end or goal. Thus, **leadership** as defined here is the ability to influence people toward the attainment of goals. This definition captures the idea that leaders are involved with other people in the achievement of goals.

Leadership is reciprocal, occurring *among* people.[6] Leadership is a "people" activity, distinct from administrative paper shuffling or problem-solving activities. Leadership is dynamic and involves the use of power to influence people and get things done.

LEADERSHIP FOR CONTEMPORARY TIMES

The environmental context in which leadership is practiced influences which approach might be most effective, as well as what kinds of leaders are most admired by society. The technology, economic conditions, labor conditions, and social and cultural mores of the times all play a role. A significant influence on leadership styles in recent years is the turbulence and uncertainty of the environment in which most organizations are operating. Ethical and economic difficulties, corporate governance concerns, globalization, changes in technology, new ways of working, shifting employee expectations, and significant social transitions have contributed to a shift in how we think about and practice leadership.

leadership The ability to influence people toward the attainment of organizational goals.

Of particular interest for leadership in contemporary times is a *post-heroic approach* that focuses on the subtle, unseen, and often unrewarded acts that good leaders perform every day, rather than on the grand accomplishments of celebrated business heroes.[7] During the 1980s and 1990s, leadership became equated with larger-than-life personalities, strong egos, and personal ambitions. In contrast, the post-heroic leader's major characteristic is humility.[8] **Humility** means being unpretentious and modest rather than arrogant and prideful. Humble leaders don't have to be in the center of things. They quietly build strong, enduring companies by developing and supporting others rather than touting their own abilities and accomplishments. Two approaches that are in tune with post-heroic leadership for today's times are Level 5 leadership and interactive leadership, a style that is commonly used by women leaders.

Go to the ethical dilemma on page 615 that pertains to post-heroic leadership for turbulent times.

■ **TAKE A MOMENT**

Level 5 Leadership

A recent five-year study conducted by Jim Collins and his research associates identified the critical importance of what Collins calls *Level 5 leadership* in transforming companies from merely good to truly great organizations.[9] As described in his book *Good to Great: Why Some Companies Make the Leap . . . and Others Don't*, Level 5 leadership refers to the highest level in a hierarchy of manager capabilities, as illustrated in Exhibit 18.1. A key characteristic of Level 5 leaders is an almost complete lack of ego, coupled with a fierce resolve to do what is best for the organization. In contrast to the view of great leaders as larger-than-life personalities with strong egos and big ambitions, Level 5 leaders often seem shy and unpretentious. Although they accept full responsibility for mistakes, poor results, or failures, Level 5 leaders give credit for successes to other people. For example, Joseph F. Cullman III, former CEO of Philip Morris, staunchly refused to accept credit for the company's long-term success, citing his great colleagues, successors, and predecessors as the reason for the accomplishments. Another example is Darwin E. Smith. When he was promoted to CEO of Kimberly-Clark, Smith questioned whether the board really wanted to appoint him because he didn't believe he had the qualifications a CEO needed.

humility Being unpretentious and modest rather than arrogant and prideful.

EXHIBIT 18.1

The Level 5 Leadership Hierarchy

SOURCE: "The Level 5 Leadership Hierarchy" from *Good to Great: Why Some Companies Make the Leap . . . and Others Don't*, by Jim Collins. Reprinted by permission of HarperCollins Publishers, Inc.

Level 5: The Level 5 Leader
Builds an enduring great organization through a combination of personal humility and professional resolve.

Level 4: The Effective Executive
Builds widespread commitment to a clear and compelling vision; stimulates people to high performance.

Level 3: Competent Manager
Sets plans and organizes people for the efficient and effective pursuit of objectives.

Level 2: Contributing Team Member
Contributes to the achievement of team goals; works effectively with others in a group.

Level 1: Highly Capable Individual
Productive contributor; offers talent, knowledge, skills, and good work habits as an individual employee.

Kimberly-Clark

Darwin Smith, who led Kimberly-Clark from 1971 to 1991, is a classic example of a Level 5 leader. Few people have ever heard of him—and that's probably just the way he wanted it.

Smith was somewhat shy and awkward in social situations, and he dressed much like a farm boy in his first JCPenney suit. He was never featured in splashy articles in *Fortune* magazine or *The Wall Street Journal*. Yet, far from being meek, Smith demonstrated an aggressive determination to revive Kimberly-Clark, which at the time was a stodgy old paper company that had seen years of falling stock prices. Anyone who interpreted his appearance and demeanor as a sign of ineptness soon learned differently, as Smith made difficult decisions that set Kimberly-Clark on the path to greatness. When Smith took over, the company's core business was in coated paper. Convinced that this approach doomed the company to mediocrity, Smith took the controversial step of selling the company's paper mills and investing all its resources in consumer products such as Kleenex and Huggies diapers.

Over his 20 years as CEO, Smith turned Kimberly-Clark into the leading consumer paper products company in the world, beating rivals Scott Paper and Procter & Gamble. The company generated cumulative stock returns that were 4.1 times greater than those of the general market. When asked about his exceptional performance after his retirement, Smith said simply, "I never stopped trying to become qualified for the job."[10]

As the example of Darwin Smith illustrates, despite their personal humility, Level 5 leaders have a strong will to do whatever it takes to produce great and lasting results for their organizations. They are extremely ambitious for their companies rather than for themselves. This goal becomes highly evident in the area of succession planning. Level 5 leaders develop a solid corps of leaders throughout the organization, so that when they leave the company it can continue to thrive and grow even stronger. Egocentric leaders, by contrast often set their successors up for failure because it will be a testament to their own greatness if the company doesn't perform well without them. Rather than an organization built around "a genius with a thousand helpers," Level 5 leaders build an organization with many strong leaders who can step forward and continue the company's success. These leaders want everyone in the organization to develop to their fullest potential.

Women's Ways of Leading

The focus on minimizing personal ambition and developing others is also a hallmark of *interactive leadership*, which has been found to be common among female leaders. Research indicates that women's style of leadership is typically different from most men's and is particularly suited to today's organizations.[11] Using data from actual performance evaluations, one study found that when rated by peers, subordinates, and bosses, female managers score significantly higher than men on abilities such as motivating others, fostering communication, and listening.[12]

Interactive leadership means that the leader favors a consensual and collaborative process, and influence derives from relationships rather than position power and formal authority.[13] For example, Nancy Hawthorne, former chief financial officer at Continental Cablevision Inc., felt that her role as a leader was to delegate tasks and authority to others and to help them be more effective. "I was being traffic cop and coach and facilitator," Hawthorne says. "I was always into building a department that hummed."[14] Similarly, Terri Kelly, who took over as CEO of W. L. Gore in 2005, says her goal is to provide overall direction and guidance, not to micromanage and tell people how to do their jobs.[15] It is important to note that men can be interactive leaders as well, as demonstrated by the example of Pat McGovern of International Data Group earlier in the chapter. For McGovern, having personal contact with employees and letting them know they're appreciated is a primary responsibility of leaders. The characteristics associated with interactive leadership are

interactive leadership A leadership style characterized by values such as inclusion, collaboration, relationship building, and caring.

INTERPERSONAL PATTERNS

The majority of a new manager's work is accomplished through interpersonal relationships. To understand your relationship pattern, consider the following verbs. These 20 verbs describe some of the ways people feel and act from time to time. Think about your behavior in groups. How do you feel and act in groups? Check the five verbs that best describe your behavior in groups as you see it.

_____ acquiesce	_____ coordinate	_____ lead
_____ advise	_____ criticize	_____ oblige
_____ agree	_____ direct	_____ relinquish
_____ analyze	_____ disapprove	_____ resist
_____ assist	_____ evade	_____ retreat
_____ concede	_____ initiate	_____ withdraw
_____ concur	_____ judge	

Two underlying patterns of interpersonal behavior are represented in the preceding list: *dominance* (authority or control) and *sociability* (intimacy or friendliness). Most individuals tend either to like to control things (high dominance) or to let others control things (low dominance). Similarly, most persons tend either to be warm and personal (high sociability) or to be somewhat distant and impersonal (low sociability). In the following diagram, circle the five verbs in the list that you used to describe yourself. The set of 10 verbs in either horizontal row (sociability dimension) or vertical column (dominance dimension) in which three or more are circled represents your tendency in interpersonal behavior.

	High Dominance	Low Dominance
High Sociability	advises	acquiesces
	coordinates	agrees
	directs	assists
	initiates	concurs
	leads	obliges
Low Sociability	analyzes	concedes
	criticizes	evades
	disapproves	relinquishes
	judges	retreats
	resists	withdraws

Your behavior pattern suggested in the diagram is a clue to your interpersonal style as a new manager. Which of the four quadrants provides the best description of you? Is that the type of leader you aspire to become? Generally speaking the high sociability and high dominance pattern reflects the type of leader to which many new managers aspire. How does your pattern correspond to the Level 5 and interactive leadership patterns described in the text?

SOURCE: David W. Johnson and Frank P. Johnson, *Joining Together: Group Theory and Group Skills,* 8th ed. (New York: Allyn and Bacon, 2003): 189–190. Used with permission.

emerging as valuable qualities for both male and female leaders in today's workplace. Values associated with interactive leadership include personal humility, inclusion, relationship building, and caring.

> As a new manager, will your interpersonal style fit the contemporary leadership approaches described above? To find out, complete the New Manager Self Test above.

TAKE A MOMENT

LEADERSHIP VERSUS MANAGEMENT

Much has been written in recent years about the leadership role of managers. Management and leadership are both important to organizations. Effective managers have to be leaders, too, because distinctive qualities are associated with management and leadership that provide different strengths for the organization, as illustrated in Exhibit 18.2. As shown in the exhibit, management and leadership reflect two different sets of qualities and skills that frequently overlap within a single

EXHIBIT 18.2

Leader and Manager Qualities

SOURCE: Based on Genevieve Capowski, "Anatomy of a Leader: Where Are the Leaders of Tomorrow?" *Management Review* (March 1994): 12.

LEADER QUALITIES

SOUL
Visionary
Passionate
Creative
Flexible
Inspiring
Innovative
Courageous
Imaginative
Experimental
Initiates change
Personal power

MANAGER QUALITIES

MIND
Rational
Consulting
Persistent
Problem solving
Tough-minded
Analytical
Structured
Deliberate
Authoritative
Stabilizing
Position power

traits Distinguishing personal characteristics, such as intelligence, values, and appearance.

© DENESE IZZARD-FERRIS/DENESE IZZARD-FERRIS PHOTOGRAPHY

CONCEPT
CONNECTION Linda St. Clair (right) has been both an artistic-director of theater productions and a personnel manager for a technology firm. Her **interactive leadership style** worked equally well in both settings. As a theater director, she articulated a clear overarching vision, supported individual artists, encouraged collaborative relationships—and then let the creative process take its course. The job of a manager isn't very different. "When I was at my best in the corporation," she recalls, "I helped people get what they needed to be effectively creative." Good leaders, St. Clair believes, know how to build relationships and act not as a commander but rather as a coach, guide, and mentor.

individual. A person might have more of one set of qualities than the other, but ideally a manager develops a balance of both manager and leader qualities.

A primary distinction between management and leadership is that management promotes stability, order, and problem solving within the existing organizational structure and systems. Leadership promotes vision, creativity, and change. In other words, "a manager takes care of where you are; a leader takes you to a new place."[16] Leadership means questioning the status quo so that outdated, unproductive, or socially irresponsible norms can be replaced to meet new challenges. Leadership cannot replace management; it should be in addition to management. Good management is needed to help the organization meet current commitments, while good leadership is needed to move the organization into the future.[17]

LEADERSHIP TRAITS

Early efforts to understand leadership success focused on the leader's personal characteristics or traits. **Traits** are the distinguishing personal characteristics of a leader, such as intelligence, values, self-confidence, and appearance. The early research focused on leaders who had achieved a level of greatness, and hence was referred to as the *Great Man* approach. The idea was relatively simple: Find out what made these people great, and select future leaders who already exhibited the same traits or could be trained to develop them. Generally, early research found only a weak relationship between personal traits and leader success.[18]

In recent years, interest in examining leadership traits has reemerged. In addition to personality traits, physical, social, and work-related characteristics of leaders have been studied.[19] Exhibit 18.3 summarizes the physical, social, and personal leadership characteristics that have received the greatest research support. However, these characteristics do not

EXHIBIT   18.3

Personal Characteristics of
Leaders

Physical Characteristics	**Personality**	**Work-Related Characteristics**
Energy	Self-confidence	Achievement drive, desire to excel
Physical stamina	Honesty and integrity	Conscientiousness in pursuit of goals
	Enthusiasm	Persistence against obstacles, tenacity
	Desire to lead	
	Independence	
Intelligence and Ability	**Social Characteristics**	**Social Background**
Intelligence, cognitive ability	Sociability, interpersonal skills	Education
Knowledge	Cooperativeness	Mobility
Judgment, decisiveness	Ability to enlist cooperation	
	Tact, diplomacy	

SOURCES: Based on Bernard M. Bass, *Bass & Stogdill's Handbook of Leadership: Theory, Research, and Managerial Applications,* 3rd ed. (New York: The Free Press, 1990): 80–81; and S. A. Kirkpatrick and E. A. Locke, "Leadership: Do Traits Matter?" *Academy of Management Executive* 5, no. 2 (1991): 48–60.

stand alone. The appropriateness of a trait or set of traits depends on the leadership situation. The same traits do not apply to every organization or situation. Further studies expand the understanding of leadership beyond the personal traits of the individual to focus on the dynamics of the relationship between leaders and followers.

BEHAVIORAL APPROACHES

The inability to define effective leadership based solely on traits led to an interest in looking at the behavior of leaders and how it might contribute to leadership success or failure. Perhaps any leader can adopt the correct behavior with appropriate training. Two basic leadership behaviors identified as important for leadership are *task-oriented behavior* and *people-oriented behavior*. These two *metacategories*, or broadly defined behavior categories, were found to be applicable to effective leadership in a variety of situations and time periods.[20] Although they are not the only important leadership behaviors, concern for tasks and concern for people must be shown at some reasonable level. Thus, many approaches to understanding leadership use these metacategories as a basis for study and comparison. Important research programs on leadership behavior were conducted at Ohio State University, University of Michigan, and University of Texas.

Ohio State Studies

Researchers at Ohio State University surveyed leaders to study hundreds of dimensions of leader behavior.[21] They identified two major behaviors, called consideration and initiating structure.

Consideration falls in the category of people-oriented behavior and is the extent to which the leader is mindful of subordinates, respects their ideas and feelings, and establishes mutual trust. Considerate leaders are friendly, provide open communication, develop teamwork, and are oriented toward their subordinates' welfare.

Initiating structure is the degree of task behavior, that is, the extent to which the leader is task oriented and directs subordinate work activities toward goal attainment. Leaders with this style typically give instructions, spend time planning, emphasize deadlines, and provide explicit schedules of work activities.

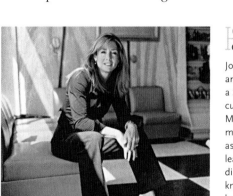

© VITO ALUIA

consideration A type of behavior that describes the extent to which the leader is sensitive to subordinates, respects their ideas and feelings, and establishes mutual trust.

initiating structure A type of leader behavior that describes the extent to which the leader is task oriented and directs subordinate work activities toward goal attainment.

595

Chapter 18 LEADERSHIP

[CONCEPT
CONNECTION]

Joanna B. Meiseles, president and founder of Snip-its Corp., a $1.5 million children's haircutting chain based in Natick, Massachusetts, demonstrates many of the **personal traits** associated with effective leadership. For example, she displayed intelligence, ability, knowledge, and judgment by knowing that to make her company successful, it had to be unique. Everything about Snip-its is tailored to children. Snip-its characters perch on a hot pink and lime green entry arch, games and stories are loaded on funky quasi-anthropomorphic computers at every cutting station, and the Magic Box dispenses a prize in exchange for a swatch of hair at the end of a visit.

Consideration and initiating structure are independent of each other, which means that a leader with a high degree of consideration may be either high or low on initiating structure. A leader may have any of four styles: high initiating structure–low consideration, high initiating structure–high consideration, low initiating structure–low consideration, or low initiating structure–high consideration. The Ohio State research found that the high consideration–high initiating structure style achieved better performance and greater satisfaction than the other leader styles. The value of the high-high style is illustrated by Brigadier General Michael P. Mulqueen, who retired from the U.S. Marine Corps to head up the Greater Chicago Food Depository. Mulqueen runs the depository like a business rather than a typical nonprofit. He stresses efficiency and is as demanding as any corporate CEO in organizing and directing people toward achieving the organization's goals. Yet Mulqueen knows that leaders don't get people to rally around them simply by issuing orders. He's never intimidating, and he's always willing to listen to other people's ideas, allow people autonomy in how they accomplish goals, and show appreciation and respect. Mulqueen's high consideration–high initiating structure leadership approach has turned the Greater Chicago Food Depository into one of the nation's most effective hunger-relief agencies.[22] Successful pro football coaches also often use a high–high style.[23] For example, coaches have to keep players focused on winning football games by scheduling structured practices, emphasizing careful planning, and so forth. However, the best coaches are those who genuinely care about and show concern for their players. This chapter's Unlocking Innovative Solutions Through People box profiles Bob Ladouceur, the coach of an extraordinary high school football team, who personifies the high-high leadership style.

Some research, however, indicates that the high–high style is not necessarily the best. These studies suggest that effective leaders may be high on consideration and low on initiating structure or low on consideration and high on initiating structure, depending on the situation.[24]

Michigan Studies

Studies at the University of Michigan at about the same time took a different approach by comparing the behavior of effective and ineffective supervisors.[25] The most effective supervisors were those who focused on the subordinates' human needs in order to "build effective work groups with high performance goals." The Michigan researchers used the term *employee-centered leaders* for leaders who established high performance goals and displayed supportive behavior toward subordinates. The less-effective leaders were called *job-centered leaders*; these leaders tended to be less concerned with goal achievement and human needs in favor of meeting schedules, keeping costs low, and achieving production efficiency.

The Leadership Grid

leadership grid A two-dimensional leadership theory that measures the leader's concern for people and for production.

Building on the work of the Ohio State and Michigan studies, Blake and Mouton of the University of Texas proposed a two-dimensional leadership theory called the **leadership grid**.[26] The two-dimensional model and five of its seven major management styles are depicted in Exhibit 18.4. Each axis on the grid is a nine-point scale, with 1 meaning low concern and 9 high concern.

Team management (9,9) often is considered the most effective style and is recommended for managers because organization members work together to accomplish tasks. *Country club management* (1,9) occurs when primary emphasis is given to people rather than to work outputs. *Authority-compliance management* (9,1) occurs when efficiency in operations is the dominant orientation. *Middle-of-the-road management* (5,5) reflects a moderate amount of concern for both people and production. *Impoverished management* (1,1) means the absence of a management philosophy; managers

PEOPLE

THE DE LA SALLE SPARTANS WIN WITH SOUL

The last time the De La Salle Spartans lost a football game was December 7, 1991. Since then, coach Bob LaDouceur has led his team of players, many of whom are derided as "undersized" and "untalented," to one victory after another, year after year. Despite competing against bigger schools and tougher players, the De La Salle Spartans just keep on winning.

De La Salle is a small, private parochial school in Concord, California. Years ago, LaDouceur sized up his team of a few, small demoralized players and made a decision. He was going to teach these guys what it takes to win, and then make it a day-to-day process. LaDouceur directs close attention to the tasks needed to accomplish the goal of winning. He keeps his players on a year-round strength and conditioning program. Each practice is methodical, and LaDouceur constantly tells his players to leave every practice just a little bit better than they were when it started. He teaches players to make up for what they lack in size and talent with intelligence and wit.

However, the coach hasn't just institutionalized the process of drills, workouts, and practices. He has also institutionalized a process of building bonds and intimacy among his players. "If a team has no soul," LaDouceur says, "you're just wasting your time."

Tasks are important, but for LaDouceur, people always come first. "It's not about how we're getting better physically, it's about how we're getting better as people," he says. During the off season, players go camping and rafting together and volunteer for community service. When the season starts, the team attends chapel together for readings and songs. After every practice, a dinner is held at a player's home.

Then comes what LaDouceur's considers his central task and his main goal for the team. As tensions build during the season, players are encouraged to speak their hearts, to confess their fears and shortcomings, and to talk about their commitments and expectations of themselves for the next game. On Thursday night before Friday games, LaDouceur doesn't give a typical locker room speech. He talks about the "L word." "*Love.* Why is that word so hard to say?" he asks his players. And then he waits—as long as it takes—until a few players overcome their embarrassment enough to say it.

SOURCE: Don Wallace, "The Soul of a Sports Machine," *Fast Company* (October 2003): 100–102; and Neil Hayes, *When the Game Stands Tall. The Story of the De La Salle Spartans and Football's Longest Winning Streak* (Berkeley, CA: Frog, Ltd./North Atlantic Books, 2005).

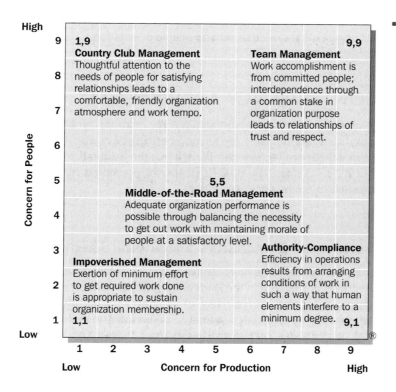

EXHIBIT 18.4

The Leadership Grid® Figure

SOURCE: The Leadership Grid® figure, Paternalism figure and Opportunism from *Leadership Dilemmas-Grid Solutions,* by Robert R. Blake and Anne Adams McCanse (formerly the Managerial Grid by Robert R. Blace and Jase S. Mouton). Houston: Gulf Publishing Company. (Grid figure: p. 29, Paternalism figure: p. 30, Opportunism figure: p. 31). Copyright © 1991, by Blake and mouton, and Scientific Methods, Inc. Reproduced by permission of the owners.

exert little effort toward interpersonal relationships or work accomplishment. Consider these examples.

TruServ and Tires Plus

When Pamela Forbes Lieberman learned that her subordinates called her *the dragon lady*, she embraced the moniker and hung a watercolor of a dragon in her office. Lieberman makes no apologies for her hard-driving leadership style. Her emphasis on ambitious goals, tough standards, and bottom-line results has brought renewed health and vitality to hardware cooperative TruServ, which supplies inventory to True Value hardware stores. As soon as Lieberman became CEO, she began slashing costs and setting tough performance targets. "If [people] succeed, they will be rewarded, but if they don't, then we're going to have to look for new people sitting in their chairs," Lieberman says.

Compare Lieberman's hard-nosed approach to that of Tom Gegax, who calls himself the head coach of Tires Plus, a fast-growing chain of retail tire stores. Gegax believes that you cannot manage people the same way as you manage fixed assets. His emphasis is on treating employees just as well as they are expected to treat their customers. Gegax personally leads classes at Tires Plus University, where employees learn not just about changing tires but about how to make their whole lives better. Gegax also makes sure stores are clean, bright, and airy, so that employees have a pleasant work environment. He believes all these details translate into better service. Employees, as well as customers, like the approach. "The last thing the world needs is another chain of stores," Gegax says. "What it does need is a company with a new business model—one that embraces customers and employees as whole people."[27]

The leadership style of Pamela Lieberman is characterized by high concern for tasks and production (task-oriented behavior) and low-to-moderate concern for people (people-oriented behavior). Tom Gegax, in contrast, is high on concern for people and moderate on concern for production. Both leaders are successful, although they display different leadership styles, because of their different situations. The next group of theories builds on the leader-follower relationship of behavioral approaches to explore how organizational situations affect the leader's approach.

▓ TAKE A MOMENT

As a new manager, realize that both task-oriented behavior and people-oriented behavior are important, although some situations call for a greater degree of one over the other. Go to the experiential exercise on page 614 to measure your degree of task-orientation and people-orientation.

CONTINGENCY APPROACHES

Several models of leadership explain the relationship between leadership styles and specific situations. They are termed **contingency approaches** and include the situational theory of Hersey and Blanchard, the leadership model developed by Fiedler and his associates, the path–goal theory presented by Evans and House, and the substitutes-for-leadership concept.

contingency approach A model of leadership that describes the relationship between leadership styles and specific organizational situations.

situational theory A contingency approach to leadership that links the leader's behavioral style with the task readiness of subordinates.

Hersey and Blanchard's Situational Theory

The **situational theory** of leadership is an interesting extension of the behavioral theories summarized in the leadership grid (see Exhibit 18.4). Hersey and Blanchard's approach focuses a great deal of attention on the characteristics of followers in determining appropriate leadership behavior. The point of Hersey and Blanchard is that subordinates vary in readiness level. People low in task readiness, because of little ability or training, or insecurity, need a different leadership style than those who are high in readiness and have good ability, skills, confidence, and willingness

EXHIBIT 18.5

Hersey and Blanchard's
Situational Theory of
Leadership

LEADER STYLE

Share ideas and facilitate in decision making

PARTICIPATING S3

SELLING S2

Explain decisions and provide opportunity for clarification

DELEGATING

Turn over responsibility for decisions and implementation

S4

Provide specific instructions and closely supervise performance

TELLING S1

(Supportive Behavior) RELATIONSHIP BEHAVIOR

(HIGH)

(LOW) ◄——— TASK BEHAVIOR ———► (HIGH)
(Guidance)
FOLLOWER READINESS

HIGH	MODERATE		LOW
R4	**R3**	**R2**	**R1**
Able and Willing or Confident	Able but Unwilling or Insecure	Unable but Willing or Confident	Unable and Unwilling or Insecure

FOLLOWER DIRECTED   LEADER DIRECTED

to work.[28] According to the situational theory, a leader can adopt one of four leadership styles, based on a combination of relationship (concern for people) and task (concern for production) behavior. The appropriate style depends on the readiness level of followers.

Exhibit 18.5 summarizes the relationship between leader style and follower readiness. The *telling style* reflects a high concern for tasks and a low concern for people and relationships. This highly directive style involves giving explicit directions about how tasks should be accomplished. The *selling style* is based on a high concern for both people and tasks. With this approach, the leader explains decisions and gives subordinates a chance to ask questions and gain clarity and understanding about work tasks. The next leader behavior style, the *participating style*, is based on a combination of high concern for people and relationships and low concern for production tasks. The leader shares ideas with subordinates, gives them a chance to participate, and facilitates decision making. The fourth style, the *delegating style*, reflects a low concern for both relationships and tasks. This leader style provides little direction and little support because the leader turns over responsibility for decisions and their implementation to subordinates.

The bell-shaped curve in Exhibit 18.5 is called a prescriptive curve because it indicates when each leader style should be used. The readiness level of followers is indicated in the lower part of the exhibit. R1 is low readiness and R4 represents high readiness. The telling style is for low readiness followers because people are unable or unwilling, because of poor ability and skills, little experience, or insecurity, to take responsibility for their own task behavior. The leader is specific, telling people exactly what to do, how to do it, and when. The selling and participating styles work for followers at moderate readiness levels. For example, followers might lack some education and experience for the job but have high confidence, interest, and willingness to learn. As shown in the exhibit, the selling style is effective in this situation because it involves giving direction but also includes seeking input from others and clarifying tasks rather than simply instructing that they be performed. When followers have the necessary skills and experience but are somewhat insecure in their abilities or lack high willingness, the participating style enables the leader to guide followers' development and act as a resource for advice and assistance. When followers demonstrate high readiness, that is, they have high levels of education, experience, and readiness to accept responsibility for their own task behavior, the delegating style can effectively be used. Because of the high readiness level of followers, the leader can delegate responsibility for decisions and their implementation to subordinates who have the skills, abilities, and positive attitudes to follow through. The leader provides a general goal and sufficient authority to do the task as followers see fit.

To apply the Hersey and Blanchard model, the leader diagnoses the readiness level of followers and adopts the appropriate style—telling, selling, participating, or delegating. Using the incorrect style can hurt morale and performance. When president of Harvard University, former U.S. Treasury Secretary Lawrence Summers, tried to use a primarily telling style with followers who were at high readiness levels, it led to serious conflict with some faculty members and eventual demands for his ouster. Summers employed an assertive top-down style with followers who think of themselves not as employees but as partners in an academic enterprise. Faculty members at Harvard have long been accustomed to decentralized, democratic decision making and having a say in matters such as department mergers or new programs of study. Summers made many decisions on his own that followers thought should be put to a faculty vote. Although students in general supported Summers, the conflicts and a vote of no-confidence from some faculty convinced Summers to resign with many of his goals and plans for the university unrealized.[29]

Fiedler's Contingency Theory

Whereas Hersey and Blanchard focused on the characteristics of followers, Fiedler and his associates looked at some other elements of the organizational situation to assess when one leadership style is more effective than another.[30] The starting point for Fiedler's theory is the extent to which the leader's style is task oriented or relationship (people) oriented. Fiedler considered a person's leadership style to be relatively fixed and difficult to change; therefore, the basic idea is to match the leader's style with the situation most favorable for his or her effectiveness. By diagnosing leadership style and the organizational situation, the correct fit can be arranged.

SITUATION: FAVORABLE OR UNFAVORABLE?

The suitability of a person's leadership style is determined by whether the situation is favorable or unfavorable to the leader. The favorability of a leadership situation can be analyzed in terms of three elements: the quality of relationships between leader and followers, the degree of task structure, and the extent to which the leader has formal authority over followers.[31]

For example, a situation would be considered *highly favorable* to the leader when leader-member relationships are positive, tasks are highly structured, and the leader has formal authority over followers. In this situation, followers trust, respect, and have confidence in the leader. The group's tasks are clearly defined, involve specific procedures, and have clear, explicit goals. In addition, the leader has formal authority to direct and evaluate followers, along with the power to reward or punish. A situation would be considered *highly unfavorable* to the leader when leader-member relationships are poor, tasks are highly unstructured, and the leader has little formal authority. In a highly unfavorable situation, followers have little respect for or confidence and trust in the leader. Tasks are vague and ill-defined,

© KEN HAWKINS

CONCEPT

CONNECTION At Earnest Partners, an asset management firm in Atlanta, Georgia, the quality of **leader-member relationships** is high. CEO Paul Viera has gained the respect and trust of colleagues and followers because he has proven that he has the integrity, skills, and commitment to keep the company thriving. Viera can be characterized as a **task-oriented leader** because he is focused, prepared, and competitive, and he expects others to be as well. According to Fiedler's contingency theory, Viera's style succeeds at Earnest because of positive leader-member relations, strong leader position power, and jobs that contain some degree of task structure.

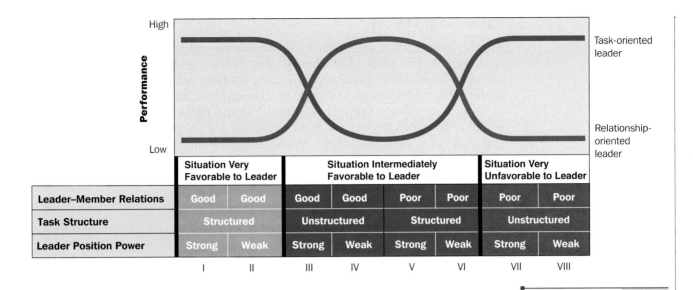

	Situation Very Favorable to Leader		Situation Intermediately Favorable to Leader				Situation Very Unfavorable to Leader	
Leader–Member Relations	Good	Good	Good	Good	Poor	Poor	Poor	Poor
Task Structure	Structured		Unstructured		Structured		Unstructured	
Leader Position Power	Strong	Weak	Strong	Weak	Strong	Weak	Strong	Weak
	I	II	III	IV	V	VI	VII	VIII

EXHIBIT   18.6

How Leader Style Fits the Situation

SOURCE: Based on Fred E. Fiedler, "The Effects of Leadership Training and Experience: A Contingency Model Interpretation," *Administrative Science Quarterly* 17 (1972): 455.

lacking in clear-cut procedures and guidelines. The leader has little formal authority to direct subordinates and does not have the power to issue rewards or punishments.

Matching Leader Style to the Situation

Combining the three situational characteristics yields a variety of leadership situations, ranging from highly favorable to highly unfavorable. When Fiedler examined the relationships among leadership style and situational favorability, he found the pattern shown in Exhibit 18.6. Task-oriented leaders are more effective when the situation is either highly favorable or highly unfavorable. Relationship-oriented leaders are more effective in situations of moderate favorability.

The task-oriented leader excels in the favorable situation because everyone gets along, the task is clear, and the leader has power; all that is needed is for someone to lead the charge and provide direction. Similarly, if the situation is highly unfavorable to the leader, a great deal of structure and task direction is needed. A strong leader will define task structure and establish authority over subordinates. Because leader-member relations are poor anyway, a strong task orientation will make no difference in the leader's popularity.

The relationship-oriented leader performs better in situations of intermediate favorability because human relations skills are important in achieving high group performance. In these situations, the leader may be moderately well liked, have some power, and supervise jobs that contain some ambiguity. A leader with good interpersonal skills can create a positive group atmosphere that will improve relationships, clarify task structure, and establish position power.

A leader, then, needs to know two things in order to use Fiedler's contingency theory. First, the leader should know whether he or she has a relationship- or task-oriented style. Second, the leader should diagnose the situation and determine whether leader-member relations, task structure, and position power are favorable or unfavorable.

Fiedler believed fitting leader style to the situation can yield big dividends in profits and efficiency.[32] On the other hand, the model has also been criticized.[33] For one thing, some researchers have challenged the idea that leaders cannot adjust their styles as situational characteristics change. Despite criticisms, Fiedler's model has continued to influence leadership studies. Fiedler's research called attention to the importance of finding the correct fit between leadership style and the situation.

■ TAKE A MOMENT

As a new manager, remember that different situations and different followers may require different approaches to leadership. Pay attention to the situation and the followers to determine how much structure and direction followers need.

Path–Goal Theory

Another contingency approach to leadership is called the path–goal theory.[34] According to the **path–goal theory**, the leader's responsibility is to increase followers' motivation and clarify the path to attain personal and organizational goals.[35] This model includes two sets of contingencies: leader behavior and the use of rewards to meet subordinates' needs.[36] In the Fiedler theory the assumption would be to switch leaders as situations change, but the path–goal theory suggests that leaders can switch their behaviors to match the situation.

LEADER BEHAVIOR

The path–goal theory suggests a fourfold classification of leader behaviors.[37] These classifications are the types of leader behavior the leader can adopt and include supportive, directive, achievement-oriented, and participative styles.

Supportive leadership involves leader behavior that shows concern for subordinates' well-being and personal needs. Leadership behavior is open, friendly, and approachable, and the leader creates a team climate and treats subordinates as equals. Supportive leadership is similar to the consideration, people-centered, or relationship-oriented leadership described earlier.

Directive leadership occurs when the leader tells subordinates exactly what they are supposed to do. Leader behavior includes planning, making schedules, setting performance goals and behavior standards, and stressing adherence to rules and regulations. Directive leadership behavior is similar to the initiating-structure, job-centered, or task-oriented leadership style described earlier.

Participative leadership means that the leader consults with his or her subordinates about decisions. Leader behavior includes asking for opinions and suggestions, encouraging participation in decision making, and meeting with subordinates in their workplaces. The participative leader encourages group discussion and written suggestions.

Achievement-oriented leadership occurs when the leader sets clear and challenging goals for subordinates. Leader behavior stresses high-quality performance and improvement over current performance. Achievement-oriented leaders also show confidence in subordinates and assist them in learning how to achieve high goals.

The four types of leader behavior are not considered ingrained personality traits as in the Fiedler theory; rather, they reflect types of behavior that every leader is able to adopt, depending on the situation.

USE OF REWARDS

Recall that the leader's responsibility is to clarify the path to rewards for subordinates or to increase the value of rewards to enhance satisfaction and job performance. In some situations, the leader works with subordinates to help them acquire the skills and confidence needed to perform tasks and achieve rewards already available. In others, the leader may develop new rewards to meet the specific needs of subordinates.

© SOUTHWEST AIRLINES/PR NEWSWIRE PHOTO SERVICE

CONCEPT

CONNECTION Southwest Airlines co-founder and chairman Herb Kelleher (shown here celebrating Southwest's new Philadelphia service with Ben Franklin) firmly believes that it's free-flowing communication that makes **participative leadership** possible. Southwest encourages employees to talk to anyone at anytime about anything on their minds. In addition to sending notes or e-mails, workers get the chance to share their opinions and ask questions when executives drop in on them periodically. When Gary Kelly, Kelleher's successor as CEO, visited an employee lounge at Chicago's Midway Airport, a mechanic who owns Southwest stock took him aside. "What's happening here?" he asked, pointing to stock quotes on a computer screen. "That's my retirement, and it's not moving."

Example Situation	Leader Behavior	Impact on Follower	Outcome
Follower lacks self-confidence	Supportive leadership	Increase confidence to achieve work outcome	More effort; improved satisfaction and performance
Ambiguous job	Directive leadership	Clarify path to reward	More effort; improved satisfaction and performance
Lack of job challenge	Achievement-oriented leadership	Set high goals	More effort; improved satisfaction and performance
Incorrect reward	Participative leadership	Clarify follower's needs and change rewards	More effort; improved satisfaction and performance

Exhibit 18.7 illustrates four examples of how leadership behavior is tailored to the situation. In the first example situation, the subordinate lacks confidence; thus, the supportive leadership style provides the social support with which to encourage the subordinate to undertake the behavior needed to do the work and receive the rewards. In the second situation, the job is ambiguous, and the employee is not performing effectively. Directive leadership behavior is used to give instructions and clarify the task so that the follower will know how to accomplish it and receive rewards. In the third situation, the subordinate is unchallenged by the task; thus, an achievement-oriented behavior is used to set higher goals. In the fourth situation, an incorrect reward is given to a subordinate, and the participative leadership style is used to change this situation. By discussing the subordinates' needs, the leader is able to identify the correct reward for task accomplishment and help people know how to achieve the reward. In all four cases, the outcome of fitting the leadership behavior to the situation produces greater employee effort by either clarifying how subordinates can receive rewards or changing the rewards to fit their needs.

At The Home Depot, CEO Bob Nardelli reinvigorated employee morale—and retail sales—with his achievement-oriented leadership, which cascades down from headquarters to the store level.

E X H I B I T   18.7

Path–Goal Situations and Preferred Leader Behaviors

SOURCE: Adapted from Gary A. Yukl, *Leadership in Organizations* (Englewood Cliffs, NJ: Prentice Hall, 1981): 146–152.

Things seemed a little shaky when new CEO Bob Nardelli first started imposing high goals, order, and discipline at The Home Depot, the nation's second-largest retailer next to Wal-Mart. Many store managers, who were used to a more relaxed approach, left the company, and investors sent the stock price plummeting.

But Nardelli knew what he was after. Instead of a retail chain where employees were becoming complacent and bored, he wanted a company full of enterprising people who thrive on challenge, responsibility, and recognition. Nardelli slowly began building a cadre of talented people, from top to bottom, and instituting a "no-bull performance culture" that gives people challenging goals and generous rewards for achieving them. Rigorous talent assessments, new approaches to hiring, new performance measurement systems, and programs such as the Store Leadership Program and Accelerated Leadership Program have enhanced employee skills and reduced turnover. Nardelli can monitor stores in real time via computer, and he spends one week a quarter as a "mystery shopper," popping in unannounced to as many as 10 stores a day. He makes clear to employees that he's not trying to "catch anybody," he just wants to see the store from the eyes of customers and help people do a better job of serving them.

Nardelli's achievement-oriented leadership has helped to increase sales from $45.7 billion to about $80 billion within five years, increase earnings per share by 20 percent annually and giving the retailer an edge in new segments such as the $410 billion professional construction market. "His real ability," says Jack Welch, who was Nardelli's boss at General Electric, "is to motivate lots of people around a mission, excite them about it, and make it happen."

The Home Depot

603

Chapter 18 LEADERSHIP

Variable		Task-Oriented Leadership	People-Oriented Leadership
Organizational variables	Group cohesiveness	Substitutes for	Substitutes for
	Formalization	Substitutes for	No effect on
	Inflexibility	Neutralizes	No effect on
	Low position power	Neutralizes	Neutralizes
	Physical separation	Neutralizes	Neutralizes
Task characteristics	Highly structured task	Substitutes for	No effect on
	Automatic feedback	Substitutes for	No effect on
	Intrinsic satisfaction	No effect on	Substitutes for
Group characteristics	Professionalism	Substitutes for	Substitutes for
	Training/experience	Substitutes for	No effect on

EXHIBIT 18.8

Substitutes and Neutralizers for Leadership

Nardelli's achievement-oriented leadership is successful because it encourages every manager in the organization to focus on keeping people challenged and motivated to reach goals.[38] Path–goal theorizing can be complex, but much of the research on it has been encouraging.[39] Using the model to specify precise relationships and make exact predictions about employee outcomes may be difficult, but the four types of leader behavior and the ideas for fitting them to situational contingencies provide a useful way for leaders to think about motivating subordinates.

Substitutes for Leadership

The contingency leadership approaches considered so far focus on the leaders' style, the subordinates' nature, and the situation's characteristics. The final contingency approach suggests that situational variables can be so powerful that they actually substitute for or neutralize the need for leadership.[40] This approach outlines those organizational settings in which a leadership style is unimportant or unnecessary.

Exhibit 18.8 shows the situational variables that tend to substitute for or neutralize leadership characteristics. A **substitute** for leadership makes the leadership style unnecessary or redundant. For example, highly professional subordinates who know how to do their tasks do not need a leader who initiates structure for them and tells them what to do. A **neutralizer** counteracts the leadership style and prevents the leader from displaying certain behaviors. For example, if a leader has absolutely no position power or is physically removed from subordinates, the leader's ability to give directions to subordinates is greatly reduced.

Situational variables in Exhibit 18.8 include characteristics of the group, the task, and the organization itself. When followers are highly professional and experienced, both leadership styles are less important. People do not need much direction or consideration. With respect to task characteristics, highly structured tasks substitute for a task-oriented style, and a satisfying task substitutes for a people-oriented style. With respect to the organization itself, group cohesiveness substitutes for both leader styles. Formalized rules and procedures substitute for leader task orientation. Physical separation of leader and subordinate neutralizes both leadership styles.

The value of the situations described in Exhibit 18.8 is that they help leaders avoid leadership overkill. Leaders should adopt a style with which to complement the organizational situation. Consider the work situation for bank tellers. A bank teller performs highly structured tasks, follows clear written rules and procedures, and has little flexibility in terms of how to do the work. The head teller should not adopt a task-oriented style, because the organization already provides structure and direction. The head teller should concentrate on a people-oriented style to provide a more pleasant work environment. In other organizations, if group cohesiveness or intrinsic satisfaction meets employees' social needs, the leader is free to concentrate on task-oriented behaviors. The leader can adopt a style complementary to the organizational situation to ensure that both task needs and people needs of the work group will be met.

substitute A situational variable that makes a leadership style unnecessary or redundant.

neutralizer A situational variable that counteracts a leadership style and prevents the leader from displaying certain behaviors.

As a new manager, avoid leadership overkill. Don't use a task-oriented style if the job already provides clear structure and direction. Concentrate instead on people and relationships. Remember that professional employees typically need less leadership.

LEADING CHANGE

In Chapter 1, we defined management to include the functions of leading, planning, organizing, and controlling. But recent work on leadership has begun to distinguish leadership as something more: a quality that inspires and motivates people beyond their normal levels of performance. We are living in an era when leadership is needed more than ever. The environment today is turbulent, and organizations need to shift direction quickly to keep pace.[41] Leaders in many organizations have had to reconceptualize almost every aspect of how they do business to meet the needs of increasingly demanding customers, keep employees motivated and satisfied, and remain competitive in a rapidly changing global environment.

Research finds that some leadership approaches are more effective than others for bringing about change in organizations. Two types of leadership with a substantial impact are charismatic and transformational. These types of leadership are best understood in comparison to *transactional leadership*.[42] **Transactional leaders** clarify the role and task requirements of subordinates, initiate structure, provide appropriate rewards, and try to be considerate to and meet the social needs of subordinates. The transactional leader's ability to satisfy subordinates may improve productivity. Transactional leaders excel at management functions. They are hardworking, tolerant, and fair minded. They take pride in keeping things running smoothly and efficiently. Transactional leaders often stress the impersonal aspects of performance, such as plans, schedules, and budgets. They have a sense of commitment to the organization and conform to organizational norms and values. Transactional leadership is important to all organizations, but leading change requires a different approach.

© RYSTED/GETTY

CONCEPT CONNECTION The real magic behind e-tailing company Amazon.com is the **visionary leadership** of founder and CEO Jeff Bezos. His passion and enthusiasm was the key to getting investors to give him millions of dollars in financing. Bezos continued to inspire employees with his vision of a new kind of retailer as the company struggled for years before finally achieving profitability. He keeps Amazon innovative with bold moves, such as his new vision to use Amazon's technological, operations, and logistics expertise to provide services to other companies and entrepreneurs. The company plans to rent out just about everything it uses to run its own business, from warehouse space to spare computing capacity and data storage.

Charismatic and Visionary Leadership

Charismatic leadership goes beyond transactional leadership techniques. Charisma has been referred to as "a fire that ignites followers' energy and commitment, producing results above and beyond the call of duty."[43] The **charismatic leader** has the ability to inspire and motivate people to do more than they would normally do, despite obstacles and personal sacrifice. Followers transcend their own self-interests for the sake of the team, department, or organization. The impact of charismatic leaders is normally from (1) stating a lofty vision of an imagined future that

transactional leader A leader who clarifies subordinates' role and task requirements, initiates structure, provides rewards, and displays consideration for subordinates.

charismatic leader A leader who has the ability to motivate subordinates to transcend their expected performance.

employees identify with, (2) shaping a corporate value system for which everyone stands, and (3) trusting subordinates and earning their complete trust in return.[44] Charismatic leaders tend to be less predictable than transactional leaders. They create an atmosphere of change, and they may be obsessed by visionary ideas that excite, stimulate, and drive other people to work hard.

Charismatic leaders are often skilled in the art of *visionary leadership*. A **vision** is an attractive, ideal future that is credible yet not readily attainable. Vision is an important component of both charismatic and transformational leadership. Visionary leaders speak to the hearts of employees, letting them be part of something bigger than themselves. Where others see obstacles or failures, they see possibility and hope. Bill Strickland, who built a center of hope in a crumbling Pittsburgh area neighborhood, is the epitome of a visionary and charismatic leader.

Manchester Bidwell

Bill Strickland was a rootless teenager about to flunk out of high school when he met a special teacher, Frank Ross, who changed his life by turning him on to the power of art and music. When Ross took the 16-year-old to see Fallingwater, the famous Frank Lloyd Wright-designed house that has a creek running through the middle of it, Strickland's life changed forever. "It was a very interesting way of looking at water," Strickland tells people now, "and a very interesting way of looking at light. I said to myself, if I could ever bring that light to my neighborhood. . . . I thought, before I die, I am going to build that kind of place in Manchester."

Thus were planted the seeds of a vision that eventually turned into Manchester Bidwell, a nonprofit corporation that is a center of light in the crumbling Pittsburgh area community of Manchester, Pennsylvania. One division, the Manchester Craftsman's Guild, is a bright, clean, attractive center that provides after-school and summer programs in ceramics, photography, digital imaging, drawing, and painting to mostly at-risk middle and high school kids. Under the same gracefully-designed roof is the Bidwell Training Center, which gives low-income adults training in fields such as culinary arts, horticultural technology, and medical coding, placing about 90 percent of students in full-time jobs with area employers such as Bayer, Heinz, and the Pittsburgh Medical Center.

The way Strickland built Machester-Bidwell's state-of-the-art greenhouse is a lesson in the power of vision. Rep. Melissa Hart, a U.S. congresswoman from Pennsylvania recalls: "Ten years ago, he and I stood together in this bombed-out industrial area, and Bill was saying, 'This is where we're going to have the irrigation system, and this is going to be the computerized control room, and we're going to sell our orchids to [supermarket chain] Giant Eagle.' I said, Sure, uh-huh, Bill. But he actually saw that greenhouse standing in that bombed-out field. He was absolutely convinced it was a done deal." Giant Eagle helped finance the construction of the greenhouse and now buys top-grade orchids cultivated by Bidwell students, with all the revenue plowed back into training programs.

By spreading his vision of hope, Strickland established smaller Manchester Bidwell centers in San Francisco, Cincinnati, and Grand Rapids, Michigan. His long-term goal is to open 25 more such centers in inner-city neighborhoods around the country. Strickland isn't shy about admitting that he's out to save the world. Practically every member of every audience he speaks to hears the passion in his voice and wants to help make that vision a reality.[45]

An associate of Bill Strickland's said his power is that he doesn't just overcome obstacles, he refuses to even recognize them. Leaders like Bill Strickland see beyond current realities and problems and help followers believe in a brighter future as well.

Charismatic leaders typically have a strong vision for the future, almost an obsession, and they can motivate others to help realize it.[46] These leaders have an emotional impact on subordinates because they strongly believe in the vision and can communicate it to others in a way that makes the vision real, personal, and meaningful. Charismatic and transformational leaders are passionate about a vision. This chapter's Manager's Shoptalk provides a short quiz to help you determine whether you have the potential to be a charismatic leader.

vision An attractive, ideal future that is credible yet not readily attainable.

ARE YOU A CHARISMATIC LEADER?

If you were the head of a major department in a corporation, how important would each of the following activities be to you? Answer yes or no to indicate whether you would strive to perform each activity.

1. Help subordinates clarify goals and how to reach them.
2. Give people a sense of mission and overall purpose.
3. Help get jobs out on time.
4. Look for the new product or service opportunities.
5. Use policies and procedures as guides for problem solving.
6. Promote unconventional beliefs and values.
7. Give monetary rewards in exchange for high performance from subordinates.
8. Command respect from everyone in the department.
9. Work alone to accomplish important tasks.
10. Suggest new and unique ways of doing things.
11. Give credit to people who do their jobs well.
12. Inspire loyalty to yourself and to the organization.
13. Establish procedures to help the department operate smoothly.
14. Use ideas to motivate others.
15. Set reasonable limits on new approaches.
16. Demonstrate social nonconformity.

The even-numbered items represent behaviors and activities of charismatic leaders. Charismatic leaders are personally involved in shaping ideas, goals, and direction of change. They use an intuitive approach to develop fresh ideas for old problems and seek new directions for the department or organization. The odd-numbered items are considered more traditional management activities, or what would be called *transactional leadership*. Managers respond to organizational problems in an impersonal way, make rational decisions, and coordinate and facilitate the work of others. If you answered yes to more even-numbered than odd-numbered items, you may be a potential charismatic leader.

SOURCES: Based on "Have You Got It?" a quiz that appeared in Patricia Sellers, "What Exactly Is Charisma?" *Fortune* (January 15, 1996): 68–75; Bernard M. Bass, *Leadership and Performance Beyond Expectations* (New York: Free Press, 1985); and Lawton R. Burns and Selwyn W. Becker, "Leadership and Managership," in S. Shortell and A. Kaluzny (eds.), *Health Care Management* (New York: Wiley, 1986).

Charismatic leaders include Mother Theresa, Adolf Hitler, Sam Walton, Alexander the Great, Ronald Reagan, David Koresh, Martin Luther King Jr., and Osama bin Laden. Charisma can be used for positive outcomes that benefit the group, but it can also be used for self-serving purposes that lead to deception, manipulation, and exploitation of others. When charismatic leaders respond to organizational problems in terms of the needs of the entire group rather than their own emotional needs, they can have a powerful, positive influence on organizational performance.[47]

Transformational Leaders

Transformational leaders are similar to charismatic leaders, but are distinguished by their special ability to bring about innovation and change by recognizing followers' needs and concerns, helping them look at old problems in new ways, and encouraging them to question the status quo. Transformational leaders inspire followers not just to believe in the leader personally, but to believe in their own potential to imagine and create a better future for the organization. Transformational leaders create significant change in both followers and the organization.[48] They have the ability to lead changes in the organization's mission, strategy, structure, and culture, as well as to promote innovation in products and technologies. Transformational

transformational leader A leader distinguished by a special ability to bring about innovation and change.

CONCEPT CONNECTION UPS employees joke that when Mike Eskew became CEO, he'd only worked for the company for 30 years. This bit of office humor reflects UPS's long-standing promote-from-within approach to management development. Most UPS managers gain **expert power** by working their way up from the bottom. For example, when Eskew arrived as a young industrial engineer, his first assignment was to re-draw a parking lot so it could accommodate more trucks. Today, he's using his thorough understanding of the business to help move the $43 billion company from package delivery into global supply chain management.

leaders do not rely solely on tangible rules and incentives to control specific transactions with followers. They focus on intangible qualities such as vision, shared values, and ideas to build relationships, give larger meaning to diverse activities, and find common ground to enlist followers in the change process.[49]

A recent study confirmed that transformational leadership has a positive impact on follower development and follower performance. Moreover, transformational leadership skills can be learned and are not ingrained personality characteristics.[50] However, some personality traits may make it easier for a leader to display transformational leadership behaviors. For example, studies of transformational leadership have found that the trait of agreeableness, as discussed in the previous chapter, is positively associated with transformational leaders.[51] In addition, transformational leaders are typically emotionally stable and positively engaged with the world around them, and they have a strong ability to recognize and understand others' emotions.[52] These characteristics are not surprising considering that these leaders accomplish change by building networks of positive relationships.

Richard Kovacevich, who steered midsized Norwest Corp. (now Wells Fargo & Co.) through numerous acquisitions to make it one of the largest and most powerful banking companies in the United States, is an excellent example of a transformational leader.

Kovacevich's leadership style puts accountability for success in the hands of each and every employee. He leads with slogans such as, "Mind share plus heart share equals market share." Although some people might think it sounds hokey, Kovacevich and his employees don't care. It is the substance behind the slogans that matters. Kovacevich believes it's not what employees know that is important, but whether they care. Employees are rewarded for putting both their hearts and minds into their work. Kovacevich spends a lot of time out in the field, meeting employees, patting backs, and giving pep talks. He likes to personally remind people on the front lines that they are the heart and soul of Wells Fargo, and that only through their efforts can the company succeed.[53]

POWER AND INFLUENCE

Recall our definition of leadership, which is the ability to influence people to achieve goals. Particularly for leaders involved in major change initiatives, the effective and appropriate use of power is crucial. One way to understand how leaders get things done is to look at the sources of leader power and the interpersonal influence tactics leaders use.

Power is the potential ability to influence the behavior of others.[54] Sometimes the terms *power* and *influence* are used synonymously, but the two are distinct in important ways. Basically, **influence** is the effect a person's actions have on the attitudes, values, beliefs, or behavior of others. Whereas power is the capacity to cause a change in a person, influence may be thought of as the degree of actual change.

Power results from an interaction of leader and followers. Some power comes from an individual's position in the organization. Power may also come from personal sources that are not as invested in the organization, such as a leader's personal interests, goals, and values. Within organizations, five sources of power are typical: legitimate, reward, coercive, expert, and referent.

power The potential ability to influence others' behavior.

influence The effect a person's actions have on the attitudes, values, beliefs, or behavior of others.

Position Power

The traditional manager's power comes from the organization. The manager's position gives him or her the power to reward or punish subordinates in order to influence their behavior. Legitimate power, reward power, and coercive power are all forms of position power used by managers to change employee behavior.

LEGITIMATE POWER

Power coming from a formal management position in an organization and the authority granted to it is called **legitimate power**. Once a person has been selected as a supervisor, most workers understand that they are obligated to follow his or her direction with respect to work activities. Subordinates accept this source of power as legitimate, which is why they comply.

REWARD POWER

Another kind of power, **reward power**, stems from the authority to bestow rewards on other people. Managers may have access to formal rewards, such as pay increases or promotions. They also have at their disposal such rewards as praise, attention, and recognition. Managers can use rewards to influence subordinates' behavior.

COERCIVE POWER

The opposite of reward power is **coercive power**: It refers to the authority to punish or recommend punishment. Managers have coercive power when they have the right to fire or demote employees, criticize, or withdraw pay increases. For example, if Sanjay, a salesperson, does not perform as expected, his supervisor has the coercive power to criticize him, reprimand him, put a negative letter in his file, and hurt his chance for a raise.

Personal Power

In contrast to the external sources of position power, personal power most often comes from internal sources, such as a person's special knowledge or personal characteristics.

A good example of personal power is Charles Firneno, math teacher and football coach at Benjamin Franklin High School in New Orleans. After the school was devastated by Hurricane Katrina in 2005 and no one could get through to inspect the damage, Firneno took it upon himself to get things rolling. A former U.S. Marine helicopter pilot, Firneno put on his uniform and convinced National Guardsmen to let him through. Firneno laid out a plan for fixing the building and began mobilizing people to help. Although before the flood, Firneno had been held in rather low esteem by his faculty colleagues with more advanced degrees, his commitment, knowledge, skills, and ability to mobilize people in a crisis quickly won the support and respect of teachers, parents, and community volunteers. Soon, Firneno was handed an extra set of keys to the building and the principal's authorization to spend school funds as he saw fit, helping to get the school open in record time.[55] Firneno's power came from his special knowledge and skills and from his personal commitment to the school, rather than from a formal position of authority.

Personal power is the primary tool of the leader, and it is becoming increasingly important as more businesses are run by teams of workers who are less tolerant of authoritarian management.[56] Two types of personal power are expert power and referent power.

EXPERT POWER

Power resulting from a leader's special knowledge or skill regarding the tasks performed by followers is referred to as **expert power**. When the leader is a true expert, subordinates go along with recommendations because of his or her superior

legitimate power Power that stems from a formal management position in an organization and the authority granted to it.

reward power Power that results from the authority to bestow rewards on other people.

coercive power Power that stems from the authority to punish or recommend punishment.

expert power Power that stems from special knowledge of or skill in the tasks performed by subordinates.

knowledge. Leaders at supervisory levels often have experience in the production process that gains them promotion. At top management levels, however, leaders may lack expert power because subordinates know more about technical details than they do.

REFERENT POWER

The last kind of power, **referent power**, comes from a leader's personal characteristics that command followers' identification, respect, and admiration so they wish to emulate the leader. Referent power does not depend on a formal title or position. When workers admire a supervisor because of the way she deals with them, the influence is based on referent power. Referent power is most visible in the area of charismatic leadership. In social and religious movements, for example, we often see charismatic leaders who emerge and gain a tremendous following based solely on their personal power.

■ TAKE A MOMENT | As a new manager, you may not have a lot of position power. Build your personal power by strengthening your knowledge and skills and by developing positive relationships. Interpersonal influence tactics will serve you well throughout your career, even as your position power increases.

Interpersonal Influence Tactics

The next question is how leaders use their power to implement decisions and facilitate change. Leaders often use a combination of influence strategies, and people who are perceived as having greater power and influence typically are those who use a wider variety of tactics. One survey of a few hundred leaders identified more than 4,000 different techniques these people used to influence others.[57]

However, these tactics fall into basic categories that rely on understanding the principles that cause people to change their behavior and attitudes. Exhibit 18.9 lists seven principles for asserting influence. Notice that most of these involve the use of personal power rather than relying solely on position power or the use of rewards and punishments.[58]

1. *Use rational persuasion.* The most frequently used influence strategy is to use facts, data, and logical argument to persuade others that a proposed idea, request, or decision is appropriate. Using rational persuasion can often be highly effective, because most people have faith in facts and analysis.[59] Rational persuasion is most successful when a leader has technical knowledge and expertise related to the issue at hand (expert power), although referent power is also used. That is, in addition to facts and figures, people also have to believe in the leader's credibility.

referent power Power that results from characteristics that command subordinates' identification with, respect and admiration for, and desire to emulate the leader.

EXHIBIT 18.9

Seven Interpersonal Influence Tactics for Leaders

1. Use rational persuasion.
2. Make people like you.
3. Rely on the rule of reciprocity.
4. Develop allies.
5. Be assertive—ask for what you want.
6. Make use of higher authority.
7. Reward the behaviors you want.

2. *Make people like you.* Recall our discussion of *likeability* from the previous chapter. People would rather say yes to someone they like than to someone they don't. Effective leaders strive to create goodwill and favorable impressions. When a leader shows consideration and respect, treats people fairly, and demonstrates trust in others, people are more likely to want to help and support the leader by doing what he or she asks. In addition, most people like a leader who makes them feel good about themselves, so leaders should never underestimate the power of praise.

3. *Rely on the rule of reciprocity.* Leaders can influence others through the exchange of benefits and favors. Leaders share what they have—whether it be time, resources, services, or emotional support. The feeling among people is nearly universal that others should be paid back for what they do, in one form or another. This unwritten "rule of reciprocity" means that leaders who do favors for others can expect that others will do favors for them in return.[60]

4. *Develop allies.* Effective leaders develop networks of allies, people who can help the leader accomplish his or her goals. Leaders talk with followers and others outside of formal meetings to understand their needs and concerns as well as to explain problems and describe the leader's point of view. They strive to reach a meeting of minds with others about the best approach to a problem or decision.[61]

5. *Ask for what you want.* Another way to influence others is to make a direct and personal request. Leaders have to be explicit about what they want, or they aren't likely to get it. An explicit proposal is sometimes accepted simply because others have no better alternative. Also, a clear proposal or alternative will often receive support if other options are less well-defined.

6. *Make use of higher authority.* Sometimes to get things done leaders have to use their formal authority, as well as gain the support of people at higher levels to back them up. However, research has found that the key to successful use of formal authority is to be knowledgeable, credible, and trustworthy—that is, to demonstrate expert and referent power as well as legitimate power. Managers who become known for their expertise, who are honest and straightforward with others, and who inspire trust can exert greater influence than those who simply issue orders.[62]

7. *Reward the behaviors you want.* Leaders can also use organizational rewards and punishments to influence others' behavior. The use of punishment in organizations is controversial, but negative consequences almost always occur for inappropriate or undesirable behavior. Leaders should not rely solely on reward and punishment as a means for influencing others, but combined with other tactics that involve the use of personal power, rewards can be highly effective. At General Electric, for example, CEO Jeff Immelt is having success in shifting managers' behavior by using rewards for managers who demonstrate an ability to come up with innovative ideas and improve customer service and satisfaction.[63]

Research indicates that people rate leaders as "more effective" when they are perceived to use a variety of influence tactics. But not all managers use influence in the same way. Studies have found that leaders in human resources, for example, tend to use softer, more subtle approaches such as building goodwill, using favors, and developing allies, whereas those in finance are inclined to use harder, more direct tactics such as formal authority and assertiveness.[64]

ENDURING LEADERSHIP APPROACHES

To close our chapter, let's look at two timeless leadership approaches that are gaining renewed attention in today's environment of ethical scandals and weakened employee trust. Characteristics of servant leadership and moral leadership can be successfully used by leaders in all situations to make a positive difference.

Servant Leadership

Some leaders operate from the assumption that work exists for the development of the worker as much as the worker exists to do the work.[65] For example, a young David Packard, who cofounded Hewlett-Packard, made a spectacle of himself in 1949 by standing up in a roomful of business leaders and arguing that companies had a responsibility to recognize the dignity and worth of their employees and share the wealth with those who helped to create it.[66]

The concept of servant leadership, first described by Robert Greenleaf, is leadership upside down, because leaders transcend self-interest to serve others and the organization.[67] **Servant leaders** operate on two levels: for the fulfillment of their subordinates' goals and needs and for the realization of the larger purpose or mission of their organization. Servant leaders give things away—power, ideas, information, recognition, credit for accomplishments, even money. Harry Stine, founder of Stine Seed Company in Adel, Iowa, casually announced to his employees at the company's annual post-harvest luncheon that they would each receive $1,000 for each year they had worked at the company. For some loyal workers, that amounted to a $20,000 bonus.[68] Servant leaders truly value other people. They are trustworthy and they trust others. They encourage participation, share power, enhance others' self-worth, and unleash people's creativity, full commitment, and natural impulse to learn and contribute. Servant leaders can bring their followers' higher motives to the work and connect their hearts to the organizational mission and goals.

Servant leaders often work in the nonprofit world because it offers a natural way to apply their leadership drive and skills to serve others. But servant leaders also succeed in business. George Merck believed the purpose of a corporation was to do something useful. At Merck & Co., he insisted that people always come before profits. By insisting on serving people rather than profits, Merck shaped a company that averaged 15 percent earnings growth for an amazing 75 years.[69]

Moral Leadership

Another enduring issue in leadership is its moral component. Because leadership can be used for good or evil, to help or to harm others, all leadership has a moral component. Leaders carry a tremendous responsibility to use their power wisely and ethically. Sadly, in recent years, too many have chosen to act from self-interest and greed rather than behaving in ways that serve and uplift others. The disheartening ethical climate in American business has led to a renewed interest in moral leadership. **Moral leadership** is about distinguishing right from wrong and choosing to do right. It means seeking the just, the honest, the good, and the decent behavior in the practice of leadership.[70] Moral leaders remember that business is about values, not just economic performance.

Distinguishing the right thing to do is not always easy, and doing it is sometimes even harder. Leaders are often faced with right-versus-right decisions, in which several responsibilities conflict with one another.[71] Commitments to superiors, for example, may mean a leader feels the need to hide unpleasant news about pending layoffs from followers. Moral leaders strive to find the moral answer or compromise, rather than taking the easy way out. Consider Katherine Graham, the long-time leader of *The Washington Post*, when she was confronted with a decision in 1971 about what to do with the Pentagon Papers, a leaked Defense Department study that showed Nixon administration deceptions about the Vietnam War. Graham admitted she was terrified—she knew she was risking the whole company on the decision, possibly inviting prosecution under the Espionage Act, and jeopardizing thousands of employees' jobs. She decided to go ahead with the story, and reporters Bob Woodward and Carl Bernstein made Watergate—and *The Washington Post*—a household name.[72]

Clearly, moral leadership requires **courage**, the ability to step forward through fear and act on one's values and conscience. Leaders often behave unethically simply because they lack courage. Most people want to be liked, and it is easy to do the

servant leader A leader who works to fulfill subordinates' needs and goals as well as to achieve the organization's larger mission.

moral leadership Distinguishing right from wrong and choosing to do right in the practice of leadership.

courage The ability to step forward through fear and act on one's values and conscience.

wrong thing in order to fit in or impress others. One example might be a leader who holds his tongue in order to "fit in with the guys" when colleagues are telling sexually or racially offensive jokes. Moral leaders summon the fortitude to do the right thing, even if it is unpopular. Standing up for what is right is the primary way in which leaders create an environment of honesty, trust, and integrity in the organization.

MANAGER'S SOLUTION

This chapter covered several important ideas about leadership. The concept of leadership continues to evolve and change with the changing times. Of particular interest in today's turbulent environment is a post-heroic leadership approach. Two significant concepts in line with the post-heroic approach are Level 5 leadership and interactive leadership, which is common among women leaders. Level 5 leaders are characterized by personal humility combined with a strong determination to build a great organization that will thrive beyond the leader's direct influence. Interactive leadership emphasizes relationships and helping others develop to their highest potential, and may be particularly well-suited to today's workplace.

The early research on leadership focused on personal traits such as intelligence, energy, and appearance. Later, research attention shifted to leadership behaviors that are appropriate to the organizational situation. Behavioral approaches dominated the early work in this area; task-oriented behavior and people-oriented behavior were suggested as essential behaviors that lead work groups toward high performance. The Ohio State and Michigan approaches and the managerial grid are in this category. Contingency approaches include Hersey and Blanchard's situational theory, Fiedler's theory, the path–goal model, and the substitutes-for-leadership concept.

Leadership concepts have evolved from the transactional approach to charismatic and transformational leadership behaviors. Charismatic leadership is the ability to articulate a vision and motivate followers to make it a reality. Transformational leadership extends charismatic qualities to guide and foster dramatic organizational change. Leadership involves the use of power to influence others. Five types of power are legitimate, reward, coercive, expert, and referent. Leaders rely more on personal power than position power, and they use a variety of interpersonal influence tactics to implement decisions and accomplish goals. Two enduring leadership approaches are servant leadership and moral leadership. Servant leaders facilitate the growth, goals, and development of others to liberate their best qualities in pursuing the organization's mission. Moral leadership means seeking to do the honest and decent thing in the practice of leadership. Leaders can make a positive difference by applying characteristics of servant and moral leadership.

Returning to our opening example, Roy Pelaez wanted to create an organization where people cared about each other and about the customer and willingly gave their best. To do so meant breaking some "unwritten management rules" about not getting involved with followers' personal problems. Pelaez quickly realized that his subordinates (many of whom were immigrants) had low levels of skill, ability, and confidence, along with tremendous personal needs that consumed much of their attention and motivation. In terms of the theories discussed in the chapter, Pelaez combined a *telling leadership style*, as indicated by the Hersey and Blanchard theory for followers at a low readiness level, with a *supportive leadership approach*, as defined by the path–goal theory. Pelaez had to use a telling style because if he didn't, many of his workers simply didn't know what to do. However, he also knew he needed to be supportive to help build the pride and confidence of employees.

In addition, Pelaez acted as a servant leader by being deeply committed to helping his followers grow and improve in their personal as well as their work lives, such as setting up classes for anyone interested in improving their English language skills. He instituted an Employee of the Month recognition program, which provided a reward beyond a weekly paycheck. Anyone who had perfect attendance over a six-week period or who turned in a purse or wallet with cash and credit cards got a day off. Members of the "Top Crew of the Month" were rewarded with free movie passes, calling cards, or "burger bucks." These forms of recognition and reward were a real boost to workers who had received little attention and appreciation in their lives. The outcome of Pelaez's leadership was a drop in the turnover rate from 100 percent a year to 12 percent a year and an increase in revenue from $5 million to $14 million. Employees began turning in large amounts of money found on planes, returning some 250 wallets with more than $50,000 in cash to passengers who had left them on board. By genuinely caring about his employees, Pelaez tremendously increased his personal power and built a community of highly satisfied and committed employees. According to one observer, Pelaez "created a group of people who will do anything in the world for him."[73]

DISCUSSION QUESTIONS

1. Do you think leadership style is fixed and unchangeable for a leader or flexible and adaptable? Discuss.

2. Suggest some personal traits that you believe would be useful to a business leader today. Are these traits more valuable in some situations than in others?

3. What is the difference between trait theories and behavioral theories of leadership?

4. Suggest the sources of power that would be available to a leader of a student government organization. What sources of power may not be available? To be effective, should student leaders keep power to themselves or delegate power to other students?

5. What skills and abilities does a manager need to lead effectively in a virtual environment? Do you believe a leader with a consideration style or an initiating-structure style would be more successful as a virtual leader? Explain your answer.

6. What is transformational leadership? Give examples of organizational situations that would call for transformational, transactional, or charismatic leadership.

7. How does Level 5 leadership differ from the concept of servant leadership? Do you believe anyone has the potential to become a Level 5 leader? Discuss.

8. Do you think leadership is more important or less important in today's flatter, team-based organizations? Are some leadership styles better suited to such organizations as opposed to traditional hierarchical organizations? Explain.

9. Consider the leadership position of a senior partner in a law firm. What task, subordinate, and organizational factors might serve as substitutes for leadership in this situation?

10. Do you see yourself as having leader qualities or manager qualities? Do you think you will become a better leader/manager by developing the characteristics you already have or by trying to develop the characteristics you don't have? Discuss.

MANAGEMENT IN PRACTICE: EXPERIENTIAL EXERCISE

T–P Leadership Questionnaire: An Assessment of Style

Some leaders deal with general directions, leaving details to subordinates. Other leaders focus on specific details with the expectation that subordinates will carry out orders. Depending on the situation, both approaches may be effective. The important issue is the ability to identify relevant dimensions of the situation and behave accordingly. Through this questionnaire, you can identify your relative emphasis on two dimensions of leadership: task orientation (T) and people orientation (P). These approaches are not opposites; and an individual can rate high or low on either or both.

Directions: The following items describe aspects of leadership behavior. Respond to each item according to the way you would most likely act if you were the leader of a work group. Circle whether you would most likely behave in the described way: always (A), frequently (F), occasionally (O), seldom (S), or never (N).

1. I would most likely act as the   **A F O S N** spokesperson of the group.

2. I would encourage overtime work.   **A F O S N**

3. I would allow members complete freedom in their work. Ⓐ Ⓕ Ⓞ Ⓢ Ⓝ

4. I would encourage the use of uniform procedures. Ⓐ Ⓕ Ⓞ Ⓢ Ⓝ

5. I would permit members to use their own judgment in solving problems. Ⓐ Ⓕ Ⓞ Ⓢ Ⓝ

6. I would stress being ahead of competing groups. Ⓐ Ⓕ Ⓞ Ⓢ Ⓝ

7. I would speak as a representative of the group. Ⓐ Ⓕ Ⓞ Ⓢ Ⓝ

8. I would needle members for greater effort. Ⓐ Ⓕ Ⓞ Ⓢ Ⓝ

9. I would try out my ideas in the group. Ⓐ Ⓕ Ⓞ Ⓢ Ⓝ

10. I would let members do their work the way they think best. Ⓐ Ⓕ Ⓞ Ⓢ Ⓝ

11. I would be working hard for a promotion. Ⓐ Ⓕ Ⓞ Ⓢ Ⓝ

12. I would tolerate postponement and uncertainty. Ⓐ Ⓕ Ⓞ Ⓢ Ⓝ

13. I would speak for the group if visitors were present. Ⓐ Ⓕ Ⓞ Ⓢ Ⓝ

14. I would keep the work moving at a rapid pace. Ⓐ Ⓕ Ⓞ Ⓢ Ⓝ

15. I would turn the members loose on a job and let them go to it. Ⓐ Ⓕ Ⓞ Ⓢ Ⓝ

16. I would settle conflicts when they occur in the group. Ⓐ Ⓕ Ⓞ Ⓢ Ⓝ

17. I would get swamped by details. Ⓐ Ⓕ Ⓞ Ⓢ Ⓝ

18. I would represent the group at outside meetings. Ⓐ Ⓕ Ⓞ Ⓢ Ⓝ

19. I would be reluctant to allow the members any freedom of action. Ⓐ Ⓕ Ⓞ Ⓢ Ⓝ

20. I would decide what should be done and how it should be done. Ⓐ Ⓕ Ⓞ Ⓢ Ⓝ

21. I would push for increased production. Ⓐ Ⓕ Ⓞ Ⓢ Ⓝ

22. I would let some members have authority that I could keep. Ⓐ Ⓕ Ⓞ Ⓢ Ⓝ

23. Things would usually turn out as I had predicted. Ⓐ Ⓕ Ⓞ Ⓢ Ⓝ

24. I would allow the group a high degree of initiative. Ⓐ Ⓕ Ⓞ Ⓢ Ⓝ

25. I would assign group members to particular tasks. Ⓐ Ⓕ Ⓞ Ⓢ Ⓝ

26. I would be willing to make changes. Ⓐ Ⓕ Ⓞ Ⓢ Ⓝ

27. I would ask the members to work harder. Ⓐ Ⓕ Ⓞ Ⓢ Ⓝ

28. I would trust the group members to exercise good judgment. Ⓐ Ⓕ Ⓞ Ⓢ Ⓝ

29. I would schedule the work to be done. Ⓐ Ⓕ Ⓞ Ⓢ Ⓝ

30. I would refuse to explain my actions. Ⓐ Ⓕ Ⓞ Ⓢ Ⓝ

31. I would persuade others that my ideas are to their advantage. Ⓐ Ⓕ Ⓞ Ⓢ Ⓝ

32. I would permit the group to set its own pace. Ⓐ Ⓕ Ⓞ Ⓢ Ⓝ

33. I would urge the group to beat its previous record. Ⓐ Ⓕ Ⓞ Ⓢ Ⓝ

34. I would act without consulting the group. Ⓐ Ⓕ Ⓞ Ⓢ Ⓝ

35. I would ask that group members follow standard rules and regulations. Ⓐ Ⓕ Ⓞ Ⓢ Ⓝ

T_____ P_____

Scoring and Interpretation

The T–P Leadership Questionnaire is scored as follows:

a. Circle the statements numbered 8, 12, 17, 18, 19, 30, 34, and 35.

b. Write the number 1 in front of the circled number if you responded S (seldom) or N (never) to that statement.

c. Also write a number 1 in front of the statement numbers not circled if you responded A (always) or F (frequently).

d. Circle the number 1s that you have written in front of the following statements: 3, 5, 8, 10, 15, 18, 19, 22, 24, 26, 28, 30, 32, 34, and 35.

e. Count the circled number 1s. This total is your score for concern for people. Record the score in the blank following the letter P at the end of the questionnaire.

f. Count uncircled number 1s. This total is your score for concern for task. Record this number in the blank following the letter T.

SOURCE: The T–P Leadership Questionnaire was adapted by J. B. Ritchie and P. Thompson in *Organization and People* (New York: West, 1984). Copyright 1969 by the American Educational Research Association. Adapted by permission of the publisher.

MANAGEMENT IN PRACTICE: ETHICAL DILEMMA

Too Much of a Good Thing?

Not long ago, Jessica Armstrong, vice president of administration for Delaware Valley Chemical Inc., a New Jersey-based multinational company, made a point of stopping by department head Darius Harris's office and lavishly praising him for his volunteer work with an after-school program for disadvantaged children in a nearby urban neighborhood. Now she was about to summon him to her office so she could take him to task for dedication to the same volunteer work.

It was Carolyn Clark, Harris's secretary, who'd alerted her to the problem. "Darius told the community center he'd take responsibility for a fundraising mass mailing. And then he asked me to edit the letter he'd drafted, make all the copies, stuff the envelopes, and get it into the mail—most of this on my own time," she reported, still obviously indignant. "When I told him, 'I'm sorry, but that's not my job,' he looked me straight in the eye and asked when I'd like to schedule my upcoming performance appraisal."

Several of Harris's subordinates also volunteered with the program. After chatting with them, Armstrong concluded most were volunteering out of a desire to stay on the boss's good side. It was time to talk to Harris.

"Oh, come on," responded Harris impatiently when Armstrong confronted him. "Yes, I asked for her help as a personal favor to me. But I only brought up the appraisal because I was going out of town, and we needed to set some time aside to do the evaluation." Harris went on to talk about how important working for the after-school program was to him personally. "I grew up in that neighborhood, and if it hadn't been for the people at the center, I wouldn't be here today," he said. Besides, even if he had pressured employees to help out—and he wasn't saying he had—didn't all the emphasis the company was putting on employee volunteerism make it okay to use employees' time and company resources?

After Harris left, Armstrong thought about the conversation. There was no question Delaware Valley actively encouraged employee volunteerism—and not just because it was the right thing to do. It was a chemical company with a couple of unfortunate accidental spills in its recent past that caused environmental damage and community anger.

Volunteering had the potential to help employees acquire new skills, create a sense of camaraderie, and play a role in recruiting and retaining talented people. But most of all, it gave a badly needed boost to the company's public image. Recently, Delaware Valley took every opportunity to publicize its employees' extracurricular community work on its Web site and in company publications. And the company created the annual Delaware Prize, which granted cash awards ranging from $1,000 to $5,000 to outstanding volunteers.

So now that Armstrong had talked with everyone concerned, just what was she going to do about the dispute between Darius Harris and Carolyn Clark?

What Would You Do?

1. Tell Carolyn Clark that employee volunteerism is important to the company and that while her performance evaluation will not be affected by her decision, she should consider helping Harris because it is an opportunity to help a worthy community project.

2. Tell Darius Harris that the employee volunteer program is just that: a volunteer program. Even though the company sees volunteerism as an important piece of its campaign to repair its tarnished image, employees must be free to choose whether to volunteer. He should not ask for the help of his direct reports with the after-school program.

3. Discipline Darius Harris for coercing his subordinates to spend their own time on his volunteer work at the community after-school program. This action will send a signal that coercing employees is a clear violation of leadership authority.

CASE FOR CRITICAL ANALYSIS

Mountain West Health Plans Inc.

"Be careful what you wish for," thought Martin Quinn, senior vice president for service and operations for the Denver-based health insurance company, Mountain West Health Plans, Inc. When there was an opening for a new director of customer service last year due to Evelyn Gustafson's retirement, he'd seen it as the perfect opportunity to bring someone in to control the ever-increasing costs of the labor-intensive department. He'd been certain he had found just the person in Erik Rasmussen, a young man in his late twenties with a shiny new bachelor's degree in business administration.

A tall, unflappable woman, Evelyn Gustafson consistently showed warmth and concern toward her mostly female, non-unionized employees as they sat in their noisy cubicles, fielding call after call about Mountain West's products, benefits, eligibility, and claims. Because she had worked her way up from a customer service representative position herself, she could look her subordinates right in the eye after they'd fielded a string of stressful calls and tell them she knew exactly how they felt. She did her best to offset the low pay by accommodating the women's needs with flexible scheduling, giving them frequent breaks, and offering plenty of training opportunities that kept them up-to-date in the health company's changing products and in the latest problem-solving and customer service techniques.

Her motto was: "Always put yourself in the subscriber's shoes." She urged representatives to take the time necessary to thoroughly understand the subscriber's problem and do their best to see that it was completely resolved by the call's completion. Their job was important, she told them. Subscribers counted on them to help them negotiate the often Byzantine complexities of their coverage. Evelyn's subordinates adored her, as demonstrated by the 10 percent turnover rate, compared to the typical 25 to 45 percent rate for customer service representatives. Mountain West subscribers were generally satisfied, although Quinn did hear some occasional grumbling about the length of time customers spent on hold.

However, whatever her virtues, Gustafson firmly resisted all attempts to increase efficiency and lower costs in a department where salaries accounted for close to 70 percent of the budget. That's where Erik Rasmussen came in. Upper-level management charged him with the task of bringing costs under control. Eager to do well in his first management position, the hard-working, no-nonsense young man made increasing the number of calls per hour each representative handled a priority. For the first time ever, the company measured the representatives' performance against statistical standards that emphasized speed, recorded the customer service calls, and used software that generated automated work schedules based on historical information and projected need. Efficient, not flexible, scheduling was the goal. In addition, the company cut back on training.

The results, Martin Quinn had to admit, were mixed. With more efficient scheduling and clear performance standards in place, calls per hour increased dramatically, and subscribers spent far less time on hold. The department's costs were finally heading downwards, but department morale was spiraling downwards as well, with the turnover rate currently at 30 percent and climbing. And Quinn was beginning to hear more complaints from subscribers who'd received inaccurate information from inexperienced or representatives who sounded rushed.

It was time for Rasmussen's first performance review. Quinn knew the young manager was about to walk into his office ready to proudly recite the facts and figures that documented the department's increased efficiency. What kind of an evaluation was he going to give Rasmussen? Should he recommend some mid-course corrections?

Questions

1. How would you describe Evelyn Gustafson's leadership style? What were its strengths and weaknesses? What were the sources of her influence?

2. How would you describe Erik Rasmussen's leadership style as he tried to effect change? What are its strengths and weaknesses? What are the sources of his influence?

3. If you were Martin Quinn, would you recommend modifications in Erik Rasmussen's leadership style that you would like him to adopt? Do you think it will be possible for Rasmussen to make the necessary changes? If not, why not? If you do think change is possible, how would you recommend the desired changes be facilitated?

SOURCES: Based on Gary Yukl, *Leadership in Organizations,* 4th ed. (Englewood Cliffs, NJ: Prentice Hall, 1998): 66–67; and "Telephone Call Centers: The Factory Floors of the 21st Century," *Knowledge @ Wharton* (April 10, 2002): http://knowledge.wharton.upenn.edu/index.cfm?fa=viewArticle&ID=540.

ENDNOTES

1. John A. Bryne, "How to Lead Now: Getting Extraordinary Performance When You Can't Pay For It," *Fast Company* (August 2003): 62–70.

2. Leigh Buchanan, "Pat McGovern . . . For Knowing the Power of Respect," segment in "25 Entrepreneurs We Love," *Inc Magazine* (April 2004): 110–147; Melanie Warner, "Confessions of a Control Freak," *Fortune* (September 4, 2000): 130–140.

3. Greg Jaffe, "Change of Command; A Marine Captain Trains Iraqi Colonel to Take Over Fight," *The Wall Street Journal* (February 24, 2005): A1, A6; and Jackie Spinner, "Training a New Army from the Top Down; U.S. Military Struggles to 'Build Leaders,'" *Washington Post* (November 1, 2005): A19.

4. Kevin Kelleher, "How To . . . Spot Great Chief Executives," *Business 2.0* (April 2005): 42.

5. Gary Yukl, "Managerial Leadership: A Review of Theory and Research," *Journal of Management* 15 (1989): 251–289.

6. James M. Kouzes and Barry Z. Posner, "The Credibility Factor: What Followers Expect from Their Leaders," *Management Review* (January 1990): 29–33.

7. Joseph L. Badaracco, Jr. "A Lesson for the Times: Learning From Quiet Leaders," *Ivey Business Journal* (January–February 2003): 1–6; and Matthew Gwyther, "Back to the Wall," *Management Today* (February 2003): 58–61.

8. See J. Andrew Morris, Céleste M. Brotheridge, and John C. Urbanski, "Bringing Humility to Leadership: Antecedents and Consequences of Leader Humility," *Human Relations* 58, no. 10 (2005): 1323–1350; Linda Tischler, "The CEO's New Clothes," *Fast Company* (September 2005): 27–28; James C. Collins, *From Good to Great: Why Some Companies Make the Leap . . . And Others Don't* (New York: HarperCollins 2001); Charles A. O'Reilly III and Jeffrey Pfeffer, *Hidden Value: How Great Companies Achieve Extraordinary Results with Ordinary People* (Boston, MA: Harvard Business School Press, 2000); Rakesh Khurana, "The Curse of the Superstar CEO," *Harvard Business Review* (September 2002): 60–66, excerpted from his book, *Searching for a Corporate Savior: The Irrational Quest for Charismatic CEOs* (Princeton University Press, 2002); and Joseph Badaracco, *Leading Quietly* (Boston, MA: Harvard Business School Press, 2002).

9. Jim Collins, "Level 5 Leadership: The Triumph of Humility and Fierce Resolve," *Harvard Business Review* (January 2001): 67–76; Collins, "Good to Great," *Fast Company* (October 2001): 90–104; A. J. Vogl, "Onward and Upward" (an interview with Jim Collins), *Across the Board* (September–October 2001): 29–34; and Jerry Useem, "Conquering Vertical Limits," *Fortune* (February 19, 2001): 84–96.

10. Collins, "Level 5 Leadership."

11. Alice H. Eagly and Linda L. Carli, "The Female Leadership Advantage: An Evaluation of the Evidence," *The Leadership Quarterly* 14 (2003): 807–834; Judy B. Rosener, *America's Competitive Secret: Utilizing Women as a Management Strategy* (New York: Oxford University Press, 1995); Rosener, "Ways Women Lead," *Harvard Business Review* (November–December 1990): 119–125; Sally Helgesen, *The Female Advantage: Women's Ways of Leadership* (New York: Currency/Doubleday, 1990); and Bernard M. Bass and Bruce J. Avolio, "Shatter the Glass Ceiling: Women May Make Better Managers," *Human Resource Management* 33, no. 4 (Winter 1994): 549–560.

12. Rochelle Sharpe, "As Leaders, Women Rule," *BusinessWeek* (November 20, 2000): 75–84.

13. Rosener, *America's Competitive Secret*, 129–135.

14. Sharpe, "As Leaders, Women Rule."

15. Alan Deutschman, "What I Know Now" (interview with Terri Kelly), *Fast Company* (September 2005): 96.

16. James E. Colvard, "Managers Vs. Leaders," *Government Executive* 35, no. 9 (July 2003): 82–84.

17. Richard L. Daft, *The Leadership Experience*, 3rd ed. (Cincinnati, OH: South-Western, 2005): 15–22.

18. G. A. Yukl, *Leadership in Organizations* (Englewood Cliffs, NJ: Prentice Hall, 1981); and S. C. Kohs and K. W. Irle, "Prophesying Army Promotion," *Journal of Applied Psychology* 4 (1920): 73–87.

19. R. Albanese and D. D. Van Fleet, *Organizational Behavior: A Managerial Viewpoint* (Hinsdale, IL: The Dryden Press, 1983).

20. Gary Yukl, Angela Gordon, and Tom Taber, "A Hierarchical Taxonomy of Leadership Behavior: Integrating a Half Century of Behavior Research," *Journal of Leadership and Organizational Studies* 9, no. 1 (2002): 13–32.

21. C. A. Schriesheim and B. J. Bird, "Contributions of the Ohio State Studies to the Field of Leadership," *Journal of Management* 5 (1979): 135–145; and C. L. Shartle, "Early Years of the Ohio State University Leadership Studies," *Journal of Management* 5 (1979): 126–134.

22. Joseph Weber, "Waging War on Hunger," *BusinessWeek* (May 16, 2005): 94, 96.

23. Patrick J. Sauer, "Are You Ready for Some Football Clichés?" *Inc.* (October 2003): 96–99.

24. P. C. Nystrom, "Managers and the High-High Leader Myth," *Academy of Management Journal* 21 (1978): 325–331; and L. L. Larson, J. G. Hunt, and Richard N. Osborn, "The Great High-High Leader Behavior Myth: A Lesson from Occam's Razor," *Academy of Management Journal* 19 (1976): 628–641.

25. R. Likert, "From Production- and Employee-Centeredness to Systems 1–4," *Journal of Management* 5 (1979): 147–156.

26. Robert R. Blake and Jane S. Mouton, *The Managerial Grid III* (Houston: Gulf, 1985).

27. Jo Napolitano, "No, She Doesn't Breathe Fire," *The New York Times* (September 1, 2002): Section 3, 2; Katharine Mieszkowski, "Changing Tires, Changing the World," *Fast Company* (October 1999): 58–60.

28. Paul Hersey and Kenneth H. Blanchard, *Management of Organizational Behavior: Utilizing Human Resources*, 4th ed. (Englewood Cliffs, NJ: Prentice Hall, 1982).

29. Robert Tomsho and John Hechinger, "Crimson Blues; Harvard Clash Pits Brusque Leader Against Faculty," *The Wall Street Journal* (February 18, 2005): A1, A8; and Ruth R. Wisse, "Cross Country; Coup d"Ecole," *The Wall Street Journal* (February 23, 2006): A17.

30. Fred E. Fiedler, "Assumed Similarity Measures as Predictors of Team Effectiveness," *Journal of Abnormal and Social Psychology* 49 (1954): 381–388; F. E. Fiedler, *Leader Attitudes and Group Effectiveness* (Urbana, Ill.: University of Illinois Press, 1958); and F. E. Fiedler, *A Theory of Leadership Effectiveness* (New York: McGraw-Hill, 1967).

31. Fred E. Fiedler and M. M. Chemers, *Leadership and Effective Management* (Glenview, IL: Scott, Foresman, 1974).

32. Fred E. Fiedler, "Engineer the Job to Fit the Manager," *Harvard Business Review* 43 (1965): 115–122; and F. E. Fiedler, M. M. Chemers, and L. Mahar, *Improving Leadership Effectiveness: The Leader Match Concept* (New York: Wiley, 1976).

33. R. Singh, "Leadership Style and Reward Allocation: Does Least Preferred Coworker Scale Measure Tasks and Relation Orientation?" *Organizational Behavior and Human Performance* 27 (1983): 178–197; and D. Hosking, "A Critical Evaluation of Fiedler's Contingency Hypotheses," *Progress in Applied Psychology* 1 (1981): 103–154.

34. M. G. Evans, "The Effects of Supervisory Behavior on the Path–Goal Relationship," *Organizational Behavior and Human Performance* 5 (1970): 277–298; M. G. Evans, "Leadership and Motivation: A Core Concept," *Academy of Management Journal* 13 (1970): 91–102; and B. S. Georgopoulos, G. M. Mahoney, and N. W. Jones, "A Path–Goal Approach to Productivity," *Journal of Applied Psychology* 41 (1957): 345–353.

35. Robert J. House, "A Path–Goal Theory of Leader Effectiveness," *Administrative Science Quarterly* 16 (1971): 321–338.

36. M. G. Evans, "Leadership," in *Organizational Behavior*, ed. S. Kerr (Columbus, OH: Grid, 1974): 230–233.

37. Robert J. House and Terrence R. Mitchell, "Path–Goal Theory of Leadership," *Journal of Contemporary Business* (Autumn 1974): 81–97.

38. Jennifer Reingold, "Bob Nardelli Is Watching," *Fast Company* (December 2005): 76–83.

39. Charles Greene, "Questions of Causation in the Path–Goal Theory of Leadership," *Academy of Management Journal* 22 (March 1979): 22–41; and C. A. Schriesheim and Mary Ann von Glinow, "The Path–Goal Theory of Leadership: A Theoretical and Empirical Analysis," *Academy of Management Journal* 20 (1977): 398–405.

40. S. Kerr and J. M. Jermier, "Substitutes for Leadership: Their Meaning and Measurement," *Organizational Behavior and Human Performance* 22 (1978): 375–403; and Jon P. Howell and Peter W. Dorfman, "Leadership and Substitutes for Leadership among Professional and Nonprofessional Workers," *Journal of Applied Behavioral Science* 22 (1986): 29–46.

41. Anthony J. Mayo and Nitin Nohria, "Double Edged Sword," *People Management* (October 27, 2005).

42. The terms *transactional* and *transformational* come from James M. Burns, *Leadership* (New York: Harper & Row, 1978); and Bernard M. Bass, "Leadership: Good, Better, Best," *Organizational Dynamics* 13 (Winter 1985): 26–40.

43. Katherine J. Klein and Robert J. House, "On Fire: Charismatic Leadership and Levels of Analysis," *Leadership Quarterly* 6, no. 2 (1995): 183–198.

44. Jay A. Conger and Rabindra N. Kanungo, "Toward a Behavioral Theory of Charismatic Leadership in Organizational Settings," *Academy of Management Review* 12 (1987): 637–647; Walter Kiechel III, "A Hard Look at Executive Vision," *Fortune* (October 23, 1989): 207–211; and William L. Gardner and Bruce J. Avolio, "The Charismatic Relationship: A Dramaturgical Perspective," *Academy of Management Review* 23, no. 1 (1998): 32–58.

45. John Brant, "What One Man Can Do," *Inc.* (September 2005): 145–153.

46. Robert J. House, "Research Contrasting the Behavior and Effects of Reputed Charismatic vs. Reputed Non-Charismatic Leaders" (paper presented as part of a symposium, "Charismatic Leadership: Theory and Evidence," Academy of Management, San Diego, 1985).

47. Robert J. House and Jane M. Howell, "Personality and Charismatic Leadership," *Leadership Quarterly* 3, no. 2 (1992): 81–108; and Jennifer O'Connor, Michael D. Mumford, Timothy C. Clifton, Theodore L. Gessner, and Mary Shane Connelly, "Charismatic Leaders and Destructiveness: A Historiometric Study," *Leadership Quarterly* 6, no. 4 (1995): 529–555.

48. Bernard M. Bass, "Theory of Transformational Leadership Redux," *Leadership Quarterly* 6, no. 4 (1995): 463–478; Noel M. Tichy and Mary Anne Devanna, *The Transformational Leader* (New York: John Wiley & Sons, 1986); and Badrinarayan Shankar Pawar and Kenneth K. Eastman, "The Nature and Implications of Contextual Influences on Transformational Leadership: A Conceptual Examination," *Academy of Management Review* 22, no. 1 (1997) 80–109.

49. Richard L. Daft and Robert H. Lengel, *Fusion Leadership: Unlocking the Subtle Forces that Change People and Organizations* (San Francisco: Berrett-Koehler, 1998).

50. Taly Dvir, Dov Eden, Bruce J. Avolio, and Boas Shamir, "Impact of Transformational Leadership on Follower Development and Performance: A Field Experiment," *Academy of Management Journal* 45, no. 4 (2002): 735–744.

51. Robert S. Rubin, David C. Munz, and William H. Bommer, "Leading From Within: The Effects of Emotion Recognition and Personality on Transformational Leadership Behavior," *Academy of Management Journal* 48, no 5 (2005): 845–858; and Timothy A. Judge and Joyce E. Bono, "Five-Factor Model of Personality and Transformational Leadership," *Journal of Applied Psychology* 85, no. 5 (October 2000): 751ff.

52. Rubin et al., "Leading from Within."

53. Paul Nadler, "The Litttle Things That Help Make Wells a Giant," *American Banker* (December 10, 2003): 4; John R. Enger, "Cross-Sell Campaign," *Banking Strategies* 77, no. 6 (November–December 2001): 34; Bethany McLean, "Is This Guy the Best Banker in America?" *Fortune* (July 6, 1998): 126–128; and Jacqueline S. Gold, "Bank to the Future," *Institutional Investor* (September 2001): 54–63.

54. Henry Mintzberg, *Power In and Around Organizations* (Englewood Cliffs, NJ: Prentice Hall, 1983); and Jeffrey Pfeffer, *Power in Organizations* (Marshfield, MA: Pitman, 1981).

55. George Anders, "Back to Class; How a Principal in New Orleans Saved Her School," *The Wall Street Journal* (January 13, 2006): A1, A6.

56. Jay A. Conger, "The Necessary Art of Persuasion," *Harvard Business Review* (May–June 1998): 84–95.

57. D. Kipnis, S. M. Schmidt, C. Swaffin-Smith, and I. Wilkinson, "Patterns of Managerial Influence: Shotgun Managers, Tacticians, and Politicians," *Organizational Dynamics* (Winter 1984): 58–67.

58. These tactics are based on Kipnis et al., "Patterns of Managerial Influence"; and Robert B. Cialdini, "Harnessing the Science of Persuasion," *Harvard Business Review* (October 2001): 72–79.

59. Ibid.; and Pfeffer, *Managing with Power: Politics and Influence in Organizations* (Boston: Harvard Business School Press, 1992): Chapter 13.

60. Ibid.

61. V. Dallas Merrell, *Huddling: The Informal Way to Management Success* (New York: AMACOM, 1979).

62. Robert B. Cialdini, *Influence: Science and Practice,* 4th ed. (Boston: Pearson Allyn & Bacon, 2000).

63. Diane Brady, "The Immelt Revolution," *BusinessWeek* (March 28, 2005): 64–71.

64. Harvey G. Enns and Dean B. McFarlin, "When Executives Influence Peers, Does Function Matter?" *Human Resource Management* 4, no. 2 (Summer 2003): 125–142.

65. Daft and Lengel, *Fusion Leadership.*

66. Jim Collins, "The 10 Greatest CEOs of All Time," *Fortune* (July 21, 2003): 54–68.

67. Robert K. Greenleaf, *Servant Leadership: A Journey into the Nature of Legitimate Power and Greatness* (Mahwah, NJ: Paulist Press, 1977).

68. Anne Fitzgerald, "Christmas Bonus Stuns Employees," *The Des Moines Register* (December 20, 2003), http://www.desmoinesregister.com.

69. Collins, "The 10 Greatest CEOs of All Time."

70. Richard L. Daft, *The Leadership Experience*, 3rd ed. (Cincinnati, OH: South-Western, 2005): Chapter 6.

71. Badaracco, "A Lesson for the Times: Learning From Quiet Leaders."

72. Jim Collins, "The 10 Greatest CEOs of All Time."

73. Byrne, "How to Lead Now."

CHAPTER OUTLINE

Manager's Challenge

The Concept of Motivation

Foundations of Motivation

Traditional Approach

Human Relations Approach

Human Resource Approach

Contemporary Approach

Content Perspectives on Motivation

Hierarchy of Needs Theory

ERG Theory

Two-Factor Theory

Acquired Needs Theory

Process Perspectives on Motivation

Equity Theory

Expectancy Theory

Goal-Setting Theory

Reinforcement Perspective on Motivation

Reinforcement Tools

Schedules of Reinforcement

Job Design for Motivation

Job Simplification

Job Rotation

Job Enlargement

Job Enrichment

Job Characteristics Model

Innovative Ideas for Motivating

Empowering People to Meet Higher Needs

Giving Meaning to Work

LEARNING OBJECTIVES

After studying this chapter, you should be able to:

1. Define *motivation* and explain the difference between current approaches and traditional approaches to motivation.

2. Identify and describe content theories of motivation based on employee needs.

3. Identify and explain process theories of motivation.

4. Describe reinforcement theory and how it can be used to motivate employees.

5. Discuss major approaches to job design and how job design influences motivation.

6. Explain how empowerment heightens employee motivation.

7. Describe ways that managers can create a sense of meaning and importance for employees at work.

MOTIVATION

MANAGER'S CHALLENGE

Darrell Owens just got out of the hospital. What put him there, he believes, was staying up three days straight to finish a report that was unexpectedly due for his employer, Best Buy, the nation's largest and highly successful consumer electronics retailer. Owens got a big bonus and a vacation for his extraordinary efforts, but now he's wondering whether it was worth it. Traci Tobias, who manages travel reimbursements, is sneaking out the door in the mornings to avoid the guilt she feels when her young children beg her to stay for breakfast and cry when she can't. She is feeling less commitment to her job as the sacrifices she makes for it seem greater and greater. Jennifer Janssen in finance recently discovered she is pregnant and is considering leaving her job. A manager in the human resources department, Cali Ressler, noticed an alarming trend at Best Buy: increasing turnover, signs of weakening organizational commitment, and more employees, especially women, accepting the reduced pay and prestige of part-time positions because they need more flexibility than a full-time position allows. Best Buy expects a lot from its people, and the company culture has always glorified long hours and personal sacrifice. Like other companies, Best Buy is searching for an edge in an increasingly competitive global environment. If these trends continue, Ressler believes, Best Buy could lose its most valuable asset: the motivation and commitment of its workforce.[1]

> Would this issue concern you if you were a manager at Best Buy? Long hours and hard work are often a part of corporate life. If people are paid good wages and rewarded with bonuses when they put in extra effort, shouldn't managers expect them to remain satisfied, motivated, and productive?

■ **TAKE A MOMENT**

The problem at Best Buy headquarters is that many experienced employees are losing their drive. Best Buy executives are continually looking for ways to do things better, faster, and cheaper than the competition, but they realize that simply pushing for greater productivity is not the key to reviving employee morale and motivation. This situation can be a problem even for the most successful and admired of organizations, when experienced, valuable employees lose the motivation and commitment they once felt, causing a decline in their performance. One secret for success in organizations is motivated and enthusiastic employees. The challenge for Best Buy and other companies is to keep employee motivation consistent with organizational goals.

Motivation is a challenge for managers because motivation arises from within employees and typically differs for each person. For example, Janice Rennie makes $350,000 a year selling residential real estate in Toronto; she attributes her success to the fact that she likes to listen carefully to clients and then find houses to meet their needs. Greg Storey is a skilled machinist who is challenged by writing programs for numerically controlled machines. After dropping out of college, he swept floors in a machine shop and was motivated to learn to run the machines. Frances Blais sells educational books and software. She is a top salesperson, but she doesn't care about the $50,000-plus commissions: "I'm not even thinking money when I'm selling. I'm really on a crusade to help children read well." In stark contrast, Rob Michaels gets sick to his stomach before he goes to work. Rob is a telephone salesperson who spends all day trying to get people to buy products they do not need, and the rejections are painful. His motivation is money; he earned $120,000 in the past year and cannot make nearly that much doing anything else.[2]

Rob is motivated by money, Janice by her love of listening and problem solving, Frances by the desire to help children read, and Greg by the challenge of mastering numerically controlled machinery. Each person is motivated to perform, yet each has different reasons for performing. With such diverse motivations, it is a challenge for managers to motivate employees toward common organizational goals.

This chapter reviews theories and models of employee motivation. First we examine various perspectives on motivation and consider several models that describe the employee needs and processes associated with motivation. We discuss goal-setting theory and the reinforcement perspective on motivation, as well as examine how *job design*—changing the structure of the work itself—can affect employee satisfaction and productivity. Finally, we discuss the trend of *empowerment*, where authority and decision making are delegated to subordinates to increase employee motivation, and look at how managers can imbue work with a sense of meaning to inspire and motivate employees to higher performance.

THE CONCEPT OF MOTIVATION

Most of us get up in the morning, go to school or work, and behave in ways that are predictably our own. We respond to our environment and the people in it with little thought as to why we work hard, enjoy certain classes, or find some recreational activities so much fun. Yet all these behaviors are motivated by something. **Motivation** refers to the forces either within or external to a person that arouse enthusiasm and persistence to pursue a certain course of action. Employee motivation affects productivity, and part of a manager's job is to channel motivation toward the accomplishment of organizational goals.[3] The study of motivation helps managers understand what prompts people to initiate action, what influences their choice of action, and why they persist in that action over time.

A simple model of human motivation is illustrated in Exhibit 19.1. People have basic *needs*—for food, achievement, or monetary gain—that translate into an internal tension that motivates specific behaviors with which to fulfill the need. To the extent that the behavior is successful, the person is rewarded in the sense that the need is satisfied. The reward also informs the person that the behavior was appropriate and can be used again in the future.

Rewards are of two types: intrinsic and extrinsic. **Intrinsic rewards** are the satisfactions a person receives in the process of performing a particular action. The completion of a complex task may bestow a pleasant feeling of accomplishment, or solving a problem that benefits others may fulfill a personal mission. For example, Frances Blais sells educational materials for the intrinsic reward of helping children read well. **Extrinsic rewards** are given by another person, typically a manager, and include promotions, pay increases, and bonuses. They originate externally, as a result of pleasing others. Rob Michaels, who hates his sales job, nevertheless is motivated by the extrinsic reward of high pay. Although extrinsic rewards are important, good managers strive to help people achieve intrinsic rewards as well. The most talented and innovative employees are rarely motivated exclusively by

motivation The arousal, direction, and persistence of behavior.

intrinsic reward The satisfaction received in the process of performing an action.

extrinsic reward A reward given by another person.

EXHIBIT 19.1

A Simple Model of Motivation

| NEED Creates desire to fulfill needs (food, friendship, recognition, achievement) | BEHAVIOR Results in actions to fulfill needs | REWARDS Satisfy needs; intrinsic or extrinsic rewards |

FEEDBACK Reward informs person whether behavior was appropriate and should be used again.

EMPLOYEE ENGAGEMENT

The term *employee engagement* is becoming popular in the corporate world. To learn what engagement means, answer the following questions twice—(1) once for a course you both enjoyed and performed well and (2) a second time for a course you did not enjoy and performed poorly. Please mark a "1" to indicate whether each item is Mostly True or Mostly False for the course you enjoyed and performed well. Please mark a "2" to indicate whether each item is Mostly True or Mostly False for the course you did not enjoy and performed poorly.

	Mostly True	Mostly False
1. I made sure to study on a regular basis.	___	___
2. I put forth effort.	___	___
3. I found ways to make the course material relevant to my life.	___	___
4. I found ways to make the course interesting to me.	___	___
5. I raised my hand in class.	___	___
6. I had fun in class.	___	___

	Mostly True	Mostly False
7. I participated actively in small group discussions.	___	___
8. I helped fellow students.	___	___

INTERPRETATION AND SCORING. Engagement means that people involve and express themselves in their work, going beyond the minimum effort required. Engagement typically has a positive relationship with both personal satisfaction and performance. If this relationship was true for your classes, the number of "1s" in the Mostly True column will be higher than the number of "2s." You might expect a score of 6 or higher for a course in which you were engaged, and possibly 3 or lower if you were disengaged.

The challenge for a new manager is to learn to engage subordinates in the same way your instructors in your favorite classes were able to engage you. Teaching is similar to managing. What techniques did your instructors use to engage students? Which techniques can you use to engage your people when you become a new manager?

SOURCE: Questions based on Mitchell M. Handelsman, William L. Briggs, Nora Sullivan, and Annette Towler, "A Measure of College Student Course Engagement," *Journal of Educational Research* 98 (January/February 2005): 184–191.

rewards such as money and benefits, or even praise and recognition. Instead, they seek satisfaction from the work itself.[4] For example, at Google, people are motivated by an idealistic goal of providing "automated universal transference," which basically means unifying data and information around the world and totally obliterating language barriers via the Internet. People are energized by the psychic rewards they get from working on intellectually stimulating and challenging technical problems, as well as by the potentially beneficial global impact of their work.[5]

> As a new manager, remember that people will be more engaged when they do things they really like. Take the New Manager Self-Test above to understand what engages you in a class. You will read more about engagement later in the chapter.

■ TAKE A MOMENT

The importance of motivation as illustrated in Exhibit 19.1 is that it can lead to behaviors that reflect high performance within organizations. Studies have found that high employee motivation goes hand-in-hand with high organizational performance and profits.[6] Managers can use motivation theory to help satisfy employees' needs and simultaneously encourage high work performance. With massive layoffs in many U.S. organizations in recent years and a decline in trust of corporate leadership, managers are struggling to keep employees focused and motivated. Finding and keeping talented workers is a growing challenge. Managers have to find the right combination of motivational techniques and rewards to keep people satisfied and productive in a variety of organizational situations.

FOUNDATIONS OF MOTIVATION

A manager's assumptions about employee motivation and the use of rewards depend on his or her perspective on motivation. Four distinct perspectives on employee motivation have evolved: the traditional approach, the human relations approach, the human resource approach, and the contemporary approach.[7]

Traditional Approach

The study of employee motivation really began with the work of Frederick W. Taylor on scientific management. Recall from Chapter 2 that scientific management pertains to the systematic analysis of an employee's job for the purpose of increasing efficiency. Economic rewards are provided to employees for high performance. The emphasis on pay evolved into the notion of the *economic man*—people would work harder for higher pay. This approach led to the development of incentive pay systems, in which people were paid strictly on the quantity and quality of their work outputs.

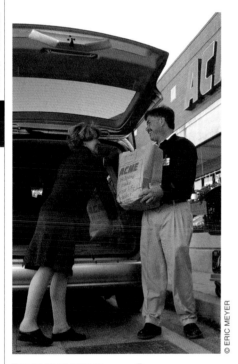

CONCEPT CONNECTION Managers at Albertson's believe that creating a work environment that is rich in opportunity, challenge, and reward **motivates employees** and is key to the company's success. By providing clear goals and objectives, performance reviews, formal and informal education programs, functional training, lateral promotions, and individual mentoring, managers help employees such as Raymond Harlan (photo), find both **intrinsic** and **extrinsic rewards** in their work. Harlan has been assisting shoppers and winning hearts at Albertson's Acme supermarket in Philadelphia since the store opened in 1999. "He's the 'Mayor of Acme,'" says store director Dan Houck.

Human Relations Approach

The economic man was gradually replaced by a more sociable employee in managers' minds. Beginning with the landmark Hawthorne studies at a Western Electric plant, as described in Chapter 2, noneconomic rewards, such as congenial work groups that met social needs, seemed more important than money as a motivator of work behavior.[8] For the first time, workers were studied as people, and the concept of *social man* was born.

Human Resource Approach

The human resource approach carries the concepts of economic man and social man further to introduce the concept of the *whole person*. Human resource theory suggests that employees are complex and motivated by many factors. For example, the work by McGregor on Theory X and Theory Y described in Chapter 2 argued that people want to do a good job and that work is as natural and healthy as play. Proponents of the human resource approach believed that earlier approaches had tried to manipulate employees through economic or social rewards. By assuming that employees are competent and able to make major contributions, managers can enhance organizational performance. The human resource approach laid the groundwork for contemporary perspectives on employee motivation.

Contemporary Approach

The contemporary approach to employee motivation is dominated by three types of theories, each of which will be discussed in the following sections. The first are *content theories*, which stress the analysis of underlying human needs. Content theories provide insight into the needs of people in organizations and help managers understand how needs can be satisfied in the workplace. *Process theories* concern the thought processes that influence behavior. They focus on how people seek rewards in work circumstances. *Reinforcement theories* focus on employee learning of desired work behaviors. In Exhibit 19.1, content theories focus on the concepts in the first box, process theories on those in the second, and reinforcement theories on those in the third.

CONTENT PERSPECTIVES ON MOTIVATION

Content theories emphasize the needs that motivate people. At any point in time, people have basic needs such as those for monetary reward, achievement, or recognition. These needs translate into an internal drive that motivates specific behaviors in an attempt to fulfill the needs. In other words, our needs are like a hidden catalog of the things we want and will work to get. To the extent that managers understand employees' needs, they can design reward systems to meet them and direct employees' energies and priorities toward attaining organizational goals.

Hierarchy of Needs Theory

Probably the most famous content theory was developed by Abraham Maslow.[9] Maslow's **hierarchy of needs theory** proposes that people are motivated by multiple needs and that these needs exist in a hierarchical order, as illustrated in Exhibit 19.2. Maslow identified five general types of motivating needs in order of ascendance:

1. *Physiological needs.* These most basic human physical needs include food, water, and oxygen. In the organizational setting, they are reflected in the needs for adequate heat, air, and base salary to ensure survival.

2. *Safety needs.* These needs include a safe and secure physical and emotional environment and freedom from threats—that is, for freedom from violence and for an orderly society. In an organizational workplace, safety needs reflect the needs for safe jobs, fringe benefits, and job security.

3. *Belongingness needs.* These needs reflect the desire to be accepted by one's peers, have friendships, be part of a group, and be loved. In the organization, these needs influence the desire for good relationships with coworkers, participation in a work group, and a positive relationship with supervisors.

4. *Esteem needs.* These needs relate to the desire for a positive self-image and to receive attention, recognition, and appreciation from others. Within organizations, esteem needs reflect a motivation for recognition, an increase in responsibility, high status, and credit for contributions to the organization.

content theories A group of theories that emphasize the needs that motivate people.

hierarchy of needs theory A content theory that proposes that people are motivated by five categories of needs—physiological, safety, belongingness, esteem, and self-actualization—that exist in a hierarchical order.

EXHIBIT 19.2

Maslow's Hierarchy of Needs

625

Chapter 19 MOTIVATION

5. *Self-actualization needs.* These needs include the need for self-fulfillment, which is the highest need category. They concern developing one's full potential, increasing one's competence, and becoming a better person. Self-actualization needs can be met in the organization by providing people with opportunities to grow, be creative, and acquire training for challenging assignments and advancement.

According to Maslow's theory, low-order needs take priority—they must be satisfied before higher-order needs are activated. The needs are satisfied in sequence: Physiological needs come before safety needs, safety needs before social needs, and so on. A person desiring physical safety will devote his or her efforts to securing a safer environment and will not be concerned with esteem needs or self-actualization needs. Once a need is satisfied, it declines in importance and the next higher need is activated.

A study of employees in the manufacturing department of a major health care company in the United Kingdom provides some support for Maslow's theory. Most line workers emphasized that they worked at the company primarily because of the good pay, benefits, and job security. Thus, employees' lower level physiological and safety needs were being met. When questioned about their motivation, employees indicated the importance of positive social relationships with both peers and supervisors (belongingness needs) and a desire for greater respect and recognition from management (esteem needs).[10]

■ **TAKE A MOMENT**

As a new manager, recognize that some people are motivated primarily to satisfy lower-level physiological and safety needs, while others want to satisfy higher-level needs. Learn which lower- and higher-level needs motivate you by completing the experiential exercise on page 650.

ERG Theory

Clayton Alderfer proposed a modification of Maslow's theory in an effort to simplify it and respond to criticisms of its lack of empirical verification.[11] His **ERG theory** identified three categories of needs:

1. *Existence needs.* The needs for physical well-being.
2. *Relatedness needs.* The needs for satisfactory relationships with others.
3. *Growth needs.* The needs that focus on the development of human potential and the desire for personal growth and increased competence.

The ERG model and Maslow's need hierarchy are similar because both are in hierarchical form and presume that individuals move up the hierarchy one step at a time. However, Alderfer reduced the number of need categories to three and proposed that movement up the hierarchy is more complex, reflecting a **frustration-regression principle**, namely, that failure to meet a high-order need may trigger a regression to an already fulfilled lower-order need. Thus, a worker who cannot fulfill a need for personal growth may revert to a lower-order need and redirect his or her efforts toward making a lot of money. The ERG model therefore is less rigid than Maslow's need hierarchy, suggesting that individuals may move down as well as up the hierarchy, depending on their ability to satisfy needs.

Need hierarchy theory helps explain why organizations find ways to recognize employees, encourage their participation in decision making, and give them opportunities to make significant contributions to the organization and society. For example, Sterling Bank, with headquarters in Houston, Texas, no longer uses *bank tellers*. These positions are now front-line managers who are expected to make decisions and contribute ideas for improving the business.[12] USAA, which offers insurance, mutual funds, and banking services to 5 million members of the military and their families, provides another example.

ERG theory A modification of the needs hierarchy theory that proposes three categories of needs: existence, relatedness, and growth.

frustration-regression principle The idea that failure to meet a high-order need may cause a regression to an already satisfied lower-order need.

USAA's customer service agents are on the front lines in helping families challenged by war and overseas deployment manage their financial responsibilities. Managers recognize that the most important factor in the company's success is the relationship between USAA members and these front-line employees.

To make sure that relationship is a good one, USAA treats customer service reps, who are often considered the lowest rung on the corporate ladder, like professionals. People have a real sense that they're making life just a little easier for military members and their families, which instills them with a feeling of pride and accomplishment. Employees are organized into small, tightly knit "expert teams" and are encouraged to suggest changes that will benefit customers. One service rep suggested that the company offer insurance premium billing timed to coincide with the military's biweekly paychecks. Service reps don't have scripts to follow, and calls aren't timed. Employees know they can take whatever time they need to give the customer the best possible service.

Giving people the opportunity to make real contributions has paid off. In a study by Forrester Research, 81 percent of USAA customers said they believe the company does what's best for them, rather than what's best for the bottom line. Compare that to about 20 percent of customers for financial services firms such as JPMorgan Chase and Citibank.[13]

USAA

A recent survey found that employees who contribute ideas at work, such as those at USAA, are more likely to feel valued, committed, and motivated. In addition, when employees' ideas are implemented and recognized, a motivational effect often ripples throughout the workforce.[14]

Many companies are finding that creating a humane work environment that allows people to achieve a balance between work and personal life is also a great high-level motivator. Flexibility in the workplace, including options such as telecommuting, flexible hours, and job sharing, is highly valued by today's employees because it enables them to manage their work and personal responsibilities. Flexibility is good for organizations too. Employees who have control over their work schedules are significantly less likely to suffer job burnout and are more highly committed to their employers, as shown in Exhibit 19.3. This idea was supported by a survey conducted at Deloitte, which found that client service professionals cited workplace flexibility as a strong reason for wanting to stay with the firm. Another study at Prudential Insurance found that work-life satisfaction and work flexibility directly correlated to job satisfaction, organizational commitment, and employee retention.[15]

Making work fun can play a role in creating this balance. One psychologist recently updated Maslow's hierarchy of needs for a new generation and included the need to have fun as a substantial motivator for today's employees.[16] Having fun at work relieves stress and enables people to feel more "whole," rather than feeling that

Commitment Score

Burnout Score

8.7

7.3

4.0

1.7

☐ Employees who have control over their work schedules

☐ Employees who lack control over their work schedules

EXHIBIT 19.3

The Motivational Benefits of Job Flexibility

SOURCE: WFD Consulting data, as reported in Karol Rose, "Work-Life Effectiveness," *Fortune* (September 29, 2003): S1–S17.

627

Chapter 19 MOTIVATION

their personal lives are totally separate from their work lives. Something as simple as a manager's choice of language can create a lighter, more fun environment. Research suggests the use of phrases such as "Play around with this . . . Explore the possibility of . . . Have fun with . . . Don't worry about little mistakes . . . View this as a game . . ." and so forth can effectively build elements of fun and playfulness into a workplace.[17]

Two-Factor Theory

Frederick Herzberg developed another popular theory of motivation called the *two-factor theory*.[18] Herzberg interviewed hundreds of workers about times when they were highly motivated to work and other times when they were dissatisfied and unmotivated at work. His findings suggested that the work characteristics associated with dissatisfaction were quite different from those pertaining to satisfaction, which prompted the notion that two factors influence work motivation.

The two-factor theory is illustrated in Exhibit 19.4. The center of the scale is neutral, meaning that workers are neither satisfied nor dissatisfied. Herzberg believed that two entirely separate dimensions contribute to an employee's behavior at work. The first, called **hygiene factors**, involves the presence or absence of job dissatisfiers, such as working conditions, pay, company policies, and interpersonal relationships. When hygiene factors are poor, work is dissatisfying. However, good hygiene factors simply remove the dissatisfaction; they do not in themselves cause people to become highly satisfied and motivated in their work.

The second set of factors does influence job satisfaction. **Motivators** focus on high-level needs and include achievement, recognition, responsibility, and opportunity for growth. Herzberg believed that when motivators are absent, workers are neutral toward work, but when motivators are present, workers are highly motivated and satisfied. Thus, hygiene factors and motivators represent two distinct factors that influence motivation. Hygiene factors work only in the area of dissatisfaction. Unsafe working conditions or a noisy work environment will cause people to be dissatisfied, but their correction will not lead to a high level of motivation and satisfaction. Motivators such as challenge, responsibility, and recognition must be in place before employees will be highly motivated to excel at their work.

The implication of the two-factor theory for managers is clear. On one hand, providing hygiene factors will eliminate employee dissatisfaction but will not motivate

hygiene factors Factors that involve the presence or absence of job dissatisfiers, including working conditions, pay, company policies, and interpersonal relationships.

motivators Factors that influence job satisfaction based on fulfillment of high-level needs such as achievement, recognition, responsibility, and opportunity for growth.

EXHIBIT 19.4

Herzberg's Two-Factor Theory

Part 6 LEADING

628

workers to high achievement levels. On the other hand, recognition, challenge, and opportunities for personal growth are powerful motivators and will promote high satisfaction and performance. The manager's role is to remove dissatisfiers—that is, to provide hygiene factors sufficient to meet basic needs—and then to use motivators to meet higher-level needs and propel employees toward greater achievement and satisfaction. Consider how Vision Service Plan (VSP), the nation's largest provider of eye care benefits, uses both hygiene factors and motivators.

Based in Sacramento, California, VSP has seen its workforce nearly triple over the past decade. Despite the challenges of rapid growth, employee satisfaction levels have climbed to an astonishing high of 98 percent.

VSP doesn't offer outrageous salaries and stock options; it does make sure people are paid fairly and provided with solid benefits. The real key to high motivation and satisfaction at VSP, though, is that people feel valued and respected. The process starts the minute someone is hired. Managers use a checklist of items that should be waiting for the new hire upon arrival. Having such basics as a computer, voice mail and e-mail accounts, a nameplate, and business cards helps the newcomer feel like a member of the team. Supervisors give each new employee a picture frame with a note from the CEO encouraging them to use it to display the important people in their lives. A career development program gives employees opportunities to examine their personal priorities, develop their skills, and discuss their career objectives. If someone wants a new job in the company that he or she is not qualified for, VSC sets up an individualized training program to help bridge the gap.

Open communication is another high-level motivator. Issues are raised, debated, and dealt with openly, and people have all the information they need to do their best work. CEO Roger Levine personally answers e-mails from any employee, randomly sits with employees in the company cafeteria, and holds biannual employee meetings where he shares all company information and answers any employee question on the spot. This openness is motivating to employees, who appreciate the higher responsibility and the respect and trust that it implies.[19]

By incorporating both hygiene factors and motivators, managers at VSC have created an environment where people are highly motivated and want to stay. The company regularly shows up on *Fortune* magazine's list of the 100 Best Companies to Work For, moving from number 10 in 2005 to number 7 in 2006.[20]

Acquired Needs Theory

The final content theory was developed by David McClelland. The *acquired needs theory* proposes that certain types of needs are acquired during the individual's lifetime. In other words, people are not born with these needs but may learn them through their life experiences.[21] The three needs most frequently studied are these:

1. *Need for achievement.* The desire to accomplish something difficult, attain a high standard of success, master complex tasks, and surpass others.

2. *Need for affiliation.* The desire to form close personal relationships, avoid conflict, and establish warm friendships.

3. *Need for power.* The desire to influence or control others, be responsible for others, and have authority over others.

© RAJESH NIRGUD/ASSOCIATED PRESS

CONCEPT CONNECTION According to General Electric CEO Jeffrey Immelt, people who succeed at GE are usually those who have a strong **need for achievement** or **need for affiliation.** "We lose people who just want to make a lot of money, or just want to be powerful. But if you like building stuff, and you like who you work with, this is a pretty energizing place to work." Immelt is counting on those highly motivated employees as he tries to steer the multinational conglomerate toward unprecedented growth by transforming it into a customer-driven company that thrives on innovation as well as superior productivity.

Early life experiences determine whether people acquire these needs. If children are encouraged to do things for themselves and receive reinforcement, they will acquire a need to achieve. If they are reinforced for forming warm human relationships, they will develop a need for affiliation. If they get satisfaction from controlling others, they will acquire a need for power.

For more than 20 years, McClelland studied human needs and their implications for management. People with a high need for achievement are frequently entrepreneurs. The parents of social entrepreneur Bill Strickland, the charismatic leader who established Manchester Bidwell, described in the previous chapter, always encouraged him to follow his dreams. When he wanted to go south to work with the Freedom Riders in the 1960s, they supported him. His plans for tearing up the family basement and making a photography studio were met with equal enthusiasm. Strickland thus developed a need for *achievement* that enabled him to accomplish amazing results later in life.[22] People who have a high need for *affiliation* are successful integrators, whose job is to coordinate the work of several departments in an organization.[23] Integrators include brand managers and project managers who must have excellent people skills. People high in need for affiliation are able to establish positive working relationships with others.

A high need for *power* often is associated with successful attainment of top levels in the organizational hierarchy. For example, McClelland studied managers at AT&T for 16 years and found that those with a high need for power were more likely to follow a path of continued promotion over time. More than half of the employees at the top levels had a high need for power. In contrast, managers with a high need for achievement but a low need for power tended to peak earlier in their careers and at a lower level. The reason is that achievement needs can be met through the task itself, but power needs can be met only by ascending to a level at which a person has power over others.

In summary, content theories focus on people's underlying needs and label those particular needs that motivate behavior. The hierarchy of needs theory, the ERG theory, the two-factor theory, and the acquired needs theory all help managers understand what motivates people. In this way, managers can design work to meet needs and hence elicit appropriate and successful work behaviors.

PROCESS PERSPECTIVES ON MOTIVATION

Process theories explain how people select behavioral actions to meet their needs and determine whether their choices were successful. The two basic process theories are equity theory and expectancy theory.

Equity Theory

Equity theory focuses on individuals' perceptions of how fairly they are treated compared with others. Developed by J. Stacy Adams, equity theory proposes that people are motivated to seek social equity in the rewards they expect for performance.[24]

According to equity theory, if people perceive their compensation as equal to what others receive for similar contributions, they will believe that their treatment is fair and equitable. People evaluate equity by a ratio of inputs to outcomes. Inputs to a job include education, experience, effort, and ability. Outcomes from a job include pay, recognition, benefits, and promotions. The input-to-outcome ratio may be compared to another person in the work group or to a perceived group average. A state of **equity** exists whenever the ratio of one person's outcomes to inputs equals the ratio of another's outcomes to inputs.

Inequity occurs when the input-to-outcome ratios are out of balance, such as when a person with a high level of education or experience receives the same salary as a new, less-educated employee. Interestingly, perceived inequity also occurs in the other direction. Thus, if an employee discovers she is making more money than

process theories A group of theories that explain how employees select behaviors with which to meet their needs and determine whether their choices were successful.

equity theory A process theory that focuses on individuals' perceptions of how fairly they are treated relative to others.

equity A situation that exists when the ratio of one person's outcomes to inputs equals that of another's.

other people who contribute the same inputs to the company, she may feel the need to correct the inequity by working harder, getting more education, or considering lower pay. Studies of the brain have shown that people get less satisfaction from money they receive without having to earn it than they do from money they work to receive.[25] Perceived inequity creates tensions within individuals that motivate them to bring equity into balance.[26]

The most common methods for reducing a perceived inequity are these:

:: *Change inputs.* A person may choose to increase or decrease his or her inputs to the organization. For example, underpaid individuals may reduce their level of effort or increase their absenteeism. Overpaid people may increase effort on the job.

:: *Change outcomes.* A person may change his or her outcomes. An underpaid person may request a salary increase or a bigger office. A union may try to improve wages and working conditions in order to be consistent with a comparable union whose members make more money.

:: *Distort perceptions.* Research suggests that people may distort perceptions of equity if they are unable to change inputs or outcomes. They may artificially increase the status attached to their jobs or distort others' perceived rewards to bring equity into balance.

:: *Leave the job.* People who feel inequitably treated may decide to leave their jobs rather than suffer the inequity of being under- or overpaid. In their new jobs, they expect to find a more favorable balance of rewards.

The implication of equity theory for managers is that employees indeed evaluate the perceived equity of their rewards compared to others'. An increase in salary or a promotion will have no motivational effect if it is perceived as inequitable relative to that of other employees.

At Meadowcliff Elementary School in Little Rock, Arkansas, principal Karen Carter used the ideas of equity theory to devise a bonus system for teachers. Carter implemented several new programs designed to improve student learning, and she wanted to reward teachers for their efforts. To avoid fears of bias or favoritism, Carter and the Public Education Foundation of Little Rock decided to use Stanford achievement test results as a basis for bonuses. For each student whose Stanford score rose up to 4 percent over the course of the year, the teacher involved would get $100; 5 percent to 9 percent, $200; 10 percent to 14 percent, $300; and more than 15 percent, $400. The school's scores on the test rose by an average of 17 percent over the course of the year. The base line test gave teachers a way to analyze individual students' strengths and weaknesses and tailor instruction for each student. And because teachers felt the bonus system was equitable, it proved to be a powerful incentive. Administrators think the bonus system is helping to retain the best teachers at Meadowcliff, which serves primarily low-income students.[27] If bonuses were based on subjective judgment, some teachers would likely be concerned that rewards were not being distributed equitably.

Inequitable pay puts pressure on employees that is sometimes almost too great to bear. They attempt to change their work habits, try to change the system, or leave the job.[28] Consider Deb Allen, who went into the office on a weekend to catch up on work and found a document accidentally left on the copy machine. When she saw that some new hires were earning $200,000 more than their counterparts with more experience, and that "a noted screw-up" was making more than highly competent people, Allen began questioning why she was working on weekends for less pay than many others were receiving. Allen became so demoralized by the inequity that she quit her job three months later.[29]

As a new manager, be aware of equity feeling on your team. Don't play favorites, such as regularly praising some while overlooking others making similar contributions. Keep equity in mind when you make decisions about compensation and other rewards.

■ TAKE A MOMENT

© BARBARA LAING

CONCEPT CONNECTION Circuit City managers are using **expectancy theory** principles to help meet employee's needs while attaining organizational goals. By creating an incentive program that is a commission-based plan designed to provide the highest compensation to sales counselors who are committed to serving every customer, Circuit City achieves its volume and profitability objectives. The incentive program is also used in other areas such as distribution, where employees are recognized for accomplishment in safety, productivity, and attendance.

expectancy theory A process theory that proposes that motivation depends on individuals' expectations about their ability to perform tasks and receive desired rewards.

E → P expectancy Expectancy that putting effort into a given task will lead to high performance.

P → O expectancy Expectancy that successful performance of a task will lead to the desired outcome.

valence The value or attraction an individual has for an outcome.

Expectancy Theory

Expectancy theory suggests that motivation depends on individuals' expectations about their ability to perform tasks and receive desired rewards. Expectancy theory is associated with the work of Victor Vroom, although a number of scholars have made contributions in this area.[30] Expectancy theory is concerned not with identifying types of needs but with the thinking process that individuals use to achieve rewards. Consider Amy Huang, a university student with a strong desire for a B in her accounting course. Amy has a C+ average and one more exam to take. Amy's motivation to study for that last exam will be influenced by (1) the expectation that hard study will lead to an A on the exam and (2) the expectation that an A on the exam will result in a B for the course. If Amy believes she cannot get an A on the exam or that receiving an A will not lead to a B for the course, she will not be motivated to study exceptionally hard.

ELEMENTS OF EXPECTANCY THEORY

Expectancy theory is based on the relationship among the individual's *effort*, the individual's *performance*, and the desirability of *outcomes* associated with high performance. These elements and the relationships among them are illustrated in Exhibit 19.5. The keys to expectancy theory are the expectancies for the relationships among effort, performance, and the value of the outcomes to the individual.

E → P expectancy involves determining whether putting effort into a task will lead to high performance. For this expectancy to be high, the individual must have the ability, previous experience, and necessary machinery, tools, and opportunity to perform. For Amy Huang to get a B in the accounting course, the E → P expectancy is high if Amy truly believes that with hard work, she can get an A on the final exam. If Amy believes she has neither the ability nor the opportunity to achieve high performance, the expectancy will be low, and so will be her motivation.

P → O expectancy involves determining whether successful performance will lead to the desired outcome. In the case of a person who is motivated to win a job-related award, this expectancy concerns the belief that high performance will truly lead to the award. If the P → O expectancy is high, the individual will be more highly motivated. If the expectancy is that high performance will not produce the desired outcome, motivation will be lower. If an A on the final exam is likely to produce a B in the accounting course, Amy Huang's P → O expectancy will be high. Amy might talk to the professor to see whether an A will be sufficient to earn her a B in the course. If not, she will be less motivated to study hard for the final exam.

Valence is the value of outcomes, or attraction to outcomes, for the individual. If the outcomes that are available from high effort and good performance are not valued by employees, motivation will be low. Likewise, if outcomes have a high value, motivation will be higher.

Expectancy theory attempts not to define specific types of needs or rewards but only to establish that they exist and may be different for every individual. One employee might want to be promoted to a position of increased responsibility, and another might have high valence for good relationships with peers. Consequently, the first person will be motivated to work hard for a promotion and the second for the opportunity of a team position that will keep him or her associated with a group. Recent studies by the Gallup Organization substantiate the idea that rewards need to be individualized to be motivating. A recent finding from the U.S. Department of Labor shows that the number 1 reason people leave their jobs is because they "don't feel appreciated." Yet Gallup's analysis of 10,000 workgroups in 30 industries found that making people feel appreciated depends on finding the right kind of reward for each individual. Some people prefer tangible rewards or gifts, while others place high value on words of recognition. In addition, some want public recognition while others prefer to be quietly praised by someone they admire and respect.[31] Many of today's managers are also finding that praise and recognition from one's peers often means more than a pat on the back from a supervisor, so they are implementing peer-recognition programs that encourage employees to applaud one another for accomplishments.[32]

A simple sales department example illustrates how the expectancy model in Exhibit 19.5 works. If Carlos, a salesperson at the Diamond Gift Shop, believes that increased selling effort will lead to higher personal sales, we can say that he has a high E → P expectancy. Moreover, if Carlos also believes that higher personal sales will lead to a promotion or pay raise, we can say that he has a high P → O expectancy. Finally, if Carlos places a high value on the promotion or pay raise, valence is high and he will have a high motivational force. On the other hand, if either the E → P or P → O expectancy is low, or if the money or promotion has low valence for Carlos, the overall motivational force will be low. For an employee to be highly motivated, all three factors in the expectancy model must be high.[33]

IMPLICATIONS FOR MANAGERS

The expectancy theory of motivation is similar to the path–goal theory of leadership described in Chapter 18. Both theories are personalized to subordinates' needs and goals. Managers' responsibility is to help subordinates meet their needs and at the same time attain organizational goals. Managers try to find a match between a subordinate's skills and abilities, job demands, and available rewards. To increase motivation, managers can clarify individuals' needs, define the outcomes available from the organization, and ensure that each individual has the ability and support (namely, time and equipment) needed to attain outcomes.

Some companies use expectancy theory principles by designing incentive systems that identify desired organizational outcomes and give everyone the same shot at getting the rewards. The trick is to design a system that fits with employees' abilities and needs.

Goal-Setting Theory

Recall from Chapter 7 our discussion of the importance and purposes of goals. Numerous studies have shown that people are more motivated when they have specific targets or objectives to work toward.[34] You have probably noticed in your own life that you are more motivated when you have a specific goal, such as making an A on a final exam, losing 10 pounds before spring break, or earning enough money during the summer to buy a used car.

Goal-setting theory, described by Edwin Locke and Gary Latham, proposes that managers can increase motivation by setting specific, challenging goals that are accepted as valid by subordinates, then helping people track their progress toward goal achievement by providing timely feedback. The four key components of goal-setting theory include the following:[35]

:: *Goal specificity* refers to the degree to which goals are concrete and unambiguous. Specific goals such as "Visit one new customer each day," or "Sell $1,000 worth of merchandise a week" are more motivating than vague goals such as "Keep in touch with new customers" or "Increase merchandise sales." The first, critical step in any pay-for-performance system is to clearly define exactly what managers want people to accomplish. Lack of clear, specific goals is a major cause of the failure of incentive plans in many organizations.[36]

:: In terms of *goal difficulty*, hard goals are more motivating than easy ones. Easy goals provide little challenge for employees and don't require them to increase their output. Highly ambitious but achievable goals ask people to stretch their abilities.

:: *Goal acceptance* means that employees have to "buy into" the goals and be committed to them. Managers often find that having people participate in setting goals is a good way to increase acceptance and commitment. At Aluminio del Caroni, a state-owned aluminum company in southeastern Venezuela, plant workers felt a renewed sense of commitment when top leaders implemented a *co-management* initiative that has managers and lower-level employees working together to set budgets, determine goals, and make decisions. "The managers and the workers are running this business together," said one employee who spends his days shoveling molten aluminum down a channel from an industrial oven to a cast. "It gives us the motivation to work hard."[37]

:: Finally, the component of *feedback* means that people get information about how well they are doing in progressing toward goal achievement. It is important for managers to provide performance feedback on a regular, ongoing basis. However, self-feedback, where people are able to monitor their own progress toward a goal, has been found to be an even stronger motivator than external feedback.[38] Managers at Advanced Circuits of Aurora, Colorado, which makes custom-printed circuit boards, steer employee performance toward goals by giving everyone ongoing numerical feedback about every aspect of the business. Employees are so fired up that they check the data on the intranet throughout the day as if they were checking the latest sports scores. The system enables people to track their progress toward achieving goals, such as reaching sales targets or solving customer problems within specified time limits. "The more goals we get, the better it is for us," says employee Barb Frevert. "The more we do for Ron, the more he does for us."[39]

goal-setting theory A motivation theory in which specific, challenging goals increase motivation and performance when the goals are accepted by subordinates and these subordinates receive feedback to indicate their progress toward goal achievement.

Why does goal setting increase motivation? For one thing, it enables people to focus their energies in the right direction. People know what to work toward, so they can direct their efforts toward the most important activities to accomplish the goals. Goals also energize behavior because people feel compelled to develop plans and strategies that keep them focused on achieving the target. Specific, difficult goals provide a challenge and encourage people to put forth high levels of effort. In addition, when goals are achieved, pride and satisfaction increase, contributing to higher motivation and morale.[40]

■ **TAKE A MOMENT** As a new manager, use specific, challenging goals to keep people focused and motivated. Have team members participate in setting goals and determining how to achieve them. Give regular feedback on how people are doing.

REINFORCEMENT PERSPECTIVE ON MOTIVATION

The reinforcement approach to employee motivation sidesteps the issues of employee needs and thinking processes described in the content and process theories. **Reinforcement theory** simply looks at the relationship between behavior and its consequences. It focuses on changing or modifying employees' on-the-job behavior through the appropriate use of immediate rewards and punishments.

Reinforcement Tools

Behavior modification is the name given to the set of techniques by which reinforcement theory is used to modify human behavior.[41] The basic assumption underlying behavior modification is the **law of effect**, which states that behavior that is positively reinforced tends to be repeated, and behavior that is not reinforced tends not to be repeated. **Reinforcement** is defined as anything that causes a certain behavior to be repeated or inhibited. The four reinforcement tools are positive reinforcement, avoidance learning, punishment, and extinction. Each type of reinforcement is a consequence of either a pleasant or unpleasant event being applied or withdrawn following a person's behavior. The four types of reinforcement are summarized in Exhibit 19.6.

© CLAY PETERSON/THE CALIFORNIAN/ASSOCIATED PRESS

CONCEPT CONNECTION Farm managers often use a **fixed-rate reinforcement schedule** by basing a fruit or vegetable picker's pay on the amount he or she harvests. A variation on this individual piece-rate system is a relative incentive plan that bases each worker's pay on the ratio of the individual's productivity to average productivity among all co-workers. A study of Eastern and Central European pickers in the United Kingdom found that workers' productivity declined under the relative plan. Researchers theorized that fast workers didn't want to hurt their slower colleagues, so they reduced their efforts. The study authors suggested a team-based scheme—where everyone's pay increased if the team did well—would be more effective.

POSITIVE REINFORCEMENT

Positive reinforcement is the administration of a pleasant and rewarding consequence following a desired behavior. A good example of positive reinforcement is immediate praise for an employee who arrives on time or does a little extra work. The pleasant consequence will increase the likelihood of the excellent work behavior occurring again. Studies have shown that positive reinforcement does help to improve performance. In addition, nonfinancial reinforcements such as positive feedback, social recognition, and attention are just as effective as financial incentives.[42] Indeed, many people consider factors other than money to be more important. Nelson Motivation Inc. conducted a survey of 750 employees across various industries to assess the value they placed on various rewards. Cash and other monetary awards came in dead last. The most valued rewards involved praise and manager support and involvement.[43]

AVOIDANCE LEARNING

Avoidance learning is the removal of an unpleasant consequence following a desired behavior. Avoidance learning is sometimes called *negative reinforcement*. Employees learn to do the right thing by avoiding unpleasant situations. Avoidance learning occurs when a supervisor stops criticizing or reprimanding an employee once the incorrect behavior has stopped.

reinforcement theory A motivation theory based on the relationship between a given behavior and its consequences.

behavior modification The set of techniques by which reinforcement theory is used to modify human behavior.

law of effect The assumption that positively reinforced behavior tends to be repeated, and unreinforced or negatively reinforced behavior tends to be inhibited.

reinforcement Anything that causes a given behavior to be repeated or inhibited.

| | Positive Reinforcement
Increases likelihood that
behavior will be repeated |
| Praise employee
Recommend pay raise | |
| Employee increases work rate | |
| | Avoidance Learning
Increases likelihood that
behavior will be repeated |
| Avoid reprimands,
negative statements | |
| Slow work rate
Supervisor requests faster work | |
| | Punishment
Reduces likelihood that
behavior will be repeated |
| Reprimand employee
Make negative statements | |
| Employee continues slow work | |
| | Extinction
Reduces likelihood that
behavior will be repeated |
| Withhold raises, merit
pay, praise | |

EXHIBIT 19.6

Changing Behavior with
Reinforcement

SOURCE: Based on Richard
L. Daft and Richard M. Steers,
*Organizations: A Micro/Macro
Approach* (Glenview, IL; Scott,
Foresman, 1986): 109.

PUNISHMENT

Punishment is the imposition of unpleasant outcomes on an employee. Punishment typically occurs following undesirable behavior. For example, a supervisor may berate an employee for performing a task incorrectly. The supervisor expects that the negative outcome will serve as a punishment and reduce the likelihood of the behavior recurring. The use of punishment in organizations is controversial and often criticized because it fails to indicate the correct behavior. However, almost all managers report that they find it necessary to occasionally impose forms of punishment ranging from verbal reprimands to employee suspensions or firings.[44]

EXTINCTION

Extinction is the withdrawal of a positive reward. Whereas with punishment, the supervisor imposes an unpleasant outcome such as a reprimand, extinction involves withholding pay raises, bonuses, praise, or other positive outcomes. The idea is that behavior that is not positively reinforced will be less likely to occur in the future. For example, if a perpetually tardy employee fails to receive praise and pay raises, he or she will begin to realize that the behavior is not producing desired outcomes. The behavior will gradually disappear if it is continually not reinforced.

Executives can use aspects of reinforcement theory to shape employees' behavior. Garry Ridge, CEO of WD-40 Company, which makes the popular lubricant used for everything from loosening bolts to removing scuff marks from floors, wanted to encourage people to talk about their failures so the company could learn from them. He offered prizes to anyone who would e-mail and share their "learning moments," and each respondent would have the chance to win an all-expenses paid vacation. The positive reinforcement, combined with the company's "blame-free" policy, motivated people to share ideas that have helped WD-40 keep learning and growing.[45]

Schedules of Reinforcement

schedule of reinforcement
The frequency with which
and intervals over which
reinforcement occurs.

A great deal of research into reinforcement theory suggests that the timing of reinforcement has an impact on how quickly employees learn and respond with the desired behavior. **Schedules of reinforcement** pertain to the frequency with which and intervals over which reinforcement occurs. A reinforcement schedule can be selected to have maximum impact on employees' job behavior. Five basic types of reinforcement schedules include continuous and four types of partial reinforcement.

CONTINUOUS REINFORCEMENT

With a **continuous reinforcement schedule**, every occurrence of the desired behavior is reinforced. This schedule can be especially effective in the early stages of learning new types of behavior, because every attempt has a pleasant consequence. Some companies use a continuous reinforcement schedule by offering people cash, game tokens, or points that can be redeemed for prizes each time they perform the desired behavior. LDF Sales & Distributing tried a program called "The Snowfly Slots," developed by management professor Brooks Mitchell, to cut inventory losses. Workers received tokens each time they double-checked the quantity of a shipment. Since it started using Snowfly, the company saved $31,000 a year when inventory losses fell 50 percent. Many companies are developing continuous reinforcement programs so that employees make a clear connection between their behavior and the desired reward.[46]

PARTIAL REINFORCEMENT

However, in the real world of organizations, it is often impossible to reinforce every correct behavior. With a **partial reinforcement schedule**, the reinforcement is administered only after some occurrences of the correct behavior. The four types of partial reinforcement schedules are fixed interval, fixed ratio, variable interval, and variable ratio.

1. *Fixed-interval schedule.* The fixed-interval schedule rewards employees at specified time intervals. If an employee displays the correct behavior each day, reinforcement may occur every week, for example. Regular paychecks or quarterly bonuses are examples of fixed-interval reinforcement. At Leone Ackerly's Mini Maid franchise in Marietta, Georgia, workers are rewarded with an attendance bonus each pay period if they have gone to work every day on time and in uniform.[47]

2. *Fixed-ratio schedule.* With a fixed-ratio schedule, reinforcement occurs after a specified number of desired responses, say, after every fifth. For example, paying a field hand $1.50 for picking 10 pounds of peppers is a fixed-ratio schedule. Most piece-rate pay systems are considered fixed-ratio schedules.

3. *Variable-interval schedule.* With a variable-interval schedule, reinforcement is administered at random times that cannot be predicted by the employee. An example would be a random inspection by the manufacturing superintendent of the production floor, at which time he or she commends employees on their good behavior.

4. *Variable-ratio schedule.* The variable-ratio schedule is based on a random number of desired behaviors rather than on variable time periods. Reinforcement may occur sometimes after 5, 10, 15, or 20 displays of behavior. One example is random monitoring of telemarketers, who may be rewarded after a certain number of calls in which they perform the appropriate behaviors and meet call performance specifications. Employees know they may be monitored but are never sure when checks will occur and when rewards may be given.

The schedules of reinforcement are illustrated in Exhibit 19.7. Continuous reinforcement is most effective for establishing new learning, but behavior is vulnerable to extinction. Partial reinforcement schedules are more effective for maintaining behavior over extended time periods. The most powerful is the variable-ratio schedule, because employee behavior will persist for a long time due to the random administration of reinforcement only after a long interval.[48]

continuous reinforcement schedule A schedule in which every occurrence of the desired behavior is reinforced.

partial reinforcement schedule A schedule in which only some occurrences of the desired behavior are reinforced.

Schedule of Reinforcement	Nature of Reinforcement	Effect on Behavior When Applied	Effect on Behavior When Withdrawn	Example
Continuous	Reward given after each desired behavior	Leads to fast learning of new behavior	Rapid extinction	Praise
Fixed-interval	Reward given at fixed time intervals	Leads to average and irregular performance	Rapid extinction	Weekly paycheck
Fixed-ratio	Reward given at fixed amounts of output	Quickly leads to very high and stable performance	Rapid extinction	Piece-rate pay system
Variable-interval	Reward given at variable times	Leads to moderately high and stable performance	Slow extinction	Performance appraisal and awards given at random times each month
Variable-ratio	Reward given at variable amounts of output	Leads to very high performance	Slow extinction	Sales bonus tied to number of sales calls, with random checks

EXHIBIT　19.7

Schedules of Reinforcement

PinnacleHealth System provides an excellent, though somewhat controversial, example of the successful use of reinforcement theory.

PinnacleHealth System

Federal health regulations in the United States are carefully designed to prevent hospitals from paying doctors to skimp on care. But one hospital system in Pennsylvania obtained special approval for an innovative program.

Administrators at PinnacleHealth System wanted to make doctors cost-sensitive and reward them for saving money. So, they developed an incentive plan that allows doctors to share in any money they save the hospital, which is positive reinforcement to doctors for using cost-efficient procedures or less-expensive medical devices. For example, in the past, many cardiologists at PinnacleHealth hospitals would inflate a new artery-opening balloon each time they inserted a stent into a patient's clogged arteries. Now, when possible, they use a single balloon throughout the procedure. The doctors say this poses no risk to the patient, and the simple step cuts a couple of hundred dollars per procedure, amounting to big savings over time. When they can, PinnacleHealth doctors also use stents, pacemakers, and other medical devices that the hospital buys at a negotiated volume discount, rather than using more costly products. Doctors can use any device they feel is in the best interest of the patient, but incentives focus doctors on manufacturers with whom the company has low-cost supplier contracts.

It's working. Annual savings in 2004 amounted to about $1 million, with participating physicians each earning an estimated $10,000 to $15,000 from the payouts that year.[49]

Reinforcement also works at such organizations as Campbell Soup Co., Emery Air Freight, Emerald Packaging, Michigan Bell, and PSS World Medical, because managers reward the desired behaviors. They tell employees what they can do to receive rewards, tell them what they are doing wrong, distribute rewards equitably, tailor rewards to behaviors, and keep in mind that failure to reward deserving behavior has an equally powerful impact on employees.

Reward and punishment motivational practices dominate organizations. According to the Society for Human Resource Management, 84 percent of all companies in the United States offer some type of monetary or nonmonetary reward system, and 69 percent offer incentive pay, such as bonuses, based on an employee's performance.[50] However, in other studies, more than 80 percent of employers with incentive programs have reported that their programs are only somewhat successful or not working at all.[51] Despite the testimonies of organizations that enjoy successful incentive programs, criticism of these "carrot-and-stick" methods is growing, as discussed in the Manager's Shoptalk.

THE CARROT-AND-STICK CONTROVERSY

Everybody thought Rob Rodin was crazy when he decided to wipe out all individual incentives for his sales force at Marshall Industries, a large distributor of electronic components based in El Monte, California. He did away with all bonuses, commissions, vacations, and other awards and rewards. All salespeople would receive a base salary plus the opportunity for profit sharing, which would be the same percent of salary for everyone, based on the entire company's performance. Six years later, Rodin says productivity per person has tripled at the company, but still he gets questions and criticism about his decision.

Rodin is standing right in the middle of a big controversy in modern management. Do financial and other rewards really motivate the kind of behavior organizations want and need? A growing number of critics say no, arguing that carrot-and-stick approaches are a holdover from the Industrial Age and are inappropriate and ineffective in today's economy. Today's workplace demands innovation and creativity from everyone—behaviors that rarely are inspired by money or other financial incentives. Reasons for criticism of carrot-and-stick approaches include the following:

1. *Extrinsic rewards diminish intrinsic rewards.* When people are motivated to seek an extrinsic reward, whether it be a bonus, an award, or the approval of a supervisor, generally they focus on the reward rather than on the work they do to achieve it. Thus, the intrinsic satisfaction people receive from performing their jobs actually declines. When people lack intrinsic rewards in their work, their performance stays just adequate to achieve the reward offered. In the worst case, employees may cover up mistakes or cheat in order to achieve the reward. One study found that teachers who were rewarded for increasing test scores frequently used various forms of cheating, for example.

2. *Extrinsic rewards are temporary.* Offering outside incentives may ensure short-term success, but not long-term high performance. When

employees are focused only on the reward, they lose interest in their work. Without personal interest, the potential for exploration, creativity, and innovation disappears. Although the current deadline or goal may be met, better ways of working and serving customers will not be discovered and the company's long-term success will be affected.

3. *Extrinsic rewards assume people are driven by lower-level needs.* Rewards such as bonuses, pay increases, and even praise presume that the primary reason people initiate and persist in behavior is to satisfy lower-level needs. However, behavior also is based on yearnings for self-expression and on feelings of self-esteem and self-worth. Typical individual incentive programs don't reflect and encourage the myriad behaviors that are motivated by people's need to express themselves and realize their higher needs for growth and fulfillment.

As Rob Rodin discovered at Marshall Industries, today's organizations need employees who are motivated to think, experiment, and continuously search for ways to solve new problems. Alfie Kohn, one of the most vocal critics of carrot-and-stick approaches, offers the following advice to managers regarding how to pay employees: "Pay well, pay fairly, and then do everything you can to get money off people's minds." Indeed some evidence indicates that money is not primarily what people work for. Managers should understand the limits of extrinsic motivators and work to satisfy employees' higher, as well as lower, needs. To be motivated, employees need jobs that offer self-satisfaction in addition to a yearly pay raise.

SOURCES: Alfie Kohn, "Incentives Can Be Bad for Business," *Inc.* (January 1998): 93–94; A. J. Vogl, "Carrots, Sticks, and Self-Deception" (an interview with Alfie Kohn), *Across the Board* (January 1994): 39–44; Geoffrey Colvin, "What Money Makes You Do," *Fortune* (August 17, 1998): 213–214; and Jeffrey Pfeffer, "Sins of Commission," *Business 2.0* (May 2004): 56.

> As a new manager, remember that reward and punishment practices are partial motivational tools because they focus only on extrinsic rewards and lower-level needs. Using intrinsic rewards to meet higher level needs is important too.

■ **TAKE A MOMENT**

JOB DESIGN FOR MOTIVATION

A *job* in an organization is a unit of work that a single employee is responsible for performing. A job could include writing tickets for parking violators in New York City, performing MRIs at Salt Lake Regional Medical Center, reading meters for Pacific

Gas and Electric, or doing long-range planning for The WB Television Network. Jobs are an important consideration for motivation because performing their components may provide rewards that meet employees' needs. An assembly-line worker may install the same bolt over and over, whereas an emergency room physician may provide each trauma victim with a unique treatment package. Managers need to know what aspects of a job provide motivation as well as how to compensate for routine tasks that have little inherent satisfaction. **Job design** is the application of motivational theories to the structure of work for improving productivity and satisfaction. Approaches to job design are generally classified as job simplification, job rotation, job enlargement, and job enrichment.

Job Simplification

Job simplification pursues task efficiency by reducing the number of tasks one person must do. Job simplification is based on principles drawn from scientific management and industrial engineering. Tasks are designed to be simple, repetitive, and standardized. As complexity is stripped from a job, the worker has more time to concentrate on doing more of the same routine task. Workers with low skill levels can perform the job, and the organization achieves a high level of efficiency. Indeed, workers are interchangeable, because they need little training or skill and exercise little judgment. As a motivational technique, however, job simplification has failed. People dislike routine and boring jobs and react in a number of negative ways, including sabotage, absenteeism, and unionization. Job simplification is compared with job rotation and job enlargement in Exhibit 19.8.

Job Rotation

Job rotation systematically moves employees from one job to another, thereby increasing the number of different tasks an employee performs without increasing the complexity of any one job. For example, an autoworker might install windshields one week and front bumpers the next. Job rotation still takes advantage of engineering efficiencies, but it provides variety and stimulation for employees. Although employees might find the new job interesting at first, the novelty soon wears off as the repetitive work is mastered.

Companies such as The Home Depot, Motorola, 1-800-Flowers, and Dayton Hudson have built on the notion of job rotation to train a flexible workforce. As companies break away from ossified job categories, workers can perform several jobs, thereby reducing labor costs and giving people opportunities to develop new skills. At The Home Depot, for example, workers scattered throughout the company's vast chain of stores can get a taste of the corporate climate by working at in-store support centers, while associate managers can dirty their hands out on the sales floor.[52] Job rotation also gives companies greater flexibility. One production

job design The application of motivational theories to the structure of work for improving productivity and satisfaction.

job simplification A job design whose purpose is to improve task efficiency by reducing the number of tasks a single person must do.

job rotation A job design that systematically moves employees from one job to another to provide them with variety and stimulation.

EXHIBIT   19.8

Types of Job Design

worker might shift among the jobs of drill operator, punch operator, and assembler, depending on the company's need at the moment. Some unions have resisted the idea, but many now go along, realizing that it helps the company be more competitive.[53]

Job Enlargement

Job enlargement combines a series of tasks into one new, broader job. This type of design is a response to the dissatisfaction of employees with oversimplified jobs. Instead of only one job, an employee may be responsible for three or four and will have more time to do them. Job enlargement provides job variety and a greater challenge for employees. At Maytag, jobs were enlarged when work was redesigned so that workers assembled an entire water pump rather than doing each part as it reached them on the assembly line. Similarly, rather than just changing the oil at a Precision Tune location, a mechanic changes the oil, greases the car, airs the tires, checks fluid levels, battery, air filter, and so forth. Then, the same employee is responsible for consulting with the customer about routine maintenance or any problems he or she sees with the vehicle.

© JEFF ZARUBA

CONCEPT CONNECTION At the Frito-Lay plant in Lubbock, Texas, Julia Garcia used to just pack bags of chips into cardboard cartons. Today, she's interviewing new hires, refusing products that don't meet quality standards, and sending home excess workers if machines shut down. Hourly workers have been enjoying the benefits of **job enlargement** and **job enrichment** since Frito-Lay introduced work teams six years ago. Garcia's 11-member potato chip team is responsible for everything from potato processing to equipment maintenance.

Job Enrichment

Recall the discussion of Maslow's need hierarchy and Herzberg's two-factor theory. Rather than just changing the number and frequency of tasks a worker performs, **job enrichment** incorporates high-level motivators into the work, including job responsibility, recognition, and opportunities for growth, learning, and achievement. In an enriched job, employees have control over the resources necessary for performing it, make decisions on how to do the work, experience personal growth, and set their own work pace. Research shows that when jobs are designed to be controlled more by employees than by managers, people typically feel a greater sense of involvement, commitment, and motivation, which in turn contributes to higher morale, lower turnover, and stronger organizational performance.[54]

Many companies have undertaken job enrichment programs to increase employees' involvement, motivation, and job satisfaction. At Ralcorp's cereal manufacturing plant in Sparks, Nevada, for example, managers enriched jobs by combining several packing positions into a single job and cross-training employees to operate all of the packing line's equipment. In addition, assembly-line employees screen, interview, and train all new hires. They are responsible for managing the production flow to and from their upstream and downstream partners, making daily decisions that affect their work, managing quality, and contributing to continuous improvement. Enriched jobs have improved employee motivation and satisfaction, and the company has benefited from higher long-term productivity, reduced costs, and happier, more motivated employees.[55]

Job Characteristics Model

One significant approach to job design is the job characteristics model developed by Richard Hackman and Greg Oldham.[56] Hackman and Oldham's research concerned **work redesign**, which is defined as altering jobs to increase both the quality of employees' work experience and their productivity. Hackman and Oldham's research into the design of hundreds of jobs yielded the **job characteristics model**, which is illustrated in Exhibit 19.9. The model consists of three major parts: core job dimensions, critical psychological states, and employee growth-need strength.

641

Chapter 19 MOTIVATION

job enlargement A job design that combines a series of tasks into one new, broader job to give employees variety and challenge.

job enrichment A job design that incorporates achievement, recognition, and other high-level motivators into the work.

work redesign The altering of jobs to increase both the quality of employees' work experience and their productivity.

job characteristics model A model of job design that comprises core job dimensions, critical psychological states, and employee growth-need strength.

Core Job Dimensions	Critical Psychological States	Personal and Work Outcomes
Skill variety Task identity Task significance Autonomy Feedback	Experienced meaningfulness of the work Experienced responsibility for outcomes of the work Knowledge of the actual results of the work activities	High internal work motivation High-quality work performance High satisfaction with the work Low absenteeism and turnover

Employee Growth-Need Strength

EXHIBIT 19.9

The Job Characteristics Model

SOURCE: Adapted from J. Richard Hackman and G.R. Oldham, "Motivation through the Design of Work: Test of a Theory," *Organizational Behavior and Human Performance* 16 (1976): 256.

CORE JOB DIMENSIONS

Hackman and Oldham identified five dimensions that determine a job's motivational potential:

1. *Skill variety.* The number of diverse activities that compose a job and the number of skills used to perform it. A routine, repetitive assembly-line job is low in variety, whereas an applied research position that entails working on new problems every day is high in variety.

2. *Task identity.* The degree to which an employee performs a total job with a recognizable beginning and ending. A chef who prepares an entire meal has more task identity than a worker on a cafeteria line who ladles mashed potatoes.

3. *Task significance.* The degree to which the job is perceived as important and having impact on the company or consumers. People who distribute penicillin and other medical supplies during times of emergencies would feel they have significant jobs.

4. *Autonomy.* The degree to which the worker has freedom, discretion, and self-determination in planning and carrying out tasks. A house painter can determine how to paint the house; a paint sprayer on an assembly line has little autonomy.

5. *Feedback.* The extent to which doing the job provides information back to the employee about his or her performance. Jobs vary in their ability to let workers see the outcomes of their efforts. A football coach knows whether the team won or lost, but a basic research scientist may have to wait years to learn whether a research project was successful.

The job characteristics model says that the more these five core characteristics can be designed into the job, the more the employees will be motivated and the higher will be performance, quality, and satisfaction.

CRITICAL PSYCHOLOGICAL STATES

The model posits that core job dimensions are more rewarding when individuals experience three psychological states in response to job design. In Exhibit 19.9, skill variety, task identity, and task significance tend to influence the employee's psychological state of *experienced meaningfulness of work.* The work itself is satisfying and provides intrinsic rewards for the worker. The job characteristic of autonomy influences the worker's *experienced responsibility.* The job characteristic of feedback provides the worker with *knowledge of actual results.* The employee thus knows how he or she is doing and can change work performance to increase desired outcomes.

PERSONAL AND WORK OUTCOMES

The impact of the five job characteristics on the psychological states of experienced meaningfulness, responsibility, and knowledge of actual results leads to the personal and work outcomes of high work motivation, high work performance, high satisfaction, and low absenteeism and turnover.

EMPLOYEE GROWTH-NEED STRENGTH

The final component of the job characteristics model is called *employee growth-need strength*, which means that people have different needs for growth and development. If a person wants to satisfy low-level needs, such as safety and belongingness, the job characteristics model has less effect. When a person has a high need for growth and development, including the desire for personal challenge, achievement, and challenging work, the model is especially effective. People with a high need to grow and expand their abilities respond favorably to the application of the model and to improvements in core job dimensions.

One interesting finding concerns the cross-cultural differences in the impact of job characteristics. Intrinsic factors such as autonomy, challenge, achievement, and recognition can be highly motivating in countries such as the United States. However, they may contribute little to motivation and satisfaction in a country such as Nigeria, and might even lead to *demotivation*. A recent study indicates that the link between intrinsic characteristics and job motivation and satisfaction is weaker in economically disadvantaged countries with poor governmental social welfare systems, and in high power distance countries, as defined in Chapter 4.[57] Thus, the job characteristics model would be expected to be less effective in these countries.

INNOVATIVE IDEAS FOR MOTIVATING

Despite the controversy over carrot-and-stick motivational practices discussed in the Shoptalk box earlier in this chapter, organizations are increasingly using various types of incentive compensation as a way to motivate employees to higher levels of performance. Exhibit 19.10 summarizes several popular methods of incentive pay.

Program	Purpose
Pay for performance	Rewards individual employees in proportion to their performance contributions. Also called *merit pay*.
Gain sharing	Rewards all employees and managers within a business unit when predetermined performance targets are met. Encourages teamwork.
Employee stock ownership plan (ESOP)	Gives employees part ownership of the organization, enabling them to share in improved profit performance.
Lump-sum bonuses	Rewards employees with a one-time cash payment based on performance.
Pay for knowledge	Links employee salary with the number of task skills acquired. Workers are motivated to learn the skills for many jobs, thus increasing company flexibility and efficiency.
Flexible work schedule	*Flextime* allows workers to set their own hours. *Job sharing* allows two or more part-time workers to jointly cover one job. *Telecommuting*, sometimes called *flex-place*, allows employees to work from home or an alternative workplace.
Team-based compensation	Rewards employees for behavior and activities that benefit the team, such as cooperation, listening, and empowering others.
Lifestyle awards	Rewards employees for meeting ambitious goals with luxury items, such as high-definition televisions, tickets to big-name sporting events, and exotic travel.

EXHIBIT 19.10

New Motivational Compensation Programs

Unlocking Innovative Solutions Through PEOPLE

NUCOR: GIVING PEOPLE A STAKE IN THE BUSINESS

Since Daniel R. DiMicco took over as CEO of Nucor in 2000, sales jumped from $4.6 billion to $12.7 billion in 2005, income grew from $311 million to $1.3 billion for the same period, and the company shipped more steel in 2005 than any other company in the United States. Yet DiMicco, a 23-year veteran of Nucor, keeps everyone focused on long-term success, not short-term results. Nucor's goal is to be "the safest, highest-quality, lowest cost, most productive, and most profitable steel-products company in the world," he says. To realize that goal, the Charlotte, North Carolina-based minimill follows the path blazed by its legendary CEO, the late F. Kenneth Iverson. Iverson's employee-centered, egalitarian management philosophy helped the floundering company he inherited in 1965 not only survive the implosion of the U.S. steel industry that began in the 1970s but also emerge as one of the largest, most profitable steel producers in the country. Under his leadership, Nucor created an empowered workforce and devised a radical, performance-based compensation system.

Nucor searches for job candidates with an entrepreneurial bent. Once hired, the nonunionized workers join teams in a decentralized, flattened, four-level organization. With most decision-making authority pushed down to the division level, employees run their part of the business as if it were their own. Managers continue to practice Iverson's approach: "Instead of telling people what to do and then hounding them to do it, our managers focus on shaping an environment that frees employees to determine what they can do and should do, to the benefit of themselves and the business. We've found that their answers drive the progress of our business faster than our own."

Under Nucor's performance-based compensation system, all employees, from the CEO on down, have both responsibility for performance and an unusual chance to share in corporate wealth. Essentially, as Iverson explained, "The more they produce, the more they earn. They have a simple stake in the business." Nucor measures performance in clear-cut ways. For the rank and file, Nucor determines productivity weekly by measuring defect-free steel output against plant equipment capabilities. For department managers, professional, and clerical personnel, the company gauges performance against return on assets; for senior executives, it looks at annual return on equity. Although base pay at Nucor is relatively low, weekly bonuses based on production can average 80 to 150 percent of a steelworker's base pay, and a manager's annual bonus can amount to roughly 80 percent of his or her salary. Even though base pay starts at about $10 an hour, for example, the average Nucor steelworker took home approximately $100,000 in 2005. In a bad year, everyone—the CEO included—shares the pain. In addition, because a plant manager's bonus depends on the entire corporation's performance, the system fosters a companywide team mind-set.

The results speak for themselves. Nucor led the United States in steel shipments in 2005 as well as boasted a five-year 387 percent return on equity and 7 to 10 percent profit margins. And it accomplishes these achievements with a work environment that longtime employees (including engineers, not usually given to flights of fancy) have called magical.

SOURCES: Nanette Byrnes with Michael Arndt, "The Art of Motivation," *BusinessWeek* (May 1, 2006): 57; "About Us," www.nucor.com/indexinner.aspx?finpage=aboutus (accessed June 20, 2006); Patricia Panchak, "Putting Employees First Pays Off," *Industry Week* (June 2002): 14; and "Nucor CEO: Instill Your Culture, Empower Workers to Reach Goal," *Charlotte Business Journal* (November 22, 2002): http://charlotte.bizjournals.com/charlotte/stories/2002/11/25/editorial2.

■ **TAKE A MOMENT** Go to the ethical dilemma on page 651 that pertains to the use of incentive compensation as a motivational tool.

Variable compensation and forms of "at risk" pay are key motivational tools and are becoming more common than fixed salaries at many companies. These programs can be effective if they are used appropriately and combined with motivational ideas that also provide employees with intrinsic rewards and meet higher-level needs. Effective managers don't use incentive plans as the sole basis of motivation. At steelmaker Nucor, for example, the amount of money employees and managers take home depends on company profits and how effective the plants are at producing defect-free steel. However, as described in the Unlocking Innovative Solutions Through People box, Nucor doesn't rely on incentives alone. The company has created one of the most motivated and dynamic workforces in the United States by meeting people's higher level needs.

Some organizations give employees a voice in how pay and incentive systems are designed, which boosts motivation by increasing people's sense of involvement and control.[58] Managers at Premium Standard Farms' pork-processing plant hired a consultant to help slaughterhouse workers design and implement an incentive program. Annual payouts to employees in one recent year were around $1,000 per employee. More important, though, is that workers feel a greater sense of dignity and purpose in their jobs, which has helped to reduce turnover significantly. As one employee put it, "Now I have the feeling that this is my company, too."[59] The most effective motivational programs typically involve much more than money or other external rewards. Two recent motivational trends are empowering employees and framing work to have greater meaning.

Empowering People to Meet Higher Needs

One significant way managers can meet higher motivational needs is to shift power down from the top of the organization and share it with employees to enable them to achieve goals. **Empowerment** is power sharing, the delegation of power or authority to subordinates in an organization.[60] Increasing employee power heightens motivation for task accomplishment because people improve their own effectiveness, choosing how to do a task and using their creativity.[61] Most people come into an organization with the desire to do a good job, and empowerment releases the motivation that is already there. Research indicates that most people have a need for *self-efficacy*, which is the capacity to produce results or outcomes, to feel that they are effective.[62] By meeting this higher-level need, empowerment can provide powerful motivation.

Empowering employees involves giving them four elements that enable them to act more freely to accomplish their jobs: information, knowledge, power, and rewards.[63]

1. *Employees receive information about company performance.* In companies where employees are fully empowered, all employees have access to all financial and operational information. At Reflexite Corporation, for example, which is largely owned by employees, managers sit down each month to analyze data related to operational and financial performance and then share the results with employees throughout the company. In addition to these monthly updates, employees have access to any information about the company at any time they want or need it.[64]

2. *Employees have knowledge and skills to contribute to company goals.* Companies use training programs to help employees acquire the knowledge and skills they need to contribute to organizational performance. For example, when DMC, which makes pet supplies, gave employee teams the authority and responsibility for assembly-line shutdowns, it provided extensive training on how to diagnose and interpret line malfunctions, as well as data related to the costs of shutdown and start-up. People worked through several case studies to practice decision making related to line shutdowns.[65]

3. *Employees have the power to make substantive decisions.* Empowered employees have the authority to directly influence work procedures and organizational performance, such as through quality circles or self-directed work teams. At Venezuela's Aluminio del Caroní, employees participate in roundtable discussions and make recommendations to management regarding new equipment purchases or other operational matters. In addition, workers vote to elect managers and board members.[66] The Brazilian manufacturer Semco, described in the Chapter 3 Unlocking Innovative Solutions Through People box, pushes empowerment to the limits by allowing its employees to choose what they do, how they do it, and even how they get compensated for it. Many employees set their own pay by choosing from a list of 11 different pay options, such as set salary or a combination of salary and incentives.[67]

empowerment The delegation of power and authority to subordinates.

4. *Employees are rewarded based on company performance.* Organizations that empower workers often reward them based on the results shown in the company's bottom line. For example, at Semco, in addition to employee-determined compensation, a company profit-sharing plan gives each employee an even share of 23 percent of his or her department's profits each quarter.[68] Organizations may also use other motivational compensation programs described in Exhibit 19.10 to tie employee efforts to company performance.

Many of today's organizations are implementing empowerment programs, but they are empowering workers to varying degrees. At some companies, empowerment means encouraging workers' ideas while managers retain final authority for decisions; at others it means giving employees almost complete freedom and power to make decisions and exercise initiative and imagination.[69] Current methods of empowerment fall along a continuum, as illustrated in Exhibit 19.11. The continuum runs from a situation in which front-line workers have almost no discretion, such as on a traditional assembly line, to full empowerment, where workers even participate in formulating organizational strategy. Studies indicate that higher-level empowerment programs, where employees have input and decision-making power related to both everyday operational issues and higher-level strategic decisions, are still relatively rare.[70]

Giving Meaning to Work

Another way to meet higher-level motivational needs and help people get intrinsic rewards from their work is to instill a sense of importance and meaningfulness. *Fortune* magazine finds that one of the primary characteristics shared by companies on its annual list of "The 100 Best Companies to Work For" is that they are *purpose-driven*, that is, people have a sense that what they are doing matters and makes a

EXHIBIT   19.11

A Continuum of Empowerment

SOURCES: Based on Robert C. Ford and Myron D. Fottler, "Empowerment: A Matter of Degree," *Academy of Management Executive 9*, no. 3 (1995), 21–31; Lawrence Holpp, "Applied Empowerment," *Training* (February 1994), 39–44; and David P. McCaffrey, Sue R. Faerman, and David W. Hart, "The Appeal and Difficulties of Participative Systems," *Organization Science 6*, no. 6 (November–December 1995), 603–627.

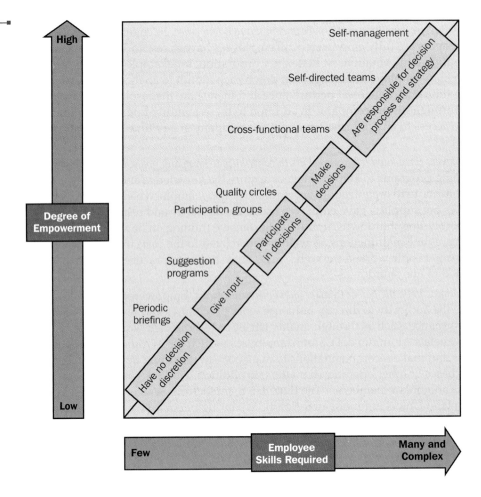

positive difference in the world.[71] Consider the motivation of employees at Genentech, which topped the list in 2006.

> Genentech was the world's first biotechnology company, and after 29 years is the brightest star in the burgeoning industry. The company's culture, which imbues employees with idealism, has a lot to do with its success. Genentech's motto, for example, is *In Business for Life*.
>
> Genentech offers plenty of extrinsic rewards, such as generous stock options, free cappuccino and made-to-order sushi, and an on-site daycare center and concierge service. But employees like Domagoj Vucic, Cynthia Wong, and Napoleone Ferrara say they work at the company because it gives them a chance to make a difference. Scientists and researchers have the time, freedom, and support at Genentech to answer big research questions that could have a big impact on curing diseases such as cancer. Genentech puts great effort into attracting people with a passion for science and a commitment to improving human life. It can take several visits and as many as 20 interviews to land a job. Part of the process is designed to screen out those who are preoccupied with salary, title, and personal advancement. CEO Art Levinson emphasizes that people who need to feel special with assigned parking spaces and executive dining rooms won't fit in at Genentech.
>
> Having said that, Genentech makes *all* of its workers feel special, treating them less like employees and more like partners in a great cause. People don't get "work assignments" at Genentech; they get "appointments." They travel around the grounds, which have the feel of a college campus, on shuttle buses and company-provided bicycles. There's a party every Friday night. To keep creativity alive, Genentech encourages scientists and engineers to spend 20 percent of their time working on their own pet projects, and the company awards sabbaticals to stave off burnout.
>
> Genentech managers by no means consider the company a philanthropy. They are focused on growth and profits as much as any other business. However, as Levinson puts it: "At the end of the day, we want to make drugs that really matter. That's the transcendent issue." Levinson believes that, as long as the company does the right thing and keeps its people motivated, the sales and profits will follow.[72]

It is easy to understand why employees at Genentech feel they are serving an important cause. But managers in any organization can tap into people's desire to contribute and make a difference. Former Coca-Cola CEO Roberto Goizueta spent a lot of time talking to employees about the company's charitable work and emphasized that millions of small merchants could make a living because they sold Coca-Cola. Employees at FedEx take pride in getting people the items they need on time, whether it be a work report that is due, a passport for a holiday trip to Jamaica, or an emergency order of medical supplies.[73]

Another example is Les Schwab Tire Centers, where employees feel like partners united toward a goal of making people's lives easier. Stores fix flats for free, and some have been known to install tires hours before opening time for an emergency trip. Employees frequently stop to help stranded motorists. Schwab rewards people with a generous profit-sharing plan for everyone and promotes store managers solely from within. However, these external rewards only supplement, not create, the high motivation employees feel.[74]

In recent years, managers have focused on employee *engagement*, which has less to do with extrinsic rewards such as pay and much more to do with fostering an environment in which people can flourish. Engaged employees are more satisfied and motivated because they feel appreciated by their supervisors and the organization, and they thrive on work challenges rather than feeling frustrated by them.[75] Engaged employees are motivated, enthusiastic, and committed employees. In addition, there is a growing recognition that it is the behavior of managers that makes the biggest difference in whether people feel engaged at work. When David A. Brandon took over as CEO of Domino's Pizza, he commissioned research to identify the factors that contributed to a store's success. What he learned was that the quality of the manager and how he or she treats employees has a much greater impact than neighborhood demographics, packaging, marketing, or other factors.[76] Indeed, a Gallup Organization study conducted over 25 years found that the single most important variable in whether employees feel good about their work is the relationship between employees and their direct supervisors.[77]

The role of today's manager is not to control others but to organize the workplace in such a way that each person can learn, contribute, and grow. Good managers channel employee motivation toward the accomplishment of organizational goals by tapping into each individual's unique set of talents, skills, interests, attitudes, and needs. By treating each employee as an individual, managers can put people in the right jobs and provide intrinsic rewards to every employee every day. Then, managers make sure people have what they need to perform, clearly define the desired outcomes, and get out of the way.

One way to evaluate how a manager or a company is doing in engaging employees by meeting higher-level needs is a metric developed by the Gallup researchers called the Q12. When a majority of employees can answer these 12 questions positively, the organization enjoys a highly motivated and productive workforce:

1. Do I know what is expected of me at work?
2. Do I have the materials and equipment that I need in order to do my work right?
3. At work, do I have the opportunity to do what I do best every day?
4. In the past seven days, have I received recognition or praise for doing good work?
5. Does my supervisor, or someone at work, seem to care about me as a person?
6. Is there someone at work who encourages my development?
7. At work, do my opinions seem to count?
8. Does the mission or purpose of my company make me feel that my job is important?
9. Are my coworkers committed to doing quality work?
10. Do I have a best friend at work?
11. In the past six months, has someone at work talked to me about my progress?
12. This past year, have I had opportunities to learn and grow?[78]

Results of the Gallup study show that organizations where employees give high marks on the Q12 have less turnover, are more productive and profitable, and enjoy greater employee and customer loyalty.[79] Many companies have used the Q12 to pinpoint problems with motivation in the organization. Best Buy, for example, uses the survey and includes employee engagement as a key item on each manager's scorecard. Eric Taverna, the general manager of a Best Buy store in Manchester, Connecticut, took to heart the finding that his employees didn't think their opinions mattered. Taverna responded by implementing significant changes based on employee ideas and suggestions. The Manchester store's engagement levels improved significantly, as did the store's financial performance, while turnover has been substantially reduced.[80] When employees are more engaged and motivated, they—and their organizations—thrive.

MANAGER'S SOLUTION

This chapter introduced a number of important ideas about the motivation of people in organizations. Rewards are of two types: intrinsic rewards that result from the satisfactions a person receives in the process of performing a job, and extrinsic rewards such as promotions that are given by another person. Managers work to help employees receive both intrinsic and extrinsic rewards from their jobs. The content theories of motivation focus on the nature of underlying employee needs. Maslow's hierarchy of needs, Alderfer's ERG theory, Herzberg's two-factor theory, and McClelland's acquired needs theory all suggest that people are motivated to meet a range of needs. Process theories examine how people go about selecting rewards with which to meet needs. Equity theory says that people compare their contributions and outcomes with others' and are motivated to maintain a feeling of equity. Expectancy theory suggests that people calculate the probability of achieving certain outcomes. Managers can increase motivation by treating employees fairly and by clarifying employee paths toward meeting their needs. Goal-setting theory indicates that employees are more motivated if they have clear, specific goals and receive regular feedback concerning their progress toward meeting goals. Still another motivational approach is reinforcement theory, which says that employees learn to behave in certain ways based on the use of reinforcements.

The application of motivational ideas is illustrated in job design and other motivational programs. Job design approaches include job simplification, job rotation, job enlargement, job enrichment, and the job characteristics model. Managers can change the structure of work to meet employees' high-level needs. The recent trend toward empowerment motivates by giving employees more information and authority to make decisions in their work while connecting compensation to the results. Managers can instill employees with a sense of importance and meaningfulness to help them reap intrinsic rewards and meet higher level needs for esteem and self-fulfillment. Managers create the environment that determines employee motivation. One way to measure the factors that determine whether people have high levels of engagement and motivation is the Q12, a list of 12 questions about the day-to-day realities of a person's job.

At Best Buy headquarters, described in the chapter opening, experienced employees were beginning to lose their motivation, and managers wisely recognized this situation as a danger to Best Buy's competitiveness. The answer was an innovative work-life balance initiative known as ROWE (Results-Oriented Work Environment), which means that people can work when and where they like, as long as they get the job done. The experiment started in one division where morale and motivation were dismal. Hourly employees, such as data entry clerks and claims processors, were disgruntled, saying that punching a time clock made them feel like unruly children who had to be kept in line. Under the ROWE system, those employees now focus on how many forms they can process in a week, rather than on the time it takes them to do it (they still keep track of their hours because of federal overtime regulations). The experiment in that division showed some remarkable results. Under ROWE, turnover in the first three months of employment fell from 14 percent to zero, job satisfaction increased 10 percent, and team-performance scores rose 13 percent. These results spurred executives to make the ROWE system available companywide. ROWE has proved to be a great high-level motivator at Best Buy.[81]

DISCUSSION QUESTIONS

1. In response to security threats in today's world, the U.S. government federalized airport security workers. Many argued that simply making screeners federal workers would not solve the root problem: bored, low-paid, and poorly trained security workers have little motivation to be vigilant. How might these employees be motivated to provide the security that travel conditions now demand?

2. One small company recognizes an employee of the month, who is given a parking spot next to the president's space near the front door. What theories would explain the positive motivation associated with this policy?

3. Campbell Soup Company reduces accidents with a lottery. Each worker who works 30 days or more without losing a day for a job-related accident is eligible to win prizes in a raffle drawing. Why has this program been successful?

4. If an experienced secretary discovered that she made less money than a newly hired janitor, how would she react? What inputs and outcomes might she evaluate to make this comparison?

5. What intrinsic rewards do you experience in your role as a student? Extrinsic rewards? Are intrinsic or extrinsic rewards generally more important motivators for you?

6. Would you rather work for a supervisor high in need for achievement, need for affiliation, or need for power? Why? What are the advantages and disadvantages of each?

7. A survey of teachers found that two of the most important rewards were the belief that their work was important and a feeling of accomplishment. Is this consistent with Hackman and Oldham's job characteristics model? Explain.

8. The teachers in question 7 also reported that pay and benefits were poor, yet they continue to teach. Use Herzberg's two-factor theory to explain this finding.

9. What theories explain why employees who score high on the Q12 questionnaire are typically highly motivated and productive?

10. How can empowerment lead to higher motivation? Could a manager's empowerment efforts sometimes contribute to demotivation as well? Discuss.

11. Why might intrinsic factors such as achievement and recognition be less motivating in a poor country such as Nigeria than they are in the United States?

MANAGEMENT IN PRACTICE: EXPERIENTIAL EXERCISE

What Motivates You?

Indicate how important each characteristic is to you. Answer according to your feelings about the most recent job you had or about the job you currently hold. Circle the number on the scale that represents your feeling—1 (very unimportant) to 7 (very important).

1. The feeling of self-esteem a person gets from being in that job   ① ② ③ ④ ⑤ ⑥ ⑦

2. The opportunity for personal growth and development in that job   ① ② ③ ④ ⑤ ⑥ ⑦

3. The prestige of the job inside the company (i.e., regard received from others in the company)   ① ② ③ ④ ⑤ ⑥ ⑦

4. The opportunity for independent thought and action in that job   ① ② ③ ④ ⑤ ⑥ ⑦

5. The feeling of security in that job   ① ② ③ ④ ⑤ ⑥ ⑦

6. The feeling of self-fulfillment a person gets from being in that position (i.e., the feeling of being able to use one's own unique capabilities, realizing one's potential)   ① ② ③ ④ ⑤ ⑥ ⑦

7. The prestige of the job outside the company (i.e., the regard received from others not in the company)   ① ② ③ ④ ⑤ ⑥ ⑦

8. The feeling of worthwhile accomplishment in that job   ① ② ③ ④ ⑤ ⑥ ⑦

9. The opportunity in that job to give help to other people   ① ② ③ ④ ⑤ ⑥ ⑦

10. The opportunity in that job for participation in the setting of goals   ① ② ③ ④ ⑤ ⑥ ⑦

11. The opportunity in that job for participation in the determination of methods and procedures   ① ② ③ ④ ⑤ ⑥ ⑦

12. The authority connected with the job   ① ② ③ ④ ⑤ ⑥ ⑦

13. The opportunity to develop close friendships in the job   ① ② ③ ④ ⑤ ⑥ ⑦

Scoring and Interpretation

Score the exercise as follows to determine what motivates you:

Rating for question 5 = _____.
Divide by 1 = _____ security.

Rating for questions 9 and 13 = _____.
Divide by 2 = _____ social.

Rating for questions 1, 3, and 7 = _____.
Divide by 3 = _____ esteem.

Rating for questions 4, 10, 11, and 12 = _____.
Divide by 4 = _____ autonomy.

Rating for questions 2, 6, and 8 = _____.
Divide by 3 = _____ self-actualization.

Your instructor has national norm scores for presidents, vice presidents, and upper middle-level, lower middle-level, and lower-level managers with which you can compare your mean importance scores. How do your scores compare with the scores of managers working in organizations?

SOURCE: Lyman W. Porter, *Organizational Patterns of Managerial Job Attitudes* (New York: American Foundation for Management Research, 1964): 17, 19. Used with permission.

To Renege or Not to Renege?

Federico Garcia, vice president of sales for Tacoma, Washington-based Puget Sound Building Materials, wasn't all that surprised by what company president Michael Otto and CFO James Wilson had to say during their meeting that morning.

Last year, launching a major expansion made sense to everyone at Puget, a well-established company that provided building materials as well as manufacturing and installation services to residential builders in the Washington and Oregon markets. Puget looked at the record new housing starts and decided it was time to move into the California and Arizona markets, especially concentrating on San Diego and Phoenix, two of the hottest housing markets in the country. Federico carefully hired promising new sales representatives and offered them hefty bonuses if they reached the goals set for the new territory over the next 12 months. All of the representatives had performed well, and three of them had exceeded Puget's goal—and then some. The incentive system he'd put in place had worked well. The sales reps were expecting handsome bonuses for their hard work.

Early on, however, it became all too clear that Puget had seriously underestimated the time it took to build new business relationships and the costs associated with the expansion, a mistake that was already eating into profit margins. Even more distressing were the most recent figures for new housing starts, which were heading in the wrong direction. As Michael said, "Granted, it's too early to tell if this is just a pause or the start of a real long-term downturn. But I'm worried. If things get worse, Puget could be in real trouble."

James looked at Federico and said, "Our lawyers built enough contingency clauses into the sales reps' contracts that we're not really obligated to pay those bonuses you promised. What would you think about not paying them?" Federico turned to the president, who said, "Why don't you think about it, and get back to us with a recommendation?"

Federico felt torn. On the one hand, he knew the CFO was correct. Puget wasn't, strictly speaking, under any legal obligation to pay out the bonuses, and the eroding profit margins were a genuine cause for concern. The president clearly wanted to not pay the bonuses. But Federico had created a first-rate sales force that had done exactly what he'd asked them to do. He prided himself on being a man of his word, someone others could trust. Could he go back on his promises?

What Would You Do?

1. Recommend to the president that a meeting be arranged with the sales representatives entitled to a bonus and tell them that their checks were going to be delayed until the Puget's financial picture clarified. The sales reps would be told that the company had a legal right to delay payment and that it may not be able to pay the bonuses if its financial situation continues to deteriorate.

2. Recommend a meeting with the sales representatives entitled to a bonus and tell them the company's deteriorating financial situation triggers one of the contingency clauses in their contract so that the company won't be issuing their bonus checks. Puget will just have to deal with the negative impact on sales rep motivation.

3. Recommend strongly to the president that Puget pay the bonuses as promised. The legal contracts and financial situation don't matter. Be prepared to resign if the bonuses are not paid as you promised. Your word and a motivated sales team mean everything to you.

SOURCE: Based on Doug Wallace, "The Company Simply Refused to Pay," *Business Ethics* (March–April 2000): 18; and Adam Shell, "Overheated Housing Market Is Cooling," *USA Today* (November 2, 2005): www.usatoday.com/money/economy/housing/2005-11-01-real-estate-usat_x.htm.

Kimbel's Department Store

Frances Patterson, Kimbel's CEO, looked at the latest "Sales by Manager" figures on her daily Web-based sales report. What did these up-to-the-minute numbers tell her about the results of Kimbel's trial of straight commission pay for its salespeople?

A regional chain of upscale department stores based in St. Louis, Kimbel's faces the challenge shared by most department stores these days: how to stop losing share of overall retail sales to discount store chains. A key component of the strategy the company formulated to counter this long-term trend is the revival of great customer service on the floor, once a hallmark of upscale stores. Frances knows Kimbel's has its work cut out for it. When she dropped in on several stores incognito a few years ago, she was dismayed to discover that finding a salesperson actively engaged with a customer was rare. In fact, finding a salesperson when a customer wanted to pay for an item was often difficult.

About a year and a half ago, the CEO read about a quiet revolution sweeping department store retailing. At stores such as Bloomingdale's and Bergdorf Goodman, managers put all salespeople on straight commission. Frances decided to give the system a year long try in two area stores.

Such a plan, she reasoned, would be good for Kimbel's if it lived up to its promise of attracting better salespeople, improving their motivation, and making them more customer-oriented. It could also potentially be good for employees. Salespeople in departments such as electronics, appliances, and jewelry, where expertise and highly personalized services paid off, had long worked solely on commission. But the majority of employees earn an hourly wage plus a meager 0.5 percent commission on total sales. Under the new scheme, all employees earn a 7 percent commission on sales. When she compared the two systems, she saw that a new salesclerk in women's wear would earn $35,000 on $500,000 in sales, as opposed to only $18,000 under the old scheme.

Now, with the trial period about to end, Frances notes that while overall sales in the two stores have increased modestly, so also has employee turnover. When the CEO examined the sales-by-manager figures, it was obvious that some associates had thrived and others had not. Most fell somewhere in the middle.

For example, Juan Santore is enthusiastic about the change—and for good reason. He works in women's designer shoes and handbags, where a single item can cost upwards of $1,000. Motivated largely by the desire to make lots of money, he's a personable, outgoing individual with an entrepreneurial streak. Ever since the straight commission plan took effect, he has put even more time and effort into cultivating relationships with wealthy customers, and it shows. His pay has increased an average of $150 per week.

It's a different story in the lingerie department, where even luxury items have more modest price tags. The lingerie department head, Gladys Weinholtz,

said salespeople in her department are demoralized. Several valued employees had quit, and most miss the security of a salary. No matter how hard they work, they cannot match their previous earnings. "Yes, they're paying more attention to customers," conceded Gladys, "but they're so anxious about making ends meet, they tend to pounce on the poor women who wander into the department." Furthermore, lingerie sales associates are giving short shrift to duties such as handling complaints or returns that don't immediately translate into sales. "And boy, do they ever resent the sales superstars in the other departments," said Gladys.

The year is nearly up. It's time to decide. Should Frances declare the straight commission experiment a success on the whole and roll it out across the chain over the next six months?

Questions

1. What theories about motivation underlie the switch from salary to commission pay?

2. What needs are met under the commission system? Are they the same needs in the shoes and handbag department as they are in lingerie? Explain.

3. If you were Frances Patterson, would you go back to the previous compensation system, implement the straight commission plan in all Kimbel's stores, or devise and test some other compensation method? If you decided to test another system, what would it look like?

SOURCES: Based on Cynthia Kyle, "Commissions question—to pay . . . or not to pay?" *Michigan Retailer* (March 2003): www.retailers.com/news/retailers/03mar/mr0303commissions.html; "Opinion: Effective Retail Sales Compensation," *Furniture World Magazine* (March 7, 2006): www.furninfo.com/absolutenm/templates/NewsFeed.asp?articleid=6017; Terry Pristin, "Retailing's Elite Keep the Armani Moving Off the Racks," *The New York Times* (December 22, 2001): D1; Francine Schwadel, "Chain Finds Incentives a Hard Sell," *The Wall Street Journal* (July 5, 1990): B4; and Amy Dunkin, "Now Salespeople Really Must Sell for Their Supper," *BusinessWeek* (July 31, 1989): 50–52.

ENDNOTES

1. Jyoti Thottam, "Reworking Work," *Time* (July 25, 2005): 50–55.

2. David Silburt, "Secrets of the Super Sellers," *Canadian Business* (January 1987): 54–59; "Meet the Savvy Supersalesmen," *Fortune* (February 4, 1985): 56–62; Michael Brody, "Meet Today's Young American Worker," *Fortune* (November 11, 1985): 90–98; and Tom Richman, "Meet the Masters. They Could Sell You Anything," *Inc.* (March 1985): 79–86.

3. Richard M. Steers and Lyman W. Porter, eds., *Motivation and Work Behavior*, 3rd ed. (New York: McGraw-Hill, 1983); Don Hellriegel, John W. Slocum, Jr., and Richard W. Woodman,

Organizational Behavior, 7th ed. (St. Paul, MN: West, 1995): 170; and Jerry L. Gray and Frederick A. Starke, *Organizational Behavior: Concepts and Applications*, 4th ed. (New York: Macmillan, 1988): 104–105.

4. Carol Hymowitz, "Readers Tell Tales of Success and Failure Using Rating Systems," *The Wall Street Journal* (May 29, 2001): B1.

5. Alan Deutschman, "Can Google Stay Google?" *Fast Company* (August 2005): 62–68.

6. See Linda Grant, "Happy Workers, High Returns," *Fortune* (January 12, 1998): 81; Elizabeth J. Hawk and

Garrett J. Sheridan, "The Right Stuff," *Management Review* (June 1999): 43–48; Michael West and Malcolm Patterson, "Profitable Personnel," *People Management* (January 8, 1998): 28–31; Anne Fisher, "Why Passion Pays," *FSB* (September 2002): 58; and Curt Coffman and Gabriel Gonzalez-Molina, *Follow This Path: How the World's Great Organizations Drive Growth By Unleashing Human Potential* (New York: Warner Books, 2002).

7. Steers and Porter, *Motivation*.

8. J. F. Rothlisberger and W. J. Dickson, *Management and the Worker* (Cambridge, MA: Harvard University Press, 1939).

9. Abraham F. Maslow, "A Theory of Human Motivation," *Psychological Review* 50 (1943): 370–396.

10. Sarah Pass, "On the Line," *People Management* (September 15, 2005).

11. Clayton Alderfer, *Existence, Relatedness, and Growth* (New York: Free Press, 1972).

12. Robert Levering and Milton Moskowitz, "2004 Special Report: The 100 Best Companies To Work For," *Fortune* (January 12, 2004): 56–78.

13. Jena McGregor, "Employee Innovator; Winner: USAA," *Fast Company* (October 2005): 57.

14. Jeff Barbian, "C'mon, Get Happy," *Training* (January 2001): 92–96.

15. Karol Rose, "Work-Life Effectiveness," *Fortune* (September 29, 2003): S1–S17.

16. W. Glaser, *The Control Theory Manager* (New York: Harper-Business, 1994); and John W. Newstrom, "Making Work Fun: An Important Role for Managers," *SAM Advanced Management Journal* (Winter 2002): 4–8, 21.

17. Newstrom, "Making Work Fun."

18. Frederick Herzberg, "One More Time: How Do You Motivate Employees?" *Harvard Business Review* (January 2003): 87–96.

19. Elaine Leuchars, Shauna Harrington, and Carrie Erickson, "Putting People First: How VSP Achieves High Employee Satisfaction Year After Year," *Journal of Organizational Excellence* (Spring 2003): 33–41; Levering and Moskowitz, "The 100 Best Companies to Work For 2004."

20. Robert Levering and Milton Moskowitz, "And the Winners Are . . .," *Fortune* (January 23, 2006): 89–108; and Geoff Colvin, "The 100 Best Companies to Work For 2006," *Fortune* (January 23, 2006): 71ff.

21. David C. McClelland, *Human Motivation* (Glenview, IL: Scott, Foresman, 1985).

22. John Brant, "What One Man Can Do," *Inc.* (September 2005): 145–153.

23. David C. McClelland, "The Two Faces of Power," in *Organizational Psychology*, ed. D.A. Colb, I.M. Rubin, and J.M. McIntyre (Englewood Cliffs, NJ: Prentice Hall, 1971): 73–86.

24. J. Stacy Adams, "Injustice in Social Exchange," in *Advances in Experimental Social Psychology*, 2d ed., ed. L. Berkowitz (New York: Academic Press, 1965); and J. Stacy Adams, "Toward an Understanding of Inequity," *Journal of Abnormal and Social Psychology* (November 1963): 422–436.

25. "Study: The Brain Prefers Working Over Getting Money for Nothing," *TheJournalNews.com* (May 14, 2004), www.thejournalnews.com/apps/pbcs.dll/frontpage.

26. Ray V. Montagno, "The Effects of Comparison to Others and Primary Experience on Responses to Task Design," *Academy of Management Journal* 28 (1985): 491–498; and

Robert P. Vecchio, "Predicting Worker Performance in Inequitable Settings," *Academy of Management Review* 7 (1982): 103–110.

27. Daniel Henninger, "How One School Found a Way to Spell Success," *The Wall Street Journal* (October 14, 2005): A10.

28. James E. Martin and Melanie M. Peterson, "Two-Tier Wage Structures: Implications for Equity Theory," *Academy of Management Journal* 30 (1987): 297–315.

29. Jared Sandberg, "Why You May Regret Looking at Papers Left on the Office Copier," *The Wall Street Journal* (June 20, 2006): B1.

30. Victor H. Vroom, *Work and Motivation* (New York: Wiley, 1964); B. S. Gorgopoulos, G. M. Mahoney, and N. Jones, "A Path-Goal Approach to Productivity," *Journal of Applied Psychology* 41 (1957): 345–353; and E. E. Lawler III, *Pay and Organizational Effectiveness: A Psychological View* (New York: McGraw-Hill, 1981).

31. Studies reported in Tom Rath, "The Best Way to Recognize Employees," *Gallup Management Journal* (December 9, 2004).

32. Erin White, "Theory & Practice: Praise from Peers Goes a Long Way—Recognition Programs Help Companies Retain Workers as Pay Raises Get Smaller," *The Wall Street Journal* (December 19, 2005): B3.

33. Richard L. Daft and Richard M. Steers, *Organizations: A Micro/Macro Approach* (Glenview, IL: Scott, Foresman, 1986).

34. See Edwin A. Locke and Gary P. Latham, "Building a Practically Useful Theory of Goal Setting and Task Motivation: A 35-Year Odyssey," *The American Psychologist* 57, no. 9 (September 2002): 705+; Gary P. Latham and Edwin A. Locke, "Self-Regulation through Goal Setting", *Organizational Behavior and Human Decision Processes* 50, no. 2 (1991): 212+; G. P. Latham and G. H. Seijts, "The Effects of Proximal and Distal Goals on Performance of a Moderately Complex Task," *Journal of Organizational Behavior* 20, no. 4 (1999): 421+; P. C. Early, T. Connolly, and G. Ekegren, "Goals, Strategy Development, and Task Performance: Some Limits on the Efficacy of Goal Setting," *Journal of Applied Psychology* 74 (1989): 24–33; E. A. Locke, "Toward a Theory of Task Motivation and Incentives," *Organizational Behavior and Human Performance* 3 (1968): 157–189; Gerard H. Seijts, Ree M. Meertens, and Gerjo Kok, "The Effects of Task Importance and Publicness on the Relation Between Goal Difficulty and Performance," *Canadian Journal of Behavioural Science* 29, no. 1 (1997): 54+.

35. Locke and Latham, "Building a Practically Useful Theory of Goal Setting and Task Motivation."

36. Edwin A. Locke, "Linking Goals to Monetary Incentives," *Academy of Management Executive* 18, no. 4 (2005): 130–133.

37. Brian Ellsworth, "Making a Place for Blue Collars in the Boardroom," *The New York Times* (August 3, 2005), www.nytimes.com.

38. J. M. Ivanecevich and J. T. McMahon, "The Effects of Goal Setting, External Feedback, and Self-Generated Feedback on Outcome Variables: A Field Experiment," *Academy of Management Journal* (June 1982): 359+; G. P. Latham and E. A. Locke, "Self-Regulation Through Goal Setting," *Organizational Behavior and Human Decision Processes* 50, no. 2 (1991): 212+.

39. Ellyn Spragins, "The Best Bosses," *FSB* (October 2004): 39–57.

40. Gary P. Latham, "The Motivational Benefits of Goal-Setting," *Academy of Management Executive* 18, no. 4 (2004): 126–129.

41. Alexander D. Stajkovic and Fred Luthans, "A Meta-Analysis of the Effects of Organizational Behavior Modification on Task Performance, 1975–95," *Academy of Management Journal* (October 1997): 1122–1149; H. Richlin, *Modern Behaviorism* (San Francisco: Freeman, 1970); and B. F. Skinner, *Science and Human Behavior* (New York: Macmillan, 1953).

42. Stajkovic and Luthans, "A Meta-Analysis of the Effects of Organizational Behavior Modification on Task Performance, 1975–95," and Fred Luthans and Alexander D. Stajkovic, "Reinforce for Performance: The Need to Go Beyond Pay and Even Rewards," *Academy of Management Executive* 13, no. 2 (1999): 49–57.

43. Reported in Charlotte Garvey, "Meaningful Tokens of Appreciation," *HR Magazine* (August 2004): 101–105.

44. Kenneth D. Butterfield and Linda Klebe Treviño, "Punishment from the Manager's Perspective: A Grounded Investigation and Inductive Model," *Academy of Management Journal* 39, no. 6 (December 1996): 1479–1512; and Andrea Casey, "Voices from the Firing Line: Managers Discuss Punishment in the Workplace," *Academy of Management Executive* 11, no. 3 (1997): 93–94.

45. Gwendolyn Bounds, "Boss Talk: No More Squeaking By—WD-40 CEO Garry Ridge Repackages a Core Product," *The Wall Street Journal* (May 23, 2006): B1.

46. Jaclyn Badal, "New Incentives for Workers Combine Cash, Fun," *The Wall Street Journal* (June 19, 2006): B3.

47. Roberta Maynard, "How to Motivate Low-Wage Workers," *Nation's Business* (May 1997): 35–39.

48. L. M. Sarri and G. P. Latham, "Employee Reaction to Continuous and Variable Ratio Reinforcement Schedules Involving a Monetary Incentive," *Journal of Applied Psychology* 67 (1982): 506–508; and R. D. Pritchard, J. Hollenback, and P. J. DeLeo, "The Effects of Continuous and Partial Schedules of Reinforcement on Effort, Performance, and Satisfaction," *Organizational Behavior and Human Performance* 25 (1980): 336–353.

49. Reed Abelson, "To Fight Rising Costs, Hospitals Seek Allies in the Operating Room," *The New York Times* (November 18, 2005), www.nytimes.com.

50. Amy Joyce, "The Bonus Question; Some Managers Still Strive to Reward Merit," *The Washington Post* (November 13, 2005): F6.

51. Survey results from WorldatWork and Hewitt Associates, reported in Karen Kroll, "Benefits: Paying for Performance," *Inc.* (November 2004): 46; and Kathy Chu, "Firms Report Lackluster Results from Pay-for-Performance Plans," *The Wall Street Journal* (June 15, 2004): D2.

52. Barbian, "C'mon, Get Happy."

53. Norm Alster, "What Flexible Workers Can Do," *Fortune* (February 13, 1989): 62–66.

54. Christine M. Riordan, Robert J. Vandenberg, and Hettie A. Richardson, "Employee Involvement Climate and Organizational Effectiveness," *Human Resource Management* 44, no. 4 (Winter 2005): 471–488.

55. Glenn L. Dalton, "The Collective Stretch," *Management Review* (December 1998): 54–59.

56. J. Richard Hackman and Greg R. Oldham, *Work Redesign* (Reading, MA: Addison-Wesley, 1980); and J. Richard Hackman and Greg Oldham, "Motivation through the Design of Work: Test of a Theory," *Organizational Behavior and Human Performance* 16 (1976): 250–279.

57. Xu Huang and Evert Van de Vliert, "Where Intrinsic Job Satisfaction Fails to Work: National Moderators of Intrinsic Motivation," *Journal of Organizational Behavior* 24 (2003): 157–179.

58. Ann Podolske, "Giving Employees a Voice in Pay Structures," *Business Ethics* (March–April 1998): 12.

59. Rekha Balu, "Bonuses Aren't Just for the Bosses," *Fast Company* (December 2000): 74–76.

60. Edwin P. Hollander and Lynn R. Offermann, "Power and Leadership in Organizations," *American Psychologist* 45 (February 1990): 179–189.

61. Jay A. Conger and Rabindra N. Kanungo, "The Empowerment Process: Integrating Theory and Practice," *Academy of Management Review* 13 (1988): 471–482.

62. Jay A. Conger and Rabindra N. Kanungo, "The Empowerment Process: Integrating Theory and Practice," *Academy of Management Review* 13 (1998): 471–482.

63. David E. Bowen and Edward E. Lawler III, "The Empowerment of Service Workers: What, Why, How, and When," *Sloan Management Review* (Spring 1992): 31–39; and Ray W. Coye and James A. Belohav, "An Exploratory Analysis of Employee Participation," *Group and Organization Management* 20, no. 1, (March 1995): 4–17.

64. William C. Taylor, "Under New Management; These Workers Act Like Owners (Because They Are)," *The New York Times* (May 21, 2006), www.nytimes.com.

65. Russ Forrester, "Empowerment: Rejuvenating a Potent Idea," *Academy of Management Executive* 14, no. 3 (2000): 67–80.

66. Ellsworth, "Making a Place for Blue Collars in the Boardroom."

67. Ricardo Semler, "How We Went Digital Without a Strategy," *Harvard Business Review* (September–October 2000): 51–58.

68. Podolske, "Giving Employees a Voice in Pay Structures."

69. This discussion is based on Robert C. Ford and Myron D. Fottler, "Empowerment: A Matter of Degree," *Academy of Management Executive* 9, no. 3 (1995): 21–31.

70. Bruce E. Kaufman, "High-Level Employee Involvement at Delta Air Lines," *Human Resource Management* 42, no. 2 (Summer 2003): 175–190.

71. Geoff Colvin, "The 100 Best Companies to Work For."

72. Betsy Morris, "The Best Place to Work Now," *Fortune* (January 23, 2006): 78–86.

73. Colvin, "The 100 Best Companies to Work For"; Levering and Moskowitz, "And the Winners Are . . ."; and Daniel Roth, "Trading Places," *Fortune* (January 23, 2006): 120–128.

74. Cheryl Dahle, "Four Tires, Free Beef," *Fast Company* (September 2003): 36.

75. Jerry Krueger and Emily Killham, "At Work, Feeling Good Matters," *Gallup Management Journal* (December 8, 2005).

76. Erin White, "New Recipe; To Keep Employees, Domino's Decides It's Not All About Pay," *The Wall Street Journal* (February 17, 2005): A1, A9.

77. This discussion is based on Tony Schwartz, "The Greatest Sources of Satisfaction in the Workplace are Internal and Emotional," *Fast Company* (November 2000): 398–402; Marcus Buckingham and Curt Coffman, *First, Break All the Rules: What the World's Greatest Managers Do Differently* (New York: Simon and Schuster, 1999); and Krueger and Killham, "At Work, Feeling Good Matters."

78. The Gallup Organization, Princeton, NJ. All rights reserved. Used with permission.

79. Curt Coffman and Gabriel Gonzalez-Molina, *Follow This Path: How the World's Greatest Organizations Drive Growth by Unleashing Human Potential* (New York: Warner Books, 2002), as reported in Anne Fisher, "Why Passion Pays," *FSB* (September 2002): 58.

80. Rodd Wagner, "'One Store, One Team' at Best Buy," *Gallup Management Journal* (August 12, 2004).

81. Thottam, "Reworking Work."

CHAPTER OUTLINE

Manager's Challenge

Communication and the Manager's Job

What Is Communication?

The Communication Process

Communicating Among People

Communication Channels

Communicating to Persuade and Influence Others

Nonverbal Communication

Listening

Organizational Communication

Formal Communication Channels

Team Communication Channels

Personal Communication Channels

Communicating During Turbulent Times

Open Communication

Dialogue

Crisis Communication

Feedback and Learning

Managing Organizational Communication

Barriers to Communication

Overcoming Communication Barriers

LEARNING OBJECTIVES

After studying this chapter, you should be able to:

1. Explain why communication is essential for effective management and describe how nonverbal behavior and listening affect communication among people.

2. Explain how managers use communication to persuade and influence others.

3. Describe the concept of channel richness, and explain how communication channels influence the quality of communication.

4. Explain the difference between formal and informal organizational communications and the importance of each for organization management.

5. Identify how structure influences team communication outcomes.

6. Explain why open communication, dialogue, and feedback are essential approaches to communication in a turbulent environment.

7. Identify the skills managers need for communicating during a crisis situation.

8. Describe barriers to organizational communication, and suggest ways to avoid or overcome them.

COMMUNICATION

MANAGER'S CHALLENGE

As a doctor, Peter Plantes knows first hand what it's like to lose patients that he thought could be saved. As vice president of VHA, Inc., an alliance of more than 2,400 not-for-profit health care organizations across the United States, he knows what it's like to see hospitals losing millions of dollars due to inefficiencies and waste. Because the two issues come together most dramatically in the operating room, that's where VHA administrators are looking to see what issues contribute to inefficiencies and errors in patient care. They decide to conduct a survey at 20 hospitals, based on recent studies suggesting that the intense atmosphere of operating rooms, where surgeons typically call all the shots, is a big part of the problem. Administrators—and most surgeons—are stunned by the results. As many as 60 percent of nurses and support staff members say they find it difficult to speak up if they perceive a problem with patient care in the operating room. Something has to be done to improve communications between surgeons and support staff or hospitals will continue to unnecessarily lose patients' lives, as well as waste money due to mistakes that could have been prevented.[1]

> If you were a manager at VHA, Inc., what steps would you take to improve communications between surgeons and hospital support staff? How would you overcome the communication barriers that exist and get people to communicate across functional and hierarchical boundaries?

■ **TAKE A MOMENT**

Effective communication, both within the organization and with people outside the company, is a major challenge and responsibility for managers. Although in most companies, poor communication doesn't risk people's lives, as it does in hospital operating rooms, ineffective communication can cause significant problems, including poor employee morale, lack of innovation, decreased performance, and a failure to respond to new threats or opportunities in the environment. Many managers are trying to improve their communications knowledge and skills.

To stay connected with employees and customers and shape company direction, managers must excel at personal communications. At Dallas-based Brinker International, CEO Doug Brooks set up numerous processes to make sure he stays in touch with employees, including surveys, leadership discussion groups, and small quality circles that involve people from all levels of the company. Guidant Corporation, now owned by Eli Lilly, has a "reverse mentoring" program in which each top manager is assigned a mentor from lower organizational levels to help them stay in touch with what's going on in the organization. James E. Rogers, CEO of Cinergy Corp., encourages employees to send him e-mails, and he reads every one. They often alert him to such issues as festering problems in the organization, what the competition is doing, or pending legislation that could affect energy prices. Rogers is by no means alone. A survey for *The Wall Street Journal* found that 39 out of 44 companies responding said their CEOs personally read and answer employees' e-mails.[2]

Nonmanagers often are amazed at how much energy successful executives put into communication. Consider the comment about Robert Strauss, former chairman of the Democratic National Committee and former ambassador to Russia:

> One of his friends says, "His network is everywhere. It ranges from bookies to bank presidents. . . ."
>
> He seems to find time to make innumerable phone calls to "keep in touch"; he cultivates secretaries as well as senators; he will befriend a middle-level White House aide whom other important officials won't bother with. Every few months, he sends candy to the White House switchboard operators.[3]

This chapter explains why executives such as Robert Strauss, Doug Brooks, and James Rogers are effective communicators. First, we examine communication as a crucial part of the manager's job and describe a model of the communication process. Next, we consider the interpersonal aspects of communication, including communication channels, persuasion, listening skills, and nonverbal communication that affect managers' ability to communicate. Then, we look at the organization as a whole and consider formal upward, downward, and horizontal communications as well as personal networks and informal communications. We discuss the importance of keeping multiple channels of communication open and examine how managers can effectively communicate during times of turbulence, uncertainty, and crisis. Finally, we examine barriers to communication and how managers can overcome them.

COMMUNICATION AND THE MANAGER'S JOB

How important is communication? Consider this: Managers spend at least 80 percent of every working day in direct communication with others. In other words, 48 minutes of every hour is spent in meetings, on the telephone, communicating online, or talking informally while walking around. The other 20 percent of a typical manager's time is spent doing desk work, most of which is also communication in the form of reading and writing.[4]

Exhibit 20.1 illustrates the crucial role of managers as communication champions. Managers gather important information from both inside and outside the organization and then distribute appropriate information to others who need it.

EXHIBIT 20.1

The Manager as Communication Champion

SOURCES: Adapted from Henry Mintzberg, *The Nature of Managerial Work* (New York; Harper and Row, 1973); and Richard L. Daft, *The Leadership Experience,* 3rd ed. (Cincinnati, OH: South-Western, 2005): 346.

Managers' communication is *purpose-directed*, in that it directs everyone's attention toward the vision, values, and desired goals of the team or organization and influences people to act in a way to achieve the goals. Managers facilitate *strategic conversations* by using open communication, actively listening to others, applying the practice of dialogue, and using feedback for learning and change. **Strategic conversation** refers to people talking across boundaries and hierarchical levels about the team or organization's vision, critical strategic themes, and the values that help achieve important goals.[5] For example, at Royal Philips Electronics, president Gerald Kleisterlee defined four strategic technology themes that he believes should define Philips's future in the industry: display, storage, connectivity, and digital video processing. These themes intentionally cross technology boundaries, which requires that people communicate and collaborate across departments and divisions to accomplish goals.[6] Effective managers use many communication methods, including selecting rich channels of communication; facilitating upward, downward, and horizontal communication; understanding and using nonverbal communication; and building informal communication networks that cross organization boundaries.

Communication permeates every management function described in Chapter 1.[7] For example, when managers perform the planning function, they gather information; write letters, memos, and reports; and meet with other managers to formulate the plan. When managers lead, they communicate to share a vision of what the organization can be and motivate employees to help achieve it. When managers organize, they gather information about the state of the organization and communicate a new structure to others. Communication skills are a fundamental part of every managerial activity.

What Is Communication?

A professor at Harvard once asked a class to define communication by drawing pictures. Most students drew a manager speaking or typing on a computer keyboard. Some placed "speech balloons" next to their characters; others showed pages flying from a printer. "No," the professor told the class, "none of you has captured the essence of communication." He went on to explain that communication means "to share"—not "to speak" or "to write."

Communication thus can be defined as the process by which information is exchanged and understood by two or more people, usually with the intent to motivate or influence behavior. Communication is not just sending information. Honoring this distinction between *sharing* and *proclaiming* is crucial for successful management. A manager who does not listen is like a used-car salesperson who claims, "I sold a car—they just did not buy it." Management communication is a two-way street that includes listening and other forms of feedback. Effective communication, in the words of one expert, is as follows:

> When two people interact, they put themselves into each other's shoes, try to perceive the world as the other person perceives it, try to predict how the other will respond. Interaction involves reciprocal role-taking, the mutual employment of empathetic skills. The goal of interaction is the merger of self and other, a complete ability to anticipate, predict, and behave in accordance with the joint needs of self and other.[8]

It is the desire to share understanding that motivates executives to visit employees on the shop floor, hold small informal meetings, or eat with employees in the company cafeteria. The things managers learn from direct communication with employees shape their understanding of the organization.

The Communication Process

Many people think communication is simple. After all, we communicate every day without even thinking about it. However, communication usually is complex, and the opportunities for sending or receiving the wrong messages are innumerable. No

strategic conversation Dialogue across boundaries and hierarchical levels about the team or organization's vision, critical strategic themes, and the values that help achieve important goals.

communication The process by which information is exchanged and understood by two or more people, usually with the intent to motivate or influence behavior.

EXHIBIT 20.2

A Model of the Communication Process

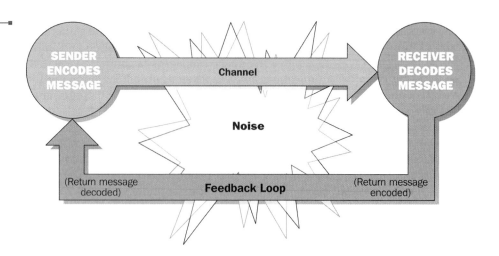

doubt, you have heard someone say, "But that's not what I meant!" Have you ever received directions you thought were clear and yet still got lost? How often have you wasted time on misunderstood instructions?

To more fully understand the complexity of the communication process, note the key elements outlined in Exhibit 20.2. Two essential elements in every communication situation are the sender and the receiver. The *sender* is anyone who wishes to convey an idea or concept to others, to seek information, or to express a thought or emotion. The *receiver* is the person to whom the message is sent. The sender **encodes** the idea by selecting symbols with which to compose a message. The **message** is the tangible formulation of the idea that is sent to the receiver. The message is sent through a **channel**, which is the communication carrier. The channel can be a formal report, a telephone call or e-mail message, or a face-to-face meeting. The receiver **decodes** the symbols to interpret the meaning of the message. Encoding and decoding are potential sources for communication errors, because knowledge, attitudes, and background act as filters and create *noise* when translating from symbols to meaning. Finally, **feedback** occurs when the receiver responds to the sender's communication with a return message. Without feedback, the communication is *one-way*; with feedback, it is *two-way*. Feedback is a powerful aid to communication effectiveness, because it enables the sender to determine whether the receiver correctly interpreted the message.

■ **TAKE A MOMENT**

As a new manager, be a communication champion by communicating across boundaries, actively listening to others, and using feedback to make improvements. Remember that effective communication requires sharing and achieving mutual understanding.

encode To select symbols with which to compose a message.

message The tangible formulation of an idea to be sent to a receiver.

channel The carrier of a communication.

decode To translate the symbols used in a message for the purpose of interpreting its meaning.

feedback A response by the receiver to the sender's communication.

Managers who are effective communicators understand and use the circular nature of communication. Consider Nortel Networks' *Virtual Leadership Academy*, a monthly televised program hosted by Dan Hunt, president of Nortel's Caribbean and Latin American operations, and Emma Carrasco, vice president of marketing and communications. Hunt and Carrasco use a talk-show format to get people talking. Employees from about 40 different countries watch the show from their regional offices and call in their questions and comments. "We're always looking for ways to break down barriers," says Carrasco. "People watch talk shows in every country, and they've learned that it's okay to say what's on their minds."[9] The television program is the channel through which Hunt and Carrasco send their encoded message. Employees decode and interpret the message and encode their feedback, which is sent through the channel of the telephone hookup. The communications circuit is complete.

COMMUNICATING AMONG PEOPLE

The communication model in Exhibit 20.2 illustrates the components of effective communication. Communications can break down if sender and receiver do not encode or decode language in the same way.[10] We all know how difficult it is to communicate with someone who does not speak our language, and today's managers are often trying to communicate with people who speak many different native languages. However, communication breakdowns can also occur between people who speak the same language.

Many factors can lead to a breakdown in communications. For example, the selection of communication channel can determine whether the message is distorted by noise and interference. The listening skills of both parties and attention to nonverbal behavior can determine whether a message is truly shared. Thus, for managers to be effective communicators, they must understand how factors such as communication channels, nonverbal behavior, and listening all work to enhance or detract from communication.

© POLYCOM, INC./PR NEWSWIRE PHOTO SERVICE

CONCEPT CONNECTION Videoconferencing systems, such as the Polycom high-definition system shown here, use increasingly sophisticated hardware and software to transmit both visual and verbal cues and provide feedback. On large screens in the front of the room, managers not only see and hear colleagues thousands of miles away, but they can also scrutinize displays of relevant information. These new systems provide **channel richness** once characteristic of only face-to-face meetings. Analysts expect that terrorism threats, possible pandemics, and expensive business travel will fuel at least a 20 percent annual increase in spending on videoconferencing systems in the foreseeable future.

Communication Channels

Managers have a choice of many channels through which to communicate to other managers or employees. A manager may discuss a problem face-to-face, make a telephone call, use instant messaging, send an e-mail, write a memo or letter, or put an item in a newsletter, depending on the nature of the message. Research has attempted to explain how managers select communication channels to enhance communication effectiveness.[11] The research has found that channels differ in their capacity to convey information. Just as a pipeline's physical characteristics limit the kind and amount of liquid that can be pumped through it, a communication channel's physical characteristics limit the kind and amount of information that can be conveyed through it. The channels available to managers can be classified into a hierarchy based on information richness.

THE HIERARCHY OF CHANNEL RICHNESS

Channel richness is the amount of information that can be transmitted during a communication episode. The hierarchy of channel richness is illustrated in Exhibit 20.3. The capacity of an information channel is influenced by three characteristics: (1) the ability to handle multiple cues simultaneously; (2) the ability to facilitate rapid, two-way feedback; and (3) the ability to establish a personal focus for the communication. Face-to-face discussion is the richest medium, because it permits direct experience, multiple information cues, immediate feedback, and personal focus. Face-to-face discussions facilitate the assimilation of broad cues and deep, emotional understanding of the situation. Telephone conversations are next in the richness hierarchy. Although eye contact, posture, and other body language cues are missing, the human voice can still carry a tremendous amount of emotional information.

channel richness The amount of information that can be transmitted during a communication episode.

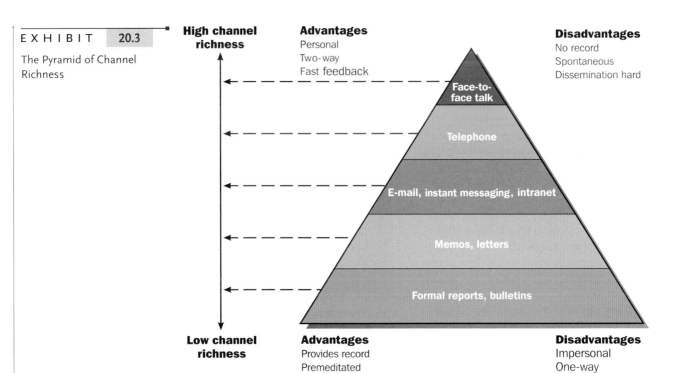

EXHIBIT 20.3

The Pyramid of Channel Richness

High channel richness

Advantages
Personal
Two-way
Fast feedback

Disadvantages
No record
Spontaneous
Dissemination hard

Face-to-face talk

Telephone

E-mail, instant messaging, intranet

Memos, letters

Formal reports, bulletins

Low channel richness

Advantages
Provides record
Premeditated
Easily disseminated

Disadvantages
Impersonal
One-way
Slow feedback

Electronic messaging, such as e-mail and instant messaging, is increasingly being used for messages that were once handled via the telephone. However, in a survey by researchers at The Ohio State University, most respondents said they preferred the telephone or face-to-face conversation for communicating difficult news, giving advice, or expressing affection.[12] Because e-mail messages lack both visual and verbal cues and don't allow for interaction and feedback, messages can sometimes be misunderstood. Using e-mail to discuss disputes, for example, can lead to an escalation rather than a resolution of conflict.[13] Studies have found that e-mail messages tend to be much more blunt than other forms of communication, even other written communications. This bluntness can cause real problems when communicating cross-culturally, because some cultures consider directness rude or insulting.[14] Instant messaging alleviates the problem of miscommunication to some extent by allowing for immediate feedback. **Instant messaging (IM)** allows users to see who is connected to a network and share short-hand messages or documents with them instantly. A growing number of managers are using IM, indicating that it helps people get responses faster and collaborate more smoothly.[15] Overreliance on e-mail and IM can damage company communications because people stop talking to one another in a rich way that builds solid interpersonal relationships. However, some research indicates that electronic messaging can enable reasonably rich communication if the technology is used appropriately.[16] Organizations are also using interactive meetings over the Internet, sometimes adding video capabilities to provide visual cues and greater channel richness.

Still lower on the hierarchy of channel richness are written letters and memos. Written communication can be personally focused, but it conveys only the cues written on paper and is slower to provide feedback. Impersonal written media, including fliers, bulletins, and standard computer reports, are the lowest in richness. These channels are not focused on a single receiver, use limited information cues, and do not permit feedback.

SELECTING THE APPROPRIATE CHANNEL

It is important for managers to understand that each communication channel has advantages and disadvantages, and that each can be an effective means of communication in the appropriate circumstances.[17] Channel selection depends on

instant messaging (IM)
Electronic communication that allows users to see who is connected to a network and share information instantly.

whether the message is routine or nonroutine. *Nonroutine messages* typically are ambiguous, concern novel events, and involve great potential for misunderstanding. They often are characterized by time pressure and surprise. Managers can communicate nonroutine messages effectively by selecting rich channels. *Routine* messages are simple and straightforward. They convey data or statistics or simply put into words what managers already agree on and understand. Routine messages can be efficiently communicated through a channel lower in richness, such as e-mail or memorandum. Written communications should also be used when the communication is official and a permanent record is required.[18]

Consider the alert to consumers issued by the FDA following a widespread e.coli outbreak in September 2006. Tainted bagged spinach sickened 199 people in at least 26 states and resulted in one death. Grocers immediately pulled the product from shelves, and widespread news coverage warned the public not to consume any bagged spinach until the cause of the contamination could be identified. An immediate response was critical. This type of nonroutine communication forces a rich information exchange. The group will meet face-to-face, brainstorm ideas, and provide rapid feedback to resolve the situation and convey the correct information. If, in contrast, an agency director is preparing a press release about a routine matter such as a policy change or new department members, less information capacity is needed. The director and public relations people might begin developing the press release with an exchange of memos, telephone calls, and e-mail messages.

■ **TAKE A MOMENT**

As a new manager, take care in choosing how to send a message. Don't use e-mail for difficult or emotional conversations that should be dealt with face-to-face or via the telephone. E-mail is preferable for more routine communications.

The key is to select a channel to fit the message. During a major acquisition, one firm decided to send top executives to all major work sites of the acquired company, where most of the workers met the managers in person, heard about their plans for the company, and had a chance to ask questions. The results were well worth the time and expense of the personal face-to-face meetings because the acquired workforce saw their new managers as understanding, open, and willing to listen.[19] Communicating their nonroutine message about the acquisition in person prevented damaging rumors and misunderstandings. The choice of a communication channel can also convey a symbolic meaning to the receiver; in a sense, the medium becomes the message. The firm's decision to communicate face-to-face with the acquired workforce signaled to employees that managers cared about them as individuals.

Communicating to Persuade and Influence Others

Communication is not just for conveying information, but to persuade and influence people. Although communication skills have always been important to managers, the ability to persuade and influence others is even more critical today. Businesses are run largely by cross-functional teams who are actively involved in making decisions. Issuing directives is no longer an appropriate or effective way to get things done.[20]

To persuade and influence, managers have to communicate frequently and easily with others. Yet some people find interpersonal communication experiences unrewarding or difficult and thus tend to avoid situations where communication is required. The term **communication apprehension** describes this avoidance behavior, and is defined as "an individual's level of fear or anxiety associated with either real or anticipated communication." With training and practice, managers can overcome their communication apprehension and become more effective communicators.

communication apprehension An individual's level of fear or anxiety associated with interpersonal communications.

Go to the experiential exercise on page 685 that pertains to your level of communication apprehension.

Effective persuasion doesn't mean telling people what you want them to do; instead, it involves listening, learning about others' interests and needs, and leading people to a shared solution.[21] Managers who forget that communication means *sharing*, as described earlier, aren't likely to be as effective at influencing or persuading others, as the founder and president of the executive coaching firm Valuedance learned the hard way.

Valuedance

When Susan Cramm was asked by a client to help persuade the client's boss to support an initiative she wanted to launch, Cramm readily agreed. They scheduled a meeting with the boss, then held a series of planning sessions where the two discussed the current situation at the client's firm, weighed the options, and decided on the best approach for launching the initiative. Filled with enthusiasm and armed with a PowerPoint presentation, Cramm was sure the client's boss would see things their way.

An agonizing 15 minutes later, she was out the door, PowerPoint deck and all, having just had a lesson about the art of persuasion. What went wrong? Cramm had focused on the hard, rational matters and ignored the soft skills of relationship building, listening, and negotiating that are so critical to persuading others. "Never did we consider the boss's views," Cramm said later about the planning sessions she and her client held to prepare for the meeting. "Like founding members of the 'it's all about me' club, we fell upon our swords, believing that our impeccable logic, persistence, and enthusiasm would carry the day."

With that approach, the meeting was over before it even began. The formal presentation shut down communications because it implied that Cramm had all the answers and the boss was just there to listen and agree.[22]

As this example shows, people stop listening to someone when that individual isn't listening to them. By failing to show interest in and respect for the boss's point of view, Cramm and her client lost the boss's interest from the beginning, no matter how suitable the ideas they were presenting. To effectively influence and persuade others, managers have to show they care about how the other person feels. Persuasion requires tapping into people's emotions, which can only be done on a personal, rather than a rational, impersonal level.

Managers who use symbols, metaphors, and stories to deliver their messages have an easier time influencing and persuading others. Stories draw on people's imaginations and emotions, which helps managers make sense of a fast-changing environment in ways that people can understand and share. If we think back to our early school years, we may remember that the most effective lessons often were couched in stories. Presenting hard facts and figures rarely has the same power. Evidence of the compatibility of stories with human thinking was demonstrated by a study at Stanford Business School.[23] The point was to convince MBA students that a company practiced a policy of avoiding layoffs. For some students, only a story was used. For others, statistical data were provided that showed little turnover compared to competitors. For other students, statistics and stories were combined, and yet other students were shown the company's official policy statements. Of all these approaches, the students presented with a vivid story alone were most convinced that the company truly practiced a policy of avoiding layoffs. Managers can learn to use elements of storytelling to enhance their communication.[24] Stories need not be long, complex, or carefully constructed. A story can be a joke, an analogy, or a verbal snapshot of something from the manager's own past experiences.[25]

Nonverbal Communication

Managers also use symbols to communicate what is important. Managers are watched, and their behavior, appearance, actions, and attitudes are symbolic of what they value and expect of others.

Most of us have heard the saying that "actions speak louder than words." Indeed, we communicate without words all the time, whether we realize it or not. **Nonverbal communication** refers to messages sent through human actions and behaviors rather than through words.[26] Most managers are astonished to learn that words themselves carry little meaning. A significant portion of the shared understanding from communication comes from the nonverbal messages of facial expression, voice, mannerisms, posture, and dress.

Nonverbal communication occurs mostly face to face. One researcher found three sources of communication cues during face-to-face communication: the *verbal*, which are the actual spoken words; the *vocal*, which include the pitch, tone, and timbre of a person's voice; and *facial expressions*. According to this study, the relative weights of these three factors in message interpretation are as follows: verbal impact, 7 percent; vocal impact, 38 percent; and facial impact, 55 percent.[27] To some extent, we are all natural *face readers*, but facial expressions can be misinterpreted, suggesting that managers need to ask questions to make sure they're getting the right message. Managers can hone their skills at reading facial expressions and improve their ability to connect with and influence followers. Studies indicate that managers who seem responsive to the unspoken emotions of employees are more effective and successful in the workplace.[28]

This research also strongly implies for managers that "it's not what you say but how you say it." Nonverbal messages and body language often convey our real thoughts and feelings with greater force than do our most carefully selected words. Thus, while the conscious mind may be formulating a vocal message such as "Congratulations on your promotion," body language may be signaling true feelings through blushing, perspiring, or avoiding eye contact. When the verbal and nonverbal messages are contradictory, the receiver will usually give more weight to behavioral actions than to verbal messages.[29]

A manager's office sends nonverbal cues as well. For example, what do the following seating arrangements mean? (1) The supervisor stays behind her desk, and you sit in a straight chair on the opposite side. (2) The two of you sit in straight chairs away from her desk, perhaps at a table. (3) The two of you sit in a seating arrangement consisting of a sofa and easy chair. To most people, the first arrangement indicates, "I'm the boss here," or "I'm in authority." The second arrangement indicates, "This is serious business." The third indicates a more casual and friendly, "Let's get to know each other."[30] Nonverbal messages can be a powerful asset to communication if they complement and support verbal messages. Managers should pay close attention to nonverbal behavior when communicating. They can learn to coordinate their verbal and nonverbal messages and at the same time be sensitive to what their peers, subordinates, and supervisors are saying nonverbally.

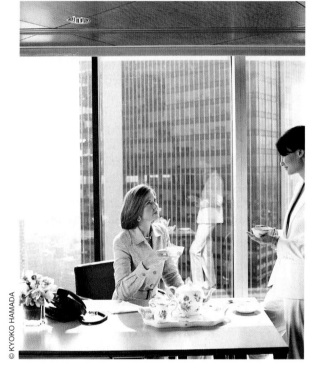

© KYOKO HAMADA

CONCEPT CONNECTION About a year ago, Hillary Johnson became the editor of a small newspaper in California. Describing her new responsibilities, Johnson emphasizes the importance of **listening**. "Whenever someone walks into my office with a knitted brow and an open mouth, I say, preemptively, 'Would you like a cup of tea?' Whatever the answer, this creates a pause and sets the tone for the discussion to follow." Johnson is convinced that listening to employees, although time consuming, is essential to her success as a manager.

Listening

One of the most important tools of manager communication is listening, both to employees and customers. Most managers now recognize that important information flows from the bottom up, not the top down, and managers had better be tuned in.[31] This chapter's Unlocking Innovative Solutions Through People box describes how

nonverbal communication A communication transmitted through actions and behaviors rather than through words.

Unlocking Innovative Solutions Through | P E O P L E

MANAGERS AT KWIK-FIT LEARN THAT IT PAYS TO LISTEN

When Keren Edwards took over as human resources director at Kwik-Fit Financial Services, the work environment was dour indeed. Staff turnover at the insurance company call center, located near Glasgow, was 52 percent. So Edwards rolled up her sleeves and got to work.

Her efforts have clearly paid off. The Chartered Institute of Personnel and Development (CIPD) awarded Kwik-Fit its prestigious 2005 People Management Award, and *The Sunday Times* named it one of Britain's 100 best places to work. Kwik-Fit's 2005 turnover rate dropped to about 34 percent, profits nearly doubled, and more than 7 out of 10 employees said they enjoyed working there. What accounts for this turnaround? According to Edwards, it all comes down to listening: "Listening to your people and making changes based on their views, opinions, and feedback is very powerful."

With the support of new managing director Martin Oliver, who vowed to make Kwik-Fit a "fantastic place to work," Edwards supervised a series of one-day workshops that called on the entire workforce to tackle the company's human resource problems. She and her staff primed the idea pump by making it a competition, posting the number of suggestions generated by each session outside the company cafeteria. In all, 32 workshops generated 6,500 proposals, some admittedly more fanciful than practical—for example, a pet day care and a rooftop helicopter pad. But there were plenty of potentially workable suggestions. The company then charged teams consisting of both senior managers and rank-and-file volunteers with the task of implementing selected employee-generated ideas.

As a result, Kwik-Fit employees now work in a completely renovated building and enjoy bonuses, performance-based pay, flextime, flexible benefits, and an onsite day care. In addition, they counter job stress by taking advantage of the free corporate gym; a cheerful chill-out room complete with TV, pool tables, and computer games; yoga and tai chi classes; and a massage service. And then there's Rob Hunter, the company's first "minister of fun," who organizes special theme days, social evenings, and the holiday party, not to mention the annual sales awards he hosts in a sparkly jacket. "Staff needs to work hard and play hard to be motivated and productive," he observes.

Kwik-Fit has gone from being perceived as a company that doesn't care about its workers to one where employees feel they matter. Its "Mail Martin" program, which encourages people to send ideas straight to the managing director by awarding £250 monthly for the best idea, guarantees that Kwik-Fit call center employees will continue to feel they're being heard.

SOURCES: Steve Crabb,"You Can't Get Better," *www.peoplemanagement.co.uk* (November 10, 2005): 28–30; "Meet the Winner," www.onrec.com/content2/news.asp?ID=9527; and "Kwik-Fit Financial Services," *The Sunday Times* (March 06, 2005): http://business.timesonline.co.uk/article/0,12190-1501501,00.html.

a new managing director and human resources director transformed Kwik-Fit Financial Services by listening to employees who were tired of feeling as though no one in the organization cared about them. Some organizations use innovative techniques for finding out what's on employees' and customers' minds. Cabela's, a retailer for outdoor enthusiasts, lets employees borrow and use any of the company's products for a month, as long as they provide feedback that helps other employees better serve customers. The employee fills out a form detailing the product's pros and cons, gives a talk to other employees or customers about the product, and provides feedback in the form of "Item Notes" that are fed into a knowledge sharing system.[32]

In the communication model in Exhibit 20.2, the listener is responsible for message reception, which is a vital link in the communication process. **Listening** involves the skill of grasping both facts and feelings to interpret a message's genuine meaning. Only then can the manager provide the appropriate response. Listening requires attention, energy, and skill. Although about 75 percent of effective communication is listening, most people spend only 30 to 40 percent of their time listening, which leads to many communication errors.[33] One of the secrets of highly successful salespeople is that they spend 60 to 70 percent of a sales call letting the customer talk.[34] However, listening involves much more than just not talking. Many people

listening The skill of receiving messages to accurately grasp facts and feelings to interpret the genuine meaning.

Keys	Poor Listener	Good Listener
1. Listen actively.	Is passive, laid back	Asks questions, paraphrases what is said
2. Find areas of interest.	Tunes out dry subjects	Looks for opportunities, new learning
3. Resist distractions.	Is easily distracted	Fights or avoids distraction, tolerates bad habits, knows how to concentrate
4. Capitalize on the fact that thought is faster.	Tends to daydream with slow speakers	Challenges, anticipates, mentally summarizes; weighs the evidence; listens between the lines to tone of voice
5. Be responsive.	Is minimally involved	Nods, shows interest, give and take, positive feedback
6. Judge content, not delivery.	Tunes out if delivery is poor	Judges content; skips over delivery errors
7. Hold one's fire.	Has preconceptions, starts to argue	Does not judge until comprehension is complete
8. Listen for ideas.	Listens for facts	Listens to central themes
9. Work at listening.	Shows no energy output; fakes attention	Works hard, exhibits active body state, eye contact
10. Exercise one's mind.	Resists difficult material in favor of light, recreational material	Uses heavier material as exercise for the mind

SOURCES: Adapted from Sherman K. Okum, "How to Be a Better Listener," *Nation's Business* (August 1975): 62; and Philip Morgan and Kent Baker, "Building a Professional Image: Improving Listening Behavior," *Supervisory Management* (November 1985): 34–38.

EXHIBIT 20.4

Ten Keys to Effective Listening

do not know how to listen effectively. They concentrate on formulating what they are going to say next rather than on what is being said to them. Our listening efficiency, as measured by the amount of material understood and remembered by subjects 48 hours after listening to a 10-minute message, is, on average, no better than 25 percent.[35]

> **TAKE A MOMENT** As a new manager, use stories and metaphors to tap into people's imagination and emotions. When influencing or persuading, first listen and strive to understand the other person's point of view. And pay attention to nonverbal communication.

What constitutes good listening? Exhibit 20.4 gives 10 keys to effective listening and illustrates a number of ways to distinguish a bad from a good listener. A good listener finds areas of interest, is flexible, works hard at listening, and uses thought speed to mentally summarize, weigh, and anticipate what the speaker says. Good listening means shifting from thinking about self to empathizing with the other person and thus requires a high degree of emotional intelligence, as described in Chapter 17. Dr. Robert Buckman, a cancer specialist who teaches other doctors, as well as businesspeople, how to break bad news, emphasizes the importance of listening. "The trust that you build just by letting someone say what they feel is incredible," Buckman says.[36]

Few things are as maddening to people as not being listened to. Executives at health-insurer Humana Inc. realized they could grab a bigger share of the Medicare drug benefits business simply by listening to America's senior citizens.

Sixty-eight-year-old Helen Arnold tells how she spent hours trying to research a Medicare drug benefit plan over the phone without ever being able to get through to a person. "This recorded voice just kept giving me all these numbers to punch," she said, her voice rising as she recalled the frustration. It's a frustration that was shared by seniors all over the United States as they struggled to comprehend the new Medicare plans.

Humana, Inc.

> Arnold is part of a consumer gripe session, sponsored by Humana, Inc., the nation's number 5 health insurer. Humana decided to take an approach unique in the health insurance industry—listening to what customers want and designing products and services around their needs. The company holds consumer focus groups, solicits the input of employees, and observes people in their homes as they make health-care decisions. Humana learned for example, that many people got frustrated researching the new Medicare plans online or over the phone, so it set up kiosks at Wal-Marts, hired sales representatives to sell the plans in people's homes, and made a deal with 17,000 State Farm insurance agents to offer Humana's Medicare plans through their offices.
>
> Listening has paid off. In early 2006, Humana had signed up 2.4 million people to its Medicare plans, second only to much-larger United Health Group. The company is using listening to better serve other customers as well, such as by setting up kiosks at employers' offices so people can talk to someone face-to-face.[37]

Humana is the first major health insurer to create a culture that emphasizes actively listening to customers. Consumer products company Procter & Gamble effectively used these techniques for finding out what people want. P&G also learned that listening to employees translates into business success. Managers emphasize the importance of listening to both internal as well as external customers. "Gaining the hearts and minds of every employee . . . is no small challenge, and it's one that managers have to wrestle with every day to succeed," says P&G's global marketing officer James Stengel. "That's what we do with our customers—and now we're making sure we do it with our own employees."[38]

ORGANIZATIONAL COMMUNICATION

Another aspect of management communication concerns the organization as a whole. Organization-wide communications typically flow in three directions—downward, upward, and horizontally. Managers are responsible for establishing and maintaining formal channels of communication in these three directions. Managers also use informal channels, which means they get out of their offices and mingle with employees.

Formal Communication Channels

Formal communication channels are those that flow within the chain of command or task responsibility defined by the organization. The three formal channels and the types of information conveyed in each are illustrated in Exhibit 20.5.[39] Downward and upward communications are the primary forms of communication used in most traditional, vertically organized companies. However, many of today's organizations emphasize horizontal communication, with people continuously sharing information across departments and levels.

Electronic communication such as e-mail and instant messaging have made it easier than ever for information to flow in all directions. For example, the U.S. Army is using technology to rapidly transmit communications about weather conditions, the latest intelligence on the insurgency, and so forth to lieutenants in the field in Iraq. Similarly, the Navy uses instant messaging to communicate within ships, across Navy divisions, and even back to the Pentagon in Washington. "Instant messaging has allowed us to keep our crew members on the same page at the same time," says Lt. Cmdr. Mike Houston, who oversees the Navy's communications program. "Lives are at stake in real time, and we're seeing a new level of communication and readiness."[40]

DOWNWARD COMMUNICATION

The most familiar and obvious flow of formal communication, **downward communication**, refers to the messages and information sent from top management to subordinates in a downward direction.

formal communication channel A communication channel that flows within the chain of command or task responsibility defined by the organization.

downward communication Messages sent from top management down to subordinates.

Upward Communication
- Problems and exceptions
- Suggestions for improvement
- Performance reports
- Grievances and disputes
- Financial and accounting information

Downward Communication
- Implementation of goals, strategies
- Job instructions and rationale
- Procedures and practices
- Performance feedback
- Indoctrination

Horizontal Communication
- Intradepartmental problem solving
- Interdepartmental coordination
- Change initiatives and improvements

Coordinate

Interpret

Influence

Managers can communicate downward to employees in many ways. Some of the most common are through speeches, messages in company newsletters, e-mail, information leaflets tucked into pay envelopes, material on bulletin boards, and policy and procedures manuals. Managers sometimes use creative approaches to downward communication to make sure employees get the message. Mike Olson, plant manager at Ryerson Midwest Coil Processing, noticed that workers were dropping expensive power tools, so he hung price tags on the tools to show the replacement cost. Employees solved the problem by finding a way to hook up the tools so they wouldn't be dropped. Olson's symbolic communication created a climate of working together for solutions.[41]

Managers also have to decide what to communicate about. It is impossible for managers to communicate with employees about everything that goes on in the organization, so they have to make choices about the important information to communicate.[42] Unfortunately, many U.S. managers could do a better job of effective downward communication. The results of one survey found that employees want open and honest communication about both the good and the bad aspects of the organization's performance. But when asked to rate their company's communication effectiveness on a scale of 0 to 100, the survey respondents' score averaged 69. In addition, a study of 1,500 managers, mostly at first and second management levels, found that 84 percent of these leaders perceive communication as one of their most important tasks, yet only 38 percent believe they have adequate communications skills.[43]

Managers can do a better job of downward communication by focusing on specific areas that require regular communication. Recall our discussion of purpose-directed communication from early in this chapter. Downward communication usually encompasses these five topics:

1. *Implementation of goals and strategies.* Communicating new strategies and goals provides information about specific targets and expected behaviors. It gives direction for lower levels of the organization. *Example:* "The new quality campaign is for real. We must improve product quality if we are to survive."

2. *Job instructions and rationale.* These directives indicate how to do a specific task and how the job relates to other organizational activities. *Example:* "Purchasing should order the bricks now so the work crew can begin construction of the building in two weeks."

3. *Procedures and practices.* These messages define the organization's policies, rules, regulations, benefits, and structural arrangements. *Example:* "After your first

90 days of employment, you are eligible to enroll in our company-sponsored savings plan."

4. *Performance feedback.* These messages appraise how well individuals and departments are doing their jobs. *Example:* "Joe, your work on the computer network has greatly improved the efficiency of our ordering process."

5. *Indoctrination.* These messages are designed to motivate employees to adopt the company's mission and cultural values and to participate in special ceremonies, such as picnics and United Way campaigns. *Example:* "The company thinks of its employees as family and would like to invite everyone to attend the annual picnic and fair on March 3."

A major problem with downward communication is *drop off*, the distortion or loss of message content. Although formal communications are a powerful way to reach all employees, much information gets lost—25 percent or so each time a message is passed from one person to the next. In addition, the message can be distorted if it travels a great distance from its originating source to the ultimate receiver. A tragic example is the following historical example:

> A reporter was present at a hamlet burned down by the U.S. Army 1st Air Cavalry Division in 1967. Investigations showed that the order from the Division headquarters to the brigade was: "On no occasion must hamlets be burned down."
>
> The brigade radioed the battalion: "Do not burn down any hamlets unless you are absolutely convinced that the Viet Cong are in them."
>
> The battalion radioed the infantry company at the scene: "If you think there are any Viet Cong in the hamlet, burn it down."
>
> The company commander ordered his troops: "Burn down that hamlet."[44]

Information drop off cannot be completely avoided, but the techniques described in the previous sections can reduce it substantially. Using the right communication channel, consistency between verbal and nonverbal messages, and active listening can maintain communication accuracy as it moves down the organization.

UPWARD COMMUNICATION

Formal **upward communication** includes messages that flow from the lower to the higher levels in the organization's hierarchy. Most organizations take pains to build in healthy channels for upward communication. Employees need to air grievances, report progress, and provide feedback on management initiatives. Coupling a healthy flow of upward and downward communication ensures that the communication circuit between managers and employees is complete.[45] Five types of information communicated upward are the following:

1. *Problems and exceptions.* These messages describe serious problems with and exceptions to routine performance in order to make senior managers aware of difficulties. *Example:* "The printer has been out of operation for two days, and it will be at least a week before a new one arrives."

2. *Suggestions for improvement.* These messages are ideas for improving task-related procedures to increase quality or efficiency. *Example:* "I think we should eliminate step 2 in the audit procedure because it takes a lot of time and produces no results."

3. *Performance reports.* These messages include periodic reports that inform management how individuals and departments are performing. *Example:* "We completed the audit report for Smith & Smith on schedule but are one week behind on the Jackson report."

4. *Grievances and disputes.* These messages are employee complaints and conflicts that travel up the hierarchy for a hearing and possible resolution. *Example:* "The manager of operations research cannot get the cooperation of the Lincoln plant for the study of machine utilization."

5. *Financial and accounting information.* These messages pertain to costs, accounts receivable, sales volume, anticipated profits, return on investment, and other

upward communication
Messages transmitted from the lower to the higher levels in the organization's hierarchy.

matters of interest to senior managers. *Example:* "Costs are 2 percent over budget, but sales are 10 percent ahead of target, so the profit picture for the third quarter is excellent."

Many organizations make a great effort to facilitate upward communication. Mechanisms include suggestion boxes, employee surveys, open-door policies, management information system reports, and face-to-face conversations between workers and executives. Consider how one entrepreneur keeps the upward communication flowing.

Pat Croce is involved in several business ventures, including the development of Pirate Soul, "the ultimate pirate museum," in Key West, Florida. Like many entrepreneurs, Croce spends a lot of time on the road, traveling all across the country from his home office in Philadelphia.

To make sure he stays in touch with what's going on in his various businesses, Croce implemented a key communication tool he calls the Five-Fifteen. Each Friday, all employees and managers take 15 minutes to write brief progress reports and forward them to their immediate supervisors. Within a few days, all the information trickles up to Croce in a sort of "corporate Cliff Notes" version. The idea is that the reports take Croce only five minutes to read (hence the name Five-Fifteen). Croce says the Five-Fifteens have enabled him to keep in touch with the little details that make a big difference in the success of his businesses.

Employees typically look at the Five-Fifteens as a chance to be heard, while Croce looks at them as a way to keep his finger on the pulse of each business. In addition, the reports give him a chance to compliment and thank people for their accomplishments and offer questions or suggestions in areas that need improvement.[46]

In today's fast-paced world, many managers find it hard to maintain constant communication. Ideas such as the Five-Fifteen help keep information flowing upward so managers get feedback from lower levels.

Despite these efforts, however, barriers to accurate upward communication exist. Managers might resist employee feedback because they don't want to hear negative information, or employees might not trust managers sufficiently to push information upward.[47] At *The New York Times*, for example, poor upward communication was partly to blame for the Jayson Blair scandal. Some people in the newsroom knew or suspected that the rising reporter was fabricating elements of his news stories, but the environment of separation between reporters and editors prevented the information from being transmitted upward.[48] Innovative companies search for ways to ensure that information gets to top managers without distortion. A report reviewing the Blair scandal at the *Times*, for instance, recommended techniques such as cross-hierarchical meetings, office hours for managers, and informal brainstorming sessions among reporters and editors to improve upward communication.[49] At Golden Corral, a restaurant chain with headquarters in Raleigh, North Carolina, top managers spend at least one weekend a year in the trenches—cutting steaks, rolling silverware, setting tables, and taking out the trash. By understanding the daily routines and challenges of waiters, chefs, and other employees at their restaurants, Golden Corral executives increase their awareness of how management actions affect others.[50]

HORIZONTAL COMMUNICATION

Horizontal communication is the lateral or diagonal exchange of messages among peers or coworkers. It may occur within or across departments. The purpose of horizontal communication is not only to inform but also to request support and coordinate activities. Horizontal communication falls into one of three categories:

1. *Intradepartmental problem solving.* These messages take place among members of the same department and concern task accomplishment. *Example:* "Kelly, can you help us figure out how to complete this medical expense report form?"

2. *Interdepartmental coordination.* Interdepartmental messages facilitate the accomplishment of joint projects or tasks. *Example:* "Bob, please contact marketing and production and arrange a meeting to discuss the specifications for the new subassembly. It looks like we might not be able to meet their requirements."

horizontal communication
The lateral or diagonal exchange of messages among peers or coworkers.

The National Oceanic and Atmospheric Administration (NOAA)—a decentralized, geographically dispersed agency with a mission to observe and describe changes in the entire earth's ecosystem—serves other coastal resource management groups with information, technology, and training. NOAA recently established the Office of Program Planning and Integration to improve **horizontal communication** and create a more coherent organization. For example, the new office solicits input during the strategic planning process from partners, stakeholders, and employees, such as oceanographers Michelle Zetwd and Chris Walters, shown here.

© ALAN DIAZ/ASSOCIATED PRESS

3. *Change initiatives and improvements.* These messages are designed to share information among teams and departments that can help the organization change, grow, and improve. *Example:* "We are streamlining the company travel procedures and would like to discuss them with your department."

Horizontal communication is particularly important in learning organizations, where teams of workers are continuously solving problems and searching for better ways of doing things. Recall from Chapter 10 that many organizations build in horizontal communications in the form of task forces, committees, or even a matrix or horizontal structure to encourage coordination. At Chicago's Northwestern Memorial Hospital, two doctors created a horizontal task force to solve a serious patient health problem.

Northwestern Memorial Hospital

We've all heard of it happening—a patient checks into the hospital for a routine procedure and ends up getting sicker instead of better. Hospital-borne infections afflict about 2 million patients—and kill nearly 100,000—each year. Greater antibiotic use causes the germs to develop greater resistance. The infection epidemic is growing worse worldwide, but a task force at Northwestern Memorial Hospital has reversed the trend by breaking down communication barriers.

When a cancer patient became Northwestern's first victim of a new strain of deadly bacteria, infectious-disease specialists Lance Peterson and Gary Noskin realized it would take everyone's help to defeat the insidious enemy. As infection spread throughout the hospital, they launched a regular Monday morning meeting to plot countermoves. Although some physicians and staff members were offended at having their procedures questioned, the goal of preventing needless deaths overrode their concerns. Absolute candor was the rule at the Monday morning meetings, which involved not only doctors and nurses, but also lab technicians, pharmacists, computer technicians, and admissions representatives. One pharmacist, for example, recognized that antibiotics act as fertilizer for many bacteria, which encouraged physicians to decrease their use of antibiotics in favor of alternative treatments. Computer representatives and admissions people got together to develop software to identify which returning patients might pose a threat for bringing infection back into the hospital. Eventually, the task force even included maintenance staff when studies showed that a shortage of sinks was inhibiting hand-washing.

Increasing horizontal communication paid off at Northwestern, saving millions in annual medical costs and at least a few lives. Over three years, Northwestern's rate of hospital-borne infections plunged 22 percent. In a recent fiscal year, such infections totaled 5.1 per 1,000 patients, roughly half the national average.[51]

Team Communication Channels

A special type of horizontal communication is communicating in teams. Teams are the basic building block of many organizations. Team members work together to accomplish tasks, and the team's communication structure influences both team performance and employee satisfaction.

SOURCES: Adapted from A. Bavelas and D. Barrett, "An Experimental Approach to Organization Communication," *Personnel* 27 (1951): 366–371; M. E. Shaw, *Group Dynamics: The Psychology of Small Group Behavior* (New York: McGraw–Hill, 1976); and E. M. Rogers and R. A. Rogers, *Communication in Organizations* (New York: Free Press, 1976).

Research into team communication has focused on two characteristics: the extent to which team communications are centralized and the nature of the team's task.[52] The relationship between these characteristics is illustrated in Exhibit 20.6. In a **centralized network**, team members must communicate through one individual to solve problems or make decisions. In a **decentralized network**, individuals can communicate freely with other team members. Members process information equally among themselves until all agree on a decision.[53]

In laboratory experiments, centralized communication networks achieved faster solutions for simple problems. Members could simply pass relevant information to a central person for a decision. Decentralized communications were slower for simple problems because information was passed among individuals until someone finally put the pieces together and solved the problem. However, for more complex problems, the decentralized communication network was faster. Because all necessary information was not restricted to one person, a pooling of information through widespread communications provided greater input into the decision. Similarly, the accuracy of problem solving was related to problem complexity. The centralized networks made fewer errors on simple problems but more errors on complex ones. Decentralized networks were less accurate for simple problems but more accurate for complex ones.[54]

The implication for organizations is as follows: In a highly competitive global environment, organizations typically use teams to deal with complex problems. When team activities are complex and difficult, all members should share information in a decentralized structure to solve problems. Teams need a free flow of communication in all directions.[55] Teams that perform routine tasks spend less time processing information, and thus communications can be centralized. Data can be channeled to a supervisor for decisions, freeing workers to spend a greater percentage of time on task activities.

Personal Communication Channels

Personal communication channels exist outside the formally authorized channels. These informal communications coexist with formal channels but may skip hierarchical levels, cutting across vertical chains of command to connect virtually anyone in the organization. In most organizations, these informal channels are the primary way information spreads and work gets accomplished. Three important types of personal communication channels are *personal networks*, *management by wandering around*, and the *grapevine*.

centralized network A team communication structure in which team members communicate through a single individual to solve problems or make decisions.

decentralized network A team communication structure in which team members freely communicate with one another and arrive at decisions together.

personal communication channels Communication channels that exist outside the formally authorized channels and do not adhere to the organization's hierarchy of authority.

PERSONAL NETWORKING

How good are you at personal networking? Having sources of information and support helps a new manager gain career traction. To learn something about your networking, answer the following questions. Please indicate whether each item is Mostly True or Mostly False for you in school or at work.

	Mostly True	Mostly False
1. I learn early on about changes going on in the organization and how they might affect me or my position.	___	___
2. I network as much to help other people solve problems as to help myself.	___	___
3. I am fascinated by other people and what they do.	___	___
4. I frequently use lunches to meet and network with new people.	___	___
5. I regularly participate in charitable causes.	___	___

	Mostly True	Mostly False
6. I maintain a list of friends and colleagues to whom I send Christmas cards.	___	___
7. I maintain contact with people from previous organizations and school groups.	___	___
8. I actively give information to subordinates, peers, and my boss.	___	___

INTERPRETATION AND SCORING: Many good things flow from active networking, which will build a web of personal and organizational relationships for a new manager. Networking builds social, work, and career relationships that facilitate mutual benefit. People with active networks tend to be more effective managers and have broader impact on the organization.

Give yourself 1 point for each item marked as Mostly True. A score of 6 or higher suggests active networking and a solid foundation on which to begin your career as a new manager. If you scored 3 or less, you may want to focus more on building relationships if you are serious about a career as a manager.

■ **TAKE A MOMENT** | As a new manager, it is essential to build and nurture a personal communication network. Take the New Manager Self-Test on page 674 to learn how you are as a networker. Networking plugs you into the grapevine, and supplements your formal communication channels.

DEVELOPING PERSONAL COMMUNICATION NETWORKS

Personal networking refers to the acquisition and cultivation of personal relationships that cross departmental, hierarchical, and even organizational boundaries.[56] Smart managers consciously develop personal communication networks and encourage others to do so. In a communication network, people share information across boundaries and reach out to anyone who can further the goals of the team and organization. Exhibit 20.7 illustrates a communication network. Some people are central to the network while others play only a peripheral role. The key is that relationships are built across functional and hierarchical boundaries.

The value of personal networks for managers is that people who have more contacts have greater influence in the organization and get more accomplished. For example, in Exhibit 20.7, Sharon has a well-developed personal communication network, sharing information and assistance with many people across the marketing, manufacturing, and engineering departments. Contrast Sharon's contacts with those of Mike or Jasmine. Who do you think is likely to have greater access to

personal networking The acquisition and cultivation of personal relationships that cross departmental, hierarchical, and even organizational boundaries.

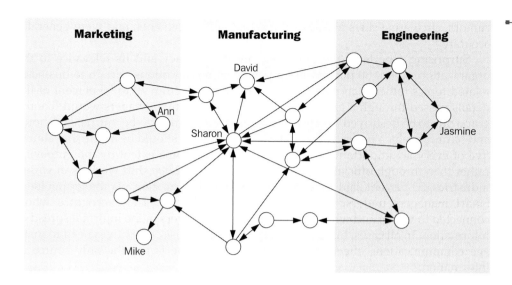

EXHIBIT 20.7

An Organizational
Communication Network

resources and more influence in the organization? Here are a few tips from one expert networker for building a personal communication network:[57]

1. *Build it before you need it.* Smart managers don't wait until they need something to start building a network of personal relationships—by then, it's too late. Instead, they show genuine interest in others and develop honest connections.

2. *Never eat lunch alone.* People who excel at networking make an effort to be visible and connect with as many people as possible. Master networkers keep their social as well as business conference and event calendars full.

3. *Make it win-win.* Successful networking isn't just about getting what *you* want; it's also about making sure other people in the network get what *they* want.

4. *Focus on diversity.* The broader your base of contacts, the broader your range of influence. Build connections with people from as many different areas of interest as possible (both within and outside of the organization).

Most of us know from personal experience that "who you know" sometimes counts for more than what you know. By cultivating a broad network of contacts, managers can significantly extend their influence and accomplish greater results.

THE GRAPEVINE

One type of informal, person-to-person communication network that is not officially sanctioned by the organization is referred to as the **grapevine**.[58] The grapevine links employees in all directions, ranging from the CEO through middle management, support staff, and line employees. The grapevine will always exist in an organization, but it can become a dominant force when formal channels are closed. In such cases, the grapevine is actually a service because the information it provides helps makes sense of an unclear or uncertain situation. Employees use grapevine rumors to fill in information gaps and clarify management decisions. One estimate is that as much as 70 percent of all communication in a firm is carried out through its grapevine.[59] The grapevine tends to be more active during periods of change, excitement, anxiety, and sagging economic conditions. For example, a survey by professional employment services firm Randstad found that about half of all employees reported first hearing of major company changes through the grapevine.[60] Consider what happened at Jel, Inc., an auto supply firm that was under great pressure from Ford and GM to increase quality. Management changes to improve quality—learning statistical process control, introducing a new compensation system, buying a fancy new screw machine from Germany—all started out as

grapevine An informal, person-to-person communication network of employees that is not officially sanctioned by the organization.

rumors, circulating days ahead of the actual announcements, and were generally accurate.[61]

Surprising aspects of the grapevine are its accuracy and its relevance to the organization. About 80 percent of grapevine communications pertain to business-related topics rather than personal gossip. Moreover, from 70 to 90 percent of the details passed through a grapevine are accurate.[62] Many managers would like the grapevine to be destroyed because they consider its rumors to be untrue, malicious, and harmful, which typically is not the case. Managers should be aware that almost five of every six important messages are carried to some extent by the grapevine rather than through official channels. In a survey of 22,000 shift workers in varied industries, 55 percent said they get most of their information via the grapevine.[63] Smart managers understand the company's grapevine. They recognize who's connected to whom and which employees are key players in the informal spread of information. In all cases, but particularly in times of crisis, executives need to manage communications effectively so that the grapevine is not the only source of information.[64]

MANAGEMENT BY WANDERING AROUND

The communication technique known as **management by wandering around (MBWA)** was made famous by the books *In Search of Excellence* and *A Passion for Excellence*.[65] These books describe executives who talk directly with employees to learn what is going on. MBWA works for managers at all levels. Managers mingle and develop positive relationships with employees and learn directly from them about their department, division, or organization. The president of ARCO had a habit of visiting a district field office. Rather than schedule a big strategic meeting with the district supervisor, he would come in unannounced and chat with the lowest-level employees. In any organization, both upward and downward communications are enhanced with MBWA. Managers have a chance to describe key ideas and values to employees and, in turn, learn about the problems and issues confronting employees.

When managers fail to take advantage of MBWA, they become aloof and isolated from employees. For example, Peter Anderson, president of Ztel, Inc., a maker of television switching systems, preferred not to personally communicate with employees. He managed at arm's length. As one manager said, "I don't know how many times I asked Peter to come to the lab, but he stayed in his office. He wasn't that visible to the troops." This formal, impersonal management style contributed to Ztel's troubles and eventual bankruptcy.[66]

USING THE WRITTEN WORD

Not all manager communication is face-to-face, or even verbal. Managers frequently have to communicate in writing, via memorandums, reports, or everyday e-mails. The memo, whether it is sent on paper or electronically, remains a primary way of communicating within companies, and e-mail has become the main way most organizations communicate with customers and clients. Yet evidence shows that the writing skills of U.S. employees and managers in general are terrible. One study found that at least a third of workers in the United States don't have the writing skills they need to perform their jobs. A report from The National Commission on Writing says that states spend nearly $250 million a year on remedial writing training for government workers.[67]

Good writing matters. Consider this story told by the president of Opus Associates, a written communications consulting company: After attorney Brian Puricelli won a major case for a client, he petitioned the court to recover his fees. Magistrate Judge Jacob Hart agreed, but he deemed the petition so full or errors and

management by wandering around (MBWA) A communication technique in which managers interact directly with workers to exchange information.

misspellings that he declared it disrespectful to the court and slashed the amount due to Puricelli by nearly $30,000.[68]

Managers can learn to be good writers. Here are a few tips from experts on how to effectively communicate in written form:[69]

:: *Respect the reader.* The reader's time is valuable; don't waste it with a rambling, confusing memo or e-mail that has to be read several times to try to make sense of it. Pay attention to your grammar and spelling. Sloppy writing indicates that you think your time is more important than that of your readers. You'll lose their interest—and their respect.

:: *Know your point and get to it.* What is the key piece of information that you want the reader to remember? Many people just sit and write, without clarifying in their own mind what it is they're trying to say. To write effectively, know what your central point is and write to support it.

:: *Write clearly rather than impressively.* Don't use pretentious or inflated language, and avoid jargon. The goal of good writing for business is to be understood the first time through. State your message as simply and as clearly as possible.

:: *Get a second opinion.* When the communication is highly important, such as a formal memo to the department or organization, ask someone you consider to be a good writer to read it before you send it. Don't be too proud to take their advice. In all cases, read and revise the memo or e-mail a second and third time before you hit the send button.

A former manager of communication services at consulting firm Arthur D. Little Inc. has estimated that around 30 percent of all business memos and e-mails are written simply to get clarification about an earlier written communication that didn't make sense to the reader.[70] By following these guidelines, you can get your message across the first time.

COMMUNICATING DURING TURBULENT TIMES

During turbulent times, communication becomes even more important. To build trust and promote learning and problem solving, managers incorporate ideas such as open communication, dialogue, and feedback and learning. In addition, they develop crisis communication skills for communicating with both employees and the public in exceptionally challenging or frightening circumstances.

Open Communication

A recent trend that reflects managers' increased emphasis on empowering employees, building trust and commitment, and enhancing collaboration is open communication. **Open communication** means sharing all types of information throughout the company, across functional and hierarchical levels. Many companies, such as Springfield Remanufacturing Corporation, AmeriSteel, and Whole Foods Markets, are opening the financial books to workers at all levels and training employees to understand how and why the company operates as it does. At Wabash National Corporation, one of the nation's leading truck-trailer manufacturers, employees complete several hours of business training and attend regular meetings on the shop floor to review the company's financial performance.[71]

Open communication runs counter to the traditional flow of selective information downward from supervisors to subordinates. By breaking down conventional hierarchical barriers to communication, the organization can gain the benefit of all employees' ideas. The same ideas batted back and forth among a few managers do not lead to effective learning or to a network of relationships that keep companies thriving. New voices and conversations involving a broad spectrum of people

open communication
Sharing all types of information throughout the company, across functional and hierarchical levels.

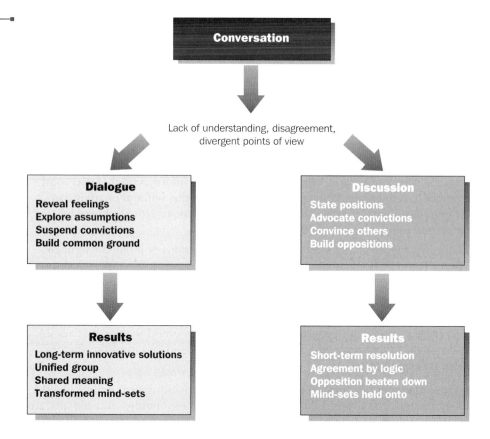

EXHIBIT   20.8

Dialogue and Discussion:
The Differences

SOURCE: Adapted from
Edgar Schein, "On Dialogue,
Culture, and Organizational
Learning," *Organizational
Dynamics* (Autumn 1993): 46.

revitalize and enhance organizational communication.[72] Open communication also
builds trust and a commitment to common goals, which is essential in organizations
that depend on collaboration and knowledge-sharing to accomplish their purpose.
Fifty percent of executives surveyed report that open communication is a key to
building trust in the organization.[73]

Dialogue

Another popular means of fostering trust and collaboration is through dialogue.
The "roots of dialogue" are *dia* and *logos*, which can be thought of as *stream of meaning*. **Dialogue** is a group communication process in which people together create a
stream of shared meaning that enables them to understand each other and share a
view of the world.[74] People may start out at polar opposites, but by talking openly,
they discover common ground, common issues, and shared goals on which they can
build a better future.

A useful way to describe dialogue is to contrast it with discussion (see
Exhibit 20.8). The intent of discussion, generally, is to deliver one's point of view
and persuade others to adopt it. A discussion is often resolved by logic or "beating down" opponents. Dialogue, by contrast, asks that participants suspend
their attachments to a particular viewpoint so that a deeper level of listening,
synthesis, and meaning can evolve from the group. A dialogue's focus is to
reveal feelings and build common ground. Both forms of communication—
dialogue and discussion—can result in change. However, the result of discussion
is limited to the topic being deliberated, whereas the result of dialogue is characterized by group unity, shared meaning, and transformed mind-sets. As new and
deeper solutions are developed, a trusting relationship is built among team
members.[75]

dialogue A group communication process aimed at
creating a culture based on
collaboration, fluidity, trust,
and commitment to shared
goals.

Crisis Communication

Over the past few years, the sheer number and scope of crises have made communication a more demanding job for managers. Organizations face small crises every day, such as charges of racial discrimination, a factory fire, or a flu epidemic. Moreover, acts of intentional evil, such as bombings or kidnappings, continue to increase, causing serious repercussions for people and organizations.[76] Managers can develop four primary skills for communicating in a crisis.[77]

© RICK RYCRAFT/ASSOCIATED PRESS

:: *Maintain your focus.* Good crisis communicators don't allow themselves to be overwhelmed by the situation. Calmness and listening become more important than ever. Managers also learn to tailor their communications to reflect hope and optimism at the same time they acknowledge the current difficulties.

:: *Maintain your focus.* Good crisis communicators don't allow themselves to be overwhelmed by the situation. Calmness and listening become more important than ever. Managers also learn to tailor their communications to reflect hope and optimism at the same time they acknowledge the current difficulties.

:: *Be visible.* Many managers underestimate just how important their presence is during a crisis.[78] As we discussed in Chapter 1, people need to feel that someone is in control. A manager's job is to step out immediately, both to reassure employees and respond to public concerns. Face-to-face communication with employees is crucial for letting people know that managers care about them and what they're going through.

:: *Get the awful truth out.*[79] Effective managers gather as much information as they can, do their best to determine the facts, and tell the truth to employees and the public as soon as possible. Getting the truth out quickly prevents rumors and misunderstandings.

:: *Communicate a vision for the future.* People need to feel that they have something to work for and look forward to. Moments of crisis present opportunities for managers to communicate a vision of a better future and unite people toward common goals.

Feedback and Learning

Feedback occurs when managers use evaluation and communication to help individuals and the organization learn and improve. It enables managers to determine whether they have been successful in communicating with others. Recall from Exhibit 20.2 that feedback is an important part of the communication process. However, despite its importance, feedback is often neglected. Giving and receiving feedback is typically difficult for both managers and employees. Yet, by avoiding feedback, people miss a valuable opportunity to help one another learn, develop, and improve.[80]

Successful managers focus their feedback to help develop the capacities of subordinates, and they encourage critical feedback from employees. When managers enlist the whole organization in reviewing the outcomes of activities, they can quickly learn what works and what doesn't and use that information to improve the organization. Consider how the U.S. Army's feedback system promotes whole-system learning.

CONCEPT CONNECTION

When an extortionist claimed to have placed seven pesticide-contaminated candy bars in Sydney area stores, manufacturer MasterFoods Australia-New Zealand's response was a textbook example of effective **crisis communication.** President Andy Weston-Webb announced, "It's not safe to eat Mars or Snickers bars" and immediately activated recall plans. MasterFoods launched a public relations campaign, which included interviews with Weston-Webb, full-page newspaper ads, a company hotline, and media access to the burial of 3 million candy bars in a deep pit. The two-month absence of the popular snacks cost the company more than $10 million. But MasterFoods emerged with its reputation intact. During the first week of the products' return, sales surged 300 percent.

At the National Training Center just south of Death Valley, U.S. Army troops engage in a simulated battle: The "enemy" has sent unmanned aerial vehicles (UAVs) to gather targeting data. When the troops fire on the UAVs, they reveal their location to attack helicopters hovering just behind a nearby ridge. After the exercise, unit members and their superiors hold an *after-action review* to review battle plans, discuss what worked and what didn't, and talk about how to do things better. Gen. William Hertzog suggests that inexpensive decoy UAVs might be just the thing to make a distracted enemy reveal its location. The observation became a "lesson learned" for the entire army, and UAVs became an important part of battle operations in Iraq.

Many researchers attribute the transformation of the army from a demoralized, dysfunctional organization following the Vietnam War into an elite force capable of effectively accomplishing Operation Iraqi Freedom to this unique feedback and learning system. In the U.S. Army, after-action reviews take just 15 minutes, and they occur after every identifiable event—large or small, simulated or real. The review involves asking four simple questions: What was supposed to happen? What actually happened? What accounts for any difference? What can we learn? It is a process of identifying mistakes, of innovating, and of continually learning from experience.

The lessons are based not only on simulated battles, but also on real-life experiences of soldiers in the field. The Center for Army Lessons Learned (CALL) sends experts into the field to observe after-action reviews, interview soldiers, and compile intelligence reports. Leaders in all army divisions are currently engaged in a detailed analysis of lessons learned during Operation Iraqi Freedom and Operation Enduring Freedom. The lessons will be used to train soldiers and develop action plans for resolving problems in future conflicts. For example, many of the problems and issues from a similar process following Operation Desert Storm had been resolved by the time of Operation Iraqi Freedom. A primary focus for current leaders is to improve training regarding the difficult shift from offensive operations to humanitarian and relief efforts.[81]

In this example, the organization is learning by communicating feedback about the consequences of field operations and simulated battles. Compiling what is learned and using communication feedback create an improved organization. After-action reviews are also used in corporate America. Steelcase Inc., an office furniture manufacturer, and oil giant BP are among the companies adapting the army's system to create a process of continuous learning and improvement. BP credits the feedback system for $700 million in cost savings and other gains.[82]

MANAGING ORGANIZATIONAL COMMUNICATION

Many of the ideas described in this chapter pertain to barriers to communication and how to overcome them. Exhibit 20.9 lists some of the major barriers to communication, along with some techniques for overcoming them.

EXHIBIT   20.9

Communication Barriers and Ways to Overcome Them

Barriers	How to Overcome
Individual	
Interpersonal dynamics	Active listening
Channels and media	Selection of appropriate channel
Semantics	Knowledge of other's perspective
Inconsistent cues	MBWA
Organizational	
Status and power differences	Climate of trust, Dialogue
Departmental needs and goals	Development and use of formal channels
Lack of formal channels	Encouragement of multiple channels, formal and informal
Communication network unsuited to task	Changing organization or group structure to fit communication needs
Poor coordination	Feedback and learning

Barriers to Communication

Barriers can be categorized as those that exist at the individual level and those that exist at the organizational level.

INDIVIDUAL BARRIERS

First, *interpersonal barriers* include problems with emotions and perceptions held by employees. For example, rigid perceptual labeling or stereotyping prevents people from modifying or altering their opinions. If a person's mind is made up before the communication starts, communication will fail. Moreover, people with different backgrounds or knowledge may interpret a communication in different ways.

Second, *selecting the wrong channel* or *medium* for sending a communication can be a problem. When a message is emotional, it is better to transmit it face to face rather than in writing. E-mail can be particularly risky for discussing difficult issues because it lacks the capacity for rapid feedback and multiple cues. On the other hand, e-mail is highly efficient for routine messages.

Third, *semantics* often causes communication problems. **Semantics** pertains to the meaning of words and the way they are used. A word such as *effectiveness* may mean achieving high production to a factory superintendent, but to a human resources staff specialist it might mean employee satisfaction. Many common words have an average of 28 definitions; thus, communicators must take care to select the words that will accurately encode ideas.[83] Language differences can also be a barrier in today's organizations. This chapter's Shoptalk offers some guidelines for how managers can better communicate with people who speak a different language.

Go to the ethical dilemma on page 686 that pertains to individual barriers to communication.

■ **TAKE A MOMENT**

Fourth, sending *inconsistent cues* between verbal and nonverbal communications will confuse the receiver. If one's facial expression does not reflect one's words, the communication will contain noise and uncertainty. The tone of voice and body language should be consistent with the words, and actions should not contradict words.

ORGANIZATIONAL BARRIERS

Organizational barriers pertain to factors for the organization as a whole. One of the most significant barriers relates to *status and power differences*. Low-power people may be reluctant to pass bad news up the hierarchy, thus giving the wrong impression to upper levels.[84] High-power people may not pay attention or may think that low-status people have little to contribute.

Second, *differences across departments in terms of needs and goals* interfere with communications. Each department perceives problems in its own terms. The production department is concerned with production efficiency whereas the marketing department's goal is to get the product to the customer in a hurry.

Third, the *absence of formal channels* reduces communication effectiveness. Organizations must provide adequate upward, downward, and horizontal communication in the form of employee surveys, open-door policies, newsletters, memos, task forces, and liaison personnel. Without these formal channels, the organization cannot communicate as a whole.

Fourth, the *communication flow* may not fit the team's or organization's task. If a centralized communication structure is used for nonroutine tasks, not enough information will be circulated to solve problems. The organization, department, or team is most efficient when the amount of communication flowing among employees fits the task.

semantics The meaning of words and the way they are used.

LEAPING OVER LANGUAGE BARRIERS

In today's global business environment, odds are good you'll find yourself conversing with an employee, colleague, or customer who has limited skills in your native language. Here are some guidelines that will help you speak—and listen—more effectively.

1. **Keep your message simple.** Be clear about what you want to communicate, and keep to the point.

2. **Select your words with care.** Don't try to dazzle with your vocabulary. Choose simple words, and look for opportunities to use cognates—that is, words that resemble words in your listener's language. For example, *banco* in Spanish means "bank" in English. Assemble those simple words into equally simple phrases and short sentences. And be sure to avoid idioms, slang, jargon, and vague terminology such as *soon, often,* or *several.*

3. **Pay close attention to nonverbals.**

   :: Don't cover your mouth with your hand. Being able to see your lips helps your listener decipher what you're saying.

   :: Speak slowly and carefully. In particular, avoid running words together. "Howyadoin?" won't make any sense to someone still struggling with the English language, for example.

   :: Allow for pauses. If you're an American, your culture has taught you to avoid silence whenever possible, but pauses give your listener time to take in what you've said, ask a question, or formulate a response.

   :: Fight the urge to shout. Speaking louder doesn't make it any easier for someone

to understand you. It also tends to be intimidating and could give the impression that you're angry.

   :: Pay attention to facial expressions and body language, but keep in mind that the meaning of such cues can vary significantly from culture to culture. For example, Americans may view eye contact as a sign you're giving someone your full attention, but the Japanese consider prolonged eye contact rude.

4. **Check for comprehension frequently, and invite feedback.** Stop from time to time and make sure you're being understood, especially if the other person laughs inappropriately, never asks a question, or continually nods and smiles politely. Ask the listener to repeat what you've said in his or her own words. If you find the other person hasn't understood you, restate the information in a different way instead of simply repeating yourself. Similarly, listen carefully when the non-native speaks, and offer feedback so the person can check your understanding of his or her message.

Above all, when communicating with someone who doesn't speak your language well, be patient with yourself and the listener, be encouraging, and be persistent.

SOURCES: "How to Communicate with a Non Native English Speaker," wikiHow, www.wikihow.com/Communicate-With-a-Non-Native-English-Speaker; Sondra Thiederman, "Language Barriers: Bridging the Gap," www.thiederman.com/articles_detail.php?id=39; "Communicating with Non-native Speakers," Magellan Health Services, www.magellanassist.com/mem/library/default.asp?TopicId=95&CategoryId=0&ArticleId=5.

A final problem is *poor coordination*, so that different parts of the organization are working in isolation without knowing and understanding what other parts are doing. Top executives are out of touch with lower levels, or departments and divisions are poorly coordinated so that people do not understand how the system works together as a whole.

Overcoming Communication Barriers

Managers can design the organization so as to encourage positive, effective communications. Designing involves both individual skills and organizational actions.

Individual Skills

Perhaps the most important individual skill is *active listening*. Active listening means asking questions, showing interest, and occasionally paraphrasing what the speaker has said to ensure accurate interpretation. Active listening also means providing feedback to the sender to complete the communication loop.

Second, individuals should select the *appropriate channel* for the message. A complicated message should be sent through a rich channel, such as face-to-face discussion or telephone. Routine messages and data can be sent through memos, letters, or e-mail, because the risk of misunderstanding is lower.

Third, senders and receivers should make a special effort to *understand* each other's perspective. Managers can sensitize themselves to the information receiver so they can better target the message, detect bias, and clarify misinterpretations. When communicators understand others' perspectives, semantics can be clarified, perceptions understood, and objectivity maintained.

The fourth individual skill is *management by wandering around*. Managers must be willing to get out of the office and check communications with others. Glenn Tilton, the CEO of United Airlines, takes every opportunity to introduce himself to employees and customers and find out what's on their minds. He logs more airplane time than many of his company's pilots, visits passenger lounges, and chats with employees on concourses, galleys, and airport terminals.[85] Through direct observation and face-to-face meetings, managers like Tilton gain an understanding of the organization and are able to communicate important ideas and values directly to others.

CONCEPT CONNECTION "I've taken an oath to serve and protect all in my county," says Clark County, Ohio, Sheriff Gene Kelly. He uses the Phraselator P2, shown here, to overcome **barriers to communication** with the county's growing Spanish-speaking population. The Phraselator is a PDA-sized translation device originally developed by Maryland-based VoxTec for the military. The hand-held computer translates English phrases such as "Halt" or "Show me where it hurts" and then broadcasts them in one of approximately 60 languages. Troops and medical personnel in Afghanistan, Iraq, Haiti, and Southeast Asia use Phraselators, and they're beginning to make their way into U.S. emergency rooms and county health departments in addition to law enforcement agencies.

Organizational Actions

Perhaps the most important thing managers can do for the organization is to create a *climate of trust and openness*. Open communication and dialogue can encourage people to communicate honestly with one another. Subordinates will feel free to transmit negative as well as positive messages without fear of retribution. Efforts to develop interpersonal skills among employees can also foster openness, honesty, and trust.

Second, managers should develop and use *formal information channels* in all directions. Scandinavian Design uses two newsletters to reach employees. Dana Corporation has developed innovative programs such as the "Here's a Thought" board—called a HAT rack—to get ideas and feedback from workers. Other techniques include direct mail, bulletin boards, and employee surveys.

Third, managers should encourage the use of *multiple channels*, including both formal and informal communications. Multiple communication channels include written directives, face-to-face discussions, MBWA, and the grapevine. For example, managers at GM's Packard Electric plant use multimedia, including a monthly newspaper, frequent meetings of employee teams, and an electronic news display in the cafeteria. Sending messages through multiple channels increases the likelihood that they will be properly received.

Fourth, the structure should *fit communication needs*. An organization can be designed to use teams, task forces, project managers, or a matrix structure as needed to facilitate the horizontal flow of information for coordination and problem solving. Structure should also reflect information needs. When team or department tasks are difficult, a decentralized structure should be implemented to encourage discussion and participation.

A system of organizational *feedback and learning* can help overcome problems of poor coordination. Harrah's created a *Communication Team* as part of its structure at the Casino/Holiday Inn in Las Vegas. The team includes one member from each department. This cross-functional team deals with urgent company problems and helps people think beyond the scope of their own departments to communicate with anyone and everyone to solve those problems.

MANAGER'S SOLUTION

This chapter described several important points about communicating in organizations. Communication takes up at least 80 percent of a manager's time. Managers' communication is purpose-directed, in that it unites people around a shared vision and goals and directs attention to the values and behaviors that achieve goals. Communication is a process of encoding an idea into a message, which is sent through a channel and decoded by a receiver. Communication among people can be affected by communication channels, nonverbal communication, and listening skills. An important aspect of management communication is persuasion. The ability to persuade others to behave in ways that help accomplish the vision and goals is crucial to good management. Managers frequently use symbols, stories, and metaphors to persuade and influence others.

At the organizational level, managers are concerned with managing formal communications in a downward, upward, and horizontal direction. Good writing skills have become even more important with the increased use of e-mail for communication.

Informal communications also are important, especially management by wandering around, developing personal networks, and understanding the grapevine. Moreover, research shows that communication structures in teams and departments should reflect the underlying tasks. Open communication, dialogue, feedback, and learning are important communication mechanisms, especially in times of turbulence and uncertainty. In addition, today's managers have to develop effective crisis communication skills. Four important skills for communicating in a crisis are to remain calm and focused, be visible, "get the awful truth out," and communicate a vision for a brighter future.

The final part of this chapter described several individual and organizational barriers to communication. These barriers can be overcome by active listening, selecting appropriate channels, engaging in MBWA, using dialogue, developing a climate of trust, using formal channels, designing the correct structure to fit communication needs, and using feedback for learning. Status and power differences can be a significant barrier to communications, as they have been at the VHA Inc. hospitals described in the chapter opening, where people are afraid to speak up to surgeons because of their status and unique skills. Administrators took the first step toward breaking down barriers with a survey that gave people a chance to be heard. VHA then launched a program called Transforming the Operating Room, which includes team-building activities, pre- and post-surgical briefing sessions where everyone is expected to participate, and required "safety pauses" to encourage anyone in the OR to delay or even suspend surgery if there is a concern. By establishing these formal mechanisms, administrators significantly improved horizontal and upward communications at VHA hospitals. However, the idea of a hierarchical system with the surgeon in charge is deeply ingrained in most hospitals, and change doesn't always come easily. Facilitators are working with surgeons and support staff to make sure people feel safe about speaking up. In addition, the program emphasizes that everyone is an essential part of the medical team, with a primary goal of providing patients with the best medical care.[86]

1. Lee's Garage is an internal Wal-Mart Web site that CEO H. Lee Scott uses to communicate with the company's 1.5 million U.S. employees. A public relations associate screens employee questions, and Scott dictates his responses to an aide, who then posts them on the Web. What would you predict are the advantages and potential problems to this method of upper-level management's connecting with employees?

2. Describe the elements of the communication process. Give an example of each part of the model as it exists in the classroom during communication between teacher and students.

3. Why do you think stories are more effective than hard facts and figures in persuading others?

4. Try to recall an incident at school or work when information was passed primarily through the grapevine. How accurate were the rumors, and how did people react to them? How can managers control information that is processed through the grapevine?

5. What is the difference between a discussion and a dialogue? What steps might managers take to transform a discussion into a constructive dialogue?

6. What do you think are the major barriers to upward communication in organizations? Discuss.

7. What is the relationship between group member communication and group task? For example, how should communications differ in a strategic planning group and a group of employees who stock shelves in a grocery store?

8. Some senior managers believe they should rely on written information and computer reports because these yield more accurate data than do face-to-face communications. Do you agree? Why or why not?

9. Why is management by wandering around considered effective communication? How might managers encourage open and honest communication, as opposed to polite conversation and best behavior, when engaging in MBWA?

10. Assume that you have been asked to design a training program to help managers become better communicators. What would you include in the program?

685

Chapter 20 COMMUNICATION

MANAGEMENT IN PRACTICE: EXPERIENTIAL EXERCISE

Personal Assessment of Communication Apprehension

The following questions are about your feelings toward communication with other people. Indicate the degree to which each statement applies to you by marking (5) Strongly agree, (4) Agree, (3) Undecided, (2) Disagree, or (1) Strongly disagree. There are no right or wrong answers. Many of the statements are similar to other statements. Do not be concerned about their similarities. Work quickly, and just record your first impressions.

Disagree Strongly	①	②	③	④	⑤	Agree Strongly

1. When talking in a small group of acquaintances, I am tense and nervous. ① ② ③ ④ ⑤

2. When presenting a talk to a group of strangers, I am tense and nervous. ① ② ③ ④ ⑤

3. When conversing with a friend or colleague, I am calm and relaxed. ① ② ③ ④ ⑤

4. When talking in a large meeting of acquaintances, I am calm and relaxed. ① ② ③ ④ ⑤

5. When presenting a talk to a group of friends or colleagues, I am tense and nervous. ① ② ③ ④ ⑤

6. When conversing with an acquaintance or colleague, I am calm and relaxed. ① ② ③ ④ ⑤

7. When talking in a large meeting of strangers, I am tense and nervous. ① ② ③ ④ ⑤

8. When talking in a small group of strangers, I am tense and nervous. ① ② ③ ④ ⑤

9. When talking in a small group of strangers, I am tense and nervous. ① ② ③ ④ ⑤

10. When presenting a talk to a group of acquaintances, I am calm and relaxed. ① ② ③ ④ ⑤

11. When I am conversing with a stranger, I am calm and relaxed. ① ② ③ ④ ⑤

12. When talking in a large meeting of friends, I am tense and nervous. ① ② ③ ④ ⑤

13. When presenting a talk to a group of strangers, I am calm and relaxed. ① ② ③ ④ ⑤

14. When conversing with a friend or colleague, I am tense and nervous. ① ② ③ ④ ⑤

15. When talking in a large meeting of acquaintances, I am tense and nervous. ❶ ❷ ❸ ❹ ❺

16. When talking in a small group of acquaintances, I am calm and relaxed. ❶ ❷ ❸ ❹ ❺

17. When talking in a small group of strangers, I am calm and relaxed. ❶ ❷ ❸ ❹ ❺

18. When presenting a talk to a group of friends, I am calm and relaxed. ❶ ❷ ❸ ❹ ❺

19. When conversing with an acquaintance or colleague, I am tense and nervous. ❶ ❷ ❸ ❹ ❺

20. When talking in a large meeting of strangers, I am calm and relaxed. ❶ ❷ ❸ ❹ ❺

21. When presenting a talk to a group of acquaintances, I am tense and nervous. ❶ ❷ ❸ ❹ ❺

22. When conversing with a stranger, I am tense and nervous. ❶ ❷ ❸ ❹ ❺

23. When talking in a large meeting of friends or colleagues, I am calm and relaxed. ❶ ❷ ❸ ❹ ❺

24. When talking in a small group of friends or colleagues, I am tense and nervous. ❶ ❷ ❸ ❹ ❺

Scoring and Interpretation

This questionnaire permits computation of four subscores and one total score. Subscores relate to communication apprehension in four common situations—public speaking, meetings, group discussions, and interpersonal conversations. To compute your scores, add or subtract your scores for each item as indicated next.

Subscore/Scoring Formula

For each subscore, start with 18 points. Then add the scores for the plus (+) items and subtract the scores for the minus (−) items.

Public Speaking

18 + scores for items 2, 5, and 21; − scores for items 10, 13, and 18. Score = _____

Meetings

18 + scores for items 7, 12, and 15; − scores for items 4, 20, and 23. Score = _____

Group Discussions

18 + scores for items 1, 8, and 24; − scores for items 9, 16, and 17. Score = _____

Interpersonal Conversations

18 + scores for items 14, 19, and 22; − scores for items 3, 6, and 11. Score = _____

Total Score

Sum the four subscores for Total Score = _____

This personal assessment provides an indication of how much apprehension (fear or anxiety) you feel in a variety of communication settings. Total scores may range from 24 to 120. Scores above 72 indicate that you are more apprehensive about communication than the average person. Scores above 85 indicate a high level of communication apprehension. Scores below 59 indicate a low level of apprehension. These extreme scores (below 59 and above 85) are generally outside the norm. They suggest that the degree of apprehension you may experience in any given situation may not be associated with a realistic response to that communication situation.

Scores on the subscales can range from a low of 6 to a high of 30. Any score above 18 indicates some degree of apprehension. For example, if you score above 18 for the public speaking context, you are like the overwhelming majority of people.

To be an effective communication champion, you should work to overcome communication anxiety. The interpersonal conversations create the least apprehension for most people, followed by group discussions, larger meetings, and then public speaking. Compare your scores with another student. What aspect of communication creates the most apprehension for you? How do you plan to improve it?

SOURCES: J. C. McCroskey, "Measures of Communication-Bound Anxiety," *Speech Monographs* 37 (1970): 269–277; J. C. McCroskey and V. P. Richmond, "Validity of the PRCA as an Index of Oral Communication Apprehension," *Communication Monographs* 45 (1978): 192–203; J. C. McCroskey and V. P. Richmond, "The Impact of Communication Apprehension on Individuals in Organizations," *Communication Quarterly* 27 (1979): 55–61; J. C. McCroskey, *An Introduction to Rhetorical Communication* (Englewood Cliffs, NJ: Prentice Hall, 1982).

MANAGEMENT IN PRACTICE: ETHICAL DILEMMA

On Trial

When Werner and Thompson, a Los Angeles business and financial management firm, offered Iranian-born Firoz Bahmani a position as an accountant assistant one spring day in 2002, Bahmani felt a sense of genuine relief, but his relief was short-lived.

With his degree in accounting from a top-notch American university, he knew he was more than a little overqualified for the job. But time after time, he'd been rejected for suitable positions. His language difficulties were the reason most often given for his unsuccessful candidacy. Although the young man had grown up speaking both Farsi and French in his native land, he'd only begun to pick up English shortly before his arrival in the United States a few years ago. Impressed by his educational credentials and his quiet, courtly manner, managing partner Beatrice Werner overlooked his heavy accent and actively recruited him for the position, the only one available at the time. During his interview, she assured him he would advance in time.

It was clear to Beatrice that Firoz was committed to succeeding at all costs. But it soon also became apparent that Firoz and his immediate supervisor, Cathy Putnam, were at odds. Cathy was a seasoned account manager who had just transferred to Los Angeles from the New York office. Saddled with an enormous workload, she let Firoz know right from the start, speaking in her rapid-fire Brooklyn accent, that he'd need to get up to speed as quickly as possible.

Shortly before Cathy was to give Firoz his three-month probationary review, she came to Beatrice, expressed her frustration with Firoz's performance, and suggested that he be let go. "His bank reconciliations and financial report preparations are first-rate," Cathy admitted, "but his communication skills leave a lot to be desired. In the first place, I simply don't have the time to keep repeating the same directions over and over again when I'm trying to teach him his responsibilities. Then there's the fact that public contact is part of his written job description. Typically, he puts off making phone calls to dispute credit card charges or ask a client's staff for the information he needs. When he does finally pick up the phone . . . well, let's just say I've had more than one client mention how hard it is to understand what he's trying to say. Some of them are getting pretty exasperated."

"You know, some firms feel it's their corporate responsibility to help foreign-born employees learn English," Beatrice began. "Maybe we should help him find an English-as-a-second-language course and pay for it."

"With all due respect, I don't think that's our job," Cathy replied, with barely concealed irritation. "If you come to the United States, you should learn our

language. That's what my mom's parents did when they came over from Italy. They certainly didn't expect anyone to hold their hands. Besides," she added, almost inaudibly, "Firoz's lucky we let him into this country."

Beatrice had mixed feelings. On one hand, she recognized that Werner and Thompson had every right to require someone in Firoz's position be capable of carrying out his public contract duties. Perhaps she had made a mistake in hiring him. But as the daughter of German immigrants herself, she knew firsthand both how daunting language and cultural barriers could be and that they could be overcome in time. Perhaps in part because of her family background, she had a passionate commitment to the firm's stated goals of creating a diverse workforce and a caring, supportive culture. Besides she felt a personal sense of obligation to help a hard-working, promising employee realize his potential. What will she advise Cathy to do now that Firoz's probationary period is drawing to a close?

What Would You Do?

1. Agree with Cathy Putnam. Despite your personal feelings, accept that Firoz Bahmani is not capable of carrying out the accountant assistant's responsibilities. Make the break now, and give him his notice on the grounds that he cannot carry out one of the key stated job requirements. Advise him that a position that primarily involves paperwork would be a better fit for him.

2. Place Firoz with a more sympathetic account manager who is open to finding ways to help him improve his English and has the time to help him develop his assertiveness and telephone skills. Send Cathy Putnam to diversity awareness training.

3. Create a new position at the firm that will allow Firoz to do the reports and reconciliations for several account managers, freeing the account assistants to concentrate on public contact work. Make it clear that he will have little chance of future promotion unless his English improves markedly.

SOURCES: Mary Gillis,"Iranian Americans,"*Multicultural America:* www.everyculture.com/multi/Ha-La/Iranian-Americans.html (accessed September 19, 2006); and Charlene Marmer Solomon, "Managing Today's Immigrants,"*Personnel Journal* 72, no. 3 (February 1993): 56–65.

CASE FOR CRITICAL ANALYSIS

Hunter-Worth

Christmas was fast approaching. Just a short while ago, Chuck Moore, national sales manager for Hunter-Worth, a New York–based multinational toy manufacturer, was confident the coming holiday was going to

be one of the company's best in years. At a recent toy expo, Hunter-Worth unveiled a new interactive plush toy that was cuddly, high-tech, and tied into a major holiday motion picture expected to be a smash hit. Chuck had thought the toy would do well, but frankly, the level of interest took him by surprise. The buyers at the toy fair raved, and the subsequent pre-order volume was extremely encouraging. It had all looked so promising, but now he couldn't shake a sense of impending doom.

The problem in a nutshell was that the Mexican subsidiary that manufactured the toy couldn't seem to meet a deadline. Not only were all the shipments late so far, but they fell well short of the quantities ordered. Chuck decided to e-mail Vicente Ruiz, the plant manager, about the situation before he found himself in the middle of the Christmas season with parents clamoring for a toy he couldn't lay his hands on.

In a thoroughly professional e-mail that started with a friendly "Dear Vicente," Chuck inquired about the status of the latest order, asked for a production schedule for pending orders, and requested a specific explanation as to why the Mexican plant seemed to be having such difficulty shipping orders out on time. The reply appeared within the hour, but to his utter astonishment, it was a short message from Vicente's secretary. She acknowledged the receipt of his e-mail and assured him the Mexican plant would be shipping the order, already a week late, in the next ten days.

"That's it," Chuck fumed. "Time to take this to Sato." He prefaced his original e-mail and the secretary's reply with a terse note expressing his growing concern over the availability of what could well be this season's must-have toy. "Just what do I have to do to light a fire under Vicente?" he wrote. He then forwarded it all to his supervisor and friend, Michael Sato, the executive vice president for sales and marketing.

Next thing he knew, he was on the phone with Vicente—and the plant manager was furious. "Signor Moore, how dare you go over my head and say such things about me to my boss?" he sputtered, sounding both angry and slightly panicked. It seemed that Michael had forwarded Chuck's e-mail to Hunter-Worth's vice president of operations, who had sent it on to the Mexican subsidiary's president.

That turn of events was unfortunate, but Chuck wasn't feeling all that apologetic. "You could have prevented all this if you'd just answered the questions I e-mailed you last week," he pointed out. "I deserved more than a form letter—and from your secretary, no less."

"My secretary always answers my e-mails," replied Vicente. "She figures that if the problem is really urgent, you would pick up the phone and talk to me directly. Contrary to what you guys north of the border might think, we do take deadlines seriously here. There's only so much we can do with the supply problems we're having, but I doubt you're interested in hearing about those." And Vicente hung up the phone without waiting for a response.

Chuck was confused and disheartened. Things were only getting worse. How could he turn the situation around?

Questions

1. Based on Vicente Ruiz's actions and his conversation with Chuck Moore, what differences do you detect in cultural attitudes toward communications in Mexico as compared with the United States? Is understanding these differences important? Explain.

2. What was the main purpose of Chuck's communication to Vicente? To Michael Sato? What factors should he have considered when choosing a channel for his communication to Vicente? Are they the same factors he should have considered when communicating with Michael Sato?

3. If you were Chuck, what would you have done differently? What steps would you take at this point to make sure the supply of the popular new toy is sufficient to meet the anticipated demand?

SOURCES: Based on Harry W. Lane, *Charles Foster Sends an E-mail,* (London, Ontario: Ivey Publishing, 2005); Frank Unger and Roger Frankel, *Doing Business in Mexico: A Practical Guide on How to Break into the Market* (Council on Australia Latin America Relations and the Department of Foreign Affairs and Trade, 2002): 24–27; and Ignacio Hernandez, "Doing Business in Mexico—Business Etiquette—Understanding U.S.–Mexico Cultural Differences," *MexGrocer.com:* www.mexgrocer.com/business-in-mexico.html (accessed September 18, 2006).

ENDNOTES

1. Laura Landro, "Making It OK to Challenge Surgeons," *The Wall Street Journal* (November 16, 2005): D1, D4; "VHA is Transforming the Hospital Operating Room," VHA, Inc. press release, http://www.vha.com.

2. Joann S. Lublin, "The 'Open Inbox'," *The Wall Street Journal* (October 10, 2005): B1, B3.

3. Elizabeth B. Drew, "Profile: Robert Strauss," *The New Yorker* (May 7, 1979): 55–70.

4. Henry Mintzberg, *The Nature of Managerial Work* (New York: Harper & Row, 1973).

5. Phillip G. Clampitt, Laurey Berk, and M. Lee Williams, "Leaders as Strategic Communicators," *Ivey Business Journal* (May–June 2002): 51–55.

6. Ian Wylie, "Can Philips Learn to Walk the Talk?" *Fast Company* (January 2003): 44–45.

7. Fred Luthans and Janet K. Larsen, "How Managers Really Communicate," *Human Relations* 39 (1986): 161–178; and Larry E. Penley and Brian Hawkins, "Studying Interpersonal Communication in Organizations: A Leadership Application," *Academy of Management Journal* 28 (1985): 309–326.

8. D. K. Berlo, *The Process of Communication* (New York: Holt, Rinehart and Winston, 1960): 24.

9. Paul Roberts, "Live! From Your Office! It's . . . ," *Fast Company* (October 1999): 150–170.

10. Bruce K. Blaylock, "Cognitive Style and the Usefulness of Information," *Decision Sciences* 15 (Winter 1984): 74–91.

11. Robert H. Lengel and Richard L. Daft, "The Selection of Communication Media as an Executive Skill," *Academy of Management Executive* 2 (August 1988): 225–232; Richard L. Daft and Robert H. Lengel, "Organizational Information Requirements, Media Richness and Structural Design," *Managerial Science* 32 (May 1986): 554–572; and Jane Webster and Linda Klebe Treviño, "Rational and Social Theories as Complementary Explanations of Communication Media Choices: Two Policy-Capturing Studies," *Academy of Management Journal* 38, no. 6 (1995): 1544–1572.

12. Research reported in "E-mail Can't Mimic Phone Calls," *Johnson City Press* (September 17, 2000): 31.

13. Raymond E. Friedman and Steven C. Currall, "E-Mail Escalation: Dispute Exacerbating Elements of Electronic Communication, http://www.mba.vanderbilt.edu/ray.friedman/pdf/emailescalation.pdf; Lauren Keller Johnson, "Does E-Mail Escalate Conflict?" *MIT Sloan Management Review* (Fall 2002): 14–15; and Alison Stein Wellner, "Lost in Translation," *Inc. Magazine* (September 2005): 37–38.

14. Wellner, "Lost in Translation"; Nick Easen, "Don't Send the Wrong Message; When E-Mail Crosses Borders, a Faux Pas Could Be Just a Click Away," *Business 2.0* (August 2005): 102.

15. Scott Kirsner, "IM Is Here. RU Prepared?" *Darwin Magazine* (February 2002): 22–24.

16. John R. Carlson and Robert W. Smud, "Channel Expansion Theory and the Experiential Nature of Media Richness Perceptions," *Academy of Management Journal* 42, no. 2 (1999): 153–170; R. Rice and G. Love, "Electronic Emotion," *Communication Research* 14 (1987): 85–108.

17. Ronald E. Rice, "Task Analyzability, Use of New Media, and Effectiveness: A Multi-Site Exploration of Media Richness," *Organizational Science* 3, no. 4 (November 1992): 475–500; and M. Lynne Markus, "Electronic Mail as the Medium of Managerial Choice," *Organizational Science* 5, no. 4 (November 1994): 502–527.

18. Richard L. Daft, Robert H. Lengel, and Linda Klebe Treviño, "Message Equivocality, Media Selection and Manager Performance: Implication for Information Systems," *MIS Quarterly* 11 (1987): 355–368.

19. Mary Young and James E. Post, "Managing to Communicate, Communicating to Manage: How Leading Companies Communicate with Employees," *Organizational Dynamics* (Summer 1993): 31–43.

20. Jay A. Conger, "The Necessary Art of Persuasion," *Harvard Business Review* (May–June 1998): 84–95.

21. Ibid.

22. Susan Cramm, "The Heart of Persuasion," *CIO* (July 1, 2005): 28–30.

23. J. Martin and M. Powers, "Organizational Stories: More Vivid and Persuasive than Quantitative Data," in B. M. Staw, ed., *Psychological Foundations of Organizational Behavior* (Glenview, IL: Scott Foresman, 1982): 161–168.

24. Bronwyn Fryer, "Storytelling that Moves People: A Conversation with Screenwriting Coach Robert McKee," *Harvard Business Review* (June 2003): 51–55.

25. Bill Birchard, "Once Upon a Time," *Strategy & Business* no. 27 (Second Quarter 2002): 99–104; and Laura Shin, "You Can Be a Great Storyteller," *USA Weekend* (January 16–18, 2004): 14.

26. I. Thomas Sheppard, "Silent Signals," *Supervisory Management* (March 1986): 31–33.

27. Albert Mehrabian, *Silent Messages* (Belmont, CA: Wadsworth, 1971); and Albert Mehrabian, "Communicating without Words," *Psychology Today* (September 1968): 53–55.

28. Meridith Levinson, "How to Be a Mind Reader," *CIO* (December 1, 2004): 72–76; Mac Fulfer, "Nonverbal Communication: How to Read What's Plain as the Nose . . . ," *Journal of Organizational Excellence* (Spring 2001): 19–27; Paul Ekman, *Emotions Revealed: Recognizing Faces and Feelings to Improve Communication and Emotional Life* (New York: Time Books, 2003).

29. Sheppard, "Silent Signals."

30. Arthur H. Bell, *The Complete Manager's Guide to Interviewing* (Homewood, IL: Richard D. Irwin, 1989).

31. C. Glenn Pearce, "Doing Something about Your Listening Ability," *Supervisory Management* (March 1989): 29–34; and Tom Peters, "Learning to Listen," *Hyatt Magazine* (Spring 1988): 16–21.

32. Michael A. Prospero, "Leading Listener; Winner: Cabela's," *Fast Company* (October 2005): 53.

33. M. P. Nichols, *The Lost Art of Listening* (New York: Guilford Publishing, 1995).

34. "Benchmarking the Sales Function," a report based on a study of 100 salespeople from small, medium, and large businesses, conducted by Ron Volper Group Inc. Sales Consulting and Training, White Plains, NY (1996), as reported in "Nine Habits of Highly Successful Salespeople," *Inc. Small Business Success.*

35. Gerald M. Goldhaber, *Organizational Communication*, 4th ed. (Dubuque, IA: Brown, 1980): 189.

36. Curtis Sittenfeld, "Good Ways to Deliver Bad News," *Fast Company* (April 1999): 58, 60.

37. Vanessa Fuhrmans, "Bedside Manner; An Insurer Tries a New Strategy: Listen to Patients," *The Wall Street Journal* (April 11, 2006): A1.

38. James R. Stengel, Andrea L. Dixon, and Chris T. Allen, "Listening Begins at Home," *Harvard Business Review* (November 2003): 106–116.

39. Richard L. Daft and Richard M. Steers, *Organizations: A Micro/Macro Approach* (New York: Harper Collins, 1986); and Daniel Katz and Robert Kahn, *The Social Psychology of Organizations*, 2d ed. (New York: Wiley, 1978).

40. Greg Jaffe, "Tug of War: In the New Military, Technology May Alter Chain of Command," *The Wall Street Journal* (March 30, 2001): A3; and Aaron Pressman, "Business Gets the Message," *The Industry Standard* (February 26, 2001): 58–59.

41. Roberta Maynard, "It Can Pay to Show Employees the Big Picture," *Nation's Business* (December 1994): 10.

42. Phillip G. Clampitt, Robert J. DeKoch, and Thomas Cashman, "A Strategy for Communicating about Uncertainty," *Academy of Management Executive* 14, no. 4 (2000): 41–57.

43. Reported in Louise van der Does and Stephen J. Caldeira, "Effective Leaders Champion Communication Skills," *Nation's Restaurant News* (March 27, 2006): 20.

44. J. G. Miller, "Living Systems: The Organization," *Behavioral Science* 17 (1972): 69.

45. Michael J. Glauser, "Upward Information Flow in Organizations: Review and Conceptual Analysis," *Human Relations* 37 (1984): 613–643; and "Upward/ Downward Communication: Critical Information Channels," *Small Business Report* (October 1985): 85–88.

46. Pat Croce, "Catching the 5:15: A Simple Reporting System Can Help You Keep Tabs on Your Business," *FSB* (March 2004): 34.

47. Dennis Tourish, "Critical Upward Communication: Ten Commandments for Improving Strategy and Decision Making," *Long Range Planning* 38 (2005): 485–503; Mary P. Rowe and Michael Baker, "Are You Hearing Enough Employee Concerns?" *Harvard Business Review* 62 (May–June 1984): 127–135; W. H. Read, "Upward Communication in Industrial Hierarchies," *Human Relations* 15 (February 1962): 3–15; and Daft and Steers, *Organizations*.

48. Jena McGregor, "Gospels of Failure," *Fast Company* (February 2005): 61–67.

49. Ibid.

50. Barbara Ettorre, "The Unvarnished Truth," *Management Review* (June 1997): 54–57; and Roberta Maynard, "Back to Basics, From the Top," *Nation's Business* (December 1996): 38–39.

51. Thomas Petzinger, "A Hospital Applies Teamwork to Thwart An Insidious Enemy," *The Wall Street Journal* (May 8, 1998): B1.

52. E. M. Rogers and R. A. Rogers, *Communication in Organizations* (New York: Free Press, 1976); and A. Bavelas and D. Barrett, "An Experimental Approach to Organization Communication," *Personnel* 27 (1951): 366–371.

53. This discussion is based on Daft and Steers, *Organizations*.

54. Bavelas and Barrett, "An Experimental Approach"; and M. E. Shaw, *Group Dynamics: The Psychology of Small Group Behavior* (New York: McGraw-Hill, 1976).

55. Richard L. Daft and Norman B. Macintosh, "A Tentative Exploration into the Amount and Equivocality of Information Processing in Organizational Work Units," *Administrative Science Quarterly* 26 (1981): 207–224.

56. This discussion of informal networks is based on Rob Cross, Nitin Nohria, and Andrew Parker, "Six Myths About Informal Networks," *MIT Sloan Management Review* (Spring 2002): 67–75; and Rob Cross and Laurence Prusak, "The People Who Make Organizations Go—or Stop," *Harvard Business Review* (June 2002): 105–112.

57. Tahl Raz, "The 10 Secrets of a Master Networker," *Inc.* (January 2003).

58. Keith Davis and John W. Newstrom, *Human Behavior at Work: Organizational Behavior*, 7th ed. (New York: McGraw-Hill, 1985).

59. Suzanne M. Crampton, John W. Hodge, and Jitendra M. Mishra, "The Informal Communication Network: Factors Influencing Grapevine Activity," *Public Personnel Management* 27, no. 4 (Winter 1998): 569–584.

60. Survey results reported in Jared Sandberg, "Ruthless Rumors and the Managers Who Enable Them," *The Wall Street Journal* (October 29, 2003): B1

61. Joshua Hyatt, "The Last Shift," *Inc.* (February 1989): 74–80.

62. Donald B. Simmons, "The Nature of the Organizational Grapevine," *Supervisory Management* (November 1985): 39–42; and Davis and Newstrom, *Human Behavior*.

63. Barbara Ettorre, "Hellooo. Anybody Listening?" *Management Review* (November 1997): 9.

64. Lisa A. Burke and Jessica Morris Wise, "The Effective Care, Handling, and Pruning of the Office Grapevine," *Business Horizons* (May–June 2003): 71–74; "They Hear It Through the Grapevine," in Michael Warshaw, "The Good Guy's Guide to Office Politics," *Fast Company* (April–May 1998): 157–178 (p. 160); and Carol Hildebrand, "Mapping the Invisible Workplace," *CIO Enterprise*, Section 2 (July 15, 1998): 18–20.

65. Thomas J. Peters and Robert H. Waterman Jr., *In Search of Excellence* (New York: Harper & Row, 1982); and Tom Peters and Nancy Austin, *A Passion for Excellence: The Leadership Difference* (New York: Random House, 1985).

66. Lois Therrien, "How Ztel Went from Riches to Rags," *BusinessWeek* (June 17, 1985): 97–100.

67. Reported in "Employers Want Better Writing," *News for You* (December 8, 2004): 2.

68. Jonathan Hershberg, "It's Not Just What You Say," *Training* (May 2005): 50.

69. Based on Michael Fitzgerald, "How to Write a Memorable Memo," *CIO* (October 15, 2005): 85–87; and Hershberg, "It's Not Just What You Say."

70. Mary Anne Donovan, "E-Mail Exposes the Literacy Gap," *Workforce* (November 2002): 15.

71. John Case, "Opening the Books," *Harvard Business Review*, (March–April 1997): 118–127.

72. Gary Hamel, "Killer Strategies That Make Shareholders Rich," *Fortune* (June 23, 1997): 70–84.

73. "What Is Trust?" results of a survey by Manchester Consulting, reported in Jenny C. McCune, "That Elusive Thing Called Trust," *Management Review* (July–August 1998): 10–16.

74. David Bohm, *On Dialogue* (Ojai, CA: David Bohm Seminars, 1989).

75. This discussion is based on Glenna Gerard and Linda Teurfs, "Dialogue and Organizational Transformation," in *Community Building: Renewing Spirit and Learning in Business*, ed. Kazinierz Gozdz (New Leaders Press, 1995): 142–153; and Edgar H. Schein, "On Dialogue, Culture, and Organizational Learning," *Organizational Dynamics* (Autumn 1993): 40–51.

76. Ian I. Mitroff and Murat C. Alpaslan, "Preparing for Evil," *Harvard Business Review* (April 2003): 109–115.

77. This section is based on Leslie Wayne and Leslie Kaufman, "Leadership, Put to a New Test," *The New York Times* (September 16, 2001): Section 3, 1, 4; Ian I. Mitroff, "Crisis Leadership," *Executive Excellence* (August 2001): 19; Jerry Useem, "What It Takes," *Fortune* (November 12, 2001): 126–132; Andy Bowen, "Crisis Procedures That Stand the Test of Time," *Public Relations Tactics* (August 2001): 16; and Matthew Boyle, "Nothing Really Matters," *Fortune* (October 15, 2001): 261–264.

78. Stephen Bernhut, "Leadership, with Michael Useem," *Ivey Business Journal* (January–February 2002): 42–43.

79. Mitroff, "Crisis Leadership."

80. Jay M. Jackman and Myra H. Strober, "Fear of Feedback," *Harvard Business Review* (April 2003): 101–108; and Tourish, "Critical Upward Communication."

81. Thomas E. Ricks, "Army Devises System to Decide What Does, and Does Not, Work," *The Wall Street Journal* (May 23, 1997): A1, A10; Stephanie Watts Sussman, "CALL: A Model for Effective Organizational Learning," *Strategy* (Summer 1999): 14–15; John O'Shea, "Army: The Leader as Learner-in-Chief," *The Officer* (June 2003): 31; Michael D. Maples, "Fires

First in Combat—Train the Way We Fight," *Field Artillery* (July–August 2003): 1; Thomas E. Ricks, "Intelligence Problems in Iraq Are Detailed," *The Washington Post* (October 25, 2003): A1; and Richard W. Koenig, "Forging Our Future: Using Operation Iraqi Freedom Phase IV Lessons Learned," *Engineer* (January–March 2004): 21–22.

82. Thomas A. Stewart, "Listen Up, Maggots! You *Will* Deploy a More Humane and Effective Managerial Style!" *Ecompany* (July 2001): 95.

83. James A. F. Stoner and R. Edward Freeman, *Management*, 4th ed. (Englewood Cliffs, NJ: Prentice Hall, 1989).

84. Janet Fulk and Sirish Mani, "Distortion of Communication in Hierarchical Relationships," in *Communication Yearbook*, vol. 9, ed. M. L. McLaughlin (Beverly Hills, CA: Sage, 1986): 483–510.

85. "CEO Stopping Descent of Airline That's in Trouble," *Johnson City Press* (June 20, 2004): 7D.

86. Landro, "Making It OK to Challenge Surgeons."

CHAPTER 21

CHAPTER OUTLINE

Manager's Challenge

Teams at Work

What Is a Team?

Model of Work Team Effectiveness

Types of Teams

Formal Teams

Self-Directed Teams

Teams in the New Workplace

Team Characteristics

Size

Diversity

Member Roles

Team Processes

Stages of Team Development

Team Cohesiveness

Team Norms

Managing Team Conflict

Balancing Conflict and Cooperation

Causes of Conflict

Styles to Handle Conflict

Negotiation

Work Team Effectiveness

Productive Output

Satisfaction of Members

Capacity to Adapt and Learn

LEARNING OBJECTIVES

After studying this chapter, you should be able to:

1. Identify the types of teams in organizations.

2. Discuss new applications of teams to facilitate employee involvement.

3. Identify roles within teams and the type of role you could play to help a team be effective.

4. Explain the general stages of team development.

5. Identify ways in which team size and diversity of membership affects team performance.

6. Explain the concepts of team cohesiveness and team norms and their relationship to team performance.

7. Understand the causes of conflict within and among teams and how to reduce conflict, including the importance of negotiation.

8. Define the outcomes of effective teams and how managers can enhance team effectiveness.

TEAMWORK

MANAGER'S CHALLENGE

Employees at United Airlines could use a lift. They've suffered years of declining organizational performance, resulting in a demoralizing bankruptcy that cut wages, laid off thousands of employees, and forced remaining workers to do more with less. Ramp workers, those who wave in jets, load baggage, and push planes around with tractors and tow bars, have one of the toughest—and often one of the most underappreciated—jobs in the industry. At United, ramp workers typically work in teams of four. The work can be chaotic, with missing equipment, lousy weather, machinery breakdowns, and potentially dangerous debris on the tarmac. If someone calls in sick, an understaffed team has to handle the myriad ramp chores in the allotted time to get planes back in the air. Unfortunately, even fully staffed teams at United have trouble turning planes quickly. United began a campaign to standardize ramp functions, but operations managers know it isn't enough. They have to improve team effectiveness or the new procedures will do little to help workers meet an accelerated schedule.[1]

> If you were an airport operations manager, how would you improve work team effectiveness for ramp workers at United? What team characteristics do you think are essential for a team to function smoothly and effectively?

■ TAKE A MOMENT

In recent years, teams have become the primary way in which many companies accomplish their work, from the assembly line to the executive suite. Hypertherm, Inc., a maker of metal-cutting equipment in Hanover, New Hampshire, uses teams of researchers, engineers, marketers, and salespeople focused on updating and improving the company's five product lines.[2] Cirque du Soleil's top executives, including the CEO, chief operating officer, chief financial officer, and vice president of creation, function as a team to coordinate, develop, and oversee 13 acrobatic troupes that travel to 100 cities on four continents.[3] And Lassiter Middle School in Jefferson County, Kentucky, uses teams of teachers to prepare daily schedules and handle student discipline problems.

Some companies use global virtual teams composed of managers and employees working in different countries.[4] Steelcase International, a furniture manufacturer based in Strasburg, France, has 14,000 employees and manufacturing facilities in 20 countries. Steelcase has been using teams for 30 years. In the past, they were aligned according to geography, with U.S. teams for the United States, French teams for France, and so on. Today, though, Steelcase teams have evolved into cross-functional and cross-geographical virtual teams that communicate and collaborate electronically.[5]

However, as at United Airlines, teams aren't always effective. In a survey of manufacturing organizations, about 80 percent of respondents said they used some kind of teams, but only 14 percent of those companies rated their teaming efforts as highly effective. Just over half of the responding manufacturers said their efforts were only "somewhat effective," and 15 percent considered their efforts not effective at all.[6]

This chapter focuses on teams and their applications within organizations. We define various types of teams, explore the stages of team development, and examine how characteristics such as size, cohesiveness, diversity, and norms influence team effectiveness. We also discuss how individuals can make contributions to teams, look at techniques for managing team conflict, and describe how negotiation can facilitate cooperation and teamwork. The final sections of the chapter focus on the outcomes of effective work teams within organizations. Teams are a central aspect of organizational life, and the ability to manage them is a vital component of manager and organization success.

TEAMS AT WORK

Some organizations have had great success with teams, including increased productivity, quality improvements, greater innovation, and higher employee satisfaction. FedEx, for example, cut service problems such as incorrect bills and lost packages by 13 percent by using teams. At Xerox, production plants using teams reported a 30 percent increase in productivity.[7] A study of team-based organizations in Australia supports the idea that teams provide benefits to both employees and organizations.[8] However, simply organizing people into teams does not guarantee their effectiveness. Managers are responsible for creating and nurturing the conditions and processes that enable teams to be successful.

In this section, we first define teams and then discuss a model of team effectiveness that summarizes the important concepts.

What Is a Team?

team A unit of two or more people who interact and coordinate their work to accomplish a specific goal.

A **team** is a unit of two or more people who interact and coordinate their work to accomplish a specific goal.[9] This definition has three components. First, two or more people are required. Teams can be quite large, although most have fewer than 15 people. In the survey of manufacturing organizations referred to earlier in the chapter, for example, the average size of teams decreased from 12.7 in 2003 to 10.5 in 2004.[10] Second, people in a team have regular interaction. People who do not interact, such as when standing in line at a lunch counter or riding in an elevator, do not compose a team. Third, people in a team share a performance goal, whether to design a new handheld computing device, build a car, or write a textbook. Students often are assigned to teams to do class assignments, in which case the purpose is to perform the assignment and receive an acceptable grade.

Although a team is a group of people, the two terms are not interchangeable. An employer, a teacher, or a coach can put together a *group* of people and never build a *team*. The team concept implies a sense of shared mission and collective responsibility. Exhibit 21.1 lists the primary differences between groups and teams. One example of a true team comes from the military, where U.S. Navy surgeons, nurses, anesthesiologists, and

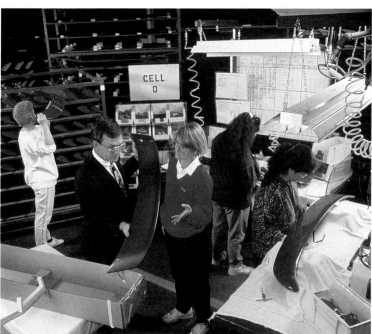

COURTESY OF TRINOVA CORPORATION

CONCEPT CONNECTION Teams are emerging as a **powerful management tool** and are popping up in the most unexpected places, such as this manufacturing cell at TRINOVA'S Aeroquip Inoac facility in Fremont, Ohio. The facility uses more than 40 teams that cross operations and job functions, helping the company eliminate non-value-added activities, lower costs, improve customer responsiveness, and increase quality.

EXHIBIT   21.1

Group	Team
• Has a designated strong leader • Holds individuals accountable • Sets identical purpose for group and organization • Has individual work products • Runs efficient meetings • Measures effectiveness indirectly by influence on business (such as financial performance) • Discusses, decides, delegates work to individuals	• Shares or rotates leadership roles • Holds team accountable to each other • Sets specific team vision or purpose • Has collective work products • Runs meetings that encourage open-ended discussion and problem solving • Measures effectiveness directly by assessing collective work • Discusses, decides, shares work

Differences Between
Groups and Teams
SOURCE: Adapted from Jon
R. Katzenbach and Douglas
K. Smith, "The Discipline of
Teams," *Harvard Business
Review* (March–April 1995):
111–120.

technicians make up eight-person forward surgical teams that operated for the first time ever in combat during Operation Iraqi Freedom. These teams were scattered over Iraq and were able to move to new locations in four trucks and be set up within an hour. With a goal of saving the 15 to 20 percent of wounded soldiers and civilians who will die unless they receive critical care within 24 hours, members of these teams smoothly coordinated their activities to accomplish a critical shared mission.[11] The sports world also provides many examples of the importance of teamwork. The 2004 U.S. Olympic basketball team was made up entirely of superstar players, yet the members never coalesced as a team, instead functioning as a group of individual players. The team came in third and lost to Lithuania. In contrast, the 1980 U.S. hockey team that beat the Soviets to win gold at the Lake Placid Olympics consisted of a bunch of no-name players. Coach Herb Brooks picked players based on their personal chemistry—how they worked together as a team—rather than on their individual abilities and egos.[12]

Model of Work Team Effectiveness

Some of the factors associated with team effectiveness are illustrated in Exhibit 21.2. Work team effectiveness is based on three outcomes—productive output, personal satisfaction, and the capacity to adapt and learn.[13] *Satisfaction* pertains to the team's ability to meet the personal needs of its members and hence maintain their membership and commitment. *Productive output* pertains to the quality and quantity of task outputs as defined by team goals. *Capacity to adapt and learn* refers to the ability of teams to bring greater knowledge and skills to job tasks and enhance the potential of the organization to respond to new threats or opportunities in the environment.

EXHIBIT   21.2

Work Team Effectiveness
Model

The factors that influence team effectiveness begin with the organizational context.[14] The organizational context in which the team operates is described in other chapters and includes such factors as structure, strategy, environment, culture, and reward systems. Within that context, managers define teams. Important team characteristics are the type of team, the team structure, and team composition. Managers must decide when to create permanent teams within the formal structure and when to use a temporary task team. Factors such as the diversity of the team in terms of gender and race, as well as knowledge, skills, and attitudes, can have a tremendous impact on team processes and effectiveness.[15] Team size and roles also are important. Managers strive for the right mix of knowledge and skills for the task to be performed and consider whether a team is the best way to accomplish the task. If costs outweigh benefits, managers may wish to assign an individual employee to the task.

These team characteristics influence processes internal to the team, which, in turn, affect output, satisfaction, and the team's contribution to organizational adaptability. Good team leaders understand and manage stages of team development, cohesiveness, norms, and conflict in order to build an effective team. These processes are influenced by team and organizational characteristics and by the ability of members and leaders to direct these processes in a positive manner.

The model of team effectiveness in Exhibit 21.2 is the basis for this chapter. In the following sections, we will examine types of organizational teams, team structure, internal processes, and the benefits of effective work teams.

TYPES OF TEAMS

Many types of teams can exist within organizations. The easiest way to classify teams is in terms of those created as part of the organization's formal structure and those created to increase employee participation.

Formal Teams

Formal teams are created by the organization as part of the formal organization structure. Two common types of formal teams are vertical and horizontal, which typically represent vertical and horizontal structural relationships, as described in Chapter 10. These two types of teams are illustrated in Exhibit 21.3. A third type of formal team is the special-purpose team.

formal team A team created by the organization as part of the formal organization structure.

EXHIBIT 21.3

Horizontal and Vertical Teams in an Organization

- - - - Horizontal team for L21 modification
——— Vertical engineering team

Vertical Team

A **vertical team** is composed of a manager and his or her subordinates in the formal chain of command. Sometimes called a *functional team* or a *command team*, the vertical team may in some cases include three or four levels of hierarchy within a functional department. Typically, the vertical team includes a single department in an organization. The third-shift nursing team on the second floor of St. Luke's Hospital is a vertical team that includes nurses and a supervisor. A financial analysis department, a quality control department, an accounting department, and a human resource department are all vertical or command teams. Each is created by the organization to attain specific goals through members' joint activities and interactions.

Horizontal Team

A **horizontal team** is composed of employees from about the same hierarchical level but from different areas of expertise.[16] A horizontal team is drawn from several departments, is given a specific task, and may be disbanded after the task is completed. The two most common types of horizontal teams are cross-functional teams and committees.

As described in Chapter 10, a *cross-functional team* is a group of employees from different departments formed to deal with a specific activity and existing only until the task is completed. Sometimes called a *task force*, the team might be used to create a new product in a manufacturing organization or a new history curriculum in a university. Georgetown Preparatory School created a task force made up of teachers, coaches, administrators, support staff, and outside consultants to develop a preparedness plan to address the threat of seasonal influenza and other potentially devastating epidemics.[17] When several departments are involved, and many views have to be considered, tasks are best served with a horizontal, cross-functional team.

A **committee** generally is long-lived and may be a permanent part of the organization's structure. Membership on a committee usually is decided by a person's title or position rather than by personal expertise. A committee often needs official representation, compared with selection for a cross-functional team, which is based on personal qualifications for solving a problem. Committees typically are formed to deal with tasks that recur regularly. For example, a grievance committee handles employee grievances; an advisory committee makes recommendations in the areas of employee compensation and work practices; a worker-management committee may be concerned with work rules, job design changes, and suggestions for work improvement.[18]

As part of the horizontal structure of the organization, cross-functional teams and committees offer several advantages: (1) They allow organization members to exchange information; (2) they generate suggestions for coordinating the organizational units that are represented; (3) they develop new ideas and solutions for existing organizational problems; and (4) they assist in the development of new organizational practices and policies.

Special-Purpose Team

Special-purpose teams, sometimes called *project teams*, are created outside the formal organization structure to undertake a project of special importance or creativity. Special-purpose teams focus on a specific purpose and expect to disband once the specific project is completed.[19] Examples include the team that developed the first IBM ThinkPad and the project team for the Motorola RAZR cell phone. A special-purpose team still is part of the formal organization and has its own reporting structure, but members perceive themselves as a separate entity.[20]

Many of today's companies are using special-purpose teams to dramatically speed up development of a special product or execute a highly important project. These *fast-cycle teams*, as described in Chapter 11, are set up to work on projects that

vertical team A formal team composed of a manager and his or her subordinates in the organization's formal chain of command.

horizontal team A formal team composed of employees from about the same hierarchical level but from different areas of expertise.

committee A long-lasting, sometimes permanent team in the organization structure created to deal with tasks that recur regularly.

special-purpose team A team created outside the formal organization to undertake a project of special importance or creativity.

© BERND AUERS

⌐CONCEPT
⌐CONNECTION⌐ James Frankel, James McLurkin, and Jennifer Smith serve on the SwarmBot team, a **special purpose team** at iRobot in Burlington, Massachusetts, that is researching how SwarmBots can benefit mankind. SwarmBots are small robots in the form of cubes with rechargeable batteries that can potentially collaborate like a colony of ants to accomplish difficult tasks, such as disposing of land mines or taking over buildings held by bad guys. The team is perfecting software that can work with as few as 10 robots or as many as 10,000, and asking the critical question: "If you could make small robots cheaply, what would you use them for?"

problem-solving team
Typically 5 to 12 hourly employees from the same department who meet to discuss ways of improving quality, efficiency, and the work environment.

self-directed team A team consisting of 5 to 20 multi-skilled workers who rotate jobs to produce an entire product or service, often supervised by an elected member.

top management deems highly important. They are provided the freedom and resources to bring projects to closure quickly.[21]

Self-Directed Teams

Employee involvement through teams is designed to increase the participation of workers in decision making and the conduct of their jobs, with the goal of improving performance. Employee involvement started out simply with techniques such as information sharing with employees or asking employees for suggestions about improving the work. Gradually, companies moved toward greater autonomy for employees, which led first to problem-solving teams and then to self-directed teams.[22]

Problem-solving teams typically consist of 5 to 12 hourly employees from the same department who voluntarily meet to discuss ways of improving quality, efficiency, and the work environment. Recommendations are proposed to management for approval. Problem-solving teams usually are the first step in a company's move toward greater employee participation. The most widely known application is *quality circles*, first used by Japanese companies, in which employees focus on ways to improve quality in the production process. USX adopted this approach in several of its steel mills, recognizing that quality takes a team effort. Under the title All Product Excellence program (APEX), USX set up APEX teams of up to 12 employees who met several times a month to solve quality problems.[23]

As a company matures, problem-solving teams can gradually evolve into self-directed teams, which represent a fundamental change in how work is organized. Self-directed teams enable employees to feel challenged, find their work meaningful, and develop a strong sense of identity with the company.[24] **Self-directed teams** typically consist of 5 to 20 multiskilled workers who rotate jobs to produce an entire product or service or at least one complete aspect or portion of a product or service (e.g., engine assembly, insurance claim processing). The central idea is that the teams themselves, rather than managers or supervisors, take responsibility for their work, make decisions, monitor their own performance, and alter their work behavior as needed to solve problems, meet goals, and adapt to changing conditions.[25] For example, at Ralston Foods plant in Sparks, Nevada, which produces cereals, production workers are divided into teams of about 10 people. Some of the teams function entirely without designated leaders and handle all issues and problems that arise in their areas, including hiring and firing, scheduling, budgeting, quality, and disciplinary problems. Other teams have leaders assigned by management as they continue to learn how to work in a team environment, but the teams that have progressed to total self-direction actually outperform teams with assigned leaders.[26]

Self-directed teams are permanent teams that typically include the following elements:

:: The team includes employees with several skills and functions, and the combined skills are sufficient to perform a major organizational task. A team may include members from the foundry, machining, grinding, fabrication, and sales departments, with members cross-trained to perform one another's jobs. The team eliminates barriers among departments, enabling excellent coordination to produce a product or service.

:: The team is given access to resources such as information, equipment, machinery, and supplies needed to perform the complete task.

:: The team is empowered with decision-making authority, which means that members have the freedom to select new members, solve problems, spend money, monitor results, and plan for the future.[27]

In a self-directed team, team members take over managerial duties such as scheduling or ordering materials. They work with minimum supervision, perhaps electing one of their own as supervisor, who may change each year. The most effective self-directed teams are those that are fully empowered, as described in the discussion of empowerment in Chapter 19. In addition to having increased responsibility and discretion, empowered teams are those that have a strong belief in their team's capabilities, find value and meaning in their work, and recognize the impact the team's work has on customers, other stakeholders, and organizational success.[28] Managers create the conditions that determine whether self-directed teams are empowered by giving teams true power and decision-making authority, complete information, knowledge and skills, and appropriate rewards. The manager to whom the team and team leaders report, sometimes referred to as the *external leader*, has a tremendous impact on the team's success. In addition to creating conditions for empowerment, effective external leaders serve as an active link between the team and the organization, building constructive relationships and getting the team what it needs to do its best work.[29] An interesting example of the use of self-directed teams is the Orpheus Orchestra of New York City.

> Most orchestras are strongly hierarchical and structured around a conductor who wields almost complete power and control. Not Orpheus, a world-renowned chamber orchestra started in the 1970s by a small group of musicians committed to democratic power sharing.
>
> Orpheus operates completely without a conductor! Teams of musicians determine the repertoire, schedule concerts, select new musicians, interpret musical works, and handle all the other artistic and performance duties a conductor usually controls. The instrument sections constitute natural, specialized self-directed teams. Leadership rotates among different members, who are elected by their teammates.
>
> The actual structure of teams at Orpheus is quite complex and is designed to facilitate participative leadership, avoid hierarchical control, and allow everyone to participate in decision making.[30]

Orpheus Orchestra

The Orpheus Orchestra has found that using self-directed teams provides a number of advantages. The greater information flow and diverse artistic input contributes to a superb performance. In addition, members typically feel a high degree of commitment, and turnover is quite low. One business organization that succeeds with teamwork is Consolidated Diesel's engine factory in Whitakers, North Carolina. In its 20 or so years of operation as a team-based organization, the plant has had higher revenues, lower turnover, and significantly lower injury rates than the industry average. In addition, while most plants average 1 supervisor for every 25 workers, Consolidated Diesel has 1 for every 100 employees because the plant workers themselves handle many supervisory duties. The difference yields a savings of about $1 million a year.[31]

Teams in the New Workplace

Some exciting new approaches to teamwork have resulted from advances in information technology, shifting employee expectations, and the globalization of business. Two types of teams that are increasingly being used are virtual teams and global teams.

VIRTUAL TEAMS

A **virtual team** is made up of geographically or organizationally dispersed members who are linked primarily through advanced information and telecommunications technologies.[32] Although some virtual teams may be made up of only organizational members, virtual teams often include contingent workers, members of partner

virtual team A team made up of members who are geographically or organizationally dispersed, rarely meet face to face, and do their work using advanced information technologies.

CONCEPT
C O N N E C T I O N When commercial air traffic was grounded immediately after September 11, 2001, Dreamworks CEO Jeffrey Katzenbach had to assemble a **virtual team** of creative designers. He discovered that existing videoconferencing technology didn't allow team members to hold multiple conversations or get a good look at an object's details. The experience inspired the animation studio to join forces with Hewlett-Packard to produce the Halo Collaboration Studio, pictured here. In addition to HP, companies such as Cisco Systems and Polycom are now offering these high-end "telepresence" systems that use studio-quality cameras and sound equipment, high-speed data transmission, and rooms carefully designed to be identical, giving geographically dispersed teams a lifelike virtual meeting room.

organizations, customers, suppliers, consultants, or other outsiders. Team members use e-mail, instant messaging, voice mail, videoconferencing, Internet and intranet technologies, and various types of collaboration software to perform their work, although they might also sometimes meet face to face. Many virtual teams are cross-functional teams that emphasize solving customer problems or completing specific projects. Others are permanent self-directed teams.

With virtual teams, team leadership is typically shared or rotated, depending on the area of expertise needed at each stage of the project.[33] In addition, team membership in virtual teams may change fairly quickly, depending on the tasks to be performed. One of the primary advantages of virtual teams is the ability to rapidly assemble the most appropriate group of people to complete a complex project, solve a particular problem, or exploit a specific strategic opportunity. Virtual teams present unique challenges. Managers as team leaders should consider these critical issues when building virtual teams:[34]

:: *Select the right team members.* The first step is creating a team of people who have the right mix of technical and interpersonal skills, task knowledge, and personalities to work in a virtual environment. Interviews with virtual team members and leaders indicate that the ability to communicate and a desire to work as a team are the most important personal qualities for virtual team members.[35]

:: *Manage socialization.* People need to get to know one another and understand the appropriate behaviors and attitudes. Smart team leaders establish team norms and ground rules for interaction early in the team's formation.

:: *Foster trust.* Trust might be the most important ingredient in a successful virtual team. Teams that exhibit high levels of trust tend to have clear roles and expectations of one another, get to know one another as individuals, and maintain positive action-oriented attitudes.

:: *Effectively manage communications.* Frequent communication is essential. Team leaders need to understand when and how to use various forms of communication to best advantage. Some experts suggest regular face-to-face meetings, while others believe virtual teams can be successful even if they interact only electronically. One time when face-to-face communication might be essential is when misunderstandings, frustrations, or conflicts threaten the team's work.[36]

GLOBAL TEAMS

global team A work team made up of members of different nationalities whose activities span multiple countries; may operate as a virtual team or meet face-to-face.

Virtual teams are also sometimes global teams. **Global teams** are cross-border work teams made up of members of different nationalities whose activities span multiple countries.[37] Generally, global teams fall into two categories: intercultural teams, whose members come from different countries or cultures and meet face-to-face, and virtual global teams, whose members remain in separate locations around the world and conduct their work electronically.[38] For example, global teams

MySQL: Creating a Twenty-First-Century Global Team

How do you instill esprit de corps in a far-flung virtual team? It's a challenge managers at MySQL, a Swedish software maker, face daily. MySQL, which produces a database management system used in Web applications, employs about 320 people scattered in 25 countries. The majority of them work from home.

For MySQL, building an effective virtual global team begins with hiring the right people. Interestingly, though, managers don't consider being a "team player" in the conventional sense all that important. What the company looks for are people with the right technical skills and a real love for their work. It doesn't mean all aspects of teamwork are ignored, however. It just looks different. Thomas Basil, MySQL's director of support, works in a basement office next to his family's washing machine, so he knows from experience that people working virtually can feel isolated. When he signs in to the MySQL chat room each day, he greets each support team member by name. Basil even staged an online Christmas party, gathering staffers from places as far apart as Russia, England, and Germany into a cyber get-together, where he played Santa and dispensed virtual drinks and gifts. "When a company is as spread out as this one," he points out, "you have to think of virtual ways to imitate the dynamics of what goes on in a more familiar work situation." Occasionally, top executives get the entire MySQL staff together online through a system dubbed "Radio Sakila," which combines a typical conference call with instant messaging.

MySQL managers have built-in numerous communication channels to keep people talking across time and space. Team leaders recognize the limitations of text-based electronic communication, such as how easily miscommunication can occur in the absence of nonverbal cues. It's their responsibility to help people develop and follow guidelines for communication. As Basil found, sometimes an old-fashioned telephone conversation works best. "Voice is more personal than text and more helpful in building real understanding," he points out.

Managers have to think about performance evaluation and feedback differently too. Controls such as weekly performance reports keep people focused on tasks, yet managers have to be comfortable with the informality and loose structure of a virtual environment. "I'm not the kind of CEO who needs to see everybody sweat and work hard," says CEO Mårten Mickos. "These are passionate people who aren't going to stop because somebody isn't looking."

SOURCES: Josh Hyatt, "The Soul of a New Team," *Fortune* (June 12, 2006): 134–143; and Victoria Murphy Barret, "A Chat With . . . Oracle's New Enemy," *Forbes.com* (February 15, 2006): www.forbes.com/technology/2006/02/15/oracle-yahoo-google-cz_vmb_0215Mysql.html.

of software developers at Tandem Services Corporation coordinate their work electronically so that the team is productive around the clock. Team members in London code a project and transmit the code each evening to members in the United States for testing. U.S. team members then forward the code they've tested to Tokyo for debugging. The next morning, the London team members pick up with the code debugged by their Tokyo colleagues, and another cycle begins.[39] The trend toward creating virtual teams that cross geographical boundaries has grown tremendously in recent years. In some organizations, such as open-source software maker MySQL, described in this chapter's Unlocking Innovative Solutions Through Technology box, most employees are scattered around the world and never see one another face-to-face.

Global teams present enormous challenges for team leaders, who have to bridge gaps of time, distance, and culture. In some cases, members speak different languages, use different technologies, and have different beliefs about authority, decision making, and time orientation. For example, some cultures, such as the United States, are highly focused on "clock time," and tend to follow rigid schedules, whereas many other cultures have a more relaxed, cyclical concept of time. These different cultural attitudes toward time can affect work pacing, team communications, and the perception of deadlines.[40] Members from different countries may also have varied attitudes about teamwork itself. Multinational organizations have found that many team phenomena are culture-specific. Some countries, such as Mexico, value high power distance, as described in Chapter 4, meaning that differences in power and status are seen as appropriate and desirable. This viewpoint conflicts with the American idea of teamwork, which emphasizes shared power and authority. Thus, the acceptance and effectiveness of team-based systems can vary widely across different cultures, which makes implementing and evaluating teams quite complex.[41]

Organizations using global teams invest the time and resources to adequately educate employees. Managers make sure all team members appreciate and understand cultural differences, are focused on goals, and understand their responsibilities to the team. For a global team to be effective, all team members must be willing to deviate somewhat from their own values and norms and establish new norms for the team.[42] As with virtual teams, carefully selecting team members, building trust, and sharing information are critical to success.

TEAM CHARACTERISTICS

The next issue of concern to managers is designing the team for greatest effectiveness. One factor is *team characteristics*, which can affect team dynamics and performance. Characteristics of particular concern are team size, diversity, and member roles.

Size

More than 30 years ago, psychologist Ivan Steiner examined what happened each time the size of a team increased, and he proposed that team performance and productivity peaked at about 5—a quite small number. He found that adding additional members beyond 5 caused a decrease in motivation, an increase in coordination problems, and a general decline in performance.[43] Since then, numerous studies have found that smaller teams perform better, though most researchers say it's impossible to specify an optimal team size. One recent investigation of team size based on data from 58 software development teams found that the five best-performing teams ranged in size from 3 to 6 members.[44] Results of a recent Gallup poll in the United States show that 82 percent of employees agree that small teams are more productive.[45]

Teams need to be large enough to incorporate the diverse skills needed to complete a task, enable members to express good and bad feelings, and aggressively solve problems. However, they should also be small enough to permit members to feel an intimate part of the team and to communicate effectively and efficiently. In general, as a team increases in size, it becomes harder for each member to interact with and influence the others.

A summary of research on group size suggests the following:[46]

1. Small teams (2–5 members) show more agreement, ask more questions, and exchange more opinions. Members want to get along with one another. Small teams report more satisfaction and enter into more personal discussions. They tend to be informal and make few demands on team leaders.

2. Large teams (10 or more) tend to have more disagreements and differences of opinion. Subgroups often form, and conflicts among them occur. Communication becomes more difficult, and demands on leaders are greater because of the need for stronger coordination, more centralized decision making, and less member participation. Large teams also tend to be less friendly. Turnover and absenteeism are higher in a large team, especially for blue-collar workers. Because less satisfaction is associated with specialized tasks and poor communication, team members have fewer opportunities to participate and feel like an important part of the team.

3. As teams increase in size, so does the number of *free riders*. The term **free rider** refers to a team member who attains benefits from team membership but does not actively participate in and contribute to the team's work. The problem of free riding has likely been experienced by people in student project groups, where some students put more effort into the group project but everyone benefits from the result. Free riding is sometimes called *social loafing* because members do not exert

free rider A person who benefits from team membership but does not make a proportionate contribution to the team's work.

equal effort.[47] A classic experiment by German psychologist Ringelmann found that the pull exerted on a rope was greater by individuals working alone than by individuals in a group.[48] Similarly, experiments have found that when people are asked to clap and make noise, they make more noise on a per person basis when working alone or in small groups than they do in a large group.[49]

As a general rule, large teams make need satisfaction for individuals more difficult; thus, people feel less motivation to remain committed to their goals. Large projects can be split into components and assigned to several smaller teams to keep the benefits of small team size. At Amazon.com, CEO Jeff Bezos established a "two-pizza rule." If a team gets so large that members can't be fed with two pizzas, it needs to be split into smaller teams.[50]

Diversity

Because teams require a variety of skills, knowledge, and experience, it seems likely that heterogeneous teams would be more effective than homogeneous ones. In general, research supports this idea, showing that diverse teams produce more innovative solutions to problems.[51] Diversity in terms of functional area and skills, thinking styles, and personal characteristics is often a source of creativity. In addition, diversity may contribute to a healthy level of disagreement that leads to better decision making. At Southern Company, a new CIO made a conscious effort to build a diverse senior leadership team, recruiting people to build in gender, racial, educational, religious, cultural, and geographical diversity. "The differences we bring to the table sometimes mean we have long, heated discussions," says Becky Blalock. "But once we make a decision, we know we've viewed the problem from every possible angle."[52]

Research studies have confirmed that both functional diversity and gender diversity can have a positive impact on work team performance.[53] Racial, national, and ethnic diversity can also be good for teams, but in the short term these differences might hinder team interaction and performance. Teams made

© PRNEWSFOTO/NEWSCOM

CONCEPT CONNECTION "As demographic shifts sweep our nation and our community, **diversity** in public relations is not just a good thing to do, but a necessary business reality," declares Judy Iannaccone, Rancho Santiago Community College District communications director. Her professional organization agrees. The Public Relations Society of America (PSRA) promotes inclusion among work teams with a diversity tool kit, career Web site, and speakers list. Each year, the Society recognizes individual chapters for outstanding diversity promotion efforts. The Orange County, California, PSRA diversity committee was one of the 2005 recipients. Iannaccone, a committee member, is second from the right.

up of racially and culturally diverse members tend to have more difficulty learning to work well together, but, with effective leadership, the problems fade over time.[54]

> As a new manager, remember that team effectiveness depends on selecting the right type of team for the task, getting people with the right mix of knowledge and skills, and balancing the team's size and diversity.

■ **TAKE A MOMENT**

Member Roles

For a team to be successful over the long run, it must be structured so as to both maintain its members' social well-being and accomplish its task. In successful teams, the requirements for task performance and social satisfaction are met by the emergence of two types of roles: task specialist and socioemotional.[55]

People who play the **task specialist role** spend time and energy helping the team reach its goal. They often display the following behaviors:

:: *Initiate ideas.* Propose new solutions to team problems.

:: *Give opinions.* Offer opinions on task solutions; give candid feedback on others' suggestions.

:: *Seek information.* Ask for task-relevant facts.

:: *Summarize.* Relate various ideas to the problem at hand; pull ideas together into a summary perspective.

:: *Energize.* Stimulate the team into action when interest drops.[56]

People who adopt a **socioemotional role** support team members' emotional needs and help strengthen the social entity. They display the following behaviors:

:: *Encourage.* Are warm and receptive to others' ideas; praise and encourage others to draw forth their contributions.

:: *Harmonize.* Reconcile group conflicts; help disagreeing parties reach agreement.

:: *Reduce tension.* Tell jokes or in other ways draw off emotions when group atmosphere is tense.

:: *Follow.* Go along with the team; agree to other team members' ideas.

:: *Compromise.* Will shift own opinions to maintain team harmony.[57]

Exhibit 21.4 illustrates task specialist and socioemotional roles in teams. When most individuals in a team play a social role, the team is socially oriented. Members do not criticize or disagree with one another and do not forcefully offer opinions or try to accomplish team tasks, because their primary interest is to keep the team happy. Teams with mostly socioemotional roles can be satisfying, but they also can be unproductive. At the other extreme, a team made up primarily of task specialists will tend to have a singular concern for task accomplishment. This team will be effective for a short period of time but will not be satisfying for members over the long run. Task specialists convey little emotional concern for one another, are unsupportive, and ignore team members' social and emotional needs. The task-oriented team can be humorless and unsatisfying.

As Exhibit 21.4 illustrates, some team members may play a dual role. People with **dual roles** both contribute to the task and meet members' emotional needs. Such people often become team leaders. A study of new-product development teams in high-technology firms found that the most effective teams were headed by leaders who balanced the technical needs of the project with human interaction issues, thus meeting both task and socioemotional needs.[58] Exhibit 21.4 also shows the final type of role, called the **nonparticipator role**, in which people contribute

task specialist role A role in which the individual devotes personal time and energy to helping the team accomplish its task.

socioemotional role A role in which the individual provides support for team members' emotional needs and social unity.

dual role A role in which the individual both contributes to the team's task and supports members' emotional needs.

nonparticipator role A role in which the individual contributes little to either the task or members' socioemotional needs.

EXHIBIT 21.4

Team Member Roles

	Low — Member Social Behavior — High
High / Member Task Behavior	**Task Specialist Role** Focuses on task accomplishment over human needs — Important role, but if adopted by everyone, team's social needs will not be met • **Dual Role** Focuses on task and people — May be a team leader — Important role, but not essential if members adopt task specialist and socioemotional roles
Low	**Nonparticipator Role** Contributes little to either task or people needs of team; also called free riding — Not an important role—if adopted by too many members, team will disband • **Socioemotional Role** Focuses on people needs of team over task — Important role, but if adopted by everyone, team's tasks will not be accomplished

little to either the task or the social needs of team members. These people are free riders, as defined earlier, and typically are held in low esteem by the team.

The important thing for managers to remember is that effective teams must have people in both task specialist and socioemotional roles. Humor and social concern are as important to team effectiveness as are facts and problem solving. Managers also should remember that some people perform better in one type of role; some are inclined toward social concerns and others toward task concerns. A well-balanced team will do best over the long term because it will be personally satisfying for team members as well as permit the accomplishment of team tasks.

TEAM PROCESSES

Now we turn our attention to internal team processes. Team processes pertain to those dynamics that change over time and can be influenced by team leaders. In this section, we discuss the team processes of stages of development, cohesiveness, and norms. The fourth type of team process, conflict, will be covered in the next section.

Stages of Team Development

After a team has been created, it develops through distinct stages.[59] New teams are different from mature teams. Recall a time when you were a member of a new team, such as a fraternity or sorority pledge class, a committee, or a small team formed to do a class assignment. Over time the team changed. In the beginning, team members had to get to know one another, establish roles and norms, divide the labor, and clarify the team's task. In this way, each member became part of a smoothly operating team. The challenge for leaders is to understand the stages of team development and take action that will help the group improve its functioning.

Research findings suggest that team development is not random but evolves over definitive stages. One useful model for describing these stages is shown in Exhibit 21.5. Each stage confronts team leaders and members with unique problems and challenges.[60]

FORMING

The **forming** stage of development is a period of orientation and getting acquainted. Members break the ice and test one another for friendship possibilities and task orientation. Team members find which behaviors are acceptable to others. Uncertainty is high during this stage, and members usually accept whatever power or authority is offered by either formal or informal leaders. Members are dependent on the team until they find out what the ground rules are and what is expected of them. During this initial stage, members are concerned about such things as "What is expected of me?" "What is acceptable?" "Will I fit in?" During the forming stage, the team leader should provide time for members to get acquainted with one another and encourage them to engage in informal social discussions.

STORMING

During the **storming** stage, individual personalities emerge. People become more assertive in clarifying their roles and what is expected of them. This stage is marked by conflict and disagreement. People may disagree over their perceptions of the team's mission. Members may jockey for position, and coalitions or subgroups based on common interests may form. One subgroup may disagree with another over the total team's goals or how to achieve them. Unless teams can successfully move beyond this stage, they may get bogged down and never achieve high performance. During the storming stage, the team leader should encourage participation by each team member. Members should propose ideas, disagree with one another, and work through the uncertainties and conflicting perceptions about team tasks and goals.

forming The stage of team development characterized by orientation and acquaintance.

storming The stage of team development in which individual personalities and roles, and resulting conflicts, emerge.

EXHIBIT 21.5

Five Stages of Team Development

Forming:
Orientation, break the ice
Leader:
Facilitates social
interchanges

Storming:
Conflict, disagreement
Leader:
Encourages participation,
surfaces differences

Norming:
Establishment of order
and cohesion
Leader:
Helps clarify team roles,
norms, values

Performing:
Cooperation,
problem solving
Leader:
Facilitates task
accomplishment

Adjourning:
Task completion
Leader:
Brings closure, signifies
completion

NORMING

During the **norming** stage, conflict is resolved, and team harmony and unity emerge. Consensus develops on who has the power, who are the leaders, and members' roles. Members come to accept and understand one another. Differences are resolved, and members develop a sense of team cohesion. This stage typically is of short duration. During the norming stage, the team leader should emphasize unity within the team and help to clarify team norms and values.

PERFORMING

During the **performing** stage, the major emphasis is on problem solving and accomplishing the assigned task. Members are committed to the team's mission. They are coordinated with one another and handle disagreements in a mature way. They confront and resolve problems in the interest of task accomplishment. They interact frequently and direct their discussions and influence toward achieving team goals. During this stage, the leader should concentrate on managing high task performance. Both socioemotional and task specialists contribute to the team's functioning.

norming The stage of team development in which conflicts developed during the storming stage are resolved and team harmony and unity emerge.

performing The stage of team development in which members focus on problem solving and accomplishing the team's assigned task.

■ TAKE A MOMENT

As a new manager, help people on a new team get to know one another, clarify expectations, work out differences, and learn to work together. Encourage team members to both accomplish the task and meet the social needs of team members.

ADJOURNING

The **adjourning** stage occurs in committees and teams that have a limited task to perform and are disbanded afterward. During this stage, the emphasis is on wrapping up and gearing down. Task performance is no longer a top priority. Members may feel heightened emotionality, strong cohesiveness, and depression or regret over the team's disbandment. They may feel happy about mission accomplishment and sad about the loss of friendship and associations. At this point, the leader may wish to signify the team's disbanding with a ritual or ceremony, perhaps giving out plaques and awards to signify closure and completeness.

The five stages of team development typically occur in sequence. In teams that are under time pressure or that will exist for only a short period of time, the stages may occur quite rapidly. The stages may also be accelerated for virtual teams. For example, bringing people together for a couple of days of team building can help virtual teams move rapidly through the forming and storming stages. McDevitt Street Bovis, one of the country's largest construction management firms, uses an understanding of the stages of team development to put teams on a solid foundation.

CONCEPT CONNECTION To accomplish their goals—whether in the business world or on the basketball court—teams have to successfully advance to the **performing stage of team development.** The WNBA's Phoenix Mercury teammates shown here blend their talents and energies so effortlessly that they play the game not like separate people but like a coordinated piece of a whole. Phoenix recently began using psychological testing as part of the appraisal of new coaches and potential draft picks. Managers think testing gives them another tool for building a high-performance team. As part-owner Anne Mariucci puts it, "If a person isn't dotting the I's and crossing the T's, we know why, and we can surround that person with people who complement that. . . ."

The team-building process at McDevitt Street Bovis is designed to take teams to the performing stage as quickly as possible by giving everyone an opportunity to get to know one another; explore the ground rules; and clarify roles, responsibilities, and expectations. The company credits this process for quickly and effectively unifying teams, circumventing damaging and time-consuming conflicts, and preventing lawsuits related to major construction projects.

Rather than the typical construction project characterized by conflicts, frantic scheduling, and poor communications, Bovis wants its collection of contractors, designers, suppliers, and other partners to function like a true team—putting the success of the project ahead of their own individual interests. The team is first divided into separate groups that may have competing objectives—such as the clients in one group, suppliers in another, engineers and architects in a third, and so forth—and asked to come up with a list of their goals for the project. Although interests sometimes vary widely in purely accounting terms, common themes almost always emerge. By talking about conflicting goals and interests, as well as what all the groups share, facilitators help the team gradually come together around a common purpose and begin to develop shared values that will guide the project. After jointly writing a mission statement for the team, each party says what it expects from the others, so that roles and responsibilities can be clarified. The intensive team-building session helps take members quickly through the forming and storming stages of development. "We prevent conflicts from happening," says facilitator Monica Bennett. Leaders at McDevitt Street Bovis believe building better teams builds better buildings.[61]

McDevitt Street Bovis

Team Cohesiveness

Another important aspect of the team process is cohesiveness. **Team cohesiveness** is defined as the extent to which members are attracted to the team and motivated to remain in it.[62] Members of highly cohesive teams are committed to team activities, attend meetings, and are happy when the team succeeds. Members of less

adjourning The stage of team development in which members prepare for the team's disbandment.

team cohesiveness The extent to which team members are attracted to the team and motivated to remain in it.

cohesive teams are less concerned about the team's welfare. High cohesiveness is normally considered an attractive feature of teams.

DETERMINANTS OF TEAM COHESIVENESS

Characteristics of team structure and context influence cohesiveness. First is *team interaction*. The greater the contact among team members and the more time spent together, the more cohesive the team. Through frequent interactions, members get to know one another and become more committed to the team.[63] Second is the concept of *shared goals*. If team members agree on goals, they will be more cohesive. Agreeing on purpose and direction binds the team together. Third is *personal attraction to the team*, meaning that members have similar attitudes and values and enjoy being together.

Two factors in the team's context also influence group cohesiveness. The first is the presence of competition. When a team is in moderate competition with other teams, its cohesiveness increases as it strives to win. Finally, team success and the favorable evaluation of the team by outsiders add to cohesiveness. When a team succeeds in its task and others in the organization recognize the success, members feel good, and their commitment to the team will be high.

CONSEQUENCES OF TEAM COHESIVENESS

The outcome of team cohesiveness can fall into two categories—morale and productivity. As a general rule, morale is higher in cohesive teams because of increased communication among members, a friendly team climate, maintenance of membership because of commitment to the team, loyalty, and member participation in team decisions and activities. High cohesiveness has almost uniformly good effects on the satisfaction and morale of team members.[64]

With respect to team performance, research findings are mixed, but cohesiveness may have several effects.[65] First, in a cohesive team, members' productivity tends to be more uniform. Productivity differences among members are small because the team exerts pressure toward conformity. Noncohesive teams do not have this control over member behavior and therefore tend to have wider variation in member productivity.

With respect to the productivity of the team as a whole, research findings suggest that cohesive teams have the potential to be productive, but the degree of productivity depends on the relationship between management and the working team. Thus, team cohesiveness does not necessarily lead to higher team productivity. One study surveyed more than 200 work teams and correlated job performance with their cohesiveness.[66] Highly cohesive teams were more productive when team members felt management support and less productive when they sensed management hostility and negativism. Management hostility led to team norms and goals of low performance, and the highly cohesive teams performed poorly, in accordance with their norms and goals.

The relationship between performance outcomes and cohesiveness is illustrated in Exhibit 21.6. The highest productivity occurs when the team is cohesive and also has a high performance norm, which is a result of its positive relationship with management. Moderate productivity occurs when cohesiveness is low, because team members are less committed to performance norms. The lowest productivity

EXHIBIT 21.6

Relationship Among Team Cohesiveness, Performance Norms, and Productivity

	Team Cohesiveness	
Team Performance Norms High	**Moderate Productivity** Weak norms in alignment with organization goals	**High Productivity** Strong norms in alignment with organization goals
Low	**Low/Moderate Productivity** Weak norms in opposition to organization goals	**Low Productivity** Strong norms in opposition to organization goals
	Low Team Cohesiveness High	

occurs when cohesiveness is high and the team's performance norm is low. Thus, cohesive teams are able to attain their goals and enforce their norms, which can lead to either very high or very low productivity. A good example of team cohesiveness combined with high performance norms occurred at Motorola, where a highly cohesive team created a new cell phone that revived the company.

Motorola

The mood inside Motorola was bleak. Managers and engineers alike knew the company needed a hot new product to regain its reputation—and maybe even some of its lost market share. In the concept phone unit, engineers started talking about building an impossibly thin clamshell phone that would be as beautiful as a piece of fine jewelry and just as desirable—and they wanted it done in a year.

Engineer Roger Jellicoe aggressively promoted himself to lead the team and quickly put together a group of engineers, designers, and other specialists who were fired up by the ambitious project. The "thin clam" team, as they came to be known, rapidly became viewed almost as a rebellious cult within Motorola. The team worked at a facility 50 miles from Motorola's central research unit and kept the details of the project top-secret, even from their colleagues within the company. The need for secrecy and speed, as well as the relative isolation, contributed to the quick, tight bond that developed among team members. Time and again, the thin clam team flouted Motorola's rules for developing new products and followed their own instincts. Top management looked the other way. They wanted the team to have the freedom to be creative and take chances. Because Motorola badly needed a hit, money was not an object; top management gave the team whatever they needed in terms of support and resources to accomplish their goal.

The result was the RAZR, named as such based on the team's humorous reference to it as *siliqua patula*, Latin for razor clam. Unlike any other cell phone the world had seen, the RAZR wowed the industry and consumers alike—and rejuvenated the company in the process.[67]

At Motorola, a combination of team cohesiveness and management support that created high performance norms led to amazing results. The phone wasn't originally conceived to be a blockbuster, but it proved to be just that. Between the time the RAZR was launched in late 2004 and mid-2006, the stylish phone sold almost as many units as the red-hot Apple iPod.[68]

■ **TAKE A MOMENT**

As a team leader, build a cohesive team by focusing people on shared goals, giving team members time to know one another, and do what you can to help people enjoy being together as a team. Manage key events and make explicit statements to help the team develop norms of productivity. The experiential exercise on page 720 shows a way to evaluate team cohesiveness.

Team Norms

A **team norm** is a standard of conduct that is shared by team members and guides their behavior.[69] Norms are informal. They are not written down, as are rules and procedures. Norms are valuable because they define boundaries of acceptable behavior. They make life easier for team members by providing a frame of reference for what is right and wrong. Consider norms associated with the grueling three-week-long Tour de France. Each team is out to win the 2,700-mile bike race, but cooperation among competing teams is necessary for survival. When a team leader crashes, informal norms dictate that everyone slows down and waits. And when someone calls for a bathroom break, no formal rule says other riders have to pull to the side or slow down, but norms suggest they do so. When Dante Coccolo decided instead to go on the attack, putting a large time gap between him and the group, he learned the power of norms. When it came his own turn for a break, several other riders slowed down— but their purpose was to grab Coccolo's bike and toss it into a ditch. The chastened rider finished second to last, and never again rode in the Tour de France.[70]

team norm A standard of conduct that is shared by team members and guides their behavior.

EXHIBIT 21.7

Four Ways Team Norms
Develop

Norms identify key values, clarify role expectations, and facilitate team survival. Norms begin to develop in the first interactions among members of a new team.[71] Thus, it is important for leaders, especially those of virtual teams, to try to shape early interactions that will lead to norms that help the team succeed. Norms that apply to both day-to-day behavior and employee output and performance gradually evolve, letting members know what is acceptable and directing their actions toward acceptable performance. Four common ways in which norms develop for controlling and directing behavior are illustrated in Exhibit 21.7.[72]

CRITICAL EVENTS

Often, *critical events* in a team's history establish an important precedent. One example occurred when an employee at a forest products plant was seriously injured while standing too close to a machine being operated by a teammate. This incident led to a norm that team members regularly monitor one another to make sure all safety rules are observed. Any critical event can lead to the creation of a norm.

PRIMACY

Primacy means that the first behaviors that occur in a team often set a precedent for later team expectations. For example, at one company a team leader began his first meeting by raising an issue and then "leading" team members until he got the solution he wanted. The pattern became ingrained so quickly into an unproductive team norm that members dubbed meetings the "Guess What I Think" game.[73]

CARRYOVER BEHAVIORS

Carryover behaviors bring norms into the team from outside. One current example is the strong norm against smoking in many management teams. Some team members sneak around, gargling with mouthwash, and fear expulsion because the team culture believes everyone should kick the habit. Carryover behavior also influences small teams of college students assigned by instructors to do class work. Norms brought into the team from outside suggest that students should participate equally and help members get a reasonable grade.

EXPLICIT STATEMENTS

With *explicit statements*, leaders or team members can initiate norms by articulating them to the team. Explicit statements symbolize what counts and thus have considerable impact. Making explicit statements can be a highly effective way for leaders to influence or change team norms. One division of ABB was about to go bankrupt partly because team members had developed norms of politeness that made people hesitant to express disagreement or bring up negative information. The unit's leader turned things around by making an explicit statement that everyone was expected to speak their minds about problems. Similarly, Ameritech CEO Bill Weiss established a norm of cooperation and mutual support among his top leadership team by telling them bluntly every week that if he caught anyone trying to undermine the others, the guilty party would be fired.[74]

MANAGING TEAM CONFLICT

The final characteristic of team process is conflict. Of all the skills required for effective team management, none is more important than handling the conflicts that inevitably arise among members. Conflict can arise among members within a team or between one team and another. **Conflict** refers to antagonistic interaction in which one party attempts to block the intentions or goals of another.[75] Competition, which is rivalry among individuals or teams, can have a healthy impact because it energizes people toward higher performance.[76]

Whenever people work together in teams, some conflict is inevitable. Bringing conflicts out into the open and effectively resolving them is one of the team leader's most challenging jobs. For example, studies of virtual teams indicate that how they handle internal conflicts is critical to their success, yet conflict within virtual teams tends to occur more frequently and take longer to resolve because people are separated by space, time, and cultural differences. Moreover, people in virtual teams tend to engage in more inconsiderate behaviors such as name-calling or insults than do people who work face-to-face.[77]

Balancing Conflict and Cooperation

Some conflict can actually be beneficial to teams.[78] A healthy level of conflict helps to prevent **groupthink**, in which people are so committed to a cohesive team that they are reluctant to express contrary opinions. Author and scholar Jerry Harvey tells a story of how members of his extended family in Texas decided to drive 40 miles to Abilene on a hot day when the car's air conditioning didn't work. Everyone was miserable. Later, each person admitted they hadn't wanted to go but went along to please the others. Harvey used the term *Abilene paradox* to describe this tendency to go along with others for the sake of avoiding conflict.[79] Similarly, when people in work teams go along simply for the sake of harmony, problems typically result. Thus, a degree of conflict leads to better decision making because multiple viewpoints are expressed. Among top management teams, for example, low levels of conflict have been found to be associated with poor decision making.[80]

However, conflict that is too strong, that is focused on personal rather than work issues, or that is not managed appropriately can be damaging to the team's morale and productivity. Too much conflict can be destructive, tear relationships apart, and interfere with the healthy exchange of ideas and information.[81] Team leaders have to find the right balance between conflict and cooperation, as illustrated in Exhibit 21.8. Too little conflict can decrease team performance because the team doesn't benefit from a mix of opinions and ideas—even disagreements—that might lead to better solutions or prevent the team from making mistakes. At the other end of the spectrum, too much conflict outweighs the team's cooperative efforts and leads to a decrease in employee satisfaction and commitment, hurting team performance. A moderate amount of conflict that is managed appropriately typically results in the highest levels of team performance.

conflict Antagonistic interaction in which one party attempts to thwart the intentions or goals of another.

groupthink The tendency for people to be so committed to a cohesive team that they are reluctant to express contrary opinions.

Go to the ethical dilemma on page 721 that pertains to team cohesiveness and conflict.

■ **TAKE A MOMENT**

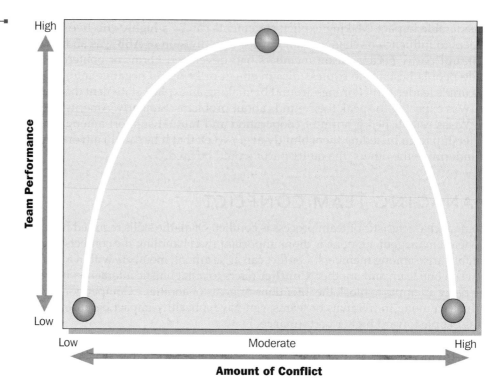

Causes of Conflict

Several factors can cause people to engage in conflict:[82]

SCARCE RESOURCES

Resources include money, information, and supplies. Whenever individuals or teams must compete for scarce or declining resources, conflict is almost inevitable. The introduction of fast-cycle teams, as described earlier, for example, frequently leads to conflict because it creates a new competition for resources.[83] Some projects may be delayed because managers reallocate resources to fast-cycle projects, potentially creating conflicts.

COMMUNICATION BREAKDOWN

Poor communication results in misperceptions and misunderstandings of other people and teams. In some cases, information is intentionally withheld, which can jeopardize trust among teams and cause long-lasting conflict. Faulty communication can occur in any team, but virtual and global teams are particularly prone to communication breakdowns. For one thing, the lack of nonverbal cues, as described in the previous chapter, leads to more misunderstandings among virtual team members. In addition, trust issues are a major source of conflict in virtual teams because members may fear that they are being left out of important communication interactions.[84]

PERSONALITY CLASHES

A personality clash occurs when people simply do not get along or do not see eye-to-eye on any issue. Personality clashes are caused by basic differences in personality, values, and attitudes. In one study, personality conflicts were the number-one reported cause preventing front-line management teams from working together effectively.[85] Some personality differences can be overcome. However, severe personality clashes are difficult to resolve. Often, it is a good idea to simply separate the parties so that they need not interact with one another.

MANAGING CONFLICT

Conflicting opinions and perspectives occur in every team. The ability to handle conflict and disagreement is one mark of a successful new manager. To understand your approach to managing conflict, think about disagreements you have had with people on student teams or in other situations, then answer each of the following items as Mostly True or Mostly False for you.

	Mostly True	Mostly False
1. I typically assert my opinion to win a disagreement.	___	___
2. I often suggest solutions that combine others' points of view.	___	___
3. I prefer to not argue with team members.	___	___
4. I raise my voice to get other people to accept my position.	___	___
5. I am quick to agree when someone makes a good point.	___	___
6. I tend to keep quiet rather than argue with other people.	___	___
7. I stand firm in expressing my viewpoints during a disagreement.	___	___

	Mostly True	Mostly False
8. I try to include other people's ideas to create a solution they will accept.	___	___
9. I like to smooth over disagreements so people get along.	___	___

SCORING AND INTERPRETATION: Three categories of conflict-handling strategies are measured in this instrument: competing, accommodating, and collaborating. By comparing your scores you can see your preferred conflict-handling strategy.

Give yourself 1 point for each item marked Mostly True.

Competing: Items 1, 4, 7

Accommodating: Items 2, 5, 8

Collaborating: Items 3, 6, 9

For which conflict-handling strategy do you score highest? New managers may initially be accommodating to get along with people until they size up the situation. A too-strong competing style may prevent subordinates from having a say in important matters. The collaborating style tries for a win-win solution and has the long-run potential to build a constructive team. How would your strategy differ if the other people involved in a disagreement were family members, friends, subordinates, or bosses?

GOAL DIFFERENCES

Conflict often occurs simply because people are pursuing conflicting goals. Goal differences are natural in organizations. Individual salespeople's targets may put them in conflict with one another or with the sales manager. Moreover, the sales department's goals might conflict with those of manufacturing. When team members don't have a clear understanding of and commitment to the team goal and how their individual tasks contribute, they may be pursuing their own agendas, which can lead to conflicts.

> As a new manager, appreciate that some conflict can be healthy, but don't let conflict reduce the team's effectiveness and well-being. Take the New Manager Self-Test above to learn about your personal style for handling conflict.

■ **TAKE A MOMENT**

Styles to Handle Conflict

Teams as well as individuals develop specific styles for dealing with conflict, based on the desire to satisfy their own concern versus the other party's concern. A model that describes five styles of handling conflict is in Exhibit 21.9. The two major dimensions are the extent to which an individual is assertive versus cooperative in his or her approach to conflict.

EXHIBIT 21.9

A Model of Styles to Handle Conflict

SOURCE: Adapted from Kenneth Thomas, "Conflict and Conflict Management," in *Handbook of Industrial and Organizational Behavior,* ed. M. D. Dunnette (New York: John Wiley, 1976): 900.

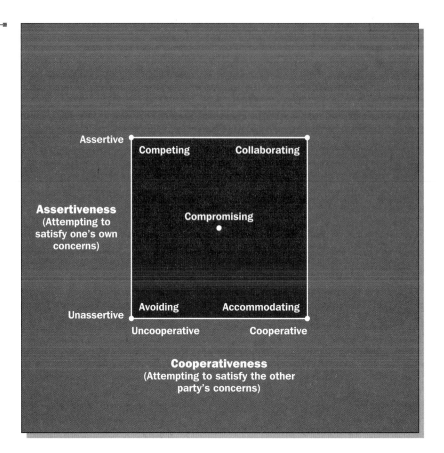

Effective team members vary their style of handling conflict to fit a specific situation. Each of these five styles is appropriate in certain cases.[86]

1. The *competing style* reflects assertiveness to get one's own way, and should be used when quick, decisive action is vital on important issues or unpopular actions, such as during emergencies or urgent cost cutting.

2. The *avoiding style* reflects neither assertiveness nor cooperativeness. It is appropriate when an issue is trivial, when there is no chance of winning, when a delay to gather more information is needed, or when a disruption would be costly.

3. The *compromising style* reflects a moderate amount of both assertiveness and cooperativeness. It is appropriate when the goals on both sides are equally important, when opponents have equal power and both sides want to split the difference, or when people need to arrive at temporary or expedient solutions under time pressure.

4. The *accommodating style* reflects a high degree of cooperativeness, which works best when people realize that they are wrong, when an issue is more important to others than to oneself, when building social credits for use in later discussions, and when maintaining harmony is especially important.

5. The *collaborating style* reflects both a high degree of assertiveness and cooperativeness. The collaborating style enables both parties to win, although it may require substantial bargaining and negotiation. The collaborating style is important when both sets of concerns are too important to be compromised, when insights from different people need to be merged into an overall solution, and when the commitment of both sides is needed for a consensus.

These various styles of handling conflict are especially effective when an individual disagrees with others. But what does a manager or team leader do when a conflict erupts among others within a team or among teams for which the manager is responsible? Research suggests that several techniques can be used as strategies for resolving conflicts among people or departments. These techniques might also be used when conflict is formalized, such as between a union and management.

SUPERORDINATE GOALS

The larger objective that cannot be attained by a single party is identified as a **superordinate goal**.[87] It is similar to the concept of vision. A powerful vision often compels people to overcome conflicts and cooperate for the greater good. Similarly, a superordinate goal requires the cooperation of conflicting team members for achievement. People must pull together. To the extent that employees can be focused on team or organization goals, the conflict will decrease because they see the big picture and realize they must work together to achieve it.

MEDIATION

Using a third party to settle a dispute is referred to as **mediation**. A mediator could be a supervisor, a higher-level manager, an outside consultant, or someone from the human resource department. The mediator can discuss the conflict with each party and work toward a solution. If a solution satisfactory to both sides cannot be reached, the parties might be willing to turn the conflict over to the mediator and abide by his or her solution.

Negotiation

One distinctive type of conflict management is **negotiation**, whereby people engage in give-and-take discussions and consider various alternatives to reach a joint decision that is acceptable to both parties. Conflicting parties may embark upon negotiation from different perspectives and with different intentions, reflecting either an *integrative* approach or a *distributive* approach.

Integrative negotiation is based on a win-win assumption, in that all parties want to come up with a creative solution that can benefit both sides of the conflict. Rather than viewing the conflict as a win-lose situation, people look at the issues from multiple angles, consider trade-offs, and try to "expand the pie" rather than divide it. With integrative negotiation, conflicts are managed through cooperation and compromise, which fosters trust and positive long-term relationships. **Distributive negotiation**, on the other hand, assumes the "size of the pie" is fixed and each party attempts to get as much of it as they can. One side wants to win, which means the other side must lose. With this win-lose approach, distributive negotiation is competitive and adversarial rather than collaborative, and does not typically lead to positive long-term relationships.[88]

In recent years, books, software, newsletters, and training seminars on negotiating have proliferated. Most emphasize the value of integrative negotiation

> **superordinate goal** A goal that cannot be reached by a single party.
>
> **mediation** The process of using a third party to settle a dispute.
>
> **negotiation** A conflict management strategy whereby people engage in give-and-take discussions and consider various alternatives to reach a joint decision that is acceptable to both parties.
>
> **integrative negotiation** A collaborative approach to negotiation that is based on a win-win assumption, whereby the parties want to come up with a creative solution that benefits both sides of the conflict.
>
> **distributive negotiation** A competitive and adversarial negotiation approach in which each party strives to get as much as it can, usually at the expense of the other party.

© NEUCEL SPECIALTY CELLULOSE/PRNEWSFOTO (NEWSCOM)

CONCEPT CONNECTION The closing of the pulp mill in Port Alice on Canada's Vancouver Island put 350 people out of work in a community of only 700. "There was no one in the village who didn't suffer," said employee Stu Roper. In late 2005, foreign investors bought the plant after British Columbia absolved the new owners of responsibility for past environmental damage, the community approved a five-year reduction in property taxes, and union members and Neucel management, pictured here, reached an agreement after contentious **distributive negotiation.** The newly christened Neucel mill will produce high-purity cellulose used in a variety of industries.

for today's collaborative business environment. That is, the key to effectiveness is to see negotiation not as a zero-sum game but as a process for reaching a creative solution that benefits everyone.[89]

RULES FOR REACHING A WIN-WIN SOLUTION

Achieving a win-win solution through integrative negotiation is based on four key strategies:[90]

1. Separate the people from the problem. For successful integrative negotiation, people stay focused on the problem and the source of conflict rather than attacking or attempting to discredit each other.

2. Focus on interests, not current demands. Demands are what each person wants from the negotiation, whereas interests are why they want them. Consider two sisters arguing over the last orange in the fruit bowl. Each insisted she should get the orange and refused to give up (demands). Then, the girls' aunt walks in and asks each of them *why* they want the orange (interests). As it turned out, one wanted to eat it and the other wanted the peel to use for a class project. By focusing on the interests, the sisters arrived at a solution that got each person what she wanted.[91] Demands create yes-or-no obstacles to effective negotiation. Interests present problems that can be solved creatively.

3. Generate many alternatives for mutual gain. Both parties in an integrative negotiation come up with a variety of options for solving the problem and engage in give-and-take discussions about which alternatives can get each side what it wants.

4. Insist that results be based on objective standards. Each party in a negotiation has its own interests and would naturally like to maximize its outcomes. Successful negotiation requires focusing on objective criteria and maintaining standards of fairness rather than using subjective judgments about the best solution.

IN THE BARGAINING ZONE

The **bargaining zone** is the zone between one party's minimum reservation point (the point beyond which the party is willing to accept a deal) and the other party's maximum reservation point. Exhibit 21.10 illustrates the bargaining zone for two students negotiating for the purchase of a used textbook. Samantha wants to buy a used *Health Standards* textbook. She would like to get one for $60, but is willing to pay up to $85. Bailey has advertised a used book for sale at $90. He knows he can sell it back to the bookstore for $65, so he won't go lower than that price. As shown in the exhibit, the bargaining zone is the range between $65 (the lowest Bailey will accept) and $85 (the highest Samantha is willing to pay). It is a *positive bargaining zone* because the reservation points overlap by a $20 amount, allowing room for negotiation.[92]

bargaining zone The range between one party's minimum reservation point (the point beyond which the party is willing to accept a deal) and the other party's maximum reservation point.

EXHIBIT   21.10

The Bargaining Zone

SOURCE: "Negotiation: Distributive Bargaining," Culture at Work, http://www.culture-at-work.com/distribute.html

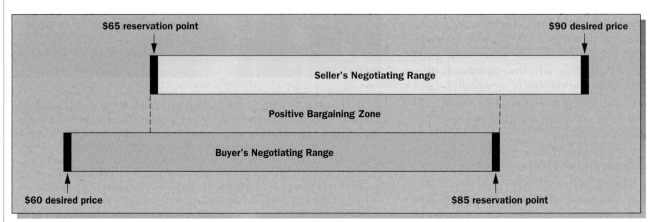

A *negative bargaining zone* occurs when the ranges do not overlap, for instance if Bailey would not accept less than $65 and Samantha would go no higher than $60. This situation leaves no room for negotiation, and the parties have to fall back on their best alternative to a negotiated agreement, or **BATNA**. Prior to negotiation, each party decides what it will do if a mutual agreement cannot be reached. In the example of Samantha and Bailey, Samantha's BATNA might be to check out a copy of the textbook from the library and share a text with a classmate. Bailey's BATNA might be to wait for another buyer who will pay a higher price or sell the book to the bookstore for $65.

A key aspect of any negotiation is for each party to determine its BATNA and to ascertain the other party's reservation point. With a positive bargaining zone, successful negotiation is possible if both parties follow the strategies for effective integrative negotiation.

WORK TEAM EFFECTIVENESS

Teams are the building blocks of today's organizations, but not all teams are effective. Teams often do not live up to their potential or to the dreams managers have for them. Good leaders help teams be successful.

In this section, we look at the positive outcomes of effective teams. By assessing teams in terms of productive output, personal satisfaction, and the capacity to adapt and learn, managers can better identify actions that will enhance work team effectiveness.[93]

Productive Output

One aspect of effectiveness relates to whether the team's output (such as decisions, products, or services) meets the requirements of customers or clients in terms of quality, quantity, and timeliness. An IBM team made up of members in the United States, Germany, and the United Kingdom, for example, used collaboration software as a virtual meeting room to solve a client's technical problem resulting from Hurricane Katrina within the space of just a few days.[94] Whether online or in physical space, effective meetings are essential to effective teamwork. The Manager's Shoptalk gives some tips for running a great meeting.

Effective employee teams often unleash enormous energy and creativity from workers. Research has found that working in a team often increases an individual's motivation and performance. **Social facilitation** refers to the tendency for the presence of others to enhance one's motivation and performance. Simply being in the presence of other people has an energizing effect.[95] This benefit of teams is often lost in virtual and global teams because people are working in isolation from their teammates. Organizations such as MySQL, described earlier in the Unlocking Innovative Solutions Through Technology box, build in communication mechanisms that keep team members interacting.

Satisfaction of Members

Another important question is whether the team experience contributes to the well-being, personal satisfaction, and development of its members. Effective teams provide multiple opportunities for people to satisfy their individual needs and to develop both personally and professionally.[96] As described in Chapter 19, employees have needs for belongingness and affiliation, and working in teams can help meet these needs. Participative teams can also reduce boredom, increase individuals' feeling of dignity and self-worth, and contribute to skill development because the whole person is employed. At Radius, a Boston restaurant, for example, two-person kitchen teams have full responsibility for their part of a meal, which gives them a greater sense of accomplishment and importance and enables them to expand their culinary and organizational skills.[97] People who have a satisfying team

BATNA The "best alternative to a negotiated agreement"; a previously determined choice of what a party will do if an acceptable agreement cannot be reached through negotiation.

social facilitation The tendency for the presence of others to influence an individual's motivation and performance.

HOW TO RUN A GREAT MEETING

A recent survey of nearly 700 employees in the United States and Britain found that people spend an average of 5.6 hours a week in meetings. Unfortunately, too much of this time is wasted in meetings where people doodle, drink coffee, tap away on their laptops, and think about what they could be doing back in their offices.

Effective meetings help people process important information, solve problems, and most importantly, feel actively involved in the organization's tasks or goals. But good meetings don't just happen. They are the result of careful planning. Here are a few tips from the experts:

PREPARE IN ADVANCE

Advance preparation is the single most important tool for running an efficient, productive meeting. Advance preparation should include the following:

:: *Define the purpose.* Not all meetings have the same purpose. Their goal can be to draw on participants' expertise and skills; elicit their commitment to a project, program, or goal; teach them new skills; or coordinate the efforts required to accomplish a specific task. The leader needs to be clear about what the meeting's purpose is and then communicate it clearly to others. Remember, if a meeting isn't essential, don't have it.

:: *Prepare an agenda.* The agenda, a simple list of the topics to be discussed, is important because it lets people know what to expect and keeps the meeting focused.

:: *Issue invitations selectively.* If the group gets too big, the meeting will not be productive. However, be sure every department with a stake in the topic is represented.

:: *Set a strict time limit.* Announce the ending time for the meeting in advance, and then make sure the discussion stays on track.

BRING OUT THE BEST DURING THE MEETING

During the meeting, certain techniques will bring out the best in people and ensure a productive session:

:: *Start on time.* Although this sounds obvious, many meetings get started 10 or 15 minutes late. Starting on time has symbolic value, because it tells people that the topic is important and that the leader values their time.

:: *Outlaw cell phones, BlackBerry devices, and laptops.* A ringing cell phone can throw a meeting completely off-track. Ban laptops unless they'll be used during a meeting activity.

:: *State the purpose, and review the agenda.* Begin by stating the meeting's explicit purpose and clarifying what should be accomplished by its conclusion.

:: *Create involvement.* If the leader merely wants to present one-way information, he or she should send a memo. Some subtle techniques go a long way toward getting people involved:

:: *Give everyone a voice.* Good leaders draw out the silent and control the talkative so that the meeting isn't dominated by one or two assertive people. One organization has a rule called NOSTUESO (No one speaks twice until everyone speaks once).

:: *Encourage the clash of ideas.* A good meeting is a cross-current of discussion and debate. The leader listens, guides, mediates, stimulates, and summarizes this discussion.

:: *Stick to the purpose.* Encouraging a free flow of ideas does not mean allowing participants to waste time by sidetracking the meeting into discussions of issues not on the agenda.

ATTEND TO THE END AS MUCH AS THE BEGINNING

Review and follow-up is important to summarize and implement agreed-upon points.

:: *End with a call to action.* Review the decisions made during the meeting, and make sure everyone understands his or her assignments.

:: *Follow up.* Send a short memo to summarize the meeting's key accomplishments, outline agreed-upon activities, and suggest schedules for implementation.

SOURCES: Based on Phred Dvorak, "Corporate Meetings Go Through a Makeover," *The Wall Street Journal* (March 6, 2006): B3; Richard Axelrod, Emily M. Axelrod, Julie Beedon, and Robert Jacobs, "Creating Dynamic, Energy-Producing Meetings," *Leader to Leader* (Spring 2005): 53–58; Antoney Jay, "How to Run a Meeting," *Harvard Business Review* (March–April 1976): 120–134; Edward Michaels, "Business Meetings," *Small Business Reports* (February 1989): 82–88; and Jeffrey L. Seglin, "We've Got to Start Meeting Like This," *CIO* (March 1, 2001): 168–170.

MANAGER'S SHOPTALK

environment cope better with stress, enjoy their jobs, and have a higher level of organizational commitment.

Capacity to Adapt and Learn

A professor of management at Santa Clara University analyzed 14 years of National Basketball Association results and found that teams that had played together longer won more games. By playing together over a period of time, members learned to anticipate their teammates' moves and adapt their own behavior to defeat the competition.[98] The same thing happens in effective work teams, where members can anticipate one another's actions and respond appropriately. A good example is the emergency room trauma team at Massachusetts General Hospital, which functions so smoothly that the team switches leaders seamlessly depending on the crisis at hand. With each new emergency, direction may come from a doctor, nurse, intern, or technician—whoever is particularly experienced with the problem.[99] Over time, effective teams learn from experience and use that learning to revitalize and regenerate themselves, smoothly adapting to shifting organizational and competitive demands.[100]

MANAGER'S SOLUTION

Several important concepts about teams were described in this chapter. Organizations use teams both to achieve coordination as part of the formal structure and to encourage employee involvement. Formal teams include vertical teams along the chain of command and horizontal teams such as cross-functional teams and committees. Special-purpose teams are used for special, large-scale creative projects. Employee involvement via teams is designed to bring lower-level employees into decision processes to improve quality, efficiency, and job satisfaction. Companies typically start with problem-solving teams, which may evolve into self-directed teams that take on responsibility for management activities. Innovative approaches to teamwork include virtual teams and global teams.

Most teams go through systematic stages of development: forming, storming, norming, performing, and adjourning. Team characteristics that influence organizational effectiveness are size, diversity, cohesiveness, norms, and members' roles. All teams experience some conflict because of scarce resources, ambiguous responsibilities, communication breakdown, personality clashes, power and status differences, and goal conflicts. Some conflict is beneficial, but too much can hurt the team and the organization. Techniques for managing and resolving conflicts include superordinate goals, bargaining, mediation, and negotiation. To identify ways to improve work team effectiveness, managers can assess teams in terms of productive output, personal satisfaction, and the capacity to adapt and learn.

Returning to the example of United Airlines, described in the chapter opening, a major problem was that teams of ramp workers were functioning more like a group of individuals rather than a cohesive and coordinated team. United took an innovative approach to team-building and sent more than 1,200 "lead" ramp workers through training at "Pit Crew U," where they learned the split-second techniques and teamwork practices of NASCAR pit crews. At Pit Instruction & Training LLC, in Mooresville, North Carolina, teams of people who had never before worked together had to quickly coalesce into a high-performing team in order to handle the various pit exercises thrown their way. The training course emphasizes the importance of teamwork, preparedness, and safety, issues that are as important on an airport tarmac as they are in a NASCAR pit. United wants people to translate what they learned into helping build cohesive teams that can quickly reach the performing stage of team development. At the same time, top executives are striving to improve relationships between management and workers, so that teams will be more likely to establish high-performance norms. With a combination of more cohesive teams and high-performance norms, United hopes to cut the time it takes to turn a plane by eight minutes and allow it to run more daily flights without buying new planes, thus increasing revenues and helping to pull United out of its slide.[101]

DISCUSSION QUESTIONS

1. Volvo went to self-directed teams to assemble cars because of the need to attract and keep workers in Sweden, where pay raises are not a motivator (high taxes) and many other jobs are available. Are these factors good reasons for using a team approach? Discuss.

2. Trust is an important characteristic of a successful team. If you were a team leader, how would you go about building a culture of trust?

3. What factors in today's environment are contributing to an increasing use of virtual teams and global teams? Would you like to be part of a virtual team? Why or why not?

4. Suppose you are the leader of a team that has just been created to develop a new registration process at your college or university. How can you use an understanding of the stages of team development to improve your team's effectiveness?

5. Imagine yourself as a potential member of a team responsible for designing a new package for breakfast cereal. Do you think interpersonal skills would be equally important if the team is organized face-to-face versus a virtual team? Why or why not? Might different types of interpersonal

skills be required for the two types of teams? Be specific.

6. If you were the leader of a special-purpose team developing a new computer game, and conflicts arose related to power and status differences among team members, what would you do? How might you use the various conflict-resolution techniques described in the chapter?

7. When you are a member of a team, do you adopt a task specialist or socioemotional role? Which role is more important for a team's effectiveness? Discuss.

8. Some people argue that the presence of an outside threat correlates with a high degree of team cohesion. Would you agree or disagree? Explain your answer. What is the relationship between team cohesiveness and team performance?

9. Describe the advantages and disadvantages of teams. In what situations might the disadvantages outweigh the advantages?

10. One company had 40 percent of its workers and 20 percent of its managers resign during the first year after reorganizing into teams. What might account for this dramatic turnover? How might managers ensure a smooth transition to teams?

MANAGEMENT IN PRACTICE: EXPERIENTIAL EXERCISE

Is Your Group a Cohesive Team?

Think about a student group with which you have worked. Answer the following questions as they pertain to the functioning of that group.

| Disagree Strongly | ❶ | ❷ | ❸ | ❹ | ❺ | Agree Strongly |

1. Group meetings were held regularly and everyone attended. ❶ ❷ ❸ ❹ ❺

2. We talked about and shared the same goals for group work and grade. ❶ ❷ ❸ ❹ ❺

3. We spent most of our meeting time talking business, but discussions were open-ended and active. ❶ ❷ ❸ ❹ ❺

4. We talked through any conflicts and disagreements until they were resolved. ❶ ❷ ❸ ❹ ❺

5. Group members listened carefully to one another. ❶ ❷ ❸ ❹ ❺

6. We really trusted each other, speaking personally about what we really felt. ❶ ❷ ❸ ❹ ❺

7. Leadership roles were rotated and shared, with people taking initiative at appropriate times for the good of the group. ❶ ❷ ❸ ❹ ❺

8. Each member found a way to contribute to the final work product. ❶ ❷ ❸ ❹ ❺

9. I was really satisfied being a member of the group. ❶ ❷ ❸ ❹ ❺

10. We freely gave each other credit for jobs well done. ❶ ❷ ❸ ❹ ❺

11. Group members gave and received feedback to help the group do even better. ❶ ❷ ❸ ❹ ❺

12. We held each other accountable; each member was accountable to the group. ❶ ❷ ❸ ❹ ❺

13. Group members really liked and respected each other. ❶ ❷ ❸ ❹ ❺

Scoring and Interpretation

The questions here are about team cohesion. Add your scores for all 13 questions to obtain your total score: _____. If you scored 52 or greater, your group experienced authentic teamwork. Congratulations. If you scored between 39 and 51, you reached a positive group identity that might have been developed even further. If you scored between 26 and 38, group identity was weak and probably not all that satisfying. If you scored below 26, it was hardly a group at all, resembling a loose collection of individuals.

Remember, teamwork does not happen by itself. Individuals like you have to understand what a team is and then work to make it happen. What can you do to make a student group more like a team? Do you have the courage to take the initiative?

MANAGEMENT IN PRACTICE: ETHICAL DILEMMA

One for All and All for One?

Melinda Asbel watched as three of her classmates filed out of the conference room. Then she turned back to the large wooden table and faced her fellow members (a student and three faculty members) of the university's judiciary committee.

The three students—Joe Eastridge, Brad Hamil, and Lisa Baghetti—had just concluded their appeal against a plagiarism conviction stemming from a group project for an international marketing course. Melinda, who happened to be in the class with the students on trial, remembered the day the professor, Hank Zierden, had asked Joe, Brad, and Lisa, along with the group's leader, Paul Colgan, to stay after class. She happened to walk by the classroom a half hour later to see four glum students emerge. Even though Paul had a chagrined expression on his face, Joe was the one who looked completely shattered. It didn't take long for word to spread along the ever-active grapevine that Paul had admitted to plagiarizing his part of the group paper.

At the hearing, the students recounted how they'd quickly and unanimously settled on Paul to lead the group. He was by far the most able student among them, someone who managed to maintain a stellar GPA even while taking a full course load and holding down a part-time job. After the group worked together for weeks analyzing the problem and devising a marketing plan, Paul assigned a section of the final paper to each member. With the pressure of all those end-of-the-semester deadlines bearing down on them, everyone was delighted when Paul volunteered to write the company and industry background, the section that typically took the most time to produce. Paul gathered in everyone's contributions, assembled them into a paper, and handed out the final draft to the other members. They each gave it a quick read. They liked what they saw and thought they had a good chance for an A.

Unfortunately, as Paul readily admitted when Professor Zierden confronted them, he had pulled the section he'd contributed directly off the Internet. Pointing out the written policy he had distributed at the beginning of the semester stating that each group member was equally responsible for the final product, the professor gave all four students a zero for the project. The group project and presentation counted for 30 percent of the course grade.

Joe, Brad, and Lisa maintained they were completely unaware that Paul had cheated. "It just never occurred to us Paul would ever need to cheat," Brad said. They were innocent bystanders, the students argued. Why should they be penalized? Besides, the consequences weren't going to fall on each of them equally. Although Paul was suffering the embarrassment of public exposure, the failing group project grade would only put a dent in his solid GPA. Joe, on the other hand, was already on academic probation. A zero probably meant he wouldn't make the 2.5 GPA he needed to stay in the business program.

At least one of the faculty members of the judiciary committee supported Professor Zierden'a actions. "We're assigning more and more group projects because increasingly that's the way these students are going to find themselves working when they get real jobs in the real world," he said. "And the fact of the matter is that if someone obtains information illegally while on the job, it's going to put the whole corporation at risk for being sued, or worse."

Even though she could see merit to both sides, Melinda was going to have to choose. If you were Melinda, how would you vote?

What Would You Do?

1. Vote to exonerate the three group project members who didn't cheat. You're convinced they had no reason to suspect Paul Colgan of dishonesty. Exonerating them is the right thing to do.

2. Vote in support of Hank Zierden's decision to hold each individual member accountable for the entire project. The professor clearly stated his policy at the beginning of the semester, and the students should have been more vigilant. The committee should not undercut a professor's explicit policy.

3. Vote to reduce each of the three students' penalties. Instead of a zero, each student will receive only half of the possible total points for the project, which would be an F. You're still holding students responsible for the group project, but not imposing catastrophic punishment. This compromise both undercuts the professor's policy and punishes "innocent" team members to some extent, but not as severely.

SOURCE: Based on Ellen R. Stapleton, "College to Expand Policy on Plagiarism," *The Ithancan Online* (April 12, 2001): www.ithaca.edu/ithacan/articles/0104/12/news/0college_to_e.htm.

CASE FOR CRITICAL ANALYSIS

Acme Minerals Extraction Company

Several years ago, Acme Minerals Extraction Company introduced teams in an effort to solve morale and productivity problems at its Wichita plant. Acme used highly sophisticated technology, employing geologists, geophysicists, and engineers on what was referred to as the "brains" side of the business, as well as skilled and semiskilled labor on the "brawn" side to run the company's underground extracting operations. The two sides regularly clashed, and when some engineers locked several operations workers out of the office in 100-degree heat, the local press had a field day. The company hired Suzanne Howard to develop a program that would improve productivity and morale at the Wichita plant. The idea was that it would then be implemented at other Acme sites.

In Wichita, Howard had a stroke of luck in the form of Donald Peterson, a long-time Acme employee who was highly respected at the Wichita plant and was looking for one final challenging project before he retired. Peterson had served in just about every possible line and staff position at Acme over his 39-year career, and he understood the problems workers faced on both the brains and the brawn sides of the business. Howard was pleased when Peterson agreed to serve as leader for the Wichita pilot project.

Three functional groups at the Wichita plant included operations, made up primarily of hourly workers who operated and maintained the extracting equipment; the "below ground" group, consisting of engineers, geologists, and geophysicists who determined where and how to drill; and the "above ground" group of engineers in charge of cursory refinement and transportation of the minerals. Howard and Peterson decided the first step was to get these different groups talking to one another and sharing ideas. They instituted a monthly "problem chat," an optional meeting to which all employees were invited to discuss unresolved problems. At the first meeting, Howard and Peterson were the only two people who showed up. However, people gradually began to attend the meetings, and after about six months, they became lively problem-solving discussions that led to many improvements. For example, a maintenance worker complained that a standard piece of equipment failed repeatedly due to high levels of heat and sand contamination. Peterson listened carefully and then drew a facilities engineer into the discussion. The engineer came up with a new configuration better suited to the conditions, and downtime virtually disappeared.

Next, Howard and Peterson introduced teams to "select a problem and implement a tailored solution," or SPITS. These ad hoc groups were made up of members from each of the three functional areas. They were formed to work on a specific problem identified in a chat meeting and were then disbanded when the problem was solved. Acme gave SPITS the authority to address problems without seeking management approval. Some rocky moments occurred when engineers resented working with operations personnel, and vice versa. However, over time, and with Peterson's strong leadership, the groups eventually began to come together and focus on the issues rather than spending most of their time arguing.

Eventually, workers in Wichita were organized into permanent cross-functional teams that were empowered to make their own decisions and elect their own leaders. After a year and a half, things were really humming. The different groups weren't just working together; they had also started socializing together. At one of the problem chats, an operations worker jokingly suggested that the brains and the brawn should duke it out once a week to get rid of the tensions so they could focus all their energy on the job to be done. Several others joined in the joking, and eventually, the group decided to square off in a weekly softball game. Peterson had T-shirts printed up that said BRAINS and BRAWN. The softball games were well attended, and both sides usually ended up having a few beers together at a local bar afterward. Productivity and morale soared at the Wichita plant, and costs continued to decline.

The company identified the Lubbock plant as the next facility where Suzanne Howard and her team needed to introduce the cross-functional teams that had proven so successful in Kansas. Howard's team felt immense pressure from top management to get the team-based productivity project up and running smoothly and quickly at Lubbock. Top executives believed the lessons learned at Wichita would make implementing the program at other sites less costly and time-consuming. However, when Howard and her team attempted to implement the program at the Lubbock plant, things didn't go well. Because people weren't showing up for the problem chat meetings, the team made attendance mandatory. However, the meetings still produced few valuable ideas or suggestions. Although a few of the SPITS teams solved important problems, none of them showed the kind of commitment and enthusiasm Howard had seen in Wichita. In addition, the Lubbock workers refused to participate in the softball games and other team-building exercises that the team developed for them. Howard finally convinced some workers to join in the softball games by bribing them with free food and beer.

"If I just had a Donald Peterson in Lubbock, things would go a lot more smoothly," Howard thought. "These workers don't trust us the way workers in Wichita trusted him." It seemed that no matter how hard Howard and her team tried to make the project work in Lubbock, morale continued to decline and conflicts between the different groups of workers actually seemed to increase.

Questions

1. Suzanne Howard and Donald Peterson phased in permanent cross-functional teams in Wichita. What types of teams are the "problem chats" and SPITS groups? What stage or stages of team development did these groups evolve through?

2. What role did Donald Peterson play in the success of the Wichita team-based productivity project? What style did he employ to help reduce conflict between labor and the professionals? Do you agree with Suzanne Howard that if she just had a Donald Peterson in Lubbock, the project would succeed? Explain your answer.

3. What advice would you give Suzanne Howard and her team for improving the employee involvement climate, containing costs, and meeting production goals at the Lubbock plant?

SOURCES: Based on Michael C. Beers, "The Strategy That Wouldn't Travel," *Harvard Business Review* (November–December 1996): 18–31.

ENDNOTES

1. Susan Carey, "Racing to Improve; United Airlines Employees Go to School for Pit Crews to Boost Teamwork, Speed," *The Wall Street Journal* (March 24, 2006): B1.

2. Scott Thurm, "Theory & Practice: Teamwork Raises Everyone's Game—Having Employees Bond Benefits Companies More Than Promoting 'Stars'," *The Wall Street Journal* (November 7, 2005): B8.

3. Telis Demos, "Cirque du Balancing Act," *Fortune* (June 12, 2006): 114.

4. "Team Goal-Setting," *Small Business Report* (January 1988): 76–77; Frank V. Cespedes, Stephen X. Dole, and Robert J. Freedman, "Teamwork for Today's Selling," *Harvard Business Review* (March–April 1989): 44–55; Victoria J. Marsick, Ernie Turner, and Lars Cederholm, "International Managers as Team Leaders," *Management Review* (March 1989): 46–49; and Terry Adler, Janice A. Black, and John P. Loveland, "Complex Systems: Boundary-Spanning Training Techniques," *Journal of European Industrial Training* 27, no. 2–4 (2002): 111+.

5. Purdum, "Teaming, Take 2."

6. Industry Week/Manufacturing Performance Institute's Census of Manufacturers for 2004, reported in Traci Purdum, "Teaming, Take 2," *Industry Week* (May 2005): 41–43.

7. J. D. Osburn, L. Moran, E. Musselwhite, and J. H. Zenger, *Self-Directed Work Teams: The New American Challenge* (Homewood, IL: Business One Irwin, 1990).

8. Linda I. Glassop, "The Organizational Benefits of Teams," *Human Relations* 55, no. 2 (2002): 225–249.

9. Carl E. Larson and Frank M. J. LaFasto, *TeamWork* (Newbury Park, CA: Sage, 1989).

10. Purdum, "Teaming, Take 2."

11. "'Golden Hour' Crucial Time for Surgeons on Front Line," *Johnson City Press* (April 1, 2003): 9.

12. Geoffrey Colvin, "Why Dream Teams Fail," *Fortune* (June 12, 2006): 87–92.

13. Eric Sundstrom, Kenneth P. DeMeuse, and David Futrell, "Work Teams," *American Psychologist* 45 (February 1990): 120–133.

14. Deborah L. Gladstein, "Groups in Context: A Model of Task Group Effectiveness," *Administrative Science Quarterly* 29 (1984): 499–517.

15. Dora C. Lau and J. Keith Murnighan, "Demographic Diversity and Faultlines: The Compositional Dynamics of Organizational Groups," *Academy of Management Review* 23, no. 2 (1998): 325–340.

16. Thomas Owens, "Business Teams," *Small Business Report* (January 1989): 50–58.

17. Margaret Frazier, "Flu Prep," *The Wall Street Journal* (March 25, 2006): A8.

18. "Participation Teams," *Small Business Report* (September 1987): 38–41.

19. Susanne G. Scott and Walter O. Einstein, "Strategic Performance Appraisal in Team-Based Organizations: One Size Does Not Fit All," *Academy of Management Executive* 15, no. 2 (2001): 107–116.

20. Larson and LaFasto, *TeamWork*.

21. V. K. Narayanan, Frank L. Douglas, Brock Guernsey, and John Charnes, "How Top Management Steers Fast-Cycle Teams to Success," *Strategy & Leadership* 30, no. 3 (2002): 19–27.

22. James H. Shonk, *Team-Based Organizations* (Homewood, IL: Business One Irwin, 1992); and John Hoerr, "The Payoff from Teamwork," *BusinessWeek* (July 10, 1989): 56–62.

23. Gregory L. Miles, "Suddenly, USX Is Playing Mr. Nice Guy," *BusinessWeek* (June 26, 1989): 151–152.

24. Jeanne M. Wilson, Jill George, and Richard S. Wellings, with William C. Byham, *Leadership Trapeze: Strategies for Leadership in Team-Based Organizations* (San Francisco: Jossey-Bass, 1994).

25. Ruth Wageman, "Critical Success Factors for Creating Superb Self-Managing Teams," *Organizational Dynamics* (Summer 1997): 49–61.

26. Daniel R. Kibbe and Jill Casner-Lotto, "Ralston Foods: From Greenfield to Maturity in a Team-Based Plant," *Journal of Organizational Excellence* (Summer 2002): 57–67.

27. Thomas Owens, "The Self-Managing Work Team," *Small Business Report* (February 1991): 53–65.

28. Bradley L. Kirkman and Benson Rosen, "Powering Up Teams," *Organizational Dynamics* (Winter 2000): 48–66.

29. Vanessa Urch Druskat and Jane V. Wheeler, "Managing from the Boundary: The Effective Leadership of Self-Managing Work Teams," *Academy of Management Journal* 46, no. 4 (2003): 435–457.

30. Donald Vredenburgh and Irene Yunxia He, "Leadership Lessons from a Conductorless Orchestra," *Business Horizons* (September–October 2003): 19–24.

31. Curtis Sittenfeld, "Powered by the People," *Fast Company* (July–August 1999): 178–189.

32. The discussion of virtual teams is based on Wayne F. Cascio and Stan Shurygailo, "E-Leadership and Virtual Teams," *Organizational Dynamics* 31, no. 4 (2002): 362–376; Anthony M. Townsend, Samuel M. DeMarie, and Anthony R. Hendrickson, "Virtual Teams: Technology and the Workplace of the Future," *Academy of Management Executive* 12, no. 3 (August 1998): 17–29; and Deborah L. Duarte and Nancy Tennant Snyder, *Mastering Virtual Teams* (San Francisco: Jossey-Bass, 1999).

33. Jessica Lipnack and Jeffrey Stamps, "Virtual Teams: The New Way to Work," *Strategy & Leadership* (January–February 1999): 14–19.

34. Based on Bradley L. Kirkman, Benson Rosen, Cristina B. Gibson, Paul E. Tesluk, and Simon O. McPherson, "Five Challenges to Virtual Team Success: Lessons from Sabre, Inc.," *Academy of Management Executive* 16, no. 3 (2002): 67–79; Wayne F. Cascio and Stan Shurygailo, "E-Leadership and Virtual Teams," *Organizational Dynamics* 31, no. 4 (2002): 362–376; Ilze Zigurs, "Leadership in Virtual Teams: Oxymoron or Opportunity?" *Organizational Dynamics* 31, no. 4 (2002): 339–351; and Manju K. Ahuja and John E. Galvin, "Socialization in Virtual Groups," unpublished manuscript.

35. Kirkman et al., "Five Challenges to Virtual Team Success."

36. Terri L. Griffith and Margaret A. Neale, "Information Processing in Traditional, Hybrid, and Virtual Teams: From Nascent Knowledge to Transactive Memory," *Research in Organizational Behavior* 23 (2001): 379–421.

37. Vijay Govindarajan and Anil K. Gupta, "Building an Effective Global Business Team," *MIT Sloan Management Review* 42, no. 4 (Summer 2001): 63–71.

38. Charlene Marmer Solomon, "Building Teams Across Borders," *Global Workforce* (November 1998): 12–17.

39. Carol Saunders, Craig Van Slyke, and Douglas R. Vogel, "My Time or Yours? Managing Time Visions in Global Virtual Teams," *Academy of Management Executive* 18, no. 1 (2004): 19–31.

40. Saunders et al., "My Time or Yours?"

41. Cristina B. Gibson, Mary E. Zellmer-Bruhn, and Donald P. Schwab, "Team Effectiveness in Multinational Organizations: Evaluation Across Contexts," *Group and Organizational Management* 28, no. 4 (December 2003): 444–474.

42. Sylvia Odenwald, "Global Work Teams," *Training and Development* (February 1996): 54–57; and Debby Young, "Team Heat," *CIO* (September 1, 1998): 43–51.

43. Reported in Jia Lynn Yang, "The Power of Number 4.6," part of a special series, "Secrets of Greatness: Teamwork," *Fortune* (June 12, 2006): 122.

44. Martin Hoegl, "Smaller Teams—Better Teamwork: How to Keep Project Teams Small," *Business Horizons* 48 (2005): 209–214.

45. Reported in "Vive La Difference," box in Julie Connelly, "All Together Now," *Gallup Management Journal* (Spring 2002): 13–18.

46. For research findings on group size, see M. E. Shaw, *Group Dynamics*, 3d ed. (New York: McGraw-Hill, 1981); G. Manners, "Another Look at Group Size, Group Problem-Solving and Member Consensus," *Academy of Management Journal* 18 (1975): 715–724; and Martin Hoegl, "Smaller Teams—Better Teamwork: How to Keep Project Teams Small," *Business Horizons* 48 (2005): 209–214.

47. Robert Albanese and David D. Van Fleet, "Rational Behavior in Groups: The Free-Riding Tendency," *Academy of Management Review* 10 (1985): 244–255.

48. D. A. Kravitz and B. Martin, "Ringelmann Rediscovered: The Original Article," *Journal of Personality and Social Psychology* 50, no. 5 (1986): 936–941.

49. Baron, *Behavior in Organizations*.

50. Yang, "The Power of Number 4.6."

51. Warren E. Watson, Kamalesh Kumar, and Larry K. Michaelsen, "Cultural Diversity's Impact on Interaction Process and Performance: Comparing Homogeneous and Diverse Task Groups," *Academy of Management Journal* 36 (1993): 590–602; Gail Robinson and Kathleen Dechant, "Building a Business Case for Diversity," *Academy of Management Executive* 11, no. 3 (1997): 21–31; and David A. Thomas and Robin J. Ely, "Making Differences Matter: A New Paradigm for Managing Diversity," *Harvard Business Review* (September–October 1996): 79–90.

52. Becky Blalock, "Peer to Peer: Playing Nice in the Sandbox," *CIO* (December 15, 2005): 32–34.

53. J. Stuart Bunderson and Kathleen M. Sutcliffe, "Comparing Alternative Conceptualizations of Functional Diversity in Management Teams: Process and Performance Effects," *Academy of Management Journal* 45, no. 5 (2002): 875–893; and Marc Orlitzky and John D. Benjamin, "The Effects of Sex Composition on Small Group Performance in a Business School Case Competition," *Academy of Management Learning and Education* 2, no. 2 (2003): 128–138.

54. Watson et al. "Cultural Diversity's Impact on Interaction Process and Performance."

55. George Prince, "Recognizing Genuine Teamwork," *Supervisory Management* (April 1989): 25–36; K. D. Benne and P. Sheats, "Functional Roles of Group Members," *Journal of Social Issues* 4 (1948): 41–49; and R. F. Bales, *SYMOLOG* Case Study Kit (New York: Free Press, 1980).

56. Robert A. Baron, *Behavior in Organizations*, 2d ed. (Boston: Allyn & Bacon, 1986).

57. Ibid.

58. Avan R. Jassawalla and Hemant C. Sashittal, "Strategies of Effective New Product Team Leaders," *California Management Review* 42, no. 2 (Winter 2000): 34–51.

59. Kenneth G. Koehler, "Effective Team Management," *Small Business Report* (July 19, 1989): 14–16; and Connie J. G. Gersick, "Time and Transition in Work Teams: Toward a New Model of Group Development," *Academy of Management Journal* 31 (1988): 9–41.

60. Bruce W. Tuckman and Mary Ann C. Jensen, "Stages of Small-Group Development Revisited," *Group and Organizational Studies* 2 (1977): 419–427; and Bruce W. Tuckman, "Developmental Sequences in Small Groups," *Psychological Bulletin* 63 (1965): 384–399. See also Linda N. Jewell and H. Joseph Reitz, *Group Effectiveness in Organizations* (Glenview, IL: Scott, Foresman, 1981).

61. Thomas Petzinger Jr., "Bovis Team Helps Builders Construct a Solid Foundation" *The Wall Street Journal* (March 21, 1997): B1.

62. Shaw, *Group Dynamics*.

63. Daniel C. Feldman and Hugh J. Arnold, *Managing Individual and Group Behavior in Organizations* (New York: McGraw-Hill, 1983).

64. Dorwin Cartwright and Alvin Zander, *Group Dynamics: Research and Theory*, 3d ed. (New York: Harper & Row, 1968); and Elliot Aronson, *The Social Animal* (San Francisco: W. H. Freeman, 1976).

65. Peter E. Mudrack, "Group Cohesiveness and Productivity: A Closer Look," *Human Relations* 42 (1989): 771–785. Also see Miriam Erez and Anit Somech, "Is Group Productivity Loss the Rule or the Exception? Effects of Culture and Group-Based Motivation," *Academy of Management Journal* 39, no. 6 (1996): 1513–1537.

66. Stanley E. Seashore, *Group Cohesiveness in the Industrial Work Group* (Ann Arbor, MI: Institute for Social Research, 1954).

67. Adam Lashinsky, "RAZR's Edge," *Fortune* (June 12, 2006): 124–132.

68. Ibid.

69. J. Richard Hackman, "Group Influences on Individuals," in *Handbook of Industrial and Organizational Psychology*, ed. M. Dunnette (Chicago: Rand McNally, 1976).

70. Paul Hochman, "Pack Mentality," *Fortune* (June 12, 2006): 145–152.

71. Kenneth Bettenhausen and J. Keith Murnighan, "The Emergence of Norms in Competitive Decision-Making Groups," *Administrative Science Quarterly* 30 (1985): 350–372.

72. The following discussion is based on Daniel C. Feldman, "The Development and Enforcement of Group Norms," *Academy of Management Review* 9 (1984): 47–53.

73. Wilson et al., *Leadership Trapeze*, 12.

74. Colvin, "Why Dream Teams Fail."

75. Stephen P. Robbins, *Managing Organizational Conflict: A Nontraditional Approach* (Englewood Cliffs, NJ: Prentice Hall, 1974).

76. Daniel Robey, Dana L. Farrow, and Charles R. Franz, "Group Process and Conflict in System Development," *Management Science* 35 (1989): 1172–1191.

77. Yuhyung Shin, "Conflict Resolution in Virtual Teams," *Organizational Dynamics* 34, no. 4 (2005): 331–345.

78. Dean Tjosvold, Chun Hui, Daniel Z. Ding, and Junchen Hu, "Conflict Values and Team Relationships: Conflict's Contribution to Team Effectiveness and Citizenship in China," *Journal of Organizational Behavior* 24 (2003): 69–88; C. De Dreu and E. Van de Vliert, *Using Conflict in Organizations* (Beverly Hills, CA: Sage, 1997); and Kathleen M. Eisenhardt, Jean L. Kahwajy, and L. J. Bourgeois III, "Conflict and Strategic Choice: How Top Management Teams Disagree," *California Management Review* 39, no. 2 (Winter 1997): 42–62.

79. Jerry B. Harvey, "The Abilene Paradox: The Management of Agreement," *Organizational Dynamics* (Summer 1988): 17–43.

80. Eisenhardt et al., "Conflict and Strategic Choice."

81. Koehler, "Effective Team Management"; and Dean Tjosvold, "Making Conflict Productive," *Personnel Administrator* 29 (June 1984): 121.

82. This discussion is based in part on Richard L. Daft, *Organization Theory and Design* (St. Paul, MN: West, 1992): Chapter 13; and Paul M. Terry, "Conflict Management," *The Journal of Leadership Studies* 3, no. 2 (1996): 3–21.

83. Narayanan et al., "How Top Management Steers Fast-Cycle Teams to Success."

84. Shin, "Conflict Resolution in Virtual Teams."

85. Clinton O. Longenecker and Mitchell Neubert, "Barriers and Gateways to Management Cooperation and Teamwork," *Business Horizons* (September–October 2000): 37–44.

86. This discussion is based on K. W. Thomas, "Towards Multidimensional Values in Teaching: The Example of Conflict Behaviors," *Academy of Management Review* 2 (1977): 487.

87. Robbins, *Managing Organizational Conflict*.

88. "The Negotiation Process: The Difference Between Integrative and Distributive Negotiation," La Piana Associates Inc., http://www.lapiana.org/resources/tips/negotiations.

89. Rob Walker, "Take It or Leave It: The Only Guide to Negotiating You Will Ever Need," *Inc.*, (August 2003): 75–82.

90. Based on Roger Fisher and William Ury, *Getting to Yes: Negotiating Agreement Without Giving In* (New York: Penguin, 1983).

91. This familiar story was reported in "The Difference Between Integrative and Distributive Negotiation."

92. This discussion and example is adapted from "Distributive Bargaining," *Culture at Work* http://www.culture-at-work.com/distribute/html.

93. Based in part on "A Note for Analyzing Work Groups," prepared by Linda A. Hill, Harvard Business School Publishing, http://www.hbsp.harvard.edu.

94. "Big and No Longer Blue," *The Economist* (January 21–27, 2006), http://www.economist.com.

95. R. B. Zajonc, "Social Facilitation," *Science* 149 (1965): 269–274; and Erez and Somech, "Is Group Productivity Loss the Rule or the Exception?"

96. Claire M. Mason and Mark A. Griffin, "Group Task Satisfaction; The Group's Shared Attitude to Its Task and Work Environment," *Group and Organizational Management* 30, no. 6 (2005): 625–652.

97. Gina Imperato, "Their Specialty? Teamwork," *Fast Company* (January–February 2000): 54–56.

98. Reported in Thurm, "Theory & Practice: Teamwork Raises Everyone's Game."

99. Kenneth Labich, "Elite Teams Get the Job Done," *Fortune* (February 19, 1996): 90–99.

100. "A Note for Analyzing Effective Work Groups."

101. Carey, "Racing to Improve"; and Patrick J. Kiger, "Unite or Die," *Workforce* (February 2003): 26.

COSTCO WHOLESALE CORPORATION PART FIVE: PROVIDING LEADERSHIP IN BULK

When Costco Wholesale procured land to construct a new warehouse in Cuernavaca, Mexico in 2001, it had no idea that the purchase would spark a two-year clash between anti-globalization protesters and senior management. The leading U.S. warehouse club operator was looking to continue its international expansion, and the Mexican government's auctioning of a site occupied by a dilapidated hotel and casino known as the *Casino de la Selva* presented a strategic opportunity.

But what started out as a business-as-usual transaction for Costco soon turned into a public relations crisis. Opponents of the land development staged human blockades to stop chainsaw crews from clearing the way for the superstore and surrounding facilities. Numerous protestors were arrested, and the conflict received widespread media attention.

Despite overwhelming support in Cuernavaca for the new Costco store and its promise of new jobs and economic prosperity, accusations that Costco was paving a parking lot overtop the city's civic, artistic, and national heritage were beginning to create the perception of Costco as an insensitive multinational corporation. To demonstrate environmental and cultural sensitivity to the citizens of the region, and to offer an olive branch to anti-growth opponents, Costco set aside millions of dollars beyond its original budget to preserve much of the area's natural landscape and to restore the dilapidated murals of the *Casino de la Selva*, the site's once-thriving hotel and gaming casino. In cooperation with the Mexican National Institute of Fine Arts and Literature, the Vergel Foundation, and regional city planners, Costco built a cultural center and museum that now displays the hotel frescos as well as the esteemed Gelman Collection of Mexican art, featuring works by Frida Kahlo and Diego Rivera. Today, the site serves as a valuable international attraction for Cuernavaca, preserving the city's cultural heritage and providing a boost to the city's economy.

The Cuernavaca story illustrates the exemplary moral leadership that has come to characterize Costco's senior management. From the very beginning, Costco had a different way of seeing its own mission. While many businesses measure success in strictly financial terms—Are we profitable?—the world's leading membership warehouse chain has always gauged achievement according to broader criteria: Are we creating greater value for the consumer? Are we more efficient? Are we doing the right thing for employees and other stakeholders? This holistic approach to business has made Costco not only wildly profitable but also vitally relevant to the issues and trends shaping the future of business today.

Led by co-founder and CEO James Sinegal, Costco forged a new model of retailing that combined wholesale-styled bulk efficiencies with brand-name merchandising, delivering high-end products to club members at the lowest possible prices. As a result of Sinegal's strong leadership and vision, Costco finds itself at the forefront of big box retailing, occupying a seat among top chains like Wal-Mart, Target, and Home Depot.

On its way to becoming the No.1 warehouse club in the nation, Costco launched timely ancillary businesses that changed the way people shop. To its core warehouse club business Costco has added gas stations, home furnishing stores, pharmacies, drive-through car washes, optical centers, photo labs, fresh-food departments, and business centers. These ancillary businesses have contributed $7 billion to Costco's $60 billion in annual sales and stimulated a growing market demand for one-stop shopping.

In some instances, Costco's side ventures have risen to the top of their associated retail categories. In 2006, Costco's fast-growing pharmacy division generated sales of $2.6 billion, making Costco one of the nation's largest pharmacy chains—an astounding accomplishment that took only 20 years. With their staggering prescription drug sales and recent entry into low-priced generic drugs, Costco pharmacies are turning up the heat on category leaders CVS Corp. and Walgreen Co. and demonstrating effective positioning to meet the needs of the aging baby-boomer population.

Costco's innovative leadership has also extended to the private label enterprise. At a time when many retailers are struggling to sell private labels alongside national brands, Costco's Kirkland Signature label has evolved into one of the most successful and recognized own-brands in the country. Designed to be of equal or better quality than national brands, Kirkland Signature products make up 400 of Costco's approximately 4,000 SKUs, with items ranging from diapers manufactured by Kimberly-Clark to tires produced by Michelin—offered at a minimum of 20 percent savings compared to leading national brands. Applying high-volume leverage on the distribution channel helped to create Kirkland Signature's more-for-less reputation—Costco buyers famously exclude suppliers that fail to meet their demands. "This is not the Little Sisters of the Poor," Sinegal declares with usual dry wit. "We have to be competitive in the toughest marketplace in the world against the biggest competitor in the world. We cannot afford to be timid."

From its development of Cuernavaca to its transformational impact upon the retail industry, Costco's legacy of innovation and success is owed to the company's motivational leadership, and especially to James Sinegal, a visionary CEO that *Time* magazine named as one of the 100 most influential people of 2006.

Questions

1. What is moral leadership, and why is it increasingly important for global business?

2. What types of leadership are necessary for leading change? In what ways has Costco's management demonstrated such leadership?

3. What motivational impact might Costco's handling of the Cuernavaca expansion have on employees, both in Mexico and internationally? Explain.

SOURCES: Mya Frazier, "The Private Label Powerhouse; With Booming Kirkland Signature Line, Costco Controls National Brands Like No Other Retailer," *Advertising Age,* August 21, 2006; Mike Duff, "A Private Label Success Story," *DSN Retailing Today,* December 19, 2005; Doug Desjardins, "Presence Builds Rapidly Amid Rx Top Tier," *Retailing Today,* November 6, 2006; David Pinto, "Costco Named Retailer of the Year," *MMR,* January 9, 2006; "Costco to Match $4 Generics Price as Rx Sales Continue to Rise," *Drug Store News,* November 6, 2006; Investor Relations Web site, *http://phx.corporate-ir.net/phoenix.zhtml?c=83830&p=irol-irhome,* accessed November 21, 2006; "Ancillary Businesses Continue to Drive Through Sales," *Retailing Today,* September 25, 2006; "Mix Includes Everything From Cosmetics to Caskets," *MMR,* January 9, 2006; Alyce Lomax, "Most Foolish CEO: Jim Sinegal," *The Motley Fool,* September 28, 2006, *http://www.fool.com;* Mya Frazier, "Chic Costco beauty line displayed-in cardboard; Warehouse chain offers Borghese, undercutting department store rivals," *Advertising Age,* May 22, 2006; Steven Greenhouse, "How Costco Became the Anti-Wal-Mart, *The New York Times,* July 17, 2005; Mac Greer, "Is Costco Giving Away the Store?", *The Motley Fool,* November 22, 2006, *http://www.fool.com;* "A Culture of Commitment: The Story of Costco in Cuernavaca," Company Web site, *http://www.costco.com/Service/FeaturePage.aspx?ProductNo=11004800;* Daren Fonda, "Jim Sinegal: Costco's Discount CEO," *Time,* May 8, 2006.

■ ON THE JOB VIDEO CASES   730

1   Original Penguin Rides Out Turbulence   730
2   Original Penguin Becomes a Learning Organization   731
3   Lonely Planet Creates an Adventurous Culture   732
4   Lonely Planet Travels the World   733
5   Organic Valley Plants the Seeds of Social Responsibility   734
6   Organic Valley Grows Up   735
7   Timbuk2: The Message Is in the Bag   736
8   Timbuk2: Make the Swirl as Famous as the Swoosh   737
9   Timbuk2: CEO Sets a Course   738
10 Lonely Planet: Structure That Makes Sense   739
11 Original Penguin Spreads Its Wings   740
12 PepsiCo Puts People First   741
13 Diversity at PepsiCo   742
14 Control Is Key to Peapod's Online Grocery Service   743
15 Peapod Takes Grocery Shopping Online   744
16 Peapod Delivers Convenience and Quality   745
17 P.F. Chang Serves Its Workers Well   746
18 Leadership at P.F. Chang's   747
19 P.F. Chang's Employees Taste the Fruits of Motivation   748
20 NEADS Creates Partnerships between People and Dogs   749
21 The NEADS Team: People and Dogs   750

■ BIZFLIX VIDEO CASES   751

8 Mile   751
Backdraft   751
Mr. Baseball   751
Emperor's Club   752
The Bourne Identity   752
Blue Crush   752
Dr. Seuss' How the Grinch Stole Christmas   753
The Paper   753
Apollo 13   753
Bowfinger   754
The Breakfast Club   754
U-571   754
For Love of the Game   754
Patch Adams   755

Apollo 13   755

Scent of a Woman   755

Lorenzo's Oil   755

Casino   756

ON THE JOB VIDEO CASES   757

1   Managing in Turbulent Times at Second City Theater   757

2   The Evolution of Management Thinking   758

3   The Environment and Corporate Culture at Caterpillar   759

4   Managing in a Global Environment at Yahoo!   760

5   Ethics and Social Responsibility at British Petroleum   761

6   Managing Small Business Start Ups at The Little Guys Home Electronics   762

7   Managerial Planning and Goal Setting at Cold Stone Creamery   763

8   Strategy Formulation and Implementation at Yahoo!   764

9   Managerial Decision-making, Organizational Planning, and Goal Setting at McDonald's   765

10   Designing Adaptive Organizations at Boyne USA Resorts   766

11   Managing Change and Innovation at Hard Rock   767

12   Human Resource Management at Allstate   768

13   Meeting the Challenge of Diversity at Whirlpool Corporation   769

14   Managerial and Quality Control at Honda   770

15   Information Technology and E-Business at Peet's Coffee & Tea   771

16   Operation and Service Management at Washburn Guitar   772

17   Dynamics of Behavior in Organizations at Zingerman's   773

18   Leadership at McDonald's   774

19   Motivation at Washburn Guitar   775

20   Communication at Navistar International   776

21   Teamwork at Cold Stone Creamery   777

CHAPTER 1: ORIGINAL PENGUIN RIDES OUT TURBULENCE

Penguins have always been cool. But golf shirts with a little flapping bird printed on them experienced a lull in coolness. In fact, their popularity remained frozen for two decades largely because they were worn by aging golfers. Now the penguins are back, flapping furiously—and, many would argue, coolly—not just on golf shirts but also on a wide array of men's and women's clothing and accessories, including shirts, shoes, hats, belts, neckties, handbags, and even bathing suits. These items represent the extreme makeover of a 50-year-old brand of clothing called Original Penguin. Now owned by Perry Ellis International, the Original Penguin brand of clothing is experiencing rejuvenation—thanks largely to Penguin's vice president, Chris Kolbe.

Chris Kolbe knows that thawing out an old brand is a daunting task under the best circumstances. But the fashion industry is particularly difficult—the pace is dizzying, and the turbulence is sometimes terrifying. Kolbe's activities as a manager are clearly characterized by variety, fragmentation, and brevity. For example, in a single day, Kolbe may be expecting several hundred samples from sources around the globe to arrive in time for a fashion show. He may have to decide whether to extend credit to a retailer or whether to drop one retailer in favor of another. He may have to review ad copy, return calls from fashion magazines, thumb through swatches of fabric, welcome sales reps arriving for a meeting, and fix his own computer. "We are always way behind and scrambling," he says with a chuckle. But Kolbe thrives on these activities because he is convinced that the time is right for his penguins to regain their place in the market among other legendary figures such as alligators and polo ponies—and he intends to make it happen.

Because the Penguin division is a tiny component of the much larger Perris Ellis company, Kolbe serves all the management functions of planning, organizing, leading, and controlling—often during the course of one work day. "I take personal responsibility and accountability for everything that has the Penguin brand on it," Kolbe notes.

Kolbe also fulfills all the roles of a top manager. He considers himself a hands-on manager, communicating constantly with his staff and keeping himself "involved in every detail so I don't lose sight" of things. He develops relationships with employees so that they can work well together. "My job is really the A to Z in assembling a team of people who can focus on certain pieces of that business and deliver on the strategic goals for the company," he explains. "I feel very fortunate to have such a good team." He makes decisions about where to take the brand. Right now, he has his sights set on a more upscale market. He envisions his customers as comfortable suburbanites who want high-quality, fashionable casual clothing. But he doesn't worry too much about direct competitors in the clothing industry. Instead, he focuses on how Original Penguin can compete for consumer dollars. "My role as vice president of Penguin really is . . . I'm acting president of a very small division—a start-up company attached to a larger company," Kolbe observes. "So I really took on the A to Z of running a brand or running a company, from the . . . creative vision of the brand, to marketing the brand, to the business operations and sales of the brand."

As for that turbulence? Kolbe shrugs it off. "In every business there are roadblocks. So your ability to focus on the roadblock or work around the roadblock sometimes comes down to your ability to be successful." This is true even when the roadblock happens to be a shipment of women's flip-flops that hasn't arrived in time for the fashion show.

Questions

1. Describe the conceptual skills you think Chris Kolbe needs for his job as vice president of Original Penguin.

2. Suppose those flip-flops—or other components of the upcoming fashion show—don't arrive in time. Describe how Chris Kolbe might manage the situation.

3. What do you think is the most difficult part of Kolbe's job? Why?

SOURCES: Company Web site, *http://www.originalpenguin.com*, accessed July 30, 2004; "Pick up an Original Penguin," *Fashion UK*, July 8, 2004, *http://www.widemedia.com/fashionuk/news/2004*; Carl Swanson, "A Senior Moment," *The New York Times*, Spring 2004, p. 44; Stephanie Thomson, "Perry Ellis Banks on Brand Resurrections," *Advertising Age*, March 15, 2004, p. 14; Rima Sugi, "The Bird Is the Word," *New York Metro.com*, December 8, 2003, *http://www.newyorkmetro.com*.

CHAPTER 2: ORIGINAL PENGUIN BECOMES A LEARNING ORGANIZATION

Taking charge of a company is both a challenge and a dream for any young manager. Chris Kolbe, vice president of Original Penguin, a division of Perry Ellis International, is no exception. Original Penguin is experiencing a total makeover, courtesy of Chris Kolbe and a small staff of designers, marketers, and finance managers. Once the domain of middle-aged golfers, the penguin logo now graces hats, neckties, shoes, and an entire line of fashionable women's clothing and accessories ranging from T-shirts and skirts to belts, shoes, handbags, and bathing suits. Original Penguin clothing now appears in such upscale department stores as Barney's and Saks—as well as its own retail store in midtown Manhattan. This hip new brand of clothing has come a long way from the golf courses of half a century ago.

Remaking a brand involves remaking an organization. In 1955, marketers for Munsingwear Penguin approached celebrities such as Bing Crosby and Bob Hope with the request to provide shirts for their golf tournaments. Then they contacted the Golf Association, asking for a list of its members—all men—to whom they sent sample golf shirts. The penguin logo quickly became associated with the men's pro golf tour. The company was run as a traditional organization, manufacturing a traditional product. But not any more.

Perry Ellis has made a strategy of acquiring languishing brands, such as Jantzen bathing suits and Penguin golf wear, and breathing new life into them. When Chris Kolbe was hired by the company to turn Original Penguin around, he was given a small New York office and two staffers. There was no way he could run the company as a traditional large corporation, nor did he want to. Original Penguin was about to become a learning organization, complete with teams, empowered employees, and a free flow of information.

Kolbe relies on collaboration and communication across departments—usually just across cubicles—among team members. He helps them set goals, makes sure they have the information they need, and then allows them to take responsibility for their own performance. "If you have a team, you have to give them ownership of what they do," Kolbe explains. He communicates regularly with the design team and marketing team but says that he prefers to limit the time everyone spends in meetings. "I'm a one-on-one guy. I try not to schedule a lot of meetings because meetings can be stifling."

Kolbe believes firmly in empowering employees with the freedom and resources to initiate their own ideas, make their own decisions, and perform their best. "Chris is easy to work with," says marketing manager Laura Bellafronto. "He makes you feel comfortable and secure . . . he makes you want to be here and be working with him." Kolbe is happy that he inspires that kind of loyalty. "I try to respect and treat everybody as I wish to be treated, but also I'm very comfortable with pushing people and asking a lot of them," he remarks.

The free flow of information between Kolbe and his staff is key to the rejuvenation of Original Penguin. Kolbe makes sure he communicates with every employee the goals and needs of the company. "He has a vision that he makes clear to everyone," says Laura Bellafronto.

Today, Original Penguin products sport an updated, more youthful look. "[They are] fashionably new, but not avant-garde," says Kolbe. If the clothes are vintage inspired, Penguin's new customers are too young to remember leisure suits or wall-to-wall shag carpeting. Kolbe's management style is as deceptively casual as the clothing itself—comfortable but made to last. "My authority [really derives] from what I do and how I communicate with people, my directness. I know when to have fun and I know when to be serious. I try to strike that balance."

Questions

1. As the organization has grown from just three employees, Chris Kolbe has had to delegate more decisions to others. How important is this transition to Original Penguin's success as a learning organization? Explain.

2. Do you think that Kolbe views knowledge among his employees as an important resource? Why or why not?

3. What steps might Original Penguin as a company take to ensure the satisfaction of its employees?

SOURCES: Company Web site, *http://www.originalpenguin.com,* accessed July 30, 2004; Carl Swanson, "A Senior Moment," in "Men's Fashions of the Times," *The New York Times,* spring 2004, p. 44; Mary Lisa Gavenas, "Brands on the Run," *DNR,* April 28, 2004, p. 17; Stephanie Thompson, "Perry Ellis Banks on Brand Resurrections," *Advertising Age,* March 15, 2004, p. 14.

CHAPTER 3: LONELY PLANET CREATES AN ADVENTUROUS CULTURE

When you think of corporate culture, the image of suits and ties, pantyhose and pumps often springs to mind. But at Lonely Planet, the values, beliefs, understandings, and norms of the firm are expressed by staff members and managers who wear T-shirts, khakis, soft skirts, and sandals or clogs to work. Lonely Planet is a publishing company based in Australia with offices in several other countries—including the United States—that produces series of travel books, guides, and language phrasebooks for people who want adventure.

Founded in 1971 by Tony and Maureen Wheeler, who admit that they started the company as a way to fund their own travel dreams, Lonely Planet has grown to become a major force in the travel publishing industry. The company publishes books—like *South America on a Shoestring*—for travelers who want to visit off-beat places, often on a budget. To do so, Lonely Planet employs people who love to travel and who love books. They are happy wending their way through a jungle path or along an ancient, cobblestone street as part of the job. They also delight in putting together the photos and text that will entice other travelers to explore. "I would say that the culture of Lonely Planet is sort of embodied in a sense of pioneering," observes Cindy Cohen of Lonely Planet's public relations department. "We like to give people a scoop on the 'inside' places to be." Lonely Planet describes trips for the curious, nonmainstream traveler.

Lonely Planet fosters an internal culture in which employees are free to be themselves—to exchange ideas and try new approaches to problems. The work space itself is informal and open, so that people can communicate easily with each other. Successes are celebrated by everyone with office parties, and employees are naturally friends who socialize together outside of work. In addition, although there is a Lonely Planet approach and format to the guides, the voices of individual travel writers are valued, which is unusual among travel publishers.

Lonely Planet's informal culture lends itself readily to adapting quickly to an ever-changing external environment. Not only do staff members have a broader view of the world because of their travel experience, but they are also sensitive to changes in the environment that signal changes Lonely Planet should make to capture new markets. For instance, Lonely Planet's books were originally geared toward Australian, European, and Asian markets, where travelers tend to take longer trips. Europeans often have a month to six weeks of vacation, so they take off on long jaunts. But Americans take shorter trips, for a variety of reasons. One is that they only get an average of two weeks' vacation from work per year. Another factor is the economy—only recently have American consumers begun to show confidence in the U.S. economy after the recession. A third factor is the practice of "cocooning," or staying close to home in the wake of the terrorist attacks of September 11, 2001, and the ensuing war on terrorism.

In addition, Americans still love to drive their cars—despite a recent spike in gasoline prices. Even if gasoline is more expensive than it used to be, it is still less expensive—at least for a family—to drive to a destination than to fly to it. So, Lonely Planet has refocused in the United States, developing a series of guidebooks to the National Parks, including the Grand Canyon, Yosemite, Yellowstone, and the Grand Tetons. In addition, the series includes popular parks in Canada that are accessible by car, such as Banff, Glacier, and Jasper. Then there are the *Road Trip Guides*—a series of guides to destinations around the United States that are off the beaten path but still accessible for weekend getaways. Travelers can drive the famous Route 66 or California Highway 1; they can cruise up the Hudson River Valley; or they can follow one of Lonely Planet's hottest new guides—*Blues and Barbecue*—through the South. In short, just about anywhere a traveler wants to go, Lonely Planet is ready to guide.

Questions

1. Describe the task environment for Lonely Planet.
2. Describe factors in the external environment that could create uncertainty for Lonely Planet.
3. Give an example of Lonely Planet's corporate culture at each of the three levels identified in Exhibit 3.5.

SOURCES: Company Web site, *http://www.lonelyplanet.com,* accessed August 5, 2004; "Lonely Planet Publications Company Profile," *Hoover's Online, http://biz.yahoo.com,* accessed July 30, 2004; Lonely Planet press packet.

CHAPTER 4: LONELY PLANET TRAVELS THE WORLD

For a company such as Lonely Planet, the idea of a borderless world is nothing new. Founded in Australia by Tony and Maureen Wheeler so that they could fund their own travel dreams, the travel publisher now has offices in Australia, the United States, the United Kingdom, and France, with a total of about 450 employees. Its writers, photographers, and marketers span the globe on a regular basis in search of the best destinations for their customers to explore. However, despite the fact that the idea of globalization is built into the firm's culture, its managers face international challenges every day.

Howard Ralley, director of global marketing and promotions, is now based in Australia, after having worked at the Lonely Planet office in the United Kingdom. He's a decisive manager who says what he means and means what he says. "You can get caught up in a lot of navel gazing, asking, 'What does *global* really mean?'" he quips. "Global doesn't really exist in a lot of senses. When you talk about global marketing, marketing is really all about talking with [a particular] customer, and that customer isn't global. [He or she] is concerned about the immediate environment." Thus, when Ralley and his staff get together to discuss a particular project, they consider the features of the destination, the characteristics of its culture, and the needs of the traveler as they relate to the location. The focus of a book on weekend escapes for the European traveler will be much different from the focus of a book on China.

Still, Ralley and his staff, along with the rest of the Lonely Planet employees around the world, strive to achieve consistency in the message they convey to consumers and other members of the travel industry. "There is a lot of 'globalness' that we achieve," says Ralley. "It's not about product . . . we're talking to an audience which shares many things, including a passion for travel. They believe that travel can change the world. So we work that message into individual markets." In addition, Lonely Planet employees around the world need to achieve consistency in the messages they convey to each other. The Internet has proved to be an excellent tool for handling both types of audiences. For instance, an image representing a specific book or series of books can be transmitted anywhere in the world, among Lonely Planet offices, to travel industry professionals, and to the home computers of consumers. This consistency in messages helps reinforce the Lonely Planet brand worldwide.

Ralley emphasizes the importance of conveying a unique message about Lonely Planet to distinguish the publisher from its competitors. "If a brand tries to work in all kinds of markets and you try to dumb down to the lowest common denominator," he notes, then you get "blanding" instead of branding. "We all agree that travel is important," Ralley continues. "If we just did a message on that, it would make us no different from National Geographic, Fodor's, or Discovery—so that is blanding. You have to get brave in saying something new to the world. Branding is all about that distinction." Ralley doesn't mind that not every consumer likes Lonely Planet books. He feels that it is more important to speak with a decisive, distinctive voice.

To that end, Ralley is a decisive manager. "The world is not all happy," he said during one recent meeting when discussing with his staff the selection of representative photos for a pictorial book covering 230 countries. Ralley wanted to include a potentially controversial photo of an Ethiopian woman whose facial expression did not appear to be welcoming. His staff expressed concern that the photo would be interpreted as too political. But Ralley insisted that the photo was consistent with Lonely Planet's direct, frank approach to the world. "You face different challenges every day," he later explained when discussing his role as an international manager. "Everything you thought you knew . . . all your assumptions [about a certain culture or market] . . . you have to rethink that." And in the end, he makes the decisions. "At some point," Ralley says, "you have to call the shot."

Questions

1. Identify at least three ways that Lonely Planet can benefit from the use of technology around the world.
2. Why is a global presence particularly important for Lonely Planet?
3. Describe at least two personal challenges that Howard Ralley faces as a manager.

SOURCES: Company Web site, *http://www.lonelyplanet.com,* accessed August 5, 2004; "Lonely Planet Publications Company Profile," *Hoover's Online, http://biz.yahoo.com,* accessed July 30, 2004; Lonely Planet press packet.

CHAPTER 5: ORGANIC VALLEY PLANTS THE SEEDS OF SOCIAL RESPONSIBILITY

Many organizations treat social responsibility as if it were a separate division—the department of good deeds. They support volunteerism among employees, use environmentally friendly packaging, and sponsor special programs in the community. All of these activities are to be commended. But very few commercial organizations can actually claim to be based on the principles of social responsibility. The Organic Valley Cooperative is an exception. Based in Wisconsin, Organic Valley is a cooperative of small farmers whose products are certified to be produced without pesticides, synthetic hormones, or antibiotics, including organic milk, cheese, butter, spreads, creams, eggs, vegetables, juice, and meat.

Nearly two decades ago, a few farmers who believed strongly in the value to society of practicing organic agriculture and saving family farms got together to form a cooperative. By acting together, these farmers could better control their fate. They could control supply, negotiate with larger customers, and reach more consumers who wanted their products. And they could set their own milk prices. Instead of being forced to accept prices subject to wild fluctuations in the open marketplace, these farmers began to set their own. This practice alone may be the single most important factor in the ability of family farms to survive. In one recent year, the milk price paid to Organic Valley farmers was 60 percent higher than the price paid to conventional dairy farmers. Organic Valley has actually received criticism for this practice, particularly from its creditors. But the cooperative holds firm. "Lowering the milk price would have been as easy as falling off a log," argues Organic Valley's CEO George Siemon. "But one of our objectives is to pay our farmers a good price. . . . We have a pay program the farmers expect us to deliver on. These relationships are the most important thing."

Today, Organic Valley is being called the most successful organic cooperative in the world. The cooperative has 630 members farming 100,000 acres in 16 states, with a waiting list. Sales are hitting upwards of $200 million per year and growing. Member farmers are the cooperative's major stakeholders. With assistance from Organic Valley employees, the farmers govern the cooperative by serving on the board and executive committees. Organic Valley's structure is designed so it will be able to sustain itself from one generation to the next, ensuring the survival of family farms and sustainable, organic agriculture.

Sweet Ridge Organic Dairy is one of the cooperative's farms, operated by Paul Deutsch in Westby, Wisconsin. Deutsch owns twenty-six cows that are milked twice a day and allowed to graze over pastureland the rest of the time—unlike cows in many larger, conventional dairy farms, which are kept in stalls 24 hours a day and may be given hormones or antibiotics. It costs more to run an organic dairy farm, where in addition to grass the cows are fed organic corn, alfalfa, and other grains, and the cows need more grazing land. But Deutsch isn't spending money on chemicals or vet bills. He estimates that he makes about 30 percent profit each year because consumers are happy to pay more for products they know are more healthful for themselves and their families. "Many parents have read the *Consumer Reports* studies and the National Academy of Science reports and know that organic for their kids is like seatbelts in a car," notes Theresa Marquez, Organic Valley's director of sales and marketing. "The organic category has been growing steadily at 20 percent, and organic milk, with 27+ percent annual growth, is driving the growth of the category. The implementation of the National Organic Program in the U.S. . . . further established the organic market as one that is here to stay. Consumers want organic."

Organic Valley has helped the economies of several rural areas. When a large federal dam project in southwestern Wisconsin was cancelled after displacing more than 140 local farmers from their land, many lost their livelihoods. As Organic Valley became established, it created employment opportunities—both on the farms and in the cooperative offices—for hundreds of residents in the area. "Going organic saved our farm," says cooperative farmer Mike Gehl, whose family has operated a Wisconsin farm for 154 years and five generations. Now Gehl and others like him can look forward to the next generation of farming.

Questions

1. In addition to the farmers, who are Organic Valley's other stakeholders?

2. Where does Organic Valley fit in the *shades of green* illustration in Exhibit 5.6? Give reasons for your answer.

3. Describe at least one ethical challenge that Organic Valley may face during turbulent times.

SOURCES: Company Web site, *http://www.organicvalley.coop.com*, accessed August 2, 2004; Judy Ettenhofer, "Organic Valley a Big Success," *The Capital Times*, July 29, 2004, *http://www.madison.com*; "Organic Valley Posts Record Level Pay Price to Farmers," *OFARM*, December 30, 2003, *http://www.ofarm.org*; Organic Valley press kit.

CHAPTER 6: ORGANIC VALLEY GROWS UP

Every business starts small. Sometimes it begins in a garage or a basement. Sometimes it starts in a small storefront. Organic Valley Cooperative planted its seeds in the lands and barns of half a dozen family farmers in Wisconsin nearly 20 years ago. And despite the alarming trend in which more than 6 million U.S. family farms have closed during this time period, Organic Valley is growing. Starting a business like this, building it, and growing into a larger organization is a process filled with all kinds of challenges and setbacks. The conventional challenges include the search for financial resources, an uncertain market, potential competitors, changing regulations, and issues of supply and demand. But farming comes with its own set of potential setbacks—drought, flooding, tornadoes, and disease among animals, just to name a few. Organic Valley has managed to face these challenges and grow from a few dairy farms to more than 630 organic farms on 100,000 acres in 16 states across the United States. Here is how they did it.

Driven by their belief that food—meat, produce, and dairy products—should be free of pesticides, antibiotics, and synthetic hormones, the first group of Organic Valley farmers set up a cooperative with an office in tiny LaFarge, Wisconsin, whose population is still less than 800. Even as a small group, Organic Valley was able to provide a consistent, stable price to farmers for their products, particularly milk. This consistency allowed the farmers to pay off debts and grow their own businesses. The cooperative obtained financing from bank loans and private stock that was available to select investors (mostly the cooperative farmers themselves), with set returns on profits. As more and more farmers joined the cooperative— and as consumer demand for organic products increased—sales increased, organizational staff increased by 30 to 50 employees per year, and ultimately the cooperative itself needed more office space.

Committed to remaining in LaFarge, Organic Valley searched for ways to expand. LaFarge is so small that there isn't much land available to lease or buy, so the cooperative spread out among mobile office trailers, houses, the town community center, an unused feed mill, and several abandoned business offices around town. Since the cooperative didn't have a single room that could accommodate more than twelve people, it had to rent a room from the town for larger meetings. Workers were scattered around town, packed into tiny rooms, riding bicycles from office to office when they needed to meet with each other. But

this fragmented, frugal way of doing business bought Organic Valley time—and money—to build a real headquarters. And just when it seemed that the cooperative was about to burst at the seams, construction on One Organic Way in LaFarge was completed.

The new office looks like a barn. The 49,210-square-foot structure also has plenty of room for more growth. Constructed of many recycled materials, it contains a state-of-the-art energy recovery system that exchanges warm and cool air throughout the building, as well as systems for using natural light and solar power. As the staffers pour in and spread out, enjoying their new-found elbow room, Organic Valley plans to hire even more employees, helping to bolster the local economy. Employees now get to enjoy organic foods served in the cafeteria, a mile-long nature path around the property, and locker rooms with showers. They still ride bikes as their major on-site transportation—but now it is for fun.

There are some risks involved in Organic Valley's growth. For example, other businesses aren't stampeding LaFarge to join the cooperative's lead. So if the cooperative falters or fails, or if Organic Valley decides to leave town, the $5.9 million headquarters has little or no resale or rental value. And agriculture is always a risky business. But Organic Valley's founders, members, and investors already know this. Organic Valley's CEO George Siemon sums it up by saying that in business, entrepreneurs must be prepared for three things: what happens if they are wildly successful, what happens if they are moderately successful, and what happens if they fail. If they are ready for all three, they'll do all right.

Questions

1. Farmers are natural entrepreneurs. What personal traits would you say Organic Valley's farmers must have in order to succeed?

2. Two methods of financing were mentioned in the case. What other types of financing might Organic Valley and its farmers obtain?

3. At what stage of growth would you place Organic Valley, according to Exhibit 6.9 in the chapter? Why?

SOURCES: Company Web site, *http://www.organicvalley.coop*; accessed August 2, 2004; Judy Ettenhofer, "Organic Valley a Big Success," *The Capital Times*, July 29, 2004, *http://www.madison.com*; "Organic Valley to Hold Ribbon-Cutting Ceremony for New $5.9 Million Green Design Headquarters," press release, July 20, 2004, *http://www.organicvalley.coop*; "Organic Valley Posts Record Level Pay Price to Farmers," *OFARM*, December 30, 2003, *http://www.ofarm.org/news*.

CHAPTER 7: TIMBUK2: THE MESSAGE IS IN THE BAG

Picture yourself on a bike, weaving in and out of city traffic, pedaling as fast as you can through a maze of streets, dodging taxicabs and pedestrians, carrying your cargo on your back. Now picture yourself making dozens of deliveries in a day, pedaling an eight- or nine-hour shift in blazing sun, pouring rain, stinging sleet, or even blowing snow. This is the life of a bicycle messenger. Timbuk2, founded in San Francisco more than 15 years ago by former bicycle messenger Rob Honeycutt, manufactures what seems to be a specialized product: messenger bags for cyclists who make their living delivering documents door to door. Today, Timbuk2 still manufactures professional bags for bike messengers. But the firm has expanded its offerings to include fashion bags for other consumers—and its goals and plans are much broader than they were fifteen years ago.

"Our goal for the future is to remain faithful to our working-class urban roots, while expanding our unique qualities and design sensibilities to a broader range of products and a wider audience," states Timbuk2's Web site. Mark Dwight, CEO of the firm, echoes this sentiment. Dwight's job as CEO is to focus on the big picture—overall goals and how to achieve them. "The difference between strategy and goals is, goals are the endpoint and strategy is the way to get there. The actual steps you take would be the tactics," Dwight explains. Timbuk2's current goal is to move from a tiny, specialized market into a broader market. "Our roots are in the bicycle messenger market . . . a subculture that is very interesting. . . . However, it isn't really a market; there's no growth there. So what we're trying to do is build from that heritage, that authenticity that gives value to our brand as a lifestyle brand," says Dwight.

Formulating the strategies to achieve the goals requires careful planning. "We are building a lifestyle brand; we are [also] trying to build brand equity because that ultimately is the value of this company," notes Dwight. "Then, when we go to sell the company or take it public, there's value there." So every effort, from the development of new products to the marketing of existing ones, focuses on strengthening the Timbuk2 brand in consumers' minds. Dwight and his staff plan to "develop a product portfolio that asserts our position in existing markets, moves into new markets, and really creates a sense of lifestyle . . . so when you think of Timbuk2 . . . you think of an emotional concept, a brand, a lifestyle."

Timbuk2 is already moving rapidly toward its goals. Sit in on a Timbuk2 planning meeting, and you'll hear lots of ideas and opinions flying back and forth—how to design a new bag, how to market it, how to offer it over the Web. "I don't want to see any of this hardware," says Dwight, pointing to a sketch in one design meeting. "That's Coach. We're not Coach." When reminded that chrome hardware is popular among today's consumers, he does not back down. He wants Timbuk2's bags to have a look that is distinctive. So far, they have managed to offer a variety of bags for a variety of needs—without chrome hardware. Consumers can pick up a water-resistant bag with quick-release buckles that allow yoga followers to snap out their practice mats with ease, weatherproof travel bags with destination stickers superimposed on the flaps, and colorful, messenger-style laptop computer bags for commuters who want to blend durability with style. The bags don't come cheap; with the addition of custom features, consumers can pay $100 or more for their Timbuk2 bags. But a good purse or travel bag from another maker can cost just as much or more.

Timbuk2 hasn't forgotten bicycle messengers, even with its new focus. The professionals can still visit the Timbuk2 Web site and "build" customized professional bags—selecting from four different sizes, several fabrics, and an array of colors. In addition, as part of a celebration of the firm's heritage, Timbuk2 has planned to collaborate with Joe Urich, San Francisco bike messenger and design student at the California College of Arts (CCA), to design two new, industrial-strength messenger bags for his colleagues. These new bags will be designed specifically to meet requirements of working messengers. "I hope it goes well," says Urich. The project should succeed—after all, who knows better how to design a messenger bag than the messenger himself?

Questions

1. Do Timbuk2's goals have the characteristics of effective goals? Why or why not?
2. Does Timbuk2 represents a high performance approach to planning? Why or why not?
3. Using what you know about Timbuk2, write a brief mission statement for the organization.

SOURCES: Company Web site, *http://www.tumbuk2.com,* accessed August 13, 2004; "Timbuk2's Groovy Bag," *Yoga Journal,* July/August 2004, *http://www.yogajournal com;* Larry Armstrong, "Green with Envy," *BusinessWeek,* [no pub info], *http://www.businessweek.com;* "In Style Every Mile," Organic Style, May 2004, *www.organicstyle.com.*

CHAPTER 8: TIMBUK2: MAKE THE SWIRL AS FAMOUS AS THE SWOOSH

"We want to make the *Swirl* as famous as the *Swoosh*," says Timbuk2's CEO Mark Dwight with a chuckle. While he may be joking by comparing his firm's logo to the Nike *Swoosh,* Dwight isn't kidding. When Dwight took over as head of Timbuk2 a few years ago, the company was on a downward slide, losing money because it had only one product to offer to a narrow market—a bag for bicycle messengers. Granted, the bag came in several sizes and colors—but Dwight realized that Timbuk2 couldn't survive, let alone grow, on the strength of one messenger bag. So Dwight and his managers developed corporate- and business-level strategies to achieve the goal of turning the company around and then achieving growth: increasing and broadening the product line to reach into new markets, developing the brand while remaining true to the company's heritage, finding new distribution channels, creating alliances with other firms, and outsourcing some production to maintain quality but reduce costs.

To achieve the sales goal of $25 million in five years, the Timbuk2 design, production, and marketing teams set about developing new products. Meanwhile, the sales staff renewed their efforts with Timbuk2's existing bags and customers. The expanded product line now includes yoga bags, CD cases, travel bags, duffels, graphic-arts totes, and laptop/commuter bags, among others. "We now have a [product] portfolio that you can shake the trees with," says Geoff Sacco. "It's not just about asking customers, 'Can you buy some more messenger bags?'" More products means more potential sales to more markets. For instance, a chic traveler might want to carry a Timbuk2 bag; a yoga student might choose a Timbuk2 bag for her yoga mat, water bottle, and other gear; a cyclist might choose the new Shortcut, a convertible waist pack that contains easy-access pockets and reflective patches for night riding.

However, Mark Dwight and his staff are determined to remain true to Timbuk2's original customers, the bicycle messengers. They are the firm's long-standing customers, and Dwight wants to be careful not to leave them behind. To that end, Timbuk2 is developing the new professional messenger bag called the Tag Junkie—referring to a term used by messengers—in collaboration with a California design student who also happens to be a bike messenger. Whenever new designs are reviewed in meetings, Dwight and his staff discuss the elements of a bag that make it stand out as a Timbuk2 brand—so that each bag is consistent with the image of the Timbuk2 brand.

Developing new distribution channels is an important strategy for Timbuk2. One is the Internet. The firm's Web site is already profitable, so building on that strength makes sense. A current popular feature of the site is "Build Your Own Bag," where customers can combine sizes, fabrics, colors, and features to create their own customized bags.

Developing products that can be used successfully with other firms' products is a creative strategy. Recently, Timbuk2 has begun manufacturing bags specifically to fit Apple laptops—much to the delight of Apple users. One reviewer who tried the Commute XL Laptop Messenger Bag for his Apple Macintosh 17" Powerbook was pleased with several features, including the strap, padded back, durable construction (a Timbuk2 hallmark), and waterproof interior (making it a good all-weather commuter bag).

Timbuk2's decision to outsource production of some of its bags to China—most are made in a factory near the company's offices in San Francisco—drew criticism from a few customers. However, the firm defended the move by explaining that doing so actually allowed the San Francisco factory to remain open and active. The laptop bags, explains their Web site, "are much more complex to build and require substantially more labor and a variety of very expensive machines we don't have here in our factory." So the bags are made in China to strict quality specifications—and can be sold in the United States at a more reasonable price.

To make certain that each of these strategies is being implemented effectively, Mark Dwight meets weekly with his management staff and daily with his operations staff. We "look at performance on an ongoing basis," says Dwight. "How do I know if we picked the right strategy? The results that we've seen so far indicate that we're on the right path. There are examples of other [firms] that have done the same thing and they created substantial, lasting enterprises on this strategy."

Questions

1. In which category would you place Timbuk2's grand strategy? Why?
2. How would you define Timbuk2's core competency?
3. Identify one strength, weakness, opportunity, and threat for Timbuk2.

SOURCES: Company Web site, *http://www.timbuk2.com,* accessed August 13, 2004; "Timbuk2—New Stuff," *Cross Country Skier,* January 2004, *http://www.findarticles.com*; product review, *mymac.com,* January 2004, *http://www.mymac.com.*

Chapter 9: Timbuk2: CEO Sets a Course

Making decisions is a big part of any manager's job. Making the decisions that determine the direction a company will take is the job of a CEO. Mark Dwight, CEO of Timbuk2, is comfortable with this role, even though it means sometimes making unpopular decisions—or even making mistakes. Timbuk2's 45 workers tend to be young, so Dwight sees himself as the senior manager in more ways than one. "I'm the experienced executive here, and it's my charter to manage the company," he explains. "It's not a democracy. I ask the people that I think have a good perspective on [an] issue, who are affected by the issue, we discuss it, and I make a command decision based on those inputs. Hopefully, people think I make educated, informed decisions. That's my job."

Most of the decisions Dwight is referring to are nonprogrammed decisions—such as the design of a new product or the type of fabric to use. These decisions can affect sales, the brand image, and even the overall performance of the company. During one recent meeting on the new Tag Junkie bags (whose working name may be changed, requiring another decision), Dwight and his managerial staff discussed whether to invest in a costly, high-performance fabric for the bag. The cost of the fabric could potentially put the price of the bag out of reach for the average professional bike messenger. But in talking about it, the group speculated that the bag could successfully reach the motorcycle market. With night reflectors and highly durable, weatherproof fabric, the bag could be very appealing to motorcyclists—and could be offered at a higher price. Then the group discussed the working name of the product line—Tag Junkie, a term used by bike messengers and also the name of the original Timbuk2 messenger bag. Did they want to resurrect the name for the final product or try something new? The group tossed around the name Pro Series—and everyone liked the ring of it. "It sounds fast," observed marketing manager Macy Allatt. But the decision was not yet final, since the group wanted to weigh the consequences of a name change in the bike messenger market.

"Mark is the guy with the vision," says Allatt. "He will drive the decision making, but he's very open to taking input from other people. When decisions need to be made, everyone sits down and we hash it out, and when we come out of the room, we feel like we're going to make some progress."

Just about every decision facing Mark Dwight has some degree of uncertainty. He knows that he wants Timbuk2 to achieve $25 million in sales in five years; he knows he wants the firm to reach new markets such as motorcycle riders and yet rejuvenate the bike messenger market; he knows the firm needs to find new distribution channels. But there's no guarantee that a single decision is the right one. Still, Dwight believes he is ultimately responsible for deciding which way to go. "We have to make a decision and move on," he remarks. "Sometimes we make mistakes, but it's better to move to a new place than sit around and talk about it." One recent decision involved moving the production of certain bags to China to cut production costs. Despite receiving criticism for the move, particularly because so many textile factories surrounding Timbuk2's hometown of San Francisco have been closed, Dwight hung tight to his decision, insisting that transferring some production overseas would actually help the San Francisco factory stay open. So far, Dwight has been able to maintain the San Francisco plant. Increased orders for the firm's artistic Graphic Messenger Bags have actually resulted in hiring more employees at the San Francisco facility.

As a leader, Dwight doesn't mind taking the heat. "I'm a strong personality. . . . It's my job to call the shots, and I can be very dictatorial about it." If he's right, future success for Timbuk2 is in the bag.

Questions

1. What part do you think intuition plays in Mark Dwight's decision making? Why?
2. How would you categorize Dwight's leadership participation style on the Vroom-Jago model? Why?
3. Which of the new "decision approaches for turbulent times" that are described in the chapter does Dwight use?

SOURCES: Company Web site, *http://www.timbuk2.com,* accessed August 13, 2004; Brad Stone, "Homegrown," *Newsweek,* April 19, 2004, *http://www.msnbc.com.*

CHAPTER 10: LONELY PLANET: STRUCTURE THAT MAKES SENSE

When travelers Tony and Maureen Wheeler founded Lonely Planet in the early 1970s, they didn't intend to create a globe-spanning company. They didn't necessarily plan to start a publishing company. As newlyweds, they had just completed an overland trip from London through Asia, winding up in Australia. All they really wanted to do was finance their next trip—it never occurred to them to stop traveling around the world. So they wrote and published the first Lonely Planet guidebook, *Across Asia on the Cheap;* it was an instant best-seller among world wanderers.

With just two people, the Wheelers naturally didn't think about organization. They traveled, wrote, and published whatever they wanted. By the mid 1970s, they had completed *Nepal and Trekking in the Himalayas* and were working on a group of guides covering Australia, Europe, Africa, and New Zealand. In 1981, *Lonely Planet India* was published and became a travel best-seller. By then, Lonely Planet had a staff of ten. It was time to get organized.

Today, Lonely Planet publishes more than 650 guidebooks, including specialized activity guides, "shoestring" or budget guides, international food guides, and phrasebooks. The firm is still owned by the Wheelers, employing 400 workers in offices in Melbourne; London; Paris; and Oakland, California. In addition, there are about 150 authors traveling and writing around the world. Lonely Planet has people to create maps, take photos, design book covers, sell books, and create marketing campaigns. There are also finance people and people who work with and manage the freelancers who are roaming the world. Managing all of these activities in four countries on three continents requires communication and coordination.

For example, each office is responsible for all sales and marketing efforts for its own region in order to address cultural and other environmental differences. In addition, a regional warehouse distributes all of that office's book titles to booksellers within the geographical area. Because Lonely Planet publishes books about world travel, having a presence in several key countries enhances the firm's credibility among readers. This organization gives the individual offices more flexibility in directing marketing messages to specific audiences and ensures that workers in each office know their region thoroughly. In addition, one of Lonely Planet's greatest assets is its local writers, according to David Zingarelli, managing editor for Lonely Planet USA. Being able to meet with them in person and cultivate a relationship is a great advantage. Despite their relative independence, the offices must communicate with each other. So, managers rely on the Internet for regular communication and to create consistency among marketing messages.

Although regional offices may commission books for their areas—Lonely Planet USA commissions all the books for North and South America, as well as Central America—the headquarters in Australia actually produces all of the books. This centralization streamlines the production process, reduces costs by keeping cartographers and designers under one roof, and ensures that the books are designed and produced in a consistent fashion. In addition, negotiations with the printers in Hong Kong are more efficient and effective if they are conducted from a single location.

People who work at Lonely Planet love to travel, and they like the way the company is organized. "It's got all the excitement of working for a multinational . . . but without any of the . . . complexity of bureaucracy," explains one employee. "Working with other offices—Melbourne, Paris, London—as a global company and still being independently owned" is a positive experience, notes another. "It's a large company, but it's really small," he continues. Tony and Maureen Wheeler are still very much a presence in the company, visiting its worldwide offices and maintaining contact with many employees. There are some drawbacks to this far-flung method of managing; sometimes staffers grumble about the challenges of dealing with time differences, but they concede that this is a minor inconvenience. After all, if you work at a travel publisher because you love to travel, think about the possibilities. Perhaps you'll work in Australia this year and Paris next year. Maybe you've got the urge to set up shop in London. At Lonely Planet, there's almost always an opportunity to hit the road—and get paid for it.

Questions

1. In what ways is Lonely Planet decentralized? In what ways is it centralized?

2. Does Lonely Planet have a tall structure or a flat structure? Explain briefly.

3. In what ways does Lonely Planet achieve horizontal coordination across departments or offices?

SOURCES: Company Web site, *http://www.lonelyplanet.com,* accessed July 30, 2004; Lonely Planet press kit.

CHAPTER 11: ORIGINAL PENGUIN SPREADS ITS WINGS

Change is hard for companies—especially for large companies, which have large numbers of people and systems to manage. But in many cases, change can be positive, especially when it is in response to an opportunity for growth. Chris Kolbe is a master of change. Now vice president of Original Penguin, Chris essentially runs the division for its parent company, Perry Ellis International. He got there by finding himself in the unique position of rediscovering a languishing bird—and bringing it back to life.

Original Penguin was a 1950s icon—the penguin logo appeared on Munsingwear Penguin knit sport shirts for men, mostly golfers. Eventually, its popularity faded, and Perry Ellis International later acquired the brand. Chris Kolbe was working in merchandising at retailer Urban Outfitters when he conceived the idea of rejuvenating the penguin—but with a new twist and for a new market. Starting with a few new shirts, which sold out almost immediately, the "new" Original Penguin began to grow, and Perry Ellis tapped Kolbe to complete the transformation as head of a new venture team.

Despite the fact that the Original Penguin flagship store in New York boasts an oversized vintage photo of Kolbe's family, including his father wearing one of the "original" Munsingwear Penguin golf shirts, Kolbe recognizes that the fashion industry is a hotbed of change—and any clothing company that wants to survive must embrace innovation. "The fashion business is a young business," observes Kolbe. "It's about having fresh ideas. . . . What can happen is, if you stop having those brands in your pipeline, things start to dry up. . . . We realized Penguin could be one of those brands." So Kolbe and his team have focused on designs and clothing items that appeal to a younger market, both men and women, between the ages of 17 and 30.

While Kolbe could certainly be called the idea champion for this project, he does not work alone. He has a team of highly creative fashion-industry professionals, including David Bedwell, Creative Director. "We changed the brand a bit to really reach out to a different market today than maybe the market it was reaching in the past . . . yet keeping a classic twist on it," says Bedwell.

Consumers who wander into the new Original Penguin store will find an entire line of trendy, yet classic clothing and accessories. "We try to create an environment that our clothes will live in," explains Bedwell. Store displays show quirky, unconventional clothing combinations—such as a striped top with plaid pants. And visitors may wander through the "garden" or the "bedroom" to look at different outfits. Yes, shoppers can still buy knit sport shirts—in new colors and designs—but they can also pick up belts, shoes, and even bikinis.

If it sounds as though Kolbe and his team have free rein from Perry Ellis, they don't. Instead, they have a loose rein. They have a great deal of freedom to take risks, be creative, and make decisions. But Perry Ellis is taking the ultimate risk, and Kolbe knows that. The company does require regular updates on key financial and sales numbers. "The best thing about being young is you don't know the odds you're up against. . . . The risk for Perry Ellis was equally significant because they finance everything," says Kolbe.

Kolbe envisions the current fashion lines as the beginning of more innovation for Original Penguin and Perry Ellis. He also understands that change takes time and patience. "It takes a couple of years to see results, so it takes a certain amount of perseverance," he acknowledges. But he is excited about the future. "We've been able to bring a lot of influence and fresh ideas to a company that was searching. You can start to be a catalyst for a larger business."

Questions

1. In what ways might creativity be designed into the Original Penguin division of Perry Ellis International?

2. Why has it been important for Perry Ellis to give freedom to a new venture team in order to relaunch Original Penguin?

3. In what respects does Original Penguin represent a cultural change for Perry Ellis?

SOURCE: Company Web site, *http://www.originalpenguin.com*, accessed July 30, 2004.

CHAPTER 12: PEPSICO PUTS PEOPLE FIRST

Whether a company employs five or five thousand people, its greatest resource is those workers. Many of today's companies view their workforces as part of their overall competitive strategy—the best people producing the best products. Human resource managers at large firms such as PepsiCo may be viewed as strategic business partners. No longer do they simply sign paychecks, approve vacations, and process health benefit claims. At PepsiCo, HR managers play an integral role in the day-to-day success of the business.

Headquartered in Purchase, New York, PepsiCo is a global organization, with more than 143,000 employees worldwide. The company produces and markets such brands as PepsiCo beverages, Frito-Lay snacks, Gatorade and Tropicana drinks, and Quaker Foods. PepsiCo brand products are available in nearly 200 countries and territories. But recruiting, selecting, training, and managing more than 100,000 workers requires planning to meet the career needs of so many people. To foster long-term career growth, PepsiCo offers a variety of programs and has created its own PepsiCo Career Growth Model, which offers job opportunities to promote employees' knowledge and skills, and abilities in leadership capability, functional excellence, knowing the business, and critical experiences.

PepsiCo's HR managers follow their own Human Resources Competency Model, which defines four key roles played by the HR department:

- As a *strategic partner,* the HR department is charged with aligning the human resource strategy with the business strategy of PepsiCo.

- As a *change agent,* the department focuses on facilitating and leading organization transformation and change initiatives.

- As a *technical functional expert,* the HR department emphasizes mastering and driving efficiency and effectiveness in the core information and administrative processes.

- As an *employee champion,* the department drives employee satisfaction, commitment, and engagement.

Both of these models indicate a high degree of structure within PepsiCo, and the structure helps ensure that everyone's career, benefits, and other needs are met. Employees have a choice of flexible benefits. At Quaker Oats, workers may select time off for adoption, apply for a student loan, or take a leave of absence under the QuakerFlex benefits program.

At many locations, they may even enjoy free oatmeal in the morning!

Regardless of job level or brand, PepsiCo looks for the best workers to contribute to the overall performance of the company. "Excellent performance . . . does not happen on its own," writes chairman and CEO Steve Reinemund on the company's Web site. "Our people make it happen. In order to sustain this level of success, we need to ensure that we continue to attract, retain, and develop great people in all of our businesses." At PepsiCo's online Career Center, potential job candidates will find information on what the company looks for in its employees. In turn, PepsiCo offers its workers opportunities such as "exciting career challenges," "world-class training and development," and "excellent compensation." This, in essence, is PepsiCo's social contract with its employees.

Keeping all of this in mind, consider the job of Darryl Claiborne, HR manager for regional sales at PepsiCo's Frito-Lay division. Claiborne works with Frito-Lay's route sales reps, who sell and deliver their products directly to retailers. Claiborne and his reps understand that their success correlates directly with Frito-Lay's profitability. So, as an HR strategic partner, Claiborne looks for ways to help his reps manage and grow their business. Claiborne communicates regularly with his reps, on how well they are doing and where they need help. He continually reengineers their routes to make sure they can steadily increase sales. Claiborne embraces the company's "Know the Business" principles, the set of guidelines created to help managers understand the company, its mission, and the way its employees achieve success. "PepsiCo—Taste the Success!" invites the company Web site. Claiborne, his route sales reps, and more than 140,000 other employees intend to do just that.

Questions

1. In what ways could Darryl Claiborne be considered an employee champion?

2. Why is this important to PepsiCo's efforts to build human capital?

3. In essence, Darryl Claiborne engages in on-the-job training as he communicates with and accompanies his reps on their sales rounds. How is this an important part of their effectiveness as a workforce?

SOURCES: Company Web sites, *http://www.pepsico.com* and *http://www.pepsicojobs.com,* accessed August 19, 2004; PepsiCo career and HR materials, "Knowing the Business: Resources Guide" and "Career Framework: Functional Competency Model."

CHAPTER 13: DIVERSITY AT PEPSICO

Imagine trying to manage and accommodate the needs of more than 140,000 people at once. Imagine a variety of voices, languages, cultures, ethnic backgrounds, families, lifestyles, ages, and geographies all vying for attention, all bearing the name PepsiCo. That's the challenge of managers throughout PepsiCo. From the top down, PepsiCo embraces diversity and inclusion in its worldwide workforce. Top executives, including CEO Steve Reinemund, believe that nurturing diversity in the organization is not only a matter of responsible ethics but also good business. Because PepsiCo offers products to such a diverse array of customers, it makes sense for the PepsiCo workforce to mirror the market. In addition, a facility's workforce will likely reflect the local population. However, embracing a philosophy of diversity is entirely different from implementing it. Here is how PepsiCo takes on this global task.

Although some of the divisions may use different program models, the Frito-Lay North American Diversity/Inclusion Model is a good example of how PepsiCo builds a measurable framework for diversity. The model was developed so that managers could implement and track diversity programs under their jurisdictions. It addresses five key areas, ranging from "evolving the culture" to "leveraging our people systems." By following a structure, the human resource department and other managers can develop and implement specific programs to meet the needs of their employees.

One such program is the development of employee networks throughout divisions. PepsiCo's employee networks are usually grassroots groups created on the basis of a common characteristic, such as gender or ethnic background. These networks provide opportunities for support and mentoring as employees develop their careers at PepsiCo. But the networks also help PepsiCo reach its diverse customer base. Ideas for new products, marketing efforts, and other projects grow out of the employee networks. For example, a new guacamole chip came from the Hispanic employee network, Adelante. In one recent year, Frito-Lay sold $100 million Lay's guacamole chips.

Regardless of the characteristics of a particular network, all PepsiCo employee networks have similar missions and goals:

- to become business partners that are focused on key organizational issues

- to offer resources to PepsiCo based on their unique perspectives and experiences

- to pave the way for employees to grow in their careers

- to provide opportunities for group members to network with each other and business leaders

- to become ambassadors for PepsiCo, creating opportunities for community involvement

Each division sponsors its own networks, depending on its population of workers. For example, Frito-Lay has the Black Employees Association (BEA), Adelante (Hispanic employee network), Asians in Motion (AIM), EQUAL (gay, lesbian, bisexual, and transgender employee network), and Women's Initiative Network (WIN).

In addition to the formation of employee networks, PepsiCo has established a formal, three-level inclusion training program. At level 1, division presidents and their teams participate in a course that covers issues of cultural differences and similarities; components of culture such as values and communication styles; models for individual and organizational change; and exercises. Level 2 training aimed at all business managers throughout the United States businesses, is designed to provide managers with the skills to lead teams of diverse workers. It focuses on enhancing self-awareness, conducting difficult conversations, recognizing people's strengths, and managing conflict. Level 3 training is intended to reinforce the previous two levels of training for ongoing efforts to promote diversity and inclusion throughout the company.

PepsiCo believes that diversity can be harnessed as a powerful tool for growth, even during turbulent times. It's more than coming up with an idea for a new chip; it brings together groups of people who can work to meet the needs of consumers.

Questions

1. Would you describe PepsiCo as being ethnocentric, ethnorelativistic, or somewhere in between? Why?

2. Why is it important for upper-level managers at PepsiCo to receive diversity and inclusion training?

3. Do you think that PepsiCo's encouragement of employee networks actually works against diversity and the formation of multicultural teams? Why or why not?

SOURCE: Company Web site, *http://www.pepsico.com,* accessed August 16, 2004.

CHAPTER 14: CONTROL IS KEY TO PEAPOD'S ONLINE GROCERY SERVICE

Imagine a big food fight—tomatoes, peanut butter, eggs, bread flying across the room. The grocery industry is a like a food fight without the mess. It is so competitive that only the strongest survive. Now imagine trying to survive in the online grocery industry, where customers can't see, smell, or touch the goods, and they expect their orders to be accurate and arrive on time. Finally, picture being one of the few companies to ride out the original dot.com storm. Those are daunting challenges for any firm. But Peapod, the online grocery service founded in 1989 by brothers Andrew and Thomas Parkinson, is succeeding on all three fronts.

Peapod introduced a new concept 15 years ago: the convenience of shopping for groceries online. Plenty of skeptics said the idea wouldn't fly, but some consumers and businesses were intrigued and began to order their groceries online. When many dot.coms of the era began to fail, Peapod hung on. Mike Brennan, vice president of marketing for Peapod, explains that the firm was able to survive because its founders focused on controlling the quality of their goods and services, as well as their costs. Meanwhile, competitors that entered the market with far more investor funding fell by the wayside. A company called Webvan actually raised $1 billion in capital—and is nowhere to be seen today. HomeRuns.com and Streamline.com are also gone.

Quality and service have been Peapod's highest priorities since the beginning. "The biggest hurdle was convincing consumers they could shop online and still maintain control over the quality of their picks," notes CEO Marc van Gelder. "That's been Peapod's cornerstone all along. Today, customers see us for what we are: a lifestyle solution for their busy lives." Whether an order is fulfilled through one of Peapod's own freestanding warehouses or in any of its eight smaller "warerooms," which are adjacent to Peapod's supermarket partners Stop & Shop and Giant Food, it must be accurate; contain the highest quality meats, seafood, and produce; and be completed quickly. Peapod works closely with its suppliers to select the best fresh foods and store them in controlled climates to ensure the longest freshness with minimal waste.

Customer service is controlled on a daily basis. When a call comes in from a customer, it is immediately routed to the department best equipped to deal with it. If there is a problem, it is corrected within 24 hours, which reduces the number of subsequent calls. Fewer customer service calls means more satisfied customers, better service, and less money spent on staffing the customer service department.

Transportation is one of Peapod's largest costs. Mike Brennan explains that when a delivery truck goes out on a route, the costs are fixed no matter how many deliveries the truck actually makes. That's because the truck requires maintenance and fuel, and the driver needs to be paid. So, it is more cost effective to send out a truck with 10 customer orders than it is to send out the same truck with 4 orders. To control some of these fixed transportation costs, Peapod developed the Smart Mile program, which sets a minimum number of deliveries each truck must make. Under the program, each truck must have on board between 14 and 25 deliveries before it can leave the distribution center. However, Peapod must still coordinate delivery times with its customers, or its service will begin to falter. That's why Peapod offers customers a discount in delivery fees if they agree to choose certain time slots. Mike Brennan believes that the Smart Mile program is vital to Peapod's profitability and ultimate success.

Finally, Peapod's growth must be controlled. Although the firm is still based in Chicago, it has expanded into markets where its grocery partners are located. Peapod began serving the Washington, D.C., area several years ago, in partnership with Giant Food. Recently, delivery was expanded to the Baltimore area, making the service available to nearly 250,000 additional households. With industry research revealing that online grocery shopping is a growing trend, Peapod plans to grow, too. By keeping its costs, quality, and service in control, this dot.com survivor could win the ultimate food fight.

Questions

1. What types of feedforward controls might Peapod use in the next few years?

2. Using the feedback control model, identify at least two standards that Peapod might establish.

3. Do you think decentralized control would be effective at Peapod? Why or why not?

SOURCES: Company Web site, *http://www.peapod.com*, accessed September 8, 2004; "Peapod Grocery Delivery Service Coming to Baltimore," *Baltimore Business Journal*, August 11, 2004, *http://baltimore. bizjournals.com*; "Online Groceries Keep Expanding, Quietly," *MSNBC News*, May 16, 2004, *http://www.msnbc.com*; "Online Grocery Shopping Finally Becoming Profitable," *Food & Drink Weekly*, April 28, 2003, *http://www. findarticles.com*.

CHAPTER 15: PEAPOD TAKES GROCERY SHOPPING ONLINE

It's hard to imagine a time before e-commerce. The dot.com boom and bust seems to be ancient history, particularly because so many start-up firms didn't survive. But a few of them did, and one that not only survived—but thrived—is a company with the unlikely name of Peapod. Peapod was founded in 1989 by brothers Andrew and Thomas Parkinson, several years before the dot.com boom began. Both brothers stayed with the firm after its sale to Royal Ahold. Thomas Parkinson remains with the company today as its chief technology officer (CTO) and vice president. Peapod offers consumers a relatively simple service—online grocery shopping with delivery—but its success depends on a great deal more.

Peapod wouldn't exist without Internet technology, the vehicle for e-commerce. But this technology alone isn't enough for a business to run smoothly, satisfy customers, and grow. Thomas Parkinson explains that Peapod isn't selling goods, or whiz-bang technology; it sells time to busy consumers. A customer who logs onto Peapod for grocery shopping spends an average of 15 minutes instead of the 1 to 2 hours usually spent at the local supermarket. That's a huge savings of time. It means that a parent with a sick child doesn't have to leave home to shop for groceries, that a professional with a deadline doesn't have to take time off work to buy food, or that a person without a car doesn't have to wait for public transportation.

How does the typical shopping experience at Peapod work? The Peapod Web site is set up to guide new visitors through the process with ease. On the second visit, shoppers encounter a different interface that streamlines the process. Subsequent visits are tailored to meet the needs of each customer, with coupons, targeted marketing messages, and the like. Registered shoppers may receive e-mail reminders and other direct-mail promotions. When shoppers are ready to check out, they have the option to pay by credit card or with an electronic check that automatically withdraws the correct amount from an authorized checking account. Either choice is convenient for the customer.

Parkinson explains that Peapod's information technology (IT) department continually tries to balance a streamlined interface with a sophisticated one that provides loyal customers with more options. For example, customers can select thick or thin deli slices, or yellow or green bananas. They can browse through weekly specials or supermarket "aisles," read recipes, or find out about new products. In the end, however, speed and simplicity are the highest priorities, because those features are valued most by customers. Even those who are on strictly regulated diets, such as low sugar or low carbohydrates, can use a special search tool to streamline their selection process so they don't have to scroll through endless foods they don't need or want. The site also increases the efficiency of grocery shopping by creating a list of previously purchased items—a kind of ongoing grocery list. Consumers can access the list and check off the items they need. Then they can add or subtract from the order until the night before their order is scheduled to be delivered. In addition, the IT team is working on technology that will remind regular customers when to replenish milk or eggs or cat food.

Skeptics who can't imagine ordering fresh tomatoes, sirloin steak, or milk online because they can't squeeze or sniff or see the goods may be surprised when they visit the Peapod site for the first time. Parkinson says his team's goal is to make the site as "luscious" as the real thing. Shoppers can scroll through delicious photos of inventory—colorful produce, protein-rich meats, fresh-baked bread. When they realize they can have any of those products with a click of the mouse, they're sold.

Questions

1. What type of data might the Peapod IT department obtain about consumers who visit the Web site?
2. In what ways might Peapod managers use a decision-support system?
3. In what ways might Peapod use a CRM system to maintain its competitive advantage in the marketplace?

SOURCE: Company Web site, *http://www.peapod.com*; accessed September 8, 2004.

CHAPTER 16: PEAPOD DELIVERS CONVENIENCE AND QUALITY

From the company's beginning, Peapod cofounder Thomas Parkinson insisted that his firm's Web site be inviting—packed with images of bright carrots, fresh-baked bread, deep red tomatoes, flavorful beef. But none of these images would have credibility if the food delivered to customers who shopped online at Peapod didn't live up to expectations. All it would take to turn a customer away from placing a second order would be one overripe banana, one slightly gray piece of meat, or a carton of ice cream with freezer burn. So Peapod has to get it right the first time and every time.

Peapod decided to start from the ground up, designing and building a state-of-the art warehouse for its fresh-foods inventory. The company hired Tony Stallone, vice president of Fresh Markets, to handle the process. Stallone has worked with produce for 40 years, and his family has been in the produce business for a century. This history made him a good choice for Peapod. Stallone also happens to be a stickler for perfection. When the warehouse design plans were nearly finalized and the financing secured, he stopped everything. He informed Peapod's executives that the warehouse needed a "pepper room" because peppers, cucumbers, and other vegetables need to be kept in a consistent 45-degree temperature to maintain their freshness and avoid mold. Peapod's executives ordered the pepper room.

Peapod's two freestanding, 75,000-square-foot warehouses located in Illinois and Maryland now contain five separate refrigerated areas designated exclusively for produce. Bananas and bread share their own room—and it's not because they both begin with the letter *b*. It's because they both require the exact same conditions. Strawberries, grapes, and melons are stored in another area. Tomatoes and other vegetables that do best at warmer temperatures are in still another room. Each room is set to a specific temperature and humidity level, so produce items ripen more slowly and therefore stay fresh longer. Produce sold in traditional grocery stores is usually kept at room temperature so that consumers can examine each item. But that is not optimal for the fruits and vegetables, and much of this produce will ripen and go bad quickly. Stallone notes that Peapod's new customers are surprised at how long their produce lasts—usually a week after delivery. Once they experience this kind of value, they come back for more. Being able to serve customers well—offering greater convenience and

more superior products than the conventional supermarket—is a great source of pride for Stallone and Peapod's managers.

Produce isn't the only product that gets special treatment from Peapod. Frozen foods such as ice cream, frozen yogurt, popsicles, and frozen juices all get their own freezer area to ensure that nothing melts or softens. The company has a separate section for frozen dinners, pizza, vegetables, and the like. "Our warehouses and warerooms maintain different climate zones for each food category," explains Peapod CEO Marc van Gelder. "It is quality assurance that frozen items like ice cream will arrive rock hard but that delicate perishables like produce won't."

Part of managing operations successfully is keeping costs down. In the produce business, waste is typically a significant contributor to costs. But at Peapod, Stallone and his staff keep waste to a minimum by selecting the very best produce and storing it in optimal conditions. Achieving this high quality also requires developing good relationships with distributors who cull the best products from those available on the market. In addition, Peapod partners with two major supermarket chains, Giant Food and Stop & Shop, to fulfill orders quickly and efficiently. Peapod and its supermarket partners operate special warerooms—smaller than warehouses—adjacent to the supermarkets themselves so that customers get the same quality and value they receive when orders are filled from the giant Peapod warehouses.

Peapod's operations—from pepper room to wareroom—are tied closely to customer service. When shoppers click onto Peapod's Web site, they can be assured that they will receive the best bananas, broccoli, and bread available today.

Questions

1. How does Peapod combine characteristics of manufacturing and service organizations?

2. At which stage would you place Peapod in the evolution of operations strategy? Why?

3. Peapod has two freestanding warehouses and eight warerooms located in the Midwest, Mid-Atlantic, and southern New England states. What factors might the firm's managers consider in selecting a site for a new warehouse or wareroom in California?

SOURCE: Company Web site, *http://www.peapod.com,* accessed September 8, 2004; "Peapod Grocery Delivery Service Coming to Baltimore," *Baltimore Business Journal,* August 11, 2004.

CHAPTER 17: P.F. CHANG SERVES ITS WORKERS WELL

Have you ever sat down in a restaurant and immediately thought, "This place is great?" You can tell by the atmosphere that diners are happy and staff members enjoy their jobs. Your server seems genuinely glad to see you. On the flip side, you've probably been to at least one restaurant where the staff was rushed or surly, the service slow—and you don't even recall the food because the service was so poor. You're likely to return to the first restaurant and recommend it to others. However, you're unlikely to give the second restaurant another chance. Restaurant managers face the challenge every day of putting the right person in the right job, creating a team that works well together, fostering positive work attitudes, and helping employees manage stress. Managers at P.F. Chang's, which owns and operates 97 full-service, casual dining Asian bistros and 33 contemporary Chinese diners across the country, greet these challenges with gusto.

Founded in 1993, P.F. Chang's prides itself in being able to offer "fresh, contemporary, and consistently outstanding" fare at every one of its restaurants. Selections of rice, noodles, grains, dumplings, vegetables, meat, poultry, and seafood are served at each restaurant, with mixtures of traditional Chinese foods and innovative dishes from Southeast Asia. P.F. Chang's strives to create an exceptional dining experience for every customer—and that includes a friendly, knowledgeable staff. Whether guests choose the full-service casual dining experience at P.F. Chang's bistros or the quick-service, limited-menu option of the Pei Wei Asian diners, they receive the same high quality of food and service.

How does an organization this large—and spread out—foster positive attitudes and high performance among its workers? Roxanne Pronk, Regional Vice President of Operations, explains P.F. Chang's approach. First, she notes, restaurant workers are typically young, working for hourly wages (and tips), and struggling to establish themselves in their lives and careers. So, when they arrive at work, they are not necessarily thinking about the needs of customers but are thinking about themselves. According to Pronk, most restaurants deal with these problems through the use of discipline and negative reinforcement—which results in unhappy employees and a high degree of turnover. But P.F. Chang's takes a different approach. If a worker begins to exhibit a pattern of poor behavior, such as arriving late to work, his or her manager sits down with the employee, asks whether everything is all right and how the manager might be able to help turn things around. Pronk notes that this caring and respectful treatment has a profound effect on workers' attitudes about their jobs.

By treating employees with respect, restaurant managers find that they can expect more from their staffs—and get it. Unlike many hourly restaurant employees, those at P.F. Chang's have the authority to make decisions that benefit customers. For example, if a customer is dissatisfied with a meal, the server has the authority to offer a replacement or a free meal. If a customer requests butter—which is not an ingredient found in Asian cuisine—the server can ask a busboy to run to the nearest market to buy butter for the customer's meal. Giving employees the freedom to make decisions has had a huge impact on their attitude and performance, says Pronk. Of course, workers are also held accountable for their behavior and their performance, but they welcome the responsibility.

Managers at P.F. Chang's restaurant receive extensive training in how to create and nurture a positive attitude among their employees, and all workers receive an employee handbook, which clearly spells out exactly what is expected of them. In addition, every work shift at P.F. Chang's begins with a staff meeting which acts as a sort of pep rally to motivate workers to head into their shifts with an upbeat outlook.

The Chang's culture is made up of trust, respect, accountability, commitment, and passion. "We believe that every employee and member of our management team must embody our messages as well as our values," explains the Web site. That's a recipe for some delicious dining.

Questions

1. Managers at P.F. Chang's address the affective component of workers' attitudes. Why is this an important step for them to take?

2. In what ways does P.F. Chang's create organizational commitment among its workers?

3. How might a manager at P.F. Chang's use the Big Five personality factors to assess whether a candidate for a position on the wait staff would be suitable?

SOURCES: Company Web site, *http://www.pfchangs.com,* accessed August 26, 2004; "Work Force Still Top Concern for CEOs," *The Phoenix Business Journal,* May 24, 2004, *http://phoenix.bizjournals.com.*

CHAPTER 18: LEADERSHIP AT P.F. CHANG'S

How do you manage 97 bistros and 33 diners at once? This isn't a riddle, it is actually the daily challenge of Rick Federico, chairman and CEO of P.F. Chang's, which owns and operates a chain of Asian restaurants across the country. During the time he has been head of the company, Federico has taken on the huge tasks of taking the company public and launching Pei Wei, the firm's chain of diners. In addition, he has developed management teams and laid out clear expectations for his employees. He has earned the respect of his managers, his workers, his customers, and even his competitors. He has won accolades and leadership awards. "Rick has done a great job of building a strong team culture and has built an organization that is based upon quality of execution," notes one colleague. "He has built P.F. Chang's into a concept that is craved and loved by its customers and team members." These characteristics are the attributes of a leader.

Rick Federico knows the restaurant industry. He began his career as a dishwasher for a steak house and worked his way up the management chain. So he understands everyone's job, from busboy to chef to manager. Perhaps that is why he feels comfortable fostering a team atmosphere at P.F. Chang's, giving employees the authority to make decisions to please customers and ultimately benefit the restaurant. And because he has so many contacts throughout the industry, he is able to attract the best staff, from hourly employees to restaurant managers. At the same time, he maintains a clear vision for the company as a whole. He believes that restaurants based on an Asian menu will continue to grow in popularity—and that developing a recognizable Asian brand is a huge opportunity. Everything at P.F. Chang's two types of restaurants—bistros and diners—is designed with this vision of growth in mind. From tableside cooking to replicas of 12th-century Chinese murals, the entire P.F. Chang's dining experience is intended to leave a strong impression on customers, which is exactly what Federico wants.

While the restaurant industry in general has suffered during the past few years, P.F. Chang's has managed to grow. Federico is both philosophical and practical about the obstacles that every restaurant faces during uncertain times. "While so many of the challenges that face our industry are out of our control, our greatest challenge is also our greatest opportunity: our people," he says. "We are in the hospitality service industry, and our business is to provide our customers with an outstanding dining experience each and every time they walk through our doors." One way he accomplishes this goal is by empowering employees to make decisions, such as fulfilling special requests from customers. And because of its success, P.F. Chang's has been able to create hundreds of jobs across the country while other restaurant chains are laying off workers.

Federico expects results from every team, manager, and worker. But he expects no less from himself. "I'm a reflection of our employees," he muses. "I surround myself with people better than I am in certain areas." He believes his greatest tasks as a leader involve remaining focused on his customers, his workers, and the food they serve. As P.F. Chang's grows, he wants to be sure that the quality of service, atmosphere, and food are always at their highest. He's not afraid to look in the mirror for the solution to a problem. "I suppose the day I'm not an effective leader, I'll be out of here," he admits. For now, he'll be busy coming up with ways to make P.F. Chang's bigger, better, and eventually, a household name.

Questions

1. Describe some of Rick Federico's personal leadership traits.

2. Would you characterize Rick Federico as a charismatic or transformational leader? Why?

3. Which of the five sources of power does Rick Federico use most?

SOURCES: Company Web site, *http://www.pfchangs.com,* accessed August 26, 2004, Charles Bernstein, "Chief Execution Officer," *Chain Leader,* September 2004, 62–68; "Work Force Still Top Concern for CEOs," *The Phoenix Business Journal,* May 24, 2004, *http://phoenix. bizjournals.com.*

CHAPTER 19: P.F. CHANG'S EMPLOYEES TASTE THE FRUITS OF MOTIVATION

What motivates you? Do you run every morning to get fit, lose weight, or slide into that special pair of jeans? Do you study because you love what you are learning, or because you want good grades? Do you work every weekend for money to pay for college or for money to eat out with your friends? All of these motives are real and legitimate—they are what drive you to do the things you do. The same is true for workers everywhere, including P.F. Chang's bistros. It's easy to see what motivates managers and executives at P.F. Chang's: they want customers to love the food and atmosphere, they want their business to succeed and grow, and they want to earn a good living in return for their investment and hard work. "We are truly glad you are here," says P.F. Chang's motto, "and we will do everything possible to make you want to come back again." This is the biggest motivation of all—to have customers come back.

But what motivates employees at P.F. Chang's—the wait staff, bartenders, hosts, chefs and kitchen crew, bus boys, and dishwashers? Historically, the restaurant industry has relied on a rigid hierarchy, with managers meting out punishments and rewards to hourly workers. The result has been a low degree of job satisfaction and a high degree of turnover. There might be some use of job rotation or job enlargement, but it is not an industry that is generally known for its embrace of a new workplace. P.F. Chang's, however, is different—and some may argue that the way its workers are treated is a major factor in the company's success.

Throughout the firm, Chairman and CEO Rick Federico introduced the concept of partnerships, rather than layers of management. Because they are empowered to hire their own team of workers, from the kitchen to the dining room, operating partners have a major stake in their restaurant's success. "Managers have a passion for the business," explains operating partner Jennifer Olson Hicks, "and we instill that in our employees." Hicks also notes that it is important for managers to be wherever they are needed in the restaurant—whether it is hosting, taking orders, or washing dishes. Setting this kind of example of commitment to the success of the organization can be a powerful motivator to employees.

All of P.F. Chang's restaurant workers are trained to understand more than just their jobs. They know the food and the way it is prepared; they know the wine list; they know what their guests want and how to provide it for them; and they know how P.F. Chang's operates as a company. In addition, the workers themselves are empowered to do just about whatever it takes to satisfy their customers. For example, wait staff are trained to guide new visitors through the Asian menu—termed the "limo ride" in company lingo—so they can select the food they will enjoy. Waiters don't just take orders, they provide a service through their knowledge of the menu, the food, and its preparation. In the kitchen, although workers may have specific jobs, ranging from line cook to sous chef, all employees understand the total picture. "Everyone knows what's going on in the kitchen," explains Paul Muller, corporate executive chef. He likens the performance of the kitchen staff to "a great baseball team."

P.F. Chang's also motivates by providing opportunity for advancement. Its continued growth "enables us to promote from within and offer members of our team the opportunity to enter management and further develop their business skills," notes CEO Federico. Finally, the firm offers a generous array of benefits, ranging from meal discounts to bonus plans to various retirement savings plans. P.F. Chang's sounds like a great place to eat—and an even better place to work.

Questions

1. P.F. Chang's offers a menu of extrinsic rewards to its workers. What are some of the intrinsic rewards?

2. In what ways might managers at P.F. Chang's use positive reinforcement for their kitchen crew or wait staff?

3. In what ways can P.F. Chang's employees use the four elements of empowerment to achieve the highest level of performance in their jobs?

SOURCES: Company training materials and company Web site, http://www.pfchangs.com, accessed September 8, 2004; Charles Bernstein, "Chief Execution Officer," *Chain Leader,* September 2004, pp. 62–68; "Work Force Still Top Concern for CEOs," *The Phoenix Business Journal,* May 24, 2004, http://phoenix.bizjournals.com.

Chapter 20: NEADS Creates Partnerships between People and Dogs

Suppose you woke up one day and couldn't see. Or perhaps you couldn't hear, couldn't speak, or couldn't walk. How would you communicate and interact with the world around you? Today's technology provides solutions to some of these challenges, but there is a live solution as well: assistance dogs. The National Education for Assistance Dog Services (NEADS) acquires, trains, and matches dogs with people who need assistance. Founded in 1976 as a nonprofit organization, NEADS is based in the rural community of Princeton, Massachusetts, where it adopts and trains dogs to serve their new owners.

Communication is central to success at NEADS. Communication between trainer and dog; between interviewer and client; between trainer and interviewer; and among the trio of client, trainer, and dog is a well-established process. Executive director Sheila O'Brien describes the importance of the process this way. "The match of client and dog is the most important thing that we do, because if we make a bad match, we can't salvage it in any way, shape, or form." Thus, while a trainer begins to work with a dog, developing the skills it will need in its new role—such as responding to a doorbell, ringing telephone, or activated smoke alarm—an interviewer reviews a client's application and conducts an in-person interview to learn as much about the client as possible. If the person has a hearing loss, the interviewer will ask how the loss occurred, how severe it is, and what the prognosis might be. Clients answer questions about lifestyle: Do they live in the city or the country? Do they work outside the home? How many people live in the home? Do they travel a lot? and so forth. They also have a chance to describe their expectations and preferences—whether they want a large or small dog, an energetic or quiet dog, a male or female dog. "The interviewer does have to listen on many levels," notes Shelia O'Brien. "[The interviewer must] ask questions and listen to the answers." Once the interview is complete, the interviewer and trainers meet to try to match dogs with clients.

The match meeting is lively. By now, the trainers know the characteristics of the dogs, and the interviewers know the personalities of their clients. "Match meetings have a lot of give and take," says O'Brien. "The lines of communication have got to be open." Sometimes, a match may seem close—but needs some tweaking. So a trainer will work further with the dog, and ultimately the client-dog pair, to create a smooth relationship.

Because NEADS staffers deal with different types of individuals, ranging from hearing-impaired clients to dogs in need of training, they are open to all kinds of communication. They don't view communication barriers as an obstacle. "I think my staff is of the opinion that the sky is the limit when it comes to communication," says O'Brien. If hearing or speaking is an issue, she explains, "We don't necessarily rely on voice . . . we rely on body language." Hand signals are often the best means of communication between a dog and a hearing-impaired client, so both are trained for their new language. Clients who will be receiving dogs live at the NEADS facility for two weeks while they learn how to communicate with their new partners. "We have to be open to a wide variety of communication skills," says O'Brien. "We'll do what works. We'll use any kind of communication we can."

In its three decades of existence, NEADS has trained more than 650 client-dog teams. Because the program has been so successful, there is currently a two-year waiting period for clients who have been accepted into NEADS to receive their dogs. But when the match is made, it lasts a lifetime.

Questions

1. How would you describe the capacity and richness of the NEADS match meeting as a communication channel?
2. According to one study, the impact of facial expressions on message interpretation is 55 percent. How might this finding be used at NEADS?
3. Why are listening skills so important at NEADS?

SOURCE: Organization Web site, *http://www.neads.org,* accessed September 2, 2004.

CHAPTER 21: THE NEADS TEAM: PEOPLE AND DOGS

All the teams you have encountered in this chapter have been teams of people. NEADS, the National Education for Assistance Dog Services, functions with teams of people as well. But another type of teamwork is central to the mission of NEADS: the team of human and dog. NEADS acquires, raises, trains, and matches service dogs to meet the needs of people with limited physical mobility or deafness. A typical service dog may be trained to respond to a blaring smoke alarm or ringing telephone, nudge a light switch on or off with its nose, or retrieve items for an owner. Since this partnership is intended to last a lifetime, it is important for the match to be perfect.

It takes about two years to train a service dog—and that requires a lot of teamwork. Since NEADS is a nonprofit organization, it must be creative in the way it recruits and uses volunteers. These volunteers include high school students, families, and prisoners. High school students may help NEADS puppy trainers begin to expose the youngest dogs to experiences they will encounter in their lives as service dogs, such as sitting by a wheelchair or walking next to a cane. Families become part of the team when, at four months of age, the puppies are placed in foster care for the next part of their education. Volunteer families agree to feed, love, and raise the puppies so they become accustomed to the distractions and energy of the real world. Professional dog trainers from NEADS visit regularly to work with the families and dogs to ensure that the dogs receive the proper training in preparation for their later work. Since 1998, prison inmates in Massachusetts and Connecticut have participated in a foster care program as well. While a puppy lives at the prison, a small team from NEADS visits regularly to monitor the puppy's development. Another set of volunteers participate in a program called Pups on Parole, during which they take the puppies outside the prison for field trips to shopping malls, supermarkets, business districts, parks, and the like. In addition, a professional trainer works with the prisoners and puppies. The partnership with prisons has required another level of teamwork, with state agencies. NEADS executive director Sheila O'Brien says this

relationship has been highly successful. "The commissioner felt very strongly that inmates should give back to the society that they violated, in a safe way." Working with the dogs has proved to be a safe and effective program for inmates. In fact, the dogs who live with prisoners return to NEADS more advanced in their readiness for formal training than those who live with families.

The puppies live in their foster homes until they are about a year and a half old—then they return to the NEADS farm to continue their education. Here, they receive advanced training from professional dog trainers. When a dog's training is complete, its new owner arrives on campus for a two-week stay, during which the person and dog become a team. The dog and person have been matched through an extensive process that involves a team of people interviewers and dog trainers. During this intensive get-acquainted and training period, "they learn to love each other, respect each other, and work together," explains O'Brien.

O'Brien emphasizes that, "Even though the concentration at this point is on the team, meaning two—the dog and the person—there are still many team members working behind the stage to facilitate this coming together." She refers to volunteers who raise funds to cover the cost of receiving a dog, as well as those who greet new clients and help them become familiar and comfortable with the NEADS campus. "What makes these teams work so cohesively is that everyone knows what the outcome should be," says O'Brien. "Everyone is working toward getting a dog and person together and making sure this dog provides the independence that this disabled or deaf person needs. Everyone has that in sight. Everyone just works toward that end."

Questions

1. Describe the characteristics of a typical NEADS team, using the criteria discussed in the chapter.

2. What factors determine the cohesiveness of NEADS teams?

3. Describe a situation in which conflict might arise in a NEADS team.

SOURCE: Organization Web site, *http://www.neads.org.*

8 MILE

Jimmy "B-Rabbit" Smith, Jr. (Eminem) wants to be a successful rapper and to prove that a white man can create moving sounds. He works days at a plant run by the North Detroit Stamping Company and pursues his music at night, sometimes on the plant's grounds. The film's title refers to Detroit's northern city boundary which divides Detroit's white and African American populations. This film gives a gritty look at Detroit's hip-hop culture in 1995 and Jimmy's desire to be accepted by it. Eminem's original songs "Lose Yourself" and "8 Mile" received Golden Globe and Academy Award nominations.

This scene is an edited composite of two brief sequences involving the stamping plant. The first half of the scene appears early in the film as part of "The Franchise" sequence. The second half appears in the last 25 minutes of the film as part of the "Papa Doc Payback" sequence. In the first part of the scene, Jimmy's car won't start so he rides the city bus to work and arrives late. The second part occurs after he is beaten by Papa Doc (Anthony Mackie) and Papa Doc's gang. Jimmy's mother (Kim Basinger) returns to their trailer and tells him she won $3,200 at bingo. The film continues to its end with Jimmy's last battle (a rapper competition).

What to Watch for and Ask Yourself

1. What is your perception of the quality of Jimmy's job and his work environment?
2. What is the quality of Jimmy's relationship with Manny, his foreman (Paul Bates)? Does it change? If it does, why?
3. How would you react to this type of work experience?

BACKDRAFT

Two brothers follow in the footsteps of their late father, a legendary Chicago firefighter, and join the department. Stephen "Bull" McCaffrey (Kurt Russell) joins first and rises to the rank of lieutenant. Younger brother Brian (William Baldwin) joins later and becomes a member of Bull's Company 17. Sibling rivalry tarnishes their work relationships, but they continue to successfully fight Chicago fires. Add a plot element about a mysterious arsonist and you have the basis of an ordinary film. The film, however, rises above its otherwise formulaic plot thanks to great acting and amazing special effects. The intense, unprecedented special effects give the viewer an unparalleled experience of what it is like to fight a fire. Chicago firefighters applauded the realism of the fire scenes.[1]

This scene appears early in the film as part of "The First Day" sequence. Brian McCaffrey has graduated from the fire academy, and the fire department has assigned him to his brother's company. This scene shows him fighting his first real fire at a garment factory. The film continues with Company 17 fighting the fire and Brian receiving some harsh first-day lessons.

What to Watch for and Ask Yourself

1. What elements of the Chicago fire department culture does this scene show? Does the scene show any cultural artifacts or symbols? If it does, what are they?
2. Does the scene show any values that guide the firefighters' behavior?
3. What does Brian McCaffrey learn on his first day at work?

[1] J. Craddock, Ed. *VideoHound's Golden Movie Retriever*, (Farmington Hills, MI: The Gale Group, Inc.), 2000.

MR. BASEBALL

The New York Yankees trade aging baseball player Jack Elliot (Tom Selleck) to the Chunichi Dragons, a Japanese team. This lighthearted comedy traces Elliot's bungling entry into Japanese culture where he almost loses everything including Hiroko Uchiyama (Aya Takanashi). As Elliot slowly begins to understand Japanese culture and Japanese baseball, he finally is accepted by his teammates. This film shows many examples of Japanese culture, especially their love for baseball.

Unknown to Hiroko's father, she and Jack develop an intimate relationship. Meanwhile, Jack does not know that Hiroko's father is "The Chief" (Ken Takakura), the manager of the Chunichi Dragons. This scene takes place after "The Chief" has removed Jack from a baseball game. The scene shows Jack dining with Hiroko and her grandmother (Mineko Yorozuya), grandfather (Jun Hamamura), and father.

What to Watch for and Ask Yourself

1. Does Jack Elliot behave as if he had had cross-cultural training before arriving in Japan?
2. Is he culturally sensitive or insensitive?
3. What do you propose that Jack Elliot do for the rest of his time in Japan?

EMPEROR'S CLUB

William Hundert (Kevin Kline), a professor at Saint Benedict's preparatory school, believes in teaching his students about living a principled life as well as teaching them his beloved classical literature. Hundert's principled ways are challenged, however, by a new student, Sedgewick Bell (Emile Hirsch). Bell's behavior during the 73rd annual Julius Caesar competition causes Hundert to suspect that Bell leads a less than principled life.

Years later Hundert is the honored guest of his former student Sedgewick Bell (Joel Gretsch) at Bell's estate. Depaak Mehta (Rahul Khanna), Bell, and Louis Masoudi (Patrick Dempsey) compete in a reenactment of the Julius Caesar competition. Bell wins the competition, but Hundert notices that Bell is wearing an earpiece. Earlier in the film Hundert had suspected that the young Bell also wore an earpiece during the competition, but Headmaster Woodbridge (Edward Herrmann) had pressed him to ignore his suspicion.

This scene appears at the end of the film. It is an edited portion of the competition reenactment. Bell announced his candidacy for the U.S. Senate just before talking to Hundert in the bathroom. He carefully desribed his commitment to specific values that he would pursue if elected.

What to Watch for and Ask Yourself

1. Does William Hundert describe a specific type of life that one should lead? If so, what are its elements?
2. Does Sedgewick Bell lead that type of life? Is he committed to any specific ethical view or theory?
3. What consequences or effects do you predict for Sedgewick Bell because of the way he chooses to live his life?

THE BOURNE IDENTITY

Jason Bourne (Matt Damon) cannot remember who he is, but others believe he is an international assassin. Bourne tries to learn his identity with the help of his new friend and lover Marie (Franka Potente). Meanwhile, while CIA agents pursue him across Europe trying to kill him, Bourne slowly discovers that he is an extremely well-trained and lethal agent. The story, which is loosely based on Robert Ludlum's 1981 novel, was previously filmed in 1988 as a television miniseries starring Richard Chamberlain.

This scene is an edited version of the "Bourne's Game" sequence near the end of the film. Jason Bourne kills the hired assassin who tried to kill him the day after Jason and Marie arrived at the home of Eamon (Tim Dutton). Eamon is Marie's friend but is a stranger to Jason. Jason uses the dead man's cell phone after returning to his apartment in Paris, France. He presses the redial button, which connects him to Conklin (Chris Cooper), the CIA manager who is looking for him. Listen carefully to Jason's conversation with Conklin as he walks along the right bank of the Seine River in Paris.

What to Watch for and Ask Yourself

1. Does Jason Bourne describe a plan to Conklin? If he does, what are the plan's elements? What is Bourne's goal?
2. Does Bourne assess the plan's execution to determine if it conforms to his goal? If so, what does he do?
3. Was Bourne's plan successfully carried out? Why or why not? How does this scene relate to organizational strategic planning?

BLUE CRUSH

Anne Marie Chadwick (Kate Bosworth) and her friends Eden (Michelle Rodriguez) and Lena (Sanoe Lake) work as hotel maids to support their commitment to surfing the magnificent waves of Hawaii's North Shore. They live in a simple beach shack where Anne Marie also cares for her sister Penny (Mika Boorem). Anne Marie trains daily to compete in the Pipe Masters surf competition. She also must fight off nagging fears from a nearly fatal surfing accident. Professional quarterback Matt Tollman (Matthew Davis) asks her to teach him to surf, and their romance soon presents another distraction for Anne Marie. *Blue Crush* is easy to watch and features some extraordinary surfing sequences including many with professional surfers.

This scene comes from the "No Fear" sequence near the end of the film. Anne Marie was thrown from her board during her first ride, almost re-creating her earlier accident. The judges gave her a score of 4.6, enough to move her into this second round. She now competes against top surfer Keala Kennelly (herself). Anne Marie has not yet had a scoring ride in this round. Kennelly has more points than Anne Marie but encourages and coaches her to catch a wave and have no fear. This section of the scene follows Kennelly's efforts to encourage Anne Marie to successfully ride "The Pipe."

What to Watch for and Ask Yourself

1. Describe the level of risk in Anne Marie's strategy.
2. What level of competitive advantage does Anne Marie have?

3. What parallels do you see between Anne Marie's involvement in the competition and a modern manager's experience in the competitive business environment? Perform a SWOT analysis for Anne Marie.

DR. SEUSS' HOW THE GRINCH STOLE CHRISTMAS

Readers and lovers of Dr. Seuss's original tale may be put off by Ron Howard's loose adaptation of the story. Whoville, a magical, mythical land that exists inside a snowflake, features two types of life: the Whos who love Christmas and the Grinch (Jim Carrey) who hates it. Cindy Lou Who (Taylor Momsen) tries to bring the Grinch back to Yuletide celebrations, an effort that backfires on all involved. Sparkling special effects will dazzle most viewers and likely distract them from the film's departures from the original story.

This scene is an edited version of the "Second Thoughts" sequence early in the film. Just before this scene, fearless Cindy Lou entered the Grinch's lair to invite him to be the Holiday Cheermeister at the Whobilation One-thousand Celebration. In typical Grinch fashion, he pulls the trap door on Cindy Lou who unceremoniously slides out of his lair to land on a snowy Whoville street. The Grinch now must decide whether to accept the invitation. The film continues with the Cheermeister award ceremony.

What to Watch for and Ask Yourself

1. What are the Grinch's decision alternatives or options?
2. What decision criteria does the Grinch use to choose from the alternatives?
3. Describe the steps in the Grinch's decision-making process.

THE PAPER

This engaging film shows the ethical dilemmas and stress of producing the *New York Sun*, a daily metropolitan newspaper. Metro Editor Henry Hackett (Michael Keaton) races against the clock to publish a story about a major police scandal that could send two young African American men to jail. He is in constant conflict with Managing Editor Alicia Clark (Glenn Close) who is more concerned about controlling the budget than about running accurate stories. Hackett is also under constant pressure from his wife Marty (Marisa Tomei), who is pregnant with their first child. While Hackett tries to get his story, Marty urges him to take a less demanding job at *The Sentinel*.

This scene is an edited version of the "The Managing Editor" sequence, which occurs early in *The Paper*.

It shows a staff meeting that takes place the day after the *Sun* missed a story about a murder and other shootings with racial overtones. Instead, the *Sun* ran a front-page story about parking problems. At the meeting, Senior Editor Bernie White (Robert Duvall) discusses his preferences in front-page stories.

What to Watch for and Ask Yourself

1. Senior Editor Bernie White wants to reach a specific goal with the next edition of the *New York Sun*. What is this goal?
2. What method of departmentalization best describes the organizational structure at the *Sun*: functional, product, customer, geographic, or matrix? Explain your choice.
3. Is the organizational structure of the *Sun* appropriate for reaching White's goal? Why or why not?

APOLLO 13

This film dramatically portrays the Apollo 13 mission to the moon that almost ended in disaster. Only innovative problem solving and decision making amid massive ambiguity saved the crew. Almost any scene dramatically makes this point. Flight Director Gene Kranz wrote a book describing the mission and the actions that prevented disaster.

A zero gravity simulator, a KC-135 four-engine jet aircraft (NASA's "Vomit Comet"), helped create the film's realistic weightless scenes. These scenes required 600 parabolic loops over 10 days of filming.[1] See the later Biz Flix exercise for a discussion of another scene from *Apollo 13*.

This scene is a composite built from portions of the "Carbon Dioxide Problem" sequence, which occurs a little after the midway point of the film, and parts of the "With Every Breath . . ." sequence, which appears about seven minutes later. The scene's first part follows the nearly complete shutdown of the Apollo 13 module to save battery power. Mission Control has detected rising carbon dioxide levels in the module, which could kill the astronauts if NASA engineers on the ground cannot solve the problem. The film continues with the Apollo 13 crew building a carbon dioxide filter designed by the engineers.

What to Watch for and Ask Yourself

1. What is the problem in this scene?
2. What are the engineers' options for solving the problem?
3. Does this scene show innovation and innovative behavior? If so, in what form?

---

[1] J. Craddock, Ed. *VideoHound's Golden Movie Retriever*, (Farmington Hills, MI: The Gale Group, Inc.), 2000.

BOWFINGER

This film, which brought Steve Martin and Eddie Murphy together for the first time, offers a funny look at Hollywood film-making. Bobby Bowfinger (Martin), perhaps the least successful director in films, wants to produce a low-budget film with top star Kit Ramsey (Murphy). Bowfinger's problem: how to recruit a crew and cast with almost no budget while tricking Kit into appearing in his film.

Bowfinger interviews several candidates for the Kit Ramsey lookalike role. He rejects everyone until Jifferson (Jiff) Ramsey (also played by Murphy) auditions. This scene is an edited version of "The Lookalike" sequence early in the film. It includes Jiff's audition, interview, and a brief look at his first day at work.

What to Watch for and Ask Yourself

1. Does Bobby Bowfinger have a set of valid selection criteria for filling the role of a Kit Ramsey look-alike? Does Bowfinger apply the criteria uniformly to each applicant?
2. Is Jiff Ramsey a good person-job fit in the screen role of Kit Ramsey?
3. Do you predict that Jiff Ramsey will be successful as a Kit Ramsey substitute?

THE BREAKFAST CLUB

John Hughes's careful look at teenage culture in a suburban high school outside Chicago focuses on a group of teenagers from the school's subcultures. They start their Saturday detention with nothing in common. Over the day they learn each others' most inner secrets. The highly memorable characters—the Jock, the Princess, the Criminal, the Kook, and the Brain—leave lasting impressions. (If you have seen the film, try to recall which actor or actress played each character.)

This scene shows the detainees at lunchtime. It is an edited version of the "Lunch Time" sequence that appears in the first third of the film. Carefully study each character's behavior to answer the questions below.

What to Watch for and Ask Yourself

1. Which Big Five personality dimensions describe each character in this scene?
2. Which characters show positive affectivity? Which show negative affectivity?
3. Are any of these characters Type A personalities or Type B personalities? If so, which ones?

U-571

This action-packed thriller deals with a U.S. submarine crew's efforts to retrieve an Enigma encryption device from a disabled German submarine during World War II. After the crew gets the device, the U.S. submarine sinks, and they must use the German submarine to escape from enemy destroyers. The film's almost nonstop action and extraordinary special effects will look and sound best with a home theater system.

This scene is an edited composite of the "To Be a Captain" sequence early in the film. The S33, an older U.S. submarine, is embarking on a secret mission. Before departure, the S33's officers receive a briefing on their mission from Office of Naval Intelligence representatives on board. Executive officer Lt. Andrew Tyler (Matthew McConaughey) reports on the submarine's status to Lt. Commander Mike Dahlgren (Bill Paxton). The film continues with the S33 finding the disabled German submarine.

What to Watch for and Ask Yourself

1. What aspects of leadership does Dahlgren say are important for a submarine commander?
2. Which leadership behaviors or traits does he emphasize?
3. Are these traits or behaviors right for this situation? Why or why not?

FOR LOVE OF THE GAME

Billy Chapel (Kevin Costner), a 20-year veteran pitcher with the Detroit Tigers, learns just before the season's last game that the team's new owners want to trade him. He also learns that his partner Jane Aubrey (Kelly Preston) intends to leave him. Faced with these daunting blows, Chapel wants to pitch a perfect final game. Director Sam Raimi's love of baseball shines through in some striking visual effects.

This scene is a slightly edited version of the "Just Throw" sequence, which begins the film's exciting closing scenes in which Chapel pitches his last game. In this scene, the Tigers' catcher Gus Sinski (John C. Reilly) comes out to the pitching mound to talk to Billy.

What to Watch for and Ask Yourself

1. What is Billy Chapel's level of esteem needs at this point in the game?
2. Do you expect Gus Sinski's talk to have any effect on Chapel? If it will, what will be the effect?
3. What rewards potentially exist for Billy Chapel? Remember, this is the last baseball game of his career.

PATCH ADAMS

Hunter "Patch" Adams (Robin Williams), a maverick medical student, believes that laughter is the best medicine. The rest of the medical community believes that medicine is the best medicine. Unlike traditional doctors who remain aloof, Patch Adams wants to be close to his patients. Williams's wackiness comes through clearly in this film, which is based on a true story.

This scene comes from the film's early sequence "The Experiment," which takes place after the students' medical school orientation. Patch Adams and fellow medical student Truman Schiff (Daniel London) leave the University Diner. They begin Patch's experiment for changing the programmed responses of people they meet on the street. Along the way, they stumble upon a meat packers' convention where this scene occurs.

What to Watch for and Ask Yourself

1. What parts of the communication process appear in this scene? Note each part of the process that you see in the scene.
2. What type of communication does this scene show: Small group, large audience, or persuasive?
3. Do you think Patch Adams is an effective communicator? Why or why not?

APOLLO 13

This film re-creates the heroic efforts of astronaut Jim Lovell (Tom Hanks), his crew, NASA, and Mission Control to return the damaged Apollo spacecraft to earth. Examples of both problem solving and decision making occur in almost every scene. See the earlier Biz Flix exercise for more information about this film and a discussion of another scene.

This scene takes place during day five of the mission about two-thirds of the way through the film. Early in Apollo 13's mission Jack Swigert (Kevin Bacon) stirred the oxygen tanks at the request of Mission Control. After this procedure, an explosion occurred, causing unknown damage to the command module. Before the scene takes place, the damage has forced the crew to move into the LEM (Lunar Exploration Module), which becomes their lifeboat for return to earth.

What to Watch for and Ask Yourself

1. What triggers the conflict in this scene?
2. Is this intergroup conflict or intragroup conflict? What effects can such conflict have on the group dynamics on board Apollo 13?

3. Does mission commander Jim Lovell successfully manage the group dynamics to return the group to a normal state?

SCENT OF A WOMAN

Young Charlie Simms (Chris O'Donnell) wants to earn extra money over Thanksgiving weekend so that he can afford the airfare to go home during Christmas break. He becomes a guide and caretaker for ill-tempered, retired Lt. Col. Frank Slade (Al Pacino) who is blind. Charlie, from Gresham, Oregon, is quiet and reserved and has had little experience with the opposite sex. He attends the exclusive Baird Preparatory School on a scholarship. His wild New York City weekend with Frank Slade bonds them forever. This film is a remake of *Profumo di Donna*, a 1974 Italian film.

This scene follows Slade's morose moments in their hotel suite after the first day and night in Manhattan. Slade wants to sleep in and perhaps even die. Charlie convinces him to venture out on this beautiful day and go for a ride. They go to a Ferrari dealership where Slade convinces salesman Freddie Bisco (Leonard Gaines) to allow a 17-year-old driver and a blind man to take the Ferrari Cabriolet T for a test drive. This scene appears in the last third of the film and defines the continued bonding of Frank Slade and Charlie Simms.

What to Watch for and Ask Yourself

1. What pattern of control do these scenes show?
2. What are the control system's elements?
3. Do these scenes show a periodic or a continuous type of performance measurement?

LORENZO'S OIL

This film tells the true story of young Lorenzo Odone who suffers from adrenoleukodystrophy (ALD), an incurable degenerative brain disorder. (Six actors and actresses play Lorenzo throughout the film.) Physicians and medical scientists offer little help to Lorenzo's desperate parents, Michaela (Susan Sarandon) and Augusto (Nick Nolte). They use their resources to learn about ALD to try to save their son. Director George Miller co-wrote the script, which benefited from his medical training as a physician.

Six months after Lorenzo's ALD diagnosis, his condition fails to improve with a restricted diet. Michaela and Augusto continue their research at the National Institutes of Health library in Bethesda, Maryland. Michaela finds a report of a critical Polish experiment that showed positive effects of fatty acid manipulation in rats. Convinced that a panel of experts could systematically focus on their problem, they help organize the First International ALD Symposium. This scene is an edited version of the symposium sequence that appears about midway through the film. The film continues with the Odones' efforts to save their son.

What to Watch for and Ask Yourself

1. Do the scientists present data or information during the symposium?

2. If it is information, who transformed the data into information? Speculate about how such data became information.

3. What do you predict will be the next course of action for the Odones?

CASINO

Martin Scorsese's lengthy, complex, and beautifully filmed *Casino* offers a close look at the gambling casinos of Las Vegas and their organized crime connections in the 1970s. It completes his trilogy that began with *Mean Streets* (1973) and continued with *Goodfellas* (1990). In *Casino*, ambition, greed, drugs, and sex ultimately destroy the mob's gambling empire. The film includes strong performances by Robert De Niro, Joe Pesci, and Sharon Stone. The violence and expletive-filled dialogue give *Casino* an R rating.

This scene, which comes from the beginning of "The Truth about Las Vegas" sequence, opens the film and establishes important background about casino operations. Listen carefully to Sam Rothstein's (De Niro) voice-over. He quickly describes the casino's operation and explains how it tries to reach its goals.

What to Watch for and Ask Yourself

1. What type of operations management does this scene show—manufacturing operations management or service operations management?

2. Are the customers directly involved in this operation? If they are, in what way? What likely effects does their involvement have on the casino's operation and its management?

3. Does the casino have independent or interdependent operations processes?

SOURCE: J. Craddock, Ed. *VideoHound's Golden Movie Retriever,* (Farmington Hills, MI: The Gale Group, Inc.), 2000.

CHAPTER 1: MANAGING IN TURBULENT TIMES AT SECOND CITY THEATER

Imagine you have prepared for weeks for this moment. All eyes are on you and everyone is counting on you to make the most of this meeting. You must respond instantly and effectively to the changes in the interaction, affirm all participants and their ideas, and direct it towards a successful conclusion. And your partner is asking you to bark like a dog.

While many business meetings contain elements of this scenario, the most likely context is a Second City Theater production of improvisational and sketch comedy. Managers today are expected to deal with uncertainty, unexpected events, diversity, and change. They must demonstrate flexibility, foster trust, and engage the hearts and minds of employees. The managers at Second City have a leg up in developing these skills and dealing with these situations because Second City has been doing it for years . . . on stage.

Since its inception in 1953, Second City has been the nation's most renowned creator of improvisational comedy acts based on the spontaneous interaction of actors and audience, and sketch comedy akin to those seen on television shows such as Saturday Night Live. Its accolades include the production of an Emmy Award winning TV series, multiple, national touring groups, and a long list of infamous alumni including Chris Farley, Tina Fey, Mike Meyers, Halle Barry, Bill Murray, and many others who have gone on to prominent careers in TV, theater, and film.

One key to Second City's success is the unified goal of furthering the art form of improvisational, satire, and revue comedy. From that goal, the managers of Second City have taken the organization many places, diversifying its reach. In 1975, owner and executive producer, Andrew Alexander, started the Second City television series (SCTV) in response to the new trend of television sketch comedy and the creation of Saturday Night Live in 1975. Later, the company opened the Second City Training Center, an educational center offering classes in improvisation, acting, writing, and other skills, as well as a summer camp. In addition to its theater in Chicago, Second City has theaters in Toronto, Vegas, Detroit, Denver, and Los Angeles, as well as national touring companies. Most recently, managers at Second City saw a need within corporations for staff trainings grounded in building trust, communication, presentation, team-building, and improvisational skills. Understanding Second City's background and specialization in just these areas, they opened the corporate communications division which provides trainings in the areas of internal communications, external marketing and branding, and learning development.

With its focus on human skills, Second City demonstrates all of the qualities of a learning organization. The managers at Second City foster a climate where experimentation and learning is encouraged. As Andrew Alexander says, "there is a culture of encouraging failure." Just like the actors on stage, employees at Second City are expected to share their thoughts and opinions and in turn, to support and build on the ideas of others. This non-traditional environment inspires trust, innovation, and teamwork amongst the many levels of the organization. Through careful planning and management, Second City has directed this unleashing of creative energy to take the company to the next level. As Kelly Leonard, Vice President of Second City Theater said, "Don't stop the creativity."

Questions

1. Many students of the Second City Training Center are businesspeople looking to gain skills for the corporate context. What skills from the world of improvisational comedy would be valuable to a business manager?

2. In what way does the focus of a learning organization address the transition to a new workplace as outlined in exhibit 1.6?

3. What do you think would be the challenges of a manager in a learning organization? Why?

CHAPTER 2: THE EVOLUTION OF MANAGEMENT THINKING

The world is a very different place than it was 100 years ago. Ford's assembly lines look very little like the office of an e-business. But managers, then as now, still have the task of coordinating and motivating employees to meet the goals of an organization. An understanding of the evolution of management helps managers learn from what has come before and shape their strategies for the future. Management philosophies are shaped by the environment and the times. Social forces, or the influence of social values, political forces, or the influence of political and legal institutions, and economic forces, affect manager's understanding about how individual employees relate to business as a whole as well as the overall organization of the business. By understanding these philosophies and the forces that shaped them, managers can better spot trends and patterns as well as gain valuable tools and techniques for use in their own companies.

One of the biggest challenges to creating a superior management strategy is the need to respond to an ever-changing set of problems and needs. Successful managers learn early that there is no one answer to all of the questions they will be presented with. The managers at Allstate know they have a diverse workforce with varying needs. Allstate's benefits package is designed as a cafeteria plan where employees can pick and choose which benefits best apply to them. They can plan for a family, pursue higher education, or augment their retirement plan, depending on their stage in life. While Allstate's benefits package is influenced by the humanistic perspective, like any real-world situation, the perspective informs the managers about the decisions they make. It is not a hard and fast rule to which they ascribe.

Peet's Coffee and Tea uses systems theory as a better way to understand the complexities of their multiple channel operation. System's theory allows them to see that a change in one element of the organization would have an impact on various different parts which, in turn, will reverberate back effects that may help or hinder the initial goal. With this understanding, they could better organize their operation and ensure that any changes to the roasting, packaging,

and shipping would not have unintended repercussions.

The contingency theory informs most managers today. In today's rapidly changing business environment, every challenge that a manager faces is unique from the rest. Thus management strategies that might work in one situation may not work in another, but it is the exposure to many different kinds of situations, that managers gain a strong toolset. By asking their employees to develop personalized strategies for implementing the Team Production system, managers at American Apparel broadened that toolset and accommodated the diversity of their workforce.

The learning organization and a technology-driven workplace are becoming ubiquitous in today's businesses. Nowadays, information and ideas have become more important than physical capital. There had been a large shift from employees using their bodies and physical labor for designated tasks to employees using their minds and creativity to problem-solve and create new opportunities. The learning organization promotes the flexibility, knowledge sharing, problem solving, and employee empowerment needed to succeed today. It is through strategies like Second City's promotion of experimentation and tolerance for failure, that companies are able to capitalize on the creativity of their employees. Similarly, managers at Zingerman's had to embrace changes in technology to take their business to the next level. By moving towards an e-business distribution base, Zingerman's could become more than just a deli in Ann Arbor and reach customers across the nation. Like many successful companies, these organizations have found success because they understood where they had come from and adapted to meet the changes of today's marketplace.

Questions

1. What are the challenges that are the same for managers today as they were 100 years ago? What are some new challenges?

2. What are the benefits to American Apparel's strategy to go to their employees for solutions? What are the drawbacks?

3. What kind of steps do you think Zingerman's had to take to transition from a traditional storefront to an e-business?

CHAPTER 3: THE ENVIRONMENT AND CORPORATE CULTURE AT CATERPILLAR

Not satisfied with merely watching the External Environment shift and change at ever-increasing speed, Caterpillar's top management saw the need for both stability and flexibility within their Internal Environment. Despite their industry-leading position, management was not content to sit back and wait for the next big externally-driven change to hit, so they began to explore the company's internal dynamics.

In January 2003, Caterpillar launched a key 6 Sigma project which found compelling evidence that having Enterprise Values, and putting them into practice, would make for a better performing company. They determined that the values outlined in their existing Code of Conduct fit the bill nicely, but management realized that simply having an official Code of Conduct would not ensure its universal buy-in throughout the organization.

The next step was to bring Caterpillar's core values to the fore by reinforcing them with a fresh coat of paint, and greatly increasing employee access to the message. If the values were a background hum before, CAT cranked up the volume so that none could ignore it. Their plan to create a global recipe for values-based behavior ultimately led to company-wide distribution of the booklet *Our Values in Action—Caterpillar's Worldwide Code of Conduct*. To help support this lynchpin of their newly-redefined culture, they put up a dedicated website, and printed the Code in 14 languages, to reflect and embrace the diversity of their global workforce. Management at all levels spread the message, and positively reinforced the supporting behaviors increasingly displayed among employees. Upper management stayed visible and on-message throughout. They believed that if employees saw them "walk the talk" consistently, it would motivate and inspire them.

In preparation for launching their new ad campaign, Caterpillar issued something new to all of its employees, amidst an atmosphere of celebration: *The CAT Manifesto*. It drew a direct correlation between CAT employees just doing their job, and the easing of human suffering through progress. They wanted their employees to feel that each of them was personally responsible for making the world a better place, and to feel pride when they experienced the new billboards, print ads, and radio spots. Caterpillar's "The World: In Progress" campaign carried this notion into the External Environment, with graphic images that powerfully suggested moving toward the future, and sparse but effective copy such as "Caterpillar: Today's Work. Tomorrow's World."

These initiatives served to redefine Caterpillar's values for both management and employees, and continue to encourage the kind of corporate culture that upper management has envisioned. When organization members feel that their employer's actions are clearly aligned with its stated values, it is reflected in increased returns and retention. A quick look at Caterpillar's numbers suggests that they are indeed "walking the talk."

Questions

1. Caterpillar went to a great deal of effort to clarify its organizational values, and get employees from 120 facilities in 23 countries on the same page. Why did they do this?

2. How can Caterpillar's corporate culture, which springs from the organization's internal environment, impact the external environment?

3. What are the most essential core values that should be integrated into your organization's corporate culture? Why?

CHAPTER 4: MANAGING IN A GLOBAL ENVIRONMENT AT YAHOO!

The internet provides a way to connect with people the world over that is unlike any other. Traditional methods of reaching a potential customer, such as print, radio, and television ads, simply can't match its scale or versatility. Managers face a formidable challenge in creating e-business models for their companies that take full advantage of the opportunities that the medium provides, while building in some measure of flexibility to cope with technological change. As a business model exists to establish an organization's position within the value chain, an e-business model establishes the value chain position in terms of the way operations are integrated with the web.

Yahoo! (www.yahoo.com) is a true e-business model implementation success story. What started as the hobby of two grad students in 1994 has become the most trafficked Internet destination in the world, with half of all internet users having visited at least one of Yahoo!'s global network of branded properties.

The company's e-business model is, as of this writing, in transition. Yahoo! has long attracted users by offering enticing free content in 13 different languages, paid for by advertising that appears with the content. Most of Yahoo!'s revenue has been driven by its marketing services, like Yahoo! Search Marketing. This pioneering arm of the company came up with the Pay-Per-Click (PPC) idea in 1998, which revolutionized the way advertising is implemented online. The advertiser supported free content model has worked well for them for quite some time.

Since 2001, Yahoo! has been implementing a subscription-based model under the banner of Premium Services, while gradually transforming free content into pay content. By November 2006, there were 250 million email users with a yahoo.com account, making up half of all web-based mail users worldwide. Anyone with internet access has been able to get an ad-supported basic account for free, but Yahoo! offers premium features for those willing to pay for an upgraded account. Most do not upgrade. As more of its services go pay-to-play, the question must be asked: Can Yahoo! add enough value to its content to convince users to stick and subscribe in force, rather than migrate to a free alternative?

There are over a billion internet users worldwide, divided roughly in thirds between English speakers, non-English European language speakers, and those who speak an Asian tongue. 50 percent of them have visited at least one Yahoo! site—that's a lot of impressions, and a tremendous opportunity to gain new regular users. In January 2007, Yahoo! implemented a sweeping reorganization to address this opportunity. As competitors like Google continue to take bites out of Yahoo!'s pie while seizing hot properties like YouTube and MySpace, the Yahoo! management team faces perhaps the most critical decisions in the company's history.

Questions

1. What are some of the ways that businesses, both domestically and abroad, can take advantage of the internet's inherently global nature?

2. As Yahoo! shifts focus from free content toward gaining paid subscribers, what do you predict the outcome will be?

3. What are some strategies that Yahoo!, or any other top-ranked business, can use to keep its edge and remain in a top market slot amid increased global competition?

CHAPTER 5: ETHICS AND SOCIAL RESPONSIBILITY AT BRITISH PETROLEUM

While stories of greedy and unscrupulous business executives have dominated the business news during the last few years, one innovative leader for BP (BP) has been at the forefront of social responsibility by demonstrating a commitment to preserving the world's fragile environment. Lord John Browne, Group Chief Executive to the second largest company in the world, earning him more than $30,000 a day, is consistently recognized as one of the 100 most influential British executives, according to the British Newspaper *The Times*. Browne is keenly aware of BP's responsibility to protect and preserve the earth's fragile environment. As a top executive, he sets the tone for BP's culture of environmental responsibility.

Environmental issues are a growing concern among businesses worldwide. In particular, energy companies face tough scrutiny by their customers and stakeholders to make socially and ethically responsible decisions. But environmental responsibility represents a realm in which varying stakeholders have differing beliefs as to what constitutes an improvement in social welfare. A crucial question is whether energy companies are responsible for encouraging the energy conservation and sustainable alternatives that are necessary to reducing environmental degradation in any meaningful way. When making decisions about the future of BP, Lord Browne must weigh BP's legal, ethical, economic, and discretionary responsibilities. Recognizing a rapidly increasing demand for energy worldwide, Browne is committed to taking BP "beyond petroleum," although the burden of this increased demand still falls to hydrocarbon-based sources, such as oil and natural gas. And while BP continues to grow its oil and gas production by 5% per year, Browne's concerns are clear: "The real challenge is the potential impact of burning ever greater volumes of hydrocarbons on the world's climate." But Browne feels, "business is at the heart of the process of taking scientific advances and transforming them into technology . . . which can alter the lives of individuals and whole communities, and which can protect the environment." And he is putting his—and BP's—money where his mouth is.

In 2002, under Lord Browne's leadership, BP succeeded in reducing its carbon emissions by 10%, well beyond the 5.2% suggested by the Kyoto treaty. But, this is still far less than the 60% reductions recommended by scientists as necessary to stabilize climate change. Since 2002, BP has begun several innovative initiatives to help preserve the environment and reverse damaging trends. These include using a process called carbon sequestration in which carbon, produced by natural gas production, is trapped before it can be released into the atmosphere. It then is injected back into reservoirs below ground where it does less harm to the environment. BP estimates this project will prevent the release of 17 million tons of CO_2. Further, BP has created an emissions trading system, similar to market-driven emissions exchanges, to allocate resources as efficiently as possible.

While BP is the leading investor of solar energies at 17% of the world market, its investment in renewable energies is still well below that of its investment in hydrocarbon based sources. BP has made great strides in furthering socially and environmentally responsible practices. Whether these efforts are considered enough are up for personal and community ethical debate.

Questions

1. Who are BP's stakeholders? How might each view BP's environmental practices?

2. Where does BP fall on the Shades of Corporate Green chart in exhibit 5.6? Why?

3. With oil and gas production growing by 5% a year, BP will not be able to keep its emissions at the 2002 level. In the video, one BP executive argues that BP should be allowed to increase its emission levels based on 'credit' from its sizable emission reductions and its promotion of 'cleaner' energy forms such as natural gas in previously coal-based markets. Do you think this is socially responsible? Why or why not?

CHAPTER 6: MANAGING SMALL BUSINESS START UPS AT THE LITTLE GUYS HOME ELECTRONICS

Have you ever had an idea of how to do something better, but no one would listen to you? For 23 years, David and Evie Wexler of The Little Guys Home Electronics had many ideas about how to improve the home electronics store in which they were working, but could not put them into action. So, they decided to go out and start their own business. And 12 year later, their many ideas have met with widespread success.

Like many entrepreneurs, the Wexlers felt blocked by their old positions, so they sought new avenues for their ideas. They fall into the category of idealists who thrive on new and creative enterprises. The Little Guys was the production of their creative energies. In starting their business, the Wexlers responded to the fast-changing world of home electronic technology. They saw the need for a store that could provide hands-on, personalized customer service that could explain to customers the complexities of new products. Essentially, they wanted to do things differently from "the big guys."

The Wexlers started with a good idea that filled a niche. But it took a lot more than that to make The Little Guys the success that it is. Crucially, the Wexlers possessed many of the characteristics of successful entrepreneurs. They had an internal locus of control, believing success was possible but also the self-confidence in their own abilities to make it happen. They were driven by a need to succeed and chose goals that were challenging but attainable. It is a risky venture starting a new business, but they knew they had the experience, the knowledge, and the motivation to take on the challenge. In those first difficult years, it was their tolerance for ambiguity and awareness of passing time that helped them weather trials such as delays in acquiring space and the rush to open before the Christmas season.

Aside from being idealists, the Wexlers are also hard workers who thrive on the challenges of growth and jugglers who have the high-energy and the love of managing the details of their business. These characteristics led in part to their decision to form The Little Guys as a partnership with a long-time associate, Pal Gerrity. As a partnership, the three maintained control and responsibility of the entire company, but could share the burden of responsibility amongst themselves. They also believed that a combining of their skills and talents would be a greater asset than each of them acting alone. This desire to retain control and self-confidence in their abilities carried into their choice of how to finance the company. Instead of choosing equity financing, which would have forced them to turn over a percentage of ownership, the Wexlers and Gerrity financed The Little Guys solely through debt financing. Family, friends, and everyone else chipped in to make it happen, which, coupled with high-interest loans, set them on their way.

Now The Little Guys has moved beyond the start-up phase and is moving past survival to success. The Wexlers are affirmed by all that has come from implementing their ideas. While they have benefited from the growth of their business, they feel more personally rewarded by the success of their creativity and hard work. But there is no rest for these high achievers. They constantly look forward to the next challenge.

Questions

1. What would the Wexler's have gained from buying the business in which they were originally employed? What would they have lost?

2. What do you think were the sources of Entrepreneurial motivation from exhibit 6.6? Give reasons for your answer.

3. Think about what the business plan for The Little Guys might have looked like. What might they have put in the Critical-Risks Segment?

CHAPTER 7: MANAGERIAL PLANNING AND GOAL SETTING AT COLD STONE CREAMERY

Cake batter mixed with sprinkles and chocolate chips, doused with marshmallows. Did you ever think something as fun as ice cream could be so serious? Donald and Susan Sutherland, founders of Cold Stone Creamery are very serious about providing the "Ultimate Ice Cream Experience." They started in 1988 with a passion to serve the world's best ice cream, opening the first Cold Stone Creamery in Tempe, Arizona. Now, with more than 1,300 stores, people everywhere have become serious about ice cream.

Cold Stone Creamery isn't just selling ice cream, it is creating an experience. Freshly made ice cream in a dizzying array of unique flavors is folded together with any topping: nuts, fruits, candy, cookies, brownies, or others on a frozen granite stone while staff sing and dance for tips, mixing to the beat of the tune. These are not servers but artists. You can customize your "Creation" to any combination you can dream up, or choose from a menu of Cold Stone Original Creations, wild concoctions of ice cream decadence. Today, Cold Stone is the number 3 scoop shop chain, outselling Ben & Jerry's and Haagen-Dazs. It got there with a song and a dance and a careful plan.

Cold Stone started with a mission: "We will make people happy around the world by selling the highest quality, most creative ice cream experience with passion, excellence, and innovation." This is what drives every member of the company and defines their daily activity. It is the reason people come to work at Cold Stone. From that mission, the company's top executives set a company-wide goal of becoming America's number 1 best selling ice cream by December 31st, 2009. With careful planning, they created a strategic plan, their Pyramid of Success 2010, and broke this down into what it would mean for every member of the company to reach this goal. From the marketing department, to the creamery, to the staff 'on the stone,' they translated this goal into tactical and operational plans. In doing so, Cold Stone ensured that every employee knows what he or she is working towards and is empowered to make decisions that support that goal. The singing staff know that whatever they can do to get one more customer and 'make them happy' contributes to making Cold Stone #1.

The purpose of Cold Stone's Pyramid of Success 2010 is, as with all goal setting, to achieve high performance. But it is particularly successful because of a number of its characteristics. From the company-wide goal to the organizational goals, each one is numerically defined and measurable. The marketing team can track its progress towards increasing sales by $100,000 over the next three years, the developers know how close they are to opening another 600 stores, and the front-line staff can count how many customers they brought in that day. Besides being measurable, each of these goals is meaningful to the employee and speaks to their area of focus. They are also within a defined time period, which helps in planning and resource allocation. The management of Cold Stone conducted large amounts of research and market analysis in determining these goals. They are a challenge to the company as a whole, but realistic and reachable. And further, the goals are linked to rewards, so every employee knows what waits for them on the other side of success.

Throughout their race to be #1, Cold Stone Creamery remains true to the "ice cream dram" of the Sutherlands to provide the "Ultimate Ice Cream Experience." They continue to be ice cream innovators, "redefining plain old regular ice cream into something truly extraordinary." In the works is a line of breakfast flavors that includes French Toast, Cinnabon, and Blueberry Muffin. In this culture of experimentation, they are also toying with Twinkie ice cream and Pop-Tart ice cream sandwiches. Each new flavor, like those before it, will continue to produce smiles and move Cold Stone ever closer to being #1.

Questions

1. Does Cold Stone Creamery represent a high performance approach to planning? Why or why not?

2. Cold Stone's Pyramid of Success 2010 represents an example of a single use plan. What might be a standing plan for a procedure for a staff 'on the stone'?

3. Locate Cold Stone's Pyramid of Success 2010 on their website and explain how it provides each of the benefits listed under "Purposes of Goals and Plans".

CHAPTER 8: STRATEGY FORMULATION AND IMPLEMENTATION AT YAHOO!

2006 was an interesting year for Yahoo, in terms of strategic planning. Facing increased pressure from both competitors and investors, Yahoo! formally announced its 5 year plan in May of that year. To create a "superior user experience," the company stated that it intends "to build robust platforms, develop key strategic relationships, maximize user content, and build core brand extensions." Throughout the year, Yahoo! forged new strategic alliances with a long list of companies, adding to an already impressive line-up of strategic partners.

In an apparent bid to become the biggest power player in the advertising industry, Yahoo! announced a partnership with a nationwide consortium of 176 newspapers in the U.S. The newspapers, having experienced declining industry growth, would benefit from Yahoo!'s advertising technology and distribution network. Yahoo! would strengthen its brand, sell more advertising, and gain more localized content. Both sets of parties benefit from a cross-pollination of Yahoo! Hotjobs (Yahoo!'s online job search network) with job listings posted in local papers.

Partnerships with the Big 4 U.S. TV networks, and the BBC, leaned toward providing integration with, and support for, broadcast news. Another intriguing move united the online presence of Telemundo, NBC Universal, and Yahoo! en español to create a comprehensive online presence for the U.S. Hispanic community. Yahoo also signed agreements with both the NFL and the FIFA World Cup, to put games up on Yahoo! for those otherwise unable to watch them. The extra ad revenue these deals generate could spell big bucks for all parties.

New partnerships with leading mobile content delivery platforms, on both the tech and service side, illustrated a clear desire to become the key access portal for wireless devices. In addition to providing more built-in functionality for handsets and palmtops, integration with Yahoo!'s online services increases the chance that users will visit Yahoo! properties from their PCs as well.

New agreements with Intel, IBM, Acer, Siemens and Linksys attempt to position Yahoo! media content in new ways, to take advantage of the unique technologies inherent in the tech companies' products. Intel's Viv technology, for example, allows Yahoo! to integrate itself into the media-PC driven television experience. As Nielsen studies show that TVs in the average American household are tuned in for over 8 hours a day, Yahoo! could reinforce its brand exposure significantly.

Reception to this laundry list of strategic alliances has been mixed. While some feel that greater exposure can only be a good thing, others see the company moving in too many directions to stay focused on what it does best. One thing's for sure: Yahoo! will be worth keeping an eye on as it continues implementation over the next 5 years.

Questions

1. Effective strategic planning not only carries a company toward an objective, it anticipates changes in the External Environment, and positions a company to adapt. What are some of the changes Yahoo! may be anticipating, based on the case study above?

2. Does this group of strategic alliances suggest that Yahoo! is focusing on the "superior user experience" objective, or is Yahoo! expanding at the cost of its stated vision?

3. How can Yahoo!'s competitors benefit from all the attention Yahoo! has received regarding its strategic alliances?

CHAPTER 9: MANAGERIAL DECISION-MAKING, ORGANIZATIONAL PLANNING, AND GOAL SETTING AT MCDONALD'S

The "hit by a bus scenario" is something that any company's board of directors must consider carefully. The idea is that a successor must be agreed upon; someone well equipped to take the reigns of the company, should a CEO die suddenly. Most companies plan for an interim successor, a substitute CEO who can occupy the spot until a permanent appointee is chosen. It is understandable that a company might not have a permanent replacement in the wings, as the "hit by a bus" scenario is possible, but certainly seems improbable. The likelihood of losing the newly appointed CEO shortly thereafter seems downright unthinkable. How many companies would have a *second* succession candidate in mind?

Jim Cantalupo, favoring improvement over expansion, was the superstar who brought McDonald's back into the light after a dark period for the company's earnings. He died suddenly at a big McDonald's conference in April 2004, prompting the board that had appointed him just the year before to quickly assemble. Hours later, they announced that COO Charlie Bell was the new CEO. Conference attendees, shocked and saddened by the news of Cantalupo's passing, were nevertheless impressed that the board had acted so quickly and decisively. Two weeks later, Bell was diagnosed with colon cancer. Both his family and the board of directors hoped for the best, but prepared for the worst. In January 2005, Jim Skinner became the third CEO in under a year.

By immediately appointing new successors, McDonald's managed to avoid the fallout that often accompanies the sudden loss of a leader. The organization kept its momentum going, and was rewarded with a confident internal environment and continued earnings growth. What is especially impressive about this scenario is not just that both successors were decided on without interruption to the business, but that they were so capable of stepping into the role. Jim Cantalupo had been with the organization since 1974, and rose from entry-level accountant to head of International Operations before he took the top spot. Charlie Bell had been with the company for almost thirty years himself, and had made history by fast-tracking through the company's ranks in Australia at a young age. Skinner joined McDonald's in 1971 as a manager trainee, and had eventually become a key player in McDonald's global presence. These men were not only qualified for the role, they were prepared to excel in it at a moment's notice.

The fact that McDonald's was so well prepared for the unthinkable made a lot of organizations re-examine their own leadership development efforts. Cultivating internal talent in a focused, meaningful way can provide essential strength in the darkest of times.

Questions

1. When a company's succession plan names an interim CEO, it buys time to decide on a permanent replacement. What are some of the risks a company might face during this process?

2. When an organization is faced with unexpected change, what can managers do to help insure that they make the right choices?

3. During Jim Cantalupo's brief tenure as CEO, McDonald's stock shot up 49 percent. When the company announced his replacement within a day of losing him, the share price rose again. With Cantalupo gone, why would stock go up again so soon?

CHAPTER 10: DESIGNING ADAPTIVE ORGANIZATIONS AT BOYNE USA RESORTS

What did it take for a one-man operation to expand into the largest privately owned ski and golf corporation in the country? The answer is vision, passion, and the persistence of one special entrepreneur.

Detroit native, Everett Kircher, moved to northern Michigan in 1947 and purchased the land (for the price of $1) necessary to start his first ski resort known today as Boyne Mountain. His roles as president and CEO were not eclipsed by his roles as chief engineer, head chef and director of marketing and finance. His success was also fueled by his inventions of many industry "firsts" in snowmaking, snow-grooming equipment and ski lift technology.

He practiced a traditional **chain of command** in a vertical organizational structure. Like most entrepreneurs, every decision came from Everett Kircher's desk. As his company expanded during the 1950's and 60's from skiing to golf resorts and real estate, additional people were needed to manage the different locations. For Everett, it was the very beginnings of a partial decentralization of his leadership and decision-making. Over the next 50 years of expansion, this change would prove profitable.

Today, Boyne USA Resorts hosts seven major four-season resorts across America from Michigan to Washington State. The natural beauty of each resort continues to draw sport and travel enthusiasts nationally and internationally. Through excellence in management practices, sport and leisure enthusiasts of all ages embrace the Boyne "way of life."

In 2002, Everett Kircher died at the age of 85 but his legacy lives on. Their reorganization in 2004 paved the way for the "Boyne Brand" to grow while maintaining organizational integrity. This system was designed with key managers for accountability, control, and information flow in order to make critical decisions.

General managers known as "Mayors of Towns" were hired at each resort location to oversee operations. In addition, Vice Presidents known as "subject matter experts," were also hired. These experts are passionate and knowledgeable in their specific fields of expertise, for example, food and beverage, retail, etc. The VP's share critical information with the general managers to help each resort operation. The general managers fold these experts into the decision-making process and help provide policy.

This streamlining of information helps general managers integrate the VP's knowledge in any areas of weakness. In addition, if one resort was doing well in a particular area, that knowledge could be also be shared and applied throughout branches of Boyne East and West.

Boyne's projections for the future are as ambitious as Everett Kircher's dream. By diversifying their resorts throughout North America they are stronger than many of their competitors. Weather dependent industries must constantly adapt new marketing strategies. The launch of a new attraction, Boyne Mountain's indoor *"Avalanche Waterpark,"* is designed to increase the year-round market accustomed to Boyne's state of the art facilities.

This family-owned company grew from revenues of $40 million in 1990 to over $200 million in 2005. Now entering their 60th year, Boyne USA Resorts' approach to organizational structure is intentional, proactive, and always subject to change.

Questions

1. Why was further decentralization necessary to Boyne's future in spite of the success with Everett Kircher at the helm of a vertical structure?

2. What do you think Boyne's organizational structure formally became after Everett Kircher's death in 2002.

3. Give an example of how Boyne USA's organizational structure supports three key areas: (a) strategy, (b) environment, and (c) technology.

CHAPTER 11: MANAGING CHANGE AND INNOVATION AT HARD ROCK

At the close of 2006, British gaming company Rank Group made a deal with the Seminole Tribe of Florida to sell its stake in the Hard Rock business, to the tune of $965 million dollars. The deal covered ownership of the Hard Rock brand name, 124 Hard Rock Cafes and stores located around the world, 8 hotels, and two Hard Rock Live concert venues.

The Rank Group was going through tough times before it put its stake in the Hard Rock business on the auction block. It was swimming in debt, and Rank stock had taken a beating on the market. Although the chain had been profitable, the Rank Group felt its demands had taken too much focus off of their gambling interests, and that selling it would give them renewed focus. The money Rank made from the sale put the company into the black again, enabled a dividend payout to its investors, and better prepared them financially to take advantage of the UK's recent deregulation of the gambling industry.

The Hard Rock acquisition marks the first time on record that a Native American tribe has purchased such a large international corporation. It was not the first time the Seminole tribe made history. Despite efforts in the early 1800s by U.S. Army and militia forces to destroy the tribe or force them to yield, they never surrendered, and remain the only American Indian tribe who never signed a peace treaty. The Seminole Tribe was the first to win the right to build a tax-free gambling hall on Indian land, a move that changed the economic landscape for Native American tribes forever. Ownership of Hard Rock now gives the savvy tribe a full-blown international presence.

The Hard Rock Cafe business stands to truly benefit from the change. It has always turned a profit, and the most impressive earnings by far have been driven by the two Seminole Hard Rock Casino hotels that the Seminole Tribe opened in 2004. The Tribe stated that it intends to expand operations into new territory, and will look into adding casinos to existing Hard Rock hotels.

All parties involved in the deal can expect big changes in the near future. The Rank Group got less for Hard Rock than many analysts and investors expected, and it may take a while for the company's stock, and investor confidence, to improve. Being newly in the black, however, gives them options. The Seminole Tribe of Florida now runs a large international operation, and must learn a new suite of best practices in order to propel the brand, and the tribe, into the future. Hard Rock's current staff and patrons must adapt to any changes the company's new owners throw at them.

Questions

1. The Seminole Tribe of Florida has had a long history of overcoming adversity in their little corner of the world. What sort of resistance might Hard Rock's new owners face when initiating organizational change?

2. What measures can Hard Rock's new owners take to reassure staff and investors that they are in good hands?

3. Name some basic steps that upper management should take as they assess the best possible direction in which to take the company.

CHAPTER 12: HUMAN RESOURCE MANAGEMENT AT ALLSTATE

Most successful companies agree that their greatest asset is their employees. It is the knowledge, skills, experience, and creativity of their human capitol that keeps successful companies at the forefront of their industries. Talented employees, performing to their full potential, are what give these companies their competitive edge. To attract, retain, and develop this crucial capital, takes comprehensive human resource management. And with today's swiftly changing labor culture, human resource managers must stay on top of management and compensation trends to remain competitive.

We all know "you're in good hands with Allstate." And Allstate has a lot of hands. With over 70,000 employees, Allstate is committed to attracting and retaining the top professionals in their industry while creating a workforce that reflects the diversity of their customer base. Of Allstate's many employees, 29.4% are minorities, 58.9% are women, and within management, over 40 percent are women and nearly 20 percent come from one of five minority groups. As Ed Liddy, Allstate's chairman and CEO said, "Our competitive advantage is our people and our people are diverse . . . Diversity is a strength and a strategy through which the company will continue to realize its growth goals."

Allstate's human resource management philosophy reflects the change in the social contract of today's workforce. Their challenging and collaborative work environment encourages individual accountability, innovative thinking, and continuous learning. They provide challenging positions that are engaging and meaningful to their employees and reward employees' efforts on a pay for performance basis. Allstate also offers a comprehensive compensation package that encourages employees to balance their work and personal life and pursue career opportunities.

Allstate makes a huge investment in their employees. In 2005, Allstate spent $3.3 billion on employee compensation, payroll taxes, welfare, and benefits. In addition to the standard benefits package of insurance, retirement, profit-sharing, and time off compensation, Allstate has a number of other benefits that contribute to their overall Work/Life Strategy. These include the option for flexible work arrangements, on-site childcare at headquarters, adoption reimbursement, and other perks such as on-site dry-cleaning, oil change, salon, postal and catering services at their headquarters. Not only is Allstate committed to attracting and retaining quality employees, they also foster personal and professional growth. Allstate has numerous education programs which include mentoring programs, on-site undergraduate, MBA and professional courses, tuition reimbursement, and education loans for employees and their families. They also have in-house training such as the Talent Acceleration Program, which develops leadership early in employee's careers, and the Learning Resource network which connects employees to more than 6,000 learning activities that help them develop new business, interpersonal, technical, and leadership skills. Allstate encourages their employees to live complete lives, giving back to their families and communities. More than 50% of Allstate employees participate in the company's Helping Hands program and the Allstate Foundation awards $500 grants to non-profit organizations where Allstate employees volunteer. With a donation matching program, Allstate also contributed $9.5 million to various community development agencies.

Allstate's investment in its human resources has met with great success. Not only is Allstate the nation's largest publicly held personal lines insurer, but the satisfaction rate from its annual employee satisfaction survey was 88%. The employees of Allstate are clearly in good hands.

Questions

1. Imagine you are considering a job at Allstate, use the matching model to determine if it would be good fit. Why or why not?

2. In what way does Allstate's human resource management philosophy adhere to the new social contract between organization and employee?

3. What are the benefits for a pay-for-performance based system versus a seniority-based pay system?

CHAPTER 13: MEETING THE CHALLENGE OF DIVERSITY AT WHIRLPOOL CORPORATION

Every day the relative size of our world shrinks. We can eat Thai food for lunch, sit in an office chair made in Taiwan, and take Kenyan drumming classes after work. We can travel to far-flung places in a matter of hours and can communication with people around the globe instantaneously. The global marketplace has arrived and with it all of the joys and challenges of a huge population of people with different languages, cultures, beliefs, values, and styles of communication. Organizations are facing an ever-diversifying customer base as well as a multicultural employee pool. In order to take advantage of the many benefits globalization offers, managers must learn to create a work environment that incorporates and supports difference. Most traditional theories of management assume all workers share the same values, beliefs, and motivations. Successful managers in today's world must create systems flexible enough to take into account varying perspectives and to utilize varying ideas.

Since 1911, Whirlpool Corporation has grown from a small company to a global corporation with manufacturing locations on every major continent and over 68,000 employees worldwide. Approximately 60 percent of Whirlpool's employees are outside of North America and those within North America represent a diverse mix of cultures. Whirlpool has made a commitment to supporting diversity within its workforce to the highest degree. The corporate values listed on its website include respect and diversity, stating, "We've built an employee culture where all beliefs, perspectives and opinions are welcomed and valued . . . By constantly seeking fresh approaches, new ideas and different outlooks, we build our success and secure our future." Whirlpool was named one of the top 50 companies for African-American MBAs to work by Black MBA magazine. Part of Whirlpool's motivation to increase diversity is a desire to better understand the needs and desires of their global customer base. It feels this is best done by creating a workforce of people making business decisions that is reflective of the customer population. Another part of its motivation is to encourage innovation, a key to Whirlpool's success. In developing a diverse workforce at every level of the organization, Whirlpool ensures that a variety of ideas and opinions are brought together to foster broad-reaching innovative solutions to problems. Their

Web site states, "Inclusion is about the respectful involvement of all people and making use of everyone's talents. We believe that differences create value. And we practice inclusion throughout our organization, not only because we believe it's the right thing to do, but also because it's a winning strategy." As evidence by this statement, Whirlpool is committed not only to creating a diverse workforce but to eliminating the bias and glass ceilings that discourage the full participation of many different kinds of people.

Like many organizations, one of Whirlpool's strategies for creating a culture of pluralism and ethnorelativism is encouraging the formation of employee network groups. These are voluntary groups formed around primary dimensions such as gender, ethnicity, and sexuality, and which meet regularly to focus on business issues. The groups are forums to discuss diversity issues and company progress, heighten the awareness within the organization of all cultural issues, and to cultivate key communications by making recommendations to the management about how to enhance the pluralistic environment.

The groups are also a resource to the employees by providing a supportive community, decreasing social isolation, and promoting career development. Further, they help retain employees by providing them a forum for expressing ideas. These discussions often spark new ideas that benefit the company as a whole.

Every day, Whirlpool is working towards fostering a culture that celebrates difference. Former Whirlpool Chairman and CEO David R. Whitwam formed the Council for World-Class Communities (CWCC), a nonprofit group that works to remove barriers to diversity and inclusion, in addition to barriers to economic prosperity in Southwest Michigan. Many Whirlpool Corporation employees are active members on the Council and the number of CWCC supporters continues to grow as the group makes more steps to improve the quality of life for all.

Questions

1. Using the Whirlpool Corporation Web site, what are the employee network groups at Whirlpool and what is the mission of each?

2. Do you think Whirlpool's encouragement of employee networks works for or against the creating a culture of diversity and the formation of multicultural teams? Why or why not?

3. What are three things a manager at Whirlpool could do to eliminate bias and glass ceilings?

CHAPTER 14: MANAGERIAL AND QUALITY CONTROL AT HONDA

In 1982 when Honda announced they were building the first Japanese auto assembly plant in North America, many Japanese were skeptical that North American labor could produce the same quality as their Japanese counterpart. Quality had been the key strategic factor for the Japanese, who were rebuilding their industry following World War II. Edward Demming was the architect behind the quality-based strategy and was honored by having the nation's highest award named after him. The strategy was simple: build a better product and build it right the first time. The Japanese spent many years perfecting this concept and were not optimistic that it could be easily transplanted to another culture, especially one like the U.S.

By having assembly plants in North America, Honda not only saved transportation costs, but was also insulated from changing exchange rates that were raising the price of goods sourced from Japan. But could the small Japanese company hold on to the market share it earned from its reliable and well-made Civics and Accords? While not a large factor in the Japanese auto market, Honda had done very well exporting their cars to the United States. This success was due primarily to the extremely high reputation Honda had for reliability and quality. If they lost that edge, they were probably out of business.

Honda realized that quality is a systemic process. By creating the right systems and infusing the culture of quality, there was no reason why the quality in North America should be any different that Japan. Sam Kennedy was given the responsibility of managing quality at Honda's Marysville plant. Some of the tools Sam uses are weekly manager's meetings; daily quality circle meetings, statistical process control, and a philosophy of continuous improvement. But the key factor was a systematic discipline for measuring quality, correcting procedure to improve quality, and making sure every employee knew that quality was Honda's biggest priority.

Honda's success has been enormous. They will open their sixth plant in North America this year. Their employment numbers in North America have grown to over 25,000, but the reputation for quality is unchanged. Honda was the first Japanese company to build a plant in North America and now every Japanese, German, and Korean automotive company has facilities in North America. Quality has been and will continue to be Honda's competitive advantage.

Questions

1. How has Honda used quality to promote its products?
2. What are some of the techniques used by Honda to ensure quality?
3. What is a QC circle?

CHAPTER 15: INFORMATION TECHNOLOGY AND E-BUSINESS AT PEET'S COFFEE & TEA

A morning fix of freshly brewed coffee has become a necessity for most Americans. The source of the fix—home brewed, national chain, or local coffee shop—differs for everyone, but the desire for high-quality, fresh, and widely available coffee does not change. Peet's Coffee & Tea has been making good mornings for people since it opened its store in 1966 in Berkeley, California. With the expansion into e-business, Peet's has been able to enlarge its market beyond California to reach people across the country. But, in order to do this, Peet's relies on a strong network of information technology.

Peet's still calls Berkely home with its original retail store and roasting facility nearby. But, it has grown considerably since 1966 with retail stores in several other cities. In, addition, there are many other ways to enjoy Peet's coffees and teas. They are available online at Peets.com or through their mail order service; can be purchased at specialty food and grocery stores; and can be found in offices, fine restaurants, and hotels. Within these many channels, Peet's strives to deliver a consistent, high-quality product.

Part of what makes Peet's unique is its high standards for quality and freshness. Unlike other coffee distributors, Peet's coffees are roasted by hand, in small batches, by roasters trained over the course of 10 years. Beans are only roasted as orders come in and are shipped out the next day to ensure freshness. While Peet's does not use a computer for its roasting, it heavily relies on technology for its packaging and distribution. Orders come in from the retail stores, the website,

the catalog, and through the handheld devices of the drivers delivering to grocery and specialty stores. Peet's offers 32 types of coffee with options for singe bean, blends, ground or whole bean, and decaffeination, as well as different packaging types for every channel. In total, Peet's processes over 40,000 lbs of coffee that are all packaged and shipped the same day.

These many variables require a complex operations information system. Peet's uses an enterprise resource planning system developed in-house called a roasting spreadsheet. At the end of every day, the roasting spreadsheet compiles all of the orders taken over the various channels and breaks them down by type of coffee, type of grind, and channel. In the morning, via an intranet, roasters are given a breakdown of how much of each bean needs to be roasted. The program produces worksheets given to each machine operators which tell them which of each package type and coffee need to be produced. The roasting spreadsheet also produces labels which layout which coffee should be placed in which package and how many packages need to be bundled for shipping, as well as what type of shipping means (e.g. ground versus airmail) should be used. It is only through the use of this sophisticated technology that Peet's is able to maintain its tradition of high-quality, artesian coffee that so many people enjoy every day.

Questions

1. What part of Peet's roasting spreadsheet processes data? What part processes information?

2. In what ways might Peet's use a CRM system to assist them?

3. What other types of information technology systems might be useful to Peet's?

771

On the Job Video Case

CHAPTER 16: OPERATION AND SERVICE MANAGEMENT AT WASHBURN GUITAR

The music industry is a tough business—just ask any of the thousands of garage bands, weekend DJs, and shower soul-singers that are struggling to make it. However, musicians are not the only ones fighting to make it big in the world of music. The people at Washburn Guitar see the music scene from another side, that of music equipment and instrument manufacturers. Manufacturers of music equipment, just like the contestants on American Idol, are constantly vying to be considered number one, and Washburn Guitar is no exception.

In the heart of Chicago, a city known for its wailing blues and strumming rock music, Washburn Guitar has been making quality products since 1883. As the music industry is increasingly flooded with equipment manufacturers trying to make a name for themselves, Washburn wants everyone to know that they continue to produce the world's best guitars. To stay competitive, they know that they must keep manufacturing quality high. As Gil Vasquez, production manager at Washburn Guitar, puts it: "You can have the prettiest guitar out there, but if it doesn't play and if it doesn't sound good, nobody's going to care."

How does Washburn Guitar ensure its high production standards? One key to their success is in their ability to keep up with the ever-changing environment of the music industry. Not comfortable with simply maintaining the status quo, the management at Washburn Guitar is constantly looking to initiate and implement organizational change that will improve their overall production. For example, over the past few years they have acquired Vasquez as their production manager and Parker Guitars, another manufacturer of specialty high-end guitars and a former competitor.

Having worked with guitar manufacturers across the country, including the world-famous Fender, Vasquez brings a meticulous eye for perfection to the production floor. He brings an open and creative managerial style that ensures both quality and efficiency. From the initial computer drawings of the guitar to the final installation of its components, Vasquez makes sure that the process is smooth, consistent, and of the highest quality.

Washburn's acquisition of Parker Guitars was another move to inject its business with new life, creativity and growth potential. Since doing so, they have increased the production of their custom guitars fifteen times—from 20 a month to 300! And the strengths of Parker's manufacturing techniques have been incorporated into both Parker and Washburn guitars. The synergy of the two companies have increased both quality and efficiency.

Overall, Washburn recognizes that the music industry is cut-throat, no matter what side of it you are on. Staying on top requires creativity and willingness to change. To continue its long tradition of success, they are committed to the organizational development that will allow them to remain one of the best names in guitars.

Questions

1. What are some environmental influences specific to Washburn that you imagine might lead to the initiation of organizational change?

2. Discuss some possible forms of resistance that you can see Washburn Guitars encountering, particularly as they merge with other manufacturers and bring on new management members like Gil Vasquez.

3. If you were brought in to revive a guitar manufacturing business that was having difficulty, how would you go about making organizational changes? Use the sequence of four change activities as a guide.

CHAPTER 17: DYNAMICS OF BEHAVIOR IN ORGANIZATIONS AT ZINGERMAN'S

The people who create the delightful Zingerman's Experience in Ann Arbor, Michigan for their customers' dining pleasure are on a mission: To make customers' lives more enjoyable with remarkably flavored food, great service, great finances, and a great work environment. The masterful mixing, stirring, and blending of the talents, skills, passion, and behavior of 400 people (closer to 1000 people during the peak holiday season) has created the legendary Zingerman's Community of Businesses, named "The Coolest Small Business in America" by Inc. Magazine.

The people of Zingerman's are not only students and connoisseurs of traditional foods, from which they craft remarkably flavored recipes. They are also students and connoisseurs of people. Ari Weinzweig, one of the co-founders of the original Zingerman's Deli in 1982, puts it this way: "People don't need our food at the price point that is required to prepare and serve it. They have to be educated to appreciate traditional recipes and foods. We not only have a passion for food, we have a passion for education and we have a passion for service."

To build and lead this level of service to their customers, the leaders, managers, and staff of all of Zingerman's Community of Businesses believe that outstanding service to customers is the result of outstanding service to one another. Zingerman's subscribes to Servant Leadership, which means that the managing partners are in service to all the managers. The managers are in service to all the people on the staff. They all feel that the staff will not provide a better service experience to customers than that which they themselves experience with one another.

What it takes to lead, inspire, and organize this level of dedication to service in every cell of the Zingerman's Experience is a passion that begins with the founders and is taught, nurtured, and developed in the hearts of everyone who is on the Zingerman's team. Zingerman's seeks to recruit people with an easy smile and a high level of emotional intelligence: self awareness, self management, social awareness, and relationship awareness, which leads to high work ethic, interest in learning, self direction and ownership ability, and enthusiasm for what they are doing.

Zingerman's is an organization that then gives people an opportunity to make a difference, an impact on the organization. They ask people to get involved. When people think they are making a difference, they are making a difference. That is the recipe that inspires the organizational behavior in the Zimmerman's Community of Businesses.

Questions

1. What is the connection between great work environment and organizational behavior at Zingerman's?

2. Why is there a high premium placed on staff education and on customer education at Zingerman's?

3. Why does Zingerman's seek to recruit emotionally intelligent people?

CHAPTER 18: LEADERSHIP AT McDONALD'S

Do you want fries with that? This ubiquitous phrase is heard by nearly 50 million people in more than 119 countries each day. McDonald's has achieved the status of one of the most recognizable franchises across the globe through a mixture of successful marketing, consistent service and products, and strong leadership.

Ray Kroc was a visionary leader. He saw the potential for standardizing an efficient, systematized restaurant model and replicating it across the country. He began as the distributor of the mechanized milk shake maker, the Multimixer. At the McDonald's hamburger stand in California, Kroc saw a restaurant that used not one, but eight Multimixers and served a record number of people in the shortest amount of time imaginable. He proposed the idea of opening up several such restaurants to the brothers Dick and Mac McDonald, and in 1955, Kroc opened the first Mc Donald's in Des Plaines, Illinois. The rest is history.

Not only was Kroc a visionary leader who inspired others with his charisma, he possessed a strong initiating structure. He is quoted as saying, "If you've got time to lean, you've got time to clean," which highlights his goal-oriented and task-focused leadership style that still exists today. McDonalds' global business strategy—Plan to Win—encompasses five areas: place, products, price, promotion, and people. Part of the commitment to people is providing employees the resources to get their jobs done. This includes adequately staffing restaurants to allow for a good customer experience as well as to provide schedule flexibility, providing employees the proper tools to serve the customer, and training employees in job skills including customer service, responsibility, teamwork, time management, problem-solving, and communication at Hamburger University. Such a philosophy follows the Path-Goal theory of increasing employee motivation through clarifying desired behaviors and company goals. This philosophy has proven successful in producing future leadership for McDonald's, as over 40% of its top management started as crew members, including CEO Jim Skinner.

Another side of McDonalds' Plan to Win embodies the more people-oriented facet of consideration-based leadership. McDonald's espouses a commitment to investing in the growth and job satisfaction of its employees so they can realize their full potential. This includes a commitment to an inclusive, supportive workplace environment that recognizes and rewards good performance. Managers are encouraged to treat employees as they would want to be treated, act as coaches as opposed to policemen, promote teamwork, and communicate openly, listening to understand, and valuing others' opinions.

Like many successful organizations, McDonald's has found great success by promoting a corporate leadership style that combines a high initiating structure and high consideration. Such a combination will allow them to weather the next 50 years of selling Big Macs.

Questions

1. Where does the leadership at McDonald's fall on the Leadership Grid in figure 15.3? Explain your answer.

2. What are the benefits of a corporate leadership strategy?

3. As a leader in the first years of McDonald's, what kind of power did Ray Kroc have?

CHAPTER 19: MOTIVATION AT WASHBURN GUITAR

"It's a labor of love," said Gil Vasquez, Washburn Guitar Production Manager.

"It's a piece of art," says Eric Karol, Washburn Floor Manager. "I tell them to treat each guitar they're working on like they're making it for themselves."

"I would say 95% of the employees that work at U.S. Music (parent of Washburn Guitar) play an instrument and it really improves the quality of all of our instruments because they have a passion for what they are doing." said Kevin Lello, Washburn Guitar VP of Marketing.

Having a motivated workforce is essential because guitar making is labor intensive, and requires attention to detail. Quality materials combined with quality craftsmanship are necessary to produce quality guitars. The Washburn Guitar workforce is motivated because they love music and care about the instruments.

Founded in the late 1800s in Chicago, Washburn boasts a rich tradition of fine instrument making. Today they sell more than 50,000 guitars annually, totaling about $40 million dollars in revenue. Washburn Guitar produces a wide variety of acoustic and electric guitars.

Over the years an impressive list of artists have played Washburn guitars, including: Greg Allman, George Harrison, and Robert Plant. Today, Washburn artists include members of Weezer, Rascal Flats, Fall Out Boy, All American Rejects, and Modest Yahoo. They also produce signature guitars for leading guitarists such as Washburn's Maya Pro DD75, which is made for Dan Donegan. He's lead guitarist for Disturbed, a very popular hard rock band.

Signature models like the Maya Pro confirms Washburn's capability for producing quality and style. It also strengthens Washburn's relationship with Dan Donegan, his band Disturbed, and their huge fan base. It also motivates their staff. Employees get more satisfaction out of creating these special guitars.

"Some are motivated by the fact of music, and some are motivated by being able to work on an instrument." Gil Vasquez says "One of the biggest motivational factors for me is when you're done with a guitar . . . you've taken it from the drawing board to the manufacturing point, given it to the artist . . . watching him play it on stage, it's like validation."

Washburn craftsman also enjoy making custom guitars. In recent years their custom shop production has grown dramatically from 20 guitars per month to 300 guitars per month.

Questions

1. What motivates most Washburn Guitar employees?
2. What kinds of guitars do employees most like to produce?
3. What is the connection between quality guitars and workforce motivation?

CHAPTER 20: COMMUNICATION AT NAVISTAR INTERNATIONAL

The decision to dedicate the resources needed to fund and support the Department of Communications within Navistar International sends a signal that Corporate Communication is seen as vital to the health of this $12 billion truck and engine manufacturing and financial services corporation.

The Department of Communications functions as a business partner with the three major business units. Each plant has a communications manager or communicator who dual reports to the plant manager and the Corporate Director of the Department of Communications. The role of the Communications Manager is to drive the message to the target audience. They use different approaches depending on the audience and the direction of the message, whether it's heading up or down the corporate ladder, or across business units.

Typically, in any successful business organization, skilled and talented people within each business unit develop and execute planning, production, and measurement with precision. Skill and talent within the business unit does not always translate into skill and talent for communicating outside the business unit, across business units, up and down the corporate ladder. In a business organization, lack of communication, poor communication, or miscommunication can be deadly and costly.

This is where skilled and talented communications professionals can add value to the organization. High quality corporate communication needs to be clearly and accurately delivered. Choosing and using the right combination of channels and media to create the best climate for reception and response is the province of communications professionals.

Some channels of communication require multiple senses to receive the message. Face to face communication is one channel of communication that uses several senses, but it may not assure accurate recall, and a conversation cannot be mass distributed without some kind of recording. Other channels of communication like telephone, TV, radio, email, memos, letters, formal reports, and bulletins enable effective recall and mass distribution, but involve fewer senses and learning styles.

Communications professionals are skilled and trained to know how to mix and match all the available communication media to the learning and communication styles and needs of the variety of audiences within the corporation. The customary communication styles that are effective within a business unit are often not the same styles that are required to communicate across business units or up and down the corporate ladder. The customary communication styles that are effective in everyday work situations are often not the same styles that are required to resolve conflict or manage crisis situations. This is the value add within Navistar International that results from the role the Department of Communications plays in the corporation.

Questions

1. Explain why the communication skills and techniques used within a business unit (department) are not always effective in communicating across business units or up and down the corporate ladder.

2. Explain why conflict resolution communication skills are not always present in everyday workplace situations and how a skilled communications professional would add value to that workplace.

3. How would a Communications Plan effectively handle a crisis in the workplace, such as violence, sexual abuse, scandal, etc? What would likely happen in a crisis situation without a communications plan in place?

CHAPTER 21: TEAMWORK AT COLD STONE CREAMERY

Freshly baked brownies and cones, handmade ice cream in a pantheon of flavors, and an array of toppings from cookies to fruit, sprinkles to marshmallow, all folded together into the perfect blend. This Ultimate Ice Cream Experience is not the work of one person, but the many teams that make up Cold Stone Creamery.

From the crew members to the managers to the franchisees, area developers, and Creamery members, Cold Stone Creamery is focused on facilitating teamwork. Their list of core values includes the statement "Win as a Team." Doug Ducey, CEO and chairman, is in charge of guiding the future direction of the business. As a leader, he is willing to embrace change and think creatively. He empowers people and believes in his team, challenging them to perform and deliver results. For Doug, individual success is measured by success of the team as a whole. It is through the building of teams that Cold Stone creates a cohesive, unified workforce committed to making Cold Stone Creamery the #1 selling ice cream in the U.S. by 2010. The front line of Cold Stone's service are the in-store crew members, mostly 17 year olds in their first job. Huge amounts of effort and the team norming go into supporting these employees and ensuring they have all of the knowledge and skill to make the next customer happy.

Within Cold Stone are a series of team structures: vertical, horizontal, special purpose, and global.

Vertical teams include members from the Creamery down to the managers, who together strategize about the newest efforts to make Cold Stone #1. Within the store, crew members form horizontal teams based on different specialties, including entertainment, daily prep, fruit prep, and baking. Together, they create the celebratory experience customers enjoy within the store. As part of the Pyramid for Success, 2010, special purpose teams have been assembled to help develop more stores, increase the customer base, adapt marketing, and, ultimately, increase sales. With stores in Japan, South Korea, Taiwan, Mainland China, and the Middle East, many global teams must meet and work virtually to deliver the Ultimate Ice Cream Experience internationally.

Cold Stone Creamery's use of teams has brought them extensive success. They have amplified the effort of their employees, unleashing their creative energies; increased employee satisfaction; expanded job knowledge; and augmented organizational responsiveness. The company has an excellent shot at making Cold Stone #1. And a little extra hot sauce does not hurt.

Questions

1. What are some norms that might be important to develop in a Cold Stone team?

2. Describe a situation in which conflict might arise in a horizontal team of Crew Members.

3. What might be some of the challenges in creating a global team?

GLOSSARY

360-degree feedback A process that uses multiple raters, including self-rating, to appraise employee performance and guide development.

A

achievement culture A results-oriented culture that values competitiveness, personal initiative, and achievement.

activity-based costing (ABC) A control system that identifies the various activities needed to provide a product and allocates costs accordingly.

activity ratio A financial ratio that measures the organization's internal performance with respect to key activities defined by management.

adaptability culture A culture characterized by values that support the company's ability to interpret and translate signals from the environment into new behavior responses.

adjourning The stage of team development in which members prepare for the team's disbandment.

administrative model A decision-making model that describes how managers actually make decisions in situations characterized by nonprogrammed decisions, uncertainty, and ambiguity.

administrative principles A subfield of the classical management perspective that focuses on the total organization rather than the individual worker, delineating the management functions of planning, organizing, commanding, coordinating, and controlling.

affirmative action A policy requiring employers to take positive steps to guarantee equal employment opportunities for people within protected groups; government-mandated programs that focus on providing opportunities to women and members of minority groups who previously experienced discrimination.

angel financing Financing provided by a wealthy individual who believes in the idea for a start-up and provides personal funds and advice to help the business get started.

application form A device for collecting information about an applicant's education, previous job experience, and other background characteristics.

assessment center A technique for selecting individuals with high managerial potential based on their performance on a series of simulated managerial tasks.

attitude A cognitive and affective evaluation that predisposes a person to act in a certain way.

attributions Judgments about what causes a person's behavior—either characteristics of the person or of the situation.

authoritarianism The belief that power and status differences should exist within the organization.

authority The formal and legitimate right of a manager to make decisions, issue orders, and allocate resources to achieve organizationally desired outcomes.

B

balance sheet A financial statement that shows the firm's financial position with respect to assets and liabilities at a specific point in time.

balanced scorecard A comprehensive management control system that balances traditional financial measures with measures of customer service, internal business processes, and the organization's capacity for learning and growth.

bargaining zone The range between one party's minimum reservation point (the point beyond which the party is willing to accept a deal) and the other party's maximum reservation point.

BATNA The "best alternative to a negotiated agreement"; a previously determined choice of what a party will do if an acceptable agreement cannot be reached through negotiation.

B2B marketplace An electronic marketplace set up by an intermediary where buyers and sellers meet.

BCG matrix A concept developed by the Boston Consulting Group that evaluates strategic business units with respect to the dimensions of business growth rate and market share.

behavior modification The set of techniques by which reinforcement theory is used to modify human behavior.

behavioral sciences approach A subfield of the humanistic management perspective that applies social science in an organizational context, drawing from economics, psychology, sociology, and other disciplines.

behaviorally anchored rating scale (BARS) A rating technique that relates an employee's performance to specific job-related incidents.

benchmarking The continuous process of measuring products, services, and practices against major competitors or industry leaders.

biculturalism The sociocultural skills and attitudes used by racial minorities as they move back and forth between the dominant culture and their own ethnic or racial culture.

Big Five personality factors Dimensions that describe an individual's extroversion, agreeableness, conscientiousness, emotional stability, and openness to experience.

blog Web log that allows individuals to post opinions and ideas.

bottom-up budgeting A budgeting process in which lower-level managers budget their departments' resource needs and pass them up to top management for approval.

boundary-spanning roles Roles assumed by people and/or departments that link and coordinate the organization with key elements in the external environment.

bounded rationality The concept that people have the time and cognitive ability to process only a limited amount of information on which to base decisions.

brainstorming A technique that uses a face-to-face group to spontaneously suggest a broad range of alternatives for decision making.

bureaucratic control The use of rules, policies, hierarchy of authority, reward systems, and other formal devices to influence employee behavior and assess performance.

bureaucratic organizations A subfield of the classical management perspective that emphasizes management on an impersonal, rational basis through such elements as clearly defined authority and responsibility, formal recordkeeping, and separation of management and ownership.

business incubator An innovation that provides shared office space, management support services, and management advice to entrepreneurs.

business intelligence (BI) The high-tech analysis of data from multiple sources to identify patterns and relationships that might be significant.

business-level strategy The level of strategy concerned with the question "How do we compete?" Pertains to each business unit or product line within the organization.

business performance dashboard A system that pulls data from a variety of organizational systems and databases; gauges the data against key performance metrics; pulls out the right nuggets of information; and delivers information to managers in a graphical, easy-to-interpret format.

business plan A document specifying the business details prepared by an entrepreneur prior to opening a new business.

C

CAD A production technology in which computers perform new-product design.

CAM A production technology in which computers help guide and control the manufacturing system.

capacity planning The determination and adjustment of the organization's ability to produce products and services to match customer demand.

capital budget A budget that plans and reports investments in major assets to be depreciated over several years.

cash budget A budget that estimates and reports cash flows on a daily or weekly basis to ensure that the company has sufficient cash to meet its obligations.

cellular layout A facilities layout in which machines dedicated to sequences of production are grouped into cells in accordance with group-technology principles.

central planning department A group of planning specialists who develop plans for the organization as a whole and its major divisions and departments and typically report to the president or CEO.

centralization The location of decision authority near top organizational levels.

centralized network A team communication structure in which team members communicate through a single individual to solve problems or make decisions.

ceremony A planned activity at a special event that is conducted for the benefit of an audience.

certainty The situation in which all the information the decision maker needs is fully available.

chain of command An unbroken line of authority that links all individuals in the organization and specifies who reports to whom.

change agent An OD specialist who contracts with an organization to facilitate change.

changing An intervention stage of organization development in which individuals experiment with new workplace behavior.

channel The carrier of a communication.

channel richness The amount of information that can be transmitted during a communication episode.

charismatic leader A leader who has the ability to motivate subordinates to transcend their expected performance.

chief ethics officer A company executive who oversees ethics and legal compliance.

classical model A decision-making model based on the assumption that managers should make logical decisions that will be in the organization's best economic interests.

classical perspective A management perspective that emerged during the nineteenth and early twentieth centuries that emphasized a rational, scientific approach to the study of management and sought to make organizations efficient operating machines.

closed system A system that does not interact with the external environment.

coalition An informal alliance among managers who support a specific goal.

code of ethics A formal statement of the organization's values regarding ethics and social issues.

coercive power Power that stems from the authority to punish or recommend punishment.

cognitive dissonance A condition in which two attitudes or a behavior and an attitude conflict.

collectivism A preference for a tightly knit social framework in which individuals look after one another and organizations protect their members' interests.

committee A long-lasting, sometimes permanent team in the organization structure created to deal with tasks that recur regularly.

communication The process by which information is exchanged and understood by two or more people, usually with the intent to motivate or influence behavior.

communication apprehension An individual's level of fear or anxiety associated with interpersonal communications.

compensation Monetary payments (wages, salaries) and nonmonetary goods/commodities (benefits, vacations) used to reward employees.

compensatory justice The concept that individuals should be compensated for the cost of their injuries by the party responsible and also that individuals should not be held responsible for matters over which they have no control.

competitive advantage What sets the organization apart from others and provides it with a distinctive edge in the marketplace.

competitors Other organizations in the same industry or type of business that provide goods or services to the same set of customers.

conceptual skill The cognitive ability to see the organization as a whole and the relationships among its parts.

concurrent control Control that consists of monitoring ongoing activities to ensure that they are consistent with standards.

conflict Antagonistic interaction in which one party attempts to thwart the intentions or goals of another.

consideration A type of behavior that describes the extent to which a leader is sensitive to subordinates, respects their ideas and feelings, and establishes mutual trust.

consistency culture A culture that values and rewards a methodical, rational, orderly way of doing things.

content theories A group of theories that emphasize the needs that motivate people.

contingency approach A model of leadership that describes the relationship between leadership styles and specific organizational situations.

contingency plans Plans that define company responses to specific situations, such as emergencies, setbacks, or unexpected conditions.

contingency view An extension of the humanistic perspective in which the successful resolution of organizational problems is thought to depend on managers' identification of key variations in the situation at hand.

contingent workers People who work for an organization, but not on a permanent or full-time basis, including temporary placements, contracted professionals, or leased employees.

continuous improvement The implementation of a large number of small, incremental improvements in all areas of the organization on an ongoing basis.

continuous process production A type of technology involving mechanization of the entire workflow and nonstop production.

continuous reinforcement schedule A schedule in which every occurrence of the desired behavior is reinforced.

controlling The management function concerned with monitoring employees' activities, keeping the organization on track toward its goals, and making corrections as needed.

coordination The quality of collaboration across departments.

core competence A business activity that an organization does particularly well in comparison to competitors.

corporate governance The system of governing an organization so the interests of corporate owners are protected.

corporate-level strategy The level of strategy concerned with the question "What business are we in?" Pertains to the organization as a whole and the combination of business units and product lines that make it up.

corporate social responsibility The obligation of organization management to make decisions and take actions that will enhance the welfare and interests of society as well as the organization.

corporate university An in-house training and education facility that offers broad-based learning opportunities for employees.

corporation An artificial entity created by the state and existing apart from its owners.

cost leadership A type of competitive strategy in which the organization aggressively seeks efficient facilities, cuts costs, and employs tight cost controls to be more efficient than competitors.

countertrade The barter of products for other products rather than their sale for currency.

courage The ability to step forward through fear and act on one's values and conscience.

creativity The generation of novel ideas that may meet perceived needs or offer opportunities for the organization.

cross-functional team A group of employees from various functional departments that meet as a team to resolve mutual problems.

cultural intelligence (CQ) A person's ability to use reasoning and observation skills to interpret unfamiliar gestures and situations and devise appropriate behavioral responses.

cultural leader A manager who uses signals and symbols to influence corporate culture.

culture The set of key values, beliefs, understandings, and norms that members of a society or an organization share.

culture change A major shift in the norms, values, attitudes, and mind-set of the entire organization.

culture shock Feelings of confusion, disorientation, and anxiety that result from being immersed in a foreign culture.

customer relationship management (CRM) systems Systems that help companies track customers' interaction with the firm and allow employees to call up information on past transactions.

customers People and organizations in the environment who acquire goods or services from the organization.

cycle time The steps taken to complete a company process.

D

data Raw, unsummarized, and unanalyzed facts and figures.

data warehousing The use of a huge database that combines all of a company's data and allows users to access

the data directly, create reports, and obtain answers to what-if questions.

debt financing Borrowing money that has to be repaid at a later date in order to start a business.

decentralization The location of decision authority near lower organizational levels.

decentralized control The use of organization culture, group norms, and a focus on goals, rather than rules and procedures, to foster compliance with organizational goals.

decentralized network A team communication structure in which team members freely communicate with one another and arrive at decisions together.

decentralized planning Managers working with planning experts to develop their own goals and plans.

decision A choice made from available alternatives.

decision making The process of identifying problems and opportunities and then resolving them.

decision styles Differences among people with respect to how they perceive problems and make decisions.

decision support system (DSS) An interactive, computer-based system that uses decision models and specialized databases to support organization decision makers.

decode To translate the symbols used in a message for the purpose of interpreting its meaning.

delegation The process managers use to transfer authority and responsibility to positions below them in the hierarchy.

departmentalization The basis on which individuals are grouped into departments and departments into total organizations.

dependent demand inventory Inventory in which item demand is related to the demand for other inventory items.

descriptive An approach that describes how managers actually make decisions rather than how they should.

devil's advocate A decision-making technique in which an individual is assigned the role of challenging the assumptions and assertions made by the group to prevent premature consensus.

diagnosis The step in the decision-making process in which managers analyze underlying causal factors associated with the decision situation.

dialogue A group communication process aimed at creating a culture based on collaboration, fluidity, trust, and commitment to shared goals.

differentiation A type of competitive strategy with which the organization seeks to distinguish its products or services from that of competitors.

digital technology Technology characterized by use of the Internet and other digital processes to conduct or support business operations.

direct investing An entry strategy in which the organization is involved in managing its production facilities in a foreign country.

discretionary responsibility Organizational responsibility that is voluntary and guided by the organization's desire to make social contributions not mandated by economics, law, or ethics.

discrimination The hiring or promoting of applicants based on criteria that are not job relevant.

distribution Moving finished products to customers; also called *order fulfillment*.

distributive justice The concept that different treatment of people should not be based on arbitrary characteristics. In the case of substantive differences, people should be treated differently in proportion to the differences among them.

distributive negotiation A competitive and adversarial negotiation approach in which each party strives to get as much as it can, usually at the expense of the other party.

diversity training Special training designed to educate employees about the importance of diversity, make people aware of their own biases, and teach them skills for communicating and working in a diverse workplace.

divisional structure An organization structure in which departments are grouped based on similar organizational outputs.

downsizing Intentional, planned reduction in the size of a company's workforce.

downward communication Messages sent from top management down to subordinates.

dual role A role in which the individual both contributes to the team's task and supports members' emotional needs.

E

e-business Work an organization does by using electronic linkages; any business that takes place by digital processes over a computer network rather than in a physical space.

e-commerce Business exchanges or transactions that occur electronically.

E → P expectancy Expectancy that putting effort into a given task will lead to high performance.

economic dimension The dimension of the general environment representing the overall economic health of the country or region in which the organization operates.

economic forces Forces that affect the availability, production, and distribution of a society's resources among competing users.

economic order quantity (EOQ) An inventory management technique designed to minimize the total of ordering and holding costs for inventory items.

economic value-added (EVA) system A control system that measures performance in terms of after-tax profits minus the cost of capital invested in tangible assets.

effectiveness The degree to which the organization achieves a stated goal.

efficiency The use of minimal resources—raw materials, money, and people—to produce a desired volume of output.

electronic brainstorming Bringing people together in an interactive group over a computer network to suggest alternatives, sometimes called *brainwriting*.

electronic data interchange (EDI) A network that links the computer systems of buyers and sellers to allow the transmission of structured data primarily for ordering, distribution, and payables and receivables.

employee network groups Groups based on social identity, such as gender or race, and organized by employees to focus on concerns of employees from that group.

employment test A written or computer-based test designed to measure a particular attribute such as intelligence or aptitude.

empowerment The delegation of power and authority to subordinates.

encode To select symbols with which to compose a message.

enterprise resource planning (ERP) Systems that unite a company's major business functions—order processing, product design, purchasing, inventory, and so on; a networked information system that collects, processes, and provides information about an organization's entire enterprise, from identification of customer needs and receipt of orders to distribution of products and receipt of payments.

entrepreneur Someone who recognizes a viable idea for a business product or service and carries it out.

entrepreneurship The process of initiating a business venture, organizing the necessary resources, and assuming the associated risks and rewards.

entropy The tendency for a system to run down and die.

equity A situation that exists when the ratio of one person's outcomes to inputs equals that of another's.

equity financing Financing that consists of funds that are invested in exchange for ownership in the company.

equity theory A process theory that focuses on individuals' perceptions of how fairly they are treated relative to others.

ERG theory A modification of the needs hierarchy theory that proposes three categories of needs: existence, relatedness, and growth.

escalating commitment Continuing to invest time and resources in a failing decision.

ethical dilemma A situation that arises when all alternative choices or behaviors are deemed undesirable because of potentially negative ethical consequence, making it difficult to distinguish right from wrong.

ethics The code of moral principles and values that governs the behaviors of a person or group with respect to what is right or wrong.

ethics committee A group of executives assigned to oversee the organization's ethics by ruling on questionable issues and disciplining violators.

ethics training Training programs to help employees deal with ethical questions and values.

ethnocentrism A cultural attitude marked by the tendency to regard one's own culture as superior to others; the belief that one's own group or subculture is inherently superior to other groups or cultures.

ethnorelativism The belief that groups and subcultures are inherently equal.

euro A single European currency that replaced the currencies of 12 European nations.

event-driven planning Evolutionary planning that responds to the current reality of what the environment and the marketplace demand.

executive information system (EIS) A management information system designed to facilitate strategic decision making at the highest levels of management by providing executives with easy access to timely and relevant information.

exit interview An interview conducted with departing employees to determine the reasons for their termination.

expatriates Employees who live and work in a country other than their own.

expectancy theory A process theory that proposes that motivation depends on individuals' expectations about their ability to perform tasks and receive desired rewards.

expense budget A budget that outlines the anticipated and actual expenses for each responsibility center.

expert power Power that stems from special knowledge of or skill in the tasks performed by subordinates.

exporting An entry strategy in which the organization maintains its production facilities within its home country and transfers its products for sale in foreign countries.

external locus of control The belief by individuals that their future is not within their control but, rather, is influenced by external forces.

extranet An external communications system that uses the Internet and is shared by two or more organizations.

extrinsic reward A reward given by another person.

F

fast-cycle team A multifunctional team that is provided with high levels of resources and empowerment to accomplish an accelerated product development project.

feedback A response by the receiver to the sender's communication; using communication and evaluation to help the organization learn and improve.

feedback control Control that focuses on the organization's outputs; also called *postaction* or *output control.*

feedforward control Control that focuses on human, material, and financial resources flowing into the organization; also called *preliminary* or *preventive control.*

femininity A cultural preference for relationships, cooperation, group decision making, and quality of life.

finished-goods inventory Inventory consisting of items that have passed through the complete production process but have yet to be sold.

first-line manager A manager who is at the first or second management level and is directly responsible for the production of goods and services.

fixed-position layout A facilities layout in which the product remains in one location and the required tasks and equipment are brought to it.

flat structure A management structure characterized by an overall broad span of control and relatively few hierarchical levels.

flexible manufacturing system A small- or medium-sized automated production line that can be adapted to produce more than one product line.

focus A type of competitive strategy that emphasizes concentration on a specific regional market or buyer group.

force-field analysis The process of determining which forces drive and which resist a proposed change.

formal communication channel A communication channel that flows within the chain of command or task responsibility defined by the organization.

formal team A team created by the organization as part of the formal organization structure.

forming The stage of team development characterized by orientation and acquaintance.

franchising A form of licensing in which an organization provides its foreign franchisees with a complete package of materials and services; an arrangement by which the owner of a product or service allows others to purchase the right to distribute the product or service with help from the owner.

free rider A person who benefits from team membership but does not make a proportionate contribution to the team's work.

frustration-regression principle The idea that failure to meet a high-order need may cause a regression to an already satisfied lower-order need.

functional-level strategy The level of strategy concerned with the question "How do we support the business-level strategy?" Pertains to all of the organization's major departments.

functional manager A manager who is responsible for a department that performs a single functional task and has employees with similar training and skills.

functional structure The grouping of positions into departments based on similar skills, expertise, and resource use.

fundamental attribution error The tendency to underestimate the influence of external factors on another's behavior and to overestimate the influence on internal factors.

G

general environment The layer of the external environment that affects the organization indirectly.

general manager A manager who is responsible for several departments that perform different functions.

glass ceiling Invisible barrier that separates women and minorities from top management positions.

global outsourcing Engaging in the international division of labor so as to obtain the cheapest sources of labor and supplies regardless of country; also called *global sourcing.*

global team A work team made up of members of different nationalities whose activities span multiple countries; may operate as a virtual team or meet face to face.

globalization The standardization of product design and advertising strategies throughout the world.

goal A desired future state that the organization attempts to realize.

goal-setting theory A motivation theory in which specific challenging goals increase motivation and performance when the goals are accepted by subordinates and these subordinates receive feedback to indicate their progress toward goal achievement.

grand strategy The general plan of major action by which an organization intends to achieve its long-term goals.

grapevine An informal, person-to-person communication network of employees that is not officially sanctioned by the organization.

greenfield venture The most risky type of direct investment, whereby a company builds a subsidiary from scratch in a foreign country.

groupthink The tendency for people to be so committed to a cohesive team that they are reluctant to express contrary opinions.

groupware Software that works on a computer network or the Internet to facilitate information sharing, collaborative work, and group decision making.

H

halo effect An overall impression of a person or situation based on one characteristic, either favorable or unfavorable; a type of rating error that occurs when an employee receives the same rating on all dimensions regardless of his or her performance on individual ones.

Hawthorne studies A series of experiments on worker productivity begun in 1924 at the Hawthorne plant of Western Electric Company in Illinois; attributed employees' increased output to managers' better treatment of them during the study.

hero A figure who exemplifies the deeds, character, and attributes of a strong corporate culture.

hierarchy of needs theory A content theory that proposes that people are motivated by five categories of needs—physiological, safety, belongingness, esteem, and self-actualization—that exist in a hierarchical order.

high-context culture A culture in which communication is used to enhance personal relationships.

high-performance culture A culture based on a solid organizational mission or purpose that uses shared adaptive values to guide decisions and business practices and to encourage individual employee ownership of both bottom-line results and the organization's cultural backbone.

horizontal communication The lateral or diagonal exchange of messages among peers or coworkers.

horizontal linkage model An approach to product change that emphasizes shared development of innovations among several departments.

horizontal team A formal team composed of employees from about the same hierarchical level but from different areas of expertise.

human capital The economic value of the knowledge, experience, skills, and capabilities of employees.

human relations movement A movement in management thinking and practice that emphasizes satisfaction of employees' basic needs as the key to increased worker productivity.

human resource information system An integrated computer system designed to provide data and information used in HR planning and decision making.

human resource management (HRM) Activities undertaken to attract, develop, and maintain an effective workforce within an organization.

human resource planning The forecasting of human resource needs and the projected matching of individuals with expected job vacancies.

human resources perspective A management perspective that suggests jobs should be designed to meet higher-level needs by allowing workers to use their full potential.

human skill The ability to work with and through other people and to work effectively as a group member.

humanistic perspective A management perspective that emerged near the late nineteenth century and emphasized understanding human behavior, needs, and attitudes in the workplace.

humility Being unpretentious and modest rather than arrogant and prideful.

hygiene factors Factors that involve the presence or absence of job dissatisfiers, including working conditions, pay, company policies, and interpersonal relationships.

I

idea champion A person who sees the need for and champions productive change within the organization.

idea incubator An in-house program that provides a safe harbor where ideas from employees throughout the organization can be developed without interference from company bureaucracy or politics.

implementation The step in the decision-making process that involves using managerial, administrative, and persuasive abilities to translate the chosen alternative into action.

income statement A financial statement that summarizes the firm's financial performance for a given time interval; sometimes called a profit-and-loss statement.

individualism A preference for a loosely knit social framework in which individuals are expected to take care of themselves.

individualism approach The ethical concept that acts are moral when they promote the individual's best long-term interests, which ultimately leads to the greater good.

influence The effect a person's actions have on the attitudes, values, beliefs, or behavior of others.

information Data that have been converted into a meaningful and useful context for the receiver.

information reporting system A system that organizes information in the form of prespecified reports that managers use in day-to-day decision making.

information technology The hardware, software, telecommunications, database management, and other technologies used to store, process, and distribute information.

infrastructure A country's physical facilities that support economic activities.

initiating structure A type of leader behavior that describes the extent to which the leader is task oriented and directs subordinates' work activities toward goal attainment.

instant messaging Electronic communication that allows users to see who is connected to a network and share information instantly.

integrative negotiation A collaborative approach to negotiation that is based on a win-win assumption, whereby the parties want to come up with a creative solution that benefits both sides of the conflict.

interactive leadership A leadership style characterized by values such as inclusion, collaboration, relationship building, and caring.

internal environment The environment that includes the elements within the organization's boundaries.

internal locus of control The belief by individuals that their future is within their control and that external forces have little influence.

international dimension Portion of the external environment that represents events originating in foreign countries as well as opportunities for U.S. companies in other countries.

international human resource management (IHRM) A subfield of human resource management that addresses the complexity that results from recruiting, selecting, developing, and maintaining a diverse workforce on a global scale.

international management The management of business operations conducted in more than one country.

Internet A global collection of computer networks linked together for the exchange of data and information.

intranet An internal communications system that uses the technology and standards of the Internet but is accessible only to people within the organization.

intrinsic reward The satisfaction received in the process of performing an action.

intuition The immediate comprehension of a decision situation based on past experience but without conscious thought.

inventory The goods that the organization keeps on hand for use in the production process up to the point of selling the final products to customers.

involvement culture A culture that places high value on meeting the needs of employees and values cooperation and equality.

ISO certification Certification based on a set of international standards for quality management, setting uniform guidelines for processes to ensure that products conform to customer requirements.

J

job analysis The systematic process of gathering and interpreting information about the essential duties, tasks, and responsibilities of a job.

job characteristics model A model of job design that comprises core job dimensions, critical psychological states, and employee growth-need strength.

job description A concise summary of the specific tasks and responsibilities of a particular job.

job design The application of motivational theories to the structure of work for improving productivity and satisfaction.

job enlargement A job design that combines a series of tasks into one new, broader job to give employees variety and challenge.

job enrichment A job design that incorporates achievement, recognition, and other high-level motivators into the work.

job evaluation The process of determining the value of jobs within an organization through an examination of job content.

job rotation A job design that systematically moves employees from one job to another to provide them with variety and stimulation.

job satisfaction A positive attitude toward one's job.

job simplification A job design whose purpose is to improve task efficiency by reducing the number of tasks a single person must do.

job specification An outline of the knowledge, skills, education, and physical abilities needed to adequately perform a job.

joint venture A strategic alliance or program by two or more organizations; a variation of direct investment in which an organization shares costs and risks with another firm to build a manufacturing facility, develop new products, or set up a sales and distribution network.

justice approach The ethical concept that moral decisions must be based on standards of equity, fairness, and impartiality.

just-in-time (JIT) inventory system An inventory control system that schedules materials to arrive precisely when they are needed on a production line.

K

knowledge management The efforts to systematically find, organize, and make available a company's intellectual capital and to foster a culture of continuous learning and knowledge sharing; the process of systematically gathering knowledge, making it widely available throughout the organization, and fostering a culture of learning.

knowledge management portal A single point of access for employees to multiple sources of information that provides personalized access on the corporate intranet.

L

labor market The people available for hire by the organization.

large-group intervention An approach that brings together participants from all parts of the organization (and may include key outside stakeholders as well) to discuss problems or opportunities and plan for major change.

law of effect The assumption that positively reinforced behavior tends to be repeated, and unreinforced or negatively reinforced behavior tends to be inhibited.

leadership The ability to influence people toward the attainment of organizational goals.

leadership grid A two-dimensional leadership theory that measures a leader's concern for people and concern for production.

leading The management function that involves the use of influence to motivate employees to achieve the organization's goals.

lean manufacturing Manufacturing process using highly trained employees at every stage of the production process to cut waste and improve quality.

learning A change in behavior or performance as the result of experience.

learning organization An organization in which everyone is engaged in identifying and solving problems, enabling the organization to experiment continuously, improve, and increase its capability.

legal-political dimension The dimension of the general environment that includes federal, state, and local government regulations and political activities designed to influence company behavior.

legitimate power Power that stems from a formal management position in an organization and the authority granted to it.

licensing An entry strategy in which an organization in one country makes certain resources available to companies in another in order to participate in the production and sale of its products abroad.

line authority A form of authority in which individuals in management positions have the formal power to direct and control immediate subordinates.

liquidity ratio A financial ratio that indicates the organization's ability to meet its current debt obligations.

listening The skill of receiving messages to accurately grasp facts and feelings to interpret the genuine meaning.

locus of control The tendency to place the primary responsibility for one's success or failure either within oneself (internally) or on outside forces (externally).

logistics The activities required to physically move materials into the company's operations facility and to move finished products to customers.

long-term orientation A greater concern for the future and high value on thrift and perseverance.

low-context culture A culture in which communication is used to exchange facts and information.

M

Machiavellianism The tendency to direct much of one's behavior toward the acquisition of power and the manipulation of others for personal gain.

management The attainment of organizational goals in an effective and efficient manner through planning, organizing, leading, and controlling organizational resources.

management by objectives (MBO) A method of management whereby managers and employees define goals for every department, project, and person and use them to monitor subsequent performance.

management by wandering around (MBWA) A communication technique in which managers interact directly with workers to exchange information.

management information system (MIS) A computer-based system that provides information and support for effective managerial decision making.

management science perspective A management perspective that emerged after World War II and applied mathematics, statistics, and other quantitative techniques to managerial problems.

manufacturing organization An organization that produces physical goods.

market entry strategy An organizational strategy for entering a foreign market.

market value-added (MVA) system A control system that measures the stock market's estimate of the value of a company's past and expected capital investment projects.

masculinity A cultural preference for achievement, heroism, assertiveness, work centrality, and material success.

mass production A type of technology characterized by the production of a large volume of products with the same specifications.

matching model An employee selection approach in which the organization and the applicant attempt to match each other's needs, interests, and values.

material requirements planning (MRP) A dependent demand inventory planning and control system that schedules the precise amount of all materials required to support the production of desired end products.

matrix approach An organization structure that utilizes functional and divisional chains of command simultaneously in the same part of the organization.

matrix boss A product or functional boss, responsible for one side of the matrix.

mediation The process of using a third party to settle a dispute.

mentor A higher-ranking, senior organizational member who is committed to providing upward mobility and support to a protégé's professional career.

merger The combination of two or more organizations into one.

message The tangible formulation of an idea to be sent to a receiver.

middle manager A manager who works at the middle levels of the organization and is responsible for major departments.

mission The organization's reason for existence.

mission statement A broadly stated definition of the organization's basic business scope and operations that distinguishes it from similar types of organizations.

modular approach The process by which a manufacturing company uses

outside suppliers to provide large components of the product, which are then assembled into a final product by a few workers.

monoculture A culture that accepts only one way of doing things and one set of values and beliefs.

moral leadership Distinguishing right from wrong and choosing to do right in the practice of leadership.

moral-rights approach The ethical concept that moral decisions are those that best maintain the rights of those people affected by them.

most favored nation A term describing a GATT clause that calls for member countries to grant other member countries the most favorable treatment they accord any country concerning imports and exports.

motivation The arousal, direction, and persistence of behavior.

motivators Factors that influence job satisfaction based on fulfillment of high-level needs such as achievement, recognition, responsibility, and opportunity for growth.

multicultural teams Teams made up of members from diverse national, social, ethnic, and cultural backgrounds.

multidomestic strategy The modification of product design and advertising strategies to suit the specific needs of individual countries.

multinational corporation (MNC) An organization that receives more than 25 percent of its total sales revenues from operations outside the parent company's home country; also called *global corporation* or *transnational corporation*.

Myers-Biggs Type Indicator (MBTI) Personality test that measures a person's preference for introversion vs. extroversion, sensation vs. intuition, thinking vs. feeling, and judging vs. perceiving.

N

need to achieve A human quality linked to entrepreneurship in which people are motivated to excel and pick situations in which success is likely.

negotiation A conflict management strategy whereby people engage in give-and-take discussions and consider various alternatives to reach a joint decision that is acceptable to both parties.

neutralizer A situational variable that counteracts a leadership style and prevents the leader from displaying certain behaviors.

new-venture fund A fund providing resources from which individuals and groups can draw to develop new ideas, products, or businesses.

new-venture team A unit separate from the mainstream of the organization that is responsible for developing and initiating innovations.

nonparticipator role A role in which the individual contributes little to either the task or members' socioemotional needs.

nonprogrammed decision A decision made in response to a situation that is unique, is poorly defined and largely unstructured, and has important consequences for the organization.

nonverbal communication A communication transmitted through actions and behaviors rather than through words.

normative An approach that defines how a decision maker should make decisions and provides guidelines for reaching an ideal outcome for the organization.

norming The stage of team development in which conflicts developed during the storming stage are resolved and team harmony and unity emerge.

O

office automation systems Systems that combine modern hardware and software to handle the tasks of publishing and distributing information.

on-the-job training (OJT) A type of training in which an experienced employee "adopts" a new employee to teach him or her how to perform job duties.

open-book management Sharing financial information and results with all employees in the organization.

open communication Sharing all types of information throughout the company, across functional and hierarchical levels.

open innovation Extending the search for and commercialization of new ideas beyond the boundaries of the organization.

open system A system that interacts with the external environment.

operational goals Specific, measurable results expected from departments, work groups, and individuals within the organization.

operational plans Plans developed at the organization's lower levels that specify action steps toward achieving operational goals and that support tactical planning activities.

operations information system A computer-based information system that supports a company's day-to-day operations.

operations management The field of management that focuses on the physical production of goods or services and uses specialized techniques for solving manufacturing problems.

operations strategy The recognition of the importance of operations to the firm's success and the involvement of operations managers in the organization's strategic planning.

opportunity A situation in which managers see potential organizational accomplishments that exceed current goals.

organization A social entity that is goal directed and deliberately structured.

organization chart The visual representation of an organization's structure.

organization development (OD) The application of behavioral science techniques to improve an organization's health and effectiveness through its ability to cope with environmental changes, improve internal relationships, and increase learning and problem-solving capabilities.

organization structure The framework in which the organization defines how tasks are divided, resources are deployed, and departments are coordinated.

organizational behavior An interdisciplinary field dedicated to the study of how individuals and groups tend to act in organizations.

organizational change The adoption of a new idea or behavior by an organization.

organizational citizenship Work behavior that goes beyond job requirements and contributes as needed to the organization's success.

organizational commitment Loyalty to and heavy involvement in one's organization.

organizational control The systematic process through which managers regulate organizational activities to make them consistent with expectations established in plans, targets, and standards of performance.

organizational environment All elements existing outside the organization's boundaries that have the potential to affect the organization.

organizing The management function concerned with assigning tasks, grouping tasks into departments, and allocating resources to departments; the deployment of organizational resources to achieve strategic goals.

outsourcing Contracting out selected functions or activities of an organization to other organizations that can do the work more cost-efficiently.

P

P → O expectancy Expectancy that successful performance of a task will lead to the desired outcome.

partial productivity The ratio of total outputs to the inputs from a single major input category.

partial reinforcement schedule A schedule in which only some occurrences of the desired behavior are reinforced.

partnership An unincorporated business owned by two or more people.

path–goal theory A contingency approach to leadership specifying that the leader's responsibility is to increase subordinates' motivation by clarifying the behaviors necessary for task accomplishment and rewards.

pay-for-performance Incentive pay that ties at least part of compensation to employee effort and performance.

peer-to-peer (P2P) file sharing File sharing that allows PCs to communicate directly with one another over the Internet, bypassing central databases, servers, control points, and Web pages.

people change A change in the attitudes and behaviors of a few employees in the organization.

perception The cognitive process people use to make sense out of the environment, by selecting, organizing, and interpreting information.

perceptual defense The tendency of perceivers to protect themselves by disregarding ideas, objects, or people that are threatening to them.

perceptual distortions Errors in perceptual judgment that arise from inaccuracies in any part of the perceptual process.

perceptual selectivity The process by which individuals screen and select the various stimuli that vie for their attention.

performance The organization's ability to attain its goals by using resources in an efficient and effective manner.

performance appraisal The process of observing and evaluating an employee's performance, recording the assessment, and providing feedback to the employee.

performance gap A disparity between existing and desired performance levels.

performing The stage of team development in which members focus on problem solving and accomplishing the team's assigned task.

permanent teams A group of participants from several functions who are permanently assigned to solve ongoing problems of common interest.

person-job fit The extent to which a person's ability and personality match the requirements of a job.

personal communication channels Communication channels that exist outside the formally authorized channels and do not adhere to the organization's hierarchy of authority.

personal networking The acquisition and cultivation of personal relationships that cross departmental, hierarchical, and even organizational boundaries.

personality The set of characteristics that underlie a relatively stable pattern of behavior in response to ideas, objects, or people in the environment.

plan A blueprint specifying the resource allocations, schedules, and other actions necessary for attaining goals.

planning The management function concerned with defining goals for future organizational performance and deciding on the tasks and resource use needed to attain them; the act of determining the organization's goals and the means for achieving them.

planning task force A group of managers and employees who develop a strategic plan.

pluralism An environment in which the organization accommodates several subcultures, including employees who would otherwise feel isolated and ignored.

point-counterpoint A decision-making technique in which people are assigned to express competing points of view.

political forces The influence of political and legal institutions on people and organizations.

political instability Events such as riots, revolutions, or government upheavals that affect the operations of an international company.

political risk A company's risk of loss of assets, earning power, or managerial control due to politically based events or actions by host governments.

portfolio strategy The organization's mix of strategic business units and product lines that fit together in such a way as to provide the corporation with synergy and competitive advantage.

power The potential ability to influence others' behavior.

power distance The degree to which people accept inequality in power among institutions, organizations, and people.

pressure group An interest group that works within the legal-political framework to influence companies to behave in socially responsible ways.

problem A situation in which organizational accomplishments have failed to meet established goals.

problem-solving team Typically 5 to 12 hourly employees from the same department who meet to discuss ways of improving quality, efficiency, and the work environment.

procedural justice The concept that rules should be clearly stated and consistently and impartially enforced.

process An organized group of related tasks and activities that work together to transform inputs into outputs and create value.

process control system A computer system that monitors and controls ongoing physical processes, such as temperature or pressure changes.

process layout A facilities layout in which machines that perform the same function are grouped together in one location.

process theories A group of theories that explain how employees select behaviors with which to meet their needs and determine whether their choices were successful.

procurement Purchasing supplies, services, and raw materials for use in the production process.

product change A change in the organization's product or service outputs.

product layout A facilities layout in which machines and tasks are arranged according to the sequence of steps in the production of a single product.

product life-cycle management Manufacturing software that manages a product from creation through development, manufacturing, testing, and even maintenance in the field.

productivity The organization's output of products and services divided by its inputs.

profitability ratio A financial ratio that describes the firm's profits (for example, sales or total assets).

programmed decision A decision made in response to a situation that has occurred often enough to enable decision rules to be developed and applied in the future.

project manager A manager responsible for a temporary work project that involves the participation of other people from various functions and levels of the organization; a person responsible for coordinating the activities of several departments on a full-time basis for the completion of a specific project.

projection The tendency to see one's own personal traits in other people.

Q

quality circle (QC) A group of 6 to 12 volunteer employees who meet regularly to discuss and solve problems affecting the quality of their work.

R

raw materials inventory Inventory consisting of the basic inputs to the organization's production process.

realistic job preview (RJP) A recruiting approach that gives applicants all pertinent and realistic information about the job and the organization.

recruiting The activities or practices that define the desired characteristics of applicants for specific jobs.

reengineering The radical redesign of business processes to achieve dramatic improvements in cost, quality, service, and speed; bringing together all elements of a single business process to eliminate waste and delays.

referent power Power that results from characteristics that command subordinates' identification with, respect and admiration for, and desire to emulate the leader.

refreezing The reinforcement stage of organization development in which individuals acquire a desired new skill or attitude and are rewarded for it by the organization.

reinforcement Anything that causes a given behavior to be repeated or inhibited.

reinforcement theory A motivation theory based on the relationship between a given behavior and its consequences.

reorder point (ROP) The most economical level at which an inventory item should be reordered.

responsibility The duty to perform the task or activity an employee has been assigned.

responsibility center An organizational unit under the supervision of a single individual who is responsible for its activity.

revenue budget A budget that identifies the forecasted and actual revenues of the organization.

reward power Power that results from the authority to bestow rewards on other people.

risk A situation in which a decision has clear-cut goals and good information is available, but the future outcomes associated with each alternative are subject to chance.

risk propensity The willingness to undertake risk with the opportunity of gaining an increased payoff.

role A set of expectations for one's behavior.

role ambiguity Uncertainty about what behaviors are expected of a person in a particular role.

role conflict Incompatible demands of different roles.

S

satisficing To choose the first solution alternative that satisfies minimal decision criteria, regardless of whether better solutions are presumed to exist.

scenario building Looking at trends and discontinuities and imagining possible alternative futures to build a framework within which unexpected future events can be managed.

schedule of reinforcement The frequency with which and intervals over which reinforcement occurs.

scientific management A subfield of the classical management perspective that emphasized scientifically determined changes in management practices as the solution to improving labor productivity.

selection The process of determining the skills, abilities, and other attributes a person needs to perform a particular job.

self-directed team A team consisting of 5 to 20 multiskilled workers who rotate jobs to produce an entire product or service, often supervised by an elected member.

self-serving bias The tendency to overestimate the contribution of internal factors to one's successes and the contribution of external factors to one's failures.

semantics The meaning of words and the way they are used.

servant leader A leader who works to fulfill subordinates' needs and goals as well as to achieve the organization's larger mission.

service organization An organization that produces nonphysical outputs that require customer involvement and cannot be stored in inventory.

service technology Technology characterized by intangible outputs and direct contact between employees and customers.

short-term orientation A concern with the past and present and a high value on meeting social obligations.

single-use plans Plans that are developed to achieve a set of goals that are unlikely to be repeated in the future.

situation analysis Analysis of the strengths, weaknesses, opportunities, and threats (SWOT) that affect organizational performance.

situational theory A contingency approach to leadership that links the leader's behavioral style with the task readiness of subordinates.

Six Sigma A quality control approach that emphasizes a relentless pursuit of higher quality and lower costs.

skunkworks A separate small, informal, highly autonomous, and often secretive group that focuses on breakthrough ideas for the business.

slogan A phrase or sentence that succinctly expresses a key corporate value.

small-batch production A type of technology that involves the production of goods in batches of one or a few products designed to customer specification.

social entrepreneurs Entrepreneurial leaders who are committed to both good business and changing the world for the better.

social facilitation The tendency for the presence of others to influence an individual's motivation and performance.

social forces The aspects of a culture that guide and influence relationships among people—their values, needs, and standards of behavior.

social networking Online interaction in a community format where people share personal information and photos, produce and share all sorts of information and opinions, or unify activists and raise funds.

sociocultural dimension The dimension of the general environment representing the demographic characteristics, norms, customs, and values of the population within which the organization operates.

socioemotional role A role in which the individual provides support for team members' emotional needs and social unity.

sole proprietorship An unincorporated business owned by an individual for profit.

span of management The number of employees reporting to a supervisor; also called *span of control.*

special-purpose team A team created outside the formal organization to undertake a project of special importance or creativity.

staff authority A form of authority granted to staff specialists in their areas of expertise.

stakeholder Any group within or outside the organization that has a stake in the organization's performance.

standing plans Ongoing plans that are used to provide guidance for tasks performed repeatedly within the organization.

stereotyping Placing an employee into a class category based on one or a few traits or characteristics; the tendency to assign an individual to a group or broad category and then attribute generalizations about the group to the individual.

storming The stage of team development in which individual personalities and roles, and resulting conflicts, emerge.

story A narrative based on true events and repeated frequently and shared among organizational employees.

strategic business unit (SBU) A division of the organization that has a unique business mission, product line, competitors, and markets relative to other SBUs in the same corporation.

strategic conversation Dialogue across boundaries and hierarchical levels about the team or organization's vision, critical strategic themes, and the values that help achieve important goals.

strategic goals Broad statements of where the organization wants to be in the future; pertain to the organization as a whole rather than to specific divisions or departments.

strategic management The set of decisions and actions used to formulate and implement strategies that will provide a competitively superior fit between the organization and its environment so as to achieve organizational goals.

strategic plans The action steps by which an organization intends to attain its strategic goals.

strategy The plan of action that prescribes resource allocation and other activities for dealing with the environment, achieving a competitive advantage, and attaining organizational goals.

strategy formulation The stage of strategic management that involves the planning and decision making that lead to the establishment of the organization's goals and of a specific strategic plan.

strategy implementation The stage of strategic management that involves the use of managerial and organizational tools to direct resources toward achieving strategic outcomes.

stress A physiological and emotional response to stimuli that place physical or psychological demands on an individual.

structural changes Any change in the way in which the organization is designed and managed.

substitute A situational variable that makes a leadership style redundant or unnecessary.

subsystems Parts of a system that depend on one another for their functioning.

superordinate goal A goal that cannot be reached by a single party.

suppliers People and organizations who provide the raw materials the organization uses to produce its output.

supply chain management Managing the sequence of suppliers and purchasers, covering all stages of processing from obtaining raw materials to distributing finished goods to final customers.

survey feedback A type of OD intervention in which questionnaires on organizational climate and other factors are distributed among employees and the results reported back to them by a change agent.

sustainability Economic development that meets the needs of the current population while preserving the environment for the needs of future generations.

symbol An object, act, or event that conveys meaning to others.

synergy The condition that exists when the organization's parts interact to produce a joint effect that is greater than the sum of the parts acting alone; the concept that the whole is greater than the sum of its parts.

system A set of interrelated parts that function as a whole to achieve a common purpose.

systems theory An extension of the humanistic perspective that describes organizations as open systems characterized by entropy, synergy, and subsystem interdependence.

T

tactical goals Goals that define the outcomes that major divisions and departments must achieve in order for the organization to reach its overall goals.

tactical plans Plans designed to help execute major strategic plans and to accomplish a specific part of the company's strategy.

tall structure A management structure characterized by an overall narrow span of management and a relatively large number of hierarchical levels.

task environment The layer of the external environment that directly influences the organization's operations and performance.

task force A temporary team or committee formed to solve a specific short-term problem involving several departments.

task specialist role A role in which the individual devotes personal time and energy to helping the team accomplish its task.

team A unit of two or more people who interact and coordinate their work to accomplish a specific goal.

team-based structure Structure in which the entire organization is made up of teams that coordinate their activities and work directly with customers to accomplish the organization's goals.

team building A type of OD intervention that enhances the cohesiveness of departments by helping members learn to function as a team.

team cohesiveness The extent to which team members are attracted to the team and motivated to remain in it.

team norm A standard of conduct that is shared by team members and guides their behavior.

technical complexity The degree to which complex machinery is involved in the production process to the exclusion of people.

technical core The heart of the organization's production of its product or service.

technical skill The understanding of and proficiency in the performance of specific tasks.

technological dimension The dimension of the general environment that includes scientific and technological advancements in the industry and society at large.

technology change A change that pertains to the organization's production process.

telecommuting Using computers and telecommunications equipment to perform work from home or another remote location.

tolerance for ambiguity The psychological characteristic that allows a person to be untroubled by disorder and uncertainty.

top-down budgeting A budgeting process in which middle- and lower-level managers set departmental budget targets in accordance with overall company revenues and expenditures specified by top management.

top leader The overseer of both the product and the functional chains of command, responsible for the entire matrix.

top manager A manager who is at the top of the organizational hierarchy and is responsible for the entire organization.

total factor productivity The ratio of total outputs to the inputs from labor, capital, materials, and energy.

total quality management (TQM) A concept that focuses on managing the total organization to deliver quality to customers. Four significant elements of TQM are employee involvement, focus on the customer, benchmarking, and continuous improvement. An organization-wide commitment to infusing quality into every activity through continuous improvement.

traits Distinguishing personal characteristics, such as intelligence, values, and appearance.

transaction processing system A type of operations information system that records and processes data resulting from routine business transactions such as sales, purchases, and payroll.

transactional leader A leader who clarifies subordinates' role and task requirements, initiates structure, provides rewards, and displays consideration for subordinates.

transformational leader A leader distinguished by a special ability to bring about innovation and change.

transnational strategy A strategy that combines global coordination to attain efficiency with flexibility to meet specific needs in various countries.

two-boss employee Employees who report to two supervisors simultaneously.

Type A behavior Behavior pattern characterized by extreme competitiveness, impatience, aggressiveness, and devotion to work.

Type B behavior Behavior pattern that lacks Type A characteristics and includes a more balanced, relaxed lifestyle.

U

uncertainty The situation that occurs when managers know which goals they wish to achieve, but information about alternatives and future events is incomplete.

uncertainty avoidance A value characterized by people's intolerance for uncertainty and ambiguity and resulting support for beliefs that promise certainty and conformity.

unfreezing The stage of organization development in which participants are made aware of problems in order to increase their willingness to change their behavior.

upward communication Messages transmitted from the lower to the higher levels in the organization's hierarchy.

utilitarian approach The ethical concept that moral behaviors produce the greatest good for the greatest number.

V

valence The value or attraction an individual has for an outcome.

validity The relationship between an applicant's score on a selection device and his or her future job performance.

venture capital firm A group of companies or individuals that invests money in new or expanding businesses for ownership and potential profits.

vertical team A formal team composed of a manager and his or her subordinates in the organization's formal chain of command.

virtual network structure An organization structure that disaggregates major functions to separate companies that are brokered by a small headquarters organization.

virtual team A team made up of members who are geographically or organizationally dispersed, rarely meet face to face, and do their work using advanced information technologies.

vision An attractive, ideal future that is credible yet not readily attainable.

Vroom-Jago model A model designed to help managers gauge the amount of subordinate participation in decision making.

W

wage and salary surveys Surveys that show what other organizations pay incumbents in jobs that match a sample of "key" jobs selected by the organization.

whistle-blowing The disclosure by an employee of illegal, immoral, or illegitimate practices by the organization.

wholly owned foreign affiliate A foreign subsidiary over which an organization has complete control.

wiki Web site that allows anyone with access, inside or outside the organization, to create, share, and edit content through a simple, browser-based user interface.

workforce diversity Hiring people with different human qualities or who belong to various cultural groups.

workforce optimization Implementing strategies to put the right people in the right jobs, make the best use of employee talent and skills, and develop human capital for the future.

work-in-process inventory Inventory composed of the materials that still are moving through the stages of the production process.

work redesign The altering of jobs to increase both the quality of employees' work experience and their productivity.

work specialization The degree to which organizational tasks are subdivided into individual jobs; also called division of labor.

World Wide Web (WWW) A collection of central servers for accessing information on the Internet.

NAME INDEX

A

Aaron, Hank, 555
Abebe, Michael, 546n32, 546n36
Abelson, Reed, 170n58, 444n3, 446n73, 654n49, 514n1
Abrahamson, Eric, 63n4
Abrams, John, 163
Abramson, Gary, 101n34
Ackerly, Leone, 637
Adair, John G., 64n32
Adam, Everett E. Jr., 545n7
Adams, J. Stacy, 630, 653n24
Adamy, Janet, 234n15, 268n34
Adan, Halima, 443
Adler, Nancy J., 107, 135n13
Adler, Terry, 723n4
Adorno, T. W., 586n42
Advani, Deepak, 438
Aeppel, Timothy, 136n83
Aggarwal, Sumer C., 546n37
Agle, Bradley, 170n65, 170n67, 170n68
Agor, Weston H., 299n23
Agres, Carole E., 344n50
Agüero, Ana, 171n84
Ahuja, Manju K., 724n34
Aken, Eileen M. Van, 235n34
Akhter, Syed H., 235n37
Alban, Billie T., 361, 376n60, 376n61, 376n62
Albanese, Robert, 618n19, 724n47
Aldag, Ramon J., 64n35
Alderfer, Clayton, 626, 648, 653n11
Aldrich, Howard E., 35n53
Alexander, Francine, 404
Alexander, John O., 234n24
Alexander, Whit, 349
Alexander the Great, 607
Allen, Chris T., 689n38
Allen, Deb, 631
Allers, Kimberly L., 445n28, 446n88
Allio, Michael K., 260
Alon, Ilan, 137n87
Alpaslan, Murat C., 33n3, 235n41, 235n44, 235n46, 690n76
Alster, Norm, 654n53
Alstyne, Marshall Van, 345n70
Alterman, Eric, 136n74
Altier, William J., 345n56
Alvord, Valerie, 24
Amabile, Teresa M., 375n9, 375n11
Amari, David, 484n45
Amelio, Bill, 105
Amichai-Hamburger, Yair, 377n83
Ammeter, Anthony P., 446n69
Anagnos, Gus, 235n40
Anand, N., 344n39, 344n50
Anders, George, 34n10, 376n40, 619n55
Anderson, Brad, 264
Anderson, Peter, 676
Anderson, Terry H., 445n43
Andre, Rae, 444
Andrea Warfield, 447n93
Andriopoulos, Constantine, 375n12
Ang, Soon, 128, 137n87
Angle, Harold L., 355, 376n41

Anglos, Don, 298
Angwin, Julia, 64n61, 101n26, 269n64
Ante, Spencer E., 35n71, 269n73, 497, 514n25, 514n34
Anthony, Robert N., 484n16, 484n18
Antonellis, Domenic, 13
Apcar, Leonard M., 377n78
Appleby, Julie, 483n7
Aquirre, Fernando, 108
Archer, Earnest R., 299n14
Areddy, James T., 135n29
Argenti, Paul, 35n77, 235n48
Ariely, Dan, 284
Armour, Stephanie, 63n7, 412n43
Armstrong, Jessica, 615–616
Arndt, Michael, 135n34, 268n54, 300n43, 344n37, 374n2, 375n25, 444n2, 514n3, 644
Arnold, Helen, 667
Arnold, Hugh J., 725n63
Arnold, W. J., 63n22, 63n24
Aronson, Amy, 445n25, 445n28
Aronson, Elliot, 725n64
Arrizurieta, Jorge L., 136n77
Arthur, Michelle M., 446n69
Arvey, R. D., 404
Asbel, Melinda, 721
Ashford, S. J., 98
Ashkenas, Ronald N., 345n61, 376n62
Asinof, Lynn, 413n113
Asmus, Peter, 163, 168n4, 170n37, 170n44
Astor, Adam, 101n12
Athitakis, Mark, 299n4
Austen, Ian, 33n2, 80, 101n29
Austin, Larry M., 64n41
Austin, Nancy, 376n46, 690n65
Avolio, Bruce J., 83, 446n68, 618n11, 619n44, 619n50
Axelrod, Emily M., 718
Axelrod, Richard, 718
Ayers, Charlie, 436
Azria, Max, 216

B

Baardwijk, Nicole van, 349, 375n8
Bacharach, Samuel B., 375n6
Badal, Jaclyne, 486n21, 654n46
Badaracco, Joseph L., 170n64, 170n71, 617n7, 617n8, 619n71
Badawy, M. K., 35n43
Baghetti, Lisa, 721
Bagley, Constance E., 169n13
Bahmani, Firoz, 686
Bailey, Diane E., 412n39
Bailey, Phil, 167–168
Baird, Inga Skromme, 299n8
Baker, Dianne, 16
Baker, Kent, 667
Baker, Michael, 690n47
Baker, Stephen, 101n12, 514n20
Balaji, Y., 515n65, 515n74
Balan, Peter, 203n83
Baldwin, Larry, 19
Bales, R. F., 724n55
Baligia, B. R., 484n26
Ballmer, Steven, 97, 311
Balu, Rekha, 102n67, 654n59

Banham, Russ, 483n6, 514n34, 515n42, 515n51, 546n19
Banks, Jennifer, 298
Bansal, Pratima, 170n48
Baquet, Dean, 245
Barad, Jill, 240
Barbaro, Michael, 481, 514n1, 514n19, 515n76
Barbian, Jeff, 653n14, 654n52
Barista, Dave, 360
Barkdull, C. W., 343n15
Barkema, Harry G., 35n63, 35n66
Barnard, C. I., 343n8
Barnard, Chester I., 44–46
Barnes, Brooks, 299n2
Barnes, Frank C., 484n44
Barnes-Vieyra, Pamela, 515n53
Barney, Jonathan, 135n49
Barnwell, Greg, 373
Baron, James N., 411n12
Baron, Robert A., 724n49, 724n56, 725n57
Baron, Ron, 490
Barret, Victoria Murphy, 701
Barreto, Hector Jr., 182
Barrett, Amy, 136n73, 483n12
Barrett, Craig, 357, 376n50
Barrett, D., 673, 690n52, 690n54
Barrick, M. R., 586n25
Barrier, Michael, 170n64
Barrionuevo, Alexei, 168n7
Barrios, Sergio, 475
Barron, Kelly, 63n21
Bart, C. K., 376n43
Bartholomew, Doug, 235n58, 413n83, 413n86, 497, 514n34
Bartlett, Christopher A., 34n31, 108, 135n17
Bartol, Kathryn M., 446n68
Bartosiewicz, Petra, 100n2
Basil, Thomas, 701
Bass, Bernard M., 83, 446n68, 595, 607, 618n11, 618n42, 619n48
Bass, Robert E., 64n43
Bass, Steedman, 322
Bastianutti, L. M., 301n61
Bateman, Thomas S., 268n24
Bates, James, 546n44
Bateson, Gregory, 377n74
Bauerlein, Valerie, 546n31
Baum, Joel A. C., 35n63, 35n66
Baveja, Alok, 268n26
Bavelas, A., 673, 690n52, 690n54
Baxendale, Sidney J., 484n50
Baxter, Stephen, 21
Bazerman, Max H., 284, 299n7
Beach, Mary Ellen, 235n33, 485n61
Beard, Luciana, 546n51
Beatty, R. W., 413n101, 413n102
Beaudan, Eric, 35n74, 35n76
Bechtold, David J., 136n56
Becker, Helmut, 170n57
Becker, S., 377n81
Becker, Selwyn W., 607
Beckford, Rita, 521
Beckhard, Richard, 376n56, 377n81
Beckman, Howard, 453, 479
Beddoe, Clive, 96
Bedeian, Arthur G., 343n15
Bedford, Norton M., 484n16, 484n18

Beecher, S., 411n22
Beedon, Julie, 718
Beehr, T. A., 587n60
Beers, Michael C., 723
Begley, Sharon, 137n90, 137n97
Begley, Thomas M., 241, 269n81
Begum, Monwara, 115
Belker, Loren B., 34n43, 35n46
Belkin, Lisa, 445n51, 446n55
Bell, Arthur H., 689n30
Bell, Cecil H., Jr., 64n39, 376n56, 376n57
Bellows, Frank, 512
Belohav, James A., 654n63
Benavides, Lisa, 202n74
Benham, Barbara, 201n34
Benjamin, John D., 724n53
Benne, K. D., 724n55
Bennet, Bill, 322
Bennett, Amanda, 421
Bennett, Julie, 586n33
Bennett, Monica, 433, 445n22, 707
Bennett, Steve, 358
Berger, David, 133
Berk, Laurey, 688n5
Berkman, Eric, 485n60, 485n61
Berkowitz, L., 653n24
Berlo, D. K., 689n8
Berman, Dennis K., 170n69, 269n66, 299n6
Bernardin, H. J., 413n101, 413n102
Berner, Robert, 202n39, 234n8, 266, 344n37, 374n2, 376n35
Berners-Lee, Tim, 498
Bernhut, Stephen, 690n78
Bernstein, Aaron, 136n78, 411n27, 444n2
Bernstein, Carl, 612
Berry, John, 484n47
Bertrand, Marianne, 445n20
Bettenhausen, Kenneth, 725n71
Betzell, Ray, 133
Beyer, Janice M., 102n57
Beyerlein, Michael M., 515n66
Bezos, Jeff, 197, 605, 703
Bhagat, R. S., 587n60
Bhawuk, D. P. S., 136n56
Bianchi, Alessandra, 201n22
Bilodeau, Barbara, 33n4, 63n10, 64n50, 65n70, 375n31
Birch, David, 39, 180
Birchard, Bill, 35n62, 689n25
Birger, Jon, 103n85, 234n17
Blace, Robert R., 597
Blacharczyk, E., 412n67
Black, J., 446n89
Black, Janice A., 723n4
Black, J. T., 527
Black, Pam, 345n74
Black, Wendy, 354
Blackford, Mansel G., 64n40
Blackwell, Charles W., 63n11
Blai, Boris, Jr., 299n14
Blair, Jayson, 13, 671
Blais, Frances, 621–622
Blake, Robert R., 596, 618n26
Blake, Stacy, 423
Blakeslee, Jerry, 484n36
Blalock, Becky, 703, 724n52
Blanchard, Kenneth H., 598–600, 613, 618n28

Blank, Renee, 445n19
Blase, Frank, 528
Blaylock, Bruce K., 689n10
Block, Caryn J., 445n44
Bloodgood, James M., 411n19, 485n2
Bloomberg, 279
Blostrom, Robert L., 169n31
Blow-Mitchell, Pamela, 431
Blumenthal, Robin Goldwyn, 484n25
Bohl, Don L., 484n46, 484n50
Bohlander, George, 397, 412n73, 412n75
Bohm, David, 690n74
Bolino, Mark C., 411n19, 585n2
Bollander, George, 411n16
Bollapragada, Srinivas, 299n17, 299n18
Bolton, Alfred A., 63n30, 64n33
Bommer, William H., 619n51
Bonabeau, Eric, 300n29
Bonamici, Kate, 34n22
Bond, M. H., 136n55
Bono, Joyce E., 177, 619n51
Bonoma, Thomas V., 14
Boone, Garrett, 393
Boorstin, Julia, 201n23
Boot, Alistair, 15, 34n38
Boquist, John A., 484n17
Bordia, Rakesh, 375n22
Bornstein, David, 202n55
Borrus, Amy, 136n75
Borsheim, Derrick, 49
Boudette, Neal E., 377n70, 546n39
Boudreau, J. W., 412n52
Boudreau, Marie-Claude, 514n38
Boulding, Kenneth E., 64n43
Boulgaides, J. D., 300n50
Bounds, Gregory M., 63n27
Bounds, Gwendolyn, 654n45
Bourgeois, L. J. III, 100n7, 725n78
Boutellier, Roman, 101n41
Boutin, Paul, 373
Bovée, C. L., 121
Bowen, Andy, 35n74, 235n43, 690n77
Bowen, David E., 654n63
Bowen, Stuart, 457–458
Boyatzis, Richard E., 586n35
Boyd, David P., 241, 269n81
Boyle, Gertrude, 574–575
Boyle, Matthew, 63n5, 267n1, 413n94, 569, 690n77
Braam, Geert J. M., 485n59, 485n63
Bracsher, Keith, 375n3
Brady, Diane, 267n11, 268n47, 269n76, 374n2, 376n52, 619n63, 619n73
Brady, John, 530
Brady, Simon, 171n92
Branch, Shelly, 268n43
Brandon, David A., 647
Branham, Leigh, 411n1, 411n2, 412n33, 412n34
Brannigan, Martha, 34n17
Branson, Richard, 185
Brant, John, 619n45, 653n22
Brechu, Mauricio Brehm, 136n58
Breckler, S. J., 586n7
Breen, Bill, 374n1, 377n87
Bremer, Paul, 458
Bremmer, Ian, 135n45, 135n46
Brewster, Mike, 413n116
Brief, Arthur P., 445n45
Briggs, Tony, 233

Briggs, William L., 623
Brignall, Miles, 34n38
Brin, Sergey, 181
Brock, Paula, 462
Brockner, Joel, 412n46
Broderick, Renée F., 413n105
Brodsky, Norm, 201n13
Brodwin, David R., 269n69
Brody, Michael, 652n2
Brokaw, Leslie, 187, 202n58
Brooks, Doug, 657–658
Brooks, Herb, 695
Brooks, Rick, 101n25
Brotheridge, Céleste M., 617n8
Brown, Andrew D., 102n46
Brown, Carolyn M., 202n60
Brown, Erika, 546n22
Brown, Eryn, 34n15
Brown, Karen A., 546n29
Brown, Michael, 158, 170n61, 170n66
Brown, Robert M., 171n85
Brown, Stuart F., 375n4
Browne, Cynthia, 375n13
Brownell, Peter, 484n19
Bruggeman, Kent, 209
Bryant, Quinne, 202n76
Brygay, Marge, 232
Bryne, John A., 617n1
Brynjolfsson, Erik, 345n70
Buchanan, Leigh, 284, 517n2
Buckingham, Marcus, 655n77
Buckley, George, 245
Buckley, M. Ronald, 35n63
Buckman, Robert, 667
Buechner, Maryanne Murray, 546n34
Bulkeley, William M., 267n3, 267n14
Buller, Paul F., 376n58
Bunderson, Stuart, 724n53
Bunker, Barbara Benedict, 361, 376n60, 376n61, 376n62
Burger, J. M., 570
Burgess, Jennifer R. D., 445n42, 445n45
Buri, John R., 331
Burke, Debbie, 376n62
Burke, Lisa A., 690n64
Burke, W. Warner, 376n56, 376n59
Burns, Greg, 269n77
Burns, James M., 618n42
Burns, James R., 64n41
Burns, Lawton R., 344n29, 507
Burns, Tom, 345n77
Burrows, Peter, 80, 101n29, 134n1, 268n53
Burton, John, 268n60, 269n67
Burton, Thomas M., 169n17
Bush, George W., 126, 245, 405
Bush, Ryan, 182
Buss, Dale, 135n14
Butler, Stephen A., 546n51
Butterfield, Kenneth D., 654n44
Buzzotta, V. R., 413n101, 413n102
Byham, W. C., 413n77
Bylinsky, Gene, 546n40, 546n41
Byrne, John A., 345n69, 413n85, 446n56, 483n3
Byrne, Patrick, 191
Byrnes, Nanette, 412n55, 413n80, 413n115, 644

C
Caddy, Adrian, 321
Cage, Jack H., 300n55
Caldeira, Stephen J., 689n43

Caldwell, David F., 587n51
Caldwell, Jacqueline A., 235n33, 485n61
Callea, Donna, 587n66
Cameron, Kim S., 412n46
Caminiti, Susan, 412n42, 412n43
Campbell, Andrew, 268n30, 344n45
Campbell, Chuck, 199
Campbell, Jeff, 526
Campbell, J. P., 404
Canabou, Christine, 102n50
Capell, Kerry, 268n33
Caplan, Jeremy, 101n21
Capowski, Genevieve, 594
Cardinal, Laura B., 234n6, 267n4
Carey, Eliza Newlin, 376n51
Carey, John, 101n22
Carey, Scott, 725n101
Carey, Susan, 344n32, 723n1
Carli, Linda L., 446n61, 446n64, 618n11
Carlos, 633
Carlson, John R., 689n16
Carlson, Kathleen A., 411n29
Carlton, Jim, 436
Carmody, Elinore, 501
Carney, Eliza Newlin, 344n26
Carns, Ann, 100n3
Carpenter, Andrew, 297
Carr, David, 33n5
Carr, J. Robert, 428
Carr, Nicholas, 511
Carrasco, Emma, 660
Carroll, Archie B., 155, 170n50
Carr-Rufino, Norma, 444
Carruth, Paul J., 484n19
Carter, Karen, 631
Carter, Lee, 410
Carton, Barbara, 447n99
Cartwright, Dorwin, 725n64
Cascio, Wayne F., 412n45, 724n32, 724n34
Case, John, 201n4, 201n8, 201n19, 202n41, 690n71
Casey, Albert, 34n25, 34n26
Casey, Andrea, 654n44
Cashman, James E., 269n85
Cashman, Thomas, 689n42
Casner-Lotto, Jill, 724n26
Castagna, Vanessa, 427
Castro, Ida L., 445n49
Castro, José Luis, 163
Catapano-Friedman, Robert S., 413n114
Cauchon, Dennis, 33n1, 343n19
Caudron, Shari, 137n96, 412n46
Caulfield, Brian, 201n27, 201n28, 515n62
Caulkin, Simon, 33, 95
Cavanagh, Gerald F., 169n15
Cavender, J. W., 586n8
Cederholm, Lars, 723n4
Cespedes, Frank V., 723n4
Cha, Sandra Eunyoung, 102n71
Chaharbaghi, Kazem, 269n70
Challenger, John, 412n42
Chambers, John, 568
Chan, Karen, 343n2
Chandler, Alfred D., Jr., 63n13
Chandler, Clay, 169n34, 344n22
Chao, Steven, 279
Chappell, Tom, 286
Charan, Ram, 34n25, 34n26
Charnes, John, 375n29, 723n21
Chase, Richard B., 345n85, 545n6, 586n23

Chatman, Jennifer A., 102n60, 102n71, 587n51
Chatterjee, Sayan, 234n23
Chazan, Guy, 484n31
Checa, Nicolas, 135n49
Chemers, M. M., 618n31, 618n32
Chen, Christine Y., 201n29
Chen, Kathy, 101n28
Chen, Thomas, 139, 165
Chen, Winston, 56
Cheng, Hong, 299n18
Chenoweth, Ross, 481
Chesbrough, Henry W., 375n31, 375n34, 376n43
Chesonis, Arunas, 9
Chew, W. Bouce, 547n64
Chigos, Philip, 191
Child, John, 343n5
Childre, Doc, 587n60, 587n61
Chin, Ed, 182–183
Chow, Chee W., 477, 485n57, 485n58
Chozick, Amy, 446n76
Christie, Richard, 587n44, 587n46
Chu, Kathy, 654n51
Chuan, Tan Kay, 64n55, 235n53
Chung, Amber, 64n65
Churchill, Neil C., 194, 484n19
Cialdini, Robert B., 619n58, 619n59, 619n62
Clair, Lynda St., 447n93
Clampitt, Phillip G., 688n5, 689n42
Clark, Carolyn, 616
Clark, Dwayne, 406
Clark, Timothy, 63n11, 125
Clarkson, Max B. E., 170n36
Claycomb, Cindy, 515n53
Clayton, Joseph, 274
Cleveland, Joseph, 431
Clifford, Lee, 484n35, 484n43
Clifford, Stephanie, 34n12
Clifton, Timothy C., 619n47
Cloyd, G. Gil, 375n35
Coccolo, Dante, 709
Cochran, Philip L., 171n85
Coffin, Charles, 7
Coffman, Curt, 653n6, 655n77, 655n79
Cohen, Dan S., 377n83
Cohen, Laurie P., 34n27
Cohen, Mark A., 170n39
Cohen, Robin R., 445n45
Cohen, Susan G., 344n35
Coin, Heather, 6–7, 12, 17
Colb, A., 653n23
Colbert, Barry, 152, 169n35
Cole, Kristin, 584
Coleman, Garry D., 235n34
Coleman, Henry J., Jr., 344n36
Coles, Ayishia, 341–342
Colgan, Paul, 721
Collins, Art, 377n67
Collins, Bill, 233–234
Collins, David, 63n11
Collins, E. G., 447n92
Collins, James C., 102n69, 235n53, 617n8
Collins, Jim, 396, 591, 618n9, 618n10, 619n66, 619n69, 619n72
Collins, Kathleen, 201n14
Collins, Paul D., 343n15
Collins, Roland G. Jr., 578
Colvard, James E., 618n16

Colvin, Geoffrey, 34n7, 34n19, 34n34, 35n48, 35n72, 63n19, 64n66, 103n84, 235n37, 301n60, 638, 653n20, 654n71, 654n73, 723n12, 725n73
Comer, Gary, 366
Concini, Paolo, 388
Conger, Jay A., 619n44, 619n56, 654n61, 654n62, 689n20, 689n21
Conklin, David W., 135n43, 135n49, 135n50
Conley, Lucas, 102n63, 102n76
Conlin, Michelle, 101n17, 168n4, 376n54, 413n108, 446n66, 446n67
Connelly, Mary Shane, 619n47
Conners, John, 311
Connolly, T., 653n34
Constantine, Mark, 91
Cook, John D., 558
Cook, Morgan, 19
Cook, Steve, 358
Cooke, Robert A., 345n81
Cooker, 301n62
Coombs, W. Timothy, 225, 235n42
Cooper, W. H., 301n61
Copeland, Lennie, 444n11, 444n13, 445n41, 446n75
Copeland, Michael V., 268n27, 299n3, 299n4, 301n64
Corbin, Stampp, 178
Corcoran, Jack, 447n98
Cornfield, Daniel B., 447n120
Cornwell, John M., 446n53
Corrigan, Eric, 139, 165
Cortese, Amy, 514n25
Cosgrove, Lorraine, 457
Coubrough, J. A., 63n22
Coulter, Mary, 421
Courtney, Hugh, 299n9
Coutright, John A., 345n78
Covin, Jeffrey G., 269n69
Covrig, Duane M., 169n28
Cowart, James, 544–545
Cowen, Scott, 28
Cox, Jim, 530
Cox, JulieWolfram, 411n22
Cox, Taylor H., 42, 423, 444n6
Coy, Peter, 35n73, 80, 101n14, 101n15, 413n108
Coye, W., 654n63
Crabb, Steve, 360, 666
Cramm, Susan, 664, 689n22
Crampton, Suzanne M., 690n59
Crandall, Richard E., 483n13, 483n14
Crandall, Robert, 293
Crimaldi, Laura, 101n19
Croce, Pat, 571, 690n46
Crockett, Roger O., 35n71, 101n29
Cronbaugh, Tara, 196
Cronin, Michael P., 186
Crosby, P. B., 547n66
Cross, Rob, 690n56
Crotts, John C., 234n21
Cruz, Hector, 339
Cryer, Bruce, 587n60, 587n61
Cullen, John B., 167, 169n30
Cullen, Lisa Takeuchi, 586n29, 587n50
Cummings, T. G., 376n63
Currall, Steven C., 689n13
Curtis, Kent, 442
Czinkota, Michael R., 136n63

D

Daft, Richard L., 83, 100n6, 101n30, 101n42, 102n62, 234n7, 269n79, 299n11, 300n38, 343n7, 344n24, 345n63, 375n6, 375n23, 375n24, 377n81, 485n55, 512, 520, 618n17, 619n49, 619n65, 619n70, 636, 653n33, 658, 689n11, 689n18, 689n39, 690n47, 690n53, 690n55, 725n82
Dahl, Darren, 202n79, 202n80, 394
Dahle, Cheryl, 202n53, 202n55, 202n57, 654n74
Daley, Kevin, 145
Dalton, Glenn L., 654n55
D'Amico, Carol, 445n41, 447n101
Daniels, Cora, 183, 202n47, 202n48, 586n32, 587n63
Daniels, Chip, 301n59
Dannemiller, Kathleen D., 376n60
Danville, Tess, 409
Darger, Henry, 99–100
Darroch, Valerie, 35n56
Dastmalchian, Ali, 137n93
Dasu, Sriram, 586n23
Datta, Deepak K., 300n36
Datz, Todd, 65n69
Davenport, Thomas H., 64n51, 299n16, 514n28
David, Forest R., 234n13
David, Fred R., 234n13
Davis, Keith, 132, 169n31, 586n6, 690n58, 690n62
Davis, Stanley M., 344n30
Davison, Barbara, 343n15, 343n17
Day, George S., 100n4, 101n38
Deagon, Brian, 170n46
Deakins, Keith, 512–513
Deal, Terrence E., 102n55
Dean, James W., Jr., 300n36
Dean, Jason, 134n4
Dearden, John, 484n16, 484n18
Debow, Yvette, 413n117
Dechant, Kathleen, 447n108, 724n51
DeCieri, Helen, 411n22
Deck, Stewart, 546n16
Dedrick, Jason, 546n16
DeGeorge, Gail, 447n94
DeGrauwe, Paul, 137n84
Dehoff, Kevin, 375n22
DeKoch, Robert J., 689n42
Delaney, John T., 411n9
Delaney, Kevin J., 100n1, 103n85, 514n22, 514n23
Delbecq, Andre L., 377n65
DeLeo, P. J., 654n48
Dell, Michael, 9, 105, 181
DeMarie, Samuel M., 724n32
DeMeuse, Kenneth P., 723n13
Deming, W. Edwards, 54, 468, 541, 547n66
Demos, Telis, 545n3
Denison, Daniel R., 90, 102n62, 136n58, 558
Dennis, Priscilla, 543–544
Dent, David J., 202n47, 202n69
Denzler, David R., 64n62, 546n14
Deschamps, Isabelle, 377n79
Dess, Gregory G., 268n58, 344n41, 344n50, 345n76
Deutsch, Claudia H., 168n4, 170n59, 171n83, 268n31, 446n62, 446n70
Deutsch, J. A., 586n22
Deutschman, Alan, 376n49, 618n15, 652n5

Devanna, Mary Anne, 411n6, 619n48
Diaper, Gordon, 64n32
Dickson, Duncan R., 234n21
Dickson, W. J., 64n31, 64n34, 653n8
Dietel, H. M., 202n63
Dietel, P. J., 202n63
Dietz, Joerg, 445n45
Digh, Patricia, 100n9
Digman, J. M., 586n25
Diller, Barry, 279
DiMicco, Daniel R., 644
Ding, Daniel Z., 725n78
Distefano, Joseph J., 447n107, 447n111, 447n113
DiTomaso, Nancy, 445n35
Dive, Brian, 343n10, 343n17
Dixon, Andrea L., 689n38
Dobbins, Gregory H., 63n27
Dobni, Brooke, 260
Dodd, R., 153, 170n40
Doh, Jonathan P., 171n83, 171n86
Doktor, Robert, 445n18
Dolan, Carrie, 203n84
Dole, Stephen X., 723n4
Dolezalek, Holly, 400
Dollinger, Marc J., 101n31
Domenico, Mary, 191
Donahue, Sean, 412n35
Donaldson, Thomas, 169n24, 169n33
Donavan, Dennis, 382
Donovan, Mary Anne, 690n70
Donovan, Priscilla, 491
Doraisamy, Vani, 587n66
Doran, George T., 300n32, 301n72
Dorfman, Peter W., 136n57, 618n40
Dougherty, Deborah, 34n43, 375n7
Douglas, Ceasar, 524
Douglas, Frank L., 375n29, 723n21
Douglas, Susan P., 137n85
DougWallace, Barton,, 32
Dow, Jim, 413n88
Downey, Diane, 345n52
Doyle, Chris, 474
Dragoon, Alice, 268n61, 515n67
Draper, Ralph, 443–444
Dreazen, Yochi J., 483n2, 483n11
Dreu, C. De, 725n78
Drew, Elizabeth B., 688n3
Drezner, Daniel W., 135n18
Drickhamer, David, 514n38
Droege, Scott B., 268n58
Drost, Ellen A., 383, 411n22, 411n23
Drucker, Peter F., 7, 34n9, 35n60, 64n68, 255, 376n43
Druskat, Vanessa Urch, 724n29
Duarte, Deborah L., 724n32
Duffau, Catherine, 506–507
Duffy, Tom, 101n33
Dumaine, Brian, 202n56, 343n17, 375n26, 412n54
Dumont, Darrell, 539
Duncan, Robert B., 101n30, 344n23, 345n76, 377n77
Dunfee, Thomas W., 169n24
Dunham, Richard S., 101n22
Dunkin, Amy, 652
Dunn, Julie, 101n19
Dunnette, M. D., 22, 404, 714, 725n64
Durrani, Anayat, 443
Dutton, Jane E., 98, 300n37
Dvir, Taly, 619n50
Dvorak, Phred, 135n15, 718
Dwyer, Paula, 344n44, 344n45

Dyer, Nicole, 585
Dykstra, Chris, 481
Dyne, Lynn Van, 128

E

Eagly, Alice H., 446n64, 618n11
Earley, P. Christopher, 128, 137n87, 653n34
Easen, Nick, 95, 689n14
Eastman, Kenneth K., 619n48
Eastridge, Joe, 721
Ebbers, Bernard, 149
Eden, Dov, 619n50
Edmondson, Gail, 267n15, 344n37, 374n2, 505
Edmunds, Lary, 266
Edwards, Catherine, 413n99
Edwards, Cliff, 35n65, 35n71, 101n11, 446n53
Edwards, John, 515n68
Edwards, Keren, 666
Egodigwe, Laura, 446n90, 447n105
Eichenwald, Kurt, 170n56
Eilon, Samuel, 299n7
Einhorn, Bruce, 134n1
Einstein, Walter O., 723n19
Eisenhardt, Kathleen M., 301n58, 301n69, 301n73, 725n78, 725n80
Eisner, Michael, 13
Ekegren, G., 653n34
Ekman, Paul, 689n28
Elashmawi, D. Farid, 444n13
Elgin, Ben, 375n15
Eliezer, Christie, 33n2
Elkind, Peter, 483n4
Elkins, Linda, 202n60
Eller, Claudia, 543n44
Ellis, Caroline, 35n64, 343n18
Ellison, Sarah, 267n11, 268n40, 376n36
Ellsworth, Brian, 653n37, 654n66
Elmuti, Dean, 546n32, 546n36
Ely, Robin J., 447n108, 724n51
Emshwiller, John R., 168n7
End, William T., 366
Eng, Sherry, 376n50
Engardio, Peter, 100n8, 100n10, 135n5, 135n9, 135n31, 136n78, 344n44, 514n37
Engargio, Pete, 135n34, 135n41
Enger, John R., 619n53
Enns, Harvey G., 619n64
Ensher, Ellen A., 411n25
Enthoven, Dan, 182
Epstein, Edwin M., 101n36
Epstein, Jeffrey, 501
Epstein, Marc J., 170n43
Erez, Miriam, 234n28, 725n65, 725n95
Erickson, Carrie, 653n19
Ernest, M., 421
Esfahani, Elizabeth, 136n62
Eskew, Mike, 608
Esterson, Emily, 547n63
Ettling, Jennifer T., 300n55
Ettorre, Barbara, 345n63, 690n50, 690n63
Etzioni, Amitai, 234n3, 234n4, 299n19
Evans, Janet Q., 167
Evans, M. G., 598, 618n34, 618n36
Everest, A., 437, 447n104
Ewing, Jack, 235n31
Ezrin, Hershell, 280

F

Fabish, Lisa, 102n75
Fackler, Martin, 377n88
Faerman, Sue R., 646
Fairey, Shepard, 308
Fairhurst, Gail T., 345n78
Falk, Charles F., 411n29
Falvey, J., 35n43
Farnham, Alan, 63n16, 102n59, 586n31, 586n36
Farrow, Dana L., 725n76
Fass, Allison, 35n78
Fatsis, Stefan, 35n75
Faux, Jeff, 136n74
Fawcette, Deborah, 530
Fayol, Henri, 44–45, 63n22
Fedarko, Kevin, 34n14
Feder, Barnaby J., 546n33, 546n35
Feigenbaum, A. V., 468, 484n32
Feldman, Daniel C., 725n63, 725n72
Feldman, Martin, 167
Fenwick, Marilyn S., 411n22
Ferrara, Napoleone, 647
Ferraro, Gary, 135n35
Ferrell, O. C., 136n63
Ferris, Gerald R., 446n69, 524
Ferris, Nancy, 64n67
Festinger, Leon A., 559, 586n19
Feurer, Rainer, 269n70
Fey, Carl F., 136n58
Feyerherm, Ann E., 376n57, 376n58
Fiedler, Fred E., 598, 600–601, 613, 618n30, 618n31, 618n32
Field, Andrew, 573
Field, Anne, 202n78
Field, R. H. G., 300n54
Fielder, Fred E., 600–601
Fields, Gary, 234n11
Fierman, Jaclyn, 412n38
Filho, Antonio Carlos, 239
Filkins, Dexter, 344n47
Fillippelli, Phil, 394
Finch, Byron J., 520
Fine, M., 444n5
Finkelstein, Sydney, 34n25, 34n26
Finley, Bob, 585
Finn, Bridget, 203n86, 350
Finney, Paul Burnham, 169n26
Finnigan, Annie, 445n51, 446n80, 447n119
Fiojas, Alma Morales, 175
Fiorina, Carly, 13, 416
Firneno, Charles, 609
Fisher, Anne, 202n77, 653n6, 655n79
Fisher, Cynthia D., 411n13
Fisher, Helen, 566
Fisher, Lawrence M., 95, 484n23
Fisher, Roger, 725n90
Fishman, Charles, 34n30, 169n34, 268n51, 321, 344n33
Fishman, Ted C., 135n7, 135n11, 135n19, 135n30
Fitzgerald, Anne, 619n68
Fitzgerald, Michael, 690n69
Fitzpatrick, Mark, 135n45
Flamholtz, Eric, 102n78
Flanigan, James, 135n33
Fleet, David D. Van, 63n26, 343n15, 618n19, 724n47
Fletcher, Joyce K., 445n49, 445n51
Fletcher, Winston, 421
Flight, Georgia, 268n36
Flint, Perry, 277

Florian, Ellen, 376n50, 377n67, 377n76
Fluhr, Jeff, 178
Follett, Mary Parker, 7, 44–45, 60, 63n22, 63n23, 63n25
Fombrun, Charles J., 411n6
Fontaine, Michael A., 514n7
Foote, Nathaniel, 300n57
Ford, D. J., 484n34
Ford, Henry, 42, 181
Ford, Robert C., 234n21, 344n44, 646, 654n69
Ford, Robert N., 61
Forelle, Charles, 134n1, 267n11, 413n89, 413n90
Forrester, Russ, 654n65
Forsythe, Jason, 445n25, 445n50
Foster, Jessica B., 445n13
Fottler, Myron D., 646, 654n69
Foust, Dean, 377n85
Fowler, Oscar S., 63n27
Fox, Adam, 443–444
Fox, Harold W., 269n68
Fox, Justin, 136n69
Fox, Shaul, 377n83
Foy, Norman, 447n97
Fraley, Dan, 513
France, Mike, 483n3
Francis, Suzanne C., 345n61
Frangos, Alex, 102n51
Frankel, James, 698
Frankel, Roger, 688
Franklin, 342–343
Franz, Charles R., 725n76
Frazee, Valerie, 137n92
Frazer, Mike, 584–585
Frazier, Greg, 546n24, 546n25, 546n48, 547n56
Frazier, Margaret, 723n17
Fred, Edward J., 418
Frederick, William C., 169n31
Fredrickson, James W., 300n36
Freed, Larry, 24
Freedman, Robert J., 723n4
Freeman, R. Edward, 34n8, 152–153, 169n35, 170n40, 691n83
Freeman, Sholnn, 484n42
Freidheim, Cyrus F., Jr., 101n40
French, Wendell L., 64n39, 376n56, 376n57
Frenkel-Brunswick, E., 586n42
Freudenheim, Milt, 412n66
Frevert, Barb, 634
Friedland, Jonathan, 136n61
Friedman, Milton, 155, 170n52, 587n62
Friedman, Raymond A., 447n114, 447n117, 447n120
Friedman, Raymond E., 689n13
Friedman, Rose, 170n52
Friedman, Thomas L., 488, 514n5, 514n6
Friel, Brian, 413n109
Frieswick, Kris, 413n93, 413n94
Frink, Dwight D., 446n69, 702
Fritsch, Mark J., 234n25
Fritsch, Peter, 169n35
Fritzsche, David J., 170n57
Frost, Taggart F., 377n84
Frucco, Giuseppe, 352
Fry, Fred L., 445n42, 445n45
Fry, Ronald E., 35n57
Fryer, Bronwyn, 689n24
Fuchsberg, Gilbert, 447n103
Fuhrmans, Vanessa, 377n71, 689n37

Fuld, Leonard M., 692n16
Fulfer, Mac, 689n28
Fulk, Janet, 691n84
Fuller, Scott, 92
Fulmer, Robert M., 376n58
Funk, Karina, 170n49
Futrell, David, 723n13

G

Gabarino, James, 427
Gabarro, John J., 20
Gaither, Norman, 546n24, 546n25, 546n48, 547n56
Galbraith, Jay R., 258, 269n72, 344n23, 345n52, 355
Gallace, Larry J., 484n39
Gallupe, R. B., 301n61, 301n62
Galvin, John E., 724n34
Galvin, Tammy, 400
Gandz, Jeffrey, 102n62
Ganti, Prasanthi, 299n17
Gantt, Henry, 42
Garaventa, Eugene, 171n79
Garbinas, Marc, 299n18
Garcia, Federico, 651
Garcia, Julia, 641
Gardner, William L., 619n44
Garfield, 342
Garino, Jason, 515n48, 515n49
Garrett, Echo Montgomery, 202n74
Garvey, Charlotte, 654n43
Garvin, David A., 301n69, 301n74, 345n65
Gates, Bill, 7, 71, 178, 181, 565
Gatewood, Robert D., 136n63
Geber, Beverly, 171n75
Geffen, David, 426
Gegax, Tom, 598
Gehrke, Garry, 49
Gehrke, Julie, 50, 64n38
Gehrke, Larry, 49
Geis, Florence, 587n44, 587n46
Gelfand, Michele J., 136n56
Gellene, Denise, 513
Gellerman, Saul W., 170n60
George, Claude S., Jr., 63n15, 63n18
George, Jill, 724n24
George, Thomas, 300n27
Georgopoulos, B. S., 618n34
Gerard, Glenna, 690n75
Gerkovich, Paulette R., 445n48, 445n49
Gersick, Connie J. G., 725n59
Gessner, Theodore L., 619n47
Gett, Bob, 56
Ghobadian, Abby, 269n82
Ghoshal, Sumantra, 34n31, 484n16
Ghosn, Carlos, 307, 339, 343n1, 345n88
Gibbs, Tim, 299n18
Gibson, Cristina B., 724n34, 724n41
Gibson, David G., 170n65
Gibson, Jane Whitney, 63n11
Gibson, Richard, 192
Giegold, W., 235n30
Gilbert, Jacqueline A., 444, 446n74
Gilbreth, Frank B., 42
Gilbreth, Lillian M., 42
Gilkey, Roderick, 376n58
Gilligan, Carol, 147, 169n23
Gillis, Mary, 687
Gilmour, Allan D., 426
Gingrich, Bryan, 445n39
Girard, Kim, 101n35
Glader, Paul, 101n27

Gladstein, Deborah L., 723n14
Gladwell, Malcolm, 299n26
Glaser, W., 653n16
Glasser, Perry, 342
Glassman, Edward, 373
Glassop, Linda I., 723n8
Glater, Jonathan D., 446n71
Glauser, Michael J., 690n45
Gluck, Frederick W., 268n44
Godfrey, Paul C., 171n86
Goding, Jeff, 484n36
Goerzen, Anthony, 135n27
Gogoi, Pallavi, 268n43, 300n43
Goizueta, Roberto, 647
Gold, Jacqueline S., 619n53
Golden, Daniel, 300n35
Golden, Marita, 439
Goldenberg, David, 546n21
Goldhaber, Gerald M., 689n35
Goldsmith, Marshall, 586n12
Goldsmith, Ronald E., 375n9
Goleman, Daniel, 586n35, 586n37, 586n38
Golopulos, Frank, 341
Gomes, Lee, 24, 40, 394, 506
Gomez-Mejia, L. R., 413n104
Gonzalez-Molina, Gabriel, 653n6, 655n79
Goode, Kathy, 63n21
Goold, Michael, 268n30, 344n45
Gordon, Angela, 618n20
Gordon, Bruce, 422
Gordon, David T., 587n74
Gordon, Edward E., 413n85, 413n87
Gordon, John Steele, 40
Gore, W. L., 592
Gorgopoulos, B. S., 653n30
Goslin, D. A., 169n22
Gossage, Bobbie, 201n1, 203n91
Gottlieb, Lori, 566, 586n34
Gottlieb, Mark, 483
Gould, Steven, 143
Govindarajan, Vijay, 268n23, 269n69, 269n75, 724n37
Gozdz, Kazinierz, 690n75
Graham, Bette Nesmith, 416
Graham, Jill W., 146, 169n22
Graham, Katherine, 612
Graham, Lawrence Otis, 429
Grant, Elaine Appleton, 201n21, 202n42
Grant, Linda, 652n6
Grant, Lorrie, 135n23, 135n28, 202n40
Grant, Peter, 375n4
Grant-Vallone, Elisa, 411n25
Gray, Jerry L., 652n3
Gray, Steven, 377n66
Grealish, Alenka, 342
Greco, Susan, 201n21, 202n42
Greehey, Bill, 91–92, 96
Green, David, 185
Green, Heather, 514n3, 514n17, 514n20
Green, Marnie E., 63n7
Green, Willard P., 100
Greenberg, Herb, 483
Greenberg, Maurice R., 485n64
Greenberg, Paul, 515n64
Greenberger, Robert S., 135n22
Greene, Charles, 618n39
Greene, Jay, 344n25, 413n112
Greene, R. J., 413n106
Greengard, Samuel, 64n47, 412n59
Greening, Daniel W., 171n91
Greenleaf, Robert K., 612, 619n67

Greenlees, Donald, 135n28
Greenspan, Alan, 136n82
Greenwell, Rachel, 62
Greenwood, Regina A., 63n30, 64n33
Greenwood, Ronald G., 63n30
Greis, Noel P., 546n53
Griffin, Jennifer J., 171n85
Griffin, Mark A., 725n96
Griffin, Martin, 33
Griffith, Terri L., 724n36
Griffith, Victoria, 392, 411n17, 411n18, 412n57
Grimsley, 235n47
Grise, M. L., 301n61
Grittner, Peter, 101n41
Groner, Alex, 64n40
Gross, N., 80
Grossman, Allen, 35n61
Grossman, Robert J., 445n44, 586n20
Grote, Dick, 413n94, 413n95
Grover, Ron, 102n44
Grow, Brian, 101n19, 229
Gruner, Stephanie, 587n57
Gryna, Frank M., 484n32
Guernsey, Brock, 375n29, 723n21
Guerrizio, Maria, 189
Guillén, Mauro F., 64n48, 515n52
Gulati, Ranjay, 515n48, 515n49
Gumpert, David E., 375n12
Gunn, Jack, 300n32, 301n72
Gunther, Marc, 170n43, 170n45, 170n47, 234n11, 300n51
Gupta, Anil K., 268n23, 269n69, 269n75, 724n37
Gupta, Rajat Kumar, 416, 420
Gupta, Udayan, 203n89
Gupta, Vipin, 136n57
Gustafson, Evelyn, 616–617
Guth, Robert A., 100n1, 103n85, 343n13, 344n25, 377n68
Gutierrez, Carlos, 108
Guyon, Janet, 102n66, 103n84, 299n10, 300n45
Gwyther, Matthew, 617n7

H

Hackman, J. Richard, 641–642, 650, 654n56, 725n69
Haddad, Charles, 170n46, 343n19
Haddad, Kamal M., 477, 485n57, 485n58
Hafner, Katie, 168n4, 170n59, 171n83
Hagerty, James R., 515n50
Hahn, Betty, 63n21
Hale, Jr., N. Wayne, 22
Hales, Colin P., 35n53
Haley, Usha C. V., 75
Hall, Douglas T., 386, 412n32
Hall, Edward T., 437
Hall, James, 515n50
Hall, Kenji, 344n37, 374n2
Hallinan, Joseph T., 268n38
Hamel, Gary, 267n5, 690n72
Hamil, Brad, 721
Hamilton, Booz Allen, 94
Hamilton, Joan O'C., 101n22
Hamm, Steve, 223, 269n74, 269n80, 344n37, 374n2, 375n27, 375n28, 375n30, 447n94, 514n37, 515n54
Hammer, Michael, 345n63, 345n64, 345n65, 345n67, 345n86, 484n36
Hammond, John, 284

Hammonds, Keith H., 35n67, 267n7, 268n58, 411n1, 413n118
Hampshire, Kristen, 202n70
Handelsman, Mitchell M., 623
Haneberg, Lisa, 34n33, 34n34
Hanges, Paul J., 136n57
Hannan, Robert L., 34n40
Hanrahan, Ted, 443–444
Hansell, Saul, 203n90
Hansen, Morten T., 515n73
Harari, Oren, 65n72, 234n2, 235n52, 284, 411n14
Hardy, Cynthia, 375n7
Harlan, Raymond, 624
Harmsen, Richard, 136n64
Harnett, 342
Harney, Alexandra, 547n57
Harper, Stephen C., 260
Harreld, Heather, 514n30, 546n13
Harrigan, Betty, 62
Harrigan, Kathryn Rudie, 135n24
Harrington, Ann, 63n17, 64n47, 64n68, 100n2, 412n65
Harrington, Shauna, 653n19
Harrington, Tom, 341
Harris, Darius, 615–616
Harris, Jeanne G., 299n16, 514n28
Harris, Jonathan, 300n34
Harris, Roy, 444n7, 445n32, 445n36
Harris, Walker, 395
Harrison, Jeffrey S., 169n33
Harrison, Margaret, 370
Harrison-Walker, L. Jean, 514n39
Hart, David W., 646
Hart, Jacob, 676
Hartman, Laura Pincus, 158, 170n61, 170n66
Harvey, Jerry B., 711, 725n79
Harvey, Michael, 35n63
Hasek, G., 484n35
Hassan, Abraham, 133
Hassan, Palwasha, 17
Hastings, Donald, 483
Hatlestad, Luc, 229
Haughom, John L., 577, 587n63, 587n64
Hawk, Elizabeth J., 652n6
Hawkins, Brian, 688n7
Hawkins, Lee Jr., 299n6, 300n41
Hawthorne, Nancy, 592, 624
Hayes, Neil, 597
Hayes, Robert H., 545n8
Hays, Scott, 412n59
Heath, Chip, 301n67
Heath, Thomas, 139, 165
Hebl, Michelle R., 445n33
Hechinger, John, 618n29
Hecht, William, 77
Heifetz, Ronald A., 64n52
Heilman, Madeline E., 300n55, 445n44
Heimlich, John, 277
Heintz, Nadine, 201n10, 485n52, 485n53
Heinzl, Mark, 80, 101n29
Heiselman, Maria, 442
Heising, Angela, 34n37
Heiter, Stefanie, 177
Helgesen, Sally, 446n64, 618n11
Hellervik, L. V., 404
Hellmann, Curtis, 293
Hellriegel, Don, 570, 652n3, 466
Hemp, Paul, 299
Hempel, Carl G., 64n43
Hempel, Jessi, 101n23, 168n4

Henderson, A. M., 43, 63n20
Henderson, Richard I., 413n103
Hendrickson, Anthony R., 724n32
Henkoff, Ronald, 546n52
Henninger, Daniel, 653n27
Hennings, Jasper, 99–100
Henricks, Mark, 174, 201n11
Hepworth, Susan J., 558
Hequet, Marc, 447n109
Herbert, Theodore T., 343
Hernandez, Henry, 435
Hernandez, Ignacio, 688
Herschlag, Judith K., 300n55
Hersey, Paul, 598–600, 613, 618n28
Hershberg, Jonathan, 690n68, 690n69
Hertzog, William, 680
Herzberg, Frederick, 628, 641, 648, 650, 653n18
Heskett, James L., 90, 102n61, 102n78
Hewlett, Sylvia Ann, 446n54
Heymans, Brian, 545n5
Higbie, Andrea, 587n70
Higgins, James M., 137n87, 234
Hildebrand, Carol, 690n64
Hill, Charles W. L., 546n9
Hill, Linda A., 17, 20, 35n45, 725n93
Himelstein, Linda, 101n22, 514n3
Hines, Charlotte, 61
Hira, Nadira A., 445n28
Hisrich, Robert D., 202n43
Hitler, Adolf, 607
Hitt, Michael A., 241, 253, 268n22
Hjorten, Lisa, 92
Hochman, Paul, 725n70
Hochwarter, Wayne A., 524
Hockett, Homer C., 63n6
Hockwarter, Wayne A., 235n55
Hodge, John W., 342–343, 690n59
Hodgetts, Richard M., 201n9, 202n37, 202n60, 484n46, 484n50, 544
Hoegl, Martin, 724n44, 724n46
Hoekstra, Joel, 234n27
Hoenig, Christopher, 376n46, 376n47
Hoerr, John, 723n22
Hof, Robert D., 375n33, 376n35, 514n3, 515n56
Hofer, Charles W., 268n35
Hoff, Ted, 412n51
Hoffman, Hugh J., 329
Hofstede, Geert, 117–119, 129, 136n54, 136n55
Hollander, Edwin P., 654n60
Hollenback, J., 654n48
Hollenbeck, George P., 137n86
Holmes, Stanley, 267n12, 376n44
Holpp, Lawrence, 646
Holson, Laura M., 235n51
Holstein, William J., 64n61, 135n13
Holstrom, Leslie, 171n92
Holt, David H., 136n64
Holt, Jim, 135n36, 135n37
Holt, Sandra, 339
Holtom, Brooks, 447n117
Hooijberg, Robert, 90, 102n64, 445n35
Hopper, Carolyn, 491
Hoque, Ekramul, 587n61
Hornstein, Harvey A., 300n55
Horowitz, Adam, 299n4
Horowitz, Shel, 233
Horton, Thomas R., 312
Horwitt, Elizabeth, 514n11

Hosking, D., 618n33
Hoskisson, Robert E., 241, 253, 268n22
Houck, Keith, 233–234
House, R. J., 136n56, 136n57
House, Robert J., 119, 136n57, 598, 618n35, 618n37, 619n43, 619n46, 619n47
Houston, Mike, 668
Hovanesian, Mara Der, 234n16
Howard, Janet, 19
Howard, Suzanne, 722–723
Howe, Jeff, 373
Howell, Jane M., 376n39, 619n47
Howell, Jon P., 618n40
Hrebiniak, Lawrence G., 268n42
Hu, Junchen, 725n78
Huang, Xu, 137n95, 654n57
Hubbard, Gwen, 423
Huey, John, 62n3
Hughes, Jack, 394
Hughes, Rob, 394
Hui, Chun, 725n78
Hui, Khoo Hsien, 64n55, 235n53
Hull, Frank, 343n15
Hult, G. Tomas M., 269n69, 269n71, 345n73
Humphreville, Mark, 299n18
Hunger, J. David, 268n52
Hunt, Albert R., 202n52
Hunt, Dan, 660
Hunt, J. G., 618n24
Hunter, Rob, 666
Hurwitz, Alan, 344n51
Huse, E. F., 376n63
Huselid, Mark A., 411n9
Huy, Quy Nguyen, 34n32, 34n34
Hyatt, Joshua, 102n45, 690n61, 701
Hyer, Nancy Lea, 546n29
Hymowitz, Carol, 34n35, 35n62, 135n15, 136n60, 171n84, 234n8, 234n26, 344n29, 344n45, 413n94, 413n96, 447n94, 483n8, 546n11, 586n27, 652n4

I

Iacocca, Lee, 326–327, 345n54
Iaffaldano, M. T., 586n8
Ian, 514n38
Iannaccone, Judy, 703
Ice, T, 279
Iger, Robert A., 227, 272
Ihlwan, Moon, 344n37, 374n2
Immelt, Jeffrey, 7, 11, 18, 27, 250, 261, 357, 497, 611, 629
Imperato, Gina, 725n97
Ingersoll, Minnie, 15
Ingrassia, Paul, 344n22
Inkson, Kerr, 34n37, 137n87
Ioannou, Lori, 171n86
Ireland, R. Duane, 241, 253, 268n22, 299n24, 300n29
Irle, K. W., 618n18
Irwin, Richard D., 268n26
Isabella, Lynn A., 101n40
Islam, Mayenul, 587n61
Ittner, Christopher D., 483n13
Ivancevich, John M., 235n32, 444, 446n74, 653n38
Iverson, F. Kenneth, 644
Iwai, Masaki, 531

J

Jackman, Jay M., 690n80
Jackofsky, Ellen F., 136n58, 137n94
Jackson, Brad, 63n11

Jackson, John H., 397, 411n3
Jackson, Roderick, 164
Jackson, Susan E., 137n94, 300n37, 411n9, 466
Jackson, Terence, 136n59
Jacob, Jay, 256
Jacobs, Robert W., 376n60, 440
Jacobs, Roger, 32
Jacobson, Henry, 111
Jaeger, Alfred M., 484n26
Jaffe, Greg, 301n59, 617n3, 689n40, 514n12
Jaffrey, Syed Hasan, 484n44
Jagger, Mick, 21
Jago, Arthur G., 288, 291, 295–296, 299, 300n52, 300n55
Jaj, Amal Kumar, 135n40
James, Brent, 490
James, Don, 484n45
James, Erika H., 445n45
Jamil, Mamnoon, 268n26
Janney, Jay J., 171n85
Janssen, Jennifer, 621
Jardins, Jory Des, 445n51, 446n61
Jaruzelski, Barry, 375n22
Jassawalla, Avan R., 725n58
Javidan, Mansour, 119, 136n57, 137n93
Jay, Antoney, 718
Jehn, Karen A., 102n60
Jemison, David B., 101n31
Jenks, James M., 398
Jensen, Mary Ann C., 725n60
Jermier, J. M., 618n40
Jerry, 202n60
Jett, Joe, 513
Jewell, Linda N., 725n60
Jobs, Steve, 7, 181
Jobson, Tom, 500, 514n35, 546n15
John, Caron H. St., 169n33
John, Warren St., 102n44
Johnson, Art, 233
Johnson, David W., 593
Johnson, F., 444n5
Johnson, Frank P., 593
Johnson, Hillary, 665
Johnson, Homer H., 171n85, 171n86
Johnson, Jim, 557
Johnson, L. A., 445n20
Johnson, Lauren Keller, 689n13
Johnson, Nora, 298
Johnson, Rob, 443
Johnston, Lynne, 585
Johnston, William B., 101n13
Jonas, Hans, 64n43
Jonas, Harry S., 35n57
Jones, Daniel T., 547n59
Jones, Del, 446n64, 585n3, 586n17, 586n26
Jones, E., 586n24
Jones, Gareth R., 546n9
Jones, Jack William, 35n50
Jones, Jerry, 279
Jones, John E., 61
Jones, Kathryn, 546n16
Jones, N. W., 618n34, 653n30
Jones, Patricia, 102n56
Jones, Thomas M., 168n6, 169n11
Jordan, Miriam, 345n55
Jovi, Jon Bon, 282
Joyce, Amy, 654n50
Joyce, Christopher, 100n5
Joyce, Kevin E., 234n9
Joyce, William F., 268n42, 268n57
Judge, Timothy A., 619n51
Judy, Richard W., 445n41, 447n101

Jung, Andrea, 416
Jung, Carl, 570, 583, 587n47
Juran, J. M., 468, 484n32
Jusko, Jill, 547n61

K

Kacmer, Charles J., 524
Kahaner, Larry, 102n56
Kahn, Jeremy, 102n69
Kahn, Robert, 689n39
Kahwajy, Jean L., 725n78
Kakuda, Cara, 9
Kalogeris, T. J., 586n22
Kamenetz, Anya, 514n17, 514n18, 514n21
Kane, Kate, 484n40
Kane, Melinda, 447n120
Kanigel, Robert, 63n16
Kanter, James, 136n68
Kanter, Rosabeth Moss, 34n32, 102n74, 375n13, 376n53, 587n71
Kanungo, Rabindra N., 619n44, 654n61, 654n63
Kaplan, David M., 446n69
Kaplan, Robert E., 34n40, 485n56, 485n57, 485n58, 485n59
Kaplan, Robert S., 477–478
Kapstein, Jonathan, 135n13
Kaptein, Muel, 168n3, 170n62
Karp, Jonathan, 345n55
Kasarda, John D., 546n53
Kashlak, Roger, 34n41
Kast, Fremont E., 64n44, 64n46
Katel, Peter, 62n1, 65n72
Kates, Amy, 345n52
Katz, Daniel, 689n39
Katz, L., 135n26, 343
Katz, Robert L., 34n18
Katzenbach, Jeffrey, 700
Katzenbach, Jon R., 695
Kaucic, Lou, 413n100
Kauffman, Stuart, 277
Kaufman, Bruce E., 654n70
Kaufman, Leslie, 35n74, 690n77
Kautz, Brian, 398
Kavovit, Barbara, 178–179
Kawamoto, Nobuhiko, 314
Kazanas, H. C., 413n81
Kazanjian, Robert K., 258, 269n72
Kee, Micah R., 103n79
Keenan, Faith, 514n37, 547n58
Keeney, Ralph L., 284, 300n44
Kehoe, William J., 136n65
Keighley, Geoff, 344n46
Kekes, John, 169n18
Kelleher, Herb, 602
Kelleher, Kevin, 617n4, 515n71, 515n72
Kelley, H. H., 586n24
Kelly, Gary, 602
Kelly, Kevin, 64n58, 170n58, 553, 580, 585n1, 587n75
Kelly, Sheriff Gene, 683
Kelly, Terri, 592
Kemske, Floyd, 411n15
Kennedy, Allan A., 102n55
Kennedy, J., 437, 447n104
Kepler, Nick, 358
Kepner, C., 282, 300n40
Kerr, Jean, 135n21
Kerr, K. Austin, 64n40
Kerr, Steven, 235n54, 376n62, 618n40
Kerwin, Kathleen, 344n43
Keys, Bernard, 413n79
Kharif, Olga, 101n29

Kher, Umesh, 170n53
Khermouch, Gerry, 101n19, 377n85
Khurana, Rakesh, 617n8
Kibbe, Daniel R., 724n26
Kidder, Rushworth M., 169n9
Kiechel, Walter III, 619n44
Killham, Emily, 585n4, 654n75, 655n77
Killing, J. Peter, 122
Kilmann, Ralph H., 102n47
Kilmas, Molly, 203n89
Kimble, Linda, 161
Kimmel, Michael S., 445n19
Kin, W. Chan, 586n16
King, Dave, 233
King, Marsha, 203n91
King, Martin Luther, Jr., 166, 507
King, Paula J., 169n33
King, Randall, 229
Kinni, Theodore, 64n51
Kipnis, D., 619n57, 619n58, 619n59
Kirchhoff, Sue, 100n5
Kirkman, Bradley L., 724n28, 724n34, 724n35
Kirkpatrick, David, 134n2, 375n16
Kirkpatrick, S. A., 595
Kirsner, Scott, 35n73, 63n21, 229, 375n4, 375n5, 689n15
Klass, Leslie Gross, 587n72
Klayman, Joshua, 301n67
Klein, Gary, 279, 299n25
Klein, Katherine J., 619n43
Klein, Mark M., 345n63
Klein, Richard, 515n39, 515n46
Kleiner, Art, 64n54, 547n59, 547n62
Kleisterlee, Gerald, 659
Klemm, Mary, 234n13
Klineberg, S. L., 586n20
Kneale, D., 411n10
Knight, Chuck, 294
Knight, Frank H., 63n20
Knight, Jennifer L., 445n33
Knopper, Steve, 33n2
Koch, Christopher, 546n23, 546n28
Kodama, Mitsuru, 376n37
Koehler, Kenneth G., 725n59, 725n81
Koenig, Richard W., 691n81
Koerper, Gary, 354
Kogut, Bruce, 135n44
Kohlberg, L., 146, 169n22
Kohn, Alfie, 638
Kohs, S. C., 618n18
Kok, Gerjo, 653n34
Kolata, Gina, 133, 483n1, 485n65
Kolb, David A., 587n54, 587n56
Kolenda, Konstanian, 169n18
Kolodinsky, Robert W., 524
Kolodny, Lora, 135n25
Konrad, Alison M., 34n41
Kontzer, Tony, 515n75
Koonce, Richard, 345n68
Koontz, Katy, 376n38
Koresh, David, 607
Kosdrosky, Terry, 546n12
Kotter, John P., 34n40, 35n50, 90, 102n61, 102n78, 366, 368, 376n64, 377n72, 377n75, 377n81, 377n83
Kouzes, James M., 102n78, 617n6
Kovacevich, Richard, 608
Kraemer, Harry Jansen, 428
Kraemer, Kenneth L., 546n16
Kramer, Robert J., 344n27

Kranhold, Kathryn, 169n12, 171n76
Krass, Peter, 411n26
Kratz, Ellen Florian, 235n36, 545n2
Kraut, A. I., 22
Kravetz, Dennis J., 412n49
Kravitz, D. A., 586n20, 724n48
Krazit, Tom, 394
Kreme, Krispy, 34n11
Kreps, David M., 411n12
Kreuze, Jerry G., 171n81
Krim, Jonathan, 103n85
Krishnan, Sanjay, 110
Kroll, Karen, 654n51
Kromkowski, Julie A., 446n68
Kronholz, June, 35n75, 100n5
Kropf, Marcia Brumit, 445n48, 445n49
Krueger, Jerry, 585n4, 654n75, 655n77
Kuehl, Charles R., 183, 202n49
Kumar, Kamalesh, 447n108, 447n112, 724n51
Kuratko, Donald F., 188, 201n9, 202n37, 202n60, 544
Kurk, Thomas, 345n84
Kurke, Lance B., 35n53
Kurland, Nancy B., 412n39
Kurschner, Dale, 171n86
Kurtz, Kevin, 13
Kurtzman, Joel, 476
Kuzmits, Frank E., 413n113
Kyle, Cynthia, 652

L

Laabs, Jennifer J., 411n23, 586n18
LaBarre, Polly, 235n60
Labich, Kenneth, 444n2, 725n99
Laden, Osama bin, 607
LaDouceur, Bob, 597
LaFasto, Frank M. J., 723n9, 723n20
Lafley, A. G., 353, 565
Lahti, Ryan K., 515n66
Lakshmi, Rama, 587n68
Lam, Long W., 514n39
Lambert, Art, 100
Lambing, Peggy A., 183, 202n49
Lancaster, H., 412n37
Lancourt, Joan, 95
Land, Edwin, 349
Landau, Meryl Davids, 413n84
Landauer, Steffan, 235n54
Landro, Laura, 688n1, 691n86
Lane, Harry W., 688
Lane, Henry W., 136n58
Langley, Ann, 300n30
Langley, Monica, 299n6
LaPolice, Christelle, 235n33, 485n61
LaPotin, Perry, 299n11
Larcker, David F., 483n13
Laroche, Lionel, 447n110
Larrick, Richard P., 301n67
Larsen, Janet K., 688n7
Larson, Carl E., 723n9, 723n20
Larson, L. L., 618n24
Lashinsky, Adam, 135n12, 483n15, 725n66, 725n67
Lasswell, Mark, 299n4
Latham, Gary P., 234n28, 634, 653n34, 653n35, 653n38, 654n40, 654n48
Lathbury, Emma, 200–201
Latour, Almar, 269n66, 377n73
Lau, Alan W., 35n53

Lau, Dora C., 723n15
Laurie, Donald L., 64n52
Lauster, Steffan M., 344n21
Lawler, E. F., III, 413n106
Lawler, Edward E. III, 411n7, 653n30, 654n63, 484n33
Lawler, Joseph C., 14
Lawrence, Paul R., 344n30, 345n60, 345n75
Lay, Kenneth, 454
Lazere, Cathy, 485n58, 546n47
Lea, Wendy, 202n71
Leahy, Tad, 497
Leana, Carrie R., 343n12
Leavitt, Harold J., 345n71, 375n17
Leavy, Brian, 375n9
Leder, Michelle, 586n30, 587n53
Ledford, Gerald E., Jr., 235n53
Ledvinka, J., 412n70
Lee, Bob, 196
Lee, Chris, 447n109
Lee, Cindy, 465
Lee, Jennifer S., 483n9
Lee, Kun-Hee, 347
Lee, Louise, 134n1, 136n61, 137n98
Lee, Reggie Van, 102n75
Lee, Stan, 196
Lehn, K., 484n48
Lei, David, 344n35
Leibs, Scott, 413n89, 546n27
Lemann, Nicholas, 445n43
Lencioni, Patrick M., 102n52, 102n65, 103n82
Lengel, R. M., 83
Lengel, Robert H., 299n11, 619n49, 619n65, 689n11, 689n18
Lengnick-Hall, Cynthia A., 411n6
Lengnick-Hall, Mark L., 411n6
Leonard-Barton, Dorothy, 377n79
Leonhardt, David, 444n17
Leontiades, Milton, 268n35, 268n41
Lesser, Eric, 62
Letts, Christine W., 35n61
Leuchars, Elaine, 653n19
Leung, Shirley, 546n42
Levering, Robert, 300n45, 653n12, 653n19, 653n20
Levin, Doron, 484n42
Levine, Andrew, 475
Levine, J. B., 80
Levine, Roger, 629
Levinson, Art, 647
Levinson, D. J., 586n42
Levinson, Meridith, 267n1, 269n88, 398, 413n76, 514n13, 514n31, 515n67, 546n32, 689n28,
Levitt, Theodore, 267n17
Levy, Sandra, 530
Lewin, Kurt, 367, 376n63, 377n80
Lewis, Neil A., 344n48
Lewis, Peter, 374n1
Lewis, Virginia L., 194
Liberman, Vadim, 169n14
Lickona, T., 146, 169n22
Lieberman, Pamela Forbes, 598
Lienert, Anita, 35n52
Likert, R., 618n25
Lilly, Eli, 657
Lindblad, Cristina, 136n74
Lipka, Sara, 345n53
Lipman, Joanne, 267n19
Lipnack, Jessica, 724n33
Lisser, Eleena De, 34n17
Littlefield, Greg, 175

Livengood, Scott, 34n11
Lizotte, Ken, 375n11
Lobel, Sharon A., 447n93
Loch, Karen D., 514n38
Locke, Edwin A., 234n28, 595, 634, 653n34, 653n35, 653n36, 653n38
Locklear, Lynn, 213
Loden, Marilyn, 418, 444n15
Lodge, Sam, 298–299
Loewenberg, Samuel, 101n20
Logue, Ann C., 447n115
London, M., 35n43
Longenecker, Clinton O., 725n85
Longenecker, Justin G., 169n15
Loomis, Carol J., 267n14, 299n6, 300n41, 512n30, 546n10, 546n13
Lopez, Julie Amparano, 445n49
Lorinc., John, 484n32
Lorsch, Jay W., 34n43, 345n60, 345n75
Love, G., 689n16
Love, Thomas, 193
Loveland, John P., 723n4
Loveman, Gary, 496, 514n31
Lownes-Jackson, Millicent, 444
Lowry, Karen, 61
Lowry, Tom, 515n40
Lowson, Robert H., 545n7
Loyalka, Michelle Dammon, 75
Lubart, Todd I., 375n11
Lublin, Joann S., 375n15, 447n94, 447n102, 688n2
Luce, Carolyn Buck, 446n54
Lucier, Charles E., 547n67
Luebbe, Richard L., 520
Luffman, George, 234n13
Lumpkin, G. T., 268n58, 268n59, 269n86
Lunsford, J. Lynn, 234n10, 268n45, 546n30
Luqmani, Mushtaq, 171n81
Luqmani, Zahida, 171n81
Luthans, Brett C., 412n45
Luthans, Fred, 64n46, 484n46, 484n50, 654n41, 654n42, 688n7
Lyles, Marjorie A., 300n37

M

Ma, L., 411n30
Mabert, Vincent A., 515n59, 546n50
Mackey, John, 293
Martel, Jeri Dawn, 573
McBain, Richard, 411n14, 412n48
McCafferty, Joseph, 223, 514n15
McCaffrey, David P., 646
McCall, Morgan W., Jr., 34n40, 137n86
McCann, J., 344n23
McCanse, Anne Adams, 597
McCarthy, Michael J., 169n16
McCaulley, Mary H., 587n48
McClanaghan, Lillian, 134
McClandon, Thurrell O., 484n19
McClelland, David C., 202n50, 586n37, 629–630, 648, 653n21, 653n23
McClenahan, J. S., 125, 136n72, 484n37
McCollough, Allen, 237
McConnell, Troy, 196
MacCormack, Alan David, 546n43
McCoy, Kevin, 483n7
McCracken, Jack, 15

McCracken, Jeffrey, 546n18
McCracken, Mike, 484n35
McCraty, Rollin, 587n60, 587n61
McCroskey, J. C., 686
McCullough, Stacie, 299n16
McCune, Jenny C., 34n34, 103n81, 234n19, 300n49, 515n73, 690n73
McDonald, Paul, 102n62
McFarlin, Dean B., 619n64
McGaw, Nancy, 102n75
McGee, G. W., 586n8
McGee, Marianne Kolbasuk, 394
McGinn, Daniel, 514n1
McGovern, Pat, 589–590, 492
McGrath, M. R., 300n50
McGregor, Douglas, 47, 49, 64n37
McGregor, Eng,, 375n21
McGregor, Eugene B., 411n6
McGregor, Jena, 34n27, 135n10, 202n70, 300n39, 344n37, 374n2, 375n31, 375n32, 376n45, 376n50, 413n95, 413n97, 413n98, 530, 624, 653n13, 690n48, 690n49
McGuinness, Paul, 6–7
McGuire, Jean B., 171n89
Machiavelli, Niccolo, 569, 587n43
Macht, Joshua, 513
Maciariello, Joseph, 483
Macintosh, Norman B., 690n55, 512
MacIntosh, Sara, 584
McIntyre, J. M., 587n56, 653n23
McKeever, Jeffrey, 294
McKenna, D. D., 22
McKinley, William, 412n45
McKinnell, Henry, 108
McKinney, Joseph A., 169n15
Mckinnon, Dan, 198
McKinstry, Nancy, 108, 274
McLaughlin, Kevin J., 344n41
McLaughlin, M. L., 691n84
McLean, Bethany, 168n2, 483n4, 619n53
McLemore, Clinton W., 169n8
McLurkin, James, 698
McMahon, J. Timothy, 235n32, 653n38
McMillen, Steve, 442
McNeilly, Mark, 101n37, 300n46, 300n47
McNerney, James, 363–364
McPherson, Simon O., 724n34
McQuaid, Sara J., 136n58
McShane, Steven L., 121
MacVicar, Jinnett,, 202n62
McWilliams, Gary, 134n1, 137n98
Magnan, Michelle, 103n83
Magner, Marge, 426
Magnet, Myron, 101n41
Magnusson, Paul, 136n81
Maguire, John, 135n49
Mahar, L., 618n32
Maher, Cyrus, 410
Maher, Kris, 457, 587n67
Mahon, John F., 171n85
Mahoney, G. M., 618n34, 653n30
Maidment, Fred, 134n3
Mailvaganam, Stefan, 6
Main, Jeremy, 35n73, 64n49
Mainardi, 267n18
Mair, Johanna, 202n52
Mak, Paul, 242
Maker, Guitar, 268n57
Makes, Harvard Guru, 267n19
Makhija, A. K., 484n48

Makhija, Mahesh, 515n65, 515n74
Maleskowski, Jim, 374
Malka, Ben, 216
Malkin, Elisabeth, 135n20, 135n26, 136n81
Mallinger, Mark, 169n15
Mallory, Maria, 101n22
Mandal, Sumant, 268n21
Mandell, Mel, 485n54
Maney, Kevin, 35n71
Manganelli, Raymond L., 345n63
Mani, Sirish, 691n84, 465
Manjeet, 136n78
Mankin, Don, 344n35
Mannes, George, 201n26, 203n85, 724n46
Manning, George, 442
Mannix, Elizabeth A., 35n63, 35n66
Mannix, Laura M., 445n33
Manson, Marshall, 510
Manville, Brook, 344n50
Mapes, Timothy, 169n35
Maples, Michael D., 690n81
March, James G., 299n8, 299n20, 412n47
Marcic, Dorothy, 32, 118, 259, 512, 583
Mariucci, Anne, 707
Markels, Alex, 64n56
Markides, Costantinos, 267n9
Marklein, Mary Beth, 446n65
Marks, Joel, 181
Markus, M. Lynne, 344n50, 689n17
Marley, Cathy, 484n45
Marley, Patrick, 100
Marr, Merissa, 135n15
Mars, Betty, 199
Marsick, Victoria J., 723n4
Martel, Leon, 64n55
Martin, B., 724n48
Martin, Chuck, 228, 235n56, 235n57
Martin, David C., 446n68
Martin, J., 689n23
Martin, James E., 653n28
Martin, Joanne, 102n47, 102n54
Martin, Justin, 135n15, 135n16, 186
Martin, Kenneth R., 484n39
Martin, Lockheed, 355
Martínez, Juan Luis, 171n84
Martins, Luis I., 444n16
Masarech, Mary Ann, 93, 102n72, 102n73, 102n77, 103n80, 269n84
Mascarenhas, Briance, 268n26
Maslow, Abraham F., 47, 49, 625–627, 641, 648, 653n9
Mason, Claire M., 725n96
Mason, Richard O., 297, 299n12, 300n50
Masuch, Michael, 299n11
Matheny, Sam, 585
Matherly, Timothy A., 375n9
Mathews, Anna Wilde, 483n9, 484n28
Mathias, P. F., 34n43
Mathis, Robert L., 397, 411n3
Mathys, Nicholas J., 235n55
Matson, Eric, 34n24, 300n57
Matthews, John A., 344n36
Mattis, Mary, 446n63
Mauborgne, Renée, 586n16
Maxwell, Jennifer, 202n70
Mayer, Caroline E., 24
Mayer, Peter, 300n44

Maynard, Micheline, 268n54
Maynard, Roberta, 193, 202n78, 257, 268n60, 654n47, 689n41, 690n50
Mayo, Andrew, 65n69
Mayo, Anthony J., 618n41
Mayo, Elton, 46–47
Mayor, Tracy, 470, 484n35
Maznevski, Martha L., 447n107, 447n111, 447n113
Mead, R., 121
Meek, V. Lynne, 102n46
Meertens, Ree M., 653n34
Mehrabian, Albert, 689n27
Mehta, Stephanie N., 300n33, 445n31, 445n34, 586n40
Meiseles, Joanna B., 595
Meising, Paul, 234n18
Meister, Jeanne C., 413n84, 413n85
Melendez, Antonio, 167–168
Mello, John P. Jr., 514n29
Melnyk, Steven A., 64n62, 546n14
Mendenhall, M., 446n89
Mendes, Decio, 343n16, 345n59
Menzer, John, 112
Menzies, Hugh D., 134n3
Merck, George, 612
Meredith, Jack R., 545
Merrell, V. Dallas, 619n61
Mestral, George de, 349
Metcalf, Henry C., 63n24, 63n25
Meyerson, Debra E., 445n49, 445n51
Miceli, Marcia Parmarlee, 171n78, 171n79
Michaels, Daniel, 546n30
Michaels, Edward, 718
Michaels, Rob, 621–622
Michaelsen, Larry K., 447n108, 447n112, 724n51
Mickos, Mårten, 701
Middelhoff, Thomas, 106
Mieskowski, Katharine, 102n74, 301n60, 618n27
Milbourn, Todd T., 484n17
Miles, Grant, 344n36
Miles, Gregory L., 724n23
Miles, Raymond E., 344n36, 344n38, 344n49
Milkovich, George T., 413n105
Miller, C. Chet, 234n6, 267n4, 299n24, 300n29
Miller, Danny, 268n48
Miller, David, 514n7
Miller, Janice S., 446n53, 689n44
Miller, Jonathan, 280
Miller, Naomi, 442
Miller, William, 65n69, 259
Milliken, Frances J., 444n16
Mills, Peter K., 345n84, 377n65
Milstein, Howard, 157
Mintxberg, Henry, 269n70
Mintz, Jessica, 412n60
Mintzberg, Henry, 16, 19–21, 34n39, 35n49, 35n50, 35n51, 35n54, 345n58, 619n54, 658, 688n4
Mirvis, Philip H., 411n14
Mishra, Aneil K., 90, 102n62
Mishra, Jitendra M., 690n59
Mitchell, Brooks, 637
Mitchell, Terrence R., 618n37
Mitchener, Brandon, 135n52
Mitroff, Ian I., 33n3, 235n40, 235n41, 235n43, 235n44, 235n46, 235n48, 299n12, 690n76, 690n77, 690n79

Moberg, Dennis J., 169n15, 345n84
Moffett, Michael H., 136n63
Moffett, Sebastian, 101n18
Mohan, Raymond, 6
Mohrman, Susan A., 484n33
Monroe, Marilyn, 245
Montagno, Ray V., 188, 653n26
Montemayor, E., 413n104
Monti, Roberto, 189
Moore, Carlos W., 169n15
Moore, Chuck, 687
Moore, Diane, 145
Moore, Karl, 137n89
Moore, L. Gordon, 525
Moore, Pamela L., 100n2
Moore, Sarah, 101n32
Moore, Signor, 688
Moran, Bill, 244
Moran, L., 723n7
Moran, Robert T., 137n91
Moravec, Bruce, 12
Moreno, Jenalie, 136n76
Morgan, Philip, 667
Morgan, Ronald B., 170n71
Morgenson, Gretchen, 171n88
Mornell, Pierre, 398
Morrill, Kimberly, 234n21
Morris, Betsy, 100n2, 554n72
Morris, David, 424
Morris, J. Andrew, 617n8
Morris, James R., 412n45
Morrisette, Hubert S., 446n69
Morrison, Ann M., 34n40
Morrison, E. W., 98
Mortenson, Greg, 9
Mosakowski, Earley, P., 137n88
Mosakowski, Elaine, 128, 137n87
Moses, Jeffrey, 297
Moses, Todd, 181
Moskowitz, Milton, 300n45, 653n12, 653n19, 653n20
Moss, Jonathan E., 386, 412n32
Moulton, Donalee, 587n69, 587n73
Mount, Ian, 201n36, 375n31, 376n35, 514n38
Mount, M. K., 586n25
Mouton, Jane S., 596–597, 618n26
Moynihan, Eugene O., 136n63
Muchinsky, P. M., 586n8
Muczyk, Jan P., 235n30
Mudrack, Peter E., 725n65
Mulally, Alan R., 285
Mulcahy, Anne, 71
Mullainathan, Sendhil, 445n20
Mullaney, Timothy J., 514n3, 514n4, 514n10, 515n43, 515n45, 515n53
Muller, Amy, 375n34
Muller, Rob, 377n82
Mulligan, Jim, 447n97
Mulqueen, Michael P., 596
Mumford, Michael D., 619n47
Munroe, Tapan, 136n72, 136n74, 136n75
Munter, Mary, 445n18
Munz, David C., 619n51
Muoio, Anna, 587n52
Muralidar, Krishnamurty, 171n85
Murnighan, J. Keith, 723n15, 725n71
Murphy, Cait, 299n1, 301n75
Murphy, Elizabeth A., 171n86, 171n87
Murphy, Hugh, 19
Murphy, Patrice, 376n62
Murray, Matt, 18
Musselwhite, E., 723n7

Myers, David, 149
Myers, Randy, 484n23

N
Nadler, David, 376n43
Nadler, Paul, 619n53
Nance-Nash, Sheryl, 202n73
Napier, N., 411n22
Napolitano, Jo, 618n27
Narayanan, Terry, Paul, 725n83
Narayanan, V. K., 375n29, 723n21
Nardelli, Bob, 382, 603
Neale, Margaret A., 724n36
Near, Janet P., 171n78, 171n79
Neely, J., 344n21
Neilson, Gary L., 343n11, 343n16, 345n59
Nelson, Bill, 490
Nelson, Bob, 412n46
Nelson, Diane, 263
Nelson, Katherine A., 169n10
Nelton, Sharon, 445n19
Neubert, Mitchell, 725n85
Neuborne, Ellen, 515n63
Newman, Lawrence James III, 546n43
Newstrom, John W., 132, 586n6, 653n16, 653n17, 690n58, 690n62
Nguyen, Ai-Lan, 373
Nicholls, Chantell E., 136n58
Nichols, M. P., 689n33
Nicoson, Robert D., 410
Nielson, Troy R., 411n25
Nijssen, Edwin J., 485n59, 485n63
Nisbett, Richard E., 137n90
Nishii, Lisa H., 136n56
Nix, John, 402
Nixon, Judy C., 445n25
Noah, 629
Nocera, Joseph, 586n27
Nohria, Nitin, 268n57, 269n78, 269n84, 515n73, 618n41, 690n56
Nooyi, Indra, 426
Normand, Troy, 149
Northcraft, Gregory B., 345n85, 545n6
Norton, David P., 477–478, 485n56, 485n57, 485n58, 485n59
Norton-Taylor, Richard, 360
Noskin, Gary, 672
Novak, William, 345n54
Nussbaum, Bruce, 374n2, 412n44
Nutt, Paul C., 269n72, 299n22, 300n42, 377n81
Nyberg, Alix, 376n55
Nystrom, P. C., 344n23, 618n24

O
O'Brien, Timothy L., 35n70, 375n31
O'Connor, Jennifer, 619n47
Odenwald, Sylvia, 724n42
Odiorne, George S., 234n29
O'Donnell, Jayne, 171n80
O'Farrell, Grace, 377n83
Offermann, Lynn R., 654n60
O'Flanagan, Maisie, 344n28
Ogiale, Stella, 173, 197–198
O'Hara, Linda A., 375n11
Ohmae, Kenichi, 267n16
O'Keefe, Brian, 135n48, 135n51
Okum, Sherman K., 667

Myers, David, 149

Oldham, Greg R., 641–642, 650, 654n56
O'Leary, Laurie P., 344n51
Oliver, Martin, 666
O'Loughlin, Michael G., 343n10
Olson, Elizabeth, 201n2, 201n3, 201n12, 201n24, 202n44, 202n47, 202n66
Olson, Eric M., 269n69, 269n71, 345n73, 485n60, 485n61
Olson, J. M., 586n7
Olson, Mike, 669
Olve, Nils-Göran, 485n60, 485n61, 485n62
O'Neal, Stanley, 416
O'Regan, Nicholas, 269n82
O'Reilly, Brian, 202n59, 343n20, 413n92
O'Reilly, Charles A. III, 301n63, 587n51, 617n8
Oringel, Amy, 202n82
Orlitzky, Marc, 724n53
Orna, Daniel, 267n10
O'Rourke, Ray, 29
Osborn, Mark, 299n17
Osborn, Richard N., 618n24
Osburn, J. D., 723n7
O'Shea, John, 690n81
Ostroff, C., 586n8
Ostroff, Frank, 345n66
Ostro-Landau, Nilly, 134n3
Otto, Michael, 651
Ouchi, William G., 484n26
Overby, Stephanie, 342
Overhold, Alison, 587n49
Owens, Darrell, 621
Owens, Thomas, 723n16, 724n27
Owens-Jones, Lindsay, 238

P
Pacanowsky, Michael, 299n13
Packard, David, 612
Paine, Lynn Sharp, 169n20, 181
Palmer, Ann Therese, 413n108
Palmeri, Christopher, 267n3, 267n13, 268n37, 268n39, 376n44, 514n3, 566
Palmisano, Sam, 260
Panchak, Patricia, 644
Parch, Lorie, 586n37
Pare, Terence C., 484n50
Parise, Salvatore, 514n7
Park, Andrew, 268n53
Parker, Andrew, 690n56
Parks, Don, 300n38
Parnell, John A., 484n30
Parson, H. M., 64n32
Parsons, Doug, 107
Parsons, Talcott, 43, 63n20
Pascale, Richard Tanner, 51, 412n31
Pascarella, Perry, 485n51
Pasmore, W., 150, 169n29, 169n30
Pass, Sarah, 653n10
Pasternack, Bruce A., 343n11, 343n16, 345n59
Patmore, Kim, 358
Patterson, Frances, 651–652
Patterson, Gregory A, 366
Patterson, Malcolm, 653n6
Patton, Susannah, 515n61, 545n1, 546n17, 547n68
Paul, Karen, 171n85
Paulhus, D. L., 570
Pavett, Cynthia M., 35n53
Pawar, Badrinarayan Shankar, 619n48

Peak, Martha H., 398
Pearce, C. Glenn, 689n31
Pearce, J. L., 411n30
Pearce, John A. II, 171n83, 171n86,
     234n13, 267n8, 267n10,
     375n27
Pearson, Christine, 35n74, 235n45
Pedigo, P. R., 22
Pei, I. M., 254
Pelaez, Roy, 589, 613–614
Penley, Larry E., 688n7
Perez, Francisco, 60
Perlmutter, Howard V., 137n85
Perot, H. Ross, 88
Perrow, Charles, 345n81
Persaud, Joy, 377n86, 411n4,
     411n24
Peters, Thomas J., 103n80, 690n65
Peters, Tom, 376n46, 689n31,
     690n65
Peterson, Donald, 722–723
Peterson, Lance, 672
Peterson, Melanie M., 653n28
Petri, Carl-Johan, 485n60, 485n61
Petro, Ray, 191
Petrock, Frank, 90, 102n64
Petty, M. M., 586n8
Petzinger, Thomas, 65n72, 690n51
Petzinger, Thomas, Jr., 62n1, 63n8,
     63n9, 725n61
Pfeffer, Jeffrey, 64n55, 102n68,
     301n63, 411n11, 617n8,
     619n54, 619n59, 638
Pfeiffer, J. William, 61
Pfeiffer, Kevin, 167–168
Phalen, Earl Martin, 185
Phelps, C. C., 98
Phillips, Carl, 100n9
Phillips, Mary, 299n18
Phillips, Sally, 585
Phumiwasana, Triphon, 476
Picard, Michele, 447n109
Piderit, S. K., 98
Piechowski, Frank, 442–443
Pierce, Jon L., 153, 170n40, 300n31
Pincus, A. L., 586n25
Pinkard, Marshall, 341–342
Pinson, Linda, 202n60
Pitroda, Salil S., 136n64
Plank, Kevin, 256
Plantes, Peter, 657
Plotkin, Hal, 484n35, 484n37
Podolske, Ann, 654n58, 654n68
Poernomo, Ardian, 394
Poet, Jonathan, 411n5
Point, Sébastien, 444n8, 444n14
Polek, David, 168n4
Pollack, Andrew, 343n4
Pool, Robert, 345n79, 345n80
Poole, Marshall Scott, 355, 376n41
Porras, Jerry I., 102n69, 235n53
Porter, Lyman W., 300n31, 411n30,
     650, 652n3, 653n7
Porter, Michael E., 251–253, 255,
     263, 265, 267n20, 268n25,
     268n48, 268n49, 268n58, 331,
     345n72
Porter, Thomas W., 260
Posner, Barry Z., 102n78, 617n6
Posner, Bruce G., 484n22
Post, James E., 152, 169n31,
     169n35, 689n19
Pottruck, David, 13
Poulos, Steve, 22
Poundstone, William, 412n71
Powell, Colin, 210
Power, Stephen, 484n31

Powers, M., 689n23
Powers, Vicki, 412n63, 412n74
Pratt, Michael G., 102n49
Prescott, John E., 267n8
Pressman, Aaron, 689n40
Preston, Lee E., 152, 169n33,
     169n35
Prewitt, Edward, 65n70, 344n31
Price, Ann, 387
Priem, Richard L., 344n41
Prince, C. J., 444n7, 445n21,
     445n23, 445n30, 446n57,
     446n79
Prince, Charles O., 214–215
Prince, George, 724n55
Pristin, Terry, 652
Pritchard, R. D., 654n48
Procter, William Cooper, 38
Prospero, Michael A., 375n14,
     689n32
Prusak, Laurence, 62, 64n51,
     690n56
Pucik, Vladimir, 134
Pulliam, Susan, 169n27
Purcell, Philip, 565
Purdum, Traci, 723n5, 723n6,
     723n10
Puricelli, Brian, 676
Putin, Vladimir, 29
Putnam, Arnold O., 375n22
Putnam, Cathy, 687
Puttnam, David, 202n52, 202n54

Q

Quadir, Iqbal, 115
Quaile, James, 299n17
Quimby, Roxanne, 195
Quinn, J., 376n62
Quinn, James Brian, 350, 375n12
Quinn, Martin, 616–617
Quinn, Robert E., 90, 102n53,
     447n93

R

Radjou, Navi, 375n34, 376n37
Radosevich, Lynda, 136n70
Rafaeli, Anat, 102n49
Ragan, Cass, 34n25, 34n26
Ragan, James W., 299n12
Ragins, B., 446n82
Ragins, Belle Rose, 446n53,
     446n63
Rai, Saritha, 343n4
Raiffa, Howard, 284
Raines, Howell, 13
Rajagopalan, Nandini, 300n36
Rajan, Raghuram G., 343n18
Ramanathan, Kannan, 299n17
Ramirez, Marc, 436
Ramstad, Evan, 134n1, 137n98,
     546n45
Rancour, Tom, 484n35
Randall, Laura, 201n5
Randolph, W. Alan, 344n44,
     345n76
Rangapriya, Kannan-Narasimhan,
     102n78
Rankin, Henry, 584–585
Ranky, Paul, 546n37
Rasheed, Abdul M. A., 300n36,
     344n41
Rasmussen, Erik, 616–617
Rath, Tom, 653n31
Raul, Alan Charles, 136n67
Ray, J. J., 469
Raz, Tahl, 690n57
Re, Daniel Del, 377n69

Read, Jim, 351
Read, W. H., 690n47
Reagan, Ronald, 607
Reason, Tim, 484n20, 484n21
Reed, Stanley, 135n13, 344n44,
     375n25
Reed, Steve, 266
Reimann, Bernard C., 235n30
Reimann, Kathryn, 159
Reinemund, Steve, 426
Reingold, Jennifer, 35n69
Reinhardt, Andy, 64n60, 65n71,
     80, 101n29, 344n37, 374n2,
     484n24
Reinhold, Barbara, 446n61, 446n69
Reinmoeller, Patrick, 349, 375n8
Reithel, Brian, 446n69
Relin, David Oliver, 34n14
Rennie, Janice, 621–622
Renshaw, Amy Austin, 345n70
Repass, Randy, 517
Research, Forrester, 190
Ressler, Cali, 621
Revesz, Therese R., 135n24
Revkin, Andrew C., 170n42
Rewards, Even, 654n42
Reynolds, George W., 496
Reynolds, Paul, 202n59
Ricciardi, Larry, 575
Rice, Faye, 444n6
Rice, Paul, 74
Rice, Ronald E., 689n16, 689n17
Rich, Motoko, 101n26, 269n64
Richards, Max D., 234n5
Richardson, Hettie A., 654n54
Richardson, Marvin, 530
Richlin, H., 654n41
Richman, Louis S., 135n39
Richman, Tom, 652n2
Richmond, V. P., 686
Richtel, Matt, 202n72, 514n9
Ricks, Thomas E., 690n81, 691n81
Ridge, Garry, 636
Riesenberger, John R., 137n91
Rifkin, Glenn, 375n7
Rigby, Darrell, 33n4, 63n10, 64n50,
     65n70, 375n31
Riggs, Joy, 234n26
Rimer, Ned, 187
Ring, Peter Smith, 101n41
Ringelmann, 703
Riordan, Christine M., 654n54
Rioux, Sheila, 411n20, 411n21
Ripley, David E., 412n50
Ripon, Jack, 374
Ritchie, J. B., 615
Rivlin, Gary, 202n68
Robbins, Dave, 291
Robbins, Stephen P., 421, 725n75,
     725n87
Roberson, Bruce, 268n8
Roberti, Mark, 514n26
Roberto, Michael A., 301n68,
     301n69, 301n70, 301n74
Roberts, Allen P. Jr., 135n22,
     201n30
Roberts, Dan, 547n57
Roberts, Nancy C., 169n33
Roberts, Paul, 587n59, 689n9
Robey, Daniel, 514n38, 725n76
Robichaux, Mark, 184
Robin, Raizel, 102n74, 515n57
Robinson, Edward, 64n61
Robinson, Gail, 447n108, 724n51
Robinson, Richard B., Jr., 267n8
Robinson, Robert K., 446n69
Robinson, Todd, 458

Rocks, David, 546n26, 547n54
Rodgers, T. J., 155
Rodin, Rob, 638
Rodriguez, Nancy, 181–182
Roethlisberger, F. J., 64n31, 64n34
Roethlisberger, Fritz, 46–47
Roger, Engineer, 709
Rogers, E. M., 673, 690n52
Rogers, James E., 657–658
Rogers, L. Edna, 345n78
Rogers, R. A., 673, 690n52
Roney, Curtis W., 235n35
Ronkainen, Ilkka A., 136n63
Roper, Doc Otis, 244
Roper, Stu, 715
Rose, Karol, 627, 653n15
Rose, Matthew, 34n27
Rose, Taryn, 191, 202n70
Rosen, Benson, 724n28, 724n34
Rosen, Robert, 100n9
Rosenbaum, Joshua, 268n56
Rosener, Judy B., 418, 444n15,
     618n11, 618n13
Rosenfeld, Jill, 411n5
Rosenfield, Donald B., 546n43
Rosenman, R., 587n62
Rosenthal, Jeff, 93, 102n72,
     102n73, 102n77, 103n80,
     269n84
Rosenzweig, James E., 64n44,
     64n46
Roshan, Maer, 501
Rosillo, Nathan, 167
Ross, Frank, 606
Roth, Daniel, 33n2, 254, 654n73
Roth, John, 80
Rothbard, N. P., 98
Rothlisberger, J. F., 653n8
Rothstein, Lawrence R., 33
Rothwell, William J., 413n81
Rotter, J. B., 586n39
Rousseau, Denise M., 34n37,
     345n81
Row, Heath, 18, 34n29
Rowe, Alan J., 297, 300n50
Rowe, Mary P., 690n47
Rowley, Daniel James, 63n11
Rowley, Ian, 344n37, 374n2,
     375n27
Rowling, J. K., 537
Roy, Jan, 485n60, 485n61
Roy, Marie-Josée, 170n43
Roy, Sofie, 485n60, 485n61
Rubin, Bonnie Miller, 586n12
Rubin, I. M., 587n56, 653n23
Rubin, Robert S., 619n51, 619n52
Rucker, Eva, 544–545
Rudolph, Barbara, 136n71
Ruf, Bernadette M., 171n85
Ruffolo, Robert, 458, 459
Ruiz, Vicente, 688
Rull, Harry, 32
Rummler, Geary A., 234n21
Rush, Andra, 174
Russell, Barbara, 32–33
Rutherford, Emelie, 345n86
Ryan, M. S., 444n5
Ryan, William P., 35n61
Ryans, John K., Jr., 268n46, 375n22
Rynes, S. L., 412n52

S

Sabatine, Frank J., 188
Sachs, Sybille, 152, 169n35
Sacks, Danielle, 101n15, 413n111
Sadler-Smith, Eugene, 300n30
Sager, Ira, 587n58

Sains, Ariane, 375n25
Sally, 32
Salter, Chuck, 343n3, 528
Salva, 267n18
Sanchez, Carol M., 412n45
Sandberg, Jared, 18, 653n29, 690n60, 484n29
Sandberg, William R., 299n12, 301n71
Sanders, Tim, 586n28
Sanderson, Stuart, 234n13, 267n18
Sanford, R. N., 586n42
Sanger, Steve, 558
Santore, Juan, 652
Santosus, Megan, 62, 412n53
Sapsford, Jathon, 101n39
Sapsford, Jothan, 135n29
Sarri, L. M., 654n48
Sashittal, Hemant C., 725n58
Sashkin, M., 376n56
Sato, Michael, 688
Sauer, Patrick J., 618n23
Saunders, Carol, 35n50, 724n39, 724n40
Saunders, Charles B., 234n7
Savage, Charles, 95
Saveri, Gabrielle, 413n108
Sawhney, Mohanbir, 268n21
Saxton, Mary J., 102n47
Scarborough, Jack, 137n92
Scarbrough, Harry, 411n11, 411n16
Schaefer, George, 310
Schatz, Amy, 375n4
Schay, Brigitte W., 235n33, 485n61
Schein, Edgar H., 102n48, 376n51, 678, 690n75
Schellhardt, Timothy D., 18
Schendel, Dan E., 268n35
Schering-Plough, 108
Schick, Allen G., 412n45
Schiffer, Jack, 410
Schiller, Zachary, 267n15, 344n44
Schilling, Melissa A., 344n34
Schlender, Brent, 102n58
Schlesinger, L. A., 368, 377n75, 377n81
Schlorman, Bob, 442
Schlosser, Julie, 299n17, 514n32, 515n69, 515n70
Schmenner, Roger W., 345n84
Schmidt, Eric, 13
Schmidt, Jeffrey A., 235n59
Schmidt, S. M., 619n57
Schmit, Julie, 133
Schnaars, Steven, 235n37, 235n38
Schneeweis, Thomas, 171n89
Schoemaker, Paul J. H., 100n4, 101n38, 300n36
Scholes, Michael, 299n18
Scholey, Cam, 485n59
Schonberger, Richard J., 527, 534, 546n46
Schonfeld, Erick, 35n72
Schoonover, Philip, 237, 264
Schriesheim, C. A., 618n21, 618n39
Schroeder, Michael, 136n83
Schubert, Siri, 202n38
Schuler, Randall S., 137n94, 411n9
Schultz, Randall L., 269n69
Schulze, Richard M., 574
Schwab, Charles, 565
Schwab, Donald P., 724n41
Schwadel, Francine, 652
Schwartz, Andrew E., 312
Schwartz, Mark S., 155, 170n50
Schwartz, Pepper, 566

Schwartz, Tony, 586n11, 655n77
Schwarz, Eric, 187
Schweiger, David M., 299n12, 301n71
Scott, H. Lee, 88, 685
Scott, Susanne G., 723n19
Searcey, Dionne, 269n66
Searles, Joseph L., 416
Seashore, Stanley E., 725n66, 725n67
Seelos, Christian, 202n52
Seelye, Katharine Q., 515n41
Seglin, Jeffrey L., 169n16, 298, 618
Seibert, Cindy, 63n21
Seibert, Jerry, 62
Seijts, Gerard H., 377n83, 653n34
Seligman, Martin, 555
Sellers, Patricia, 35n58, 35n72, 64n64, 102n43, 376n35, 446n56, 446n57, 607
Seltzer, Joe, 259
Semler, Ricardo, 95, 654n67
Sempione, Piazza, 189
Senge, Peter, 55, 64n53
Serpa, Roy, 102n47
Serwer, Andrew E., 135n42
Serwer, Andy, 35n55, 277, 586n40
Setz, Karen, 233
Seubert, Eric, 515n65, 515n74
Sewell, Dan, 101n25
Shafer, Scott M., 545
Shamir, Boas, 619n50
Shane, Scott, 344n48
Shanklin, William L., 268n46, 375n22
Shannon, Kyle, 78
Shapira, Zur, 299n8
Shapiro, Marc, 24
Sharfman, Mark P., 300n36
Sharp, A. M., 88
Sharpe, Rochelle, 446n64, 446n68, 618n12, 618n14
Shartle, C. L., 618n21
Shaw, Karyll N., 234n22
Shaw, M. E., 673, 724n46, 725n62
Shea, Gordon F., 168n5
Sheats, P., 724n55
Sheehan, Orla, 136n61
Shefy, Erella, 300n30
Shein, Esther, 411n26
Shell, Adam, 665n9
Shellenbarger, Sue, 34n23, 469, 586n9
Sheppard, I. Thomas, 689n26, 689n29
Sheridan, Eileen, 34n28
Sheridan, Garrett J., 653n6
Sherman, Ann, 457
Sherman, Arthur, 397, 411n16, 412n73, 412n75
Sherry, 375n19
Sherwin, Douglas S., 169n32, 454, 483n5, 484n27
Sherwood, John J., 102n46
Shin, Laura, 689n25
Shin, Yuhyung, 725n77, 725n84
Shirouzu, Norihiko, 101n39, 545n5
Shonk, James H., 723n22
Shroeger, Jennifer, 379, 407–408
Shultz, Howard, 279
Shurygailo, Stan, 724n32, 724n34
Siebel, Tom, 589–590
Siekman, Philip, 344n42
Sierra, Mimi Cauley de Da La, 135n24
Siklos, Richard, 102n44

Silberstein, Irving, 265
Silburt, David, 652n2
Silveri, Bob, 500, 514n35, 546n15
Simmons, Donald B., 690n62
Simmons, Russell, 279
Simon, Bernard, 101n29, 343n3
Simón, Cristina, 171n84
Simon, Herbert A., 234n7, 299n5, 299n19, 299n20, 299n21, 299n23, 412n47
Simons, John, 101n24, 101n32
Simpson, Glenn R., 545n2
Sims, C., 136n77
Sinetar, Marsha, 375n12
Singer, Marshall, 100n9
Singh, R., 618n33
Singh, Val, 444n8, 444n14
Singletary, Michelle, 64n64
Sisodia, Raj, 12
Sittenfeld, Curtis, 343n14, 689n36, 724n31
Skivington, James E., 269n79
Slater, Derek, 514n27, 515n60
Slater, Stanley F., 269n69, 269n71, 345n73, 485n60, 485n61
Slavenski, Lynn, 401
Slayter, Mary Ellen, 34n42
Slevin, Dennis P., 269n69
Slipp, Sandra, 445n19
Sloan, Paul, 234n12
Slocum, John W., Jr., 34n25, 34n26, 136n58, 137n94, 344n35, 466, 484n46, 484n50, 570, 652n3
Slyke, Craig Van, 724n39
Smet, Bob, 154
Smircich, Linda, 102n47
Smith, Adam, 343n6
Smith, Chris, 300n28
Smith, Chyanne, 467
Smith, Darwin E., 591–592
Smith, Dick, 484n36
Smith, Douglas K., 695
Smith, Fred, 369, 377n76
Smith, Geri, 136n74
Smith, Jennifer, 698
Smith, Katie, 111
Smith, Lee, 444n12, 445n38, 446n72, 447n91
Smith, N. Craig, 170n51
Smithburg, William, 278
Smud, Robert W., 689n16
Snell, Scott, 397, 411n16, 412n73, 412n75
Snow, Charles C., 344n36, 344n38, 344n49
Snyder, Nancy Tennant, 724n32
Snyder, Naomi, 444n1, 447n121
Soderberg, Mark, 524
Soderquist, Don, 88
Soeken, Don, 168
Solomon, Charlene Marmer, 446n63, 587, 724n38
Solomon, Deborah, 170n55
Solso, Theodore M., 113
Somech, Anit, 725n65, 725n95
Sommer, Steven M., 412n45
Songer, N., 445n21
Soni, Ashok, 515n59, 546n50
Soper, Barlow, 484n30
Sormumen, Juhani, 300n38
Sorrells, Nancy, 209, 231
Sotal, Dan, 584
Sparshott, Jeffrey, 136n74, 136n75
Spector, P. E., 586n41
Speer, Larry, 402
Spencer, Craig, 282
Spielberg, Steven, 565

Spielberg, Susan, 34n6, 34n20, 35n47
Spinner, Jackie, 617n3
Spragins, Ellyn, 101n15, 202n48, 202n60, 412n43, 413n91, 653n39
Spreitzer, Gretchen M., 102n53
Squeo, Anne Marie, 170n55
Srivastva, Suresh, 35n57
St. Clair, Linda, 594
Stair, Ralph M., 496
Stajkovic, Alexander D., 654n41, 654n42
Stalk, George, Jr., 171n82, 375n26
Stalker, G. M., 345n77
Stamm, Bettina von, 35n72, 376n35
Stamps, David, 447n109
Stamps, Jeffrey, 724n33
Stanton, Steven, 345n63, 345n64, 345n67
Stapleton, Ellen R., 722
Starbuck, W., 344n23
Stark, Melvyn J., 269n83
Starke, Frederick A., 652n3
Starkey, Ken, 102n46
Stathatos, Peter, 445n44
Staw, B. M., 689n23
Stayer, Ralph, 15
Stearns, Timothy M., 64n35
Stecklow, Steve, 201n25, 300n35, 483n10
Steenbergen, Ronnie, 471
Steensma, H. Kevin, 344n34
Steers, Richard M., 234n7, 636, 652n3, 653n7, 653n33, 689n39, 690n47, 690n53
Stefanko, John, 471
Stein, Sharman, 586n12
Steinbuhler, K., 202n63
Steiner, Gary A., 350
Steiner, Ivan, 702
Stemberg, Tom, 83
Stengel, James R., 668, 689n38
Stepanek, Marcia, 64n42, 223
Stephens, Carroll, 169n30
Stern, Howard, 274
Sternberg, Robert J., 375n11
Stevenson, Howard H., 375n12
Stevenson, Thomas H., 484n44
Stevenson, William B., 300n31
Stewart, Martha, 162, 224
Stewart, Rosemary, 34n40
Stewart, Thomas A., 300n27, 301n60, 343n9, 345n87, 691n82
Stine, Harry, 612
Stires, David, 103n85, 234n17
Stodghill, Ron, 203n88, 267, 412n64
Stoka, Ann Marie, 63n16
Stone, Christie, 193
Stonecipher, Harry, 434
Stoner, James A. F., 34n8, 691n83
Storey, Greg, 621–622
Storrs, Constance, 63n22
Straberg, Hans, 352
Strahley, James T., 235n53
Straub, Detmar, 514n38, 515n39, 515n46
Strauss, Robert, 658
Streidl, J. William, 235n32
Strickland, A. J., 268n26, 268n46, 268n53
Strickland, Bill, 606, 630
Strifler, Steve, 474
Stringer, Howard, 108

Strober, Myra H., 690n80
Strozniak, Peter, 547n60
Su, Lisa, 245
Suffredini, Mike, 22
Sujansky, Joanne, 446n86
Sullivan, Kevin, 135n47
Sullivan, Nora, 623
Sullivan, Scott, 149
Summers, Lawrence, 280, 600
Sundgren, Alison, 171n89
Sundstrom, Eric, 723n13
Sunoo, Brenda Paik, 412n37
Suresh, Kotha, 267n10
Sussman, Stephanie Watts, 690n81
Sutcliffe, Kathleen M., 83, 724n53
Sutton, Robert I., 293, 350, 376n42, 376n48
Svatko, James E., 102n45
Swaffin-Smith, C., 619n57
Swamidass, Paul M., 545n7
Swanson, Diane L., 170n50
Swartz, Jeffrey, 12
Swogger, Kurt, 572
Sykes, Claire, 587n70
Symonds, William C., 80, 268n50, 447n94, 586n13
Szilagyi, Andrew D., 235n32
Szwajkowski, Eugene W., 169n31, 170n54
Szygenda, Ralph, 319–320

T

Taber, Tom, 618n20
Tait, Richard, 349
Taliento, Lynn K., 344n28
Taninecz, George, 484n41
Tannenbaum, Jeffrey A., 203n89, 345n62
Tanner, Lindsey, 110
Tanninecz, George, 547n61
Tanski, David A., 345n85, 545n6
Tanz, Jason, 546n20
Tanzer, Joshua, 168n4
Tao, Amy, 168
Tapscott, Don, 269n62, 344n39
Taub, Stephen, 484n48, 484n49
Tausky, Curt, 63n28, 64n36
Taverna, Eric, 648
Taylor, Alex III, 375n4
Taylor, Frederick Winslow, 41–42, 56, 58, 624
Taylor, Robert R., 136n63, 373
Taylor, S., 411n22
Taylor, T. Shawn, 201n15
Taylor, William C., 654n64
Teagarden, Mary B., 383, 411n22, 411n23
Tedeschi, Bob, 515n52
TedWatson, F. C., Jr., 546n49
TedWeston, F. C., Jr., 515n59
Teece, David J., 267n8, 344n50
Teitelbaum, Richard, 268n55
Teresa, Mother, 185
Teresko, John, 546n32
Terhune, Chad, 545n4
Terrell, Fred, 191
Tesluk, Paul E., 724n34
Tesone, Dana V., 63n11
Tetenbaum, Toby J., 35n63, 35n68, 62n3
Teurfs, Linda, 690n75
Thach, Liz, 514n11
Thakor, Anjan V., 484n17
Thatcher, Mike, 413n78
Thayer, P. W., 412n69
Theresa, Mother, 607
Therrien, Lois, 690n66

Thill, J. V., 121
Thomas, David A., 424, 446n84, 447n108, 724n51
Thomas, David C., 137n87
Thomas, Howard, 299n8, 300n37
Thomas, Kenneth, 614
Thomas, K. W., 725n86
Thomas, Landon, Jr., 168n1
Thomas, Owen, 299n4
Thomas, Patrick, 63n11
Thomas, Paulette, 202n51, 269n87
Thomas, Philip R., 484n39
Thomas, R. Roosevelt, 429, 446n77
Thomas, Roosevelt, Jr., 445n43
Thome, Mark, 178
Thompson, Arthur A., Jr., 268n26, 268n46, 268n53
Thompson, James D., 545n3
Thompson, Joe, 509
Thompson, John, 229
Thompson, Kenneth R., 235n55
Thompson, P., 615
Thompson, Philip C., 484n33
Thompson, Rachel, 447n96, 447n100
Thottam, J., 412n37
Thottam, Jyoti, 136n78, 652n1, 655n81
Thottam, Kripalani, 136n80
Thurm, Scott, 723n2, 725n98
Tichy, Noel M., 411n6, 619n48
Tierney, Christine, 170n46
Tierney, Thomas, 515n73
Tihany, Adam, 238
Tilton, Glenn, 683
Tindell, Kip, 393
Tischler, Linda, 34n21, 617n8
Tjosvold, Dean, 725n78, 725n81
Tobias, Traci, 621
Tobins, Jordan, 239
Toffler, Barbara Ley, 170n65
Tomlinson, Richard, 267n6
Tompkins, Jonathan, 411n6, 411n8
Tomsho, Robert, 618n29
Topchik, Gary S., 34n43, 35n46
Toppo, Greg, 170n41
Toren, Nina, 34n41
Tornow, Walter W., 413n92
Torre, Joe, 27
Torsilieri, Janet D., 547n67
Tourish, Dennis, 690n47
Towler, Annette, 623
Townsend, Anthony M., 724n32
Townsend, Bickley, 446n63
Treacy, Michael, 253
Treadway, Darren C., 524
Tregoe, B., 282, 300n40
Treviño, Linda Klebe, 150, 158, 168n5, 169n10, 169n20, 169n29, 169n30, 170n61, 170n65, 170n66, 170n67, 170n68, 170n70, 654n44, 689n11, 689n18
Trice, Harrison M., 102n57
Tripoli, A. M., 411n30
Trotter, Frank, 494
Trottman, Melanie, 446n82, 446n83
Trump, Donald, 577
Tsui, Anne S., 411n30, 412n72
Tuckman, Bruce W., 725n60
Tuggel, Francis D., 234n7
Tulega, Tad, 169n19
Tung, Rosalie, 134, 445n18
Turban, Daniel B., 171n91
Turcotte, Jim, 500, 514n35, 546n15
Turek, Melanie, 515n75

Turner, Ernie, 723n4
Turnley, William H., 411n19, 585n2
Turpin, Paula, 175
Tushman, Michael, 376n43
Tyler, Kathryn, 412n61
Tyler, M. Elisebeth, 484n38
Tynan, Dan, 34n36

U

Ucelli, Loretta, 35n74
Uchitelle, Louis, 34n16
Ulfelder, Steve, 135n8
Ulrich, Dave, 376n62, 411n14
Unger, Frank, 688
Upton, David M., 545n8
Urbanski, John C., 617n8
Urwick, Lyndall, 63n24, 63n25
Ury, William, 725n90
Useem, Jerry, 34n25, 34n26, 35n74, 63n14, 136n81, 618n9, 690n77

V

Vacassin, Priscilla, 403
Välikangas, Liisa, 375n34
Vandenberg, Robert J., 654n54
van der Does, Louise, 689n43
Van de Ven, Andrew H. 355
Vanderbilt, Cornelius, 40
Vecchio, Robert P., 653n26
Velasquez, Manuel, 169n15
Ven, Andrew H. Van de, 101n41, 375n23, 376n41, 377n74
Venkataramanan, M. A., 515n59, 546n50
Verfaillie, Hendrik, 151
Verschoor, Curtis C., 171n86, 171n87
Vessels, Gordon, 375n10
Victor, Bart, 167, 169n30
Victor, Jeff, 125
Victoria, 412n67
Viera, Paul, 600
Vinas, Tonya, 269n65, 514n14
Vincent, Robert, 354
Vinson, Barbara, 532
Vinson, Betty, 149
Vleeming, R. G., 587n45
Vliert, E. Van de, 137n95, 654n57, 725n78
Vogel, Douglas R., 724n39
Vogel, Todd, 135n13, 171n90
Vogelstein, Fred, 300n33
Vogl, A. J., 518n9, 638
Voigt, Kevin, 412n40, 412n41
von Bergen, C. W., 484n30
von Bertalanffy, Ludwig, 64n43
von Glinow, Mary Ann, 121, 383, 411n22, 411n23, 445n18, 618n39
von Pierer, Heinrich, 220
Vredenburgh, Donald, 724n30
Vroom, Victor H., 288–291, 295–296, 299, 300n52, 300n53, 300n55, 300n56, 653n30
Vucic, Domagoj, 647

W

Wageman, Ruth, 724n25
Waggoner, Rick, 320
Wagner, Rodd, 234n1, 235n61, 655n80, 467
Wagner, Stephan M., 101n41
Wah, Louisa, 171n89, 386, 412n31, 515n73
Wahl, Andrew, 102n70, 103n83
Wai, Chiu, 133–134
Waldrop, Mitchell, 277

Walker, Maggie Lena, 416
Walker, Rob, 725n89
Wall, Toby D., 558
Wallace, Don, 597
Wallace, Doug, 341, 374, 584, 651
Walleigh, Richard C., 547n55
Walmac, Amanda, 203n87
Walter, Carolyn, 297
Walters, Chris, 672
Walton, Ricahrd E., 466
Walton, Sam, 38, 88, 181, 607
Wang, D., 411n30
Wanous, J. P., 412n58
Want, Jerome H., 234n13
Ward, Andrew, 547n57
Ward, Stephen, 438
Wardle, Kelly, 321
Warnecke, Ron, 178
Warner, Fara, 547n59
Warner, Melanie, 102n65, 617n2
Warr, Peter B., 558
Warren, Neil Clark, 566
Warshaw, Michael, 690n64
Waryszak, Robert, 34n41
Wasow, Omar, 445n37
Wasserman, Elizabeth, 447n118
Waterman, Robert H. Jr., 103n80, 690n65
Watkins, David, 515n76
Watkins, William, 524
Watson, Warren E., 447n108, 447n112, 724n51, 724n54
Wattenberg, B., 421
Waxer, Cindy, 514n24
Wayne, Leslie, 35n74, 690n77
Weafer, Vincent, 229
Weaver, Gary R., 170n65, 170n67, 170n68
Weaver, Vanessa J., 446n74, 446n81
Webb, Allen P., 170n64, 170n71
Webber, R. A., 34n43
Weber, James, 80, 169n28
Weber, Joseph, 101n29, 135n13, 343n20, 376n44, 618n22
Weber, Kent, 99, 200
Weber, Max, 42–44, 63n20
Webster, Jane, 689n11
Weick, Karl E., 83
Weidenbaum, Murray, 134n3
Weil, Henry, 202n75
Weiller, Bill, 178
Weimer, De'Ann, 587n55
Weinholtz, Gladys, 652
Weinstock, Sylvia, 577
Weintraut, J. Neil, 201n6
Weisinger, Hendrie, 586n37
Weiss, Bill, 711
Weiss, Leigh, 300n57
Weisul, Kimberly, 202n81
Welch, David, 514n37, 546n38
Welch, Jack, 7, 31, 239, 267n9, 465, 470, 603
Welles, Edward O., 35n59, 64n57
Wellings, Richard S., 724n24
Wellington, Sheila, 445n48, 445n49, 446n59
Wellins, Rich, 411n20, 411n21
Wellner, Alison Stein, 301n61, 301n62, 445n40, 689n13, 689n14
Wendenhof, Jon R., 235n53
Wendling, Larry, 364
Wendt, Piotr, 178
Wenger, Etienne, 300n57
Werner, Beatrice, 687
Wessel, David, 412n36

West, Michael, 445n25, 585n2, 653n6
Westcott, Scott, 412n62
Weston-Webb, Andy, 679
Wharton, Clifton R., 416
Wheatley, Malcolm, 344n40
Wheelen, Thomas L., 268n52
Wheeler, Daniel, 13, 152
Wheeler, David, 169n35
Wheeler, Jane V., 724n29
Wheeler, Michael L., 445n24, 445n26
Whitaker, Barbara, 135n53
White, Chris, 321
White, Erin, 18, 35n44, 457, 653n32, 654n76
White, Joseph B., 135n6, 300n41
Whitman, Meg, 9, 352, 460
Wicks, Judy, 185–186
Wiener, L., 413n107
Wiener, Yoash, 102n46
Wiersema, Fred, 253
Wiesendanger, Betsy, 202n70
Wiggins, J. S., 586n25
Wiggins, Ovetta, 201n18
Wighton, David, 135n32
Wild, Russell, 312
Wiley, Carolyn, 169n15, 170n71
Wilke, John R., 101n28, 234n11
Wilkinson, I., 619n57
Williams, M. Lee, 688n5
Williamson, James E., 477, 485n57, 485n58
Willis, Jonathan L., 515n45
Wilson, James, 651
Wilson, Jeanne M., 446n24, 447n73

Wilson, Jim, 64n51
Wilson, Melvin, 5, 7, 30
Wimbush, James C., 411n6, 411n8
Wimbush, Rivkin, 412n68
Winans, Pat, 182
Wind, Youram, 137n85
Winfrey, Oprah, 22, 84–85, 147, 181
Wingfield, Nick, 40, 64n59, 269n63, 457
Winston, Terry, 409–410
Winter, Greg, 445n46
Wise, Jessica Morris, 690n64
Wisse, Ruth R., 618n29
Wolf, Thomas, 35n60
Wolf, William B., 63n26
Wolfe, Charles Jr., 134
Wolfe, Joseph, 234n18, 413n79
Womack, James P., 547n59
Wonder, Jacquelyn, 491
Wong, Cynthia, 647
Wood, Robert A., 171n85
Woodhouse, Chris, 373
Woodman, Richard W., 150, 169n29, 169n30, 514n11, 570, 652n3
Woods, Ginny Parker, 444n4
Woodward, Bob, 612
Woodward, Joan, 95, 335–337, 345n82, 345n83
Woodyard, Chris, 268n29, 268n31, 445n29
Woolley, Suzanne, 267n2, 268n32, 300n48
Worley, Christopher G., 376n57, 376n58

Worthen, Ben, 514n33
Wrege, Charles D., 63n16, 63n29
Wren, Daniel A., 63n6, 63n12, 63n15, 63n18
Wright, Frank Lloyd, 606
Wright, H. A., 64n31
Wu, Joshua B., 412n72
Wulf, Julie, 343n18
Wylie, Ian, 235n39, 688n6
Wysocki, Bernard, Jr., 64n63, 299n15

X

Xin, Katherine, 134

Y

Yago, Glenn, 476
Yang, Jia Lynn, 446n58, 724n43, 724n50
Yang, Marjorie, 271, 295
Yasai-Ardekani, Masoud, 345n76
Yates, Buford, 149
Yee, Chen May, 546n43
Yoshioka, Izumi, 34n41
Youn, Jacy L., 34n13
Young, Clifford, 412n45
Young, Debby, 724n42
Young, Derek, 440
Young, Eric, 515n58
Young, Mary, 689n19
Young, W. G., 586n22
Yuanqing, Yang, 105, 438
Yukl, Gary A., 603, 617, 617n5, 618n18, 618n20
Yun, Jong-Yong, 371

Yunus, Muhammad, 115
Yunxia, Irene, 724n30
Yuspeh, Alan, 170n73

Z

Zachary, G. Pascal, 135n29, 445n27
Zajonc, R. B., 725n95
Zaltman, G., 377n77
Zander, Alvin, 725n64
Zander, Ed, 27
Zanna, M. P., 586n7
Zaslow, Jeffrey, 62n2, 585n5
Zawacki, Robert A., 64n39, 376n56, 376n57
Zeidner, Lewis, 530
Zeithaml, Carl P., 268n24
Zellmer-Bruhn, Mary E., 724n41
Zellner, Wendy, 268n54, 444n2, 483n3, 514n37
Zenger, J. H., 723n7
Zeta-Jones, Catherine, 577
Zetwd, Michelle, 672
Zevnik, Brian L. P., 398
Zey, Mary, 446n85
Zhang, Y., 411n30
Ziamou, Paschalina, 235n37, 235n38
Zierden, Hank, 721
Zigurs, Ilze, 724n34
Zinn, Laura, 101n22
Zipkin, Amy, 171n77
Zucker, Jeff, 288
Zuckerman, Mortimer B., 501
Zygmont, Jeffrey, 64n67

0–9

1-800-Flowers, 57, 640
3M Corp., 76, 87–88, 218, 238, 356, 358, 363
7-Eleven, 242
100 Black Men of America, Inc., 415, 440

A

A. T. Kearney, 456
A. W. Chesterton Company, 558
Aahs!, 463
ABB Ltd., 470, 711
ABC Network, 272
Accentra, 181
ACCIÓN International, 186
Acme Minerals Extraction Company, 722
Adaptiv Learning Systems, 555
Adelante, 328
Adelphia, 243, 478
Adobe Systems, 351
Advanced Circuits, 634
Advanced Micro Devices (AMD), 358, 394
AEA Investors, 195
Aegis Living, 406
AFL-CIO, 10
Agency.com, 78
AH Biotech, 133
Airbus, 84, 529
AIS Corporation, 182
Ajilon Professional Staffing, 559
Al Qaeda, 282
Albertsons, 84
Albertson's Acme, 624
Alcan Aluminum, 153
Alcoa Power Generating Inc. (APGI), 154
Allen P. Roberts, Inc., 201
Allied Signal, 470
Allied Tire Stores, 240
Allstate Insurance, 430, 441
Aluminio del Caroní, 634, 645
Amazon.com, 40, 57, 93, 106, 180, 197, 256, 337, 498, 503, 605, 703
America Online, 106
American Academy of Arts and Sciences, 159
American Airlines, 293, 323
American Association of Retired Persons (AARP), 382
American Educational Research Association, 615
American Express, 159, 257, 307, 435, 578
American Greetings, 181
American Greetings Corporation, 494
American Institute for Managing Diversity, 429
American Management Association (AMA), 223
American MultiCinema (AMC), 565
American Pop Corn, 182
American Red Cross, 96, 238, 454–455
American Society for the Prevention of Cruelty to Animals, 487

American Standard Companies, 329
AmeriSteel, 677
Ameritech, 711
Anadarko, 539
Anheuser-Busch, 111, 509
Ansys, 263
Antioch College, 47
AOL Technologies, 111, 280
AOL Time Warner, 8
Apple Computer, 6–7, 78, 348–349, 709
Applebee, 403
Aramark Corporation, 589
Arby's Restaurant Group, Inc., 532
Arch Coal, 487
ARCO, 676
Arena Football League (AFL), 282
Arizona, 473
Arnold Logistics, 398
Arthur Andersen, 139
Arthur D. Little Inc., 677
Aspen Institute, 94
AT&T, 45, 61, 76, 257, 348, 398, 473, 630
AT&T Wireless, 77
AT&T's Network Systems, 330
Atkinsson Congregational Church, 393
au Bon Pain, 405
Auburn Farms, 111
Auburn University, 256
AutoTradeCenter, 504
Averitt Express, 88
Avery Dennison Corporation, 316
Avon Products, 239, 416

B

Bain & Company, 39, 59
Baker & McKenzie, 493
Ball Aerospace, 351
Bank of America, 139, 165, 395
Barbara K! Enterprises, 179
Barclays Global Investors, 510
Barnes & Noble, 85, 537
Barnesandnoble.com, 85
Baron Partners Fund, 590
Barron's, 7
Basecamp, 493
Batanga.com, 196
Baxter Healthcare, 428
Bay Networks, 81
BCBG Max Azria Group, 216
Beacon Sweets & Chocolates, 111
Beall's Sunglass Hut, 456
Bed Bath & Beyond, 179
Beijing British Embassy, 75
Bell Atlantic, 422
Bell Canada, 477
Bell Emergis, 477
BellSouth, 257, 579
Ben & Jerry's Ice Cream, 74
Benjamin Franklin High School, 609
Bentley College, 12
Bergdorf, 652
Bertelsmann AG, 85, 106
Best Buy, 237, 264, 441, 534, 574, 621, 648–649
Best Western International, 354
Bethlehem Steel, 42

BeVocal, 182
Bharti Tele-Ventures Ltd., 322
Big Brown. see United Parcel Service (UPS)
BiosGroup, 277
Black & Decker, 181, 220
Black Enterprise magazine, 392
Blackberry, 27
Blair Corporation, 502
Bloomingdale's, 265, 496, 552
Blue Bell Creameries, 316
Blue Nile, 40
BMW, 84, 355, 507, 555
BMW of North America, 255
Boat Group, 245
Boeing Co., 12, 84, 159, 212, 240, 285–286, 351, 415, 434, 462, 528–529, 531
Boise Cascade, 473
Bombardier, 323
Border's Bookstores, 395
Boston Consulting Group, 351
BP, 680
Brady Corporation, 307
Brinker International, 657
Bristol-Myers Squibb Company, 152, 213–214
British Airways, 477
Brooks Brothers, 271
Brookside Gables, 455
Brunswick, 245
Budweiser, 111
Buffalo Wild Wings Grill & Bar, 192
Building Educated Leaders for Life (BELL), 185
Burger King, 111
Burlington Northern Santa Fe (BNSF) Railway, 526
Burt's Bees, 195
BusinessWeek, 351
Butter Crisp Snack Foods, 690–691
BuyProduce.com, 506

C

Cabela's, 666
Cadillac, 272
Callaway, 177
Cambrian Systems, 81
Cambridge University, 419
Campbell Soup Co., 84, 407, 638, 649
Canada Life, 25, 567
Canadian Airlines International, 368
Canon, 71, 468
Cap Gemini Ernst & Young, 277
Capital One, 139, 400
Capital Partners, 191
Carnival Cruise Lines, 340
Carrefour, 529
Carrier Corp, 57
Catalyst, 427
Caterpillar, Inc., 94, 242, 310–311
Caterpillar University, 400
Catholic Church, The, 8
CBS Broadcasting, 500, 502
Celanese, 284
Cellon Inc., 353
Cementos Mexicanos (Cemex), 37, 59–60

Center for Army Lessons Learned (CALL), 680
Center for Creative Leadership, 430
Center for Media Education, 513
Central Asia Institute, 9
Central High, 233
CERN (Centre Européan pour la Recherche Nucléaire), 498
Charles Schwab Corp, 13
Charlotte, 644
Charter Communications, 243
Cheesecake Factory, 6
Cheetos, 249
Chemical Bank, 159
Chem-Tech Corporation, 167
Chesterfield Health Services, 173, 197–198
Chevron Texaco, 222
CHI Research, 180
Chicago electric company, 46
Chiquita Brands, 108, 150
Christian and Timbers, 279
Chrysler, 107
Chrysler Corporation, 326–327
Cigna Insurance, 477
Cinergy Corp., 657
Cingular Wireless, 10, 76, 182, 492
Circuit City, 50, 237, 256, 264, 632
Cirque du Soleil, 693
Cisco Systems, 9, 80–81, 393, 464, 568, 700
Cisco-Eagle, 474
Cisneros Group, 111
Citibank, 77, 240, 578, 627
Citigroup, 76, 214–215, 240, 256, 426, 435, 513
Citizen Schools, 187
City of Madison, the, 498
Civil Service Board, 61–62
Clarify, 81
Clark County Sheriff's department, 683
Cleveland Orchestra, 23
Clorox, 256
Cobalt Boats, 388
Coca-Cola Company, 78–79, 105, 108, 117, 224–225, 241, 252, 369, 415, 473, 647
Cognetics, Inc., 39, 180
Colgate-Palmolive Company, 318
Colors, 6
Columbia Pictures, 107
Columbia Sportswear, 574
Columbia/HCA Healthcare, 160
Columbine High School, 679
Columbus, The, 113
Comambault, 45
Comedy Central, 500
Comfort Inn, 254
Commerce Bank, 532
Computer Associates, 140
Computerworld, 589
ConAgra, 261
Conair, 407
Conexant Systems, 113
Conoco, 402
ConocoPhillips, 336
Consolidated Bank & Trust Co., 416
Consolidated Diesel, 311, 699
Container Store, 393–394

Container Store, The, 397
Continental Airlines, 489
Continental Cablevision Inc., 592
Coopers & Lybrand, 397
Coors distributor, 509
Cornell University, 427
Cox Communications, 478
CPI Aerostructures, 418
Cracker Barrel, 415, 440
Craiglist, 492
Cummins Engine, 113, 152
Cyn-Com Systems, 409
Cypress Semiconductor, 155

D

DaimlerChrysler, 84, 107, 323, 327,
    348, 364, 471
Dallas Cowboys, 279
Dallas–Fort Worth Marriott, 209,
    231, 388
Dana Corporation, 150, 471
Dataquest, 578
David's Bridal, 555
Dayton Hudson, 640
De La Salle Spartans, 597
Dee Zee, 395
Defense Acquisition
    University, 400
Del Monte Foods, 13
Delaware Valley Chemical Inc.,
    615–616
Dell Computer Corporation, 9, 58,
    71, 105–106, 131, 263, 464,
    503, 522–523, 537, 565
Dell Inc., 338
Deloitte Touche Tohmatsu,
    393, 627
Delphi Automotive Systems, 112,
    273, 471
Delta Airlines, 10, 277, 589
Democratic National
    Committee, 658
Denny's Restaurants, 430
Departments of Motor Vehicles
    (DMV), 332
Development Counsellors
    International (DCI), 475
DFW Marriott, 231
DHL Worldwide Express, 517
Diamond Gift Shop, 633
Dick's Sporting Goods Inc., 256
Directgov, 24
Dixon Ticonderoga Company, 71
DMC, 645
Dole, 538
Dollar General, 261
Domino's Pizza, 647
Dongfeng Motor Company, 113
Doritos, 249
Dow Chemical, 76, 256, 435, 572
Dr. Pepper/Seven Up, 308
Draper Manufacturing, 443–444
DreamWorks SKG, 426, 700
Duke University Hospital, 29
DuPont & Co., 54, 106, 154, 212,
    220, 284, 470, 526, 565

E

E. W. Scripps Networks, 500
E&B Marine, 517
Earnest Partners, 600
Eaton Corporation, 10
eBags, Inc., 40
eBay, 9, 58, 93, 106, 180, 337, 352,
    460, 498, 503–504
eCitizen, 24
Eckerd, 240

Edelman, 487, 510
Edmunds Corrugated Parts &
    Services, 266–267
Edun, 177
Edward Jones Investments, 255
eHarmony.com, 565–566
Electric Boat Corporation, 314
Electrolux, 352, 354
Electronic Arts, 379
Electronic Data Systems, 88
Electronics Assembly, 339
Elektra Products, Inc., 32–33
Eli Lilly, 308, 383
Emerald Packaging, 553, 580, 638
Emergency Medical
    Associates, 230
Emerson Electric, 294
Emery Air Freight, 638
Emigrant Savings, 157
Emma's Parlor, 200
Empress Luxury Lines, 167
Energizer, 252
Enron, 12–13, 96, 139–140, 143,
    155, 161, 454, 478
Enron Wind, 250
Entelos, 348
Enterprise Rent-A-Car, 254, 495
Environmental Protection
    Agency, 153
Environmental Protection Agency
    (EPA), 77
Equal Employment Opportunity
    Commission, 415, 435
Equifax, 401
Ernst & Young, 430
ESPN.com, 500
Esquel Group, 271, 295
e-Steel, 57
Ethics and Compliance Officers
    Association, 161
Everbank.com, 494
Eukanuba, 239
Excel Foundry and Machine, 107
Expedia.com, 57, 79, 256, 393, 498
Express, 308
Exxon Mobil, 114, 126, 222,
    273, 477
E-Z Pass, 529

F

Facebook.com, 78, 492
Families and Work Institute, 579
Fast Company magazine, 559
FasTrak, 529
Federal Bureau of Investigation
    (FBI), 8, 212, 423–424
Federated Department
    Stores, 555
Federation of Women Business
    Owners, 175
FedEx, 17, 79, 105–106, 223, 232,
    252, 365, 369, 400, 471, 529,
    647, 694
Fiat, 240
Figgies International Inc., 240
Financial Times, 7
Finish Line, 501
Firestone, 275
First Data Corp, 358
First Net Card, 117
First Union, 579
FirstGov.gov, 24
Five Prime Therapeutics, 178
FMB&T, 341
Food Marketing Support
    Services, 182
Food Network, 500

Ford Motor Company, 42, 57, 78,
    107, 257, 275, 307, 323,
    337–338, 402, 426, 471, 523,
    536, 675
Foreign Candy Company, 196
ForeSee Results, 24
Forrester Research Inc., 503, 627
Fortune magazine, 7, 159, 215, 417,
    430, 592, 629
Fortune 1,000, 430
Fortune 50, 416
Fortune 100, 416, 572
Fortune 100 Best Companies to
    Work For, 96, 212, 629, 646
Fortune 500, 416, 425
Fortune America's 50 Best Compa-
    nies for Minorities, 430
Fortune Small Business, 402
Four Seasons Hotels Inc., 254
Fox television network, 279
Frank Purdue, 113
Frankenstein foods, 151
Fred Meyer, 179
Freedom Riders, 630
Fresno, 115
Friendster, 492
Frito-Lay, 328, 641
Fujitsu, 354

G

Gallup Organization, 632,
    647–648, 655, 702
Gap, 162, 276, 496
Gartner Group, 507
Gartner Inc., 380
Gaylord Hotels, 243
Genentech, 237, 647
General Communications
    Headquarters (GCHQ),
    359–360
General Electric (GE), 7, 11, 18, 27,
    31, 50, 54, 57, 75, 78, 98, 107,
    109, 161, 169, 220, 238, 250,
    261, 338, 340, 348, 357–358,
    399–400, 403, 431, 465, 470,
    474, 492, 497–498, 541, 565,
    603, 611, 629
    Energy Rentals, 276
    Healthcare, 250
    Security, 250
    Work-Out, 361
General Foods, 328
General Mills, 244, 328, 558
General Motors, 16, 57, 84, 240,
    273, 282, 323, 348, 369, 468,
    471, 502, 504, 675
General Motors Information
    Systems and Services,
    319–320
    Packard Electric, 683
Gentiva Health Services, 394
George Mason University, 439
Georgetown Preparatory
    School, 697
Gerber Scientific Inc., 109
Gibson Guitar Corp, 255
GID, 531
Gillette Company, 105, 239,
    241, 252
Girl Scouts, 23, 76, 318
Glad Force Flex, 349
Glasgow Airport, 21
GlaxoSmithKline, 493
GLOBE research, 118–120, 129,
    134, 437
GMSupplyPower, 504
go2call.com, 402

Golden Corral, 671
Goldman Sachs, 148
Golfsmith International, 256
Goodman, 652
Goodyear Tire &
    Rubber Co., 370
Google, Inc., 13, 15, 71, 180, 284,
    317, 337, 351, 353, 363, 394,
    435–436, 623
Gore-Tex, 253
Governance Metrics
    International, 164
Grant J. Hunt Co., 506
Greater Chicago Food
    Depository, 596
Green Day, 6
Grokster, 58
GSI Commerce, 503
GTE, 159
Guidant Corporation, 657
Guitar Center, 212

H

H&M (Hennes & Mauritz), 352
Habitat for Humanity
    International, 318, 424
Hallmark Cards, 88, 181
Hamburger University, 400
Harley-Davidson Motor
    Company, 83, 253, 400, 533
Harmony, 194
Harpo Inc., 22, 84
Harrah's, 496
Harris Ice, 395
Harvard Business School,
    108, 424
Harvard University, 45–46, 58, 89,
    280, 600
Hasbro, 76, 111
Hatteras, 245
Hay Group, 339
HBO, 8
HealthSouth, 139, 478
Hear Music, 348
Hearst Magazines, 84
Heineken, 111
HeiterConnect, 177
Help Desk, 387
Henry Estate, 110
Herman Miller, 256
Hertz, 254
Hewlett-Packard, 13, 71, 78, 307,
    324, 416, 565, 612, 700
HGTV, 500
H.I.D., 233–234
High Tech Computer Corporation
    (HTC), 73
Hilton Hotels Corp., 256, 477
Hoilman Inc., 298–299
Holiday Inn, 209
Hollywood Video, 10
Home Depot, The, 79, 111–112,
    157, 162, 226, 252, 276, 382,
    395, 441, 496, 529, 534,
    603, 640
Home Mart, 112
Honda, 86, 314, 468, 531
Honeywell Industrial Automation
    and Control, 454
Hospitality Alliance, 440
Hotels.com, 79, 256
Hudson Institute, 435
Hughes Electronics Corp., 240
Humana, Inc., 364, 667–668
Hunter-Worth, 687–688
Hyatt Corp., 256, 420
Hypertherm, Inc., 693

I

Iams Company, 239
Ibanez, 255
IBM, 8, 27, 76, 84, 87, 105, 117, 148, 209, 245, 260–262, 307, 354, 356, 380, 391, 398–401, 416–417, 420, 434, 438, 490, 575, 578, 697, 717
igus Inc., 528
IHS, 387
IKEA, 243, 253, 498, 500
Imagination Ltd., 320–321
IMD, 121–122
Independent Beverage Group, 509
Industry Week, 471
Information Bureau, 473
Infosys Technologies, 488
InnoCentive, 353–354
Innovative Design Lab (IDS), 371
Inspire Learning Corp, 232
Intel, 76, 107, 220, 351, 357–358, 394, 400
Intel Capital, 357
Intermountain Health Care, 490
Internal Revenue Service (IRS), 215, 317
International Consulting, 298
International Data Group, 589, 592
International Monetary Fund (IMF), 78, 126
International Standards Organization, 473
International Survey Research, 557
International Truck and Engine Corporation, 257
Intuit, 351, 358
iRobot, 698
ITT Industries, 470
Ivy League colleges, 419

J

J. Crew, 271
J. D. Power & Associates, 521
JCPenney, 179, 240, 399, 427, 565, 592
Jel, Inc., 675
Jenny Craig, 574
Jet Blue, 37, 248
Jobster and JobThread, 393
John Deere, 521
John Lewis, 15
Johnson & Johnson, 76, 159, 238, 314
Johnson & Johnson Pharmaceuticals, 348
Johnson Controls, 164
Johnsonville Sausage, 15
JPMorgan Chase, 112, 139, 165, 627
Junior Achievement, 182–183

K

KaBOOM!, 157
Kaiser Permanente, 140
Kazaa, 58
Kazoo & Company, 263
Kazoo.com, 263
Kellogg, 105, 108
Kentucky, 456
KFC, 111, 116, 565
Killid magazine, 17
Kimbel's Department Store, 651
Kimberly-Clark, 591–592
Kinko's Inc., 243, 365
Kirin, 111
Kmart, 12, 37, 150, 261, 264

Kodak, 238, 240, 431
Korn Ferry International, 422
KPMG, 168
Kraft Foods, 214, 244, 248–249, 439
Krispy Kreme Doughnuts, 8
Kroger, 84
Kwik-Fit Financial Services, 666
Kyocera Wireless, 354

L

Labatt, 111
Lamprey, Inc., 373
Lancôme, 238
Lands' End Inc., 117, 256, 366
Lassiter Middle School, 693
LDF Sales & Distributing, 637
Le Creusot-Loire, 45
Lea & Perrins, 538
Learning Center, 75
LendLease, 230
Lenova Corp, 105, 131, 438
Leo Burnett, 350
Les Schwab Tire Centers, 647
Levi Strauss & Co., 93, 308, 416
LG Electronics, 122
LG&E Energy, 406
Libya's National Oil Corporation, 222
Lighthouse, 191
Lincoln Electric, 166, 482–483
Linden Lab's Second Life, 353
Linens 'n Things, 503
Little Gym International, 565
Liz Claiborne, 456
L.L.Bean, 78, 366, 470–471
Lockheed Martin, 431
L'Oreal, 238
Los Angeles
    Chinese Learning Center, 75
    County Museum of Art, 23
Los Angeles Times, 245
Louisiana State University Health Sciences Center, 157
Lowe's, 79, 252
Lucasfilm, 13
Lucent Technologies, 81
Lush Cosmetics, 91
Lutheran Health Network, 37

M

Macmillan Publishing Company, 343
Madison Manufacturing, 291
Magellan Health Services, 682
Magna Securities, 182
Malaysian Airlines, 561
Mana, a National Latina Organization, 175
Manchester Bidwell, 606, 630
Manpower Inc., 387
Marriott Hotels, 209, 254, 337
Marriott International, 256
Marshall Industries, 639
Martha Stewart Living Omnimedia, 224
Mary Kay Cosmetics Company, 89, 242
Massachusetts General Hospital, 719
Master Foods, 679
MasterCard, 83
Match.com, 566
Mattel, 71–72, 76, 238, 240
Mayo Clinic, 576
Maytag, 272, 641
McDevitt Street Bovis, 707

McDonald's, 105, 111, 113, 115, 154, 237–238, 241, 274, 283, 337, 363, 400, 489
McDonnell Douglas, 240
MCI, 257
McKinsey & Co., 25, 416, 420
McMurray Publishing Company, 161
Meadowcliff Elementary School, 631
Medecins Du Monde, 506
Mediagrif Interactive Technologies, 93, 504
Medicare, 156
Medtronic, 363
Merck & Co., 612, 462
Mercury Communications, 399
Mercury Marine, 245
Merrill Lynch, 416, 495
MetLife, 566
Mexicana Airlines, 19
MGA Entertainment, 72
Michigan Bell, 638
MicroAge, 294
MicroPhone, 584
Microsoft, 7–8, 71, 97, 116, 178, 216, 294, 307, 311, 317, 363, 397, 402, 474, 492
Miller Brewing Company, 182, 509
Milwaukee Journal Sentinel, The, 159–160
Ming Cycle Company, 322
Mini Maid, 637
Minnie Pearl Fried Chicken, 240
Mintz Levin Cohn Ferris Glovsky & Popeo, 428
Mirage Hotel, 238
Miramax, 265
Mississippi Power, 5, 7, 30, 314
Mitsubishi, 415, 441
Modern Healthcare, 490
Molex, 111
Monarch Ski & Snowboard Area, 76
Monsanto, 148, 151
Monster.com, 393
Montgomery Ward, 40
Morgan Stanley Dean Witter, 29, 226, 565
Morsal, 17
Motek Software, 387
Motel 6, 254
Motorola, 8, 27, 54, 160, 239, 347, 349, 355, 470, 640, 697, 709
MTV Networks, 85
Mulberry Neckware, 111
Multicultural Foodservice, 440
Multiplex Co., 110
MySpace, 492
MySpace.com, 78
MySQL, 701, 717

N

Nabisco, 538
Napster, 493
NASA, 22, 28, 76, 178
National, 175
National Association of Chain Drug Stores Foundation, 530
National Basketball Association (NBA), 719
National Bureau of Economic Research, 419
National Commission on Writing, 676
National Council of YMCAs, 318

National Federation of Independent Business, 184
National Football League (NFL), 503
National Oceanic and Atmospheric Administration (NOAA), 672
National PTA, 513
NationsBank, 540
Nature Conservancy, 23
Nautica, 243
NBC Entertainment, 276–277, 288
NBC Universal, 493, 500
Nelson Motivation Inc., 636
Neptune Drying Center, 272
Netgear, 109
Neucel, 715
New England Confectionary Co. (Necco), 13
New Haven, 75
New Jersey Bell, 45
New Leaf Paper Company, 154
New Line Cinemas, 8, 107
New York Stock Exchange, 416
New York Times, The, 13, 417, 435, 487, 671
New York Yankees, 27
News Corp., 492
NewsMarket, 393
Nextel Communications, 9, 257
Nextel Partners, 9
Nibco, 680
NightHawk Radiology Services, 110
Nike, 105, 162, 232
NineSigma Inc., 353
Nintendo, 294, 436
Nissan, 112, 307, 339, 352, 530–531
NitroCision, 178
Nokia, 25, 73, 347, 364
Nordstrom, 87
Norfolk Southern, 15
Nortel Networks, 79–81, 106, 660
North Face, 243
North Woods Appliance Corp, 441, 443
Northern States Power Co., 218
Northfield Laboratories, 142–144
Northrop Grumman, 160
Northwest, 277
Northwestern Memorial Hospital, 672
Norton, 159
Norwest Corp, 84, 608
Novell, 13
Nucor, 644
Nussbaum Center for Entrepreneurship, 196
NutriSystem Inc., 245–246
Nypro, Inc., 85

O

Occidental Petroleum, 222
Oceanographics, Inc., 464
Of the Hook Tees, 373
Office Depot, 10, 502
Office of Personnel Management, 405
Ogio, 177
O'Hare International Airport, 19
Ohio State University, 595, 662
Old Navy, 10
Ontario Power Generation, 153
Opus Associates, 676
Oracle Corp., 9
Orange SA, 81
Orpheus Orchestra, 699
OSI Industries, 115

Otis Elevator, 249
Overstock.com, 191
Oxford University, 419

P

Pacific Edge Software, 92
Pacific Gas and Electric, 640
PaeTec Communications, 9
Papa John's, 162
Parkland Memorial Hospital, 23
PC World, 589
PeaceHealth, 577
Peebles Hydro Hotel, 401
Pentagon, 28, 330, 668
PepsiCo Inc., 79, 249, 252, 328,
    416, 426, 519
PerfectMatch.com, 566
Periphonics, 81
Peugeot, 238
Pfizer, 108, 164
Philadelphia Soul, 282
Philip Morris, 112, 397
Philips Electronics, 364
Philips Petroleum Company, 473
Phoenix Mercury, 707
Piazza Sempione, 189
Pic n' Pay Shoe Stores, 397
Pinkerton Security, 397
Pinnacle Machine Tool Co.,
    298–299
PinnacleHealth System, 637
Pirate Soul, 671
Pit Instruction & Training LLC, 719
Pitney Bowes, 432
Pitney Bowes Management
    Services (PBMS), 540
Pizza Hut, 116, 565
Police Department's Records, 473
Polycom, 661, 700
Porsche, 521
PPG Industries, 383
PPL Corporation, 77
PrairieStone Pharmacy, 530
Pratt & Whitney Canada, 531
Precision Tune, 641
Premium Standard Farms, 645
Priceline.com, 337
Pricewaterhouse Coopers
    Consulting, 76, 171
Princecraft, 245
PrintingForLess.com, 573
Procter & Gamble (P&G), 27, 38,
    54, 107, 181, 239, 244, 246,
    252, 256, 265–266, 277, 314,
    328, 353–354, 427–428, 430,
    565, 668
Professional Facilities
    Management, 175
Progressive, 57
Project Impact, 185
Protective Life Corporation, 141
Provender Capital, 191
Prudential Insurance Company,
    392–393, 627
PSA Peugeot Citroën SA, 237
PSS World Medical, 293, 638
Public Education Foundation, 631
Puget Sound Building
    Materials, 651
Purafil, 178
Purdue University, 42

Q

Quaker Oats Co., 278, 405, 426, 473
Qualiac, 506
QVC, 246
Qwest Communication, 466–467

R

Radar magazine, 501
Radcliffe College, 45
RadioShack Corp, 87, 285
Radius, 717
Ralcorp, 641
Ralston Foods, 698
Rancho Santiago Community
    College District, 703
Random House, 106
Randstad, 675
Rawlings Sporting Goods, 240
Ray's Mountain Bike Indoor
    Park, 191
Read Corporation, 351
Rearden Commerce, 503
Redix International, 229
Reebok, 503
Reflex Systems, 584
Reflexite Corporation, 645
REI, 436
Reliable Tools, Inc., 503
Remploy Ltd., 370
Renault, 307
Resorts Worldwide Inc., 256
RetroBox, 178
RhonePoulenc Rorer (RPR), 438
Ricoh, 71
Rio Grande Supply Co., 99–100
Robinson Helicopter, 243
Robinson Jewelers, 87
Roche Holding, 308
Rochester Independent Practice
    Association, 453, 479
Rockingham Toys, 341
Rocky River Industries, 133
Rolling Stones, 6, 21
Rolm Corporation, 232
Royal Dutch/Shell Group, 127,
    209, 224
Royal Philips Electronics, 659
Rubbermaid, 12
Ruggieri & Sons, 539
Rush Communications Inc., 279
Russell Reynolds Associates, 572
Ryerson Midwest Coil
    Processing, 669

S

Safeway, 84, 502
Saint Luke Penny Savings
    Bank, 416
Saks, 456
Salt Lake Regional Medical
    Center, 639
Salvation Army, 23, 238
Samsung Electronics, 73, 76, 106,
    220, 347–348, 371
Samsung Group, 347
San Diego Zoo, 462
Santa Clara University, 719
Santa Fe Institute, 277
Sara Lee Corporation, 391
Save-A-Lot, 243–244, 255
SBC Communications
    Inc., 257
Schering-Plough, 108, 148
Schick Quattro, 252
Schlumberger, Ltd., 391
Scholastic, 537
Schneider National and
    Covenant, 456
Sea Pro, 245
Seagate, 524
Sears Roebuck, 37, 40, 160, 240,
    255, 557
SEI Investments, 27

Semco Corp, 95, 645–646
Shanghai Fabric Ltd., 133
Shawmut National
    Corporation, 327
Shell, 153, 462
Shell Group, 127
Shellington Pharmaceuticals, 32
Sherman Oaks, 6
Sherwin-Williams, 405
Shoe Stores, 397
Shui Fabrics, 133–134
SIA Corporation, 62
Siebel Systems, 91, 589
Siemens, 106, 220
Siemens Business Services, 503
Signet Painting Inc., 49–50
Sirius Satellite System, 274
Six Continents, 256
Smallworld, 543
SmartAuction, 57
Smith & Wesson, 472
Snapper, 253
Snip-its Corp., 595
Society for Human Resource
    Management, 417, 438, 638
Solectron Corp, 56
Solo Cup, 523
Sony, 84, 294, 321, 347
Sound of Music, 574
South Mountain Company,
    163–164
Southern Company, 703
Southwest Airlines, 255, 277,
    293, 602
Space & Communications
    Division, 240
Speedo FASTSKIN FSII, 349
Speedy Muffler King, 280
Spencer Stuart, 108
Spherion Corp., 454–455
Spitzer, 266
Spitzer Group, 265
Springfield Remanufacturing
    Corporation, 677
Sprint, 257, 578
St. Charles, 92
St. Luke's Hospital, 697
St. Paul Travelers, 140
Stanford Business School, 664
Stanford University, 92, 293
Staples, 83, 190, 508
Starbucks, 10, 73, 162, 253,
    279, 348
Starwood Hotels, 256
State Farm Insurance, 213, 668
Steelcase Inc., 680, 693
Sterling Bank, 626
Stine Seed Company, 612
Strategy + Business magazine, 55
Strida, 323
StubHub Inc., 178
Studio Number One, 308
Subaru, 349
Subway, 192
Sun Microsystems, 13, 358, 394
SunBright Outdoor Furniture,
    Inc., 544
Sunglass Hut, 456
Sunoco, 164
Swift Foods, 181–182
Sylvia Weinstock Cakes, 577
Symantec Corp, 229

T

Tacit Networks, 111
Taco Bell, 565
Tacoma, 651

TagWorld, 492
Tandem Services Corporation, 701
Tandy, 285
Target Stores, 78, 256, 265,
    359, 498
Taryn Rose International, 191
Tata Motors, Ltd., 113
Team Germany, 178
Teleradiology Solutions, 110
TeleService Resources, 388
Tenet Healthcare, 156
Tenneco, 220
Tennessee Valley Authority
    (TVA), 390
Tesco, 502, 523, 529
Tesco.com, 464
Texaco, 415
Texas Instruments, 54, 105,
    355, 573
Thomas Betts Corp., 539
Thos. Moser Cabinetmakers, 178
TIAA-CREF, 416
Ticobeans, 193
Timberland, 12, 503
Time Inc., 8
Time Warner Cable, 8
Time Warner, Inc., 8
Timex, 272
Tires Plus University, 598
T-Mobile, 407
TNT, 517
Tommy Hilfiger, 271
Tom's of Maine, 286
TopCoder, 394
Toronto General Hospital, 10
Toshiba, 84
Tostitos, 249
Touchstone, 265
Tower Records, 5
Toyota Motor Co., 53, 84, 107, 126,
    239, 348, 468, 518–519, 521,
    523, 531, 538
Toys 'R' Us, 565, 534
Transfair, 74
Transparency International,
    147, 169
Travelers, 76, 240
Travelweb.com, 79, 256
Treatment Products, Ltd., 125
Tri-Angle Equipment and
    Leasing, 513
Tribble Creative Group, 579
Tribune Company, 245
Tricon, 116
Trinchero Family Estates, 487
TRINOVA'S Aeroquip Inoac, 694
True Value, 598
Truly Blessed Styles, 175
TruServ, 598
Tucker Company, 342
Tulane University, 29
Turner Broadcasting, 8
Twin Cities Staffing, 441
Tyco, 12, 76, 139, 143
Tyson Foods, 224

U

U2, 6
Ubisoft, 325
Umpqua Bank, 94
Under Armour, 256
Unión Fenosa, 163
Union Pacific Railroad, 565
United Airlines, 78, 248, 683,
    693, 719
United Health Group, 668
United Methodist Church, 10

United Parcel Service (UPS), 44, 79, 87, 154, 173, 252, 285, 314, 351, 365, 379, 383, 407–408, 538, 608
  Buffalo distribution center, 379
  Capital Insurance division, 285
United Technologies Corp. (UTC), 115, 249, 462, 503
United Way, 209, 318
united.com, 78
Universal Pictures, 107
University of Chicago Graduate School of Business, 416
University of Miami, 472
University of Michigan, 595
University of Pennsylvania, 186
University of Texas, 595–596
University of Texas Medical Branch, 276
Upper Crust Pizza, 239
U.S. Air Force, 467
U.S. Airways, 320
U.S. Army, 292, 668, 679–680, 490
U.S. Army 1st Air Cavalry Division, 670
U.S. Bureau of Labor Statistics, 405, 421
U.S. Census Bureau, 101, 426, 509
U.S. Congress, 220, 405
U.S. Department of Agriculture, 72
U.S. Department of Commerce, 443
U.S. Department of Defense, 330, 400, 529
U.S. Department of Labor, 24, 632
U.S. Food and Drug Administration (FDA), 133, 142–143, 225, 663
U.S. Internal Revenue Service (IRS), 24, 349
U.S. Justice Department, 148, 156

U.S. Marine Corps, 596, 609
U.S. National Security Agency, 360
U.S. National Training Center, 680
U.S. Navy, 668
U.S. Postal Service, 44, 349, 470, 498
U.S. Securities and Exchange Commission (SEC), 148, 151, 273
U.S. Small Business Administration (SBA), 174, 179–180, 182, 190
U.S. Supreme Court, 425
USAA, 626–627
USS Dwight D. Eisenhower, 333–335
USS John F. Kennedy, 558
USX, 698

V

Valero Energy Corp, 91–92, 96, 98, 231, 283
Valuedance, 664
Vanity Fair, 243
Verizon Communications, 81–82, 243, 257, 433, 578
Verizon Wireless, 526
VHA, Inc., 56, 657, 684
Victoria's Secret, 78
Virgin Airlines, 182, 185
Virginia Power, 397
Visa, 83
Vision Service Plan (VSP), 629
Visteon Corporation, 439
Vivendi Universal, 321
Vocalpoint, 265–266
Volant, 523–524
Volkswagen, 323
Volvo, 107
Voyant Technologies, 9

W

W. L. Gore and Associates, 573
Walker Research, 164
Wall Street Journal, The, 162, 192, 466, 575, 592, 657
Wal-Mart, 37–38, 57, 73, 78, 88–89, 105, 112, 122, 126, 151, 212, 231, 244, 253, 256, 261, 265, 284, 348, 415, 441, 603, 668, 685, 487–488, 510–511, 518, 523, 529, 534
walmartsucks.com, 78
Walt Disney Company, 13, 78, 107, 227, 265, 272, 321, 503
Warner Brothers, 8
Warner Communications, 257
Washington Post, The, 612
Watergate, 612
Waterway Industries, 410
WB Television Network., 640
WD-40 Company, 636
Wells Fargo & Co., 84, 406, 608
Wendy's, 111
Werner and Thompson, 686
West Marine, 517–518, 542
Western Electric Company, 46–47, 624
WestJet Airlines, 96
Westwind Electronics, 481–482
Weyerhaeuser Company, 52
Whirlpool, 310, 462, 503, 523
White Dog
  Café, 186
  Enterprises, 185–186
Whole Foods Markets, 253, 293, 677
Wikipedia, 492
Willamette Industries, 153
Windows on the World, 6

Winegardner & Hammons Inc. (WHI), 209
Wipro Ltd., 26
Wisconsin, 498
Wm. Wrigley Jr. Co., 214
Wolters Kluwer, 108, 274
Woolworth, 40
World Bank, 78, 126
World Commission on Economic Development, 170
World Trade Center (WTC), 6, 28, 224, 372
World Trade Organization (WTO), 78, 126, 131
WorldCom, 12, 139, 143, 149, 478
Wranger, 243
WuXi Pharmatech, 308
Wyeth, 458, 459

X

Xerox Corporation, 12, 71, 356, 434–435, 469, 509–510, 694
Xerox Palo Alto Research Center (PARC), 13, 356
XM Satellite Radio, 371

Y

Yahoo!, 106, 243, 394, 498, 503
Yamaha, 255
Yankelovich Partners, 174, 201
YouTube, 492–493
YumBrands, 565

Z

Ziff Davis, 351
Zilten oilfield, 222
ZipCar, 154
Ztel, Inc., 676

807

0–9
360-degree Feedback, 402

A
Abilene paradox, 711
Acceptance theory of authority, 45
Accommodator, 574
Accountability, 310
Achievement, 630
  culture, 91
  oriented leadership, 602
Acquired needs theory, 629–630
Acquisition, 112
Action, 176
Active listening, 683
Activity ratio, 464
Activity-based costing (ABC), 474, 480
Adaptability culture, 91
Adaptive organizations. *see also* Organizations
  departmentalization, 314, 316–326
  organizing for horizontal coordination, 326–331
  organizing the vertical structure, 308–314
Adjourning, 707
Administrative
  model, 277–279
  principles, 44–46
Affiliation, 630
Affirmative action, 385, 392, 424
Age Discrimination in Employment Act (ADEA), 384
All Product Excellence program (APEX), 698
Alliances, 26
Ambiguity, 273, 275
American Airlines Flight 587 crash, 224
Americans with Disabilities Act, 384
America's Most Wanted, 279
Angel financing, 190
Application form, 395
Appropriate channel, 683
ARMS (automated rental management system), 521
Arm's-length approach, 523
Assertiveness, 119
Assessment centers, 398–399
Assimilator, 574
Association of Southeast Asian Nations (ASEAN), 125
Attitudes, 554
  components of attitudes, 555–557
  conflicts among attitudes, 559–560
  high-performance work attitudes, 557–558
  organizational commitment, 558–559
  positive attitude, 555
Attributions, 562–563
Authoritarianism, 569
Authority, 310–311
  compliance management, 596
  role models, 331
Autonomy, 642

Avoidance learning, 535
Awareness
  relationship awareness, 567
  self-awareness, 565–566
  self-management, 566
  social awareness, 567

B
B2B marketplace model, 503–504
Balance sheet, 462–463
Balanced scorecard, 476–478
Balancing conflict and cooperation, 712
Barbie doll, 72
Bargaining zone, 716–717
  negative bargaining zone, 717
  positive bargaining zone, 716
BCG matrix, 249–250
Behavior modification, 635
Behavioral sciences approach, 50
Behaviorally anchored rating scale (BARS), 403–404
Benchmarking, 54, 469
Benefits, 406
Best Alternative To a Negotiated Agreement (BATNA), 717
Biculturalism, 422
Big five personality factors
  agreeableness, 564
  conscientiousness, 564
  emotional stability, 564
  extroversion, 564
  openness to experience, 564
Bisquick, 328
Blog, 492
Borderless world, 106–108
Bottom line, 24, 463
Bottom-up budgeting, 462
Boundary spanners, 84
Boundarylessness, 338
Boundary-spanning roles, 82–84
Bounded rationality, 278
Brain hemispheric dominance, 491
Brainstorming, 292–293
Brainwriting, 292
Bratz, 72
Budgetary control, 460
Bureaucracy, 43
Bureaucratic administration, 48
Bureaucratic control, 465
Bureaucratic organizations, 42–44
Business
  growth rate, 249
  incubator, 193
  intelligence, 82
  intelligence (BI), 508–509
  level strategy, 245–246
  performance dashboard, 498
  plan, 187
  process, 476
  process reengineering, 329
Business owner
  buying a franchise, 192–193
  buying an existing business, 191–192
  participating in a business incubator, 193–194
  starting a new business, 191
  tactics for becoming a, 191
Business-to-business e-commerce (B2B), 57, 525

Business-to-consumer e-commerce (B2C), 57

C
CAD (computer-aided design), 531–532
CAM (computer-aided manufacturing), 531–532
Capacity; 533
  to adapt and learn, 695, 719
  planning, 533
Capital budget, 461–462
Career advancement, 431–432
Carrot-and-stick controversy, 639
Carryover behaviors, 710
Cash budget, 461
Cash cow, 249
Causes of conflict, 712
Cellular layout, 527–528
Central America Free Trade Agreement (CAFTA), 125
Central planning departments, 227
Centralization, 313–314
Centralized network, 673
Ceremony, 88
Certainty, 273–274
Chain of command, 309
Chairperson, 14
Challenging but realistic goals, 218
Champion, 354
Change agent, 362
Change implementation
  coercion, 369
  communication and education, 368–369
  different assessments and goals, 366–367
  force-field analysis, 367–368
  implementation, 365–370
  lack of understanding and trust, 365
  negotiation, 369
  participation, 369
  resistance to change, 365
  self-interest, 365
  tactics implementation, 368
  top management support, 369–370
  uncertainty, 366
Change management
  changing people and culture, 357–362
  implementing change, 365–370
  model of planned organization change, 362–365
  new products and technologies, 348–357
  turbulent times and changing workplace, 348
Changing, 362
  social contract, 385–386
  structures and policies, 430
Changing things, 348–349
  cooperation, 351–354
  entrepreneurship, 354–357
  exploration, 349–351
  external coordination, 353–354
  internal coordination, 351–353
Channel, 660
  richness, 661–662

Charismatic leaders, 605–607
Cheerios, 328
Chief ethics officer, 160
Chief Executive, 108
Chief executive officer (CEO), 14
Civil Rights Act
  of 1964, 384–385, 434
  of 1991, 432
  Title VII, 384
Classical model, 275–277
Classical perspective, 40
Climate of trust and openness, 683
Closed systems, 53
Coalition, 280
Coalition building, 280
Code of ethics, 159–160
Coercion, 369
Coercive power, 609
Cognitive dissonance, 559
Cohesive team, 720–721
Collaborative *relationships*, 27
Collaborative work systems, 498
Collectivism, 118
Columbia spaceshuttle crash (2003), 28, 224
Command team, 697
Commanding, 45
Commitment, 212
Committee, 697
  on Industrial Lighting (CIL), 46
Communication, 368
  apprehension, 663
  apprehension personal assessment, 685
  breakdown, 712
  channels, 661–663
  communicating among people, 661–668
  communicating during turbulent times, 677–680
  communication channels, 661–663
  communication process, 659–660
  crisis communication, 679
  definition of, 659
  dialogue, 678
  differences, 437
  feedback and learning, 679–680
  flow, 681
  listening, 665–668
  manager's job, 658–660
  managing organizational communication, 680–684
  needs, 683
  nonverbal communication, 664–665
  open communication, 677–678
  organizational communication, 668–677
  to persuade and influence others, 663–664
  team, 684
Companies
  ethnocentric, 127
  geocentric, 127
  polycentric, 127
Company ethics and, 157–162
Compensation, 404
  equity, 405
Compensatory justice, 144
Competency-based pay, 405

Competitive
　advantage, 242
　intelligence (CI), 82
　strategies, 253–255
Competitors, 78–79
Computer-based interviews, 397
Conceptual skill, 11
Concurrent, 455
Concurrent control, 456
Conflict, 711
Consensus, 563
Consideration, 595
Consistency, 563
　culture, 92
Consolidated Omnibus Budget
　Reconciliation Act
　(COBRA), 384
Consulting a group, 289
Consulting individually, 289
Consumer-to-consumer (C2C), 58
Content perspectives on
　motivation, 625
Content theories, 624
Contingencies, 331
Contingency
　approaches, 598–601
　plans, 209, 222
　view, 53–54
Contingent workers, 387
Continuous improvement, 54,
　471–472, 543
Continuous process production,
　335–336
Continuous reinforcement
　schedule, 637
Continuum of empowerment, 646
Controlling, 9–10, 45, 130
Conventional level, 146
Converger, 474
Conversion ratio, 464
Coordinating, 45
Coordination, 326
Cops, 279
Core competence, 243
Core job dimensions
　autonomy, 642
　feedback, 642
　skill variety, 642
　task identity, 642
　task significance, 642
Corporate culture, 262–263
　achievement culture, 91
　adaptive cultures, 90–91
　changing the, 428–430
　consistency culture, 92
　cultural leadership, 94–96
　environment and culture, 89–92
　internal environment, 85–89
　involvement culture, 91–92
　levels of, 86
　Performance, 94
　performance
　　combination, 93
　shaping for innovative
　　response, 92–96
　types of cultures, 90–92
Corporate governance, 478
Corporate governance reform law
　(2002). *see* Sarbanes-Oxley
　Act (2002)
Corporate social responsibility, 150
　discretionary responsibilities, 157
　economic responsibilities, 155
　ethical responsibilities, 156–157
　legal responsibilities, 156
Corporate university, 400–401
Corporate-level strategy, 245

Corporations, 189–190
　global, 126
　multinational, 126–127
　stateless, 126
　transnational, 126
Corruption Perception Index, 116
Cost, 525
Cost leadership, 254
Countertrade, 110
Country club management, 596
Courage, 612
Creative people and organizations
　characteristics, 350
Creativity, 176, 349
Creativity economy, 347
Credo, The, 159
Crisis communication, 679
Crisis EQ, 569
Crisis management
　containment of, 226
　preparation of, 225–226
　prevention of, 225
Crisis management plan
　(CMP), 226
Crisis planning, 223–224, 231
Critic, 355
Critical events, 710
Cross-functional teams, 316,
　320, 697
Crowdsourcing, 373
Cultural intelligence (CQ),
　127–129, 128, 131
Cultural leader, 95
Culture, 85, 262
Culture change, 357
Culture game, 120
Culture shock, 128
Current assets, 462
Current debt, 462
Current ratio, 464
Customer relationship
　management (CRM)
　systems, 59, 507, 510
Customer service, 476
Customers, 78
Cyberslackers, 457
Cycle time, 470

D
Daily flextime, 579
Dashboard, 498
Data, 494
Data mining, 508
Data warehousing, 508
Debt financing, 190
Debt ratio, 465
Decentralization, 313–314
Decentralized
　control, 465–466
　network, 673
　planning, 227
Decision, 272, 288
Decision biases, 284
Decision goals, 278
Decision making, 130, 272
　behavior, 287
　decision-making models,
　　275–281
　decision-making steps, 281–283,
　　285–286
　increasing participation in,
　　288–294
　nonprogrammed decisions,
　　272–273
　personal decision framework,
　　286–288
　programmed decisions, 272–273

　six steps in managerial, 281
　types of decisions and
　　problems, 272–275
Decision significance, 289
Decision styles
　analytical style, 287
　behavioral style, 288
　conceptual style, 288
　directive style, 286
　leader participation styles,
　　288–289
Decision support systems
　(DSSs), 496
Decisional roles, 21–23
Decision-making models
　administrative model, 277–279
　classical model, 275–277
　political model, 279–281
Decodes, 660
Delegation, 289, 310–311, 312
Deliberately structured, 10
Dell Computer's integrated
　supply chain, 522
Demotivation, 643
Departmentalization, 314
　advantages and disadvantages
　　of each structure, 323–326
　divisional approach, 316–317
　geographic- or customer-based
　　divisions, 317–318
　matrix approach, 318–320
　network approach to, 322
　team approach, 320–321
　vertical functional
　　approach, 316
　virtual network approach,
　　321–323
Dependent demand inventory, 536
Descriptive, 278
Design for manufacturability and
　assembly (DFMA), 524
Developing an effective
　workforce, 399–404
Devil's advocate, 294
Diagnosis, 282, 362
Dialogue, 678
Differentiation strategy, 253, 255
Digital networking, 26
Digital technology, 337–338
Dimensions of diversity, 418–419
Direct investing, 111–113
Directive leadership, 602
Disaster recovery plans, 209
Discretionary responsibility, 157
Discrimination, 385
Discussion questions, 131
Disputes, 670
Disseminator role, 21
Distinctiveness, 563
Distribution, 538
Distributive justice, 144
Distributive negotiation, 715
Disturbance handler, 22
Diverger, 474
Diversification, 239
Diversity, 26, 703
　attitudes toward, 419–420
　challenges minorities face, 422
　changing workplace, 420–424
　current debates about
　　affirmative action, 424–425
　current responses to diversity,
　　428–433
　defining new relationships in
　　organizations, 434–435
　diversity in a turbulent world,
　　438–440

　diversity training, 432–433
　glass ceiling, 425–427
　global diversity, 435–438
　management challenges,
　　422–424
　primary and secondary
　　dimensions of, 418
　skills training, 432–433
　valuing diversity, 417–420
　workforce, 418
Diversity awareness
　stages of, 433
　training, 432
Divestiture, 240
Division of labor, 309
Division of work, 45
Divisional approach, 324
Divisional structure, 316
DMAIC (Define, Measure,
　Analyze, Improve, and
　Control), 470
Dominance, 593
Dot-com bubble, 28
Downsizing, 240, 388–389
Downward communication,
　668–670
Driving, 367
Drop off, 670
Dual roles, 704

E
E → P expectancy, 632–633
EBBS and flows of management
　innovations (1950–2000), 51
E-business, 57, 498
　e-marketplaces, 503–504
　for engaging clicks with
　　bricks, 501
　going international, 503
　implementing e-business
　　strategies, 502–503
　internet and e-business, 498–510
　key components of e-business
　　for two traditional organi-
　　zations, 500
　opening page of the web site for
　　IKEA, 499
　productivity and efficiency, 502
　strategies, 500
EcoBook 100, 154
E-commerce, 498
　business-to-business e-commerce
　　(B2B), 57
　business-to-consumer e-commerce
　　(B2C), 57
　consumer-to-consumer e-commerce
　　(C2C), 58
　definition of, 57
Economic development, 115
Economic dimension, 77
Economic forces, 39
Economic man, 624
Economic order quantity (EOQ),
　535–536
Economic performance, 164
Economic responsibility, 155
Economic Value-Added (EVA),
　473, 480
E-cruiting, 392–393
Education, 368
Effective workforce, 388
Effectiveness, 10, 681
Efficiency, 10, 543
E-file, 349
Electronic brainstorming, 292
Electronic data interchange
　(EDI), 500

E-marketplaces, 503–504
Emotional intimacy, 434
Employee
  centered leaders, 596
  empowerment, 56
  growth-need strength, 643
  involvement, 54
  network groups, 439–440
  productivity, 540
Employer of choice, 387
Employment tests, 398
Empowered employees, 25
Empowerment, 45, 56, 645–646
Encodes, 660
**Enterprise resource planning
  (ERP) systems**, 58, 503–504,
  510, 536
Entrepreneurial start-up
  choosing a legal structure, 189
  corporation, 189–190
  debt financing, 190
  equity financing, 190–191
  getting financing, 190
  partnership, 189
  sole proprietorship, 189
  starting with the idea, 187
  writing the business plan,
    187, 189
Entrepreneurs, 174
  diversity of, 182–183
  glimpse of tomorrow's, 183
  high energy level, 184
  internal locus of control, 183
  personality traits of, 183
  role, 21
  self-confidence of, 184
  tolerance for ambiguity, 184–185
  who are entrepreneurs, 181–182
Entrepreneurship, 174–175, 349,
    354–357
  and the environment, 175–181
  impact of entrepreneurial
    companies, 179–181
  launching an entrepreneurial
    start-up, 186–187, 189–194
  social, 185–186
  today, 176
  world's most entrepreneurial
    countries, 177
Entropy, 53
Environment, 52
  and manager mind, 83
Environmental forces, 363
Environmental Protection Agency
  (EPA), 77
Environmental uncertainty, 81
Environments of management
  economic environment, 77,
    114–116
  environment and culture, 89–92
  external environment, 72–81
  external environment
    of Nortel, 80
  general environment, 72–73
  internal environment, 72,
    85–89
  international business
    environment, 113–114
  international environment,
    73–74
  legal-political environment,
    77–78
  organizational environment, 72
  organization–environment
    relationship, 81–85
  sociocultural environment, 76,
    117–121

task environment, 72, 78
technological environment,
  74–76
Equal Employment Opportunity
  Commission (EEOC), 385
Equal employment opportunity
  (EEO), 384, 392
Equal Pay Act, 384
Equity, 630
Equity financing, 190–191
Equity theory, 630
ERG theory, 626–628
Escalating commitment, 293
ESPN360, 500
Estimated time of arrival
  (ETA), 537
Ethical challenges in turbulent
  times, 162–165
Ethical choices affecting factors
  the manager, 145–148
  the organization, 149–150
Ethical decision making
  individualism approach, 143
  justice approach, 144
  moral-rights approach, 143–144
  utilitarian approach, 142–143
Ethical dilemma, 141
Ethical individuals, 157–158
Ethical issues, 145
Ethical leadership, 158–159
Ethical organization, three pillars
  of an, 158
Ethical responsibility, 156–157
**Ethical and socially
  responsible**, 164
Ethical structures, 160–161
Ethics, 140
  committee, 160
  and compliance officers
    association, 161
  ethical decision making criteria,
    142–144
  guide, 161
  managerial ethics, 140–142
  questions for analyzing a
    company's cultural
    impact on, 150
  three domains of human
    action, 140
  training, 161
Ethnocentric companies, 127
Ethnocentrism, 121, 419
Ethnorelativism, 419
Euro, 124
Europe '92, 124
European Union (EU), 123–124
Evaluation and feedback, 285
Event-driven planning, 229
Evergreen project, 255
Exchange rates, 116
Executive director, 14
**Executive information systems
  (EISs)**, 496
Exit interview, 406
Expatriates, 436
Expectancy theory, 632–633
Expense budget, 461
*Experienced meaningfulness
  of work*, 642
Experienced responsibility, 642
Expert power, 609–610
*Explicit
  knowledge*, 508
  statements, 710
Exporting, 109–110
External
  attribution, 562–563

leader, 699
locus of control, 568
  recruiting, 391–392
  threat, 248
Extinction, 636
Extranet, 500
Extreme telecommuting, 388
Extrinsic rewards, 622, 639
Extroversion, 571

F

Face readers, 665
Face validity, 396
Facial expressions, 665
Facilitation, 289
Family and Medical Leave
  Act, 384
Fast-cycle teams, 352, 697
Father of quality movement, 54
Federal legislation, 384–385
Feedback, 52, 285, 455, 634,
    642, 660
Feedback control model, 456, 458
  application to budgeting,
    460–461
  capital budget, 461–462
  cash budget, 461
  comparision of performance to
    standards, 459–460
  establish standards of
    performance, 458–459
  expense budget, 461
  measurement of actual
    performance, 459
  revenue budget, 461
  steps of, 458
  take corrective action, 460
Feedback and learning,
  679–680, 684
Feedforward, 455
Feedforward control, 455–456
Feeling, 571
Female advantage, 427
Femininity, 118
Fiedler's contingency theory,
  600–601
*Fifth Discipline: The Art and
  Practice of Learning
  Organizations, The*, 55
Figurehead role, 21
Financial control
  activity ratios, 464
  financial analysis, 463–465
  financial statements, 462–463
  leverage ratios, 465
  liquidity ratios, 464
  profitability ratios, 464–465
Financial performance, 476
Finished-goods inventory, 533
Firms of Endearment, 12
First-line managers, 15
Five whys practice, 294
Five-fifteen, 671
Fixed assets, 462
Fixed-interval schedule, 637
Fixed-position layout, 528–529
Fixed-ratio schedule, 637
Flat structure, 313
**Flexible manufacturing
  system**, 530
Flexible scheduling, 388
Flexible structure, 336
Focus strategy, 255
Focused on the customer, 54
Force-field analysis, 367
**Formal communication
  channels**, 668

Formal information channels, 683
Formal teams, 696–698
Forming, 705
*Frame of reference
  human resource*, 48
  political, 48
  structural, 48
  symbolic, 48
Franchising, 111, 192
Free rider, 702
Free Trade Area of the Americas
  (FTAA), 125
**Frustration regression
  principle**, 626
Functional
  approach, 323–324
  level strategy, 246
  managers, 15
  structure, 316
  team, 697
**Fundamental attribution
  error**, 563
Future orientation, 119

G

Gallup study, 648
Gantt chart, 42
Gazelles, 180
Gender differentiation, 119
General Agreement on Tariffs
  and Trade (GATT), 122
*General and Industrial
  Management*, 45
General Electric's work-out
  program, 361
General environment, 72–73
General managers, 16
Generation X employees, 38–39
Generation Y employees, 38–39,
  76, 388, 432
Genesis grants, 356
Geocentric companies, 127
Glad Force Flex Trash Bags, 256
Glad Press & Seal, 256
Glass ceiling, 425–427
Glass walls, 425
Global corporations, 126
Global Leadership and
  Organizational Behavior
  Effectiveness (GLOBE)
  project, 118–120
Global matrix structures, 319
Global mind-set, 262
Global outsourcing, 109, 111
Global strategy, 240
  global corporate strategies, 241
  globalization, 241
  multidomestic strategy,
    241–242
  transnational strategy, 242
Global teams, 700–702
Globalization, 26, 241, 476
  and increased competition,
    177–178
Globalization stages
  domestic stage, 107–108
  global stage, 107–108
  international stage, 107–108
  multinational stage, 107–108
  stateless stage, 107–108
Goal acceptance, 634
Goal differences, 713
Goal difficulty, 634
Goal setting
  characteristics of effective, 217
  levels of goals and their
    importance, 210

in organizations, 213–216
overview of, 210–211
plans and, 214–216
purposes of goals and plans,
211–213
Goal specificity, 634
Goals, 210
alignment of, 216
challenging but realistic, 218
criteria for effective, 217–219
decision, 278
hierarchy of goals for
a manufacturing
organization, 217
operational, 215
quantitative, 219
strategic, 211, 214
stretch, 218, 228
tactical, 211, 215
Goal-setting theory, 634–634
Grand strategy of growth,
238–240
Grapevine, 673, 675, 683
Great meeting, 718
Greenfield venture, 112
Grievances, 670
Gross domestic product
(GDP), 179
Gross margin, 464
Group, 694
Group expertise, 290
Groupthink, 711
Groupware, 498
Growth, 239–240
Growth and Leadership Center
(GLC), 358
Guides to action, 212

H

Halo effect, 403, 562
Hamburger helper, 328
Hard workers, 175
Harry Potter
and the Order of the Phoenix, 154
and the Prisoner of Azkaban, 321
Hat rack, 683
Hawthorne
effect, 47
studies, 46
Headhunters, 391
Health Insurance Portability
and Accountability Act
(HIPPA), 384
Health Standards textbook, 716
Helix aspera, 72
Hero, 87–88
Hersey and Blanchard's
situational theory, 598–600
Herzberg's two-factor theory,
628–629
Hierarchy of needs theory,
625–626
High-context culture, 437
High-performance culture, 94
Hofstede
study, 119
value dimensions, 117
Holding costs, 535
Horizontal communication,
671–672
Horizontal coordination
need for coordination, 326–327
project management, 327–329
reengineering, 329–331
task forces, 327–329
teams, 327–329
Horizontal linkage model, 351

Horizontal team, 697
Horses, 229
Human capital, 381–382
Human relations, 46–47
Human relations movement,
46–47, 47
**Human resource information
system,** 383
**Human resource management
(HRM),** 379
attracting an effective workforce, 389–399
changing nature of careers,
385–389
developing an effective
workforce, 399–404
environmental influences on,
381–385
maintaining an effective
workforce, 404–407
major federal laws related
to, 384
some trends in, 383
strategic role of, 380–381
Human resource planning,
390–391
Human resources, 262
Human resources perspective,
47, 49–50
Human skill, 11–12
Humane orientation, 119
Humanistic attitude, 121
Humanistic perspective, 46–47,
48–50
Humility, 591
Hurricane Katrina, 28, 30, 157,
162, 454, 609, 717
Hygiene factors, 628–629

I

Idea champion, 354
Idea incubator, 351
Idealists, 174
Implementation, 285
Impoverished management, 596
Improvisation, 176
In Search of Excellence, 676
In-basket simulation, 399
Incentive pay, 405
Income statement, 462–463
Index of Economic Freedom, 116
Individual collectivism, 119
Individualism, 118, 143
approach, 143
Indoctrination, 670
Industrial psychology, 42
Influence, 608
Informal organization, 45–46
Information, 494
Information and control
systems, 261
Information fatigue syndrome, 491
**Information reporting
systems,** 496
Information systems types, 493
data versus information, 494
management information
systems (MIS),
495–496, 498
operations information
systems, 494–495
Information technology (IT),
51, 263
e-HR, 383–384
evolving world of, 492–493
has changed everything,
488–492

types of information systems,
493–494
Informational roles, 21
Infrastructure, 115
Ingenuity, 176
Initiating structure, 595
Innovation, 180–181
coordination model for, 352
new products and technologies,
348–357
Innovative control systems, 474
balanced scorecard, 476–478
new workplace concerns,
478–479
open-book management,
474–476
Instant messaging (IM), 662
Intangible output, 337
Integrated enterprise, 521–523
Integrative negotiation, 715
Interactive leadership, 592
Interim managers, 15, 26
Internal
attribution, 562–563
environment, 72
forces, 363
locus of control, 567
recruiting, 391
**International business
environment,** 113–114
International dimension, 73
**International human resource
management (IHRM),** 383
International management, 113
International Opacity Index, 476
International Quality
Standards, 473
International trade alliances
European Union (EU), 123–124
General Agreement on Tariffs
and Trade (GATT), 122–123
globalization backlash, 126
North American Free Trade
Agreement (NAFTA),
124–125
other trade alliances, 125
World Trade Organization
(WTO), 122–123
Internet, 57, 676
Interorganizational
partnerships, 84
Interpersonal barriers, 681
Interpersonal influence tactics,
610–611
Interpersonal patterns, 593
Interpersonal roles, 21
Interview, 396–397
Intradepartmental problem
solving, 671
Intranet, 499, 509–510
Intrinsic rewards, 622
Introversion, 571
Intuition, 279, 570
Inventor, 354
Inventory, 533
Inventory management
economic order quantity
(EOQ), 535–536
importance of inventory, 534
Just-in-time (JIT) inventory,
536–537
logistics and distribution
management, 538
material requirements
planning, 536
Inventory turnover, 464
Involvement culture, 91–92

IPOs (initial public offerings), 40
ISO 14001 standards, 154
ISO certification, 473

J

Job, 639
analysis, 391
based pay, 405
centered leaders, 596
characteristics model,
641–642, 642
creation, 180
description, 391
design, 622, 640
enlargement, 641
enrichment, 641
evaluation, 405
rotation, 640–641
satisfaction, 557
sculpting, 389
simplification, 640
specification, 391
Job design for motivation
core job dimensions, 642
job characteristics model, 641
job enlargement, 641
job enrichment, 641
job rotation, 640–641
job simplification, 640
types of, 640
Joint ventures, 26, 84–85, 111
Judging, 571
Juggler, 175
Jung's typology, 581
Justice
compensatory justice, 144
distributive justice, 144
procedural justice, 144
Justice approach, 144
Just-in-time (JIT)
inventory control systems,
367–368, 536–537
shipments, 519

K

Kanban systems, 537
Knowledge economy, 347
Knowledge management; 58, 508
portal, 509
systems, 503
Knowledge of actual results, 642
Knowledge work, 58

L

Labor market, 79
Lake Placid Olympics, 695
Language barriers, 682
Large-group intervention, 360
Law of effect, 635
Laws and regulations, 117
Lead 21, a project, 360
Leader-member relationships, 600
Leaders
behavior, 602
charismatic, 605–607
employee-centered leaders, 596
expertise, 289
external, 699
hierarchical levels and
importance of a, 22
job-centered leaders, 596
path–goal situations and
preferred leader
behaviors, 603
role, 21
seven interpersonal influence
tactics for, 610–611

Leaders (*continued*)
style, 601
task-oriented, 601
transactional, 605
transformational leaders, 607–608
Leadership, 27, 259
achievement-oriented leadership, 602
behavioral approaches, 595–598
charismatic, 605–607
for contemporary times, 590–593
contingency approaches, 598–601
directive leadership, 602
grid, 596–598
interactive, 592
leadership approaches, 611–613
leadership grid, 596–598
leadership traits, 594–595
leading change, 605–608
level 5 leadership, 591–592
manager qualities, 594
moral leadership, 612–613
nature of leadership, 590
participative leadership, 602
power and influence, 608–611
servant leadership, 612
substitutes and neutralizers for, 604–605
supportive leadership, 602
T–P leadership questionnaire, 614–615
versus management, 594–595
visionary, 605–607
Leading, 9, 129–130
Lean manufacturing, 519, 538
employee productivity, 540
improving productivity, 540–541
managerial productivity, 540–541
measuring productivity, 539–540
Learn, don't punish
philosophy, 294
Learning
continuous learning, 575–576
learning style types, 575
process, 573–574
styles, 574–575
Learning organizations, 27, 48, 55
Legal approach, 153
Legal responsibility, 156
Legal-political dimension, 77
Legal-political environment, 116
Legitimacy, 212
Legitimate power, 609
Less-developed countries (LDCs), 115
Level 5 leadership hierarchy, 591
Leverage ratios, 465
Liabilities, 462
Liaison roles, 22
Licensing, 110–111
Life balance resources program, 432
Line authority, 311
Line departments, 311
Linguistic pluralism, 121
Liquidation, 240
Liquidity ratio, 464
Listening, 665–668
Locus of control, 567–570
external, 183
internal, 183
Logistics, 538

Long-term debt, 462
Long-term orientation, 118
Lord of the Rings, The, 8
Low-context culture, 437

M

Machiavellianism, 569
Machiavellianism (Mach) orientation, 569
Malware, 229
Management
authority-compliance management, 596
condensation of 14 points for, 541
contingency view of, 53–54
country club management, 596
definition of, 7–8
elements of, 45
four functions of, 8–10
horizontal differences in, 15–16
impoverished management, 596
innovative thinking for turbulent times, 54–59
levels in organizational hierarchy, 14
middle-of-the-road management, 596
new competencies, 27–28
new workplace, 25–29
open-book, 38
organization and, 38–40
organizational performance, 10–11
perspectives over time, 41
process of, 8
scientific, 41–42
skills, 11–13
team management, 596
types, 13–16
vertical differences in, 14
Management by objectives (MBO), 54, 219–221
Management by wandering around, 673, 683
Management by wandering around (MBWA), 676, 683
Management information system (MIS), 495–496, 498
Management science perspective, 50–52
Management thinking evolution
classical perspective, 40–46
humanistic perspective, 46–47, 49–50
innovative management thinking for turbulent times, 54–59
management science perspective, 50–52
recent historical trends, 52–54
Managerial planning, 209–210
Managerial productivity, 540–541
Managers
activities, 17–19
challenge, 5–7, 37–38, 71–72, 105–106, 139–140, 173–174, 209–210, 237–238, 271–272, 307–308, 347, 379–380, 415–417, 453, 487–488, 517–518, 553–554, 589–590, 621–622, 657–658, 693–694
communication champions, 658
courage, 148
first-lin, 15
functional, 15

general, 16
implications for, 633
interim, 15, 26
making the leap from individual performer to, 17
middle, 14
project, 15
reality, 20
roles, 20–23
solution, 29–30, 59–60, 96–97, 130–131, 165, 197–198, 230–231, 263–264, 295, 338–339, 371, 407, 440, 479–480, 510–511, 542, 579–580, 613–614, 648–649, 684, 719–720
ten roles of, 21
top, 14
what is it like to be a, 16
Managing
conflict, 713
cross-culturally, 129
in a global environment, 105–106, 127–130
growing business, 194–197
in small businesses and non-profit organizations, 23–25
team conflict, 711–717
the technology-driven workplace, 56–57
in turbulent times, 28–29
Manufacturing operations, 519–520
Manufacturing organizations, 519
Market approach, 153
Market entry strategies, 108
Market expansion, 502
Market share, 249
Market value-added (MVA), 473–474, 480
Masculinity, 118
Mass production, 335
Matching model, 389
Material requirements planning (MRP), 536
Matrix approach, 318, 324
Matrix boss, 319
MBO. *see* **Management by objectives (MBO)**
Means-ends chain, 216
Medecins du Monde (Doctors of the World), 506
Mediation, 715
centers, 579
Member roles, 703–705
Mentor, 431
Merger, 84–85
Message, 660
Metacategories, 595
Michigan studies, 596
Microelectromechanical systems (MEMS), 178
Microsoft
Business Solutions products, 317
Microsoft TV, 317
MSN, 317
Office, 317
Windows, 317
Windows mobile, 317
Xbox games, 317
Middle managers, 14
Middle-of-the-road management, 596
Milestones in history of corporate diversity in US, 416
Milwaukee Journal Sentinel, The, 159

Mission, 213, 230
statement, 213
statement for Bristol-Myers Squibb, 214
Modular approach, 323
Monitor role, 21
Monoculture, 419
Moral agent, 141
Moral leadership, 612–613
Moral-rights approach
right of free consent, 143
right of free speech, 144
right of freedom of conscience, 143
right to due process, 144
right to life and safety, 144
right to privacy, 143
Motivating, 130
Motivation, 212
concept of motivation, 622–624
employee engagement, 623
foundations of motivation, 624–625
Herzberg's two-factor theory, 628–629
innovative ideas for motivating, 643–648
job design for motivation, 639–643
motivational benefits of job flexibility, 627
process perspectives on, 630–634
reinforcement perspective on motivation, 635–639
simple model of motivation, 622
Motivation process perspectives
equity theory, 630–631
expectancy theory, 632–633
Motivation reinforcement perspective
avoidance learning, 635
changing behavior with reinforcement, 636
continuous reinforcement, 637
extinction, 636
partial reinforcement, 637–639
positive reinforcement, 635
punishment, 636
reinforcement tools, 635
schedules of reinforcement, 636–637
Motivators, 628
Multicultural teams, 438–439
Multidomestic strategy, 241–242
Multinational corporation (MNC), 126–127
Multiple channels, 683
Multitasking adventures, 19
My scene, 72
Myers–Briggs Type Indicator (MBTI), 570–572, 571–572, 579, 581, 583
MySpace killer, 492

N

Nanoparticles, 76
Nanotechnology, 75
Negative bargaining zone, 717
Negative reinforcement, 635
Negotiation, 369, 715–716
Negotiator role, 22
Neutralizer, 604
New workplace, 25
New-venture fund, 356
Nexters. *see* Generation X employees
Noise, 660

Nonparticipator role, 704
Nonprogrammed decisions, 272
Nonromantic love relationships, 434
Nonroutine messages, 663
Nonverbal communication, 664–665
Norming, 706
North American Free Trade Agreement (NAFTA), 124–125

O

O, The Oprah Magazine, 84
Occupational Safety and Health Administration (OSHA), 77, 384
Office automation systems, 495
Offshoring, 109
Ohio State Studies, 595–596
Old workplace, 25
One-owner operations, 173
On-the-job training (OJT), 399
Opacity index, 475
Open communication, 677
Open information, 56
Open innovation, 353
Open systems, 53
Open-book management, 38
Open-book management, 474–476
Operational goals, 215
Operational plans, 211, 215
Operational research teams, 51
Operations, 519
Operations information systems, 493
Operations management, 51, 519–521
Operations management systems
  basic production layouts, 527
  CAD/CAM, 531–532
  capacity planning, 533
  cellular layout, 527–528
  facilities layout, 526
  facility location, 532–533
  fixed-position layout, 528–529
  flexible manufacturing systems, 530–531
  process layout, 526
  procurement, 525–526
  product and service design, 523–525
  product layout, 526–527
  service technology, 529–530
  technology automation, 529
Operations research, 51
Operations strategy, 520
Opportunities, 247, 282
Oprah, 22
Optimizers, 174
Opt-out trend, 426–427
Order fulfillment, 537
Ordering costs, 535
Organization chart, 308–309
Organization development (OD), 50, 357
  activities, 359–362
  approaches to culture change, 361
  conflict management, 359
  mergers/acquisitions, 358–359
  organizational decline/revitalization, 359
  steps, 362
Organization structure, 308
Organizational behavior
  attitudes, 554–560

learning, 573–576
  perception, 560–563
  personality and behavior, 563–573
  stress and stress management, 576–579
Organizational change, 348
  forces for change, 363
  four roles in, 355
  model of planned, 362–365
  need for change, 364–365
Organizational citizenship, 554
Organizational commitment, 558
Organizational communication
  communication barriers, 680–681
  downward communication, 668–670
  formal communication channels, 668
  horizontal communication, 671–672
  individual barriers, 681
  individual skills, 683
  language barriers, 682
  network, 675
  organizational actions, 683–684
  organizational barriers, 681–682
  overcoming communication barriers, 682
  personal communication channels, 673–674
  team communication channels, 672–673
  upward communication, 670–671
Organizational control, 454
  concurrent control, 456
  feedback control, 456, 458
  feedforward control, 455–456
Organizational environment, 72
Organizational mission, 213
Organizational structures and systems, 159–161
Organizations
  bureaucratic, 42–44
  definition of an, 10
  and environment relationship, 81
  forces on, 26
  goals in, 213–216
  informal, 45–46
  learning, 27
  learning, 55
  management and, 38–40
  Quadrant A organizations, 93
  Quadrant B organizations, 93
  Quadrant C organizations, 93–94
  Quadrant D organizations, 94
  systems view of, 52
Organizing, 8–9, 45, 308
Output control, 456
Outputs, 52
Outsourcing, 26, 59, 109, 321
Overconfidence, 284
Owners' equity, 462

P

P → O expectancy, 632–633
Panel interviews, 397
PaperPro, 181
Parallel approach, 352
Partial productivity, 540
Partial reinforcement schedule, 637–639
Participating style, 599
Participation, 369

Participative leadership, 602
Partnership, 189, 502
  approach, 523
  paradigm shift, 85
  strategies, 255–257
Passion for Excellence, A, 676
Path–goal theory, 602
Pause strategy. see Stability
Pay-for-performance, 405
Peer-to-peer (P2P) file sharing networks, 58, 493
People change, 357
People-oriented behavior, 595
Per capita income, 115
Perceiving, 571
Perception
  attributions, 562–563
  perceptual distortions, 561–562
  perceptual selectivity, 560–561
  process, 560
Perceptual defense, 562
Perceptual distortions, 561
Performance, 11
  appraisal, 401–402
  assessment, 402–403
  dashboards, 230, 675
  evaluation errors, 403–404
  gap, 364
  management, 477
  measurement, 477
  orientation, 119
  review ranking system, 402
Performing, 706
Performing stage of team development, 707
Permanent teams, 320
Persistence, 176
Personal attraction to the team, 708
Personal communication channels, 673–674
Personal decision framework, 286–288
Personal moral development
  conventional level, 146
  postconventional level, 146
  preconventional level, 145
  principled level, 146
Personal networking, 673–674
Personal power, 609
Personality, 563
  assessment, 581
  attitudes and behaviors influenced by personality, 567–572
  authoritarianism, 569
  clashes, 712–713
  emotional intelligence, 565–567
  locus of control, 567–568
  machiavellianism, 569–570
  Myers–Briggs type indicator, 570–572
  personality traits, 564–565
  person–job fit, 572–573
  problem-solving styles, 570–572
Person–environment fit, 573
Person–job fit, 572
Phishers, 229
Phraselator, 683
Planning, 8, 45, 210
Planning task force, 230
Planning types
  contingency plans, 222–223
  decentralized, 227
  event-driven, 228–229
  for high performance, 226–230
  management by objectives (MBO), 219–221

single-use and standing plans, 221
  in a turbulent environment, 223–226
Plans
  operational, 211, 215
  strategic, 214
  tactical, 215
Pluralism, 419
Point-counterpoint, 294
Political forces, 39
Political instability, 116–117, 117
Political risk, 116–117, 117
Political skills, 524
Polycentric companies, 127
Poor coordination, 682
Porter's competitive forces and strategies, 251–255
Portfolio strategy, 249
Position power, 609
Positive
  attitude, 455
  bargaining zone, 716
  reinforcement, 635
Postaction control, 456
Postconventional level, 146
Post-heroic approach, 591
Potential for learning and growth, 476
Power, 608
  coercive power, 609
  distance, 117, 119
  expert power, 609–610
  legitimate power, 609
  personal power, 609
  position power, 609
  referent power, 610
  reward power, 609
Powerful management tool, 694
Preconventional level, 145
Preliminary control, 455
President, 14
Pressure, 176
Pressure groups, 78
Preventive control, 455
Primacy, 461, 710
Principled level, 146
Problem, 282
Problem statement, 290
Problem-solving styles, 571
Problem-solving teams, 698
Procedural justice, 144
Process, 329
Process control systems, 495
Process layout, 526
Process theories, 624–625, 630
Proclaiming, 659
Procurement, 525–526
Producibility, 525
Product change, 349
Product layout, 526–527
Product life-cycle management (PLM), 531
Product markets, 115
Product structure, 316
Production, 519
Productive output, 695, 717
Productivity, 539
Productivity goal, 529
Profit margin on sales, 464
Profitability ratios, 464–465
Profit-and-loss statement (P&L), 462
Profit-maximizing view, 155
Program structure, 316
Programmed decisions, 272
Project management, 387

Project manager, 15, 328
Project teams, 697
Projection, 562
Promotion from within, 391, 401
Protected groups, 392
Prudential's corporate recruiting policy, 393
Punishment, 636
Pythons, 27

Q

Q12 metric, 648–649
Quadrant A organizations, 93
Quadrant B organizations, 93
Quadrant C organizations, 93–94
Quadrant D organizations, 94
Quality, 525
Quality and financial control trends
  Activity-Based Costing (ABC), 474
  Economic Value-Added (EVA), 473
  International Quality Standards, 473
  Market Value-Added (MVA), 473–474
  new financial control systems, 473
Quality circles, 469, 698
Quality control
  changing philosophy of control, 465–468
  feedback control model, 458–462
  financial control, 462–465
  innovative control systems for turbulent times, 474–479
  meaning of control, 454
  organizational control focus, 455–458
  quality and financial control trends, 472–474
  total quality management (TQM), 468–472
Quantitative goals, 219
Quiet rooms, 579

R

Radar magazine, 501
Radio-frequency identification (RFID), 488, 529
Rational persuasion, 610
Rationale for decisions, 212
Raw materials inventory, 712
Realistic job previews (RJP), 391–392
Receiver, 660
Recency, 561
Recognition, 279
Recruiting, 391
Recruitment, 430–431
Reengineering, 329
Referent power, 610
Refreezing, 362
Reinforcement, 635
Reinforcement theory, 625, 635
Relationship awareness, 567
Relay Assembly Test Room (RATR) experiment, 46
Reliability, 525
Reorder point (ROP), 535
Resource, 115
Resource allocation, 212
Resource allocator role, 22
Resource maturity, 195
Responsibility, 310–311

Responsibility center, 461
Restraining forces, 367
Retrenchment, 240
Return on quality (ROQ), 94
Return on total assets (ROA), 465
Revenue budget, 461
Reverse discrimination, 525
Reward power, 609
Rigorous debate, 294
Risk, 273–274
Risk propensity, 283, 285
Roles
  conflict, 578
  decisional roles, 21–23
  definition of, 20
  disseminator role, 21
  dual roles, 704
  entrepreneur role, 21
  figurehead role, 21
  informational roles, 21
  interpersonal roles, 21
  leader role, 21
  liaison roles, 22
  monitor role, 21
  negotiator role, 22
  nonparticipator role, 704
  resource allocator role, 22
  socioemotional role, 704
  spokesperson role, 21
  task specialist role, 704
  team member roles, 704
Room for Improvement, 179
Rowe (results-oriented work environment), 649
Rule of reciprocity, 611

S

Sara Lee's required skills for finance executives, 392
Sarbanes-Oxley Act (2002), 23, 72, 161, 479
Satisfaction, 695
Satisficing, 278
Scalar chain, 45
Scalar principle, 309
Scarce resources, 712
Scenario building, 223–224
Scenarios, 209
Schedules of reinforcement, 636–638
Scientific management, 41–42, 48
  characteristics of, 43
  father of, 42
SEC guidelines, 223
Selection, 395
Self-awareness, 565–566
Self-confidence, 568
Self-contained unit structure, 316
Self-directed teams, 698, 698–699
Self-management, 566
Self-serving bias, 563
Selling style, 599
Semantics, 681
Sender, 660
Sensation, 570
Servant leaders, 612
Service operations, 519–520
Service organizations, 519
Service technology, 337
Sex and the City, 179
Sexual harassment, 385, 434–435
Shades of green, 153
Shared goals, 708
Sharing, 659, 664
Short-term orientation, 118
Simultaneous linkage, 352

Single-use plans, 221
Situation, 600–601
Situation analysis, 247–248
Situational theory, 598–600
Six Sigma quality, 228, 465, 470
Skill variety, 642
Skill-based pay systems, 405
Skunkworks, 355
Slogan, 88
Small business, 179
  definition of, 179
  examples of SBA definitions of, 180
  owners types, 174
Small-batch production, 335
Sociability, 593
Social
  awareness, 567
  capital, 554
  contract, 38
  entity, 10
  entrepreneur, 185
  facilitation, 717
  forces, 38
  loafing, 702
  networking, 492
  security, 406
  sustainability, 164
  values, 117
Social responsibility
  company ethics and, 157–162
  corporate social performance criteria, 155
  definition of, 150–151
  ethic of sustainability, 153–154
  evaluating corporate social responsibility, 155–157
  organizational stakeholders, 151–153
Societal collectivism, 119
Sociocultural dimension, 76
Sociocultural environment, 117–121
Socioemotional role, 704
Sole proprietorship, 189
Sole proprietorships, 173
Span of control, 311
Span of management, 311–313
Special purpose teams, 698
Specialization, 309
Special-purpose teams, 697
Spokesperson role, 21
Sponsor, 355
SportsCenter, 500
Stability, 240
Staff authority, 311
Staff departments, 311
Stakeholder, 151
Stakeholder approach, 153
Standard of performance, 213, 458
Standing plans, 221
Stated goal, 10
Stateless corporations, 126
Stereotyping, 403, 561–562
Stigma of incompetence, 525
Stockless systems, 537
Storming, 705
Story, 87
Strategic business units (SBUs), 249
Strategic conversation, 659
Strategic goals, 211, 214
Strategic management process, 238, 246
Strategic plans, 214
Strategical thinking, 11
  business-level strategy formulation, 251–257

corporate-level strategy formulation, 249–250
formulating functional-level strategy, 257–258
global strategy, 240–242
grand strategy, 239–240
levels of strategy, 244–246
purpose of strategy, 242–244
strategic management process, 239, 246–249
strategy implementation and control, 258–263
Strategies, 242
  business-level, 245–246
  competitive, 253–255
  continuum of partnership, 257
  corporate-level, 245
  differentiation, 253, 255
  effective implementation, 260
  focus, 255
  formulation, 237–238, 247
  functional-level, 246
  global, 240–242
  implementation, 237–238, 247, 258–263
  levels of, 244–246
  multidomestic, 241–242
  partnership, 255–257
  Porter's competitive forces and, 251–255
  portfolio, 249
  purpose of, 242–244
  strength, 259
  transnational, 242
Stream of meaning, 678
Strengths, 247–248
Stress, 176, 576–579
Stress management, 576–579
Stressors, 576
Stretch goals, 218, 228
Structural design approaches, 261, 315
Structures
  divisional structure, 316
  factors shaping, 331–338
  functional structure, 316
  global matrix, 319
  product structure, 316
  program structure, 316
  self-contained unit structure, 316
Styles
  participating style, 599
  selling style, 599
  telling style, 599
Submarine Kursk, sinking of, 29
Substitute, 604
Subsystems, 53
Subtle biases, 429
Superordinate goals, 715
Suppliers, 79
Supply chain management, 57, 522
Supportive leadership, 602
Supportive leadership approach, 613
Survey feedback, 359
Sustainability, 154, 178
Sustainable development, 154
Sustainer, 174
SWOT (strengths, weaknesses, opportunities, threats)
  analysis, 247–249, 364
  teams, 261
Symbol, 87
Synergy, 53, 243
System, 52
Systems theory, 48, 52–53

T

Tacit knowledge, 508
Tactical goals, 211, 215
Tactical plans, 215
Talent acquisition, 391
Tall structure, 313
Task
  demands, 577
  environment, 72
  force, 327–328, 697
  identity, 642
  oriented behavior, 595
  oriented leader, 600–601
  significance, 642
  specialist role, 704
Team norm
  carryover behaviors, 710
  critical events, 710
  explicit statements, 710–711
  primacy, 710
Team processes
  adjourning, 707
  five stages of team development, 706
  forming, 705
  norming, 706
  performing, 706
  storming, 705
  team cohesiveness, 707–708
  team development stages, 705
  team norms, 709–711
Teams, 387, 694
  approach, 325
  based structure, 56, 320
  building, 359
  building skills, 27
  cohesiveness, 707–708, 720–721
  command team, 697
  committee, 697
  communication channels, 672–673
  competence, 290
  cross-functional team, 697
  fast-cycle teams, 697–698
  formal teams, 696–698
  functional team, 697
  global teams, 700–702
  horizontal team, 697
  interaction, 708
  management, 596
  member roles, 704
  in new workplace, 699
  problem-solving teams, 698
  project teams, 697
  self-directed teams, 698, 698–699
  special-purpose teams, 697–698, 698
  task force, 697
  vertical teams, 697
  virtual teams, 699–700
Teamwork
  managing team conflict, 711–717
  team characteristics, 702–705

team processes, 705–711
teams at work, 694–696
types of teams, 696–702
work team effectiveness, 717–719
Technical complexity, 336
Technical core, 518
Technical skill, 12
Technological dimension, 74, 77
Technology, 26, 178, 388
Technology change, 349
Telecommuting, 388
Telling leadership style, 613
Telling style, 599
Temporary employees, 387
Termination, 406–407
The evolving world of, 492–498
The Prince, 569
Theories
  acquired needs theory, 629–630
  content theories, 624
  equity theory, 630–631
  ERG, 626–628
  expectancy theory, 632–633
  Herzberg's two-factor theory, 628–629
  hierarchy of needs, 625–626
  process theories, 624–625, 630
  reinforcement theories, 625
  X scale, 49, 61, 624
  Y scale, 49–50, 61, 624
Thinking, 571
Threats, 247–248
Time and motion studies, 42
Tolerance for ambiguity, 184–185
Top leader, 319
Top management support, 369
Top managers, 14
Top-down budgeting, 462
Total factor productivity, 540
Total quality management (TQM), 54
  benchmarking, 469
  continuous improvement, 471–472
  importance of quality improvement programs, 470
  quality circles, 469
  reduced cycle time, 470–471
  Six Sigma, 470
  TQM success factors, 472
  TQM techniques, 468
T–P leadership questionnaire, 614–615
Training
  classroom training, 399
  computer-based training, 399
  cross-training, 399
  e-training, 399
  mentoring, 399
  on-the-job training (OJT), 399
  orientation training, 399
  types and methods of, 400
Training and development, 357–358, 399

Traits, 594
Transactional leaders, 605
Transaction-processing systems (TPSs), 495
Transformation process, 52
Transformational leaders, 607–608
Transnational corporations, 126
Transnational strategy, 242
Transparency International Bribe Payers Index (2002), 247
Triple bottom line, 164
Trojan, 229
Turbulent times
  and changing workplace, 348
  communicating during, 677–680
  ethical challenges in, 162–165
  implementation during, 262
  innovative control systems for, 474–479
  new decision approaches for, 292
Two-boss employees, 319
Two-factor theory, 628–629
Type 2 diabetes, 152
Type A behavior, 576–577
Type B behavior, 576–577

U

Uncertainty, 273–274, 366
Uncertainty avoidance, 117
Uncertainty avoidance, 119
Undercontrol, 478
Unethical behavior, 156
Unfreezing, 362
United Nations, 439
Unity of command, 45, 309
Unity of direction, 45
Upward communication, 670
U.S. Treasury Secretary, 280
U.S.–Canada agreement (1989), 124
Use of rewards, 602
USS Dwight D. Eisenhower, 334
USS Indianapolis, 146
Utilitarian approach, 142–143

V

Valence, 632
Valero SAFE fund, 92
Validity, 395
Value, 243
Value chain management
  designing operations management systems, 523–533
  inventory management, 533–538
  lean manufacturing and productivity, 538–541
  organization as a value chain, 518–523
Variable-interval schedule, 637
Variable-ratio schedule, 637
Venture capital firm, 190

Vertical team, 697
Vietnam war, 78
Virtual incubator, 193
Virtual Leadership Academy, 660
Virtual network approach, 325–326
Virtual network structure, 322
Virtual teams, 388, 699–700
Viruses, 229
Visionary leadership, 605
Vocational Rehabilitation Act, 384
VOIP (voice over Internet protocol), 402
Vroom-Jago model, 288–294

W

Wage and salary
  surveys, 405
  systems, 404–405
Wage gap, 426
Wall Street Journal, 192
WD-40, the jet engine, 181
Weaknesses, 247
Weberian bureaucracy, 43
Whistle-blowing, 161–162
Wholly owned foreign affiliate, 112
Wicked decision problem. see Ambiguity
Wiki, 493
Winning Workplaces, 402
Win-win solution, 716
Women's ways of leading, 592–593
Woodward's manufacturing technology, 335–337
Work
  redesign, 641
  specialization, 309
  stress, 577–578
  team effectiveness model, 695
Workforce
  2020, 435
  diversity, 418
  optimization, 401
Work-in-process inventory, 534
Work/life balance, 388
Workplace
  e-mail in, 223
  HR issues in new, 386–387
  innovative technology in, 58–59
  new, 25
  old, 25
  transition to a new, 25
World Trade Organization (WTO), 122
World War II, 50–51, 54, 146
World Wide Web (WWW), 498
Worms, 229

Z

Zero inventory systems, 537